Professional Voice

The Science and Art of Clinical Care

Third Edition

Professional Voice
The Science and Art of Clinical Care

Third Edition

Robert Thayer Sataloff, MD, DMA

Plural Publishing, Inc.
SAN DIEGO   OXFORD

MW

Plural Publishing, Inc.
6256 Greenwich Drive, Suite 230
San Diego, CA 92122

e-mail: info@pluralpublishing.com
Web site: http://www.pluralpublishing.com

49 Bath Street
Abington, Oxfordshire OX14 1EA
United Kingdom

Typeset in 10/12 Palatino by So Cal Graphics

Care has been taken to confirm the accuracy of the information presented in this book and to describe generally accepted practices. However, the authors, editors, and publisher are not responsible for errors or omissions or for any consequences from application of the information in this book and make no warranty, expressed or implied, with respect to the currency, completeness, or accuracy of the contents of the publication. Application of this information in a particular situation remains the professional responsibility of the practitioner.

The authors, editors, and publisher have exerted every effort to ensure that drug selection and dosage in this text are in accordance with current recommendations and practice at the time of publication. However, in view of ongoing research, changes in government regulations, and the constant flow of information on drug therapy and drug reactions, the reader is urged to check the package insert for each drug for any change in indications and dosage and for added warnings and precautions.

Some drugs and medical devices presented in this publication have Food and Drug Administration (FDA) clearance for limited use in restricted research settings. It is the responsibility of the health care provider to ascertain the FDA status of each drug or device planned for use in their clinical practice.

ISBN 1-59756-001-4

Library of Congress Control Number: 2005924419

5/25/06

VOLUME III
Surgical Management and Special Considerations

VIII

STRUCTURAL DISORDERS AND SURGERY

80

The Evolution of Phonosurgery

Hans von Leden

Phonosurgery, or esthetic surgery of the vocal organ, became an accepted surgical modality in the late 1950s and early 1960s when the entire field of surgery experienced an interest in procedures for functional improvement. In the fall of 1963, Godfrey Arnold and I met in the bar of the Roosevelt Hotel in New York after the 68th Annual Meeting of the American Academy of Ophthalmology and Otolaryngology. We exchanged information about our personal experiences with surgical techniques for the improvement of the voice. We were enthusiastic about the surgical potential for the enhancement of vocal function, and we decided that this modality needed a comprehensive designation. In a discussion of numerous possible alternatives, I first mentioned the term *phonosurgery,* and we agreed to adopt and publicize this designation. Subsequently, I have used this term in presentations and publications around the world,[1] and phonosurgery is now an accepted medical expression in scientific circles.

Phonosurgery refers to any surgery designed primarily for the improvement or restoration of the voice. Arnold and I did not intend this designation for surgery in which the improvement and/or restoration of vocal function is of secondary consideration.

Phonosurgery represents only one aspect of laryngology, and the history of laryngology spans but a short interval in the annals of medicine. In 1854, the Spanish singing teacher Manuel García first observed his own larynx with the aid of a small dental mirror. Three years later, the Viennese neurologist Ludwig Türck adapted this technique to the examination of a few patients, and shortly thereafter the physiologist Johann Nepomuk Czermak, from Prague, popularized this indirect visualization of the larynx through-

out Europe. In 1895, Professor Alfred Kirstein, in Berlin, developed the art of direct laryngoscopy, and the stage was set for the evolution of laryngeal surgery.

During the first 100 years of our specialty, laryngeal surgery was devoted largely to the removal of neoplasms, and any potential improvement in voice was really a byproduct of this process. For many years, the fame of laryngologists was measured by the number of laryngectomies they performed, and the preservation of voice was of lesser importance. This phase, fortunately, has passed, and today the maintenance and improvement of vocal function are the goals of every practicing laryngologist.

This change in attitude has been encouraged by the urbanization of our society and by the increasing emphasis on human communications, which have placed social and economic demands on the voice. The process has been facilitated by the advances in laryngeal physiology, which have produced a better understanding of laryngeal function in health and disease. New surgical techniques have become feasible with the advent of antibiotics, the progress in anesthesiology, the adaptation of the microscope for use in laryngeal surgery, and other technical advances.

In the United States, the foundation of phonosurgery was based in the 1950s on the basic anatomic and physiologic studies by Paul Moore and me at Northwestern University[2] and on Arnold's extensive animal experiments at New York University.[3] The development of objective measures of laryngeal function at the Institute of Laryngology and Voice Disorders in Los Angeles[4] in the 1960s was an important element for accurate evaluation of the surgical results. Invaluable in this research were my colleagues Robert

This chapter is adapted from "The History of Phonosurgery" by Hans von Leden, 1991. In CN Ford & DM Bless, eds. *Phonosurgery.* Philadelphia, Pa: Raven Press, with permission.

Ringel, Nobuhiko Isshiki, William Perkins, Masaki Yanagihara, Knud Faaborg-Andersen, Minoru Hirano, Elvira Werner-Kukuk, Yasuo Koike, John Large, and Shigenobu Iwata, to name a few. From these basic investigations, visual, aerodynamic, and acoustic criteria were available for an accurate assessment of the voice before and after the projected surgery.

Advances in Phonosurgery

Phonosurgery in Vocal Fold Paralysis

Historically, a few surgical procedures had been performed solely for the improvement of voice, and these steps eventually led to my own involvement in this exciting new field.

Five decades earlier, in 1911, at the 18th Annual Meeting of the German Laryngological Society, Wilhelm Brünings (Fig 80–1) presented an ingenious and novel technique for the relief of aphonia in patients

Fig 80–1. Professor Wilhelm Brünings, MD.

with unilateral vocal fold paralysis.[5] In his stimulating presentation, Brünings described the injection of paraffin into the paralyzed vocal fold of patients with a poor voice caused by unilateral vocal fold paralysis. This procedure displaced the involved fold medially and permitted satisfactory approximation of the two folds during phonation. Brünings used a paste of hard paraffin (at a melting point of 46°C), and the patient regained his voice!

At the time, Brünings was a Privat-Dozent (or assistant professor) under Professor Wittmaak at the University of Jena in central Germany. He subsequently became professor of otolaryngology in Greifswald, Jena, and Munich. Brünings was a true pioneer in otolaryngology, an innovator who developed many of the specialized instruments still in use. An example is the Brünings laryngeal syringe (Fig 80–2), which has been used routinely over the past 30 years for the injection of prosthetics in patients with unilateral vocal fold paralysis. This instrument includes a ratchet device that emits a clicking sound after the injection of every 0.05 mL so that the surgeon knows the injected amount, even in a darkened operating room.

Other famous laryngologists, including Johannes Zange in Jena, Alfred Seiffert (at that time in Breslau, later professor in Kiel), Otto Mayer and Victor Imre in Vienna, and Samuel Iglauer in Cincinnati followed Brünings' example and reported similarly good results. This procedure could be performed under direct or indirect laryngoscopy, and the results were described as excellent. Seiffert even used a percutaneous approach for this injection (Fig 80–3).

Until his death, some 30 years later, Brünings insisted that his patients had developed no long-range complications. Other laryngologists, however, were not equally fortunate. In some cases the tissue developed a foreign-body reaction to the injection, with a resulting paraffinoma. In other patients, the paraffin liquified at body temperature and migrated from the area of injection. I have seen a patient with a subcutaneous paraffinoma of the lower neck after a paraffin injection into the larynx. This complication may have been the result of using soft paraffin, which is easier to inject through the long laryngeal needle, or of a faulty technique. In any case, the patient was left with a poor voice and an unsightly tumor of the neck. Eventually the procedure fell into disrepute and was abandoned.

I was delighted when I attended the VIth International Congress of Oto-Rhino-Laryngology in Washington in May 1957 and heard Godfrey Arnold (Fig 80–4) describe two successful vocal fold injections using diced autogenous cartilage from the nasal septum in place of paraffin.[6] A Moravian by birth, Arnold spent his early medical career as a professor of phoniatrics at

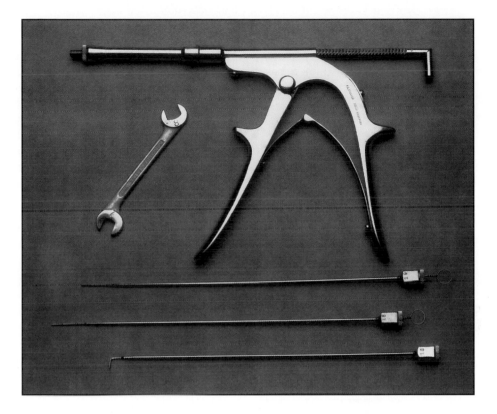

Fig 80–2. Brünings' laryngeal syringe and needles.

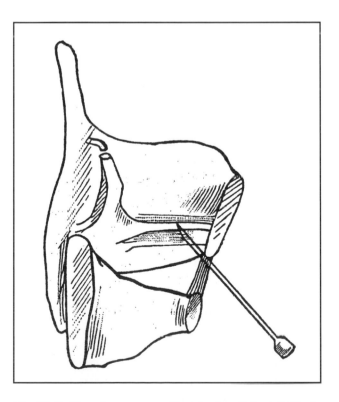

Fig 80–3. Percutaneous paraffin injection (Alfred Seiffert). (From Seiffert, *Laryngology*, 1916;8:233.)

Fig 80–4. Dr Godfrey Arnold.

the University of Vienna. When the Allies occupied Austria at the end of World War II, Arnold transferred his activities to New York. As director of research at the National Hospital for Speech Disorders and at the New York Eye and Ear Infirmary, Arnold devoted the next 15 years to impressive fundamental investigations in neurolaryngology and voice disorders. He finished his life's work as the first full-time professor of otolaryngology at the University of Mississippi in Jackson. Arnold's work was based on experiments in dogs over a 5-year period,[3] during which he employed autogenous, heterogenous, and preserved cartilage in various admixtures.

His impressive results fired my imagination, and I returned to Chicago and Northwestern University determined to help my patients with unilateral vocal fold paralysis regain their voices. We can hardly forget the problems we experienced in dicing, preparing, and sterilizing the cartilaginous paste. In the fall of 1957, after meticulous trials on living animals and human cadavers, I operated on my first patient, a law student from the University of Wisconsin, and the good results further spurred my enthusiasm. Although my colleagues were skeptical, my intuition

told me that laryngology was at the beginning of a new era—surgery for the improvement of voice.

The subsequent development of phonosurgery for unilateral vocal fold paralysis is better known.[7] Important contributions include Willard Goff's injections of bovine bone dust in Seattle, Robert B. Lewy's work with tantalum powder in Chicago, Henry Rubin's experiences with silicone in Los Angeles, and finally the successful use of Teflon paste. Teflon is a polymer of tetrafluoroethylene. Teflon powder particles, 6 to 12 μm in size, are suspended in a solution of 50% glycerine to form the paste. The availability of this substance and the lack of local reaction have rendered it an unusually effective prosthetic. Used for the correct indications and with the proper technique (Fig 80–5), the injection of Teflon paste has given new hope to countless patients with unilateral vocal fold paralysis. By 1976, Lewy reported 1039 augmentation procedures performed over a 14-year period by 38 approved investigators, with improvement of voice in 96% of the patients.[8] Nevertheless, in spite of this high success rate, some problems associated with Teflon have motivated laryngologists to search for other appropriate filler substances, such as bovine collagen and autogenous fat.

Still other laryngologists employed a different approach for the improvement of voice in patients with unilateral voice fold paralysis. Two or three years after Brünings' original discovery, Professor Erwin Payr (Fig 80–6) of Leipzig noted that the voice of younger patients with this impediment was much improved when the examiner compressed the elastic thyroid cartilage. He reasoned that this finding could be used for a new surgical application. While serving as a general in the medical department of the German Army during World War I, Payr was able to translate his theory into practice.[9] In 1915, a young soldier was referred to him because the patient could not speak after a hemithyroidectomy. For the improvement of his voice, Payr designed an ingenious thyroplasty (Fig 80–7), which forced the paralyzed vocal fold medially for better approximation. The rectangular flap of thyroid cartilage remained hinged posteriorly, and the anterior end was pressed inward. The patient's voice was restored, and the soldier returned to duty.

It is of interest for the historian to observe that the next advances in this field again occurred during a World War. In 1942, during World War II, the Finnish laryngologist Professor Yrjo Meurman (Fig 80–8) of Helsinki reported the implantation of a sliver of autogenous costal cartilage for medializing the involved vocal fold.[10] Meurman was concerned with the rehabilitation of soldiers under his care who had become

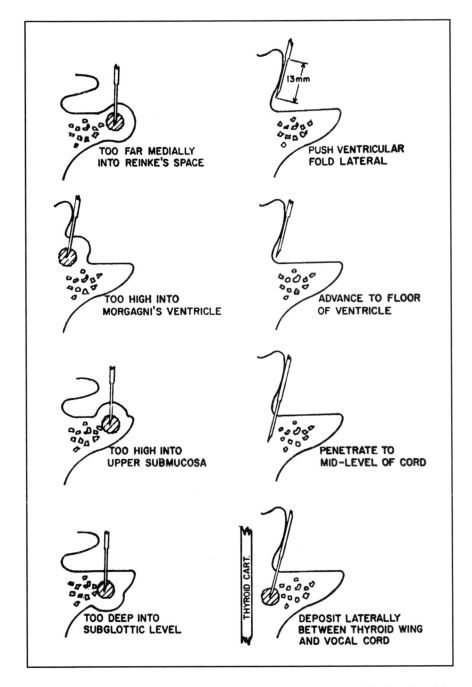

Fig 80–5. Correct procedure for intracordal injection operation (Godfrey Arnold). (From Arnold[7(p366)])

aphonic after gunshot injuries of the neck destroyed the vagus or recurrent laryngeal nerve. Meurman shaped the excised cartilage into a triangular form and inserted this sliver between the vocalis muscle and the thyroid ala by means of a laryngofissure. In the same year, Professor Gösta Dohlman of the University of Lund in Sweden also presented two similar patients. By 1952, Meurman had collected 15 patients in whom the affected fold was brought into a new, more median position by this procedure.[11] The functional results were most satisfactory, except for one patient in whom the transplanted cartilage was extruded because of infection.

In 1955, Professor Odd Opheim of Oslo presented a modification of Meurman's technique,[12] in which he implanted a section of cartilage from the ipsilateral

Fig 80–6. Professor Dr Erwin Payr.

Katgutfaden

Knorpellappen in die Tiefe gedrückt

Fig 80–7. Thyroplasty (Erwin Payr). (From Payr[9(p1265)])

Fig 80–8. Professor Dr Yrjo Meurman.

thyroid ala (Fig 80–9). Jules Waltner of Columbia University in New York was the first American to use this approach to move the cicatricial remnant of a vocal fold medially after the removal of a malignant tumor. Similar procedures were employed in the 1960s by Professor Adolf Miehlke at the University of Göttingen in Germany, Professor Masayuki Sawashima and his colleagues at the University of Tokyo, Professor Alfredo Celis Perez in Venezuela, and a former associate of mine, Dr. Andrcs Delgado, in Mexico.

Microsurgical Techniques for Phonosurgery

Without doubt, the adaptation of the surgical microscope for magnification of the laryngeal interior was the most important element in the evolution of phonosurgery in our specialty.[13] The microscopic visualization of the vocal folds was first described in 1954 by Professor Rosemarie Albrecht (Fig 80–10) of the Medical Academy in Erfurt, a city in the former East Germany.[14] Albrecht was perhaps the leading woman otolaryngologist of this century, yet her work is virtually unknown in the United States. It is of interest that Albrecht adapted the microscope for laryngeal diagnosis not through her exposure to otologic micro-

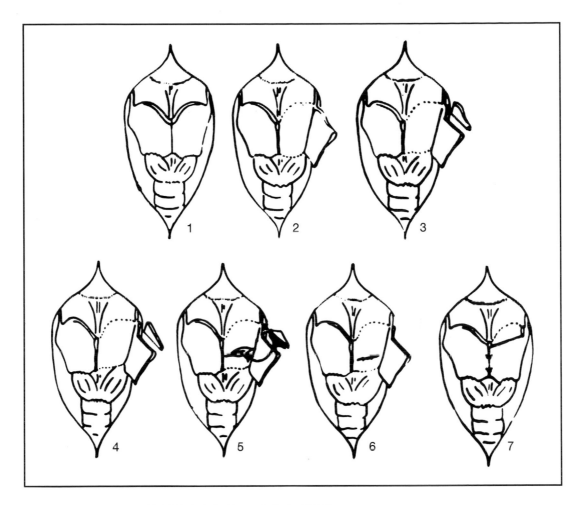

Fig 80–9. Thyroplasty (Odd Opheim). (From Opheim[12(p228)])

surgery, but because she attempted to emulate the success of her gynecologic colleagues in diagnosing early malignancies of the uterine cervix.

Albrecht continued her microscopic studies of the larynx after she had been appointed professor of otolaryngology at the University of Jena. However, the limited facilities and funds in the war-ravaged Communist sector of Germany posed a severe handicap for the further development of this approach. Since no suitable equipment was at hand or obtainable, Albrecht had to work in the department of gynecology, using a colposcope with magnification for her examinations. Apparently, not one of her colleagues on either side of the Iron Curtain paid any attention to Albrecht's novel idea. What self-respecting laryngologist would use a gynecologic speculum for a laryngoscopy? At any rate, the acceleration of the Cold War put a stop to the future exchange of ideas between East Germany and the Western world.

The credit for the perfection of this technique belongs to Professor Oskar Kleinsasser (Fig 80–11), an Austrian by birth, Kleinsasser was a trained pathologist who became interested in otolaryngology. Like Albrecht, Kleinsasser was impressed with the results of microscopic examinations of the uterine cervix and attempted to develop similar diagnostic facilities for the larynx. In the late 1950s, while serving as an assistant in the ear, nose, and throat department of the University of Cologne in Germany, Kleinsasser had an opportunity to put his ideas into practice.

At first, he used different loupes for magnification, but the results were less than desired. Gradually, he enlarged and tapered the laryngoscope until he was able to accomplish binocular vision and bimanual surgery (Fig 80–12). By 1962, Kleinsasser had adapted the Zeiss microscope for selected cases of laryngeal diagnosis.[15] Shortly thereafter, Zeiss developed a 400-mm focal lens that permitted the facile use of the long-handled laryngeal instrument for precision surgery on the vocal folds with vastly improved functional results. In 1968, Kleinsasser published his comprehensive book on microlaryngoscopy with magnifi-

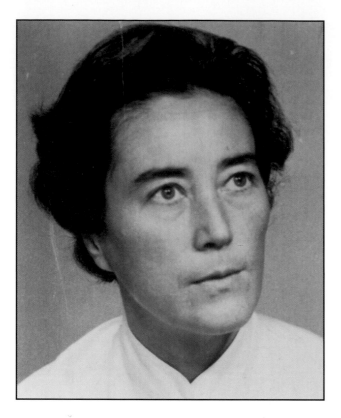

Fig 80–10. Professor Dr Rosemarie Albrecht.

Fig 80–11. Professor Dr Oskar Kleinsasser.

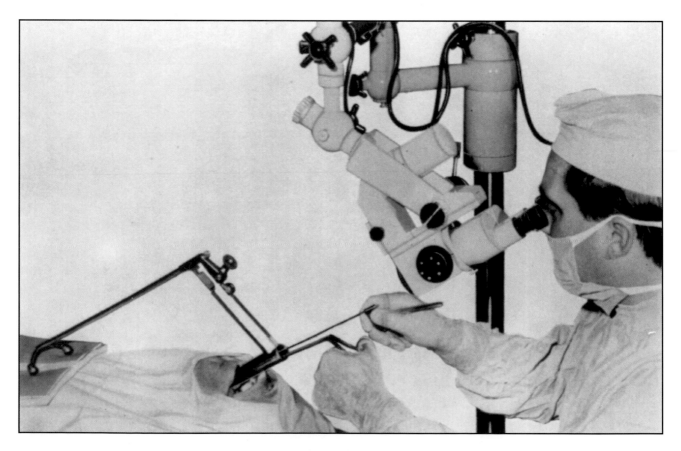

Fig 80–12. Endolaryngeal microsurgical procedure (Oskar Kleinsasser). (From Kleinsasser[16(p19)])

cent magnified photographs of the larynx in health and disease.[16]

Both during his tenure as Oberarzt (assistant professor) at the University of Cologne and later as professor of otolaryngology at the University of Marburg in Germany, Kleinsasser popularized the art and science of microlaryngoscopy. He justly deserves the honors he has been accorded for this advance.

During the same period, parallel advances were being made by laryngologists in the United States who were working in this direction.[13] As early as 1960, Anthony Scalco and his colleagues at Tulane University in New Orleans used a Zeiss microscope with a Lynch suspension laryngoscope for magnification. Other surgeons, such as Albert Andrews, Lewy, and I, employed monocular or binocular loupes for magnification. However, all of these attempts proved unsatisfactory: either the magnification was inadequate, the equipment was unwieldy, or the customary laryngoscopes were not suitable for binocular vision. A more serious obstacle was the use of local anesthesia for endoscopic laryngeal work as advocated by the renowned American laryngologist, Chevalier Jackson. As a result, involuntary movements of the patients precluded precision surgery.

Geza Jako (Fig 80–13), in Boston, surmounted these difficulties by developing an improved laryngoscope for binocular diagnosis and bimanual surgery. Jako had started his attempts with magnification in the 1950s, about the same time as Kleinsasser. He advanced from a binocular loupe to the use of the Zeiss microscope for indirect laryngoscopy and then to direct laryngoscopy with still photographs and motion pictures.[17] As early as 1962, Jako designed a series of microlaryngeal instruments with the firm Stümer in Würzburg, Germany (Fig 80–14). His skill and agility resulted in instrumentation that has not changed significantly in the past 20 years, a notable credit to this gifted inventor.

At first, most senior laryngologists frowned on this novel technique. I experienced this negative attitude after I met Kleinsasser at a medical meeting in Germany in 1963 and attempted to introduce microlaryngoscopy in the western United States.[13] It was apparent that the technique required general anesthesia for precision surgery, and most laryngologists were reluctant to deviate from the generally accepted concept of local anesthesia for direct laryngoscopies. However, the benefits of magnification were soon evident, and the increasing availability of skilled anesthesiologists facilitated the adoption of microlaryngoscopy as a routine surgical procedure. Over a period of years, microsurgery has proven a vastly improved technique for surgery on the vocal folds to restore or improve the patient's voice.

Fig 80–13. Dr Geza Jako.

Phonosurgery of the Laryngeal Nerves

One of the most exciting new ventures in the broad field of phonosurgery deals with the restoration or replacement of the injured recurrent laryngeal nerve and its potential for vocal improvement. The simplest procedure in this grouping is the liberation of the nonfunctioning nerve from adhesions and scar tissue. This neurolysis had been carried out with some measure of success by Joseph Ogura of St. Louis, Adolf Miehlke of Göttingen, Germany,[18] and other surgeons.

For decades, surgeons have attempted to perfect an end-to-end anastomosis of the recurrent laryngeal nerve, but only in recent years have these efforts been partially successful. The use of the operating microscope and the development of microsurgical techniques have permitted precise approximation of the damaged nerve. In 1969, Patrick Doyle of Portland, Oregon, reported 5 cases of functional recovery in six patients on whom he had operated within five days of their injury.[19] Doyle subsequently became professor of otolaryngology at the University of British Columbia in Vancouver, where he continued his work. Miehlke, Frank Lahey of Boston, the Portmann group

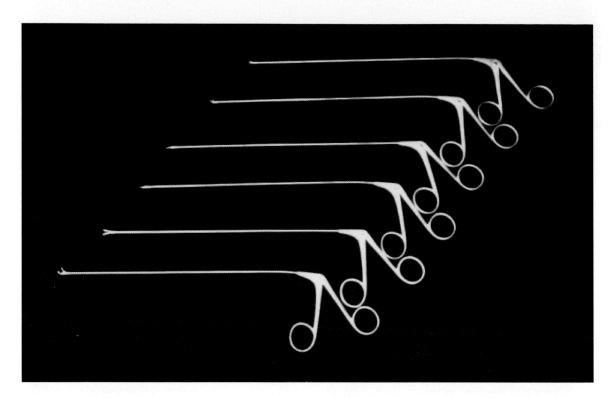

Fig 80–14. Microsurgical instruments (Jako/Stümer, 1962–1963).

of Bordeaux, and other surgeons reported successful results in selected cases. The timing of the reconstruction appears to be crucial for the success of a neurorrhaphy. The first 2 weeks are considered decisive.

Miehlke (Fig 80–15) of Göttingen and Julius Berendes of Marburg, Germany, are the only surgeons who have reported success with an autogenous transplant of the recurrent laryngeal nerve.[20] Miehlke replaced the destroyed segment of a recurrent laryngeal nerve 10 weeks after the injury with a branch of the greater auricular nerve. I was able to observe this patient during a visit to the University of Göttingen. Miehlke also developed an ingenious technique for isolating the recurrent laryngeal nerve bundle in the vagus nerve and "shunting" the liberated segment to the distal nerve stump of the severed nerve near the larynx (Fig 80–16). With his painstaking animal experiments and his successful surgery of the facial nerve as well as the recurrent laryngeal nerve, Miehlke must be considered the leading pioneer in the peripheral neurosurgery of our field.

As early as 1924, Charles Frazier of Philadelphia attempted to cure paralysis of the laryngeal nerve by anastomosing it to the descending ramus of the hypoglossal nerve. By 1926, he reported improvement in 6 of 10 patients.[21]

Other surgeons have attempted direct nerve implantation into the posterior cricoarytenoid muscle.

Fig 80–15. Professor Dr Adolf Miehlke.

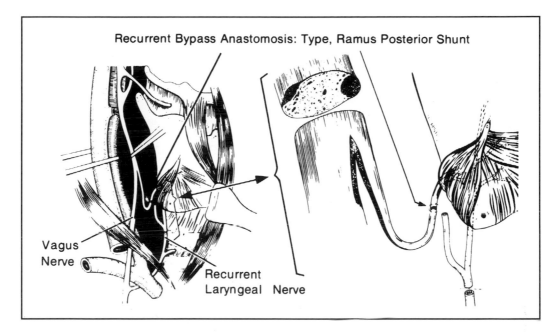

Recurrent Bypass Anastomosis: Type, Ramus Posterior Shunt

Vagus Nerve

Recurrent Laryngeal Nerve

Fig 80–18. Recurrent bypass anastomosis (Adolf Miehlke). (From Miehlke A. *Arch Otolaryngol.* 1974;100:434.)

For this purpose, Doyle has used the proximal segment of the recurrent laryngeal nerve, and Calcaterra and associates at the University of California, Los Angeles, have used the phrenic nerve. More successful has been the composite nerve/muscle transplant described in 1975 by Harvey Tucker (Fig 80–17) of the Cleveland Clinic. Originally, Tucker transplanted a nerve/muscle pedicle consisting of the branch of the ansa hypoglossi nerve to the anterior belly of the omohyoid muscle, together with the surrounding muscular segment, directly into the posterior cricoarytenoid muscle (Fig 80–18). By 1979, he reported success in 40 of a series of 45 cases (89%).[22] Edward Applebaum and colleagues at Northwestern University in Chicago confirmed Tucker's favorable results with the nerve/muscle pedicle technique. Tucker also transplanted a similar nerve/muscle pedicle into the thyroarytenoid muscle on the paralyzed side by means of a window in the thyroid ala. In a series of 10 patients, he reported some degree of success. This procedure was designed solely for the improvement of voice after destruction of the recurrent laryngeal nerve.[23]

Phonosurgery for Spastic Dysphonia

A totally different aspect of laryngeal neurosurgery is represented by efforts to improve the voice in patients with spastic dysphonia by a surgical approach. By 1970, both Arnold and I had begun to inject a local anesthetic into the laryngeal nerves of patients with spastic dysphonia. Although the dramatic improvement was transitory, the procedure was of value for the differential diagnosis.

Using the same rationale, Herbert Dedo (Fig 80–19) of the University of California, San Francisco, decided to sever the recurrent laryngeal nerve to relieve the disabling spasticity. His first patient recovered her voice, and a successful procedure for the relief of spastic dysphonia was born.[24] In a series of articles, Dedo and associates presented their favorable results and created new hope for patients with this disabling condition. Although not all patients with spastic dysphonia have benefited from neurectomy, a large percentage were able to resume their normal lifestyles. Dedo merits appreciation for his courage and determination to achieve a constructive result by a destructive surgical procedure.

Over the past 5 years, yet another surgical treatment has been adopted for the relief of spastic dysphonia. In 1986, Andrew Blitzer and Mitchell Brin and colleagues of Columbia University in New York injected a solution of botulinum toxin into the vocalis muscle to relieve spasticity.[25] Simultaneously, the treatment was tested at the National Institute of Neurological and Communicative Disorders and Stroke. Currently, testing is taking place at the National Institute for Deafness and Other Communication Disorders in Washington, DC, by Christy Ludlow and associates.[26] Although the details of the two clinical trials varied,

Fig 80–17. Dr Harvey Tucker.

the results were the same: a significant improvement in voice that lasted for several months. Further clinical investigations are in progress.

Phonosurgery After Laryngectomy

The laryngoplasty described by Professor Ryozo Asai (Fig 80–20) of Kobe University, Japan, in 1963, represented an entirely new approach for the restoration of voice after laryngectomy.[27] Asai's technique (Fig 80–21) was designed originally as a three-stage procedure. The first stage, at the completion of the laryngectomy, consisted of the construction of two tracheal stomata, separated by a thin bridge of tracheal wall. The second stage involved preparation of a pharyngeal fistula. In the third stage, a dermal tube was fashioned to connect the upper tracheal stoma and the pharyngeal fistula. In later years, various modifications of this technique were introduced in the United States by Alden Miller of the University of Southern California, William Montgomery of Harvard University, and Frederick M. Turnbull, Jr, of the University of California at Irvine. Bernhard Minnigerode of the University of Essen, Germany, and other surgeons in

Europe also modified the procedure to reduce Asai's method to two stages.

In any event, the purpose of this laryngoplasty was to retain the lower stoma for respiration. For phonation, this stoma was occluded manually, and the exhaled air was directed into the dermal tube, which formed a pseudolarynx near its junction with the hypopharynx. The sound waves were then amplified and transformed into speech by the structures of the throat, mouth, and nose in the usual fashion. This procedure could be performed primarily at the completion of the laryngectomy, or subsequently as a secondary operation, if the patient could not master esophageal speech.

During the past decade, other procedures have been devised to create a tracheopharyngeal fistula and deflect the air from the trachea into the esophagus for improved vocalization. The developers of these techniques include John Conley of New York, Thomas Calcaterra of the University of California, Los Angeles, and Miehlke of Göttingen. The most effective method to date appears to be the endoscopic technique of Mark Singer and Eric Blom of Indianapolis, which consists of tracheoesophageal puncture and maintenance of the fistula by the Blom-Singer voice prosthesis.[28] This tracheoesophageal button has been used in a large number of laryngectomized patients to improve the production of voice after the removal of the larynx. Other prosthetic implantations have been attempted in the oral cavity and in the cervical area, but these devices are still in the experimental stage.

Phonosurgery of the Laryngeal Framework

As the preceding sections have indicated, throughout the 1950s and 1960s, surgeons and scientists in the United States played a leading role in the development of phonosurgery. This trend was encouraged by the keen interest of Americans in the mass media and by the special training of Americans otolaryngologists in plastic surgery. However, in the 1970s, the professional liability crisis in the United States hampered further development of this new surgical modality for esthetic changes in the voice. The risk of legal redress increased exponentially, and most, if not all, professional liability insurance contracts excluded coverage for any procedure that was not generally accepted by the medical profession in the community. Under these circumstances, it is not surprising that highly skilled Japanese surgeons assumed the leadership in surgery for an esthetic improvement in the voice. It was this opportunity to change the pitch, intensity, and quality of the voice that Arnold and I conceptualized in our use of the term *phonosurgery* for this new surgical modality.

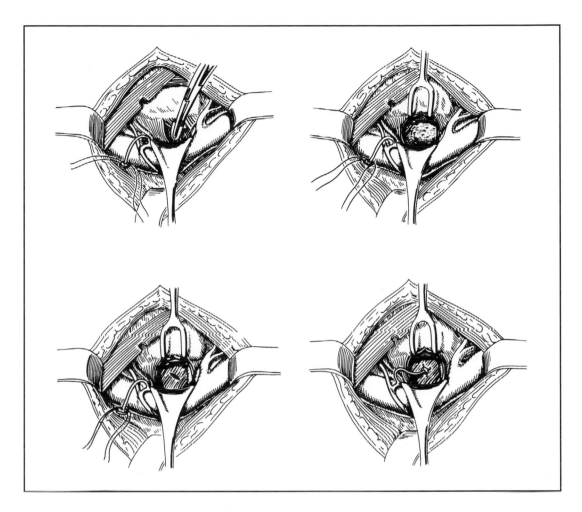

Fig 80–18. Nerve-muscle pedicle technique (Harvey Tucker). (From Tucker H. *Laryngoscope*. 1978; 88:601.)

It is true that in the 1950s Tschiassny of the University of Cincinnati recommended approximation of the cricoid and thyroid cartilages anteriorly for tensing the vocal cords and raising the vocal pitch. It is also true that in the 1960s my colleagues and I employed the injection of Teflon into the vocal folds for lowering the vocal pitch. However, it remained for Nobuhiko Isshiki (Fig 80–22) at the University of Kyoto in Japan to present a systematic approach to surgery of the vocal skeleton that holds out hope for a significant improvement in, or transformation of, the human voice. The surgical techniques described by Isshiki for alternating the framework of the larynx lead to changes in length, tension, and mass of the vocal folds and thereby permit a true transformation of the patient's voice.

During his medical education, Isshiki was exposed to postgraduate instruction at the University of Kyoto as well as to the facilities at the Institute of Laryngology and Voice Disorders and the University of California at Los Angeles. After his return to Kyoto, Isshiki became professor of plastic surgery at the University and applied the concept of this specialty to the field of laryngology.

In a seminal article,[29] Isshiki and colleagues described four basic procedures to alter the laryngeal skeleton and thereby the resulting voice. These four operations lengthen or shorten the vocal folds and compress or expand the laryngeal interior (Fig 80–23). The first procedure, thyroplasty type I, was designed to shift the fold(s) medially through lateral compression. Originally, a portion of the thyroid cartilage on the involved side was depressed inward, but more recently Isshiki created a window in the thyroid cartilage on patients with imperfect closure of the glottis (Fig 80–24). A rectangular piece of cartilage was then

Fig 80–19. Dr Herbert Dedo.

Fig 80–20. Professor Ryozo Asai, MD.

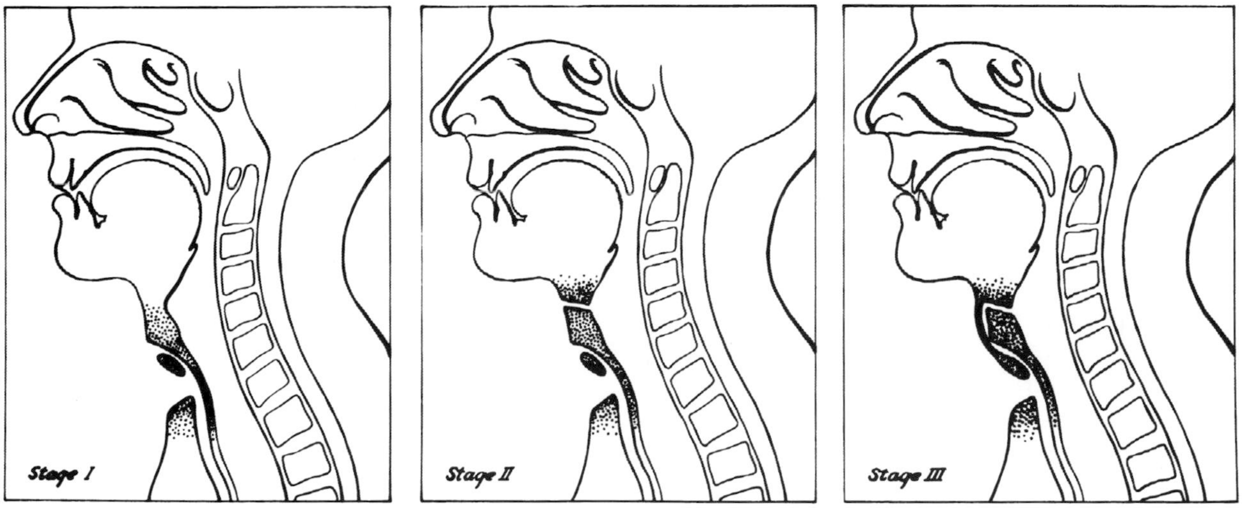

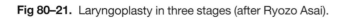

Fig 80–21. Laryngoplasty in three stages (after Ryozo Asai).

Fig 80–22. Professor Nobuhiko Isshiki, MD.

depressed inward to move the affected fold medially. This procedure is carried out under local anesthesia, and fine adjustments are performed while listening to the voice produced.

Thyroplasty type II was intended for lateral expansion of the vocal folds in patients with an abnormal glottis after injuries. This step consists of dividing the thyroid cartilage anteriorly and holding the two fragments apart with a cartilage splint. In practice, this procedure is rarely used.

Thyroplasty type III results in a shortening of the vocal folds by incising and depressing the anterior segment of the thyroid cartilage. This technique also may be used to lower the vocal pitch. For this purpose, it also may be combined with an augmentation of the mass by cordal injection.

Thyroplasty type IV is intended to lengthen and increase tension of the vocal folds and thereby raise the vocal pitch. In this procedure, the cricoid and thyroid cartilages are approximated anteriorly with nylon sutures, and the vocal folds are stretched and tightened. Deliberate scarring of the vocal folds by laser vaporization has been suggested as a possible alternative method for raising the vocal pitch, but knowledge of the delicate anatomy of the vocal folds highlights the shortcoming of this approach.

Since his original description, Isshiki has modified some of these basic steps to improve the functional results. He also has designed a series of new procedures to achieve this objective. One of these newer techniques for patients with unilateral vocal fold paralysis consists of rotating the arytenoid cartilage medially for improved adduction (Fig 80–25).

A book on the theory and practice of phonosurgery presents Isshiki's wide experience in this new subspecialty and includes an extensive bibliography on the subject.[30] At this time, Isshiki and associates continue their experimental and clinical trials of new and improved techniques in phonosurgery, and we are indebted to them for developing a promising new dimension of this modality.

Another pioneer in the development of phonosurgery, Minoru Hirano (Fig 80–26), is also a graduate of Kyoto University who continued his professional education at the Institute of Laryngology and Voice Disorders and the University of California, Los Angeles. On his return to Japan, Hirano became professor of otolaryngology at Kurume University, where he has developed one of the world's leading laryngeal centers. Many of the physiologic research concepts that Hirano and his assistants conceived have proven important in the development of phonosurgery.

Like Isshiki, Hirano devoted himself to the surgical improvement of the human voice. As early as 1975, he submitted an official report on his basic and clinical investigations of phonosurgery to the 76th Annual Convention of the Oto-Rhino-Laryngological Society of Japan.[31] The report, a comprehensive and profusely illustrated book of 213 pages, was published in Japanese. Since this report, Hirano has demonstrated his competence in phonosurgery through numerous presentations and publications on microsurgery, thyroplasty, medial displacement of the vocal fold(s), laryngoplasty, and so on.

Still another Japanese otolaryngologist, Professor Shigeji Saito of Keio University in Tokyo, deserves mention as one of the early leaders in phonosurgery. Saito presented his animal and human investigations of various innovative procedures in the form of an extensive report in 1977.[32] This material, too, was submitted in Japanese and is, therefore, a limited resource to Western scholars.

In 1983, Francis LeJeune, Jr, of the Ochsner Clinic in New Orleans described an advancement of the anterior commissure[33] to tighten the vocal ligament and strengthen the voice in patients with bowed vocal folds or weak voices. The procedure can also be used for *raising* the vocal pitch. For this purpose, LeJeune mobilized a midline strip of thyroid cartilage. The everted upper end was held in position with a sliver of tantalum fold (Fig 80–27). Clinical success was

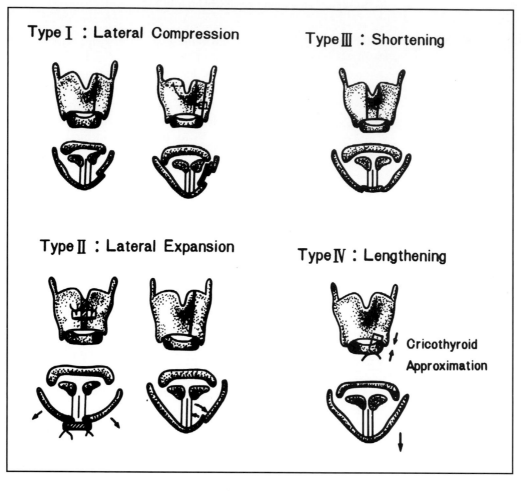

Fig 80–23. Four types of thyroplasty (Nobuhiko Isshiki). (From Isshiki N. *Folia Phoniatr.* 1980;32:135, with permission.)

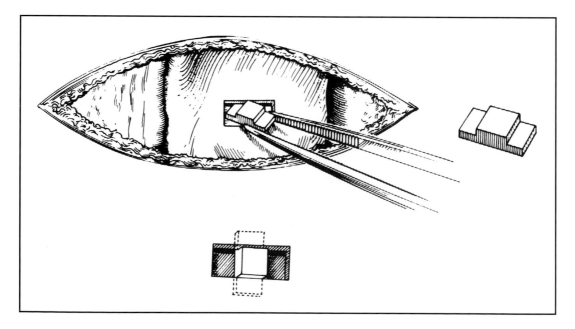

Fig 80–24. Modification of thyroplasty type I (Nobuhiko Isshiki). (From Isshiki N. *Folia Phoniatr.* 1980;32:137, with permission.)

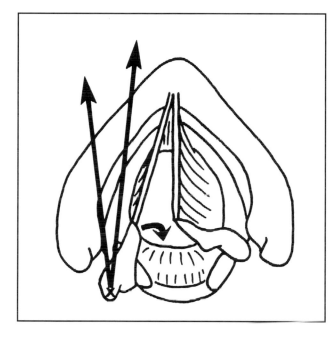

Fig 80–25. Arytenoid adduction for unilateral vocal fold paralysis (Nobuhiko Isshiki). (From Isshiki N. *Folia Phoniatr*, 1980;32:138, with permission.)

Fig 80–26. Professor Minoru Hirano, MD.

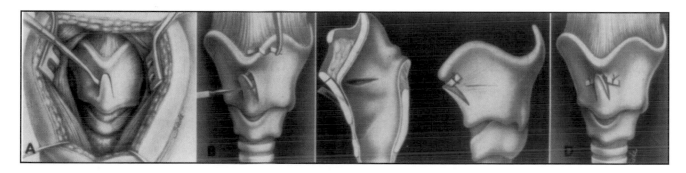

Fig 80–27. Tightening of vocal ligaments (Francis LeJeune). (From LeJeune[33] [(p476)])

achieved in the six patients on whom this technique was used. Two years later, Tucker reported nine cases involving a similar procedure, in which he based his cartilage flap superiorly to use the greater elasticity of the thyroid cartilage in that area (Fig 80–28). He also recommended depressing the incised segment for *lowering* the vocal pitch.

By 1987, LeJeune had developed an elaborate caliper for measuring tension of the vocal ligament. At the same time, he described a modification of the original procedure for additional extension of the vocal cords (Fig 80–28). In 1989, James Koufman of Bowman Gray University in Winston-Salem, North Carolina, enhanced the anterior advancement technique by Silastic implants between the thyroarytenoid muscles and the thyroid alae for the further improvement of voice in patients with bowed vocal folds. Other Amer-

ican laryngologists, including Stanley Blaugrund, Charles Cummings, Charles Ford, Wilbur James Gould, Clarence Sasaki, and Robert Sataloff, have experimented with Isshiki's thyroplasty type I for unilateral vocal fold paralysis and have confirmed the advantages of this technique in carefully selected patients. Sataloff has also proposed a modification of thyroplasty type IV that may improve long-term maintenance of elevated pitch.[34]

Transplants in Phonosurgery

The increasing use of partial and subtotal laryngectomies has created the need for reconstruction of the resected vocal fold from mucosal flaps and skin grafts. Laryngeal surgeons from various nations have participated in the development of diverse transplants,

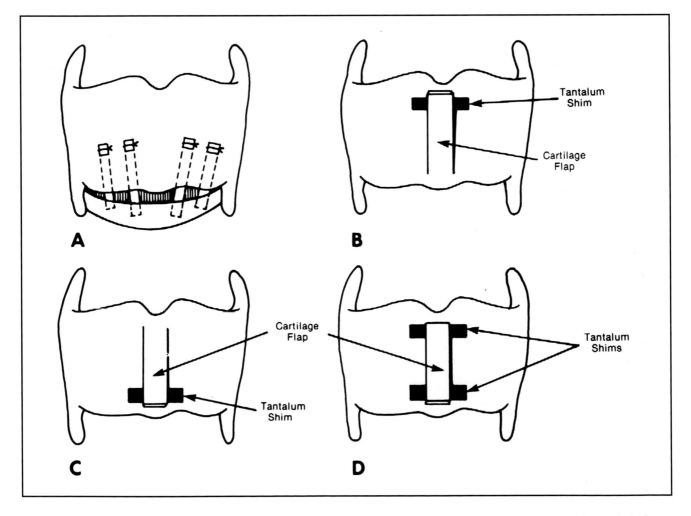

Fig 80–28. Anterior laryngoplastic procedures for correction of vocal fold bowing. **A.** Cricothyroid approximation (Isshiki). **B.** Inferiorly based anterior cartilage flap (LeJeune). **C.** Superiorly based anterior cartilage flap (Tucker). **D.** Anterior commissure advancement (LeJeune). (From Koufman JA. *Ann Otol Rhinol Laryngol*, 1989;98:42, with permission.)

including cartilage and composite grafts, as well as the transposition of the thyroid cartilage and extrinsic laryngeal muscles. Many of these innovative techniques[35] are the work of the leading head and neck surgeon of this time, John Conley (Fig 80–29) of New York. However, since these procedures form an integral part of malignant tumor surgery, I will not discuss them here.

Every laryngologist envisions transplantation of an entire larynx as the supreme goal of laryngeal transplant surgery. To date, however, only one surgeon has succeeded in this endeavor, Professor Paul Kluyskens (Fig 80–30) of the University of Ghent in Belgium.[36] Unfortunately, his patient died 4½ months after surgery. It is of special interest to note that the postoperative voice was "entirely acceptable." The quality of the voice varied with the success of the immunosuppression. The special difficulties in transplanting an entire larynx relate not only to the immune system but also to our current inability to restore the motor and sensory functions of a transplanted organ. Although

microsurgical techniques permit anastomosis of small blood vessels, success in laryngeal transplantation must await a breakthrough in immunology as well as in neurologic surgery.

Conclusion

Phonosurgery, or surgery for the improvement of voice, is one of the newer surgical modalities in the armamentarium of the otorhinolaryngologist. Although there have been sporadic attempts to improve the voice in the past, only in the last 30 years have concerted efforts by surgeons in the United States, Japan, and Germany established reliable and effective procedures for transforming the human voice. As these techniques mature, laryngologists can look forward to improving the pitch, intensity, and quality of their patients' voices. The work of each of those pathbreaking innovators will rest heavily on that of the visionaries who pioneered the field of phonosurgery.

Fig 80–29. Dr John Conley.

Fig 80–30. Professor Dr Paul Kluyskens.

References

1. von Leden H. Fono-cirujia. *Acta ORL Iber-Americ.* 1971; 22:291–299.

2. von Leden H. The mechanism of phonation—a search for a rational theory of voice production. *Arch Otolaryngol.* 1961;74:660–676.

3. Arnold GE. Vocal rehabilitation of paralytic dysphonia. I: Cartilage injection into a paralyzed vocal cord. *Arch Otolaryngol.* 1955;52:1–17.

4. von Leden H. Larynx—measurement of function. In: Harrison R, Hinchcliffe D, eds. *Scientific Foundations of Otolaryngology.* London: William Heinemann; 1976: 574–591.

5. Brünings W. Über eine Behandlungsmethode der Rekurrenslähmung. 18. *Verhandl Deutsch Laryngol.* 1911;93:151.

6. Arnold GE. Vocal rehabilitation of paralytic dysphonia. In: Abstract Section, VI. International Congress of Otolaryngology; Washington, DC: 1957;146.

7. Arnold GE. Vocal rehabilitation of paralytic dysphonia. IX: technique of intracordal injection. *Arch Otolaryngol.* 1962;76:358–368.

8. Lewy RB. Experience with vocal cord injection. *Ann Otol Rhinol Laryngol.* 1976;85:440–450.

9. Payr E. Plastik am Schildknorpel zur Behebung der Folgen einseitiger Stimmbandlähmung. *Dtsch Med Wochnschr.* 1915;43:1265–1270.

10. Meurman Y. Mediofixation der Stimmlippe bei ihrer vollständigen Lähmung. *Arch Ohren Nasen Kehlkopfheilk.* 1944;154:296–302.

11. Meurman Y. Operative mediofixation of the vocal cord in complete unilateral paralysis. *Arch Otolaryngol.* 1952; 55:544–553.

12. Opheim O. Unilateral paralysis of the vocal cord. Operative treatment. *Acta Otolaryngol.* 1955;45:226–230.

13. von Leden H. Microlaryngoscopy: a historical vignette. *J Voice.* 1987;1:314–346.

14. Albrecht R. Über den Wert kolkoskopischer Untersuchungsmethoden bei Leukoplakien und Carcinomen des Mundes und Kehlkopfes. *Arch Ohrenheilk* 1954;164: 459–463.

15. Kleinsasser O. Mikrochirurgie im Kehlkopf. *Arch Ohrenheilk.* 1964;183:428–433.

16. Kleinsasser O. *Mikrolaryngoskopie und Endolaryngeale Mikrochirurgie.* Stuttgart, Germany: Schattaure-Verlag; 1968.

17. Jako GJ. Laryngoscope for microscopic observation, surgery and photography. *Arch Otolaryngol.* 1970;91: 196–199.

18. Miehlke A. Zur Indikation und Technik der Recurrensneurolyse. *Laryngol Rhinol Otol.* 1958;37:44–54.

19. Doyle PJ. Indications and contraindications for recurrent laryngeal nerve repair. *Trans Pac Coast Oto-Ophthalm Soc.* 1969;50:354–357.

20. Berendes J, Miehlke A. Repair of recurrent laryngeal nerve and phonation: basic considerations and techniques. *Int Surg.* 1968;49:319–329.

21. Frazier CH. Treatment of recurrent laryngeal nerve paralysis by nerve anastomosis. *Surg Gynecol Obstet.* 1926;43:134–139.

22. Tucker HM. Reinnervation of the paralyzed larynx. A review. *Head Neck Surg.* 1979;1:235–242.

23. Tucker HM. Reinnervation of the unilaterally paralyzed larynx. *Ann Otol Rhinol Laryngol.* 1977;86:789–794.

24. Dedo HH. Recurrent laryngeal nerve section for spastic dysphonia. *Ann Otol Rhino Laryngol.* 1976;85:451–459.

25. Blitzer A, Brin MF, Fahn S, et al. Botulinum toxin (BOTOX) for the treatment of "spastic dysphonia" as part of a trial of toxin injection for the treatment of other cranial dystonias. *Laryngoscope.* 1986;96:1300–1301.

26. Ludlow CL, Naunton R, Bassich CJ. Effects of Botulinum toxin injection on speech in adductor spasmodic dysphonia. *Neurology.* 1988;38:1220–1225.

27. Asai R. Plastic surgery of the trachea and bronchus. *J Jap Bronchoesoph Soc.* 1963;14:69–72.

28. Singer MI, Blom ED. An endoscopic technique for restoration of voice after laryngectomy. *Ann Otol Rhinol Laryngol.* 1980;88:529–533.

29. Isshiki N, Morita H, Okamura H. Thyroplasty as a new phonsurgical technique. *Acta Otolaryngol.* 1974;78:451–457.

30. Isshiki N. *Phonosurgery—Theory and Practice.* Tokyo: Springer-Verlag; 1989.

31. Hirano M. Phonosurgery—basic and clinical investigations [in Japanese]. Berlin, Heidelberg, New York, London, Paris, Hong Kong. Official Report. 76th Annual Convention of the ORL Soc Japan. *Otologia* (Fukuoka). 1974;23:(suppl 1):239–442.

32. Saito S. Phonosurgery [in Japanese]. *Otologia* (Fukuoka). 1977;23(suppl 1):171–384.

33. LeJeune FE, Guice C, Samuels P. Early experiences with vocal ligament tightening. *Ann Otol Rhinol Laryngol.* 1983;92:475–477.

34. Sataloff R, Spiegel J, Carroll L, et al. Male soprano voice: a rare complication of thyroidectomy. *Laryngoscope.* 1992;102(1):90–93.

35. Conley JJ. Surgical techniques for the vocal rehabilitation of the postlaryngectomized patient. *Trans Am Acad Ophthalmol Otolaryngol.* 1969;73:288–299.

36. Kluyskens P, Ringoir S. A case of larynx homotransplantation in man. Proceedings IX. International Congress Otorhinolaryngology; 1969:302–305.

81

The History and Development of Phonomicrosurgery

Steven M. Zeitels

The development of phonomicrosurgery has been an evolutionary process that can be traced to the first attempts at mirror visualization of the larynx at the beginning of the 19th century.[1] Over the 50 years subsequent to Garcia's popularization of the technique (1855), the instrumentation and the procedures for indirect laryngoscopy were improved until mirror-guided surgical manipulation of the larynx became commonplace. The origin of the field of laryngology was facilitated by both laryngeal visualization and transoral laryngeal surgery.[2] Mirror laryngoscopy provided a means to both understand and treat vocal pathology. More importantly, laryngoscopy allowed for visually controlled surgical intervention for airway obstruction secondary to infectious membranous laryngeal disease, a formidable problem in the 19th and early 20th centuries. During the first 25 years of laryngology, trans-oral biopsies were often performed on lesions suspicious for cancer. The subsequent controversy surrounding the case of Crown Prince Frederick's laryngeal cancer (discussed below) in the late 19th century dissuaded many surgeons from performing biopsies of the larynx. From that case, myths were perpetuated suggesting that laryngeal biopsies would induce infection, malignant transformation, and metastasis. This view of the biopsy lasted until well into the 20th century. By the time these myths had been dispelled, direct surgical laryngoscopy had for the most part replaced indirect surgical laryngoscopy. Through the 20th century, a variety of technological developments improved direct examination of the larynx such as improved laryngoscopes, hand instruments, and lighting as well as the surgical microscope, the carbon dioxide laser, and general anesthesia. Through the last two decades, we have gained a greater understanding of the physiology underlying vocal fold oscillation. These principles have been joined with the technological developments of microlaryngeal surgery and have led to current concepts of phonomicrosurgery.

The Prelaryngology Era of Indirect Mirror Laryngoscopy

Bozzini (Fig 81–1) was the first individual (1807) to report on mirror visualization of the larynx.[1] He designed an ingenious handle (Fig 81–2) that housed a candle with a reflector as an artificial light source. A variety of specula could be attached to the universal handle for examining different body cavities, including one speculum that had a self-contained mirror for examining the larynx (Fig 81–2).[2] Bozzini's brilliant concept of employing an extracorporeal light source to illuminate internal body cavities is the guiding premise of all endoscopy.

Despite multiple descriptions of the use of mirror laryngoscopy during the subsequent 50 years, these reports had little influence on the practice of medicine at the time.[5-10] However, Babington's[6] glottiscope (Fig 81–3) and Avery's[10] laryngoscope (Fig 81–4) have attracted significant academic interest over the years. The former instrument was comprised of a mirror and a tongue spatula that retracted the tongue anteriorly. This introduced the concept of using internal distention for enhancing laryngeal exposure,[11] a concept that was further developed by Haslinger[12] in the 20th century. Avery's laryngoscope was composed of a speculum that was similar to Bozzini's and was used with artificial illumination, which was provided by a candle that was attached to a perforated concave head-mirror (a headlight).

Fig 81–1. Philipp Bozzini: self-portrait (1773–1809) From *Phillip Bozzini and Endoscopy in the 19th Century*, inside cover.

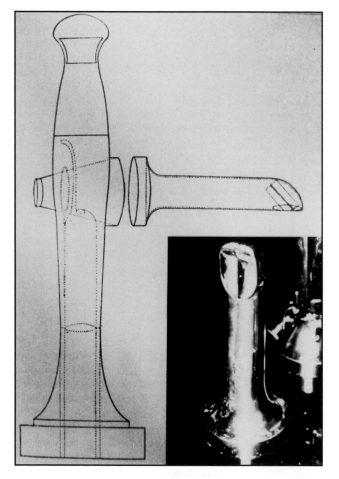

Fig 81–2. Bozzini's Lichtleiter (1807). (Courtesy of the American College of Surgeons)

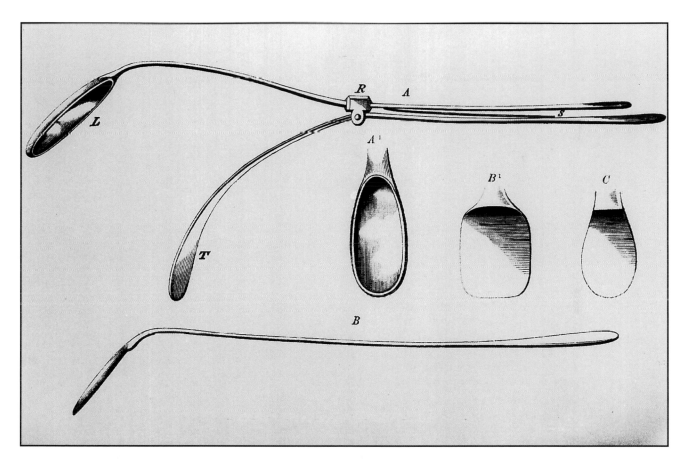

Fig 81–3. Benjamin Guy Babington's (1794–1866) glottiscope (1829). From Mackenzie[21]: *The Use of the Laryngoscope in Diseases of the Throat With an Appendix on Rhinoscopy*, p. 22.

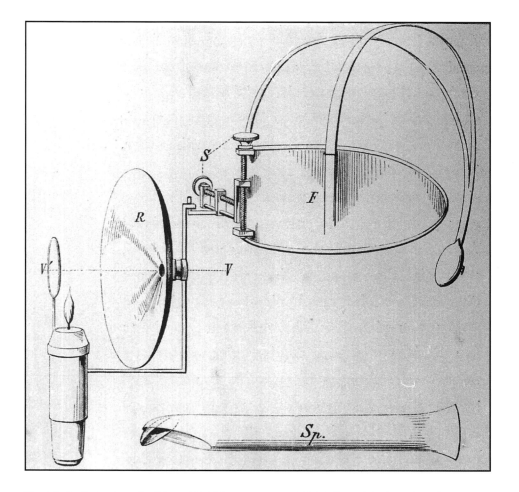

Fig 81–4. John Avery's (1807–1855) laryngoscope (1844) From Mackenzie. "The Use of the Laryngoscope in Diseases of the Throat With an Appendix on Rhinoscopy," p. 34.

In 1855, Manuel García (Fig 81–5), the renowned classic vocal pedagogist, presented his investigations with mirror autolaryngoscopy to the Royal Society of London. In that paper, "Observations on the Human Voice,"[13] García made substantive contributions toward the understanding of voice production. Medical historians have deduced that García was unaware of the previous descriptions of mirror laryngoscopy because of his limited medical background.[14,15] His independent discovery of mirror laryngoscopy stimulated new interest in the medical community in the application of this technique for the management of laryngeal disease. Unlike his medical predecessors, García primarily described what he learned about voice produc-

Fig 81–5. Manuel García (1805–1906) at the age of 100. Portrait by John Singer Sargent. (Courtesy of the Rhode Island School of Design)

tion from mirror laryngoscopy rather than emphasizing the instrumentation. It is believed that this was the key to the origin of laryngology.[15]

The Origin of Laryngology

Türck[16] was the first physician, subsequent to García's presentation, to adopt mirror laryngoscopy; however, he depended on sunlight for illumination. He became frustrated during the cloudy autumn in Budapest and abandoned the technique. Shortly thereafter, his colleague Czermak (Fig 81–6) borrowed the same mirrors, was more successful with their use, and reported those successes in 1858.[17,18] Czermak reintroduced the use of artificial light in conjunction with the fenestrated concave mirror (initially stabilized between his teeth), which greatly facilitated the technique. Türck also resumed his investigations. Ultimately, a rivalry developed between the two about who should receive academic recognition for introducing the broad application of mirror laryngoscopy to the mainstream of Western medicine. The rivalry created a great deal of

attention both in and out of the medical community, which helped stimulate interest in the fledgling field of laryngology. Czermak is recognized by most as the one most influential in fostering mirror laryngoscopy and the field of laryngology to the medical community because of the innovations (artificial light and the fenestrated mirror) he introduced.[15]

The ability to see the larynx well was catalytic for making transoral mirror-guided surgical manipulation[19] reliable and effective. Lewin[20] reported on the transoral management of 50 tumors in 1861. In addition to obtaining tissue for biopsy purposes, he excised three neoplasms and applied caustics to four. Mackenzie (Fig 81–7), in Britain,[21–23] and Elsberg (Fig 81–8), in America,[24,25] were key figures in improving laryngoscopic surgery and disseminating the techniques through their teachings.[26] In the United States, Elsberg and later Solis-Cohen (Fig 81–9) expended great effort as educators of laryngoscopy and laryngology, and they became the first and second presi-

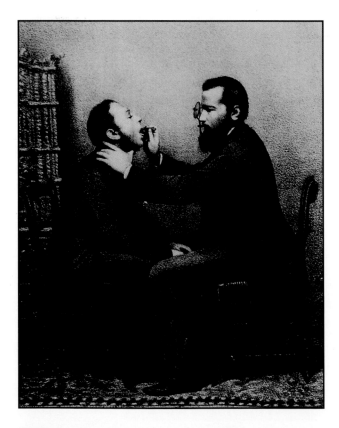

Fig 81–6. Johann Nepomuk Czermak (1828–1873) examining a patient. From *Der Kehlkopfspeigel und siene Verwerthung fur Physiologia und Medizin*. Inside cover.

Fig 81–7. Sir Morell Mackenzie (1837–1892). (Courtesy of the Francis Countway Medical Library: Harvard Medical School)

Fig 81–8. Louis Elsberg (1837–1885), first president of the American Laryngological Association. (Reprinted with permission from *Ann Otol Rhinol Laryngol.* 15:883.)

Fig 81–9. Jacob Solis-Cohen, second president of the American Laryngological Association. (Courtesy of the Mutter Medical Museum)

dents of the American Laryngological Association.[15,26–28]

Solis-Cohen who served as a general surgeon for the Union in both the army and navy during the US Civil War, was probably the first surgeon to adopt laryngology as a profession.[29] This educational model became the paradigm by which otolaryngologists are trained today. Therefore, Solis-Cohen became the first specialized head and neck surgeon in the US and possibly anywhere. Soon thereafter, he authored the definitive textbook of laryngology and head and neck surgery.[30]

Solis-Cohen is probably the first individual to cure larynx cancer, which was done by means of a hemilaryngectomy on a University of Pennsylvania's professor's son.[31] Another important contribution was his method of reconstruction of the total laryngectomy defect, in which he sutured the trachea to the neck skin, thereby separating the trachea from the pharyngo-esophagus.[32] This greatly enhanced the viability of total laryngectomy as a reliable procedure and paved the way for his description of pharyngoesophageal speech.

Transoral Management of Larynx Cancer and Crown Prince Frederick

Fraenkel (Fig 81–10), in Germany, was the first to report (1886) on the successful transoral resection of a vocal fold cancer.[33] In that article, he described performing multiple transoral excisions of recurrences in the larynx and also doing a modified neck dissection, which included the removal of a 5-cm segment of the internal jugular vein. At the time of Fraenkel's publication, more than 5 years had passed since the patient first presented with his cancer and 2 years had elapsed without a recurrence.

In that paper, Fraenkel delineated several of the current principles of laryngoscopic management of early vocal-fold cancer. He noted that early vocal fold cancer is likely to arise on the superior vocal fold surface, to be small in volume, and to cause hoarseness with only minimal changes of the epithelium. The fortuitous origin of these lesions on the superior surface of the musculomembranous vocal fold makes them easily visible during laryngoscopy. Invasion at this location frequently spared the anterior commissure and

Fig 81–10. Bernhard Fraenkel (1836–1911). (Reprinted with permission from *Ann Otol Rhinol Laryngol*. 15:606.)

the arytenoid and, therefore, facilitated endoscopic excision. Subsequent to this publication, there were other isolated reports of the transoral removal of laryngeal cancer for cure[34–37]; however, this approach did not gain significant support.

Shortly after the presentation of Fraenkel's innovative work, Crown Prince Frederick of Germany developed hoarseness, and after an initial examination, it was suspected that he had larynx cancer. The Prince's primary physician, insisted that there be a consulting laryngologist for the primary management. Remarkably, Fraenkel was practicing in Berlin, but Mackenzie was selected to be the consultant due in part to his extensive writing on laryngology.[38] Thus, the English laryngologist was summoned to Germany.[39]

Based on his mirror examination, Mackenzie transorally biopsied abnormal vocal fold tissue three times during four attempts in 5 weeks.[39] Virchow evaluated the specimens but could not establish the diagnosis of cancer.[38,39] Therefore, Mackenzie was not in favor of having the Prince undergo the perilous procedure of laryngectomy unless cancer could be documented in

the specimens. Mackenzie held to this opinion despite the urging of the Prince's surgeons that he undergo the operation. The Prince had chosen Mackenzie as his primary consultant and, therefore, refused to have the laryngectomy. Ultimately, the Prince developed airway obstruction secondary to the progressive growth of the clinically suspected, but pathologically undiagnosed, subglottic cancer. After a tracheotomy and further biopsies, the cancer diagnosis was established by Waldeyer.[40]

There were some who felt that Virchow had purposely misdiagnosed the cancer because he was aware of Van Bergman's (the Prince's surgeon) abysmal survival statistics with total laryngectomy,[41,42] which he had performed on seven prior occasions. The Prince did reign as the Emperor (Kaiser) for 3 months before succumbing to the disease. Had he undergone the laryngectomy, it is likely that he would not have lived to become the Kaiser (Caesar).

A more likely thesis is that Virchow simply erred in the diagnosis.[43] Despite creating surgical pathology, Virchow believed that cancer arose from connective tissue and invaded toward the surface to create a mucosal irregularity. Contrary to this thesis, Waldeyer formulated the epithelial theory of carcinoma, which suggests that cancer evolves in the surface and invades into deep tissues. Waldeyer's concept is the foundation for the current theory of mucosal carcinogenesis and because of this he had little difficulty diagnosing cancer.[43] Review of Virchow's detailed written descriptions of the specimens that he had observed histologically from the original biopsies reveals that his descriptions are consistent with the diagnosis of cancer.

Apart from the personal and political tragedies that evolved from this unfortunate case, a damaging oncological thesis evolved. Many believed that the Prince's cancer was precipitated by Mackenzie's biopsies. This idea, in conjunction with the international media attention attracted by the case, generated additional academic support for the thesis that a laryngeal biopsy could induce cancer (Brown, 1878[40]; Solis-Cohen, 1881[202]) and gave rise to an exaggerated cancer phobia in many parts of the world. This concept could be extrapolated to other sites in the body.

Semon realized that the fear of transoral surgical manipulation would damage and potentially cripple the young field of laryngology. He reported on an exhaustive series of over 10,000 mirror-documented cases of laryngeal lesions.[44,45] There were two groups. In one group, about 8,000 underwent biopsy with histopathologically benign pathology and cancer was ultimately diagnosed in 0.40% of the patients. In the other group, about 2,500 were observed without surgical manipulation and 0.47% of the group developed cancer. Thus, there was no significant difference in the development of cancer between the two groups. This study was extremely helpful in clearing Mackenzie's reputation and securing the practice of laryngology for the future.

Despite the evidence in Semon's article, the controversy concerning the danger of the laryngeal biopsy persisted throughout the 19th century. Strong support for performing laryngeal biopsies to obtain a histopathological diagnosis came from Butlin,[46] Fraenkel,[47] and Chiari,[48] as well as from Solis-Cohen,[49] who had previously expressed reservations about this approach. Nevertheless, misconceptions continued into the 20th century that suggested that the laryngeal biopsy would induce infection at the biopsy site, malignant transformation of benign tissue, acceleration of cancer growth, and both regional and distant metastases. Mackenzie,[50,51] an American, was vehemently against the laryngeal biopsy and suggested that naked-eye-mirror diagnosis should be followed by open cervical laryngectomy. While this position was supported by Moore[52] and Mackenty[53] well into the 1920s, it did not take into account Delevan's work[54] which indicated that infectious diseases such as tuberculosis and syphilis could mimic carcinoma. Over time, based upon diligent work by leaders such as Jackson (Fig 81–11),[55] the myths surrounding the dangers of laryngeal biopsy were dispelled. This was critical to the 20th century development of both laryngology and direct surgical laryngoscopy.

Fig 81–11. Chevalier Jackson (1865–1958). (Courtesy of the Mutter Medical Museum)

The Era of Direct Surgical Laryngoscopy

The transoral techniques used today for the management of the vocal fold evolved from the improvements that were made in direct surgical laryngoscopy. The first report of direct visualization of the laryngeal introitus was made by Horace Green (Fig 81–12) in 1852.[56] He accomplished this by means of a bent tongue spatula (similar to an intubation spatula-blade laryngoscope) and sunlight. In his textbook entitled, *On the Surgical Treatment of Polypi of the Larynx, and Oedema of the Glottis*, Green described the visually-controlled transoral excision of a polypoid mass from the ventricle region of an 11-year-old girl. The favorable elevated position that is characteristic of a child's larynx greatly facilitated the endoscopic excision of this laryngeal mass. Neither this work, nor his reports of transoral application of caustics[57,58] to alleviate airway obstructive symptoms, were considered credible at the time of their presentation.[15,27,59] However, toward the end of Green's career, his work was broadly acknowledged.[27] Seemingly unaware of Green's writings, Brünings, in his comprehensive textbook on rigid endoscopy, substantiated the concept that a bent tongue spatula could provide direct exposure of the larynx.[60]

Fig 81–12. Horace Green (1802–1866), the father of American laryngology. (Courtesy of the American Laryngological Association)

It was not until 1895, when Kirstein (Fig 81–13) rediscovered direct examination of the larynx,[61,62] that the modern era of direct surgical laryngoscopy began. Kirstein described both tubular and spatula laryngoscopy; and all current laryngoscopes are derivatives of one of those designs. Kirstein's success with the technique was facilitated by his use of the optimal head and neck position for laryngeal exposure,[63] his laryngoscope designs, and his use of artificial illumination in the form of a headlight. Unlike Green's earlier frustrating attempts at disseminating his technique, the widespread 20th-century adoption of direct laryngoscopy resulted from Kirstein's success in an era when interest was intense in the fledgling field of laryngology.

The primary principles for achieving and maintaining complete laryngeal exposure were developed during the 25-year period subsequent to Kirstein's presentation of direct laryngoscopy.[11] These principles for exposure made effective transoral resection of laryngeal cancer possible. The key reports underlying the development of these principles were that: (1) Boyce and Jackson adapted Kirstein's head and neck position for laryngeal exposure (Fig 81–14) from sitting-direct laryngoscopy to supine-direct laryngoscopy[63-65]; (2) Brünings (Fig 81–15) introduced the concept of external laryngeal counter-pressure[66,67]; (3) Haslinger[12] described internal laryngeal distention by means of a bivalved speculum; (4) Killian (Fig 81–16) introduced the "inverted-V" spatula blade to accommodate the anterior glottal commissure[67] and later joined this spatula to his suspension gallows, which freed the surgeon's hands for bimanual laryngoscopic surgery.[68-71]

Killian's elaborate suspension gallows (Fig 81–16) was an outgrowth of his 1909 cadaver studies, at the Third International Laryngo-Rhinological Congress in 1911. His experiments in laryngeal suspension were initially performed to stabilize the larynx for anatomical illustration. In Jackson's monumental textbook, *Peroral Endoscopy and Laryngeal Surgery*,[63] the only chapter not written by him was "Suspension Laryngoscopy," which was authored by Killian. Observation of Killian working with his suspension gallows reveals that the

Fig 81–13. Alfred Kirstein (1863–1922). (Reprinted with permission from C. Jackson. *Peroral Endoscopy and Laryngeal Surgery*, p. 82, the Laryngoscope Corp.)

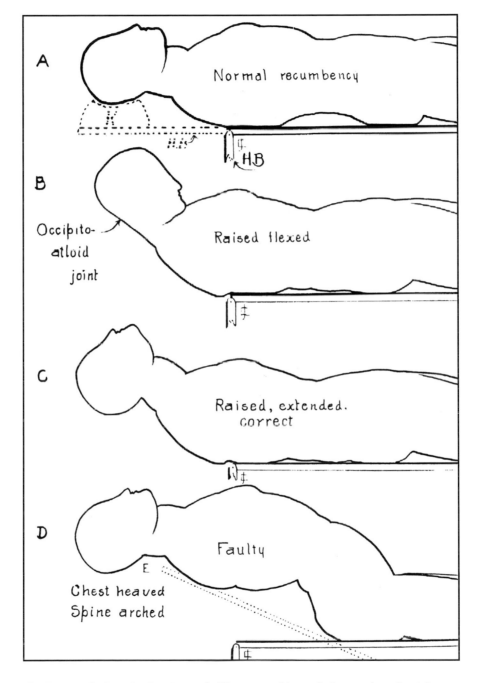

Fig 81–14. Jackson's drawings of different positions during supine direct laryngoscopy. (Reprinted from Jackson C, Jackson CW. *Bronchoscopy, Esophagoscopy, and Gastroscopy,* p. 90.)

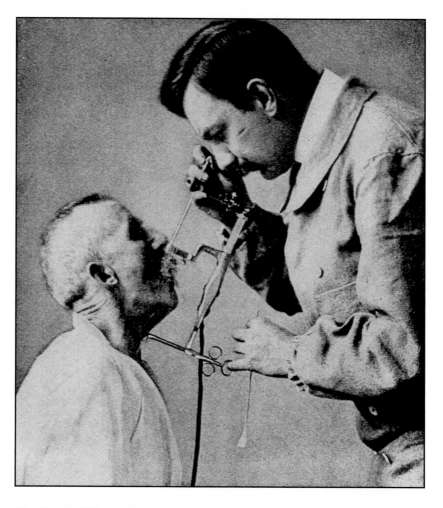

Fig 81–15. Wilhelm Brünings (1876-1958) (Reprinted from Brünings. *Direct Laryngoscopy, Bronchoscopy, and Esophagoscopy*, p. 121.)

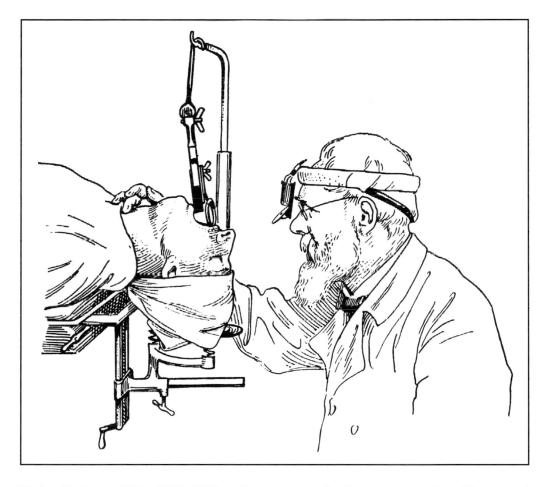

Fig 81–16. Gustav Killian (1860–1921) performing suspension laryngoscopy and applying manual external counter-pressure. (From Killian[70]: *Die Schwebelaryngoscopie und ihre praktishe*, p. 44.)

patient is not in the Boyce-Jackson position but rather in a head-hanging extension position (Figs 81–16 and 81–17). There was often inadequate anterior glottal exposure with the extended neck position during suspension laryngoscopy. Although exposure was improved by using Brüning's[66] extrinsic *counter-pressor* devices to compress the lower larynx (Fig 81–17), suspension devices that freed the surgeon's hands did not reliably expose the entire musculo-membranous vocal fold.

Jackson must not have been in favor of this technique[72] because there is little recognition or discussion of suspension devices or laryngoscope holders in his later textbooks.[73,74] It is unclear from his writings why Jackson did not build a device that would stabilize the laryngoscope in the head and neck position that he utilized. Suspension laryngoscopy done in the extended position often did not provide complete glottal exposure, but without a suspension device and two-handed tissue manipulation, successful excision of

vocal fold neoplasms was not possible. Presumably, it was because of this set of conditions that Jackson did not pursue endoscopic excision of vocal fold cancer.

Lynch[75–77] furthered Killian's techniques of bimanual transoral laryngeal surgery and reported the first transoral *en block* excisions of vocal fold cancer in 1915. He designed a suspension laryngoscope system that was a modification of Killian's. Although the modifications made it popular among some surgeons in this country, there were disadvantages to both suspension laryngoscope systems. General anesthesia was not used during laryngoscopic surgery and therefore mandated a high level of skill by the surgeon and the anesthesiologist. Also, the suspension laryngoscopes did not have self-contained illumination.

Around 1920, in an effort to overcome the difficulty in performing suspension laryngoscopy, Seiffert, a disciple of Killian, introduced the chest-support system (Fig 81–18). Seiffert altered Killian's spatula suspension-laryngoscope by rotating the distal arm,

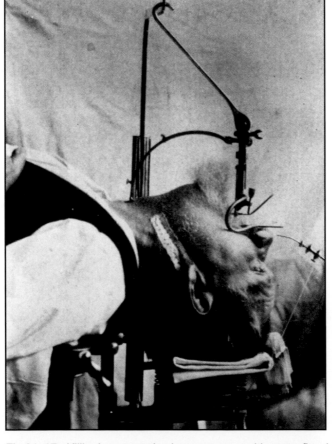

Fig 81–17. Killian's suspension laryngoscope with a retrofitted external counterpressure designed by his disciple, Brünings. (Reprinted with permission from Jackson C. *Peroral Endoscopy and Laryngeal Surgery*, p. 153. The Laryngoscope Corp.)

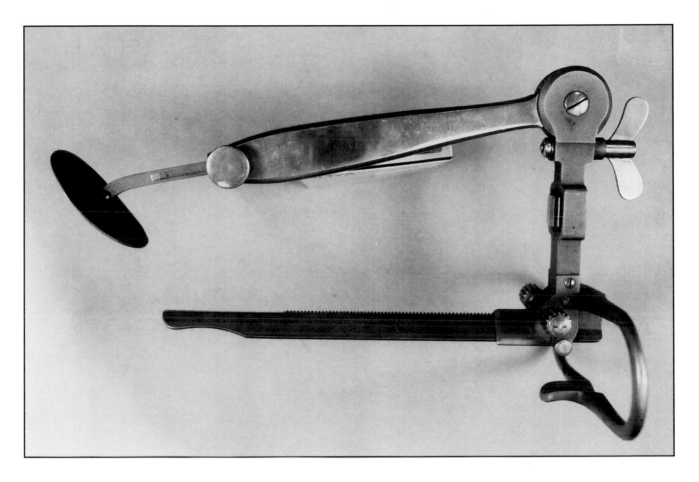

Fig 81–18. Seiffert's fulcrum chest-support spatula laryngoscope. (Courtesy of the Massachusetts Eye and Ear Infirmary)

which initially hung on the gallows, until it was resting on the chest. This modification fundamentally transformed the suspension laryngoscope into a lever laryngoscope-holder that exerted a torsion force on the upper teeth. Roberts[78, 79] further modified this instrument and thoughtfully designed special pillows to support the head in the Jackson position.

Jackson did not employ extrinsic devices to maintain his tubed laryngoscopes. King,[80] Sommers,[81] and Lewy,[82] in the 1950s, designed holders (stabilizers) for Jackson-style laryngoscopes. They were constructed to follow the chest-support fulcrum principle. Little attention was given to laryngoscopic head position. These devices employ a stable platform (chest wall or Mayo stand), an extension arm that creates a lever, and a fulcrum in which a torsional force is exerted to the maxilla, resulting in undesirable head and neck extension.[83]

Fulcrum laryngoscope-holders can precipitate iatrogenic injury because these devices produce extension forces on the neck. Cervical spine injury may occur in patients in whom degenerative kyphotic cervical fusion has occurred from osteoporosis.[84] Additionally,

the surgeon is less aware of the force being generated and less sensitive to the resistance of a particular position because of the device's gear-power advantage. In the 1950s,[85] further departure from Jackson's laryngoscopic principles was precipitated by the popularization of general endotracheal anesthesia with paralyzing agents. There was less need for orthodox laryngoscopic technique because of the use of small-lumened monocular laryngoscopes and the anesthetically induced increase in muscular compliance made possible by the neuromuscular paralyzing agents.

In 1971, Thomas[86] modified the Lewy laryngoscope holder by attaching it to a telescoping arm and an inverted U-shaped frame. His apparatus allowed for true mechanical laryngoscope stabilization in the Boyce-Jackson position. This position, where the head and neck are actually lifted off the table, will be referred to as elevated-vector suspension (Fig 81–19) to distinguish it from Killian's head-hanging extension suspension (Figs 81–16, 81–17). In 1975, as a modification of the Killian gallows, Grundfast and the Boston University group[87] developed an apparatus (Pilling Co) that also provided elevated-vector suspension

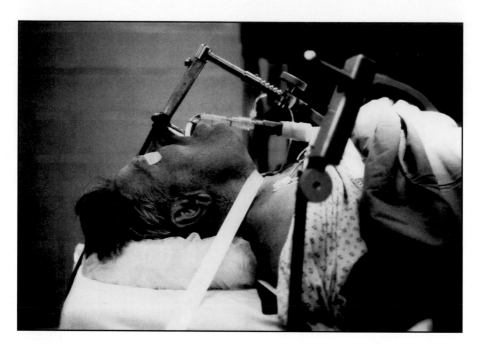

Fig 81–19. Elevated-vector suspension with the Boston University gallows and external laryngeal counterpressure facilitated by silk adhesive tape. (Courtesy of the *Annals of Otology, Rhinology and Laryngology.* 103:106)

(Fig 81–19). The classical tubed laryngoscopes were fitted with extended handles to allow application of a force equal and opposite to that needed to expose the glottis; this eliminated rotation (levers) and worked in varied head and neck positions. The suspension gallows employed a simple window crank for its works. Zeitels designed a mechanically stronger and more versatile laryngeal suspension gallows, which has caused many surgeons to reexamine the value and asssets of a true suspension system.[88]

Microlaryngoscopy

Microlaryngoscopy arose from the need and desire to perform more precise vocal fold surgery. In the early 1950s, Albrecht[89] used a colposcope for magnified indirect vocal fold examination and for photo-documentation of keratosis. The first report on suspension microlaryngoscopy was made by Scalco et al in 1960.[90] The microscope provided both a magnified stereoscopic surgical field and improved illumination that fostered a new era in precision vocal fold surgery.

In 1962, Jako (Fig 81–20) (personal communication) performed microlaryngoscopy (using a 200-mm lens) with both a monocular tubed laryngoscope and general endotracheal anesthesia. Later that year, to accompany the requirements of a magnified surgical field, Jako,

working with the Stuemer Company (in Germany), developed the first set of microlaryngeal hand-held instruments; they were otologic instruments with long handles. In 1963, he (personal communication) designed a wide lumened microlaryngoscope (Pilling Co) to enable stereoscopic visualization.[91,92] Jako also perfected microlaryngoscopic surgery with general endotracheal anesthesia. The accompanying paralysis stabilized the operative field and improved precision. During that same period, Kleinsasser[93,94] reported stereoscopic microlaryngoscopy. Soon thereafter, the Zeiss Company developed a 400-mm lens for him to facilitate the introduction of hand instrumentation into the proximal lumen of the laryngoscope.[95] After the first decade of microlaryngoscopy, DeSanto et al[96] and Strong[97] provided a review and appraisal of the American experience.

Finally, in the early 1970s, Jako,[98] Strong,[99] and Vaughan,[100] introduced the laser (Fig 81–21) to laryngology and surgical oncology.[101,102] The laser was coupled to the surgical microscope and provided precise hemostatic cutting. The delivery system consisted of a micromanipulator and a foot pedal, which also improved precision. Many surgeons had difficulty performing bimanual long-distance vocal fold surgery under high magnification, especially with their nondominant hand.[103] Therefore, the laser provided precise, stable cutting to enhance cold instruments in the contralateral hand.

Fig 81–20. Geza Jako.

Fig 81–21. The original carbon dioxide laser. (Courtesy of *Laryngoscope*. 105(suppl 67):10.)

The Body-Cover Theory of Voice Production

While a complete developmental history of voice production theory is beyond the scope of this chapter, the important contributions to body-cover mucosal wave theory that have influenced phonomicrosurgical concepts are reviewed.

The body-cover mucosal-wave theory of voice production was introduced by Bishop[104] in 1836 in his publication, "Experimental Researches into the Physiology of the Human Voice." He stated, "The true vibrating surface of the glottis is the mucous membrane. The vocal cords confer on it the tension, resistance, position, and probably other conditions necessary for vibration." This outstanding and insightful contribution was made without the use of the mirror laryngoscope or the stroboscope; he was, therefore, unable to see the moving glottis.

In 1866, in his comprehensive textbook on voice, Fournie also concluded that the vocal fold mucosa was the major component of the glottal vibration. "The voice is a sound produced by a particular reed having walls modifiable under the influence of muscular action; the vibrating part being furnished by the mucous fold which limits the borders of the glottis. The vibrations are occasioned by the passage of air through the glottis … For the membranes to vibrate, one tenses them on a frame like the skin of a drum, and they will emit their vibrations transmitting them through the air. They produce a more high pitch shrill sound according to how small and how taut they are."[105]

Hirano[106,107] further developed the body-cover theory of voice production by assimilating information from stroboscopy, gross anatomical evaluations, and his elegant scanning electron-microscopic evaluation of the vocal fold's layered anatomy. These studies of the microanatomy of the vocal fold reveal that there is a cover (epithelium, superficial lamina propria), a transition zone (vocal ligament: medial lamina propria and deep lamina propria), and a body (muscle). The superficial lamina propria is composed of an amorphous substance with few fibroblasts and allows for maximal epithelial pliability for transmission of a vibrational wave.[108] It abates anteriorly as the vocal ligament and mucosa fuse with the anterior commissure tendon, and it disappears posteriorly as the vocal ligament and mucosa join the vocal process of the arytenoid. The medial lamina propria is composed primarily of elastic fibers and the deep lamina propria is composed primarily of collagen fibers. Fibroblasts are more prevalent in the medial and deep lamina propria; as a result, there is concern that there may be excessive scarring of the vocal fold mucosa to these layers when they are surgically disturbed.

Aerodynamic principles of the mucosal wave theory were discussed by Garcia in 1855. From his experiments in laryngoscopy, he described the rhythmic release of air by the vocal folds into the supraglottal vocal tract. "The voice is formed by the periodical compressions and dilations which the air experiences when, on reaching the glottis, the latter, by alternate and regular movements, stops or permits its exit."[13]

The visualization of the oscillating vocal fold was facilitated by the laryngeal stroboscope and was first reported by Oertel[109] in 1878. However, he desribed the perfected instrument with the use of electricity in 1895.[110] In essence, a motorized perforated pin-wheel disc (Fig 81–22) was placed between the artificial light source and the examiner's head mirror. Varying the speed of revolution of the disc allowed for rhythmic interruption of the light that was transmitted from the head mirror to the laryngeal mirror. This provided the effect of slow-motion visualization of the vocal fold.

The device initially did not gain popularity or acceptance for several reasons[111]: (1) it was necessary to train the patient to duplicate and maintain a specific pitch that was coordinated with the speed of the rotating disk; (2) the disk needed to be changed for each frequency; and (3) the device generated considerable objectionable background noise. Also, whereas in Europe, speech and voice science were frequently within otolaryngology departments, in North America, these disciplines were independent and had only limited collaboration with each other.[112] As a result, few laryngostroboscopic investigations[111–118] were done in North America throughout much of the 20th century. The increase in the number of American multidisciplinary voice and laryngological studies suggests that this trend has changed.

Phonomicrosurgery: Current Concepts

Phonomicrosurgery reflects the convergence of theories that guide endoscopic vocal fold surgery with theories that explain voice production (body-cover mucosal-wave theory).[119] The underlying premise of this surgical approach is that optimal postoperative voice, which is observed as a pliable vocal fold cover, will be achieved if there is maximal preservation of the vocal fold's layered microstructure (laminae propria).[120–121]

Phonomicrosurgery is improved by safely placing the *largest* well-designed glottiscope that can be admitted from the lips to the vocal folds to provide the widest exposure of the vocal fold surgical field.[120,122-125] This should be supported by a device that will maintain the patient in Boyce-Jackson position by employing *elevated-vector suspension*.[88,126,127] The improved exposure of the operative site allows for better exposure of the lesion as well as more room to retract tissue by angulation of the hand instruments. This improved exposure, along with higher magnification and finer hand instruments[114] (such as those designed by Shapshay, Healy [K. Storz Co.] and Bouchayer [Instramentarium Co], has enhanced the precision of present phonomicrosurgical techniques.

Precision has also been improved by the technique of infusing saline and epinephrine into the superficial lamina propria (SLP) of the vocal fold.[127-130] It did so in a number of ways including vasoconstricting the microvasculature in the SLP, which improved visualization during cold-instrument tangential dissection. The technique was based on experiments by Hajek,[131] Reinke,[132,133] and Pressman.[134,135] Zeitels and coworkers have demonstrated that by using the subepithelial infusion technique, atypical vocal fold epithelium and selected early cancers can be resected transorally and that the patient will have a normal postoperative voice at conversational levels as analyzed by objective acoustic and aerodynamic measures.[136]

Today, the laryngologist must select from a variety of instrumentation to achieve the optimal surgical result. Controversy about the merits of using the carbon

Fig 81–22. Oertel's laryngostroboscope.[109] (From *Archiv für Laryngologie und Rhinologie*. 3: Tafel II)

dioxide (CO_2) laser during microlaryngoscopic surgery has arisen because of concerns about the potentially harmful effects of laser use on the delicate vocal fold microstructure. Injudicious use of the laser can lead to thermal trauma of the superficial lamina propria, resulting in vocal fold epithelium that is adherent to the vocal ligament. This leads to a stiff vocal system and disordered voice production.[126,136] The rationale to use cold instruments alone or to use the CO_2 laser in conjunction with cold instrument use is based upon which approach allows for the greatest surgical precision. For smaller lesions, this is best accomplished with cold instruments alone. The CO_2 laser facilitates hemostatic surgical dissection for selected larger glottal lesions in which bleeding would obscure visualization of the microanatomy of the musculomembranous vocal fold. Instrument selection will vary because of the surgeon's familiarity and preference, the availability of instrumentation, and the type of lesion to be resected. Typically, cold instruments alone are better suited to resect superficial and/or smaller vocal fold lesions. The CO_2 laser facilitates the use of cold instruments when resecting larger and more vascular lesions of the glottis.

The 585 nm pulsed-dye laser is capable of selective photoangiolysis of the vocal fold microcirculation. This selectivity limits trauma and fibrosis to the delicate superficial lamina propria and has made it an ideal laser to treat a variety of vocal fold lesions.[138-140]

Conclusion

Phonomicrosurgery is fundamentally rooted in the historical development of improved visualization and surgical manipulation of the vocal folds. All substantive innovations in the techniques led to improved precision. More recently, improved understanding of the physiological principles of voice production among surgeons has led to a convergence of surgical technique theory with concepts of vocal fold oscillation. The ongoing development of improved phonomicrosurgical procedures will be driven by this interdependence.

References

1. Zeitels SM. *Atlas of Phonomicrosurgery and Other Endolaryngeal Procedures for Benign and Malignant Disease.* San Diego, Calif: Singular Thomson Learning; 2001:xi–xii.
2. Zeitels SM. *Atlas of Phonomicrosurgery and Other Endolaryngeal Procedures for Benign and Malignant Disease.* San Diego, Calif: Singular Thomson Learning; 2001:1–14.
3. Bozzini P. *Der Lichtleiter oder Beschreibung einer einfachen Vorichtung, und ihrer Anwendung zur Eleuchtung innerer Hohlen, und Zwischenräume des lebenden animaschen Körpers.* Weimar, Germany: 1807.
4. Reuter HJ, Reuter MA. *Philipp Bozzini and Endoscopy in the 19th Century.* Stuttgart, Germany: 1988. Max Nitze Museum.
5. Senn. Cited by Mackenzie. The use of the laryngoscope in diseases of the throat. *Jour de Progres.* 1829: 11.
6. Babington BG. *London Medical Gazette.* 1829; 3:555.
7. Selligue. Cited by Mackenzie in The use of the laryngoscope in diseases of the throat. *Journal L'Institut.* 1832: 17.
8. Liston R. *Practical Surgery.* London, England: J & A Churchill: 1837.
9. Baumes. Compte Rendu des Travaux de la Societé de Medecine de Lyons. 19:18, 1836–1838.
10. Avery. Cited by Mackenzie. The use of the laryngoscope in diseases of the Throat. *Jour de Progres.* 1844: 25
11. Zeitels SM, Vaughan CW. "External Counter-Pressure" and "Internal Distension" for Optimal Laryngoscopic Exposure of the Anterior Glottal Commissure. *Ann Otol Rhinol Laryngol.* 1994;103:669–675.
12. Israel S. The directoscope of Haslinger in diagnosis and surgery of the larynx. *Laryngoscope.* 1923;33:945–948.
13. Garcia M. Observations on the human voice. *Proc Royal Soc London.* 1855;7:397–410.
14. Wright J. The laryngoscope: Manuel Garcia. In: *A History of Laryngology and Rhinology.* 2nd ed. Philadelphia: Lea & Febiger; 1914:207.
15. Clerf LH. Manuel Garcia's contribution to laryngology. *Bull NY Acad Med.* 1956;32:603–611.
16. Turck L. On the laryngeal mirror and its mode of employment, with engravings on wood. *Zeitschrift der Gesellschaft der Aerzte ze Wein.* 1858;26:401–409.
17. Czermak JN. Über den Kehlkopfspiegel. *Wiener Med. Wochenschrift.* 1858;8:196-198.
18. Czermak JN. On the laryngoscope and its employment in physiology and medicine. *New Sydenham Society,* 1861;11:1–79.
19. Stoerk C. On the layrngoscope. *Zeitschrift der Gesellschaft der Aerzte ze Wein.* 1859;46:721–727.
20. Lewin G. *Allgemeine Medicinische Zentral-Zeitung.* 1861; 30:654.
21. Mackenzie M. *The Use of the Laryngoscope in Diseases of the Throat with an Appendix on Rhinoscopy.* London: J & A Churchill; 1865.
22. Mackenzie M. *Growths in the Larynx.* London: J & A Churchill; 1871.
23. Mackenzie M. The laryngoscope and its accessory apparatus; laryngoscopy; autolaryngoscopy; infra-glottic laryngoscopy; the laryngoscope image; laryngeal instruments; dilators of the larynx. In: *Diseases of the Pharynx, Larynx, and Trachea.* New York: William Wood & Ct; 1880:158–195.
24. Elsberg L. *Laryngoscopal Medication or the Local Treatment of theDiseases of the Throat, Larynx, and Neighboring Organs, Under sight.* New York:William Wood & Co; 1864.

25. Elsberg L. *Laryngoscopal Surgery Illustrated in the Treatment of Morbid Growths within the Larynx.* Philadelphia: Collins; 1866.

26. Elsberg L. President's Address: Laryngological Instruction. *Trans Am Laryng Assn.* 1880;2:4–8.

27. Elsberg L. President's address: Laryngology in America. *Trans Am Laryngol Assn.* 1879;1:30–90.

28. Solis-Cohen J. President's address. *Trans Am Laryngol Assn.* 1881;3:2–4.

29. Zeitels SM. Jacob DaSilva Solis-Cohen: America's first head and neck surgeon. *Head Neck.* 1997;19:342–346.

30. Solis-Cohen J. *Diseases of the Throat: A Guide to the Diagnosis and Treatment.* New York, NY: William Wood; 1872.

31. Solis-Cohen J. Clinical history of surgical affections of the larynx. *The Medical Record.* 1869;4:244–247.

32. Solis-Cohen J. Pharyngeal voice: illustrated by presentation of a patient who phonates without a larynx and without the use of the lungs. *Trans Am Laryngol Assn.* 1893;15:114–116.

33. Fraenkel B. First healing of a laryngeal cancer taken out through the natural passages. *Archiv fur Klinische Chirurgie.* 1886;12:283–286.

34. Arslan A. Emorragia laringes. *Archivo Italiano.* 1901;11:390–411.

35. Ingals EF. Nonrecurrent carcinoma of the larynx removed from the natural passages. *Laryngoscope.* 1907;17:370–372.

36. Sendziac J. Treatment of cancer of the larynx. *NY Med J.* 1907;86:1042.

37. Thompson, SC. Intrinsic cancer of the larynx—complete excision apparently effected by the endo-laryngeal operation. *Trans Am Laryngol Assn.* 1914;36:34–44.

38. Gerhardt. Report of Dr. Gerhardt. In: *Case of Emperor Frederick III: Full Official Reports by the German Physicians and by Sir Morell Mackenzie.* New York: Edgar S Werner; New York: 1–16.

39. Mackenzie M. *The Fatal Illness of Frederick the Noble.* London: Sampson, Low, Marston, Searle and Rivington Ltd; 1888.

40. Waldeyer. Report of Dr. Waldeyer. In: *Case of Emperor Frederick III: Full Official Reports by the German Physicians and by Sir Morell Mackenzie.* New York:Edgar S Werner; 1888;72–75.

41. Delavan DB. A Consideration of the statistics of the operations for the relief of malignant disease of the larynx. *Trans Am Laryngol Assn,* 1900;22:66–74.

42. Delavan DB. A history of thyrotomy and laryngectomy. *Transactions of a Commemorative Meeting in the Honour of Dr. John Edmund Mackenty Held by the Section of Otolaryngology: The New York Academy of Medicine;* 1932.

43. Lin JI. Virchow's Pathological Reports on Frederick III's Cancer. *New Eng J Med.* 1984;311:1261–1264.

44. Semon F. Bezüglich des Überganges gutartiger Kehlkopf-Geschwülste i bosartige nach intralaryngealen Operationen. *Internationales Centralblatt für Laryngologie, Rhinologie.* 1888; 4(7):245–246.

45. Semon F. Die Frage des Überganges gutatiger Kehlkopf-Geschwülster in bosartige, speciell nach intralaryn-

gealen Operationen. *Internationales Centralblatt für Laryngologie, Rhinologie.* 1889; 4(6):271–279.

46. Butlin, HT. *Malignant Disease (Sarcoma and Carcinoma) of the Larynx.* London: J & A Churchill; 1883.

47. Fraenkel B. The anatomo pathologic diagnosis of cancer of the larynx. *Ann Otol Rhinol Laryngol.* 1900;9:276.

48. Chiari O. Contributions to the diagnosis and treatment of laryngeal cancer. *Ann Otol Rhinol Laryngol.* 1989;7:572–580, 1898.

49. Solis Cohen J. The surgical treatment of laryngeal cancer. *Trans Am Laryngol Assn.* 1900;22:75–87.

50. Mackenzie J. A plea for early naked-eye diagnosis and removal of the entire organ, with the neighboring area of possible lymphatic infection in cancer of the larynx. *Trans Am Laryngol Assn.* 1900;22:56–65.

51. Mackenzie J. Remarks of the macroscopic diagnosis and general indications for treatment of cancer of the larynx. *Ann Otol Rhinol Laryngol.* 1906;15:61–72.

52. Moore I. Diagnosis of intrinsic cancer of the larynx. In: *Intrinsic Cancer of the Larynx and the Operation of Laryngofissure.* London: University of London Press; 1921: 13–17.

53. Mackenty J. Laryngectomy for cancer, with remarks on seventy operated cases. *Trans Am Laryngol Assn.* 1922;44: 205–223.

54. Delevan DB. Recent advances in the treatment of malignant disease of the larynx. *Trans Am Laryngol Assn.* 1904; 26:150–170.

55. Jackson C, Jackson CL. A history of the laryngeal biopsy. In: *Cancer of the Larynx.* Philadelphia: WB Saunders; 1939:231–240.

56. Green H. Morbid growths within the larynx. In: *On the Surgical Treatment of Polypi of the Larynx, and Oedema of the Glottis.* New York: GP Putnam; 1852:56–65.

57. Green H. On the subject of the priority in the medication of the larynx and trachea. *Amer Med Monthly.* 1854; 1:241–257.

58. Green H. Report on the use and effect of applications of nitrate silver to the throat, either in local or general disease. *Trans Am Med Assn.* 1856;9:493–530.

59. Donaldson F. The laryngology of Trousseau and Horace Green. *Trans Am Med Assn.* 1890;12:10–18.

60. Brünings W. Direct laryngoscopy: criteria determining the applicability of autoscopy. In: *Direct Laryngoscopy, Bronchoscopy, and Esophagoscopy.* London:Bailliere, Tindall, Cox; 1912:93–95.

61. Kirstein A. Autoskopie des Larynx und der Trachea (Laryngoscopia directa, Euthyskopie, Besichtigung ohne Spiegel). *Archiv für Laryngologie und Rhinologie.* 1895;3:156–164.

62. Kirstein A. *Autoscopy of the Larynx and Trachea (Direct Examination Without Mirror).* Philadelphia, Pa: FA Davis Co; 1897.

63. Jackson C. Position of the patient for peroral endoscopy. In: *Peroral Endoscopy and Laryngeal Surgery.* St. Louis: Laryngoscope Co; 1915:77–88.

64. Boyce J W. Duties of the second assistant in endoscopy per OS. In: Jackson C, ed. *Tracheobronchoscopy, Esophagoscopy and Gastroscopy.* St. Louis, Mo: The Laryngoscope Co; 1907: 145–147.

65. Jackson C, Jackson CL. The early diagnosis of cancer of the larynx: position of the patient for direct laryngoscopy. In: *Cancer of the Larynx*. Philadelphia, Pa: WB Saunders; 1939:17–18.

66. Brunings W. Direct laryngoscopy: autoscopy by counter-pressure. In: *Direct Laryngoscopy, Bronchoscopy, and Esophagoscopy*. London: Bailliere, Tindall, & Cox; 1912: 110–115.

67. Killian G. Demonstration of an endoscopic spatula. *J Laryngol Rhinol*. 1910;25:549–550.

68. Killian G. Die Schwebelaryngoscopie. *Archiv fur Laryngologie und Rhinologie*. 1912;26:277–317.

69. Killian G. Suspension laryngoscopy. In: Jackson C, ed. *Peroral Endoscopy and Laryngeal Surgery*. St. Louis, Mo: Laryngoscope Co; 1915: 133–154.

70. Killian G. *Die Schwebelaryngoscopie und ihre praktische.* Wein, Germany: Schwarzenberg; 1920.

71. Killian G. Suspension laryngoscopy and its practical use. *J Laryngol Otol*. 1914; 24:337–360.

72. Hill W. Chevalier Jackson on per-oral endoscopy and laryngeal surgery. *J Laryngol Rhinol Otol*. 1916; 31:164–175. Book review.

73. Jackson C, Jackson CL. Chronic laryngitis, benign tumors of the larynx. In: *The Larynx and Its Diseases*. Philadelphia, Pa: WB Saunders; 1937: 136–151, 315–342.

74. Jackson C, Jackson CL. *Cancer of the Larynx*. Philadelphia, Pa: WB Saunders; 1939.

75. Lynch RC. Suspension laryngoscopy and its accomplishments. *Ann Otol Rhinol Laryngol*. 1915; 24:429–446.

76. Lynch RC. A resume of my years work with suspension laryngoscopy. 1912. 1916; 38:158–175.

77. Lynch RC. Intrinsic carcinoma of the larynx, with a second report of the cases operated on by suspension and dissection. *Trans Am Laryngol Assn*. 1920; 40:119–126.

78. Roberts SE, Forman FS. Direct laryngoscopy—a simplified technique with screw driven fulcrum lift. *Laryngoscope*. 1948; 57:245-256.

79. Roberts SE. A self retaining dual distal lighted laryngoscope with screw driven fulcrum lift. *Laryngoscope*. 1952; 62:215–221.

80. King, NE. Direct Laryngoscopy aided by a new laryngoscope "stabilizer." *Arch Otolaryngol*. 53:89–92.

81. Sommers KE. Direct laryngoscopy and description of a self-retaining attachment for the laryngoscope. *Arch Otolaryngol*. 1952; 55:484–488.

82. Lewy RE. Suspension fixation gear power laryngoscopy (with motion pictures). *Laryngoscope*. 1954; 64:693–695.

83. Vaughan CW. Vocal fold exposure in phonosurgery. *J Voice*. 1993; 7:189–194.

84. Netter FH. Osteoporosis. In: *The Ciba Collection of Medical Illustrations: Musculoskeletal System*. Summit, NJ: Ciba-Geigy Co; 1987; 216–227.

85. Priest RE. Controversial aspects of the treatment of laryngeal keratosis. *Laryngoscope*. 1958; 68:766–779.

86. Thomas GK. Suspension apparatus for laryngeal microsurgery. *Arch Otolaryngol*. 1971; 94:258–259.

87. Grundfast KM, Vaughan CW, Strong MS, De Vos P. Suspension microlaryngoscopy in the Boyce position with a new suspension gallows. *Ann Otol Rhinol Laryngol*. 1978; 87:560–566.

88. Zeitels SM, Mauri M, Burns JA, Dailey SH. Suspension laryngoscopy revisited. *Ann Otol Rhinol Laryngol*. 2004; 113:16–22.

89. Albrecht R. Über den Wert koloskopischer Untersuchungsmethoden bei Leukoplakien und Carcinomen des Mundes und Kehlkopfs. *Arch für Ohren Nasen Kehlkopfheilk*. 1954; 165:459–463.

90. Scalco, AN, Shipman, WF, Tabb, HG: Microscopic suspension laryngoscopy. *Ann Otol Rhinol & Laryngol*. 1960; 69:1134–1138.

91. Jako GJ. Laryngoscope for microscopic observation, surgery, and photography. *Arch Otolaryngol*. 1970; 91: 196–199.

92. Jako GJ. Laryngeal endoscopy and microlaryngoscopy. In: M Paparella, D Shumrick, eds. *Otolaryngology*. Philadelphia, Pa: WB Saunders; 1980: 2410–2430.

93. Kleinsasser O. Die Laryngomicroscope (Lupenlaryngoskopie) und ihre Bedeutung für die Erkennung der Vorerkrankungen und Frühformen des Stimmlipencarcinomas. *Arch für Ohren Nasen Kehlkopfheilk*. 1962: 724–727.

94. Kleinsasser O. Weitere technische Entwicklung und erste Ergebnisse der endolaryngealen Mikrochirurgie. *Z Laryng Rhinol*. 1965; 711–727.

95. Kleinsasser O. Development of microlaryngoscopy and endolaryngeal microsurgery. In: *Microlaryngoscopy und Endolaryngeal Microsurgery*. Baltimore, Md: University Park Press; 1978:3.

96. DeSanto LW, Carney FW. Microlaryngoscopic surgery. *Arch Otolaryngol*. 1970; 91:324–326.

97. Strong MS. Microscopic laryngoscopy: a review and appraisal. *Laryngoscope*. 1970; 80:1540–1552.

98. Jako GJ. Laser surgery of the vocal folds. *Laryngoscope*. 1972;82:2204–2205.

99. Strong MS, Jako GJ. Laser surgery of the larynx: early clinical experience with continuous CO2 laser. *Ann Otol Rhinol Laryngol*. 1972;81:791–798.

100. Vaughan CW. Transoral laryngeal surgery using the CO2 laser. Laboratory experiments and clinical experience. *Laryngoscope*. 1978;88:1399.

101. Vaughan CW, Strong MS, Jako GJ. Laryngeal carcinoma: transoral treatment using the CO2 laser. *Am J Surg*. 1978;136:490–493.

102. Strong MS. Laser excision of carcinoma of the larynx. *Laryngoscope*. 1975;85:1286–1278,

103. Zeitels SM. Laser excision of carcinoma of the larynx. *Laryngoscope*. 1975;85:1286–1289.

104. Bishop J. Experimental researches into the physiology of the human voice. *London & Edinburgh Philosophical Magazine and Journal of Science*; 1836.

105. Fournie E. *Physiologie de la Voix et de la Parole*. Paris: Adrien Delahaye; 1866.

106. Hirano M. Phonosurgery: basic and clinical investigations. *Otologia (Fukuoka)*. 1975; 21:239–442.

107. Hirano M. Structure of the vocal fold in normal and diseased states: anatomical and physical studies. *Proceedings of the Conference on the Assessment of Vocal Pathology*; The American Speech-Language-Hearing Association, 11:11–27, 1981.

108. Hirano M. Phonosurgical anatomy of the larynx. In: Ford C, Bless D, eds. *Phonosurgery*. New York: Raven; 1991: 25–41.

109. Oertel M. Über eine neues laryngostroboskopische Untersuchungsmethode des Kehlkopfes. *Centralblatt Medicinischen Wissenchaften*. 1878; 16:81–82.

110. Oertel M. Das Laryngo-Stroboskop und die laryngostoboskpische Üntersuchung. *Archiv für Laryngologie Rhinologie*. 1895; 3:1–16.

111. Von Leden H. The electronic synchron-stroboscope: its value for the practicing laryngologist. *Ann Oto, Rhinol Laryngol*. 1961;70:881–893.

112. Alberti PW. The diagnostic role of laryngeal stroboscopy. *Otolaryngol Clin North Am*. 1978; 11:3457–354.

113. Powell LS. The laryngostroboscope. *Arch Otolaryngol*. 1934; 19:708–710.

114. Kallen LA. Laryngostrobscopy in the practice of otolaryngology. *Arch Otolaryngol*. 1932; 16:791–807.

115. Timcke R, Von Leden H, Moore P. Laryngeal vibrations: measurement of the glottic wave: Part I. Normal vibratory cycle. *Arch Otolaryngol*. 1958; 68:1–19.

116. Timcke R, Von Leden H, Moore P. Laryngeal vibrations: measurements of the glottic wave: Part II. Physiologic variations. *Arch Otolaryngol*. 1959; 69:438–444.

117. Von Leden H, Moore P, Timcke R. Laryngeal vibrations: measurements of the glottic wave: Part III. The pathological larynx. 1960; *Arch Otolaryngol*. 1960; 71: 16–35.

118. Morrison MD. A clinical voice laboratory, videotape and stroboscopic instrumentation. *Otolaryngol Head Neck Surg*. 1984; 92:487–488.

119. Zeitels SM. Premalignant epithelium and microinvasive cancer of the vocal fold: the evolution of phonomicrosurgical management. *Laryngoscope*. 1995; (suppl 67): 1–51.

120. Zeitels SM, Hillman RE, Desloge RB, et al. Phonomicrosurgery in singers and performing artists: treatment outcomes, management theories, and future directions. *Ann Otol Rhinol Laryngol*. 2002;111(suppl 190):21–40.

121. Zeitels SM, Healy GB. Laryngology and phonosurgery: past, present and future. *N Engl J Med*. 2003;349: 882–892.

122. Zeitels SM. A universal modular glottiscope system: the evolution of a century of design and technique for direct laryngoscopy. *Ann Otol Rhinol Laryngol*. 1999;108(suppl 179):124.

123. Zeitels SM. Instrumentation. In: *Atlas of Phonomicrosurgery and Other Endolaryngeal Procedures for Benign and Malignant Disease*. San Diego, Calif: Singular Thomson Learning; 2001;23–36.

124. Zeitels SM, Hillman RE, Franco RA, Bunting G. Voice and treatment outcomes from phonosurgical management of early glottic cancer. *Ann Otol Rhinol Laryngol*. 2002;111(suppl 190):1–20.

125. Zeitels SM, Dailey SH, Burns JA. En block endoscopic fronto-lateral laryngectomy for glottic cancer. *Laryngoscope*. 2004;104:175–180.

126. Zeitels SM, Vaughan CW. External counterpressure and internal distension for optimal laryngoscopic exposure of the anterior glottal commissure. *Ann Otol Rhinol Laryngol*. 1994;103:669–675.

127. Zeitels SM. Premalignant epithelium and microinvasive cancer of the vocal fold: the evolution of phonomicrosurgical management. *Laryngoscope*. 1995;105(suppl 67):1–51.

128. Zeitels SM, Vaughan CW. A submucosal true vocal fold infusion needle. *Otolaryngol Head Neck Surg*. 1991;105:478–479.

129. Zeitels SM. Microflap excisional biopsy for atypical and microinvasive glottic cancer. *Op Techn Otolaryngol Head Neck Surg*. 1993;4:218–222.

130. Zeitels S M. Microflap excisional biopsy for atypia and microinvasive glottic cancer. *Operative Techniques in Otolaryngology—Head and Neck Surgery*. Phonosurgery ed., 1993; 4:218–222.

131. Hajek M. Anatomische Untersuchungen uber das Larynxodem. *Archiv Klin Chir*. 1891;42:46–93.

132. Reinke F. Untersuchungen uber das Menschliche Stimmband. *Fortschritte der Medcin*. 1895;13:469–478.

133. Reinke F. Uber die Funktionelle Struktur der Menschlichen Stimmlippe mit Besonderer Berucksichtigung des Elastischen Gewebes. *Anat Hefte*. 1897;9: 103–117.

134. Pressman J, Dowdy A, Libby R, Fields M. Further studies upon the submucosal lymphatics of the larynx by injection of dyes and isotopes. *Ann Otol Rhinol Laryngol*. 1956;65:963–980.

135. Pressman JJ, Bertz MB, Monell C. Anatomic studies related to the dissemination of cancer of the larynx. *Trans Am Acad Ophthalmol Otolaryngol*. 1960;64:628–638.

136. Isshiki N. Vibration of the vocal folds. In: *Phonosurgery: Theory and Practice*. Tokyo, Japan: Springer-Verlag; 1989:7–11.

137. Zeitels SM. Laser versus cold instruments for microlaryngoscopic surgery. *Laryngoscope*. 1996;106:545–552.

138. Franco RA, Zeitels SM, Farinelli WA, Anderson RR. 585-NM pulsed dye laser treatment of glottal papillomatosis. *Ann Otol Rhinol Laryngol*. 2002;111:486–492.

139. Franco RA, Zeitels SM, Farinelli WA, Anderson RR. 585-NM pulsed dye laser treatment of glottal dysplasia. *Ann Otol Rhinol Laryngol*. 2003;112:751–758.

140. Zeitels SM, Franco RA, Dailey SH, et al. Office-based treatment of glottal dysplasia and papilloma with 585-nm pulsed dye laser and local anesthesia. *Ann Otol Rhinol Laryngol*. 2004;113:265–276.

82

Voice Surgery

Robert Thayer Sataloff

Laryngeal surgery may be performed endoscopically or through an external approach. To provide optimal care, laryngologists must be familiar with the latest techniques in both approaches. Modern microsurgery of the voice is referred to widely as *phonosurgery*, although von Leden introduced that term originally in 1963 for procedures designed to alter vocal quality or pitch.[1] *Voice surgery* is a better term for delicate, precise laryngeal surgery in general, although phonomicrosurgery has also become widely used. It is usually performed using the microscope, small, modern instruments, and with great respect for the induplicatable anatomic complexity of the vibratory margin of the vocal fold.

Most surgical procedures for voice disorders can be performed endoscopically, obviating the need for external incisions and minimizing the amount of tissue disruption. Although endoscopic microsurgery seems intuitively more "conservative," this supposition holds true only when the equipment provides good exposure of the surgical site and the abnormality can be treated meticulously and thoroughly with endoscopic instruments. When endoscopic visualization is not adequate because of patient anatomy, disease extent, or other factors, the surgeon should not compromise the results of treatment or risk patient injury by attempting to complete an endoscopic procedure. In such patients, it may be safer to leave selected benign lesions untreated or to treat the pathology through an external approach.

Patient Selection and Consent

Prior to performing voice surgery, it is essential to be certain that patient selection is appropriate and that the patient understands the limits and potential com-

plications of voice surgery. Appropriate patients for voice surgery not only have voice abnormalities, but also really want to change their voice quality, effort, and/or endurance. For example, not all people with "pathological" voices are unhappy with them. Sports announcers, female trial attorneys with gruff, masculine voices, and others sometimes consult a physician only because of fear of cancer. If there is no suspicion of malignancy, restoring their voices to "normal" (eg, by evacuating Reinke's edema) may be a disservice and even jeopardize their careers. Similarly, it is essential to distinguish accurately between organic and psychogenic voice disorders before embarking on laryngeal surgery. Although breathy voice may be caused by numerous organic conditions, it is also commonly found in people with psychogenic dysphonia. The differentiation may require a very skilled voice team.

Although all reasonable efforts should be made to avoid operative intervention in professional voice users, particularly singers, there are times when surgery is appropriate and necessary. Ultimately, the decision depends on a risk-benefit analysis. If a professional is unable to continue his or her career, and if surgery may restore vocal function, surgery certainly should not be withheld. Sometimes, making such judgments can be challenging. A rock or pop singer with a vocal fold mass may have satisfactory voice quality with only minimal technical adjustments. Pop singers perform with amplification, obviating the need to sing loudly and project the voice in some cases (depending on the artist's style). Such a patient may be able to "work around" pathology safely for many years. However, even much more minor pathology may be disabling in some classical singers. For example, if a high soprano specializing in Baroque music develops a mild to moderate superior laryngeal nerve paresis, she may experience breathiness and instability. If she gives in to the temptation to compensate by slightly retracting her tongue and lowering her larynx, the breathiness will be controlled because of increased adductory forces, but she will lose the ability to perform rapid, agile runs and trills. Similar problems may occur from compensatory maladjustments in response to other lesions such as vocal fold cysts. In such instances, the artist may be served better by surgical correction of the underlying problem than by long-term use of hyperfunctional compensation (bad technique) that can itself cause other performance problems, as well as vocal fold pathology. The patient must understand all of these considerations clearly, including the risks of surgery. He or she needs to acknowledge the risk that any voice surgery may make the voice worse permanently, and the patient must consider this risk acceptable in light of ongoing vocal problems.

Even in the best hands, an undesirable scar may develop, resulting in permanent hoarseness. Also, the patient must be aware that there is a possibility that the voice may be worse following surgery. Naturally, other complications must also be discussed including (among others) complications of anesthesia, dental fracture, recurrence of laryngeal lesions, airway compromise, vocal fold webbing, and other untoward occurrences. In addition to the hospital's standard surgical consent, the author provides patients with additional written information prior to surgery. The patient keeps one copy of the "Risks and Complications of Surgery" document, and one signed copy remains in the chart. Specialized informed consent documents are used also for other selected treatments such as injection of cidofovir, topical application of mitomycin-C, injection of collagen, and injection of botulinum toxin, even though such documents are not really required. If medications are used for treatment purposes (rather than research purposes) and are off-label uses of medicines approved by the FDA for other purposes, their use does not necessarily require institutional review board (IRB) approval. However, this author believes it is helpful and prudent to provide patients with as much information as possible and to document that they have been so informed.

It is often helpful for the laryngologist, speech-language pathologist, singing voice specialist and patient to involve the patient's singing teacher in the decision-making process. Everyone must understand not only the risks of surgery, but also the risk involved in deciding against surgery and relying upon technical maladjustments. In many cases, there is no "good" or "right" choice; and the voice care team must combine great expertise with insight into the career and concerns of each individual patient to help the voice professional make the best choice.

Documentation

As has been noted elsewhere in this book, preoperative objective voice assessment and documentation are essential in addition to routine documentation of informed consent discussions. As a bare minimum, a high-quality tape recording of the patient's voice must be done before surgery. Auditory memories of physicians and patients are not good in general, and both the doctor and postoperative professional voice user are often surprised when they compare postoperative and preoperative recordings. Frequently, the preoperative voice is worse than either person remembers. In addition, such documentation is invaluable for medical-legal purposes. Photographs or videotapes of the larynx obtained during strobovideolaryngoscopy are extremely helpful. Ideally, complete objective laboratory voice assessment and evaluation by a voice team should be performed. Proper documentation is essential for assessing outcomes, even for the physician who is not interested in research or publication.

Timing of Voice Surgery

The time of voice surgery is important and can be particularly challenging in professionals with demanding voice commitments. Many factors need to be taken into account including the menstrual cycle, pre- and postoperative voice therapy, concurrent medical conditions, psychological state, professional voice commitments, and others.

Hormonal considerations may be important, especially in female patients with symptomatic laryngopathia premenstrualis. In patients who have obvious vocal fold vascular engorgement, or those who have a history of premenstrual vocal fold hemorrhages, it may be better to avoid elective surgery during the premenstrual period (unless the surgery is intended to treat vessels that have hemorrhaged repeatedly and that are only prominent prior to menses). In such patients, it may be best to perform surgery between approximately days 4 and 21 of the menstrual cycle. Although it appears unnecessary to time surgery in this way for all patients, the issue has not been fully studied.

Timing of surgery with regard to voice therapy and performance commitments can be especially difficult in busy voice professionals. The surgeon must be careful to avoid letting the patient's professional commitments and pressures dictate inappropriate surgery or surgical timing that is not in the patient's best interest. For example, some professional voice users will push for early surgery for vocal nodules and promise to appear for voice therapy after a busy concert season ends. This is not appropriate, because therapy may cure the nodules and avoid surgical risks altogether. However, professional commitments often require that appropriate surgery be delayed until a series of concerts or the run of a play is completed. In treating vocal fold cysts, polyps, and other conditions, such delays are often reasonable. They are made safer through ongoing voice therapy and close laryngologic supervision. Sometimes individualized treatments may help temporize. For example, aspiration of a cyst as an office procedure can provide temporary relief from symptoms, although the cyst is likely to return and require definitive surgery eventually.

At least a brief period of preoperative voice therapy is also helpful. Even when therapy cannot cure a lesion, it ameliorates the abuses caused by compensatory hyperfunction; and good preoperative therapy is the best postoperative voice therapy. It is also invaluable in educating the patient about vocal function and dysfunction and in making sure that he or she is fully informed about surgery and other options. Following surgery, voice therapy is medically necessary for many conditions. It is extremely important to long-term surgical outcome to time surgery so that the patient will be able to comply with postoperative voice rest and postoperative rehabilitation.

Many other conditions must be taken into account when deciding the timing of voice surgery. Concurrent medical conditions such as allergies that produce extensive coughing or sneezing (which may injure vocal folds following surgery), a coagulopathy (even temporary coagulopathy from aspirin use), and other physical factors may be important contributors to voice results. Psychological factors should also be considered. The patient must not only understand the risks and complications of surgery, but also be as psychologically prepared as possible to accept them and to commit to the therapeutic and rehabilitation process. Sometimes psychological preparation requires a delay in surgical scheduling to allow increased time for the patient to work with the voice team. There are very few indications for benign voice surgery that contraindicate a delay of several weeks. It is generally worth taking the time to optimize the patient's comfort and preparedness. Indeed, in the author's opinion, the patient is the most important part of the voice rehabilitation team. Realistic, committed collaboration by the patient is invaluable in achieving consistent, excellent surgical results.

Voice Cosmesis: The "Voice Lift"

In the modern communication age, the voice is critical in projecting image and personality and establishing credibility. Until very recently, voice has not received enough attention from the medical profession or from the general public. In fact, most people (doctors and the general public) do not realize anything can be done to improve a voice that is unsatisfactory or even one that is adequate but not optimal.

Historically, some techniques for voice improvement date back centuries. Singers, actors, and public speakers have sought out "voice lessons" for centuries. However, recently techniques for voice improvement have expanded and improved; and they have become practical for a great many more people.

Vocal weakness, breathiness, instability, impaired quality, and other characteristics can interfere with social and professional success. Many problems (particularly breathiness, softness, instability, tremor, and change in habitual pitch) are associated commonly with aging. For most people, these vocal characteristics, which lead people to perceive a voice (and its owner) as "old" or "infirm," can be improved or eliminated.

The first step for anyone seeking voice improvement is a comprehensive voice evaluation. Often, voice problems that people ascribe to aging, or even to their natural genetic makeup, are caused or aggravated by medical problems. The possibilities are numerous and include such conditions as reflux, low thyroid function, diabetes, tumors, and many others. Sometimes, voice deterioration is the first symptom of a serious medical problem; so comprehensive medical evaluation is essential before treating the voice complaints.

Once medical problems have been ruled out or treated, the next step for vocal habilitation or restoration is a program of therapy or exercise provided by a multidisciplinary team that incorporates the skills of not only a laryngologist, but also a speech-language pathologist and an acting-voice specialist. The training involves aerobic conditioning to strengthen the power source of the voice. In many cases, neuromuscular retraining (specific guided exercise) is sufficient to improve vocal strength and quality, eliminate effort, and restore youthful vocal quality. Doing so is important not only for singers, and other voice professionals (teachers, radio announcers, politicians, clergy, salespeople, receptionists, etc), but also really for almost everyone. This is especially true for the elderly. It is ironic but true that, as we age, voices get softer and weaker and at the same time our spouses and friends lose their hearing. This makes not just professional communication, but also social interaction, difficult, especially in noisy surroundings such as cars and restaurants. When people have to work too hard to communicate, it is often related to vocal deficiencies. Therefore, it is not surprising that, when exercises and medications alone do not provide sufficient improvement, many patients elect voice surgery in an attempt to strengthen their vocal quality and endurance and to improve their quality of life.

Several different procedures can be used to strengthen weak or injured voices. The selection of the operation depends on the individual's vocal condition as determined by a voice team evaluation, physical examination including strobovideolaryngoscopy, and consideration of what the person wants. Care must be taken to ensure that patient expectations are realistic. In most cases, surgery is directed toward bringing the vocal folds closer together so that they close more firmly. This eliminates the air leak between the vocal folds that occurs as a consequence of vocal aging (atrophy or wasting of vocal nodules or other tissues) or as a result of paresis or paralysis (partial injury to a nerve from a viral infection or other causes). In some cases, the operation is done by injecting a material through the mouth or neck into the tissues adjacent to the vocal folds, to "bulk up" the vocal tissues and bring the vocal folds closer together. This is called injection laryngoplasty and is performed usually using fat, collagen, or hydroxyapatite. This operation is sometimes done in the operating room under local anesthesia and, in selected patients, in the office with only local anesthesia. Alternatively, the problem can be corrected by performing a thyroplasty. This operation involves making a small incision in the neck. The skeleton of the voice box is entered, and the laryngeal tissues are compressed slightly using Gore-Tex or silastic implants. This procedure is generally done under local anesthesia with sedation. All of these procedures usually are performed on an outpatient basis.

Recovery usually takes days to weeks (depending on the procedure). Any operation can be associated with complications. Rarely, the voice can be made worse. The most likely complication is that voice improvement is not quite sufficient or that it does not hold up completely over time. When this problem occurs, it usually can be corrected easily by "fine tuning" through additional injections or surgical adjustment of the implants. However, most of the time, satisfactory results are achieved the first time.

Voice rehabilitation through medical intervention and therapy/exercise training is appropriate for anyone unhappy with his or her vocal quality (so called "voice lift surgery") and is suitable for almost anyone who does not have major, serious medical problems such as end-stage heart disease and is not on blood thinner medication that cannot be stopped safely for surgery, so long as that person has realistic vocal goals and expectations. However, "voice lift" surgery should be thought of as a comprehensive program stressing medical diagnosis and physical rehabilitation not as surgery alone.

Indirect Laryngoscopy

Laryngoscopic surgery is generally performed through direct laryngoscopy, as discussed below. However, indirect laryngoscopic surgery has been performed for many years and still has value in some circumstances. It permits gross biopsy of lesions under local anesthesia, removal of selected foreign bodies, and injection of fat, collagen, and other substances. In patients whose neck will not flex or extend enough to permit rigid direct laryngoscopy (cervical arthritis, fracture, fusion), indirect laryngoscopic surgery may provide a safe alternative to external surgery.

For indirect laryngoscopic surgery, the patient is generally seated. Topical anesthesia is applied and may be augmented by regional blocks. The larynx is visualized either with a laryngeal mirror, laryngeal telescope, or flexible fiberoptic laryngoscope. When surgery is performed solely for injection (eg, fat or collagen), either an external or transoral technique may be used. External injection may be performed by passing the needle through the cricothyroid membrane and into the desired position lateral to the vocal fold or through the thyroid lamina usually near the midpoint of the musculomembranous vocal fold, about 7 to 9 mm above the inferior border of the thyroid cartilage. Transoral injection has been used more commonly (Fig 82–1), and the transoral technique is also suitable for biopsy and other procedures. Assistance is required. The patient's tongue is held with gauze, as for routine indirect laryngoscopy. Cooperative patients may be asked to hold the tongue themselves. Angled instruments designed specifically for indirect laryngoscopic surgery are passed through the mouth and guided visually. Only a surgeon who is skilled in the necessary maneuvers should perform the procedure. The advantages of this technique include relatively easy access in anyone whose larynx can be visualized with a mirror, avoidance of the need for an operating room procedure, and ready availability when delays in getting to a hospital and waiting for an operating room might cause serious problems (eg, a chicken bone perched above the laryngeal inlet). However, the procedure also has distinct disadvantages. Precise control is not as good as that accomplished with microlaryngoscopy under sedation or general anesthesia, intraoperative loss of patient cooperation may result in injury, and the ability to handle complications such as bleeding and edema is limited. Nevertheless, at times the procedure is invaluable, and it should be in the armamentarium of the laryngological surgeon.

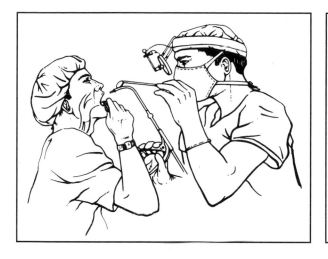
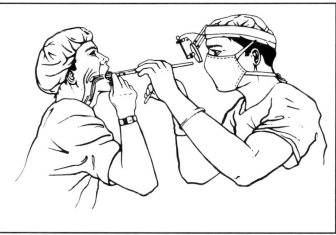

Fig 82–1. (*Left*) After topical anesthesia, the patient firmly holds his tongue extended while the mirror and indirect needle are positioned. (*Right*) The patient phonates a falsetto /i/ as the needle is inserted for injection. Similar positions may be used for biopsy and foreign body removal.

Direct Laryngoscopy

Suspension microlaryngoscopy is now the standard technique for endoscopic laryngeal surgery. The concept of direct laryngoscopy was introduced by Horace Green in 1852[2] using sunlight and supported later by Brünings.[3] The history of phonomicrosurgery is reviewed in greater detail in chapters 80 and 81. The most common light source used later with laryngoscopes was a headlight worn by the examiner. Light carriers built into laryngoscopes were first developed by Chevalier Jackson in 1915.[4] He utilized a light carrier with a tiny incandescent light bulb. Jackson's laryngoscope design included a flat, removable blade that permitted introduction of a bronchoscope. A fiberoptic version of this instrument is still in common use (Fig 82–2). Holinger modified Jackson's laryngoscope by eliminating the removable, sliding component and adding a slight lift near the tip[5] (Fig 82–3). This lifted the epiglottis, improving visualization of the anterior commissure. Holinger's design is still in common use. Kleinsasser popularized the idea of using the microscope as a light source.[6] Since that time, the use of microscope magnification has become an essential, routine part of laryngeal surgery (Fig 82–4). The microscope provides excellent stereoscopic vision and light and magnification that enhances diagnosis and helps refine surgical technique. It should be used in nearly all cases. The Holinger and Jackson laryngoscopes have such small internal diameters that stereoscopic vision cannot be obtained using the microscope. Jako solved these problems by developing a

Fig 82–2. Jackson laryngoscope.

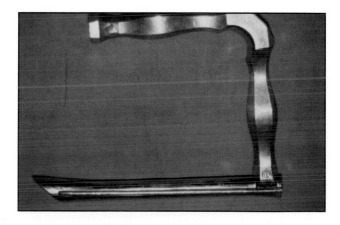

Fig 82–3. Holinger laryngoscope.

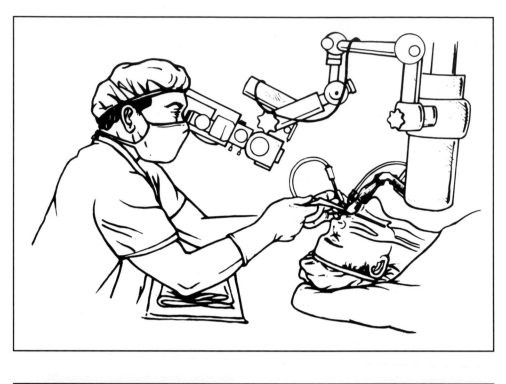

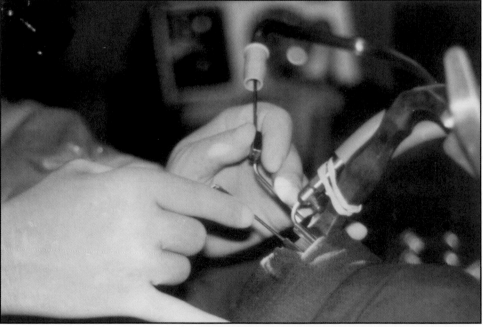

Fig 82–4. Direct microlaryngoscopy. (*Top*) Note the use of the operating microscope and the suspension device. A Mayo stand is placed under the surgeon's arms for stability, and towels cushion the elbows. (*Bottom*) Laryngoscope suspension permits bimanual surgery.

larger laryngoscope and adding two fiberoptic light bundles to improve illumination, especially for photography.[7] Jako's design was a great improvement, but it was too wide and thick to permit good visualization in many patients. Dedo designed a laryngo-scope that incorporated many of the advantages of the Jako and of the Holinger laryngoscopes,[8] permitting better visualization of the anterior commissure (Fig 82–5), and stereoscopic vision, as long as the surgeon is at least 61 cm from the patient. Using an operating

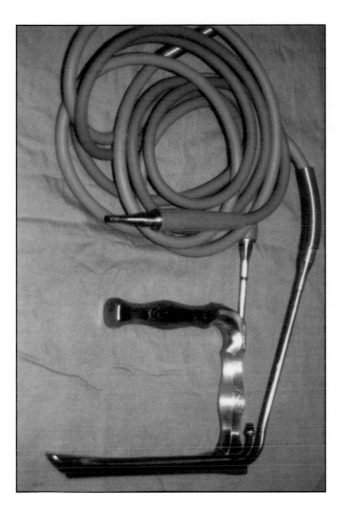

Fig 82–5. Dedo laryngoscope.

larynx to be pulled toward the ceiling (with the patient in supine position)—rather than necessitating a lever action that might fracture teeth, and that works well with the laryngoscope and head position preferred by the surgeon. It should be remembered that the suspension system should be used as a stabilizing device. That is, the surgeon should place the laryngoscope in the desired position and use the "suspension" device to keep it there, rather than using the suspension system to generate the forces necessary to obtain exposure. Adherence to this principle allows safe use of leverage systems such as the Lewy device, as well as lifting systems such as Killian's gallows or the Boston "Window Crank" (Pilling Company, Fort Washington, Pa) suspension systems. In general, the best view of the vocal folds can be obtained with the patient in "sniffing" position, with the neck flexed and the head extended (Fig 82–7). This is also the position used most commonly by anesthesiologists for intubation. When the laryngoscope is placed and suspended, the teeth must be protected from trauma by the laryngoscope; and it is essential that the patient's head be held still. Sudden motion or biting on the laryngoscope may result in patient injury. Direct laryngoscopy may be performed using local anesthesia with sedation, or general anesthesia.

In addition to choosing an appropriate laryngoscope, it is important to understand the principles not only of suspension, but also of internal distention and external counterpressure. In most cases, the laryngoscope should not only provide visualization of the entire vocal fold, but also should distend the false vocal folds and larynx in a way that optimizes visualization. Rarely, this is not desirable; and a laryngoscope positioned in the vallecula (such as the Lindholm, Karl Storz, Culver City, Calif) provides an alternative. However, this is the exception rather than the rule. In addition to internal distention, external counterpressure is important. Gentle pressure over the thyroid cartilage often can produce dramatic improvement in laryngeal visualization through the laryngoscope. Traditionally, a resident, nurse, or anesthetist has been asked to provide the counterpressure. It is better to use 1-inch tape that extends from one side of the headrest of the bed to the other and holds steady pressure on the larynx, maintaining the desired position. It is also important to realize that there can be a disadvantage to counterpressure. Although it improves visibility (especially anteriorly), it also introduces laxity in the vocal folds that may distort slightly the relationships between pathology and normal tissue. Hence, an appropriate compromise much be achieved in each case to optimize visibility of the area of interest without introducing excessive distortion.

microscope with a 400-mm objective lens permits these conditions to be met and provides adequate working room for the long instruments necessary for endolaryngeal surgery. Numerous modifications of these laryngoscopes have been designed since Jako and Dedo introduced their laryngoscopes, including the Gould laryngoscope[9] and numerous other thoughtfully designed laryngoscopes, a few of which are pictured in Figure 82–6, A-F. It is important for the surgeon to have a choice of laryngoscopes available and to select the one best suited to the patient's anatomy. The surgeon must choose an instrument that minimizes tissue damage while optimizing exposure and facilitating the manipulation of instruments.

Killian introduced the first laryngoscope suspension system in 1910.[10] Numerous suspension systems were invented subsequently. The choice is a matter of personal preference. However, in selecting a suspension system, one should look for a device that allows for two-handed surgery, that permits the tongue and

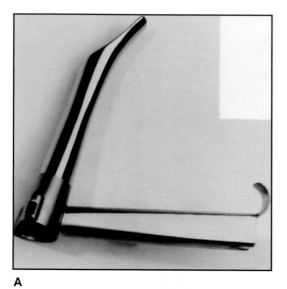

A

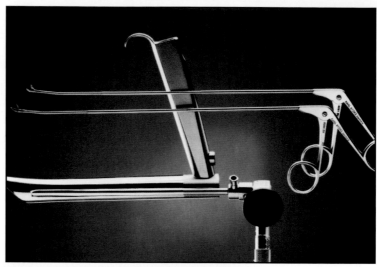

B

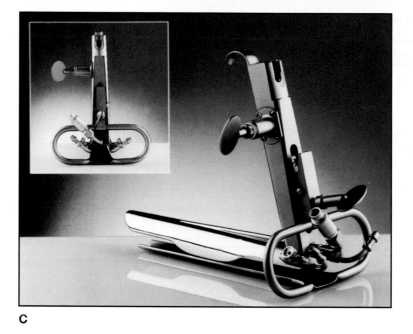

C

Fig 82–6. A. Lindholm laryngoscope (Storz), which fits in the vallecula, is ideal in combination with a Benjamin light clip and is particularly good for photography with 10 mm and other Storz telescopes. **B.** Kantor/Berci video-laryngoscope (Storz). **C.** Weerda distending operating laryngoscopes (Storz). *(continues)*

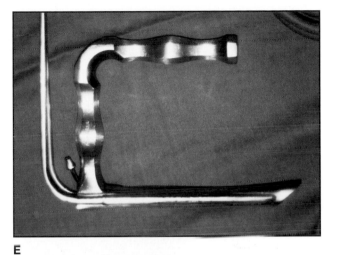

D

E

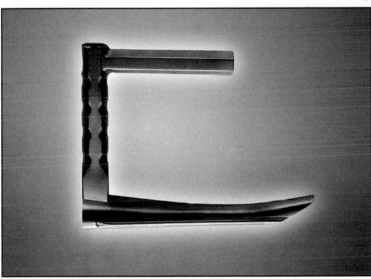

F

Fig 82–6. *(continued)* **D.** Fragen laryngoscope. **E.** Ossoff-Pilling laryngoscope, lateral view. The tip of this laryngoscope is identical to the Holinger anterior commissure laryngoscope. However, the proximal end of the larger male and even the smaller female laryngoscope is just large enough to permit binocular vision and effective laser use. This scope is invaluable for patients who are difficult to visualize, and who ordinarily would have required surgery through the Holinger laryngoscope. **F.** The Sataloff laryngoscope (Medtronics-Xomed, Jacksonville, Fla) has a triangular distal end that approximates the shape of the glottis, and enough lift near the tip to permit good exposure of the anterior commissure. It is available in large, medium (most commonly used), and pediatric sizes, as well as in a small adult anterior commissure form for patients who are particularly difficult to visualize.

Readers interested in additional information regarding counterpressure and the forces involved in laryngoscopy are advised to consult other literature.[11,12]

Anesthesia

Local Anesthesia

Local anesthesia with sedation is desirable in some cases for endoscopic laryngeal surgery, especially if fine adjustments of vocal quality are to be made, as during injection for vocal fold paralysis or reduction of a dislocated arytenoid cartilage. Many techniques of local anesthesia are used. They involve a variety of systemic, topical, and regional medications. The technique described below has proven most effective in the author's hands but should be considered only one of many options. In rare instances, direct laryngoscopy may be performed without operating room support and with topical anesthesia alone.

Generally, procedures are performed in the operating room with monitoring and sedation. Intravenous sedation is administered prior to anesthetic application. The author prefers a sedative that produces amnesia, such as midazolam. The oral cavity is sprayed with a topical anesthetic. Cetacaine, 10% xylocaine, 0.5% pontocaine, cocaine, and others have all given satisfactory results. Topical anesthetic is routinely supplemented with regional blocks and local infiltration. Bilateral superior laryngeal nerve blocks are achieved using 1% xylocaine with epinephrine 1:100,000. Superior laryngeal nerve block is accomplished by injecting 1 to 2 cc of xylocaine into the region where the nerve penetrates the thyrohyoid membrane, anterior to a line between the greater cornu of the thyroid cartilage and the greater cornu of the hyoid bone (Fig 82–8). Glossopharyngeal nerve blocks are placed using 2 cc of xylocaine in the lateral oropharyngeal wall, a few millimeters medial to the midportion of the posterior tonsillar pillar on each side. The tongue base is then infiltrated with 2 to 4 cc, using a curved tonsil needle and metal tongue depressor. Anesthesia is concluded with intratracheal application

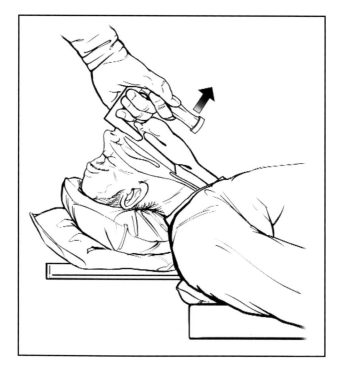

Fig 82–7. "Sniffing position," ideal for visualization during direct laryngoscopy. Note that the neck is flexed and the head is extended. Often the neck must be flexed considerably more than illustrated. The occiput is approximately 15 cm above the bed, supported by a pillow. The arrows indicate correct direction of pull during laryngoscopy.

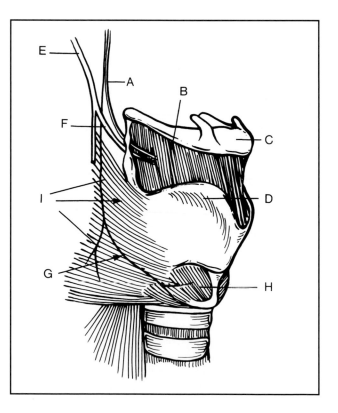

Fig 82–8. Lateral view of the larynx showing penetration of the internal branch of the superior laryngeal nerve (**A**) as it passes through the thyrohyoid membrane (**B**) between the hyoid bone (**C**) and the thyroid cartilage (**D**). Also illustrated are the superior thyroid artery (**E**), superior laryngeal artery (**F**), external branch of the superior laryngeal nerve (**G**), cricothyroid muscle (**H**), and the inferior constrictor (**I**).

of 4 cc of 4% topical xylocaine, administered through a midline injection in the cricothyroid membrane (after anesthetizing the skin with 1% of xylocaine with epinephrine 1:100,000 or by spraying topical anesthetic between the vocal folds if they can be visualized easily using a metal tongue blade). Although this anesthetic procedure can be performed very rapidly, patients frequently have difficulty managing secretions by the time the anesthesia has been applied. Suction should be available.

The adequacy of anesthesia application can be tested by placing a metal tongue depressor against the tongue base and lifting it anteriorly and inferiorly, simulating laryngoscope pressure and placement, while the hypopharynx is suctioned. If anesthesia is adequate, these maneuvers should not disturb the patient. Throughout the application of anesthesia, the physician and anesthesiologist should maintain verbal contact with the patient, carefully control the airway, and monitor vital signs including blood oxygen saturation. If adequate topical and regional anesthesia cannot be established, or if adequate sedation cannot be achieved safely, the procedure either should be discontinued or general anesthesia should be induced. Both the patient and the anesthesia team should be prepared for possible use of general anesthetic in all cases.

Most laryngeal procedures can be performed safely under local anesthesia. This choice provides not only the opportunity to monitor voice during the procedure, but also protection from the risks of endotracheal intubation. However, there are also disadvantages. When maximal precision is necessary, the motion present during local anesthesia may be troublesome. Greater accuracy is enhanced by general anesthesia with paralysis. The safety of local anesthesia during some cases of endolaryngeal surgery is questionable. In addition to mechanical surgical problems, in some patients with cardiac or pulmonary problems, the respiratory suppression caused by sedation may be more hazardous than general anesthesia. In addition, local anesthetics themselves may produce side effects. These may include mucosal irritation and inflammation (contact dermatitis) that may cause not only erythema and pruritus, but also vesiculation and oozing; dehydration of mucosal surfaces or an escharotic effect (especially from prolonged contact); hypersensitivity (rash); generalized urticaria (edema); methemoglobinemia; and anaphylaxis. Safety for use during pregnancy has not been established for most topical anesthetics used commonly in laryngology; and they should be utilized only under pressing clinical circumstances, if at all, during the first trimester of pregnancy. Methemoglobinemia may be a particularly frightening complication of local anesthesia. Methemoglobin is also called ferric protoporphyrin (IX globulin), ferrihemoglobin, and hemiglobin; because the iron in methemoglobin is trivalent (or ferric) instead of divalent (ferrous). Methemoglobinemia produces cyanosis, although skin discoloration is usually the only symptom or sign of acquired methemoglobinemia. This condition can be induced by any amine-type local anesthetic. Prilocaine and benzocaine are the drugs implicated most commonly.[13] Infants may be somewhat more susceptible, but the condition may occur in patients of any age. Methemoglobinemia is actually a misnomer because the pigment is intracellular and is not found in the plasma. Methemoglobincythemia would be more accurate; but methemoglobinemia is used commonly. Methemoglobinemia is treated by intravenous administration of methylene blue, although the condition is not life threatening and will resolve spontaneously. The notion that local anesthesia is always preferable to general anesthesia should be viewed with skepticism. The choice depends on the patient, the lesion, the surgeon, and the anesthesiologist.

General Anesthesia

Probably the most important consideration in general anesthesia for voice patients is the choice of the anesthesiologist. Laryngologists performing voice surgery must insist on the collaboration of an excellent anesthesiologist who understands vocal fold surgery and the special needs of voice patients. Those of us who work in teaching institutions recognize that medical students and first-year anesthesia residents need to practice intubation. However, this need should not be met on patients undergoing surgery for voice improvement, especially professional voice users. When a gentle, skilled, well-informed anesthesiologist and laryngologist collaborate, the choice of anesthetic depends solely on the patient and lesion, and safe effective surgery can be carried out. Such teamwork benefits the laryngologist, anesthesiologist, hospital, and especially the patient; and every effort should be made to establish the necessary professional collaboration.

The choice of agents for general anesthesia is beyond the scope of this chapter. However, in general, the regimen includes use of a short-term paralytic agent to avoid patient motion or swallowing. Intubation and extubation should be accomplished atraumatically, using the smallest possible tube. Most laryngeal endoscopic procedures are short in duration, and a 5-0 tube is generally sufficient even for most moderately obese patients. The laser may be used during many procedures, and it is best to employ a laser-resistant endotracheal tube unless the surgeon is absolutely certain that the laser will not be activated. Laser precautions are discussed in chapter 84.

Antireflux medications are prudent especially in patients with symptoms and signs of reflux, but reflux may occur under anesthesia even in patients who do not have significant clinical reflux. The combination of acid exposure and direct trauma from the endotracheal tube can lead to laryngeal mucosal injury. Intravenous steroids (eg, 10 mg of dexamethasone) may be helpful in minimizing inflammation and edema and possibly in protecting against cellular injury; and intravenous steroids should be used at the surgeon's discretion, if there is no contraindication.

Endotracheal intubation provides the safest, most stable ventilation under general anesthesia; and it generally provides adequate visibility. However, in some cases, even a small endotracheal tube may interfere with surgery. Alternatives include general anesthesia without intubation and with jet ventilation. Laryngeal microsurgery without intubation was reported by Urban.[14] The technique involves intravenous thiopental, 100% oxygen by mask initially, and manually controlled oxygen insufflation. Few anesthesiologists are comfortable with this technique, and the oxygen insufflation can be an inconvenience during surgery.

Venturi jet ventilation can be a useful technique. Anesthetic and oxygen can be delivered through a needle placed in the lumen of the laryngoscope, through a ventilation channel in specially designed laryngoscope channels, through a catheter just above or below the vocal folds, such as the Hunsicker catheter (Medtronics-Xomed, Jacksonville, Fla) used by the author Fig 82–9A) or through a Carden tube (Fig 82–9B).[15] The author uses the Hunsicker catheter because of its easy placement, security, laser resistance, and the fact that the jet ventilation initiates below the vocal folds. This seems to cause less mechanical interference at the vibratory margin during surgery. However, the catheter must be placed between the vocal folds carefully by an expert anesthesiologist or the laryngologist and removed carefully, to avoid intubation and extubation trauma as might be caused by placement of any endotracheal tube. During any surgery that employs jet ventilation, it is essential that the surgeon be a knowledgeable, cooperative part of the anesthesia team. The airway must remain unobstructed for expiration. If the laryngoscope moves or is removed obstructing the airway without a warning to the anesthesia team, pneumothorax may result.

All the care exercised in gentle intubation may be for naught unless similar caution is exercised during extubation. The most common error during extubation is failure to fully deflate the endotracheal tube cuff. This may result in vocal fold trauma or arytenoid cartilage dislocation. The anesthesia team should be aware of these problems. The surgeon should be present and attentive during intubation and extubation to help minimize the incidence of such problems.

Anesthesia is also a prime concern during surgery outside the head and neck. Laryngologists are frequently called on for guidance by professional voice users, surgeons, and anesthesiologists. The anesthesiologist must appreciate that the patient is a voice professional, and ensure that intubation and extubation are performed by the most skilled anesthesiologist available. In addition, anesthesiologists must temper their tendency to use the largest possible tube. There are very few procedures that cannot be performed safely through a size 6.5 or smaller endotracheal tube, and many can be performed with mask anesthesia or a Brain laryngeal mask without intubating the larynx at all. When possible, alternatives to general anesthesia should be considered, such as spinal blocks, regional blocks, and acupuncture. Many procedures commonly done under general anesthesia with intubation can be performed equally well using another technique. After surgery, postoperative voice assessment by the anesthesiologist, patient, and operating surgeon is essential. If voice abnormalities are present (other than very mild hoarseness that resolves within 24 hours), prompt laryngological examination should be arranged.

Instrumentation

Microlaryngeal surgery utilizes magnification, usually provided by an operating microscope, which is used through a laryngoscope (laryngoscope placement is discussed above). Many surgeons are not familiar with formulas that determine accurately the amount of magnification used, and it is often recorded incorrectly in operative reports. It is not unusual for surgeons to assume that the number on the indicator on the zoom control correlates with the number of times the image is magnified; but accurate determination is more complex than that. This author usually works with a Zeiss operating microscope (Oberkochen, Germany), and the information in this discussion refers specifically to Zeiss instruments. However, the principles are the same for microscopes manufactured by other companies. To determine the amount of magnification, the focal length of the binocular tube is divided by the focal length of the objective lens, and then multiplied by the magnification of the eyepieces.[16] That number is then multiplied by the indicator on the magnification (zoom) control of the microscope, on a modern microscope. The focal length of the binocular tube is usually a number such as F125,

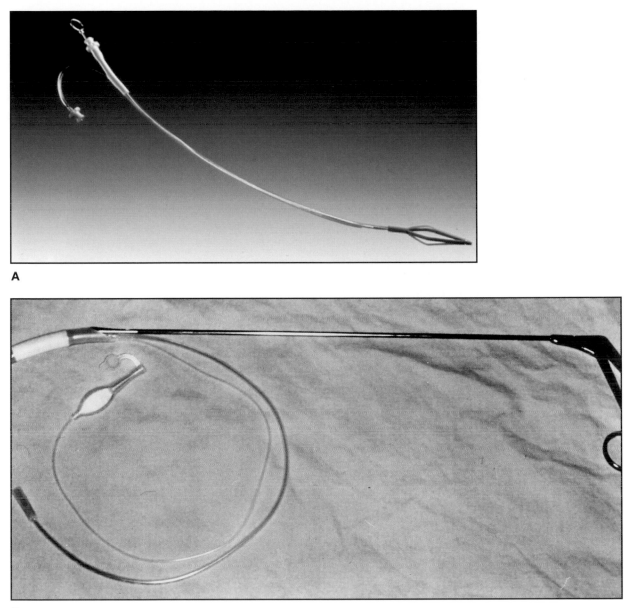

A

B

Fig 82–9. A. The Hunsicker Jet Ventilation Catheter (Medtronics-Xomed, Jacksonville, Fla). **B.** Carden tube grasped in forceps in preparation for insertion. Except for the ventilating and inflation tubes, the entire device will be positioned below the vocal folds before the cuff is inflated.

F160, or F170. For example, the Zeiss OPMI-6 microscope has a binocular tube with a focal length of F160, and the newer design with the wider angle of view has a focal length of F170. The focal length of the objective lens varies depending on the surgeon's preference. For ear surgery, it is usually 250 or 300 mm. For laryngeal surgery, a 400-mm lens is used most commonly. The usual eyepiece magnification is either 10× or 12.5×. The indicator number on a modern Zeiss operating microscope can be read through a small window next to the zoom control knob, and the number ranges from 0.4 to 2.4. The OPMI-6-S, for example, provides a continuous magnification range of 1:4. Older Zeiss operating microscopes (such as the OPMI-1) have magnification changes that are steplike rather than continuous and have numbers that range from 6 to 40 next to the dial. These provide five magnification steps in a range of 1:6. These numbers should not be used in the formula noted above, but can be converted as follows: 40 corresponds to 2.5; 25 corresponds to 1.6; 16

corresponds to 1.0; 10 corresponds to 0.6; 6 corresponds to 0.4. So, for e xample, if a surgeon is using an OPMI-1 microscope with 10× eyepieces, a 400 mm objective lens, and the magnification set at 40 (maximum), image magnification is 7.8× ($^{125}/_{400}$ × 25 × 10 = 7.8×), not 40×, as misstated commonly.

Simply changing the eyepieces from 10× to 12.5× increases the magnification from 7.8× to 9.8× and using 20× eyepieces increases the magnification to 15.6. Utilizing an objective lens with a shorter focal length also increases magnification but brings the microscope closer to the operating field. Although this approach is used during ear surgery, it is not suitable for laryngeal surgery because the decreased space between the microscope and direct laryngoscope is not sufficient to permit unimpeded manipulation of long-handled laryngeal instruments. It is important for surgeons to be familiar with these principles to optimize surgical conditions for each specific case and to document surgery accurately.

Magnifying laryngeal telescopes are also invaluable for assessing vocal fold pathology and mapping lesions for surgery. Most commonly, the author uses 10-mm 0° and 4-mm 70° telescopes (Karl Storz, Culver City, Calif); and 30° and 120° telescopes are useful in some circumstances. Laryngeal telescopes allow the surgeon to visualize lesions in great detail, to appreciate the limits of lesions in three dimensions better than can be accomplished through a microscope, and to visualize obscure areas such as the laryngeal ventricle (Fig 82–10).

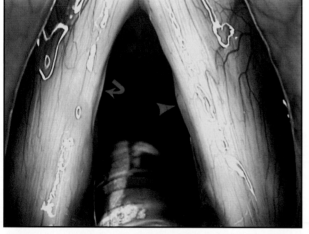

B

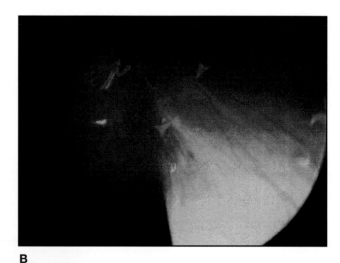

B

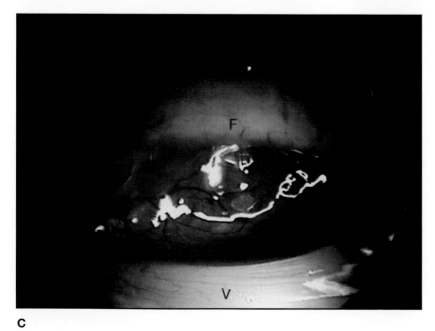

C

Fig 82–10. A. Vocal folds visualized through 10-mm 0 degree telescope (Karl Storz, Culver City, Calif.) showing a right vocal fold cyst (*arrowhead*) and left reactive swelling (*curved arrow*). **B.** Vocal folds visualized through a 70° telescope, allowing better evaluation of the vertical surface of the vibratory margin. This view shows that the cyst (*arrowheads*) involves only the superior one third to one-half of the vibratory margin. The anterior commissure can be seen, as well (*curved arrow*). **C.** The laryngeal ventricle visualized above the true vocal fold and below the false vocal fold through a 70° telescope.

A technique known as *contact endoscopy* has been used by gynecologic surgeons for many years. Its value in microlaryngeal surgery was recognized by Dr. Mario Andrea.[17] This technique uses a vital staining agent such as methylene blue. Contact endoscopy permits visualization of the cellular nature and integrity of vocal fold epithelium at any given point along the vocal fold. Cell nuclear characteristics are visible, and specific borders between pathologic, transitional, and normal epithelium can be defined, permitting precise surgical intervention. (Fig 82–11, A-F). Although this technique is relatively new and requires additional study and experience, it appears extremely valuable in selected cases.

Delicate microsurgery requires sharp, precise, small instruments. The few heavy cupped forceps and scissors that constituted a laryngoscopy tray through the early 1980s are no longer sufficient. It is now possible to obtain microlaryngeal instruments that look like ear instruments on long handles. Instruments should be long enough to be manipulated easily in the laryngoscope, but not so long that they bump into the microscope. They should include scissors (straight up, up-biting, curved left, and curved right), small grasping cupped forceps (straight, up-biting, right, and left), larger cupped forceps (straight and up-biting, at least), alligator forceps (straight, right, and left), scalpel, right-angle and oblique blunt ball-tipped dissectors, spatula, scalpel, retractors, mirrors for reflecting lasers, and suctions (Fig 82–12 and 82–13A-Z). Cutting instruments should be sharp at all times. Suctions should be thumb controlled, of several sizes, and should include both open tip and velvet eye designs. A suction/cautery tip may be valuable occasionally and should be available, as should cotton carriers. Nonreflective instruments with laser-resistant coating may be advantageous in some situations. The selection and use of lasers are discussed in chapter 84.

Powered laryngeal surgery is a relatively new concept, although powered surgery for other areas of the body has been utilized for many years.[18] Acoustic neuroma surgeons have used powered instruments such as the House-Urban Rotary Dissector (Urban Engineering, Burbank, Calif) for 3 decades; arthroscopic knee surgeons use powered instruments regularly; and powered instruments have been important to functional endoscopic sinus surgery. Their role in laryngeal surgery is not defined completely; but powered laryngeal surgery is clearly useful in the treatment of some conditions such as selected papillomas and neoplasms. The author uses the Medtronic-Xomed XPS Power System (Jacksonville, Fla) with disposable laryngeal shaver blades. To use powered instruments safely, it is important to understand the blades and instrument settings. For example, to debulk a large, exophytic or fibrous lesion, the tri-cut laryngeal blade is utilized at 3,000 rpm. To remove papilloma near the vibratory margin or anterior commissure in a controlled fashion, it is more appropriate to use a 3.5-mm laryngeal skimmer blade at a speed of 500 rpm in the "oscillate" mode. Although some surgeons prefer using powered instruments under endoscopic control rather than using a microscope (Fig 82–14), this author generally prefers using a microscope to permit binocular vision and bimanual manipulation. However, surgeons should have endoscopes available and be comfortable with their use. In some cases, difficult anatomy precludes visualization of certain regions of the larynx, especially at and above the anterior commissure. In such cases, the best way to remove pathology may be through the use of a 70° telescope for visualization and a powered skimmer blade for resection. Although delicate microdissection is still the most controlled and appropriate technique for removing most benign lesions such as cysts and polyps from the vibratory margin of the vocal fold and remains this author's preferred technique for most lesions, powered instruments used properly allow surprising precision and may be helpful especially for selected papillomas and neoplasms.

Laryngeal Microsurgery

Submucosal Infusion; Hemorrhage Control; Steroid Injection

The concept of laryngeal infusion was introduced in the 1890s for the purpose of anatomic studies.[19,20] The technique has been used intermittently over the years for a variety of purposes including infusion of steroids to disrupt adhesions in vocal fold scar, placement of collagen along the vibratory margin, and for separating benign and malignant lesions from underlying structures. The technique has been become more popular among clinicians since the 1990s.[21-23]

Submucosal infusion may be appropriate for a variety of vocal fold masses, but it has disadvantages as well as advantages. Infusion usually is performed utilizing a solution made by combining 9 cc of sterile saline with 1 cc of epinephrine 1:1,000 (a 1 to 10,000 dilution). A small amount of this mixture is infused submucosally using a 30-gauge needle to increase the fluid content of the superficial layer of the lamina propria, to separate the undersurface of the lesion more clearly from the vocal ligament, and to help define the

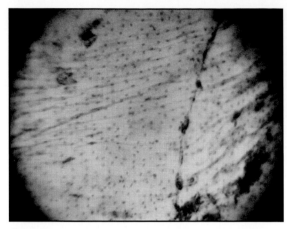

A

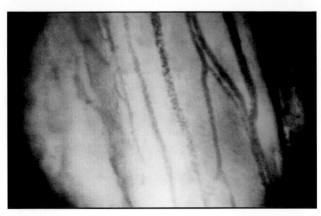

B

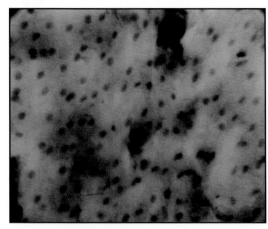

C

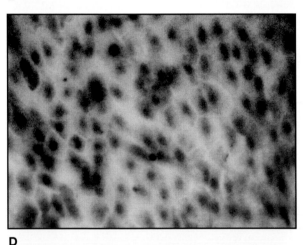

D

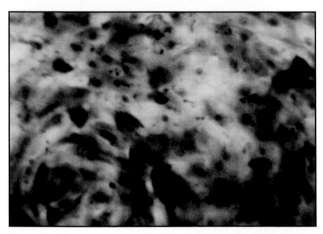

E

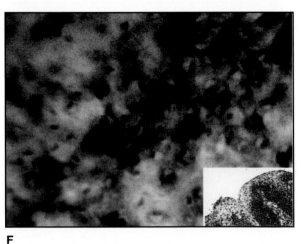

F

Fig 82–11. A. Contact endoscopy of the vocal folds (60×) revealing regular cellular characteristics, and epithelial folds. **B.** Contact endoscopy (60×) showing the normal pattern of the microvascular of the vocal fold. **C.** Contact endoscopy of normal vocal fold epithelium (150×) showing nuclear characteristics in greater detail. **D.** Contact endoscopy revealing dysplasia (150×) illustrated by the heterogeneous appearance of the epithelium, and the increased dimensions and irregular staining of the nuclei. **E.** Contact endoscopy (150×) of carcinoma, illustrating marked irregu-larity in the epithelial cellular pattern and nuclei with abnormalities of shape, size, staining characteristics, and nucleus/cytoplasmic ratio. **F.** Contact endoscopy (150×) of papilloma showing ballooning of the cells and cytoplasmic vacuoles pushing the nuclei toward the periphery of the cells. Also seen are inflammatory cells with regular, large nuclei. The insert shows a histological section of papilloma. Contact endoscopy may be helpful in identifying the boundary between papilloma and normal mucosa. (Reprinted from Andrea and Dias,[17] with permission.)

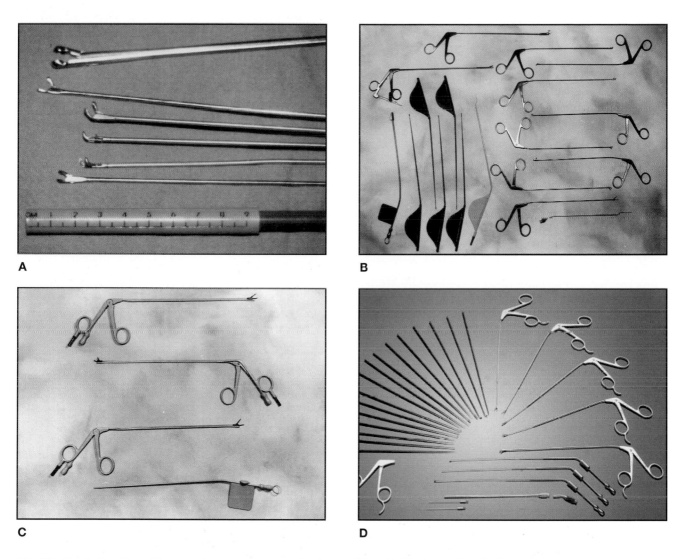

Fig 82–12. A. Traditional laryngeal cupped forceps (*top*), compared with more modern instruments designed by Dr Marc Bouchayer (Xomed-Medtronics, Jacksonville, Fla). **B.** Additional delicate Medtronics-Xomed instruments used routinely by this author. **C.** Extremely useful Medtronics-Xomed (Jacksonville, Fla) suction cautery instruments designed by J Abitbol. **D.** Selected instruments designed by the author (RT Sataloff), manufactured by Medtronics-Xomed, Jacksonville, Fla.

A

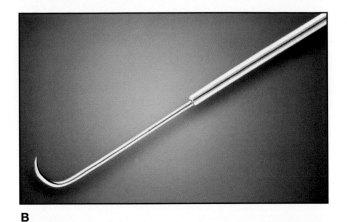

B

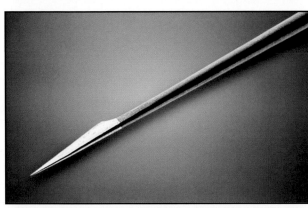

C

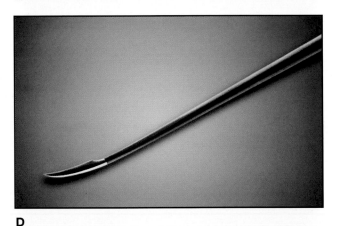

D

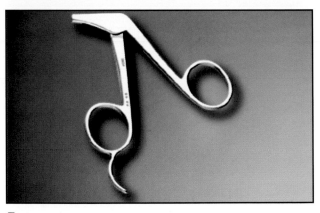

E

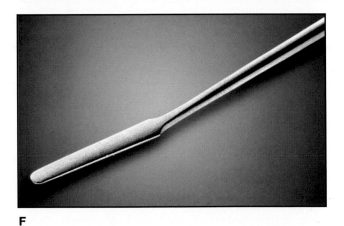

F

Fig 82–13. Selected microlaryngeal instruments (A-W are Sataloff Instruments, Medtronics-Xomed, Jacksonville, Fla). **A.** 30-gauge straight disposable needle (with cleaning stylet in place) for submucosal infusion or collagen injection. **B.** 30-gauge right-angle disposable needle with cleaning stylet in place. **C.** Sharp microknife. This and the sickle knife are disposable and screw into a handle. The vascular knife and selected other sharp instruments are designed similarly. They are intended for single use so the instruments are optimally sharp for each patient. **D.** Sickle knife. **E.** Universal scissor handle. All of the straight-handle Sataloff instruments are designed to fit in the universal scissor handle. This not only allows the instrument tip to be positioned at any angle, but it also permits case-by-case adjustments of instrument length from the handle to the tip. This allows the tip of the instrument to be on the vocal fold, while the handle is close enough to the laryngoscope to permit the surgeon's fingers to be placed against the head or laryngoscope for stabilization. **F.** Straight spatula. *(continues)*

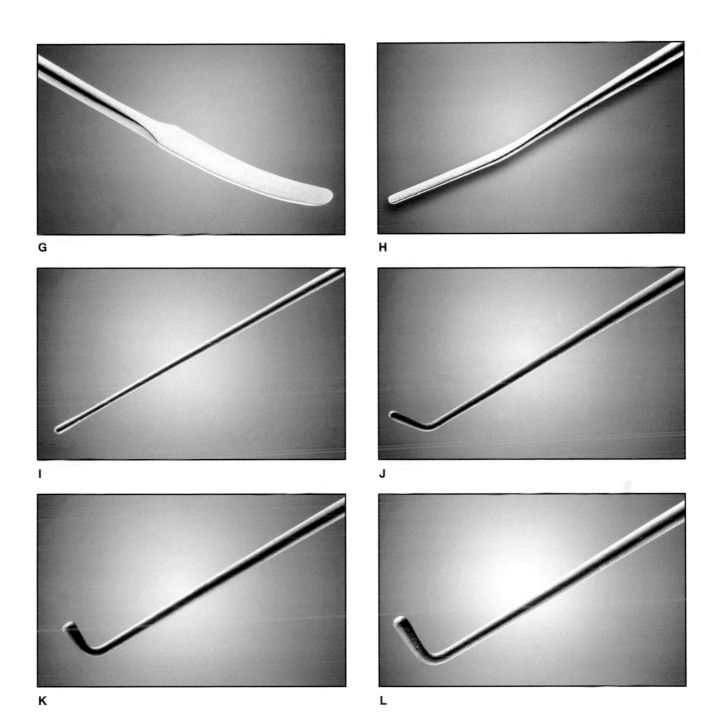

Fig 82–13. *(continued)* **G.** Curved spatula. **H.** Fine angled spatula. **I.** Straight blunt ball dissector. **J.** Oblique blunt ball dissector. **K.** Small right angle blunt ball dissector. **L.** Long right-angle blunt ball dissector. *(continues)*

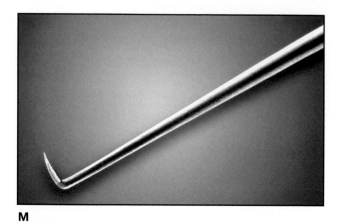

M

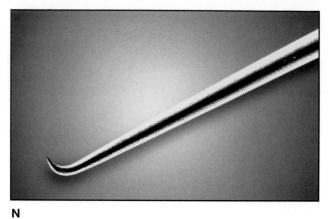

N

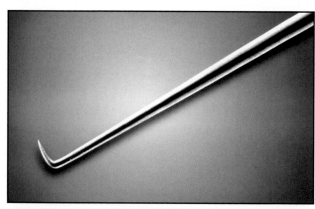

O

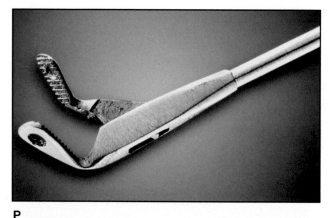

P

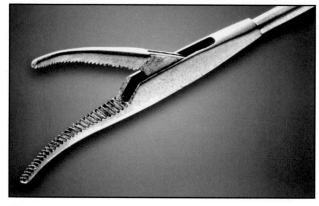

Q

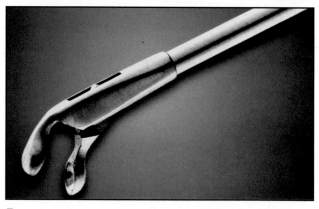

R

Fig 82–13. *(continued)* **M.** Sharp right-angle hook. **N.** Vascular knife. This 1-mm instrument is sharp on the point and blunt on the bottom. It is used for dissecting varicose blood vessels off the vocal fold. It is essential that it not be confused with the mini-microflap knife. **O.** The mini-microflap knife is similar to the sharp right-angle hook, except the mini-microflap knife is sharpened on the bottom, as well as the tip. This allows it to be placed within a mucosal pocket and to cut tissue sharply through a small access incision. If it is inadvertently confused with the vascular knife and used for vascular dissection, the sharp inferior surface of the microknife can damage the vocal fold. **P.** Small heart-shaped grasper (comes in right and left directions, left only shown). **Q.** Left alligator forceps. **R.** Down-biting forceps. *(continues)*

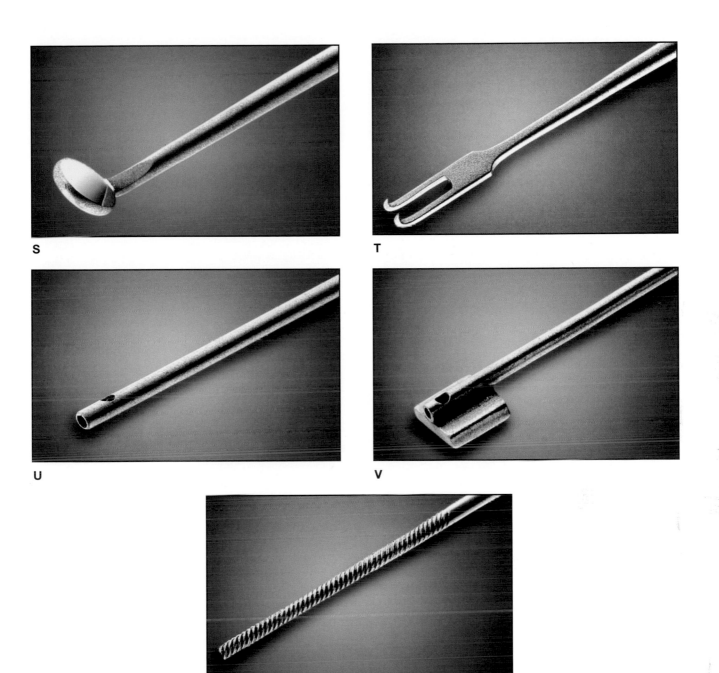

S

T

U

V

W

Fig 82–13. *(continued)* **S.** Polished mirror for reflecting and redirecting laser light (small and large mirrors are available). **T.** Fine double hook for retracting laryngeal flaps and large lesions. **U.** 3-French velvet eye suction used during microflap dissection. **V.** 3-French velvet eye suction with metal surface to retract tissue and to prevent tissue prolapse into the surgical field. **W.** Cotton carrier. *(continues)*

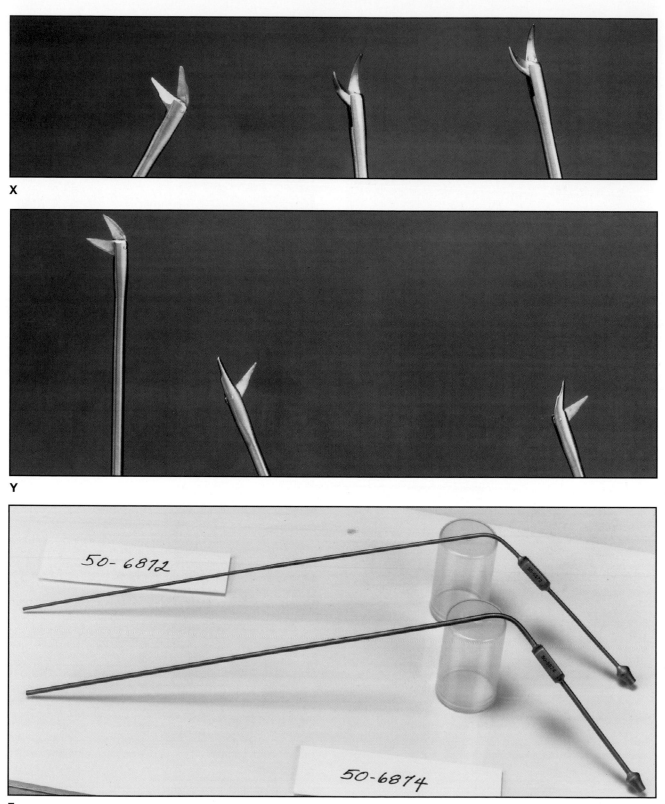

Fig 82–13. *(continued)* **X.** Blunt scissors, vertical action, angled down; blunt scissors, horizontal action, curved blades, open left; sharp scissors, horizontal action, curved blades, open left. **Y.** From left to right, sharp scissors, vertical action, angled down; blunt scissors, vertical action, straight blades; blunt scissors, vertical action, angled up (numerous other variations are available). **Z.** Suctions, 5 French and 7 French diameter.

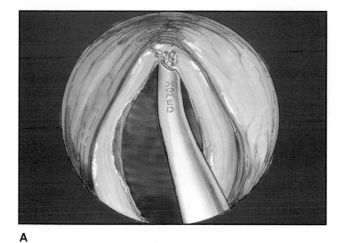

A

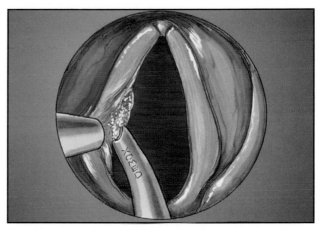

B

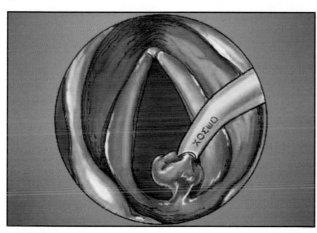

C

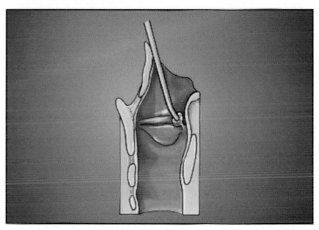

D

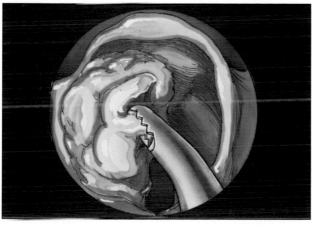

E

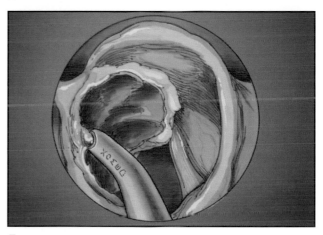

F

Fig 82–14. Powered laryngeal surgery using a skimmer blade in the right hand, endoscope in the left hand, and video monitor for visualization. **A.** 3.5-mm skimmer blade at 500 rpm, visualized through a laryngeal telescope, being used to remove papilloma from the anterior commissure. **B.** 3.5 mm skimmer blade removing papilloma from the under-surface of the left vocal fold. An operating microscope is being used, allowing use of a suction in the left hand to retract the vocal fold. **C** and **D.** 3.5-mm skimmer blade is used to remove a posterior laryngeal polyp. A collection system is placed in line with the suction tubing to collect the pathological specimen **E.** A 4-mm tri-cut blade is used at 3,000 rpm to debulk a large tumor. **F.** After most of the tumor mass has been removed, a 4-mm, angle-tip laryngeal blade can be used at 500 to 1,000 rpm to remove tumor from the margins more delicately. *(continues)*

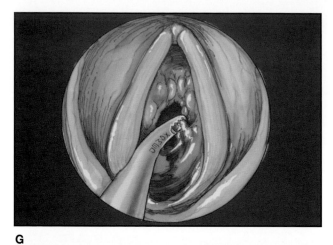

G

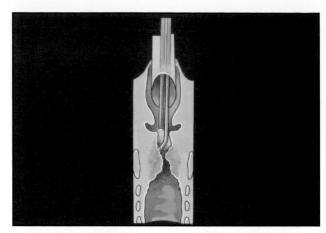

H

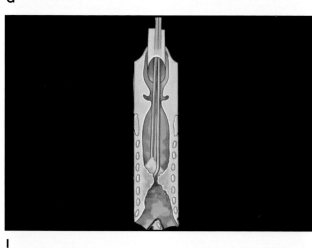

I

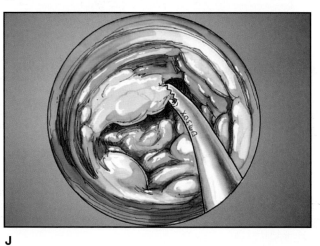

J

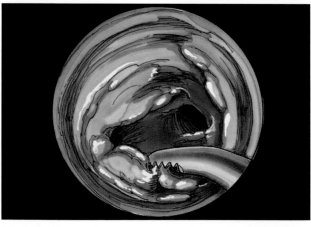

K

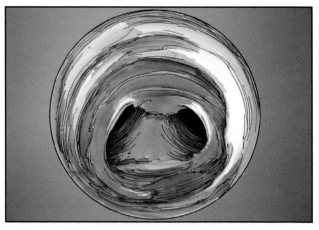

L

Fig 82–14. *(continued)* **G** and **H.** An angle-tip blade at 500 to 1,000 rpm or subglottic blade 4.0 mm or 3.5 mm in diameter can be used to remove subglottic granulation tissue. A tri-cut blade at 3,000 rpm would be more appropriate for a densely fibrotic, stenotic lesion in this region. **I-L.** A 4-mm angle-tip tri cut subglottic blade at 3,000 rpm can be invaluable for treating tracheal stenosis endoscopically. The laryngeal shaver can remove tissue that is difficult to treat with cold instruments and difficult to reach with a laser. Visualization can be provided through a microscope, or utilizing an endoscope, as illustrated in **I.** Removal of tissue (**J** and **K**) generally allows reestablishment of an appropriate tracheal lumen (**L**) with good visual and technical control. *(continues)*

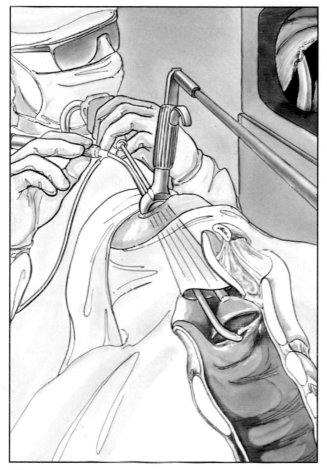

M

Fig 82–14. *(continued)* **M.** Although this author prefers to use a microscope permitting use of powered instrumentation in one hand and a suction or other instrument in the opposite hand, some surgeons prefer to operate while looking at a monitor and using an endoscope in one hand and a powered instrument in the other hand. (Courtesy of Medtronic-Xomed, Jacksonville, Fla.)

vocal ligament more clearly. In lesions such as sulcus vocalis, vocal fold scar, and papilloma, this technique is extremely helpful. In other lesions such as small vocal fold cysts, it may actually obscure the pathology making surgery more difficult. When utilized in appropriate cases, the epinephrine also causes vaso-constriction and helps minimize bleeding. When bleeding does occur, in most cases, it can be controlled with topical application of epinephrine 1:1,000 on a small cottonoid. Rarely, cauterization with a laser or cautery is required. Infusion of saline and epinephrine does not have to be limited to the vocal fold itself. Infusion also can be performed in the false vocal fold and lateral to the ventricle. This infusion technique can be

successful in everting the ventricle into the surgical field, providing direct access to lesions that involve the deep recesses of the laryngeal ventricle.

In some cases, submucosal infusion may be performed with a substance other than saline with epinephrine. For example, if the surgeon plans to inject steroid in a patient with scar or sulcus, the steroid may be used for infusion initially. It is as effective as saline and epinephrine in defining the lesion and tissue planes, but it does not provide an equally good hemostatic effect. The efficacy of steroid injection in the vocal folds is unknown. Some surgeons use it regularly. Others are concerned that it may result in muscle atrophy. If used, it is important for the surgeon to utilize an aqueous solution, not an oil-based preparation. Moreover, the author recommends against using milky-colored preparations such as Kenalog (Westwood Squibb, Buffalo, NY). Occasionally, the white suspended particles can precipitate and form a plaque that takes months to resolve.[23] *This* problem has not been encountered with clear solutions such as dexamethasone. Cidofovir can also be used sparingly as the infusion material in patients with papilloma.

Vocal Fold Cysts (with an Overview of the Evolution of Voice Microsurgery)

When submucosal cysts cause symptoms sufficient to warrant surgery, it is essential to resect them without damaging adjacent normal tissue. At the time the first edition of this book was published, the author recommended laryngeal microflaps to accomplish this goal. By the time the second edition was published, that recommendation had changed. Management of vocal fold cysts provides a particularly good window on the evolution of voice surgery.

Vast improvements in surgical care of vocal fold abnormalities occurred in the 1980s and 1990s. These changes have resulted largely because of advances in knowledge of the anatomy and physiology of the vocal tract, technological developments that have improved our ability to examine and quantify voice function, and the availability of better surgical instruments.[24-29] Because the human is the only species with a vocal ligament, there is no experimental animal for vocal fold surgery. Therefore, surgical advances have been based largely on anecdote and common sense. Consequently, it is essential to reevaluate results continually and to consider changing pronouncements about optimal techniques, especially when research provides important new information.

Through the mid-1970s (and later in some centers), the operation of choice for benign vocal fold pathology was "vocal cord stripping," an operation now abandoned except perhaps in selected cases of laryngeal cancer. However, until the mid-1970s, the available facts led us to believe that the operation made sense. Not knowing the complexity of the anatomy of the vibratory margin, we reasoned that the mucosa of the vocal fold edge had become deranged. If we removed it, it seemed probable that the healing process would replace diseased mucosa with new, healthy mucosa. Mucosal healing in the oral cavity and elsewhere in the upper respiratory tract was rarely a problem; so, why should there be a problem on the vocal folds? We had no explanation for the patients who appeared to have normal vocal folds but terrible voices after this operation and we tended to diagnose their persistent dysphonia as psychogenic. In retrospect, knowing what we do now about vocal fold anatomy and physiology, we have no explanation for the fact that so many of those patients were not permanently hoarse. Nevertheless, the beginning of the end of vocal fold stripping came in 1975 when Hirano described the anatomy of the vocal fold (Fig 82–15), which led to a better understanding of vocal fold scar formation and the development of surgical techniques to try to avoid it.[25]

Hirano demonstrated that the vocal fold consisted of an epithelium; superficial, intermediate, and deep layers of the lamina propria; and thyroarytenoid muscle. Further, he pointed out that fibroblasts capable of producing scar were numerous, primarily in the intermediate and deep layers of the lamina propria and the muscle. Most benign vocal fold pathology (nodules, polyps, etc) is superficial. Moreover, research from numerous centers highlighted the importance of the complex mucosal wave created during phonation.[27-33] Consequently, although delicate microsurgery had been advocated by a small number of farsighted laryngologists in the past, the need for this approach to voice surgery quickly became generally accepted.[34] Eventually, surgeons began to think of the anatomy and function of the vocal fold in layers, of pathology in layers, and to conceptualize surgery in layers. This paradigm resulted in the current concepts and techniques of phonomicrosurgery that are designed to remove the pathology without disturbing any adjacent normal tissue.

Vocal fold microsurgery developed rapidly in the 1980s and became the new standard of care. It was based on the notion that surgery should be designed

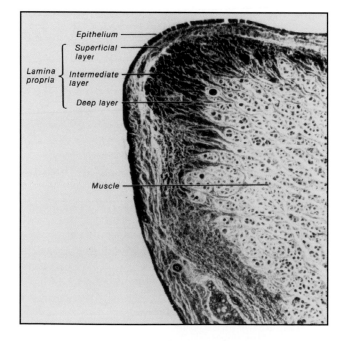

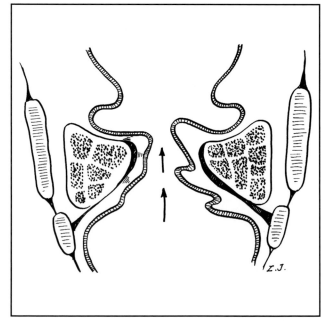

Fig 82–15. The structure of the vocal fold. The vocal fold on the right shows normal free mobility of the cover over the body of the vocal folds as air flows (*arrows*) through the glottis. The drawing on the left illustrates scarring of the epithelium to the deeper layers of the lamina propria, resulting in restriction of the mucosal wave and stiffness, as seen during stroboscopy. When the scarring is severe enough to stop vibration, the nonvibrating portion is known as an adynamic segment. Minimizing trauma to fibroblast-containing layers helps avoid this complication. (From Hirano M. *Clinical Examination of Voice*. New York, NY: Springer-Verlag, 1981:5, with permission.)

to remove pathology without provoking scar formation, that is, without stimulating fibroblasts in the intermediate layer of the lamina propria, or deeper. With this goal in mind, it seemed reasonable to protect the intermediate layer of lamina propria by preserving mucosa along the vibratory margin. If mucosa were absent, then the intermediate layer of lamina propria would be traumatized directly by contact with the contralateral vocal fold during phonation or swallowing. This contact trauma was prevented by elevating a microflap, resecting submucosal lesions, and replacing the mucosa (Fig 82–16). This technique was proposed first by the author in about 1982 and was published and illustrated in 1986.[35] It has been recommended by numerous other authors since that time.[24,34-39] This technique was attractive because the vocal folds *looked* "healed" almost immediately. However, this surgical

concept was based entirely on reasoning, not on research. Although this is unfortunate, in many ways it is unavoidable. In the absence of an animal model with a layered lamina propria, we have little alternative. Nevertheless, although it may not be reasonable to perform prospective, randomized human research on microsurgical techniques, at the very least we are obligated to look closely and critically at our results to see whether our common sense is producing consistently favorable outcomes in our patients. To be sure, laryngeal microflap surgery was a great improvement over vocal fold stripping. Since laryngologists began operating with delicate, small instruments and handling tissues gently, we have seen far fewer cases of permanent dysphonia from extensive vibratory margin scar. Nevertheless, the author was not universally happy with the results of microflap surgery. Many

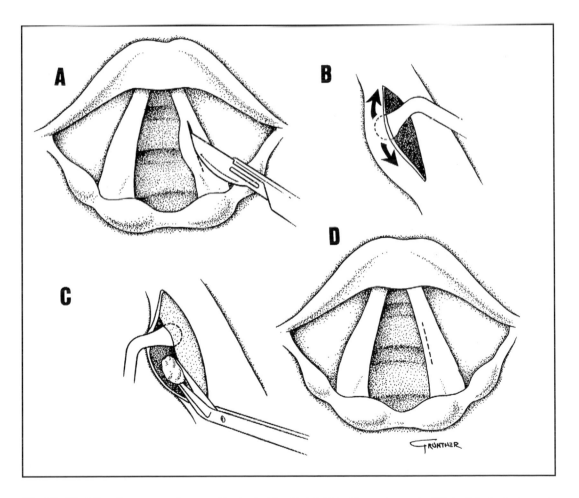

Fig 82–16. Microflap procedure, as illustrated by Sataloff in Cummings et al.[35] In this technique, a superficial incision is made in the superior surface of the true vocal fold (**A**). Blunt dissection is used to elevate the mucosa from the lesion (**B**), minimizing trauma to the fibroblast-containing layers of the lamina propria. Only pathologic tissue is excised under direct vision (**C**). Mucosa is reapproximated (**D**) without violating the leading edge. This technique is no longer recommended by this author.

were excellent (as were the results of some vocal fold strippings years ago), but careful strobovideolaryngoscopic analysis and voice assessment showed too many cases in which the final outcome was inexplicably not perfect. In fact, despite what appeared to be technically flawless operations, a small number of patients had severe, prolonged stiffness for many months after vocal fold surgery; and critical analysis revealed permanent stiffness even in some patients who were happy with their voice results. Moreover, some of this stiffness was located anterior and posterior to the region of the mass, in areas that had been normal preoperatively. This critical assessment of surgical results led the author to the uneasy feeling that we were still doing something wrong. The problem became clear immediately upon reading the basement membrane research of Dr Stephen Gray.[40]

Before Gray's landmark discovery, microflap surgery made sense. Now, it usually does not. Gray demonstrated a complex basement membrane structure between the epithelium and superficial layer of the lamina propria, as discussed in chapter 10. Moreover, he illustrated that the epithelium and basement membrane are attached to the superficial layer of the lamina propria through an intricate series of type VII collagen loops. These loops emanate from and return to basement membrane cells. Type III collagen fibers of the superficial layer of the lamina propria pass through them. This highly sophisticated architectural arrangement is probably variable from person to person, and perhaps from family to family. Basement membrane structures and the integrity of their attachments are probably related to numerous vocal fold functions, including wound healing, if we can extrapolate from basement membrane behavior elsewhere in the body. Hence, when we elevate microflaps, we are not simply manipulating structurally insignificant tissue. Rather, we are ripping apart delicate, functionally important anatomic structures.

Armed with this new anatomic knowledge and evidence that previous surgical results had not been consistently as good as desired, revised common sense suggested that the destruction of normal tissue structures involved in elevating microflaps probably rendered this technique counterproductive. Consequently, in the latter part of 1991, "traditional" microflap surgery was abandoned by this author. Since that time, the author has limited surgery strictly to the region of pathology, without elevating or disturbing any surrounding tissue. Masses are either excised with the smallest possible amount of their overlying mucosa or a mini-microflap is elevated directly over the lesion (Fig 82–17).[41] In this technique, a small mucosal incision is made anteriorly, superiorly, and

posteriorly underlying the vocal fold mass. Gentle retraction is accomplished with a small suction on the surface of the lesion; and blunt dissection is used to separate the mass from the lamina propria, reflecting it medially. The mass is then excised either with all of its overlying mucosa or, preferably, retaining a small inferiorly based medial flap of mucosa. This is generally easy to do once the mass has been reflected medially, because the mucosa is already stretched because of the lesion. The micro-miniflap is a small, medially based pedicled flap. It should not be confused with Dedo and Sooy's much larger "micro-trap-door flap" for use in supraglottic stenosis [42] or with Ossoff and colleague's larger "serial micro-trap-door flaps" used for subglottic stenosis.[42-44]

Unfortunately, for the reasons stated above, good, prospective scientific data comparing vocal fold stripping and microflap and mini-microflap surgery are not available. The author's initial anecdotal impressions, and the data presented on excision of 96 vocal fold masses in 60 patients (49 of them singers)[41] provide convincing evidence that mini-microflap surgery and limited mass excision with overlying mucosa (without disturbing any adjacent tissue) (Fig 82–18) provide substantially better results than the microflap surgery advocated originally by this author. Since abandoning microflap surgery, the author has not encountered the kind of extensive and prolonged postoperative stiffness encountered after some cases of microflap surgery. Mini-microflap is currently recommended for excision of vocal fold submucosal cysts and similar lesions. When a mini-microflap cannot be created, resection of the mass with the smallest possible amount of overlying mucosa should be performed.

Vocal Fold Polyps and Nodules

Like the vocal fold masses discussed above, vocal fold polyps and nodules should be removed conservatively, preserving normal mucosa and remaining superficial to the intermediate layer of the lamina propria. This is accomplished best by excising the lesion entirely with sharp instruments, rather than by tearing the mucosa using cupped forceps. Nodules rarely require surgery. If they are diagnosed correctly, more than 90% will resolve or become asymptomatic through voice therapy alone. However, those that persist in causing symptoms despite voice therapy should be removed with little or no trauma to the subjacent superficial layer of the lamina propria. Many vocal fold polyps are accompanied by an obvious central blood vessel that extends from the superior surface of the vocal fold. Occasionally, feeding vessels may course along the vibratory margin or originate below

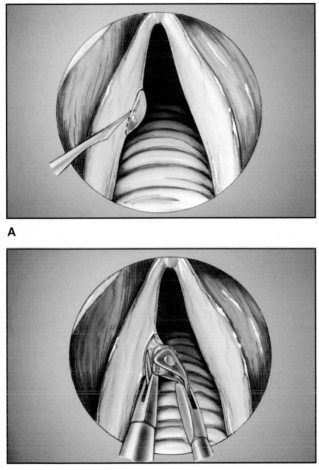

A

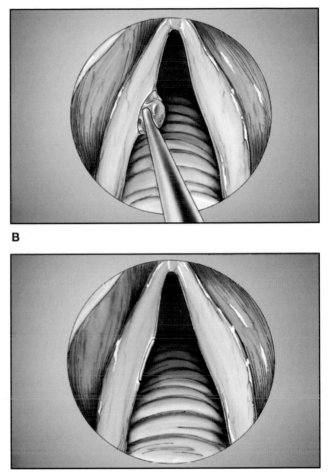

B

C

D

Fig 82–17. A. In elevating a mini-microflap, an incision is made with a straight knife at the junction of the mass and normal tissue. Small vertical anterior and posterior incisions may be added at the margins of the mass if necessary, usually using a straight scissors. **B.** The mass is separated by blunt dissection, splitting the superficial layer of the lamina propria and preserving it as much as possible. This dissection can be performed with a spatula, blunt ball dissector (illustrated), or scissors (as illustrated in **A**). **C.** The lesion is stabilized and a scissors (straight or curved) is used to excise the lesion, preserving as much adjacent mucosa as possible. The lesion itself acts as a tissue expander, and it is often possible to create an inferiorly based mini-microflap. **D.** The mini-microflap is replaced over the surgical defect, establishing primary closure and acting as a biological dressing.

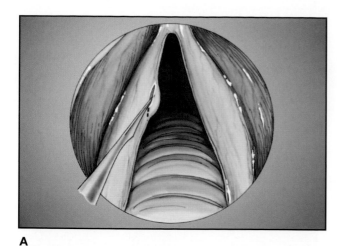

A

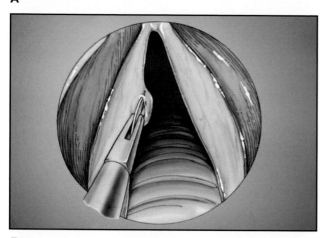

B

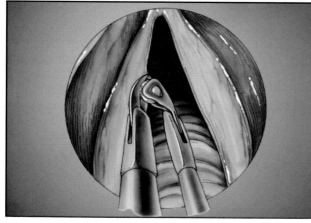

C

Fig 82–18. A. An incision is made on the superior surface of the vocal fold at the junction of the lesion and normal mucosa. **B.** Blunt dissection with the scissors is used to split the superficial layer of lamina propria. Note that the force of the side of the scissors is directed toward the base of the lesion and the glottis, not laterally toward the vocal ligament. **C.** The lesion is stabilized (not retracted) with heart-shaped forceps and excised, without adjacent normal tissue. A small mucosal gap results, but this usually heals well.

the vocal fold edge. Prominent feeding vessels should be vaporized with a carbon dioxide laser (at 1 watt, 0.1 second, defocused) or resected to help prevent recurrent hemorrhage and polyp formation (Fig 82–19). The author prefers resection in most cases. The polyp can then be removed from the vibratory margin with traditional instruments (Fig 82–20) or laser (Fig 82–21). The author uses cold instruments, but the laser can be used safely, as discussed in chapter 84.

Varicosities and Ectatic Vessels and Vocal Fold Hemorrhage

Ectatic blood vessels and varicosities are usually asymptomatic. However, occasionally, they require treatment. Usually, this is due to repeated submucosal hemorrhage emanating from the enlarged, weakened blood vessel. More rarely, it is due to dysphonia caused by engorgement of the blood vessel following the exercise of voice use (just like the veins that pump up in arms following exercise), which changes the mass of the vocal fold. This is a proven but uncommon cause of voice fatigue (Fig 82–22).

In patients with recurrent hemorrhage from a varicose or ectatic vessel, or with voice dysfunction resulting from small vessel enlargement, vaporization of the abnormal vessels used to be the treatment of choice

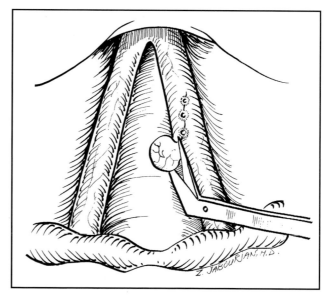

Fig 82–19 The feeding vessel of a hemorrhagic polyp may be treated with a 1-watt defocused laser burst of short duration to cauterize the vessel and prevent recurrent hemorrhage. The polyp can then be removed from the leading edge with scissors, avoiding the risk of laser injury to the vibratory margin.

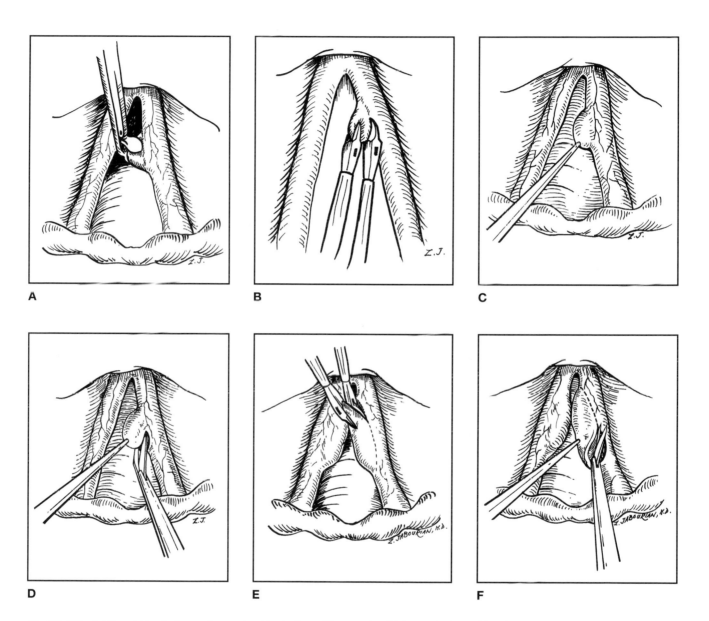

Fig 82–20. A. The old technique of grasping the lesion with a cupped forceps and evulsing the lesion from the vocal fold is not sufficiently precise. It allows for tearing of the mucosa beyond the necessary area of excision. Instead, the lesion may be grasped with a delicate forceps (**B**), or preferably stabilized with a fine suction (**C**). The lesion should not be retracted medially with forceps, as this will tent the mucosa and often result in excessive excision. The mucosa is cut sharply rather than ripped (**D**), limiting resection strictly to the area of pathology. Even with small lesions, but especially with larger lesions, it is often helpful to bluntly separate the lesion from the underlying lamina propria with a blunt dissector (**E**), or spreading with scissors (**F**). This must be done superficially, and any pressure should be directed medially (toward the portion being resected), taking care not to traumatize the intermediate layer of the lamina propria. Reinke's space is not rich in fibroblasts (although it contains some), and utilizing this technique permits resection of the diseased tissue only, while minimizing the chance of scarring.

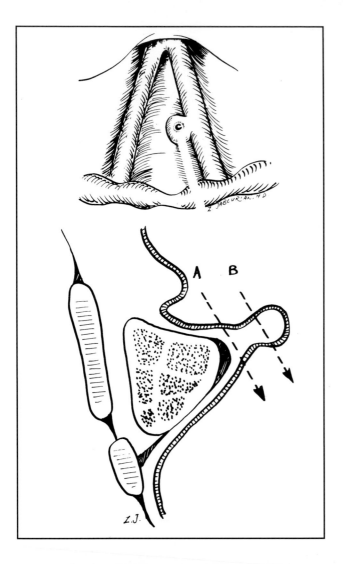

Fig 82–21. (*Top*) When a lesion on the vibratory margin is resected with laser, the center of the laser beam must be located in the body of the mass. Thus, the zone of destruction (rather than center of the laser beam) is approximately even with the vibratory margin. (*Bottom*) A cross-section of the vocal fold illustrates the same principle. Arrow B represents the center of the laser beam, and arrow A represents the outermost region of the zone of destruction around the laser beam. The zone of destruction should be superficial to the intermediate layer of the lamina propria to help prevent scar formation.

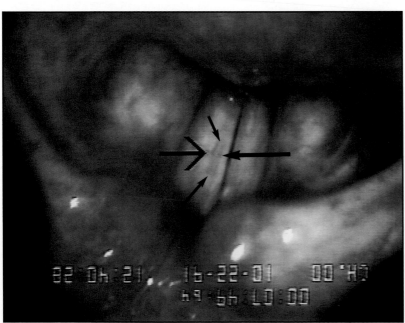

Fig 82–22. Video print revealed a prominent varicosity on the left vocal fold. The large black arrow marks the lateral margin of the varicosity, the smaller arrow marks the medial margin, and the smallest arrows mark the anterior and posterior extent of the varicosity. This vein pumped up during the singing exercises much the same as extremity veins become prominent during other forms of exercise. This added to the mass effect of the left vocal fold causing interruptions in the vibratory pattern, voice fatigue, loss of upper range, increased vocal effort, and slight hoarseness. These symptoms resolved after vaporization of the vessel. (From *Ear Nose Throat J.* 73(7):445, with permission.)

and still may be indicated in some cases. This is performed using a carbon dioxide laser, using defocused 1-watt laser bursts interrupted with single pulses at 0.1 second, and icing the vocal fold. Care should be taken not to permit heat transfer to the intermediate or deep layers of the lamina propria. Protection may be accomplished by submucosal infusion and by directing the laser beam tangentially for blood vessels directly on the vibratory margin, so that the direct impact of the laser beam is not aimed at the vibrating surface. In some cases, the mucosa may be gently retracted using alligator forceps with a cottonoid along the superior surface, stretching blood vessels onto the superior surface where they may be vaporized more safely over the body of the thyroarytenoid muscle. If the vessel is positioned over the lamina propria such that laser vaporization cannot be performed safely, delicate resection of the vessel with preservation of adjacent mucosa has proven successful in the author's hands[45] (Fig 82–23). This approach is similar to that used for symptomatic varicose vessels elsewhere in the body, and its rationale, technique and results were reviewed by Hochman, Sataloff, Hillman, et al in 1999.[45] Thirty-four of the 42 patients we reported were female, 84% of the patients with documented hemorrhages were female, and 39 of 42 of the patients were singers. Most ectasias and varices are located in the middle of the musculomembranous vocal fold, usually on the superior surface. This observation has been reported previously.[46,47] We noted that 66% of the varices and ectasias occurred in the region of the superior and lateral extent of the mucosal wave. This is probably the point at which maximum shearing forces are generated in the superficial layer of the lamina propria, as the mucosal wave reaches its superior/lateral endpoint, decelerates quickly, and reverses direction to begin the closing phase of the oscillatory cycle. We speculate that this whiplashlike effect and the limitation of the microvasculature by the basement membrane of the epithelium are probably responsible for the preponderance of hemorrhages, ectasias, and varices that occur on the superior and lateral surfaces near the middle of the musculomembranous portion of the vocal fold. The middle segment of the musculomembranous portion of the vocal fold is now referred to as the striking zone, a term coined by Zeitels and introduced in our article on ectasias and varices.[45] We believe that chronic mechanical trauma to the microvasculature is responsible for the development of varicosities and ectasias and that direct collision forces are responsible for most of the vascular abnormalities that occur on the medial surface of the vocal fold. The fact that so many such abnormalities are actually on the superior surface rather than on the

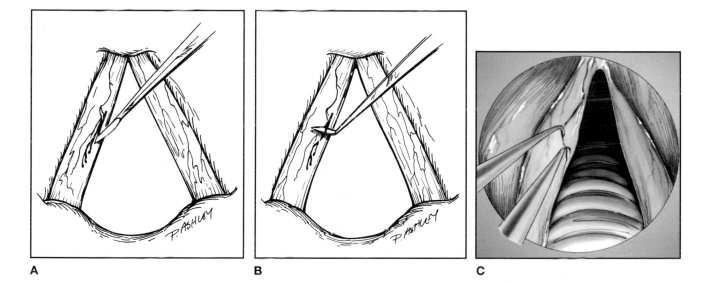

A   **B**   **C**

Fig 82–23. Ectasia. **A.** This figure illustrates the technique for elevating and resecting a varicose vessel. A superficial incision is made in the epithilium adjacent to the vessel using the sharp point of the vascular knife, or using a microknife (illustrated). **B.** The 1-mm right angle vascular knife is inserted under the vessel and used to elevate it. It may be necessary to make more than one epithelial incision in order to dissect the desired length of the vessel. **C.** Once the pathologic vessel has been elevated, it is retracted gently to provide access to its anterior and posterior limits. These can be divided sharply with a scissors or knife (bleeding stops spontaneously) or divided and cauterized with a laser, as long as there is no thermal injury to adjacent vocal ligament.

vibratory margin probably is due to the fact that the maximum shearing stresses during oscillation are on the superior surface. Because of the whiplashlike mechanism of injury, superficial vessels are more likely to be injured than deeper vessels. This is convenient, because their superficial nature facilitates surgical management. In our reported series of 42 patients for whom sufficient pre- and postoperative data were available, mucosal vibration remained the same or improved in all patients who underwent excision of ectasias or varices using cold instruments. This had not been the author's (RTS) experience with laser management of similar lesions in earlier years, prior to developing this technique. Although the author (RTS) prefers resection of vessels in most cases, laser cauterization should still be considered an acceptable option, particularly for lesions far lateral to the vibratory margin. However, regardless of location, the importance of avoiding trauma to adjacent tissues cannot be overstated.

In patients with very extensive hemorrhage distorting a vocal fold, an incision along the superior surface with evacuation of the hematoma may speed healing. In general, this is not necessary. However, if the bulging vocal fold has not flattened satisfactorily through resorption of the hematoma within a few days after the hemorrhage, evacuation may be considered. Surgery involves suction evacuation of the hematoma through a small incision on the superior surface. Vocal fold hemorrhage is discussed in detail in chapter 86.

Reinke's Edema

When surgery is performed for Reinke's edema, in this author's opinion, only one vocal fold should be operated on at a sitting in most cases, although this practice remains controversial. The vocal fold may be incised along its superior surface, and the edematous material removed with a fine suction (Fig 82–24). Redundant mucosa may be trimmed, and mucosa should be reapproximated. Care must be exercised to avoid resecting too much mucosa. The second vocal fold may be treated similarly after the first vocal fold has healed. However, the voice improvement that follows unilateral evacuation of Reinke's edema is often surprisingly good, and patients frequently elect to leave the other vocal fold undisturbed.

In addition, there is a more important reason for staging surgery for Reinke's edema. Occasionally, surgical treatment for this condition results in a stiff vocal fold, sometimes even adynamic, even though this complication theoretically should be rare with the technique advocated. Nevertheless, it can occur even when surgery has been performed well. If it occurs on one side and there is still Reinke's edema on the other side, the polypoid side usually compensates. Voice quality is generally satisfactory, and (most importantly) phonation is not effortful. If stiffness occurs bilaterally, the voice is not only hoarse, but moreover requires high phonation pressures. Patients are unhappy not only with voice quality, but especially with the fatigue that accompanies increased effort required to initiate and sustain phonation. Under these circumstances, they often feel that they are worse than they were with untreated Reinke's edema. If surgery is staged so that healing can be observed on one vocal fold before surgery is performed on the second vocal fold, this situation can be avoided in nearly all cases.

Granulomas and Vocal Process Ulcers

Prior to surgical excision, causative and contributing factors should be addressed. Reflux should be treated,

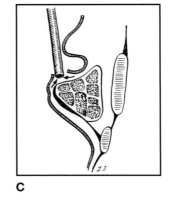 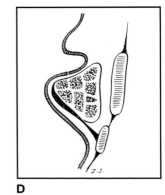

A.   **B.**   **C**   **D**

Fig 82–24. A. Bulky vocal fold showing Reinke's edema (*small dots*) in the superifical layer of the lamina propria. **B.** Incision in the superior surface opens easily into Reinke's space. **C.** Using a fine needle suction, the edema fluid is aspirated (*arrows*). **D.** The mucosal edges are reapproximated, trimming redundant mucosa if necessary.

and voice therapy instituted. If the lesions do not resolve within a few weeks, they should be excised. The laser may be helpful in removing these lesions because they are generally not on the vibratory margin. Therefore, scarring is unlikely to cause hoarseness. In addition, they are often friable; and laser excision helps minimize bleeding. However, although lasers are convenient in controlling hemorrhage in vocal fold granuloma surgery, it must be remembered that we are treating a nonhealing area. Like other thermal injury, laser burns cause substantial tissue damage. Any surgeon who has accidentally struck his or her finger with a laser beam knows that the effect is more traumatic than a sharp cut of similar size with a knife. Consequently, to minimize tissue trauma and promote healing, this author prefers to minimize or avoid laser use at the base of these lesions. The underlying perichondrium should not be traumatized. In all cases, a generous specimen should be removed for biopsy to rule out carcinoma and other possible etiologies.

In patients with recurrent granulomas, botulinum toxin injection may be considered. This can be performed as an outpatient or during surgical resection of granulomas in the operating room. In general, only a small amount of botulinum toxin is required, and it is best to place it in the lateral cricoarytenoid muscle (LCA) for recurrent granulomas near the vocal process. In these patients, there appears to be dominance of LCA activity during the adduction process, causing point-contact near the tip of the vocal process rather than the broader contact that results from a different balance of activity between the lateral cricoarytenoid and interarytenoid muscles, as noted initially by Zeitels (Steven Zeitels, MD, personal communication, 1997) and confirmed by this author's (RTS) experience. Both LCA muscles are injected usually with only 1.25 to 2.5 mouse units of Botox (Allergan, Irvine, Calif) or the equivalent, as discussed in chapter 64.

Papillomas

Laryngeal papillomatosis has been recognized as a problem for more than a century. Papilloma was described by Czermak in 1861.[48] It also was illustrated by Mackenzie, Türck, and Elsberg.[49-51] Sixty-seven of Mackenzie's first 100 mirror-guided laryngeal procedures were for papillomatous lesions.[52] Nevertheless, optimal treatment continues to elude us. Papilloma is discussed in greater detail in chapter 57.

When papillomas interfere with voice quality or airway patency, surgery is the standard treatment. To minimize the risk of seeding the lower airway with virus, intubation must be accomplished under direct vision, with a small tube that does not traumatize the papillomas as it passes through the larynx. . In general, resection of laryngeal papillomas has been performed with a carbon dioxide laser, and this instrument offers great advantages. However, it can also cause problems. When used, a smoke evaporator should be employed to avoid the risks of infecting the surgeon or other operating room personnel with viruses in the laser smoke. Only one side of the larynx should be operated on at a sitting; in many cases, multiple procedures are often necessary.

Early discouraging experience with recurrent juvenile papillomatosis, and general agreement that laser surgery is called for in papillomas, have led to a somewhat indelicate approach to laser surgery, in this author's opinion. For many surgeons, laser surgery for papilloma means directly vaporizing all the areas of papillomatous involvement on one vocal fold; this invariably means injury to underlying tissues. This produces permanent dysphonia in many patients. Moreover, recurrences tend to involve deeper structures (vocal ligament and muscle) that were not involved initially.

Anecdotally, the author believes that adult-onset laryngeal papilloma may behave differently from the virulent, juvenile papillomatosis many of us are accustomed to treating. Consequently, a method has been employed to attempt cure, rather than simply palliation, and to preserve underlying structures. The method works best when the papillomas have not been operated on previously, but it has been used effectively in recurrent cases, as well[53] (Fig 82–25). An incision is made on the superior surface of the vocal fold with the laser, leaving a small margin of grossly normal tissue around the papilloma. A microflap is then elevated in the superficial layer of the lamina propria under the papilloma. The flap and papillomas are generally retracted medially, and anterior and posterior margin incisions are made with scissors or a laser. Contact endoscopy may be helpful in determining the optimal incision site. The inferior margin can then be divided with the laser under direct vision, and the mucosa and papillomas are resected en bloc. Although elevation of a microflap does not ensure preservation of good vocal quality (as discussed above), the odds of a good result are certainly better with this technique than they are with indiscriminately "cooking" the vocal ligament. This technique appears to produce acceptable voice results, and some apparent cures in patients who have gone 5 years or more without recurrent papillomas. More research is needed, but the author continues to use this approach and recommends its consideration. In cases of frequently recurrent papilloma in which only debulking is planned, powered laryngeal instruments can be help-

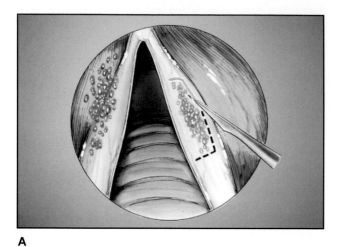

A

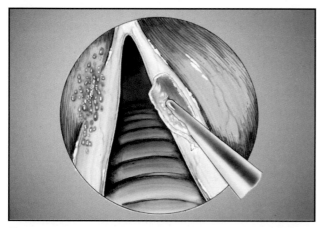

B

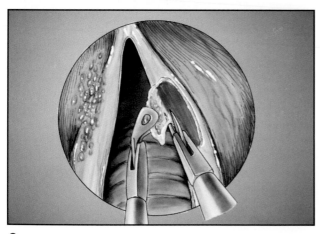

C

ful and provide surprisingly good control of the limits of tissue removal (Fig 82–26).

The use of cidofovir for laryngeal papillomatosis is promising. This antiviral agent can be injected directly into the papillomatosis lesions; and some patients respond dramatically. The use of this substance was pioneered by Wellens.[54] Although cidofovir is approved by the United States Food and Drug Administration (FDA) for other uses, laryngeal injection is an off-label use. The medication may have serious side effects, but they are not likely to occur in the doses used commonly for laryngeal surgery. Concentrations recommended most commonly for laryngeal use are in the range of 2.5 to 5 mg per ml, but higher concen-

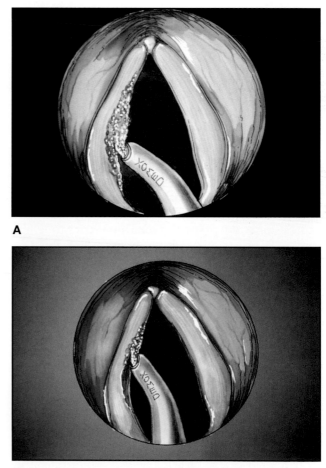

A

B

Fig 82–25. **A.** An incision is made around the area of papilloma with a sharp knife, approaching it as one might approach an area of carcinoma in situ. **B.** A microflap is elevated bluntly, sparing the underlying superficial layer of lamina propria. **C.** The region of papilloma is resected. (Courtesy of Medtronic-Xomed, Jacksonville, Fla.)

Fig 82–26 **A.** Papilloma is debulked with a 3.5- or 4.0-mm angle-tip laryngeal blade at 5,000 rpm. **B.** Final removal is performed with limited trauma to the mucosa and underlying tissues using a 3.5-mm angle-tip laryngeal skimmer blade at 500 rpm. (Courtesy of Xomed-Medtronics, Jacksonville Fla.)

trations in the range of 15 mg per cc have been used frequently without apparent adverse affect. In a few cases, concentrations as high as 75 mg per cc have been used without any adverse consequences; but there are questions about long-term effect including (onco-genicity). So, patients need to be informed fully, and this antiviral material should be used with caution in adults and children.

Ventricular Fold Cysts

Ventricular fold (false vocal fold) cysts are uncommon mucous retention cysts, frequently lined with cu-boidal cells, which generally are seen in patients over 50 years of age. They occur generally anteriorly along the ventricular fold. They must be differentiated from other lesions such as Hürthle cell tumor and oncocy-toma arising from thyroid remnants and from other lesions such as laryngoceles and cancer. Multiple cysts may occur. Surgical removal involves grasping the cyst with a cupped forceps and dissecting the base with a scissors or laser. The cyst may extend to the floor of the ventricle. If bilateral lesions are present, especially anteriorly, both sides should not be operated on at the same sitting.

Epiglottic Cysts

Epiglottic cysts occur on the lingual surface of the free edge of the epiglottis or in the area of the epiglottic folds. They may become large and cause muffling of the voice. Whenever possible, they should be removed completely. If they rupture and complete removal is not possible, they should be marsupialized.

Laryngoceles

The ventricle of Morgagni is located between the true and false vocal folds. The appendix of the ventricle of Morgagni is a blind pouch called the saccule in the anterior superior section. Laryngoceles are abnormal dilations or herniations of the laryngeal saccule.[55] They communicate with the laryngeal lumen and generally are filled with air. They become apparent clinically when they are distended after air is forced into them or when they are filled with fluid. They are connected to the ventricle by a narrow stalk and form a sac lined with pseudostratified, ciliated columnar epithelium. The appendix of the ventricle is considered abnormal if it extends above the upper border of the thyroid cartilage.

Laryngoceles limited to the interior of the larynx are called internal; those that protrude outside the thyroid cartilage into the neck are called external. They may also be mixed (internal and external). Laryngoceles should be distinguished from pharyngoceles, which are not true pouches and which generally diminish in size in the absence of pharyngeal pressure (eg, when not whistling or playing a wind instrument).[56] Out-pouchings of the laryngeal ventricle extend through the openings in the thyrohyoid membrane for the superior laryngeal vessels and nerve, and balloon outward and upward toward the submandibular triangle.[57] It should be noted that external and mixed laryngoceles are really variants of the internal laryngocele. Because laryngoceles arise from the region of the saccule within the larynx, if the lesion is a laryngocele, there must be an intralaryngeal component manifested at least as a tract connecting the lateral component with the ventricle, with or without internal dilation. Hence, pure external laryngoceles do not exist. Lesions without an intralaryngeal component should be classified differently (eg, as pharyngoceles).

There are several proposed mechanisms for laryngocele formation. In neonates, they are presumed to be remnants of the lateral air sacs seen in other primates. In adults, they can represent a congenital enlargement of the saccule or an acquired lesion associated with increased intraluminal pressure. The association of laryngoceles with laryngeal carcinoma and with occupations that involve long periods of forced expiration supports this notion.[58]

Brass and woodwind players are at risk for a variety of head and neck abnormalities as a result of increased intraluminal pressure during their musical performances.[59] Transient ischemic attacks, temporomandibular joint dysfunction, and dental malocclusion have been reported. Injury to the orbicularis oris in brass players can require surgical repair.[59] Stress velopharyngeal incompetence has been documented in trumpeters and bassoonists. Young trumpet players are at greatest risk for injury to oral and cervical tissues when they generate peak respiratory pressure averaging 151 torr.[60]

Several authors have examined laryngocele formation in woodwind players. Stephani and Tarab obtained plain x-rays on 25 wind instruments players and found laryngoceles in all of them.[61] Macfie found laryngoceles in 53 of 94%56 (56%) woodwind bandsman.[62] Subclinical laryngoceles are common among horn players, and they rarely require surgical intervention.

Surgery for laryngoceles in young musicians poses several problems. The literature offers no guidance regarding the timing of surgery, the healing period before playing can be resumed, and the risk of recurrence with continued performance. Furthermore, the cervical approach used commonly for the treatment of external laryngoceles can disrupt the normal function of the strap muscles, which are important for tone generation.[63] The risks of infection and progression of the defect must be balanced against a young performer's desire for musical growth.

Since Ward's early reports on this subject,[56] our understanding of laryngoceles and pharyngoceles has changed slightly. Both laryngoceles and pharyngoceles can change size and appearance with variations in internal pressure. Although the classical definitions of laryngocele remain valid, combinations of both can occur. Air-filled masses that arise in the pharynx (commonly in the region of the piriform sinuses) and lack a laryngeal component or origin should be called pharyngoceles. Those that arise in the laryngeal ventricle should be called laryngoceles. Considering the origins of pharyngeal pouches as reviewed in Ward's 1963 paper[56] as well as the forces involved, it appears likely that most lesions with a laryngeal component originated in the larynx and extended in the neck rather than vice versa; but it is not always possible to prove origin. It is also important to recognize that the therapeutic implications of the distinctions are not as clear-cut as they once were and that lesions that combine the features of laryngoceles and pharyngoceles occur[64] (Fig 82–27). The distinctions between laryngoceles and pharyngoceles were quite important when we still believed laryngoceles usually required surgery and pharyngoceles required surgery only rarely. However, as arts-medicine has evolved, experience has shown that in most cases neither lesion requires surgery. Contrary to our earlier understandings, the vast majority of laryngoceles are asymptomatic.

If surgery is necessary, it is commonly performed externally, particularly if the laryngocele produces a large bulge in the neck. When an external approach is used, a variety of thyrotomy techniques may be employed as discussed in this chapter and elsewhere in the literature.[65] However, in selected cases, endoscopic surgery may be adequate. This procedure usually is performed under general anesthesia. This type of surgery is most effective for internal laryngoceles or mixed laryngoceles with a large connecting neck between the internal and external components. The technique involves excising the false vocal fold. This effectively marsupializes the cyst into the larynx. The false vocal fold should be retracted toward the midline, and the incisions are made most effectively using the carbon dioxide laser (Fig 82–28). The removal of the false vocal folds may affect vocal resonance, especially in singers. Therefore, this procedure must be used with great caution, if used at all, in professional voice users.

Miscellaneous Masses

In some cases, both the surgeon and the patient must realize that health considerations sometimes have to take precedence over the preservation of optimal voice quality. Although every effort must be made to design a procedure that optimizes the voice result, sometimes a serious benign process or a neoplasm does not permit perfection. This situation is encountered commonly when treating papilloma (Fig 82–29) and other lesions. In the granular cell tumor seen in Figure 82–30, for example, the disease extended onto the posterior aspect of the membranous portion of the vocal fold. Endoscopic resection required removal of the posterior half of the vocal fold in this professional soprano. Although a good neovocal fold was formed and vocal quality was very acceptable for speech within a few months, she was not able to return to professional singing performance for more than a year following surgery.

Carcinoma

The surgical management of vocal fold carcinoma is discussed in chapter 93 and in the other sources.[66]

Surgery for Postoperative Vocal Fold Injury and Scar

This subject is covered in chapter 87.

Sulcus Vocalis

Numerous techniques have been used to treat sulcus vocalis. The mucosa can be dissected from the deeper structures to which it is adherent and simply replaced in its original position. This technique fails frequently, however. The area of the sulcus can also be resected, and mucosa can be reapproximated. This technique seems to work a little better than simple elevation, but it also does not produce consistently satisfactory results. Collagen injection has been used to treat sulcus vocalis;[67] but it, too, has not been consistently successful. Pontes and Behlau introduced a technique involving multiple crossed incisions throughout the length of the sulcus.[68] At first glance, this technique looks as if it should cause greater scarring; but it is actually a series of multiple relaxing incisions following established, classical surgical principles. Substantial voice improvement has been achieved in a majority of patients undergoing this procedure. Autologous lipoinjection and fat implantation also may be effica-

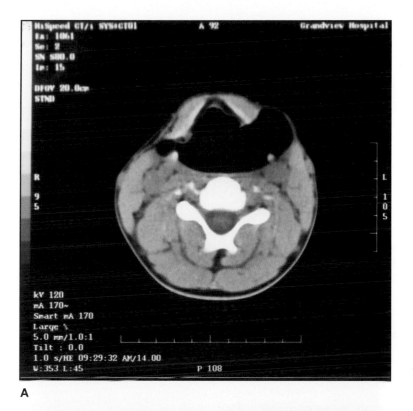

A

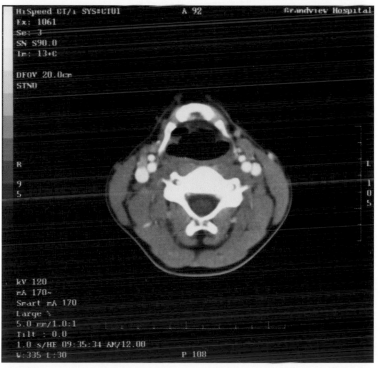

B

Fig 82–27. Laryngoceles. **A.** Bilateral dilatations that could be mistaken for pharyngoceles. **B.** Right intralaryngeal component suggesting laryngeal origin. This 16-year-old trumpet player's presentation involved features consistent with both laryngocele and pharyngocele.

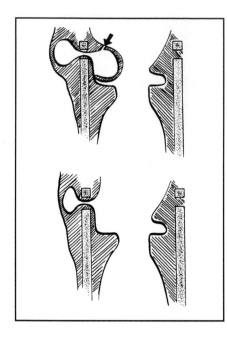

Fig 82–28. (*Top*) Depiction of a left internal laryngocele that has enlarged and displaced the false vocal fold into the glottic lumen. It has dissected through the hyothyroid space to present externally. With microsurgical techniques or a laser, the involved false vocal fold is excised. (*Bottom*) Following removal of the false vocal fold, the remaining laryngocele drains easily into the lumen of the larynx, and its external component no longer is troublesome.

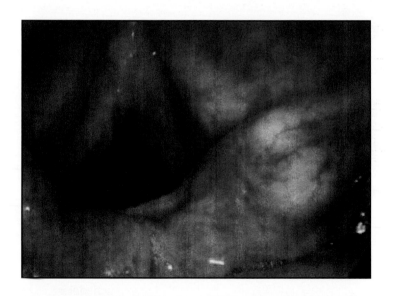

Fig 82–29. Recurrent papilloma involving the vibratory margin. Controlling the lesion and avoiding airway complications are primary treatment priorities, although it is possible to restore reasonable voice in most cases as discussed in chapter 57.

cious. They are discussed elsewhere in this book. At present, the best surgical technique has not been determined. However, it is now clear that various surgical interventions provide at least partial voice improvement in many patients. The principles of management are the same as those discussed for scar in chapter 87. It is necessary to address compensatory hyperfunction through voice therapy, failure of glottic closure through medialization, and recreation of a mucosal wave through surgery on the vibratory margin. At the time of the writing of the first edition of this book, surgical intervention was not recommended. However, developments over the last 15 years suggest that patients with significant symptoms caused by sulcus should be offered surgical options, with the clear understanding that surgical recommendations for this condition are still evolving, voice quality could be worse following voice surgery, and that there is cer-

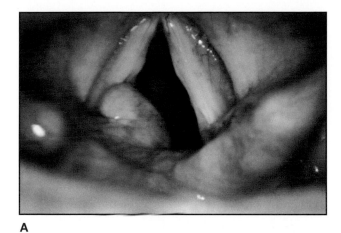

A

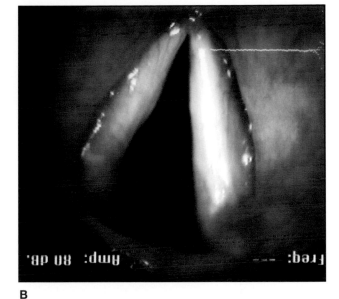

B

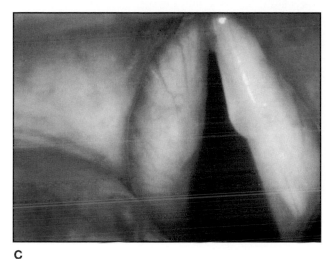

C

Fig 82–30. **A.** Preoperative granular cell tumor. **B.** Postoperative appearance 11 months after surgery. **C.** Appearance 5 years after surgery.

tainly no guarantee of improvement. The decision on whether the chances of achieving better voice are worth the risks should be made by the patient and physician on an individual basis. Surgical treatment is now good enough that it should not be denied to symptomatic and informed patients who elect it.

Laryngeal Webs

Before embarking on surgical repair, the laryngologist should determine whether the web is symptomatic and its longitudinal and vertical extent. Many webs cause no vocal or respiratory problems and should be left undisturbed. The selection of a surgical approach for symptomatic webs depends on their extent, especially subglottically. Complete assessment including strobovideolaryngoscopy and high-resolution CT scan is helpful in defining the lesion. The importance of stroboscopy cannot be overstated. When the voice is hoarse after trauma (surgical or otherwise), and a small web is present, it is essential to determine pre-operatively whether the web is truly the cause of the dysphonia. Often the web is asymptomatic, and the hoarseness is caused by scarring elsewhere in the vocal folds (an adynamic segment) that cannot be diagnosed under routine light. It is extremely helpful to make such determinations before subjecting the patient to surgery that may not only fail to improve the voice, but make it worse. For relatively small, symptomatic webs, surgery may be performed endoscopically. More extensive external approaches can be used when necessary.

Endoscopic resection of a laryngeal web may be performed with traditional instruments or laser. In a small number of cases, it may be possible to treat a web successfully endoscopically without placement of a keel. This is accomplished by dividing one edge near a vocal fold, and allowing the free edge to fold in on its base on the other side. The edge may be left free, fixed with fibrin glue, or "laser welded." This technique is minimally traumatic, but recurrences appear more frequently than they do following placement of a keel.

In general, it is necessary to place a laryngeal keel to prevent reformation of the web. A tracheotomy is rarely necessary. The keel is fashioned individually out of silastic, Teflon, metals, or other minimally reactive substances. Sutures are passed into the larynx through 16-gauge needles inserted through the cricothyroid membrane, and above the thyroid notch (Fig 82–31). The keel can be guided into position, and the sutures are fixed into the skin. Hospitalization and close observation for airway obstruction are required for the first 24 hours. The rare complications of the procedure include displacement of the keel with aspiration and obstruction and deep neck infection. Nevertheless, the procedure is less traumatic than the external approach, and frequently is effective. Whether the endolaryngeal or external approach is used, the keel should be left in position for at least 2 to 3 weeks.

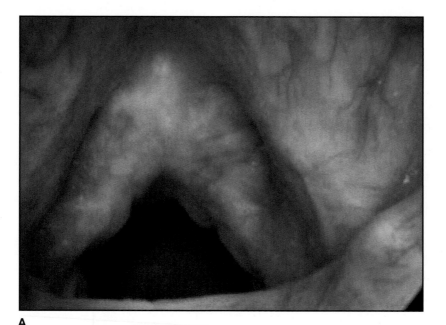

A

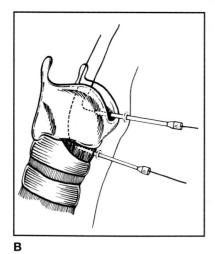

B

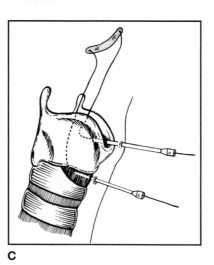

C

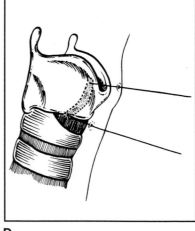

D

Fig 82–31. A. Videoprint showing a thick anterior web caused by repeated surgery for papillomas. Webs this thick often require an open procedure; but sometimes they can be repaired adequately endoscopically. **B.** Placement of 16-gauge needles above and below the thyroid cartilage in the midline, in preparation for endoscopic placement of a keel. This procedure would not generally be used in the presence of papillomas, but is useful for webs from other causes. **C.** Individually fashioned Teflon keel is attached to sutures, passed through the 16-gauge needles. **D.** The sutures are drawn through the needles in order to place the keel in final position in the anterior commissure.

A new technique was reported by Sataloff and Hawkshaw in 1998.[69] This technique permits placement of an internal laryngeal stent without external manipulation, even for placement of sutures. The original procedure was performed endoscopically using a rectangle of 0.02 inch reinforced silastic usually used in middle ear surgery. This procedure was designed originally for a patient with aggressive, active papillomatosis and a severe web. Because of the aggressiveness of the papilloma, the author (RTS) was reluctant to create even a suture tract from the larynx through

the skin to secure a keel or stent in the usual fashion, because of the risk of seeding papilloma. This entirely endoscopic, technique permits web resection without contamination of tissues outside of the endolarynx (Fig 82–32, A-D).

Postoperative management following resection of vocal fold webs can be important to ensuring success. The technique used for many years in Germany and more recently reintroduced in the United States by Stasney should be in the armamentarium of all laryngologists performing surgery for glottic web.[70] If a

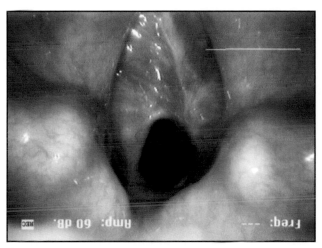

A

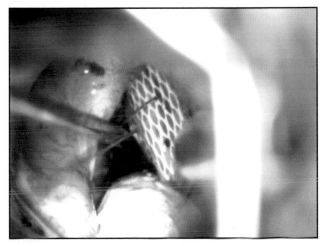

B

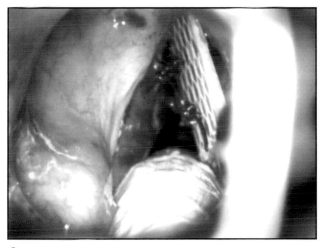

C

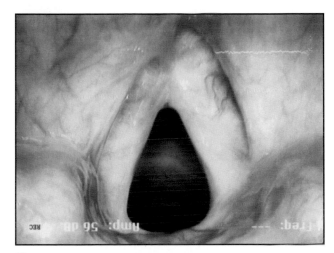

D

Fig 82–32. A. Thick anterior glottic web with significant respiratory compromise. A 38-year-old professional speaker and businesswoman with aggressive, recurrent papillomatosis developed a web severe enough to interfere with respiration. **B.** 0.02 inch silastic was sewn endoscopically through the vocal fold, without sutures being passed through the thyroid cartilage or externally. **C.** As originally described, the knots were tied medially as shown. Now, the knots are tied lateral to the silastic to avoid knot-induced trauma to the contralateral vocal fold. The sutures were left in place until the contralateral vocal fold appeared to be remucosalized. This took about 3 ½ weeks. **D.** Post-operative appearance, which has remained stable during 4 years following surgery.

web starts to re-form early in the postoperative period, it can be divided easily in the office. Under indirect laryngoscopy or nasal fiberoptic guidance, a curved indirect laryngoscopic instrument is used. The ideal instrument is a medicine applicator with a slight ball-like enlargement on the end, used in past years for dripping cocaine onto the vocal folds. Topical anesthetic can be applied with this instrument, after which the instrument is passed between the vocal folds and pulled forward to break up the web. The procedure can be repeated periodically, if necessary; and it is effective in preventing web re-formation in some cases.

Bowed Vocal Folds

As discussed previously, dysphonia from vocal fold bowing generally responds to expert voice therapy, especially if the bowing is due to "senile vocal fold atrophy." Occasionally, even this condition is so severe that therapy is insufficient. This problem is encountered more often when the bowing is due to neurological injury or dysfunction, particularly superior laryngeal nerve paresis or paralysis. In such cases, surgery is reasonable.

Injection of Teflon into mobile vocal folds is virtually never necessary or advisable. The potential complications of Teflon do not justify its use under these circumstances. However, injection of autologous fat or allogeneic collagen laterally (the same position as Teflon) may be useful. Type I thyroplasty may also be helpful in selected cases. If the larynx is not too severely ossified, the effects of medialization can be predicted to some extent by medial compression of the thyroid cartilage. If there is a significant height disparity, superficial collagen injection may be of value in selected cases. Approximately 0.2 cc is injected into the region of the lamina propria to increase the bulk of the vocal fold. Vocal lengthening procedures designed for pitch elevation have also been used. However, improvements are generally short-lived, and this approach is rarely indicated. Arytenoid adduction rotation will help restore a unilaterally bowed vocal fold to appropriate height, and this procedure is useful in the case of complete vocal fold paralysis. However, if the superior laryngeal nerve alone is paralyzed and the vocal fold is still mobile, this procedure is generally not a good choice.

Presbyphonia

The principles discussed above for management of severely bowed vocal folds may be applied in cases of profound presbyphonic changes. However, appropriate cases are uncommon. In general, medical management and voice therapy are sufficient to restore acceptable vocal quality. Occasionally, judicious medialization procedures (fat injection, collagen injection, AlloDerm injection, or thyroplasty) may be called for. Lengthening procedures are even more rarely appropriate and are often disappointing. However, in unusual cases of severe and disturbing masculinization of a female voice, as may occur with advancing age, these procedures may have a place, in conjunction with voice therapy.

Vocal Fold Paresis/Paralysis

The etiology, prevalence and evaluation of vocal fold paralysis are discussed in chapter 59. Unilateral vocal fold paralysis is common. It may be idiopathic, or it may occur after injury to the recurrent laryngeal nerve during neck or thoracic surgery, after neurosurgical procedures, or even following simple intubation. When the paralyzed fold remains in the partially abducted position, the functioning fold may be unable to cross the midline far enough to permit complete glottic closure. This will result in hoarseness, breathiness, ineffective cough, and, occasionally, in aspiration (especially after neurosurgical procedures if other cranial nerves have also been injured).

In some cases, surgery should not be performed for vocal fold paralysis until voice therapy has been tried. In many cases, strengthening vocal muscles and improving speaking technique result in good voice quality; and surgery is unnecessary. This is true especially if there is some recruitment response on EMG, even if the vocal fold is not mobile. When the paralysis is idiopathic, or when the nerve is not known to be cut, approximately 1 year of observation and therapy should usually be completed to allow time for spontaneous return of function before performing any irreversible operation. Traditionally, most surgical procedures have worked best for unilateral recurrent laryngeal nerve paralysis.

Many factors must be considered in selecting a surgical procedure for vocal fold repositioning (such as medialization). For example, the surgeon must assess the glottal configuration. It may be normal during soft phonation, but there may be insufficient lateral resistance to permit loud phonation. This scenario is amenable to injection techniques or thyroplasty. If there is a gap in the middle of the musculomembranous vocal fold but good closure at the vocal process, implantation of a traditional thyroplasty prosthesis with a straight inner edge (such as carved silastic block) is often less satisfactory than injection or use of a conformable prosthesis such as Gore-Tex. If there is a large posterior gap, injection techniques alone often do not work well, and arytenoid repositioning procedures should be considered. If there is a large posterior gap and a foreshortened vocal fold, arytenopexy may yield a more satisfactory result than traditional arytenoid reduction/rotation. Structural considerations should be weighed in light of the patient's vocal needs, his or her medical condition, and the surgeon's experience, as well as other factors such as vibratory function of the vocal fold (presence or absence of scar) and the person's phonatory skill and demands. Surgeons and patients must be prepared for changes in the surgical plan if intraoperative voice changes are not optimal. Staged surgery is appropriate in some cases (thyroplasty followed by injection laryngoplasty, or vice versa); and it is not rare to need to revise laryngoplastic surgery to optimize results. Patients and surgeons should be prepared for all possibilities.

Teflon Injection

Most surgeons inject materials for vocal fold paralysis endoscopically under local or general anesthesia. Transcutaneous and transoral injection with indirect mirror, telescopic or flexible fiberoptic laryngoscopic guidance is also possible. The most common treatment used to be injection of Teflon (Dupont, Wilmington, Del) lateral to the paralyzed vocal fold. The Teflon paste pushes the paralyzed vocal fold toward the midline, allowing the nonparalyzed vocal fold to meet it more effectively (Fig 82–33). This author has used Teflon only once since 1987. Teflon has many disadvantages, and better techniques are available. However, when used, correct technique involves injecting Teflon lateral to the vocalis muscle. The quantity of Teflon should be sufficient to move the vocal fold just to the midline. Injecting too much or injecting too superficially into the vocal fold mucosa often results in worsened voice quality. When properly placed, Teflon usually produced a foreign-body reaction locally but little or no reaction in the surrounding cartilage and muscle.[71] Teflon is usually surrounded by a fibrous capsule. However, occasionally a severe foreign-body reaction and granuloma formation may occur. Pre- and postoperative functional evaluation of

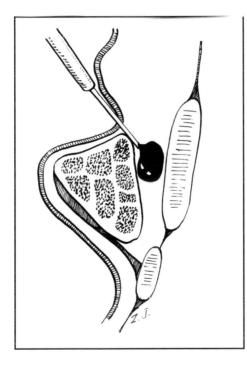
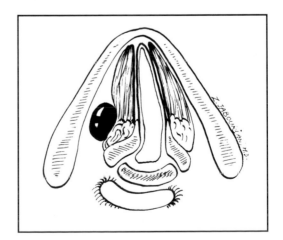

Fig 82–33. (*Left*) Injection of Teflon lateral to the vocalis muscle. (*Right*) Seen from above, the collection of Teflon lateral to the vocalis muscle displaces the vocal fold medially. Moving the vocal fold toward the median position allows the mobile vocal fold to meet it. The depth of the injected Teflon depends on the size of the larynx, but the injection is usually 3 to 5 mm. below the surface. Generally, 0.3 to 1.0 cc of Teflon paste is required. Each click of the Brünings syringe delivers approximately 0.2 cc of Teflon paste. In the author's practice, the use of Teflon injection was virtually abandoned in the mid-1980s.

the voice was advocated by von Leden et al in 1967 for all voice patients undergoing surgery for vocal fold paralysis and should now be standard practice.[72]

Gelfoam Injection

Effects of Teflon injection or other injected materials can be predicted fairly well by prior injection of Gelfoam paste, which was introduced in 1978 by Schramm et al.[73] This material is injected in the same position as Teflon, but it is temporary, resorbing in 2 to 8 weeks. In professional voice users, periodic Gelfoam injections may be appropriate early in the course of a recurrent laryngeal nerve paralysis, when recovery cannot be predicted and injection of permanent materials is not appropriate. For this technique, 1 g of sterile Gelfoam powder is mixed with 4 cc of physiologic saline. The saline must be added slowly, and the mixture should be stirred continuously. This produces 5 cc of thick paste that can be transferred to a syringe and then into the Brünings syringe. Injection technique is then identical to that of Teflon. It should be noted that, although Gelfoam injection has been used for this purpose for decades, it has never been formally approved by the FDA for this use. Gelfoam can be injected in the operating room or in the office. Office injection usually is performed per-orally, using a Brünings syringe with a curved needle. However, like injection of collagen and AlloDerm (discussed below), it also can be injected transcutaneously. Anderson and Mirza have reported success with this technique for immediate treatment of acute vocal fold immobility with aspiration.[74] Although Gelfoam is considered temporary, it usually does cause an inflammatory reaction. Scientific studies of laryngeal Gelfoam injection are wanting, and the assumption that laryngeal anatomy returns to normal following Gelfoam resorption remains unproven.

Collagen, AlloDerm, and Fascia Injection

Several other materials are still being injected to treat vocal fold paralysis, especially collagen, fat, AlloDerm (LifeCell Corporation, Branchburg, NJ), fascia and calcium hydroxyapatite (Coaptite, BioForm, Inc, Franksville, Wisc). Ford and Bless have advocated the use of collagen for many conditions including selected cases of unilateral vocal fold paralysis.[67,75,76] Collagen is in liquid form, rather than a thick paste like Teflon. These mechanical differences enhance the ease and accuracy of injection. In addition, collagen may reduce scar formation because it stimulates production of collagenase. Before injecting Bovine collagen, safety precautions such as skin testing are mandatory. However,

human autologous and allogeneic collagen are available now and appear superior to Bovine collagen for various reasons. Not only does the use of human material eliminate the severe reactions encountered occasionally with Bovine collagen (skin testing is no longer necessary), but preliminary experience suggests also that human collagen (Dermalogen, Collagenesis, Beverly, Mass) may last longer following injection,[77] potentially making it more useful for lateral injection (medialization) than Bovine collagen.[78-81] Unlike other substances, collagen is designed for superficial injection into the vocal fold margin. A special 25-, 27-, or 30-gauge laryngeal needle is inserted through the mucosa overlying the vibratory margin until the resistance of the vocal ligament is felt. Usually a 0.03 to 0.08 cc injection of collagen is injected superficially. If the standard collagen preparation (Dermalogen) is too viscous for a given clinical situation, less viscous collagen (Demalogen-lite) can be obtained from the manufacturer. However, viscosity is usually adequate with Dermalogen if it has been warmed to *body* temperature. Collagen may also be injected laterally. A peroral technique is best for superficial injection, although collagen can be injected superficially using an external approach through the cricothyroid membrane, in selected cases. For injection laterally along the vocal fold, an external approach through the thyroid lamina usually works well. The thyroid lamina is usually pierced 7 to 9 mm above its inferior border. The position of the needle can be confirmed by observing paraglottic soft tissue movement through a fiberoptic flexible laryngoscope. If the patient's gag reflex is too severe to permit peroral injection of collagen or other substances, or if the laryngeal cartilage is too ossified to allow passage of a needle through the thyroid lamina, it is often possible to inject the paraglottic space by passing a needle behind the posterior aspect of the thyroid lamina (Fig 82–34). Vocal fold injection also can be performed through the thyrohyoid membrane, using flexible nasolaryngoscopic visual guidance. This technique was developed for cidofovir injection. A 25-gauge needle is inserted into the midline at the superior border of the thyroid notch after application of topical anesthesia; and vocal injection can be performed easily (Milan R. Amin, personal communication, June 2004). Collagen injections appear to be efficacious in selected patients and are a valuable addition to the laryngologist's surgical armamentarium. Collagen is not FDA approved specifically for use in the larynx, although its use has become standard practice.

Cymetra micronized AlloDerm (LifeCell Corporation, Branchburg, NJ) is an acellular human tissue material that includes collagen, elastin, and proteogly-

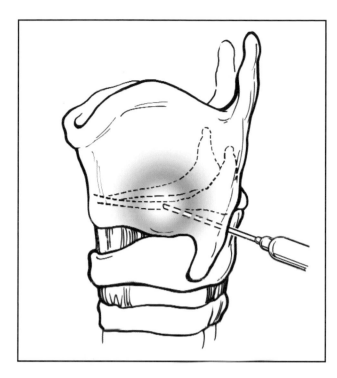

Fig 82–34. In most patients, the paraglottic space can be reached through a posterior approach, passing a needle behind the posterior border of the thyroid lamina and then angling it anteriorly and superiorly. Care should be taken to keep the needle close to the thyroid cartilage to help avoid injury to the piriform sinus or branches of the recurrent laryngeal nerve.

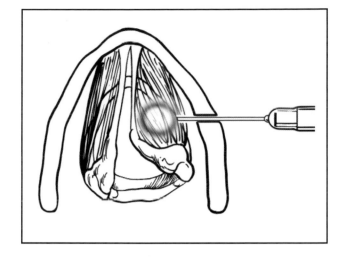

Fig 82–35. Injection of Alloderm, collagen, or other substances may be performed by passing a needle through the thyroid lamina. The point of insertion is usually about halfway between the anterior and posterior borders of the thyroid lamina and about 7 to 9 mm above the inferior border.

cans. Its use in the larynx was reported by Passalaqua et al.[82] They employed an external technique in which the thyroid lamina is pierced with a 22- or 24-gauge needle. Needle localization was confirmed using flexible nasolaryngoscopy, and AlloDerm was injected laterally to treat conditions such as bowing (Fig 82–35). Like collagen, AlloDerm can be injected either through this external technique, through a peroral indirect technique in the office, or through direct laryngoscopy in the operating room.

Autologous fascia also has been advocated for vocal fold augmentation. Rihkanen advised cutting fascia into small pieces and delivering it through a Brünings syringe.[83] This author (RTS) has tried this technique and variations of it over the years. We have used fascia alone in a manner similar to that described subsequently by Rihkanen and fascia mixed with fat to try to diminish the amount of reabsorption of augmentation material. The principal problem with fascia is technical. If all of it is not cut into tiny pieces, it is very difficult to pass through the injection syringe. In one instance, it obstructed the Brünings syringe so firmly that an attempt to pass it further forward resulted in

breakage of the metal syringe. However, if the fascia is prepared properly, it can be a good material. Relatively little is resorbed, and excessive overcorrection should be avoided.

Calcium hydroxyapatite (Coaptite, BioForm, Inc. Franksville, Wisc) is a slurry of calcium hydroxyapatite (CaHA) particles. It is approved by the FDA for use in the larynx, but there has not been enough experience with this substance to comment on its use and potential problems, yet.

Autologous Fat Injection

The first use of autologous fat in the larynx was reported by Dedo in 1975 for patients with laryngeal cancer.[84] He described the placement of a free fat graft under a mucosal advancement flap for creating a neovocal fold following vertical hemilaryngectomy. In many ways, the concept is analogous to the fat implantation reported here. Unfortunately, Dedo did not provide the number of patients or any form of objective assessment; but he reported postoperative voices with minimal hoarseness or breathiness in all cases. This technique has not been used widely, and there are no recent reports of its continued use. However, in appropriate cases, Dedo still employs a modification of this technique and has had continued good experience with it (personal communication, April 1995). Human autologous fat injection into the larynx was first reported by Mikaelian, Lowry, and Sataloff in 1991[85]—and subsequently by Brandenburg, Kirkham, and Koschkee.[86] These and subsequent reports dealt with autologous lipoinjection lateral to the vibratory margin, placing fat in the same position in which Teflon was used. The author has had continued excellent experience with fat injection, particularly in patients who need only minimal medialization. For patients with a wide posterior glottic gap, thyroplasty, or thyroplasty in combination with fat injection, and/or arytenoid adduction has been preferable.

There has been extensive experience with autologous fat transplantation in various areas of the body. In a particularly good review in 1989, Billings and May summarized the literature on this subject and addressed many of the problems that make the use of fat controversial.[87] In particular, the final bulk of the graft and fate of the fat are notoriously unpredictable. At present, the preponderance of evidence suggests that transplanted fat survives and that the relocated adipose tissue remains dynamic. However, observations in soft tissue sites such as the face and chest may or may not be applicable to the fate of fat transplanted to the larynx, especially to the vibratory margin.

Wexler et al studied the fate of fat implanted surgically in the vocal folds of five dogs.[88] The fat was introduced through a laryngofissure approach, not by injection. The fat was retrieved 2 months after the initial surgery, and in 4 of the 5 dogs was found still to be present. Moreover, the autograft produced good functional results, including greater vocal intensity, lower threshold pressures for phonation, and other improvements in the acoustic output. Hill, Meyers, and Harris used microinjection in canines after recurrent laryngeal nerve section.[89] They used an injection technique without laryngofissure and studied the experimental animals histologically at 3 weeks. The bulk of the fat was found to persist for at least that period of time.

An excellent study was reported by Archer and Banks.[90] They designed their study to evaluate the long-term viability of fat introduced submucosally into scarred vocal folds, a procedure very similar to the one the author developed independently for human use, as described in this chapter. Archer and Banks studied 15 canine subjects in three groups. The first group underwent mucosal excision of one vocal fold. The second group underwent mucosal excision of both vocal folds, one of which was augmented 6 weeks later with autologous fat by submucosal injection at three positions along the vocal fold. These two groups were sacrificed at 6 months. The third group was treated the same as the second group, but was sacrificed at 12 months. Each animal was used as its own control. The stripped vocal folds were thin as compared with normal and fat-augmented vocal folds. All

of the fat-augmented vocal folds revealed viable adipose cells in the superficial mucosa. The vocal folds in the fat-augmented group were statistically thicker when compared with the mucosally damaged, nonaugmented groups.

Although the studies cited above are important, their application to humans must be questioned, as with all canine research. Unfortunately, there is no better nonhuman alternative, because humans are the only species with a layered lamina propria and vocal ligament. Because dogs have no vocal ligament, extrapolations from dog research to human response must be made with great caution. Nevertheless, it is encouraging to note that autologous fat appears to be preserved and efficacious in the animal research performed so far. This is especially comforting considering the paucity of experience with fat implantation in human larynges.

The author has had continued good experience with autologous fat injections since our first report.[85] Several technical considerations are important in achieving success. The first is patient selection. The patients who do best with autologous fat injection are those who have only a small glottal gap or those who actually close the glottis during soft phonation but have insufficient resistance on the paralyzed side to permit loud phonation. Such conditions occur after spontaneous compensation for laryngeal paralysis or occasionally following Type I thyroplasty, especially when additional thyroarytenoid muscle atrophy occurs. Similar situations may be seen in patients with vocal fold bowing, as discussed elsewhere in this chapter. Second, the fat should be traumatized as little as possible, maintaining large globules. Third, fat should not be injected much more posteriorly than the middle third of the membranous portion of the vocal fold. A properly placed injection at this location provides adequate medial displacement and allows the medialized vocal fold to pull the arytenoid and vocal process into better position. Injecting too far posteriorly creates a mechanical impediment to passive arytenoid motion, often resulting in persistent vertical height disparity at the vocal processes and inferior voice results. Fourth, unlike Teflon, fat requires overinjection by approximately 30%. The vocal fold should be convex at the conclusion of the procedure to account for expected resorption (Fig 82–36). This overinjection causes moderate dysphonia. If the voice is excellent at the end of the surgical procedure, a good final result is unlikely. Initially, the author recommended performing these procedures under local anesthesia, in a manner similar to that used for Teflon injection. However, because overinjection of fat is performed routinely and there is no need to fine-tune the surgical procedure based on

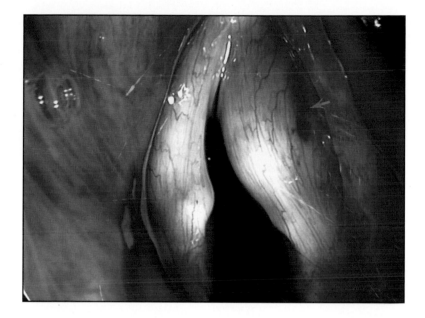

Fig 82–36. This 40-year-old marketing executive and avocational choir singer and musical theater performer had right recurrent nerve paralysis, apparently as a consequence of Lyme disease. Injection was performed near the middle of the right vocal fold (*arrow*). This intraoperative photograph shows 30 to 40% overcorrection, the desired endpoint. The apparent bowing of the left vocal fold is an artifact.

phonatory function, fat injection can be performed equally well under general anesthesia.

Until recently, it has been said that one could not inject too much fat. Although this is generally true, there are rare exceptions. After more than 10 years of utilizing the technique, the author has encountered one case in which excess fat had to be resected. Interestingly, histologically normal, viable fat was removed 1 year following the injection (Fig 82–37). However, this situation represents the exception; and surgeons tend to err by injecting too little. Overcorrection should normally be at least 30 to 40% as described above, or repeated injections will be needed in many patients. In most cases, initial fat resorption occurs fairly quickly. Patients achieve a serviceable voice within 4 to 12 weeks. Additional changes occur over 6 to 12 months. Occasionally, they may even occur later, necessitating reinjection. Such delayed changes have been observed most commonly following substantial weight loss or a severe upper respiratory infection. However, in general, if glottic closure is satisfactory, the improvement is permanent.

Removal of Teflon

One of the complications of Teflon injection is overinjection. If Teflon is injected in excessive amounts or too superficially, the voice will be substantially worse after surgery than it was before Teflon injection. Treating such complications and restoring satisfactory vocal quality are widely (and correctly) regarded as difficult. However, the otolaryngologist may be helped greatly by an accurate preoperative assessment of the problem.

Cross-sectional imaging using computed tomography (CT) of a larynx after Teflon injection documents the position of deposited Teflon easily, including its amount and depth (Fig 82–38). Although this high attenuation material (216 Houndsfield units) is seen easily, the value of radiologic assessment in these cases has been appreciated only in the later 1980s.[91]

In general, preoperative evaluation by strobovideolaryngoscopy, CT, and objective voice analysis allows for reasonably accurate definition of the problem. If the Teflon has been injected incorrectly submucosally and the vibratory margin is adynamic but fairly straight, the patient should be advised that further surgical procedures are unlikely to produce improvement, especially if the vocal fold edge is smooth. If there are multiple lumps of superficial Teflon with failure of glottic closure between them, it is usually worthwhile to remove them and smooth the vibratory margin to improve glottic closure, even if vibration is not restored. If Teflon has been injected in a correct

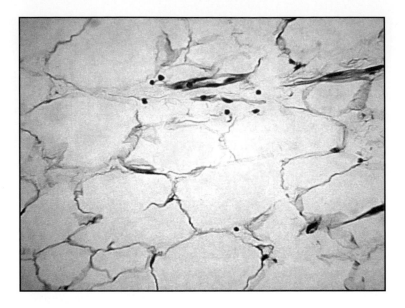

Fig 82–37. This 78-year-old corporate executive had substantial dysphonia related to bilateral superior laryngeal nerve paresis. He had undergone a fat injection 1 year previously. The usual overcorrection was performed on the right vocal fold, and a small amount of fat was injected at the same time into the left vocal fold, but without the usual excess to avoid airway obstruction. Post-operatively, he retained more fat than usual, especially anteriorly. This resulted in vocal strain and fatigue. An incision was made laterally, and the excess fat was resected 1 year following injection. The fat appeared normal and healthy grossly and microscopically, as seen above.

position, but vocal fold convexity exists because of excessive Teflon and/or granuloma formation, results are more satisfactory. It should be noted that the excess may not be due to faulty technique on the part of the surgeon. Although Teflon should not ordinarily cause a reaction, some people do form a granulomatous response or thick capsule, thus increasing mass. Consequently, the amount of Teflon may have been correct at the time of surgery but became more than was necessary after the tissue response occurred. In the author's opinion, the best way to address this problem usually is with an incision with laser laterally over the collection of Teflon. The incision should be far from the vibratory margin. When the CO_2 laser touches the Teflon, a bright white glow is noted. If there is extensive granulomatous reaction around the Teflon, it may be necessary to excise the Teflon with the laser. In other cases, exposing a small portion of the Teflon allows it to be expressed and suctioned. Gentle pressure with the side of suction against the vocal fold edge is used to milk the desired amount of Teflon out of the vocal fold and to reestablish a smooth vocal fold margin. Slight overevacuation creating a minimal concavity of the vocal fold edge seems to produce the best results. Alternatively, Teflon can be excised externally through a thyrotomy. Techniques for the external approach to resection of Teflon granuloma have been published by Netterville and coworkers.[92,93] The approach requires a thyrotomy, and the inner perichondrium is incised. In some cases, the Teflon mass can be shelled out easily. However, if Teflon and inflammatory response involve the vibratory margin, penetration into the airway can occur. If an external approach is used and it appears as if the Teflon mass has been removed safely, it may be desirable to fill part of the resulting cavity, although it is difficult to assess final phonatory outcome during these procedures. This is because Teflon often produces vocal fold stiffness and scar, and the vocal fold may not lateralize completely in the operating room. However, if a large cavity is created by the resection, some lateralization is likely to occur during healing. The cavity can be filled with a free fat graft or with a strap muscle flap. Recently, Netterville has modified his procedure (James Netterville, MD, personal communication, 2001). Rather than using a lateral cartilage flap, he approaches the paraglottic space now through a vertical thyrotomy incision made approximately 4 mm from the midline of

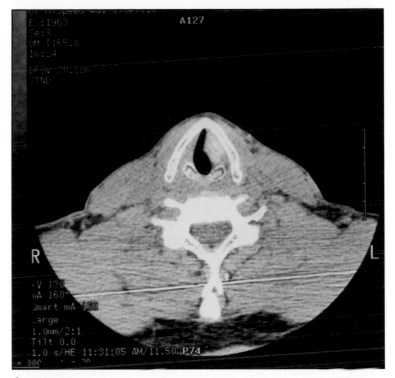

A

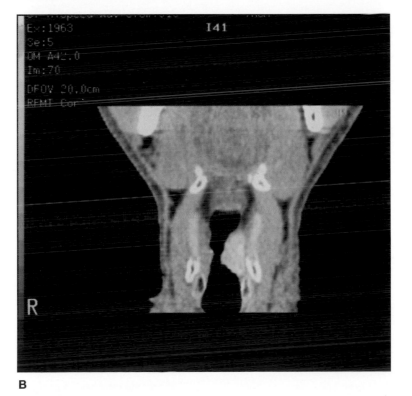

B

Fig 82–38. Axial (**A**) and coronal (**B**) CT scans of patient with left Teflon granuloma, illustrating the value of CT imaging in mapping the position of the Teflon prior to surgery.

the thyroid cartilage. He also has abandoned the inferiorly based strap muscle flap because of a few cases of fibrosis that produced inferior-lateral scarring of the vocal fold. Instead, he is using a platysmal flap with its attached fat. This author (RTS) has had reasonable success with inferiorly based and superiorly based strap muscle flaps, so long as they are divided at the point of origin or insertion, not in the body of the muscle. An excess amount of muscle is placed, and the muscle is sutured into position with stitches through the thyroid cartilage. If the tissue deep to the vocal fold is deficient (muscle atrophy or absence), a flap including fat or a free fat graft is used. It should be noted that total removal of Teflon is difficult (often impossible) using either the external or endoscopic approach. Unless a hemilaryngectomy is performed, small Teflon particles remain often. In some cases, they may produce recurrent symptomatic granulomas months or years after successful treatment. Such problems are the primary reasons why use of Teflon was abandoned in the late 1980s in favor of injection of fat or other materials or thyroplasty.

Thyroplasty

Another excellent approach to medialization is Type I thyroplasty. This procedure was popularized by Isshi-ki et al in 1975,[94] although the concept had been introduced early in the century by Payr.[95] Thyroplasty is performed under local anesthesia. Although the author rarely uses the original technique anymore, in classical thyroplasty, with the neck extended, a 4-cm to 5-cm incision is made horizontally at the midpoint between the thyroid notch and the lower rim of the thyroid cartilage. A rectangle of thyroid cartilage is cut out on the involved side. It begins approximately 5 mm to 7 mm lateral to the midline and is usually approximately 3 mm to 5 mm by 3 mm to 10 mm. The inferior border is located approximately 3 mm above the inferior margin of the thyroid cartilage. Care must be taken not to carry the rectangle too far posteriorly, or it cannot be displaced medially. The cartilage is depressed inward, moving the vocal fold toward the midline. The wedge of silicone is then fashioned to hold the depressed cartilage in proper position (Fig 82–39). Since Isshiki's original description, many surgeons have preferred to remove the cartilage. Most preserve the inner perichondrium, although techniques that involve incisions through the inner perichondrium also have been used successfully. Surgeons have also used various or other materials including autologous cartilage, hydroxyapatite, expanded polytetrafluoroethylene, and titanium.[96-102]

Various additional technical modifications were proposed as this technique has became more popular,

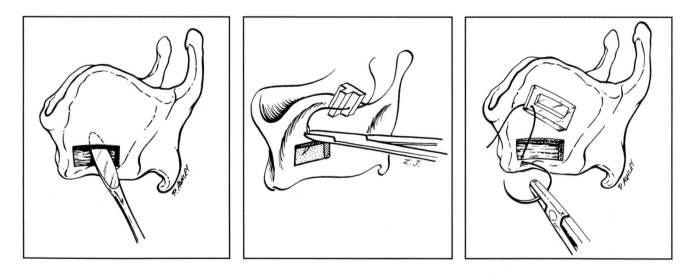

Fig 82–39. (*Left*) In Type I thyroplasty, cartilage is cut beginning 5 to 7 mm lateral to the midline. The window is about 3-5 mm × 3–10 mm. The window should be no more than 5 mm from the inferior border of the thyroid cartilage. After the cartilage cut has been completed, the inner perichondrium is elevated. This drawing illustrates correct window placement. (*Middle*) A silicone block is used to depress the cartilage into proper position, displacing the vocal fold medially. The silicone may be sutured to the cartilage. It is often necessary to taper the silicone anteriorly. This drawing also illustrates the most common errors in thyroplasty surgery, placing the window slightly too high and making the block too thick anteriorly. (*Right*) Appropriate thyroplasty window position and tapered prosthesis.

and several varieties of preformed thyroplasty implant devices have been introduced commercially. Many of these modifications have proven helpful, especially techniques that obviate the need to carve individualized silicone block implants, a technique that is often challenging for inexperienced thyroplasty surgeons. The silicone block modifications described by Dr Harvey Tucker[103] are also useful, particularly the technique of cutting out a portion of the prosthesis to allow for the placement of a nerve-muscle pedicle. However, this author has generally abandoned all of these techniques except during revision cases in favor of Gore-Tex (expanded polytetrafluoroethylene). The use of Gore-Tex in the larynx was reported initially by Hoffman and McCulloch.[100] Since then, several reports have documented its efficacy,[104-106] and others are in preparation. In our center, the author has used Gore-Tex for primary Type I almost exclusively since 1999. The material is easy to place, easy to adjust, and can be contoured to compensate for vocal fold bowing.

Our preferred technique is slightly different from procedures published previously. One of the major advantages of Gore-Tex is that it can be placed through a mini-thyrotomy, obviating the need to traumatize or transect strap muscles. A small (2 cm) horizontal incision is made centered in the midline, in a skin crease near the lower third of the vertical dimension of the thyroid cartilage. The cartilage is exposed in the midline, and the perichondrium is incised and elevated. A 4-mm diamond bur is used to drill a 4-mm mini-thyrotomy. Its anterior border is located approximately 7 mm from the midline in females and 9 mm from the midline in males; and its inferior margin is approximately 3 to 4 mm above the inferior border of the thyroid cartilage. The inner perichondrium is left intact. A fine elevator, such as a Woodson elevator or Sataloff Thyroplasty Elevator (Medtronics Xomed, Jacksonville Fla), is used to elevate the perichondrium posteriorly. In this author's opinion, it is very important that only minimal elevation be performed. A small pocket, only 2 to 3 mm in width, parallel to the inferior border of the thyroid cartilage is sufficient. This is substantially different from the extensive elevation performed during traditional thyroplasty. However, if the perichondrium is elevated excessively, it is difficult to control the position of the Gore-Tex. Any additional elevation necessary will be accomplished by the Gore-Tex during insertion. Gore-Tex is then layered through the thyrotomy incision and adjusted to optimize phonation (Fig 82–40). This procedure is performed under local anesthesia with sedation, and vocal fold position can be monitored by flexible laryngoscopy during the operation. We do not use

continuous monitoring routinely, but ordinarily we check the final position visually at conclusion of the operation. For closure, other surgeons use perichondrial flaps that are repositioned and sutured. This author has found this maneuver unnecessary and time consuming. Once Gore-Tex has been positioned optimally, it is cut a few millimeters outside the thyrotomy. The thyrotomy is then filled with a few drops of cyanoacrylate. This glue does not react with the Gore-Tex. However, it forms a customized buttonlike seal with a small inner flange of cyanoacrylate, and with a wick of Gore-Tex in the center of the cyanoacrylate block. This prevents extrusion of the Gore-Tex; and the cyanoacrylate "button" and Gore-Tex are removed easily when revision surgery is necessary, simply by pulling on the end of the Gore-Tex that extends a few millimeters beyond the cyanoacrylate. Gore-Tex thyroplasty is so expeditious and atraumatic that it can be performed bilaterally at the same sitting. This is done commonly to treat vocal fold bowing from bilateral superior laryngeal nerve paresis and other causes and to treat presbyphonia refractory to voice therapy. Bilateral thyroplasties can be accomplished ordinarily in less than 1 hour. A small drain usually is placed at the conclusion of the procedure and removed on the first postoperative day. In many cases, the procedure is performed as an outpatient, although overnight observation is appropriate if there is vocal fold swelling or any concern about airway compromise.

There have been no studies documenting the efficacy of routine use of steroids or antibiotics in thyroplasty surgery. Many surgeons use both routinely. This author does not use either antibiotics or steroids routinely. In our practice, we have encountered only one infection following thyroplasty in over 20 years and that was believed to be due to contaminated sutures recalled by the manufacturer shortly after that operation. However, because a foreign body is implanted during thyroplasty, many surgeons prefer to give antibiotics prophylactically.

Revision thyroplasty is a more complex matter. Most thyroplasties that have required revision, so far, have been performed originally using a silastic block or one of the preformed, commercially available implants. During these initial operations, a large thyroplasty window was created and perichondrium was elevated. Removing the silastic block and replacing it with Gore-Tex generally does not prove satisfactory. Gore-Tex position cannot be controlled well because of the post-surgical anatomy. In general, this author prefers to revise such cases by carving a new silastic block, or by modifying the prosthesis that had been placed originally. If revision is being performed because of insufficient medialization, it is sometimes

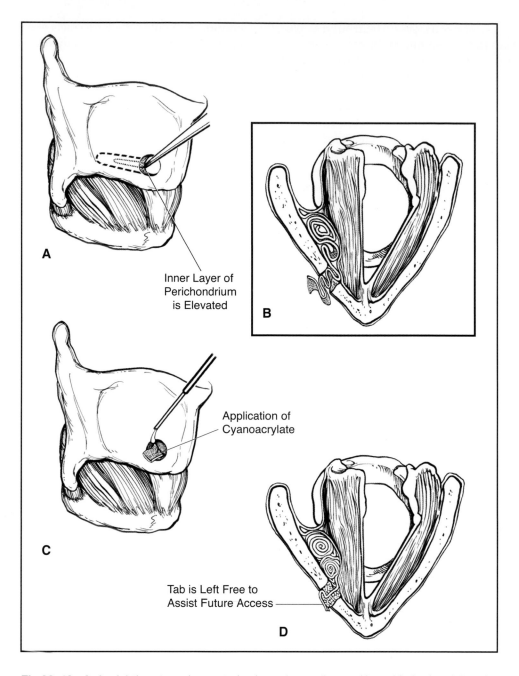

Inner Layer of
Perichondrium
is Elevated

Application of
Cyanoacrylate

Tab is Left Free to
Assist Future Access

Fig 82–40. A. A mini-thyrotomy is created using a 4-mm diamond burr. Limited perichondrial elevation is performed. **B.** Gore-Tex (W.L. Gore and Associates Incorporated, Newark, Del) is layered into the space between the cartilage and perichondrium. The patient is asked to phonate, and Gore-Tex is adjusted until phonatory output is optimal. **C.** Cyanoacrylate is used to seal the thyrotomy. **D.** A small amount of Gore-Tex is left externally.

possible to elevate the anterior aspect of the prosthesis and layer Gore-Tex medial to it. However, such cases are uncommon. More often, it is necessary to incise the fibrotic capsule in the region of the inner perichondrium with an electric cautery (which often produces momentary discomfort for the patient) and to create a new prosthesis. The most common problems that require revision are undermedialization resulting in persistent glottic insufficiency, excessive anterior medialization resulting in strained voice, excessively high placement of the original prosthesis, and inappropriate patient selection. Undermedialization can be corrected by underlaying Gore-Tex or creating a larger prosthesis as discussed above, or endoscopically by injecting fat or collagen. Excessive anterior medialization is corrected by reshaping the prosthesis. In such cases, the original implant is usually too thick and placed too far anteriorly. Excessively high placement is often associated with a cartilage window that is considerable higher than the desirable 3 to 4 millimeters above the inferior border of the thyroid cartilage. When additional cartilage is removed to place the prosthesis at the desired height, cartilage deficiency from the original operation often leaves the prosthesis unstable. In such cases, the implanted device should be secured to the thyroid cartilage by sutures. In fact, when using an implant other than Gore-Tex for primary or revision surgery, this author always secures the prosthesis to cartilage with proline suture to prevent migration or extrusion.

Another common reason for revision is inappropriate patient selection. If there is a large, symptomatic posterior glottal gap, thyroplasty alone is often insufficient. Procedures to alter arytenoid cartilage position are necessary in many such cases. Failure to recognize this need and perform the appropriate operation initially may lead to a need for revision surgery that includes arytenoid repositioning procedures. Apart from malposition of the implant, Type I thyroplasty is generally uncomplicated. Successful thyroplasty improves vibratory function.[107] However, if thyroplasty is complicated by hemorrhage with superficial hematoma along the vibratory margin, or by infection, vocal fold stiffness with permanent dysphonia can result. Hemorrhage and edema also can produce airway obstruction. Although this author has never seen a case, Weinman and Maragos[108] reported on 630 thyroplasty procedures. Seven of their patients required tracheotomy. Five of 143 patients who underwent arytenoid cartilage adduction in association with thyroplasty required tracheotomy. In the experience of Weinman and Maragos, the median interval from surgery to tracheotomy was 9 hours, with five of the seven patients requiring airway surgery within 18 hours following thyroplasty.[108] Hence, although in our experience and most other series airway obstruction has not been common, it must be recognized that this complication and the need for tracheotomy are possible.

Isshiki also described other thyroplasty techniques.[37] (Fig 82–41). The Type I thyroplasty described above was designed to medialize the vocal fold. Type II thyroplasty expands the vocal folds laterally. It is designed for patients with airway insufficiency after laryngeal trauma. The thyroid cartilage is separated anteriorly and held apart with cartilage or some other material. This uncommon procedure restores the airway at the expense of the voice. Type III thyroplasty shortens the vocal folds by incising and depressing the anterior segment of the thyroid cartilage. This may be used to lower vocal pitch. An additional decrease in fundamental frequency may be obtained by combining this procedure with vocal fold injection to increase vocal fold mass. However, it involves a fairly significant risk of dysphonia. Type III thyroplasty also has shown at least temporary efficacy in some patients with spasmodic dysphonia.

Type IV thyroplasty was designed to lengthen the vocal folds and increase their tension in order to raise vocal pitch. The cricoid and thyroid cartilages are approximated anteriorly with nylon sutures. This procedure has been used primarily for patients undergoing male to female sex-change surgery and for elderly women with excessive vocal masculinization. Unfortunately, the long-term results (beyond 6 to 12 months) have been disappointing. Sataloff et al described an alternative procedure that fuses the cricoid and thyroid (Fig 82–42), which has proven more satisfactory.[109] The position of the cricoid and thyroid cartilage can be held either with sutures as illustrated, or with miniplates. Surprisingly, these patients have maintained approximately a 1-octave frequency range despite complete cricothyroid fusion and fixation.

Pitch can also be raised by shifting the anterior commissure forward. The procedure is performed by making incisions similar to those used for Type III thyroplasty. However, the anterior segment is advanced. The advancement is maintained by interposing silastic blocks in the gaps between the cartilage edges, and fixing the cartilage with miniplates. Care must be taken not to detach the anterior commissure ligament during this procedure, and during cosmetic laryngoplasty used in sex-change patients.

If the anterior commissure tendon is detached, dysphonia usually is severe. The vocal folds become flaccid, and habitual pitch drops. The ability to change pitch diminishes and pertubation increases. Separation of the anterior commissure can occur iatrogenically, as noted above, or as a consequence of blunt trauma such as may occur from steering wheel injuries or elbow injuries during sports. Anterior commissure laryngoplasty is performed through an external approach. The technique for repair depends on the nature of the injury and the presence or absence of cartilage at the point at which the anterior commissure should be attached. If cartilage is missing following a laryngeal shave procedure or fracture, it is sometimes possible to identify the retracted anterior commissure tendon without additional trauma to the cartilage. If this is not possible, it may be necessary to perform a laryngofissure or to cut a window near the vertical midpoint of the thyroid cartilage. The vocal folds

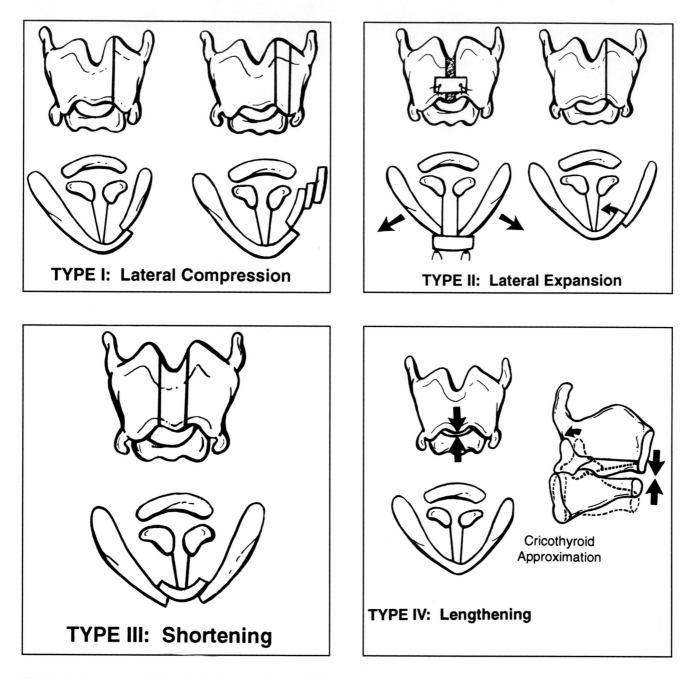

TYPE I: Lateral Compression

TYPE II: Lateral Expansion

TYPE III: Shortening

TYPE IV: Lengthening

Cricothyroid Approximation

Fig 82–41. Four types of thyroplasty described by Isshiki.[37]

should be mobilized for a distance of several millimeters bilaterally. Then, the anterior commissure ligament can be drawn forward and sutured to cartilage (if present); to a piece of cartilage harvested from the lateral aspect thyroid lamina and placed external to the midline of the thyroid cartilage; or to a miniplate. In particularly difficult cases, other technical modifications may be necessary.

Occasionally, singers and actors inquire about surgery for pitch alteration. Laryngeal framework surgery has proven successful in altering pitch in specially selected patients, such as those undergoing gender reassignment (sex-change) surgery. However, these operations do not provide consistently good enough voice quality to be performed on a professional voice user for elective pitch change. In addition, con-

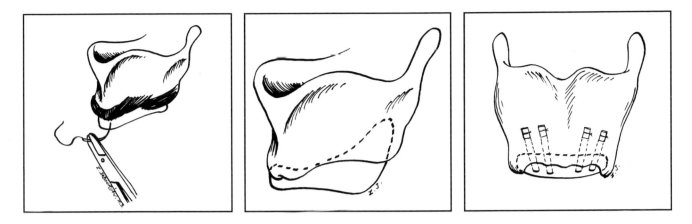

Fig 82-42. In cricothyroid approximation surgery described by Isshiki (*left*), sutures tied over bolsters are used to narrow the cricothyroid space, simulating the action of the cricothyroid muscle. In our modification (*middle*), the cricoid carti- lage is subluxed behind the thyroid cartilage. It is fixed into position (*right*) using sutures and bolsters or using mini- plates. Although the cricothyroid space is obliterated, the ability to vary pitch remains surprisingly good.

siderably more than habitual fundamental frequency is involved in the perception of voice classification, and important other factors (such as the center frequency of the singer's formant) are not modified by laryngeal surgery.

Nomenclature

In an effort to standardize the confusing nomenclature of laryngoplastic voice surgery (commonly called phonosurgery), the Committee on Speech, Voice and Swallowing Disorders of the American Academy of Otolaryngology—Head and Neck Surgery developed a nomenclature, which the author recommends using (see Table 82–1).[110]

Arytenoid Cartilage Adduction/Rotation, Cricothyroid Subluxation, Arytenoidectomy

All of the procedures discussed above work fairly well for recurrent laryngeal nerve paralysis but not nearly so well if the superior laryngeal nerve is involved or if the arytenoid cartilage is in abnormal position for some other reason. In these cases, arytenoid cartilage adduction/rotation or alternative techniques of arytenoid cartilage repositioning procedures are preferable.[111] Arytenoid adduction/rotation surgery is usually performed under local anesthesia. The thyropharyngeus muscle is divided, and the posterior margin of the thy-

roid cartilage is exposed. Subperichondrial elevation is carried onto the inferior surface of the thyroid ala. The cricothyroid joint is dislocated, and the piriform sinus is protected. When the piriform sinus has been elevated for arytenoid cartilage adduction/rotation or arytenopexy (discussed below), it is advisable to reattach the mucoperichondrial flap at the conclusion of the procedure. This helps prevent fibrosis and constriction that may interfere with swallowing. In addition, if extensive piriform sinus mucosa elevation is performed, the piriform sinus may prolapse producing airway obstruction, especially in the presence of a posterior thyroid cartilage window. This problem can be avoided by suturing the piriform sinus mucosa to the thyroid cartilage (Nicholas E. Maragos, MD, personal communication, 2003). The muscular process of the arytenoid cartilage is identified, and the joint is opened in the classic approach through a small incision over the cricoarytenoid muscle. However, in many cases, it is not necessary to open the joint; and it may even be better not to. Two 3-0 permanent sutures are fixed in soft tissue across the muscular process and tied in the directions of the lateral cricoarytenoid and lateral thyroarytenoid muscles, adjusting vocal fold position (Fig 82–43).

This author prefers not to divide the cricothyroid joint in most cases. When it is divided, it heals with scar. The resulting fixation may impair movement of the functioning on the contralateral side and is likely to impair passive movement of the ipsilateral side in response to contralateral cricothyroid muscle contraction. In addition, if the joint is divided and not re-

Table 82–1. Nomenclature for Laryngoplastic Voice Surgery.

A. Laryngeal framework surgery (LFS) with
    Arytenoid adduction (AA)
       Medialization (M)
    Lateralization (L)
    Anterior Commissure
       Retrusion (relaxation) (ACR)
       Protrusion (tensing) (ACP)
    Cricothyroid approximation (CTA)
  Medialization laryngoplasty can be qualified by method of medialization
    Medialization laryngoplasty with
    s = silicone elastoner
    c = cartilage
    e = expander
    o = other

B. Injection laryngoscopy (IL)
    D = Direct
    I = Indirect
  Injection laryngoplasty with
    t = Teflon
    g = Gelfoam
    col = collagen
    f = fat
    o = other
  Abbreviations may be used
    Laryngeal framework surgery with medialization-silicone elastomer (LFS-M-s)
    Laryngeal framework surgery with arytenoid adduction (LFS-AA)
    Injection laryngoplasty-direct-Teflon (IL-D-t)

From Benninger et al,[110] with permission.

paired, the natural forces of the neck tend to push the inferior cornu posterior to the cricothyroid joint facet, shortening the vocal fold and aggravating the dysphonia. Traditionally, this author has prevented that problem by suturing the cricothyroid joint into its normal position, if it has been divided. This prevents retrusion, but it does not result in passive mobility of the joint in most cases.

An alternate technique called cricothyroid subluxation has been described by Zeitels.[112] This technique also does not ensure passive mobility, but it has been surprisingly successful at improving frequency range and dynamic range of phonation, at least during short-term follow-up. A suture is tied around the inferior cornu of the thyroid cartilage and passed through the midline of the cricoid cartilage (Fig 82–44). The inferior cornu is pulled gently forward and adjusted in accordance with the patient's phonatory response. In Zeitels' illustrations, the inferior cornu is pictured as

fairly far anterior to the cricothyroid joint facet. In this author's experience (RTS), it is usually unnecessary to distract it so far anteriorly. Usually, optimal results are achieved when the posterior aspect of the inferior cornu is fairly close to the anterior aspect of the cricoid joint facet.

When arytenoid cartilage adduction is combined with thyroplasty, it is not always necessary to create a thyroplasty window. The author has devised a technique in which a silastic block is placed through a posterior approach. The arytenoid cartilage procedure is performed first (adduction/rotation or arytenoidopexy). The inner perichondrium is then elevated from posterior to anterior under direct vision. A silastic block is carved and adjusted to the appropriate size and shape. The position of the silastic block is noted, and the block is removed. A suture is passed through the thyroid cartilage from external to internal at approximately the position of the junction of the ante-

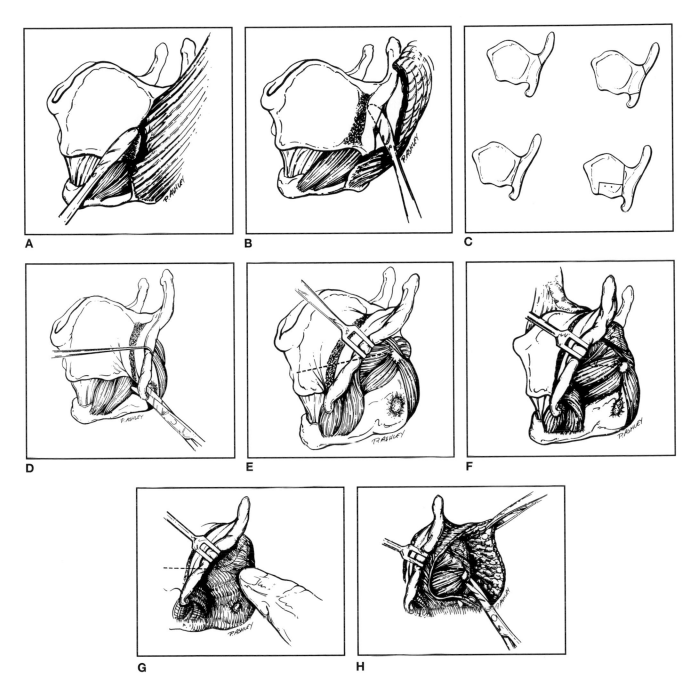

Fig 82–43. A. In arytenoid adduction/rotation surgery, the thyropharyngeus muscle is separated from the ala of the thyroid cartilage. **B.** Starting at the posterior aspect of the thyroid cartilage, the inner perichondrium is elevated to prevent entrance into the airway. **C.** Ordinarily, the procedure can continue simply with anterior retraction of the thyroid cartilage. However, especially with a large thyroid ala as encountered in some men, it is helpful to transect the thyroid cartilage in one of the patterns illustrated above by solid lines. **D.** Ordinarily, simple anterior retraction of the thyroid cartilage allows the surgeon to divide the cricothyroid joint with the scissors, exposing the cricothyroid joint surface. **E.** The muscular process of the arytenoid is located at approximately the level of the vocal fold (*dotted line*). **F.** The distance (*arrow*) between the upper margin of the cricothyroid joint and the lower margin of the cricoarytenoid joint is ordinarily less than 1 cm. The position of the muscular process (*m*) and vocal process (*v*) are also illustrated. **G.** The muscular process can often be identified by palpation. **H.** After elevating the mucosa lining the piriform sinus to avoid entering the airway, the posterior cricoarytenoid muscle fibers are divided, and the cricoarytenoid joint is entered. Entry into the joint is not necessary in every case.

(continues)

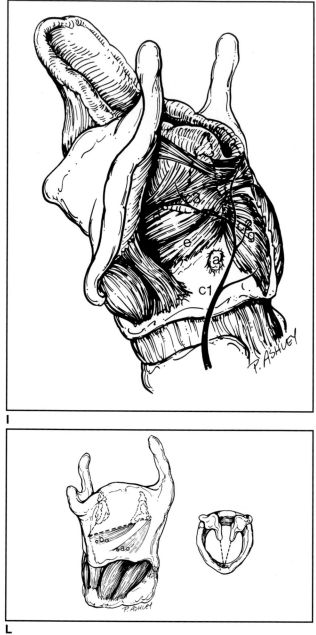

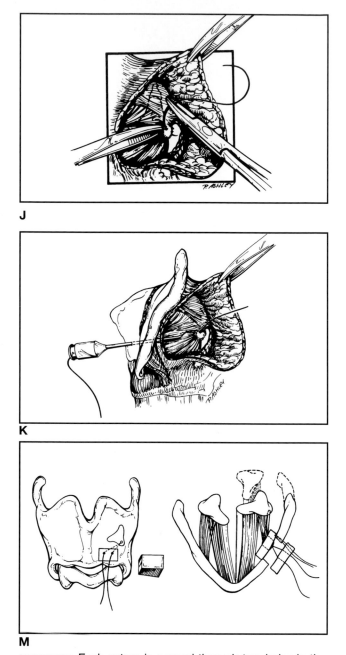

Fig 82–43. *(continued).* **I.** It is important to be familiar with the anatomic structures that may be encountered during this procedure. The most important ones include the cricothyroid joint (*a*), cricoarytenoid joint (*b*), recurrent laryngeal nerve (*c-1*), one with its abductor branches (*c-2*) and adductor branches (*c-3*); thyroarytenoid muscle (*d*), laterocricoarytenoid muscle (*e*), interarytenoid muscle (*f*) and posterior cricoarytenoid muscle (*g*). **J.** A 4-0 nylon suture is placed through the muscular process of the arytenoid. The tip of the needle is visible in the joint space. **K.** After the suture is tied to the muscular process, it is passed through the thyroid ala. An injection needle may be used if the suture cannot be passed easily using suture needles. **L.** Left, one or two sutures may be used, pulling the vocal fold in the direction of the lateral cricoarytenoid (*a*) and the direction of the thyroarytenoid (*b*). Adjusting tension between these two sutures permits proper positioning of the vocal fold. Often, only the cricoarytenoid suture is necessary. Each suture is passed through two holes in the thyroid cartilage (*circles*) and tied externally on the thyroid cartilage. Suture placement (*right*) in the arytenoid is important. If the suture is placed posteriorly (*black dot*) on the muscular process, more adduction is possible than if the suture is placed more anteriorly (*open circle*). **M.** (*Left*) Arytenoid adduction/rotation can be combined with Type I thyroplasty. Suture is passed first through the region of the intended window using either a needle, or small holes created with a drill. The suture is left untied. (*Right*) After the inner perichondrium is elevated, the cartilage may be depressed medially, and the suture can be tied. Alternatively, the suture can be passed through a silastic block and tied over the prosthesis. The suture is then passed through another implant placed lateral to the window and tied again to maintain secure position and prevent the internal prosthesis or cartilage from pulling medially away from the inner aspect of the thyroid lamina.

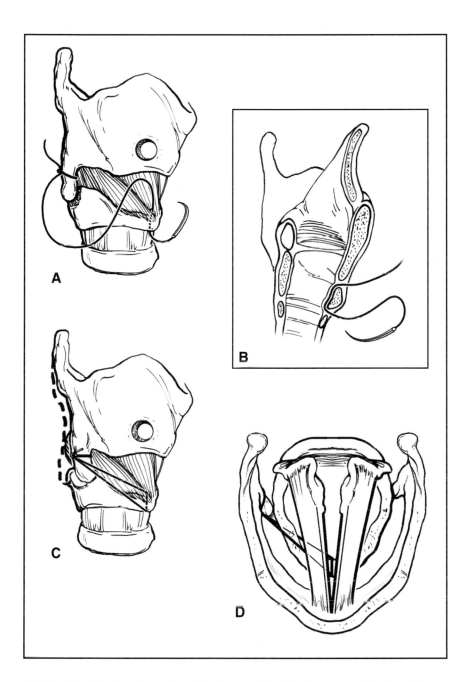

Fig 82–44. A. 2-0 proline suture is tied around the inferior cornu of the thyroid cartilage and (**B**) passed circumferentially around the cricoid arch in the midline. **C** and **D.** The suture is adjusted to pull the inferior cornu forward, lengthening the vocal fold. The patient is asked to phonate. When frequency and dynamic range are optimal, it is best to overcorrect slightly (approximately 1 mm) and fix the inferior cornu in that position.

rior and middle thirds of the final position of the silastic block. The needle is then passed through the outer surface of the junction of the anterior and middle thirds of the silastic block near its upper border and brought back through the silastic block from medial to lateral near its lower border. It is then passed from the inner surface of the thyroid lamina through the outer surface, below the initial suture entry point. The suture is then tied on the outside of the thyroid cartilage. As the suture is tightened, the silastic block is reinserted and anchored into position. If the position is not completely stable, a second suture can be used.

This procedure has proven extremely fast and effective. Gore-Tex (Newark, Del) has not been used in this scenario, because the Gore-Tex would probably extrude through the posterior opening unless it were sutured into position; and, even then, maintaining optimal Gore-Tex position would be challenging. When Gore-Tex is preferred in combination with an arytenoid cartilage procedure, it is performed in the usual fashion through an anterior mini-thyrotomy.

Zeitels also introduced adduction arytenopexy (Fig 82–45) as an alternative to classical arytenoid cartilage adduction/rotation.[113] This is an interesting and effective procedure, although it can be challenging technically for inexperienced laryngeal framework surgeons. It often is necessary to divide the cricothyroid joint to obtain adequate exposure, so that the procedure is combined routinely either with suture repair of the joint or cricothyroid subluxation. In adduction arytenopexy, it is easiest to exposure the cricoid cartilage at the cricothyroid joint, follow the cartilage from the joint to the superior surface of the cricoid, and dissect along the superior surface of cricoid cartilage. This allows easy identification of the cricoarytenoid joint, particularly after the lateral cricoarytenoid and posterior cricoarytenoid muscles have been divided from the muscular process. The cricothyroid joint is opened during this procedure, a maneuver not always necessary in classic arytenoid cartilage adduction/rotation. A suture is placed initially through the medial aspect (near the midline) of the posterior face of the cricoid cartilage and through the medial aspect of the cricoarytenoid joint. The suture is then passed through the arytenoid cartilage, looped around the lateral aspect of the arytenoid, and then brought back through the joint and posterior face of the cricoid cartilage where it is tied. This technique pulls the arytenoid cartilage up the cricoid facet, closing the posterior glottic gap. It also eliminates sutures that extend anteriorly and, in some cases, may interfere with thyroplasty. In addition, this technique tends to pull the vocal process posteriorly, lengthening the vocal fold. However, optimizing vocal process height can be difficult. To facilitate vocal process alignment, the patient should be asked to phonate at his or her habitual pitch (not at high pitch, as used commonly during mirror examination). This author (RTS) sometimes finds it necessary to place an additional proline suture or two to stabilize the arytenoid cartilage in the positioned desired.

Woodson et al have also recognized the problem of controlling the vertical position of the vocal process and have proposed a technique to help control this variable factor during arytenoid cartilage adduction/rotation surgery.[114] Their technique works better with arytenoid cartilage adduction/rotation (for which it was designed) than with arytenopexy because of the degree of joint instability created during arytenopexy and because of the final position of the inferior cornu of the thyroid cartilage when arytenoidopexy is combined with cricothyroid subluxation. However, the principle can be applied during either operation. Woodson noted that, in flaccid laryngeal paralysis, the vocal process often is displaced superiorly and laterally. She observed correctly that arytenoid cartilage adduction tends to move the vocal process medially and caudally, but that its position often ends up more caudal than normal. She hypothesized that this was due to the absence of the normal action of the posterior cricoid arytenoid muscle and proposed a posterior anchoring suture to replace posterior cricoarytenoid support. She used sutures from the arytenoid cartilage to the inferior cornu of the thyroid cartilage or to the posterior midline of the cricoid cartilage. Tension on these sutures decreased caudal displacement, but the sutures anchored near the midline widened the glottic gap. Consequently, anchoring the sutures to the inferior cornu of the thyroid cartilage is preferable when using this approach. Although classical arytenoid adduction/rotation is substantially easier and provides excellent results in some cases, adduction arytenoidopexy has clear advantages in selected cases and should be used especially in patients with complete unilateral vocal fold paralysis when there is a large posterior glottic gap and the arytenoid cartilage is tipped far laterally.

Iwamura has described yet another procedure for arytenoid cartilage repositioning called the lateral cricoarytenoid muscle pull procedure.[115,116] This operation is performed under local anesthesia through a 10 × 8 mm thyrotomy window. The window is placed immediately in front of the oblique line, over the lateral cricoarytenoid muscle (Fig 82–46). Sutures are passed through several points along the atrophic lateral cricoarytenoid (LCA) muscle bundle and tied first around the muscle, and then to the thyroid cartilage. The sutures are adjusted according to intraoperative voice improvement.

Nerve Anastomosis

Reanastomosing divided or injured recurrent laryngeal nerves has not resulted in the restoration of normal motion in most cases and traditionally has been considered not helpful. Failures may be due to abnormal intermingling of abductor and adductor fibers or to other causes. Attempts have been made to improve the results, optimizing abduction by dividing intralaryngeal adductor nerve branches.[117] However, this

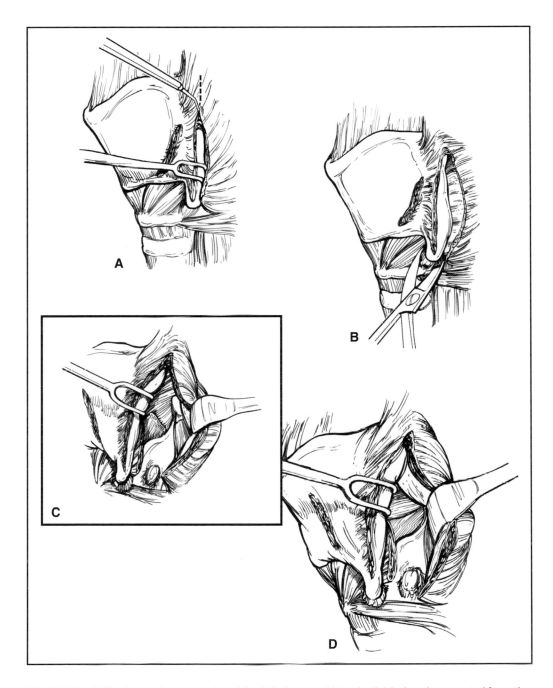

Fig 82–45. A. The larynx is exposed, and the inferior constrictor is divided and separated from the thyroid lamina. **B.** The cricothyroid joint is separated with scissors. **C.** Dissection follows the cricoid cartilage from the cricothyroid joint facet to the superior rim of the cricoid cartilage. The piriform sinus is dissected gently posteriorly. The cricothyroid muscle is cut during this dissection. **D.** The lateral cricoarytenoid and posterior cricoarytenoid muscles are divided from the muscular process.

(continued)

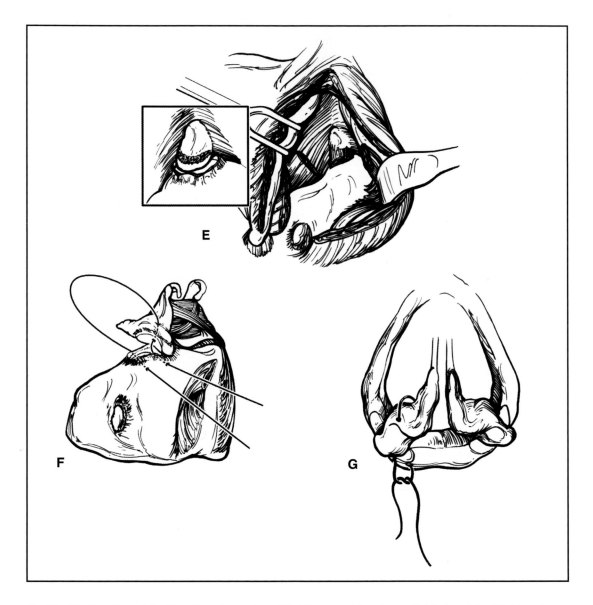

Fig 82–45. *(continued)* **E.** After the cricoarytenoid joint capsule has been divided and the joint has been opened widely, the posterior cricoarytenoid muscle is dissected off of the posterior aspect of the cricoid cartilage. **F.** 4-0 proline suture on a cutting needle is passed through the posterior face of the cricoid cartilage and through the cricoarytenoid joint. It is then wrapped around the anterolateral aspect of the arytenoid and brought back through the joint and posterior cricoid plate. **G.** Arytenoid position is adjusted by the tension on the suture as it is tied along the posterior face of the cricoid cartilage. In some cases, additional simple sutures through the arytenoid and cricoid may be necessary to adjust vocal process position optimally.

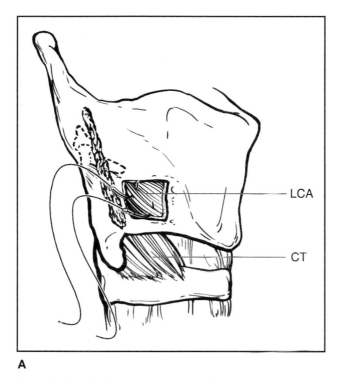

A

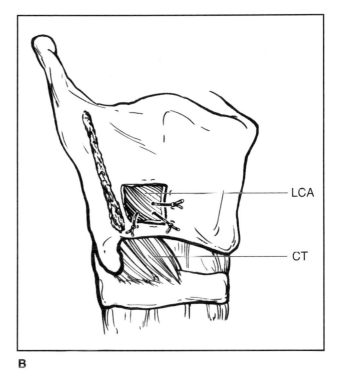

B

Fig 82–46. A. Sutures are placed through the lateral cricoarytenoid muscle. **B.** The tension on the sutures is adjusted to optimize phonatory output, and they are fixed to the thyroid cartilage anteriorly and inferiorly.

technique has limited applicability. Procedures using various other nerves, including vagus nerve bypass, split vagus nerve, phrenic nerve, and other nerves in the region, have been tried. Results have been variable.

However, research on reinnervation suggests that the technique may be much more valuable than previously appreciated. In at least some patients with vocal fold paralysis, there appears to be some degree of vocal fold atrophy after long-term denervation. Although some vocal folds show return of normal function even after complete recurrent laryngeal nerve section, reestablishing neural supply may be important to maintain vocal fold bulk (hence the effectiveness of medialization surgery) and to help control vocal fold pitch.[118-121] If a recurrent laryngeal nerve is known to have been cut during surgery, it is worthwhile for the surgeon to suture the cut ends, even though this is not likely to result in normal abduction and adduction (Fig 82–47). This subject is discussed at greater length in chapter 59.

Nerve Muscle Pedicle Surgery

Nerve muscle pedicle surgery involves implanting a portion of the omohyoid or other muscle with its intact motor branch from the ansa hypoglossi into a paralyzed laryngeal abductor muscle (Fig 82–48A-D) or a

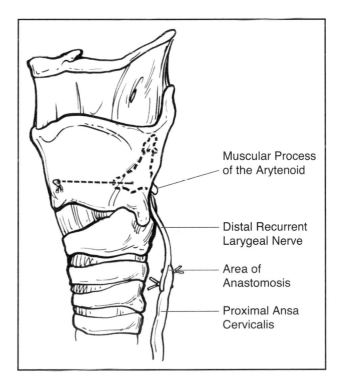

Fig 82–47. Anastomosis between ansa cervicalis and distal recurrent laryngeal nerve. Primary end-to-end recurrent laryngeal nerve reanastomosis may be performed when both portions of the severed nerve are available

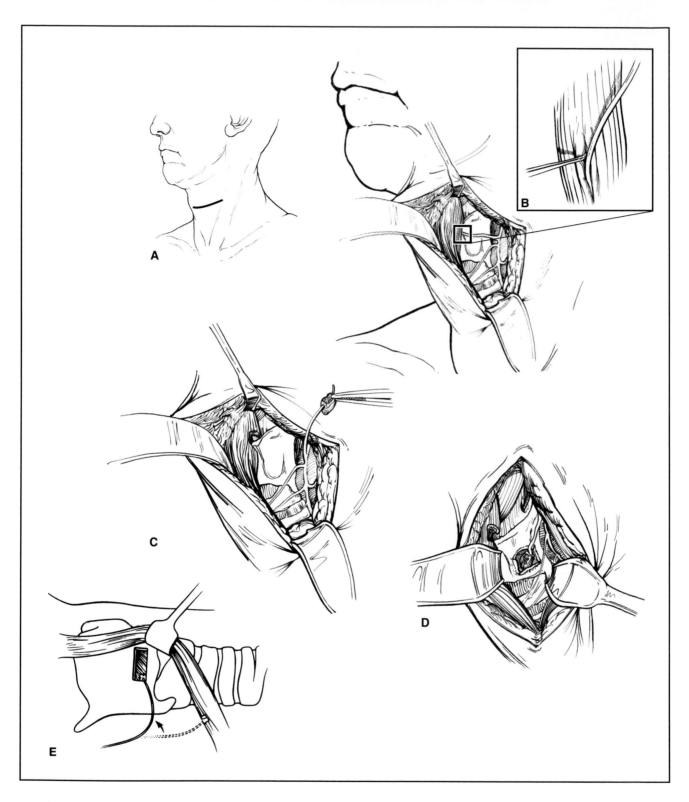

Fig 82–48. A. The ansa hypoglossi is seen entering the omohyoid muscle. **B.** The nerve is followed 2 to 3 cm into the muscle to the point at which it branches and is included in a muscle block that leaves the nerve-muscle junctions untraumatized. **D.** The nerve-muscle pedicle is sutured to the desired intrinsic laryngeal muscle. **E.** Nerve-muscle pedicle using the ansi hypoglossi branch to the anterior belly of the omohyoid muscle. After using Tucker's technique of rotating the nerve-muscle pedicle and suturing it to the exposed thyroarytenoid muscle through a thyroplasty window, the thyroplasty prosthesis must then be notched in order to prevent injury to the nerve-muscle pedicle.

portion of the cricothyroid muscle with its motor branch of the superior laryngeal nerve into a paralyzed adductor muscle. The concept was originally reported by Takenouchi and Sato in 1968,[122] and was popularized by Tucker et al in 1970,[123] and described in numerous publications thereafter. Success rates have varied, and the operation certainly has not been universally satisfactory. Probably, the small improvement that is often seen results more from change in mass or position than from return of mobility. Avoidance of atrophy may occur also. This subject is discussed later in this chapter in the section in bilateral vocal fold paralysis and in chapter 59. Failure of reinnervation after this procedure has been demonstrated histochemically in some patients. This procedure is often most effective when it is combined with a medialization procedure such as Type I thyroplasty that can be performed through the same incision (Fig 82–48E).

Other Techniques

Numerous other techniques have been tried to restore voice quality in patients with vocal fold paralysis. They include switching of intact muscles, implantation of artificial muscles, cartilage implantation, and other methods. None of the techniques available is entirely satisfactory, although interest in laryngeal pacing is particularly encouraging.[124,125] It shows promise for management of both unilateral and bilateral vocal fold paralysis along with other exciting advances undergoing research.

Treatment of Cricoarytenoid and Cricothyroid Subluxation

Treatment of cricoarytenoid and cricothyroid joint injuries is discussed in chapter 89.

Arytenoidectomy

Arytenoidectomy remains the most reliable technique for reestablishing a good airway in patients with bilateral vocal fold paralysis or arytenoid fixation. Unfortunately, it generally does so at the expense of voice quality. However, it results in voice quality superior to the operation it replaced, which was total cordectomy.[125] Traditionally, arytenoidectomy has been performed through an external incision. The procedure was introduced initially in 1946 by Woodman. He described removing the arytenoid cartilage with preservation of the vocal process.[126] Endoscopic ary-

tenoidectomy was described 2 years later by Thornell.[127] Endoscopic arytenoidectomy has been successful and effective, and has proven a particularly satisfactory approach since use of the carbon dioxide laser was introduced for this operation.[128-131]

The procedure is performed using suspension microlaryngoscopy. A 400-mm objective lens is usually optimal. Lasers with a spot size of 0.4 mm are generally used at 6 to 10 watts in repeat mode with 0.1-second pulses. The corniculate cartilage and mucosa over the apex of the arytenoid are vaporized, as is the mucoperiosteum of the apex and body of the arytenoid cartilage. The upper portion of the body of the arytenoid is ablated using continuous mode. Repeat mode is then used to vaporize the mucoperichondrium of the lower body, which is then vaporized from lateral to medial. The lateral ligament is transected, and the cricoid cartilage is exposed. The vocal process is vaporized, as is the muscular process preserving the attachment of the arytenoideus muscle (Fig 82–49). Vaporization is continued lateral to the vocalis muscle to create a scar that will assist in lateralization of the vocal fold (Fig 82–50). Because of cartilage exposure, antibiotics are generally recommended. If there is no tracheotomy in place, intraoperative corticosteroids are also used by many surgeons. There are no data proving the efficacy of either antibiotics or steroids during this procedure. Their use at present depends on the surgeon's judgment. There are various modifications of arytenoidectomy procedures. Many surgeons (including this author) preserve a mucosal flap, suturing it over the resection site. Closing mucosa helps avoid granuloma formation, a troublesome complication of arytenoidectomy. Arytenoidectomy pa-

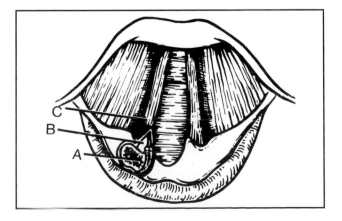

Fig 82–49. Intermittent step during laser arytenoidectomy, showing exposure of the cricoid cartilage (A), vocal process of the arytenoid cartilage (B), and vocalis muscle (C).

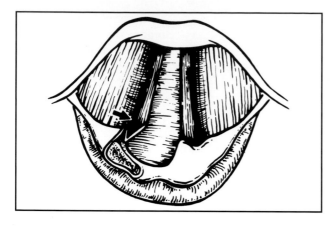

Fig 82–50. Completed arytenoidectomy with remnant of muscular process and arytenoideus attachment, and laser-induced trauma lateral to the vocal muscle to help lateralization (*arrow*).

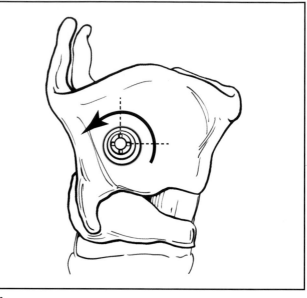

A

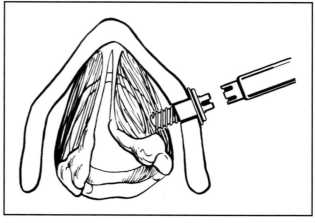

B

Fig 82–51. A. The Cummings device is snapped into a 1-cm hole cut in the thyroid cartilage, which stabilizes the device and provides access for adjustment. **B.** Once the device is attached to the region of the vocal process, the outer cam is retracted lateralizing the true vocal fold. The double-helix, double-cam, stainless steel/polythene device is attached to the vocal process through a 1-cm window in the thyroid cartilage. This screwlike device can be adjusted incrementally to lateralize the vocal fold precisely, establishing an optimal balance between airway and voice.

tients also should be treated prophylactically for larynogopharyngeal reflux. This appears to expedite healing and does not appear to interfere with formation of lateralizing scar.

It also is possible to resect only portions of the arytenoid cartilage. Medial arytenoidectomy (preserving a thin, lateral shell of arytenoid cartilage) often provides an adequate airway and minimizes collapse of the posterior laryngeal anatomy. Medial arytenoidectomy was popularized by Crumley.[131] This procedure may be advantageous particularly in patients who are likely to aspirate after complete arytenoidectomy. Medial arytenoidectomy also has been used in unusual circumstances, such as bilateral pseudoparalysis.[132]

Other Techniques for Bilateral Vocal Fold Paralysis

Bilateral vocal fold paralysis still places the patient and surgeon in a most difficult position. No good treatment is available, yet. Arytenoidopexy is an alternative to arytenoidectomy. In this procedure, no tissue is removed; but the arytenoid cartilage is sutured into the abducted position.[133,134] Unfortunately, this procedure is less consistent than arytenoidectomy in producing a good airway. However, suture lateralization (passing a stitch through the skin in the lateral neck, around the vocal fold, and back out through the skin) can be a useful adjunct to arytenoidectomy, helping to lateralize the posterior aspect of the vocal fold.

An interesting alternative to placement of a suture or arytenoidectomy was proposed by Cummings et al[135] (Fig 82–51). They developed a double-helix, dou-

ble-cam, stainless steel/polythene device that is attached to the vocal process through a 1-cm window in the thyroid cartilage. This screwlike device can be adjusted incrementally to lateralize the vocal fold precisely, establishing an optimal balance between airway and voice. This minimally invasive technique was reported after studies in sheep; and human efficacy studies are pending. However, the technique appears promising.

Although arytenoidectomy provides a good airway, as discussed above, it usually results in a breathy, somewhat hoarse voice. The better the airway is, the worse the voice. However, if the vocal folds are near the midline, producing good voice, a tracheotomy is usually required for active individuals. Another technique proposed to reestablish adequate airway is posterior cordotomy, as described by Dennis and Kashima.[136] This procedure involves removal of the posterior third of the vocal fold. This may produce better voice quality than arytenoidectomy alone.[136] Many surgeons combine this principle with arytenoidectomy with a lateral, wedgelike resection of thyroarytenoid muscle anterior to the vocal process (posterior cordotomy).

If bilateral vocal fold paralysis presents with good voice and borderline airway, reinnervation may be worth trying; reinnervation may be worthwhile even when the vocal folds are in midline. In order to undergo reinnervation of the posterior cricoarytenoid muscles, patients must have mobile arytenoids and intact cricoarytenoid joints. Ascertaining the condition of the cricoarytenoid joints may require palpation during direct laryngoscopy with paralysis. It is advisable to palpate the arytenoid cartilages routinely on all patients, so that the surgeon knows the degree of pressure required to move a normal arytenoid cartilage. Palpation should be accomplished with the side of a suction or with a spatula placed against the medial or lateral face of the arytenoid cartilage. Pressure directly on the vocal process or its junction with the body of the arytenoid cartilage should be avoided to prevent fracturing the vocal process off the arytenoid body.

A nerve muscle pedicle 2 to 3 mm square is created from any of the strap muscles,[137,138] although the omohyoid is used most commonly. The posterior cricoarytenoid muscle is exposed by retracting the posterior aspects of the cricoid cartilage and separating the inferior constrictor muscle near the base of the inferior cornu of the thyroid cartilage. Care must be taken to reflect rather than transgress the piriform sinus. The posterior cricoarytenoid muscles are recognized easily because they run at right angles to the inferior constrictor. The nerve-muscle pedicle is sutured into the cricoarytenoid muscle. When the procedure works, there is usually a 4- to 6-month delay between surgery and active abduction and abduction. Further details are provided in chapter 59.

This author occasionally has used botulinum toxin for bilateral vocal fold paralysis. Although this seems counterintuitive, it should be remembered that at least a small amount of reinnervation is common following vocal fold paralysis. When reinnervation occurs, there is synkinesis. That is, both abductors and adductors are innervated. Consequently, if a borderline airway is present, injecting botulinum toxin into the adductor muscles may allow enough unopposed abductor function to result in an extra millimeter or two of glottic space. If this is sufficient for the patient, it is certainly less traumatic than arytenoidectomy; and usually it results in better voice quality.

Vocal Process Avulsion

Vocal process avulsion may occur with internal or external laryngeal trauma. Examination findings may be subtle. Highly magnified strobovideolaryngoscopic evaluation is helpful. Endoscopic evaluation with palpation under general anesthesia may be necessary. Voice therapy should be administered initially. Surgical options include the use of injectable materials for closed reduction, chemical tenotomy with botulinum toxin, endoscopic open reduction of the fracture via a cordotomy approach, or open reduction using a laryngofissure.

Vocal process avulsion can result from intubation or from external trauma to the larynx. These are also the most common etiologies of arytenoid dislocation, which should be included in the differential of dysphonia after such events. Discrepancy in the heights of the vocal processes may be seen with either vocal process avulsion or arytenoid dislocation. Close examination of movement of the body of the arytenoid cartilage in relation to the vocal process may help distinguish between the two. Of note, when reducing an anterior arytenoid cartilage dislocation, one should take care not to insert the laryngoscope too deeply into the laryngeal inlet so as to place the vocal process at risk for avulsion. External laryngeal trauma is a potentially life-threatening injury. Dysphonia is an ominous sign and should alert the physician to a possible laryngeal fracture or vocal fold injury.

In the author's experience, patients with vocal process avulsion have presented with persistent dysphonia weeks to months after the initial insult.[139] Some structure injury was suspected from examination and EMG results. Other symptoms in the acute setting may include pain and dysphagia. Findings of a vocal process avulsion can be subtle, and close examination of the larynx with both flexible laryngoscopy and rigid videostroboscopy is critical in the evaluation of these injuries. Signs of avulsion may include an apparent separation of the vocal process from the arytenoid body, abnormal angle or position of the vocal process, overlapping of the avulsed vocal process with the contralateral process, mobility of the vocal process independent from the body of the arytenoids, and foreshortening and decreased stretch of the vocal fold during glissando.

Treatment of the vocal process avulsion must be geared toward the severity of the injury and the expectations of the patient. A trial of voice therapy usually is warranted, as this may provide a satisfactory voice for some patients. If one proceeds with surgery, several options are available. Endoscopic open reduction of the fracture may be performed.

Laryngofissure and Lateral Thyrotomy

In some situations, it is necessary to operate on the vocal folds or paraglottic tissue through an external approach. In addition to laryngeal framework procedures discussed elsewhere in this chapter, laryngofissure and thyrotomy can be used to provide access to the area of interest.

Laryngofissure is performed through a horizontal incision in the anterior neck, centered near the vertical midpoint of the thyroid cartilage. Laryngofissure was performed initially in 1788 by Pellatone to remove a laryngeal foreign body, although it had been suggested early by Desault.[140] In 1834, Brauers in Belgium was the first surgeon to use laryngofissure to remove a neoplasm.[140] The operation also was utilized by Billoff

for eight patients between 1870 and 1884, and by many others in the later 19th and early 20th centuries.[140] Before the end of the first quarter of the 20th century, it had become the standard approach for surgical treatment of early carcinoma of the vocal folds. It is sometimes still used for that indication; but now it is used more commonly to repair vocal fold trauma, to resect other neoplasms, and in combination with other procedures such as anterior and/or posterior cricoid cartilage split. Soft tissues are divided and strap muscles are retracted, exposing the cartilage in the midline. An incision is made in the anterior midline of thyroid cartilage with a knife or saw, taking care not to damage the underlying soft tissue (Fig 82–52). Ordinarily, an incision is then made through the cricothyroid membrane. As this incision is carried superiorly, the vocal folds are visualized so that they can be divided exactly in the midline. Dissection can be performed with a knife or with straight scissors placed between the vocal folds and pulled gently forward to ensure proper position. If the cricothyroid membrane is not amenable to surgery because of pathology or previous injury, a superior approach can be used, although it is slightly more difficult because of the additional thickness of tissue that must be traversed before entering the airway. Once the cartilage, vocal folds, and soft tissue above and below the anterior commissure have been divided, the thyroid cartilage is retracted laterally to expose the interior of the larynx. When closing, it

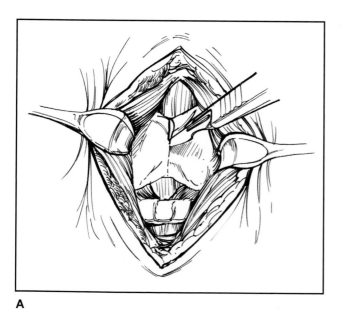

A

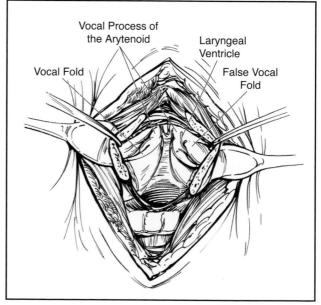

B

Fig 82–52. A. An incision is made vertically through the midline of the thyroid cartilage. **B.** After the thyroid cartilage and soft tissues have been exposed, the interior of the larynx can be visualized.

is essential to reattach the anterior commissure tendon and to suture both vocal folds at the same level. Ideally, suture (and especially suture knots) should be in the soft tissues anteriorly, not in the airway. This precaution helps avoid granuloma formation. The cartilages can be reapproximated with miniplates, but the author has found figure-of-eight sutures entirely satisfactory. If miniplates are used, it is preferable to use absorbable miniplates, which do not interfere with future imaging studies as do metal miniplates.

Lateral thyrotomy permits access to the paraglottic space and is useful for removing Teflon, excising laryngoceles, and for approaching similar lesions. Entry can be made through the thyroid cartilage using a variety of approaches. The inner perichondrium is then incised, and the operation is individualized depending on the pathology (Fig 82–53). Lateral thyrotomy was introduced in 1914 by Lewis, who divided the thyroid cartilage vertically anterior to the superior and inferior cornu of the thyroid cartilage.[141] He used

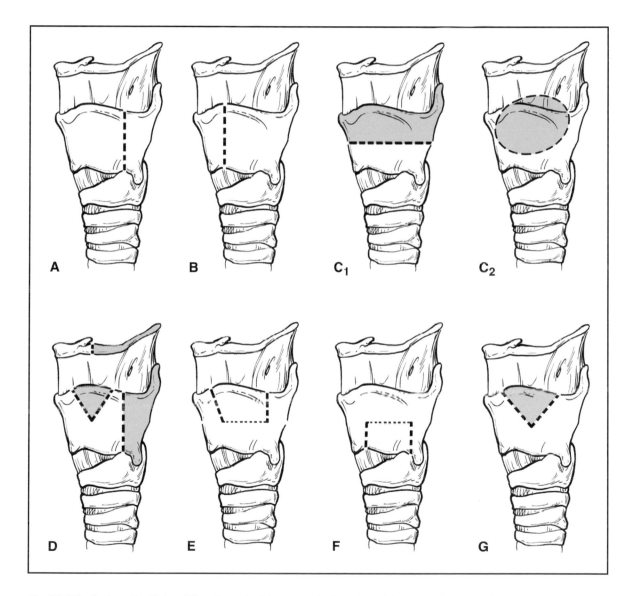

Fig 82–53. A. A vertical lateral thyrotomy incision near the junction of the posterior and middle thirds. **B.** Vertical thyrotomy near the junction of the anterior and middle thirds. **C₁.** Exposure also can be obtained through a horizontal incision with removal of the superior portion of the thyroid cartilage or (**C₂**), by biting away a portion of the thyroid cartilage; **D,** by creating a triangular thyrotomy along with removing the posterior third of the laryngeal cartilage and the greater cornu of the hyoid bone; **E,** by creating an superiorly-based trapped-door flap which can be folded inferiorly; **F,** by creating a inferiorly-based trap-door flap which can be folded superiorly; or **G,** by using a V-shaped resection of thyroid lamina.

the procedure to resect a congenital cyst in the para-glottic space. Other authors have modified the position of the cartilaginous incision, using a vertical incision at the junction of the anterior and middle third,[142,143] a horizontal incision with resection of thyroid lamina,[144-148] biting away a portion of the thyroid cartilage,[149] using a rectangular "fold down trap-door flap,"[150] or a superiorly-based trap-door fold-up flap,[151] and using a triangular resection of thyroid cartilage superiorly.[65] Keim and Livingstone enlarged the exposure by resecting a triangular segment of thyroid lamina superiorly, along with the posterior third of the thyroid lamina and the greater cornu of the hyoid bone.[152] These and other variations are useful for a variety of paraglottic lesions.

Thyroarytenoid Neurectomy

When Dedo introduced recurrent laryngeal nerve section as a treatment for spasmodic dysphonia in 1976,[153] the procedure was greeted with great enthusiasm. However, it quickly became clear that there were problems associated with this approach[154,155]; and it was abandoned by most surgeons in the 1980s. Disappointment and controversy surrounding recurrent laryngeal nerve section may be responsible in part for the delay in recognizing the value of selective thyroarytenoid neurectomy. This procedure was developed by Shinobu Iwamura in 1978 and introduced to the United States in 1979.[156] This procedure involves creating a window similar to a thyroplasty window but placed more posteriorly. The posterior aspect of the window is adjacent to the oblique line. The window should be approximately 8 × 10 mm in size. The inner perichondrium is incised, and blunt dissection is used to identify the thyroarytenoid branch of the recurrent laryngeal nerve (Fig 82–54). Iwamura describes dividing the nerve to paralyze the thyroarytenoid muscle. The procedure is actually slightly more complex, as described below.

Iwamura's procedure was reintroduced by Berke and coworkers in 1991. Their initial report described bilateral thyroarytenoid denervation in dogs, with anastomosis of the ansa cervicalis to the distal, cut end of the thyroarytenoid nerve, thereby preventing reinnervation from the proximal stump of the thyroarytenoid nerve.[157] This procedure was also believed to limit atrophy and fibrosis of the thyroarytenoid muscle. Since that time, Berke has used this approach in humans and continues to advocate anastomosis of the ansa cervicalis with the distal end of the cut thyroarytenoid nerve to prevent recurrence of symptoms.[158]

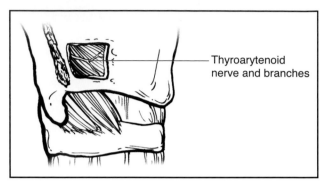

Fig 82–54. A window approximately 10 mm by 8 mm is created in the thyroid lamina, just anterior to the oblique line. Usually, after opening the inner perichondrium, the thyroarytenoid nerve can be exposed easily with blunt dissection. However, occasionally it may branch prior to this point and be more difficult to find.

Initially, the procedure advocated by Berke seems superior to Iwamura's operation because reinnervation should occur in some patients if the thyroarytenoid nerve is merely cut or even if it is cut, avulsed, and clipped. This author is familiar with cases in which that problem has occurred. Interestingly, Iwamura reports that he has not had problems with recurrence of symptoms (Shinobu Iwamura, MD, personal communication, 2000); but it was not clear to this author why the discrepancy existed until Dr. Iwamura visited Philadelphia and we had an opportunity to discuss his procedure in detail and review videotapes of the operation. In addition to performing a thyroarytenoid neurectomy, Iwamura routinely removes a large amount of thyroarytenoid muscle. The myomectomy not only helps ensure that all branches of the thyroarytenoid nerve are cut, but also removes so much muscle that normal activity cannot occur even if the residual fibers are reinnervated. In our experience with laryngeal electromyography in patients with adductor spasmodic dysphonia following botulinum toxin injection, we have found that many patients remain fluent with as little as 30 to 40% reduced recruitment in the thyroarytenoid muscle. Having observed the amount of muscle that Dr. Iwamura removes, it seems likely that muscle loss and fibrosis would result in substantially diminished TA muscle function, even if substantial reinnervation from the proximal end of the cut nerve were to occur. So, ansa anastomosis is unnecessary if the procedure is performed in this fashion. Dr. Iwamura usually operates on one side, proceeding to surgery on the contralateral side if control is insufficient (a minority of cases). This author has utilized Iwamura's approach and had similar results. Although the operation results in some dysphonia, in most patients, generally after 3 to 6 months, it is minimal and comparable to voice quality noted during successful treatment with botulinum toxin injection.

This author has been pleased with results of thyroarytenoid neurectomy and myomectomy, but both this procedure and the procedure described by Berke (ansa cervicalis anastomosis) are reasonable options. However, in this author's opinion, it is unwise to simply divide the thyroarytenoid nerve without performing either simultaneous myomectomy or nerve anastomosis.

Laryngeal Transplantation

Laryngeal transplantation is a major surgical procedure that is extremely important but has few indications. The first successful laryngeal transplantation was performed by Strome.[159] Like other transplantation procedures, laryngeal transplant requires long-term use of immunosuppressive medications. Hence, at present it is not advocated for patients with a history of malignancy. Currently, it is considered most suitable for patients with little or no voice who are dependent on tracheotomy for respiration. This scenario is most likely to occur following trauma, as in Strome's patient. The patient achieved a human-sounding voice with inflection, range, and qualities unique to him; and he was able to swallow normally. He has a tracheostoma; and at 36 months, the characteristics of his speech were considered within the normal range. He has been able to work as a motivational speaker. Laryngeal transplantation requires substantially more study and experience but represents an important option for a small, select group of patients.

Other Considerations

Voice Rest

The efficacy of voice rest as therapy is unproven. Its wide standard is based on anecdotal experience and common sense, which may or may not turn out to be correct. Voice rest may be indicated after vocal fold hemorrhage, mucosal tear, and vocal fold surgery, especially if the mucosa of the leading edge of the vocal fold has been removed. The rationale is attractive, even though it is unsubstantiated. Microsurgical techniques are designed to minimize scar formation. A scar forms when fibroblast proliferation is initiated in the intermediate and deep layers of the lamina propria. If vibratory margin mucosa has been removed,

then the lamina propria is exposed. Therefore, it seems reasonable to minimize contact trauma to this region through voice rest until the mucosal cover is restored (sometimes within 2 to 3 days, rarely more than 1 week). Although some vocal fold contact will occur inevitably because of swallowing and coughing, more (avoidable) contact occurs during speech. When a patient phonates at a pitch of A below middle C, the vocal folds make contact 220 times per second. This is close to the normal fundamental frequency of the female speaking voice. In addition, these contacts may be abusive if the patient attempts to achieve voice quality and volume after surgery. Consequently, the author recommends voice rest routinely after surgery, unless the vibratory margin mucosa has been left intact. Absolute voice rest is maintained until the vocal fold has remucosalized (rarely more than 1 week). The author's patients' first utterance is the /i/ in the examining chair approximately 1 week after surgery. Patients then have a short session with the speech-language pathologist to assist in the transition from silence to limited voice use. Relative voice rest and good vocal hygiene under the supervision of speech-language pathologists are maintained until complete healing has occurred. Details of voice rest technique are discussed in chapter 69. Preoperative voice therapy is extremely helpful in preparing patients for voice rest and voice conservation.

Related Surgery

Velopharyngeal insufficiency has also been suggested as a cause of problems for singers, actors, and instrumentalists. Damsté[160] has described push-back surgery for "congenital short palate" in a professional singer who presented with nodules and voice fatigue. The prevalence and importance of this problem await further clarification, and most of us who care for large numbers of singers and actors do not encounter it frequently.

Obstructive Sleep Apnea Syndrome

Obstructive sleep apnea syndrome in professional voice users is discussed in chapter 39.

Miscellaneous Laryngeal Procedures

Many laryngeal procedures are not included in detail in this chapter. They include operations for recreating new vocal folds, readjusting vocal fold height, and many other purposes. This chapter is not intended to be all-inclusive, and the reader is encouraged to consult other chapters, and other literature for additional information about laryngeal surgery.[26,36,37]

References

1. von Leden H. The history of phonosurgery. In: Sataloff RT. *Professional Voice: The Science and Art of Clinical Care.* 2nd ed. San Diego, Calif: Singular Publishing Group, Inc; 1997:561–580.

2. Green H. Morbid growths within the larynx. In: *On the Surgical Treatment of Polypi of the Larynx, and Oedema of the Glottis.* New York, NY: GP Putnam; 1852:56–65.

3. Brünings W. Direct laryngoscopy: criteria determining the applicability of autoscopy. In: *Direct Laryngoscopy, Bronchoscopy, and Esophagoscopy.* London: Bailliere, Tindall, Cox; 1912:93–95

4. Jackson C. *Peroral Endoscopy and Laryngeal Surgery.* St Louis, Mo: Laryngoscope Co; 1915.

5. Holinger P. An hour-glass anterior commissure laryngoscope. *Laryngoscope.* 1960;70:1570–1571.

6. Kleinsasser O. [Microlaryngoscopy and endolaryngeal microsurgery. II: A review of 2500 cases.] *HNO.* 1974;22(3):69–83

7. Jako G. Laryngoscope for microscopic observation, surgery, and photography. *Arch Otolaryngol.* 1970;91:196–199.

8. Dedo HH. A fiberoptic anterior commissure laryngoscope for use with the operating microscope. *Trans Sect Otolaryngol Am Acad Ophthalmol Otolaryngol.* 1976;82:91–92.

9. Gould WJ. The Gould laryngoscope. *Trans Sect Otolaryngol Am Acad Ophthalmol Otolaryngol.* 1973;77:139–141.

10. Killian G: Suspension laryngoscopy—a modification of the direct method. *Trans 3rd Internat Laryngol Congr.* Germany. (Part II) Transactions; 1911:12

11. Zeitels SM, Vaughan CW. "External counterpressure" and "internal distention" for optimal laryngoscopic exposure of the anterior glottal commissure. *Ann Otol Rhinol Laryngol.* 1994;103(9):669–675.

12. Hochman II, Zeitels SM, Heaton JT. Analysis of the forces and position required for direct laryngoscopic exposure of the anterior vocal folds. *Ann Otol Rhinol Laryngol.* 1999;108(8):715–724.

13. Adriani J, Naraghi M. Drug induced methemoglobinemia: local anesthetics. *Anesthesiol Rev.* 12(1):54–59.

14. Urban GE. Laryngeal microsurgery without intubation. *South-Med J.* 1976;69:828–830.

15. Carden E, Becker G, Hamood H. Percutaneous jet ventilation. *Ann Otol Rhinol Laryngol.* 1976;85:652–655.

16. Hoerenz P. The operating microscope: I. optical principles, illumination systems, and support systems. *J Microsurg.* 1980;1:364–369.

17. Andrea M, Dias O. *Atlas of Rigid and Contact Endoscopy in Microlaryngeal Surgery.* Philadelphia, Pa: Lippincott Williams and Wilkins; 1995:1–112.

18. Flint PW. Powered surgical instruments for laryngeal surgery. *Otolaryngol Head Neck Surg.* 2000;122(2):263–266.

19. Hajek M. Anatomische Untersuchungen uber das Larynxodem. *Arch Klin Chir.* 1891;42:46–93.

20. Reinke F. Uber die Funktionelle Struktur Menschlichen Stimmlippe mit Besonderer Berucksichtigung des Elastischen Geweber. *Anat Heft.* 1897;9:103–117.

21. Pressman J, Dowdy A, Libby R, Fields M. Further studies upon the submucosal compartments and lymphatics of the larynx by the injection of dyes and radioisotope. *Ann Otol Rhinol Laryngol.* 1956;65:963–980.

22. Welsh LW, Welsh JJ, Rizzo TA Jr. Laryngeal spaces and lymphatics: current anatomic concepts. *Ann Otol Rhinol Laryngol Suppl.* 1983;105:19–31.

23. Kass ES, Hillman RE, Zeitels SM. Vocal fold submucosal infusion technique in phonomicrosurgery. *Ann Otol Rhinol Laryngol.* 1996;105(5):341–347.

24. Rosen C. Kenalog laryngoscope.

25. Hirano M. Phonosurgery. Basic and clinical investigations. *Otologia Fukuoka.* 1975;21:239–442.

26. Sataloff RT. *Professional Voice: The Science and Art of Clinical Care.* New York, NY: Raven Press; 1991.

27. Gould WJ, Sataloff RT, Spiegel JR. *Voice Surgery.* Chicago, Ill: Mosby Year Book; 1993.

28. Sataloff RT. The human voice. *Sci Am.* 1992;267(6):108–115.

29. Sundberg J. *The Science of the Singing Voice.* DeKalb, Ill: Northern Illinois University Press; 1987.

30. Titze IR, Strong WJ. Normal modes in vocal cord tissues. *J Acoustic Soc Am.* 1975;57(3):736–744.

31. Titze IR, Talkin DT. A theoretical study of the effects of various laryngeal configurations on the acoustics of phonation. *J Acoustic Soc Am.* 1979;66(1):60–74.

32 Titze IR. Comments on the myoelastic-aerodynamic theory of phonation. *J Speech Hear Res.* 1980;23(3):495–510.

33. Titze IR. The physics of small-amplitude oscillation of the vocal folds. *J Acoustic Soc Am.* 1988;83(4):1536–1552.

34. von Leden H. The history of phonosurgery. In: Gould WJ, Sataloff RT, Spiegel JR eds. *Voice Surgery.* Chicago, Ill: Mosby Year Book; 1993:65–96.

35. Sataloff RT: The professional voice. In: Cummings CW, Frederickson JM, Harker LA, et al, eds. *Otolaryngology—Head and Neck Surgery.* St. Louis, Mo: CV Mosby; 1986; 3:2029–2056.

36. Gould WJ, Lawrence VL: Surgical care of voice disorders. In: Arnold GE, Winckel F, Wyke BD, eds. *Disorders of Human Communication.* New York NY: Springer-Verlag; 1984.

37. Isshiki N. *Phonosurgery—Theory and Practice.* New York, NY: Springer-Verlag; 1989.

38. Ford CN, Bless DM. *Phonosurgery: Assessment and Surgical Management.* New York, NY: Raven Press; 1992.

39. Sataloff RT. Endoscopic microsurgery. In: Gould WJ, Sataloff RT, Spiegel JR, eds. *Voice Surgery.* Chicago, Ill: Mosby Year Book; 1993:227–267.

40. Gray S. Basement membrane zone injury in vocal nodules. In: Gauffin J, Hammarberg B, eds. *Vocal Fold Physiology.* San Diego, Calif: Singular Publishing Group; 1991.

41. Sataloff RT, Spiegel JR, Heuer RJ, et al. Laryngeal minimicroflap: a new technique and reassessment of the microflap saga. *J Voice.* 1995;9(2):198–204.

42. Dedo HH, Sooy CD. Endoscopic laser repair of posterior glottic, subglottic, and tracheal stenosis by division or micro-trap-door flap. *Laryngoscope.* 1984;94:445–450.

43. Duncavage JA, Ossoff RH, Toohill RJ. Carbon dioxide laser management of laryngeal stenosis. *Ann Otol Rhinol Laryngol.* 1985;94:565–569.

44. Werkhaven J, Ossoff RH. Surgery for benign lesions of the glottis. *Otolaryngol Clin North Am.* 1991;24(5):1179–1199.

45. Hochman I, Sataloff RT, Hillman R, Zeitels S. Ectasias and varices of the vocal fold: clearing the striking zone. *Ann Otol Rhinol Laryngol.* 1999;108(1):10–16.

46. Baker DC Jr. Laryngeal problems in singers. *Laryngoscope.* 1962;72:902–908.

47. Feder RJ. Varix of the vocal cord in the professional voice user. *Otolaryngol Head Neck Surg.* 1983;91:435–436.

48. Czermak JN. On the laryngoscope and its employment in physiology and medicine. *N Sydenham Soc.* 1861:11: 1–79

49. Mackenzie M. *The Use of the Laryngoscope in Diseases of the Throat with an Appendix on Rhinoscopy.* London, England: J & A Churchill; 1865.

50. Turck L. *Atlas zur Klinik der Kehlkopfkrankheiten.* Wien, Austria: Willhelm Braumuller; 1860.

51. Elsberg L. *Laryngoscopal Surgery Illustrated in the Treatment of Morbid Growths Within the Larynx.* Philadelphia, Pa: Collins; 1866.

52. Mackenzie M. *Growths in the Larynx.* London, England: J & A Churchill; 1871.

53. Zeitels SM, Sataloff RT. Phomicrosurgical resection of glottal papillomatosis. *J Voice.* 1999;13:123–127.

54. Wellens W, Snoeck R, Desloovere C, et al. Treatment of severe laryngeal papillomatosis with intralesional injections of Cidofovir® [(S)-1-(3-Hydroxy-Phosphonylmethoxypropyl) Cytosine, HPMPC Vistide®] Transactions of the XVI World Congress of Otorhinolaryngology—Head and Neck Surgery; March 2–7, 1997; Sydney, Australia.

55. Holinger LD, Barnes DR, Smid LJ, Holinger PH. Laryngocele and saccular cysts. *Ann Otol Rhinol Laryngol.* 1978; 87:675–685.

56. Ward PH, Frederickson J, Strandjord NM, Valvessori GE. Laryngeal and pharyngeal pouches. Surgical approach and the use of cinefluorographic and other radiologic techniques as diagnostic aids. *Laryngoscope.* 1963;73:564–582.

57. DeSanto LW. Laryngocele, laryngeal mucocele, large saccules, and laryngeal saccular cysts: a developmental spectrum. *Laryngoscope.* 1974;84:1291–1296.

58. Norris CW. Pharyngoceles of the hypopharynx. *Laryngoscope.* 1979;89:1788–1807.

59. Papsin BC, Maaske LA, McGrail JS. Orbicularis oris muscle injury in brass players. *Laryngoscope.* 1996; 106:757–760.

60. Fiz JA, Aguilar J, Carreras A, et al. Maximum respiratory pressure in trumpet players. *Chest.* 1993;104:1203–1204.

61. Stephani A, Tarab S. [Obscure and ventricular laryngocele.] *Schweiz Rundsch Med Prax.* 1972;61:1520–1523.

62. Macfie DD. Asymptomatic laryngoceles in wind-instrument bandsmen. *Arch Otolaryngol.* 1966;83:270–275.

63. Backus J. The effect of the player's vocal tract on woodwind instrument tone. *J Acoust Soc Am.* 1985;78:17–20.

64. Isaacson G, Sataloff RT. Bilateral laryngoceles in a young trumpet player: case report. *Ear Nose Throat J.* 2000;4: 272–274.

65. Thome R, Thome DC, De La Cortina RA. Lateral thyrotomy approach on the paraglottic space for laryngocele resection. *Laryngoscope.* 2000;110:447–450.

66. Stern SJ, Sven JY. Conservation surgery of the larynx and its relationship to voice result. In: Rubin JS, Sataloff RT, Korovin GS, Gould WJ, eds. *Diagnosis and Treatment of Voice Disorders.* New York, NY: Igaku-Shoin; 1995:445–467.

67. Ford CN, Bless DM, Loftus JM. The role of injectable collagen in the treatment of glottic insufficiency: a study of 119 patients. *Ann Otol Rhinol Laryngol.* 1992;101(3):237–247.

68. Pontes P, Behlau M. Treatment of sulcus vocalis: auditory perceptual and acoustic analysis of the slicing mucosa surgical technique. *J Voice.* 1993;7(4):365–376.

69. Sataloff RT, Hawkshaw MJ. Endoscopic internal stent: a new procedure for laryngeal webs in the presence of papilloma. *Ear Nose Throat J.* 1998;77(12):949–950.

70. Stasney CR. Laryngeal webs: a new treatment for an old problem. Presented at the 22nd Annual Symposium: Care of the Professional Voice; June 12, 1993; The Voice Foundation, Philadelphia, Pa.

71. Stone JW, Arnold GE. Human larynx injected with Teflon paste. Histological study of innervation and tissue reaction. *Arch Otolaryngol.* 1967;86:550–561.

72. von Leden H, Yanagihara N, Kukuk-Werner E. Teflon in unilateral vocal cord paralysis. *Arch Otolaryngol.* 1967; 85(6):666–674.

73. Schramm V, May M, Lavorato AS, Gelfoam paste injection for vocal fold paralysis: temporary rehabilitation of glottic incompetence. *Laryngoscope.* 1978;88:1268–1273.

74. Anderson TD, Mirza N. Immediate percutaneous medialization for acute vocal fold immobility with aspiration. *Laryngoscope.* 2001;111:1318–1321.

75. Ford CN, Bless DM. Collagen injected in the scarred vocal fold. *J Voice.* 1988;1:116–118.

76. Ford CN, Bless DM. Selected problems treated by vocal fold injection of collagen. *Am J Otolaryngol.* 1993;14(4): 257–261.

77. Cendron M, DeVore DP, Connolly R, et al. The biological behavior of autologous collagen injected into the rabbit bladder. *J Urol.* 1995;154:808–811.

78. Ford CN, Staskowski PA, Bless DM. Autologous collagen vocal fold injection: a preliminary clinical study. *Laryngoscope.* 1995;105(9):944–948.

79. DeVore DP, Hughes E, Scott JB. Effectiveness of injectable filler materials for smoothing wrinkle lines and depressed scars. *Med Prog Technol.* 1994;20:243–250.

80. Burstyn DG, Hagerman TC. Strategies for viral removal and inactivation. *Dev Biol Stand.* 1996;88:73–79.

81. DeVore DP, Kelman C, Fagien S, Casson P. Autologen: autologous, injectable dermal collagen. In: Bosniak S, ed.

Ophthalmic Plastic and Reconstructive Surgery. vol 1. Philadelphia, Pa: WB Saunders Company; 1996:670–675.

82. Passalaqua P, Pearl A, Woo P, Ramospizarro CA. Direct transcutaneous translaryngeal injection laryngoplasty with AlloDerm. Presented at the 30th Annual Symposium: Care of the Professional Voice; June 16, 2001; Philadelphia, Pa.

83. Rihkanen H. Vocal fold augmentation by injection of autologous fascia. *Laryngoscope.* 1998;108(1):51–54.

84. Dedo H. A technique for vertical hemilaryngectomy to prevent stenosis and aspiration. *Laryngoscope.* 1975;85:978–984.

85. Mikaelian D, Lowry LD, Sataloff RT. Lipoinjection for unilateral vocal cord paralysis. *Laryngoscope.* 1991;101:465–468.

86. Brandenburg J, Kirkham W, Koschkee D. Vocal cord augmentation with autologenous fat. *Laryngoscope.* 1992;102:495–500.

87. Billings E Jr, May JW Jr. Historical review and present status of free fat graft autotransplantation in plastic and reconstructive surgery. *Plast Reconstr Surg.* 1989;83:368–381.

88. Wexler D, Jiang J, Gray S, et al. Phonosurgical studies: fat-graft reconstruction of injured canine vocal cords. *Ann Otol Rhinol Laryngol.* 1989;98:668–673.

89. Hill DP, Meyers AD, Harris J. Autologous fat injection for vocal cord medialization in the canine larynx. *Laryngoscope.* 1991;101:344–348.

90. Archer SM, Banks ER. Intracordal injection of autologous fat for augmentation of the mucosally damaged canine vocal fold: a long-term histological study. Presented at the Second World Congress on Laryngeal Cancer; February 24, 1994; Sydney, Australia.

91. Sataloff RT, Mayer DP, Spiegel JR. Radiologic assessment of laryngeal Teflon injection. *J Voice.* 1988;2(1):93–95.

92. Netterville JL, Coleman JR Jr, Chang S, et al. Lateral laryngotomy for the removal of Teflon granuloma. *Ann Otol, Rhinol Laryngol.* 1998;107:735–744.

93. Coleman JR, Miller FR, Netterville JL. Teflon granuloma excision via a lateral laryngotomy. *Oper Techn Otolaryngol Head Neck Surg.* 1999;10(1):29–35.

94. Isshiki N, Okamura H, Ishikawa T. Thyroplasty type I (lateral compression) for dysphonia due to vocal cord paralysis or atrophy. *Acta Otolaryngol.* 1975;80:465–473.

95. Payr E. Plastik am schildknorpel zur Behebung der Folgen einseitiger Stimmbandlahmung. *Dtsch Med Wochensch.* 1915;43:1265–1270.

96. Cummings CW, Purcell LL, Flint PW. Hydroxylapatite laryngeal implants for medialization: preliminary report. *Ann Otol Rhinol Laryngol.* 1993;102:843–851.

97. Montgomery WW. Montgomery SK, Warren MA. Thyroplasty simplified. *Operat Techn Otolaryngol Head Neck Surg.* 1993;4:223–231.

98. Montgomery WW. Montgomery SK. Montgomery thyroplasty implant system. *Ann Otol Rhinol Laryngol Suppl.* 1997;170:1–16.

99. Flint PW, Corio RL, Cummings CW. Comparison of soft tissue response in rabbits following laryngeal implantation with hydroxylapatite, silicone rubber, and Teflon. *Ann Otol Rhinol Laryngol.* 1997;106:339–407.

100. McCulloch TM, Hoffman HT. Medialization laryngoplasty with expanded polytetrafluoroethylene. Surgical technique and preliminary results. *Ann Otol Rhinol Laryngol.* 1998;107:427–432.

101. Friedrich G. Titanium vocal fold medializing implant: introducing a novel implant system for external vocal fold medialization. *Ann Otol Rhinol Laryngol.* 1999;108:79–86.

102. Giovanni A, Vallicioni JM, Gras R, Zanaret M. Clinical experience with Gore-Tex for vocal fold medialization. *Laryngoscope.* 1999;109:284–288.

103. Tucker HA. External laryngeal surgery for adjustment of the voice. In: Gould WJ, Sataloff RT, Spiegel JR, eds. *Voice Surgery.* St. Louis: CV Mosby Co; 1993:275–290.

104. Zeitels SM, Jarboe J, Hillman RE. Medialization laryngoplasty with Gore-Tex for voice restoration secondary to glottal incompetence, Presented at the Voice Foundation's Annual Symposium, Care of the Professional Voice; July 2, 2000; Philadelphia, Pa.

105. Zeitels SM. New procedures for paralytic dysphonia: adduction arytenopexy, Goretex medialization laryngoplasty, and cricothyroid subluxation. *Otolaryngol Clin North Am.* 2000;33:841–854.

106. McCulloch TM, Hoffman HT, Andrews BT, Karnell MP. Arytenoid adduction combined with Gore-Tex medialization thyroplasty. *Laryngoscope.* 2000;110:1306–1311.

107. Omori K, Slavit D, Kacker A, et al. Effects of thyroplasty type I on vocal fold vibration. *Laryngoscope.* 2000;110:1086–1091.

108. Weinman EC, Maragos NE. Airway compromise in thyroplasty surgery. *Laryngoscope.* 2000;110:1082–1085.

109. Sataloff RT, Spiegel JR, Carroll LM, Heuer RJ. Male soprano voice: a rare complication of thyroidectomy. *Laryngoscope.* 1992;102(1):90–93.

110. Benninger MS, Crumley RL, Ford CN, et al. Evaluation and treatment of the unilateral paralyzed vocal fold. *Otolaryngol Head Neck Surg.* 1994;111(4):497–508.

111. Isshiki N, Tanabe M, Sawada M. Arytenoid adduction for unilateral vocal cord paralysis. *Arch Otolaryngol.* 1978;104:555–558.

112. Zeitels SM. Adduction arytenoidopexy with medialization laryngoplasty and cricothyroid subluxation: a new approach to paralytic dysphonia. *Oper Techn Otolaryngol Head Neck Surg.* 1999;10(1):9–16.

113. Zeitels SM, Hochman I, Hillman RE. Adduction arytenopexy: a new procedure for paralytic dysphonia and the implications for medialization laryngoplasty. *Ann Otol Rhinol Laryngol Suppl.* 1998;107:2–24.

114. Woodson JE. Picerno R, Yeung D, Hengesteg A. Arytenoid adduction: controlling vertical position. *Ann Otol Rhinol Laryngol.* 2000;109:360–364.

115. Iwamura S, Curita N. A newer arytenoid adduction technique for one-vocal-fold paralysis: a direct pull of the lateral cricoarytenoid muscle. *Otolaryngol Head Neck Surg.* 1996;6(1):1–10.

116. Iwamura S, Murakawa Y. Tomographic assessment of the arytenoid body and unilateral vocal fold paralysis before and after lateral cricoarytenoid muscle-pull surgery. *Jpn J Broncoesophagol.* 1997; 48(4):310–320.

117. Murakami Y, Kirchner JA. Vocal cord abduction by regenerated recurrent laryngeal nerve. *Arch Otolaryngol.* 1971;94:64–68.

118. Tucker HM. Reinnervation of the unilaterally paralyzed larynx. *Ann Otol Rhinol Laryngol.* 1977;86:789–794.

119. Tucker HM, Rusnov M. Laryngeal reinnervation for unilateral vocal cord paralysis: long-term results. *Ann Otol Rhinol Laryngol.* 1981;90:457–459.

120. May M, Berry Q. Muscle-nerve pedicle laryngeal reinnervation. *Laryngoscope.* 1986;96:1196–1200.

121. Crumley R. New perspectives in laryngeal reinnervation. In: Bailey BJ, Biller HF, eds. *Surgery of the Larynx.* Philadelphia, Pa: WB Saunders; 1985:135–147.

122. Takenouchi S, Sato F. [Phonatory function of the implanted larynx.] *Jpn J Bronchoesophagol.* 1968;19:280–281.

123. Tucker HM, Harvey J, Ogura JH. Vocal cord remobilization in the canine larynx. *Arch Otolaryngol.* 1970;92:530–533.

124. Goldfarb D, Keane WM, Lowry LD. Laryngeal pacing as a treatment for vocal fold paralysis. *J Voice.* 1994; 8(2):179–185.

125. Lundy DS, Casiano RR, Landy HJ, Gallo J, et al. Effects of vagal nerve stimulation on laryngeal function. *J Voice.* 1993;7(4):359–364.

126. Woodman D. A modification of the extralaryngeal approach to arytenoidectomy for bilateral abductor paralysis. *Arch Otolaryngol.* 1946;43:63–65.

127. Thornell WC. Intralaryngeal approach for arytenoidectomy in bilateral abductor vocal cord paralysis. *Arch Otolaryngol.* 1948;47:505–508.

128. Eskew JR, Bailey BJ. Laser arytenoidectomy for bilateral vocal cord paralysis. *Otolaryngol Head Neck Surg.* 1983;91:294–298.

129. Strong MS, Jako GJ, Vaughan CW. The use of the CO_2 laser in otolaryngology: a progress report. *Trans Sect Otolaryngol Am Acad Ophthalmol Otolaryngol.* 1976;82: 595–602.

130. Ossoff RH, Duncavage JA, Shapshay SM, et al. Endoscopic laser arytenoidectomy revisited. *Ann Otol Rhinol Laryngol.* 1990;99:764–771.

131. Crumley RL. Endoscopic laser medical arytenoidectomy for airway management in bilateral laryngeal paralysis. *Ann Otol Rhinol Laryngol.* 1993;102:81–84.

132. Cantarella G, Neglia CB, Marzano AV, Ottaviani A. Bilateral laryngeal pseudocoparalysis in xanthoma disseminatum treated by endoscopic laser medical arytenoidectomy. *Ann Otol Rhinol Laryngol.* 2001;110:263–268.

133. Ejnell H, Mansson I, Hallen O, et al. A simple operation for bilateral vocal cord paralysis. *Larynogoscope.* 1984; 94:954–958.

134. Geterud A, Ejnell H, Stenborg R, Bake B. Long-term results with simple surgical treatment of bilateral vocal cord paralysis. *Laryngoscope.* 1990;100:1005–1008.

135. Cummings CW, Redd EE, Westra WH, Flint PW. Minimally invasive device to effect vocal fold lateralization. *Ann Otol Rhinol Laryngol.* 1999;108(9):833–836

136. Dennis DP, Kashima H. Carbon dioxide posterior cordectomy for treatment of vocal cord paralysis. *Ann Otol Rhinol Laryngol.* 1989;98:930–934.

137. Tucker HM. Human laryngeal reinnervation: long-term experience with nerve-muscle pedicle technique. *Laryngoscope.* 1978;88:598–604.

138. Tucker HM. *The Larynx.* 2nd ed. New York, NY: Thieme Medical Publishers; 1993:255–265.

139. Rubin AD, Hawkshaw M, Sataloff RT. Vocal process avulsion. *J Voice.* 2005: in press.

140. Willemot J, Naissance et developpement de l'oto-rhino-laryngologie dans l'histoire de la medicine. *Acta Otorhinolaryngol Belg.* 1981;35 (suppl 2,3,4):1–1622.

141. Lewis DD, Discussion on ventricle of larynx. *Ann Otol Rhinol Laryngol.* 1914;24:129–138.

142. New GB, Erich JB. Congenital cysts of the larynx: report of a case. *Arch Otolaryngol.* 1939;30:943–949.

143. New GB. Treatment of cysts of the larynx. *Arch Otolaryngol.* 1942;36:687–690.

144. Alonso JM, Caubarrere NL. The laryngocele. *Ann Otorinolaringol Urug.* 1944;14:38–44.

145. Schall LA. An extralaryngeal approach for certain benign lesions of the larynx. *Ann Otol Rhinol Laryngol.* 1959;68:346–355.

146. Thawley SE, Bone RC. Laryngopyocele. *Laryngoscope.* 1973;83:362–368.

147. Stell PM, Maran AG. Larynogcoele. *J Laryngol Otol.* 1975;89:915–924.

148. Gil Tutor E. [Laryngoceles: a clinical and therapeutic study.] *An Otorinolaringol Ibero Am.* 1991;18:451–464.

149. Montgomery WW. *Surgery of the Upper Respiratory System.* Vol. 2. Philadelphia: Pa: Lea & Febiger; 1971:467–479.

150. Malis DJ, Seid AB. Fold-down thyroplasty: a new approach for congenital lateral saccular cysts. *Laryngoscope.* 1998;108:941–943.

151. Netterville JL, Coleman JR Jr, Chang S, et al. Lateral laryngotomy for removal of Teflon granuloma. *Ann Otol Rhinol Laryngol.* 1998;107:735–744.

152. Keim WF, Livingstone RG. Internal laryngocele. *Ann Otol Rhinol Laryngol.* 1951;60:39–50.

153. Dedo HH. Recurrent laryngeal nerve section for spastic dysphonia. *Ann Otol Rhinol Laryngol.* 1976;85:451–459.

154. Aronson AE, DeSanto LW. Adductor spastic dysphonia: three years after recurrent laryngeal nerve resection. *Laryngoscope.* 1983;93:1–8.

155. Dedo HH, Izdebski K. Problems with surgical (RLN section) treatment of spastic dysphonia. *Laryngoscope.* 1983;93:268–271.

156. Iwamura S: Comments in spastic dysphonia: state of the art. In: Lawrence VL, ed. *Transcripts pf the Symposium: Care of the Professional Voice.* New York, NY: The Voice Foundation; 1979:26–32.

157. Sercarz JA, Berke GS, Ming YE, et al. Bilateral thyroarytenoid denervation: a new treatment for laryngeal

hyperadduction disorders studied in the canine. *Head Neck Surg.* 1992;107(5):657–668.

158. Berke GS, Blackwell KE, Gerratt BR, et al. Selective laryngeal adductor denervation-reinnervation: a new surgical treatment for adductor spasmodic dysphonia. *Ann Otol Rhinol Laryngol.* 1999;108:227–231.

159. Strome M, Stein J, Esclamado R, et al. Laryngeal transplantation and 40-month follow-up. *N Engl J Med.* 2001; 344(22):1676–1679.

160. Damsté PH. Shortness of the palate: a cause of problems in singing. *J Voice.* 1988;2(1):96–98.

83

Phonomicrosurgical Techniques

Steven M. Zeitels

Overview of the Technique

The evolution of transoral management of vocal fold lesions arose first from the ability to visualize the larynx followed by the ability to surgically manipulate it.[1,2] Since Kirstein's formal description of direct laryngoscopy a century ago,[3] phonomicrosurgical techniques[4] have developed as a result of a series of innovations that improved precision. These innovations began with concepts to improve glottic exposure.[5,6]

During the 25 years subsequent to Kirstein's description in 1895, five principles[7,8] were developed for obtaining and maintaining complete visualization of the musculomembranous vocal folds:

1. Ideal supine head and neck position, which is flexion of the neck on the chest and extension of the head on the neck at the occipito-atloid joint[9,10] (Jackson, ca 1910)
2. External counterpressure, which is a posteriorly directed force on the lower laryngeal cartilage framework. The force may be supplied by a mechanical device or by hand[11,12] (Brünings, ca 1910)
3. Conformation of the laryngoscope shape to the triangular shape of the glottis, which is the "inverted-V" concept[12] (Killian, 1910)
4. Laryngeal suspension to free the surgeon's hands[13] (Killian, 1912)
5. Internal laryngeal distension, which is the distraction of supraglottic structures peripherally to obtain the widest possible view of the true vocal folds[14,15] (Haslinger, ca 1920; Jackson 1927).

External counterpressure and internal laryngeal distension produce forces that are helpful for enhancing laryngoscopic exposure of the anterior glottis. These principles were formally described in the early 20th century but are seldom used today. Hand pressure has been the typical source for counterpressure. Since this maneuver is unstable if provided by an assistant and wasteful if provided by the surgeon, it is often neglected. Current phonomicrosurgical techniques require wider glottal exposure both to accommodate the surgical microscope and to facilitate angulation of hand instruments.[5,6]

In the 1950s, general endotracheal anesthesia stabilized the patient[16] and, therefore, the surgical field. About the same time, monocular magnified indirect laryngoscopy was described by Albrecht[17] and subsequently stereoscopic microlaryngoscopy was introduced by Scalco et al,[18] Kleinsasser,[19] and Jako.[20,21] Wide-lumen glottiscopes were designed to accommodate the visual field that was provided by the microscope. As a result of the magnified view of the stable larynx, Jako introduced microlaryngeal hand instruments in 1962. These were long-stemmed otologic instruments that facilitated the development of microlaryngeal surgery.

As fulcrum chest-wall laryngoscope holders did not incorporate Jackson's force principles for positioning the laryngoscope, these devices were not always effective for maintaining wide-bore laryngoscopes that are necessary for adequate vocal fold exposure. To solve this problem, Grundfast and the Boston University group designed a modified Killian gallows that could be married to standard glottiscopes.[22] This device maintained the patient in Jackson position by lifting the individual off of the operating table, which resulted in elevated-vector suspension. Phonomicrosurgical procedures are facilitated by the widest exposure that can be achieved, and for this reason, larger glottiscopes are being designed. Placement of these larger scopes will provide the catalyst for a return to the use of suspension gallows and elevated-vector suspension.

Finally, in the early 1970s, the carbon-dioxide (CO_2) laser was introduced to aerodigestive tract surgery by Jako,[23] Strong,[24] and Vaughn.[25] The laser further improved precise microlaryngeal surgery in some cases by means of its hemostatic properties and its delivery system. The micromanipulator and foot pedal facilitated stable bimanual cutting and tissue dissection under high magnification.[1]

Laryngeal sound-production theory developed somewhat independently[26-29] from microlaryngoscopic surgical technique theory. Mucosal wave concepts of voice production were only marginally assimilated into microlaryngeal surgical techniques until the last 10 years. During the last decade, there has been a deliberate convergence of voice-production theory with microlaryngoscopic surgical theory,[30] which has resulted in new surgical goals.[1]

Objective postoperative voice analyses (visual, acoustic, and aerodynamic) of phonomicrosurgical procedures revealed that the ideal vocal outcome is achieved with maximal preservation of the vocal fold's layered microstructure (lamina propria and epithelium).[1,31] This is facilitated in some cases by infusing a saline-epinephrine solution into the superficial lamina propria.[1,7,32,33] the compartment described by Reinke[34] and Pressman.[35,36] The need to preserve the lamina propria has led to a reevaluation of the ideal indications for employing the CO_2 laser to enhance cold-instrument microdissection. Surgeons must decide by individual case whether the assets of the laser outweigh its liabilities for achieving optimal precision and, in turn, the optimal vocal result.[37]

Method

Upper and lower teeth guards are inserted before placing the laryngoscope. Internal laryngeal distension is performed on all patients by inserting the largest-lumen glottiscope possible between the lips and the glottis. This distension occurs by intercalating the distal glottiscope between the infrapetiole region of the supraglottis and the endotracheal tube, and displacing the vocal folds laterally. Insertion of a wide-bore glottiscope is facilitated by placing the patient in Jackson position. This position is sustained with the Boston University gallows, which results in elevated-vector suspension. Endotracheal anesthesia is preferred over jet ventilation because of the improved exposure that is achieved with internal distension as well as the improved stability of the operating field.

Exposure is also improved by applying external counterpressure to the lower laryngeal framework. Manual external counterpressure is used only to test the effectiveness of this force for enhancing laryngeal exposure. When needed for the surgical procedure, external counterpressure was produced mechanically by stretching silk adhesive tape over the cricoid and lower thyroid cartilages and attaching the tape to the operating table. The tape is adjusted to provide the best possible view of the vocal folds by posteriorly displacing the glottis and, as necessary, by slightly rotating the laryngeal framework to center the vocal folds within the triangular contour of the laryngoscope. External counterpressure will enhance glottal exposure in approximately 75% of cases.[5] The use of both external counterpressure and internal distension as an adjunct to microlaryngoscopy is most helpful for the surgical management of lesions located near the anterior commissure. Seemingly, the two resultant forces are in opposition to each other, but in fact they are complementary, both to themselves and to the orthodox laryngoscopic principle of elevated-vector suspension.

The decision to use the laser is determined during the microlaryngeal examination and may be altered as the procedure progresses. Factors that affect instrument selection include size of the lesion, vascularity of the lesion, and endoscopic exposure.[8,37] Photographs of a variety of benign and malignant lesions may be helpful in illustrating surgical principles (Fig 83–1 through 83–54). The reader is encouraged to supplement these still photographs with a study of videotapes (available through the Voice Foundation, the American Academy of Otolaryngology—Head and Neck Surgery, and elsewhere), courses in phonosurgery, and site visits to the operating rooms of experienced voice surgeons.

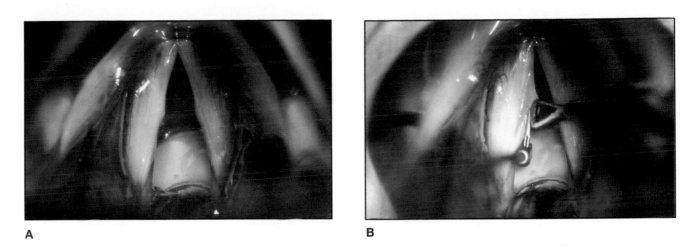

A   **B**

Fig 83–1. A. Small bilateral nodules in a classical singer. **B.** Excision is performed by means of cold instruments.

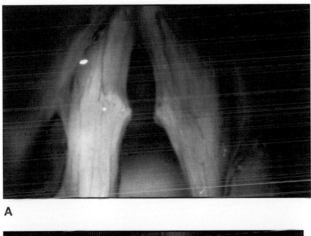

A   **B**

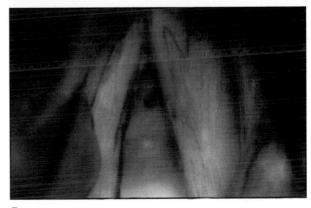

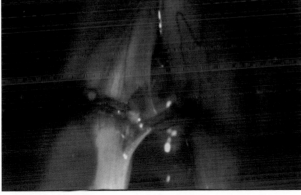

C   **D**

Fig 83–2. A. (7×) Bilateral sessile nodules are noted in this radio disc jockey. **B.** (7×) An epithelial cordotomy has been done on the right. The microflap is retracted with a mini-micro alligator forceps and a mini-microscissors is used to dissect the fibrous tissue from the underlying SLP and overly-ing epithelial basement membrane. **C.** (7×) A second alligator forceps is used to remove the fibrous tissue. **D.** (7×) The vocal folds are now smooth and straight. A small amount of blood is seen in the incision.

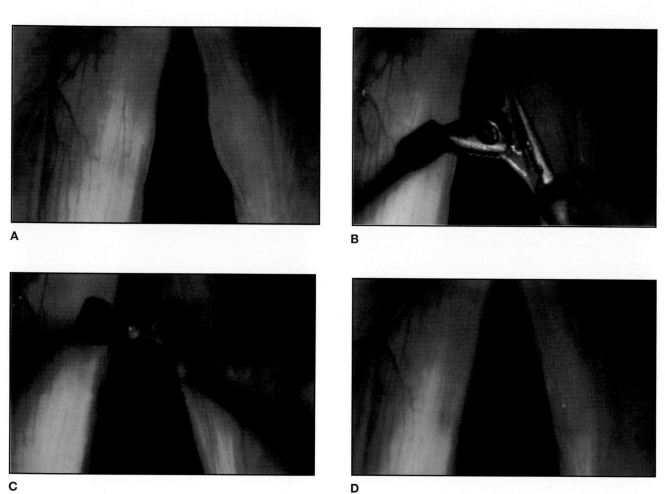

A

B

C

D

Fig 83–3. A. (10×) Bilateral sessile nodules in a classical singer. **B.** (10×) A forceps is used to retract the nodule and an epithelial cordotomy is performed. **C.** (10×) The subepithelial fibrovascular contents have been withdrawn and a curved microscissors is used to amputate the tissue. **D.** (10×) The postexcision appearance of the vocal folds revealing that the incisions are nearly imperceptible.

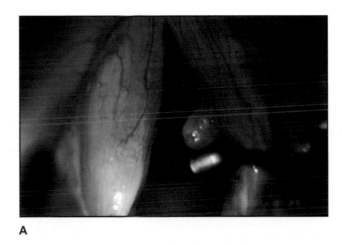

A

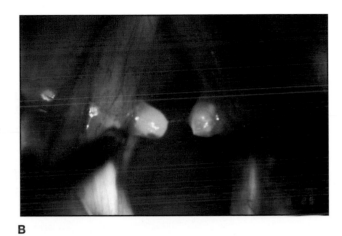

B

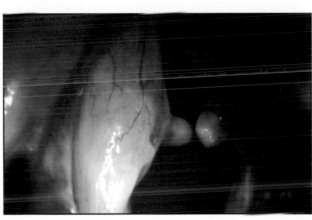

C

D

Fig 83–4. A. Larger bilateral nodules. **B.** After subepithelial infusion of saline and 1/10,000 epinephrine, there is distention of the superficial lamina propria and vasoconstriction of its microvasculature. **C.** The excision is performed by means of cold instruments. **D.** The final examination after both lesions were resected.

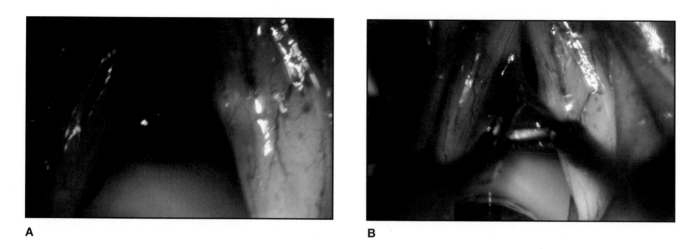

A

B

Fig 83–5. A. Small hemorrhagic polyp and a contralateral nodule. **B.** The polyp is removed by scissors amputation.

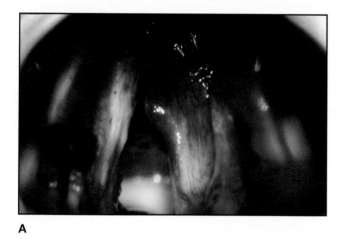
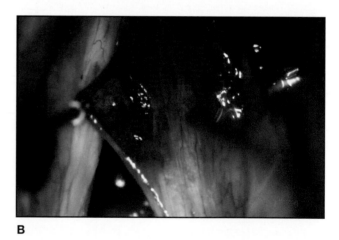

A

B

Fig 83–6. A. Small hemorrhagic polyp and a contralateral nodule in a Latin vocalist (reprinted with permission of the *Annals of Otology, Rhinology, and Laryngology*. In press).

B. The polyp is removed by subepithelial cold dissection (reprinted with permission of the *Annals of Otology, Rhinology, and Laryngology*. In press).

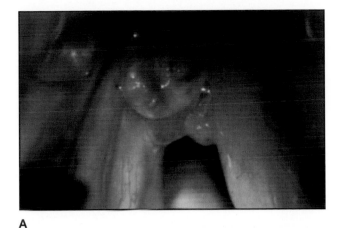

A

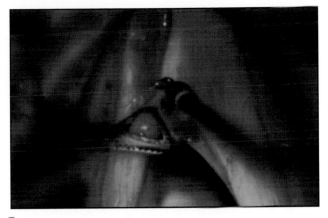

B

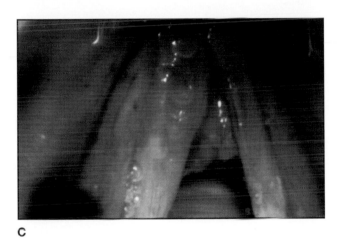

C

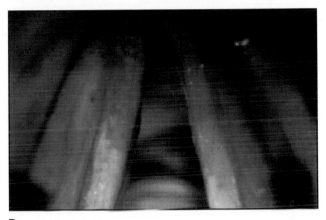

D

Fig 83–7. A. (7×) The polyps have been positioned above the level of the glottal aperture demonstrating their more extensive nature. A subepithelial infusion has been performed on the right. **B.** The right polyp is retracted and a curved microscissors is used to perform an epithelial cordotomy.

C. (7×) A subepithelial infusion has now been performed on the left. The bubbles can be seen as a result of the turbulent infusion. **D.** (7×) Both lesions have been resected and the vocal folds are smooth and straight.

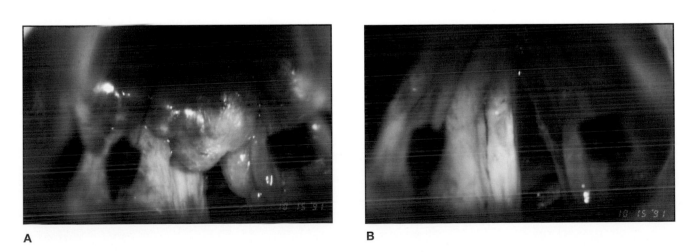

A

B

Fig 83–8. A. Large hemorrhagic polyp in a Gospel singer. **B.** The polyp is removed by carbon dioxide laser excision.

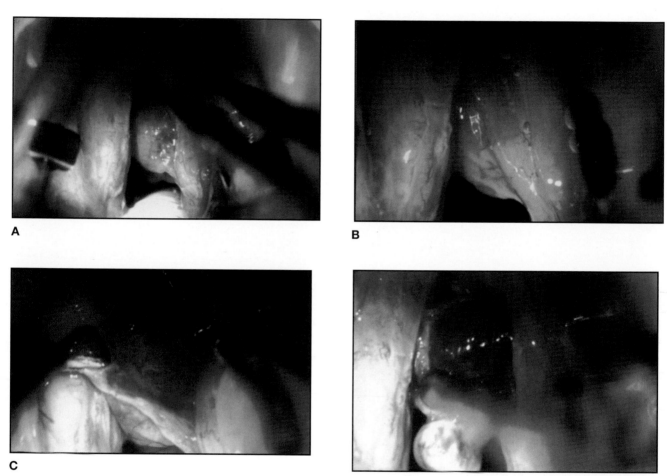

A

B

C

D

Fig 83–9. A. (4×) A large hemorrhagic polyp arising from the medial and subcordal surface of the right vocal fold is retracted so that the dimensions of the base can be better seen. The base does not extend to the anterior glottal commissure. **B.** (7×) A subepithelial infusion is performed. **C.** After dissecting the normal SLP from the normal fibrovascular mass, the dissection is advanced to better define the base of the polyp. **D.** (7×) The base of the polyp is now well seen. *(continues)*

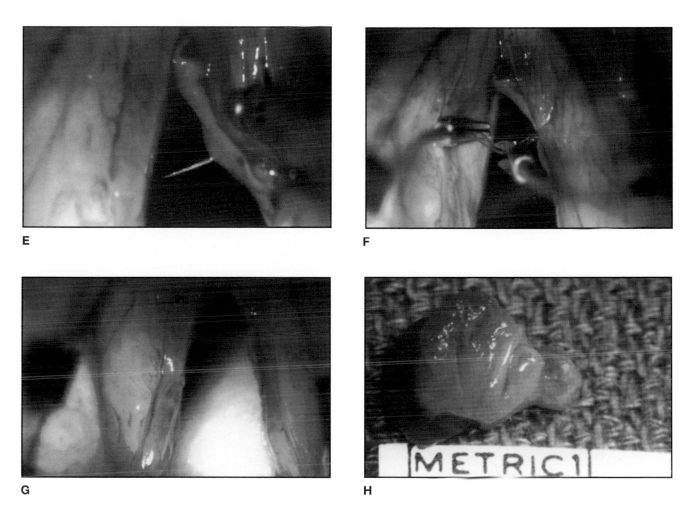

E

F

G

H

Fig 83–9. *(continued)* **E.** (10×) When the polyp is excised, an inferior microflap is preserved for coaptation of the epithelial edges due to the size of the lesion and the defect. The epithelial edges are sutured to facilitate more rapid healing.

F. (7×) The suture is retracted with an alligator forceps and trimmed. **G.** (7×) The epithelial edges are redraped now that a suture has been placed to maintain its basic favorable position. **H.** The excised specimen.

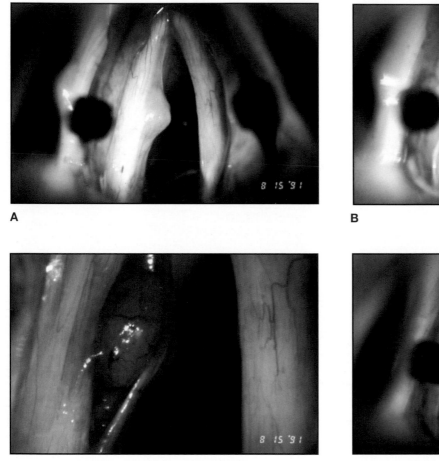

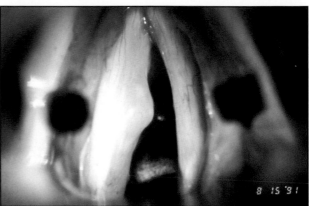

A

B

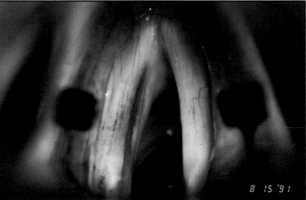

C

D

Fig 83–10. A. Subepithelial mucous cyst in the superficial lamina propria (reprinted with permission of the *Annals of Otology, Rhinology and Laryngology*). **B.** After epithelial infusion of saline and 1/10,000 epinephrine, there is distention of the superficial lamina propria and vasoconstriction of its microvasculature (reprinted with permission of the *Annals of Otology, Rhinology and Laryngology*). **C.** An atraumatic mi-croflap is developed such that the microvasculature on the thin-walled cyst can be seen (reprinted with permission of the *Annals of Otology Rhinology, and Laryngology*). **D.** The cyst is excised en bloc and the epithelial edges of the mi-croflap oppose well (reprinted with permission of the *Annals of Otology, Rhinology and Laryngology*).

A

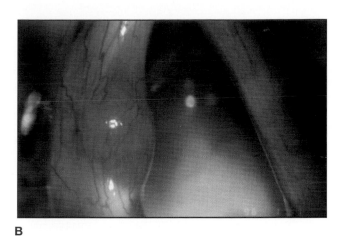

B

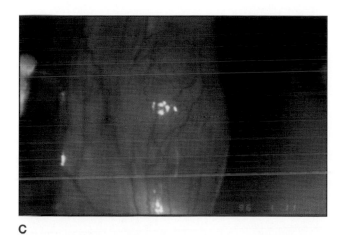

C

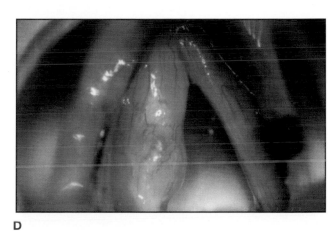

D

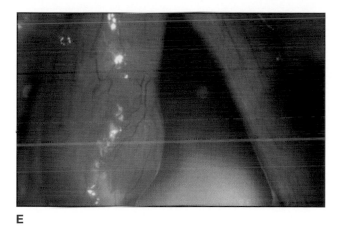

E

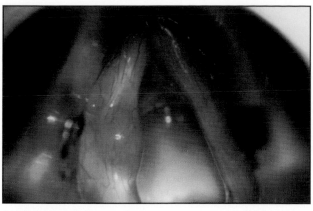

F

Fig 83–11. (4×) A sphenoid mass, which has an erythematous hue, is seen on the superior and medial surface of the left vocal fold. **B.** (7×) The mass seen at higher magnification. **C.** (10×) The mass seen at even higher magnification. Note the light reflex at the center of the lesion and note the distribution of the microvasculature overlying the lesion. **D.** (4×) A subepithelial infusion is done on the left. **E.** (7×) The infusion shown at higher magnification. **F.** (7×) An epithelial cordotomy is done overlying the lesion, and a subepithelial cyst is noted. *(continues)*

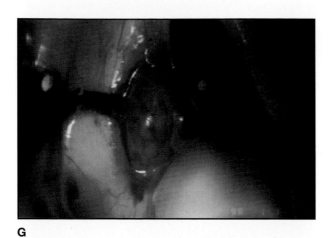

G

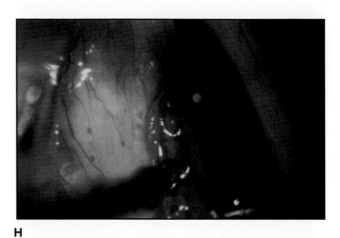

H

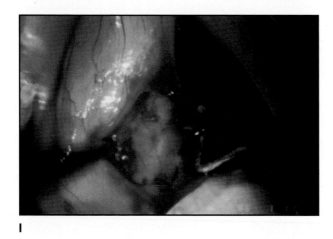

I

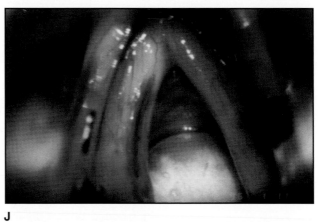

J

Fig 83–11. *(continued)* **G.** (7×) A curved left dissector is utilized to demonstrate the thin translucent epithelium that was overlying the cyst. **H.** (7×) The cyst is grasped with an angled forceps and withdrawn from the SLP. The final resection is performed by excising the base with a curved microscissors. **I.** (7×) The edges of the microflaps are retracted for visualization of the cavity where the cyst had been situated. There was maximal preservation of normal SLP and epithelium. **J.** (4×) Note the normally contoured vocal fold and minimal trauma outside the perimeter of the location of the mass.

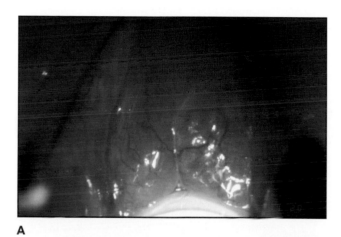

A

B

C

Fig 83–12. A. Polypoid corditis (Reinke's edema). **B.** After laser-assisted incisions, the mixoid stroma is suctioned, taking care not to remove too much superficial lamina propria. **C.** Final intraoperative examination The retraction of the microflap on the left resulted in a 2-mm area of exposed superficial lamina propria that epithelialized in 2 weeks without consequence.

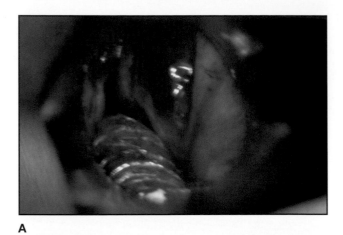

A

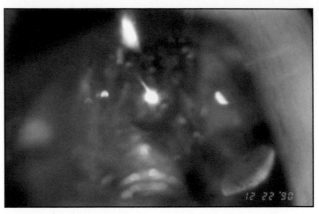

B

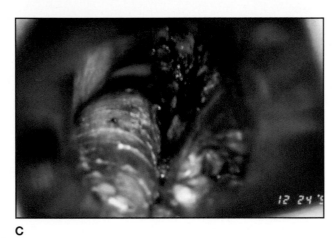

C

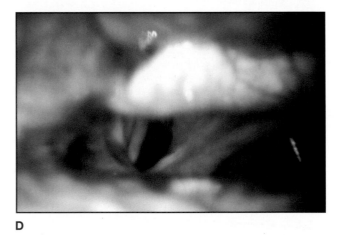

D

Fig 83–13. A. Large Teflon granuloma. **B.** Laser vaporization of the granuloma displaying the characteristic flair. **C.** The edge of the vocal fold was sculpted with the laser because a wedge resection of the granuloma did not result in lateralization of the vocal fold. **D.** As seen in the office 5 weeks later with complete epithelialization.

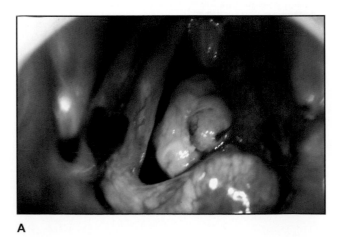

A

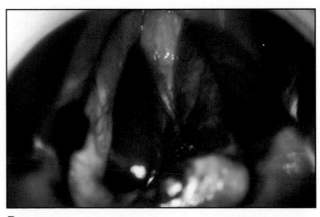

B

Fig 83–14. A. A medium-sized posterior glottic granuloma after endoscopic arytenoidectomy. **B.** The narrow pedicle was amputated with a microscissors and the laser was used to microcauterize the feeding vessel.

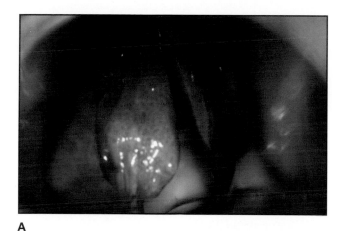

A

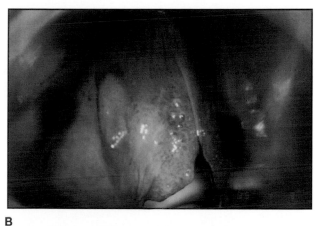

B

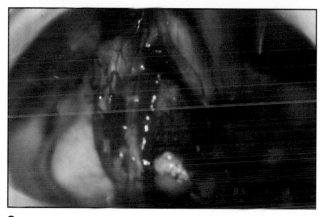

C

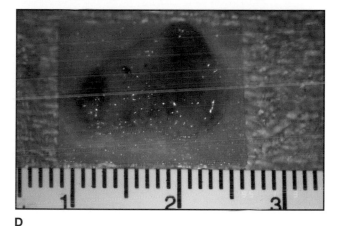

D

E

Fig 83–15. A. Initial presentation of glottic papilloma (reprinted with permission of the *Annals of Otolaryngology, Rhinology and Laryngology*, in press). **B.** Subepithelial infusion (reprinted with permission of the *Annals of Otolaryngology, Rhinology and Laryngology*, in press). **C.** Large microflap encompassing all of the epithelial disease (reprinted with permission of the *Annals of Otolaryngology, Rhinology and Laryngology*, in press). **D.** The entire vocal fold vibratory epithelium is excised and prepared on a carrier for whole-mount sectioning (reprinted with permission of the *Annals of Otolaryngology, Rhinology and Laryngology*, in press). **E.** The histopathology demonstrates clear margins and almost no superficial lamina propria in the specimen. The lesion is essentially dissected and resected at the epithelial basement membrane (reprinted with permission of the *Annals of Otolaryngology, Rhinology and Laryngology*, in press).

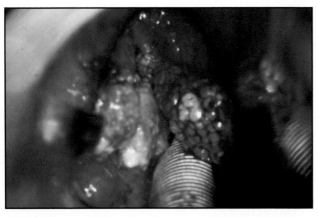

A

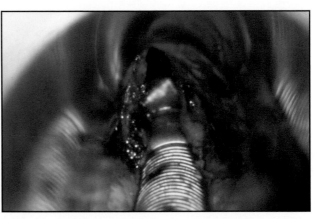

B

Fig 83–16. A. Extensive recurrent glottal papillomatosis in a patient who presented with stridor and impending airway obstruction. **B.** Laser vaporization of the papilloma. Cold dissection resulted in troublesome bleeding.

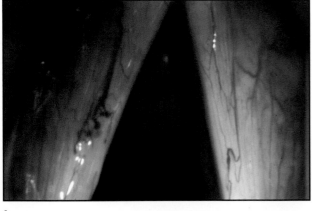

A

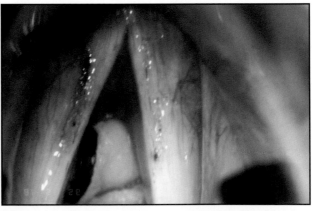

B

Fig 83–17. A. Vascular ectasia accompanied by recurrent hemorrhages in a classical singer. **B.** Precise superficial laser coagulation is performed, which eradicated the problem.

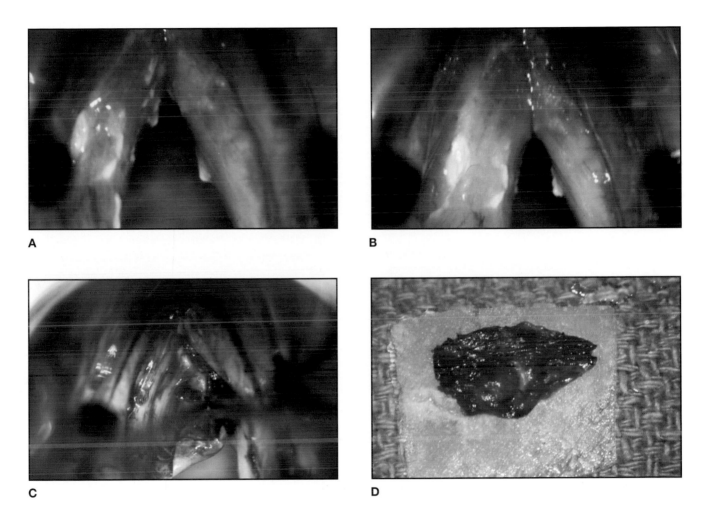

A

B

C

D

Fig 83–18. A. Keratosis with atypia (reprinted with permission from *Laryngoscope.* 1995;105[suppl 67]:28). **B.** Subepithelial infusion (reprinted with permission from *Laryngoscope.* 1995;105[suppl 67]:28). **C.** Large microflap encompassing all of the epithelial tissue (reprinted with permission from *Laryngoscope.* 1995;105[suppl 67]:28). **D.** The entire vocal fold vibratory margin epithelium is excised and prepared on a carrier for whole-mount sectioning (reprinted with permission from *Laryngoscope.* 1995;105[suppl 67]:28).

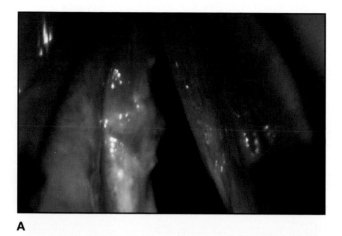

A

B

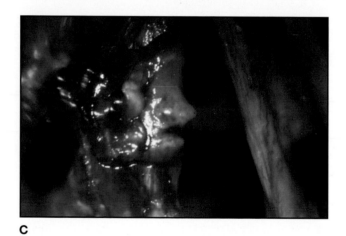

C

Fig 83–19. A. T1 vocal fold cancer. **B.** After subepithelial infusion, it could be determined that the disease was not attached to the vocal ligament. **C.** Large microflap encompassing all of the epithelial disease.

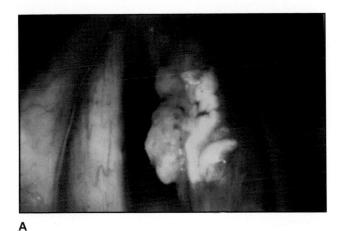

A

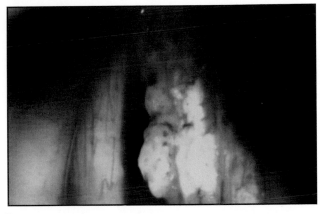

B

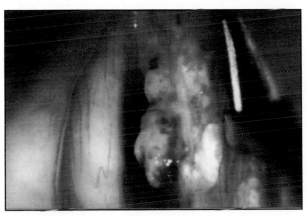

C

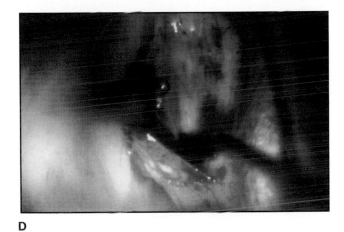

D

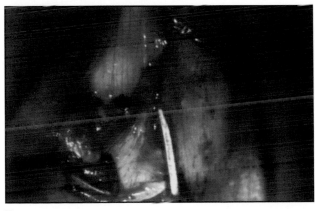

E

F

Fig 83–20. **A.** (7×) A T1, N0, M0 squamous cell carcinoma is seen on the right vocal fold in a Shakespearean actor. **B.** (7×) An infusion needle is seen lateral to the cancer margin. The lesion did not invade the vocal fold. **C.** (7×) An upturned scissors is used to perform a perimeter incision lateral to the lesion. **D.** (7×) A curved dissector is used to continue the caudal deep incision. **E.** (7×) An upturned scissors is used to complete the caudal resection of the cancer. **F.** (7×) The completed cancer resection. Note that there is residual microvasculature in the deep SLP. (All images courtesy of Endocraft LLC.)

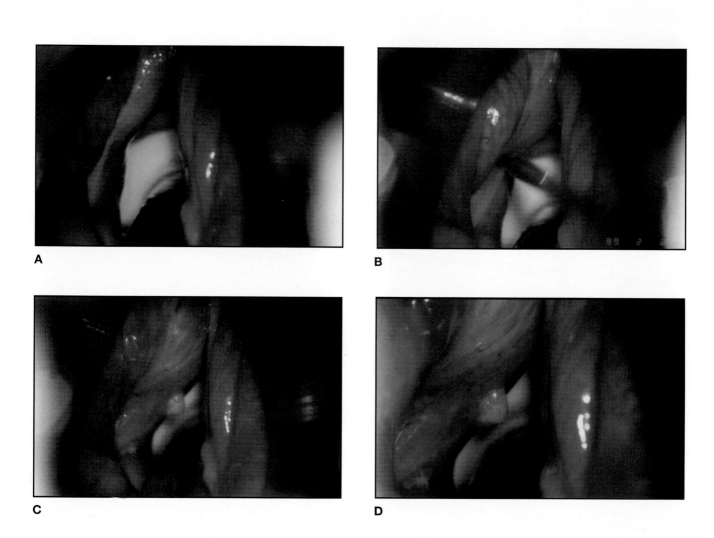

A

B

C

D

Fig 83–21. A. (4×) The patient has undergone phonomicrosurgical resection of a left T1a carcinoma and now has an excavated vocal fold in the musculomembranous region. **B.** (4×) A Brünings injection needle is placed lateral to the concavity in the paraglottic region. **C.** (4×) The vocal fold has been augmented with fat. A small amount of the graft is extruding from the puncture site and should be removed with cold instruments to avoid a granuloma. Note the new convexity of the vocal fold. **D.** (7×) The same field shown at higher magnification.

References

1. Zeitels SM. Premalignant epithelium and microinvasive cancer of the vocal fold; the evolution of phonomicrosurgical management. *Laryngoscope.* 1995;105(suppl 67): 1–51.

2. Zeitels SM. *Atlas of Phonomicrosurgery and Other Endolaryngeal Procedures for Benign and Malignant Disease.* San Diego, Calif: Singular Thomson Learning; 2001:1–14.

3. Kirstein A. Autoskopie des Larynx und der Trachea (Laryngoscopic directa, Euthyskopie, Besichtigung ohne Spiegel). *Archiv Laryngol Rhinol.* 1895;3:156–164.

4. Zeitels SM. *Atlas of Phonomicrosurgery and Other Endolaryngeal Procedures for Benign and Malignant Disease.* San Diego, Calif: Singular Thomson Learning. 2001.

5. Zeitels SM, Vaughan CW. "External counter-pressure" and "internal distension" for optimal laryngoscopic exposure of the anterior glottic commissure. *Ann Otol Rhinol Laryngol.* 1994;103:669–675.

6. Zeitels SM. A universal modular glottiscope system: the evolution of a century of design and technique for direct laryngoscopy. *Ann Otol Rhinol Laryngol.* 1999;108(suppl 179):1–24.

7. Zeitels SM. *Atlas of Phonomicrosurgery and Other Endolaryngeal Procedures for Benign and Malignant Disease.* San Diego, Calif: Singular Thomson Learning. 2001:18–20.

8. Zeitels SM. *Atlas of Phonomicrosurgery and Other Endolaryngeal Procedures for Benign and Malignant Disease.* San Diego, Calif: Singular Thomson Learning. 2001:23–36.

9. Jackson C. Position of the patient for peroral endoscopy. In: Jackson C. *Peroral Endoscopy and Laryngeal Surgery.* St. Louis, Mo: Laryngoscope Co; 1915:77–88.

10. Jackson C, Jackson CL. The early diagnosis of cancer of the larynx: position of the patient for direct laryngoscopy. In: Jackson C. *Cancer of the Larynx.* Philadelphia, Pa: WB Saunders; 1939:17–18.

11. Brünings W. Direct laryngoscopy: autoscopy by counter-pressure. In: *Direct Laryngoscopy, Bronchoscopy, and Esophagoscopy.* London: Bailliere, Tindall, & Cox; 1912:110–115.

12. Killian G. Demonstration of an endoscopic spatula. *J Laryngol Rhinol.* 1910;25:549–550.

13. Killian G. Die Schwebelaryngosckopie. *Arch Laryngol Rhinol.* 1912;26:277–317.

14. Israel S. The directoscope of Haslinger in diagnosis and surgery of the larynx. *Laryngoscope.* 1923;33:945–948.

15. Jackson C, Tucker G, Clerf LH. Laryngostasis and the laryngostat. *Arch Otolaryngol.* 1925;1:167–169.

16. Priest RE, Wesolowski S. Direct laryngoscopy under general anesthesia. *Trans Am Acad Ophthalmol Otolaryngol.* 1960;64:639–648.

17. Albrecht R. Uber den Wert koloskopischer Untersuchungsmethoden bei Leukoplakien und Carcinomen des Mundes und Kehlkopes. *Arch Ohren Nasen Kehlkopfheilkd.* 1954;165:459–463.

18. Scalco AN, Shipman WF, Tabb HG. Microscopic suspension laryngoscopy. *Ann Otol Rhinol Laryngol.* 1960; 69:1134–1138.

19. Kleinsasser O. Mikrochirurgie im kelkopf. *Arch Ohren Nasen Kehlkopfheilkd.* 1964;183:428–433.

20. Jako GJ. Laryngoscope for microscopic observation, surgery, and photography. *Arch Otolaryngol.* 1970;91: 196–199.

21. Jako GJ. Laryngeal endoscopy and microlaryngoscopy. In Paparella M, Shumrick D, eds. *Otolaryngology.* Philadelphia, Pa: WB Saunders; 1980:2410–2430.

22. Grundfast KM, Vaughan CW, Strong MS, De Vos P. Suspension microlaryngoscopy in the Boyce position with a new suspension gallows. *Ann Otol Rhinol Laryngol.* 1978; 87:560–566.

23. Jako GJ. Laser surgery of the vocal cords. *Laryngoscopy.* 1972;82:2204–2215.

24. Strong MS, Jako GJ. Laser surgery of the larynx: early clinical experience with continuous CO_2 laser. *Ann Otol Rhinol Laryngol.* 1972;81:791–798.

25. Vaughan, CW. Transoral laryngeal surgery using the CO_2 laser. Laboratory experiments and clinical experience. *Laryngoscope.* 1978;88:1399–1420.

26. Bishop J. Experimental researches into the physiology of the human voice. *The London & Ediburgh Magazine and Journal of Science.* 1836.

27. Garcia M. Observations on the human voice. *Proc Royal Soc London.* 1855;7:397–410.

28. Fournie E. *Physiologie de la Voix et de la Parole.* Paris, France: Adrien Delahaye. 1866.

29. Hirano M. Phonosurgery: basic and clinical investigations. *Otologia* (Fukuoka). 1975;21:239–442.

30. Hirano M. Phonosurgical anatomy of the larynx. In: Ford CN, Bless DM, eds. *Phonosurgery.* New York, NY: Raven Press; 1991:25–41.

31. Sataloff R, Spiegel JR, Hcuer RJ, et al. Laryngeal minimicroflap: a new technique and reassessment of the microflap saga. *J Voice.* 1995;9:198–204.

32. Zeitels SM, Vaughan CW. A submucosal vocal fold infusion needle. *Otolaryngol Head Neck Surg.* 1991;105: 478–479.

33. Kass ES, Hillman RE, Zeitels SM. The submucosal infusion technique in phonomicrosurgery. *Ann Otol Rhinol Laryngol.* 1996;105:341–347.

34. Reinke F. Uber die Funktionelle Struktur der Menschlichen Stimmlippe mit Besonderer Berucksichtigung des Elastischen Gewebes. *Anatomische Hefte.* 1897;9:103–117.

35. Pressman J, Dowdy A, Libby R, Fields M. Further studies upon the submucosal lymphatics of the larynx by injection of dyes and isotopes. *Ann Otol Rhinol Laryngol.* 1956;65:963–980.

36. Pressman JJ, Bertz MB, Monell C. Anatomic studies related to the dissemination of cancer of the larynx. *Trans Am Acad Ophthalmol Otolaryngol.* 1996;106:545–552.

37. Zeitels SM. Laser versus cold instruments for microlaryngoscopic surgery. *Laryngoscope.* 1996;106:545–552.

84

Laryngeal Laser Surgery

Jean Abitbol and Robert Thayer Sataloff

Ever since the laser was first used for laryngeal surgery in the 1960s, controversy and disappointment have accompanied its use. Because of technical advantages over lasers of other wavelengths, the carbon dioxide (CO_2) laser has become standard for laryngeal surgery. Bredemeier's invention of a micromanipulator that allowed the delivery of a CO_2 laser beam through a microscope[1] heralded the beginning of the current era of laryngeal laser surgery. The initial report by Strong and Jako[2] was encouraging. Since that time, the laser has become a routine instrument for laryngeal microsurgery. Nevertheless, although its usefulness for some laryngeal procedures is universally accepted, its efficacy for many common laryngeal applications is still controversial. In all cases, its advantages must be weighed against its potential hazards.

Lasers generate heat. Consequently, they introduce the possibility of heat-related complications. Although such complications will be seen even among patients of the best and most experienced laser surgeons, their incidence can be minimized through thorough understanding of the principles of laser surgery.

Laser surgery is complex and requires education of the anesthesiologist, the complete operating room team, and especially the surgeon.[3] The anesthesiologist must be aware that a laser will be used. A laser-resistant endotracheal tube should be selected, and high oxygen concentrations should be avoided. The operating room nurses need to understand laser use and safety. The laser is checked by the nursing staff and surgeon for proper function and alignment. Appropriate instruments and laser-resistant moist drapes must be provided, along with safety glasses. An evacuation system to remove smoke from the airway must also be employed. Both the nurse and surgeon are responsible for utilization of laser safety devices such as wet cottonoids in the airway and wet towels around

the laryngoscope. Failure to observe any of these precautions may result in injury to the patient or operating room staff.

In addition, it is essential that the surgeon understand the principles of CO_2 laser function. The concept of radiant exposure is central. This is the relation of power density and time of laser use. Power density describes the relationship between the watts of laser energy delivered and the area of tissue to which the energy is delivered. Equally important is the concept of lateral thermal energy spread. That is, heat generated by the laser spreads from the point of impact. The longer the tissue exposure, the greater the lateral thermal energy spread and the greater the risk of injuring adjacent structures (eg, the vocal ligament). Consequently, the surgeon should usually select single or intermittent pulses, using the shortest time pulse that will accomplish the surgical task. When a 400-mm focal lens is used on the microscope, and a laser spot size of 0.4 mm is employed, 4 watts to 6 watts at 0.1 seconds are generally sufficient,[4] although up to 10 watts may be appropriate for some lesions. This spot size is still in use in many operating rooms. However, it is usually preferable to use a smaller spot size (0.15 mm or smaller) to permit comparable power density and tissue effect with less laser energy and a smaller zone of destruction.

The surgeon should also understand the difference between continuous, superpulse, ultrapulse, and chopped modes of laser delivery. Newer lasers allow the surgeon to select the contour and millijoule level of each laser burst, permitting more precise control over tissue effect. In addition, if the surgeon places laser bursts immediately adjacent to each other, there is likely to be an area of thermal overlap. Therefore, even when creating a continuous incision, laser impact should be spaced slightly apart to avoid inadvertent injury to deeper tissues. This is referred to commonly as "skip technique." The surgeon must also recognize that the laser beam has width. It cuts not only with the center of the beam, but also with the edge; and there is thermal damage beyond the edge. Therefore, the surgeon must center the laser beam in the lesion, using the edge of the beam to create the margin of excision. The margin of the beam should be considered as the laser blade. The surgeon must also understand the use of a focused laser beam (for cutting or vaporization, for example), a defocused laser beam (for coagulation), and the implications of spot size. Incisions are made most precisely using a very small spot size, often with high power. Vaporization is accomplished best in many situations with a larger spot, but still with high power. A larger spot with low power is optimal for coagulation. Microspot lasers provide a beam as small as 0.1 mm in diameter, which allows more precise laryngeal microsurgery than 0.8 mm or even 0.4 mm spots. However, the surgeon must recognize that, as spot size decreases, wattage must be adjusted in order to maintain the desired power density. If the surgeon fails to appreciate these principles and techniques, thermal injury to normal tissues may result. Hydration of the tissue is also important. Serious thermal damage may occur if the tissue is dry.

The CO_2 laser has distinct advantages over traditional instruments. It permits better hemostasis, better visibility, and less tissue manipulation. For varicosities, benign friable lesions on the superior surface of the vocal folds, and selected other lesions, these advantages are compelling. However, the laser also has important disadvantages. These include loss of tissue by vaporization and the consequences of thermal injury.

The problem of tissue loss by vaporization should not be underestimated. Although clinical impressions are often accurate in benign laryngeal lesions, especially following strobovideolaryngoscopy, they are no substitute for histopathological examination. Even lesions that look like routine nodules and polyps occasionally turn out to be amyloid, rheumatoid nodules, minor salivary gland tumors, or serious malignancies. Often they are small. The lesion should be excised entirely when possible and studied microscopically. Laser vaporization deprives the patient of potentially critical histopathologic assessment. Even in laryngeal papillomatosis, a portion of the abnormal tissue should be sent for evaluation by the pathologist, although some of the disease should be treated by vaporization. With the microspot, thermal damage on the sample usually is no more than 150 microns.

Heat-induced consequences of laser surgery have received considerable attention. The most dramatic is

endotracheal tube fire. This disaster can usually be avoided by meticulous attention to laser safety precautions and accurate delivery, but it is a well recognized complication that is always possible. The risk of laser fire is also diminished by use of laser-resistant endotracheal tubes or high-flow jet ventilation.

Lateral thermal energy spread is a more common cause of laser-related complications in vocal fold surgery. As laser surgery became increasingly common, more and more anecdotal reports surfaced describing apparent delayed healing and increased scarring following laser surgery. Confirmation of these impressions was reported in separate studies by Abitbol[5] and Tapia[6] in separate studies in 1984. Histological observations by Durkin and coworkers supported anecdotal observations that laser surgery could delay healing and increase scar formation.[7] It is now clear that the most significant disadvantage of CO_2 laryngeal laser surgery is thermal injury to the intermediate and deep layers of the lamina propria, which contain significant numbers of fibroblasts, or the vocalis muscle. Such injuries may result in scarring. When an adynamic segment is created along the vibratory margin of the vocal fold, dysphonia results. This may take the form of severe hoarseness and breathiness. At the present time, there is no consistently effective treatment for adynamic segments; and dysphonia in such cases is generally permanent. Therefore, it is most important to avoid such injury whenever possible.

In general, although the laser can be used safely by an expert surgeon for nearly any laryngeal lesion, it does not offer clear advantages in the treatment of most benign masses of the vibratory margin of the vocal fold such as nodules and cysts.[8,9] They are usually not particularly friable, their limits are visualized easily, and they usually can be removed deftly without injuring underlying tissue. Laser excision adds little other than the risk of undesirable thermal spread to deeper layers, although techniques using a microspot CO_2 laser may decrease the incidence of thermal complications.[10,11]

Lasers are often helpful in coagulating the central feeding vessel of unilateral polyps. Such vessels usually are found on the superior surface of the vocal fold. However, polyps based on the vibratory margin can be excised easily and precisely with microlaryngeal scissors following central vessel coagulation. An infusion should be provided by injection of saline, then a "hydrotomy" is performed. Subsequent microsurgery is easier. If the polyp can be separated form the vocal ligament by blunt dissection, it can usually be removed safely by a laser beam directed medially and tangentially to avoid injury. However, slight motion or misdirection can result in a vocal ligament burn;

and once blunt dissection has been accomplished, the laser offers no significant advantage over traditional instruments for final removal of the polyp. Similarly, laser has been advocated for making incisions in the superior surface of the vocal fold prior to evacuation of Reinke's edema. In this case, although the risk of significant vocal fold scar is low, the laser offers no substantial advantage over scissors except that there is no bleeding; and laser surgery for this condition is also often slower than surgery with cold instruments. Its use in such cases is a matter of the individual surgeon's preferences.

Laser has been advocated for treatment of various other lesions including vocal fold webs, granulomas, vocal fold paralysis, stenosis, and carcinoma. So far, no significant advantages or disadvantages have been identified in the treatment of web. Topical contact of mitomycin for 2 minutes may improve results. The laser does not consistently obviate the need for a keel or stent, especially in larger lesions. When arytenoidectomy is necessary, endoscopic laser arytenoidectomy has proven convenient and successful. Potential laser-related disadvantages include the risk of endotracheal tube fire, especially if tracheotomy has not been performed, and thermal damage to the interarytenoid region, which might result in posterior laryngeal stenosis. These complications are avoidable in most cases. Lasers may be used in the treatment of granulomas, as long as an adequate biopsy has been obtained and the underlying perichondrium is not traumatized. Lasers may be used also for carcinoma, although the value of laser surgery in malignant lesions remains uncertain.[12-18] When the laser is used for laryngeal cancer, the surgeon must obtain adequate histological specimens from not only the tumor, but also the margins. The impact of laser use on vocal quality in laryngeal cancer patients is unknown.

At the present time, the CO_2 laser is the only laser in wide general use for laryngeal surgery, although other lasers have been tried,[19,20] as discussed below. So far, other wavelengths do not appear to be efficacious for most laryngeal surgery, for various reasons including the inability to use them through a microscope, excessive thermal injury, or the need for contact between the laser-emitting instrument and the tissue. Additional investigation of various wavelengths is needed.

History of the Laser

Laser is an acronym for light amplification by the stimulated emission of radiation. The surgical tool LASER has a specific and accurate role in surgery. The principles of the laser beam are a precise focus, precise cut-

ting effect, and a minimal thermal effect, which results in less edema with little or no bleeding of the surgical bed and a fast rate of healing.

Creation of light and fire have intrigued mankind throughout history. Pythagorus, the Greek philosopher, proposed the first theory of visible light in the sixth century BC in which he stated that an object is made visible because light waves traveled outward from the eyes. Yet visible light is only a small part of the light spectrum. Newton, in 1704, published his corpuscular theory, which held that light consisted of rapidly moving particles. Huygens, an opponent, maintained that light was a series of waves. J.C. Maxwell, an English physicist, developed the first electromagnetic theory of light. Light waves, he stated, were electrical in nature and different from the mechanical nature of sound waves. Many phenomena of light, such as propagation, reflection, refraction, interference, diffraction, and polarization were explained by the electromagnetic wave theory. But the absorption and emission of light by matter remained unexplained until 1887 when Hertz proposed the photoelectric emission theory in which he stated that a photoelectric emission is independent of the intensity of light but dependent on the wavelength of the incident light. This incident light induces the ejection of electrons from conductors of light. These effects were defined by Einstein in 1905 as the absorption of light energy by matter. Einstein also extended the Planck theory, which held that light energy transferred by matter must be transferred in discrete units, or "quanta." According to Max Planck's theory promulgated in about 1900, "Light is corpuscular in nature but apparently travels in electromagnetic waves emitting radiant energy by tiny packages of energy called quanta." Einstein later postulated that the energy of a light photon was proportional to the frequency of the light.

The equation between "quanta" and "wavelength" was defined as:

$$e = h \eta$$

(e = quantum energy, h = Planck's constant, η = wavelength)

If the electromagnetic theory is believed to be true, electrons must continually emit energy as they revolve around the nucleus or spiral inward toward the center of the atom, and collapse into the nucleus. The same theory states that all atoms emit a continuous spectrum of energy, because the frequency of radiation emitted by the revolving electrons must be equal to the frequency of revolution. This was in contradiction to the line spectra theory that had been previously described. Proposing the first postulate of the atomic theory, both held that electrons can revolve around the nucleus of an atom in certain stable orbits without emitting radiant energy. The second postulate held that an electron makes a transition from a stable orbit to a lower energy level orbit by emitting a photon. The photon emitted has an energy equal to the difference between the two orbits, and the photon is the emission of radiant energy. Bohr's model explains only the emission spectra of an atom; it does not predict what energy level elements and molecules should have, or the emissions they should give off. To explain this, an understanding of quantum mechanics is required.

The theory of quantum mechanics states that energy levels can be predicted and explains the frequency of light observed in the atomic spectrum. In 1919, Einstein presented "Zur Quantum Theorie der Stralung" (the Quantum Theory of Radiations). In his theory, electrons, atoms, molecules, and photons interact with electromagnetic radiation of quantum units by three types of radiation transitions: absorption, spontaneous emission, and stimulated emission. Absorption of a photon occurs when an electron goes from a lower orbit to a higher orbit. The electron is in an excited state, which is unstable. Light, thermal, electrical, or optical energy can induce this kind of excited state.

Spontaneous emission of a photon occurs when the electron goes down to its stable orbit. Stimulated emission was the genius idea of Albert Einstein. He discovered that one photon of a specific wavelength could interact with an excited atom to induce the emission of a second photon. Laser-produced light operates on that principle: in a stimulated emission, the second photon emitted from the excited atom has the same frequency, the same phase, and the same direction as the incident photon absorbed and immediately released.

A laser produces a beam, like a sunbeam, but with four fundamental characteristics: intensity (tremendous energy in a very focused, narrow beam), coherence (in phase spatially and temporally), high collimation (light waves are parallel with minimal divergence and thus minimal dissipation of energy), and monochromaticity (uniform wavelength). This last characteristic is fundamental from a surgical point of view, because a specific wavelength is absorbed by specific tissues such as muscle or bone. The components of human tissue absorb wavelengths selectively based on their state of hydration, temperature, color, and thickness.

Before the active medium of a laser is excited, it has more stable than unstable atoms. During amplification, it will become a tremendous source of energy. The electromagnetic emission released by stimulated emission is amplified to produce an intense beam by an external power source, which will excite the atoms, thus allowing the emissions of photons from the atoms.

In essence, it creates a chain reaction in the active medium of a laser.

Radiation emitted from a laser consists of a spectrum of wavelengths ranging from 200 (ultraviolet) to 10,000 (infrared) nanometers (nm). The seven types of surgical lasers in current use emit approximately 500 nm (Argon laser); 1060 nm (Neodymium Yttrium-Aluminium-Garnet Laser or Nd-Yag); 532 nm (KTP); 640 nm (Dye laser), diode laser, pulse dye laser; and 10,600 nm (the CO_2 laser, most commonly used in laryngeal surgery).

The idea of using light energy for surgery predates the laser. In 1945, Gerhard Meyer-Schwickerath treated detached retinas and eye tumors with sunlight.[21] The first proposed use of lasers in surgery occurred in 1958 by Schawlow and Townes.[22] Maiman built the first Ruby laser in 1960 with a wavelength of 690 nm.[23] The application of infrared emission lasers using pure carbon dioxide, nitrogen, and helium, that operated continuously at 10,600 nm, was reported in 1965 by Patel et al.[24]

Preliminary laboratory studies using a 20 watt CO_2 laser for liver surgery in dogs were reported by Yahr and Strully in 1966.[25] Their results were encouraging and led to Jako's application of the laser in laryngeal microsurgery in 1967 on a cadaver larynx.[26] Clinical application commenced in 1972 when Strong and Jako presented their first reports on use of the CO_2 laser on 12 patients.[27,28]

Characteristics of Lasers Required for Phonomicrosurgery

Lasers can be used to incise, vaporize, coagulate, or penetrate the vocal fold structures. The use of lasers in phonomicrosurgery was first described 30 years ago.[2] Absorption by water yields small penetration of a laser beam. Living tissue contains a large amount of water; therefore, absorption of CO_2 laser emissions is maximal in the superficial layers of tissue. It causes a surgical defect by the evaporation of tissue fluid and subsequent burning of organic material. A small proportion of the laser light energy penetrates deeper, partly by absorption but mostly by conduction. This causes a zone of devitalized cells due to thermal damage. The depth of this scarring, (which appears as black particles) is due to carbonization and is proportional to the energy density and temperature of the tissue. If laser is used on carbonized tissue, which is black, the heat effect increases and the scarring process is disturbed. Energy density depends on the time of exposure to the laser, the energy delivered, hand speed, the angle of delivery, and overall, the diameter of the impact point.

Types of Lasers

Argon Laser

The Argon laser, introduced in the 1960s, was the pioneering instrument in otolaryngologic laser surgery.[29-31] It is a stable gaseous laser with a continuous wave. Wavelengths range from 488 to 514.5 nm, are transmitted through clear fluid and structures, and emit light in the visible spectrum of blue-green. It can be used through flexible fibers in endoscopes. Spot size is about 100 to 200 microns. This laser is used in the treatment of pigmented and vascular lesions and is absorbed by hemoglobin, melanin, and retinal tissue. The average power is 4 to 6 watts, but it can be raised to 30 watts. It has coagulation capability and a very low cutting effect.

Nd-YAG Laser

The Neodymium Yttrium-Aluminium-Garnet Laser (Nd-YAG laser) has a wavelength of 1060 nm. It is a solid laser that emits continuous short infrared wavelengths and is usable through optical quartz fiber light guides. The Nd-YAG laser beam is transmitted through clear fluids and delivers 10 to 120 watts through a fiberoptic channel. It produces a high degree of scatter, which results in a large spot size, small cutting effect, and substantial charring effect. The thermal effect is significant, and it is capable of coagulating vessels up to 2 mm in size. Its tissue penetrating ability is 5 to 7 mm. At low powers, it shrinks tissue without any vaporization; however, the thermal effect could damage, destroy, or boil the lamina propria and ruin the voice by noncontact. With a properly placed contact tip, the cutting effect is good, but tips must be in contact with the tissue before firing; otherwise the heat will be too high due to the scattering effect. This laser alone,[32] or combined with the CO_2 laser, can be used in treating obstructing malignant laryngeal lesions.

KTP (Potassium, Titanyl, Phosphate) Crystal Laser

The KTP/532 laser is an Nd-YAG Laser. Its potential for use in surgery increased by two important improvements: doubling of the frequency of the wave length and point of contact. Frequency doubling offers a technique to change the output wavelength from 1060 nm (infrared) to 532 nm (green) by means of a special crystal that combines two infrared photons to one green photon. Contact KTP with a conical sapphire, which, due to its shape, reflects the laser energy to the tips and heats up to several hundred degrees Celsius on a very focused spot, provides almost a pure cutting effect. The KTP laser is transmitted through clear fluids and structures. It does not vaporize well and has a 200 nm spot size when delivered through fiberoptic channels in endoscopes (available fibers range from 0.2 to 0.6 mm in diameter). It can also be used through the microscope. Perkins developed the KTP laser for otosclerosis, before it was used in the larynx.[33] Since 1986, KTP/532 has been used commonly in the treatment of laryngeal pathology. It is a green beam, which may pass through the microscope by the flexible fiberoptic channel of an endoscope. The indications are numerous; however, in our hands, the thermal damages seem to be more significant than with the CO_2 laser.

Dye-Laser Photodynamic Therapy

Argon lasers, or tunable dye lasers, activate hematoprophyrin derivative (HPD), which is concentrated preferentially in tumor cells.[34] Patients receive a photosensitizing agent, which is administrated through an intravenous injection 24 hours before laser treatment. Only tumor cells less than 3 mm deep are destroyed, which seems an applicable technique for treating carcinoma in situ (CIS) or a T1N0 cancer. Moreover, in all cases, endoscopic examination and biopsy must be done prior to developing a treatment protocol. The drugs used in photodynamic therapy can cause photosensitivity. Patients so treated must remain in darkness for 30 days, beginning 24 hours after an injection, to ensure there is fluorescence of malignant cells only as laser irradiation destroys the tumor cells. The wavelength of the Argon laser is 632 microns. Light dosimetry is calculated, based on body surface. Photodynamic therapy (PDT) is performed with laryngoscopy and general anesthesia. It lasts between 20 to 45 minutes. PDT follow-up appointments are scheduled every week for 2 months and should be made for late in the afternoon to avoid sun irradiation. On the vocal folds, this technique is debatable particularly in the treatment of vocal fold cancer, which requires a very early diagnosis. Before undergoing treatment with the dye laser, a biopsy must be done. First, a piece of the vocal fold is removed to diagnose the cancer. Following dye laser treatment, a biopsy must be repeated to confirm that the margins are clear. Due to the side effects previously described, a minimal cordectomy type 1 should be the safer surgical procedure. The dye laser is potentially helpful in treating lesions of the anterior commissure, for avoiding post-operative web formation and in preserving the voice. Tunable dye lasers may prove more valuable in the future for treating selected vascular lesions of the larynx, papillomas, and other conditions. Because of the pulsed dye laser, these techniques are used less often today.

Pulsed Dye Laser

The 585 nanometer pulsed dye laser (PDL) has been used to treat vocal fold disease only recently. It was recognized by 1981 that dye lasers could be used to damage microvasculature.[35] Pulsed dye lasers can be used through a flexible laryngoscope in an office setting. Typically, the laser is passed through a 1-mm fiber and delivers a spot size of 1 to 2 mm. Typical settings include up to 5 joules per pulse, with a 450-microsecond pulse width, a 1-Hertz repetition rate, and a fluency of 19 to 76 joules per square centimeter (j/cm^2). Treatment is tolerated well. The pulsed dye laser has been used for papilloma [36,37] and dysplasia [37,38] Additional experience is necessary to determine the safety and efficacy of PDL therapy for laryngeal disease, but preliminary results have been encouraging. This laser is specifically cleared for lesions with important microvascularization. It is a "no touch" surgery performed on an outpatient basis, which changes the approach to respiratory papillomatosis.

Diode Laser

This is a newer laser technologically with a very precise focus point. It can vaporize and cut with a minimal thermal effect. It can be guided through a fiber, and used through an endoscope to vaporize papillomas and to open recurrent glottic webs.

CO_2 Laser

The carbon dioxide or CO_2 laser is a sealed gaseous laser with a mixture of CO_2, nitrogen, and helium. CO_2 lasers have a wavelength of 10,600 nm. It emits in the infrared portion of the light spectrum, which is invisible to the human eye. It requires a helium-neon light source to direct the CO_2 laser beam. It is highly absorbed in water and produces no backscatter caused by flash-boiling of the intracellular water and ablation of cells.

By focusing the CO_2 laser beam, the highest energy density is expected and the cutting effect is maximized. In laryngeal surgery, the ability to cut without instrument contact, up to a distance of 400 mm through the microscope, is an important advantage of this laser. It is an aseptic technique. The combination of a slight coagulating effect on small blood vessels without direct contact with the vocal fold muscle (as is the usual effect by cauterization) will produce minimal tissue damage and precision.

Spot size has been one of the parameters to decrease since 1972.[27] In surgery of the larynx, the original CO_2 spot size was 800 to 600 microns; currently, it is 150 microns. Hemostatic capability is limited to microcirculation. A coagulating forceps is necessary to coagulate large vocal fold blood vessels (0.6 mm or more) when encountered during cordectomy. The greatest advantage of CO_2 laser is its precision by using the tangential portion of the beam, thus enabling surgical accuracy of less than 100 microns. The time required to perform laser phonomicrosurgery is also shorter than using conventional technique.[39-41]

The properties of CO_2 lasers are particularly well suited to laryngeal surgery. The CO_2 laser produces a cone-shaped impact that has three characteristic levels including, from the center to the outer layer, an area of charring, a region of tissue dessication, and an outer layer of edema.

Electromicroscopic studies of soft tissue show that, with a spot size of 130 microns, a power of 50 watts, and an exposure of 1 second, CO_2 laser impact creates a cone-shaped defect approximately 450 microns deep and 230 microns wide with 30 microns for the center area of charring, 100 microns for the intermediate dessicated tissue layer, and 100 microns for the outer layer of the edematous tissue. CO_2 laser tissue interaction depends on the mode of impact being either a continuous mode firing or a pulsed mode firing.

In the continuous type, photons are emitted with a constant and stable delivery of energy and intensity. A constant power source is needed to keep the active medium in an excited state to stimulate emissions. In a pulsed mode, an intermittent power source is used (similar to a flash-bulb). It provides sudden bursts of energy to the active medium. A pulsed mode laser delivers a higher energy in a very short time. A continuous wave laser delivers easily 25 watts and a pulsed mode laser will deliver up to 2 watts with each pulse. Between the pulses, there is almost no energy, which is the reason a pulsed CO_2 laser has a more accurate and deeper cutting effect with less thermal damage than the continuous mode for impact spots of the same diameter.

Limitations of Laser Surgery

Laser Tissue Interaction: Four Crucial Considerations for Phonomicrosurgery

These tissue interactions may occur singularly or in combination.

1. *Reflection* occurs when the laser beam Is not absorbed and does not penetrate the tissue; it is reflected as a beam on a mirror. Reflection of the laser beam can occur off surgical instruments and can re-

sult in tissue damage of the patient or surgical team personnel.

2. *Transmission* occurs when the laser beam is not absorbed and passes through the tissue similar to a light beam through the glass. This property is especially important when treating diseases of the retina, through the cornea.

3. *Absorption* occurs when a laser beam is absorbed by the tissue (an effect similar to a sunbeam being focused by a magnifier onto a piece of dry wood), thus causing it to burn.

4. *Scatter or dispersion* is a result of a laser beam that is partially absorbed, transmitted and thus scattered through and by the tissue.

Each type of laser interacts with tissue in a specific way, producing characteristic patterns of heat conduction, coagulation, ablation, and charring. Knowledge of laser physics and typical tissue interactions allows the surgeon to select a laser best suited to the task at hand.

Limitations of Diode Laser Surgery

The diode laser has limitations that make it unsuitable for most laryngeal surgery, including the precision of fiber arrangement in the endoscopes. It is very difficult not to damage the vocal fold's free edge when treating small lesions with a diode laser. The indications for its use in the larynx, if it is used at all, are for treating large papillomas and webs.

Limitations of CO$_2$ Laser Surgery

The CO$_2$ laser also has a few disadvantages in laryngeal surgery. First, it cannot be conducted through a fiberoptic endoscope. It can also cause tissue loss, which may limit biopsy results; and by thermal injury, it can cause biopsy artifact or vocal fold scarring that can result in dysphonia for 3 to 6 months if the vocal ligament is not touched. The same complication may appear with cold instruments if the ligament is traumatized..

Phonomicrosurgical Procedures

Laser phonomicrosurgery is functional surgery. It is not surgery for life-threatening disease. There must not be any medical (cardiac, pulmonary, renal, metabolic, neurologic) conditions that would be a contraindication to operating on these patients or to subjecting them to general anesthesia. Technical problems that limit the ability to perform laryngoscopy include conditions such as arthrosis or ankylosis of cervical vertebrae, short neck, or prognathism.

Safe Laser Phonomicrosurgery Considerations

- The laser tissue interaction is affected by the duration of impact, the power of the laser, and the handspeed, which yields a power-density per second. The amount of energy absorbed by a specific area of tissue per second on initial contact (impact) is different than the second impact.

- The first laser impact at a given location will cut but also dehydrate the surgical bed. The second laser firing on the same spot will impact on dehydrated tissue, which will lead to a scattering effect and an increased possibility of thermal injury of the vocal ligament.

- Laser-safe phonomicrosurgical procedures must follow several basic rules: Cool down the lesion with an icy and moist cottonoid for 1 minute before the surgery; remove the lesion with a duration of 1/10 second .per impact; and avoid suction directly on the tissue, rather doing it through the icy and wet cottonoid, which will not traumatize the epithelium or the lesion.

Instruments Specific for Laser Phonomicrosurgery

Good positioning of the patient and good exposure of the larynx are the main requirements for performing laryngoscopy. Laser phonomicrosurgery requires few additional surgical instruments. The adapted instruments permit good surgical craftsmanship. One author's (JA) laryngeal instrument set consists of 14 microinstruments and three laryngoscopes (two for adults and one for pediatric patients). The specificity of these forceps is that both suction and cauterization are linked in one instrument, which functions for each purpose. Most are manufactured by Medtronic Xomed (Jacksonville, Fla). All of the instrument's surfaces are matted to prevent reflection of the laser beam and light. One author (RTS) has also developed laryngoscopes and instruments manufactured by Medtronic Xomed for use in laser phonomicrosurgery, including polished mirrors to redirect laser light. All laryngoscopes have channels for suction and light. The choice of laryngoscope depends on the physician's preference, patient's morphology, and the pathology to be treated:

- The pediatric laryngoscope is suitable for children, for some women, and patients with restricted access to larynx (jaw pathology, retrognathism). A laryngoscope with a long spatula (Medtronics Xomed) is used for long-necked patients.

- The A-Laryngoscope (Abitbol laryngoscope), used most frequently by the author, (JA), includes two lateral channels for light and a superior gliding probe for suction. It is used for treating pathologies of the vocal folds and the anterior commissure. One of the channels for suction can be used to adapt the Hopkins scope to have a closer view for video recording or photography. The A-Valve-laryngoscope includes a spatula with a lower articulated valve with an adjustable aperture. A tube guide, shaped as a half-ring, is fixed on the superior surface of the upper valve to facilitate placement and adjustment of the endotracheal tube; thus the tube does not slip laterally and stays fixed on the anterior commissure. This laryngoscope is used for lesions of the posterior wall or when performing an arytenoidectomy.

All of these laryngoscopes have a broad and flat surface, necessary to spread the pressure over the upper jaw teeth, which are protected by the dental plate and posterior dental shield if necessary. Distal illumination is provided by a glass fiber with a 250 watts cold light. The laryngoscope support is easy to install and is fixed to the table. To straighten the neck, a supple shaft is necessary.

The Sataloff laryngoscopes (Medtronics Xomed) have a more triangular design and more lift near the tip; and they include double light carriers and double suction smoke evacuation channels. There are also others excellent laryngoscopes available such as those designed by Jako, Dedo, Fragen, Kleinsasser, and others, as reviewed in chapter 82.

The Zeiss or Wild operating microscopes are fitted with a 350- or a 400-mm lens. The laser does most of the difficult work to "micro-cut" the lesion. Most forceps are 22 cm long and have suction for smoke removal; and forceps with a unipolar coagulating system are available. If arteries are more than about 0.6 mm in diameter, we use the forceps rather than laser to coagulate bleeding vessels. One author (JA), does not use scissors but recommends having them ready and, more importantly, knowing how to use them; because if the laser stops working, the surgeon must be prepared to proceed with traditional surgery with cold instruments. The other author (RTS) uses scissors and other cold instruments routinely, including during most cases in which the laser is used also. These instruments are a new generation—more precise, smaller, and perfectly suited to the task

Microlaryngoscopy Procedures

Good exposure of the larynx is the key to successful phonomicrosurgery, including laser surgery as discussed in chapter 83.

A disposable dental protector is placed after anesthesia is induced. Sometimes, when the teeth are very fragile, a specially designed dental guard is put between the molars on both sides and a dental plate covers the front teeth; thus, the forces that the laryngoscope induces are distributed on the entire jaw. This avoids dental accidents such as chipped or fractured teeth. Intubation is performed as discussed in chapter 82.

Anesthesia Techniques, Risks, and Complications

Anesthesia for laryngeal laser surgery has three major goals

1. To ensure good ventilation for the patient while minimizing risk such as fire.
2. To obtain muscle relaxation that prevents any motion of the vocal folds, thus increasing the surgeon's comfort with an open and immobile glottic area.
3. To choose anesthetic drugs with a rapid reversal that allows quick recovery of pharyngeal and laryngeal reflexes postoperatively.

Anesthetic Procedures

We do not prefer neuroleptic or benzodiazepine medications because of their prolonged postoperative effects. The authors advocate induction drugs that have a rapid onset of action and a short half-life, such as thiopenthal (Pentothal, Nesdonal) or propofol (Diprivan), 2 mg/kg intravenously. The use of analgesic morphinelike substances such as alfentanyl, 5 to 15 µg/kg (Alfenta) are particularly well-suited to the average duration of the procedure (10 to 45 minutes). Anesthesia is maintained with reinjections of thiopenthal or Propofol administered via an infusion pump at the rate of 6 to 12 mg/kg/hr. Muscle relaxation is obtained with short-acting potent drugs like Suxamethonium (1 mg/kg at intubation), and maintained by continuous infusion (2 to 15 mg/kg/hr). Anaphylaxis is rarely encountered with these drugs. Once the straight laryngoscope is suspended, the surgeon covers the endotracheal tube and cuff with a gauze soaked in iced water (RTS) or 2% lidocaine-epinephrine (1:100:000) (JA) solution. This prevents tube ignition and potential damage to the surrounding tissues. Wet compresses placed on the patient's face, after careful eye closure, provide protection from the laser beam. On the Abitbol laryngoscope, there is a special arch to fit the wet drapes. At the end of the procedure, dexamethasone (4 mg) may be injected intravenously. Laser surgery carries some risk for the otolaryngologic patient because of a number of challenges the anesthesiologist will have to deal with, forcing him or her to choose a technique that ensures good ventilation and complete muscle relaxation to bring as much comfort as possible to facilitate the surgery.

Anesthesia Techniques

Numerous anesthetic techniques have been developed specifically for laser phonomicrosurgery, including endotracheal tubes protected by metallic taping or coating, jet ventilation (high- or low-frequency), and neuroleptic analgesia. Spontaneous ventilation may not be acceptable for laser phonomicrosurgery because of the lack of immobility of vocal folds with this procedure. Other techniques currently used are described as follows.

Endotracheal Tubes

Metallic endotracheal tubes may be useful. For example, the Oswal-Hunton tube is flexible and appropriate.[42,43] Tubes may be coated with adhesive aluminum foil over 10 cm before the cuff, providing good protection from laser damage. However, this technique has been responsible for lacerations of the vocal folds. One author (JA) utilizes classical endotracheal intubation, with a lubricated, size 5 cuffed tube protected with a green icy and wet gauze or cottonoids. The other author (RTS) uses Medtronic Xomed's laser-resistant tube, or jet ventilation (without an endotracheal tube). Once intubated, chest auscultation is performed. The patient's ventilation is then manually assisted. A mixture of air with no more than 30% oxygen, carefully excluding nitrous oxide, helps avoids tube ignition. Alternatively, a helium/oxygen mixture may be used.

Jet Ventilation. Jet ventilation is an intermittent positive-pressure ventilation that works according to the Venturi effect. The jetted gas leaves a narrow cannula and, upon entering the trachea, entrains outside air inside the lungs, because of the depression created by the larger tracheal volume. This causes the gases to move forward. There are two techniques:

1. Manual jet ventilation or low-frequency jet ventilation was initially described by Sanders in 1967 for patients undergoing bronchoscopy.[44,45] It includes an injector connected to a gas reservoir (air or/and oxygen), a flow interrupter with a manual trigger, and a large bore catheter placed distal or proximal to the vocal folds. It allows a relatively low-frequency ventilation with 10 to 16 insufflations per minute and an insufflation time of 1 to 3 seconds.[46-48]

2. High-frequency jet ventilation: Air and oxygen (30% FiO_2) are delivered at a frequency of 100 to 300 insufflations per minute, under a pressure of 3 bars. A Venturi effect is produced at the distal end of the injector, imposing an additional air circuit with a flow of 10 to 20 l/mn. The sum of the two volumes (ventilation system plus displaced gas) equals the patient's tidal volume (ie, 5 ml/kg). One author (JA) rarely uses this technique in patients presenting with chronic obstructive pulmonary diseases, distension, and asthma, in whom it becomes more dangerous because it predisposes the patient to alveolar hypoventilation and pneumothorax. Moreover, the vocal folds "shiver" following the rhythm of the jet ventilation, and the laser may be impaired. The author (RTS), uses it fairly often, especially for lesions of the posterior larynx such as scar bands or granulomas. A 14-gauge subglottic needle or a Hunsicker jet tube (Medtronics Xomed) is used, and the laser is applied during periods of apnea. This technique requires close cooperation between the surgeon and anesthesiologist.

Transtracheal Ventilation. Used in cases of difficult or nonfeasible intubation and emergency or maxillofacial trauma, this method allows a proper access to the airway, through either tracheotomy or a 14-gauge needle inserted into the trachea through the cricothyroid membrane. Except for a few contraindications (eg, goiter, subglottic tumors), this technique uses jet ventilation.

General Anesthesia without Intubation. We virtually never use this technique because of various drawbacks and dangers. The need for urgent or repeated intubation, extubation, and reintubation may jeopardize the mucosa and lead to bleeding or regurgitation with aspiration. Furthermore, smoke exhalation prevents the surgeon from adjusting the laser beam.

Laryngeal Block. This method seems to be a technique applicable for specific cases such as immobility of the vocal folds or spastic dysphonia.

Preoperative Procedures

The success of laser surgery in laryngology depends on the skills and cohesiveness of the entire surgical team. Duration of the procedures is generally short, ranging from 10 minutes to a maximum of about 1 hour. Drugs, therefore, have to induce a rapid and deep anesthesia and, at the same time, allow a fast recovery of pharyngeal and laryngeal reflexes and cognitive function so that the patient does not injure the vocal folds through abusive phonation or coughing while disoriented after surgery.

Besides the history and physical examination, routine preoperative evaluation includes screening for any previous intubation problems and dysmorphic features or maxillofacial trauma resulting in limited mandibular or cervical vertebrae mobility. Pre-existing dental pathology is also assessed, as are general medical problems.

Allergic diseases are more and more common and may include allergies to the anesthetic drugs or to materials such as latex. It is crucial to look for such information preoperatively.

Premedication is limited to medications such as hydroxyzine (100 mg orally) and sometimes atropine (0.5 to 1 mg intramuscularly). In the operating room, a large intravenous line (14- to 18-gauge) and noninvasive monitoring are established. Gas exchanges are monitored using PO_2, SaO_2, FiO_2, and PCO_2, as well as ventilation curves and analysis of volumes, pressures, and flows. Cardiovascular function is monitored via automatic blood pressure-measuring systems, transcutaneous oximetry, and electrocardiography to detect dysrhythmia or myocardial ischemia.

Complications of Anesthesia

Ventilation-related accidents include hypoventilation and laryngeal obstruction from aspiration of blood. Regurgitation may also result in aspiration. Other incidents such as hypertension with tachycardia, due not to hypercapnia but to hypoanalgesia may occur. The richly innervated oral, pharyngeal, and laryngeal areas are exposed to very strong nociceptive stimuli. A sinus bradycardia, with regular, normal P waves and without modification of PR interval or QRS complex, may appear during laryngoscope suspension, either because of inadequate analgesia or cervical hyperextension. Flexion of the neck will usually correct this situation if the primary stimulation was reflex bradycardia from carotid sinus compression.

Phonomicrosurgical Structure and Function

Three main factors must be respected to ensure a good voice from the phonomicrosurgical point of view:

1. glottic closure,
2. vocal fold vibrations, and
3. lubrication of the vocal folds.

From Anterior to Posterior Locations on the Vocal Fold

The biomechanical aspects of the vocal folds must be well known to understand the physiopathology of vocal fold lesions. Most protruding lesions are located in the middle part of the vocal ligament where the collision forces are maximal. It is where the stresses are highest, the amplitude of the vibration is maximum, and the vocal muscle and epithelium are thicker. If the musculomembranous vocal fold is divided into three parts, it is located roughly in the middle third. When a lesion is on the first third of the vocal fold, the singing and the speaking voice are often affected severely. When the lesion is on the posterior third of the vocal fold, the speaking voice may be almost normal, but the singing voice is often impaired. When the lesion is on the middle third, the vocal consequences depend on the flexibility of the epithelium and on the type and size of lesion.

Choosing the precise surgical procedure to perform begins during the videostroboscopic examination, which shows the dynamic and functional consequences of the lesion, of the opposite side, and the behavior of the vocal folds and of the false vocal folds.

The "Lips" of the Free Edge

Usually, the vocal fold is described as having a superior surface, inferior surface, and free edge. However, in terms of dynamic vocal fold anatomy, and from a phonomicrosurgical anatomic point of view, we have distinguished three lips of the free edge: the superior lip, the middle lip, and the inferior lip. If the superior lip of the free edge is removed surgically, the mechanical vibration will continue from the inferior lip to the middle lip; and the voice is likely to recover in 2 to 6 weeks.

If we remove the superior and the middle lips, the voice will usually take at least 4 to 6 weeks to recover. However, if we have to remove all three lips of the free edge, then, phonation often takes 8 to 12 weeks to recover and the risk of permanent scar and dysphonia is increased. This may also create an iatrogenic sulcus vocalis. It is best to preserve as much epithelium as possible to minimize the risks of permanent dysphonia. For a lesion of the inferior lip, the author (JA) often observes a 3- to 4-week healing process. The explanation is simple: vibration starts at this level, so the mechanical structure takes more time to recover.

From the Superficial Layer to the Deep Layer

Most vocal fold lesions, benign or malignant, come from the epithelium. Some cysts may mimic intramuscular lesions, exerting pressure on the vocal ligament without actually invading it. Phonomicrosurgeons must respect the vocal ligament itself, not allowing scissors or the laser to touch it. Reinke's space must not be disturbed more than necessary, as well. For some intracordal cysts, laser technique may be contraindicated.

Principles of CO_2 Laser Phonomicrosurgery

The laryngoscope is put in place at a working distance of 400 mm, and the microscope used. Routinely 4 to 6 watts of delivered CO_2 energy is used in laser laryngeal surgery. The surgeon should examine the entire larynx and then focus on the lesion, placing wet and icy, moist cottonoid under the glottic space to protect the tube and the subglottic area. A checklist is used to confirm that suction, laser, and coagulation are ready to work. A ring controls the focus of the laser beam, from 100 to 500 microns. The surgeon controls the alignment of the helium-neon aiming beam and the CO_2 laser beam: a first spot is fired on the gauze or another target to align the impact with the red spot (or aiming beam). The laser incision is barely visible on the vocal fold with no visible thermal effect, because of the cutting technique. The thermal effect is seen ordinarily only on a lesion less than 150 microns in size. For angiomatous polyps, for example, the technique is to isolate the feeding vessels first, to vaporize them, and then to remove the polyp. For cysts, nodules, and micropolyps, ultrapulse or superpulse mode will provide a tremendous advantage in performing very precise surgery with controlled thermal effect, but also with little or no coagulating effect. However, because there are few vessels on these types of lesions, there is no troublesome bleeding. Surrounding tissue trauma is avoided by using higher energy density. Samples for histological documentation also are more reliable because of limited thermal artifact and tissue loss. No firing should occur twice on the same spot or on charred tissue, because this increases the thermal effect tremendously. In some cases, hydrotomy may be interesting (injection of saline in the vocal fold to isolate the lesion from the deep epithelium).

It must be remembered that the CO_2 laser is not always responsible for scar. Vocal fold epithelium is fragile. For example, traumatic suction of the vocal fold mucosa also can cause scarring and is avoided by suctioning it through a moist cottonoid placed over the mucosa. Scar also occurs after surgery with cold instruments and is also often present preoperatively from the lesion itself. The size of the microinstruments used plays an important role in avoiding these complications.

The rate of temperature rise in tissue should be achieved as rapidly as possible. The use of superpulse mode allows high peak power with each pulsed application over a very brief period of milliseconds. There is thus an immediate temperature rise at the point of impact, resulting in instant vaporization without charring of tissue. The power setting is usually 2 to 3 watts and the exposure time, 0.05 to 0.1 second. The energy is applied in single shots, repeat mode or continuous mode, depending on the nature of operation. Thus, on the one hand, while removing a lesion from the free edge of the vocal fold, it is appropriate to use single shots to limit the spread of energy to vocal ligament. On the other hand, to make an incision on the superior surface of the vocal fold to evacuate Reinke's edema, the superpulse can be used in repeat mode and moved rapidly in the line of incision. The use of continuous mode is appropriate when dealing with a malignant lesion of the vocal fold, because the spread of energy to deeper tissues will, to a limited extent, help hemostasis and seal off any lymphatics. It will also reduce the operating time.

The total spot size can be reduced further by striking the tissue tangentially. Thus, only a small part of the spot falls on the tissue, while the remaining part falls on a swab or cottonoid held in the proximity of the target tissue. This technique is extremely useful in the final stages of removal of pathological tissue from the free edge of the vocal fold. By using only a part of the spot on the tissue, the effective spot size is thus reduced to under 100 microns.

When using in the continuous or repeat mode, the slower the beam is moved on the surface, the greater is the spread of energy within the tissue. Not only will the first few hundred microns suffer irreversible thermal damage, but the next few hundred microns also will be desiccated and thus will not absorb the energy, which will then be conducted to even deeper tissue. To limit the spread of energy within the tissue, the beam should be moved rapidly and not dwell at the same spot for any length of time when using continuous or repeat modes.

Laser Phonomicrosurgical Techniques for Types of Lesions

One author (JA) uses laser routinely for lesions described below, and the other (RTS) uses laser rarely for most of these lesions. Surgical techniques with cold instruments are described elsewhere in this book. However, when the laser is used, both authors utilize similar techniques, as described below.

Protruding Lesions

Protruding lesions include nodules, cysts, polyps, granuloma, papilloma, laryngocele, and Reinke's edema. Some of them will need hydrodissection by hydrotomy.

How We Do It in Protruding Lesions (chronological order of procedure)

Secure the laryngoscope in place.

Palpation of the lesion is crucial, as well as palpation of the other side.

The surgical bed is examined with the microscope and often with 90° and 70° Storz laryngeal telescopes before and after the surgical procedure.

Place the green gauze or cottonoid under the vocal fold.

Focus the microscope.

With the grasping forceps, which hold a wet icy cottonoid, the lesion is palpated.

The icy wet cottonoid is left in place for over the surgical site to cool the vocal fold, and then removed.

The forceps holds a new cottonoid.

Push slowly from outside to inside the glottic space to isolate the protruding lesions.

The laser is aimed with a target at the root of the lesion, with the beam glancing the free edge tangentially. The beam is perpendicular to the superior surface of the fold. The laser shoots at an angle of 90° to the root of the lesion. The impact is performed on clean mucosa. Any carbonized tissue is removed with a wet icy small cotton ball to avoid increasing thermic effect of a subsequent laser strike.

The parameters of the laser are: 0.1 second, 4 watts, spot of 120 microns.

The lesion is removed almost entirely but without creating a divot in the superficial layer of the lamina propria.

Using specific forceps, for example, Monopolar Coagulating Heart-Shaped Grasper with suction, angled right for a nodule on the right vocal fold, or a Monopolar Coagulating Alligator Forceps with suction, curved left for a polyp of the left vocal fold, the sample is removed.

Frozen section is done when appropriate.

If necessary, any small epithelial irregularity is vaporized.

The inferior, then the middle, and finally the superior lips of the vocal fold are checked. This is accomplished best with a 70° telescope.

Check the opposite side.

Leave an icy wet cottonoid for 1 minute on the surgical bed and, if necessary, administer a steroid injection.

Specific modifications will be made for specific cases; for example, an angiomatous lesion may need feeding vessels coagulated before excision, as noted above.

Lesions from the middle third and the posterior third of the vocal fold such as nodules, polyps, granulomas, Reinke's space edema, laryngitis, or keratosis can be treated during the same procedure.

Bilateral Reinke's space edema involving the anterior commissure, or the anterior third of the vocal fold, and bilateral protruding lesions of the anterior third of the vocal fold should be treated one side at a time (staged procedure).

When treating lesions that involve the anterior commissure, the epithelium just above the anterior commissure and just under the anterior commissure must be protected,

Recessed Lesions

The recessed lesions are sulcus vocalis, bowed vocal folds, atrophic vocal folds, notches, and vocal fold scar. The laser or a Sharp knife will be used to open the space between the scarred epithelium and the vocal ligament.

How We Do It in Recessed Lesions

Hydrodissection is performed in treating a sulcus vocalis.

The scarred epithelium is removed with laser and is followed by injection of collagen, autologous fat, or hydroxyapatite.

Injection of these substances is also used in treatment of bowed or atrophied vocal folds.

Relatively Flat Lesions

Flat lesions include laryngitis, leukoplakia, keratosis, Reinke's edema, vascular lesions (microvarices, hemorrhages), anterior and posterior webs, papilloma, stenosis, post-irradiation edema, and submucosal lesions such as cysts and fibrosis. This type of lesion may benefit from hydrodissection.

How We Do It in Relatively Flat Lesions

Hydrodissection is utilized.

The laser is used on the superior surface of the vocal fold.

If a cyst is also present, cold instruments may be used in combination with laser dissection

Caution: For microvarices, if vessels are parallel to the free edge, excessive removal should be avoided. Excessive removal will affect the lubrication of the fold.

Pitch Modification Surgery

One may need to perform surgery on patients with excessively high or low vocal pitch. Voice therapy, and hormonal treatment in some cases, is the first step in treatment. Surgery will be performed only for those who did not improve adequately during an adequate therapeutic trial. The vocal fold pitch is regulated by four principal parameters: the static mass, the vibratory mass, the length and tension of the vocal folds, and the subglottic pressure, all of which can be modified through phonomicrosurgical procedures.

Increasing Pitch

We have developed an endoscopic technique to increase vocal pitch in selected cases. An incision is made parallel to the free edge of the vocal fold with the CO_2 laser (microspot, a power of 1.5 watts, discontinuous fire 0.1 sec), then some fibers of the thyroarytenoid muscle are removed from front to back. Only one side is operated on. An injection of cortisone is performed on both sides (atrophy was observed in one case on the opposite side). If the voice is not satisfactory, a second procedure is carried out 3 months later on the contralateral side. We eventually, or alternatively, may create a web to shorten the vocal folds as discussed in chapter 82. This web is created by excising the epithelium of the anterior commissure and suturing both vocal folds together. Isshiki's techniques, and modifications thereof, remain satisfactory procedures if the patient accepts an open laryngeal operation. Our technique is simple, with a fast rate of healing and no significant complications, so far. Fundamental frequency measured before and after laser surgery and patient satisfaction will indicate whether the second vocal fold must undergo laser surgery, at least 3 months later.

Decreasing Pitch

Collagen injection on one side, to increase the static vocal mass, has produced acceptable but temporary results. It seems that the best technique remains the Isshiki procedure described in 1977[49] and more recently by Tucker in 1985.[50] Laser surgery has not proven helpful.

Early Malignant Lesions

The treatment of laryngeal cancer is discussed in detail in chapter 93. However, a few basic principles are reviewed here to highlight applications of laser surgery. Because of the necessity to have a margin with no tumor involved, a cordectomy must be done. Abitbol has described three types of cordectomy.[51] The staging of the carcinoma is related essentially to the invasion of the basement membrane zone:

Anatomical/Pathological Classification

Carcinoma in situ or CIS: the basement membrane zone is spared; the lesion originating from the epithelium is located in the superficial layer of the lamina propria.

Microinvasive carcinoma or T_1N_0: the basement membrane zone is destroyed, the corium is invaded. The lamina propria is involved, as well as the Reinke's space with or without the entire vocal ligament being involved. The muscles are spared.

Invasive carcinoma or T_2N_0: the basement membrane zone and the superficial layer of the muscles are involved.

Verrucous carcinoma: a challenging case in that, macroscopically, it looks like an invasive lesion; but histologically, there is rarely an invasion of the vocal fold muscles.

Surgical Classification: Three Types of Cordectomy

The author (JA) has developed a personal surgical classification technique of three types of cordectomy:

1. Type 1: Mucosa and a portion of the superficial layer are removed. (for T_1N_0)
2. Type 2: Mucosa, lamina propria, and superficial muscles layers are removed, the false vocal fold may be removed to allow a better view of the floor of the ventricle. (for T_1N_0)
3. Type 3: Mucosa, lamina propria, and thyroarytenoid muscles are removed up to the perichondrium. The false vocal fold is also removed. Coagulation of posterior arteries is often necessary. The

false vocal fold may hide lesions sheltered in the ventricle, which is why the false vocal fold may have to be removed. Inspection with a 70° telescope is helpful in making judgments in this regard.

Laser techniques are the same for any type of cordectomy:

- A hydrodissection is performed first.
- The laser beam angle from the microscope to the vocal fold is 90°.
- The laser firing starts perpendicular to the free edge, in the horizontal plane from the free border to the ventricle to start and finish the cordectomy.
- A straight firing, parallel to the free border, is performed with the laser from the anterior angle to the posterior angle of the vocal fold incision. It starts: 2 mm behind the anterior commissure. It ends 2 mm anterior to the posterior glottic region. A rectangular specimen is removed.

If any area looks suspicious, a second-look laser microsurgery may be necessary 2 months later. Close follow-up using strobovideolaryngoscopy is needed. Frozen sections are necessary in many cases to identify appropriate margins.

In our experience, carcinomas of the anterior or posterior larynx are relative contraindications for laser laryngeal surgery, although safe endoscopic resection is possible in some cases, as discussed in chapters 82 and 93. A lesion of the anterior commissure or the posterior larynx may become a T_3 or T_4 even when small, because of the thinness of the tissue of these locations in the larynx. Carcinoma in situ, T_1N_0, and T_2N_0 of the middle third are good indications for laser endoscopic cordectomy and have very satisfactory results.

Impaired Mobility

Vocal fold hypomobility or immobility may be due to laryngeal nerve paresis, paralysis, or mechanical causes such as cricoarytenoid joint ankylosis, subluxation, or dislocation. The laser has little place in the management of hypomobility in which one or both vocal folds is abducted. Standard techniques for medialization include injection laryngoplasty (autologous fat, fascia, collagen and other substances), thyroplasty, arytenoid adduction/rotation and arytenoidopexy. Voice therapy before and after surgery is important to voice improvement in all such cases. The use of Teflon for vocal fold injection was abandoned by the authors in the 1980s with the advent of better techniques that are not associated with complications such as Teflon granuloma. Teflon granuloma is still encountered from time to time. In some cases, it can occur many years after Teflon injection. In others, it occurs because a few surgeons still utilize Teflon despite its substantial shortcomings and the availability of better alternatives. Laser does play a role in the treatment of Teflon granuloma, as discussed in chapter 82.

The laser plays an important role in the management of bilateral vocal fold paralysis or fixation in the adducted position. Techniques to address this challenging problem include vocal fold lateralization by suture placement through the thyroid cartilage; reinnervation (including nerve anastomosis and nerve-muscle pedicle techniques); laryngeal pacing; cordotomy, external arytenoidectomy, and laser arytenoidectomy. The laser is particularly advantageous for endoscopic arytenoidectomy and is used by both authors. The technique is discussed in chapter 82.

Complications of Laser Phonomicrosurgery

Complications of laryngoscopy are rare, but they occur, in three different areas:

1. *Pharyngeal tissue:* In addition to the general complications previously described, laryngoscopy can involve specific injuries. Tonsillar hematomas and lesions of the tongue base are difficult to prevent, because these structures cannot be seen during the surgery. They are caused by laryngoscope pressure, and only a preventive approach, consisting of a gentle introduction of the laryngoscope and perfect positioning, will help to avoid these complications. The laryngoscope must gently follow the anesthetist's tube.
2. *Dental trauma* can occur, but generally is preventable. A patient suffering from periodontal disease must be informed that teeth could be accidentally extracted during laryngoscopy. The surgeon and the anesthetist must always check the patient's teeth and inform him or her of the risks.
3. Neurologically, taste disturbances can last from 6 weeks to 6 months after surgery, as well as, a partial paralysis (hypesthesia) of the tongue.

Complications related to uncontrollable patient factors include granulomas and recurrences, both of which are uncommon. Coughing, throat clearing, sneezing, and reflux laryngitis must be controlled in the postoperative period to minimize the incidence of vocal fold trauma including tears and granuloma formation. Voice rest is used for about 1 week following the surgery. One author (JA) prescribes antibiotics, anti-inflammatory, and antireflux drugs for 8 days in association with vitamins and magnesium for 1 month. The other author (RTS) routinely prescribes only antireflux medications as indicated. Patients generally are taken off voice rest by their speech-language pathologist with whom they will continue post-operative voice therapy.

Laser-Related Accidents

Cutaneous and mucosal membrane burns of the face, tongue, lips, and eyes can be avoided by efficient protection with moist compresses on the face of the patient and the use of an appropriate laryngoscope. Protective eyeglasses must be worn by the entire surgical team. The most serious accident is the tracheal burn due to a mixture of oxygen and nitrous oxide. The use of helium helps to avoid this problem. Finally, laryngeal complications specific to this surgery, such as stenosis or synechiae, can occur.

To avoid these potential hazards, we subject ourselves to strict protocol control, including use of a checklist before each procedure. The occurrence of these complications, in our experience, is infrequent and often minor; but they can be serious if not remedied immediately. Potential hazards are detected by close clinical supervision and adequate monitoring of the patient.

Conclusion

Excellent expertise is needed in laser phonomicrosurgery. In our experience, the 10 commandments for success are:

1. Do not operate on the vocal fold if the patient doesn't ask for it (except in cancer).
2. Obtain optimal exposure of the vocal folds and the anterior commissure.
3. Touch the free edge of the vocal fold as little as possible.
4. Impact only on the superior surface of the vocal fold.
5. The angle of laser impact on the vocal fold edge must be 90°.
6. Hand speed must be steady.
7. Protect the subglottic space with icy green gauze or cottonoid, which must be changed if laser surgery lasts more than 6 to 8 minutes or anytime the material dries out.
8. Never fire on charred tissue.
9. Use a cottonoid to remove charred tissue.

10. Appropriate voice rest, medical therapy, and voice therapy should be used before and following laser phonomicrosurgery.

In summary, laser laryngeal microsurgery is a valuable addition to the laryngologist's armamentarium. Several studies have shown similar results with laser and cold instruments when surgery is performed by an experienced surgeon.[52-55] In our experience, the surgeon's experience and skill are critical to produce optimal results with laser voice surgery. Although it has many advantages, its potential hazards militate against injudicious use. Laser surgery requires a fully educated operating team so that precautions are taken routinely to avoid endotracheal tube fire or injury to adjacent tissues. In general, the laser is best suited for cases that cannot be treated equally well with traditional instruments, and great care must be exercised if it is used on the vibratory margin of the vocal fold because of the risk of injury to the vocal ligament and consequent scarring and permanent dysphonia. In addition, when serious or unusual pathology may be present, tissue vaporization may be a serious disadvantage. It must be preceded by adequate biopsy for small lesions, and surgeons must always consider the possibility that a section of tissue lost to vaporization may be the portion that contains critical histopathologic information. Nevertheless, in expert hands, the laser can facilitate precise surgery while minimizing bleeding and avoiding serious thermal injury. A skilled laser surgeon must first be a skilled classical microlaryngeal surgeon capable of performing phonomicrosurgery with cold instruments; and he or she must have excellent hand control to maintain precise placement and speed of the laser beam. The surgeon's experience and skill are crucial to obtaining optimal results with laser voice surgery.

References

1. Bredemeier HC. Laser accessory for surgical applications. US Patent 3,659,613; issued 1972.
2. Strong MS, Jako GJ. Laser surgery in the larynx. Early clinical experience with continuous CO_2 laser. *Ann Otol Rhinol Laryngol.* 1972;81:791–798.
3. Ossoff RH. Laser surgery in otolaryngology-head and neck surgery: anesthetic and educational considerations for laryngeal surgery. *Laryngoscope.* 1989,99(8 Pt 2 suppl 48):1–26.
4. Ossoff RH, Karlan MS. Instrumentation for CO_2 laser surgery of the larynx and tracheobronchial tree. *Surg Clin North Am.* 1984;64:973–980.
5. Abitbol J. Limitations of the laser in microsurgery of the larynx. In: Lawrence VL, ed. *Transactions of the Twelfth*

Symposium: Care of the Professional Voice. New York, NY: The Voice Foundation; 1984:297–301.

6. Tapia RG, Pardo J, Marigil M, Pacio A. Effects of the laser upon Reinke's space and the neural system of the vocalis muscle. In: Lawrence VL, ed. *Transactions of the Twelfth Symposium: Care of the Professional Voice.* New York, NY: The Voice Foundation; 1984:289–291.

7. Durkin GE, Duncavage JA, Toohill RJ, et al. Wound healing of true vocal cord squamous epithelium after CO_2 laser ablation and cup forceps stripping. *Otolaryngol Head Neck Surg.* 1986;95(3 Pt 1):273–277.

8. Motta G, Villari G, Motta G Jr, et al. The CO_2 laser in the laryngeal microsurgery. *Acta Otolaryngol Suppl* (Stockholm). 1986;433:1–30.

9. Bennett S, Bishop SG, Lumpkin SM. Phonatory characteristics following surgical treatment of severe polypoid degeneration. *Laryngoscope.* 1989;99(5):525–532.

10. Shapshay SM, Wallace RA, Kveton JR, et al. New microspot micromanipulator for carbon dioxide laser surgery in otolaryngology. Early clinical results. *Arch Otolaryngol Head Neck Surg.* 1988;114(9):1012–1015.

11. Shapshay SM, Rebeiz EE, Bohigan RK, Hybels RL. Benign lesions of the larynx: should the laser be used? *Laryngoscope.* 1990;100(9):953–957.

12. Krespi YP, Meltzer CJ. Laser surgery for vocal cord carcinoma involving the anterior commissure. *Ann Otol Rhinol Laryngol.* 1989;98(2):105–109.

13. Shapsay SM, Hybels RL, Bohigian RK. Laser excision of early vocal cord carcinoma: indications, limitations, and precautions. *Ann Otol Rhinol Laryngol.* 1990;99(1):46–50.

14. Eckel HE, Thumfart WF. Vorläufige Ergebnisse der endolaryngealen Laserresektionen von Kehlkopfkarzinomen. *HNO.* 1990;38(5):179–183.

15. Thumfart WF, Eckel HE. Endolaryngeale Laserchirurgie zur Behandlung von Kehlkopfkarzinomen. Das aktuelle Kölner Konzept. *HNO.* 1990;38(5):174–178.

16. Hofler H, Bigenzahn W. Die Stimmqualität nach CO_2-Laserchordektomie. *Laryngol Rhinol Otol* (Stuttg). 1986;65(11):655–658.

17. Ossoff RH, Matar SA. The advantages of laser treatment of tumors of the larynx. *Oncology* (Huntingt). 1988;2(9):58–61, 64–65.

18. Haraf DJ, Weichselbaum RR. Treatment selection in T_1 and T_2 vocal cord carcinomas. *Oncology* (Huntingt). 1988;2(10):41–50.

19. Shapshay SM, Ruah CB, Bohigian RK, Beamis JF Jr. Obstructing tumors of the subglottic larynx and cervical trachea: airway management and treatment. *Ann Otol Rhinol Laryngol.* 1988;97(5 Pt 1):487–492.

20. Tate LP, Newman HC, Cullen JM, Sweeney C. Neodymium (Nd):YAG laser surgery in the equine larynx: a pilot study. *Lasers Surg Med.* 1986;6(5):473–476.

21. Meyer S. Gerhard Meyer-Schwickerath. In: *Neue Deutsche Biographie.* vol 17. Berlin: Duncker & Humblot. 1994:372–373, 384–385.

22. Schawlow AL, Townes CH. Infrared and optical masers. *Phys Rev.* 1940;112:1940–1949.

23. Maiman TH. Stimulated optical radiation in rub. *Nature.* 1960;87:493.

24. Patel CKN, Tien PK, Mcfee JH. CW high power CO2-N2-He laser. *Appl Phys Lett.* 1965;7:290–292.

25. Yahr WZ, Strully J. Blood vessel anastomosis by laser and other biomedical applications. *J Assoc Advance Med Instrument.* 1966;1(2):1–4.

26. Jako GJ. Laser surgery of the vocal cords, *Laryngoscope.* 1972;82:2204–2216.

27. Strong MS, Jako GJ. Laser surgery in the larynx. Early clinical experience with continuous CO2 laser. *Ann Otol Rhinol Laryngol.* 1972;81:791–798.

28. Strong MS, Jako GJ, Polanyi T, Wallace RA. Laser surgery in the aerodigestive tract. *Am J Surg.* 1973;126:529–533.

29. Stahle J, Hogberg L. Laser and the labyrinthe. Some preliminary experiments on pigeons. *Acta Otolaryngol.* 1965;60:367–373.

30. Stahle J, Hogberg L, Engstrom B. The laser as a tool in inner-ear surgery. *Acta Otolaryngol.* 1972;73:27–37.

31. Sataloff J. Experimental use of the laser in otosclerotic stapes. *Arch Otolaryngol.* 1967;85:614–616.

32. Sultan R, Marinov V, Falo Kh. [The role of the laser in gastrointestinal surgery.] *Khirurgiia* (Sofiia). 1989;42(2):15–19. Bulgarian.

33. Perkins RC. Laser stapedotomy for otosclerosis. *Laryngoscope.* 1980;90:228–240.

34. Carruth JAS, McKenzie AL. Preliminary report of a pilot study of photoradiation therapy for the treatment of superficial malignancies of the skin, head and neck. *Eur J Surg Oncol.* 1985;11:47–50.

35. Anderson RR, Parrish JA. Microvasculature can be selectively damaged using dye lasers: a basic theory and experimental evidence in human skin. *Laser Surg Med.* 1987;1:263–276.

36. Cohen JT, Koufman JA, Postma GN. Pulsed-dye laser in the treatment of recurrent respiratory papillomatosis of the larynx. *Ear Nose Throat J.* 2003;83(8):558.

37. Zeitels SM, Franco R, Dailey SH, Burns JA, Hillman RE, Anderson RR. Office-based treatment of glottal dysplasia and papillomatosis with the 585-nm pulsed dye laser and local anesthesia. *Ann Otol Rhinol Laryngol.* 2004;113(4):265–275.

38. Franco RA Jr, Zeitels SM, Farinelli WA, et al. 585-nm pulsed dye laser treatment of glottal dysplasia. *Ann Otol Rhinol Laryngol.* 2003;112(9):751–758.

39. Mihashi S. [The carbon dioxide laser surgery.] *Nippon Jibiinkoka Gakkai Kaiho.* 1975;78;1244–1288.

40. Mihashi S, Jako G, Incze J, et al. Laser surgery in otolaryngology: interaction of CO2 laser and soft tissue. *Ann N Y Acad Sci.* 1976;267:263–294.

41. Hirano M, Mihashi S, Shin T, Nakajima TA. [CO2 laser apparatus for surgery.] *Nippon Jibinkoka Gakkai Kaiho.* 1979;82;34–39.

42. Hunton J, Oswal VH. Metal tube anaesthesia for ear, nose and throat carbon dioxide laser surgery. *Anaesthesia.* 1985;40:1210–1212.

43. Hunton J, Oswal VH. Anaesthesic management for carbon dioxide laser surgery in tracheobronchial lesions. *Anaesthesia.* 1987;42:1222–1225.

44. Sanders R. Two ventilating attachments for bronchoscopes. *Del Med J.* 1967;39:170–182.

45. Lee ST. A ventilating laryngoscope for inhalation anaesthesia and augmented ventilation during laryngoscopic procedures. *Br J Anaesth*. 1972;44:874–878.

46. Miyasaka K, Sloan IA, Froese AB. An evaluation of the jet injector (Sanders) technique for bronchoscopy in pediatric patients, *Can Anaesth Soc J*. 1980;27:117–124.

47. Carden E, Galido J. Foot-pedal control of jet ventilation during bronchoscopy and microlaryngeal surgery. *Anesth Analg*. 1975;54:405–406.

48. Mayne A, Joucken K, Collard E, Randour P. Intravenous infusion of propofol for induction and maintenance of anesthesia during endoscopic carbon dioxide laser ENT procedures with high frequency jet ventilation. *Anaesthesia*. 1988;43:97–100.

49. Isshiki N, Tanabe M, Ishizaka K, Board C. Clinical significance of asymmetrical tension of the vocal cords. *Ann Otol Rhinol Laryngol*. 1977;86:58–66.

50. Tucker HM. Anterior commissure laryngoplasty for adjustment of vocal fold tension. *Ann Otol Rhinol Laryngol*. 1985;94:498–501.

51. Abitbol J. *Atlas of Laser Voice Surgery*. San Diego, Calif: Singular Publishing Group; 1995:300–335.

52. Benninger MS. Microdissection on microspot CO_2 laser for limited vocal fold benign lesions: a prospective randomized trial. *Laryngoscope*. 2000;110(suppl 92):1–17.

53. Sataloff RT, Spiegel JR, Heurer RJ, et al. Laryngeal mini-microflaps: a new technique and reassessment of the microflap saga. *J Voice*. 1995;9:198–204.

54. Remacle M, Lawson G, Watelet JB. Carbon dioxide laser microsurgery of benign vocal fold lesions: indications techniques, and results in 251 patients. *Ann Otol Rhinol Laryngol*. 1999,108:156–164.

55. Zeitels SM. Laser versus cold instruments for microlaryngoscopic surgery. *Laryngoscope*. 1996,106:545–552.

85

Structural Abnormalities of the Larynx

Robert Thayer Sataloff

This chapter discusses selected common and/or important structural abnormalities of the larynx that may affect the voice. There are many others, of course; but those discussed in this chapter have been selected for their relevance to professional singers and actors or because of their incidence, unusual presentation, or special rehabilitation problems. A few selected structural abnormalities and their surgical treatment are discussed in subsequent chapters. This chapter briefly addresses principles and selected details of nonsurgical treatments.

Vocal Nodules

Vocal fold nodules are ordinarily caused by voice abuse. Normally, they are bilateral, fairly symmetrical, solid benign masses at the junctions of the anterior and middle thirds of the vocal folds (Figs 85–1, 85–2, 85–3). Functionally, this is the midpoint of the musculomembranous portion of the vocal fold, the area known as the "striking zone." It is the area of maximal excursion and most forceful contact during phonation. Typically, these whitish masses increase the mass and stiffness of the vocal fold cover, interfering with the vibration and causing hoarseness and breathiness. They may be fibrotic, and thickening or reduplication of the basement membrane is common (Dr. Steven Gray, personal communication, June 1995). These and other consequences of vocal fold trauma are discussed more fully in chapter 10. Occasionally, laryngoscopy reveals asymptomatic vocal fold nodules that do not appear to interfere with voice production. In such cases, the nodules should not be treated surgically. Some famous and successful singers have had untreated vocal nodules. However, in most cases, nodules are associated with hoarseness, breathiness, loss of range, and vocal fatigue. They may be due to abuse of the voice during speaking or singing. Caution must be exercised in diagnosing small nodules in patients who have been singing actively. Many singers develop bilateral, symmetrical, soft swellings in the striking zone following heavy voice use. There is no evidence to suggest that singers with such "physiologic swellings" are predisposed toward development of vocal nodules. At present, the condition is generally considered to be within normal limits. The physiologic swelling usually disappears during 24 to 48 hours of rest from heavy voice use. Care must be taken not to frighten the patient or embarrass the physician by misdiagnosing physiologic swelling as vocal nodules. Strobovideolaryngoscopy is essential for accurate diagnosis of vocal nodules.[1-5] Without strobovideolaryngoscopy, vocal fold cysts and other lesions will be misdiagnosed routinely as vocal nodules. Because the conditions respond differently to treatment, accurate differentiation is essential.

Nodules carry a great stigma among singers and actors, and the psychological impact of the diagnosis should not be underestimated. When nodules are present, the patient should be informed with the same gentle caution used in telling a patient that he or she has cancer. Voice therapy always should be tried as the initial therapeutic modality and will cure the vast majority of patients, even if the nodules look firm and have been present for many months or years. Even for those who eventually need surgical excision of their nodules, preoperative voice therapy is essential to help prevent recurrence of the nodules.

Surgery for vocal fold nodules should be avoided whenever possible and should virtually never be performed without an adequate trial of expert voice therapy including patient compliance with therapeutic suggestions. A minimum of 6 to 12 weeks of observa-

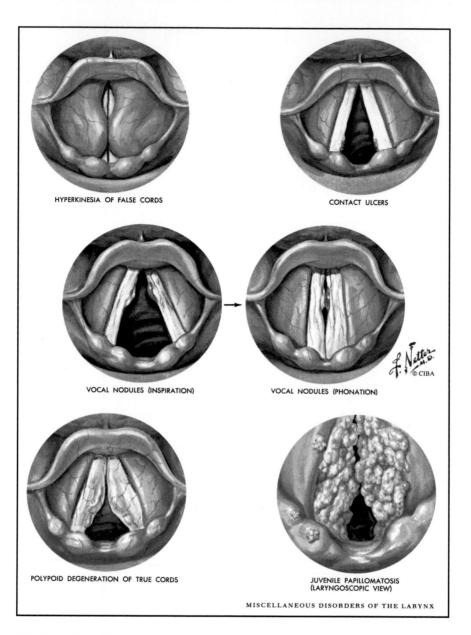

HYPERKINESIA OF FALSE CORDS

CONTACT ULCERS

VOCAL NODULES (INSPIRATION)

VOCAL NODULES (PHONATION)

POLYPOID DEGENERATION OF TRUE CORDS

JUVENILE PAPILLOMATOSIS
(LARYNGOSCOPIC VIEW)

MISCELLANEOUS DISORDERS OF THE LARYNX

Fig 85–1. Miscellaneous disorders of the larynx. Hyperkinesia of the false vocal folds is seen in hyperfunctional voice abuse. In its more severe form, phonation may actually occur primarily with the false vocal folds. This condition is known as *dysphonia plica ventricularis.* Contact ulcers occur in the posterior portion of the vocal folds, generally in the cartilaginous portion. *Vocal fold nodules* are smooth, reasonably symmetrical benign masses at the junction of the anterior and middle thirds of the vocal folds. Although Netter's classic drawing is labeled "vocal nodules," the mass on the right appears hemorrhagic in origin. It may be a hemorrhagic cyst or fibrotic hematoma from hemorrhage of one of the prominent blood vessels on the superior surface. The mass on the left has the typical appearance of a reactive vocal nodule. The illustration of vocal nodules during phonation shows failure of glottic closure anterior and posterior to the masses. This is responsible for the breathiness heard in the voices of patients with nodules. Polypoid degeneration, *Reinke's edema,* has a typical floppy "elephant ear" appearance. *Juvenile papillomatosis* is a viral disease. This disease and its treatment frequently result in permanent disturbance of the voice. (From The larynx. In: *Clinical Symposia.* Summit, NJ: CIBA Pharmaceutical Company; 1964:16[3]: Plate VIII. Copyright 1964 Icon Learning Systems, LLC, a subsidiary of MediMedia USA, Inc. Reprinted with permission from ICON Learning Systems, LLC, illustrated by Frank Netter, MD. All rights reserved.)

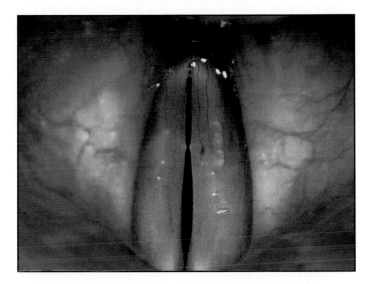

Fig 85–2. Typical appearance of vocal nodules.

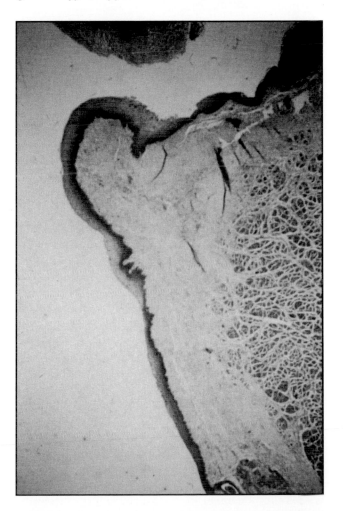

Fig 85–3. Typical histological appearance of a vocal fold nodule. The lesion is sessile and involves the epithelium and superficial layer of the lamina propria. The lesion contains collagenous fibers and edema. Intermediate and deep layers of the lamina propria are not involved. (Courtesy of Minoru Hirano, MD.)

tion should be allowed while the patient is using therapeutically modified voice techniques under the supervision of a speech-language pathologist and ideally a singing voice specialist. Proper voice use rather than voice rest (silence) is correct therapy. It has been recognized for many years and is effective in curing vocal nodules.[1,2,4,6-19] In our hands, nodules are cured by therapy alone in more than 90% of cases. However, this success rate depends on accurate diagnosis (eg, differentiating nodules from cysts), which cannot be accomplished without strobovideolaryngoscopy.[20,21]

Vocal nodules in children represent a special case. There are differing opinions on management, and especially on the efficacy of voice therapy. In the United States, the consensus has been that nodules should generally not be operated on until after puberty. In the author's opinion, children with vocal nodules should be treated, especially if they are bothered by their dysphonia. Dysphonia commonly results in teasing by other children, exclusion from activities such as plays and choirs, and other hardships that should not be allowed to mar childhood. Treatment begins with accurate diagnosis. Stroboscopy can be performed easily on most children over the age of 6, and we have used this diagnostic technique successfully on children as young as 6 months. Once it is clear that the masses are nodules rather than cysts, treatment should start with voice therapy. Successful therapy generally requires treating the whole family, not just the child. Frequently, voice abuses are learned behavior. The patient should be instructed to monitor the vocal behavior of other family members (gold stars for mom when she doesn't yell) just as other family members help monitor his or her vocalization and remind the child about proper voice use and avoidance of abuse. If the voice therapy results in behavioral modification and proper voice use is carried over into daily life but the nodules persist and symptoms remain disturbing, surgical excision is reasonable. If the child is close to puberty and not terribly disturbed by the phonatory quality, waiting until after voice mutation is also reasonable and often results in spontaneous voice improvement. It should be noted that there may be at least a theoretical advantage to operating on younger children, although it has not been tested or even explored clinically. Hirano has shown that the layered structure of the vocal ligament (layered structure of the lamina propria)[22] does not begin to develop until approximately 6 to 8 years of age. One might suspect, then, that the risk if scarring and permanent dysphonia might be lower if surgery were performed prior to that time. However, this notion must be considered purely speculative. Permanent destruction of voice quality is not a rare complication of surgery on the vocal fold. Even after expert surgery, this may be caused by submucosal scarring, resulting in an adynamic segment along the vibratory margin of the vocal fold. This situation results in a hoarse voice with vocal folds that appear normal with regular light, although under stroboscopic light the adynamic segment is obvious. There is no reliable cure for this complication. Consequently, even large, apparently fibrotic nodules of long standing should be given a chance to resolve without surgery. In some cases, the nodules remain but become asymptomatic, with voice quality returning to normal. Stroboscopy in these patients usually reveals that the nodules are on the superior surface rather than the leading edge of the vocal folds during proper, relaxed phonation (although they may be on the contact surface and symptomatic when hyperfunctional voice technique is used and the larynx is forced down).

Vocal Fold Cysts

Vocal fold cysts are generally unilateral, although they can cause contact swelling on the contralateral side (Fig 85–4). They may also be bilateral (Fig 85–5). They are frequently misdiagnosed as vocal nodules initially. Cysts commonly protrude onto the vibratory margin (Fig 85–6), increase the mass of the cover, and sometimes increase stiffness (particularly when they were associated with hemorrhage initially; Fig 85–7). Whether they are unilateral or bilateral, they may cause bilateral vibratory interference. Usually, they involve the superficial layer of the lamina propria, but in uncommon cases they may be attached to the vocal ligament. Cysts are often caused by trauma that blocks a mucous gland duct. However, other etiologies are possible. Cysts may be congenital or acquired. Acquired cysts may have epithelial linings and can be glandular, ciliary, or oncolytic. Most are probably retention cysts and are filled with mucoid fluid. Congenital cysts are generally epidermoid, lined with squamous or respiratory epithelium (Fig 85–8). They may contain caseous material. Cysts are generally easy to differentiate from nodules by strobovideolaryngoscopy. This examination reveals the mass to be fluid-filled. A cyst should also be suspected when "nodules" are diagnosed and only one side resolves after voice therapy. The persistent lesion frequently turns out to be a fluid-filled cyst. Cysts generally require surgery, although the patient should undergo a trial of voice therapy first. The author generally tentatively schedules surgery to be performed 4 to 6 weeks after the time of diagnosis, with a preoperative examination following the trial of voice therapy. Occasion-

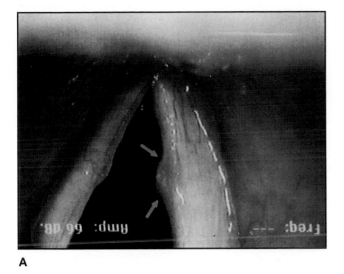

A

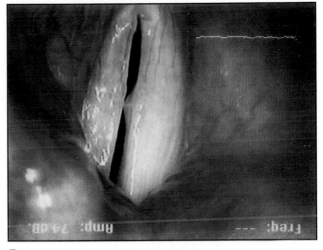

B

Fig 85–4. Videoprint showing right vocal fold fluid-filled cyst (*white arrows*) and a left reactive nodule in abduction (**A**) and adduction (**B**), in a 52-year-old singing teacher and former Metropolitan Opera lead singer. In adduction, the shape of the mass is slightly different from that in abduction, due to shifting the fluid within the mass. Both masses required microsurgical removal, although in some cases the reactive mass will resolve following voice therapy and excision of the cyst.

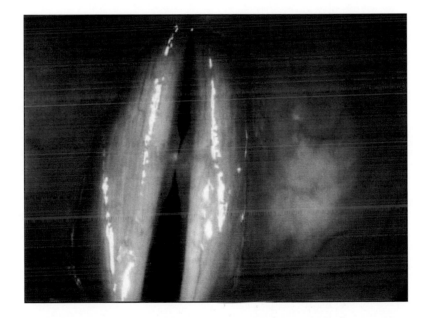

Fig 85–5. This 29-year-old female is a high school mathematics teacher, aerobics instructor, sales representative, cheerleader, and cheerleading coach. She has a 5-year history of hoarseness. Her voice worsened following extensive use. She had previously been told that she had vocal nodules. Strobovideolaryngoscopy revealed bilateral, slightly asymmetric, fluid-filled masses that deformed with contact. However, they were large enough to interfere with vibration and prevent glottic closure. The left mass was clearly a cyst or a soft reactive nodule. Voice therapy resulted in no significant improvement. The above videoprint was taken at the time of microlaryngoscopy. At the time of surgery, both masses were found to be fluid-filled cysts. She healed well after resection of both masses, and her voice is within normal limits.

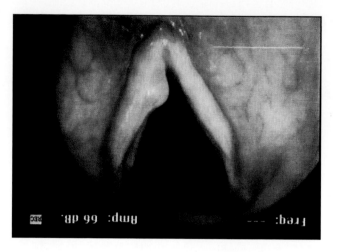

Fig 85–6. This 47-year-old professional popular singer has a 17-year history of hoarseness. In January 1994, he developed gradually worsening hoarseness, raspiness, and inability to sing. His vocal deterioration plateaued several months before our examination in August 1995. The videoprint reveals a left vocal cyst, which did not respond to voice therapy. The patient underwent excision of the left vocal fold cyst, which contained milky fluid. The cyst was removed with overlaying mucosa, but without disturbing any normal surrounding tissues. He recovered well and was able to resume his professional career.

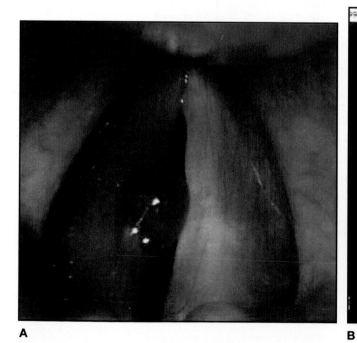

A

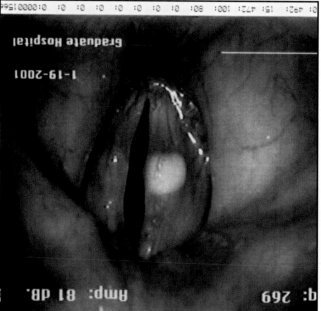

B

Fig 85–7. A. Videoprint showing left post-hemorrhagic vocal fold cyst and resolving hemorrhage with minimal contact-induced swelling of the right vocal fold. Following complete resolution of the hemorrhage, mild stiffness remained persistent anterior and posterior to the mass, but severe at the base of the mass. However, phonation improved to normal for this patient's purpose as a university professor and a lecturer. **B.** This figure shows the typical appearance of a right epithelial cyst involving the superior surface and vibratory margin.

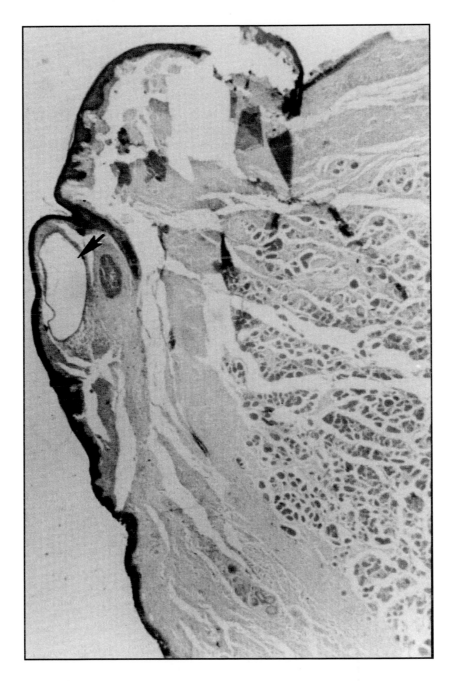

Fig 85–8. Typical histological appearance of a vocal fold cyst (*arrow*). It involves the superficial layer of the lamina propria and epithelium, probably extended into deeper layers. They generally have a squamous epithelial cyst wall. Cysts of epidermoid origin have caseous contents. Retention cysts are filled with mucoid material; and posthemorrhagic cysts contain evidence of blood products. (Courtesy of Minoru Hirano, MD.)

ally, the cyst disappears and does not recur or becomes asymptomatic. Although most diagnosed cysts occur on the vocal fold, it should also be recognized that cysts occur commonly on the ventricular fold and epiglottis, as well. Cysts in these areas are probably more common than appreciated, but they often go unrecognized because they are asymptomatic. Histologically, they are generally similar to acquired vocal fold cysts, although epiglottic cysts may also contain lymphoid stroma.

Vocal Fold Polyps

Many other structural lesions may appear on the vocal folds, of course, and not all respond to nonsurgical therapy. Polyps are usually unilateral, and they often have a prominent feeding blood vessel coursing along the superior surface of the vocal fold and entering the base of the polyps (Figs 85–1, 85–9, 85–10, 85–11, 85–12, 85–13, 85–14, 85–15). The etiology of vocal fold polyps often remains unknown. Some appear to be traumatic. Some are clearly preceded by localized vocal fold hemorrhage.

Polyps may be loose, gelatinous masses, fibrinoid, or hyaline. Polyps have also been classified as angiomatous, mucoid, and myxomatous. They are generally unilateral and may be extremely small, or in-

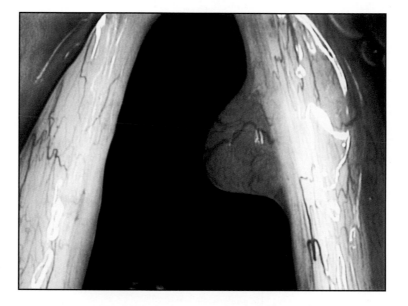

Fig 85–9. Intraoperative videoprint showing typical appearance of a sessile, unilateral polyp of the right vocal fold.

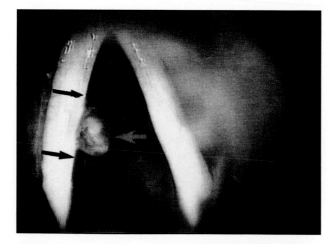 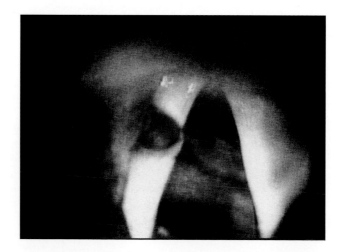

Fig 85–10. This figure was taken intraoperatively and shows (*left*) a pedunculated hemorrhagic polyp (*white arrow*), with prominent feeding vessel on the vibratory margin of the vocal fold (*straight black arrows*). The pedunculated nature of the lesion can be seen (*right*) as the lesion is displaced onto the superior surface of the vocal fold. (From *ENT J* 1993:72[7] with permission.)

Fig 85–11. Intraoperative videoprint showing right post-hemorrhagic vocal fold polyp with a vascular blush in its base anteriorly and with jagged vessels feeding it from anterior. There are also varicosities on the superior surface of the right vocal fold. The left vocal fold shows a varicosity and large ectasia on the superior surface, and a cyst on the left vibratory margin (partially obscured by the right polyp).

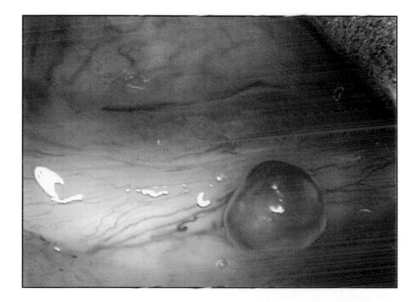

Fig 85–12. Left post-hemorrhagic vocal fold polyp as seen intraoperatively through a 70° telescope. The polyp is located on the vibratory margin. The metal laryngoscope can be seen anteriorly, and the laryngeal ventricle is visualized well above the vocal fold.

A

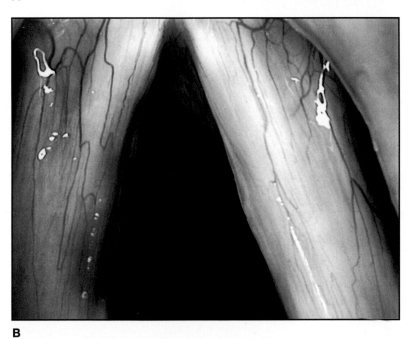

B

Fig 85-13. **A.** Some polyps are clearly associated with hemorrhage. Residual blood can be seen within the left vocal fold polyp, in a videoprint taken through a 70 degree laryngeal telescope. A feeding vessel along the vibratory also is seen clearly. Such vessels are often difficult to visualize from above, or using a 0 degree telescope. **B.** Even a broad-based sessile polyp that is inseparable from overlying epithelium can be excised without extensive mucosal resection. This intraoperative photograph shows that the mucosal edges meet spontaneously almost completely, forming a fairly linear epithelial deficit. The indentation in the area of resection reflects dissection along the medial aspect of the lesion in an area that was adynamic preoperatively. No uninvolved tissue was disturbed. This approach is useful in many cases, although in some instances it is better to transect fibrotic tissue and leave a straight vocal fold edge.

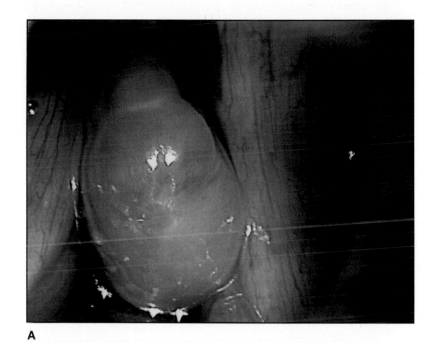

A

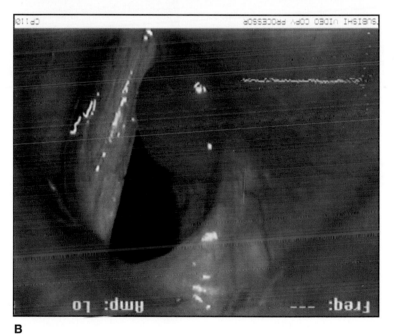

B

Fig 85–14. **A.** Although this is a large polyp, it is based on a relatively small area along the vocal fold. Consequently, excision involves a risk of scarring to only a small area of the vibratory margin. This risk is reduced further because of the amount of redundant mucosa seen anterior to the mass and the relatively enlarged Reinke's space. **B.** Polyp located on the right false vocal fold. When the mass was not in contact with the vocal folds, the voice was normal. As the mass enlarged slightly, it touched the superior surfaces of the vocal folds intermittently causing irregular dysphonia. Resecting a polyp from this region of the false vocal fold generally is not associated with a substantial risk of hoarseness.

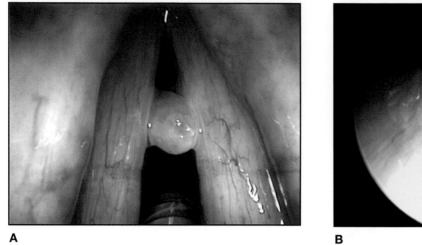

A

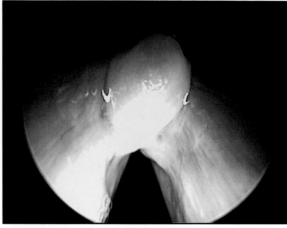

B

Fig 85–15. From above, this intraoperative videoprint shows a broad-based left vocal fold polyp partially obscuring a right vocal fold mass in a 42-year-old rabbi with a 1½- year history of gradually progressive dysphonia (**A**). A 70° laryngeal telescope (**B**) clarifies the relation between the right mass and the overlying left polyp. The right contact lesion was much more firm and fibrotic than the larger left polyp. Both lesions were removed, and the voice improved substantially.

volve an entire vocal fold. Larger polyps frequently extend into the subglottic area. The functional effect of polyps depends on whether they are unilateral or bilateral, sessile or pedunculated, symmetrical or asymmetrical, and situated on the margin or elsewhere. Functional effect depends also on the pathology. With edematous polyps, the mass of the cover layer may function as if it were decreased. If polyps contain blood and/or fibrosis, the mass is increased. Polyps may interfere with vibration unilaterally or bilaterally; or, in some cases, they may not interfere with vibration at all (if they are not located on the vibratory margin; Figs 85–15 and 85–16). Historical characteristics generally allow for the differentiation of polyps from nodules and cysts (Fig 85–16). However, it must be recognized that not all lesions that look clinically like polyps are simple, benign polyps. Some may be neoplastic (Figs 85–17, 85–18, 85–19).

In some cases, even sizable polyps resolve with relative voice rest and a few weeks of low-dose steroid therapy such as methylprednisolone 4 mg twice a day. However, most of them require surgical removal. If polyps are not treated, they may produce contact injury on contralateral vocal fold. Voice therapy should be used to ensure good relative voice rest and to avoid voice abusive behaviors before and after surgery.

"Contact" Granulomas and Vocal Process Ulcers

Granulomas usually occur on the posterior aspect of the vocal folds, often in or above the cartilaginous por-

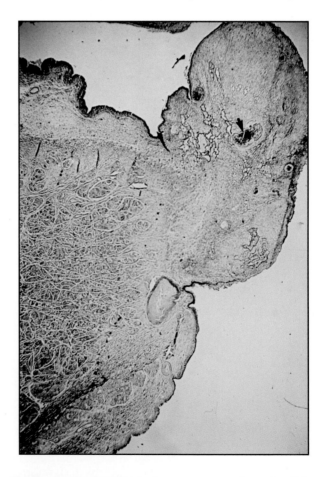

Fig 85–16. Typical histologic appearance of a polyp. It involves the epithelium and superficial layers of the lamina propria. Evidence of bleeding into the tissue is apparent (*arrow*), and hyaline degeneration, thrombosis, edema, collagen fibrous proliferation, and cellular infiltration are common. (Courtesy of Minoru Hirano, MD.)

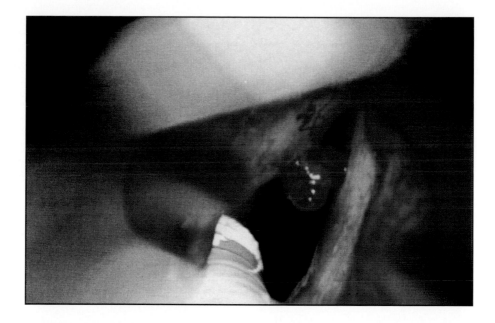

Fig 85–17. Intraoperative photograph from a 35-year-old male with a 6-month history of hoarseness. Although the lesion looks like a hemorrhagic polyp, histologic assessment revealed it to be a hemangioma. This was suspected intraoperatively, because of unusually profuse hemorrhage. The possibility of neoplasm should always be kept in mind, and biopsy should not be unduly delayed when a lesion fails to respond promptly to noninvasive therapy.

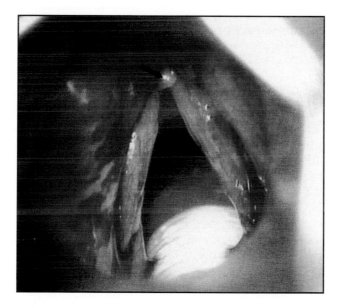

Fig 85–18. This 79-year-old female had a 3-month history of hoarseness. She has smoked at least one pack of cigarettes daily for 70 years. She has no history of throat pain or otalgia, and she denied dysphagia. The intraoperative videoprint above reveals a mass that might have been mistaken for a benign polyp (*arrow*). Erythema and fullness are present anteriorly. Actually, this "polyp" is the tip of a squamous cell carcinoma extending into the supraglottic and infraglottic regions, with cartilage invasion. It involves the true and false vocal folds bilaterally. The tumor was stage $T_4N_0M_0$.

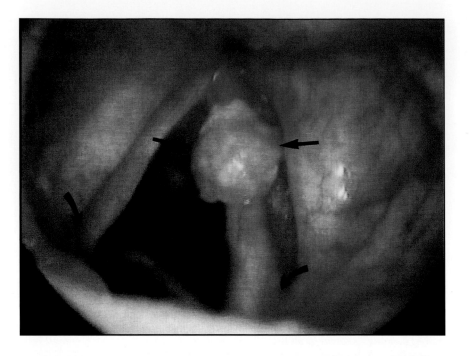

Fig 85–19. This videoprint shows an irregular, polypoid, right vocal fold mass (*arrows*). There is also arytenoid erythema associated with reflux. The arytenoids are not visible in this picture, but acid-induced erythema extending into the cartilaginous portion of the vocal folds can be seen (*curved arrows*). This patient had not smoked for more than 10 years. This pedunculated mass was $T_1N_0M_0$ well differentiated squamous cell carcinoma, which was excised with adequate margins. The patient is being monitored closely, and no further treatment is planned unless the tumor recurs (From *ENT J* 1994;73[8], with permission.).

tion (Figs 85–20, 85–21, 85–22, 85–23, 85–24, 85–25, 85–26, 85–27). Granulomas may be unilateral. They occur commonly on the medial surface of the arytenoids. Histopathologic evaluation reveals fibroblasts, collagenous fibers, proliferated capillaries, leukocysts, and sometimes ulceration. Thus, they are actually chronic inflammatory tissue, not true granulomas such as those seen in tuberculosis or sarcoidosis. Granulomas and ulcers in the region of the vocal process traditionally have been associated with trauma, especially intubation injury. However, they are also seen in young, apparently healthy professional voice users with no history of intubation or obvious laryngeal injury. Previous teachings have held that the lesion should be treated surgically but that the incidence of recurrence is high. In fact, the vast majority of granulomas and ulcerations (probably even those from intubation) are aggravated or caused by acid reflux; and voice abuse and misuse are associated commonly. Ylitalo has published an extensive review of granuloma, including its relationship to reflux.[23] In our experience, when the reflux is controlled and voice therapy is begun, the le-

sions usually resolve within a few weeks. If they do not, they should be removed for biopsy to rule out other possible causes. So long as a good specimen is obtained, the laser may be used in this surgery, because the lesions usually are not on the vibratory margin, and they are often friable. However, this author usually uses traditional instruments, wishing to avoid the third-degree burn caused by the laser in the treatment of this condition.

Occasionally, patients present with multiply recurrent granulomas, which may present even after excellent reflux control (including fundoplication), surgical removal including steroid injection into the base of the granuloma, and voice therapy. Medical causes other than reflux and muscle tension dysphonia must be ruled out, particularly granulomatous diseases including sarcoidosis and tuberculosis. When it has been established that the recurrent lesions are typical granulomas occurring in the absence of laryngopharyngeal reflux, the cause is almost always phonatory trauma. When voice therapy is insufficient to permit adequate healing, some of these uncommon and diffi-

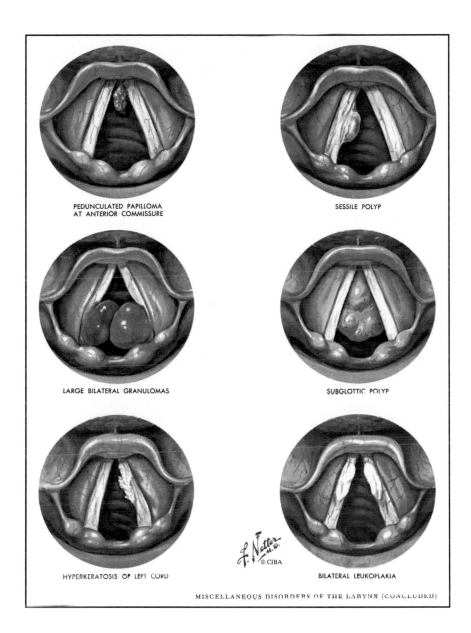

PEDUNCULATED PAPILLOMA
AT ANTERIOR COMMISSURE

SESSILE POLYP

LARGE BILATERAL GRANULOMAS

SUBGLOTTIC POLYP

HYPERKERATOSIS OF LEFT CORD

BILATERAL LEUKOPLAKIA

MISCELLANEOUS DISORDERS OF THE LARYNX (CONCLUDED)

Fig 85–20. Miscellaneous disorders of the larynx. An isolated papilloma such as that illustrated in the top left usually has less grave implications than the papillomatosis illustrated in Figure 85–1. Nevertheless, careful removal with a laser is appropriate. The broad-based sessile polyp illustrated has typically prominent vascularity at its base and along the superior surface of the vocal fold. The contact granulomas illustrated are considerably large than those shown in Figure 85–1. Even granulomas of this size sometimes resolve with antireflux therapy and low-dose steroids, although more often excision is required. Subglottic lesions such as the polyp illustrated usually can be removed safely without adverse effect on the voice. Potentially malignant or premalignant lesions are discussed elsewhere in this book. (From The larynx. In: *Clinical Symposia.* Summit, NJ: CIBA Pharmaceutical Company; 1964:16[3]: Plate IX. Copyright 1964 Icon Learning Systems, LLC, a subsidiary of MediMedia USA, Inc. Reprinted with permission from ICON Learning Systems, LLC, illustrated by Frank Netter, MD. All rights reserved.)

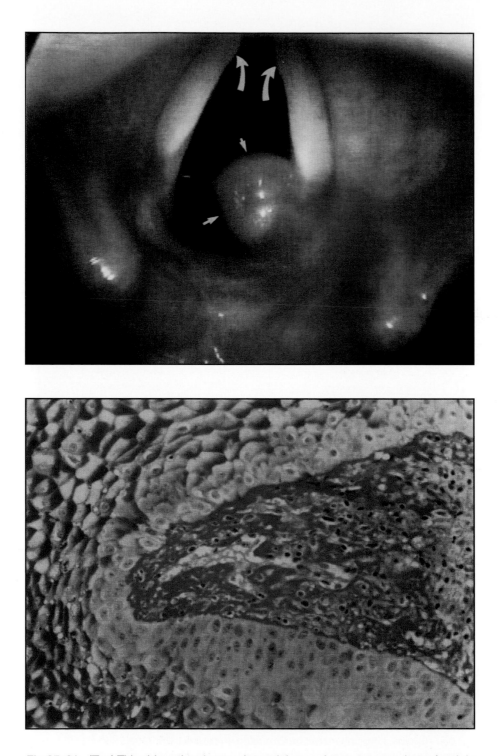

Fig 85–21. (*Top*) This videoprint shows a large right vocal process granuloma *(straight arrows)*, bilateral prenodular swellings *(curved arrows)*, and marked diffuse erythema of both regions consistent with gastroesophageal reflux laryngitis. (From *ENT J.* 1994;73[7], with permission.) (*Bottom*) Typical appearance of a laryngeal granuloma composed primarily of fibroblasts, proliferated capillaries, collagenous fibers, and leukocysts. An epithelial covering may or may not be present.

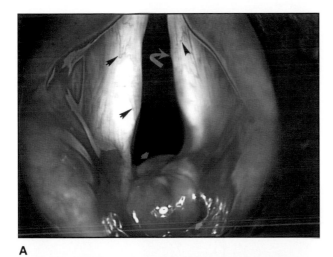

A

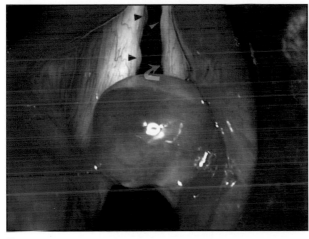

B

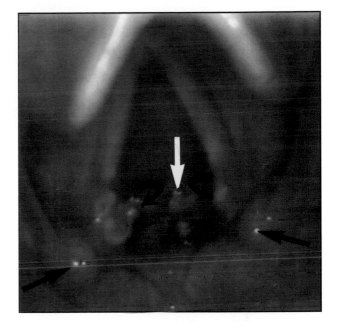

Fig 85–23. Videoprint from a 45-year-old male with recurrent laryngospasm. He had undergone tracheotomy prior to referral to the author (RTS). Strobovideolaryngoscopy revealed bilateral laryngeal granulomas (*curved arrows*). A Montgomery T tube (*white arrow*) was visible in the subglottic area. He also had marked erythema of his arytenoids (*straight arrows*) and posterior laryngeal mucosa consistent with reflux laryngitis. The reflux was confirmed by 24-hour pH monitor. Vigorous therapy was instituted. The laryngospasm, cough, and other reflux symptoms stopped. The granulomas resolved spontaneously, and the patient was decannulated. He has had no difficulty in the subsequent 7 years. (From *ENT J.* 1995;74[10], with permission.)

Fig 85–22. A. During gentle inspiration, a large right pyogenic granuloma fills the posterior glottis (*solid white arrow*) of this 42-year-old executive. The mass is based on a stalk attached to the base of the right vocal process. There are varicosities on the superior surfaces of both folds (*black arrows*), including a vessel that crosses toward the vibratory margin into a small cyst (*curved white arrow*) on the right. **B.** On expiration, the small cyst (*curved white arrow*) and its associated vessels are seen more easily. There are also contact swellings more anteriorly on the right (*white arrowhead*) and two left vocal fold cysts (*black arrowheads*). During exhalation, the large pyogenic granuloma is displaced superiorly out of the posterior glottis. The severe erythema of the posterior portion of the larynx is due to reflux. The pyogenic granuloma and cysts were excised. The granuloma recurred despite voice therapy and reflux control. Botulinum toxin was injected at the time of repeat excision, and he had no recurrence in the subsequent 4 years.

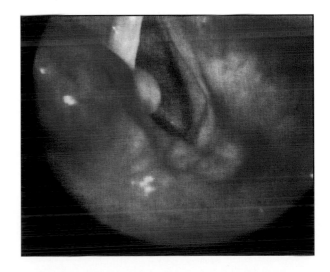

Fig 85–24. Typical appearance of a laryngeal granuloma occurring near the region of the medial surface of the arytenoids above the level of the glottis.

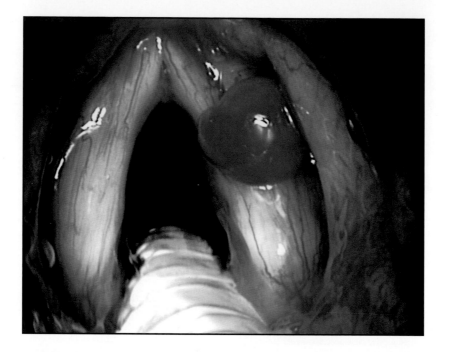

Fig 85-25. Although granulomas typically occur near the vocal process and medial surface of the arytenoid, they may be seen elsewhere. This videoprint reveals a granuloma arising from the right vocal false vocal fold and ventricle in an area of previous trauma. There is also varicosity anteriorly along the right vocal fold, as well as a small anterior web.

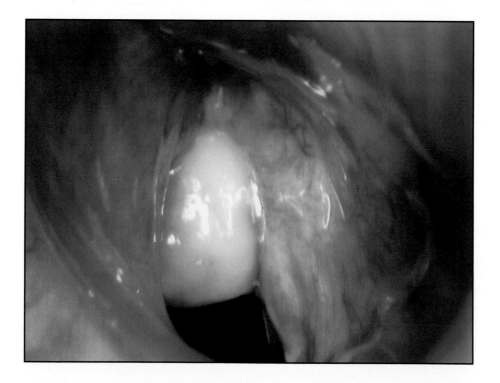

Fig 85–26. Granulomas also can occur in the musculomembranous portion of the vocal fold, although this is relatively uncommon. This large right granuloma occurred following removal of a mass from the right vocal fold. Excision of the granuloma was required.

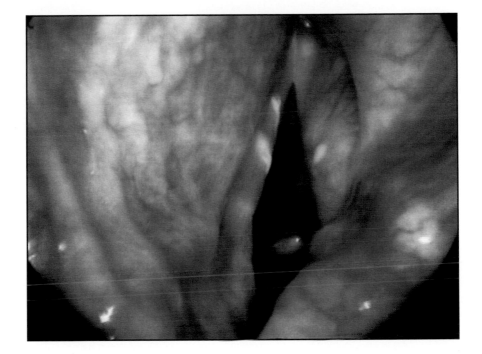

Fig 85–27. Granulomas may be iatrogenic. This videoprint shows a right Teflon granuloma that occurred in a 52-year-old male. He had right recurrent laryngeal nerve paresis. After reviewing all surgical options, he elected Teflon injection in 1988. He was the last patient for whom the author (RTS) utilized Teflon. His voice improved and stayed satisfactory for 2 years. Thereafter, he developed a Teflon granuloma. It was excised with a CO_2 laser resulting in satisfactory voice. However, he has had recurrent Teflon granulomas, requiring surgical re-excision six times over the ensuing 12 years. Teflon granuloma development even long after successful injection is one of the problems that led to the abandonment of this procedure for vocal fold medialization in the late 1980s.

cult patient problems can be solved by chemical tenotomy using Botulinum toxin. Although most other laryngologists have injected Botulinum toxin to the thyroarytenoid (TA) muscle, this author treats the lateral cricoarytenoid (LCA) muscle in most cases. If patients with multiply recurrent granulomas are observed closely using frame-by-frame analysis of strobovideolaryngoscopic images, or using high-speed video, many will make initial contact during adduction near the point of the vocal process, closing the rest of the posterior glottis slightly later. This is a lateral cricoarytenoid-dominant closing pattern, and it is different from the normal closing pattern in which LCA and interarytenoid muscle activity are balanced so that there is a broader area of initial contact. Weakening the LCA with Botulinum toxin prevents this forceful point contact and allows resolution of the granulomas. Usually, only 2.5 mouse units in LCA are necessary. Although this treatment approach has been effective, it is not recommended as initial therapy and is appropriate only for selected recalcitrant cases.

Reinke's Edema

Reinke's edema is characterized by mucoid, gelatinous fluid in the superficial layer of the lamina propria (Reinke's space), creating a typical floppy "elephant ear," polypoid appearance of the vocal fold (Figs 85–1, 85–28, 85–29, 85–30, 85–31). It is generally seen in adults. The condition is more common in women than in men.[24] It was named after Reinke who described the compartment now known as the superficial layer of the lamina propria while studying membraneous edema of the larynx.[25] Reinke's space is defined anteriorly by Broyle's ligament, posteriorly by the arytenoid cartilage; and it is superficial to the vocal ligament. It has been associated with increased subglottic driving pressure in aerodynamic studies by Zeitels et al.[26] It has been suggested that patients with mucosal irritation and muscle tension dysphonia are likely to develop Reinke's edema due to aerodynamically induced unopposed distention of the lamina propria and overlying epithelium.

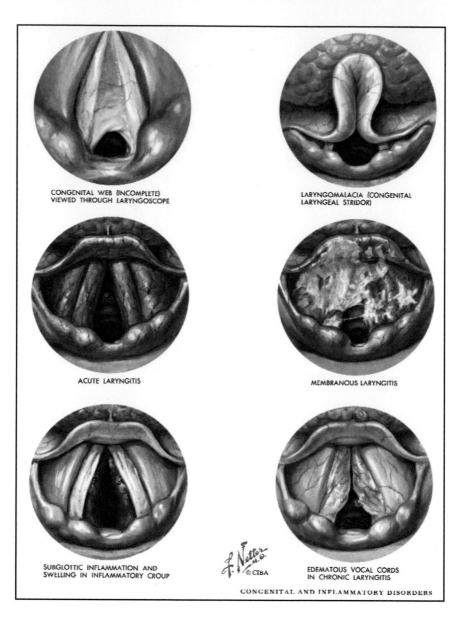

CONGENITAL WEB (INCOMPLETE) VIEWED THROUGH LARYNGOSCOPE

LARYNGOMALACIA (CONGENITAL LARYNGEAL STRIDOR)

ACUTE LARYNGITIS

MEMBRANOUS LARYNGITIS

SUBGLOTTIC INFLAMMATION AND SWELLING IN INFLAMMATORY CROUP

EDEMATOUS VOCAL CORDS IN CHRONIC LARYNGITIS

CONGENITAL AND INFLAMMATORY DISORDERS

Fig 85–28. Congenital and inflammatory disorders. The erythema, edema, and vascular congestion illustrated in the case of acute laryngitis are typical of a moderate to severe infection. With vocal folds this inflamed, performance could be justified only under the most extraordinary circumstances. The subglottic inflammation illustrated from a case of croup is similar to that seen in adults with severe respiratory infections, which are difficult to control in short periods of time, although in adult performers a lesser degree of inflammation, swelling, and airway compromise is usually present. The edematous vocal folds seen in chronic laryngitis have fluid collections in Reinke's space. Vocal folds with this appearance may be diagnosed as erythematous vocal folds, Reinke's edema, polypoid corditis, or polypoid degeneration. In some cases the edema reverses when the chronic irritant is removed. The congenital web illustrated is extensive. Smaller webs may occur congenitally or following trauma (including surgery). The illustration of laryngomalacia shows an omega-shaped epiglottis. This shape is common in normal larynges before puberty and may persist in some adults, making visualization difficult. Membranous laryngitis is uncommon and severe, necessitating cancellation of performance commitments. (From The larynx. In: *Clinical Symposia.* Summit, NJ: CIBA Pharmaceutical Company; 1964:16[3]: Plate VI. Copyright 1964 Icon Learning Systems, LLC, a subsidiary of MediMedia USA, Inc. Reprinted with permission from ICON Learning Systems, LLC, illustrated by Frank Netter, MD. All rights reserved.)

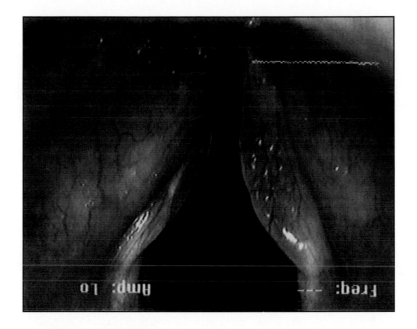

Fig 85–29. Typical appearance of Reinke's edema, worse on the right than on the left. The hypervascularity seen on the superior surface of the right vocal fold is associated with chronic Reinke's edema routinely. This patient was a smoker and had muscle tension dysphonia.

Reike's edema is uncommon in classical professional singers, but it is seen more frequently among pop singers, radio and sports announcers, attorneys, and salespeople. The association of Reinke's edema with voice abuse[27] and smoking[28] dates back more than a half century. Although the etiology is unproven, the condition is almost always related to cigarette smoking and/or other metabolic problems such as hypothyroidism and to voice abuse. Reinke's edema is also known as polypoid degeneration, polypoid corditis, and edematous hypertrophy. It is usually bilateral, involves the entire membranous vocal fold, and may be asymmetrical. Vibration is impaired bilaterally. The mass of the cover is increased, but stiffness is decreased. It causes a low, gruff, husky voice. If it does not resolve after smoking has been discontinued and all irritants (including voice abuse) have been removed, it may be treated surgically. Extreme care must be taken to be certain that the patient wants voice quality restored to normal. Reinke's edema is found commonly in sports announcers, businesswomen, female trial attorneys, and others who may like the low, masculine vocal quality associated with this pathology. When this is the case, and the appearance of the vocal folds does not suggest mailignancy, close follow-up rather than surgery is reasonable.

Unilateral Reinke's edema deserves special attention. The laryngologist should always seek an underlying cause. This condition has not been studied well, but it should be. The author (RTS) has seen malignancy present as unilateral Reinke's edema. More commonly, it occurs secondary to other vocal fold pathology. In some cases, the pathology is obvious, such as a contralateral lesion causing edema in the superficial layer of lamina propria induced by vocal fold contact. However, even more commonly, the pathology is subtler. In the author's (RTS) experience, unilateral Reinke's edema is usually due to vocal paresis, commonly involving the superior laryngeal nerve. The paresis may be on the ipsilateral or contralateral side. Koufman has made similar observations (James A. Koufman, MD, personal communication, 2000) and has termed localized compensatory Reinke's edema that develops in response to paresis a "paresis podule."

Vocal Fold Hemorrhage

Hemorrhage in the vocal folds and mucosal disruption (Fig 85–32) are contraindications to singing, acting, or speaking. When these are observed, the therapeutic course initially includes strict voice rest in addition to correction of any underlying disease. Vocal fold hemorrhage is of such importance that it is discussed in detail in chapter 86.

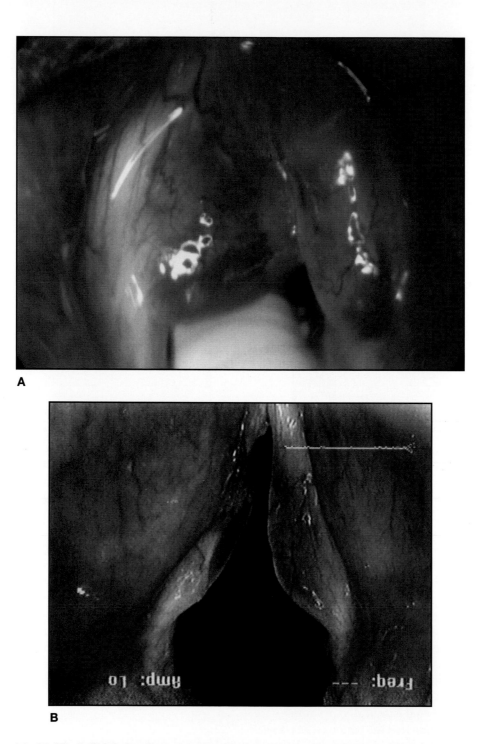

Fig 85-30. A. Reinke's edema can sometimes be severe enough to cause not only dysphonia but also stridor, and occasionally airway obstruction. Surprisingly, the patient whose vocal folds are pictured had a low, masculine voice (she is female), but denied airway difficulties. **B.** This videoprint shows typical, bilateral Reinke's edema. This condition is most often seen in smokers, but it is also often associated with reflux, voice abuse, and sometimes hypothyroidism.

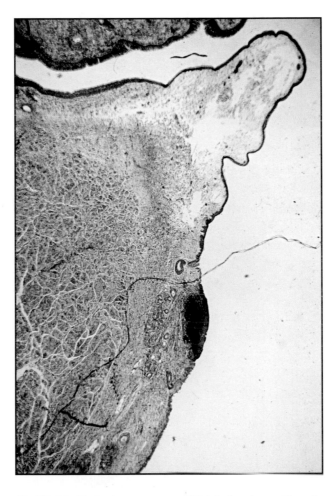

Fig 85–31. Typical appearance of Reinke's edema. There is edema in the superficial layer of the lamina propria. Note that the lesion does not display degeneration, hypertrophy, or inflammation. (Courtesy of Minoru Hirano, MD.)

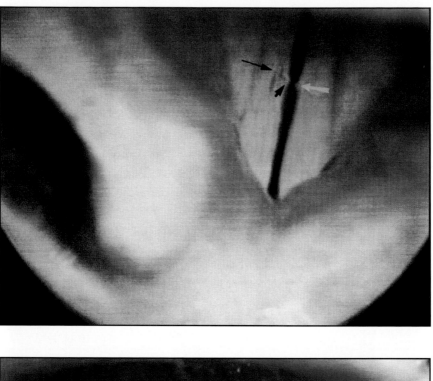

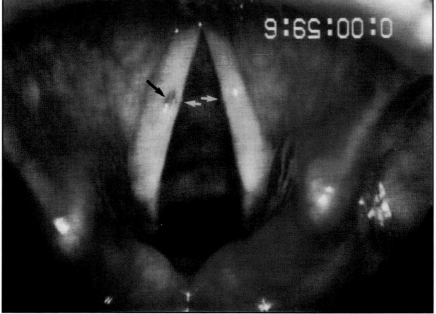

Fig 85–32. Videoprint from a 36-year-old professional singer who developed sudden hoarseness while coughing. Strobovideolaryngoscopy (*top*) revealed an acute right vocal fold tear (*white arrow*) and new left vocal fold varicosities with a surrounding blush of resolving mucosal hemorrhage (*black arrows*) and a small left vibratory margin mass. Re-examination 3 months later (*bottom*) showed smaller residual bilateral vocal fold masses (*white arrows*) and a persistent area of raised, ectatic/varicose vessels (*black arrow*). There was also mild stiffness in the region where the left vocal fold hemorrhage had occurred. (From *ENT J.* 1994;73[9], with permission.)

Sulcus Vocalis

Sulcus vocalis is a groove in the surface of the membranous portion of the vocal fold, usually extending throughout its length (Figs 85–33, 85–34). The lesion is usually bilateral. In sulcus vocalis, the epithelium invaginates through the superficial layer of the lamina propria and adheres to the vocal ligament. This results in a groove running longitudinally along the vocal fold. The apparent groove is actually a sac lined with stratified squamous epithelium, and hyperkeratosis is common near the deepest aspects of the sac or pocket. Some authors believe this represents an open epidermal cyst. There are a deficiency of capillaries and an increase in collagenous fibers in the region of the sulcus. Sulcus vocalis increases the stiffness of the cover layer and is often associated with hoarseness, breathiness, and decreased vocal efficiency. However, it may be asymptomatic if it occurs below the contact edge. The mass of the cover layer is reduced. Invaginated cover layer may adhere to the vocal ligament, causing increased stiffness.

Pseudosulcus vocalis and *sulcus vergeture* may occur in patients with similar dysphonia. Sulcus vergeture has similar appearance, but is not a true sulcus vocalis. Sulcus vergeture is caused by atrophic epithelial changes along the medial margin of the vocal fold. It is often also associated with a bowed appearance. Usually, the superior edge of the groove appears quite mobile, but the inferior edge is generally stiff. The superior layer of the lamina propria is usually deficient, and the epithelium may be closely apposed to the vocal ligament; but it is an atrophic depression of epithelium

rather than an invagination of variable thickness and scattered hyperkeratosis, as seen in a true sulcus vocalis. The term pseudosulcus vocalis often is used interchangeably with sulcus vergeture but actually is a different entity. Pseudosulcus is a longitudinal groove that may appear similar to sulcus vocalis or sulcus vergeture, except that it may extend beyond the limit of the musculomembranous portion of the vocal fold, involving the cartilaginous portion, as well. Commonly, it is associated with chronic inflammation and edema, usually caused by laryngopharyngeal reflux. Pseudosulcus vocalis is managed by treating the underlying reflux and any other related conditions. Treatment of sulcus vocalis is controversial and is discussed elsewhere in this book.

Fig 85–34. Histologically, sulcus vocalis involves the superficial layer of the lamina propria. Dense, collagenous fibers with scant capillaries and thickened epithelium are common. The epithelium may adhere to the vocal ligament, but otherwise the transitional layer is uninvolved. (Courtesy of Minoru Hirano, MD.)

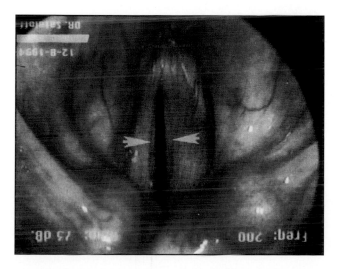

Fig 85–33. Typical appearance of bilateral sulcus vocalis (*arrows*).

A mucosal bridge involves a longitudinal separation between the mucosa covering the vibratory margin and the rest of the vocal fold (Fig 85–35). Mucosal bridges usually are congenital, but they may be posttraumatic. They have been associated with sulcus vocalis, as well. Ordinarily they are thin strips of mucosa (much less dramatic than the case shown in Fig 85–35), but they are challenging therapeutically. Removal of the mucosal bridge does not always result in improvement in vocal quality. In some cases, there is atrophy of the epithelial surface of the remaining vocal fold, which becomes the vibratory margin after the bridge has been removed. It is often not possible to predict phonatory outcome following excision, rendering intraoperative decision-making difficult.

Laryngeal Webs

Webs connecting the vocal folds may be congenital, or they may follow trauma (Fig 85–36). They are particularly likely to form when mucosa is disrupted in the anterior thirds of both vocal folds simultaneously, especially near the anterior commissure. They are dis-

cussed in greater detail in chapter 82 on Voice Surgery. Posterior glottic webs and stenosis also occur and are discussed in chapter 90.

Bowed Vocal Folds

The term *bowed vocal fold* is commonly applied when the vocal folds appear to be slightly concave and when glottic closure seems incomplete. Sulcus vergeture is present commonly, as well. Under stroboscopic light, many such cases reveal complete glottic closure but some thinning of the cover. Bowing of this sort is often associated with advanced age. In the past, many patients with this condition have been told either that it is incurable or that surgery to increase vocal fold bulk or tension is advisable. In the author's experience, neither statement is true for most patients. Unless there is neurological damage, the breathiness, slight hoarseness, and voice fatigue associated with apparent bowing in these patients can be corrected with specially designed voice therapy, ideally including both speaking and singing exercises. Such measures result in satisfactory improvement in the vast majority of cases.

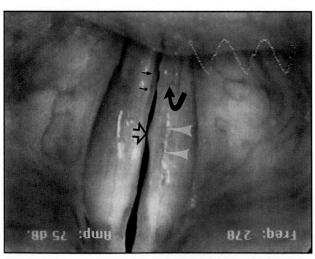

A

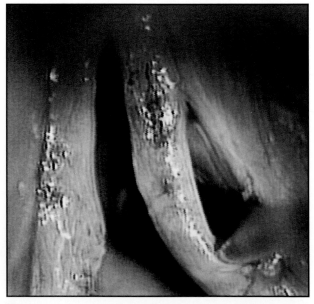

B

Fig 85–35. A. Strobovideolaryngoscopy of this 33-year-old singer revealed bilateral vocal fold stiffness, evidence of previous hemorrhage, left sulcus vocalis (*small arrows*), right vocal fold mass (*open arrow*), ectatic vessels on the superior surfaces of both vocal folds with a prominent vessel running at 90° to the vibratory margin (*curved arrow*), a small anterior glottic web (not shown), and muscular tension dysphonia. The importance of a line on the superior surface of the right vocal fold (*white arrowheads*) was not appreciated preoperatively. It appeared to be simply a light reflex. **B.** Intraoperatively, this was found to be the opening into an unusually large mucosal bridge. The mucosal bridge was removed, and autologous fat was injected laterally to medialize the right vocal fold and improve glottic closure.

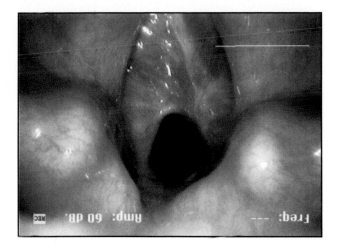

Fig 85–36. Typical appearance of an anterior glottic web.

True vocal fold bowing occurs with neurologic injury, particularly superior laryngeal nerve paralysis. This condition creates a deficit in longitudinal tension, causing the vocal fold to be at a lower level and to bow laterally. When the condition is unilateral and incomplete, voice therapy usually is helpful but rarely restores normalcy. When the superior laryngeal nerve is completely paralyzed, treatment is much more difficult. Collagen injections have been advocated for this situation, as have autologous fat injection, thyroplasty, and other procedures. Treatment for true vocal fold bowing due to vocal fold paralysis is discussed in chapter 82, Voice Surgery.

Laryngeal Trauma

Laryngeal trauma may cause many problems in addition to the webs discussed above. Trauma may be internal or external. It may result in vocal fold hemorrhage or mucosal tears, either of which may produce permanent scars. Trauma may also fracture the laryngeal skeleton, dislocate the arytenoids, or paralyze the laryngeal nerves. The principles of treatment in a professional voice user are the same as those for anyone else, and they are discussed in detail in chapter 88 and in other literature. A safe airway should be established. If intubation is required, immediate or early tracheotomy should be performed to minimize the risk of iatrogenic trauma of the vocal folds.

Whenever possible, a complete diagnostic voice evaluation including strobovideolaryngoscopy and objective voice analysis should be carried out to map and document the injury as well as possible. When there is a question as to whether vocal fold motion is impaired because of paralysis or mechanical causes,

laryngeal electromyography should be used. High-resolution axial and coronal CT scans are often extremely helpful. High resolution allows not only an excellent view of the larynx, but also clear visualization of the cricoarytenoid and cricothyroid joints.

When major injuries occur in professional voice users, it is advisable to involve a speech-language pathologist in the patient's care as soon as the medical condition permits, preferably prior to surgery. After surgery, the speech-language pathologist should participate in the patient's rehabilitation as soon as the patient is allowed to speak. Early involvement of the patient's professional voice teacher is also helpful, so long as the singing or acting teacher is interested in and comfortable with training of injured voices. Close collaboration among all members of the voice team is particularly important in rehabilitating such patients.

Cricoarytenoid and Cricothyroid Joint Injury

Injuries to the cricoarytenoid and cricothyroid are discussed in detail in chapter 89.

Papilloma

Treatment of laryngeal papilloma is discussed in chapter 57.

Precancerous Lesions

Precancerous lesions are discussed in detail in chapter 92. Two common terms are worthy of extra emphasis here, however. The term *leukoplakia* is used for abnormalities that look like white plaques. Patchy white areas may occur anywhere on the mucous membrane, including on the true vocal folds. Although leukoplakia is commonly thought of as premalignant, the term is descriptive and carries no histological implication. Leukoplakia may be caused by cancer, hyperkeratosis, tuberculosis, prolonged ulcerative laryngitis, and other conditions. However, because precancerous lesions and some cancers often present as leukoplakia, white lesions of this sort generally require biopsy if they do not resolve promptly. *Erythroplakic* lesions are red patches, and their implications are similar to those of leukoplakia.

Hyperkeratosis is an abnormality in which keratinized cells build up upon each other in a layered fashion. This causes a mass-effect, and it may cause increased stiffness of the vocal fold cover. It is considered precancerous. However, hyperkeratosis does not generally cause adynamic segments. If hyperkeratosis progresses to invasive carcinoma, the invading tumor essentially attaches the epithelium to the vocal ligament and muscle. This does produce an adynamic region. However, it must also be recognized that early superficial cancers may be present without causing adynamic regions on the vocal fold, so malignancy cannot be ruled out by strobovideolaryngoscopy alone.

Carcinoma of the Vocal Fold

When cancer (Fig 85–37) occurs in professional voice users, a great effort must be made to choose a treatment modality that preserves good voice function while providing the best chance for cure of the cancer. At present, there are no indisputable controlled studies on post-treatment vocal quality to help guide the laryngologist and patient. Initially, it seems as if radiation therapy is "obviously" better for vocal quality than surgery. However, postradiation changes in the mucosa, lubrication, and muscle may be significant. Controlled studies comparing radiation with various surgical techniques are needed, and such studies must consider not only early results, but also vocal quality 5 and 10 years after the treatment. Laser surgery has become popular for treatment of selected vocal lesions including cancer. However, Hirano[22] has pointed out that "tissue is much thicker after laser surgery than after radiation therapy," and critical comparisons of surgery with laser versus traditional instruments also

need to be done. For advanced cancer, treatment in professional voice users varies little from that in other patients, as discussed in chapter 93.

Granular Cell Tumor

Granular cell tumor is a rare neoplasm that may involve the larynx (see Fig 85–38). The tumor can be mistaken easily for a laryngeal granuloma. However, it is important for laryngologists to recognize this neoplasm and treat it appropriately.[29]

Granular cell tumor is rare, usually benign neoplasm that can occur in various parts of the body. Granular cell tumors may be single or multiple. They are most commonly seen in black population and have slightly higher incidence in females. Half of all granular cell tumors occur in the head or neck, with 33% of these occurring in the tongue. Tumors of the larynx are rare, accounting for only 7 to 10% of all reported cases of granular cell tumor.[30] Granular cell tumors present generally between the third and sixth decades of life, with a mean age for laryngeal tumors of 34 years. More than 50% of laryngeal granular cell tumors involve the true vocal folds, but involvement of the arytenoid cartilages, anterior commissure, false vocal folds, subglottis, and posterior cricoid region has been reported.[31] In adults, the posterior portion of the true vocal folds and arytenoid areas are the most common laryngeal sites affected. Although pediatric granular cell tumors are rare, they tend to involve the anterior and subglottic areas.[30]

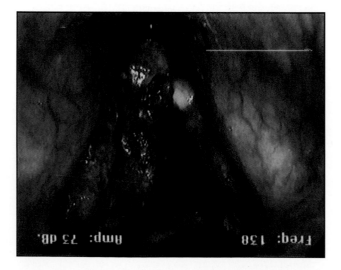

Fig 85–37. T1$_b$ squamous cell carcinoma involving both true vocal folds and the anterior commissure, but not involving cartilage or causing vocal fold fixation.

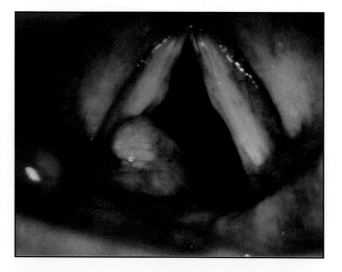

Fig 85–38. Left posterior granular cell tumor.

Granular cell tumors were first described by Abrikossoff in 1926.[32] He called them myoblastomas because he believed that the tumor was of skeletal muscle origin. Since then, it has become evident that the lesion arises more frequently in tissue other than muscle, and there is often a relationship between its cells and peripheral nerves.[31] The research of Sobel and Marquet using microscopic and cytochemical staining techniques[33] has not supported Abrikossoff's theory of muscle origin but rather suggests a derivation from undifferentiated mesenchymal cells or Schwann cells. Although the cause remains unknown, inflammatory, degenerative, regenerative, and congenital etiologies have been proposed. Currently, granular cell tumors generally are accepted to be of neurogenic origin, although it continues to be difficult to confirm the neural origin of some granular cell tumors.[34]

There are two clinicopathologic forms of granular cell tumor in the upper aerodigestive tract. The congenital epulis form occurs in the gum pads of newborns. The nonepulis form is primarily a lesion found in adults. Over 1200 cases have been reported in the literature.[33] However, only 209 of these reported cases occurred in the larynx.[30,34-125]

Macroscopically, granular cell tumors are firm, sessile, and covered with mucosa that usually is intact. They are typically small (< 2 cm) and well circumscribed but not encapsulated.[30] A covering of pseudoepitheliomatous hyperplasia overlies the mucosa in 50 to 65% of granular cell tumors. This epithelial finding may lead to the misdiagnosis of squamous cell carcinoma when a shallow biopsy is performed.

Granular cell tumors are distinctive histologically. They are polymorphic and range from polyhedral-shaped cells to a bizarre spindle form. They have abundant pale-staining acidophilic and granular cytoplasm. Cell nuclei are small, densely chromatic, vesicular, and centrally located. The cytoplamic granules react positively to Sudan black B and also to periodic acid-Schiff (PAS). Myelinated nerve fibers commonly are found in granular cell tumors. Ultrastructurally, these tumors have many fragmented, dense cytoplasmic lysosomes that are responsible for the granularity seen by the light microscopy.[126]

The diagnosis of laryngeal granular cell tumor usually is made on the basis of its histopathology. A diagnosis rarely is established preoperatively unless granular cell tumors have occurred in other sites before the development of laryngeal symptoms.[125] Typically, the tumors are painless.[126] The most common presenting symptom is hoarseness, with some patients also reporting dysphasia, otalgia, stridor, or hemoptysis.[30] Larger tumors can present with breathing difficulty.[122] Some tumors also may be asymptomatic and discovered incidentally. Tumor growth usually is slow.[33]

The preferred treatment is local excision using a cold knife or laser. Larger lesions may require laryngofissure or laryngectomy.[30] Treatment usually is curative with a recurrence rate between 2 and 8%.[31] It is possible that some of these "recurrences" actually may be new primary lesions because multiple lesions in various parts of the body occur in approximately 10% of patients.[30] Granular cell tumors are radio-resistant, and therefore radiation therapy generally is not indicated.

Although the literature states that a maximum of 3% of laryngeal granular cell tumors may be malignant, there is actually only one reported case[31] of the 209 (including this study) that the authors have identified. This suggests 0.6% incidence of malignancy in laryngeal granular cell tumors. Considering all sites, only 33 malignant granular cell tumors have been reported, and only 6 of these were in the head and neck.[126] These tumors usually result in death within 2 years of diagnosis, and 5 of the 6 reported patients died within 5 years. Malignancy in granular cell tumor is notoriously difficult to diagnose. There are two types of malignancy in granular cell tumor.[127,128] The first type is histologically and biologically malignant. The second and more common type is biologically malignant but may be histologically impossible to differentiate from benign granular cell tumor. The malignant tumors are typically larger (often over 4 cm), invasive, and grow rapidly. Metastases may occur in regional lymph nodes, lungs, bones, and viscera; and metastasis to areas that are not ordinarily involved with multiple primary granular cell tumors is the only certain criterion for diagnosis of malignancy.[126] To date, the mean age of patients with malignant tumors is 48 years, 16 years older than the mean age of patients with benign tumors at the time of diagnosis.[129]

Granular cell tumors of the larynx are uncommon but not rare. It is important for all otolaryngologists to be familiar with this entity and current concepts in management. Complete surgical resection usually is possible, and in most cases, a serviceable voice can be preserved. Although the length of follow-up has varied substantially in the literature, the author recommends long-term surveillance, including clinical examination and periodic imaging using magnetic resonance imaging (MRI) with gadolinium, at least until additional study has established the natural history and recurrence patterns of granular cell tumor with greater certainty.

Chondroma and Chondrosarcoma

Cartilaginous tumors of the larynx are uncommon. When they occur, they are most likely to be chondromas or low-grade chonodrosarcomas. Three quarters of these cartilaginous tumors arise from the posterior lamina of the cricoid cartilage on the endolaryngeal surface.[130-133] Twenty percent of tumors or less involve the thyroid cartilage, and only about 10% of tumors involve the body of the arytenoids cartilage.[134] Laryngeal chondromas are extremely uncommon, although the true incidence is difficult to determine from the literature. Chondromas must be placed in a spectrum of cartilaginous lesions including chondroma, chondrometaplasia, chondrosarcoma, and cartilage within a lesion classified otherwise. Chondrosarcomas represent between 30 and more than 50% of cartilaginous tumors in the larynx.[132,135-137] Because the majority of laryngeal chondrosarcomas are histologically low grade and grow slowly, they are misdiagnosed commonly (clinically) as chondromas. Chondromas can occur in children or adults. In general, at the time of presentation they tend to be small (< 3 cm in diameter). Chondrosacomas are often larger than 3 cm in diameter and generally are found in adults in the sixth and seventh decades of life. There is a male-to-female preponderance of 3 or 4 to 1.[138] Most cartilaginous tumors arise below the level of the vocal folds. Dyspnea, stridor, and dysphonia are common presenting complaints. In addition to the usual presentations of condrosarcoma, Koufman has described chondrosarcoma of the cricoid cartilage (low grade) presentations as "arytenoids hypertelorism" (excessively wide spacing between the arytenoids cartilages). Treatment with hemicricoidectomy is usually sufficient, although laryngectomy may be required (Jaime Koufman, MD, personal communication, 2003).

Histologically, vascular invasion occurs with both benign chondromas and malignant chondrosarcomas. The differentiation is made based on the presence of many cells with plump nuclei or clumps of chromatin in malignant lesions.[139] The differentiation between chondromas and low-grade chondrosarcomas is difficult, and it is often useful to obtain a second opinion from a pathologist who is expert in these tumors. The increased cellularity and nuclear pleomorphism in high-grade chondrosarcomas make them more distinct. Chondrosarcomas metastasize by hematogenous spread, usually to the lungs, kidney, cervical spine, or as subcutaneous nodules; metastasis occurs in 8% of the cases.[140]

Diagnosis usually is made initially by CT scan. Chondromas typically show coarse calcifications in a smooth soft tissue mass. Chondromas are treated by surgical excision, as well. Low-grade chondrosarcomas usually are treated by conservative surgical excision, as well. Lavertu and Tucker found no difference between radical surgery and conservative surgery followed by salvage therapy.[136] Nevertheless, because

local occurrence rates are high and few cases are reported, optimal treatment remains uncertain. High-grade chondrosarcomas are treated by laryngectomy, as are anaplastic tumors, recurrent tumors, and tumors that have destroyed substantial amounts of the laryngeal skeleton.

Osteoma and Osteosarcoma

Osteomas are slow-growing benign neoplasms that form dense, sclerotic bone. They have been described only once in the larynx.[141]

Osteogenic sarcoma of the larynx is also an uncommon tumor.[142] Osteosarcoma will not be discussed in detail in this chapter. It is a potentially lethal tumor that requires aggressive therapy.

Lipoma

Lipoma of the larynx and hypopharynx is rare.[143] These benign fatty tumors can involve hypopharynx or larynx and can be misdiagnosed as laryngoceles, pharyngoceles, or retention cysts. MRI scan is helpful in defining the lesion and in recognizing the typical fatty tissue appearance of a lipoma. Only six cases of laryngeal lipoma have been reported in the literature, five of them in 2000 by Jungehülsing.[143]

Amyloidosis

Amyloidosis is a condition characterized by the accumulation of insoluble fibrillar protein (amyloid) in tissues and organs throughout the body. Some deposition processes are local and some are systemic. Of the several types of amyloidosis, nodular amyloidosis is most commonly found in the larynx and nasopharynx, as well as trachea and lungs.

An illustrative case was reported by Sataloff et al,[144] and is discussed here to highlight the nature of this condition. A 48-year-old basketball coach presented with a 2½-year history of progressive hoarseness, vocal fatigue, loss of high and low range, and pain on speaking. The problems were severe enough to cause his retirement from coaching. His otolaryngologists had diagnosed him recently with amyloidosis of the larynx. Histopathologic evaluation by H&E staining revealed a soft-tissue mass with normal surface squamous epithelium, chronic subepithelial inflammatory infiltrate, and diffuse eosinophilic intercellular deposits (some causing pressure necrosis of surrounding stroma) (Fig 85–39). Congo red dye stained sections showed the characteristic yellow and apple green

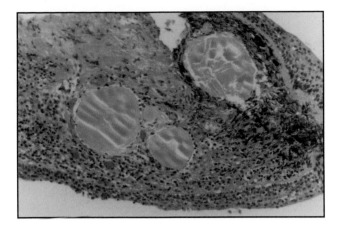

Fig 85–39. Amyloidosis showing normal surface epithelium, with subepithelial inflammatory infiltrate and eosinophilic intracellular deposits.

birefringence caused by cross-beta-pleated configuration of the amyloid fibrils (Fig 85–40).

He was referred to the author (RTS) for further treatment. A thorough system workup showed no evidence of amyloid elsewhere. Physical examination and videostroboscopy revealed a large left supraglottic mass (Fig 85–41) obscuring visualization of the anterior two thirds of the left vocal fold, with partial supraglottic obstruction of the airway and a good subglottic airway, despite evidence of a tracheal mass (Fig 85–42). A pharyngeal mass (Fig 85–43 and a tongue base mass (Fig 85–44) were also found. Surgical resection of the supraglottic mass resulted in an improved voice.

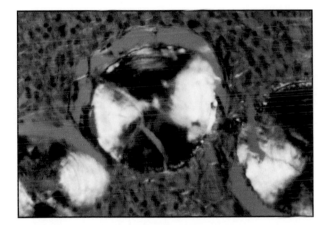

Fig 85–40. Yellow and apple green birefringence typical of amyloidosis stained with Congo red dye.

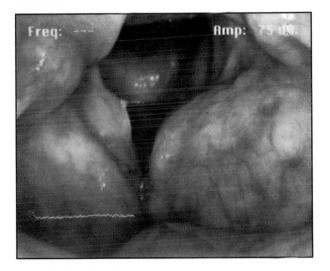

Fig 85–42. Amyloid tracheal mass.

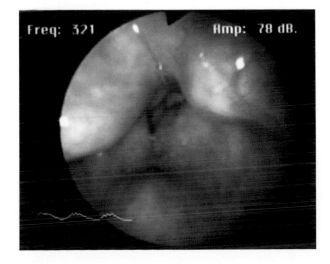

Fig 85–41. Left supraglottic amyloid mass.

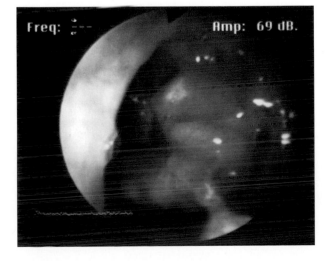

Fig 85–43. Pharyngeal mass of amyloid.

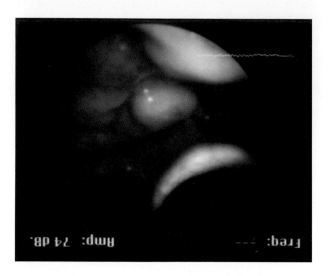

Fig 85–44. Amyloid involving the tongue base.

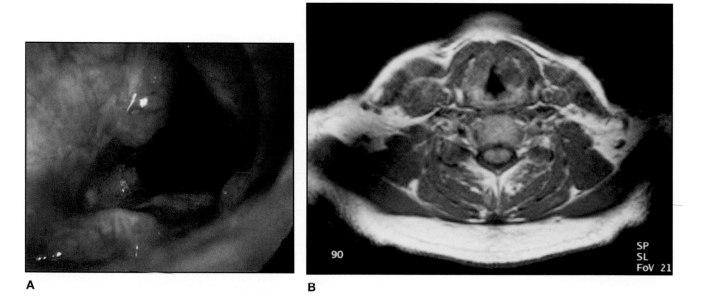

A   B

Fig 85–45. This patient is a minister who was referred because of severe dysphonia due to supraglottic amyloidosis. The amyloidosis is apparent in the left supraglottic area (**A**) and extending transglottally into the subglottic region. However, CT and MRI (**B**) revealed amyloidosis involving both false vocal folds, and (not shown) extending into tongue base and pharynx. The amyloidosis was resected extensively from the region of the left false vocal fold, removing the bulk of amyloid that was compressing and invading the left true vocal fold. Excellent voice improvement resulted. Additional surgery has been and will be required periodically.

Surgery is the mainstay of treatment for laryngeal amyloidosis. However, the surgeon must guard against the tendency to try to cure the amyloidosis with total resection, unless it is delimited clearly within nonvital structures. Amyloidosis tends to involve areas larger than apparent from clinical inspection (Fig 85–45). Its boundaries can be detected more accurately by CT and MRI. Until better therapy is devised, surgery should be directed toward optimizing phonatory and respiratory function in most cases, rather than toward eradication of disease.

Laryngeal amyloidosis has been recognized for many years.[145-147] Laryngeal amyloidosis is most common in the false vocal fold. Amyloid is a substance composed of protein and starch that accumulates in body tissues. Secondary amyloidosis, the more common form, may be associated with multiple myeloma (a malignancy of bone marrow), collagen vascular disease such as rheumatoid arthritis, infections such as chronic osteomyelitis, and other conditions. Primary amyloidosis occurs for no discernible reason. Amyloidosis may affect the heart, kidney, liver, spleen, tongue, stomach, intestines, larynx, and virtually any other body tissue. The involved areas generally enlarge and develop a pink or gray color, and waxy or raised areas are found commonly in the axial, groin, face, and neck. Amyloidosis usually is not hereditary, but there is also an inherited form. Hereditary amyloidosis frequently involves the nervous system, causing peripheral neuropathy, incontinence, decreased sweating, postural hypertension, and renal failure. When the larynx is involved, hoarseness and decreased vocal range are common. Regardless of the tissue affected, diagnosis depends on biopsy with special stains. It is helpful if the surgeon suspects the condition so that the pathologist can be warned to stain the tissues appropriately. In secondary amyloidosis, treatment of the underlying disease often results in stabilization or even reversal of amyloid deposits. However, there is no other specific treatment for secondary amyloidosis and no known treatment for primary amyloidosis other than surgical resection if resectable amyloid deposits cause symptoms. Amyloidosis is discussed also in chapter 52.

Miscellaneous Structural Lesions

Other masses, neoplasms, and other structural abnormalities may occur in the larynx. Some of these are covered in other chapters in this text, vocal fold scar in chapter 87 and ventricular fold cysts, epiglottic cysts, and laryngoceles in chapter 82. Others are discussed in other literature. The principles of management for the more uncommon lesions are similar to those discussed in this chapter and the chapters that follow.

References

1. Curtis HH. The cure of singers' nodules. *NY Med J.* January 8, 1898:37–39.
2. Rubin HJ, Lehrhoff I. Pathogenesis and treatment of vocal nodules. *J Speech Hear Dis.* 1962;27(2):150–161.
3. Brodnitz FS. Goals, results, and limitations of vocal rehabilitation. *Arch Otolaryngol.* 1963;77:148–156.
4. Deal RE, McClain B, Sudderth JF. Identification, evaluation, therapy, and follow-up for children with vocal nodules in a public school setting. *J Speech Hear Dis.* 1976;41(3):390–397.
5. Lancer JM, Sider D, Jones AS, LeBoutillier A. Vocal cord nodules: a review. *Clin Otolaryngol.* 1988;13:43–51.
6. Knight FI. Singer's nodes. *Trans Am Laryngol Assoc.* 1894;16:118–123.
7. Curtis HH. The cure of singers' nodules. *Trans Am Laryngol Rhinol Otolog Soc.* 1897;3:95–101.
8. Zerffi AC. Voice reeducation. *Arch Otolaryngol.* 1948;48: 521–526.
9. Brodnitz FS. *Keep Your Voice Healthy.* New York, NY: Harper & Brothers; 1953.
10. Withers B,. Dawson MH. Treatment of vocal nodule cases: psychological aspects. *Texas J Med.* 1960;56:43–46.
11. Wilson KD. Voice reeducation of adolescents with vocal nodules. *Laryngoscope.* 1962;72:45–53.
12. Wilson KD. Voice reeducation of adults with vocal nodules. *Arch Otol Rhinol Laryngol.* 1962;76:68–73.
13. Fisher HB, Logemann JA. Objective evaluation of therapy for vocal nodules: a case report. *J Speech Hear Dis.* 1970;35:277–285.
14. Fisher HB, Logemann JA. Voice diagnosis and therapy. *Otolaryngol Clin North Am.* 1970;35:639–663.
15. Brodnitz FS. *Vocal Rehabilitation.* Rochester, Minn: American Academy of Ophthalmology and Otolaryngology; 1971.
16. Drudge MK, Philips BJ. Shaping behavior in voice therapy. *J Speech Hear Dis.* 1976;41:398–411.
17. Reed CG. Voice therapy; a need for research. *J Speech Hear Dis.* 1980;45:157–169.
18. Barnes JE. Voice therapy for nodules and vocal polyps. *Rev Laryngol Rhinol.* 1981;102:99–103.
19. Vaughan CW. Current concepts in otolaryngology: diagnosis and treatment of organic voice disorders. *New Engl J Med.* 1982;307:333–336.
20. Sataloff RT, Spiegel JR, Hawkshaw MJ. Strobovideolaryngocopy: results and clinical value. *J Voice.* 1988;1: 359–364.
21. Sataloff RT, Spiegel JR, Hawkshaw MJ. Strobovideolaryngocopy in professional voice users: results and clinical value. *Ann Otol Rhinol Laryngol.* 1991;100:725–757.
22. Hirano M. Surgical anatomy and physiology of the vocal folds. In: Gould WJ, Sataloff RT, Spiegel JR, eds. *Voice Surgery.* New York, NY: Mosby-Yearbook, Inc; 1993: 135–158.
23. Ylitalo R. Clinical studies of contact granuloma in posterior laryngitis with special regard to esophagopharyngeal reflux. Stockholm, Sweden: Karolinska Institute; 2000.
24. Fritzell B, Hertegard S. A retrospective study of treatment of vocal fold edema: a preliminary report. In: Kirchner JA, ed. *Vocal Fold Histopathology: A Symposium.* San Diego, Calif: College-Hill Press; 1986:57–64.
25. Reinke F. Uber die funktionelle Struktur der menschlichen Stimmlippe mit besonderer berucksichtigung des elastischen Gewebes [About the functional structure of the human vocal cord with special reference to the elastic tissue]. *Anat Hefte.* 1897;9:103–117.
26. Zeitels SM, Hillman RE, Bunting GW, Vaughn T. Reinke's edema: phonatory mechanisms and manage-

ment strategies. *Ann Otol Rhinol Laryngol.* 1997;106: 533–543.

27. Putney FJ, Clerf LH. Treatment of chronic hypertrophic laryngitis. *Arch Otolaryngol.* 1940;31:925–929.

28. Myerson MC. Smoker's larynx. A clinical pathological entity. *Ann Otol Rhinol Laryngol.* 1940;31:925–929.

29. Sataloff RT, Ressue JC, Portell M, et al. Granular cell tumors of the larynx. *J Voice.* 2000;14(1):119–134.

30. Lazar RH, Younis RT, Kluka EA, et al. Granular cell tumor of the larynx: report of two pediatric cases. *Ear Nose Throat J.* 1992:440–443.

31. Conley SF, Milbrath M, Beste D. Pediatric laryngeal granular cell tumor. *J Otolaryngol.* 1992;21:450–453.

32. Abrikossoff AJ. Uber myome. *Virchow Arch* (A). 1926; 260:215–233.

33. Sobel HJ, Marquet E. Granular cells and granular cell lesions. *Pathol Ann.* 1974;9(0):43–79.

34. Batsakis JG. *Tumors of the Head and Neck.* 2nd ed. Baltimore, Md: Williams & Wilkins; 1979:327–331.

35. Dawydow C. Zur Frage der unausgereiften rhabdomyome des kehlkopfes. *Zeitschriff Fur Hals, Nasen und Ohren.* 1931;30:221–227.

36. Derman GL, Golbert ZW. Uber unreife, aus der quergestreifteb muskulatur hervorgehende myome. *Virchows Archiv.* 1931;282:172–180.

37. Glasunow M. Uber nreife, begrenzt und destruierend wachsende rhabdomyoblastome. *Frankf Zeitschr Pathol.* 1933;45:328–345.

38. Geschelin AI. Fall von myoblastom des kehlkopfs. *Zur Klinik Seltener Kehlkopfgeschwulste.* 1934;21:66–70.

39. Kleinfeld L. Myoblastoma of the larynx. *Arch Otolaryngol.* 1934;19:551–555.

40. Kernan JD, Cracovaner AJ. Rhabdomyoma of the vocal cord—report of a case. *Laryngoscope.* 1935;45:891–893.

41. Bobbio A. Mioblastoma ad elementi granulose (mioblastoma di Abrikossoff) della laringe. *Arch Sci Med.* 1936; 61:583–589.

42. Frenckner P. The occurrence of so-called myoblastomas in the mouth and upper air passages. *Acta Otolaryngol* (Stockh). 1938;26:689–701.

43. Iglauer S. Myoblastoma of the larynx. *Ann Otol Rhinol Laryngol.* 1942;51:1089–1093.

44. Fust JA, Custer RP. On the neurogenesis of so-called granular cell myoblastoma. *Am J Clin Pathol.* 1949;19: 522–535.

45. Maguda TA, Young JM. Granular cell myoblastoma of the vocal cord. *Ann Otol Rhinol Laryngol.* 1953;62:1035–1038.

46. Somers K, Farinacci CJ. Granular cell myoblastoma of the vocal cord. *Laryngoscope.* 1953;63:422–429.

47. MacNaughtan IP, Fraser MS. Myoblastoma of the larynx. *J Laryngol Otol.* 1954;68:680–688.

48. Keohane J. Myoblastoma of the larynx: a case report. *J Laryngol Otol.* 1956;70:544–545.

49. Busanny-Caspari W, Hammar CH. Zur malignitat der sogenannten myoblastenmyome. *Zentralbl Allg. Pathol.* 1958;98:401–406.

50. Hinton CD, Weinberger MA. Granular cell myoblastoma of the larynx. *Arch Otolaryngol.* 1958;68:497–500.

51. Bertogalli D. Mioblastoma della corda vocale. *Arch Ital Otol Rinol Laringol.* 1959;70:748–759.

52. Slywanowicz L, Mioduszewska O. Myoblastoma laryngis. *Pol Tyg Lek.* 1959,14:1155–1158.

53. Balshi SF. Myoblastoma of the larynx. *Ann Otol Rhinol Laryngol.* 1960;69:115–120.

54. Beekhuis GJ. Granular-cell myoblastoma of the larynx: report of three cases. *Arch Otolaryngol.* 1960;72:314–320.

55. Walter WL. Granular myoblastoma of the larynx with the presentation of two cases. . *Ann Otol Rhinol Laryngol.* 1960;69:328–340.

56. Chiappe LC. Mioblastoma laringeo. [Laryngeal myoblastoma. Abrikossoff's tumor.] *Prensa Med Argent.* 1961;48:3215–3217.

57. Lyons GD, Haindel C, Blatt IM. Myoblastoma of the larynx. A report of five cases. *Laryngoscope.* 1962;72:909–914.

58. Ward PH, Oshiro H. Laryngeal granular-cell myoblastoma. Appearance with pseudoepitheliomatous hyperplasia. *Arch Otolaryngol.* 1962;76:239–244.

59. Gosavi DK, Bond WM. Granular cell myoblastoma of vocal cord. *J Laryngol Otol.* 1964;78:79–81.

60. Halperin D. Granular cell myoblastoma of the vocal cord. Report of a case. *Ann Otol Rhinol Laryngol.* 1964;73: 184–185.

61. Ottosson BG. Myoblastoma of the larynx. *Acta Otolaryngol* (Stockh). 1964;58:86–93.

62. Von Westernhagen BV. Die sogenannten myoblastenmyome des Kehlkopfes und ihre haufige Fehldeutung als Carcinom. *HNO.* 1964;12:49–50.

63. Pope TH. Laryngeal myoblastoma. *Arch Otolaryngol.* 1965;81:80–82.

64. Andre P. Renault P, Laccourreye H, et al. Tumeur d'Abrikossoff du larynx. *Ann Otolaryngol Chir Cervicofac.* 1966;83(6):437–440.

65. Cracovaner AJ, Opler SR. Granular cell myoblastoma of the larynx. *Laryngoscope.* 1967;77(6):1040–1046.

66. Sedee GA. Granular cell myoblastoma of the larynx. *J Laryngol Otol.* 1967;81:557–559.

67. Guerrier Y, Dejean Y, Galy G, Serrou B. Myoblastome du larynx ou tumeur d'Abrikossoff. *J Fr Otorhinolaryngol Audiophonol Chir Maxillofac.* 1968;17:477–489.

68. Otto HD, Rose AM. Granularzellenmyoblastom mit pseudokarzinomatoser epithelproliferation an der stimmlippe. *Z Laryngol Rhinol Otol.* 1968;47:228–233.

69. Bhatnagar HN, Schawarz HJ. Granular cell myoblastoma of larynx with papillary adenocarcinoma of thyroid. *Arch Otolaryngol.* 1969;90:156–158.

70. Lacomme Y, Galaup J. Volumineuse tumeur d'Abrikossoff du larynx. *J Fr Otorhinolaryngol Audiophonol Maxillofac.* 1969;9:708–712.

71. Piquet JJ, Blondy G, Leduc M, Decroix G. Les tumeurs d'Abrikossoff du larynx. *Ann Otolaryngol Chir Cervicofac.* 1969;86:79–85.

72. Sardana DS, Yadav YC. Granular cell myoblastoma of the laryngopharynx. *J Laryngol Otol.* 1969;83:1023–1025.

73. Schneider C, Gould WJ, Mirani R. Granular cell myoblastoma of larynx. *Arch Otolaryngol.* 1969;89:95–99.

74. Vance SF, Hudson RP. Granular cell myoblastoma. Clinicopathologic study of forty-two patients. *Am J Clin Pathol.* 1969;52:208–211.

75. Booth JB, Osborn DA. Granular cell myoblastoma of the larynx. *Acta Otolaryngol.* 1970;70:279–293.

76. Canalis RF, Cohn AM. Granular cell myoblastoma of the larynx. *Arch Otolaryngol.* 1970; 91:125–127.

77. Goldstein A, Thaler S, Rozycki D. Granular cell myoblastoma and carcinoma of the larynx. *Arch Otolaryngol.* 1971;94:366–368.

78. Miglets AW, Gebhart DE, Gregg LO. Airway obstruction due to a large laryngeal granular cell myoblastoma. *Laryngoscope.* 1971;81:971–978.

79. Wolfowitz BL, Jaffe A. Granular cell myoblastoma of the larynx. *J Laryngol Otol.* 1972;86:643–646.

80. Thawley SE, May M, Oruga JH. Granular cell myoblastoma of the larynx. *Laryngoscope.* 1974;84:1545–1551.

81. Thawley SE, Oruga JH. Granular cell tumor of the trachea. *Arch Otolaryngol.* 1974;100:393–394.

82. Compagno J, Hyams VJ, Ste-Marie P. Benign granular cell tumors of the larynx: a review of 36 cases with clinicopathologic data. *Ann Otol Rhinol Laryngol.* 1975;84: 308–314.

83. Michaels L. Neurogenic tumors, granular cell tumor, and paraganglioma. *Can J Otolaryngol.* 1975;4(2):319–327.

84. Coates HL, Devine KD, McDonald TJ, Weiland LH. Granular cell tumors of the larynx. *Ann Otol Rhinol Laryngol.* 1976;85(4 Pt 1): 504–507.

85. Frable MA, Fisher RA. Granular cell myoblastomas. *Laryngoscope.* 1976;86(1):36–42.

86. Helidonis E, Dokianakis G, Pantazopoulos P. Granular cell myoblastoma of the larynx. *J Laryngol Otol.* 1978; 92:525–528.

87. Kenefick C. Granular cell myoblastoma of the larynx. *J Laryngol Otol.* 1978;92(6):521–523.

88. Agarwal RK, Blitzer A, Perzin KH. Granular cell tumors of the larynx. *Otolaryngol Head Neck Surg.* 1979;87: 807–814.

89. Lulenski GC. Granular cell myoblastoma of the larynx. *Arch Otolaryngol.* 1979;105:296–298.

90. Fechner RE. Pathologic Quiz Case 1. Granular cell tumor. *Arch Otolaryngol.* 1979;105(4):226–228.

91. Lack EE, Worsham GF, Callihan MD, Crawford BE, et al. Granular cell tumor: a clinicopathologic study of 110 patients. *J Surg Oncol.* 1980;13:301–316.

92. Majmudar B, Thomas J, Gorelkin L, Symbas PN. Respiratory obstruction caused by a multicentric granular cell tumor of the laryngotracheobronchial tree. *Hum Pathol.* 1981;12(3):283–286.

93. Shevchenko AM, Egorov VP, Gladkii NI, Miroshnichenko SV. [Abrikosov's granular cell tumor localized on the vocal fold.] *Vestn Otorhinolaringol.* 1981;5:77–78.

94. Tomeckova A, Odehnal F, Cerny K. Abrikosovuv tumor (granularne bunecny myoblastom) lokalozaci v hrtanu. Sdeleni o dvou pripadech. *Cesk Otolaryngol.* 1981;5:296–302.

95. El-Ghazali AMS, El-Ghazali TMS. Granular cell myoblastoma of the larynx. *J Laryngol Otol.* 1982;96:1177–1180.

96. Ivatury R, Shah D, Ascer E, et al. Granular cell tumor of the larynx and bronchus. *Ann Thorac Surg.* 1982;33(1): 69–73.

97. Lapena AM, Caballero T. Mioblastoma de celulas granulosas o tumor de Abrikossof de localizacion laringea. A proposito de un caso. *Acta Otorrinolaringol Esp.* 1982; 164–168.

98. Lopez-Cortijo C, Gonzalez F, Vergara J, Aranda FI. Tumor de celulas granulares (mioblastoma) de la laringe. *Acta Otorrinolaringol Esp.* 1983;34(3):315–320.

99. Garud O, Bostad L, Elverland HH, Mair IW. Granular cell tumor of the larynx in a 5-year-old child. *Ann Otol Rhinol Laryngol.* 1984;93:45–47.

100. Bedbeder P, Gehanno P. Localisations orl des tumeurs d'Abrikossoff a propos de 5 observations une tumeur qui n'est pas toujours anodine. *Ann Otolaryngol Chir Cervicofac.* 1985;102:169–173.

101. Har-El G, Shviro J, Avidor I, et al. Laryngeal granular cell tumor in children. *Am J Otolaryngol.* 1985;6:32–36.

102. Toncini C, Pesce C. Granular cell tumours of the oesophagus and larynx. *J Laryngol Otol.* 1985;99:1301–1304.

103. Broniatowski M. Pathologic Quiz Case 2. Granular cell myoblastoma. *Arch Otolaryngol Head Neck Surg.* 1986; 112:108–109.

104. DeBonis M, Montserrart JR, Mendez R, et al. Mioblastoma de celulas granulosas o tumor de Abrikossoff de localizacion laringea: a proposito de un caso. *Acta Otorrinolaringol Esp.* 1986;37(6):414–417.

105. Gangemi P, Arcidiacono A, Puzzo L. Tumore a cellule granulose (mioblastoma) della corda vocale. *Pathologica.* 1986;78:641–646.

106. Schottenfeld R, Marsh B. Granular cell tumor of the larynx. *Ear Nose Throat J.* 1987;66:415–418.

107. Alessi DM, Zimmerman MC. Granular cells tumors of the head and neck. *Laryngoscope.* 1988;98:810–814.

108. Goldofsky E, Hirschfield LS, Abramson AL. An unusual laryngeal lesion in children: granular cell tumor. *Int J Pediatr Otorhinlaryngol.* 1988;15(3):263–267.

109. Solomons NB. Extensive granular cell tumor of the larynx and trachea (a case of report). *J Laryngol Otol.* 1988; 102(7):658–660.

110. Fliss DM, Puterman M, Zirkin H, Leiberman A. Granular cell lesions in head and neck: a clinicopathological study. *J Surg Oncol.* 1989;42:154–160.

111. Manos PM, Garces GE, Casalots J, et al. Tumor de celulas granulares de laringe. *An Otorrinolaringol Ibero Am.* 1989;16(6):595–606.

112. Robb PJ, Girling A. Granular cell myoblastoma of the supraglottis. *J Laryngol Otol.* 1989;103:328–330.

113. Wight RG, Variend S, Bull PD. Granular cell tumor of the larynx in childhood. *J Laryngol Otol.* 1989;103:880–881.

114. Brandwein M, LeBenger J, Strauchen J, Biller H. Atypical granular cell tumor of the larynx: an unusually aggressive tumor clinically and microscopically. *Head Neck.* 1990;12:154–159.

115. Cree IA, Bingham BJ, Ramesar KC. Granular cell tumor of the larynx. *J Laryngol Otol.* 1990;104:159–161.

116. Falcioni M, Vighi V, Ferri T, Caruana P. Tumore a cellule granulose della laringe: a proposito di un caso. *Acta Biomed Ateneo Parmense.* 1990;61:179–184.

117. Watkins GL, Clark D, Foss D. Pathologic Quiz Case 1. Granular cell tumor of the larynx. *Arch Otolaryngol Head Neck Surg.* 1990;116:1448–1450.

118. Zamarro MT, Lopez JR, Ruiz JV, et al. Tumor de celulas granulosas de laringe. *Acta Otorrinolaringol Esp.* 1990; 41:133–135.

119. Del Toro AJJ, Marques VB, Rocher PF, et al. Tumor de celulas granulares de localizacion glotica. *Acta Otorrinolaringol Esp.* 1991;42(2):117–120.

120. Martinez Martinez CJ, Fogue Calvo L. Tumor de celulas granulares laringeo. *Rev Clin Esp.* 1991;189(4):181–182.

121. Conley SF, Milbrath MM, Beste DJ. Pediatric laryngeal granular cell tumor. *J Otolaryngol.* 1992;21(6):450–453.

122. Zietek E, Ptaszynski K, Jach K, Sienicki J. [Cases of granular cell tumor (myoblastoma) in the larynx.] *Otolaryngol Pol.* 1992;46:71–75.

123. Hamid AM, Alshaikhly A. Granular cell tumor of the larynx in an eight-year-old girl. *J Laryngol Otol.* 1993; 107(10):940–941.

124. Elo J, Arato G, Koppany J. Granular cell (Abrikosov) tumors treated with CO2 laser. *Orv Hetil.* 1994;135(12): 635–637.

125. Mukherji SK, Castillo M, Rao V, Weissler M. Granular cell tumors of the subglottic region of the larynx: CT and MRI findings. *Am J Roentgenol.* 1995;164:1492–1494.

126. Holland RS, Abaza N, Balsara G, Lesser R. Granular cell tumor of the larynx in a six-year-old child: case report and review of literature. *Ear Nose Throat J.* 1998; 77(8):652–660.

127. Kershisnik M, Batsakis JG, Makay B. Granular cell tumors. *Ann Otol Rhinol Laryngol.* 1994;103:416–419.

128. Batsakis JG, Manning JT. Soft tissue tumors: unusual forms. *Otolaryngol Clin N Am.* 1986;19:659–683.

129. Klima M, Peters J. Malignant granular cell tumor. *Arch Pathol Lab Med.* 1987;111:1070–1073.

130. Neis PR, McMahon MF, Norris CW. Cartilaginous tumors of the trachea and larynx. *Ann Otol Rhinol Laryngol.* 1989;98:31–36.

131. Weise J, Viner T, Rinehart RJ, Dolan K. Imaging case of the month—cartilaginous tumor of the larynx. *Ann Otol Rhinol Laryngol.* 1987;101:617–619.

132. Tiwari RM, Snow GB, Balm AJ, et al. Cartilaginous tumours of the larynx. *J Laryngol Otol.* 1987;101:266–275.

133. Damiani K, Tucker H. Chondroma of the larynx. *Arch Otolaryngol.* 1981;107:399–402.

134. Huizenga C, Balogh K. Cartilaginous tumors of the larynx. *Cancer.* 1979;26:201–210.

135. Cantrell RW, Reibel JF, Jahrsdoerfer RA, Johns ME. Conservative surgical treatment of chondrosarcoma of the larynx. *Ann Otol Rhinol Laryngol.* 1980;89:567–571.

136. Lavertu P, Tucker HM. Chondrosarcoma of the larynx. Case report and management philosophy. *Ann Otol Rhinol Laryngol.* 1984;93:452–456.

137. Neel HB III, Unni KK. Cartilaginous tumors of the larynx: a series of 33 patients. *Otolaryngol Head Neck Surg.* 1982;90:201–207.

138. Franco RA Jr, Singh B, Har-El G. Laryngeal chondroma. *J Voice.* 2002;16(1):92–95.

139. Lichtenstein L, Jaffe HL. Chondrosarcoma of bone. *Am J Pathol.* 1943;19:553–573.

140. Ferlito A, Nicola P, Montaguti A, et al. Chondrosarcoma of the larynx: review of the literature and report of 3 cases. *Am J Otolaryngol.* 1984;5:350–359.

141. Batti JS, Abramson A. First report of a case of osteoma of the larynx. *Ear Nose Throat J.* 2000;79(8):564–566, 568.

142. Pinsolle J, LeChise I, Demeauz H, et al. Osteosarcoma of the soft tissue of the larynx: report of a case with electron microscopic studies. *Otolaryngol Head Neck Surg.* 1990;102:276–280.

143. Jungehülsing M, Fischbach R, Pototschnig C, et al. Rare benign tumors: laryngeal and hypopharyngeal lipomata. *Ann Otol Rhinol Laryngol.* 2000;109:301–305.

144. Sataloff RT, Abaza M, Abaza NA, et al. Amyloidosis of the larynx. *Ear Nose Throat J.* 2001;80(6):369–370.

145. Stark DB, New GB. Amyloid tumors of larynx and trachea or bronchi. *Med Clin North Am.* 1950;34:1145–1150.

146. Epstein SS, Winston P, Friedmann I, Ormerod FC. The vocal cord polyp. *J Laryngol Otol.* 1957;71:673–688.

147. Michaels L, Hyams VJ. Amyloid in localised deposits and plasmacytomas of the respiratory tract. *J Pathol.* 1979;128:29–38.

86

Vocal Fold Hemorrhage

Robert Thayer Sataloff and Mary J. Hawkshaw

Vocal fold hemorrhages result from the rupture of a blood vessel within the vocal fold. They can be caused by internal or external laryngeal trauma and produce a wide range of voice complaints. The consequences of vocal fold hemorrhage may be serious, especially in a professional voice user. Hemorrhage may cause not only acute dysphonia, but also permanent voice change if submucosal scarring develops as the hematoma resolves. Laryngologists, speech-language pathologists, and voice professionals should be familiar with the presenting symptoms, precipitating and predisposing factors, physical and stroboscopic findings, treatment course, and possible consequences of a vocal fold hemorrhage.

Review of Literature

Submucosal hemorrhage of the vocal fold has been considered an uncommon lesion. Hemorrhages have been reported in small numbers and almost exclusively in professional voice users.[1-4] Only Abitbol[2] (14 cases), Lin et al[3] (44 cases), and Spiegel et al[5] (31 cases) have reported on substantial numbers of patients. The authors' patient population is dominated by professional voice users, many of whom are singers. Vocal fold hemorrhage may have a greater incidence in singers and other professional voice users because of the strain of their vocal demands. However, it may simply be diagnosed more frequently in this population because even minor changes in vocal quality lead the singer to seek medical attention. Moreover, some people (particularly nonsingers) may suffer vocal fold hemorrhage and recover without ever consulting a laryngologist.

In 1990, 31 patients who had suffered vocal fold hemorrhage were studied.[5] The average age of the 20 females and 11 males was 35 years. Twenty-five of the patients were professional voice users, and 23 of these were singers. Sixteen patients presented with sudden voice change, 10 had progressive hoarseness, 9 complained of reduction in upper vocal range, 6 reported voice fatigue, and 1 patient denied vocal symptoms (the hemorrhage was discovered serendipitously). Thirteen of the patients developed hemorrhage while they were singing, and 9 hemorrhaged in association with extensive public speaking. Three ruptured blood vessels occurred while sneezing, 2 while coughing, and 2 patients hemorrhaged after blunt external laryngeal trauma. Ten patients had vocal fold masses, although it was not generally possible to determine whether the masses developed before or after the hemorrhage (Figs 86–1 to 86–6). Two patients had bilateral vocal fold hemorrhages. One of these had sustained external trauma with laryngeal fracture, and the other hemorrhaged while she was singing. Three patients developed recurrent vocal fold hemorrhages within 4 months of the time of their original presentation, and a fourth patient hemorrhaged again 24 months after her first hemorrhage (Figs 86–7, 86–8, and 86–9). Nine of the 31 patients eventually required vocal fold surgery.

The most common presenting symptom of vocal fold hemorrhage is *sudden* change in vocal quality. The sudden onset of symptoms is evident because blood dissects in the submucosal plane, altering the vibratory motion of the vocal fold. However, many patients note the progressive development of hoarseness or voice fatigue or minor vocal changes such as loss of range in the upper register. Patients with slowly progressive symptoms may have small hemorrhages that restrict vibratory motion in a limited segment of the vocal fold or, conceivably, progressive hemorrhage due to the slow extravasation of blood from the ruptured

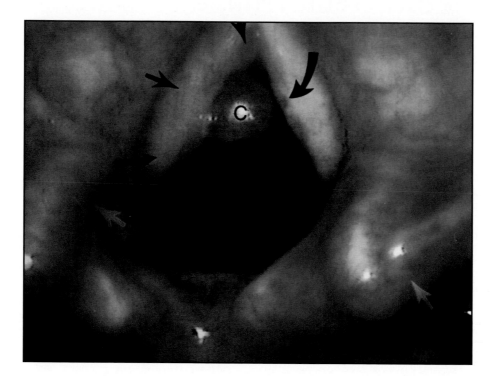

Fig 86–1. This 36-year-old male had a 10-month history of hoarseness, worse during the last 4–6 weeks. He had been examined elsewhere with a laryngeal mirror alone and was told that his problem was "functional" and that his vocal folds were normal. Indirect laryngoscopy revealed a moderately hyperactive gag reflex and an epiglottis that obscured the anterior position of the vocal folds. Nevertheless, even on indirect laryngoscopy, it was possible to see the red and yellow discoloration of the left vocal fold, increased vocal fold thickness, and the posterior portion of the left vocal fold mass. Arytenoid erythema (*white arrows*) was also apparent. Examination with a laryngeal telescope and strobovideolaryngoscopy revealed a large hemorrhagic cyst (c), hemorrhage extending throughout the length of the left vocal fold (*straight black arrows*), and contact ecchymosis on the right vocal fold (*curved arrow*). The submucosal extent of the hemorrhage and the stiffness seen under stroboscopic examination indicate a guarded prognosis for return to normal vibratory function, although improvement following surgery can certainly be expected. The presence of a mass associated with vocal fold hemorrhage is a bad prognostic sign and is the most common finding associated with poor voice recovery from hemorrhage, and the need for surgery. (From *ENT J.* 1993;72[4]:252, with permission.)

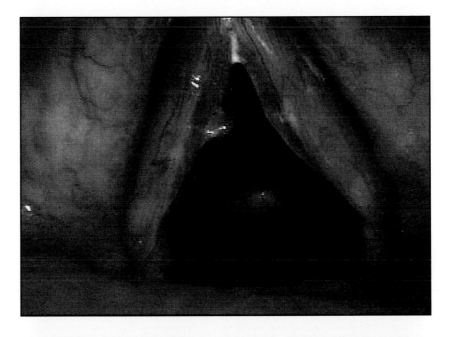

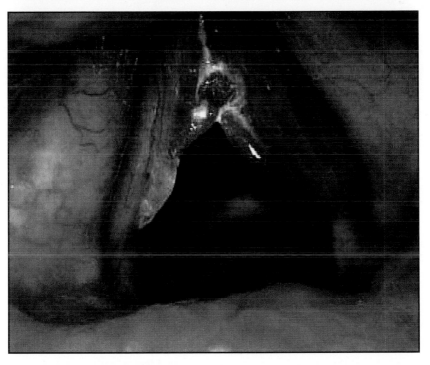

Fig 86-2. (*Top*) This 36-year-old prison guard had a long history of low husky voice. He was referred because of his family physician's concern about his hoarseness. He had smoked one pack of cigarettes a day for 18 years (and still smoked) and consumed approximately 12 beers per week. He had undergone direct laryngoscopy twice, performed by another physician, and his hoarseness had recurred. At the time of his initial examination, he was diagnosed with bilateral Reinke's edema, varicosities, a left polypoid mass, and laryngopharyngeal reflux. He was started on antireflux ther-apy and voice therapy. (*Bottom*) He was not consistently compliant with therapy, and he abused his voice. He returned 1 month later with recently worsened hoarseness, new right vocal fold hemorrhage, and markedly increased bilateral Reinke's edema. After his hemorrhage resolved and he had undergone a successful course of voice therapy (with compliance), he underwent excision of his left vocal fold mass, evacuation of his Reinke's edema, Decadron injection, and resection of the varicosities (visible on both vocal folds in A) that had led to his hemorrhage.

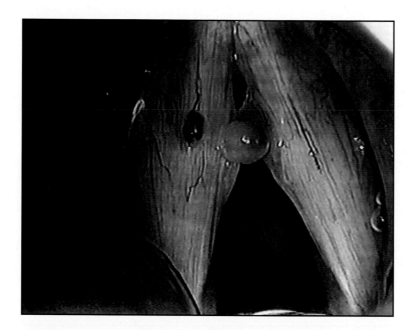

Fig 86-3. This 33-year-old female professional actor and singer presented with a 1-year history of hoarseness and vocal inconsistency. Strobovideolaryngoscopy revealed bilateral masses, varicosities, and stiffness. She had a bilobed right post-hemorrhagic polyp with a persistent blush at the base anteriorly. There is a left pseudocyst, probably caused by contact trauma. She has bilateral superior surface varicosities with a left superior surface vascular mass, as well.

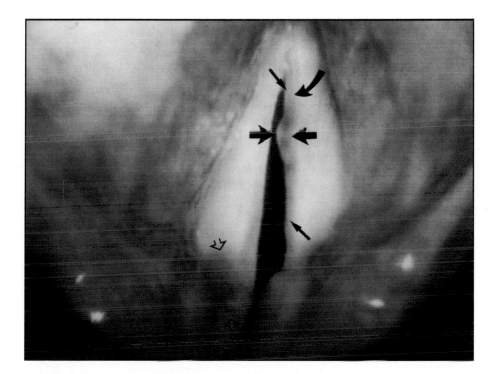

Fig 86–4. The hemorrhagic mass illustrated in this videoprint developed after an episode of sudden hoarseness 14 months prior to this evaluation. The patient was a physician. He had already undergone voice therapy for 1 year. He had been using nonsteroidal antiinflammatory medications for tennis elbow. Strobovideolaryngoscopy revealed a red, hemorrhagic mass at the junction of the anterior and middle thirds of the right vocal fold (*thick solid arrows*). There was also erythematous discoloration extending from the vocal fold process to within 2 mm of the anterior commissure (*small thin arrows*). Strobovideolaryngoscopy showed stiffness throughout this entire area caused by fibrosis of the submucosal hemorrhage. Anteriorly, there was also a prominent vessel, the contours of which became indistinct and widened to the point at which it had hemorrhaged on at least two occasions (*curved arrow*). There is also prominent arytenoid erythema extending onto the posterior aspect of the vocal folds (*open arrow*) caused by gastroesophageal reflux laryngitis. Surgery resulted in improvement, but not restoration to normal voice quality, as predicted because of extensive preoperative right vocal fold stiffness. (From *ENT J.* 1995;74[1]:11, with permission.)

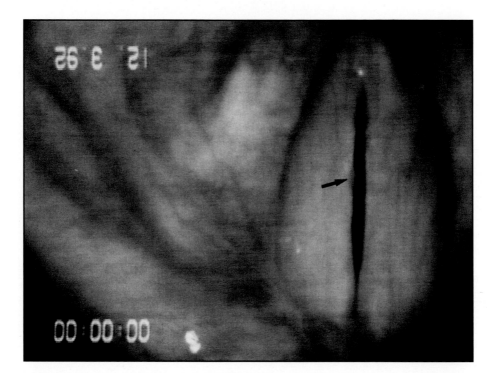

Fig 86–5. Sometimes, even small posthemorrhagic masses can produce dysphonia. The small left erythematous vocal fold mass illustrated above (*arrow*) was difficult to see even with stroboscopy. However, strobovideolaryngoscopy showed that its base was broader than it appeared under continuous light and that the region beneath and adjacent to the mass was stiff. Moreover, the mass caused failure of glottic closure when this rock singer sang the upper half of his range. Voice therapy and singing lessons were insufficient. Surgery resulted in normal glottic closure and restoration of excellent voice quality. In addition to excising the mass, the associated vessel (on the undersurface, and not seen in this picture) was cauterized. (From *ENT J.* 1994; 73[1]:11, with permission.)

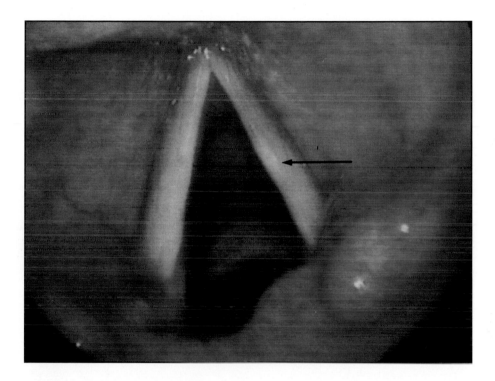

Fig 86–6. A small, persistent right vocal fold mass (*arrow*). Strobovideolaryngoscopy revealed stiffness throughout the entire, edematous right vocal fold. The mass caused slight failure of glottic closure. Voice therapy was insufficient. Surgery 11 months after injury resulted in substantial voice improvement, complete glottic closure, and improvement in the mucosal wave; the patient has resumed singing. (From *ENT J.* 1994;73[10]:717, with permission.)

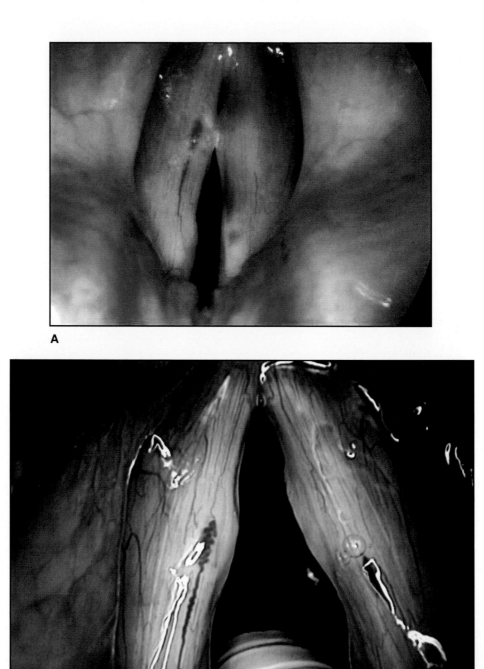

Fig 86-7. A. Videoprint illustrating bilateral varicosities and bilateral striking zone masses. The left superior surface varicosity can be seen clearly. Recent hemorrhage in the right vocal fold obscures definition of the borders. **B.** The vessel was clearly defined after the hemorrhage had resolved. Surgical treatment included resection of the varicosities using cold instruments.

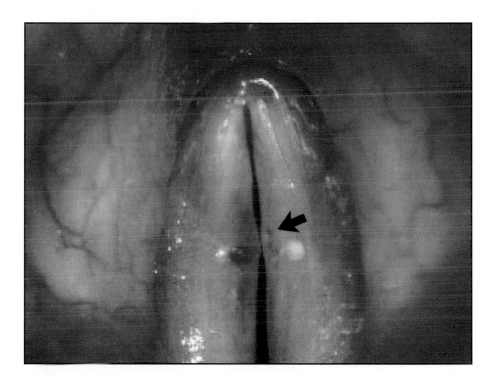

Fig 86-8. This figure shows a sequela of left vocal fold hemorrhage, a left post-hemorrhagic mass. The mass appears to involve the superior surface primarily. However, strobovideolaryngoscopy reveals stiffness and mass offset extending on the vibratory margin and striking zone. There is also an area of discoloration extending for several millimeters anterior and posterior to the center of the mass. The post-hemorrhagic discoloration is sometimes permanent. On the right vocal fold, there is a contact mass, and there are adjacent areas of ectasia (*arrow*).

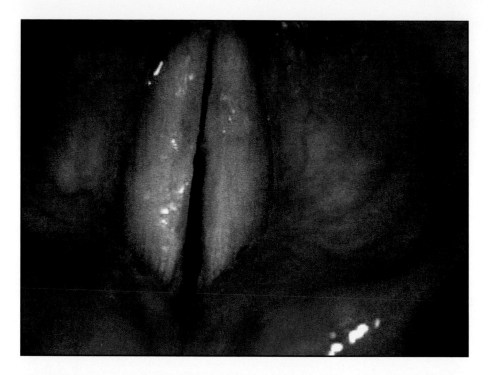

Fig 86-9. Although the vocal folds shown in this figure may initially look better than those in the previous figure where the mass is somewhat more prominent, this patient's voice is actually worse than that of the patient illustrated in the previous figure. The post-hemorrhagic vascular mass on the right in the vocal fold above is on the vibratory margin. There is scalloping at its base which is accompanied by stiffness on stobovideolaryngscopy. The stiffness extends throughout the middle of the musculomembranous vocal fold. The contact lesion on the left is also associated with stiffness involving the striking zone, and hypervascularity on the superior surface.

vessel; or they may manifest symptoms only after contralateral contact swelling of the vocal fold develops. Laryngologists have long been wary of potentially dangerous lesions such as vocal fold hemorrhage and mucosal tears in singers who develop sudden dysphonia. However, it appears that in some cases slowly progressive dysphonia and minor alterations in voice quality can also be symptoms of vocal fold hemorrhage and thus require prompt, comprehensive laryngologic evaluation.

The influence of predisposing infectious, anatomic, hormonal, and metabolic factors in the development of vocal fold hemorrhages must be considered. Ten (33%) of the patients studied related the onset of symptoms to the presence of an upper respiratory infection.[5] This is consistent with the 36% association reported by Lin et al.[3] Infection in some patients results in laryngeal mucosal dehydration from mouth breathing necessitated by reduced nasal airflow and the thickening and/or reduction in the amount of normal mucus. In other patients, there is an increase in the amount of mucus resulting in throat clearing, inflam-

matory changes of the laryngeal and pharyngeal mucosa, and/or reduced breath support from lower respiratory impairment. The risks are undoubtedly greater in people who have used aspirin, ibuprofen, or other medicines that alter blood-clotting abilities.

The influence of hormonal factors in the development of vocal fold hemorrhage is of great interest. Isolated cases of injuries in female voices related to menstruation have been reported for many years.[6-8] Cyclical variations in laryngeal architecture related to hormonal cycles have been documented.[9] Lin et al[3] reported "hormonal imbalances" in 8 of 30 women in their series of 44 patients. These hormonal imbalances included abnormal menstrual cycles, use of estrogen supplements, gynecological surgery, and the use of oral contraceptives. Four of their patients had single episodes of vocal fold hemorrhage while singing during menses, and a fifth patient with irregular menstrual cycles had three episodes of vocal fold hemorrhage while singing during menstrual periods. One patient hemorrhaged while singing 2 days after an abortion, and one patient had undergone bilateral oophorectomy and had recurrent hemorrhages when she missed her estrogen replacement pills. Menstrual cycle phase was not specified for the other patients, for the patients in Abitbol's report,[2] nor those in Baker's study of several patients with recurrent vocal fold hemorrhage treated by excision of visible lesions.[10] Anecdotally, premenstrual and early menstrual hormonal changes have been associated with an increased risk of vocal fold hemorrhage.[11] This is presumed to be due to increased capillary fragility. Lacina noted a 42% incidence of hoarseness and submucosal vocal fold hemorrhage in opera singers in this phase of the menstrual cycle.[8] In our study, one patient was noted to be symptomatically premenstrual and another was pregnant at the time she developed the hemorrhage.[5] Unfortunately, menstrual phase was not specified for all patients, so there are insufficient data to draw conclusions about hormonal effect. However, the approximately 2:1 female to male ratio (67% females) suggests that hormonal influence may be a factor. Interestingly, 68% of Lin's patients with vocal fold hemorrhages were women,[3] as were 93% of Abitbol's.[2] Ongoing, prospective studies are aimed at determining conclusively whether there is an increased risk of vocal fold hemorrhage associated with cyclical hormonal variations. Anecdotally, the authors believe that the association is present and important. The use of anticoagulants such as aspirin and ibuprofen for premenstrual cramps increases the risk of hemorrhage. Physicians and voice professionals must be familiar with these risk factors, and must be particularly careful to advise professional voice users on simultaneous multiple risk factors such as premenstrual hormonal changes, aspirin use, and singing with impaired support techniques owing to the pain of menstrual cramps.

Most of the hemorrhages diagnosed occur on the musculomembranous portion of the vocal fold. In most cases, those that cause substantial symptoms involve the vibratory margin. However, hematomas can occur elsewhere. Posterior laryngeal hematomas are much more common than recognized or reported, because they rarely cause symptoms that trigger consultation with an otolaryngologist. If they are not large enough to cause failure of glottic closure, they commonly do not produce hoarseness. Mild to moderate sore throat and dysphagia are accepted as "expected" following some intubations. Patients with these symptoms who are discharged within 24 hours of surgery do not raise concern in the medical profession; the symptoms usually are gone by the time they return for follow-up a week or two later. People who are hospitalized for longer periods of time following intubation frequently are medicated or recovering from more serious illnesses, so the laryngeal symptoms are considered inconsequential, or are not reported. Although we are aware of no systematic study of the incidence of posterior laryngeal ecchymosis, edema, or hematoma following intubation, the author (RTS) has observed these conditions on several occasions in patients without laryngeal complaints who were seen in consultation for other problems. Dysphagia associated with a large hematoma of the arytenoid, posterior larynx, or posterior pharyngeal wall is less common, but can occur. Ordinarily, such hematomas resolve spontaneously. However, it is not surprising that some do not. Some form persistent masses or scar. In some cases, the masses are cystic; and in other cases, they are fibrotic. Hematomas of the arytenoids, posterior larynx, and even true vocal folds also may occur as a result of nasogastric tube placement, diagnostic endoscopy (ie, esophagoscopy or bronchoscopy), or in response to external trauma. Rarely, symptoms of dysphagia can be prolonged. If the damage is limited to the posterior larynx, swallowing complaints may remain more prominent than dysphonia.

Stroboscopic examination is invaluable in the diagnosis and follow-up of vocal fold hemorrhage. When stroboscopy is not used, some of these hemorrhages go unrecognized, and subsequent treatment may be inappropriate. A reduction in the amplitude and/or wave form is noted in the involved vocal fold during the initial stroboscopic examination in nearly all patients (Table 86–1). The authors' reported findings support the observations of Abitbol[2] and Lin et al.[3] The only exceptions were in small hemorrhages isolated in the superior surface of the vocal folds. Follow-up stroboscopic examination revealed improvement of the mucosal wave in all patients who recovered functionally. In many cases, the examination returned to normal. The majority of the remaining cases had only "minimal" residual stiffness of the vocal fold. Reduced amplitude and wave form of the involved vocal fold were noted in all patients who did not have total functional recovery. Voice rest is prescribed routinely for acute vocal fold hemorrhage. Stroboscopic findings are critical in assessing the speed of resolution of the hemorrhages and in giving recommendations regarding voice use.

Theoretically, voice rest should help prevent recurrent hemorrhage from the involved blood vessel, limit dissection of blood in the submucosal plane, and minimize vocal fold trauma that might provoke fibroblast proliferation and scar formation. Absolute voice rest is usually prescribed for about 1 week. It is thought that many patients who suffer sudden symptoms of vocal fold hemorrhage instinctively reduce or cease voice use quickly, preventing sequelae and

Table 86–1. Comparative Stroboscopic Findings in Patients Who Had Initial and Follow-up Examinations.

Stroboscopic Findings	Initial (N = 23)	Follow-up (N = 23)
Decreased Amplitude	20	15
Decreased Waveform	19	12
Incomplete Glottic Closure	12	4
Vocal Fold Mass	7	7
Varicosity	4	6
Normal Examination	0	7

Note: Patients demonstrated multiple indicators of vocal fold dysfunction. Seven patients demonstrating residual decreases in amplitude and/or waveform had only minimal stiffness.

speeding recovery. The total recovery of almost all patients with sudden onset of symptoms provides additional anecdotal support for the use of voice rest in the treatment of vocal fold hemorrhage (Table 86–2). These patients have done much better than those with gradual onset of symptoms and continued voice use. Although the efficacy of voice rest remains unproven, the authors believe it to be valuable and prescribe it routinely for patients with hemorrhage. Absolute voice rest can usually be discontinued after about 1 week, and limited, supervised speaking can be resumed. After voice rest has been discontinued, voice therapy and singing lessons are advised routinely in an effort to reduce any abuse patterns that may have contributed to the development of hemorrhage or developed as compensatory strategies after vocal injury and to assist in the patients' recovery from a period of vocal rest. It may take 6 weeks or more before singing lessons can be instituted safely. In such cases, it is not unusual for patients to have curtailed unrestricted singing performance for close to 3 months from the time of injury.

Nine patients in the study group had coexisting vocal fold masses at the time of diagnosis of the submucosal hemorrhage. Vocal fold hemorrhage can be caused by voice abuse, as can mass lesions. It is not clear whether the vocal fold masses contributed to the bleeding episode, were caused by the bleeding episode, or both conditions simply resulted from voice abuse. When surgical removal of the masses is performed, it is primarily to improve voice quality but also to reduce the risk of recurrent hemorrhage in some patients. The persistence of a symptomatic vocal fold mass was the leading cause of surgery among our patients (Table 86–3). One patient required two surgical procedures 1 year apart. In 4 of the 10 operative cases, the patients noted posthemorrhagic, preoperative recovery of the voice to its "abnormal" prehemorrhage quality, but elected surgery to improve their persistent dysphonia. In the other 6 cases (20%), including the patient who had two operations, the patients never recovered their prehemorrhagic voice quality. In Abitbol's study,[2] 9 of the 12 vocal fold hemorrhage patients (75%) underwent surgery within 6 months of presentation, 2 at 5 weeks to evacuate persistent hematomas, and 7 at 5 months. In Lin's series,[3] only 34 of the 44 patients with vocal fold hemorrhage were available for follow-up after diagnosis. Of this 34, 13 patients had visible polyps or nodules, and 9 had varicosities. At the time of publication, only 2 of the 34 (6%) had undergone surgery.

Summary of Current Concepts in Clinical Management

Submucosal vocal fold hemorrhage usually follows trauma. In the authors' opinion, it is more likely to occur following ingestion of aspirin and other anticoagulants and in women prior to menses, although that was not proven definitively (or studied specifically) in the research. Hemorrhage in the vocal folds is a contraindication to singing, acting, and speaking. When hemorrhage is observed, the therapeutic course should include strict voice rest initially, as well as correction of any underlying disease or predisposing factor. The potential gravity of vocal fold hemorrhage must be stressed, for singers and actors are generally reluctant to cancel a performance. As von Leden observed, it is a pleasure to work with "people who are determined that the show must go on when everyone else is determined to goof off."[12(p64)] However, patient compliance is essential when serious damage has occurred.

Table 86–2.—Outcome Assessment.

	Total Recovery	Near-total Recovery	Voice Change
Sudden Onset	16	1	0
Progressive Onset	6	2	5
No Symptoms	1	0	0
Total	23	3	5

Table 86–3. Surgical Intervention.

Patient	Interval to Surgery (months)	Findings	Postoperative Stroboscopy
P.O.	20	Bilateral varices	Normal
B.B.	3½	Bilateral masses Bilateral varices	Minimal stiffness
W.S.	2	Contralateral cyst	Minimal stiffness
K.D.	6	Bilateral masses	Asymmetric stiffness
R.S.	5	Ipsilateral mass	None
N.B.	5	Contralateral mass	Minimal stiffness (contralateral)
A.B.	2	Bilateral nodules (present > 18 months)	None
A.B.	8 months after new hemorrhage	Ipsilateral mass varix	Minimal to moderate stiffness
E.G.	15	Ipsilateral mass varix	None
S.H.	21	Bilateral masses	Normal

Ten surgical procedures on nine patients.

Submucosal vocal fold hemorrhage appears to be a more prevalent injury than previously recognized. It is more commonly reported in professional voice users, especially singers, due to their extreme vocal demands. The diagnosis of vocal fold hemorrhage requires a high index of suspicion. Patients can present with sudden *or* progressive changes in vocal quality and may not be able to discern a specific event that led to the voice change. Occasionally, acute hemorrhage is seen in a patient with little or no dysphonia. Such hemorrhages are nearly always isolated to the superior surface of the vocal fold (Fig 86–10A).

Stroboscopic examination is essential to diagnosis and treatment planning. Reduced vibratory motion in the affected vocal fold is a consistent finding, and improvement in the mucosal wave corresponds with functional recovery of the voice.

In most cases, hemorrhages resolve spontaneously. Even in extensive hemorrhage, substantial resolution should be noted within a few days, and the vocal fold should be flat, although still discolored (Fig 86–10B). Proper therapy usually involves only close observation, voice rest for the first week, and relative voice rest until vibration returns to the vibratory margin (usually at least 3 to 6 weeks following significant hemorrhage). However, not all hemorrhages resolve completely. In some cases, the hematoma within the layers of the vocal fold organizes and fibroses, resulting in

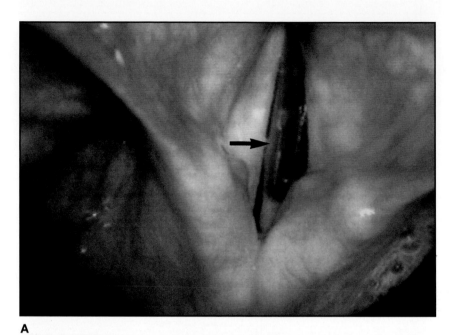

A

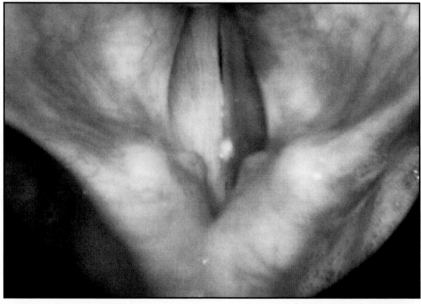

B

Fig 86–10. This 36-year-old police officer was struck in the larynx during an altercation. Although he had extremely mild hoarseness, we were consulted because he had sustained direct trauma to his larynx. He had a prominent hematoma involving his right vocal fold, However, stroboscopy revealed that the vibratory margin had been spared (*arrow*), explaining why his focal fold looked so much worse than his voice sounded. The hematoma was a raised mass (**A**). Within 1 week, the vocal fold was flat (**B**), although still discolored. When the bulk of the hematoma resolves in this fashion, complete recovery generally occurs, as it did in this case. If a large mass of submucosal blood persists for more than a few days, incision and evacuation of the clot should be considered.

scar and permanent dysphonia. In others, hemorrhage may be followed by persistent, enlarged, varicose vessels. In some patients, particularly professional singers, the increased bulk and engorgement of these vessels associated with heavy voice use produce subtle but disturbing changes (Fig 86–11). In addition, in a small number of cases, recurrent vocal fold hemorrhage may occur from repeated traumatic rupture of a varicose vessel, generally on the superior or leading surface of the vocal folds.

Most patients can be expected to return to their pre-hemorrhage vocal quality. Those who present after the sudden onset of dysphonia have the best chance for total recovery. The presence of a vocal fold mass(es) makes it more likely that they will not recover totally normal voice and may require surgical intervention if improved vocal quality is desired. Masses should be recognized as prognostic of inferior recovery (Fig 86–12). Most singers can be expected to be restricted from singing, even in the studio, for about 6 weeks following diagnosis of a vocal fold hemorrhage without a mass in order to optimize long-term, full functional recovery.

Vocal rest appears to be important in promoting recovery from vocal fold hemorrhage. A prospective, randomized study of the efficacy of voice rest is not available, and probably will be impossible due to the risks of permanent voice change in patients who develop persistent vocal fold scarring. However, it is the opinion of the authors that the spontaneous decrease in voice use beginning at the time of injury and compliance with voice rest instructions after medical diagnosis prompted faster and more complete recovery in most patients.

In some cases, surgery may be efficacious. In patients with very extensive hemorrhage distorting the

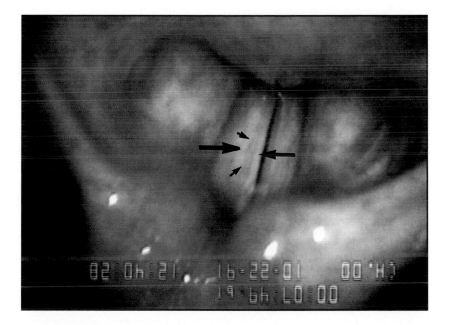

Fig 86–11. This 20-year-old conservatory voice major had been singing seriously for 5 years and had had no voice problems until 10 months prior to examination. Initially, he noted voice fatigue and loss of his lower range after singing for approximately one-half hour. Strobovideolaryngoscopy was performed on two occasions, 1 hour apart. The initial examination was normal. He then sang for approximately 1 hour and was reexamined when his voice was fatigued. The video print above was taken at the time of the second examination. It revealed a prominent varicosity on the left vocal fold. The largest black arrow marks the lateral margins of the varicosity, the smaller arrow marks the medial margin, and the smallest arrows point towards the anterior and posterior extent of the varicosity. This vein "pumped up" during singing, much as extremity veins become prominent during other forms of exercise. Following surgical obliteration of the vein, his voice returned to normal. Today, the vein would be resected rather than cauterized with a laser.

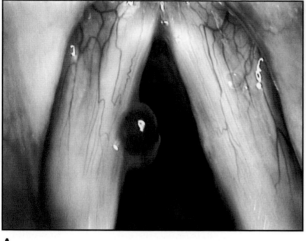

A

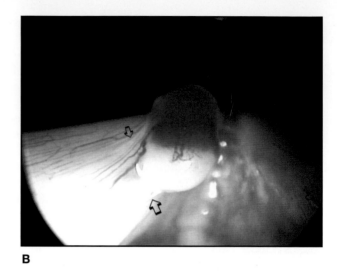

B

Fig 83–12. This 37-year-old female nonsmoker was examined 2 months following the sudden onset of hoarseness. Strobovideolaryngoscopy revealed a hemorrhagic polyp of the left vibratory margin in the striking zone (**A**).There were also enlarged, irregular vessels on the superior surfaces of both vocal folds. This video print was taken through a Storz 10 mm 0° rod. An asymptomatic anterior microweb is also present. Examination of the same lesion taken through a Storz 70° 4 mm rod (**B**), illustrates the vertical extent of the mass and shows the mass's vasculature and the anatomy of its attachment to the vocal fold (*open arrows*) more clearly. The anterior commissure and its web can also be seen (slightly out of focus) (*solid arrow*).

vocal fold, an incision along the superior surface with suction evacuation of the hematoma may speed healing. However, if the bulging fold has not flattened satisfactorily through resorption of the hematoma within 2 to 3 days after the hemorrhage, evacuation may be considered.

In patients with recurrent hemorrhage from a varicose vessel, or with voice dysfunction resulting from small vessel enlargement, resection or cauterization of the abnormal vessels is indicated. This is performed with a vascular knife, as described in chapter 82, or with a carbon dioxide laser, using defocused 1-watt laser bursts interrupted or singly at 0.1 second after icing the vocal fold. Care should be taken not to permit heat transfer to the intermediate or deep layers of the lamina propria. Protection may be accomplished by directing the laser beam tangentially for blood vessels directly on the vibratory margin so that the direct impact of the laser beam is not aimed at the vibratory surface, and by submucosal infusion. In some cases, the mucosa may be gently retracted using an alligator forceps with a cottonoid along the superior surface, stretching blood vessels onto the superior surface where they may be vaporized safely over the body of the thyroarytenoid muscle. Laser-associated risks of thermal injury are avoided if the vessels are resected using cold instruments, as preferred by the author (RTS).[13]

The development of a vocal fold hemorrhage is potentially disastrous in a professional voice user. It leads not only to dysphonia that can persist for weeks or longer, but also has the potential to cause permanent voice change. Professional voice users should be educated by their laryngologists, voice teachers, and professional publications regarding predisposing factors and common presenting symptoms of submucosal vocal fold hemorrhage. With accurate early diagnosis, institution of voice rest, and follow-up with appropriate voice and singing therapy, total functional recovery can be achieved in most cases.

References

1. Sataloff RT, Spiegel JR, Hawkshaw MJ. Strobovideo-laryngoscopy: results and clinical value. *Ann Otol Rhinol Laryngol.* 1991;100(9):725–727.
2. Abitbol J. Vocal cord hemorrhages in voice professionals. *J Voice.* 1988;2:261–266.
3. Lin PT, Stern JC, Gould WJ. The risk factors and management of vocal cord hemorrhages: an experience with 44 cases. *J Voice.* 1991;5(1):74–77.
4. Feder RJ. Varix of the vocal cord in a professional voice user. *Otolaryngol Head Neck Surg.* 1983;91:435–436.
5. Spiegel JR, Sataloff RT, Hawkshaw M, et al. Vocal fold hemorrhage: diagnosis and clinical implications. Presented at the Nineteenth Annual Symposium: Care of the Professional Voice; June 7, 1990; Philadelphia, Pa.
6. Brodnitz FS. Hormones and the human voice. *Bull N Y Acad Med.* 1971;47:183–191.
7. Smith FM. Hoarseness, a symptom of premenstrual tension. *Arch Otolaryngol.* 1962;75:66–68.
8. Lacina VO. Der Einfluss der Menstruation auf die Stimme der Sängerinnen. *Folia Phoniatr.* 1968;20:13–24.

9. Abitbol J, de Brux J, Millot G, et al. Does a hormonal vocal cord cycle exist in women? Study of vocal premenstrual syndromes in voice performers by videostroboscopy-glottography and cytology on 38 women. *J Voice.* 1989;2:157–162.

10. Baker DC. Laryngeal problems in singers. *Laryngoscope.* 1962;72:902–908.

11. Sataloff RT. *Professional Voice: The Science and Art of Clinical Care.* New York, NY: Raven Press; 1991:201–202.

12. von Leden H, In: Brodnitz F, Andrews A, Gould WJ, Lawrence VL, von Leden H, Winer H. Medical problems and treatment (in singers). *Transcripts of the Seventh Symposium: Care of the Professional Voice, part III.* New York, NY: The Voice Foundation; 1978:64.

13. Hochman I, Sataloff RT, Hillman RE, Zeitels SM. Ectasias and varicies of the vocal fold: clearing the striking zone. *Ann Otol Rhinol Laryngol.* 1999;108(1):10–16.

87

Vocal Fold Scar

Robert Thayer Sataloff

Vocal fold scar poses great therapeutic challenges in treatment of voice professionals. Unfortunately, laryngologists frequently are confronted with patients who have remained or become dysphonic after laryngeal surgery. Occasionally, a cause such as arytenoid dislocation can be found and treated. More often, however, the problem is scar producing and adynamic segment, decreased bulk of one vocal fold following "stripping," bowing caused by superior laryngeal nerve paralysis, or some other serious complication in a mobile vocal fold. None of the surgical procedures available for these conditions is effective consistently. If surgery is considered at all in such patients, it should be discussed pessimistically. The patient should be aware that the chances of returning the voice to normal or professional quality are slight and there is a chance of making it worse. However, advances in the management of vocal fold scar have increased our therapeutic options.

Symptomatic vocal fold scarring alters phonation by interfering with the mucosal wave. This may be due to the obliteration of the layered structure of the vibratory margin, as seen commonly after vocal fold stripping, or, to a limited extent, after other vocal fold surgery trauma. Similar disruption of the layered structure and mucosal wave function may also occur congenitally, as in some cases of sulcus vocalis. Scarring may also cause dysphonia by mechanical restriction of vibration or glottic closure, as seen in some cases of dense vocal fold web, or fibrotic masses on the membranous vocal fold, as may form subsequent to vocal fold hemorrhage. It is also necessary to distinguish raised scar that causes failure of glottic closure by mass effect from the more common scar that effectively thins the vocal fold edge and causes failure of glottic closure by adhering the epithelium to the vocal ligament or muscle. In the former case, treatment must include resection of the scar tissue mass to reestablish a straight vocal fold edge. However, most of this chapter will discuss the even more challenging problem of vocal scar that has obliterated the layered structure and mucosal wave. A scar involving the posterior, subglottic, and arytenoid regions may also be troublesome, but this discussion will be limited to scarring involving membranous portion of the vocal folds.

Reliable, valid, objective voice assessment is essential in diagnosing vocal fold scar, as well as in the assessment of other voice disorders. Accurate assessment of vibration is critical, and strobovideolaryngoscopy is virtually indispensable to proper diagnosis and management of vocal fold scar.[1,2] Integrity of the vibratory margin of the vocal fold is essential for the complex motion required to produce good vocal quality. Under continuous light, the vocal folds vibrate approximately 250 times per second while phonating at middle C. Naturally, the human eye cannot discern necessary details during such rapid motion. Assessment of the vibratory margin may be performed through high-speed photography, strobovideolaryngoscopy, electroglottography, or photoglottography. Only strobovideolaryngoscopy provides the necessary clinical information in a practical fashion. For example, in a patient with poor voice following laryngeal surgery and a normal looking larynx, stroboscopic light reveals adynamic segments (scar) that explain the problem even to an untrained observer (such as the patient). In most instances, stroboscopy provides all of the clinical information necessary to assess vibration. However, objective voice analysis, particularly aerodynamic and acoustic assessment, is extremely valuable for diagnosis, therapy, and evaluation of treatment efficacy.

Therapy for Vocal Fold Scar

Therapy for vocal fold scar depends on the size, location, and severity of the scar; the vocal needs of the individual patient, the patient's motivation; and the skill of the voice team. In general, once the vibratory margin of the vocal fold has been scarred (the layered structure obliterated), it is not possible to return the voice to normal. However, several options are available to improve the voice.

Voice therapy is essential for anyone interested in obtaining optimal results. Most patients do not use their vocal mechanisms optimally. Consequently, even in the presence of vocal fold scar, teaching the individual to make effective use of the support and resonator systems generally improves vocal intensity and ease and helps diminish fatigue. Nearly everyone with significant vocal fold injury develops compensatory behaviors. These gestures are usually hyperfunctional, counterproductive, and in some cases dangerous. Such unconscious adjustments are seen even in the most skilled voice professionals after sustaining a vocal fold injury and scar. Expert voice therapy eliminates this compensatory muscular tension dysphonia, further decreasing fatigue and allowing a more accurate assessment of vibratory margin function. After voice technique has been optimized, and the vocal fold scar has matured (usually about 6 to 12 months), judgments can be made about the acceptability of the final voice result. If voice function is not satisfactory to the patient, then surgery may be considered. However, it is essential for the laryngologist to be sure that the patient's expectations are reasonable. These do not include restoration to normalcy. However, in some cases, it is possible to decrease hoarseness and breathiness substantially.

Surgery for Vocal Fold Scar

Vocal fold scar causes dysphonia by disrupting or obliterating the mucosal wave and by interfering with glottic closure. Clear understanding of these facts is necessary if one is to design rational surgical intervention. At present, there is no generally accepted, highly successful surgical treatment for vocal fold scar. However, numerous procedures have been tried, and some are useful in selected cases. Although there is very little information published on older attempts at surgical procedures to correct vocal fold scar, anecdotally, many experienced voice surgeons admit to having attempted surgery in a very small number of patients. Procedures to restore the mucosal wave have included injection of steroids into the vibratory margin, elevation of a microflap to "lyse adhesions," followed by simply replacing the microflap, elevation of microflap with the placement of steroids under the flap, and other procedures. Although none of these procedures produces consistently excellent results, they may help

somewhat. Microflap elevation with steroids is sometimes helpful and is still used (M. Bouchayer, personal communication, April 1995); but the results are not consistently excellent. Pontes and Behlau have suggested a unique approach to the treatment of sulcus vocalis that essentially involves multiple releasing incisions.[3] The voice results have been surprisingly good, considering the limited success achieved by previous procedures for this condition. These principles have been applied to iatrogenic vocal fold scar and appear to have some merit in severe, extensive scarring (P. Pontes, personal communication, April 1995).

The problem of glottic incompetence is generally addressed through medialization surgery. Most medialization procedures in the past have involved injection of Teflon. Because this substance can itself cause profound scarring, many otolaryngologists have abandoned its use in most cases since the mid- to late 1980s. At present, the medialization techniques of choice are generally thyroplasty or injection of a substance other than Teflon. For extensive failure of glottic closure, the author has found Type I thyroplasty with Gore-Tex to be the most effective. For limited medialization, lateral injection of autologous fat (in the same place where Teflon used to be injected) has proven successful.[4] Approximately 30% overinjection is necessary to account for resorption. Other injection materials are discussed in chapter 82. Techniques to manage vibratory margin scar are worthy of more complete discussion.

Collagen injection was investigated most-extensively by Ford and coworkers.[5-7] Long-term results from skin injections of collagen have shown a reduction of scar tissue in the treated areas. Collagen is a thin liquid that can easily be injected in small quantities. Consequently, collagen injections are ideally suited for small adynamic segments. The ease and accuracy of injection allow for attempts at augmentation in areas of scar, as well as for managing difficult problems such as persistent posterior glottic incompetence and combined recurrent and superior laryngeal nerve paralysis. Former concerns about efficacy and safety of this material[8] seem to be less warranted, and experience using collagen has been most encouraging. When used, collagen is injected into the region of the vocal ligament and appears particularly appropriate for treating limited vocal fold scarring. Such cases are common, for example, after laser resection of vocal nodules. For more extensive scarring, as may be seen following stripping of an entire vocal fold, collagen appears less effective. However, since autologous and allogeneic human collagen have come into use, results appear to have been better than they were with allogeneic collagen, as discussed in chapter 82. The author

(RTS) uses collagen more frequently than he did at the time of the last edition of this book; but it is still generally not satisfactory as the sole treatment for severe, extensive scarring.

In 1995, the author introduced a technique for autologous fat implantation into the vibratory margin of the vocal fold as a treatment for vocal fold scar.[9] The technique involves implantation into the vibratory margin, not injection.

To recreate a mobile vibratory margin, a mucosal pocket is created and filled with fat in order to prevent readherence of the mucosa to the vocal ligament and vocalis muscle. An incision is made on the superior surface (Fig 87–1A), and a small access tunnel is elevated toward the vibratory margin. The superior incision is placed in a position that will permit angled instruments to be passed through the tunnel to reach the anterior and posterior limits of the vocal fold scar.

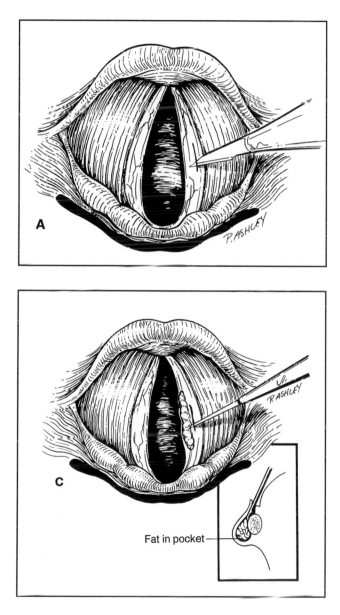

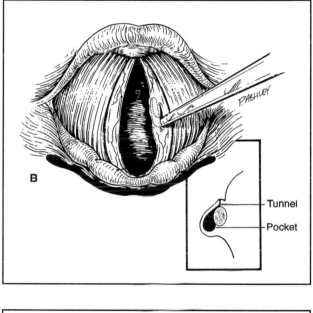

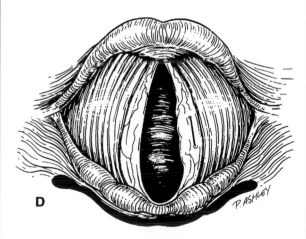

Fig 87–1. A. A small incision is made on the superior surface of the scarred vocal fold, and a narrow access tunnel is excavated to provide access to the medial edge. **B.** Through the access tunnel, an angled instrument is used to elevate a pocket. It is essential that the mucosa along the medial and inferior margins be kept intact. **C.** A Brünings syringe with the largest needle is passed through the tunnel and used to deposit fat in the pocket. **D.** When the needle is removed, the small access tunnel closes spontaneously, preventing extrusion of the fat. Fat should not extrude even when pressure is placed against the medial margin. If fat extrusion occurs, a suture can be placed.

Although working through a small access tunnel is technically more difficult than elevating a large flap, we believe that it is advantageous because it closes spontaneously upon removal of instruments and prevents fat extrusion from the surgically created pocket. If a larger incision is made along the superior surface, sutures are necessary to prevent fat extrusion; and even small sutures create additional tissue trauma.[10] A pocket is created along the medial margin using a right-angle dissector and an angled knife or scissors, as needed (Fig 87–1B). The pocket extends to the superior aspect of the vibratory margin and inferiorly for at least 3 to 5 mm to encompass all of the medial surface ordinarily involved in creating the mucosal wave vertical phase difference during phonation. Fat harvested at the beginning of the surgery to fill the tunnel (Fig 87–1C). Instruments are then withdrawn, and the access tunnel closes and provides sufficient resistance against fat extrusion (Fig 87–1D). The procedure is performed under local anesthesia. At the conclusion of the procedure, the patient is asked to phonate briefly and to cough in order to be certain that the implant is secure. Although no problems preventing closure of the mucosal flap have occurred to date, if extrusion occurred, fibrin glue would be tried (if available) or a suture would be placed.

Previous experience with lipoinjection has provided convincing evidence that it is important to avoid extensive manipulation or trauma to the fat. The fat is harvested in large globules either by resecting a small amount of fat (usually from the abdomen) with traditional instruments or by harvesting it with the largest available liposuction cannula. The fat is gently rinsed with saline, but it is not morselized. Packing the fat through the access tunnel with microinstruments has been attempted, but it is technically difficult to pack the fat tightly and evenly; and this method appears to cause more trauma to the access tunnel, flap, and fat than delivering the implant through a Brünings syringe. At present, the fat globules are loaded into the Brünings syringe and the largest Brünings needle is used to deliver the fat into the preformed vibratory margin pocket. Gross examination with a microscope indicates that passing the fat through the Brünings syringe certainly elongates the fat globules and must traumatize them to some degree, but they appear to be largely intact and not too badly traumatized. At present, this seems to be the best available method, although technical improvements are tested regularly. In a recent review, Neuenschwander, Sataloff, Abaza, et al[11] reported on the first eight patients who had undergone vocal fold fat implantation for severe scar and dysphonia. Their mean follow-up time was 23 months. Analysis of strobovideolaryngoscopy revealed statistically significant improvement in glottic closure, mucosal wave, and stiffness. In perceptual studies, there was statistically significant improvement in all five parameters of the GRBAS rating scale. All eight patients had undergone more than one surgical procedure, including fat injection in all eight, thyroplasty in one, scar excision in two, lysis of adhesions in two, and steroid injection in two. The senior author (RTS) continues to utilize this procedure. However, it should still be considered one among various options for the treatment of dysphonia caused by vocal fold scar.[12]

Occasionally, surgeons are faced with extreme cases of vibratory margin scar. These are especially common after major trauma or extensive cancer surgery. When a nonvibrating scarred vocal fold is lateralized so that glottic closure is impossible, and when the involved hemilarynx is so densely scarred that the vocal fold cannot be adequately medialized even with thyropasty, occasionally more extensive surgery for vocal fold scar may be appropriate. For example, some such cases may be improved through resection of the scarred hemilarynx and creation of a pseudovocal fold using modifications of strap muscle techniques employed routinely for cordectomy or vertical hemilaryngectomy.[13] Certainly, this is an unusual and extreme approach for the treatment of vocal fold scar, but it is an option that should be in the surgeon's armamentarium for the rare, appropriate patient.

Familiarity with the latest concepts in vocal fold anatomy and physiology is essential in understanding the consequences of vocal fold scar.

References

1. Sataloff RT, Spiegel JR, Carroll LM, et al. Strobovideolaryngoscopy in professional voice users: results and clinical value. *J Voice*. 1988;1:359–364.

2. Sataloff RT, Spiegel JR, Hawkshaw MJ. Strobovideolaryngoscopy: results and clinical value. *Ann Otol Rhinol Laryngol*. 1991;100:725–757.

3. Pontes P, Behlau M. Treatment of sulcus vocalis: auditory perceptual and acoustic analysis of the slicing mucosa surgical technique. *J Voice*. 1993;7(4):365–376.

4. Mikaelian D, Lowry LD, Sataloff RT. Lipoinjection for unilateral vocal cord paralysis. *Laryngoscope*. 1991;101: 465–468.

5. Ford CN, Bless DM, Loftus JM. The role of injectable collagen in the treatment of glottic insufficiency: a study of 119 patients. *Ann Otol Rhinol Laryngol*. 1973;101(3):237–247.

6. Ford CN, Bless DM. Collagen injected in the scarred vocal fold. *J Voice*. 1988;1:116–118.

7. Ford CN, Bless DM. Selected problems treated by vocal fold injection of collagen. *Am J Otolaryngol*. 1993;14(4): 257–261.

8. Spiegel JR, Sataloff RT, Gould WJ. The treatment of vocal fold paralysis with injectable collagen. *J Voice.* 1987;1: 119–121.

9. Sataloff RT, Spiegel JR, Hawkshaw M, et al. Autologous fat implantation for vocal fold scar: a preliminary report. *J Voice.* 1997;11(2):238–246.

10. Feldman MD, Sataloff RT, Epstein G, Ballas SK. Autologous fibrin tissue adhesive for peripheral nerve anastomosis. *Arch Otolaryngol Head Neck Surg.* 1987;113:963–967.

11. Neuenschwander MC, Sataloff RT, Abaza M, et al. Management of fold scar with autologous fat implantation: perceptual results. *J Voice.* 2001;15(2):295–304.

12. Benninger MS, Alessi D, Archer S, et al. Vocal fold scarring: current concepts and management. *Otolaryngol Head Neck Surg.* 1996;115(5):474–482.

13. Spiegel JR, Sataloff RT. Surgery for carcinoma of the larynx. In: Gould WJ, Sataloff RT, Spiegel JR, eds. *Voice Surgery.* St. Louis, Mo: CV Mosby Co; 1993:307–338.

88

Laryngotracheal Trauma

Yolanda D. Heman-Ackah and Robert Thayer Sataloff

The incidence of laryngotracheal trauma is estimated to be 1 in 14,000 to 30,000 emergency department visits yearly in the United States.[1,2] Trauma to the laryngotracheal complex can be classified as blunt, penetrating, caustic, thermal, and iatrogenic injuries. The morbidity associated with these injuries ranges from chronic airway obstruction to voice compromise, with complication rates as high as 15 to 25%.[3-5] Because of their potential for airway compromise, these injuries can be lethal, with mortality rates of 2 to 15%.[3,5] Injuries to the larynx and trachea often accompany other severe injuries, and the neck can appear to be deceptively normal even in cases of serious laryngotracheal disruption.

Laryngotracheal injuries can be caused by external or internal trauma. External insults include blunt and penetrating injuries. In the past, most external laryngeal trauma was the result of motor vehicle accidents. Studies have shown that, due to improved car safety features such as seat belts, shoulder harnesses, child safety seats, padded dashboards, and reduced speed limits, laryngeal trauma is seen less frequently. Many laryngeal injuries still occur, however, in other types of accidents and in sports. Baseball bats, hockey sticks, and lacrosse sticks, hockey pucks, elbows, shoulders, and knees have all been sources of blunt laryngeal trauma. In addition, penetrating injuries are becoming more prevalent due to increasing urban violence.[6-8]

The majority of internal laryngeal injuries are iatrogenic. Intubation and flexible and rigid endoscopy can lead to injuries of the upper airway.[9,10] Noniatrogenic internal injuries can result from foreign-body aspiration, caustic ingestion and toxin inhalation, and, occasionally, voice abuse or trauma (including phonation, coughing, and sneezing).

Despite some excellent retrospective reviews and ongoing studies with animal models, many points of controversy remain in the surgical treatment of laryngeal trauma.[2,4,7,11-15] This chapter focuses on the state-of-the-art methods for evaluation and surgery that seem to lead to the most consistently acceptable results: a stable airway with good vocal quality.

Blunt Injury

Blunt injury to the larynx and trachea is the most common cause of laryngotracheal injury in the United States today, accounting for 60% of all injuries to the laryngotracheal complex.[2,4] These injuries result from motor vehicle collisions in the adult population and from accidents involving all-terrain vehicles, bicycles, contact sports, and hanging type injuries in the young adult, adolescent, and pediatric populations. Adults and children differ not only in the mechanisms of injury, but also in the types of injuries experienced. These differences can be accounted for, at least in part, by differences in the relative size, position, and degree of calcification of the larynx and trachea.

Adult Framework Injuries from Blunt Trauma

In the adult, the inferior border of the cricoid cartilage sits at the level of the sixth and seventh cervical vertebrae.[16] Thus, in the normal upright position, the larynx is relatively protected from trauma by the overhang of the mandible superiorly, the bony prominence of the clavicles and sternal manubrium inferiorly, and by the mass of the sternocleidomastoid muscles laterally. Laryngeal injuries are relatively rare except when there is a direct blow to the neck. The usual victim of laryngotracheal trauma in a motor vehicle collision is an unbelted front seat passenger or driver in a vehicle without protective airbags. Upon collision, the front seat passenger or driver is propelled forward with the neck in extension, eliminating the mandible as a protective shield. The laryngotracheal complex hits the dashboard or steering wheel with a posterior-superiorly based vector of force, and the thyroid and cricoid cartilages are crushed against the cervical vertebrae (Fig 88–1).[17,18] Direct blows to the larynx can also occur during athletic competition, while falling forward onto a blunt object, or with hanging of the neck from a suspended rope or wire.

A wide spectrum of predictable injuries occurs. The thyroid and cricoid cartilages interact dynamically to protect the airway from blunt injury.[18] Forces to the anterior larynx often are encountered first by the thyroid prominence, which bends against the cervical vertebrae on impact. The thyroid cartilage eventually reaches a point of maximal flexibility, and a single median or paramedian fracture occurs (Fig 88–2).

The force then impacts the cricoid ring, which was previously shielded by the anterior projection of the thyroid cartilage. In a patient with a marked laryngeal prominence, multiple fractures of the thyroid cartilage in both the vertical and horizontal planes may occur prior to the distribution of force onto the cricoid cartilage (Fig 88–3).[18] The cricoid has a relatively thin anterior arch that blends laterally into rigidly buttressed tubercles. Lower level impacts result in a single median fracture or multiple paramedian vertical fractures. The airway is maintained by the lateral buttresses (Fig 88–4). With higher impact forces, secondary lateral arch fractures can occur in the cricoid cartilage, resulting in airway collapse and possible injury to the recur-

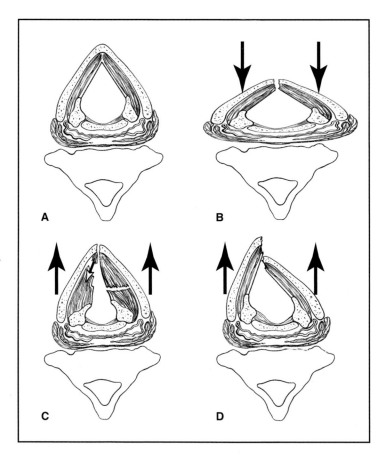

Fig 88–1. Mechanism of blunt laryngeal trauma. **A.** Normal laryngeal position; **B.** Posteriorly directed force crushing thyroid ala against cervical vertebrae, resulting in a midline fracture; **C.** Recovery of larynx from force resulting in detachment of the vocal ligament on the left, tear in the right thyroarytenoid muscle, and bilateral arytenoid dislocation; **D.** Recovery of larynx from force resulting in overlapping, displaced thyroid lamina fracture and malposition of the vocal fold. (Illustrations courtesy of Sabrina M. Heman-Ackah.)

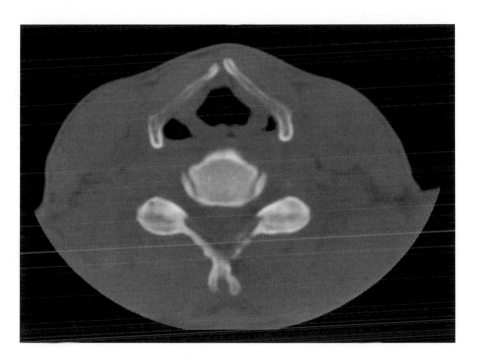

Fig 88–2. Axial CT scan of the thyroid ala. There is a midline thyroid ala fracture with diastasis of fracture segments.

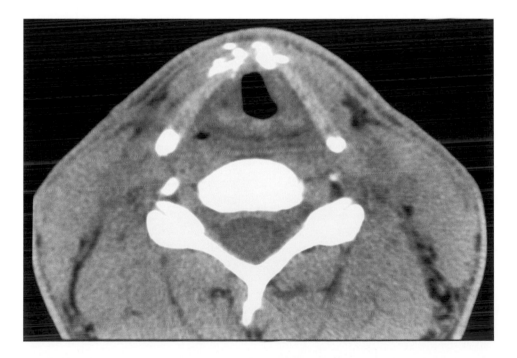

Fig 88–3. Axial CT scan of the thyroid ala demonstrating an anterior comminuted thyroid ala fracture sustained by the patient in a motor vehicle collision.

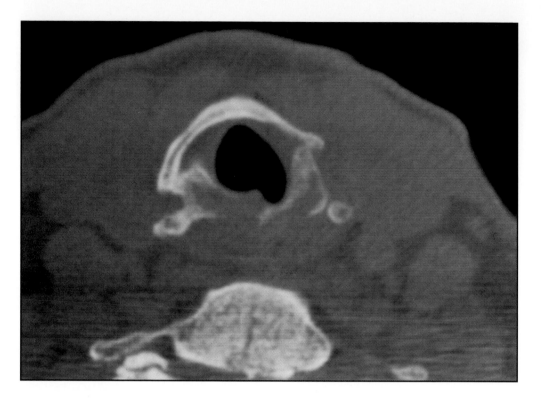

Fig 88–4. Axial CT scan at the level of the thyroid and cricoid cartilages. There is a vertical, displaced posterior cricoid lamina fracture with fusion of the right cricothyroid joint. The airway is maintained by the lateral buttresses.

rent laryngeal nerve due to impingement at the level of the cricothyroid joint (Figs 88-5 and 88-6).

If the force is severe or low in the neck, complete laryngotracheal separation may occur.[19] Separation usually occurs between the cricoid cartilage and the first tracheal ring, resulting in displacement of the trachea inferiorly and soft tissue collapse into the airway, with consequent airway obstruction.[19-22] The strap musculature and surrounding cervical fascia can serve as a temporary conduit for air until edema and hematoma formation result in obstruction of this temporary airway.

Pediatric Framework Injuries from Blunt Trauma

Fractures of the thyroid and cricoid cartilage from blunt trauma are uncommon in the pediatric population. The pediatric larynx sits higher in the neck than in the adult, and depending on age, can lie between the second and seventh cervical vertebrae. The mandible serves more as a protective shield in the child than it does in the adult.[23] The greater elasticity of the pediatric cartilaginous framework makes it more resilient to external stresses, and the mobility of the supporting tissues tends to protect the laryngotracheal complex more effectively. Children are likely to sustain soft tissue injuries resulting in edema and hematoma formation.[22,23] This is of particular concern in a child because of the relatively smaller diameter of the pediatric airway.

The pediatric patient is more likely than an adult to sustain transection and telescoping injuries. An individual who falls onto the handlebar of a bicycle may suffer a telescoping injury in which the cricoid cartilage is dislocated superiorly underneath the thyroid lamina (Fig 88–7).[22-25] With more forceful blows, complete laryngotracheal separation may occur. The adolescent and young adult riding a snowmobile or an all-terrain vehicle may sustain a "clothes-line" type injury to the neck upon collision with a cable or wire. A horizontal, linear force is applied low in the neck, compressing the cricotracheal complex against the anterior cervical vertebrae and resulting in cricotracheal separation.[25] The elasticity of the intercartilaginous ligaments contributes to substernal retraction of the trachea. These are often fatal injuries, but occasionally there is enough fascial stenting to maintain an adequate airway until an artificial airway can be established. There may be an associated injury and possibly transection of both recurrent laryngeal nerves, which

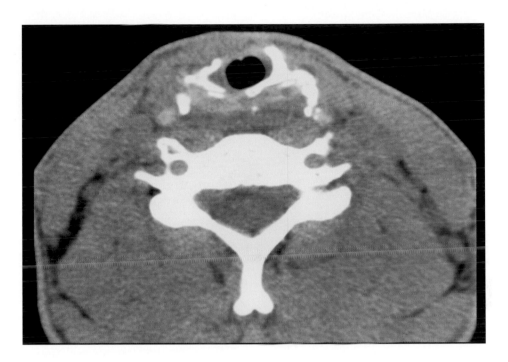

Fig 88–5. Axial CT scan of the cricoid cartilage. The airway is narrowed secondary to anterior and posterior vertical, displaced cricoid lamina fractures.

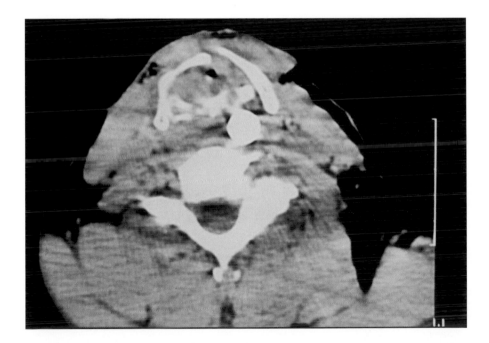

Fig 88–6. Axial CT scan at the level of the thyroid and cricoid cartilages. There are midline and left lateral fractures of the thyroid ala and comminuted fractures of the posterior cricoid lamina with loss of the airway space. The airway was secured below the fracture segments with tracheostomy.

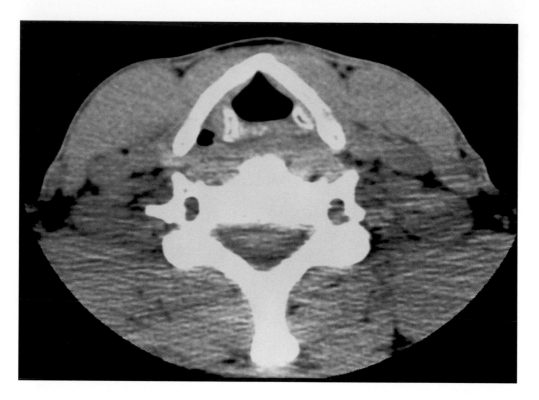

Fig 88–7. Axial CT scan at the level of the thyroid and cricoid cartilages. There is subluxation of the cricoid cartilage under the thyroid ala after the patient sustained an elbow injury to the neck while playing basketball.

are also compressed against the cervical vertebrae during the injury.[22,25]

Young children may accidentally hang themselves while playing, and adolescents may do so intentionally in suicide attempts. In these instances, the fall to hanging position is usually less than 1 to 2 feet. The rope around the neck tightens usually in the region of the thyrohyoid membrane, resulting in airway obstruction as the epiglottis closes over the glottis. The distinction between this and the injury that results from hanging inflicted by a second party is that in self-inflicted or accidental injuries, death is not necessarily imminent; and in those who survive, there is usually injury, possibly avulsion, at the level of the thyrohyoid membrane. In homicidal hanging (professional execution), the victim is usually dropped a distance of several feet, resulting in death secondary to tracheal transection or spinal cord injury from C1–C2 dislocation.[25]

Soft Tissue Injuries from Blunt Trauma

Blunt trauma to the larynx may result in soft tissue injuries with or without associated framework injuries. Rupture of the thyroepiglottic ligament can be associated with either horizontal or vertical fractures of the thyroid cartilage. Narrowing of the laryngeal lumen can occur secondary to herniation of pre-epiglottic tissue or posterior displacement of the epiglottic petiole.[17,21]

Vocal fold injuries result from vertical fractures of the thyroid ala (see Fig 88–1). As the thyroid cartilage snaps back from its compression against the cervical vertebrae, the thyroarytenoid muscle and ligament may tear, resulting in a separation at any point along its length. This may be evident as mucosal lacerations or hemorrhage of one or both vocal folds. The mucosa on the arytenoids may be denuded or avulsed. Because of the traction on the arytenoids from this springlike motion of the thyroid cartilage, the arytenoid cartilages may also become displaced from the cricoarytenoid joint into a more posterior and lateral or anterior position (Fig 88–8). If one segment of the thyroid cartilage fails to return to its normal position, an overlapping fracture may occur, resulting in malposition of the vocal fold (Figs 88–9 and 88–10). Lacerations of the piriform sinus and upper esophagus may occur as the thyroid cartilage rubs against the cervical vertebrae.[17,21]

Soft tissue injuries associated with cricoid, tracheal, and cricotracheal separation injuries within the cartilaginous framework usually involve crushed or lacerated mucosa. Both recurrent laryngeal nerves are fre-

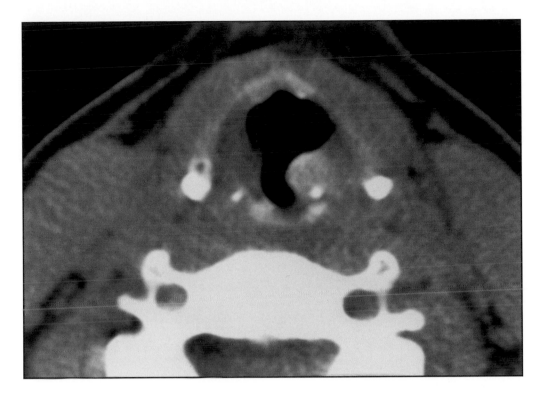

Fig 88–8. Axial CT scan of the larynx at the level of the arytenoids demonstrating anterior dislocation of the right arytenoid cartilage.

quently injured and can be severed by blunt trauma that results in cricoid fractures and/or cricotracheal separation. The phrenic nerve can also be injured, especially in cases of cricotracheal separation.[17,19,21,22,25] Associated esophageal lacerations and perforations are common.

Assessment of Blunt Injuries

Initial evaluation and assessment of the blunt trauma patient is similar for adults and children. It is important to obtain an understanding of the mechanism of injury. A high index of suspicion for blunt neck injury should be maintained in motor vehicle collisions, even without obvious external signs. Knowledge of the speed of the vehicle at the time of collision, the use of seatbelts by the trauma victim, and the presence and deployment of airbags can also be helpful in estimating the amount of force involved. In the patient with short stature, the force of deceleration against a locking "shoulder" strap that is draped over the neck may also produce significant injury. Assessment of the patient begins with evaluation and stabilization of the airway, paying particular attention to the status of the cervical spine. Assessment then proceeds with evaluation and stabilization of respiratory, cardiovascular,

cervical spine, neurologic, and other emergent organ system injuries. Management of aerodigestive tract injuries varies depending upon the presence of acute airway distress (Fig 88–11).

Evaluation of the Blunt Trauma Patient Without Airway Distress

In the patient without immediate signs of upper airway compromise, the evaluation can proceed with a complete examination, including palpation of the neck, assessment of voice quality, and flexible fiberoptic evaluation of the larynx and upper airway. Fiberoptic laryngoscopy allows assessment of the mobility of the vocal folds, patency of the upper airway, and integrity of the mucosa. If there is an adequate airway, intubation is not necessary. Because of the potential for the development of worsening laryngeal edema and airway compromise, serial examinations of the airway should be performed during the first 24 to 48 hours after injury if intubation is initially deemed unnecessary.

Adequate visualization of the endolarynx is imperative in completing the physical examination. Indirect laryngoscopy is the easiest method but can be dangerous in a patient with airway compromise. Flexible

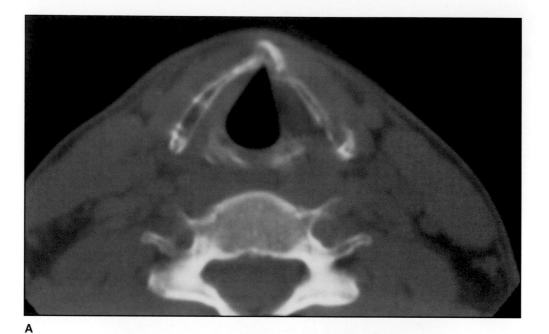

A

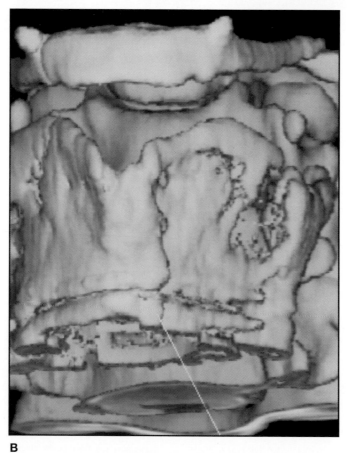

B

Fig 88–9. **A.** Axial CT scan of the subglottic larynx demonstrating a displaced, paramedian fracture of the left thyroid ala. The vocal folds (not shown) are malpositioned. **B.** Three-dimensional CT reconstruction of the left paramedian thyroid ala fracture demonstrating overlapping of the fracture segments.

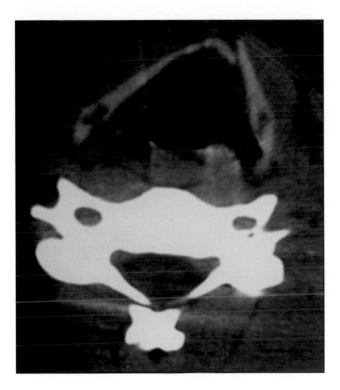

Fig 88–10. Axial CT of the supraglottic larynx. There is a displaced paramedian fracture of the right thyroid ala.

laryngoscopy has almost completely obviated this risk and is currently the preferred method of initial laryngeal examination. In patients with concomitant facial trauma or severe airway trauma, a flexible bronchoscope is sometimes preferred due to the presence of a suction channel. Strobovideolaryngoscopy can be invaluable in assessing injuries involving vocal fold mobility and integrity. Microscopic direct laryngoscopy continues to provide the most detailed evaluation of the larynx (except for determinations of dynamic function, which must be made by stroboscopy). However, advances in flexible endoscopy and the availability of stroboscopy have limited the use of direct laryngoscopy to the last step in assessment, usually at the time of the operative repair.

Management is based on the severity of the initial signs and symptoms.[7]

Patients with any sign of endolaryngeal injury (Table 88–1) should undergo radiologic imaging to evaluate for possible laryngeal framework injury.[7,24,26] Minimally displaced fractures of the thyroid cartilage can be present with very mild endolaryngeal signs and should be evaluated to determine the likelihood of fracture stability. Radiologic evaluation is best preformed by high-resolution CT scanning in multiple planes.[24] Thyroid and cricoid cartilage integrity,

cricoarytenoid joint status, cricothyroid joint status, and even soft tissue laryngeal injuries can all be assessed by an experienced radiologist if fine-cut, 1-mm, multiplanar techniques are used. MRI scanning may provide additional information about the degree of soft-tissue injury, but the CT scan remains the study of choice in laryngeal trauma.

When exposed cartilage is noted on endolaryngeal examination, or when the CT scan reveals a multiply comminuted thyroid cartilage fracture, the need for open reduction and stabilization is unquestioned (Fig 88–12) Studies by Hirano et al and Stanley et al also have shown that reduction of a single, linear, even minimally displaced, thyroid cartilage fracture is important in obtaining an adequate post-injury voice.[27,28] Although no comparative studies are available, the authors believe that only stable, nondisplaced thyroid cartilage fractures with normal endolaryngeal architecture should be treated without operative intervention. Table 88–2 lists CT findings that suggest fracture stability and instability.

Fractures that appear to have the potential for instability should be evaluated further with direct laryngoscopy and open exploration for repair. Patients with minimally displaced fractures that are associated with significant endolaryngeal injuries also require direct laryngoscopy, open exploration, and repair of the soft tissue injuries (Table 88–3). Because of the high potential for concomitant cervical spine injuries, assessment of the cervical spine is always performed prior to operative intervention of the laryngeal injuries. The presence of a cervical spine injury may preclude the ability to perform a direct laryngoscopy, and repair is begun based on findings on CT scan and flexible endoscopic examination (Fig 88–13).

Dislocation of the cricoarytenoid joint is now being recognized as a fairly common component of laryngeal trauma.[29,30] It can be seen as the only significant lesion after blunt neck trauma, in combination with nondisplaced laryngeal fractures, or as part of a complex laryngeal surgery. It must be suspected by the laryngologist if proper diagnosis and treatment are to be obtained. If a posterior dislocation is present, the involved side may appear to be paralyzed, and the involved vocal process is high. In anterior dislocations, the involved vocal process is below the normal side, and the vocal fold may appear to be short. In many acute cases, edema prohibits good assessment by indirect laryngoscopy. Stroboscopic assessment may reveal asymmetry of the mucosal wave or level of vocal fold apposition, particularly during pitch sliding maneuvers. The "jostle sign" is often absent on the dislocated side, helping to differentiate arytenoid dislocation from vocal fold paralysis. However, arytenoid

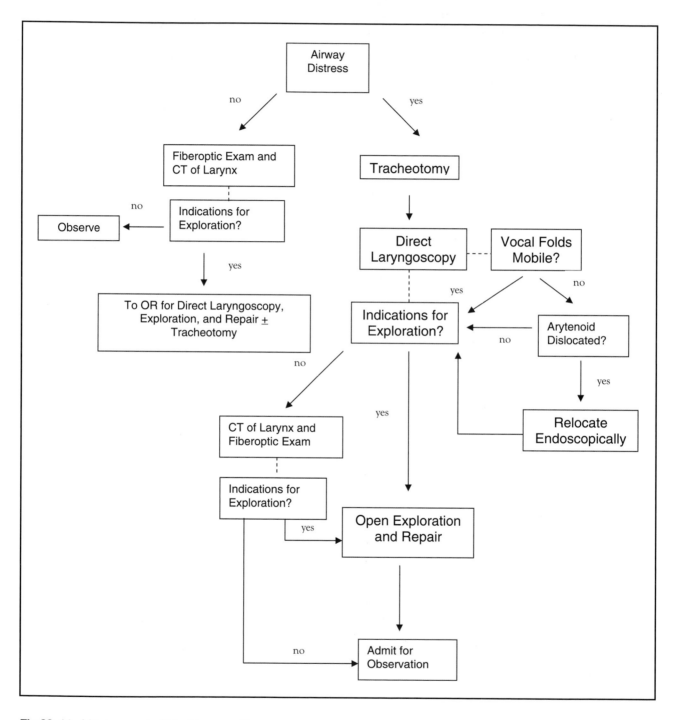

Fig 88–11. Management of blunt laryngeal trauma.

Table 88–1. Signs and Symptoms of Laryngeal Injury.

Hoarseness/dysphonia	Dyspnea
Stridor	Endolaryngeal edema
Endolaryngeal hematoma	Subcutaneous emphysema
Endolaryngeal laceration	Neck pain/point tenderness
Dysphagia	Loss of laryngeal landmarks
Odynophagia	Impaired vocal fold mobility
Hemoptysis	Arytenoid dislocation
Ecchymosis/abrasions of anterior neck	Exposed endolaryngeal cartilage

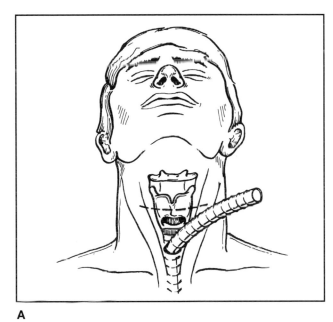

A

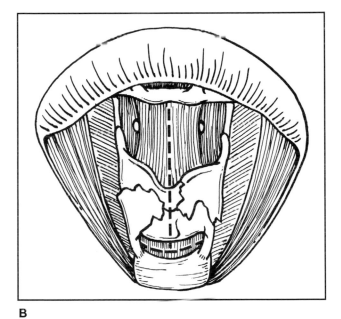

B

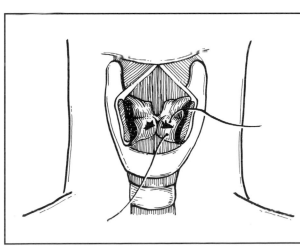

C

Fig 88–12. A. Surgical access for repair of laryngeal trauma is best obtained through a transverse incision superior to the tracheotomy site. **B.** In cases of comminuted thyroid cartilage fractures, the larynx must be entered through the thyrohyoid or cricothyroid membranes so the mucosal incision can be made accurately under direct vision at the anterior commissure. **C.** Mucosal lacerations are meticulously closed using fine absorbable sutures.

Table 88–2. CT Findings That Suggest Fracture Stability.

Fracture Type	Displacement	Stable	Suggested Management
Single Vertical, Unilateral	Nondisplaced	yes	Observe, fixate if symptoms or exam worsen
	Minimally displaced (<1 cartilage width)	yes	Fixate if immediate or delayed voice change, otherwise observe
	Displaced (>1 cartilage width)	no	Reduce and fixate
Single Horizontal, Unilateral	Nondisplaced	yes	Observe, fixate if symptoms or exam worsen
	Minimally displaced	yes	Observe, fixate if symptoms or exam worsen
	Displaced	no	Reduce and fixate
Multiple Unilateral	Nondisplaced	no	Reduce and fixate
	Displaced	no	Reduce and fixate
Multiple Bilateral	Nondisplaced	no	Reduce and fixate
	Displaced	no	Reduce and fixate

Table 88–3. Indications for Operative Repair After Blunt Laryngeal Trauma.

Laceration of vibrating edge of true vocal fold

Laceration of anterior commissure

Deep laceration of thyroarytenoid muscle

Exposed cartilage

Impaired vocal fold mobility

Arytenoid dislocation

Epiglottis displacement

Herniation of pre-epiglottic contents

Unstable/displaced laryngeal fractures

Airway compromise

Extensive endolaryngeal edema

dislocation does not necessarily imply immobility, especially acutely. A recently dislocated arytenoid may still be mobile, but close observation reveals abnormal speed, smoothness, and direction of arytenoid motion. Stroboscopic assessment may reveal asymmetry of the mucosal wave or level of vocal fold apposition. A laryngeal EMG may be useful in distinguishing between cricoarytenoid subluxation and recurrent laryngeal nerve paralysis. Diagnosis is facilitated by noting the asymmetric position of the arytenoid on laryngoscopy and on CT scan.

In the case of severe injury, inspection and palpation of the arytenoid at the time of surgery is necessary to determine joint integrity. Anterior dislocations occur most commonly and usually result from blunt external trauma compressing the larynx against the cervical spine or from traumatic intubations. Posterior dislocations occur from prolonged intubation, traumatic intubation and extubation, and traumatic endoscopy. Arytenoid dislocations should be reduced as soon as possible. Even when they are discovered long after the initial injury, reduction should be attempted because improve-

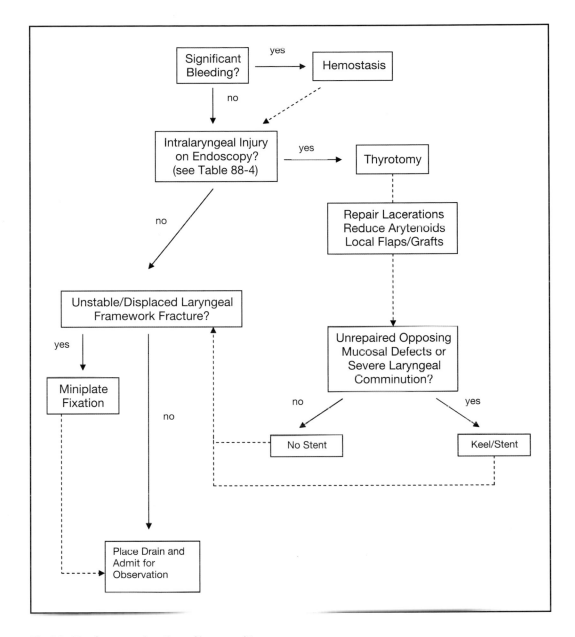

Fig 88-13. Open exploration of laryngeal trauma.

ment in vocal quality can be obtained in most cases.[30]

Patients without fractures on CT scanning and those with minimally displaced, stable fractures can be observed closely. Soft tissue injuries that consist of isolated mucosal lacerations of the supraglottic larynx, superficial lacerations of the nonvibrating edge of the true vocal fold, small hematomas of the true vocal fold, and/or mild mucosal edema may also be observed. Management of these patients includes the use of antibiotics, antireflux medications, reflux precautions, elevation of the head of bed, voice rest, and humidity. The use of antireflux medications and reflux

precautions, including elevation of the head of the bed, helps to limit additional inflammation and delays in wound healing caused by laryngopharyngeal reflux. Humidity helps to maintain lubrication of the vocal folds, which aids in the re-epithelialization process. The benefit of steroids in this scenario is controversial. The disadvantage of corticosteroids is that their anti-inflammatory action may interfere with and prolong the natural process of wound healing. The advantage of using steroids is that they may minimize the formation of granulation tissue and decrease laryngeal edema.[7,11,13,28,29,31] In the patient with mild to moderate mucosal edema, high dose steroids are given during the first 24 to 48 hours to minimize mucosal edema acutely.

Evaluation of the Blunt Trauma Patient with Airway Distress

Signs of upper airway distress include stridor, sternal retraction, and dyspnea. The patient should be examined for signs of upper aerodigestive tract injury. In the presence of immediate post-traumatic airway distress, significant laryngotracheal injury is likely. The neck is stabilized to prevent worsening of unrecognized cervical spine injuries, and the airway is secured with a tracheotomy fashioned at least two rings below the injured segments or through the distal transected segment under local anesthesia.[1,2,15,17,19,22,32-36] Tracheotomy prevents further laryngeal injury, and may expose an unnoticed laryngotracheal separation. Orotracheal and/or nasopharyngeal intubation in the presence of severe laryngotracheal trauma can lead to further laryngeal injury and airway compromise.

In the child with upper airway distress, the airway is secured in the operating room if time permits. General anesthesia is induced using an inhalational agent that is unlikely to cause laryngospasm. During spontaneous respiration, a rigid bronchoscope is passed gently through the injured larynx and trachea to a point distal to the sites of injury. Tracheotomy is performed over the bronchoscope followed by repair of the injuries.[20,23]

Operative evaluation of the larynx with direct laryngoscopy is performed after securing the airway. If direct laryngoscopy reveals significant endolaryngeal injuries (see Table 88–3), open exploration and repair are performed. The presence of palpable laryngeal fractures is also an indication for open exploration and repair. If direct laryngoscopy does not reveal a need for open exploration, then a postoperative CT of the larynx is obtained to complete the evaluation.

Surgical Evaluation

Full evaluation and determination of the need for surgical intervention should begin as soon as a laryngeal injury is suspected. Schaefer and Leopold both have reported better results when treatment is initiated in the first 24 hours.[2,11] Although many patients who suffer multiple trauma must have the evaluation delayed, it should still proceed as soon as their general condition allows. Indications for surgery can be divided into three groups: the need to restore cartilaginous integrity, the need to restore mucosal integrity, and the need to restore normal cricoarytenoid joint function.

Intraoperative evaluation begins with direct laryngoscopy to assess the extent of endolaryngeal injury, esophagoscopy to assess for esophageal lacerations, and bronchoscopy to assess for subglottic and tracheobronchial injuries. The arytenoid cartilages are palpated for possible dislocation. In the patient with isolated cricoarytenoid joint dislocation, reduction can usually be accomplished endoscopically, especially if the dislocation is noted early. With delays in diagnosis beyond even a week, joint ankylosis can begin, making reduction more difficult. Nonetheless, an attempt should be made to relocate the arytenoid cartilage back to its normal position on the cricoid regardless of the interval from the time of injury. In cases of posterior dislocation, this can be accomplished by inserting the anterior lip of an intubating laryngoscope into the posterior aspect of the cricoarytenoid joint while exerting a lifting motion in an antero-medial direction on the arytenoid cartilage. Anterior dislocations can be reduced by exerting a posteriorly directed force on the cricoarytenoid joint using the tip of a rigid laryngoscope.[33,37] Anterior dislocations can also be reduced by direct manipulation of the arytenoid body or with a blunt right-angle hook or right-angle cup forceps placed under the anteriorly displaced arytenoid body. Care must be taken not to fracture the vocal process during this maneuver. If no other injuries that require repair are noted on CT scan or on direct laryngoscopy, then open exploration is not necessary.

Open Exploration and Repair

Open exploration is performed to repair mucosal lacerations involving the anterior commissure and/or the vibratory edge of the vocal fold; to repair deep lacerations of the thyroarytenoid muscle; to restore mucosal cover over exposed cartilage; to reposition the vocal ligament and anterior commissure; to reposition a displaced epiglottis or herniated preepiglottic contents; to reanastomose separated segments; and to reduce and fixate displaced and/or unstable fractures (Fig 88–13). If not previously done, tracheotomy is performed to allow intraoperative access to the larynx and postoperative airway management.

Principles of Repair

The basic principles of repair follow the primary principles of wound healing elsewhere in the body. Repair within the first 24 hours after injury is most desirable to prevent granulation tissue formation from occurring prior to closure.[7,19] An attempt should be made to repair all mucosal lacerations and defects to promote healing by primary intention. Healing by secondary intention predisposes to a greater deposition of collagen and an increased likelihood of granulation tissue and scar formation, which may result in vibratory dysfunction, stenosis, or webbing of the vocal folds. All de-epithelialized areas that cannot be closed primarily without tension should be covered with local mucosal flaps to minimize scar formation. Free mucosal grafts can be used to cover de-epithelialized areas when local flaps cannot be fashioned; however, these are rarely needed. Fine, absorbable suture on an atraumatic needle seems to help minimize granulation tissue formation also.

Exposure

For open exploration, a horizontal neck incision is made and subplatysmal skin flaps are elevated. To expose the thyroid and cricoid cartilages, the strap muscles may be divided in the midline and retracted laterally. When endolaryngeal repair of soft tissue injuries is necessary, entry into the larynx is gained through fractures of the thyroid cartilage that are median or those that are paramedian and less than 0.5 cm from the midline. In patients with lateral or horizontal fractures of the thyroid cartilage, a midline thyrotomy is performed. A midline cut is then made through the anterior commissure under direct visualization, with care not to further disrupt the architecture of the vocal fold. Above the level of the glottis, the endolaryngeal incision is curved lateral to the epiglottis on one side to avoid cutting through its cartilage or mucosa. Care is taken during the exposure to avoid further injury to the recurrent and superior laryngeal nerves.

Endolaryngeal Repair

The functional goal of repair is to realign glottic tissues to their premorbid anteroposterior and transverse planes, beginning posteriorly and proceeding in an anterior direction to maximize exposure. The arytenoid is repositioned with meticulous closure of overlying mucoperichondrial defects. If the arytenoid mucosa is damaged badly, local rotation flaps can be developed from the piriform sinus or postcricoid region. Regardless of the extent of the injuries, an attempt should be made to repair severe unilateral and bilateral arytenoid injuries. Consideration of arytenoidectomy as a secondary procedure can be made at a later date after healing has occurred, and the wounds have matured.[17] This approach allows for the possibil-

ity of vocalization and respiration if at least one of the arytenoids retains some function.

Lacerations in the thyroarytenoid muscle or mucosa may be repaired with fine, absorbable suture. Avascular and crushed mucosal injuries are debrided prior to closure. If primary closure of mucosal disruptions is difficult, local advancement or rotational flaps should be performed. Local advancement or rotational flaps from the piriform sinus or postcricoid region usually provide adequate coverage of the arytenoid and its vocal process. A sternohyoid muscle flap can fill small defects, but does not provide cartilaginous support (Fig 88–14). Adequate mucosa for coverage of the anterior commissure region usually can be obtained from the epiglottis. If an extensive amount of mucosa is needed, the epiglottic mucosa can be elevated off the laryngeal and lingual surfaces of the epiglottis with removal of the cartilage to allow for a large superiorly based epiglottic flap (Fig 88–15).[38] It is important to ensure meticulous closure and re-epithelialization of the anterior commissure region, as this is the region most likely to develop a web or stenosis as a late complication.

Mucosal defects on the false vocal fold and epiglottis are less likely to pose significant problems with stenosis. If primary repair or a local flap cannot be accomplished, this area can be left open to granulate and mucosalize by secondary intention. A ruptured thyroepiglottic ligament should be reattached anteriorly to reposition the epiglottis to its more anatomical position. Herniated contents of the pre-epiglottic space should be removed or replaced anterior to the epiglottis and the thyroepiglottic ligament.

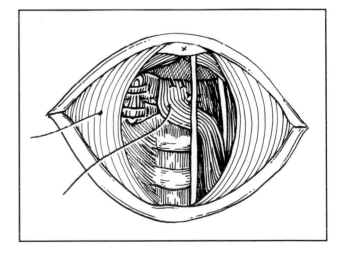

Fig 88–14. An inferiorly based sternohyoid muscle flap is utilized to cover a posterior mucosal defect.

The attachment of the vocal ligament at the anterior commissure is inspected. If torn, it is repaired by placing a slow-absorbing monofilament suture through the anterior aspect of the ligament and bringing it through a midline fracture to secure to the thyroid cartilage. If the fracture is paramedian, the suture is brought through the midline of the cartilage and secured. It is important to re-establish the appropriate height of the vocal fold as well as the appropriate midline placement for optimal post-operative voice results. Proper placement of the vocal ligament helps to ensure the proper position of the remainder of the vocal fold.

Endolaryngeal Stenting

Questions regarding when and how to utilize stents in acute trauma repair have not yet been answered adequately. However, there are some definitive and relative guidelines. Definitive indications for stenting include severely comminuted fractures where direct fixation is inadequate (to maintain) cartilaginous integrity; severe disruption of the anterior commissure; severe endolaryngeal mucosal disruption; and large mucosal defects that require application of skin or mucosal grafts. If bilateral mucosal lacerations produce webbing or if a web has been resected, a stent may also be employed. Although stenting may seem to promote a more consistent restoration of the laryngeal airway, it may also be harmful. Stents have been shown to cause local inflammatory reaction in almost all cases.[39] The wires and sutures used to fix the stent to the cervical skin also produce chronic irritation from the shearing caused by vertical laryngeal motion during swallowing (Fig 88–16).

Thus, in cases where the anterior commissure is the major problem, a keel that will prevent anterior webbing while not having contact with most of the endolaryngeal mucosa is preferred. The keel can be formed of Silastic, Teflon, or tantalum (Fig 88–17).[40,41]

Keels can be placed through an open incision or endoscopically. In cases where a patient has normal vo-

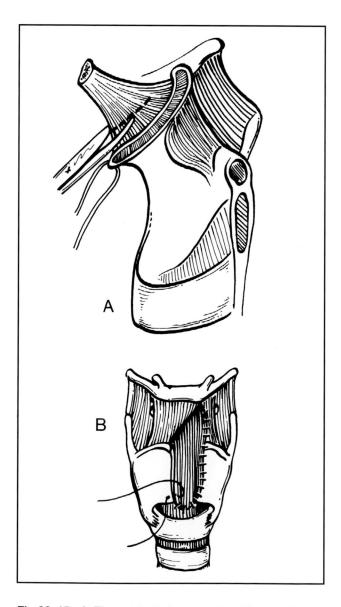

Fig 88–15. A. The epiglottis is grasped and its anterior attachments are severed so that it can be advanced inferiorly into the laryngeal defect. **B.** The epiglottic flap is sutured in the laryngeal defect using interrupted, permanent sutures.

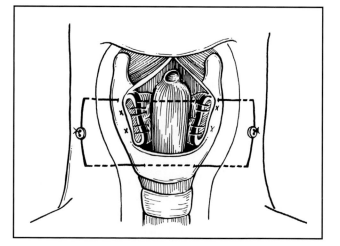

Fig 88–16. Wires sutured over buttons on the external skin hold a soft stent in place. The wires also restrict vertical laryngeal motion in the neck.

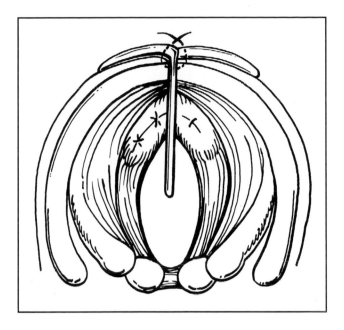

Fig 88–17. A tantalum keel is utilized to reduce scarring at the anterior commissure.

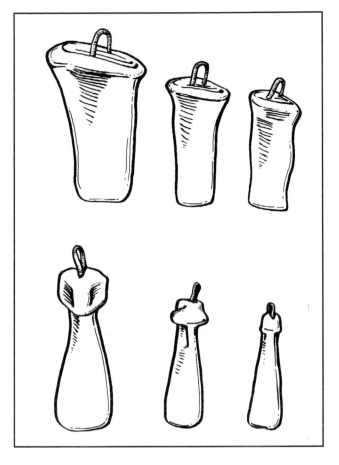

Fig 88–18. Montgomery premolded laryngeal stents come in male, female, and pediatric sizes.

cal fold motion or undergoes cricoarytenoid reduction, stents are avoided if at all possible. Whenever stents are utilized, they are removed as soon as possible. Two weeks is adequate for most patients unless other medical problems that may delay healing (eg, diabetes, malnutrition, or advanced age) coexist. Stents are rarely left in place longer than 4 weeks. Both prefabricated molded stents and soft stents have been used with success. Molded stents are available in varying sizes and conform to the endolaryngeal surfaces, presumably reducing frictional trauma (Fig 88–18).

Both Silastic and Gore-Tex varieties are available. Soft stents, usually a latex finger cot filled with gauze or a rubber sponge, allow for mucosal swelling and may be less traumatic than molded materials. Mucosal or split-thickness skin grafts can be fixed circumferentially to either type of stent with the epidermis away from the laryngeal mucosa as a biological dressing (Fig 88–19).

Laryngeal Fixation

Reduction and fixation of the cartilaginous framework is performed after all mucosal injuries have been addressed. If a stent is deemed necessary, it is placed prior to repair of the framework injuries. The fractures are reduced and fixated to ensure a stable reduction. Traditionally, stabilization has been achieved using stainless steel wire or nonabsorbable suture. However, because these provide only two-dimensional fixation, there can be some movement of the laryngeal fragments with head turning, flexion, and swallowing. The recent availability of titanium and absorbable miniplates has allowed more rigid fixation of the laryngeal framework in three-dimensional planes (Fig 88–20). This has the advantage over wire or suture fixation in that it allows for immediate immobility of the fracture segments, can be used effectively in most comminuted fractures and can decrease the need for endolaryngeal stenting.[42,43] The miniplates can be bent to conform to the geometry of the laryngeal framework, thus preserving the anteroposterior and transverse dimensions of the larynx. Usually, low profile plates in the 1.2 mm to 1.4 mm size range provide adequate fixation of the laryngeal framework and are less prominent than larger profile systems. In patients without significant ossification of the thyroid cartilage, it is often necessary to use drill bits that are two sizes smaller than the screw in order to prevent prob-

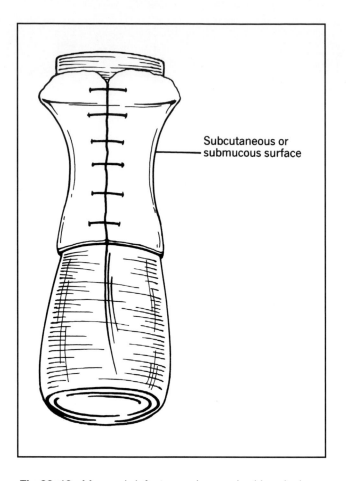

Fig 88–19. Mucosal defects can be repaired by placing a skin graft circumferentially around the laryngeal stent with the dermis facing out.

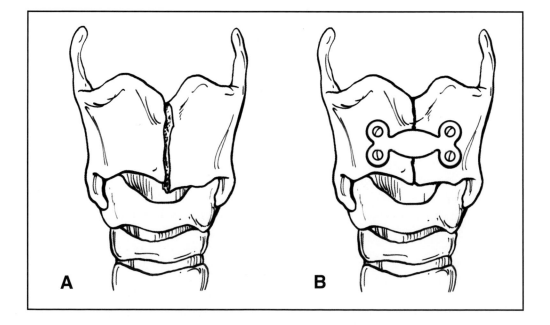

Fig 88–20. Miniplate fixation of a vertical thyroid lamina fracture. (llustrations courtesy of Sabrina M. Heman-Ackah.)

lems with overdrilling of the soft cartilage.[42-44] For example, if one were to use a 1.3-mm plating system, the hole would be drilled with a 0.8-mm drill bit instead of the usual 1.0-mm drill bit. Alternatively, one may use the 1.0-mm drill bit with the wider threaded "emergency" screws (1.5-mm diameter) from the 1.3 mm-plating set or self-drilling screws.

Laryngotracheal Reanastomosis

In patients with cricotracheal separation, initial intubation is through the distal segment. Any avulsed or badly bruised mucosa or cartilage is resected prior to reanastomosis to decrease the incidence of granulation tissue formation. Repair is begun with placement of sutures from the posterior tracheal mucosa to the inner cricoid perichondrium using 3-0 absorbable suture or fine wire. The repair then proceeds anteriorly, tying all knots extraluminally. The cricoid and tracheal perichondria and cartilages are then repaired using a 2-0 or 3-0 absorbable suture.[17] The use of absorbable suture decreases the incidence of anastomotic granulation tissue formation and late stenosis.[45] In the presence of cricoid injury and/or in patients in whom post-operative edema seems likely, a T-tube may be placed as a temporary stent. Post-operatively, the neck is kept in flexion for 7 to 10 days to prevent traction on the anastomotic closure.

Recurrent Laryngeal Nerve Repair

Laryngotracheal separation injuries may be accompanied by bilateral recurrent laryngeal nerve injuries. An attempt should be made to locate the nerves if the vocal folds exhibit evidence of immobility preoperatively. Crushed or otherwise damaged but intact nerves should be left alone to regenerate on their own. If a severed nerve is found, the severed ends should be freshened; and an attempt should be made to reanastomose the epineurium using a fine monofilament suture under tension-free closure. If a tension-free closure cannot be obtained or if the proximal end cannot be located and the opposite nerve is intact, unilateral ansa-cervicalis to recurrent laryngeal nerve transfer is an option. Recurrent laryngeal nerve repair is unlikely to restore full abductor or adductor function to the vocal fold, but it should provide enough tone to the thyroarytenoid muscle for long-term vocalization purposes.[46,47] If soft-tissue injury in the neck is extensive and ansa cervicalis to recurrent laryngeal nerve transfer cannot to be performed, hypoglossal to recurrent laryngeal nerve transfer or cable grafting using a greater auricular or sural nerve graft are other possibilities for nerve repair. In general, better results are obtained with nerve transfer than with cable grafting procedures.

Post-operative Management

The goal of post-operative management is to promote wound healing and limit granulation tissue formation. Patients who undergo mucosal repair of the vocal folds should exercise strict voice rest for the first few days to allow the initial phases of epithelialization to occur. Consideration should be given to the placement of a small flexible nasogastric feeding tube intraoperatively to allow enteral feeding in the early post-operative period. All patients with mucosal injuries are placed on an aggressive antireflux protocol, even in the absence of a history of gastroesophageal reflux, to minimize delays in wound healing associated with reflux-induced laryngeal injury. Prophylactic antibiotics are given to patients with open wounds to minimize the risk of chondritis. Routine tracheotomy care is performed gently to minimize excessive coughing.

Penetrating Injuries

Penetrating injuries are the second most common cause of laryngotracheal injuries in adults and the most common cause in the pediatric population.[1,4,22] These injuries result from accidental or deliberate stab wounds and from gunshot wounds. It is important to understand the mechanism of the injury, the direction of the force, as well as the instrument used to create the injury. If the path has traversed the midline, an injury to the upper aerodigestive tract is likely.

In victims of gunshot wounds, in addition to noting both the entry and exit wounds, it is also helpful to know the caliber and velocity of the weapon used. The kinetic energy ($KE = \frac{1}{2} mv^2$, where KE is kinetic energy, m is mass of the projectile, and v is projectile velocity) released from the bullet on impact determines the degree of tissue damage. Thus, small caliber, high velocity bullets tend to produce greater tissue damage than do larger caliber, low velocity bullets. The long bullet of the shotgun produces a different type of injury than the short bullet of the pistol or handgun. Because of their shorter length, handgun bullets fly with a straight trajectory, resulting in tissue damage at the site of impact. The bullets of the shotgun are longer and unstable in their trajectory. They, thus, tumble as they leave the barrel of the weapon. This "tumbling" produces significant circumferential "shock wave" damage to surrounding tissue that may extend several centimeters from the site of impact.[48]

In victims of stab wounds, the location and direction of the entrance wound are particularly important to note. Long penetrating objects can create injuries to structures at a significant distance from the entrance wound. As in the blunt trauma patient, victims of penetrating injuries to the larynx and trachea can appear to be comfortable; however, complications from airway compromise, vascular injuries, and esophageal perforations can result in mortality rates as high as 19%.[5,40,50] Therefore, a high index of suspicion coupled with a thorough physical examination is necessary.

Assessment of Penetrating Injuries

The initial concerns in evaluating and treating patients with penetrating injuries are the assessment and establishment of a patent airway and the evaluation and control of vascular and cervical spine injuries, as these are often major contributing factors to early morbiditiy and mortality in penetrating neck injuries.[49] In patients who require emergent airway control, the decision to perform orotracheal intubation versus tracheotomy must be individualized. The patient with a minor injury

is less likely to have an occult laryngotracheal separation, making attempts at intubation less problematic.[49]

Examination of the patient who has sustained a penetrating neck injury involves assessment of all of the neck structures. Signs and symptoms of disruption of the upper aerodigestive tract are the same as in the blunt trauma patient (see Table 88–1). If they are stable, patients with penetrating neck injuries that cross the midline should have a flexible laryngoscopic examination and CT scan of the neck and larynx to evaluate for possible endolaryngeal injury (Fig 88–21). The patient without any symptoms or signs on flexible endoscopic examination or CT scan of laryngeal injury may be observed closely for development of airway, voice, or esophageal abnormalities. Patients with mild laryngeal inflammation and no other signs of endolaryngeal injury may also be observed. Because of the potential for esophageal injuries, an esophagram with water-soluble contrast should be obtained in patients with minor injuries who do not require rigid endoscopy. The false negative rate with esophagrams has been reported as high as 21%.[50,51] Thus, patients with a negative esophagram who begin to develop

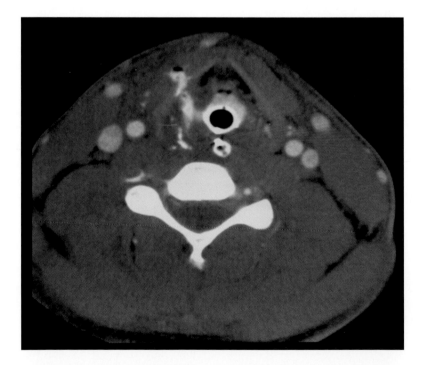

Fig 88–21. Axial CT of the larynx at the level of the false vocal folds after gunshot wound to the left neck. There is shrapnel debris along the trajectory of the bullet from the soft tissues of the left neck anterior to the sternocleiodmastoid muscle, through the left thyroid ala, and within the soft tissues of the endolarynx. An endotracheal tube is surrounded by significant endolaryngeal soft tissue edema.

odynophagia, fever, or back or chest pain should be evaluated for possible esophageal perforation with flexible or rigid esophagoscopy.

Patients who are noted to have signs and symptoms of a significant aerodigestive tract injury (Table 88–4) should undergo rigid direct laryngoscopy with consideration for possible open neck exploration and repair.[49] Because associated esophageal injuries have been reported in as many as 20 to 50% of the patients with laryngeal injuries, esophagoscopy should also be performed at the time of rigid endoscopy.[5,49]

Repair of Penetrating Injuries

Repair of penetrating laryngeal injuries and postoperative management is accomplished in a similar fashion as would be done with the blunt trauma patient. In patients with combined esophageal and posterior tracheal wall injuries, consideration should be given to placing a muscle interposition flap between the trachea and esophagus to prevent the formation of a tracheoesophageal fistula. This can be accomplished with the use of a nearby pedicled strap or sternocleidomastoid muscle flap.

Caustic and Thermal Injuries

Caustic and thermal injuries to the larynx can cause significant acute and chronic airway compromise as well as late vocal complications. Caustic injuries occur in both the adult and pediatric populations. Caustic injuries can result from ingestion of bases, acids, or bleaches. The most severe injuries are caused by bases,

Table 88–4. Indications for Operative Evaluation of Penetrating Laryngeal Injury.

Endolaryngeal lacerations

Expanding neck hematoma

Subcutaneous emphysema

Audible air leak from neck wound

Hemoptysis

Laryngeal framework disruption

Impaired vocal fold mobility

Endolaryngeal edema

Dysphagia/odynophagia

Stridor/dyspnea

which produce a liquefaction necrosis of muscle, collagen, and lipids with progressively worsening injury over time. Acids cause a coagulation necrosis that occurs more rapidly and tends to damage superficial structures only. In children under age 5, these tend to be accidental ingestions. Adolescent and adult ingestions usually are suicide attempts and thus tend to produce the most severe injuries.[53,54]

Caustic ingestions most often affect the oral cavity, pharynx, and esophagus, but can occasionally contact the larynx and result in edema and mucosal disruption secondary to burn injury. Because the epiglottis and false vocal folds are the initial barriers in preventing aspiration, the laryngeal edema typically seen in caustic ingestions involves the epiglottis and supraglottic larynx, often sparing the true vocal folds.[53,55] The larynx is examined in all caustic ingestions. Of particular concern is the ingestion of low phosphate or nonphosphate detergents. Ingestions of even small amounts of these may cause severe upper airway edema and airway compromise 1 to 5 hours after ingestion and warrant admission to the hospital for airway observation even in the absence of other significant injuries.[55] If significant edema or stridor is present, the airway should be stabilized with tracheotomy. Because of the potential for exacerbating the laryngeal injuries, nasotracheal and orotracheal intubation are avoided; tracheotomy is the preferred method of airway stabilization. The mouth, pharynx, and laryngeal inlet should be irrigated with water to remove any remnants of the offending agent. The use of steroids and antibiotics remains common but controversial. Further evaluation and management of esophageal injuries should then proceed. A discussion of the protocol for evaluation and treatment of esophageal injuries is beyond the scope of this chapter but can be found elsewhere.[53,54,56,57]

Thermal laryngeal injuries are usually encountered in patients who have experienced significant burn injuries from closed-space fires.[58] The laryngeal injuries most often result from thermal insult to the supraglottic and glottic larynx.[59] Because inhalational injuries may affect the larynx, tracheobronchial tree, or the lung parenchyma, all patients experiencing significant inhalational injuries should undergo flexible laryngoscopy and bronchoscopy. The diagnosis of laryngeal or tracheal injury is made by the presence of carbonized materials with inflammation, edema, or necrosis.[58] In patients with hypovolemic shock, as commonly occurs in patients with significant burn injuries, there may be severe injury to the larynx or trachea without signs of edema initially. The edema usually ensues with cardiovascular resuscitation.[60] The epiglottis, aryepiglottic folds, and hypopharynx are most prone to edema, which is usually progressive in the first few hours after injury.[60]

The primary concern is protection of the airway. The decision to perform tracheotomy versus orotracheal intubation is controversial. Orotracheal and nasotracheal intubation carry the risk of causing further mucosal injury. Several studies have suggested that tracheotomy in the burn patient places the patient at increased risk of long-term sequelae such as tracheal stenosis and sepsis.[59,61,62] In general, tracheotomy is recommended in patients who cannot be endotracheally intubated due to significant laryngeal injury, those who fail extubation, and/or those in whom prolonged respiratory support will be necessary.[58,60,62]

Late complications associated with thermal and caustic injuries include stenosis and webbing. Scar formation may continue for several months following the initial insult.[58] Thus, the larynx and trachea should be serially evaluated over the course of several months. Repair is delayed until scar formation has stabilized. This helps to minimize the incidence of recurrent scar formation and enhances the likelihood for successful repair.[58,60]

Iatrogenic Injuries

Iatrogenic injuries to the larynx include radiation injuries and injuries that result from intubation. Doses of radiation used to treat head and neck cancer (6000 cGy–7000 cGy) can result in injury to the mucosa and cartilaginous framework of the larynx if it is included in the radiation field. These injuries are an expected outcome of radiation therapy and can include mucosal drying, soft tissue edema, and laryngeal radionecrosis. The treatment of mucosal drying is symptomatic, encouraging frequent water ingestion. Several preparations are available to minimize xerostomia in patients receiving radiation therapy to the head and neck. These work with variable success. Laryngeal edema from radiation can become problematic, resulting in narrowing of the airway. In some patients, this can be treated effectively with intermittent steroid use. In others, tracheotomy is necessary to help maintain an adequate airway.[69]

The incidence of radionecrosis of the larynx is approximately 1% of patients who receive doses in the range of 6000 cGy to 7000 cGy and increases with larger daily fractions.[70] Patients who continue to smoke or drink alcohol during and after radiation therapy are at increased risk. The presence of laryngopharyngeal reflux may contribute to the development and exacerbation of radionecrosis. Radionecrosis can pose a diagnostic dilemma to the clinician, because the symptoms are similar to the symptoms of recurrent cancer; and there is often associated edema and/or ulceration overlying the devitalized tissue. It is often difficult to distinguish between recurrent or persistent tumor and radionecrosis. These patients should undergo direct laryngoscopy and biopsy. Biopsy of radiation-damaged tissue often shows necrotic debris. However, in an inadequately biopsied area, a similar specimen can be obtained in the face of recurrent tumor. Although deep biopsies may exacerbate necrosis, tumor recurrence must be ruled out.[65] Hyperbaric oxygen treatments can be offered to patients with radionecrosis of the larynx, as the increased tissue oxygenation induced by such treatments may promote healing and prevent further damage to the laryngeal framework.[66,67] If the signs and symptoms worsen or are not improved with conservative treatment, partial or total laryngectomy should be considered because of the risk of a life-threatening infection with a retained necrotic larynx and because of the high risk of malignancy in this scenario.[65-67]

The most common iatrogenic injury to the larynx results from intubation trauma.[68] Because children are more often subjected to prolonged intubation as premature infants and neonates in the intensive care unit, they are more likely to experience complications as a result of being intubated.[69] The reported incidence of intubation injury in adults and children has decreased in the last 20 years from 18% to 3% due to improved equipment and methods of intubation.[21] The advent of low-pressure cuffed endotracheal tubes of uniform diameter has significantly decreased the incidence of subglottic stenosis in adults. In addition, the development of ventilator adapters to prevent excessive movement of the endotracheal tube has also contributed to a decrease in the incidence of intubation trauma.[21,68]

In neonates, prolonged intubation often leads to circumferential granulation tissue, scarring, and eventual stenosis of the subglottis. This region is most often affected because the cricoid is the narrowest portion of the airway in the neonate and is, thus, most traumatized by the endotracheal tube. The posterior tilt of the cricoid cartilage in neonates likely helps to prevent damage to the interarytenoid region, which is the most common site of injury in the adult.

Subglottic stenosis from intubation injury in the infant can be managed similarly to congenital subglottic stenosis. For stenoses that are less than 50% obstructing, management can consist of observation, dilatation, or CO_2 laser excision. If CO_2 laser is used for a circumferential stenosis, it is done serially with no more than 30% of the circumference resected during any one procedure to prevent restenosis. If the stenosis is

50 to 70% obstructing, one may consider either endoscopic procedures or open procedures, depending on the location and potential ease of an endoscopic procedure. Stenotic regions that are more than 70% obstructing are managed best using open techniques. Lesions isolated to the subglottic region may be treated with an anterior cricoid split procedure. Longer stenotic regions may be treated with either cartilage grafting or resection with end-to-end anastomosis. Completely stenotic regions require resection and reanastomosis.[70]

In the adult, the glottis is the narrowest portion of the airway, and the posterior glottis often supports the endotracheal tube in the adult. Movement of the arytenoids against the endotracheal tube with respiration often contributes to ischemic necrosis of the thin mucosa overlying the vocal process. This can be followed by ulceration, chondritis, granulation, granuloma formation, and scarring. Often, removal of the endotracheal tube will allow for normal healing in the absence of gastroesophageal reflux, which should be treated presumptively during the healing process.

Scarring of the posterior glottis uncommonly causes problems with airway compromise. Attempts to release posterior glottic scar bands usually should be avoided to prevent worsening stenosis unless substantial symptoms justify the risks. In cases of significant airway compromise and minimal posterior scar-

ring, treatment with microscopic direct laryngoscopy and carbon dioxide laser division of the scar band is usually successful.[71] Care should be taken during these divisions to protect the normal mucosa of the interarytenoid region.[72] Occasionally, repeat microscopic direct laryngoscopy with repeat laser division is needed. In cases with moderate to severe interarytenoid scarring, a laryngofissure with a mucosal advancement flap from the interarytenoid notch or from an aryepiglottic fold or a similar endoscopic procedure can be performed (Fig 88–22).[73] The value of adjunctive treatment with topical mitomycin-C to prevent restenosis is being studied currently, but preliminary results are encouraging.[74] Posterior glottic stenosis is discussed in chapter 90.

Conclusion

Injury to the laryngotracheal complex can result from blunt, penetrating, caustic, thermal, and iatrogenic insults. The primary concern in the initial management of these injuries is the establishment and maintenance of an adequate airway. Treatment can then address the reconstruction of the normal anatomical relationships of the larynx and trachea in an attempt to restore the normal phonatory, respiratory, and protective functions of the larynx.

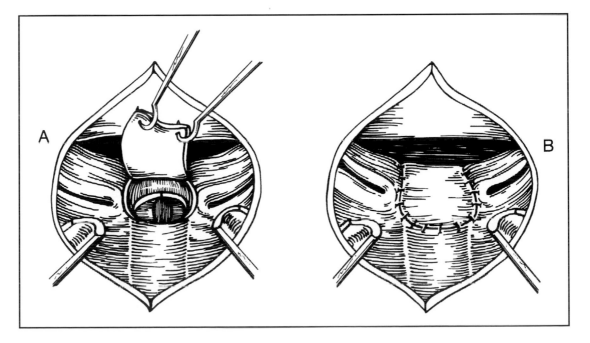

Fig 88–22. A. After resection of posterior glottic stenosis, a superiorly based mucosal flap is elevated. **B.** The mucosal flap is advanced into the defect and fixed with fine, absorbable sutures.

References

1. Bent JP III, Silver JR, Porubsky ES. Acute laryngeal trauma: a review of 77 patients. *Otolaryngol Head Neck Surg.* 1993;109:441–449.
2. Schaefer SD. The treatment of acute external laryngeal injuries. *Arch Otolaryngol Head Neck Surg.* 1991;117:35–39.
3. Jewett BS, Shockley WW, Rutledge R. External laryngeal trauma analysis of 392 patients. *Arch Otolaryngol Head Neck Surg.* 1999;125:877–880.
4. Gussack GS, Jurkovich GJ, Luterman A. Laryngotracheal trauma: a protocol approach to a rare injury. *Laryngoscope.* 1986;96:660–665.
5. Minard G, Kudsk KA, Croce MA, Butts JA, et al. Laryngotracheal trauma. *Am Surg.* 1992;58:181–187.
6. Angood PB, Attia EL, Brown RA, Mudder DS. Extrinsic civilian trauma to the larynx and cervical trachea—important predictors of long-term morbidity. *J Trauma.* 1986;26:869–873.
7. Schaefer SD, Close LG. Acute management of laryngeal trauma. *Ann Otol Rhinol Laryngol.* 1989;98:98–104.
8. Komisar A, Blaugrund SM, Camins M. Head and neck trauma in taxicabs. *Arch Otolaryngol Head Neck Surg.* 1991;117:442–445.
9. Blanc VF, Tremblay NA. The complications of tracheal intubation: a new classification with a review of the literature. *Anesth Analg.* 1974;53:202–213.
10. Whited RE. A prospective of laryngotracheal sequelae in long-term intubation. *Laryngoscope.* 1984;94:367–377.
11. Leopold DA. Laryngeal trauma: a historical comparison of treatment methods. *Arch Otolaryngol.* 1983;109:106–112.
12. Cohn AM, Larson DL. Laryngeal injury: a critical review. *Arch Otolaryngol.* 1976;102:166–170.
13. Olson NR. Surgical treatment of acute blunt laryngeal injuries. *Ann Otol Rhinol Laryngol.* 1978;87:716–721.
14. Potter LR, Sessions DG, Ogura JH. Blunt laryngotracheal trauma. *Otolaryngology.* 1978;86:909–923.
15. Trone TH, Schaefer SD, Carder HM. Blunt and penetrating laryngeal trauma: a 13-year review. *Otolaryngol Head Neck Surg.* 1980;88:257–261.
16. Holinger PH, Schild JA. Pharyngeal, laryngeal, and tracheal injuries in the pediatric age group. *Ann Otol Rhinol Laryngol.* 1972;81:538–545.
17. Pennington CL. External trauma of the larynx and trachea: immediate treatment and management. *Ann Otol Rhinol Laryngol.* 1972;81:546–554.
18. Travis LW, Olson NR, Melvin JW, Snyder RG. Static and dynamic impact trauma of the human larynx. *Am Acad Ophthamol Otolaryngol.* 1975;80:382–390.
19. Ashbaugh DG, Gordon JH. Traumatic avulsion of the trachea associated with cricoid fracture. *J Thorac Cardiovasc Surg.* 1975;69:800–803.
20. Gold SM, Gerber ME, Shott SR, Myer CM III. Blunt laryngotracheal trauma in children. *Arch Otolaryngol Head Neck Surg.* 1997;123:83–87.
21. Bryce DP. Current management of laryngotracheal injury. *Adv Otorhinolaryngol.* 1983;29:27–38.
22. Ford HR, Gardner MJ, Lynch JM. Laryngotracheal disruption from blunt pediatric neck injuries: impact of early recognition and intervention on outcome. *J Pediatr Surg.* 1995;30:331–334.
23. Myer CM III, Orobello P, Cotton RT, Bratcher GO. Blunt laryngeal trauma in children. *Laryngoscope.* 1987;97:1043–1048.
24. Offiah CJ, Endres D. Isolated laryngotracheal separation following blunt trauma to the neck. *J Laryngol Otol.* 1997;111:1079–1081.
25. Alonso WA, Caruso VG, Roncace EA. Minibikes, a new factor in laryngotracheal trauma. *Ann Otol Rhinol Laryngol.* 1973;82:800–804.
26. Schild JA, Denneny EC. Evaluation and treatment of acute laryngeal fractures. *Head Neck.* 1989;11:491–496.
27. Hirano M, Kurita S, Terasawa R. Difficulty in high-pitched phonation by laryngeal trauma. *Arch Otolaryngol.* 1985;111:59–61.
28. Stanley RB Jr, Cooper DS, Florman SH. Phonatory effects of thyroid cartilage fractures. *Ann Otol Rhinol Laryngol.* 1987;96:493–496.
29. Hoffman HT, Brunberg JA, Winter P, et al. Arytenoid subluxation: diagnosis and treatment. *Ann Otol Rhinol Laryngol.* 1991;100:1–9.
30. Sataloff RT, Feldman M, Darby KS, et al. Arytenoid dislocation. *J Voice.* 1988;1:368–377.
31. Sataloff RT, Spiegel JR, Hawkshaw MJ, Rosen DC. Vocal fold hemorrhage: diagnosis and treatment. *NATS J.* 1995;51(5):45–48.
32. Reece CP, Shatney CH. Blunt injuries to the cervical trachea: review of 51 patients. *South Med J.* 1988;81:1542–1547.
33. Chodosh PL. Cricoid fracture with tracheal avulsion. *Arch Otolaryngol.* 1968;87:461–467.
34. Harris HH. Management of injuries to the larynx and trachea. *Laryngoscope.* 1972;82:1924–1929.
35. Ogura J. Management of traumatic injuries of the larynx and trachea including stenosis. *J Laryngol Otol.* 1971;85:1259–1261.
36. Fuhrman GM, Stieg FH, Buerk CA III. Blunt laryngeal trauma: classification and management protocol. *J Trauma.* 1990;30:87–92.
37. Sataloff RT, Bough ID, Spiegel JR. Arytenoid dislocation: diagnosis and treatment. *Laryngoscope.* 1994;104:1353–1361.
38. Olson NR. Laryngeal suspension and epiglottic flap in laryngopharyngeal trauma. *Ann Otol Rhinol Laryngol.* 1976;85:533–537.
39. Thomas GK, Stevens MH. Stenting in experimental laryngeal injuries. *Arch Otolaryngol.* 1975;101:217–221.
40. Dedo HH. Endoscopic Teflon keel for anterior glottic web. *Ann Otol Rhinol Laryngol.* 1979;88:467–473.
41. McNaught RC. Surgical correction of anterior web of the larynx. *Trans Am Laryngol Rhinol Otol Soc.* 1950:232–242.
42. Woo P, Kellman R. Laryngeal framework reconstruction with miniplates: indications and extended indications in 27 cases. *Oper Techn Otolaryngol Head Neck Surg.* 1972;3:159–164.

43. Woo P. Laryngeal framework reconstruction with miniplates. *Ann Otol Rhinol Laryngol.* 1990;99:772–777.

44. Pou AM, Shoemaker DL, Carrau RL, et al. Repair of laryngeal fractures using adaptation plates. *Head Neck.* 1998;20:707–713.

45. Grillo HC, Donahue DM, Mathisen DJ, et al. Postintubation tracheal stenosis: treatment and results. *J Thorac Cardiovasc Surg.* 1995;109:486–492.

46. Crumley RL. Teflon versus thyroplasty versus nerve transfer: a comparison. *Ann Otol Rhinol Laryngol.* 1990; 99:759–763.

47. Crumley RL. Update: ansa cervicalis to recurrent laryngeal nerve anastomosis for unilateral recurrent laryngeal nerve paralysis. *Laryngoscope.* 1991;100:384–387.

48. Harrison DF. Bullet wounds of the larynx and trachea. *Arch Otolaryngol.* 1984;110:203–205.

49. Grewal H, Rao PM, Mukerji S, Ivatury RR. Management of penetrating laryngotracheal injuries. *Head Neck.* 1995;17:494–502.

50. Feliciano DV, Bitondo CG, Mattox KL, et al. Combined tracheoesophageal injuries. *Am J Surg.* 1985;150:710–715.

51. Defore WW Jr, Mattox KL, Hansen HA, et al. Surgical management of penetrating injuries to the esophagus. *Am J Surg.* 1977;134:734–738.

52. Glatterer MS Jr, Toon RS, Ellestad C, et al. Management of blunt and penetrating external esophageal trauma. *J Trauma.* 1985;25:784–792.

53. Hawkins DB, Demeter MJ, Barnett TE. Caustic ingestion: controversies in management. A review of 214 cases. *Laryngoscope.* 1980;90:98–109.

54. Schild JA. Caustic ingestion in adult patients. *Laryngoscope.* 1985;95:1199–1201.

55. Einhorn A, Horton L, Altieri M, et al. Serious respiratory consequences of detergent ingestions in children. *Pediatrics.* 1989;84:472–474.

56. Holinger LD. Caustic ingestion, esophageal injury and stricture. In: Holinger LD, Lusk RP, Green CG, eds. *Pediatric Laryngology and Bronchoesophagology.* Philadelphia, Pa: Lippincott Williams and Wilkins; 1996:295–304.

57. Wijburg FA, Beukers MM, Heymans HS, et al. Nasogastric intubation as sole treatment of caustic esophageal lesions. *Ann Otol Rhinol Laryngol.* 1985;94:337–341.

58. Jones JE, Rosenberg D. Management of laryngotracheal thermal trauma in children. *Laryngoscope.* 1995;105:540–542.

59. Moylan JA. Smoke inhalation and burn injury. *Surg Clin North Am.* 1980;60:1533–1540.

60. Miller RP, Gray SD, Cotton RT, Myer CM III. Airway reconstruction following laryngotracheal thermal trauma. *Laryngoscope.* 1988;98:826–829.

61. Lund T, Goodwin CW, McManus WF, et al. Upper airway sequelae in burn patient requiring endotracheal intubation or tracheostomy. *Ann Surg.* 1985;201:374–382.

62. Eckhauser FE, Billote J, Burke JF, Quinby WC. Tracheotomy complicating massive burn injury. *Am J Surg.* 1974;127:418–423.

63. Calhoun KH, Deskin RW, Garza C, et al. Long-term airway sequelae in a pediatric burn population. *Laryngoscope.* 1988;98:721–725.

64. Calcaterra TC, Stern F, Ward PH. Dilemma of delayed radiation injury of the larynx. *Ann Otol Rhinol Laryngol.* 1972;81:501–507.

65. Parsons JT. The effect of radiation on normal tissues of the head and neck. In: Million RR, Cassisi NJ, eds. *Management of Head and Neck Cancer: A Multidisciplinary Approach.* Philadelphia, Pa: JB Lippincott; 1984:183–184.

66. Feldmeier JJ, Heimbach RD, Davolt DA, Brakora MJ. Hyperbaric oxygen as an adjunctive treatment for severe laryngeal necrosis: a report of nine consecutive cases. *Undersea Hyperb Med.* 1993;20:329–335.

67. Ferguson BJ, Hudson WR, Farmer JC Jr. Hyperbaric oxygen therapy for laryngeal radionecrosis. *Ann Otol Rhinol Laryngol.* 1987;69:1–6.

68. Richardson MA. Laryngeal anatomy and mechanisms of trauma. *Ear Nose Throat J.* 1981;60:346–351.

69. Cotton RT, Seid AB. Management of the extubation problem in the premature child: anterior cricoid split as an alternative to tracheotomy. *Ann Otol Rhinol Laryngol.* 1980;89:508–511.

70. Lusk RP, Wooley AL, Holinger LD. Laryngotracheal stenosis. In: Holinger LD, Lusk RP, Green CG, eds. *Pediatric Laryngology and Bronchoesophagology.* Philadelphia, Pa: Lippincott Williams & Wilkins; 1996:172–184.

71. Dedo HH, Rowe LD. Laryngeal reconstruction in acute and chronic injuries. *Otolaryngol Clin North Am.* 1983; 16:373–389.

72. Dedo HH, Sooy FA. Endoscopic laser repair of posterior glottic, subglottic, and tracheal stenosis by division or micro-trapdoor flap. *Laryngoscope.* 1984;94:445–450.

73. Dedo HH, Sooy FA. Surgical repair of late glottic stenosis. *Ann Otol Rhinol Laryngol.* 1968;77:435–441.

74. Correa AJ, Reinisch L, Sanders DL, et al. Inhibition of subglottic stenosis with mitomycin-C in the canine model. *Ann Otol Rhinol Laryngol.* 1999;108:1053–1060.

89

Cricoarytenoid and Cricothyroid Joint Injury: Evaluation and Treatment

Robert Thayer Sataloff

Cricoarytenoid Joint Injury

Vocal fold hypomobility immobility may occur following internal or external neck trauma. The impaired mobility may be due to vocal fold paresis or paralysis, cricoarytenoid joint fixation, or arytenoid dislocation or subluxation. Dislocation is the displacement of a structure, particularly a disarrangement of the normal relation of bones or cartilages entering into the formation of a joint. Dislocation and luxation are synonymous. Subluxation is an incomplete dislocation, such that there is still contact between joint surfaces, although the relationship is altered. Subluxation is synonymous with semiluxation, and it constitutes a specific form of dislocation. Most arytenoid dislocations are actually subluxations; but the term dislocation encompasses partial and complete malposition and will be used throughout this chapter. Arytenoid dislocation is misdiagnosed commonly as vocal fold paralysis. When accurate diagnosis is delayed, surgical repair becomes more difficult, although not impossible as previously thought.[1,2] Many laryngologists were taught that arytenoid reduction was impossible or inappropriate beyond the first or second week following injury. Our experience suggests that reasonably good results are common so long as the arytenoid is reduced within about 10 weeks.[2] Although reduction can be performed even many years following arytenoid dislocation, late reductions usually result in correction of the vertical height disparity without restoration of joint motion.

Embryology and Anatomy

Understanding the complicated embryology and anatomy of the arytenoid cartilages is helpful in clari-

fying surgical principles and avoiding complications. The primordium of the larynx, trachea, bronchi, and lungs arises as an outgrowth of the pharynx during the third week of embryonic life, forming a laryngotracheal groove.[3] This anterior groove lies immediately posterior to the hypobranchial eminence and becomes the primitive laryngeal aditus. The aditus lies between the sixth branchial arches. The laryngotracheal groove fuses in a caudocranial direction at about the fourth week. The ventral ends of the sixth branchial arches grow and form the arytenoid eminences. During the seventh week, a fissure appears on each arytenoid eminence extending into the primitive vestibule. This is the laryngeal ventricle. The last portion of laryngotracheal groove to be obliterated is the intra-arytenoid sulcus at about 11 weeks.

Laryngeal hyaline cartilages develop from branchial arch mesoderm, and elastic cartilages are derived from mesoderm of the floor of the pharynx.[4] Most of the arytenoid is composed of hyaline cartilage. However, the vocal processes are developed separately in association with the vocal folds and consist of elastic cartilage. "Arytenoid" comes from the Greek word *arytainoeides*, meaning ladle-shaped. The cartilages are pyramidal, consisting of an apex, base, and two processes. The base articulates with the cricoid cartilage. The apex attaches to the corniculate cartilage of Santorini and to the aryepiglottic fold. The vocal process projects anteriorly to connect with the vocal ligament, and the muscular process is the point of insertion for most of the muscles that move the arytenoid.[5] The cricoarytenoid facets are well defined, smooth, and symmetrical. Each arytenoid articulates with an elliptical facet on the posterior superior margin of the cricoid ring. The cricoid facet is about 6 mm long and is cylindrical.[6] Traditional teaching holds that the cricoarytenoid joint motion includes rotating, gliding, and rocking. Most of the cricoarytenoid motion is rocking. However, along the long axis of the cricoid facet, gliding also occurs.[7] Limited rotary pivoting is permitted as well. More recent studies suggest that these traditional descriptions are not fully accurate and that complex revolution may more succinctly describe arytenoid behavior.[8] The arytenoid cartilages and the cricoarytenoid facets are extremely symmetric and consistent.[9] The cricoarytenoid joint is an arthrodial join, supported by a capsule lined with synovium. The capsule is strengthened posteriorly by the cricoarytenoid ligament.[9] This ligament is strong and ordinarily prevents anterior subluxation. The axis of the joint is at an angle of about 45 degrees from the sagittal plane and 40 degrees from the horizontal plane. The cricoarytenoid joint controls abduction and adduction of the true vocal folds, thereby facilitating respiration, protection of the airway, and phonation.

Arytenoid motion is controlled directly by intrinsic laryngeal muscles, including the posterior cricoarytenoid, lateral cricoarytenoid, interarytenoid, and thyroarytenoid. It is also affected by the cricothyroid muscle, which increases longitudinal tension of the vocal fold (which attaches to the vocal process of the arytenoid), and to a lesser degree by the thyroepiglottic muscle, which tenses the aryepiglottic fold.

Arytenoid Dislocation: Diagnosis

Traditionally, arytenoid dislocation has been suspected on the basis of history and absence of the jostle phenomenon present in many cases of unilateral vocal fold paralysis.[10] Often it is not diagnosed until direct laryngoscopy reveals impaired passive mobility of the vocal fold. Preoperative differentiation between vocal fold paralysis and arytenoid dislocation should be possible in virtually all cases. However, if not considered specifically, it will often be missed. Disparity in height between the vocal fold processes is much easier to see in slow motion under stroboscopic light at various pitches than with continuous light. In posterior dislocations, the vocal process and vocal fold are usually higher on the dislocated side[11] (Fig 89–1). In anterior dislocations, generally they are lower on the abnormal side[12] (Fig 89–2). In either case, the injured vocal fold may move sluggishly or be immobile. Rarely, abduction and adduction may appear almost normal under continuous light. Video documentation

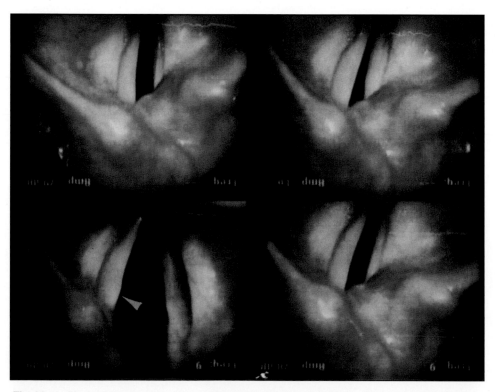

Fig 89–1. Typical appearance of a posterior arytenoid dislocation. The dislocated left arytenoid lifts the vocal process (*arrowhead*) so the abnormal side overlaps the mobile vocal fold.

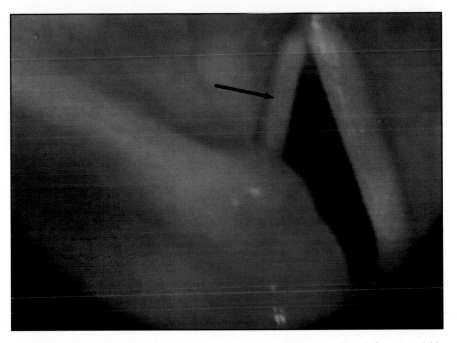

Fig 89–2. Typical appearance of a severe anterior dislocation. The left arytenoid is tilted forward, and the vocal process pulls the vocal fold to a lower level (*arrow*), so the mobile right vocal fold overlaps the abnormal side during adduction.

of the pre- and postoperative appearance can prove particularly helpful in cases of arytenoid dislocation not only diagnostically, but also because many of these patients are involved in litigation related to their injuries.

The most valuable tests are the stroboscopic examination to visualize differences in vocal process height; CT scan of the larynx, which should image the arytenoid dislocation and reveal clouding or obliteration of the cricoarytenoid joint space; and laryngeal electromyography to differentiate an immobile dislocated arytenoid joint from vocal fold paralysis. Airflow analysis is also helpful in documenting changes before and after therapy. Strobovideolaryngoscopy is also important to assess other vocal fold injuries. Stiffness and scar of the musculomembranous portion of the vocal folds are found commonly in association with arytenoid dislocation. The trauma causing dislocation frequently involves considerable force that results in vocal fold hemorrhage. It is important to recognize the presence of vocal fold scar prior to reducing an arytenoid dislocation so that the patient can be informed about reasonable expectations for surgical outcome.

When the author reported his series of 26 cases in 1994, only 31 additional cases had been reported in the literature.[2] Since that time, additional cases have been documented.[10-22] Although anterior and posterior dislocations are described most commonly, the arytenoid can be dislocated in any direction.[2] Complex disloca-

tions have been observed in some of the more than two dozen cases cared for by the author since our last report.[2]

Posterior dislocation is commonly an extubation injury. The arytenoid is displaced posterolaterally, and the vocal process is high and laterally positioned. Anterior dislocation is commonly most caused by intubation. The laryngoscope engages the posterior lip of the arytenoid, tearing the posterior cricoarytenoid ligament and tipping the arytenoid anteromedially (Fig 89–3). The vocal process ordinarily is lower than normal in such cases. Complex arytenoid dislocations also occur and can be particularly challenging. In our more recent (unreported) cases, direct anterior dislocation was seen in two patients. In these cases, the arytenoid was displaced anteriorly, but the vocal process was high. This injury requires considerable trauma, with disruption of cartilage. Both cases followed intubation. With injury of this severity, endoscopic reduction has been less satisfactory than with more typical anterior or posterior dislocations. In rare instances, even more complicated situations can be encountered, including bilateral arytenoid dislocation (Fig 89–4).

Techniques for Surgical Reduction of Arytenoid Dislocation

Although early spontaneous reduction of arytenoid dislocation has been reported,[2] surgical reduction

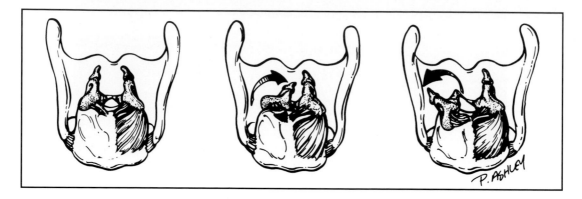

Fig 89–3 On the left, a normal larynx can be visualized from the back. The cricoarytenoid ligament is seen on both sides. The interarytenoid muscle has been removed. The posterior cricoarytenoid muscle is preserved on the right. In posterior arytenoid dislocation (*center image*), the posterior cricoarytenoid ligament is generally made more lax, and it is not torn. In an anterior dislocation (*right image*), the posterior cricoarytenoid ligament is generally torn (as illustrated) or avulsed from its insertion into the cricoid or arytenoid cartilage.

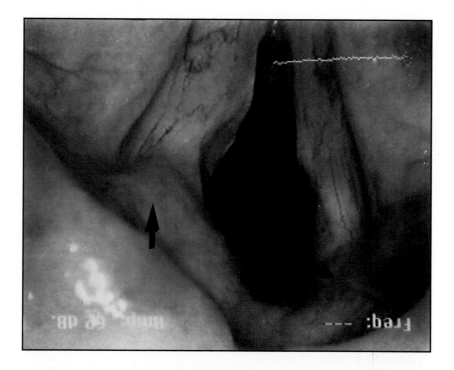

Fig 89–4. This 62-year-old artist and teacher awoke from abdominal surgery with severe hoarseness, breathiness, and sore throat 10 months prior to our evaluation. Both vocal folds were immobile, and laryngeal electromyography was normal. Note the very unusual position of the arytenoids. They are at different heights. The right arytenoids (*curved arrow*) is dislocated posteriorly. The left arytenoid has suffered a complex anterior arytenoid dislocation (*straight arrow*) with the vocal process displaced straight forward and high. Note the bowing and laxity of the left vocal fold.

generally is required. Voice therapy for at least a brief period may be helpful in some cases, and preoperative evaluation by a speech-language pathologist is generally recommended. Surgeons also should be aware that nonsurgical approaches have been suggested. For example, Rontal and Rontal have introduced the concept of chemical tenotomy using Botulinum toxin to enhance spontaneous reductions.[23] In some cases, adjunct procedures performed at the time of arytenoid reduction may also be advisable, as discussed below.

Closed Reduction for Posterior Arytenoid Dislocation

The author has found the anesthesiologist's old-fashioned, straight, Miller-3 laryngoscope blade to be the most useful instrument for posterior arytenoid dislocation (Fig 89–5). Newer models do not have the distal rolled lip. The instrument is placed in the piriform sinus with the rolled tip of the laryngoscope against the infralateral edge of the dislocated cartilage (Fig 89–6). The surgeon's other hand is placed on the opposite side of the larynx externally to apply counterpressure. The arytenoid is distracted cranially, then manipulated anteromedially to pop the arytenoid back into position. Substantial force is often necessary, sometimes the full strength of the author's right arm.

A Holinger laryngoscope usually is used to reduce anterior dislocations. More delicate instruments such as cupped forceps are not strong enough and are more likely to lacerate the mucosa and expose cartilage to the risk of infection. No instrument should be placed under the vocal process because of the risk of fracture at the embryologic fusion plane between the vocal process and body of the arytenoid. The Holinger laryngoscope is rotated so that its supralateral surface makes broad contact with the anteromedial face of the arytenoid. The surgeon's other hand is placed against the larynx externally and posteriorly for manipulation and counterpressure (Fig 89–7).

For complex dislocations, a combination of these techniques is used. It may be necessary to refracture the cartilage and/or separate the joint in order to manipulate the arytenoid. For example, in lateral and anterolateral dislocations, it has been helpful to use the Holinger laryngoscope to disrupt the cartilage and fibrosis, bringing the arytenoid posteriorly. Then, a combination of the Holinger laryngoscope and Miller-3 laryngoscope is used to return the arytenoid to optimal position.

When endoscopic closed reduction is not successful or is so unstable that dislocation recurs, open reduc-

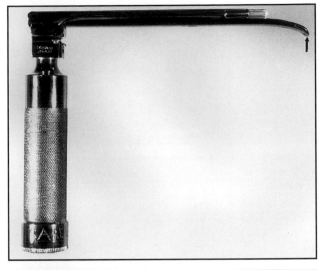

Fig 89–5. Straight Miller-3 laryngoscope blade (*top*) used by anesthesiologists. Below, the curved tip with a slight lip (*arrow*) has proven ideal for the reduction of posterior arytenoid dislocation.

tion and fixation should be considered. The procedure is performed using a standard arytenoid adduction/rotation approach. Usually, the joint is entered. If the joint has been obliterated by scar, a "joint" is created sharply, usually using an iris scissors. The arytenoid is moved to optimize vocal process position. The surgery is performed with the patient awake, and it is important to adjust vocal process position while the patient is phonating at his or her habitual frequency, rather than using a high-pitch /i/. If the arytenoid is unstable or hypermobile, it is sometimes possible to stabilize it with three to six fine sutures placed through the soft tissue attached to the cricoid and arytenoid cartilages. This approach has not been discussed prior to this publication; but the author has found it useful to stabilize a hypermobile cartilage in selected cases, particularly if the arytenoid is tending to fall anteriorly. Essentially, the sutures replace the posterior cricoarytenoid ligament.

Special situations and challenging clinical conditions sometimes demand other solutions to the problems of arytenoid dislocation. On three occasions, the

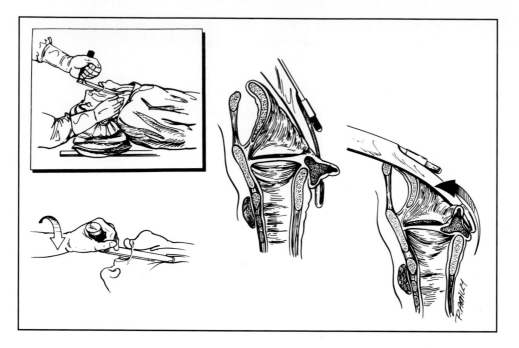

Fig 89–6. To reduce a posterior arytenoid dislocation, the tip of a Miller-3 blade is placed in the piriform sinus (*upper left*). To reduce a left posterior dislocation, the laryngoscope is rotated medially (*lower left*) so that the lip on the laryngoscope engages the dislocated arytenoids as the laryngoscope is drawn superiorly out of the piriform sinus. Digital external counterpressure (*upper left*) is required; and the right hand ordinarily needs to be placed more anteriorly than illustrated in this figure. If illustrated in proper position, the hand would block visualization of the tip of the laryngoscope. Once the arytenoid has been hooked by the lip of the laryngoscope (*center*), considerable force is necessary to distract the arytenoid in a cephalad direction and then to rotate it anteromedially, reducing it (right).

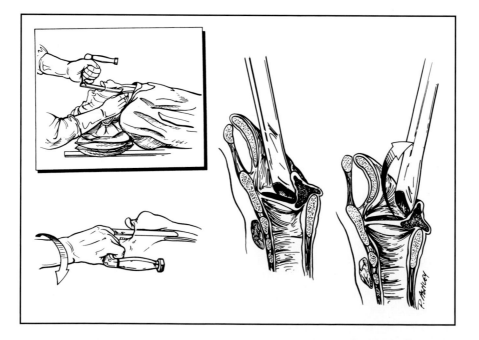

Fig 89–7. To reduce an anterior dislocation, a Holinger laryngoscope is positioned (*upper left*). To reduce a right arytenoid dislocation, the laryngoscope is rotated about 130° (*lower left*) so that the upper surface of the laryngoscope makes broad contact with the medial surface of the dislocated arytenoid (*center*). The surgeon's contralateral hand is placed externally, posteriorly on the larynx (*upper left*), so that the arytenoid is manipulated between the laryngoscope tip and the fingers of the surgeon's right hand, to reduce this right arytenoid anterior dislocation. Considerable force is required to reduce the arytenoid (*right*); and care must be taken not to injure or avulse the vocal process.

author has used digital reduction (Fig 89–8). The first was on an edentulous patient in an intensive care unit who had extubated herself repeatedly. Her physicians were concerned about even the risk of transporting her to the operating room, let alone sedating her. Yet, she had respiratory problems, and it was important to restore the efficiency of her cough. Her tongue was held with gauze in the manner of indirect laryngoscopy, at the bedside. An assistant helped stabilize her larynx externally. A finger was placed in her piriform sinus, and her posterior arytenoid dislocation was manually reduced. It maintained good position and mobility returned. This technique has been used on two other patients whose arytenoids redislocated within 48 hours following surgical reduction.

Most recently, another new technique was utilized. The author was called to see a patient who had awakened with a hoarse, weak, breathy voice and ineffective cough following anterior cervical fusion. Posterior arytenoid dislocation was diagnosed easily, and good vocal fold innervation was confirmed by electromyography. However, the patient had a short, thick neck and was flexed in a halo, and on full-dose coumadin. In the operating room, the arytenoid was reduced indirectly under nasal fiberoptic laryngoscopic control. A right angle bayonet forceps was used. This is the instrument that used to be utilized routinely for holding cocainized cotton in the piriform sinuses to provide local anesthesia to the larynx. The tip of the forceps was covered with a red rubber catheter. The instrument was placed in the piriform sinus, and the arytenoid was lifted cranially, anteriorly and medially; and it popped back into position easily (Fig 89–9).

It is worthwhile attempting endoscopic reduction even long after the injury.[1,2,22] In 1998 (not yet reported in detail), the author successfully reduced an anterior arytenoid dislocation that had occurred 38 years previously, restoring vertical symmetry of the vocal process and fold, although thyroplasty was necessary to provide adequate medialization.

Adjunctive Measures

Several adjunctive measures should be considered when performing arytenoid reduction. For a long-standing posterior dislocation, especially when the reduction seems unstable, simultaneous medialization should be considered. Thyroplasty or injection of autol-

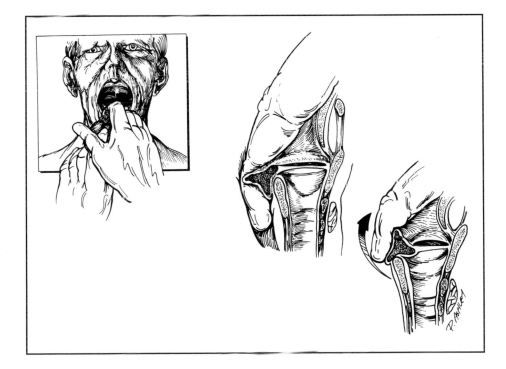

Fig 89–8. Digital reduction can be accomplished occasionally, especially for patients who are edentulous and who have had recent posterior dislocation or redislocation following recent arytenoid reduction. The patient's tongue is retracted by the patient or an assistant, leaving the surgeon's other hand free for external counterpressure (*left*). The surgeon's index or middle finger is placed in the piriform sinus, engaging the dislocated arytenoid (*center*). The surgeon's other hand applies external counterpressure, and the arytenoid is reduced digitally (*right*).

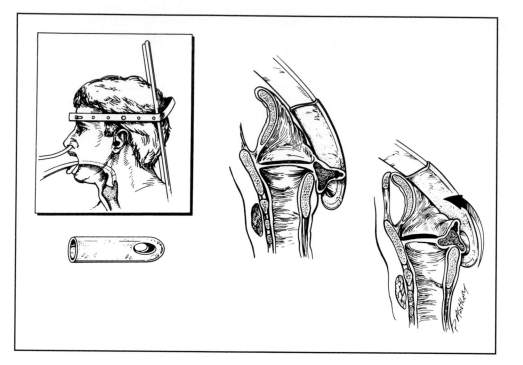

Fig 89–9. This previously undescribed procedure can be used for patients with posterior arytenoid dislocation and difficult anatomical constraints, such as this patient in a halo. A flexible laryngoscope is placed in the nostril to observe the larynx. A right-angle instrument such as a laryngeal bayonet forceps is covered with a shortened red rubber cathe-ter. The hole in the red rubber catheter (*lower left*) assists in making stable contact with the dislocated arytenoid. The posterior aspect of the dislocated arytenoid is engaged (*center*) and then drawn superiorly, and anteromedially, to reduce the dislocated cartilage (*right*).

ogous fat or collagen not only helps medialize the vocal fold, but also tends to pull the vocal process forward. This helps maintain the desired arytenoid position.

Following anterior dislocation, Rontal and Rontal have suggested Botulinum toxin injection into adductor muscles that tend to pull the arytenoid forward.[23] In fact, they have suggested that Botulinum toxin alone may result in "spontaneous" reduction without the need for surgical intervention. In this author's opinion, although this may be true in rare cases, it is not likely to occur once the joint has been fibrosed. More investigation of this novel concept is certainly warranted. However, the author (RTS) has used Botulinum toxin intraoperatively on several occasions when arytenoid reductions have appeared somewhat unstable. If a posterior dislocation can be reduced but tends to redislocate posteriorly when the patient is asked to cough in the operating room, Botulinum toxin can be injected into the posterior cricoarytenoid muscle. This permits unopposed pull from the adductor muscle, which tends to move the arytenoid in the desired direction. When combined with autologous fat injection, this technique has proven very effective.

Cricothyroid Joint Injury

Although injuries to the cricoarytenoid joint have been discussed in considerable detail, as noted above, dysphonia related to injury of the cricothyroid joint has been reported only rarely. [24,25] Otolaryngologists should be aware that injury to this structure can occur and cause severe voice dysfunction. The cricothyroid joint is a synovial articulation between the inferior cornu of the thyroid cartilage and the side of the cricoid cartilage, as described previously in chapter 6. In 1978, Schultz-Coulon described a 44-year-old professional singer who suffered a severe laryngeal contusion following a sports accident.[24] He recovered from the acute injury but complained of persistent loss of his falsetto voice. Left unilateral subluxation of the cricothyroid joint was diagnosed by xero-radiography. At lower pitches, his voice reportedly returned to normal, but he failed to recover his falsetto despite more than 12 months of intensive voice therapy. The authors attributed this permanent impairment to disturbance of the tilting mechanism between the cricoid and thyroid cartilages.

In 1998, Sataloff et al reported two patients with cricothyroid joint dysfunction.[25] Case 1 was a 38-year-old retired professional basketball player. He had been struck in the anterior neck 12 times during his ca-

reer. The last injury resulted in immediate and persistent breathiness, decreased volume, hoarseness, very low pitch, and inability to project his voice. His cricothyroid joint was fused and ossified (Fig 89–10);

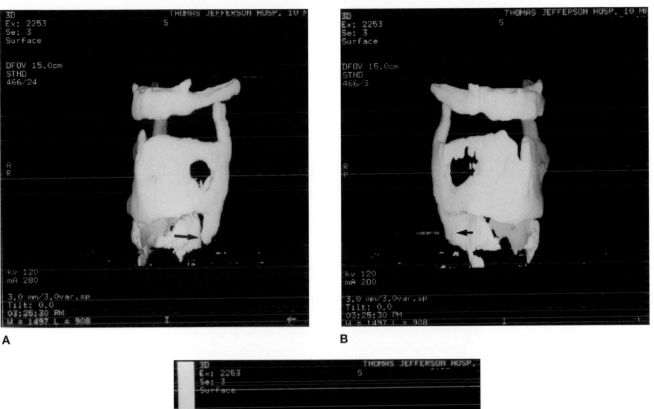

A   **B**

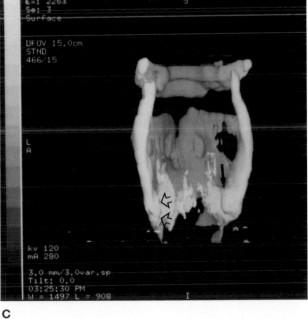

C

Fig 89–10. A. Anterior oblique CT scan of larynx showing normal left cricothyroid joint (*arrow*). **B.** Anterior oblique 3-D CT scan showing fusion of cricoid and thyroid in region of obliterated cricothyroid joint (*arrow*). **C.** Posterior-anterior 3-

D CT scan showing the left cricothyroid joint intact (*open arrows*) and fusion with new cartilage formation in the right cricothyroid joint region (*straight arrow*).

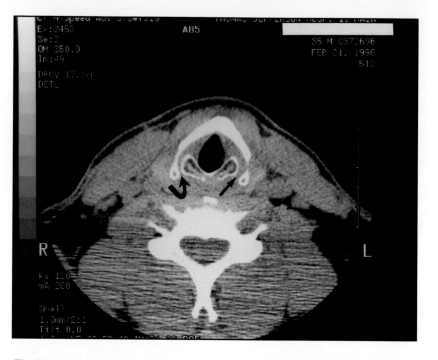

Fig 89–11. Axial CT scan showing normal right cricothyroid joint (*curved arrow*) and separated left cricothyroid joint (*straight arrow*). This appearance was consistent throughout the CT scans and is not due to rotation.

and his cricothyroid space was widened, fixing his voice in vocal fry. Case 2 was a 36-year-old male who had been involved in an altercation. He complained of dysphagia, mild vocal weakness, and laryngeal pain that was most pronounced during sneezing and coughing. His left cricothyroid joint was separated (Fig 89–11). Both patients had significant dysphonia due to impairment of the tilting mechanism between the cricoid and thyroid cartilages. In Case 1, motion between the cricoid and thyroid cartilages was eradicated completely. Voice therapy alone was not adequate, and surgery was necessary to restore mobility. In Case 2, motion was impaired but still present. Voice therapy permitted restoration of vocal quality and endurance adequate for the patient's purposes. If the patient had greater professional voice demands, surgery to realign the cricoid and thyroid cartilages (reduction of the joint separation) would have been offered.

Conclusion

Arytenoid dislocation is not rare, although it often is misdiagnosed as vocal fold paralysis. Although the goal of treatment is restoration of normal position and function, this cannot always be achieved. However, even correcting the vertical height abnormality is worthwhile. Essentially, this simplifies the problem,

converting it to one that can be managed easily by standard medialization surgery. It is essential for the surgeon to understand the anatomy and surgical principles involved, because visualization during surgical manipulation is extremely limited and considerable force is required. In virtually all cases, the patient's voice can be improved; and airway problems and other significant complications have not been encountered thus far.

Injury to the cricothyroid joint has been reported rarely, although it is certain that it has occurred more frequently but not been recognized. Laryngologists should be familiar with the nature and the importance of the cricothyroid joint and the potential for symptomatic injury of this structure. Additional experience is needed to determine optimal treatment.

References

1. Sataloff RT, Feldman M, Darby KS, et al. Arytenoid dislocation. *J Voice.* 1987;1(4):368–377.
2. Sataloff RT, Bough ID Jr, Spiegel JR. Arytenoid dislocation: diagnosis and treatment. *Laryngoscope.* 1994;104(10): 1353–1361.
3. Lee GJ. *Essential Otolaryngology.* 3rd ed. New York, NY: Medical Examination Publishing; 1983:306–310.
4. Langman J. *Medical Embryology.* 3rd ed. Baltimore, Md: Williams and Wilkins; 1975:269, 272.
5. Hollinshead WH. *Anatomy for Surgeons.* Vol 1. 3rd ed. New York, NY: Harper and Row; 1982:423–427.

6. Maue W, Dickson DR. Cartilages and ligaments of the adult human larynx. *Arch Otolaryngol.* 1971;94:432–439.

7. von Leden H, Moore P. The mechanics of the cricoarytenoid joint. *Arch Otolaryngol.* 1961;73:541–550.

8. Letson JA, Jr, Tatchell R. Arytenoid joint. In Sataloff RT. *Professional Voice: Science and Art of Clinical Care.* 2nd ed. San Diego, Calif: Singular Publishing Group, Inc; 1997: 131–146.

9. Pennington CL. External trauma of the larynx and trachea. Immediate treatment and management. *Ann Otol Rhinol Laryngol.* 1972;81:546–554.

10. Jackson C, Jackson CL. *Disease and Injuries of the Larynx.* New York, NY: Macmilian; 1942:321.

11. Sataloff RT, McCarter AA, Hawkshaw M. Posterior arytenoid dislocation. *Ear Nose Throat J.* 1998;77(1):12.

12. Sataloff RT, Spiegel JR, Heuer RJ, Hawkshaw M. Pediatric anterior arytenoid dislocation. *Ear Nose Throat J.* 1995;74(7):454–456.

13. Szigeti CL, Baeuerle JJ, Mongan PD. Arytenoid dislocation with lighted stylet intubation: case report and retrospective review. *Anesth Analg.* 1994;78(1):185–186.

14. Alexander AE, Jr, Lyons GD, Fazekas-May MA, et al. Utility of helical computed tomography in the study of arytenoid dislocation and arytenoid subluxation. *Ann Otol Rhinol Laryngol.* 1997;160(12):1020–1023.

15. Gauss A, Treiber HS, Haehnel J, Johannsen HS. Spontaneous reposition of a dislocated arytenoid cartilage. *Br J Anaesth.* 1993;70(5):591–592.

16. Hsu CS, Huang CT, So EC, et al. [Arytenoid subluxation following endotracheal intubation—a case report.] *Acta Anaesthesiol Sin.* 1995;33(1):45–52.

17. Rieger A. Hass I, Gross M, et al. [Intubation trauma of the larynx—a literature review with special reference to arytenoid cartilage dislocation.] *Anasthesiol Intensivmed Notfallmed Schmerzther.* 1996;31(5):281–287.

18. Friedberg J, Giberson W. Failed tracheotomy decannulation in children. *J Otolaryngol.* 1992;21(6):404–408.

19. Talmi YP, Wolf M, Bar-Ziv J, et al. Postintubation arytenoid subluxation. *Ann Otol Rhinol Laryngol.* 1996;105(5): 384–390.

20. Stack BC Jr, Ridley MB. Arytenoid subluxation from blunt laryngeal trauma. *Am J Otolaryngol.* 1994;15(1):68–73.

21. Hiong YT, Fung CF, Sudhaman DA. Arytenoid subluxation: implications for the anaesthetist. *Anaesth Intensive Care.* 1996;24(5):609–610.

22. Sataloff RT. Arytenoid dislocation. *Oper Techn Otolaryngol Head Neck Surg.* 1998;9(4):196–202.

23. Rontal E, Rontal M. Laryngeal rebalancing in the treatment of anteromedial dislocation of the arytenoids. *J Voice.* 1998;12(3):383–388.

24. Schultz-Coulon J, Brase A. [Clinical and roentgenological manifestations of unilateral subluxation of the cricothyroid joint.] *HNO.* 1978;26(2):68–72.

25. Sataloff RT, Rao VM, Hawkshaw M, et al. Crycothyroid joint injury. *J Voice.* 1998;12(1):112–116.

90

Posterior Glottic Stenosis

Joseph R. Spiegel and Robert Thayer Sataloff

The posterior glottis consists of the posterior third (cartilaginous portion) of the vocal folds, the posterior portion of the larynx (commonly called the "posterior commissure") with its interarytenoid muscle, the cricoid lamina, the cricoarytenoid joints, the arytenoid cartilages, and the overlying mucosa. Although the term posterior commissure is used frequently to describe the interarytenoid region, it is actually a misnomer. A commissure is a "coming together," as occurs anteriorly, and there is no "posterior commissure." Other terminology has been preferred in recent years.

Stenosis of the posterior glottis arises most often as a result of the trauma of endotracheal intubation. Factors that affect the development of postintubation complications include traumatic intubation, prolonged intubation, repeated intubations, large endotracheal tube size, motion of the endotracheal tube, and the presence of reflux or local infection. Occasionally, posterior glottic stenosis may result from other traumatic etiologies such as inhalation burns, caustic ingestion, and surgical misadventure.

Patients who develop posterior glottic stenosis (PGS) often fail extubation and require tracheotomy. Patients who are extubated successfully may present with airway distress and/or dysphonia at various intervals during their recuperation. The classification system used most commonly for PGS was published by Bogdasarian and Olson[1] (Table 90–1). Type I stenosis is a scar band between the vocal folds that is anterior to and separate from the posterior laryngeal mucosa. Type II stenoses involve the mucosa and/or musculature of the interarytenoid region. Types III and IV stenoses are defined by unilateral and bilateral cricoarytenoid joint fixation, respectively.

Evaluation of a patient with suspected PGS begins with a detailed history and thorough visualization of the larynx. Strobovideolaryngoscopy is optimal. Flexible laryngoscopy provides the best assessment of laryngeal motion, and video recording can be extremely valuable. Some patients can provide only short bursts of phonation or breathing with their tracheotomy occluded, and replay of these portions of the examination is quite helpful in diagnosis. Stroboscopy is useful specifically in determining the relative vertical height and tenseness of the vocal folds for assessing cricoarytenoid function and in evaluating scarring of the vocal folds.

Many patients will benefit from electromyography (EMG) of the intrinsic laryngeal muscles. It is critical to establish the potential laryngeal function by EMG before embarking on planned repair to restore cricoary-

Table 90–1. Posterior Glottic Stenosis Grading System.

Type	Pathology
I	Interarytenoid scar, posterior larynx normal
II	Posterior laryngeal scarring
III	Posterior laryngeal scarring with unilateral cricoarytenoid fixation
IV	Posterior laryngeal scarring with bilateral cricoarytenoid fixation

tenoid mobility. In the presence of severe paresis or paralysis, the entire effort could be futile. In a case of suspected paralysis, a normal EMG may signal an arytenoid dislocation or ankylosis. A fine cut computed tomography (CT) of the larynx can be helpful to determine arytenoid position. CT of the neck and chest can be utilized to examine other levels of airway stenosis. Pulmonary function testing, specifically a flow volume loop, can provide objective measurement of the airway obstruction; and objective voice analysis with airflow studies can quantify and document the effect of PGS on the voice.[2]

After initial evaluation, all patients in reasonable medical condition undergo endoscopic examination under general anesthesia. Microscopic examination of the glottic surfaces, palpation of the cricoarytenoid complex and posterior glottic region, and examination of the subglottis and trachea complete the assessment. In cases of simple, type I stenosis, endoscopic procedures may suffice for treatment. When endoscopic mucosal resurfacing and stenting are feasible, even more involved problems can also be approached without laryngotomy. However, many patients with advanced stages of PGS will require open laryngeal procedures to obtain adequate laryngeal function.

Endolaryngeal Procedures

Endoscopic laryngeal procedures are most useful in the simplest (type I) and the most severe (type IV)

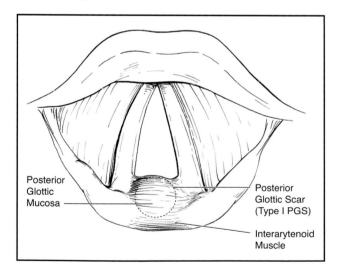

Fig 90–1. Type I posterior glottic stenosis, with a typical scar band.

forms of PGS. The simplest form of PGS (type I) is a scar band that prevents full abduction of the vocal folds but spares the posterior laryngeal mucosa (Fig 90–1). The level of the scar can be determined by passing an instrument between the band and the posterior larynx. The band can be excised with cold instruments or a laser. Recurrences have not been reported.[3,4]

Endolaryngeal procedures are used to reestablish a glottic airway in patients with type IV PGS when mobility of the cricoarytenoid joints cannot be restored. Some of these patients have failed closed and open attempts at repair. Perhaps the most important prognostic factor in PGS is mobility of the cricoarytenoid joints. When the joints are mobile and severe paresis or paralysis is present bilaterally, direct treatment of the posterior laryngeal scarring is rarely warranted. If dislocation of an arytenoid cartilage is encountered, reduction should be attempted endoscopically. Even if the joint remains fixed, the airway may be improved and appropriate vocal fold height may be restored. If any vocal fold mobility can be regained, it greatly improves the chances for a successful repair. Arytenoidectomy is utilized primarily in the treatment of bilateral vocal fold paralysis. However, in cases of PGS involving midline fixation of both cricoarytenoid joints, endoscopic laser arytenoidectomy may be adequate primary treatment to restore an adequate airway and permit decannulation.[5] Posterior transverse cordotomy has also been utilized successfully to relieve airway obstruction in a patient with PGS who had failed a prior endoscopic procedure.[6]

When the posterior mucosa and interarytenoid muscle are scarred, the value of endoscopic techniques is controversial. Some authors, such as Kleinsasser,[7] feel that open methods should be used whenever scarring involves the muscle. It is clear that any endoscopic method of PGS repair must provide adequate mucosal coverage of the posterior glottic region. The microtrapdoor flap technique that was first described by Dedo and Sooy in 1984 provides a method of mucosal preservation with scar excision.[8] Using the carbon dioxide laser, a transverse incision is made superiorly in the posterior laryngeal mucosa. Vertical relaxing incisions are made bilaterally and scar tissue can be excised posteriorly to the level of the cricoid lamina. The flap is redraped over the resection site. Although contraction of the flap prevents total coverage, the flap can resurface small areas well enough to allow adequate healing[9-11] (Fig 90–2). Most patients treated with the microflap trapdoor technique have type II stenosis, but occasionally patients with unilateral cricoarytenoid joint fixation also can be treated endo-

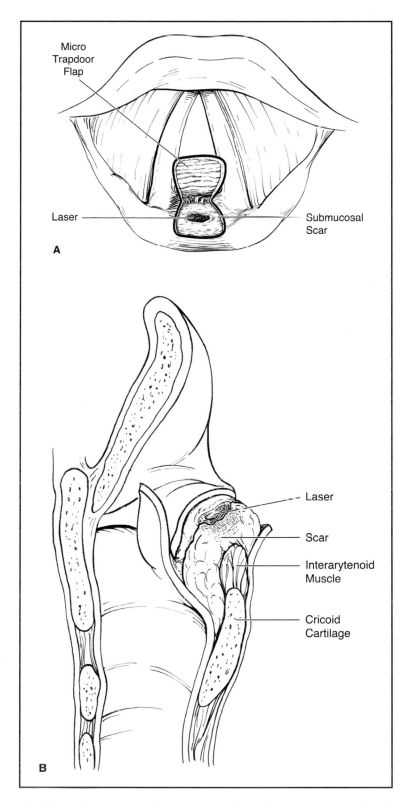

Fig 90–2. Microtrapdoor flap technique illustrating transverse and vertical incision (*top*), permitting laser vaporization of the posterior glottic scar (*bottom*) (**A, B**).

scopically. In the small number of patients with PGS treated endoscopically with mucosal flaps, most achieve decannulation. However, Duncavage et al have noted even better results in their patents with subglottic stenosis.[9] Newer methods of endolaryngeal suturing and laser welding may allow attempts at endoscopic repair of large areas of scarring in the future.[12]

In an attempt to reduce scarring after endoscopic repair, recent reports have demonstrated the safety and efficacy of topically applied mitomycin-C.[13,14] Mitomycin-C is an antineoplastic antibiotic that acts as an alkylating agent by inhibiting DNA and protein synthesis. It can inhibit cell division and fibroblast proliferation and may be helpful in treating PGS.

Open Laryngeal Procedures

Most patients with advanced stages of PGS involving dense mucosal and deep scarring will require an open surgical procedure to achieve decannulation and optimal airway. An aggressive approach to the treatment of PGS is warranted, as it has been shown to be the most important site of stenosis resulting in prolonged tracheotomy.[15] Open procedures for PGS often are combined with treatment of subglottic stenosis and should be completed prior to surgically addressing areas of lower tracheal stenosis.

Resection and repair of PGS using a laryngofissure approach have been reported for many years.[16] The scar tissue is excised sparing the interarytenoid muscle, if possible, and the capsules of the cricoarytenoid joints. When scarring is limited to the interarytenoid area, mucosal coverage is obtained with local mucosal flaps. The most useful is a posteriorly based flap advanced from the postcricoid area. A transposition flap from the aryepiglottic fold also can be utilized. When adequate local mucosa cannot be mobilized to cover the laryngeal wound, free graft tissue is utilized. Buccal mucosa, full thickness grafts, and perichondrocutaneous grafts (harvested from the auricular concha) have been used successfully.[17]

When free mobility of the cricoarytenoid joints cannot be established, the arytenoids can be held apart with a cartilage. This procedure has been described using a small window of cartilage from the thyroid ala or a portion of costal cartilage[18] (Fig 90–3). Stents are used to hold the arytenoids laterally during initial healing and to provide soft pressure on any mucosal flaps and grafts. Stenting is advocated in many procedures for posterior glottic reconstruction. Both soft and rigid stents can be utilized depending on the surgeon's preference.

Conclusion

Posterior glottic stenosis is a particularly difficult problem to treat in long-term airway injuries. The outcome of treatment will determine the patient's ability to live without a tracheotomy, the voice quality, and the ability to maintain airway protection during swallowing. Simple scar bands are excised endoscopically. Deeper scars can be treated using endolaryngeal procedures if mucosal coverage is possible, but most patients with PGS involving cricoarytenoid fixation require an open procedure. Severe PGS involving cricoarytenoid fixation usually requires an open procedure. Severe PGS is approached by laryngotomy with cartilage interposition between the arytenoids, coverage by a local mucosal flap or graft, and postoperative stenting. Arytenoidectomy and cordotomy may be used to open the airway when laryngeal mobility cannot be reestablished.

References

1. Bogdasarian RS, Olson NR. Posterior glottic laryngeal stenosis. *Otolaryngol Head Neck Surg.* 1980;88:765–772.
2. Smith ME, Marsh JH, Cotton RT, Myer CM III. Voice problems after pediatric laryngotracheal reconstruction: videolaryngostroboscopic, acoustic, and perceptual assessment. *Int J Pediatr Otorhinolaryngol.* 1993;25:173–181.
3. Strong MS, Healy GB, Vaughan CW, et al. Endoscopic management of laryngeal stenosis. *Otolaryngol Clin North Am.* 1979;12(4):797–805.
4. McCombe AW, Phillips DE, Rogers JH. Inter-arytenoid glottic bar following intubation. *J Laryngol Otol.* 1990; 104:727–729.
5. Lim RY. Endoscopic CO2 laser arytenoidectomy for postintubation glottic stenosis. *Otolaryngol Head Neck Surg.* 1991;105:662–666.
6. Gaboriau H, Laccourreye O, Laccourreye H, Brasnu D. CO2 laser posterior transverse cordotomy for isolated type IV posterior glottic stenosis. *Am J Otolaryngol.* 1995; 16:350–353.
7. Kleinsasser O. *Microlaryngoscopy and Endolaryngeal Microsurgery: Technique and Typical Findings.* Philadelphia, Pa: Hanley & Belfus, Inc; 1980:84.
8. Dedo HH, Sooy CD. Endoscopic laser repair of posterior glottic, subsglottic and tracheal stenosis by division or microtrapdoor flap. *Laryngoscope.* 1984;94:445–450.
9. Duncavage JA, Piazza LS, Ossoff RH, Toohill RJ. The microtrapdoor flap technique for the management of laryngeal stenosis. *Laryngoscope.* 1987;97:825–828.
10. Beste DJ, Toohill RJ. Microtrapdoor flap repair of laryngeal and tracheal stenosis. *Ann Otol Rhinol Laryngol.* 1991;100:420–423.
11. Werkhaven JA, Weed DT, Ossoff RH. Carbon dioxide laser serial microtrapdoor flap excision of subglottic stenosis. *Arch Otolaryngol Head Neck Surg.* 1993;119:676–679.

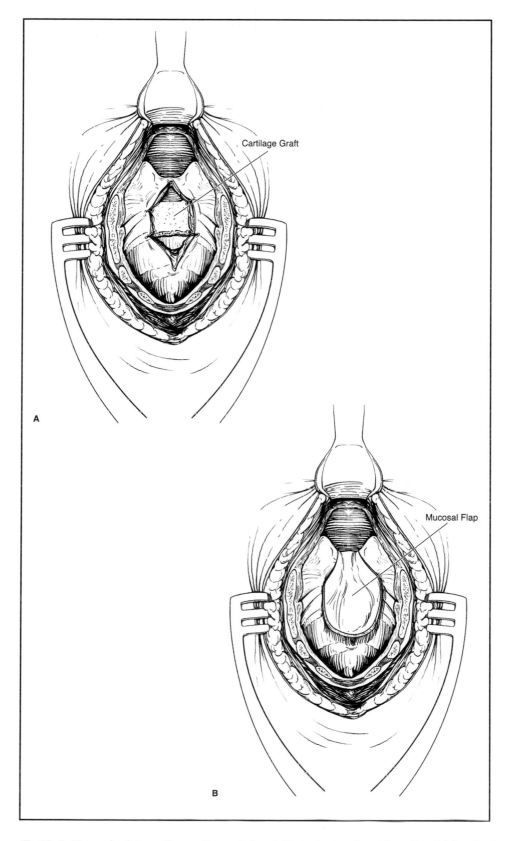

Fig 90–3. Through a laryngofissure, the posterior glottic region can be widened by dividing the cricoid and holding the arytenoids apart with cartilage (*top*), which is then covered with a posteriorly based mucosal flap (*bottom*).

12. Shapshay SM, Wang Z, Volk M, et al. Resurfacing of a large laryngeal wound with mucosa grafting: a combined technique using endoscopic suture and laser soldering. *Ann Otol Rhinol Laryngol.* 1995;104:919–923.

13. Rahbar R, Valdez TA, Shapshay SM. Preliminary results of intraoperative mitomycin-C in the treatment and prevention of glottic and subglottic stenosis. *J Voice.* 2000; 14:282–286.

14. Rahbar R, Shapshay SM, Healy GB. Mitomycin: effects on laryngeal and tracheal stenosis, benefits, and complications. *Ann Otol Rhinol Laryngol.* 2001;110:1–6.

15. McCaffrey TV. Classification of laryngotracheal stenosis. *Laryngoscope.* 1992;102:1335–1340.

16. Montgomery WW. Posterior and complete laryngeal (glottic) stenosis. *Arch Otolaryngol.* 1973;98:170–175.

17. Hoasjoe DK, Franklin SW, Aarstad RF, et al. Posterior glottic stenosis mechanism and surgical management. *Laryngoscope.* 1997;107:675–679.

18. Cummings CW, Sessions DG, Weymuller WA, Wood P. Posterior glottic split cartilage perichondrial graft. In: Cummings CW et al, eds. *Atlas of Laryngeal Surgery.* St. Louis, Mo: CV Mosby Co; 1984:179.

91

Management of Gender Reassignment (Sex Change) Patients

Reinhardt J. Heuer, Margaret M. Baroody, and Robert Thayer Sataloff

Transsexualism is a gender dysphoric disorder characterized by persistent feelings of inappropriateness of biologic sex and preoccupation with eliminating primary and secondary sexual characteristics. Male-to-female transsexualism is encountered more commonly than female-to-male transsexualism and demonstrates more difficult communication problems. In most cases, these patients benefit from communication therapy. Female-to-male transsexuals, due to the influence of hormonal treatment on the larynx and related structures, are less likely to have vocal problems. Male-to-female transsexualism occurs in approximately 1 out of 37,000 births.[1,2] Other related groups of individuals require similar communication assistance. Transgenderists are men who wish to live full time as women but are not so concerned with body issues. Interestingly, in the American culture, it is easier for women to live full time in a masculine role. Cross-dressers are men who enjoy part-time dressing and behaving as women. However, individuals frequently will vacillate from one classification to another over a lifetime. Persons who are primarily cross-dressers will move toward transsexualism or will abandon (purge) their feminine accoutrements. Most males falling into these categories report periods of rejection of the entire issue and work toward becoming hypermasculine, usually early in their lives. Most are married, and many have children. The authors believe that therapy for voice and communication issues is most appropriate when the patient has been diagnosed with gender dysphoria and is living 90 to 100% of the time as a woman. When working with cross-dressers, treatment should be behaviorally based and focus on developing "stage" accent and scripts for use during social events. Other subgroups, such as transvestites and female impersonators, are less likely to look to voice and communication specialists for assistance; but they can be helped similarly when they do.

When developing a program of therapy for the male-to-female transsexual (M/FT), it is important to keep in mind which aspects of communication are based in biology/genetic structure (male/female) and which aspects are based in learned/social behavior (masculine/feminine). Biologic and genetic aspects include, of course, primary and secondary sexual characteristics. Specifically related to communication are lung size and capacity, laryngeal size and configuration, vocal fold mass, resonating cavity sizes, muscle mass of the tongue, and oral orifice size and thickness. These differences affect the pitch, loudness, quality, and resonance of the voice and some aspects of articulation. Learned or social aspects of communication include melody/intonation in voicing, patterns of syllabic emphasis/stress, word choice, sentence structure, semantic structure, gestural communication, and dress.

The major goal for most M/FTs is sexual reassignment surgery with modification of the primary sexual characteristics. This surgery is expensive ($20,000) and is considered elective by many insurance companies. Most responsible sexual reassignment surgeons require psychiatric proof of gender dysphoria and practical evidence of the patient's ability to live successfully in a feminine role prior to consenting to do the surgery.

There are no really good surgical procedures to lower the voice in female-to-male transsexuals. The mass of the vocal folds can be increased by injection of substances, and the vocal folds can be shortened by type III thyroplasty; but neither technique results consistently in both substantial decrease in habitual pitch and retention of good vocal quality. Procedures to feminize the biologically male voice are more successful.

Nonsurgical Therapy for Pitch Modification

Ninety-five percent of the more than 400 M/FTs the author (RJH) has seen had a primary complaint of excessively low pitch. Although this is a male/female trait, the patient frequently elects to work on pitch behaviorally. Surgical considerations for pitch change are discussed later in this chapter.

Gelfer and Schofield[3] report that speech fundamental frequencies above 155 Hz (D3) are more likely to be perceived as feminine. Oates and Dacakis[4] are more generous in reporting a gender ambiguous range between 128 and 260 Hz. The goal of pitch modification in M/FTs is to develop a speaking fundamental frequency high enough to allow down-glides that remain above the masculine/feminine cutoff. Initial evaluation of the M/FT involves determining current speech fundamental frequency and the patient's frequency comfortable range. It would be difficult to modify the pitch range upward for an individual who has little flexibility in the upper voice ranges. Behavioral modification of habitual pitch is not easy. It involves development of vocal flexibility, breath support, relaxation, and practice. General breath support and relaxation exercises can be found in chapters 68 and 73. Several approaches have been successful in raising speech fundamental frequency, hopefully allowing the patient to continue using modal voice. Again, this is possible only if the patient has an adequate range. A series of up, down, and up-and-down glide exercises is helpful in extending the patient's range and flexibility. Exercises may include glides on the vowels /ɑ/, /i/, and /u/. One would like to establish a pitch range of at least four semitones above 155 Hz. Drills on words and phrases following upglides are very helpful. Visual feedback using the Kay Visi-Pitch or Kay Real-Time Pitch programs is also very helpful. The majority of patients who seek help do so because they are unable to modify or monitor their own voices acoustically. A program of practice with and upglide + phrase with visual cues, upglide + phrase without visual cues, followed by fading of the upglide and visual cues has been effective in our clinic.

Patients with limited upper ranges are not good candidates for behavioral modification of modal voice or for surgical modification of voice. A voice modification program called "Melanie Speaks" advocated the use of low falsetto voice.[5] The author describes exercises gliding down from natural falsetto to lower falsetto pitches and modifying pharyngeal tension. This is similar to a classical Bel Canto exercise used for centuries by singers to integrate registers into a "mixed" voice.

Surgery for Pitch Modification

Once the diagnosis has been established, the patient is living as a female, psychiatry clearance has been obtained, and voice therapy has been completed, pitch modification surgery may be reasonable. Transsexuals often request this surgery even if they have been extremely successful at modifying voice gender recognition through voice therapy. If such patients are awakened suddenly, talk in their sleep, or are startled, they are often "revealed" through unthinking, sudden bursts of masculine phonation. This can be extremely embarrassing; and surgical correction in such patients is appropriate.

Many techniques have been proposed, and none is ideal for all cases. Isshiki's type IV thyroplasty, which is described in chapter 82, has been used for this indication. Unfortunately, even with overcorrection, vocal pitch tends to drop over time. The author's (RTS) cricothyroid fusion procedure (also described in the thyroplasty section of chapter 82) produces better long-term results. However, it is only suitable for use in young transsexuals. The cricoid cartilage must be sufficiently flexible to permit its placement just inside the lower border of the thyroid cartilage. When pulling the cricoid toward the thyroid cartilage, it is extremely important to exert all forces under the cricoid arch laterally. The cricoid arch is thin in the midline. If attempts are made to pull the cricoid superiorly with hooks placed in or near the midline, midline fracture is likely to occur. In patients under 40, this operation tends to work well. In patients over 60, ossification is usually too advanced to permit subluxation of the cricoid arch behind the thyroid cartilage. In those between 40 and 60 years old, success depends on the degree of ossification. In such patients, Isshiki's technique can be used as described originally or with suture placement as modified by Lee et al.[6] Anterior commissure advancement was described by LeJeune and coworkers in 1983.[7] LeJeune created a cartilage window that was pulled forward, along with the vocal folds. The space between the advanced cartilage and the rest of the thyroid cartilage was maintained with a titanium splint. Tucker modified the procedure by placing the cartilage window in a more cranial position.[8] However, both of these procedures result in increased prominence of the thyroid cartilage. Because many transsexual patients have already undergone laryngeal shave to reduce the thyroid prominence, this cosmetic disadvantage may be unacceptable to the patient.

A few authors have used scarring obtained by parallel cuts near the vibratory margin[9] or vocal fold stripping[10] to elevate pitch. Although increased stiffness does elevate pitch, it is also associated with decreased volume and substantial hoarseness. This author (RTS) does not advocate these procedures. Abitbol has utilized endoscopic thyroarytenoid myomectomy successfully (Jean Abitbol, MD, Paris, France, personal communication, 2001). In this operation, a large ellipse of thyroarytenoid muscle is removed using a CO_2 laser through an incision placed laterally on the superior surface of the vocal fold. The vibratory margin is not disturbed. This procedure results in decreased mass and, consequently, elevated pitch. The voices are slightly breathy but clear. This procedure can be done unilaterally or bilaterally and has a place in the management of these patients.

Another approach to pitch elevation involves shortening of the vocal folds. Initially, Donald proposed performing such surgery through an external approach.[11] The anterior commissure was divided, the anterior portion of the vocal folds was de-epithelialized, and the vocal folds were sutured together. This procedure was modified by Wendler[12] and Gross[13,14] and more recently by the author (RTS, unpublished data). The procedure described by Wendler and by Gross essentially creates a web, as did Donald; but it is created endoscopically. The anterior portion of the vocal fold is de-epithelialized, and the vocal fold are sutured together firmly through the laryngoscope, creating a V-shaped anterior commissure but a shorter vibrating vocal fold. As in patients who have vocal fold webs for other reasons, this usually results in a clear voice of higher pitch; because the remaining vibrating segment is short, but the vibratory margin has not been disturbed. This author (RTS) has modified the procedure slightly, preserving approximately 2 mm of mucosa adjacent to the anterior commissure. This small area does not interfere with the result. However, although it is unlikely that anyone would elect to have this procedure reversed, should it ever be necessary to try to correct the surgically created web, retaining the anterior commissure will probably prove helpful. To elevate pitch substantially, it has been necessary to de-epithelialize at least one-third to one-half of the musculomembranous vocal fold. This author prefers to accomplish this procedure by marking the anterior and posterior limits of the intended resection with a CO_2 laser. Submucosal infusion is then performed. Flaps of mucosa can be elevated bilaterally using cold instruments or the CO_2 laser. However, because the intention is to scar the vocal fold together, there is no disadvantage to using the laser during this procedure. The vocal folds are approximated using one or two Vicryl sutures. The procedure can be performed under local or general anesthesia. This operation has proven useful both as a primary procedure and as a secondary procedure when cricothyroid approximation has proven insufficient for the patient's needs. Following successful pitch modification surgery, it is reasonable to expect an increase in pitch of about 5 to 9 semitones (about one-fourth to one-sixth of an octave). Pitch elevations as low as 3 or 4 semitones and as high as about 12 semitones occur occasionally. With the increase in pitch, there usually is some decrease in pitch range, particularly loss of a one-fourth or one-fifth of an octave on the lower end of the pitch range. The highest notes that can be produced do not tend to change much as a result of the surgery.

Therapy for Other Aspects of Voice Gender Identification

Speech fundamental frequency is not the sole answer to a more feminine voice, even following surgical modification. As noted above, Oates and Dacakis[4] reported the gender ambiguous frequency range as quite large. Probably of more importance to gender identification is the inclusion of increased melody within the spoken syllable. This voice attribute appears to be learned and is an aspect of the masculine/feminine continuum not the male/female continuum. The more feminine individual tends to utilize increased intrasyllabic melody on vowels within the syllable. The more masculine individual tends to utilize a flatter, less melodic pattern. Listen to the way masculine individuals say "Hello" or "Good morning," and this difference is obvious immediately. Pitch modification does not change this voicing attribute and may only create the impression of a masculine individual with a high-pitched voice.

Practice in melodic intonation should include visual feedback using a device such as the Kay Visi-Pitch overwrite feature for short phrases and sentences. Initially, vowels may need to be elongated, and consonants may have to be shortened and made more precise to allow time to shift pitch on each vowel. Extensive drill is necessary. Practice on varying intonation patterns (particularly upglides) within phrases is also helpful. Over time, visual feedback should be faded, speaking rate increased, and carryover procedures should be initiated. Matching melody to emotional content should be encouraged once the patient is able to free herself from the more monotone masculine pattern. Phrases and sentences taken from the patient's own corpus of frequently said sentences should be used for practice purposes. Melanie Phillips[5] suggests pharyngeal constrictions similar to that obtained when mimicking "the wicked witch of the west" voice and then relaxing the throat to the point of resonance desired. Moya Andrews[15] discusses elevation of the larynx and pharyngeal constriction as another possibility. Currently, there is no evidence of safety from vocal discomfort or disorders in developing these vocal misuse patterns.

Using a relaxed jaw and gentle smile is very effective in reducing the strength of the lower partials in the voice. More feminine individuals are found to smile more frequently during speech in any case. Better oral resonance and a relaxed open jaw can be facilitated by an exercise that involves clenching the jaw while monitoring the masseter muscles with the fingertips and then relaxing the jaw until the muscle bulk has diminished but the muscle is not stretched. Mirrors and videotapes are helpful feedback devices for practicing smiling speech. Over-rounding of the lips or a chimneylike anterior resonance chamber should be avoided.

The female oral cavity is somewhat smaller in most cases than the male oral cavity. Tongue bulk is also less. More feminine articulation is characterized by lighter contacts and shorter articulatory gesture distances that result in less impact on contact. The patient should practice reducing the vowel triangle both posteriorly/anteriorly and inferiorly/superiorly; moving the posteriorly articulated consonants /k/ and /g/ and /ŋ/ forward may create a more feminine articulatory production. Utilizing a modified paired-stimuli approach is helpful. The target consonant-vowel (CV) syllable /ki/ can be contrasted with /ku/ and other back vowels, striving to keep the place of articulation of /k/ and the vowel in the forward position. These modifications in articulation tend to change the positioning of formant II, which is correlated with more feminine speech. Extensive practice at home is necessary to modify these basic speech patterns. Drilling on words from the Thorndike/Lorge Lists of the 1000 Most Frequently Used Words[16] may be helpful.

In addition to working on anteriorizing vowels and consonants, narrowing the productions of sibilants may also improve femininity of speech. More masculine sibilants tend to be more dull and strong. All of these aspects of voicing, resonance, and articulation benefit from singing as well as speech practice.

Carol Gilligan, in her book *In a Different Voice* discusses the differences in the developmental patterns of boys and girls and how differences affect a person's worldview, what he or she talks about, and how he or she phrases speech.[17] Women develop other-orientation, oligarchical superiority, and relationship maintenance preferences. Apparently differences between boys' and girls' attitudes begin very early in life and are probably related, at least in part, to differential parental patterns. Gilligan demonstrates these differences even in the play patterns of young children. More feminine individuals tend to soften the harshness of their speaking patterns by including more tag question sentences such as, "It's time to go, isn't it?" They tend to use more psychological verbs, such as "I feel, I think," and so on. These kinds of changes are difficult to train later in life when we work with gender dysphoria, because they are related directly to the person's mindset. However, the patient should be aware of these kinds of differences, as well.

Gesture and body language also may need to be modified. More masculine individuals tend to take up all of the available space with their bodies; whereas more feminine individuals tend to compact themselves with more upright posture, crossed legs or ankles, and arms held close to the body. More masculine individuals tend to walk with a broad-based gait and the palms of the hands facing backwards; more feminine individuals walk with the feet placed in front of each other and the palms of the hands facing toward the thighs. Feminine arm gestures tend to be more lateral and less often in front of the gesturer. Arm gestures focus on the wrists and fingers of more feminine gesturers.

The major goal in behavioral therapy with male-to-female transsexuals is the development of comfort and a feeling of confidence in the patient's femininity. If a true relationship exists between communicating partners, after about 5 minutes of conversation, the voice and speech patterns of the individual become irrelevant and/or are simply part of that person's persona. A conundrum always exists within the male-to-female transsexual because of the feeling of being "female" trapped in a "male" body. "If I already feel as though I am a woman, why do I have to change my behavior?" Yet, there is an anxiety about "passing" and "being ready" as the opposite sex. The development of confidence and the ability to recognize what constitutes more feminine behavior assist patients in developing comfort and ease with whatever level of feminine voice and speech they are capable of reaching.

References

1. Brown GR. A review of clinical approaches to gender dysphoria. *J Clin Psychiatry*. 1990;51(2):57–69.

2. Landen M, Walinder J, Lundstrom B. Prevalence, incidence and sex ratio of transsexualism. *Acta Psychiatr Scand.* 1996;93:221–223

3. Gelfer MP, Schofield KJ. Comparison of acoustic and perceptual measures of voice in male-to-female transsexuals perceived as female versus those perceived as male. *J Voice.* 2000:14(1) 22–33.

4. Oates JM, Dacakis G. Speech pathology considerations in the management of transsexualism–a review. *Br J Disord Commun.* 1983:18(3) 139–151.

5. Phillips M. *Melanie Speaks!* Burbank, Calif: Heart Corp (PO Box 295, Burbank, CA 91503). [Video.]

6. Lee SY, Liao TT, Hsieh T. Extralaryngeal approach in functional phonosurgery. In: *Proceedings of the 20th Congress of the IALP.* Tokyo, Japan: The Organizing Committee of the XXth Congress of the International Association of Logopedics and Phoniatrics; 1986:482–483.

7. LeJeune FE, Guice CE, Samuels PM. Early experiences with vocal ligament tightening. *Ann Otol Rhinol Laryngol.* 1983;92:475–477.

8. Tucker HM. Anterior laryngoplasty for adjustment of vocal fold tension. *Ann Otol Rhinol Laryngol.* 1985;94: 547–549.

9. Tanabe M, Haji T, Isshiki N. Surgical treatment for androphonia. An experimental study. *Folia Phoniatr (Basel).* 1985;37:15–21.

10. Hirano M, Ohala J, Vennard W. The function of laryngeal muscles in regulating fundamental frequency and intensity of phonation. *J Speech Hear Res.* 1969;12:616–628.

11. Donald PJ, Voice change in the transsexual. *Head Neck Surg.* 1982;4:433–437.

12. Wendler J. Pitch elevation after transsexualism male to female. Presented at the XVI UEP Congress; October 10–14, 1990; Salsomaggiore, Italy.

13. Gross M, Fehland P. Ergebnisse nach operativer Anhebung der mittleren Sprechstimmlage bie Transsexuellen durch Verkurzung des schwingenden Stimmkippenanteils. In: Gross M, ed. *Aktuelle phoniatrisch-padaudiologische Aspekte 1995.* Berlin: Germany: RGV; 1996:88–89.

14. Gross M. Pitch-raising surgery in male-to-female transsexuals. *J Voice.* 1999;13(2).246–250.

15. Andrews ML. *Manual of Voice Treatment: Pediatrics through Geriatrics.* San Diego, Calif: Singular Publishing Group, Inc; 1995:391–404.

16. Thorndike E L, Lorge I. *The Teacher's Wordbook of 30,000 Words.* New York, NY: Teacher's College, Columbia University; 1944.

17. Gilligan C. *In A Different Voice: Psychological Theory and Women's Development.* Cambridge, Mass: Harvard University Press; 1982

92

Premalignant Lesions of the Larynx

Carole M. Dean and Robert Thayer Sataloff

Accurate diagnosis and management of premalignant lesions of the larynx can prevent the development of laryngeal carcinoma or allow control of malignancy in an early stage. When laryngeal examination reveals an epithelial abnormality suspicious for malignancy, biopsy is indicated to provide a histologic diagnosis. Irregular masses and ulcerations of the mucosa are most suspicious, but more subtle surface changes are often the earliest manifestations of malignancy. Suspicion of cancerous change is greatly increased when the patient has a history of known etiologic risk factors such as cigarette smoking, alcohol use, asbestos exposure, and chemical or dust exposure. After biopsy, the laryngologist must work with the pathologist, radiation oncologist, medical oncologist, and the patient to develop a management strategy based on clinical and histologic findings.

Terminology

Clinical Terms

Leukoplakia describes any white lesion of a mucous membrane (Figs 92–1, 92–2, and 92–3). According to Wenig,[1] it is not necessarily indicative of an underlying malignant tumor. *Erythroplakia*, a red lesion of a mucous membrane, is more often indicative of an underlying malignant tumor. *Erythroleukoplakia*[2] refers to a mix of red and white changes of the mucous membrane (Fig 92–4). *Pachydermia* describes abnormal thickening of the mucous membrane with or without leukoplakia (Fig 92–5).

Histologic Terms

Hyperplasia is the thickening of the epithelial surface as a result of an absolute increase in the number of cells.

Pseudoepitheliomatous hyperplasia is an exuberant reactive or reparative overgrowth of squamous epithelium (hyperplasia) displaying no cytologic evidence of malignancy. This lesion may be mistaken for an invasive carcinoma. *Keratosis* is the presence of keratin on the epithelial surface. *Parakeratosis* refers to the presence of nuclei in the keratin layer and *dyskeratosis* is abnormal keratinization of individual cells. *Metaplasia* is a change from one histologic tissue type to another. For example, squamous metaplasia denotes the replacement of respiratory epithelium by stratified squamous epithelium; it generally occurs as a result of tissue injury. *Koilocytosis* is cytoplasmic vacuolization of a squamous cell suggestive of viral infection such as human papilloma virus (HPV). *Dysplasia* is a qualitative alteration toward malignancy in the appearance of

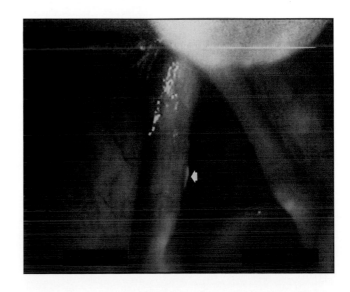

Figure 92–1. Mild leukoplakia of the left vocal fold (*arrow*).

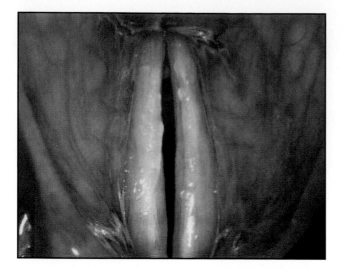

Fig 92–2. Moderate leukoplakia, worse on the left.

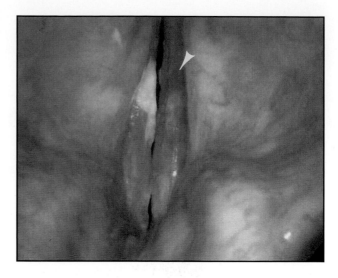

Fig 92–4. Left prominent leukoplakia with mild erythema. Right erythroplakia (*arrowhead*) with adjacent patchy white areas of leukoplakia.

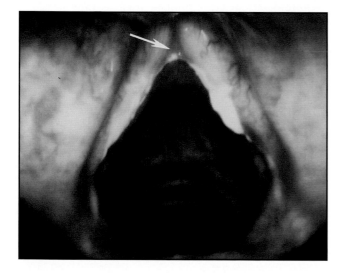

Fig 92–3. More severe leukoplakia involving both vocal folds and an anterior web (*arrow*).

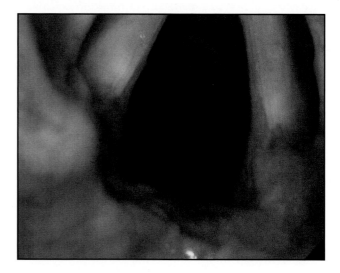

Fig 92–5. Pachydermia of the posterior larynx, most commonly associated with chronic laryngopharyngeal reflux.

cells, consisting of cellular aberrations and abnormal maturation. Cellular aberrations include nuclear enlargement, irregularity, and hyperchromatism; increased nuclear/cytoplasmic ratios; dyskeratosis; crowding of cells; loss of polarity; and increased mitotic activity. Dysplasia is graded mild if the changes are within the inner third of the surface epithelium, moderate if it involves one-third to two-thirds, and severe if it is found from two-thirds to just short of full thickness. Severe dysplasia is differentiated from *carcinoma in situ* (CIS) by normal maturation in the most superficial layers of epithelium and from *invasive carcinoma* (Fig 92–6) by the integrity of the basement membrane.

Many classifications have been used to describe laryngeal epithelial changes. Many of them are similar; some are more or less identical. However, none of the proposed classification systems is perfect. Friedman's classification[3] is modeled on gynecologic pathology for lesions of the uterine cervix. They use the term *laryngeal intraepithelial neoplasm* (LIN) to include both dysplasia and CIS. Their classification is as follows: LIN-I corresponds to mild or minimal dysplasia; LIN-II corresponds to moderate dysplasia; and LIN-III corresponds to severe dysplasia and CIS. Unlike cancer of the uterine cervix, many carcinomas of the larynx do not go through the stage of CIS and are inva-

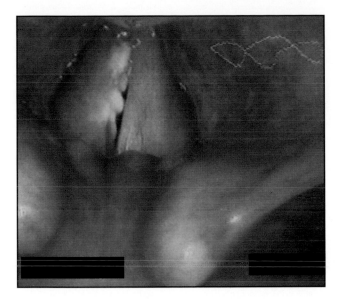

Fig 92–6. Leukoplakia associated with T1 invasive carcinoma of the left true vocal fold. From gross appearance alone, it is not distinguishable from benign leukoplakia.

sive from the start.[4] Hellqvist's classification system is also divided into three groups.[5] Group I is squamous cell hyperplasia with or without keratosis and/or mild dysplasia; Group II is squamous cell hyperplasia with moderate dysplasia; Group III is squamous cell hyperplasia with severe dysplasia or classical CIS with full thickness atypia.[6-12]

In Europe, a classification system was designed by Kleinsasser and has been widely applied throughout the world. His classification has three groups that include:

Class I = Simple Squamous Cell Hyperplasia

Class II = Squamous Cell Hyperplasia with Atypia

Class III = CIS.

Epidemiology and Etiologic Factors

Laryngeal cancer is primarily a disease of middle age with a peak incidence in the sixth and seventh decades. In the United States, in the year 2000, its incidence was much higher in men than in women with a 4:1 ratio. However, this ratio was 20:1 just twenty years prior; the trend reflects the changing pattern of tobacco use in society. This decrease in the male-to-female ratio has also been observed worldwide.[13] The incidence is also higher among black people when compared to Caucasians.[13,14]

The major etiologic factor in the development of laryngeal cancer is tobacco use. Numerous studies have shown a dose-dependent relationship between cigarette use and the development of cancer.[15,16] Smoking cigarettes has a strong association with cancer of the larynx while smoking cigars and pipes has a weaker association.[15,16] Most studies have shown that smoking cessation reduces the risk of laryngeal cancer. The importance of smoking cessation must be emphasized to patients with either premalignant or malignant lesions. One study showed that patients who continued to smoke after the diagnosis of head and neck cancer had a fourfold increase in the recurrence rate over those who never smoked, and a doubled increase for those who stopped smoking.[17]

Heavy alcohol use is also a factor in the development of laryngeal cancer and the relative risk is higher for supraglottic cancer than glottic cancer.[18] There has been a consistent finding of an interaction between cigarette smoking and alcohol consumption on laryngeal cancer risk. Yet, while studies have demonstrated that the combined effect of both cigarette smoking and alcohol consumption is greater than the sum of the individual effects, the biologic basis of this synergistic effect is still not clear. It has been reported that alcohol and tobacco account for over 80% of the squamous cell carcinomas of the mouth, pharynx, larynx, and esophagus in the United States.[19] The presence of this kind of interaction stresses the importance of eliminating at least one factor for subjects engaged in both habits.

There is increasing evidence that reflux laryngitis may be a carcinogenic cofactor in the development of laryngeal cancer. The association of reflux, Barrett's esophagus, and esophageal carcinoma is well established and can be used as an analogous model for the larynx.[20,21] Reflux of gastric acid causes acute and chronic inflammation of the larynx; that inflammation may (as in Barrett's esophagus) cause malignant transformation. Ward et al reported 19 cases of laryngeal carcinoma in lifetime nonsmokers who had moderate to severe reflux.[22] Freije et al[23] also proposed that laryngopharyngeal reflux (LPR) plays a role in the development of laryngeal carcinoma in patients without the typical risk factors.

Diet is being increasingly studied as an etiologic factor in the development of laryngeal carcinoma, and its role in the causal pathway has gained importance. It has been suggested that a high intake of fruit, salads, and dairy products may help reduce the risk of laryngeal cancer.[18] There is also evidence that deficiencies in vitamins A, C, E, beta-carotene, riboflavin, iron, zinc, and selenium have been associated with an increased risk of laryngeal cancer. The relationship between dietary factors and the occurrence of laryngeal cancer continues to be studied, as does an individual's dietary habits related to cancers elsewhere in the body.

Radiation exposure and/or avocational or occupational exposure to hazardous materials such as nickel, mustard gas, wood products, wood stove emissions, coal mines, insecticides, silica, and dry-cleaning chemicals have been implicated as etiologic factors as well.[24-27] The etiologic effect of asbestos on laryngeal cancer is still controversial, but it appears to be limited to active smokers.[16] In a study by Maier et al,[18] 92% of laryngeal squamous cell carcinoma patients were labeled as "blue-collar" workers. The risk ratio for those workers having no specialist training or higher education, compared to those with occupational training or higher educational level, was a 3.8:1 ratio. This means that subjects with low occupational training levels have a significantly increased risk of developing laryngeal cancer (after adjustment for alcohol and tobacco consumption).

The role of human papilloma virus and its relationship to the development of laryngeal cancer is discussed in detail later in this chapter.

The goal of treatment for premalignant laryngeal lesions is the prevention of malignant transformation, or the early diagnosis and treatment of laryngeal cancer. Control of potential etiologic factors, especially tobacco use, is necessary for this treatment to be complete and effective.

Malignant Transformation

Inconsistent use of terminology in reporting laryngeal cancer has hampered the collection of data that could be used to create a prognostic classification system. A clinical term such as keratosis can describe a lesion that has normal underlying epithelium or it can describe the surface of an invasive carcinoma.[28,29] There is poor consistency among pathologists in the histologic diagnoses as well. Goldman[30] studied 28 patients retrospectively with epithelial hyperplastic lesions of the larynx. Fifty-two operative biopsies were performed. Evaluation by 11 pathologists in 4 different laboratories yielded 21 different histologic diagnoses exclusive of invasive cancer. The grading of dysplasia is subjective. Blackwell et al[31] reported that one pathologist performed a blinded review of 148 laryngeal biopsies and only agreed with the original pathologic interpretation in 54% of the cases reviewed. However, the majority of cases differed by only one grade level (ie, mild vs moderate).

Although the rate of malignancy associated with a pathologic diagnosis of dysplasia varies widely, the pattern of increasing risk of malignancy with a worsening dysplasia grade is consistent. Fiorella et al[6] reported an incidence of 6% malignant transformation in keratosis without atypia and 17% when atypia was present. Kambic et al[28] reported a rate of malignant change of 0.3% for keratosis and 9.5% for keratosis with atypia. Blackwell et al[31] retrospectively reviewed 65 patients with long-term follow-up after laryngeal biopsy and found the following cancer rates: 0% (0/6) for keratosis without atypia, 12% (3/26) for mild dysplasia, 33% (5/15) for moderate dysplasia, 44% (4/9) for severe dysplasia, and 11% (1/9) for carcinoma in situ.

Although the presence and grade of dysplasia certainly have prognostic implications, the presence of keratosis has almost no predictive value. Frangeuz et al[29] reviewed 4,291 cases and reported that surface keratosis was present in simple and atypical hyperplasia in 68.8% and 85.5%, respectively. Follow-up of these patients showed malignant transformation to be 0.8% of cases with simple hyperplasia and 8.6% of those with atypical hyperplasia. Keratosis can mask epithelial changes and is not a predictor of underlying atypia. However, dyskeratosis is an important morphologic feature in the process of carcinogenesis.[29] One study revealed a transformation rate of 50% (6/12) in patients with dyskeratosis.[7]

Blackwell et al[8,31] identified five histologic parameters that were found to be significantly different when comparing dysplastic lesions that resolved or remained stable to those that progressed to invasive carcinoma. These were abnormal mitotic figures, mitotic activity, stromal inflammation, maturation level, and nuclear pleomorphism. The five factors were not statistically different when comparing severe dysplasia and carcinoma in situ. Surface morphology, nuclear prominence, and koilocytosis were not significantly different in the two groups.

Histologic examination remains the basis of diagnosis in mucosal lesions of the larynx; however, the prognostic value of the morphologic criteria is limited. Quantification of histologic parameters may become an important supplement to the traditional grading of dysplasia. Proliferation associated changes such as a count of mitotic figures, or Ki67- or PCNA-labeling index gives additional hard data which are correlated to histologic grade.[9-11] DNA histograms are being utilized as an addition to microscopic evaluation. There is evidence that lesions with abnormal DNA content are more likely to persist or progress to intraepithelial or invasive carcinoma. However, it is important to note that the same studies show that the lack of abnormal DNA content does not exclude malignant transformation and that some cancers have so few chromosomal abnormalities that they are below the threshold sensitivity of image analysis or flow cytometry.[12] The prognostic value of p53 immunohistochemistry is controversial[3] and many studies have not found any significant association between p53 immunoreactivity and the evolution of carcinoma.[3,11,32-34]

All patients found to have dysplastic lesions of the laryngeal mucosa need to be followed closely for many years. Progression to invasive carcinoma often is a slow process allowing for early diagnosis, which should yield improved cure rates. Blackwell et al[31] reported that the average interval between the first biopsy and the diagnosis of invasive carcinoma was 3.9 years, suggesting that a 5 to 10-year follow-up plan is reasonable. Velasco et al[7] also suggested a more strict follow-up of patients with dyskeratosis as a result of a 50% (6/12) malignant transformation rate. Their report was based on a retrospective study in which all pathologies were reviewed by pathologist. The period of follow-up ranged from 1 year to 130 months with a mean of 73 months follow-up. Their conclusion was that there is a longer interval between biopsy and malignant changes when you compare with patients having invasive carcinoma, the majority of whom will relapse within 2 years. The ability to provide dedicated long-term care for patients at risk for head and neck cancer is now limited by the financial constraints of managed care[30] in addition to all the other factors that have resulted in delayed diagnosis and treatment. The value of clinical examination, including strobovideolaryngoscopy, at regular intervals cannot be overstated. The senior author (RTS) follows his patients every 1 to 3 months for cancer surveillance with videostrobscopy performed at each office evaluation. Such practice allows for early diagnosis of small invasive carcinomas and use of surgical options that yield greater laryngeal preservation and better voice quality postoperatively.

The strategy of biopsy differs if there is a single area of suspicion versus broad or multifocal lesions. Single, small lesions should be excised with a small mucosal margin. This will be sufficient treatment for many dysplastic lesions and intraepithelial neoplasms. When excision requires the removal of a large area of the true vocal fold, or a critical site such as the anterior commissure or medial margin, a small incisional biopsy may be more appropriate to allow for treatment planning with optimal voice preservation. In patients with broad-based or multifocal lesions, accurate microscopic biopsy at multiple sites is required. While it is always possible for biopsy sampling to miss areas of invasive carcinomas, these techniques are usually sufficient. However, if invasion is suspected clinically and not confirmed pathologically, the surgeon and patient must be prepared to proceed with additional biopsies. The availability of high resolution micro-scopic guidance with suspension laryngoscopy permits both aggressive diagnostic biopsy and mucosal preservation. Contact endoscopy may be helpful in guiding biopsy location. Vocal fold stripping is no longer indicated in the treatment of mucosal lesions of the vocal folds.

Carcinoma in Situ (CIS)

CIS is defined as cellular dysplasia involving the entire thickness of the mucosa without compromise of the basement membrane. The dysplasia may extend into adjacent mucous glands and is still considered an in situ lesion, as long as the lesion is confined to the duct and does not extend in the periductal lamina propia.[1,35] In other words, it is a malignant epithelial neoplasm which has all the characteristics of a true carcinoma except invasiveness and the ability to metastasize.[36] It may exist as an isolated lesion, but it is frequently associated with an invasive squamous cell carcinoma (SCCa), lying either adjacent to or remote from it.[1] Unlike cervical intraepithelial neoplasia, laryngeal CIS is not a required precursor to SCCa. Pathologically, the difference between CIS and severe dysplasia may be very difficult to determine with absolute certainty and is in many ways subjective, resulting in wide differences in the reported incidence and prevalence. However, in practice, the difference between these two lesions is not critical, as both indicate a significant risk for the future development of invasive cancer.

CIS must be evaluated carefully and invasive carcinoma must be ruled out. This is even more significant in the face of CIS of the supraglottis and subglottis than on the vocal folds,[1] as those two sites are considered the "silent area" that usually presents at a later stage of disease. Thus, CIS generally is present in association with an invasive carcinoma.[37] If a small biopsy reveals CIS, then there must be a high suspicion that an adjacent invasive cancer was missed, as reported by Ferlito et al.[36]

The incidence of CIS ranges from 1% to 15% of all malignant laryngeal tumors.[36] There is a distinct male predominance, and it is most frequently seen in the sixth and seventh decades of life.[1] Although it can occur anywhere in the larynx, it most often involves the anterior portion of one or both vocal folds.[1,36,38] It may appear as leukoplakia, erythroplakia, or hyperkeratosis. CIS is a microscopic diagnosis, and its presenting signs, symptoms, and appearance are indistinguishable from other lesions of dysplasia or hyperkeratosis.[36]

The biologic behavior of this tumor is unknown. However, the main pathologic issue is whether or not all CIS will eventually develop into invasive carcinoma. Auerbach et al[15] present indirect evidence that some cases of laryngeal CIS may be reversible in an autopsy study that showed lower rates of CIS in ex-smokers than in active smokers. Stenersen et al[4] observed 41 patients with the diagnosis of CIS or severe dysplasia, but who did not develop invasive carcinoma in the first year following their initial biopsy. The average observation time was 100 months. Forty-six percent (19/41) developed invasive SCCa after a mean interval of 50 months and 54% (22/41) returned to normal mucosa following biopsy. In a literature review, Bouquot and Gnepp[39] found that an average of 29% of cases of laryngeal CIS eventually resulted in invasive carcinoma with a reported range in the different studies of 3.5 to 90%. Untreated cases of CIS were associated with higher rates of transformation: 33.3-90%. When considering all these data, it appears that some cases of CIS are cured by excisional biopsy and some lesions are reversible if the patient controls tobacco use. Yet, despite close observation and treatment, many CIS lesions will progress to invasive carcinoma.

There are some prognostic factors that can be utilized to guide treatment of patients with CIS. Myssiorek et al[37] studied 41 patients with CIS retrospectively and found a much higher rate of transformation in lesions of the anterior commissure (92%) (11/12), than of lesions on the membranous vocal fold (17%) (5/29). This may reflect understaging caused by inadequate biopsy at the anterior commissure. This study also found no association of epidermal growth factor receptors (EGFR) in predicting lesions that will progress to invasive cancer. Epidermal growth factor (EGF) may play a role in the regulation of the growth of cancer of the larynx. Some in vitro studies have shown that cancer cells are stimulated by EGF/EGFR (immunohistochemical analysis of overexpression), while others evaluated if it had any prognostic value in determining which premalignant lesion or CIS would progress to invasive carcinoma. Results concerning its usefulness are inconsistent in the literature.[3,32] In another study, 37% (7/19) of patients with CIS who developed invasive laryngeal carcinoma were found to have had the carcinoma arise at a different anatomic site from the original CIS.[4] The authors concluded that there should be a high clinical suspicion of a lesion that arises separately from the site of known CIS.

Treatment of CIS has included surgery and radiation therapy. A recent review of primary surgical treatment with microscopic laser excision showed a local recurrence rate of 8% and an ultimate control of 100%. Small's[40] et al literature review revealed that radio-therapy as the primary treatment of CIS yielded an overall recurrence rate of 20% and an ultimate local control rate of 96%, following salvage treatment. They offered two explanations for the discrepancies found in the published data. First, there may be understaging of CIS (false CIS) and second, the total doses of radiation given were inadequate. Most CIS lesions are treated surgically because the biopsy itself provides the opportunity for complete excision and because of the limitations of primary radiation therapy. Most importantly, patients with CIS are at increased risk for development of an epithelial malignancy at other laryngeal and head and/or neck sites, the mucosa field effect. Dedicating a large portion of the lifetime radiation dose to the treatment of an early premalignant lesion or superficially malignant lesion may limit severely future treatment options if an invasive malignancy arises at another site. Additionally, radiation therapy requires an extended course of treatment[41,42] and its secondary effects on the local mucosa can mask recurrent tumors.[41] Yet, radiation therapy still plays a major role in the treatment of CIS and microinvasive carcinoma. Radiation therapy is indicated in patients who are poor risks for general anesthesia, those who have recurrent lesions after previous surgical excision, lesions that cannot be adequately exposed or resected endoscopically, and patients with recurrent lesions who cannot be adequately followed.[37,40-44]

Laryngeal Papillomas

Human Papilloma Virus: Epidemiology and Molecular Biology

Human papilloma virus (HPV) is a small, non-enveloped DNA virus. More than 70 HPV types have been identified. Based on studies of cervical cancer, different HPV[16,18,31,33,35] types have been graded as high risk oncogenic viruses because they are associated with high grade dysplasia or invasive carcinoma. The low risk HPV types[6,11,13,32,34,40,42-46] are usually associated with benign lesions such as uterine cervical condylomas. HPV 6 and HPV 11 are commonly associated with genital lesions as well as with laryngeal papillomas.[45] HPV types 16 and 18 also occur in the larynx.[46]

There is a high correlation of the risk of malignant transformation of infected cells in the presence of high-risk virus types. The viral genome of the HPV includes the E6 and E7 oncogene that is responsible for the viral proteins E6 and E7, respectively. The properties of these two oncoproteins have been reported extensively. High-risk types of HPV encode E6 and E7 oncoprotein that bind the Rb-related proteins and p53 with as much as 10-fold higher affinity, than the low risk HPV types.[47] For example, the E6 oncoprotein of HPV 16, can complex with the host cell p53 tumor suppressor protein thereby inducing p53 degradation.[45,46] Loss of p53 function leads to deregulation of the cell cycle and promotes mutation, chromosomal instability, and carcinogenesis of the host genome. Nevertheless, it has been reported that p53 can still preserve the tumor suppressor activity in the presence of HPV types 6 and 11, which are the predominant types in laryngeal papillomatosis.[46]

The relationship between HPV, p53, and other cellular control genes in SCCa of the head and neck is potentially complex. Molecular epidemiologic research is needed to evaluate the independent and joint effects of tobacco, HPV, and alterations of other genes involved in carcinogenesis.

Estimates of the prevalence of HPV types in normal tissue, benign papillomas, and cancers of the larynx are inconsistent because of the ongoing evolution in typing methods. Polymerase chain reaction (PCR) is a method of amplifying target sequences from a DNA specimen thus providing a higher degree of sensitivity than traditional hybridization methodologies. A high interlaboratory agreement has been achieved on sample acquisition and processing methods, leading to concordant results. McKaig et al[45] reviewed the literature to determine HPV prevalence in head and neck cancer. Using PCR, HPV was found in 34.5% (416/1205). Forty percent contained HPV 16, 11.9% contained HPV 18, and 7% contained both types. In addition, 3.8% were positive for HPV 6, 7.4% for HPV 11, and 10.9% for both HPV 6 and HPV 11. Prevalence was also reported by site with 33% of laryngeal carcinomas found to be positive. Of those, 46% contained HPV 16 and 15.9% contained HPV 16 and HPV 18. Despite the prevalences reported, no correlation between virus infection and disease course or prognosis could be made.

The precise mechanism of malignant transformation in laryngeal papillomatosis is still unknown. In a retrospective study of 24 cases of laryngeal papillomatosis, Luzar et al[46] tried to determine any prognostic markers that might reflect the biologic behavior of the infected epithelium; they found that 23 of the 24 cases were HPV positive using PCR. All sections were immunostained for p53 protein and for c-erbB-2 oncogene product. The authors concluded that further molecular studies are needed to investigate whether increased p53 truly represents p53 overexpression or only stabilized wild type p53 gene product, and whether this possible overexpression may be a marker of malignant transformation. The staining pattern

for the c-erbB-2 oncogene changed from membranous to cytoplasmic in cells demonstrating atypical hyperplasia. The real impact of this change also requires further study.

Majoros et al[48] published a pathologic review of 101 patients with juvenile laryngeal papillomatosis treated at the Mayo Clinic between 1914 and 1960 and noted greater cellular activity from the beginning of the disease process in the 6 patients who underwent malignant transformation. This may also reflect the difficulty in histologically diagnosing malignant transformation in benign papillomas.[49-51] Majoros'[48] retrospective study of 101 patients with the juvenile form of the disease revealed no carcinoma in the 58 patients treated only with surgery and a malignancy rate of 14% (6/43) in the irradiated patients. The interval between the radiation therapy (XRT) and the diagnosis of carcinoma ranged from 6 to 21 years except in one patient with an interval of only one year.

Clinical data regarding the association of laryngeal papillomas and carcinoma are variable. The incidence of cancer is higher in patients with papillomas who have received radiation therapy (XRT). Lindeberg et al[52] found that XRT produced a 16-fold increased risk of developing subsequent carcinoma compared to nonirradiated patients. These results support the commonly accepted view that cofactors play an important role in human papilloma virus (HPV)-related cancer. Rabbett's[53] statement that the only cases of juvenile laryngeal papillomatosis at risk for malignancy are those with a history of XRT has been proven wrong in the recent literature. Shapiro et al[54] reported a case of cancer in a juvenile laryngeal papilloma (JLP) patient without a history of XRT, but with a history of heavy cigarette and alcohol use. There were three other similar cases from the literature also described in that review. In 1982, Bewtra et al[55] reported one patient with malignant transformation of JLP without any history of XRT, smoking, or alcohol use. This report also reviewed four other cases of malignant transformation in patients with longstanding diffuse papillomatosis involving the trachea and bronchi as well as the larynx. Keim[51] also reported a single case of malignant change in a patient with JLP without any history of XRT. Assessing all these reports, it is apparent that while uncommon, it is certainly possible for benign laryngeal papillomas to undergo malignant transformation without the stimulus of radiation. The possible effects of treatment of papillomas (such as repeated laser excision) on the development of malignancy are unknown, but we believe that they warrant study.

Lie et al[56] presented a retrospective study of 102 patients with laryngeal papillomas treated between 1950 and 1979 with follow-up ranging from 4 to 58 years. Eight patients developed carcinoma, seven laryngeal and one bronchial. The intervals between diagnosis of the benign papillomas and diagnosis of cancer were 4 to 55 years. Three patients had the juvenile form of disease and five had the adult type. The male to female ratio was 1:1. Two patients had received XRT, four were smokers, and one patient had received bleomycin and interferon. The authors concluded that HPV played a role in carcinogenesis, but that cofactors may also have played an important role. Klozar et al[57] reported a retrospective study of 179 HPV infected patients with a 1.7% incidence of cancer. These patients underwent 668 operations from 1982 to 1995. When he separated the patients by their clinical presentation, he found the incidence of malignancy to be 3% (3/102) in patients with the adult form and 0% (0/77) in those with the juvenile form (Table 92–1).

The concept of a possible cofactor in malignant transformation was supported by Koufman and Burke.[21] They found 21% (14/88) of patients with adult onset papillomatosis developed SCCa of the aerodigestive tract either at the site of the known papilloma or at another site after a 10-year follow-up. All the patients who developed cancer were smokers or had documented gastroesophageal reflux disease (GERD). Franceschi et al[47] reviewed HPV and cancer of the upper aerodigestive tract and found that the association of smoking, drinking, and betel nut chewing was too pervasive to permit judgment about HPV as a carcinogenic factor.

Rabkin et al[58] studied the incidence of second primary cancer in over 25,000 women with cervical cancer reported from 9 US cancer registries. There was a significantly increased risk of cancer of the oral cavity (relative risk 2.2) and of the larynx (relative risk 3.4). As HPV is a well-established risk factor for development of cervical cancer, this suggests that the cervical cancer and second primaries may share HPV as a causal agent.

Malignant transformation of laryngeal papillomas is diagnosed as a result of clinical observation, assessment of etiologic risk factors, and careful preparation and examination of biopsy specimens. Majaros et al[48] stated that as all their patients had been hoarse from the time of their original presentation with papillomas, there were no early clinical signs of malignancy. Consequently, presenting signs and symptoms are superimposed on the underlying papillomatosis and may include airway obstruction, throat pain, referred otalgia, and hemoptysis. Both Keim[51] and Fechner et al[49] report patients with progressive symptoms of malignancy but benign histology on early biopsies before invasive cancer was diagnosed. When the clinical suspicion is justified, repeated biopsy, deep biopsy, and even laryngectomy may be necessary to establish an accurate diagnosis. It is essential for the patient to be informed fully in such challenging clinical circumstances. Singh and Ramsaroop[50] reviewed 3 of 17 papilloma patients who developed cancer that revealed yet a different potential problem: simultaneous presentation of benign and malignant exophytic laryngeal lesions. All 3 cancer patients were diagnosed less than 1 year after their diagnosis of papillomas. Singh et al concluded that clinical indicators for carcinoma in patients with papillomas include gross laryngeal edema, airway obstruction, reduced vocal fold mobility, dysphagia, subglottic extension, and cervical adenopathy. When malignant transformation of laryn-

Table 92–1. Papilloma to Malignant Transformation.

Study	Number of Patients	Incidence of Malignant Transformation	Presence of Cocarcinogens	Interval Between Diagnosis of Papilloma and Malignant Transformation
Majoros et al[48] (1914-1960)	101	6%	6 radiation*	6-21 years**
Juvenile	101			
Adult	0			
Lie et al[56] (1950-1979)	102	8% (8/102)	2 previous XRT	4-55 years
Juvenile	53	6% (3/53)	2 Bleomycin ± interferon	
Adult	49	10% (5/49)	4 smokers	
Klozar et al[57] (1982-1995)	179	1.7% (3/179)	2 smokers	2-8 years
Juvenile	77	0%	1 nonsmoker	
Adult	102	3%		

*14%; 6 of 43 who received XRT; 0%; of 58 patients not treated by XRT

**except 1 case (1 year)

geal papillomas is suspected, a benign biopsy result may be misleading. Atypia can be found in both adult and juvenile papillomas and is not predictive of malignant transformation.[45] Clinical suspicion based on presenting signs and symptoms, and a complete history of risk factors should guide patient management.

Conclusion

It is important for laryngologists to be familiar with the broad spectrum of benign premalignant and malignant disease that may afflict the larynx. Premalignant lesions must be assessed histologically for malignancy and the entire larynx must be fully evaluated because of the risk of multifocal abnormalities. Adequate preoperative examination, meticulous surgical technique, and long-term surveillance are necessary in every case. Although early detection of carcinoma must be our primary goal, diagnostic and treatment strategies should be individualized with functional considerations in mind.

References

1. Wenig BM. *Atlas of Head and Neck Pathology.* Philadelphia, Pa: W.B. Saunders; 1993:221–239.
2. Silver CE, Ferlito A. *Surgery for Cancer of the Larynx and Related Structures.* 2nd ed. Philadelphia, Pa: WB Saunders; 1996:29–31.
3. Friedman I. Precursors of squamous cell carcinoma. In: Ferlito A, ed. *Surgical Pathology of Laryngeal Neoplasms.* London, UK: Chapman and Hall Medical; 1996:108–121.
4. Stenersen TC, Hoel PS, Boysen M. Carcinoma in-situ of the larynx: an evaluation of its natural clinical cause. *Clin Otolaryngol.* 1991;16(4):358–363.
5. Hellqvist H, Lundgren J, Olofson J. Hyperplasia, dysplasia and CIS of the vocal cords: a follow-up study. *Clin Otolaryngol.* 1902,7.11–27.
6. Fiorella R, DiNicola V, Resta L. Epidemiological and clinical relief on hyperplastic lesions of the larynx. *Acta Otolaryngol* (Stockh). 1997;527 (suppl):77–81.
7. Velasco JRR, Niero CS. DeBustos CP, Marcos CA. Premalignant lesions of the larynx: pathological prognostic factors. *J Otolaryngol.* 1987;16(6):367–370.
8. Blackwell KE, Fu YS, Calcaterra TC. Laryngeal dysplasia. A clinicopathologic study. *Cancer.* 1995;75(2):457–463.
9. Burkhardt A. Morphological assessment of malignant potential of epithelial hyperplastic lesions. *Acta Otolaryngol* (Stockh). 1997;527(suppl):12–16.
10. Zhao R, Hirano M, Kurita S. Expression of proliferating cell nuclear antigen in premalignant lesion of the larynx. *Am J Otolaryngol.* 1996;17(1):36–40.
11. Pignataro L, Capaccio P, Pruneri G, et al. The predictive value of p53, MDM-2, cyclin D1, and Ki67 in the progression from low-grade dysplasia towards carcinoma of the larynx. *J Laryngol Otol.* 1998;112(5):455–459.

12. Bracko M. Evaluation of DNA content in epithelial hyperplastic lesion in the larynx. *Acta Otolaryngol* (Stockh). 1997;527(suppl);62–65.
13. Cattaruzza MS, Maisonneuve P, Boyle P. Epidemiology of laryngeal cancer. *Oral Oncol Eur J Cancer.* 1996;32(5): 293–305.
14. Wasfie T, Newman R. Laryngeal carcinoma in black patients. *Cancer.* 1988;61(1):167–172.
15. Auerbach O, Hannond EC, Garfinkel L. Histologic changes in the larynx in relation to smoking habits. *Cancer.* 1970;25(1):92–104.
16. Burch JD, Howe GR, Miller AB, Semenciw R. Tobacco, alcohol, asbestos, and nickel in the etiology of cancer of the larynx: a case-control study. *J Natl Cancer Inst.* 1981;67(6):1219–1224.
17. Stevens M, Gardner JW, Parkin JL, Johnson LP. Head and neck cancer survival and life-style change. *Arch Otolaryngol.* 1983;109(11):746–749.
18. Maier H, Gewelke U, Pietz A, Heller WD. Risk factors of cancer of the larynx: results of the Heidelberg case-control study. *Otolaryngol Head Neck Surg.* 1992;107(4):577–582.
19. Thomas DB. Alcohol as a cause of cancer. *Environ Health Perspect.* 1995;103(8);153–160.
20. Sataloff RT, Castell DO, Katz, PO, Sataloff DM. *Reflux Laryngitis and Related Disorders.* San Diego, Calif: Singular Publishing Group; 1999.
21. Koufman JA, Burke AJ, The etiology and pathogenesis of laryngeal carcinoma. *Otolaryngol Clin North Am.* 1997;30(1):1–19.
22. Ward PH, Hanson DG. Reflux as an etiological factor of carcinoma of the laryngopharynx. *Laryngoscope.* 1988; 98:1195–1199.
23. Freije JE, Beatty TW, Campbell BH et al. Carcinoma of the larynx in patients with gastroesophageal reflux. *Am J Otolaryngol.* 1996;17(6):386–390.
24. Pinros J, Franco EL, Kolwalski LP, Oliveira BV, Curado MP. Use of wood stoves and risk of cancer of the upper aero-digestive tract: a case control study. *Int J Epidemiol.* 1998;27(6):936–940.
25. Haguenoer JM, Cordier S, Morel C, Lefebvre JL, Hemon D. Occupational risk factor for upper respiratory tract and upper digestive tract cancers. *Br J Ind Med.* 1990; 47:380–383.
26. Bravo MP, Espinosa J, del Rey Calero J. Occupational risk factors for cancer of the larynx in Spain. *Neoplasma.* 1990;37(4):477–487.
27. Vaughan TL, Stewart PA, Davis S, Thomas DB. Work in dry cleaning and the incidence of cancer of the oral cavity, larynx, and esophagus. *Occup Environ Med.* 1997; 54:692–695.
28. Kambic V. Epithelial hyperplastic lesions—a challenging topic in laryngology. *Acta Otolaryngol* (Stockh). 1997; 527(suppl):7–11.
29. Frangeuz I, Gale N, Luzar B. The interpretation of leukoplakia in laryngeal pathology. *Acta Otolaryngol* (Stockh). 1997;527(suppl):142–144
30. Goldman NC. Problems in outpatients with laryngeal hyperplastic lesions. *Acta Otolaryngol* (Stockh). 1997; 527(suppl):70–73.

31. Blackwell KE, Calcatura TC, Fu YS. Laryngeal dysplasia: epidemiology and treatment outcomes. *Ann Otol Rhinol Laryngol.* 1995;104:596–602.

32. Gale N, Zidar N, Kambic V, Poljak M, Cor A. Epidermal growth factor receptor, c-erbB-2 and p53 overexpression in epithelial hyperplastic lesion of the larynx. *Acta Otolaryngol* (Stockh). 1997;527(suppl);105–110.

33. Krecicki T, Jelen M, Zalesska-Krecicka M, Szkudlarek T, Szajowski K. Immunohistochemically stained markers (p53, PCNA, bcl-2) in dysplastic lesion of the larynx. *Cancer Lett.* 1999;143:23–28.

34. Ioachim E, Assimakopoulos D, Peschos D, Zissi A, Skervas A, Agnantis NJ. Immunohistochemical expression of metallothionein in benign premalignances and malignant epithelium of the larynx: correlation with p53 and proliferative cell nuclear antigen. *Pathol Res Pract.* 1999;195:809–814.

35. Fried MP. *The Larynx: A Multidisciplinary Approach.* 2nd ed. St. Louis, Mo: Mosby Year Book; 1995:470–473.

36. Ferlito A, Polidoro F, Rossi M. Pathological basis and clinical aspects of treatment policy in carcinoma-in-situ of the larynx. *J Laryngol Otol.* 1982;95(2):141–154.

37. Myssiorek D, Vambutas A, Abramson AL. Carcinoma in situ of the glottic larynx. *Laryngoscope.* 1994;104(4):463–467.

38. Myers EN, Sven JY. *Cancer of the Head and Neck.* 3rd ed. Philadelphia, Pa: W.B. Saunders; 1996:381–421.

39. Bouquot JE, Gnepp DR. Laryngeal precancer: a review of the literature, commentary, and comparison with oral leukoplakia. *Head Neck.* 1991;13(6):488–497.

40. Small W, Mittal BB, Brand WN, et al. Role of radiation therapy in the management of carcinoma in situ of the larynx. *Laryngoscope.* 1993;103(6):663–667.

41. Maran AG, Mackenzie IJ, Stanley RE. Carcinoma in situ of the larynx. *Head Neck Surg.* 1984;(7):28–31.

42. Nguyen C, Naghibzadeh B, Black MJ, Rochon L, Shenouba G. Carcinoma in situ of the glottic larynx: excision or irradiation? *Head Neck Surg.* 1996;18(3):225–228.

43. Rothfield RE, Myers EN, Johnson JT. Carcinoma in situ and microinvasive squamous cell carcinoma of the vocal cords. *Ann Otol Rhinol Laryngol.* 1991;100(10):793–796.

44. Medini E, Medini I, Lee CKK, Grapany M, Levitt SH. The role of radiotherapy in the management of carcinoma in situ of the glottic larynx. *Am J Clin Oncol.* 1998;21(3):298–301.

45. McKaig RG, Baric RS, Olshan AF. Human papillomavirus and head and neck cancer: epidemiology and molecular biology. *Head Neck.* 1998;20(3):250–265.

46. Luzar B, Gale N, Kambic V, Poljak M, Zidar N, Voobvnik A. Human papillomavirus infection and expression of p53 and c-erbB-2 protein in laryngeal papillomas. *Acta Otolaryngol* (Stockh). 1997;527(suppl):120–124.

47. Franceschi S, Munoz N, Bosch XF, Snijders PJ, Walboomers JM. Human papillomavirus and cancers of the upper aerodigestive tract: a review of epidemiological and experimental evidence. *Cancer Epidemiol, Biomarkers Prev.* 1996;5(7):567–575.

48. Majoros M, Devine KD, Parkhill EM. Malignant transformation of benign laryngeal papilloma in children after radiation therapy. *Surg Clin North Am.* 1963;43(4):1049–1061.

49. Fechner RE, Goepfert H, Alford BR. Invasive laryngeal papillomatosis. *Arch Otolaryngol.* 1974;99(2):147–151.

50. Singh B, Ramsaroop R. Clinical features of malignant transformation in benign laryngeal papillomata. *J Laryngol Otol.* 1994;108(8):642–648.

51. Keim RJ. Malignant change of laryngeal papilloma: a case report. *Otolaryngol Head Neck Surg.* 1980;88(6):773–777.

52. Lindeberg H, Elbrond O. Malignant tumors in patients with a history of multiple laryngeal papillomas: the significance of irradiation. *Clin Otolaryngol.* 1991;16:149–151.

53. Rabbett WF. Juvenile laryngeal papillomatosis: the relation of irradiation to malignant degeneration in this disease. *Ann Otol Rhinol Laryngol.* 1965;74(4):1149–1163.

54. Shapiro RS, Marlowe FI, Butcher J. Malignant degeneration of nonirradiated juvenile laryngeal papillomatosis. *Ann Otol.* 1976;85(1):101–103.

55. Bewtra C, Krishnan R, Lee SS. Malignant change in nonirradiated juvenile laryngotracheal papillomatosis. *Arch Otolaryngol.* 1982;108(2):114–116.

56. Lie ES, Engh V, Boysen M, et al. Squamous cell carcinoma of the respiratory tract following laryngeal papillomatosis. *Acta Otolaryngol (Stockh).* 1994;114(2):209–212.

57. Klozar J, Taudy M, Betka J, Kana R. Laryngeal papilloma—precancerous condition? *Acta Otolaryngol* (Stockh). 1997;527(suppl):100–102.

58. Rabkin CS, Biggar RJ, Melbye M, Curtis RE. Second primary cancers following anal and cervical carcinoma: evidence of shared etiologic factors. *Am J Epidemiol.* 1992;136(1):54–58.

93

Laryngeal Cancer

Timothy D. Anderson and Robert Thayer Sataloff

Carcinoma of the larynx represents approximately 1.3% of all new cancer diagnoses, and approximately 20% of all head and neck cancers. In 2001, the American Cancer Society estimated that in the coming year there would be approximately 10,000 new cases of laryngeal cancer with a 4:1 male to female ratio and that there would be 4,000 deaths due to laryngeal cancer.[1] Thirty-five years ago the male to female ratio was between 10:1 and 50:1, the change is probably due to increasing use of tobacco and alcohol among women.[2] Although laryngeal cancer is primarily a disease of older age with peak incidence in the sixth and seventh decades, it does occur in younger patients, including children.[3] Younger patients who present with laryngeal carcinoma most often are nonsmokers who do not have other identifiable risk factors for laryngeal cancer, suggesting a genetic predisposition.[3] Overall, the major etiologic factor in laryngeal cancer is exposure to tobacco. Studies have shown an increased incidence of both premalignant and malignant lesions in smokers and a dose-dependent relationship between cigarette use and the development of cancer.[4-6] Laryngeal cancer in nonsmokers is rare. Heavy alcohol use is also a factor in the development of laryngeal cancer, and there appears to be a synergistic effect with tobacco, especially in the development of supraglottic tumors.[7] Radiation exposure and exposure to occupational pollutants such as nickel, mustard gas, wood products, and pesticides also have been implicated as etiologic factors.[4,8,9] The etiologic effect of asbestos on laryngeal cancer is not yet well documented, but it appears to be limited to active smokers.[10,11] Laryngopharyngeal reflux and laryngeal papillomatosis may be causally related to cancer, as discussed elsewhere in this book.

Because of the larynx's unique functions of speech, swallowing, and airway protection, treatment of laryngeal cancer has always been complex and controversial. Carcinoma of the larynx is a potentially curable disease with a 5-year survival rate of over 67%. However, early detection of smaller lesions offers a much better opportunity for both survival and preservation of laryngeal function. Thus, aggressive clinical evaluation of laryngeal lesions is critical. In early lesions, treatment usually consists of either surgery or radiation therapy, with the choice based on the individual history and tumor characteristics, as well as the potential effects on laryngeal function. In advanced lesions, usually both surgery and radiation therapy are necessary to optimize long-term survival. New protocols utilizing neo-adjuvant or concomitant chemotherapy have offered some patients with advanced lesions the opportunity to be cured without the need for total laryngectomy.[12]

Supraglottic Tumors

The supraglottic larynx extends from the tip of the epiglottis to the ventricles. It includes the laryngeal surface of the epiglottis, the aryepiglottic folds, the false vocal folds, the laryngeal surface of the arytenoids, and the ventricles (Fig 93–1). The mucosa of

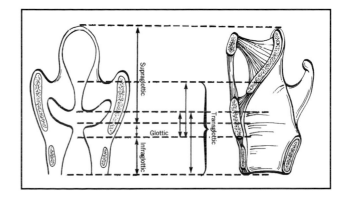

Fig 93–1. Regions of the larynx.

the lingual surface of the epiglottis is in the supraglottic larynx, but the mucosa of the vallecula is oropharyngeal. The lymphatic drainage of the supraglottis is extensive. It traverses the thyrohyoid membrane and travels with the superior laryngeal vessels to the deep jugular nodes. This lymphatic pathway is separate from the inferior drainage of glottic and subglottic tumors owing to a difference in embryologic development. Thus, surgical management of supraglottic tumors is a distinct entity.

Supraglottic cancer spreads in patterns dependent on its site of origin. It can spread over mucosal surfaces to adjacent structures, or it can traverse cartilaginous or fibrous barriers into deeper spaces. The pre-epiglottic space anteriorly is a common site for spread of the epiglottic tumors. This area is supplied richly with lymphatics and invasion of the pre-epiglottic space predisposes to neck metastases and allows unobstructed cancer extension inferiorly to the anterior commissure and subglottis. The paraglottic space, lateral to the endolarynx, is an early site of spread of false vocal fold and ventricular tumors (Fig 93–2). Paraglottic space involvement provides for rapid transglottic and subglottic extension.[13]

Most clinicians utilize the staging system based on the American Joint Committee (AJC) for Cancer Staging and End Result Reporting. Its most recent revision (1988) is seen in Table 93–1.[14] There is little emphasis on tumor size, with extent of mucosal spread determining the tumor's class. Progression to T_3 status is determined by fixation of the hemilarynx, involvement of postcricoid and piriform mucosa, or pre-epiglottic extension. Lymph node staging is standard for all head and neck cancer (Table 93–2).

Patients with supraglottic cancer can present with sore throat, voice change such as hoarseness and dysphagia, otalgia, halitosis, weight loss, or neck mass. The voice is usually muffled, but true hoarseness is usually a sign of a transglottic tumor, vocal fold fixation, or a low false vocal fold lesion. Symptoms are often subtle and insidious, and many tumors are quite extensive at presentation. The clinician must be especially suspicious of supraglottic cancer in patients with persistent complaints of sore throat and otalgia.

Lymph node metastases occur in 25 to 50% of patients with supraglottic cancer; 30 to 50% are palpable at presentation; and 20 to 40% are occult in necks with clinically negative findings.[15-19] Contralateral disease is common. The rate of metastasis increases with tumor size but ranges from 15 to 40% even in T_1 tumors.[15-18]

Treatment Considerations

Accurate assessment and staging are critical in determining treatment. Computed tomography scanning

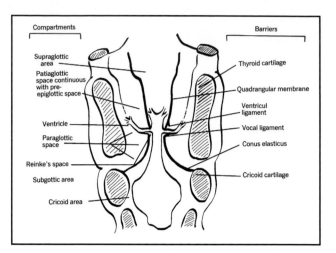

Fig 93–2. Compartments and barriers in the larynx.

Table 93–1. Staging of Primary Tumor in Laryngeal Cancer.

Supraglottis

T_1—Tumor limited to one subsite of the supraglottis with normal vocal fold mobility

T_2—Tumor invades more than one subsite of supraglottis or glottis with normal vocal fold mobility

T_3—Tumor limited to the larynx with vocal fold fixation and/or invades postcricoid area, medial wall of piriform sinus, or pre-epiglottic tissues

T_4—Tumor invades through thyroid cartilage and/or extends to other tissues beyond the larynx

with contrast infusion can help in judging the size and location of the primary tumor and the extent of lymph node involvement.[19] Magnetic resonance imaging may be useful, but in most cases CT imaging of the larynx is sufficient. All patients should undergo operative laryngoscopy to visualize and palpate the extent of the cancer. However, fiberoptic laryngoscopy, especially with stroboscopy and video documentation, can provide an excellent overall assessment and allow operative endoscopy to be reserved for the time of definitive treatment. This is especially helpful in patients with airway compromise or other significant medical conditions. A thorough search for a metachronous primary must be completed, because the incidence has been reported to be as high as 20 to 30% with aerodigestive tract tumors.[20]

In stage I lesions, cure rates with surgery and radiation therapy are equivalent (75-80%).[21,22] Radiation therapy, at least within the first year, results in less

Table 93–2. Staging of Lymphatic Metastasis in Laryngeal Cancer.

N_x— Regional lymph nodes cannot be assessed.

N_0— No regional lymph node metastasis.

N_1— Metastasis in a single ipsilateral lymph node, 3 cm or less in greatest dimension.

N_2— Metastasis in a single ipsilateral lymph node, more than 3 cm, but not more than 6 cm in greatest dimension, or multiple ipsilateral lymph nodes, none more than 6 cm in greatest dimension, or bilateral or contralateral lymph nodes none more than 6 cm in greatest dimension.

N_{2a}— Metastasis in a single ipsilateral lymph node more than 3 cm but no more than 6 cm in greatest dimension.

N_{2b}— Metastasis in multiple ipsilateral lymph nodes, none more than 6 cm in greatest dimension.

N_{2c}— Metastasis in bilateral or contralateral lymph nodes, none more than 6 cm in greatest dimension.

N_3—Metastasis in a lymph node more than 6 cm in greatest dimension.

speech and swallowing morbidity than laryngeal surgery and generally is well tolerated. Voice results following treatment (radiation vs surgery) have not been studied convincingly, and there is at least a possibility that voice results 5 and 10 years after treatment may prove superior after limited surgery than after irradiation. Surgery is advantageous in patients with limited primary lesions and in younger patients (thus reserving radiation for those who may develop another primary tumor later in life).[71,72] In stage II and III lesions, treatment options are varied. For treatment of the primary site, neither surgery nor radiation with surgical salvage has shown a superior cure rate; and the use of combined therapy is not supported clearly.[23-25] Using primary radiation therapy is an attractive alternative to surgery.[26,27] However, the cervical nodes cannot be assessed, and the morbidity of salvage surgery must be considered. Most patients undergoing salvage surgery will require total laryngectomy, although partial laryngectomies can be performed safely in selected post-irradiation patients. Primary supraglottic laryngectomy can yield local control rates as high as 90% with low morbidity.[27,28] Stage IV lesions can be treated either with combined surgery (usually a total laryngectomy) in combination with radiation therapy or with combined chemotherapy and radiation therapy in selected patients. Protocols combining chemotherapy and radiation have the advantage of laryngeal preservation in up to two-thirds of patients with equivalent survival.[12]

Treatment of metastatic neck disease is another controversial area in the care of supraglottic cancer. Patients with primary lesion T_2 or larger and N_0 neck are at risk for bilateral occult neck metastasis and should be treated. Radiation therapy and modified neck dissection are equally effective.[17] In smaller tumors that are treated with primary radiotherapy, both sides of the neck should also be radiated. Patients who are going to undergo planned postoperative radiotherapy can also be spared bilateral neck dissections through irradiation of one or both N_0 necks. However, there are significant advantages to treating the primary lesion surgically and performing simultaneous, bilateral, modified neck dissections.[27,29-32] If there are no metastases, postoperative radiation may not be warranted. The discovery of occult nodes can guide the use of postoperative radiation. Ultimately, the decision will be influenced by the patient's history and condition, the quality of radiation treatment available, and the surgeon's experience in performing conservation modified neck dissection. Recognized indications for postoperative radiotherapy include large tumors, bulky neck disease, extracapsular spread of nodal disease, and perineural or angio-lymphatic invasion.

Few data support the need for neck dissection following chemoradiation therapy for supraglottic tumors. Certainly, most residual neck masses should be treated by a neck dissection. In addition, patients who had neck disease larger than 2 to 3 cm in size prior to chemoradiation probably should undergo neck dissection following chemoradiation therapy; because there is a higher incidence of residual disease in these patients.[33,34] Local and regional recurrence rates are higher after primary chemoradiation when compared to surgery and radiation, which underscores the importance of aggressive surveillance of the primary site and the need for neck dissections in patients with poor prognostic features.[12]

Surgical Procedures

Small T_1 cancers limited to the epiglottis can be treated by transoral, subtotal supraglottic laryngectomy. Relative contraindications to this approach are involvement of the pre-epiglottic space, the petiole of the epiglottis, the free margin of the false vocal fold, or the presence of palpable neck disease. Additionally, endoscopic visualization is difficult without a large or bivalved laryngoscope designed to provide a wide field of view in the supraglottis.[35] The procedure is performed under general anesthesia usually with the carbon dioxide (CO_2) laser. A laser-safe endotracheal tube is used, and a tracheotomy is not necessary. The pre-epiglottic space is evaluated during the dissection. If pre-epiglottic space invasion is noted, the procedure is converted to an open, supraglottic laryngectomy. When endoscopic visualization is difficult, external access to the supraglottic larynx can be obtained through a transverse, suprahyoid pharyngotomy, or a lateral pharyngotomy in the piriform sinus.

Although not yet widely used, endoscopic transoral CO_2 laser resection of larger supraglottic tumors has been reported in the literature.[36-39] This technique is also performed under general anesthesia with a laser-protected endotracheal tube and wide exposure using a bivalved laryngoscope. Although various techniques have been described,[37-39] most begin with dividing the epiglottis in half and dissecting the midline pre-epiglottic space until the superior surface of the thyroid cartilage is identified. Dissection is then carried along the edge of the superior portion of the thyroid cartilage from anterior to posterior, exposing the entire top of the thyroid cartilage. The laser is then used to dissect along the inner surface of the thyroid cartilage preferably leaving the perichondrium in situ unless it is needed as a tumor margin. Dissection is carried down to the level of the vallecula. Posterior cuts are made through the false vocal folds into the ventricle distant from the tumor. The tumor is then removed through the mouth. In addition to the bivalved laryngoscope, especially designed bipolar cautery forceps and unipolar cautery instruments are needed for control of larger blood vessels. Specialized grasping instruments are desirable to provide exposure and retraction of the area to be dissected. Healing occurs over the next several weeks, and most reports indicate that swallowing function and sensation of the remucosalized larynx are excellent. Neck dissections are performed several days to weeks after the primary operation. Oncologic results have been reported to be equal or superior to open supraglottic laryngectomy.[36-39] Recurrences often can be treated adequately with repeat transoral laser excision.[40]

The standard surgical procedure for cancer isolated above the vocal folds is the horizontal supraglottic laryngectomy. It can be used for any laryngeal tumor superior to the ventricles including tumors that involve the laryngeal surface of the epiglottis, the medial wall of the piriform sinus above the apex, and the aryepiglottic folds. It is contraindicated in patients with vocal fold fixation, thyroid cartilage invasion, or if there is involvement of the arytenoid cartilage, ventricle, apex of the piriform sinus, anterior commissure,

intra-arytenoid area, base of tongue, paraglottic space, or soft tissues of the neck. Additionally, patients must be in good general health. A horizontal hemilaryngectomy allows for normal or near-normal deglutition postoperatively due to the sparing of the vocal folds, which will continue to perform their role in airway protection. However, the patient must be able to learn a new swallowing technique and must be able to sense and cough out any aspirated material. The patient must be cooperative, motivated, and strong enough to tolerate prolonged postoperative rehabilitation. Patients with inadequate pulmonary function or poor compliance may suffer life-threatening aspiration postoperatively, and total laryngectomy is indicated in this patient population.

The supraglottic laryngectomy is performed under general anesthesia with a tracheotomy in place. A separate horizontal skin incision is performed and subplatysmal flaps are raised (Fig 93–3). The strap muscles are divided in the midline, and the thyroid cartilage is exposed. The perichondrium is incised along the superior edge of the cartilage and dissected inferiorly (Fig 93–4). This dissection must be performed with care using fine elevators. The perichondrial layer is dissected halfway between the superior and inferior edges of the thyroid cartilage in males and one third of the distance from the superior edge in females. The cartilage incision is carried superiorly, medial to the

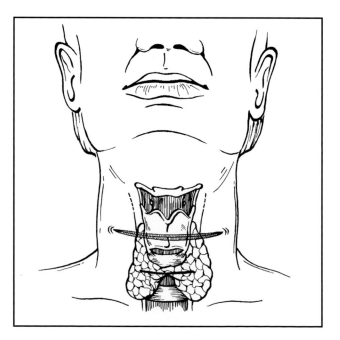

Fig 93–3. A separate transverse incision, superior to the tracheotomy site, is suitable for most partial laryngectomies, and yields the best cosmetic result.

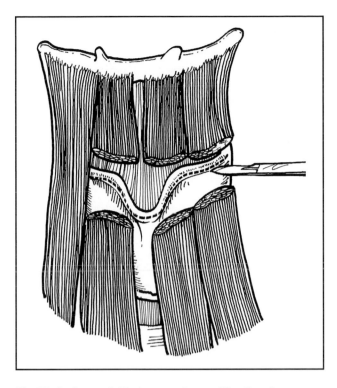

Fig 93–4. Supraglottic laryngectomy. After the strap muscles are divided, the perichondrium is incised along the superior margin of the thyroid cartilage.

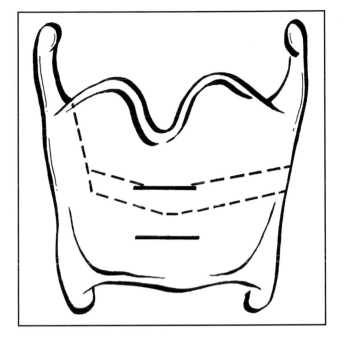

Fig 93–5. Supraglottic laryngectomy. The transverse cartilage cut is made at the presumed level of the glottis (the superior line is used for females) and angled superiorly on the unaffected side.

superior cornua on the nondominant side (Fig 93–5). The suprahyoid muscles are then transected, and the entire hyoid bone is dissected free. The superior laryngeal vessels are identified and controlled between the greater cornu of the hyoid and superior cornu of the thyroid cartilage on each side. The pharyngeal mucosa is identified superior to the hyoid bone, and the pharynx is entered through the vallecula. The epiglottis is grasped and retracted anteriorly, and incisions are extended with scissors along the lateral borders of the epiglottis. In tumors involving the tip of the epiglottis or vallecula, the larynx is entered laterally through the piriform mucosa on the side opposite the tumor. When the epiglottis is retracted anteriorly, the glottis is visualized directly and the extent of the tumor is identified. With the medial blade of the scissors in the ventricle and the lateral blade in the cartilage incision, the supraglottic larynx is excised (Fig 93–6). The perichondrium is closed to the base of the tongue using 3-0 or 4-0 absorbable sutures. Before tying the first layer of closure, the neck is flexed and the remaining larynx is suspended superiorly. The most secure suspension is accomplished by passing heavy permanent suture (prolene or stainless steel) through drilled holes in the thyroid cartilage and through the mandibular symph-

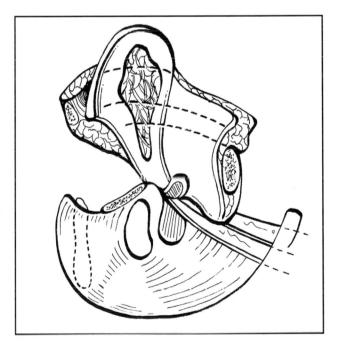

Fig 93–6. Supraglottic laryngectomy. The scissors are placed in the ventricle internally and the cartilage is cut externally in the final maneuver to remove the supraglottic larynx.

ysis (Fig 93–7). The sutures can also be fixed to the mandibular periosteum or the digastric tendons bilat-

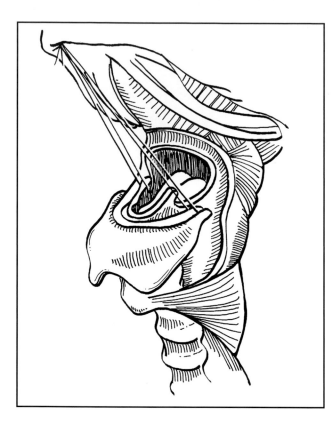

Fig 93–7. Supraglottic laryngectomy. The larynx is suspended superiorly and anteriorly by wiring to the mandibular symphysis.

erally. The larynx must be suspended as far anteriorly and superiorly as possible in order to allow it to remain under the tongue base during the oropharyngeal phase of swallowing. A cricopharyngeal myotomy should be performed before closure as well. The laryngeal closure sutures are tied and a second layer of suture is placed. The skin is closed over a small drain.

The basic supraglottic laryngectomy can be extended to include additional involved structures. When the mucosa over the arytenoid cartilages is involved, the entire cartilage can be removed. However, any extension of the resection that affects vocal fold mobility adversely increases the risk of aspiration; and the removal of additional cartilage may result in glottic stenosis.

The two most important factors in the postoperative care of a supraglottic laryngectomy patient are the healing of the laryngeal closure and mastering of the supraglottic swallowing technique. As in most partial laryngectomies, mucosal closure is not possible; thus initial healing is by secondary intention. Patients with conditions that would affect wound healing adversely, such as malnutrition, diabetes mellitus, chronic alcoholism, uncontrolled reflux laryngitis, and prior

radiation therapy, are poorer candidates for this procedure than patients who do not have such conditions. Successful supraglottic laryngectomy can be performed in previously irradiated patients, but other factors must be optimal; and there is an increased rate of complications.[41] Initial swallowing trials are accomplished best after the nasogastric tube has been removed and, if at all possible, after the tracheotomy has been removed. Patients are taught to swallow slowly, stopping to cough before each inhalation. Most nonirradiated patients can maintain adequate nutrition by an oral diet within 10 to 14 days after surgery. Irradiated patients frequently remain partially dependent on tube feedings for weeks or months following surgery.

Glottic Tumors

Glottic tumors include neoplasms involving the true vocal folds, the anterior commissure, and the posterior larynx at the level of the true vocal folds. The superior limit of the glottis is the lateral recess of the ventricles. The inferior limit extends 10 mm below the free margin of the vocal folds at the anterior commissure, decreasing to 5 mm below the free margin posteriorly (see Fig 93–1). The lymphatic channels of the glottis are quite sparse and lie in the submucosal space. Glottic tumors usually spread along the mucosa, and small lesions rarely invade deeper structures. When deep invasion occurs, violation of the inner perichondrium of the thyroid cartilage or the conus elasticus into the paralaryngeal space is the most important consideration in treatment decisions[42] (see Fig 93–2).

By far, the most common presenting symptom of glottic carcinoma is hoarseness. Sore throat, dysphagia, hemoptysis, and airway obstruction usually are present in patients with advanced tumors. Otalgia or dry cough occasionally can accompany hoarseness as early symptoms. Almost all patients with glottic cancer have a history of cigarette smoking. There is a 4:1 male predominance with a peak incidence in the sixth and seventh decades.

In early glottic carcinoma, accurate diagnosis and staging are critical. The most important factor in staging is the presence of vocal fold fixation, which makes the tumor at least T_3 (Table 93–3). The first step in evaluation is adequate laryngeal visualization to determine the indications and plan for endoscopic biopsy. With fiberoptic laryngoscopy, it should be possible to visualize most patients. The addition of video improves documentation and the patient's understanding and acceptance of future treatment. Stroboscopy can be invaluable in determining the need for biopsy

Table 93–3. Staging of Primary Tumor in Laryngeal Cancer.

Glottis

T_1— Tumor limited to vocal fold(s) (may involve anterior commissure or posterior larynx) with normal mobility.

T_{1a}—Tumor limited to one vocal fold.

T_{1b}—Tumor involves both vocal folds.

T_2— Tumor extends to supraglottis and/or subglottis and/or with impaired vocal fold mobility.

T_3— Tumor limited to larynx with vocal fold fixation.

T_4— Tumor invades through the thyroid cartilage and/or extends to other tissues beyond the larynx.

and the depth of tumor spread, especially in a professional voice user. The absence of mucosal vibration in the region of a suspicious lesion is not diagnostic for an invasive process, but it generally increases the clinical suspicion of cancer. Patients suspected of having carcinoma should undergo operative endoscopy and biopsy. Panendoscopy is recommended because, even with small glottic tumors, the risk of a metachronous primary is 15%.[20]

The differential diagnosis of a small glottic lesion includes hyperkeratosis, dysplasia, carcinoma *in situ*, and invasive carcinoma. Accuracy in pathologic diagnosis is critical. All lesions except invasive carcinoma are treated by simple excision without large margins and with close observation.[43] Invasive cancer requires either total surgical excision with free margins or radiation therapy.

For most T_1 and T_2 glottic tumors, long-term cure rates are equal after surgery or radiation.[44] The treatment decision is made by comparing the time, expense, and morbidity of radiation therapy to the operative risk and morbidity associated with surgery. It has always been assumed that radiation therapy will not alter vocal quality as much as surgical procedures. However, no study to evaluate this finding objectively has been completed. Anecdotally, in most cases, voice quality appears to be better during the first year following radiation therapy than during the first year after surgery. However, it is not certain that postradiation voice quality is better than postoperative voice quality after longer periods, because the late effects of radiotherapy become more evident. When voice is a primary concern, the location of the tumor and potential depth of the surgery must be taken into account along with other factors. The patient must be informed fully about the advantages, disadvantages, and uncertainties associated with each treatment modality

before the patient selects a therapeutic plan. Radiation failures can be salvaged by partial laryngectomy. Operative morbidity is higher than in nonirradiated patients and the need for eventual salvage with total laryngectomy may be as high as 25%.[45-47]

Surgical Treatment

Excisional Biopsy

A retrospective study of patients who had partial laryngectomy for small glottic cancers revealed no tumor in the resected specimen in as many as 20%.[48] This means that at least this percentage of tumors can be adequately removed with a generous excisional biopsy. When preoperative suspicion of cancer is high, and the patient's larynx can be visualized well by suspension laryngoscopy, excisional biopsy can be planned and accomplished safely.

Endoscopic Surgery

The indications for endoscopic excision of a vocal fold carcinoma include lesions isolated to the membranous portion of one or both vocal folds, no impairment of vocal fold mobility, and the ability to obtain adequate visualization by suspension laryngoscopy. Difficulty in obtaining adequate visualization can be expected in patients who are obese; have short necks, short mandibles, or large tongues; have a narrow dental arch with full dentition; or cervical spine disease. Tracheotomy is almost never necessary. General anesthesia is utilized with a laser-safe endotracheal tube. A Dedo, Fragen, or Sataloff suspension laryngoscope is preferred by the authors, but any large laryngoscope that provides good visibility is satisfactory. Toluidine blue may be painted on the vocal fold to reveal areas of increased DNA activity, and rigid endoscopes are helpful in visualizing the full extent of the lesion. The lesion(s) can be excised using either cold microscopic technique or a carbon dioxide laser. The laser is advantageous because of its accuracy and ability to provide ongoing hemostasis. However, when treating superficial lesions with the laser, damage to the underlying lamina propria or muscle is possible. Noninvasive lesions are removed including the full thickness of mucosa, but the vocalis muscle is not exposed. Invasive lesions are outlined with a 1-millimeter margin and are resected with underlying muscle (Fig 93–8). Contact endoscopy may be helpful in mapping the margin. With fine microscopic technique, a separate margin can be obtained to ensure adequate resection. Studies have shown endoscopic techniques to be equal to open surgery in obtaining long-term, disease-free survival in selected patients with small cancers.[48,49]

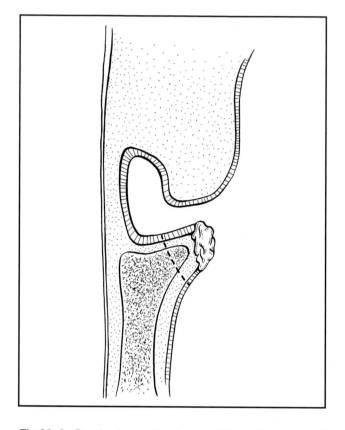

Fig 93–8. Depth of resection for a small invasive cancer of the vocal fold.

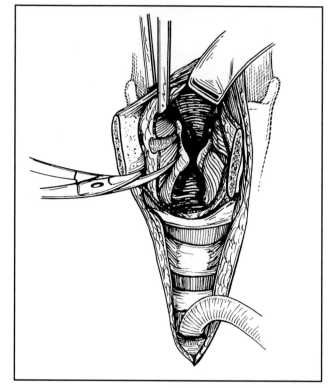

Fig 93–9. Cordectomy performed through a laryngofissure.

Photofrin-radiated photodynamic therapy has shown some promise in treating early lesions with preservation of the mucosal wave.[50] After administering a photosensitizer, intraoperative laser light activation causes irreversible cellular change to cells that concentrate the photosensitizing agent. As cancer cells concentrate porfimer sodium, they are preferentially destroyed. Small studies have had good results,[50] but larger, randomized, controlled studies have not been done.

Cordectomy

Cordectomy remains the standard by which all other surgical treatments of small glottic cancers are measured.[51] Cordectomy involves removal of the entire musculomembranous vocal fold with the vocalis muscle (Fig 93–9). The inner perichondrium of the thyroid cartilage also can be removed, either partially or completely. Cordectomy is contraindicated when vocal fold mobility is impaired, when the thyroid cartilage is invaded by the tumor, or when there is supraglottic or subglottic extension. Cordectomy can be accomplished endoscopically with a carbon dioxide laser. However,

it may be difficult to assess lateral tumor extension in many cases; and the patient should be prepared for conversion to an open procedure. Traditionally, cordectomy is performed through a laryngofissure. A tracheotomy is performed, and general anesthesia is utilized. A separate, superior transverse incision is adequate for exposure and provides a good cosmetic result, but a single vertical incision can be used. A vertical midline thyrotomy is performed in most cases; but if endoscopic examination reveals involvement of the anterior commissure, the vertical thyrotomy can be made off-center on the uninvolved side. Once the larynx is opened, the tumor's margins are defined and the involved vocal fold is resected with a 1- to 2-mm mucosal margin. Resection of the underlying vocalis muscle must be generous due to the inability to obtain reliable margins in muscle fascicles. Thus, even in cases in which some mucosa can be spared, a large bulk of the vocal fold usually is resected. Tumors that involve the inner thyroid perichondrium or abut the thyroid cartilage require vertical hemilaryngectomy in most cases. However, even with bulky disease, the cartilage can be spared in many patients with early glottic carcinoma. Most cases should be approached with the hope of performing a soft tissue resection alone. In rare cases, small lesions on both vocal folds can be resected simultaneously by this technique.[52] CT and MRI scanning may be helpful preoperatively, but examination and biopsy at the time of open surgery provide the most definitive indications for cartilage resection.

Endoscopic Laser-Assisted Vertical Hemilaryngectomy

Glottic carcinoma can be resected using a transoral CO_2 laser-assisted approach in patients in whom adequate exposure can be obtained.[36-39] Contraindications to this approach include T_4 lesions, especially in patients with invasion of thyroid cartilage, extension into the subglottis, or extensive supraglottic extension, as well as tumors with fixed vocal folds (which implies invasion of the cricoarytenoid joint). Patients in whom adequate exposure cannot be obtained are not candidates for this technique.

After obtaining adequate exposure with the bivalved laryngoscope, the false vocal fold is excised as a separate specimen in order to expose fully the lateral tumor extent. Tumors involving the anterior commissure can be exposed through excision of the petiole of the epiglottis. If the full extent of the tumor cannot be visualized easily after these maneuvers, endoscopic excision is likely to result in positive margins and generally should not be performed. Once the tumor is visualized completely, superficial marking incisions are made to outline the extent of resection. The success of this procedure requires meticulous dissection and hemostasis usually with the CO_2 laser and, occasionally, monopolar or bipolar electrocautery. Forceps are used to retract the vocal fold and tumor medially, providing counter traction, while the laser is used as a cutting instrument. The area undergoing dissection should always be under tension to aid cutting and allow identification of tissue planes and deep cancer extension. Cancer up to and including the anterior commissure can be resected using this technique, although adequate removal of the anterior commissure is technically difficult and the defect resulting from this procedure creates an extremely breathy voice that requires further surgery to improve voice quality. With this technique, intraoperative frozen sections and control of margins are essential to verify complete extirpation of the tumor.

No primary reconstruction is undertaken during this procedure. The resected areas generally mucosalize over the next few weeks. Resection of the false vocal fold and infrapetiole region has the added advantage of aiding postoperative surveillance for recurrence.

Frequent postoperative surveillance is important, because early recurrences often can be cured with a second transoral laser excision.[40] Most patients will form a scar band opposing the contralateral normal vocal fold, allowing phonation. Patients with breathy voices after this procedure can be helped by a variety of procedures to increase the bulk and size of the scar band on the operated side.

Vertical Hemilaryngectomy

When glottic carcinoma invades deeply to involve the perichondrium, removal of the thyroid cartilage is necessary. If the cartilage itself is invaded, which means a stage IV tumor, most authors recommend total laryngectomy.[53] However, when the area of cartilage involvement is small and the vocal fold is mobile, a partial laryngectomy with postoperative radiation therapy may be considered.[53]

A standard hemilaryngectomy is approached in the same way as a cordectomy (Fig 93–10). A second cartilage cut is made laterally on the involved side leaving a 3- to 4-mm strip of the posterior thyroid ala, including the superior and inferior cornua (Fig 93–11). The cartilage cuts can be tailored based on the preoperative examination and intraoperative assessments. The anterior incision can be moved off the midline to

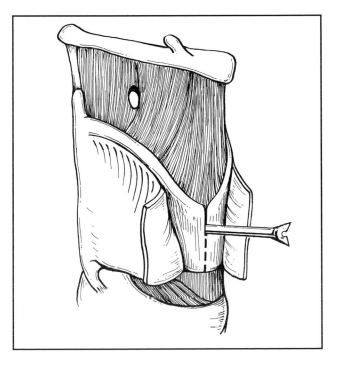

Fig 93–10. Standard midline thyrotomy approach for cordectomy or vertical hemilaryngectomy.

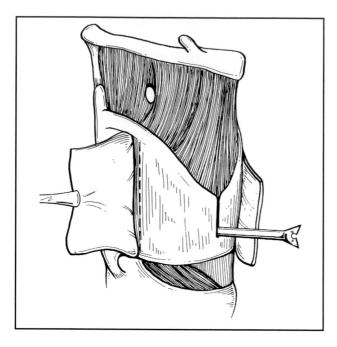

Fig 93–11. For vertical hemilaryngectomy, the second cartilage cut (*dashed line*) is made leaving a 4- to 5-mm strip of posterior thyroid ala.

include the anterior commissure, or to remove up to two thirds of the contralateral ala. The cartilage resection can also be quite narrow, involving a strip 8- to 10-mm wide, in select cases. The outer perichondrium is dissected off the cartilage to be resected and is utilized for closure. A standard hemilaryngectomy must be extended to include the anterior commissure if it is found to be involved (anterolateral laryngectomy) and can be performed to remove only the anterior commissure (anterior vertical laryngectomy).[54,55] It also can be extended to include part or all of the arytenoid cartilage. Additionally, a vertical laryngectomy can be performed with a supraglottic laryngectomy (suprahemilaryngectomy) or even in an extended fashion as a near-total laryngectomy. However, extension of the procedure increases the risks of postoperative glottic stenosis and aspiration, and decreases local control rates.[56]

Patients should be treated with perioperative prophylactic antibiotics and remain *non per os* (NPO) for 5 to 10 days postoperatively. Usually, the tracheotomy can be removed 1 to 2 weeks after surgery, but it may need to be left in place longer in patients who have extended resections, delayed healing (due to previous radiation therapy, diabetes, malnutrition, and so on) or aspiration. However, most patients swallow much more effectively after decannulation. Thus, early removal of the tracheotomy tube is encouraged.

Reconstruction After Partial Laryngectomy

Primary mucosal closure cannot be obtained after almost all forms of partial laryngectomy. In most cases, the thyroid perichondrium is used to close the operative site. In others, the area of mucosal resection is left open. In either situation, healing proceeds by granulation and epithelialization from the remaining mucosa. For this reason, most surgeons have suggested that a history of prior radiation therapy or the presence of systemic conditions that slow healing (diabetes mellitus, malnutrition, alcoholism, or renal failure) are contraindications to laryngeal conservation with a partial laryngectomy. However, with meticulous technique, a cooperative patient, and mucosal and cartilaginous reconstruction, partial laryngectomy can be considered in most cases. The simplest forms of reconstruction utilize advancement and rotation flaps of local mucosa to cover exposed areas. A posterior mucosal defect can be closed by advancing postcricoid mucosa and rotating tissue from the aryepiglottic fold or medial wall of the piriform sinus. More generous portions of piriform or posterior pharyngeal wall mucosa can be rotated to cover almost an entire hemilarynx, but this narrows or closes the piriform sinus and may increase the risk of aspiration. Amin and Koufman have described a reconstructive technique for cases in which an arytenoid is sacrificed in which the ipsilateral cricoid cartilage is resected and reconstructed with a local muscle flap and stent.[57]

Many methods have been used successfully to provide bulk to the operated side and thus improve the postoperative voice. Probably the most reliable is a bipedicled, strap muscle flap that is developed from the anterior half of the muscle and interposed deep to the perichondrium of the operated side[58] (Fig 93–12). An inferiorly based sternohyoid flap can be interposed to cover the arytenoid cartilage and provide bulk for a neo-vocal fold[59] (Fig 93–13). Portions of thyroid cartilage, especially the superior cornua, can be rotated into the defect and then covered with muscle or mucosa to provide a ridge apposing the remaining mobile vocal fold.[60]

When cartilage support and mucosal coverage are necessary, an epiglottic flap is usually the first choice for reconstruction after hemilaryngectomy or extended partial laryngectomy procedures.[61,62] The petiole must be uninvolved by tumor. The epiglottis is grasped at the petiole, and dissection is carried out superiorly along the lateral margins as the cartilage is retracted inferiorly. The mucosa over the laryngeal surface is usually left intact, and the cartilage can be released enough to suture to the cricoid cartilage inferiorly. There is no evidence of an increased risk of aspiration

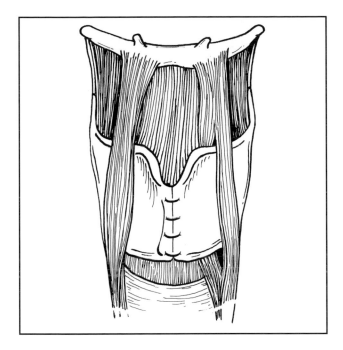

Fig 93–12. Bipedicled sternohyoid muscle flap interposed deep to the perichondrium.

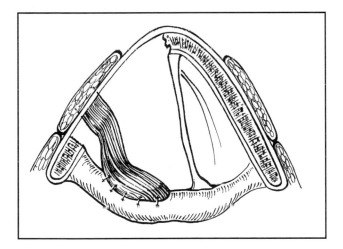

Fig 93–13. An inferiorly based sternohyoid muscle flap used to reconstruct the arytenoid bed.

after use of an epiglottic flap, and results in radiated patients are excellent.[63] Composite grafts of nasal septum or auricular cartilage and skin also can be used, but healing of these free grafts in radiated tissue is unpredictable.

Supracricoid Hemilaryngectomy

Select T_2 and T_3 glottic and supraglottic carcinomas can be treated using supracricoid hemilaryngectomy

with either cricohyoidopexy (CHP) or cricohyoepiglottopexy (CHEP) for reconstruction.[64-67] Supracricoid hemilaryngectomy provides equivalent local control to total laryngectomy in carefully selected T_3 tumors, and better local control than vertical partial laryngectomy in most T_2 carcinomas.[64-67] The technique involves removal of the entire thyroid cartilage, both vocal folds, and resection of up to one arytenoid cartilage. Voice and swallowing results are better when both arytenoid cartilages can be preserved. Contraindications to this procedure include lesions originating in the ventricle or the anterior commissure with pre-epiglottic space invasion, arytenoid cartilage fixation (indicating invasion of the cricoarytenoid joint), and subglottic extension of more than 10 mm anteriorly or 5 mm posteriorly. Patients with poor preoperative pulmonary function are not candidates as micro-aspiration is an expected consequence despite swallowing rehabilitation. The swallowing rehabilitation process after supracricoid hemilaryngectomy is very involved and patients must be able to participate actively in the rehabilitation process.

Supracricoid hemilaryngectomy is performed under general anesthesia with orotracheal intubation. A standard apron flap incision is made with elevation of the skin flap to at least 1 centimeter above the hyoid bone and down to the clavicles. Neck dissections are performed if indicated. The sternohyoid and thyrohyoid muscles are transected along the superior part of the thyroid cartilage; these muscles are then mobilized inferiorly to expose the sternothyroid muscle. The sternothyroid muscle is transected at the inferior border of the thyroid cartilage, and the pharyngeal constrictor muscles are incised along the lateral alae of the thyroid cartilage. The thyroid perichondrium is incised along the lateral border, and the piriform sinuses are dissected free of the thyroid cartilage. The cricothyroid joints are disarticulated carefully to avoid damaging the recurrent laryngeal nerves. A cricothyroidotomy is performed, and the endotracheal tube is removed from the mouth and placed through the cricothyroid membrane. For glottic tumors, the thyrohyoid membrane is incised just above the thyroid cartilage, entering the pharynx. In supraglottic cancer, the hyoid bone periosteum is incised and stripped from the deep surface of the bone. A tunnel is used to traverse the pre-epiglottic space and enter the pharynx just above the epiglottis. In either case, the tumor is visualized through the pharyngotomy; and the pharyngotomy is connected to the cricothyroidotomy on the less involved side using heavy Mayo scissors, sparing as much mucosa as is possible. This maneuver provides adequate visualization for mucosal cuts on the tumor-bearing side. If it is necessary for adequate margins, excision of the ipsilateral arytenoid cartilage may be performed. If the arytenoid is to be spared, the incision should be performed just anterior to or through the vocal process of the arytenoid. More posterior cuts are likely to violate the joint capsule and result in an immobile arytenoid. Once the tumor is released and removed, the mucosa of the upper part of the arytenoid cartilage is closed over the exposed arytenoid cartilage. No sutures are placed near the inferior portion of the arytenoid to preserve mobility. A suture is then used to pull the arytenoid cartilage anteriorly and attach it to the cricoid cartilage to prevent posterior rotation of the arytenoids due to unopposed posterior cricoarytenoid muscle pull. The primary closure of the surgical defect is then performed using three submucosal 0-Vicryl sutures that are looped around the cricoid cartilage and passed through either the remaining epiglottic cartilage and around the hyoid bone in a CHEP, or around just the hyoid bone in CHP. A large portion of the tongue base should be included in each of these sutures. The sutures are then pulled together and tied to impact the cricoid cartilage into the hyoid bone. Prior to tying these sutures, a tracheotomy is performed with the cricoid cartilage and trachea pulled up to their eventual locations.

Postoperative care includes aggressive speech and swallowing therapy. Nutrition is maintained through a feeding tube until the patient is able to tolerate a full diet. In the immediate postoperative period, the patient is instructed to expectorate all secretions forcefully in order to improve tongue mobility and future swallowing ability. As the patient is able to tolerate his or her own secretions, the diet is advanced slowly under the close supervision of the speech and swallowing therapists. Tracheotomy decannulation and full oral diet are possible in 95% of patients.[64,66]

Total Laryngectomy

In the opinion of most laryngologists, advanced tumors that impair vocal fold motion, exhibit transglottic extension, or deeply invade adjacent tissues are treated best by total laryngectomy, usually combined with postoperative radiation therapy However, Harwood et al[68] have shown the efficacy of primary radical radiotherapy with surgical salvage. The addition of chemotherapy will allow 30 to 50% of patients who are cured to retain their larynges.[12] Patients whose tumors recur after nonsurgical treatment are most often salvaged with total laryngectomy. Standard wide-field laryngectomy includes resection of the entire larynx, the hyoid bone, overlying strap muscles, and the upper trachea. The thyroid lobe on the dominant side of the tumor is usually removed, as well. The

surgery can be extended to include part or all of the hypopharyngeal mucosa, the entire esophagus, and the entire cervical trachea. Unilateral or bilateral modified or radical neck dissections are performed in combination with total laryngectomy, if indicated. Patients presenting with advanced, obstructing tumors often need airway protection prior to definitive surgery. Although tracheotomy provides a definitively safe airway, there has been some concern that performing tracheotomy before total laryngectomy increases the risk of stomal recurrence. An alternative, temporizing measure to re-establish an adequate airway is to debulk the obstructing portion of tumor, often at the time of biopsy, for definitive diagnosis. Debulking can be accomplished through the use of the CO_2 laser or with the use of powered instrumentation with specially designed laryngeal attachments.

Prior to total laryngectomy, patients should be treated with prophylactic antibiotics and are prepared for possible intraoperative transfusion. Many patients require tracheotomy under local anesthesia for airway support prior to the induction of general anesthesia. If orotracheal intubation is accomplished, the tube can be left in place until the trachea is incised.

The incision is determined by the extent of the resection. A wide, superiorly based apron flap, including a tracheal stoma, is performed for simple laryngectomies (Fig 93–14). This can be extended laterally, and an inferior limb can be added when a neck dissection is performed (Fig 93–15). A full or half "h" incision with its modifications also can provide excellent exposure. The skin flaps are elevated deep to the platysma

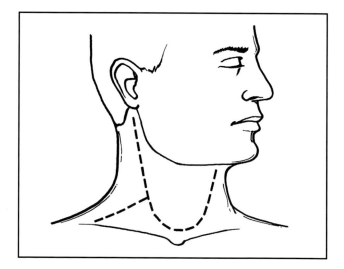

Fig 93–14. An apron flap incision as utilized for total laryngectomy. The lateral extension can be added for simultaneous radical dissection.

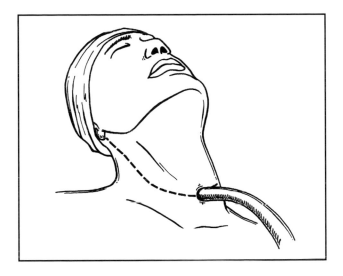

Fig 93–15. A utility incision is preferred when laryngectomy is combined with a neck dissection.

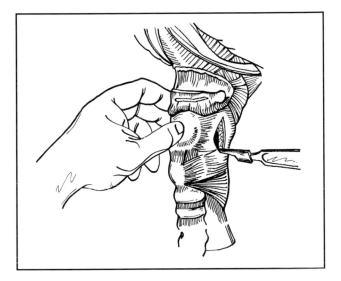

Fig 93–16. Total laryngectomy. The inferior constrictor muscle is divided form the lateral margin of the thyroid ala.

muscle. They must be handled gently, especially in radiated patients. The strap muscles are divided inferiorly, and the thyroid gland is exposed. The carotid sheath structures are identified, isolated from the larynx, and retracted laterally with the sternocleidomastoid muscle. The thyroid isthmus is divided, and the lobe on the uninvolved side is dissected sharply from the trachea. On the involved side, dissection proceeds lateral to the thyroid lobe, isolating and controlling the inferior and superior vascular pedicles. The larynx is rotated, and the inferior constrictor muscles are dissected sharply from the lateral margins of the thyroid ala on each side (Fig 93–16). The suprahyoid muscles are dissected from the hyoid bone, and the greater cornua are freed. Care must be taken to dissect close to the bone to prevent hypoglossal nerve injury. Control and ligation of the superior vascular pedicles of the larynx are the last steps in separating the larynx from external muscular structures (Fig 93–17).

The larynx is removed by separating its mucosal attachments. The trachea is divided below the second ring or one ring below a pre-existing tracheotomy. The incision in the tracheal mucosa is carried superiorly on the posterior wall to provide extra length for the stoma. Once the trachea is divided, it must be sutured to the inferior skin margin to prevent retraction into the mediastinum. Scalpel dissection proceeds through the posterior wall incision until the "gray line" between the trachea and esophagus is identified. This reveals a plane that can be opened bluntly to the level of the arytenoid cartilages. The lateral attachments along this plane are divided. The pharynx is entered superior to the hyoid bone, through the mucosa of the vallecula. If there is tumor extension into the epiglottis

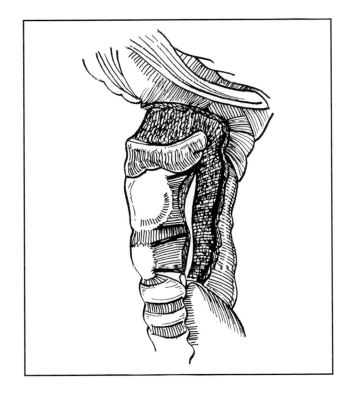

Fig 93–17. Total laryngectomy. After division of the strap muscles and the inferior constrictors, the larynx is freed from all muscular attachments.

or vallecula, the pharynx is opened through the contralateral piriform sinus (Fig 93–18). The epiglottis is grasped and mucosal incisions are carried inferiorly to allow the larynx to be opened on the contralateral side to visualize the tumor directly (Fig 93–19). Mucosal

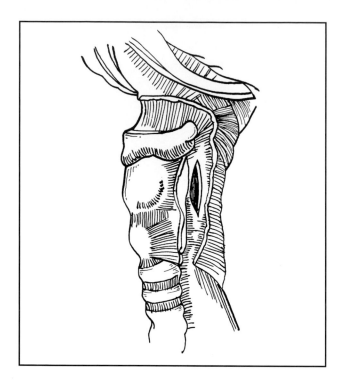

Fig 93–18. Total laryngectomy. When the pre-epiglottic space is involved, the larynx is entered through the contralateral piriform sinus, and the larynx is rotated to expose the tumor.

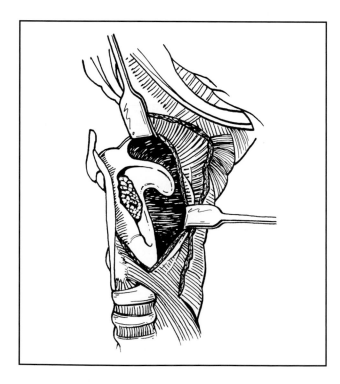

Fig. 93–19. Total laryngectomy. The final mucosal incisions are made with the tumor visualized directly to allow adequate surgical margins.

incisions proceed as medially as possible along the piriform sinus mucosa leaving at least a 2-cm mucosal margin. The incisions are connected inferiorly, and the larynx is removed. Mucosal closure of the pharynx is usually performed in a "T" fashion (Fig 93–20). When extensive pharyngectomy is required, a straight-line closure may be appropriate. The closure is in two layers: a running, inverting Connell (inverting horizontal mattress) suture in the mucosa and interrupted imbricating sutures in the muscularis. Absorbable suture is used. A nasogastric tube is placed under direct visualization prior to closure.

Creation of a stoma begins by resecting a circular ellipse of skin slightly larger than the tracheal diameter and removing subcutaneous fat from the margin. The stoma is secured with interrupted vertical mattress sutures around the distal tracheal cartilage ring. A continuous 4-0 or 5-0 absorbable suture may be placed circumferentially to closely appose the mucosa and the skin. Large suction drains are placed and the skin flaps are closed in layers.

Voice and Swallowing Rehabilitation After Total Laryngectomy

Voice rehabilitation can be accomplished with an electrolarynx (oral or neck placement), esophageal speech,

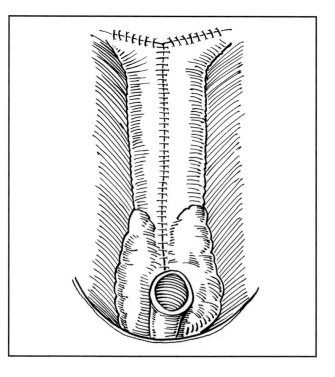

Fig 93–20. Total laryngectomy. T-closure of the pharynx.

or by means of a valve prosthesis placed in a tracheoesophageal conduit. Historically, multiple attempts have been made to create a vocal tract surgically using pharyngeal mucosal flaps placed over the tracheal air column. However, most of these methods have been abandoned due to the risk of aspiration. Almost all patients use an electrolarynx at some point during their rehabilitation, and approximately one third of laryngectomy patients can obtain good results with esophageal speech.

The valve voice prosthesis can provide a controllable, nonmechanical voice for over 90% of total laryngectomy patients.[69,70] It can be considered even after hypopharyngeal or esophageal reconstruction.[71,72] However, the prosthesis requires frequent maintenance and sometimes considerable speech training. Patient selection is based on intelligence, compliance, and manual dexterity. The fistula can be formed at the time of total laryngectomy or anytime after primary healing is completed. When prosthesis fistula creation is considered as a delayed procedure, the patient is first evaluated with a barium swallow, to rule out pharyngeal stenosis; and an air insufflation test is used to prove the patient can produce voice. Usually, the operation is performed under general anesthesia. A rigid esophagoscope is placed at the level of the superior margin of the tracheal stoma. A needle is placed 2 to 3 mm proximal to the mucocutaneous junction and visualized in the esophageal lumen. A silk suture is pulled through the esophagoscope (Fig 93–21). The suture is attached to progressively enlarging dilators (usually filiform and followers) until a 16-gauge French red rubber catheter is pulled through. The internal portion of the catheter is pushed into the distal esophagus, and the external portion is sutured to the skin superior

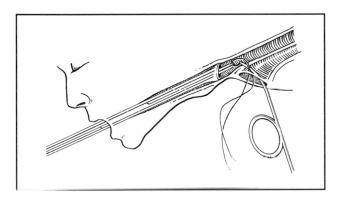

Fig 93–21. A silk suture is placed through the tracheoesophageal puncture and brought through the esophagoscope into the oral cavity. The suture is attached to dilators; and after adequate dilatation, a 16-gauge red rubber catheter is introduced in the distal esophagus and fixed to the skin.

to the stoma. Three to five days later, the catheter is removed, and the patient is fitted with a prosthesis. Kits are available with some prostheses that allow placement of the valve at the time of tracheoesophageal puncture, although surgical edema usually prevents adequate voicing for several days after placement.

The fistula also can be formed at the time of total laryngectomy. The common tracheal and esophageal walls are grasped with ring forceps, and the incision is made high on the posterior tracheal wall. A 16-gauge French red rubber catheter is placed through the incision into the esophagus directly. The distal catheter is pushed into the esophagus and used as a feeding tube postoperatively. Placement of the prosthesis within a week of laryngectomy has the advantages of providing early, excellent voice rehabilitation. Patients become more involved in their postoperative care and return to work sooner. However, the fistula can be difficult to manage during radiation therapy; and the patient may not have useful voice during that time. Additionally, the incidence of stomal stenosis is somewhat increased; and stenting with laryngectomy tubes may be necessary.[73]

Swallowing rehabilitation is easier after total laryngectomy than after partial laryngectomy due to the total separation of the digestive and respiratory passages by total laryngectomy. Most patients who do not develop pharyngocutaneous fistulae can begin oral feedings 5 to 10 days after surgery. Oral feeding is generally delayed by several weeks in previously irradiated patients due to the relatively high incidence of delayed fistulas in this patient population. A recent article demonstrated the safety of oral feedings in selected patients 48 hours after total laryngectomy.[74]

Subglottic Cancer

The cricothyroid membrane is found about 10 mm inferior to the anterior commissure and 5 mm inferior to the posterior margin of the vocal fold. Tumor extension to this membrane allows lymphatic spread to the paratracheal lymph nodes and the thyroid gland. Inferiorly, tumor may extend submucosally to involve the cricoid cartilage. Circumferential involvement and extensive posterior growth into the hypopharynx are not uncommon.[75]

Most subglottic tumors are extensions from glottic primary lesions. Primary subglottic carcinoma is rare. Patients usually present with airway obstruction, and hoarseness is common secondary to a greater than 75% incidence of vocal fold fixation.[76] Accurate diagnosis and staging are important (Table 93–4).

Table 93–4. Staging of Primary Tumor in Laryngeal Cancer.

Subglottis

T_1— Tumor limited to subglottis.

T_2— Tumor extends to vocal folds with normal or impaired mobility.

T_3— Tumor limited to larynx with vocal fold fixation.

T_4— Tumor invades the cricoid or thyroid cartilage and/or extends to other tissues beyond the larynx.

Surgical excision of primary subglottic tumors always requires a total laryngectomy, because resection of the cricoid cartilage destroys the protective function of the larynx during swallowing. However, some tumors extending from glottic cancers can be resected by vertical hemilaryngectomy with partial cricoid resection.[77] Biller and Som have described a technique of rotating the remaining posterior margin of the thyroid lamina into the cricoid defect with mucosal flap coverage.[78] Contraindicatons to vertical hemilaryngectomy with partial cricoid resection include prior radiation therapy, vocal fold fixation, and extensive invasion of the cricoid cartilage. The incidence of occult lymph node metastasis in subglottic tumors is less than 10%, so elective neck dissection is not indicated.[63]

Conclusion

Laryngeal carcinoma remains a complex clinical challenge. Intimate knowledge of anatomy, patterns of malignant spread, and diverse treatment options is essential. Treatment decisions often are difficult when attempting to balance adequate tumor control and maintenance of voice and swallowing function. The curability of laryngeal cancer has improved only minimally over the past few decades. However, functional treatment results have improved substantially thanks to adjuvant chemotherapy, radical radiotherapy, and innovative conservation and reconstructive surgical techniques.

References

1. American Cancer Society. *Cancer Facts and Figures*. Atlanta, Ga: Author; 2001:7.
2. Silverberg E. Cancer statistics, 1984. *CA*. 1984;34:7–23.
3. Albright JT, Karpti R, Topham A, et al. Second malignant neoplasms in patients under 40 years of age with laryngeal cancer. *Laryngoscope*. 2001;111:563–567.
4. Burch JD, Howe GR, Miller AB, Semenciw R. Tobacco, alcohol, asbestos, and nickel in the etiology of cancer of the larynx: a case-control study. *J Natl Cancer Inst*. 1981; 67:1219–1224.
5. Wynder EL, Bross IJ, Day E. Epidemiological approach to the etiology of cancer of the larynx. *JAMA*. 1956;160: 1384–1391.
6. Auerbach O, Hammond EC, Garfinkel L. Historic changes in the larynx in relation to smoking habits. *Cancer*. 1970;25:92–104.
7. Flanders WD, Rothman KJ. Interaction of alcohol and tobacco in laryngeal cancer. *Am J Epidemiol*. 1982;115: 371–379.
8. Wynder EL, Cover LS, Marbuchi K, Mushinski M. Environmental factors in cancer of the larynx: a second look. *Cancer*. 1976;38:1591–1601.
9. Pedersen E, Hogetveit AC, Andersen A. Cancer of respiratory organs among workers at a nickel refinery in Norway. *Int J Cancer*. 1973;12:32–41.
10. Stell PM, McGill T. Asbestos and laryngeal carcinoma. *Lancet*. 1973;2:416–417.
11. Parnes SM. Asbestos and cancer of the larynx: is there a relationship? *Laryngoscope*. 1990;100:254–261.
12. Wolf GT, Hong WK, Fisher S, et al. Induction chemotherapy plus radiation compared with surgery plus radiation in patients with advanced laryngeal cancer. *New Eng J Med*. 1991;324:1685–1690.
13. McDonald TJ, DeSanto LW, Weiland LH. Supraglottic larynx and its pathology as studied by whole laryngeal sections. *Laryngoscope*. 1976;86:635–648.
14. American Joint Committee on Cancer. *Manual for Staging Cancer*. 3rd ed. Philadelphia, Pa: JB Lippincott; 1988.
15. Coates HL, DeSanto LW, Devine KD, Elveback LR. Carcinoma of the supraglottic larynx: a review of 221 cases. *Arch Otolaryngol*. 1976;102:686–689.
16. Bocca E. Supraglottic cancer. *Laryngoscope*. 1975:85:1318–1326.
17. Shah JP, Tollefsen HR. Epidermoid carcinoma of the supraglottic larynx: role of neck dissection in initial surgical treatment. *Am J Surg*. 1974;128:494–499.
18. Som ML. Conservation surgery for carcinoma of the supraglottis. *J Laryngol Otol*. 1970;84:656–678.
19. Archer CR, Yeager VL. Computed tomography of laryngeal cancer with histopathological correlation. *Laryngoscope*. 1982;92:1173–1180.
20. Larson JT, Adams GL, Fattah HA. Survival statistics for multiple primaries in head and neck cancer. *Otolaryngol Head Neck Surg*. 1990;103:14–24.
21. Fayos JV. Carcinoma of the endolarynx: results of irradiation. *Cancer*. 1975;35:1525–1532.
22. DeSanto LW: Early supraglottic cancer. *Ann Otol Rhinol Laryngol*. 1990;99:593–597.
23. Goepfert H, Jessie RH, Fletcher GH, Hamberger A. Optimal treatment for the technically resectable squamous cell carcinoma of the supraglottic larynx. *Laryngoscope*. 1975;85:14–32.
24. Snow JB Jr, Gelber RD, Kramer S, et al. Evaluation of randomized preoperative and postoperative radiation therapy for supraglottic carcinoma. *Ann Otol Rhinol Laryngol*. 1978;87:686–691.
25. Schuller DE, McGuirt WF, Krause CJ, et al. Symposium: adjuvant cancer therapy of head neck tumors. Increased

survival with surgery alone vs. combined therapy. *Laryngoscope*. 1979;89:582–594.

26. Harwood AR. Cancer of the larynx: the Toronto experience. *J Otolaryngol*. 1982;11(suppl 11):S10–S13.

27. DeSanto LW. Cancer of the supraglottic larynx: a review of 260 patients. *Otolaryngol Head Neck Surg*. 1985;93:705–711.

28. Burstein FD, Calcaterra TC. Supraglottic laryngectomy: series report and analysis of results. *Laryngoscope*. 1985;95:833–836.

29. Mendenhall WM, Parsons JT, Stringer SP, et al. Carcinoma of the supraglottic larynx: a basis for comparing the results of radiotherapy and surgery. *Head Neck*. 1990;12:204–209.

30. Lutz CK, Jahnson JT, Wagner RL, Myers EN. Supraglottic carcinoma: patterns of recurrence. *Ann Otol Rhinol Laryngol*. 1990;99:12–17.

31. DeSanto LW, Magrina C, O'Fallon WM. The "second" side of the neck in supraglottic cancer. *Otolaryngol Head Neck Surg*. 1990;102:351–361.

32. Bocca E. Surgical management of supraglottic cancer and its lymph node metastases in a conservative perspective. Sixteenth Daniel C. Baker Jr Memorial Lecture. *Ann Otol Rhinol Laryngol*. 1991;100:261–267.

33. Boyd TS, Harari PM, Tannehill SP, et al. Planned postradiotherapy neck dissection in patients with advanced head and neck cancer. *Head Neck*. 1998;20(2):132–137.

34. Chan AW, Ancukiewicz M, Carballo N, et al. The role of postradiotherapy neck dissection in supraglottic carcinoma. *Int J Radiat Oncol Biol Phys*. 2001;50(2):367–375.

35. Zeitels SM, Vaughan CW, Domanowski GF. Endoscopic management of early supraglottic cancer. *Ann Otol Rhinol Laryngol*. 1990;99:951–956.

36. Iro H, Waldfahrer F, Altendorf-Hofmann A, et al. Transoral laser surgery of supraglottic cancer: follow-up of 141 patient. *Arch Otolaryngol Head Neck Surg*. 1998;124(11):1245–1250.

37. Rudert HH, Werner JA, Hoft S. Transoral carbon dioxide laser resection of supraglottic carcinoma. *Ann Otol Rhinol Laryngol*. 1999;108(9):819–827.

38. Quer M, Leon X, Orus C, et al. Endoscopic laser surgery in the treatment of radiation failure of early laryngeal carcinoma. *Head Neck*. 2000;22(5):520–523.

39. Eckel HE, Thumfart W, Jungehulsing M, et al. Transoral laser surgery for early glottic carcinoma. *Eur Arch Otorhinolaryngol*. 2000;257(4):221–226.

40. Eckel HE. Local recurrences following transoral laser surgery for early glottic carcinoma: frequency, management, and outcome. *Ann Otol Rhinol Laryngol*. 2001;110(1):7–15

41. DeSanto LW, Lillie JC, Devine KD. Surgical salvage after radiation for laryngeal cancer. *Laryngoscope*. 1976;86:649–657.

42. Kirchner JD. Two hundred laryngeal cancers: patterns of growth and spread as seen in serial section. *Laryngoscope*. 1977;87:474–482.

43. Maran AG, Mackenzie IJ, Stanley RE. Carcinoma in situ of the larynx. *Head Neck Surg*. 1984;7:28–31.

44. Kaplan MJ, Johns ME, Clark DA, Cantrell RW. Glottic carcinoma: the roles of surgery and irradiation. *Cancer*. 1984;53:2641–2648.

45. Nichols RD, Mickelson SA. Partial laryngectomy after irradiation failure. *Ann Otol Rhinol Laryngol*. 1991;100:176–180.

46. Shaw HJ. Role of partial laryngectomy after irradiation in the treatment of laryngeal cancer: a view from the United Kingdom. *Ann Otol Rhinol Laryngol*. 1991;100:268–273.

47. Shah JP, Loree TR, Kowalski L. Conservation surgery for radiation-failure carcinoma of the glottic larynx. *Head Neck*. 1990;12:326–331.

48. Shapshay SM, Hybels RL, Bohigan RK. Laser excision of early vocal cord carcinoma: indications, limitations, and precautions. *Ann Otol Rhinol Laryngol*. 1990;99:46–50.

49. Ossoff RH, Sisson GA, Shapshay SM. Endoscopic management of selected early vocal cord carinoma. *Ann Otol Rhinol Laryngol*. 1985;94:560–564.

50. Schweitzer VG. Photofrin-mediated photodynamic therapy for treatment of early stage oral cavity and laryngeal malignancies. *Lasers Surg Med*. 2001;29:305–313.

51. Sessions DG, Maness GM, McSwain B. Laryngofissure in the treatment of carcinoma of the vocal cord: a report of forty cases and a review of the literature. *Laryngoscope*. 1965;75:490–502.

52. Biller HF, Lawson W. Bilateral vertical partial laryngectomy for bilateral vocal cord carcinoma. *Ann Otol Rhinol Laryngol*. 1981;90:489–491.

53. Biller HF, Ogura JH, Pratt LL. Hemilaryngectomy for T2 glottic cancer. *Arch Otolaryngol*. 1971;93:238–243.

54. Kirchner JA, Som ML. The anterior commissure technique of partial laryngectomy: clinical and laboratory observations. *Laryngoscope*. 1975;85:1308–1317.

55. Sessions DG, Ogura JH, Fried MP. The anterior commissure in glottic carcinoma. *Laryngoscope*. 1975;85:1624–1632.

56. Biller HF, Lawson W. Partial laryngectomy for vocal cord cancer with marked limitation or fixation of the vocal cord. *Laryngoscope*. 1986;96:61–64.

57. Amin MR, Koufman JA. Hemicricoidectomy for voice rehabilitation following hemilaryngectomy with ipsilateral arytenoid removal. *Ann Otol Rhinol Laryngol*. 2001;110(6):514–518.

58. Bailey BJ. Partial laryngectomy and laryngoplasty: a technique and review. *Trans Am Acad Ophthalmol Otolaryngol*. 1966;70(4):559–574.

59. Biller HF, Lucente FE. Reconstruction of the larynx following vertical partial laryngectomy. *Otolaryngol Clin North Am*. 1979;12:761–766.

60. Biller HF, Lawson W. Partial laryngectomy for transglottic cancers. *Ann Otol Rhinol Laryngol*. 1984;93:297–300.

61. Schechter GL. Epiglottic reconstruction and subtotal laryngectomy. *Laryngoscope*. 1983;93:729–734.

62. Nong HU, Mo W, Huang GW, et al. Epiglottic laryngoplasty after hemilaryngectomy for glottic cancer. *Otolaryngol Head Neck Surg*. 1991;104:809–813.

63. Tucker HM, Benninger MS, Roberts JK, et al. Near-total laryngectomy with epiglottic reconstruction. *Arch Otolaryngol Head Neck Surg*. 1989;115:1314–1344.

64. Laccourreye L, Salzer SJ, Brasnu D, et al. Glottic carcinoma with a fixed true vocal cord: outcomes after neoadjuvant chemotherapy and supracricoid partial laryngectomy with cricohyoidoepiglottopexy. *Otolaryngol Head Neck Surg.* 1996;114:400–406.

65. Laccourreye O, Weinstein G, Brasnu D, et al. A clinical trial of continuous cisplatin-flurouracil induction chemotherapy and supracricoid partial laryngectomy for glottic carcinoma classified as T2. *Cancer.* 1994;74(10): 2781–2790.

66. Laccourreye O, Weinstein G, Naudo P, et al. Supracricoid partial laryngectomy after failed laryngeal radiation therapy. *Laryngoscope.* 1996;106:495–498.

67. Laccourreye O, Weinstein G, Brasnu D, et al. Vertical partial laryngectomy: a critical analysis of local recurrence. *Ann Otol Rhino Laryngol.* 1991;110:68–71.

68. Harwood AR, Bryce DP, Rider WD. Management of T3 glottic cancer. *Arch Otolaryngol.* 1980;106:697–699.

69. Wood BG, Rusnove MG, Tucker HM, et al. Tracheoesophageal puncture for alaryngeal voice restoration. *Ann Otol Rhinol Laryngol.* 1981;90:492–494.

70. Singer MI. Tracheoesophageal speech: vocal rehabilitation after total laryngectomy. *Laryngoscope.* 1983;93:1454–1465.

71. Bleach N, Perry A, Cheesman A. Surgical voice restoration with the Blom-Singer prosthesis following laryngopharyngoesophagectomy and pharyngogastric anastomosis. *Ann Otol Rhinol Laryngol.* 1991;100:142–147.

72. Kinishi M, Amatsu M, Tahara S, Makino K. Primary tracheojejunal shunt operation for voice restoration following pharyngolaryngoesophagectomy. *Ann Otol Rhinol Laryngol.* 1991;100:435–438.

73. Ho CM, Wei WI, Lau WF, Lam KH. Tracheostomal stenosis after immediate tracheoesophageal puncture. *Arch Otolaryngol Head Neck Surg.* 1991;117:662–665.

74. Medina JE, Khafif A. Early oral feeding following total laryngectomy. *Laryngoscope.* 2001;111(3):368–372.

75. Micheau C, Luboinski B, Sancho H, Cachin Y. Modes of invasion of cancer of the larynx: a statistical, histological, and radioclinical analysis of 120 cases. *Cancer.* 1976;38: 346–360.

76. Stell MP. The subglottic space. In: Alberti PW, Bryce DP, eds. *Workshops from the Centennial Conference on Laryngeal Cancer.* New York, NY: Appleton-Century-Crofts; 1976: 620.

77. Sessions DG, Ogura JH, Fried MP. Carcinoma of the subglottic area. *Laryngoscope.* 1975;85:1417–1423.

78. Biller HF, Som ML. Vertical partial laryngectomy for glottic carcinoma with posterior subglottic extension. *Ann Otol Rhinol Laryngol.* 1977;86:715–718.

94

Lymphoma: An Update on Evolving Trends in Staging and Management

Seth H. Dailey and Robert Thayer Sataloff

Because lymphoma affects young adults, it is not uncommon to encounter lymphoma in professional voice users. Treatment often involves radiation (sometimes to the neck) and chemotherapy, which may affect voice performance. Consequently, it is important for laryngologists to be familiar with the diagnosis, staging, and management of these malignancies.

There are many controversies in the management of lymphoma, ranging from categorization to staging to treatment options. Familiarity with these controversies and with the current state of the art in diagnosis and treatment is essential for the otolaryngologist to participate in a meaningful way as a member of the multidisciplinary team. Although the lymphoma management team includes oncologists, general surgeons, radiologists, radiation oncologists, and others, otolaryngologists often make the diagnosis following evaluation of a neck mass, while simultaneously establishing a relationship with the patient. Patients and referring physicians look to otolaryngologists for expertise in the management of neck masses. It is important for us to remain knowledgeable resources for both our patients and primary care physicians and to remain involved in, and familiar with, total patient management beyond the biopsy.

Disease Characteristics

Lymphoma accounts for about 4% of all new cases of cancer in the United States every year.[1] It is second only to squamous cell carcinoma as the most common head and neck cancer.[1] Lymphoma is typically categorized as either Hodgkin's or non-Hodgkin's disease.

Disease presentations vary according to their natural histories. Hodgkin's disease typically spreads by contiguity, whereas non-Hodgkin's usually does not. About 80% of Hodgkin's patients have cervical adenopathy, whereas about 33% of non-Hodgkin's patients have nodal disease in the neck.[1] Patients with both types of disease can also have hematologic disorders, mediastinal complaints, central nervous systems symptoms, gastrointestinal disorders, or other difficulties.

Hodgkin's Disease

Hodgkin's disease usually affects patients in the third and the seventh decades of life, and it is more common among men than women. The already higher relative risk of Hodgkin's disease conferred by a positive family history rises tenfold when a same-sex sibling has the disease.[1] A possible causal relationship exists between Hodgkin's disease and the presence of Epstein-Barr virus (EBV).[1]

The cell of origin in Hodgkin's disease is not yet well defined. Hodgkin's disease is characterized by the presence of the pathognomonic multinucleated Reed-Sternberg cell. The cellular background defines the four histologic subtypes: nodular sclerosis, lymphocyte predominance, mixed cellularity, and lymphocyte depletion.[2] The cellular milieu might or might not have prognostic significance.[3,4]

Non-Hodgkin's Disease

In the head and neck, non-Hodgkin's lymphoma is five times more common than Hodgkin's disease. In fact, it is the second most common head and neck malignancy in and of itself. A subtype of non-Hodgkin's disease, Burkitt's lymphoma, has been shown to be strongly associated with EBV.[1] There is also a strong association between non-Hodgkin's lymphoma and human immunodeficiency virus in patients who have adult T-cell leukemia.

In approximately 90% of cases, non-Hodgkin's lymphoma are derived from B cells; the remainder are T-cell-derived. Most patients do not have systemic symptoms ("A" status); approximately 10% of patients do ("B" status). These symptoms include unexplained fever (>38° C), unexplained weight loss (>10% of body weight), and night sweats. A patient's A or B status is routinely taken into account during staging, although this remains a subject of ongoing debate.

The immunologic status of the cells and the histology of the nodes are used to characterize non-Hodgkin's lymphoma. Over time, this categorization has taken many forms, including the simultaneous use of six different systems internationally. Among these systems are the Rappaport, Kiel, and Lukes-Collins classifications. The current classification system for non-Hodgkin's lymphoma was adopted in 1982 to provide a unifying schema (Table 94–1). In 1994, an international group of pathologists met and developed the revised European-American lymphoma (REAL) classification system for lymphoid neoplasms.[5] The REAL system was an attempt to establish a more clinically useful categorization of lymphoid neoplasms. Even so, the 1982 classification system is still widely used.

Staging

As is the case with all malignancies, the staging of lymphoma is designed to predict risk. Laparotomy and radiologic studies can help accomplish this, as can prognostic factors derived from retrospective analyses and, of course, the clinical examination. The Ann Arbor staging system is used to stratify risk for both Hodgkin's and non-Hodgkin's lymphoma (Table 94–2).[6]

Proper staging ultimately means that the patient will experience neither the morbidity of overtreatment nor the mortality of undertreatment. Even in ideal doses, treatments themselves are not benign. For example, radiation therapy can cause hypothyroidism, pneumonitis, pericarditis, sterility, and other problems. Likewise, chemotherapy can cause nausea and vomiting, neuropathies, leukopenia, sterility, and possibly the induction of acute myelogenous leukemia.[7] Clearly, these modalities should be used only when they are essential to improving outcomes.

Laparotomy Staging

Ever since its inception, staging by laparotomy has prompted much controversy. This surgical procedure is used to determine whether or not supradiaphragmatic stage I and II Hodgkin's disease has crossed the diaphragm. If it has, the disease is classified as at least

Table 94–1. Classification of non-Hodgkin's Lymphoma.

Low Grade	Intermediate Grade	High Grade
Small lymphocytic	Follicular large	Immunoblastic
Follicular small cleaved	Diffuse, small cleaved	Lymphoblastic
Follicular mixed	Diffuse, mixed Diffuse large cell	Small, noncleaved

Table 94-2. Ann Arbor Staging System for Lymphoma.

Stage	Description
I	A single lymph node or extralymphatic site
II	Two or more lymph node regions on the same side of the diaphragm or localized extralymphatic site with one or more lymph node regions on the same side of the diaphragm
III	Lymph node regions on both sides of the diaphragm and possible localized involvement of an extralymphatic site or the spleen
A or B	Denotes absence (A) or presence (B) of: unexplained weight loss of more than 10% of body weight, unexplained fever of higher than 38° C, or night sweats (*Note:* pruritus is not a B symptom.)

stage III. The essential question then becomes: Is the information gained by staging laparotomy sufficient to justify the means used to acquire it?

The rate of discovery of pathologic nodes via laparotomy can be as high as 30%.[8] Morbidity and mortality rates associated with the procedure, which vary among surgical centers, are in the range of 15% and 1%, respectively.[9] Laparotomy carries the risk of overwhelming sepsis by encapsulated organisms in both the short and long term. This risk has been reported to be about 2 to 4%.[10-20] The use of pneumococcal vaccine can decrease the risk of late infection, which makes laparotomy a more reasonable option.

In many retrospective studies, researchers have tried to identify factors that predict the positivity or negativity of staging laparotomy, and they have been successful in identifying certain subgroups of patients in whom the use or avoidance of laparotomy makes sense. Leibenhaut et al studied 915 patients with clinical stage (CS) I and II Hodgkin's disease who underwent laparotomy, and they were able to identify specific subgroups in whom laparotomy had a low yield.[14] These patients included women with CS I disease who had either lymphocyte predominance or interfollicular histologies. All of these groups had less than a 5% risk of subdiaphragmatic disease. Moreover, their B status did not correlate with advanced disease. On the other hand, males in general have histologic findings of mixed cellularity and carry an increased risk of subdiaphragmatic disease.

Likewise, Mauch et al reported on 692 patients with supradiaphragmatic disease who underwent laparotomy.[15] Again, women with CS I disease and men with CS I disease and a lymphocyte predominance had a low probability of subdiaphragmatic disease. Moreover, men with CS I disease high in the neck were also in the low-probability group. Conversely, a high probability of subdiaphragmatic disease was associated with B status, male sex, age greater than 40 years, and mixed cellularity or lymphocyte depletion on histology. Although laparotomy is still the gold-standard staging procedure, it is certainly not the only option.

Radiologic Staging

Radiologic studies also provide useful information. Lymphangiography was once the mainstay of radiologic diagnosis for lymphoma, and it is still used in some centers. However, computed tomography (CT), magnetic resonance imaging (MRI), gallium scans, and 2-[F-18]-fluoro-2-deoxy-D-glucose positron emission tomography (FDG-PET) have all come into use, and they provide physiologic as well as anatomic data.

CT is typically the primary radiologic study for lymphoma. It provides a rapid, cost-effective study for both staging and follow-up. But it is not the best choice for all patients. For example, one of the difficulties in following patients after treatment is that tumors can still be physically present but physiologically sterilized. Gallium scans and FDG-PET are especially helpful in assessing these cases.

Gallium Scans

Draisma et al compared the utility of gallium and MRI scans for detecting mediastinal lymphoma in 189 patients.[21] They found that the sensitivity and specificity of gallium were 90 and 97%, respectively, compared with 89 and 89% with MRI.

Similarly, Setoain et al studied 53 patients who were imaged with both gallium and CT after treatment.[22] They found that the sensitivity and specificity for detecting tumor recurrence were 88 and 100% with gallium, compared with 59 and 72% with CT, again demonstrating the superiority of gallium as a follow-up study. Additionally, they reported that all four of the treatment failures in their study were evident on gallium scans.

The value of gallium scans in helping guide post-chemotherapy decisions was further documented by Stroszczynski et al in their study of 28 patients who were imaged with both gallium and CT.[23] Sensitivity and specificity were 94 and 100% with gallium, compared with 83 and 93% with CT.

In a finding that is perhaps most important, Kaplan et al found that gallium scans can predict complete and lasting remissions when patients are gallium-positive before treatment and gallium-negative afterward.[24]

FDG-PET Scans

The use of FDG-PET also merits attention. Newman et al studied 16 patients who had undergone both CT and FDG-PET prior to being treated.[25] All tumor sites that were seen on CT were seen on PET, and three patients who had negative laparotomies also had negative abdominal CT and PET scans. PET thus demonstrated excellent sensitivity and specificity in this small sample.

Moog et al imaged 60 patients with both modalities to evaluate 740 lymph node regions.[26] CT identified 160 positive regions; PET identified all 160 plus 25 others that were undetected by CT. PET findings resulted in the restaging of four patients, while CT altered staging in only one. Other authors support the use of PET, particularly because of its value in detecting the activity of tumors after treatment.[27]

In view of these findings, it appears to be reasonable not to subject selected patients in low-probability categories to the morbidity of laparotomy—provided that they are followed closely with clinical, laboratory, and radiologic assessments.

Treatment

Once risk has been determined, treatment must be instituted that will attack the disease while sparing the patient. In both Hodgkin's and non-Hodgkin's disease, the more disseminated the disease, the higher the risks. Suitable therapeutic strategies have been widely agreed on for both diseases (Tables 94–3 and 94–4). Treatment options include observation, involved-field radiation, subtotal lymphoid irradiation, chemotherapy with or without radiation, and bone marrow transplant. The more advanced the disease, of course, the more aggressive and, hence, toxic the treatment. Although there are general treatment guidelines, some basic questions linger, and controversy attends the treatment of all stages of disease. The most efficacious treatment of early-stage Hodgkin's disease remains particularly controversial.

Controversy involves the avoidance of undertreatment. For example, Haybittle et al reported that undertreatment with radiation monotherapy can significantly increase mortality.[3]

To the contrary, Hoppe et al argued that salvage chemotherapy following failed radiation therapy yields survival rates that are equal to those of chemotherapy alone in early-stage disease, and therefore limited radiation as a primary treatment does not put the patient at risk for increased mortality.[28] They also reported that relapse rates are the same after chemotherapy in both groups.

Moreover, there is evidence that chemotherapy without radiation as a primary treatment of early-stage disease produces morbidity and mortality rates that are somewhat comparable to those of radiation therapy alone.[29] Other studies have shown that rates of cure and relapse-free survival following combination chemotherapy were comparable to those of radiation therapy alone in early-stage Hodgkin's disease.[30,31] Furthermore, considering that radiation therapy treats only local disease and chemotherapy treats systemic disease, staging laparotomy would become virtually useless if these data are borne out in forthcoming studies.

Prognosis

Pre- and post-treatment factors have been analyzed to help determine prognosis in non-Hodgkin's disease. One multivariate analysis of 2,031 patients identified several independent risk factors for poor survival.[32] These factors were: age more than 60 years old, late-stage disease, elevated serum lactate dehydrogenase levels, impaired performance status, and extranodal

Table 94–3. Recommended Treatment for Hodgkin's Disease.

Stage	Therapy
Favorable I, IIA	Subtotal lymphoid irradiation
Favorable I, IIB	Combination chemotherapy or lymphoid irradiation or combined modality
Favorable IIIA	Combination chemotherapy or lymphoid irradiation or combined modality
*Unfavorable I, II (A or B)	Combination chemotherapy with or without irradiation to bulky sites of disease
*Unfavorable III, IV (A or B)	Combination chemotherapy with or without irradiation to bulky sites of disease

*Bulky disease, ie, nodes >10 cm or mediastinal widening more than one third chest diameter or multiple extranodal sites.

Table 94-4. Recommended Treatment for non-Hodgkin's Lymphoma.

Stage	Low-grade	Intermediate-grade	High-grade
I	Observation or involved field radiation	Chemotherapy and involved field radiation	High-dose chemotherapy
II-IV	Observation or chemotherapy	Chemotherapy	High-dose chemotherapy with evaluation for bone marrow transplant if inadequate response

involvement. This study also found that 5-year survival rates were 73% for patients with zero or one risk factors, 51% for those with two, 43% with three risk factors, and 26% for patients with four or five. Additionally, pretreatment clinical features that predicted a relapse from complete remission included advanced stage, age greater than 60 years, and abnormal serum lactate dehydrogenase levels.

Certain treatment-related prognostic factors have also been noted. Two studies found that the faster a patient achieved a complete remission, the longer he or she survived.[33,34] However, Kwak et al reported that the administration of cyclophosphamide early during treatment decreased the chance of a complete remission and increased the chance of relapse from complete remission.[35] Of particular note was the discovery by Kaplan et al, mentioned earlier in this chapter, that gallium scans can predict prolonged complete remissions,[24] In their study, 70% of patients who were transformed from gallium-positive to gallium-negative by four to six cycles of chemotherapy had long-term complete remission remissions. Conversely, only 24% of patients who were still gallium-positive after treatment had long-term complete remissions.

Cellular and molecular features can also help stratify risk. One such method is to monitor the rate of tumor cell proliferation for the presence or absence of Ki-67, the "nuclear proliferation antigen." Grogan et al reported that patients whose tumors had Ki-67 antigen in more than 60% of cells had a median survival of 39 months.[36]

The immunology of a tumor's cells plays a strong role in predicting its aggressiveness. For example, Miller et al reported that, when the major histocompatibility complex (MHC) antigen HLA-DR was absent, median survival was only 6 months; when the antigen was present, survival exceeded 2.8 years.[37] Moreover, B-2 microglobulin—a small protein that attaches to MHC class I molecules and is detectable in serum—has been correlated directly with high tumor burdens and shortened survival in patients with aggressive non-Hodgkin's lymphoma.[38] Also, survival is correlated with the ability of a tumor to spread; and adhesion molecules can play a role in that spread. Lymphocyte homing receptors facilitate lymphocyte binding and extravasation into nodes.[39] Aggressive lymphomas that are negative for lymphocyte homing receptors have been reported to be less likely to disseminate than lymphomas with greater expression.[40-43] Furthermore, studies have shown that about half of all patients with high expressions levels had advanced disease, compared with slightly more than 10% who had low expression levels.[42-44]

Conclusion

The management of lymphoma remains dynamic. Diagnosis, staging, and treatment planning are all undergoing their own independent evolutions. We anticipate that the use of the REAL staging system will become more popular and that gallium and PET scans will replace staging laparotomy in select patient groups. We also believe that less toxic chemotherapeutic regimens will play an increasing role in the treatment of early-stage Hodgkin's disease. The effects of chemotherapy upon the voice remain unknown, although some may be predicted, as discussed in chapter 63. The effects of laryngeal radiation also have not been studied well; but radiation has been known to cause long-term alterations in laryngeal vasculature, lubrication, and voice quality. Although it is possible to avoid radiation in selected cases of early glottic squamous cell carcinoma, it may not be possible to avoid radiation treatment in a patient with lymphoma; and both the patient and the laryngologist should recognize the possibility that such treatment will alter voice function. Only through knowledge of the latest trends in therapy can we help ensure that our patients will receive treatment that will provide not only the best chance for cure, but also the best opportunity to preserve optimal voice function.

References

1. Kraut ET. Lymphoma. In: Cummings CW, et al, eds. *Otolaryngology-Head and Neck Surgery*. 3rd ed. St. Louis, Mo: Mosby; 1998:1758–1763.
2. Fauci AS, Braunwald E, Isselbacher KJ, et al. *Harrison's Principles of Internal Medicine*. 14th ed. New York, NY: McGraw Hill; 1998:695–712.
3. Haybittle JL, Hayhoe FG, Easterling MJ, et al. Review of British National Lymphoma Investigation studies of Hodgkin"s disease and development of prognostic index. *Lancet*. 1985;27:967–972.
4. Hess JL, Bodis S, Pinkus G, et al. Histopathologic grading of Hodgkin's disease: lack of prognostic significance in 254 surgically staged patients. *Cancer*. 1994;74:708.
5. Harris NL, Jaffe ES, Stein H, et al. A revised European-American classification of lymphoid neoplasms: a proposal from the International Lymphoma Study Group. *Blood*. 1994;84(5):1361–1392.
6. Carbone PP, Kaplan MS, Musshoff K, et al. Report of the Committee on Hodgkin's Disease Staging Classification. *Cancer Res*. 1971;31:1860–1861
7. Hoppe RT. Stage I-II Hodgkin's disease: current therapeutic options and recommendations. *Blood*. 1983;62(1):32–36.
8. Gill PG, Souter RG, Morris PG. Results of surgical staging in Hodgkin's disease. *Br J Surg*. 1980;67:478–481.

9. Meeker WR Jr, Richardson JD, West WO, Parker JC. Critical evaluation of laparotomy and splenectomy in Hodgkin's disease. *Arch Surg.* 1972;105:222–229.

10. Foss Abrahamsen A, Hoiby EA, Hannisdal E, et al. Systemic pneumococcal disease after staging splenectomy for Hodgkin's disease 1969–1980 without pneumococcal vaccine protection: a follow-up study 1994. *Eur J Haematol.* 1997;58:73–77.

11. Taylor MA, Kaplan HS, Nelsen TS, et al. Staging laparotomy with splenectomy from Hodgkin's disease: the Stanford experience. *World J Surg.* 1985;9:449–460.

12. Brogadir S, Fialk MA, Coleman M, et al. Morbidity of staging laparotomy in Hodgkin's disease. *Am J Med.* 1978;65:429–453.

13. Kaiser C. Complications from staging laparotomy for Hodgkin's disease. *J Surg Oncol.* 1981;16:319–325.

14. Leibenhaut MH, Hoppe RT, Efron B, et al. Prognostic indicators of laparotomy findings in clinical stage I-II supradiaphragmatic Hodgkin's disease. *J Clin Oncol.* 1989;7:81–91.

15. Mauch P, Larson D, Osteen R, et al. Prognostic factors for positive surgical staging in patients with Hodgkin's disease. *J Clin Oncol.* 1990;8:257–265.

16. Donaldson SS, Moore MR, Rosenberg SA, Vosti KL. Characteristics of postsplenectomy bacteremia among patients with and without lymphoma. *New Engl J Med.* 1972;287:69–71.

17. Chilcote RR, Baehner RL, Hammond D. Septicemia and meningitis in children splenectomized for Hodgkin's disease. *New Engl J Med.* 1976;295:798–800.

18. Coker DD, Morris DM, Coleman JJ, et al. Infection among 210 patients with surgically staged Hodgkin's disease. *Am J Med.* 1983;75:97–109.

19. Keel A, Bennett B, Sarkar TK, et al. Splenectomy and infection in Hodgkin's disease. *Br J Surg.* 1983;70:278–280.

20. Rosner F, Zarrabi MH. Late infections following splenectomy in Hodgkin's disease. *Cancer Invest.* 1983;1:57–65.

21. Draisma A, Maffioli L, Gasparini M, et al. Gallium-67 as a tumor–seeking agent in lymphomas B—a review. *Tumori.* 1998;84(4):434–441.

22. Setoain FJ, Pons F, Herranz R, et al. 67Ga scintigraphy for the evaluation of recurrences and residual masses in patients with lymphoma. *Nucl Med Commun.* 1997;18(5):405–411.

23. Stroszczynski C, Amthauer H, Hosten N, et al. [Use of Ga-67 SPECT in patients with malignant lymphoma after primary chemotherapy for further treatment planning: comparison with spiral CT]. *Rofo.* 1997;167(5):458–466. German.

24. Kaplan WD, Jochelson MS, Herman TS, et al. Gallium-67 imaging: a predictor of residual tumor viability and clinical outcome in patients with diffuse large-cell lymphoma. *J Clin Oncol.* 1990;8:1966–1970.

25. Newman JS, Francis IR, Kaminski MS, Wahl RL. Imaging of lymphoma with PET with 2-[F-18]-fluoro-2-deoxy-D-glucose: correlation with CT. *Radiology.* 1994;190(1):111–116.

26. Moog F, Bangerter M, Diederichs CG, et al. Lymphoma: role of whole-body 2-deoxy-2-[F-18] fluoro-D-glucose (FDG) PET in nodal staging. *Radiology.* 1997;203(3):795–800.

27. Stumpe KD, Urbinelli M, Steinert HC, et al. Whole-body positron emission tomography using fluorodeoxyglucose for staging of lymphoma: effectiveness and comparison with computed tomography. *Eur J Nucl Med.* 1998;25(7):721–728.

28. Hoppe RT, Coleman CN, Cox RS, et al. The management of stage I-II Hodgkin's disease with irradiation alone or combined modality therapy: the Stanford Experience. *Blood.* 1982;59:455–465

29. Longo DL, Glatstein E, Duffey PL, et al. . Radiation therapy versus combination chemotherapy in the treatment of early-stage Hodgkin's disease: seven-year results of a prospective randomized trial. *J Clin Oncol.* 1991;9(6):906–917.

30. Carde P, Burgess JM, Henry-Amar M, et al. Clinical stages I and II Hodgkin's disease: a specifically tailored therapy according to prognostic factors. *J Clin Oncol.* 1988;6(2):239–252.

31. Tubiana M, Hayat M, Henry-Amar M, et al. Five-year results of the E.O.R.T.C. randomized study of splenectomy and spleen irradiation in clinical stages I and II of Hodgkin's disease. *Eur J Cancer.* 1981;17:355–363.

32. The International Lymphoma Non-Hodgkin's Lymphoma Prognostic Factors Project. A predictive model for aggressive non-Hodgkins lymphoma. *N Engl J Med.* 1993;329:987–994.

33. Armitage JO, Weisenburger DD, Hutchins M, et al. Chemotherapy for diffuse large-cell lymphoma B. Rapidly responding patients have more durable remissions. *J Clin Oncol.* 1986;4:160–164.

34. Engelhard M, Meusers P, Brittinger G, et al. Prospective multicenter trial for the response-adapted treatment of high-grade malignant non-Hodgkin's lymphomas: updated results of the COP-BLAM/IMVP-16 protocol with randomized adjuvant radiotherapy. *Ann Oncol.* 1991;2(suppl 2):177–180.

35. Kwak LW, Halpern J, Olshen RA, Horning SJ, Prognostic significance of actual dose intensity in diffuse large-cell lymphoma: results of a tree-structured survival analysis. *J Clin Oncol.* 1990;8:963–977.

36. Grogan TM, Lippman SM, Spier CM, et al. Independent prognostic significance of a nuclear proliferation antigen in diffuse large-cell lymphomas as determined by the monoclonal antibody Ki-67. *Blood.* 1988;71:1157–1160.

37. Miller TP, Lippman SM, Spier CM, et al. HLA-DR (la) immune phenotype predicts outcome for patients with diffuse large-cell lymphoma. *J Clin Invest.* 1988;82:370–372.

38. Swan F Jr, Velasquez WS, Tucker S, et al. A new serologic staging system for large-cell lymphomas based on initial β2-microglobulin and lactate dehydrogenase levels. *J Clin Oncol.* 1989;7:1518–1527.

39. Stoolman LM. Adhesion molecules controlling lymphocyte migration. *Cell.* 1989;56:907–910.

40. Picker LJ, Medeiros LJ, Weiss LM, et al. Expression of lymphocyte homing receptor antigen in non-Hodgkin's lymphoma. *Am J Pathol.* 1988;130:496–504.

41. Pals ST, Horst E, Ossekoppele GJ, et al. Expression of lymphocyte homing receptor as a mechanism of dissemination in non-Hodgkin's lymphoma. *Blood.* 1989; 72:885–888.

42. Jalkanen S, Joensuu H, Klemi P. Prognostic value of lymphocyte homing receptor and S phase fraction in non-Hodgkin's lymphoma. *Blood.* 1990;75:1549–1556.

43. Jalkanen S, Joensuu H, Soderstrom KO, Klemi P. Lymphocyte homing and clinical behavior of non-Hodgkin's lymphoma. *J Clin Invest.* 1991;87:1835–1840.

44. Horst E, Meijer CJ, Radaszkiewicz T, Ossekoppele GJ, et al. Adhesion molecules in the prognosis of diffuse large-cell lymphoma: expression of a lymphocyte homing receptor (CD44), LFA-1 (CD11a/18), and ICAM-1 (CD54). *Leukemia.* 1990;4:595–599.

95

Facial Plastic Surgery in Professional Voice Users

Stephen A. Goldstein, Wallace K. Dyer,
Mary J. Hawkshaw, and Robert Thayer Sataloff

The desire to look and stay young has been a wish of many throughout history. Short of finding the fountain of youth, the aging process progresses with predictable changes of the face and body. As the "baby boomer" generation and general population age, the desire for both surgical and nonsurgical intervention has never been greater. As science and medicine have progressed, our understanding and treatment options for aging have also improved, and recovery time has been minimized. Surgery remains the primary tool in the armamentarium of facial plastic surgeons, who recognize that the presentation and improvement of function is as important as the aesthetic results.

Plastic surgery, derived from the Greek word *plasti-cos,* meaning to mold, refers to the correction and repair of tissues in the body. Cosmetic surgery is a branch of plastic surgery utilized to enhance one's appearance. The desire to change one's appearance is usually motivated by the desire to improve self-image. The primary goal of many patients is to look younger than their age. Others consult a facial plastic surgeon seeking improvement in function after previous surgery or traumatic event.

People, especially in the entertainment industry, are subject to public scrutiny. This heightens a performer's inherent need to look good. Such visibility fosters considerations for cosmetic surgery to enhance their appearance and maintain their careers. In a very real sense, these concerns and goals affect everyone and may prompt a consultation with a facial plastic surgeon. This chapter focuses on the general issues of facial plastic surgery. Additional attention will be given to include instrumental performers and the possible effects of facial plastic surgery.

General Considerations

The first step any patient must make when considering cosmetic surgery is deciding what he or she wants to change. The ability to verbalize exactly what concerns him or her, and to what degree, makes the initial consultation far more productive. The facial plastic surgeon is an expert in the basic pathophysiology of aging and facial anatomy. Discussion of the patient's concerns, defining his or her problem, and clarifying what is actually achievable will guide patient options and help prevent an unhappy outcome. An important part of this process is ascertaining whether the patient's hopes are realistic. A small percentage of patients may never be happy, even with a perfect result. Recognition of this patient and obtaining preoperative psychological evaluation are particularly important.

The Aging Process

As we grow older, the aging face undergoes predictable change. The physical characteristics of aging become evident in the early to mid-30s with changes in skin color. Wrinkles with motion of the face and change in skin texture soon follow as the dermal elastic fibers become disorganized.[1] "Sags and bags," or descent of the facial fat pads, typically follow in the 40s and 50s. A portion of this change is genetic and can be envisioned easily by looking at our parents and grandparents. However, in most individuals, these intrinsic (genetic) and chronologic changes constitute only a fraction of the changes brought on by aging.

Dermatoheliosis, or photoaging, is the primary culprit contributing to aging changes in the face.[2,3] The cumulative effects of environmental factors cause changes on multiple levels. Sun damage to the skin is not only seen physically as texture and color change, but also includes underlying cellular damage. The architecture breaks down, leading to dermal elastosis and degradation of the supporting collagen. Ultraviolet (UV) light exposure accelerates this process by stimulating collagenase activity. Type I collagen is broken down and replaced with type III collagen. This contributes to the development of fine rhytids (wrinkles) and skin laxity. The majority of UV light damage occurs during childhood and teenage years. By age 30, early signs of aging become visible as dyschromias and telangectasias.[1]

As we reach our 40s and 50s, the complaint of submental fullness or a "turkey gobbler" deformity is common. Submental laxity of the platysma muscle creates fullness in the neck. As the neck continues to age, midline dehiscence occurs, leading to anterior banding of the platysma fibers. The result is a diminished cervicomental angle.[2,4] Concurrently, the underlying fat pads in the cheeks also have started to descend, contributing to midface ptosis and jowling. As jawline definition decreases and becomes a concern, a face-lift is needed to restore optimal appearance.

In addition to neck complaints, people frequently first notice periorbital changes. These are recognized as puffiness and bags under the eyes or droopy upper eyelids. The etiology is most commonly pseudoherniation of the orbital fat pads. Careful examination of the eyelids is necessary for proper diagnosis and treatment. Deep rhytids of the lateral orbits, or "crow's feet," occur mostly from hyperactivity of the underlying orbicularis oculi muscles. These circular muscles around each eye contract with forceful closure of the eyes and during smiling. The combination of these changes portrays a tired, worn and aged appearance. A blepharoplasty will address the eyelids only. The crow's feet and fine wrinkles are fixed most effectively with resurfacing techniques.

The upper third of the face includes the eyebrows and forehead. The musculature of the brows can be divided into two groups. The sole brow elevator is the frontalis muscle. Contraction and hyperactivity of this muscle can occur in response to chronic brow ptosis. The resultant effect as one tries to hold the brows off of the upper eyelids is horizontal rhytids. Vertical rhytids are caused from hyperactivity of the depressor muscles. The depressor muscles cause descent of the eyebrows. Overactivity of these muscles leads to a chronically tired or angry appearance. The use of botulinium A toxin (Botox, Allergan), has been used to weaken or paralyze these muscles temporarily. This allows unopposed movement of the frontalis muscle, raising the brow. Over time, a patient should be able to retrain the forehead musculature to primarily raise the eyebrows during facial expression. Patients who are unable to do this or who have excessive ptosis may benefit from a browlift procedure.

The Procedure(s)

The choice of which procedure or procedures will be performed results from the joint discussion and evaluation by the surgeon and patient. A myriad of procedures are available to enhance physical appearance (Table 95–1); and although a patient may have a specific idea about what is necessary, the experience of the surgeon is critical in determining exactly how to reach the desired goals. It is also important for the patient to understand the substantial limits of the surgeon's ability to predict the exact outcome of surgery. Many cosmetic surgeons now utilize computer imaging in their offices to assist patients' understanding of the surgical changes that can be accomplished. This is especially helpful in demonstrating the value of adjunct procedures (ie, chin augmentations performed with rhinoplasty) to the patient. However, it must be remem-

Table 95–1. Cosmetic Facial Plastic Surgery.

Blepharoplasty

Botulinum toxin injection

Browlift

Cheiloplasty (lip augmentation)

Injectable soft tissue augmentation (ie, collagen)

Malar and chin implants

Otoplasty

Rhinoplasty

Rhytidectomy

Skin resurfacing (chemabrasion, dermabrasion, laser)

Submentoplasty

bered that computer imaging provides only an estimate of the changes that can be made and does not represent a promise of the surgical result.

Limitations

The patient's general medical condition should be reviewed prior to scheduling any surgical procedure. In most cases, age itself is not a serious limiting factor. Except in cases of severe deformity, most young patients are advised to defer cosmetic surgery until full growth and maturation are achieved. A rule of thumb is to proceed when the adolescent has reached 90% stature compared to adults in the family. By then, growth plates essentially should be closed and further change in head size should be minimal.

Chronic cardiac, pulmonary, or renal conditions may severely increase the risk of surgery, even when utilizing local anesthesia. The vascular and cutaneous changes of aging can delay the healing process, which may result in suboptimal results. A coagulopathy would restrict severely and perhaps contraindicate most cosmetic operations. Allergies to medications may limit the choice of perioperative drugs, but should rarely prohibit surgery. Finally, cigarette smoking has been proven to cause significant problems and delays in postoperative healing after many cosmetic procedures. This is due to the microvascular constriction of end arterioles. Many surgeons will refuse to operate on patients who are actively smoking.

The timing of surgery often relates to personal life events. Whether it is a family wedding, a college reunion, or an important performance commitment, obligations must be assessed and adequate time for healing must be reserved by the patient. Environmental factors or the time of year during which certain procedures are scheduled also will vary. Skin resurfacing should be considered when patients know they will be out of the sun. This is important to prevent hyperpigmentation during the healing phase.

Finances

Costs should never be the major consideration influencing a medical decision. However, most cosmetic surgery is not covered by medical insurance; thus, the patient must bear most or all of the financial responsibility. Because of this, many plastic surgeons require payment for the surgery in advance. It is best if all discussions and arrangements regarding finances are completed with the surgeon or his or her staff prior to

any detailed surgical planning so that the patient is freed of these worries. At that point, all decisions can be made with only cosmetic and medical considerations in mind.

Special Considerations

When considering cosmetic plastic surgery, performers must evaluate not only the factors discussed above, but also must consider any effects these decisions will have on their careers in general. Informed consent regarding the desired procedures is necessary so that performers can learn about possible adverse outcomes. Complications that would affect the ability to sing or limit their performance schedule obviously must be avoided.

The Surgeon

In addition to the desired technical attributes of the operating surgeon, performers must look for a physician who is sympathetic to their special needs. The surgeon must be willing to make compromises in both surgical planning and operative technique to reduce the risk of damage to the performance apparatus. Additionally, the surgeon must be willing to provide detailed information about postoperative care and limitations and how these will affect the resumption of active performance. A cosmetic surgeon who has experience in caring for professional performers is optimal. What is most important is the surgeon's willingness to work with the performer's teacher, coach, and other specialists involved. These may include a laryngologist, voice teacher, and/or speech-language pathologist, if necessary, depending on the particular needs of the patient.

Anesthesia

The management of anesthesia is especially important. Intravenous sedation with long-acting local anesthetic can limit the need for general anesthesia. General anesthesia should be avoided if possible, especially in actors, singers, and even wind instrument players, because of the need for endotracheal intubation. Endotracheal intubation for general anesthesia can have many untoward effects on the larynx. Complications of intubation include vocal fold edema, granuloma formation, arytenoid cartilage dislocation, vocal fold paralysis, and damage to teeth. Other serious voice impairments related to superior laryngeal nerve dysfunction, pulmonary complications of general anesthesia such as atelectasis and pneumonia, vocal fold hemorrhage, and injury from gastroesophageal reflux laryngitis also can ocurr. Although the risk of these potential complications is greater with prolonged intubation, they have all been noted even after brief, "easy" intubations.[5]

Certain cosmetic plastic surgical procedures outside the face such as abdominoplasty, liposuction procedures, and augmentation and reduction mammoplasty usually require general anesthesia. When these procedures are desired, it is important that the surgeon and the anesthesiologist understand these risks so that intubation is performed by a skilled anesthesiologist who is knowledgeable regarding the special needs and concerns of performers. Additionally, a preoperative laryngoscopy should be performed to document vocal health; and an early postoperative laryngologic examination should be planned, so that any laryngeal lesions incurred can be treated promptly. In certain patients, general anesthesia may be considered when multiple procedures are to be performed simultaneously and the time involved would not allow for comfortable local anesthesia. The use of a long-acting local anesthetic such as marcaine may reduce the number of procedures requiring a general anesthesia. When possible, it may be best for the performer to plan the procedures at different times, thus avoiding general anesthesia, although perhaps incurring some additional scheduling problems.

Effects on Voice and Instrumental Performance

Performers must consider also the specifics of operative procedures that will alter the airway or vocal tract in any way. The upper airway starts at the nose and continues down to the trachea. Any change in the anatomy of the upper airway that affects airflow may create a change in voice quality. Rhinoplasty is one of the most common procedures performed by the facial plastic surgeon. This operation has probably led to more questions and anxiety among singers, other professional voice users, and instrumentalists than any other cosmetic procedure. In almost all cases, rhinoplasty can be performed safely and without adverse effect on vocal performance. However, the operation must be planned meticulously so that postoperative nasal airway obstruction or sinus obstruction can be avoided.

Primary rhinoplasty surgery has changed over the past 20 years. Reduction rhinoplasty once involved aggressive resection of the nasal cartilages to alter the shape and form of the nose. Unfortunately, the underlying support structures were often over-resected leading to nasal valve collapse, supra-alar pinching, and lateral wall weakness.[6] Today's rhinoplasty surgeon generally takes a more conservative approach using suture techniques to reposition tissues while minimizing cartilage resection. The recognition of existing nasal deformities and appropriate surgical technique should leave the patient with a functional as well as aesthetically pleasing nose.

Restriction of airflow after rhinoplasty, both during inspiration and expiration, can have multiple etiologies. Weakening of the caudal septum can cause a superior over-rotation and a deprojected nose. Excessive cartilage resection in the lower portion of the nose can lead to nasal valve incompetence, thus restricting nasal airflow on inspiration. Excessive removal of the dorsal hump can cause collapse of the upper lateral cartilages and, thus, narrowing of the middle nasal vault. If not recognized and corrected during rhinoplasty, obstruction will occur. Poorly controlled osteotomies of the nasal bones can lead to narrowing of the bony vault. Further collapse of the nose can occur postoperatively from scar contracture. These restrictive changes all potentially impair nasal airflow and alter vocal resonance.

In secondary rhinoplasty, the need for structural grafting may arise when the nasal skeletal framework has been weakened, malpositioned, or both. Such deformities can be addressed using such supportive techniques as the dynamic adjustable rotational tip (DART).[7] This works especially well for patients with the triad of a deprojection, superior rotation of the nasal tip, and nasal valve collapse. In both secondary and primary rhinoplasty, midline binding of the intercrural ligaments also will restore nasal tip support and prevent internal nasal valve collapse.

Excessive and poorly controlled septal surgery can result in septal perforations. This can cause chronic irritation, crusting, and whistling as well as nasal obstruction, which are very difficult to treat.[8] Anterior perforations also may cause whistling during respiration, which is extremely problematic for vocalists and wind players. When evaluating a performing artist for rhinoplasty, these potential complications must be kept in mind and discussed. Compromises deviating from the ideal cosmetic result must be made in some cases in order to provide both an acceptable cosmetic result and a long and healthy performing career.

The effects of nasal obstruction on the voice have been described only in two patient groups. Children with cleft lip and palate have problems primarily with velopalatal insufficiency. Airflow is (limited) normally at the level of the nasal valve. Hypernasality associated with cleft patients relates to the velopharyngeal orifice size. Warren et al found no effect on the relationship between resonance balance and velopharyngeal orifice size or nasal airflow.[9] Children with adenoid hypertrophy comprise the second group. Andreassen, et al tested the perceptual changes, acoustics, and aerodynamics after adenoidectomy.[10] There is an initial period of hypernasality but no significant perceptual change could be noted at 6 months. The lack of discernible differences may be due partly to the insensitivity of vocal assessment technology.[10]

Compromise of nasal breathing is extremely problematic for singers and wind players, especially those playing double reed instruments such as the oboe and bassoon. Ordinarily, singers breathe through their noses whenever possible, thus warming, filtering, and humidifying expired air. When forced to breathe almost exclusively through their mouths, voice dysfunction may ensue. Double reed players use circular breathing, a technique that allows them to play long, uninterrupted phrases without apparently taking a breath. Nasal obstruction (or whistling) is a severe problem for these performers and, in some cases, may disable them.

Most other considerations about specific surgical techniques involve their influence on postoperative recovery. The surgeon must be very careful to explain all possible postoperative changes, even those considered minor in other patient populations. The use of fibrin-based tissue adhesives may decrease bruising and general recovery time substantially and should be considered in all patients, but especially in performers. The desired tightness of the skin of the face and neck after such procedures as face-lift, chemical peel, and liposuction must be elucidated in detail. This will allow the performer to have realistic expectations when he or she resumes performance.

Such changes may be most unsettling to a singer, violinist or violist, or woodwind or brass player (if the embouchure is affected) and may lead to substantial deleterious changes in technique unless precautions are taken. Special care also should be taken when performing procedures in the neck or chin in violinists or violists. Procedures such as face-lifts or submentoplasty may cause alterations in the way the instrument is held. Consequent neck and shoulder pain may result in performance impairment. In general, it is also not advisable to resect the skin on the neck at the point of instrument contact, even though it is commonly unsightly. Even incisions must be planned with care to avoid loss of sensation. Neck surgery in singers and actors also may lead to slight changes in technique that can be quite problematic.

Postoperative Care

A detailed, well-organized postoperative care program is essential to the recovery of the patient. A team approach to cosmetic surgery is ideal. The team should include the surgeon, a nurse, anesthesiologist, and office staff. The nurse should meet with patients and a family member prior to surgery to alleviate concerns and reaffirm realistic expectations. At this time, they can review instructions, including appropriate medications and post-operative care. The nurse can be especially helpful if he or she has had experience in dealing with professional performers.

Appropriate follow-up is sometimes more important than the actual surgery itself. The majority of cosmetic procedures are performed on an outpatient basis. Patients often are concerned about their appearance immediately after surgery. The use of drains and dressings can be minimized or even eliminated with the use of tissue adhesives. These adhesives reduce ecchymosis and edema, diminishing downtime for the patient.

Usually, 1 to 3 days are necessary to recover general strength after surgery. Restriction of activity is essential to minimize the risk of post-operative bleeding and edema. The risk for post-operative bleeding is greatest in the first 48 hours. Early recognition of hematomas or seromas is important because they compromise healing and the final result. Generally, patients are asked to fully restrict their activities for 1 week. Usually by the end of the first week, patients are asked to start taking long, easy walks. In the second week, activity is increased gradually in a fractionated manner. Normal activity should be attained by the end of the second week.

Specific performance and practice restrictions must be discussed in detail during the preoperative meeting. The artist must be advised both of the routine restrictions to ensure a smooth recovery and any additional restrictions that would result from postoperative complications. Patients who require general anesthesia must be examined for vocal fold edema and irritation prior to returning to active voice use. For most professionals, musical performance is an extremely energetic and a physically demanding activity. The usual 1 to 2 weeks of restrictions apply for most performing activities, but judgments must be individualized based on the procedure performed and the individual artist's skill and requirements. Light voice activity and exercising may be obtainable as early as 72 hours after some cosmetic procedures, but longer restrictions are prudent whenever the strain associated with supported singing may increase the risk of bleeding or when swelling, dressings, packing, or nasal obstruction alters resonance, tactile sensation or self audition (Table 95–2). Dancing should not be permitted for 2 weeks following surgery. Total abstinence from musical performance is rarely necessary. Complete voice rest is not indicated unless there is vocal fold damage from intubation or impairment of pulmonary or abdominal support functions.

The Rehabilitative Team

Treatment of professional voice users by an interdisciplinary team has now become accepted as state-of-the-art care. The team often involves more than just the laryngologist, speech-language pathologist, singing voice specialist, and acting-voice specialist. The facial plastic surgeon must be incorporated into this team to help ensure that this support structure exists for the patient. A facial plastic surgeon who has experience caring for the professional performer is optimal.[11] This is especially true if the patient is not involved with these professionals on a regular basis. This team can coordinate appointments and schedules so that the patient has adequate vocal support both before and after surgery. Similar interdisciplinary support teams for voice and nonvoice performers can be found through various arts-medicine centers and can be developed with interested specialists and performance teachers.

For singers, once the surgery and the initial healing phase are complete, unrestricted vocalization may be resumed. Vocalists should work with their teachers or coaches frequently in the postoperative period. This will assist in safe resumption of voice use with optimal technique and ensure that the vocalist does not rely on his or her own potentially altered perception of vocal quality. It is the experience of the authors (RTS, SAG) that singers who feel their voices have "changed" after facial surgery usually are noting a change primarily in their perception of their own voices rather than any objective alteration of its true quality. This is especially so after rhinoplasty. We have had similar experience with wind players. Observation and advice by the patient's vocal coach and laryngologist are critical in maintaining proper vocal technique in the face of both the perceived and any real changes in vocal quality. Scheduling performances too soon after surgery may pressure the patient and should be avoided. This requires detailed, realistic discussions between the patient, surgeon, and voice teacher and may also include the manager and a laryngologist, so that appropriate postoperative planning is made prior to surgery.

Table 95–2. Commonly Performed Cosmetic Procedures.

Procedure	Anesthesia[b]	Dressings[a]	Recovery Time[a]	Voice Restrictions[a]
Blepharoplasty	Local[b]	None	1	2–7
Botulinum toxin	Local	None	2–3 hours	None
Chemabrasion (intermediate and deep)	Local[b]	1–2	2	1
Collagen injection	Local	None	2–3 hours	None
Dermabrasion	Local[b] (sedation)	1–2	2	1
Forehead lift	Local[b] or general	None	1	None
Submental-Lipectomy	Local[b]	1	1	1–2
Liposuction	General	1–2	1	1–2
Mentoplasty	Local[b]	None	1	None
Otoplasty	Local or general	1	1	None
Rhinoplasty	Local or general	1	1	2–6
Rhytidetomy	Local or general	None	2	2–6

[a] in weeks; [b] Local anesthesia may be used in conjunction with sedation.

Voice Cosmesis

Cosmetic surgeons should be aware of issues related to vocal aging that may affect voice professionals but which are often even more prominent in patients without vocal training. Even in patients who have had excellent results following rhinoplasty, face-lift surgery, and blepharoplasty, an "old voice" can communicate chronological age and spoil the desired effect. Although research data are lacking, the author's (RTS) experience indicates that appropriate intervention can alter many of the changes associated with vocal aging. Frequently, voice therapy is sufficient. When therapy is not adequate to control breathiness and weakness associated with vocal bowing, medialization procedures many be helpful. Treatment of mild tremor is also a useful adjunct. Many of the techniques discussed throughout this book for management of voice disorders associated with disease are also relevant for vocal changes associated with aging. A program to restore youthful vocal quality (a "voice cosmesis program") should be considered for any patient undergoing cosmetic surgery for aging changes, particularly if the person can be identified as "elderly" during telephone conversations.

Conclusion

Understanding the needs of the vocal performer is essential when planning facial plastic and reconstructive surgery. Safe and effective cosmetic surgery can be performed with proper knowledge of an artist's professional requirements. If all of the performer's questions and concerns are dealt with preoperatively, cosmetic surgery can be accomplished and in fact encouraged in this population. With the priorities of general health vocal tract function and cosmesis kept in mind, in nearly all cases, the end result should be a happy, attractive, and content performing artist.

References

1. Glogau RG. Physiologic and structural changes associated with aging skin. *Dermatol Clin.* 1997;15(4):555–558.
2. Zimbler MS, Kokoska MS, Thomas JR. Anatomy and pathophysiology of facial aging. *Facial Plast Surg Clin North Am.* 2001;9(2):179–188.
3. Kligman LH. Photoaging: manifestations, prevention and treatment. *Dermatol Clin.* 1986;4:517–528.
4. Toft KM, Blackwell KE, Keller GS. Submentoplasty: an anatomical approach. *Facial Plast Surg Clin North Am.* 2000;8(2):183–193.
5. Gallivan GJ, Dawson LA, Robbins LD. Critical care perspective: videolaryngoscopy after intubation: implications for voice. *J Voice.* 1989;3:76–80.
6. Toriumi DM. Structure approach in rhinoplasty. *Facial Plast Surg Clin North Am.* 2002 10(1):1–22.
7. Dyer WK Jr, Yune M. Structural grafting in rhinoplasty. *Facial Plast Surg.* 1997;13(4):269–277.
8. Holt GR, Garner ET, McLary D. Postoperative sequelae and complcations of rhinoplasty. *Otolaryngol Clin North Am.* 1987;20:853–876.
9. Warren DW, Dalston RM, Mayo R. Hypernasality and velopharyngeal impairment. *Cleft Palate Craniofac J.* 1994;31(4):257–262.
10. Andreassen ML, Leeper HA, MacRae DL, Nicholson IR. Aerodynamic, acoustic, and perceptual changes following adnoidectomy. *Cleft Palate Craniofac J.* 1994;31(4):263–270.
11. Sataloff RT. Professional singers: the science and art of clinical care. *Am J Otolaryngol.* 1981;2:251–266.

96

Sleep-disordered Breathing: Considerations in the Surgical Management for the Professional Voice User

Mark S. Courey

The surgical management of sleep-disordered breathing is a challenging clinical problem in all patients regardless of their voice use demands. Traditionally, the surgical management of sleep-disordered breathing has been directed at the soft tissue portions of the extrathoracic airway. To trained vocal professionals, muscular control of this tissue is often considered critical to the production of their performance voice. Therefore, in professional voice users, surgical intervention on this tissue needs to be undertaken with great caution.

Briefly, the term sleep-disordered breathing refers to snoring, frank obstructive sleep apnea, and the upper airway resistance syndrome.[1] It affects as many as 40 million Americans and is due to complete or partial collapse of the extrathoracic airway structures.[2] This collapse occurs during sleep periods and results in sleep interruption or fragmentation. These interruptions lead to microarousals, which alter sleep patterns and lead to the sensations of nonrestorative sleep and excess daytime somnolence. Sleep apnea was first described as a medical condition in the middle of the 19th century. Labeled Pickwickian syndrome, surgical treatment was undertaken through tracheotomy. Subsequently, an association with pharyngeal soft tissue redundancy was uncovered; and the mainstay of surgical therapy was redirected toward reduction of excess pharyngeal soft tissue.[3] However, since the inception of pharyngeal surgery in the form of tonsillectomy and uvulopalatopharyngoplasty (UPPP) in the mid-1960s,[4] relatively little information has been obtained to support its success in the long-term management of

sleep apnea.[5] The procedure is often recommended as the initial step in surgical management in all patients with obstructive sleep apnea. However, the results are often variable and somewhat unpredictable, even when performed by the most experienced surgeons. In addition, the ability to obtain meaningful long-term follow-up is difficult secondary to poor patient compliance and cost factors of follow-up studies. Therefore, even after more than 30 years of surgical history, the true efficacy of UPPP/tonsillectomy in the management of sleep-disordered breathing remains unknown. Some studies suggest long-term efficacy rates as low as 30 to 50%.[6-10]

There are at least two reasons for the failure of UPPP to relieve obstructive apnea. First, variations in techniques among surgeons may affect postoperative airway size and second, the tonsils and palate may not be the site of airway occlusion.[1] A comparison of outcomes of UPPP with or without tonsillectomy to relieve obstructive sleep apnea syndrome (OSAS) between two large groups of surgeons, however, indicates similar success rate for both groups.[11] Therefore, it is more likely that the lack of success is due to the inadequacy of the procedure to relieve the region of airway obstruction rather than variations in surgical technique.

Sleep-disordered breathing is associated with an increased incidence of heart disease, hypertension, and stroke. A causal relationship has not been identified but is suggested through some limited studies of treatment with continuous positive airway pressure (CPAP), which have shown that treatment results in reduction of morbidity from these associated health problems.[12,13] Therefore, treatment of even mild sleep apnea is essential. There are also some indications that tendencies for sleep-disordered breathing are inherited along with the tendencies for cardiovascular disease rather than one causing the other. Population studies have demonstrated that expression of the apolipoprotein E epsilon4 allele is an independent risk factor for sleep-disordered breathing regardless of patient age, sex, body mass index, and ethnicity.[14]

Diagnosis

Sleep-disordered breathing is most commonly suspected on the basis of patient history. However, polysomnography is required to diagnose obstructive sleep apnea,[15] and a positive therapeutic response to CPAP is required to diagnose the upper airway resistance syndrome.[16] Polysomnography is the study of respiration, heart rate, arterial saturation, cardiac arrhythmia, and sleep stages during sleep. Informally called a sleep study, polysomnography testing is used to measure the number of times a patient stops breathing or experiences hypoventilation during sleep. The number of apneic and hypoxemic events per hour of sleep is determined and labeled the apnea/hypopnea index (AHI) or the respiratory disturbance index (RDI). More than 5 events per hour of sleep have been determined to represent an abnormal number.[15] Patients, however, may not report symptoms until experiencing more than 20 events per hour. Polysomnography can be accomplished with equally reliable results through either inpatient or outpatient testing depending on the clinician's and patient's preference.[17] The advantages of inpatient testing include the ability to obtain more complete EEG data and the improved likelihood of insurance coverage. In the traveling performer, outpatient studies may be easier to schedule; because they can be completed in hotel rooms and avoid a night spent in the sleep laboratory. Several centralized testing services provide reliable equipment for outpatient use.

Frequently, patients present with complaints of only simple snoring. Clinicians must determine whether snoring is an isolated problem or if more severe sleep disorders coexist. This can be accomplished through questionnaires designed to assess the degree of daytime sleepiness experienced by the patient in different situations. The Epworth Sleepiness Scale is an instrument widely used for this purpose (Fig 96–1). Total scores of 10 or greater are associated with an increased incidence of apnea; and patients with elevated scores should undergo polysomnography prior to further in-

tervention. Often patients are in denial of their illness and may, therefore, underrepresent their degree of daytime somnolence in historical information.[18] To control for patient denial, the spouse or bed-partner must be interviewed regarding witnessed apneic episodes and the patient's sleepiness in social situations. If the bed-partner discloses contradictory information, then polysomnography is most likely warranted. In addition, the existence of physical findings and comorbidities, such as obesity (more than 15% over ideal weight), neck circumference larger than 16.5 inches,[15] retrognathia, hypertension, and heart disease in patients with snoring should alert the clinician to potential obstructive apnea. Finally, a family history of apnea in first-degree relatives is also associated with an increased incidence of sleep apnea.[14] If any of these conditions exist, then it is prudent to proceed to polysomnography prior to intervention for snoring.

Physical Examination

When professional voice patients present with complaints of sleep-disordered breathing, physical examination potentially can be used to identify the source of the disorder and aid in determining surgical candidacy. Body habitus and body mass index (BMI) should be assessed first. Many Internet sites are available to determine BMI from patient weight and height. Obesity is the major disorder associated with sleep apnea.[19]

In the absence of morbid obesity, several other physical characteristics also may be associated with an increased likelihood of sleep apnea. In men, neck circumference should be measured; because a circumference larger than 16.5 inches has been shown to correlate with sleep apnea.[20] The hyoid to mental length and dental occlusion need to be assessed as indicators of retrognathia. In the oropharynx, palatal size, including Mallampati classification[21] and the presence of tonsil[22] tissue are associated with an increased incidence of apnea. Nasal and nasopharyngeal examination determining septal deviation, turbinate hypertrophy, nasopharyngeal masses, and adenoid hyperplasia as sources of nasal airflow obstruction is also critical; because nasal obstruction may exacerbate obstructive apnea or in itself interrupt sleep patterns through patient discomfort. Hypopharyngeal and laryngeal examinations need to be performed to exclude masses or stenosis as sources of airway obstruction.

Dynamic airway evaluation with flexible fiberoptic airway examination should be performed. The nose is anesthetized, and the patient placed in a comfortable, recumbent position. The fiberoptic scope is inserted through the patient's nose above the middle turbinate,

The Epworth Sleepiness Scale

Name: _____   Date: _____

Date of Birth: _____   Sex: Male / Female

How likely are you to doze off or fall asleep in the following situations, in contrast to feeling just tired? This refers to your usual way of life in recent times; even if you have not done some of these things recently, try to work out how they would have affected you. Use the following scale to choose the most appropriate number for each situation:

   0= would *never* doze

   1 = *slight* chance of dozing

   2= *moderate* chance of dozing

   3 = *high* chance of dozing

Situation   **Chance of Dozing**

1. Sitting and reading.   _____

2. Watching TV.   _____

3. Sitting, inactive in a public place (e.g., a theater or a meeting).   _____

4. As a passenger in a car for an hour without a break.   _____

5. Lying down to rest in the afternoon when circumstances permit.   _____

6. Sitting and talking to someone.   _____

7. Sitting quietly after lunch without alcohol.   _____

8. In a car, while stopped for a few minutes in the traffic.   _____

Thank you for your cooperation.

Fig 96–1. The Epworth Sleepiness Scale. For a total score greater than 10, polysomnography is recommended prior to surgical intervention.

if possible. This allows the scope to be positioned above the nasopharyngeal inlet. Relaxed respiration is observed. The patient is asked to snore while places of palatal flutter are identified and recorded. Next, the patient is asked to exhale. At the end of exhalation, the nares are gently compressed around the scope; and the patient is instructed to inhale forcibly. This portion of the examination, known as the Muller maneuver, is used to assess the degree and direction of airway collapse at the palatal level. With the nares only partially occluded, the patient is asked to snore to determine if this intensifies palatal flutter or the degree of collapse. The fiberoptic scope is then advanced into the oropharynx where the Muller maneuver is repeated to evaluate the degree and position of oropharyngeal and hypopharyngeal collapse. Finally, the scope is held in the oropharynx while the patient is asked to relax the jaw. This usually results in slight mandibular opening with separation of the teeth. The lips may or may not part. However, as the muscles of mastication are relaxed, the tongue base also relaxes; and the mandible rotates downward and posteriorly with joint space opening slightly. This more closely approximates mandibular position during the muscularly relaxed stages of sleep when apnea is more likely to occur. With the fiberoptic scope, the retrolingual airway space is evaluated.

Often, near-complete airway occlusion in the relaxed state, either due to the tongue base or epiglottis touching the posterior pharyngeal wall, can be identified (Fig 96–2).

Through repeated application of the Muller maneuver in the nasopharynx and oropharynx, the site or sites of airway obstruction can be identified. Reproducibility of the Muller maneuver has been demonstrated, and the severity of collapse is moderately correlated with the RDI.[23] Fujita described a classification system that is commonly used to refer to the level(s) of obstruction.[24] Class I indicates isolated obstruction at the palatal level, class II refers to isolated obstruction at the base of tongue region, and class III describes obstruction at both levels. In the author's experience, patients with prominent tongue base obstruction are unlikely to respond to procedures designed to reduce palatal and tonsil tissue.

Medical Management Strategies

Unfortunately, no medications have been shown to be significantly efficacious for amelioration of the sleep-disordered breathing difficulties described in the beginning of this chapter. Theoretically, medications that decrease the amount of rapid eye movement (REM) sleep could be beneficial; because apneic episodes occur more commonly during the muscle relaxation that occurs in REM sleep. The tricyclic antidepressant protriptyline has been tried with some success, but the side effects limit its usefulness.[25,26] Specifically, dry mucous membranes, a common side effect with all tricyclics, may have a negative impact on vocal fold vibratory quality in professional voice patients. Also,

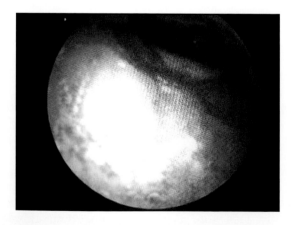

Fig 96–2. The appearance of the retrolingual airway with the patient in a relaxed, supine position. There is significant narrowing at this level.

progesterone has been tried as a respiratory stimulant with minimal benefit.[27]

For the treatment of snoring, many advertised over-the-counter products are available. One is designed to spray directly on the palate to create temporary stiffening and reduction of flutter. Only anecdotal reports of success are available.

Continuous positive airway pressure (CPAP) and/or biphasic airway pressure (BiPAP) constitute the mainstay of medical therapy for the treatment of sleep-disordered breathing.[28] The devices are designed with a pump to force air into the airway at a specified pressure. The pressure is titrated during polysomnography to be slightly greater than the minimum pressure required to prevent airway collapse. Many patients who require relatively high pressures on CPAP to maintain airway opening complain that exhalation against the machine is difficult. They can develop gastric distention. Therefore, BiPAP was designed to decrease the pressure in phasic manner to facilitate exhalation.[29] If patients tolerate CPAP or BiPAP and use it for at least 4 to 6 hours nightly, daytime hypersomnolence and the morbidity from cardiovascular disease and hypertension has been shown to be reduced. However, difficulties with patient compliance secondary to the awkward nature of the equipment, unpleasant sensations, drying and irritation of the mucous membranes, and potential insufflation of the eustachian tubes and paranasal sinuses lead to less than optimal usage. Attempts at rendering the devices more comfortable through the addition of humidifiers, gradual on mechanisms, and overall reduction to the lowest effective pressure have shown some benefit; but overall compliance and patient satisfaction remain in the range of 50 to 80%.[30] Patients often report greater usage than the amount that can be documented by computer chips placed in the appliance. For the traveling voice professional, the machine, the size of a small suitcase, must be carried with them while traveling. In foreign countries, electrical systems my not accommodate standard 110 voltage. Finally, the drying effects of the machine on the mucosal surfaces can be particularly problematic in singers.

Dental or oral appliances are designed to maintain the mandible in a forward and anterior position.[31,32] Remember that, during relaxation, the teeth come out of centric occlusion; and the mandible rotates posteriorly and downward. Secondary to this motion, the tongue base is displaced into the airway space. Dental appliances work well for patients in whom the site of airway obstruction is the tongue base and have been shown to reduce the RDI. Limited patient compliance secondary to the development of temporomandibular pain syndromes and generalized discomfort have been reported anecdotally, but rarely seen in the author's practice. In addition, reports of pain resolved when appliance usage was discontinued. Occasionally, some minor difficulty with movement of dentition has been seen; but this has not been overly problematic for the patients.

Behavioral Management Strategies

Obesity remains a large contributing factor to the development of sleep-disordered breathing. Seventy percent of patients with obstructive apnea are more than 15% over ideal body weight. Body mass index synergistically interacts with craniofacial characteristics to predispose patients to the development of sleep apnea.[33] Weight reduction, therefore, is an effective therapy for reducing or eliminating sleep-disordered breathing. Weight reduction should be accomplished through conservative dietary changes and increases in daily activity. A combined program with weight training and aerobic exercise will yield the best results. In the vocal professional rapid weight loss, which can be associated with severe muscular wasting, should be avoided. Muscle wasting can result in changes in thyroarytenoid muscle bulk, which will impact negatively on vocal characteristics. Once atrophy of musculature has been induced by prolonged starvation status, it may be difficult to regain muscle bulk, particularly in the thyroarytenoid muscles. This has been observed in the aging population that has experienced rapid weight loss due to an illness. Even though the patient regains strength in other areas, the vocal changes that occurred at the time of the illness never completely recover. Bariatric surgery, therefore, needs to be undertaken with caution in the vocal professional. Unfortunately, no studies exist on changes in voice after dramatic weight reductions of more than 150 pounds.

Some patients experience worse snoring or sleep apnea when sleeping in certain positions. Most commonly, problems occur while supine. Patients, therefore, may benefit from attempts to sleep in a lateral, prone, or semi-upright position. Some have suggested that sewing tennis balls into the back of a nightshirt may be helpful.[34] Again, specific benefits have not been studied; and patients have reported that this can be uncomfortable. When loud snoring, either with or without apnea, is disturbing to the bed-partner, serious consideration should be given to the use of separate bedrooms as one facet of treatment prior to undertaking surgical intervention.

Surgical Management Strategies

Surgical management strategies should be tailored to the needs of individual patients. No one surgical procedure offers all patients an overwhelming chance for cure. In addition, potentially negative side effects from alterations in the pharyngeal anatomy of professional singers, even in well-performed operations, may outweigh the potential benefits. Therefore, surgical therapy for sleep-disordered breathing in professional voice patients should be considered only after all medical and behavioral therapies have failed. The patient must understand and accept the chance that, even in the hands of the most experienced surgeon, his or her voice may be permanently altered in a negative manner.

If surgery is to be undertaken, then flexible fiberoptic endoscopy, as described previously, may provide some ability to identify the level of the problem within the airway and direct the choice of surgical intervention. Not all patients with sleep apnea should undergo UPPP. The success of UPPP is dependent on the amount of tissue removed, and UPPP has reduced success rates in the face of previous tonsillectomy.[22] Therefore, for patients who have small palates and minimal tonsil tissue, it may be prudent to consider tongue base procedures prior to palatal reduction procedures. This is particularly important if flexible endoscopy reveals a Fujita class II or III pattern of airway collapse. Patients with tonsil and/or adenoid hyperplasia may benefit from adenotonsillectomy alone. This has been demonstrated as efficacious in children, and is also true in adults with significant tonsillar hyperplasia.[35] Performance of adenoidectomy with simultaneous UPPP should be avoided, because the risk of velopharyngeal stenosis is increased.

With regard to palatal and tonsil surgery for the management of sleep-disordered breathing, all surgical interventions will affect the amount of palatal tissue and distensibility. In the worst case scenario, surgery could result in the inability to close the velopharyngeal port. This could occur, without medical negligence, even in the most experienced hands. The debate regarding function of the velum during singing has not been settled. Some believe that absolute closure is mandatory for the production of a well-balanced classical tone,[36] whereas others have demonstrated that at times a significant velar opening persisted.[37] In interviewing singers, most classically trained singers report that they strive for a particular and unique sensation of velar function and position during singing voice production. Therefore, alteration in velar function, short of frank insufficiency, may be enough to create problems with vocal production. Alterations in pharyngeal configuration and distensibility should at least have some theoretical impact on formant frequencies. Therefore, until this area of uncertainty is better defined, palatal intervention in trained classical singers needs to be undertaken with great caution and full informed consent.

Nasal obstruction can play a significant role in sleep-disordered breathing. The treatment of nasal obstruction has been shown to alleviate symptoms of mild apnea and snoring.[38,39] Anecdotally, patients with complete nasal obstruction due to polyposis have had complete resolution of moderate to severe sleep apnea with surgical excision of the polyps. With regard to the effects on voice, professional voice users usually respond well to septoplasty, turbinate reduction, and polypectomy. Unfortunately, voice data from this population do not exist, but patients usually report a better sense of frontal placement and less laryngeal tension.

Radiofrequency soft tissue ablation has been popularized recently for the treatment of snoring and mild sleep apnea. Radiofrequency works by heating the tissues past the point of protein denaturization. Coagulation necrosis occurs, and resorption of the injured tissue leads to volumetric reduction. Controlled, industry-sponsored clinical trials with several month follow-up have established the efficacy of this form of treatment to relieve snoring.[40] For the management of snoring, the radiofrequency probe is placed into the soft palate; and energy is delivered. As with all procedures on the palate, the procedure results in changes to the velum. Patients do not usually complain of velopharyngeal insufficiency, but reports of complications with uvular necrosis and palatal fistula do exist, and no controlled studies on the effects of voice have been published. Other procedures designed to stiffen or reduce the palatal tissue, such as injection snoreplasty, may have the same effects on vocal function as those mentioned for radiofrequency palatal reduction.[41] The effects on voice and formant structure remain unknown and should be better defined in nonprofessional voice users before using these procedure routinely in trained singers.

The effects of traditional UPPP and isolated tonsillectomy on voice have been studied at three separate institutions.[42-44] With regard to voice, two studies demonstrated no significant change in fundamental frequency (F_0); and one study on 12 adult male subjects demonstrated a significant rise in the postoperative F_0. It is unclear how surgery on the pharynx could result in changes of the vibratory function of the vocal folds. From a mechanical standpoint, oropharyngeal stiffening and reduction of mass intuitively seem too distant to directly affect laryngeal vibratory function. The same authors demonstrated a significant lowering of the second formant (F_2) in two of the five vowels studied. This change, measured by linear predictive coding (LPC) methods, was related to amount of tissue removed. In the other two studies different re-

sults were obtained. In one, the F_2 was increased while the F_1 was decreased; in the other study, no consistent changes in formant frequencies were identified. Although it is discouraging that consistent trends across all studies were not identified, some of the disparity could be secondary to one study being performed in children and varying methods of LPC analysis in the other two studies. These results represent at least an attempt to understand changes in spectral analysis of voice after pharyngeal surgery and will hopefully stimulate larger studies.

Laser assisted uvuloplasty (LAUP) was first reported by Kamami in the early 1980s and has been demonstrated as effective for the management of isolated snoring.[45] In the clinic, the carbon dioxide laser is used to sequentially shorten the palate until snoring is symptomatically abolished. The advantage of LAUP over traditional UPPP is reduction in the risk of velopharyngeal insufficiency. The disadvantage is that an average of three procedures, each 6 weeks apart, is required to obtain adequate results in the majority of patients. Each procedure is associated with significant postoperative pain, which usually requires narcotic analgesics for control. Studies on the management of mild or moderate apnea with LAUP have shown mixed results with some indicating fair relief and others showing no improvement.[46,47] The variability in results may be secondary to patient selection and technique of LAUP. With LAUP, the effects on voice have not been published. The risk of frank velopharyngeal insufficiency (VPI) is significantly reduced, but the overall change in velar function, stiffness and mass may have some effect on formant structure and spectral analysis.

In the early 1990s, recognizing that airway obstruction in sleep-disordered breathing commonly occurred at multiple levels within the airway, Riley and Powell[48,49] began reporting on the use of combined surgical techniques designed to expand the airway at multiple levels. Initially, these surgeons reported improvements in sleep-disordered breathing with multilevel interventions that were greater than improvement rates achieved with traditional UPPP/tonsillectomy alone. Multilevel airway augmentation is accomplished through the addition of hyoid advancement and genioglossal advancement procedures, which are performed in conjunction with a traditional UPPP/tonsillectomy. The procedures may be performed simultaneously or in a staged manner. The effects on voice have not been studied. In one anecdotal report, the patient, an untrained songwriter, underwent simultaneous septoplasty, hyoid advancement over the thyroid prominence, inferior boarder genioglossal advancement, and UPPP. He denied symptoms of velopharyngeal insufficiency (VPI) and reported that his voice seemed more "crisp" than it had preoperatively. He experienced a 60% reduction in his RDI and was willing to tolerate the voice changes for relief of symptoms. He could not tolerate CPAP; and as a songwriter, his performance voice was not critical in his career. Other patients experience different vocal outcomes. One patient reports increased vocal fatigue with a restriction in range. He finds articulation is difficult. This patient had UPPP/tonsillectomy, which may account for some of his problems. Simultaneous keyhole genioglossal advancement and hyoid advancement over the thyroid prominence with suture stabilization were carried out. The postoperative airway appearance can be seen in Figure 96–3. With Muller maneuver, the velopharynx closes approximately 80%; and the tongue base demonstrates near complete airway collapse. The laryngeal configuration, however, is interesting; because the anterior commissure is difficult to visualize and the supraglottis remains constricted in an anterior-to-posterior direction. This is presumed to be secondary to compression of the thyrohyoid space, which results in supraglottic constriction, as seen in muscle tension dysphonia. This patient's thyrohyoid space, however, was surgically constricted and remained so even at rest. This finding can be demonstrated in most patients in whom the hyoid bone has been advanced down and over the thyroid prominence. The effects on voice have not been studied other than previously mentioned anecdotal reports. It seems reasonable that some alteration in formant structure would occur. If enough muscular control remained, the patient could likely compensate for these changes; but the extra muscular effort required for compensation may account for the report of early vocal fatigue in our one patient.

Vocal changes from procedures designed to advance or shrink the tongue base have not been reported. These procedures include midline glossectomy, radiofrequency tongue base reduction, and maxillary/mandibular advancement. Commonly, midline glossectomy and RF tongue base ablation are undertaken only after failure of previous UPPP/tonsillectomy. Therefore, it would be difficult to obtain results of vocal changes from these procedures in isolation. However, both procedures have the risk of injury to the hypoglossal nerve and may result in reduction of overall tongue mobility from scarring alone.[50-52] This will potentially affect articulation and may alter the singer's ability to raise or lower the larynx. In the classically trained singer, this could create significant vocal difficulties.

Maxillomandibular advancement (MMA) procedures are designed to expand the airway in the anterior-to-posterior direction at all levels throughout the pharynx. The muscular slings of the velum, oropharynx, and hypopharynx are repositioned. They are not incised, nor is the amount of muscular tissue reduced. During LeForte I osteotomy for maxillary advancement, simultaneous septoplasty can be performed. Mandibular advancement is created through sagittal osteotomies. The facial segments are plated or screwed into the new position. Temporary maxillomandibular fixation with arch bars may be required. Advancements of up to 12 to 14 mm have been reported with good long-term skeletal stability even without bone grafting. Success rates of more than 90% have been reported by multiple surgeons.[53-55] In these instances, success is defined as a reduction in the RDI to less than 10. Complications include temporary, or rarely, permanent injury to sensory nerves. Neither motor deficits nor incidences of velopharyngeal insufficiency have been reported, even when performed after UPPP/tonsillectomy. In view of this information, serious consideration should be given to MMA as a primary mode of surgical treatment for patients with obstructive apnea, particularly if septal deviation and hyperplastic tonsillar and adenoid tissue are not present. At our institution, younger patients are considered for primary MMA if they fit these conditions and weight reduction has failed to alleviate their apnea. Eighty percent of patients who have undergone previous UPPP/tonsillectomy report less postoperative discomfort/pain with MMA. Unfortunately, the effects on voice have not been studied. Expansion of the pharynx theoretically could lead to changes in voice, which may be identified on spectral analysis of formant frequencies. How repositioning would change the sensation of velar function also remains unknown.

Tracheostomy with the creation of a permanent skin-lined tract remains a viable option for patients resistant to other modes of therapy.[56] The tract can be fitted with a plug for use during daily activities. The plug appliance can be removed during sleep periods. These plugs are often airtight for normal vocal activities; however, vocal activities that require high subglottal pressure may induce air leakage. In addition, suturing the neck skin to the trachea may limit laryngeal mobility; and tracheal stenosis is a potential complication. Small clear plastic devices that can be worn without ties around the neck are available. This approach has worked in nonsinging vocal professionals, such as teachers and trial attorneys. The appliance can be hidden under the high collar of a shirt or blouse. However, in a professional singer, who requires freedom of neck movement and may need elevation of subglottal pressures for performance singing, the tracheostomy could be problematic.

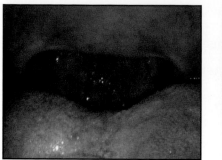

A

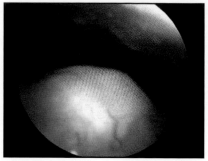

B

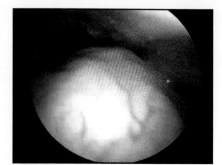

C

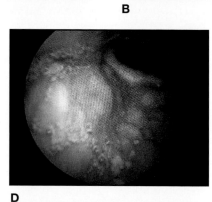

D

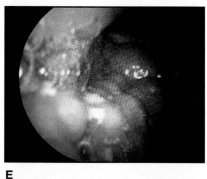

E

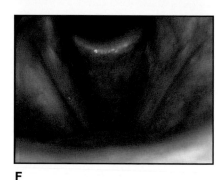

F

G

Fig 96–3. A. The oropharyngeal appearance after UPPP/tonsillectomy. The airway is expanded in the lateral dimension. It is difficult to appreciate in two-dimensional photography, but the anterior-to-posterior dimension of the oropharnyx is increased, as well. Due to removal of the distal soft palate, the number of minor salivary glands is reduced; and secretions tend to collect on the posterior wall of the pharynx from loss of the normal mechanical actions of shielding the posterior wall from dryer atmospheric conditions and cleaning the wall with swallows. Patients frequently report a globus sensation after UPPP. **B.** The velopharyngeal airway visualized from the posterior aspect of the middle meatus. In the resting position, it is widely patent. **C.** With inspiration against a closed nasal valve (Muller maneuver), the nasopharyngeal airway still collapses approximately 80%. However, it does not touch the posterior wall, and snoring is not possible. **D.** With the mouth closed, the oropharyngeal airway at the base of the tongue is visualized through the nasopharynx. **E.** The Muller maneuver shows that near complete collapse of the retrolingual airway space persists even after genioglossal advancement and hyoid suspension over the thyroid prominence. **F.** and **G.** The laryngeal configuration after hyoid suspension over the thyroid prominence. There is shortening in the anterior-to-posterior dimension in both the inspiratory (**F**) and phonatory (**G**) positions. This is secondary to mechanical compression rather than excess muscular tension.

Conclusion

Sleep-disordered breathing is usually the result of lifestyle problems creating obesity, which interacts synergistically with craniofacial structure to allow partial or complete airway obstruction. Initial therapy should be aimed at helping the patient make the lifestyle changes required to lose weight and become more physically fit. Medical intervention with CPAP to alleviate sleep apnea symptoms and lessen risk from comorbid cardiovascular disease and hypertension is beneficial, but patient compliance is relatively low. Therefore, patients often request corrective surgical therapy. Unfortunately, standard surgery, such as UPPP/tonsillectomy on the pharyngeal soft tissues, does not offer a uniformly high success rate. In addition, in singers, where fine control of the muscular tissue of the supraglottal vocal tract may be critical for maintenance of performance style, interventions on this tissue could lead to deterioration in function.

Classically trained singers usually have a definite perception of their own particular velar function. Even if surgical intervention does not create velar insufficiency it may lead to a change in the sensation that may be irreparably deleterious to the singer's performance. Postoperatively, the pharyngeal tissue will have a change in elasticity due to scarring, loss of volume, and change in shape. The effects on voice and spectral analysis of formant structure due to these changes have not been well studied. A few reports on voice changes after tonsillectomy and UPPP exist, but the results are inconclusive.

In limited series, maxillomandibular advancement procedures appear to have a high success rate in the surgical management of sleep-disordered breathing. This is likely secondary to the simultaneous adjustment of the posterior airway space throughout the entire pharynx. Although requiring long operative times, the surgery is well tolerated with few long-term complications being reported. In addition, total mass and elasticity of the pharyngeal tissues are not altered. Due to this fact and these excellent outcomes, this procedure should be considered as a primary mode of surgical management. This is particularly applicable in young, relatively thin patients without tonsillar hyperplasia. The changes in voice quality and velar sensation with MMA remain unknown. The shape of the supraglottal vocal tract is altered, and this may have an effect on formant structure; because shape is an important determinant in the resonatory characteristic of any tube. Therefore, as for all surgery for airway reconstruction, MMA should be undertaken with caution in the professional voice patient. Until proof that changes in vocal function do not occur, all patients need to be informed that irreparable vocal changes are a potential outcome.

References

1. Piccirillo JF, Thawley SE. Sleep-disordered breathing. In Cummings CW, et al, eds. *Otolaryngology—Head and Neck Surgery.* Vol 2, Pt 6. Oral Cavity/Oropharynx/Nasopharynx. St. Louis, Mo: Mosby-Yearbook. 1993: 1546–1571.
2. National Commission on Sleep Disorders Research. *Wake-up America: A National Sleep Alert.* Washington, DC: Government Printing Office; 1993.
3. Kuhl W. History of clinical research on the sleep apnea syndrome. *Respiration.* 1997;64(suppl 1):5–10.
4. Kuhlo W, Lehmann D. Das Einschlaferleben und seine neurophysiologischen Korrelate. *Arch Psychiatr Nervenkr.* 1964;205:687–716.
5. Schechtman KB, Sher AE, Piccirillo JF. Methodological and statistical problems in sleep apnea research: the literature on uvulopalatopharyngoplasty. *Sleep.* 1995;18(8): 659–666.
6. Janson C, Gislason T, Bengtsson H, et al. Long-term follow-up of patients with obstructive sleep apnea treated with uvulopalatopharyngoplasty. *Arch Otolaryngol Head Neck Surg.* 1997;123(3):257–262.
7. Senior BA, Rosenthal L, Lumley A, et al. Efficacy of uvulopalatopharyngoplasty in unselected patients with mild obstructive sleep apnea. *Otolaryngol Head Neck Surg.* 2000;123(3):179–182.
8. Larsson LH, Carlsson-Nordlander B, Svanborg E. Four-year follow-up after uvulopalatopharyngoplasty in 50 unselected patients with obstructive sleep apnea syndrome. *Laryngoscope.* 1994;104(11 Pt 1):1362–1368.
9. Piccirillo JF, Gates GA, White DL, Schectman KB. Obstructive sleep apnea: treatment outcomes pilot study. *Otolaryngol Head Neck Surg.* 1998;118(6):833–844.
10. Piccirillo JF. Outcomes research and otolaryngology. *Otolaryngol Head Neck Surg.* 1994;111(6):764–769.
11. Maisel RH, Antonelli PJ, Iber C, Mahowald M, et al. Uvulopalatopharyngoplasty for obstructive sleep apnea: a community's experience. *Laryngoscope.* 1992;102 (6):604–607.
12. Shepard JW Jr. Cardiopulmonary consequences of obstructive sleep apnea. *Mayo Clin Proc.* 1990;65(9):1250–1259.
13. Nieto FJ, Young TB, Lind BK, et al. Association of sleep-disordered breathing, sleep apnea, and hypertension in a large community-based study. *JAMA.* 2000;283(14): 1829–1836.
14. Kadotani H, Kadotani T, Young T, et al. Association between apolipoprotein E epsilon4 and sleep-disordered breathing in adults. *JAMA.* 2001;285(22):2888–2890.
15. Guilleminault C, van den Hoed J, Mitler MM. Clinical overview of the sleep apnea syndromes. In: Guilleminault C, Dement WC, eds. *Sleep Apnea Syndromes.* New York, NY: Alan R Liss; 1978:1–12.
16. Guilleminault C, Stoohs R. Upper airway resistance syndrome. *Sleep Res.* 1991;20:250–256.
17. Verse T, Pirsig W, Kroker B, Junge-Hulsing B, Zimmermann E. [Validating a 7-channel ambulatory polygraphy unit. 1: Operating instructions for the physician and patient.] *HNO.* 1999;47(4):249–255. German.
18. Uribe Echevarria EM, Alvarez D, Giobellina R, et al. [Epworth drowsiness scale value in obstructive sleep apnea syndrome.] *Medicina* (B Aires). 2000;60(6):902–906. Spanish.

19. Lopata M, Onal E. Mass loading, sleep apnea, and the pathogenesis of obesity hypoventilation, *Am Rev Respir Dis*. 1982;126:640–645.

20. Erdamar B, Suoglu Y, Cuhadaroglu C, et al. Evaluation of clinical parameters in patients with obstructive sleep apnea and possible correlation with the severity of the disease. *Eur Arch Otorhinolaryngol*. 2001;258(9):492–495.

21. Ezri T, Warters RD, Szmuk P, Saad-Eddin H. et al.: The incidence of class "zero" airway and the impact of Mallampati score, age, sex, and body mass index on prediction of laryngoscopy grade. *Anesth Analg*. 2001;93(4):1073–1075.

22. McGuirt WF Jr, Johnson JT, Sanders MH. Previous tonsillectomy as prognostic indicator for success of uvulopalatopharyngoplasty. *Laryngoscope*. 1995;105(11):1253–1255.

23. Terris DJ, Hanasono MM, Liu YC. Reliability of the Muller maneuver and its association with sleep disordered breathing. *Laryngoscope*. 2000;110(11):1819–1823.

24. Fujita S. Obstructive sleep apnea syndrome: pathophysiology, upper airway evaluation and surgical treatment. *Ear Nose Throat J*. 1993;72(1):67–72, 75–76.

25. Clark RW, Schmidt HS, Schaal SF, et al. Sleep apnea: treatment with protriptyline. *Neurology*. 1979;29:1287–1292.

26. Smith PL, Haponik EF, Allen RP, Bleecker ER. The effects of protriptyline in sleep disordered breathing. *Am Rev Respir Dis*. 1983;127:8–13.

27. Lyons HA, Huang CT. Therapeutic use of progesterone in alveolar hypoventilation associated with obesity. *Am J Med*. 1968;44:881–888.

28. American Sleep Disorders Association. Practice parameters for the treatment of obstructive sleep apnea in adults: the efficacy of surgical modifications of the upper airway. Report of the American Sleep Disorders Association. *Sleep*. 1996;19:152–155.

29. Schafer H, Ewig S, Hasper E, Luderitz B. Failure of CPAP therapy in obstructive sleep apnoea syndrome: predictive factors and treatment with bilevel-positive airway pressure. *Respir Med*. 1998;92(2):208–215.

30. Kribbs NB, Pack AI, Kline LR, et al. Objective measurement of patterns of nasal CPAP use by patients with obstructive sleep apnea. *Am Rev Respir Dis*. 1994;147:887–895.

31. Schmidt-Nowara W, Lowe A, Wiegand L, et al. Oral appliances for the treatment of snoring and obstructive sleep apnea: a review. *Sleep*. 1995;18:501–510.

32. Ichioka M, Tojo N, Yoshizawa M, et al. A dental device for the treatment of obstructive sleep apnea: a preliminary study. *Otolaryngol Head Neck Surg*. 1991;104:555–558.

33. Erdamar B, Suoglu Y, Cuhadaroglu C, et al. Evaluation of clinical parameters in patients with obstructive sleep apnea and possible correlation with the severity of the disease. *Eur Arch Otorhinolaryngol*. 2001;258(9):492–495.

34. Berger M, Oksenberg A, Silverberg DS, et al. Avoiding the supine position during sleep lowers 24 hr blood pressure in obstructive sleep apnea (OSA) patients. *J Hum Hypertens*. 1997;11(10):657–664.

35. Kravath RE, Pollack CP. Hypoventilation during sleep in children who have lymphoid obstruction treated by nasopharyngeal tube and T & A. *Pediatrics*. 1977;59:865–871.

36. Miller R. The velopharyngeal (palatopharyngeal) port during singing. *J Singing*. 1996;53:27–29.

37. Birch P, Gumoes B, Stavad H, et al. Velum behaviour in professional classic operatic singing. *KTH Speech, Music and Hearing Quarterly Status Report (TMH-QPSR)*. 1999;3–4:55–63.

38. Series F, St Pierre S, Carrier G. Effects of surgical correction of nasal obstruction in the treatment of obstructive sleep apnea. *Am Rev Respir Dis*. 1992;146(5 Pt 1):1261–1265.

39. Series F, St Pierre S, Carrier G. Surgical correction of nasal obstruction in the treatment of mild sleep apnea: importance of cephlametry in predicting outcome. *Thorax*. 1993;48(4):360–363.

40. Ferguson M, Smith TL, Zanation AM, Yarbrough WG: Radio frequency tissue volume reduction: multilesion vs single-lesion treatments for snoring. *Arch Otolaryngol Head Neck Surg*. 2001;127(9):1113–1118.

41. Brietzke SE, Mair EA. Injection snoreplasty: how to treat snoring without all the pain and expense. *Otolaryngol Head Neck Surg*. 2001;124:503–510.

42. Saida H, Hirose H. Acoustic changes in voice after tonsillectomy. *Acta Otolaryngol Suppl*. 1996;523:239–241.

43. Chuma AV, Cacace AT, Rosen R, Feustel P, Koltaii PJ. Effects of tonsillectomy and/or adenoidectomy on vocal function: laryngeal, supralaryngeal and perceptual characteristics. *Int J Pediatr Otorhinolaryngol*. 1999;47:1–9.

44. Brosch S, Matthes C, Pirsig W, Verse T. Uvulopalatopharyngoplasty changes fundamental frequency of the voice—a prospective study. *J Laryngol Otol*. 2000;114:113–118.

45. Kamami YV. Outpatient treatment of snoring with CO2 laser: laser-assisted UPPP. *J Otolaryngol*. 1994;23(6):391–394.

46. Kamami YV. Outpatient treatment of sleep apnea syndrome with CO2 laser, LAUP: laser-assisted UPPP results on 46 patients. *J Clin Laser Med Surg*. 1994;12(4):215–219.

47. Walker RP, Grigg-Damberger MM, Gopalsami C. Laser-assisted uvulopalatoplasty for the treatment of mild, moderate, and severe obstructive sleep apnea. *Laryngoscope*. 1999;109(1):79–85.

48. Powell NB, Guilleminault C, Riley RW. Surgical therapy for obstructive sleep apnea. In: Kryger MH, Roth T, Dement WC, eds. *Principles and Practice of Sleep Medicine*. 2nd ed. Philadelphia, Pa: WB Saunders; 1994:706–721.

49. Powell N, Guilleminault C, Riley RW, Smith L. Mandibular advancement and obstructive sleep apnea syndrome. *Bull Eur Physiopathol Respir*. 1983;19:607–610.

50. Fujita S, Woodson BT, Clark JL, Wittig R. Laser midline glossectomy as a treatment for obstructive sleep apnea. *Laryngoscope*. 1991;101:805–809.

51. Woodson BT, Fujita S. Clinical experience with lingualplasty as part of the treatment of severe obstructive sleep apnea. *Otolaryngol Head Neck Surg*. 1992;107:40–48.

52. Li KK, Riley RW, Powell NB, Guilleminault C. Maxillomandibular advancement for persistent obstructive sleep apnea after phase I surgery in patients without

maxillomandibular deficiency. *Laryngoscope.* 2000;110(10 Pt 1):1684–1688.

53. Riley RW, Powell NB, Guilleminault C. Maxillofacial surgery and obstructive sleep apnea: a review of 80 patients. *Otolaryngol Head Neck Surg.* 1989;101:353–361.

54. Hochban W, Brandenburg U, Peter JH. Surgical treatment of obstructive sleep apnea by maxillomandibular advancement. *Sleep.* 1994;17:624–629.

55. Prinsell JR. Maxillomandibular advancement surgery in a site-specific treatment approach for obstructive sleep apnea in 50 consecutive patients. *Chest.* 1999;116(6): 1519–1529.

56. Weitzman ED, Kahn E, Pollack CP. Quantitative analysis of sleep and sleep apnea before and after tracheostomy in patients with the hypersomnia—sleep apnea syndrome. *Sleep.* 1980;3:407–423.

IX

SPECIAL CONSIDERATIONS

97

Nursing Considerations in the Care of Professional Voice Users

Mary J. Hawkshaw and Robert Thayer Sataloff

The profession of nursing has long been in a state of transition, and nursing literature is replete with contributions that attempt to keep its practitioners abreast of the changing status and role of the professional registered nurse. Clearly, all professionals are affected by external and internal forces, including an expanding base of scientific knowledge, the changing scope of practice, and social and financial factors. These make it clear that the profession of nursing will continue to undergo redefinition. Nurses have gained an increasingly independent function in the primary care of patients in many settings, for example, the nurse practitioner's role, which is now commonplace and widely accepted. Nonetheless, the basic definition of nursing and the core of nursing care is unchanged from nursing's earliest history; nursing is a profession devoted to the prevention and relief of physical and emotional suffering. Inherent in that practice is the "control of disease, the care and rehabilitation of the sick and the promotion of health through teaching and counseling."[1,2(p3)] Nurses apply interventions with a scientific, research-based understanding of pathophysiology, clinical experience, and competence with physical procedures. Through contributions of insight and empathy, they also assist in the management of psychological distress.

It is incumbent on the nurse specialist in the field of otolaryngology to thoroughly understand the anatomy and physiology of the head and neck.[3] Pathophysiologic conditions unique to otorhinolaryngology may be present in the professional voice user, in addition to the chief presenting voice complaint. Additionally, a comprehensive knowledge of the pharmacology of the medications used in the treatment of illnesses specific to the head and neck, as well as those used in

the management of generalized medical conditions, must be acquired and frequently updated by the nurse practicing in this field.

One source of ongoing continuing education for nurses practicing in the medical-surgical subspecialty of otorhinolaryngology is the Society of Otorhinolaryngology and Head-Neck Nursing (SOHN). This society, which promotes excellence in care and nursing research, also provides certification for its practitioners.

As a member of a voice care team, the otolaryngologic nurse-clinician must develop an extensive recognition and understanding of the special problems of professional voice users. In addition to knowledge of the most common medical diagnoses, etiologies, and treatments for voice disorders, she or he must acquire extra training in technical aspects of voice production in speech and singing and work collaboratively with specialists in these disciplines as a member of a voice care team. It is especially helpful if the professional nurse functioning in this role has personal experience as a vocal performer. Not only does this permit him or her to assess the potential role demands in the patient's repertoire, it allows for greater empathy derived from experiential understanding of the professional and emotional impact of possible damage to the performer's vocal mechanism.

Functions of the Otolaryngologic Nurse-Clinician

Although many clinical voice centers function without the expertise of an otolaryngologic nurse-clinician, the role is essential in our practice model. The nurse, as a member of our multidisciplinary team, provides care for patients both directly and indirectly. Direct responsibilities involve patient care and the coordination of care provided by all members of the voice team. Indirect care includes providing and maintaining a safe physical environment in which the patient receives care and treatment from all members of the team. Additionally, our nurses devote a large percentage of their time to educating patients and their families, colleagues, and the profession as a whole.

Care of the professional voice user generally begins with triage based on telephone contact. When a patient contacts the voice center by telephone, his or her call is first taken by one of the secretarial staff who have been trained by the laryngologist (RTS) and nurse-clinician (MJH) to ask specific questions designed to elicit the information essential in deciding how urgently the patient needs evaluation. If the situation is equivocal or emergent, the secretaries are instructed to contact one of the nurse-clinicians or physicians. During clinical questioning, the nurse-clinician listens critically to the quality of the patient's voice on the telephone, as well as the description of the onset of the voice complaint and imminent performances. This allows the nurse to assess for vocal problems that require immediate, absolute voice rest, and/or an emergency evaluation. Of course, all nursing decisions involve collaboration with the laryngologist when necessary. Immediate performance demands in a professional performer with voice complaints necessitate that the patient be seen emergently. Thus, caring for professional voice users, singers, and actors is a 24-hour, 7 days a week commitment of access to laryngological care. Voice patients who seek care at our voice center for the first time are provided with our specialized questionnaire, which is included in Appendix IIb. When there is sufficient time prior to the evaluation, this form is mailed to the patient so that she or he may consider the questions carefully and answer them fully. When the patient is scheduled for an urgent evaluation, the form is completed in the waiting room once the patient arrives at the center.

Using the printed history form as a guide, the nurse will perform a complete medical and nursing history. The medical history follows the routine format: identifying data; chief complaint; history of the presenting illness; past medical and surgical history, including current medications and medication allergies; family history; social history (which includes current performance commitments in professional voice users); smoking, alcohol, and recreational drug use; and toxic exposure. The nurse should also assess the ways in which the patient's voice problem interferes with activities of daily living and how it affects emotional responses and other health problems. Once the nurse

has obtained a patient's medical and surgical history, she or he then takes a "voice" history. Questions asked include (but are not limited to): When did your voice problem begin? Is it getting better or worse? Have you had similar or any other history of voice problems? and many other questions. A more complete discussion can be found in chapter 18 on taking the history. The otolaryngologic nurse-clinician then presents the history to the laryngologist before the patient enters the room to be examined. The laryngologist reviews this information, as well as the patient's written responses. He or she will then expand the history and pursue areas relevant to the differential diagnoses.

In our center, nurses assist the physician in performing a complete head and neck physical examination. However, the nurse's role involves not only physical assistance to the physician, but also emotional support and education of the patient throughout the examination. The nurse is also responsible for thoroughly documenting the physician's physical findings on the medical record. After completion of the examination, the laryngologist may order additional laboratory tests, imaging studies, and referrals to consultants as part of the comprehensive voice evaluation. In our center, the initial evaluation of a patient with a voice disorder generally includes a strobovideolaryngoscopic evaluation of laryngeal function. This, slow-motion visual analysis of laryngeal function is the current standard of care in evaluating patients with voice disorders. Nurses interested in learning more about this procedure are encouraged to read chapters 20 and 21 in this textbook. Prior to the strobovideolaryngoscopy, the laryngologist (or the nurse-specialist on the laryngologist's order) will administer topical anesthesia to facilitate patients' comfort and a thorough endoscopic examination with optimal visualization. Among the nurse's roles is explaining to the patient the sensations associated with anesthesia in the nasopharynx, oropharynx, and hypopharynx. The patient receives both oral and written instructions for the prevention of aspiration and other problems that could occur before the anesthesia effect wears off. In our hands, the amount of topical anesthesia administered generally lasts no more than 30 to 40 minutes. The nurse then begins the first part of the videostroboscopic examination by placing a microphone and EGG (electroglottograph) leads on the patient and then records a baseline EGG and a conversational voice sample on videotape (see chapter 21).[4] The patient receives instruction and demonstration of techniques that are useful in suppressing the gag reflex (common during endoscopy); one of the nurse's responsibilities during the examination is to support and coach the patient in the use of these techniques.

The strobovideolaryngoscopic examination is performed by the laryngologist in the author's practice. Occasionally, in other voice centers, speech-language pathologists may perform and record a rigid endoscopic examination for later review by the laryngologist. In Pennsylvania (where the authors practice), registered nurses who have been specially trained are permitted to intubate and may use both flexible and rigid endoscopes under the supervision of a physician. Occasionally, it may be appropriate for the otolaryngologic nurse-clinician to perform a strobovideolaryngoscopic examination during a follow-up visit. The laryngologist subsequently reviews all of the examinations, and diagnoses are made only by the laryngologist. During the examination, the nurse will operate the computer and video equipment and document the physical findings on a standard report form. These are reviewed, amended, and expanded by the laryngologist, who prepares an operative report for the patient's medical record. At the conclusion of the examination, the nurse provides the patient with additional explanation of the diagnoses rendered by the laryngologist following his or her examination, the treatment prescribed, and explanations or instructions for additional studies the laryngologist has ordered for further assessment. Both short- and long-term plans of care are defined.

The professional nurse is responsible for supervising the implementation of the plan of care and for communication with the laryngologist and other voice team members (speech-language pathologists, singing voice specialists, and others) regarding its implementation and time frame.

We have found that patients frequently do not retain all of the information they receive during their first visit. Psychological research indicates that emotional distress radically diminishes recall of information provided during a crisis. For that reason, professional voice patients often require repetition, amplification, expansion, and documentation of information regarding their diagnoses and treatment plan. They also need the opportunity to discuss their emotional responses and the social impact they are experiencing. When the patient's emotional responses seem extreme, complex, and/or dangerous, the patient is referred to the clinical psychologist or psychiatrist for further assessment and possible treatment. The vocal rehabilitation of a professional voice user is an exquisitely slow, carefully monitored process whether or not surgery is required. For some patients, this becomes difficult to manage emotionally; and it is especially stressful for professional voice users, because their voice (treatment and outcome) and their sense of self are so closely intertwined, as discussed previously. In our setting, patients always have access to a nurse, either by telephone or in person. Supporting patients in this manner has proven to be very beneficial in allaying fears and anxiety, which, in turn, enhances voice rehabilitation. When absolute voice rest is ordered, the nurse will instruct the patient on ways to maintain communication, such as the use of writing pads, magic slates, and laptop computers. Certain types of voice surgery may require a period of absolute voice rest for 1 week following surgery. One of our patients devised a means for helping herself during this situation. A badge was suggested by this patient, and the authors' gratefully share her creativity! The badge contains the patient 's name and also the phrase, "I've had voice surgery. I can't speak but I can hear and write. Please don't shout."

Another indirect function of the nurse in an outpatient setting is the establishment of and adherence to the Occupational Safety and Health Administration (OSHA) mandated infection control policies and procedures. The nurse is responsible for ensuring that Universal Precautions are employed during the examination of any patient when contact with body fluids might be anticipated. In addition, instruments, endoscopes, and equipment are disinfected according to current OSHA guidelines. Supervision of proper disposal of medical waste also falls under the nursing purview. In-service education of other professionals on the voice team and office staff members who have a potential risk of exposure is conducted when they are newly hired and on a yearly basis. Appropriate records are maintained.

Patients cannot be examined properly without adequate lighting, instrumentation, and functioning electronic and suction equipment. The nurse is responsible for the purchasing and maintenance of equipment, as well as assisting the laryngologist in evaluating new products that might enhance the quality of patient assessment and care. In the authors' practice, the nurse-clinician is also responsible for the orientation and education of other voice team colleagues on the proper use of the equipment in the examination of the professional voice patient.

A clinical practice with quality and breadth will emphasize the need for education. This always includes education of the patient. Current nursing practice views the patient as the central participant in his or her own therapy. Nurses help direct a patient by focusing his or her energy on the goals of therapy, as designed by the laryngologist, other voice team members, and the patient. In order for this to happen, the patient must be informed of the therapeutic goals of the entire team and his or her cooperation and consent must be obtained. It is a matter of professional nursing judgment, as well as the policy of each individual medical practice, regarding which facts to impart, when, and by whom. The nurse will need to assess the patient's physical and psychological readiness to learn, and all of the factors affecting the patient's learning ability, such as educational experience, occupation, or affect. Special adaptations relating to any potential intellectual, physical, or sensory impairment must be considered. Teaching aids including written reiteration of the verbal instructions and visual aids are provided whenever possible.[3] Although voice care, as a subspeciality of laryngology, has advanced dramatically over the past two decades, new information about the voice and how it works is still being discovered. It is incumbent on all nurses involved in caring for patients with voice disorders to remain current in their knowledge of the advancements made in the diagnosis and treatment of these most interesting and challenging patients.

Continuing education for the professional staff should also be an ongoing component in any voice center. In the authors' practice, regular meetings with all members of the voice team are held to discuss the care of all voice patients. Interdisciplinary collaboration provides additional clinical insight and direction in the therapeutic goals.

Finally, the nurses in our practice devote time and energy to the growth of their professional nursing organizations, such as the Society of Otorhinolaryngology and Head-Neck Nursing. There are no graduate nursing programs that provide in-depth, additional education for the professional nurse who chooses to practice in the specialized care of voice patients. Most undergraduate nursing programs (diploma, associate nursing degrees, or baccalaureate nursing degrees) offer only minimal exposure to the anatomy and physiology, pathophysiology, medical and surgical treatment, pharmacology, and psychosocial needs in this unique patient population. Most professional nurses practicing in the field have developed their skills through on-the-job training, continuing education through the literature and seminar attendance, and networking. SOHN, with its regional education offerings and its annual Congress, provides the nurses with the most current information in otorhinolaryngology—head and neck nursing offered by colleagues who are actively working at the forefront of research, in clinical practice, and in education. The authors strongly encourage membership and attendance at SOHN educational meetings. In addition, a number of symposia dedicated to care of the professional voice offer additional training by practitioners in all disciplines in this field. The Voice Foundation offers the most extensive annual symposium, which is held yearly in June. Information may be obtained by writing to The Voice Foundation at 1721 Pine Street, Philadelphia, Pennsylvania 19103 or by calling them directly at (215) 735-7999. An internship in our voice center and others provides a unique opportunity for intense observation of all aspects of voice care and, in some centers, may also include supervised nursing intervention with these patients.

Conclusion

The face of nursing has changed since its emergence and continues to evolve rapidly. Ongoing changes in health care delivery undoubtedly will be accompanied by changes in the roles of professional nurses, particularly in the care of professional voice users. Nursing intervention is critical to the healing process in any patient as are all of the other dimensions of treatment. In professional voice users, the sense of being known, understood, and respected as an individual is critical. The laryngologist shares responsibility with the otolaryngologic nurse-clinician, for the ongoing coordination of care for professional voice patients.

References

1. Fuerst EV, Wolff L. Fundamentals of nursing. *The Humanities and Sciences in Nursing.* 4th ed. Philadelphia, Pa: JB Lippincott Co; 1969:3–8.
2. Bruner LS, Emerson CP, Ferguson LK, Suddarth DS. *Textbook of Medical Surgical Nursing.* 2nd ed. Philadelphia, Pa: JB Lippincott Co; 1970:3.
3. Sigler BA, Schuring LT. *Ear, Nose, and Throat Disorders.* Mosby's Clinical Nursing Series. St Louis, Mo: CV Mosby; 1993:18:182–186.
4. Sataloff RT, Spiegel JR, Carroll LM, et al. The clinical voice laboratory: practical design and clinical application. *J Voice.* 1990;4(3):264–279.

98

Voice Care Professionals: A Guide to Voice Care Providers

Robert Thayer Sataloff, Yolanda D. Heman-Ackah, and Mary J. Hawkshaw

Optimal voice care is delivered by an interdisciplinary team consisting of physicians and nonphysicians. The physician may be an otolaryngologist (a specialist who practices all aspects of ear, nose and throat medicine) or a laryngologist, who specializes in voice disorders. The physician commonly collaborates with other professionals, such as a speech-language pathologist, singing voice specialist, acting-voice specialist, and others who constitute the voice care team. Under the best of circumstances, all of the members of the team have received special training in not just the general aspects of their disciplines but also additional training in care of the voice. Although even the best training does not guarantee clinical excellence, it does improve the probability that a practitioner will provide superior, modern voice care. This chapter reviews the typical training and qualifications of the professionals associated most commonly with voice care teams.

The Voice Care Team

A voice care team is ordinarily under the direction of a physician who is usually an otolaryngologist or laryngologist. In addition to the physician who diagnoses and provides medical treatment for voice disorders, the team includes the speech-language pathologist, who provides voice therapy and attends to problems that affect the speaking voice; a phoniatrist in countries without speech-language pathologists; a singing voice specialist; an acting-voice specialist; a nurse and/or a physician's assistant; and consultant physicians in other specialties. It is helpful for patients to understand the background and role of each member of the voice team, as discussed below.

Otolaryngologist/Laryngologist

The leader of the voice care team is ordinarily a physician (otolaryngologist). Otolaryngologists are physicians (surgeons) who specialize in problems of the ears, nose, and throat (ENT). Laryngologists are otolaryngologists who specialize in care of disorders of the larynx and, in some cases, related problems such as swallowing. To practice laryngology, one must first complete training as an otolaryngologist. To become an otolaryngologist, a person completes college, 4 years of medical school, 1 or 2 years of training in general surgery, and 4 years of residency in otolaryngology—head and neck surgery. In the year following completion of residency, the physician takes a national, standardized board examination given in two parts (written and oral) to become a "board certified" otolaryngologist. Certification by the American Board of Otolaryngology, or the equivalent organization in other countries, is an important indicator of mastery of basic knowledge in otolaryngology and is considered a basic, minimum qualification. The only exception is "board eligibility" in the case of a physician who has finished residency but has not yet successfully passed the board examinations. Board certification is not granted until a physician has had 1 year of clinical experience following residency and demonstrated competency on the oral and written board examinations.

Most otolaryngologists' clinical practices include many or all components of the specialty, such as otology (disorders of the ear and related structures), laryngology (disorders of the voice and upper airway structures such as the throat and trachea), head and neck cancer, head and neck neoplasms (masses including benign or malignant lesions), facial plastic and reconstructive surgery, allergy and immunology, bronchoesophagology (lower airway and swallowing disorders), rhinology (nose, sinus, taste, and smell disorders), and pediatric otolaryngology (ear, nose, and throat disorders of children). Most otolaryngologists and laryngologists care for patients of all ages from early childhood through advanced years. Some otolaryngologists subspecialize, in caring for disorders in just one or two areas of otolaryngology, as described above. This subspecialization can either be a keen interest in a specific area while still providing a broad range of ear, nose, and throat care or the focused practice of only one or two of the subcomponents of otolaryngology. Laryngology is one such subspecialty.

Most of the physicians specializing in laryngology today did not receive laryngology fellowship training. That is always the case as a new field develops. Modern laryngology evolved out of an interest in caring for professional voice users, especially singers. The first comprehensive article guiding otolaryngologists on care of professional singers was published in 1981[1]; the first major modern American otolaryngology textbook with a chapter on care of the professional voice was published in 1986[2]; and the first comprehensive book on care of the professional voice was published in 1991.[3] So, most of the senior laryngologists practicing at the turn of the 21st century were involved in the evolution of the field before fellowships were developed. Most fellowship training programs started in the 1990s, although a few informal fellowship programs existed in the1980s and earlier. It is reasonable to expect most voice specialists who finished residency training in the 1990s or later to have completed a fellowship in laryngology. There are approximately a dozen laryngology fellowship-training programs in the United States, and they are highly competitive. At present, completion of a fellowship is a reasonably good indicator of superior knowledge and clinical training in laryngology. Most laryngology fellowships include training in the diagnosis and treatment of voice disorders in adults and children, neurolaryngology (neurological problems that affect the voice and larynx), swallowing disorders, airway reconstruction, and laryngeal cancer. The training includes both medical diagnosis and treatment, and sophisticated laryngeal surgery. Typically, laryngologists care for both routine and complex problems that affect the voice. Such problems include voice dysfunction associated with something as simple as a common cold,

especially when it affects the voice of a professional singer or actor. However, laryngologists also are called on to diagnose and treat structural lesions such as nodules or polyps, prolonged infections of the vocal folds, cancer, traumatic injury from fracture or internal trauma (intubation injuries from anesthesia, vocal fold injuries from previous surgery), neurological disorders, and other voice problems. The laryngologist is responsible for establishing a medical diagnosis and implementing or coordinating treatment for the patient. The laryngologist may prescribe medication, inject botulinum toxin, perform delicate microsurgery on the vocal folds, or operate through the neck on the laryngeal skeleton. He or she is also usually responsible for initiating evaluation by other members of the voice team and for generating referrals to other specialists as needed.

Laryngologists may practice in university medical centers or private offices; and in major cities in the United States, they are usually affiliated with a voice team including at least a speech-language pathologist, a singing voice specialist, and sometimes an acting-voice specialist. Laryngologists should also have, or have access to, a clinical voice laboratory with equipment to analyze the voice objectively and a stroboscope to visualize the vocal folds in slow motion. They also should be familiar with physicians in other specialties who have an understanding and interest in arts-medicine. Even for patients with a voice disorder who are not singers and actors, such knowledge and sensitivity is important. Just as nonathletes benefit from the orthopedic expertise of a sports-medicine specialist, voice patients receive more expert care from physicians trained to treat singers, the "Olympic" athletes of the voice world.

Currently, there is no official additional certification for those who have completed a laryngology fellowship. However, there are organizations (medical societies) with which many of the leading laryngologists are affiliated. Essentially all laryngologists in the United States are fellows of the American Academy of Otolaryngology—Head and Neck Surgery (http://www.entnet.org), and laryngologists in other countries are members of their nations' analogous organizations. A few are also members of the American Laryngological Association (ALA), the most senior otolaryngology society in the United States (http://www.alahns.org). The ALA also accepts "associate members" from other countries. Some laryngologists belong to the American Bronchoesophagological Association (http://www.abea.net), and the Voice Foundation (http://www.voicefoundation.org). The Voice Foundation was founded in 1969 and is the oldest organization dedicated to voice education and research. It provides seed grants for research, sponsors an annual symposium on care of the professional voice that started in 1972, and fosters voice education through conferences, educational videotapes, books, and publications such as the *Journal of Voice* and the *Voice Foundation Newsletter*. In recent years, several countries have developed organizations similar to the Voice Foundation, such as the British, Canadian, and Australian Voice Foundations. Laryngologists in such countries are usually members of their national organization, and many are also members of the Voice Foundation (Philadelphia, Pa). Although membership in these organizations is not a guarantee of excellence in practice, it suggests interest and knowledge in laryngology, particularly voice disorders.

Speech-Language Pathologist

The speech-language pathologist is a certified, licensed health care professional, ordinarily with either a master's degree (MA or MS) or doctorate (PhD). After college, speech-language pathologists generally complete a 1- or 2-year master's degree program, followed by a 9-month, supervised "clinical fellowship," which is similar to a medical internship. At the conclusion of the clinical fellowship year, speech-language pathologists in the United States are certified by the American Speech-Language-Hearing Association, and use the letters "CCC-SLP" after their names to indicate that they are certified. Like otolaryngology, speech-language pathology is a broad field that includes care of patients who have had strokes or other neurological problems affecting speech and swallowing, undergone laryngectomy (removal of the larynx), have swallowing disorders, have articulation or stuttering problems, have craniofacial disorders, or have other related fluency disorders of speech. Some speech-language pathologists subspecialize in voice, which includes the care of voice disorders and swallowing disorders. The speech-language pathologist affiliated with a voice team is usually such a subspecialist and may call him- or herself a "voice pathologist" rather than a speech-language pathologist, although "voice pathologist" is not a term recognized officially by the American Speech-Language-Hearing Association, yet. Relatively few speech-language pathology training programs provide extensive education in voice, and there are virtually no voice fellowships for speech-language pathologists. Many speech-language pathology training programs do not require even a single course on voice disorders. Thus, it cannot be assumed that all speech-language pathologists are trained in or comfortable with caring for individuals with voice problems. Most acquire the subspeciality training they need through apprenticeships, extra courses, and symposia or by obtaining doctoral degrees that include voice-related research.

Speech-language pathologists are responsible for voice therapy and rehabilitation, which is analogous to physical therapy. The speech-language pathologist analyzes voice use and teaches proper voice support, relaxation, and voice placement to optimize use of the voice during speaking. A variety of techniques are utilized to accomplish this goal. Speech-language pathologists do not ordinarily work with the singing voice, although they are involved in the treatment of speaking voices of singers.

Speech-language pathologists may be found in universities, private offices, or freestanding speech and hearing centers. In the United States, most are members of ASHA (the American Speech-Language-Hearing Association), and its voice-related special interest division (SID-3), which can be accessed on the Internet. Many speech-language pathologists with special interest in voice in the United States and elsewhere are also members of the Voice Foundation. Like otolaryngologists, speech-language pathologists who subspecialize in voice provide more incisive, state-of-the-art treatment for voice disorders than most general speech-language pathologists who care for patients with various problems encompassing the entire field. So, it is worthwhile for patients with voice disorders to seek out a subspecialist to improve the likelihood of a rapid, excellent treatment result. Referrals to speech-language pathologists specializing in voice are usually obtained through a laryngologist or otolaryngologist.

Phoniatrists

Phoniatrists do not exist in the United States, but they provide voice care in many European countries. The phoniatrist is a physician who is in some ways a hybrid of the laryngologist and speech-language pathologist. Phoniatrists receive medical training in diagnosis and treatment of voice, swallowing, and language disorders, including voice therapy; but they do not perform surgery. In countries with phoniatrists, surgery is performed by otolaryngologists. In many cases, the phoniatrist and otolaryngologist collaborate as a team, just as otolaryngologists and speech-language pathologists do in the United States and elsewhere. A physician who has completed training in phoniatry is generally well qualified to diagnose voice disorders and provide nonsurgical medical care, as well as voice therapy.

Singing Voice Specialist

The singing voice specialist is a singing teacher with special training equipping him or her to practice in a medical environment with patients who have sustained vocal injury. Most singing voice specialists have a degree in voice performance or pedagogy, although some have only extensive performing and teaching experience without a formal academic degree. Nearly all have professional performance experience, as well as extra training in laryngeal anatomy and physiology of phonation, training in the rehabilitation of injured voices, and other special education. The singing voice specialist must acquire knowledge of anatomy and physiology of the normal and disordered voice, a basic understanding of the principles of laryngology and medications, and a fundamental knowledge of the principles and practices of speech-language pathology. This information is not part of the traditional training of singing teachers. Moreover, so far there are no formal training or fellowship programs that assist singing teachers in becoming a singing voice specialist. Their training is acquired by apprenticeship and observation. Many take courses in speech-language pathology programs, but usually not as part of a formal degree or certification program[4]; because there is no certification of singing voice specialists. A few of the best singing voice specialists are also certified, licensed speech-language pathologists. This combination is optimal, provided the speech-language pathologist has sufficient experience and training not only as a performing artist but also as a teacher of singing. In patients with vocal injuries or problems, the fundamental approach to training the singing voice is different in important ways from that usually used with healthy students in a singing studio. Hence, even an excellent and experienced voice teacher may harm an injured voice if he or she is not familiar with the special considerations for this population. In addition, most voice teachers do not feel comfortable working with a singer who has had a vocal injury or surgery.

Virtually all singing voice specialists are affiliated with voice care teams. Most are members of the National Association of Teachers of Singing (NATS), or the equivalent organization in another country, and of the Voice Foundation. In many cases, their practices are limited to work with injured voices. They work not only with singers, but also with other patients with voice disorders. As a member of the voice treatment team working with nonsingers, they help teach speakers the "athletic" techniques utilized by singers for voice production. Singing is to speaking as running is to walking. When rehabilitating someone who has difficulty walking, if the person can be helped to jog or run, leg strength and endurance improve and walking rehabilitation is expedited. The singing voice specialist applies similar principles to voice rehabilitation in collaboration with the speech-language pathologist and other voice care team members.

Acting-Voice Specialist

Acting-voice trainers are also called voice coaches, drama voice teachers, and voice consultants. Traditionally, these professionals have been associated closely with the theater. Their skills have been utilized as part of a medical voice team only since the mid-1990s.[5] Consequently, few acting-voice trainers have any medical experience; but their contributions have proven invaluable.

Acting-voice trainers use a variety of behavior modification techniques designed to enhance vocal communication, quality, projection, and endurance in theatrical settings. They train actors to speak or scream through eight shows a week, and/or theatrical runs that may last years, without tiring or causing injury to their voices. They also teach techniques for adding emotional expression to vocal delivery, and they work with body language and posture to optimize vocal delivery and communication of information. They may be a great asset to the voice team in teaching people how to apply the many skills learned through the speech-language pathologist and singing voice specialist to their everyday lives. Acting-voice trainers are especially valuable for people who speak professionally such as teachers, lecturers, politicians, clergy, sales personnel, and others concerned with effective vocal delivery and with vocal endurance.

There are no formal programs to prepare voice coaches to work in a medical milieu. Those who do receive training generally do so through apprenticeships and collaboration with medical voice care teams under the direction of a laryngologist.

Acting-voice trainers interested in working with voice patients are generally members of the Voice and Speech Trainers Association (VASTA) and the Voice Foundation.

Nurse

Nurses are indispensable assets in medical offices, and they are important members of the voice team in many centers. Nurses who work closely with a laryngologist generally have vast experience in the diagnosis and treatment of voice disorders. They are wonderful information resources for patients and frequently provide much of the patient education in busy clinical settings. These nurses are usually members of the Society of Otolaryngology—Head and Neck Nurses (SOHN). Nurses with advanced knowledge and skills may be certified (by SOHN) as otolaryngology nurses and are identified as such by the initials "CORLN" (certified otolaryngologic nurse) after their names.

Nurse practitioners are advanced practice nurses with master's degrees, who are licensed to provide independent care for patients with selected medical problems. They are identified by the initials "CRNP" (certified registered nurse practitioner). They work in conjunction with a physician; but they can examine, diagnose, and treat selected problems relatively independently. A few nurse practitioners specialize in otolaryngology and work with voice teams. They ordinarily receive special training "on the job" from the otolaryngologist, and they provide care within their scope of practice. Nurse practitioners can also become members of SOHN, become certified through examination by SOHN, and on certification will also use the certification CORLN after their names.

Physician Assistants and Medical Assistants

Physician assistants, like nurse practitioners discussed above, function in association with a physician. Physician assistants graduate from a training program that usually lasts 4 years and teaches them various aspects of medical diagnosis and physical examination. They use the initials "PA" (physician assistant) after their names. They practice in conjunction with physicians but can perform examinations and treat patients independently. They are licensed in many states to write prescriptions. A few physician assistants specialize in otolaryngology, and a smaller number have had extensive training and experience in voice care. In collaboration with a laryngologist and voice teams, they are qualified to evaluate and treat patients with voice disorders.

Physician assistants should be distinguished from "medical assistants" who have less training and are qualified to assist in medical care and patient education but generally not to diagnose and treat patients independently. Medical assistants generally are trained to perform tasks such as phlebotomy (drawing blood) and perform electrocardiograms. In a laryngology office, a good medical assistant can be trained to perform many other tasks, such as taking histories, assisting with strobovideolaryngoscopy, and assisting during the performance of surgical procedures in the office, participating in research, and other tasks.

Consultant Medical Professionals

Otolaryngologists often refer voice patients for consultation with other medical professionals. Other specialists consulted commonly include neurologists, pulmonologists (lungs), gastroenterologists (stomach and intestinal system), psychologists, and psychiatrists. However, physicians in virtually any medical specialty may be called on to care for voice patients. Traditional and nontraditional ancillary medical personnel may also be involved in voice care, including nutritionists, physical therapists, chiropractors, osteopaths (for manipulation), acupuncturists, and others. Within virtually all of these fields, there are a select few professionals who have an interest in and an understanding of arts-medicine. Just as caring for voice professionals (especially singers) involves special considerations and challenges for the otolaryngologist, caring for hand problems in a pianist or ankle problems in dancers also poses challenges for the orthopedic surgeon. Orthopedic surgeons, neurologists, pulmonologists, and others who are accustomed to working with performing artists (dancers, wind instrumentalists, etc) are most likely to have the insight, sensitivities, skills, and state-of-the-art information needed to provide optimal care to voice professionals. Many such physicians tend to be associated with arts-medicine centers or are performers themselves. There is no certification or broad-based national or international organization that helps to identify such physicians, although some are members of the Performing Arts Medicine Association (PAMA). In most fields, there are no formal arts-medicine training programs or associations. Physicians acquire such training through their own interests and initiative and through apprenticeship or observation with colleagues. If there is no arts-medicine center in the area in which a patient is seeking care, arts-medicine physicians are identified best by word-of-mouth or through arts-medicine-related Web sites. Referrals can be obtained through the local laryngologist or voice specialist or by consulting with eminent performing arts teachers in the community. For example, the leading private university and conservatory violin and piano teachers often know who the best hand specialists are; the wind instrument teachers know whom to see for neurological and pulmonary problems that affect musicians; and dance teachers know the best foot-and-ankle physicians.

Conclusion

Voice care has evolved into a sophisticated, well-organized medical science. Patients with voice disorders are served best by a comprehensive voice team that coordinates the skills of professionals trained in various disciplines. It is important for health care professionals to assemble interdisciplinary teams and to affiliate with arts-medicine specialists and other disciplines in order to provide comprehensive care for voice patients. It is also important for patients to be educated about the kind of health care that is now available for voice disorders and how to evaluate and select health care providers.

References

1. Sataloff RT. Professional singers: the science and art of clinical care. *Am J Otolaryngol.* 1981;2(3):251–266.
2. Sataloff RT. The professional voice. In: Cummings CW, Frederickson JM, Harker LA, et al, eds. *Otolaryngology—Head and Neck Surgery.* Vol 3. St Louis, Mo: CV Mosby; 1986:2029–2056.
3. Sataloff RT. *Professional Voice: The Science and Art of Clinical Care.* New York, NY: Raven Press; 1991:1–542.
4. Emerich KA, Baroody MM, Carroll LM, Sataloff RT. The singing voice specialist. In: Sataloff RT. *Professional Voice: The Science and Art of Clinical Care.* 2nd ed. San Diego, Calif: Singular Publishing Group; 1997:735–753.
5. Freed SL, Raphael BN, Sataloff RT. The role of the acting-voice trainer in medical care of professional voice users. In: Sataloff RT. *Professional Voice: The Science and Art of Clinical Care.* 2nd ed. San Diego, Calif: Singular Publishing Group; 1997:765–774.

99

Voice Impairment, Disability, Handicap, and Medical-Legal Evaluation

Robert Thayer Sataloff

Medical care of singers and actors inspired the development of voice as a subspecialty of laryngology. Although the interest was originally aesthetic and scientific, the broader practical importance of voice dysfunction soon became apparent. It is intuitively obvious that dysphonia in a great singer is not only an artistic and cultural tragedy, but also a disability that may result in the loss of millions of dollars annually for some performers. However, as our discipline evolved, it became clear that singers are not the only professional voice users. Voice professionals include also actors, clergy, politicians, teachers, sales personnel, secretaries, and anyone else whose ability to make a living is diminished or interrupted by voice disturbance.

As awareness of the importance of the human voice has grown, so too have legal issues surrounding voice dysfunction. Some voice disorders arise out of an individual's employment and may be covered under workers' compensation laws in some jurisdictions. Such cases might include vocal nodules developing in a schoolteacher or dysphonia in a shop foreman who suffers a laryngeal fracture while working and can no longer be heard over the noise at his or her job site. However, workers' compensation statutes are usually quite specific and vary greatly from one jurisdiction to another. The fact that a health problem is causally related to employment does not guarantee that it will be compensable under workers' compensation statutes in any given case. Other legal avenues may be pursued in some cases, such as civil suits under tort law; and physicians should be familiar with their roles in different types of legal proceedings and the financial implications for the patient of the applicable law.

Hearing loss illustrates this issue particularly well. A given hearing loss may be compensated at the rate of $18,000 in Rhode Island, $108,940 in Pennsylvania, or at an unlimited level (depending on jury verdict) for a railroad worker subject to the Federal Employer's Liability Act. If a given injury (dysphonia, hearing loss, etc) is covered under workers' compensation law in a given jurisdiction, then compensation is determined by that statute; and the worker is generally prohibited from suing the employer outside the workers' compensation system. If the injury is not covered specifically in the applicable workers' compensation statute, then the employee may be able to file a civil suit and recover a potentially unlimited amount of compensation. Other cases are not causally related to work, such as a patient who develops dysphonia following endotracheal intubation, thoracic surgery, or laryngeal surgery. Yet, such vocal injuries may have profound effects on the patient's earning potential, and redress may be sought under tort law.

It is helpful for physicians to understand the accepted definitions of impairment, disability, and handicap. These terms are defined well by the World Health Organization.[1] An impairment is any loss or abnormality of psychological, physiological, or anatomical structure or function.[1(p47)] The abnormalities or losses that constitute an impairment may be temporary or permanent; and they involve the existence of a defect of a bodily structure, including mental defects. A disability resulting from an impairment is any restriction or lack of ability to perform an activity in the manner or within the range considered normal for a human being.[1(p143)] Disabilities are characterized by abnormalities of customarily expected performance of activities. They may be temporary or permanent; and there may be direct consequences of impairment or individual responses to an impairment (ie, psychological reactions). A handicap is any disadvantage for a given individual, resulting from an impairment or a disability, that limits or prevents the fulfillment of a role that is normal (depending on age, sex, and social and cultural factors) for that individual.[1(p183)] Handicap reflects the consequences for the individual resulting from an impairment and/or disability in terms of social, cultural, environmental, and economic impact.[2]

Voice Impairment, Disability, and Handicap

To help guide fair and reasonable determination of impairment and disability for voice, guidelines developed for other body systems and functions have been helpful. The World Health Organization's *International Classification of Functioning, Disability and Health* provides a classification scheme that is quite useful for many conditions; but it does not furnish specific compensation guidelines for most conditions. In the United States (and in some other countries) the American Medical Association's *Guides to the Evaluation of Permanent Impairment* (referred to as the *Guides*) have become the standard.[2] The *Guides* rate many impairments and disabilities throughout the body in terms of their percentage impairment of the whole person. At present, even the *Guides* do not provide a sufficient and sophisticated approach to the evaluation of voice impairment and disability. Various other publications of international repute also cover voice impairment disability in adequate depth.[2,3] This chapter contains suggestions to modify and improve existing guidelines.[2] Additional information about assessing voice handicap may be found in chapter 25.

For many years, voice and speech were treated by the medical profession (and the first four editions of the AMA *Guides*[2]) as one subject under the heading speech. In the last 20 years, voice and voice science have evolved as independent subspecialties in otolaryngology and speech-language pathology. So, technology and standards of practice now permit appropriate consideration of both aspects of verbal communication. The fifth edition of the AMA *Guides*[2] published in 2001 contains preliminary changes that acknowledge and begin to rectify this problem. *Voice* refers to production of sound of a given quality, ordinarily using the true vocal folds. *Speech* refers to the shaping of sounds into intelligible words. The disability and handicap associated with severe impairment of speech are obvious. If a person cannot speak intelligibly, verbal communication in social environments and the work place is extremely difficult or impossible. However, voice disorders have been underappreciated for so long that their significance may not be as immediately apparent. Nevertheless, if a voice disorder results in hoarseness, breathiness, voice fatigue, decreased vocal volume, or other similar voice disturbances, the worker may be unable to be heard in the presence of even moderate background noise, to carry on telephone conversations for prolonged periods, or to perform other work-related (and social) functions. Communication with hard-of-hearing family members and friends may also be particularly difficult and frustrating.

Numerous conditions, both physical and environmental, can result in voice or speech disturbances. An extensive review of their etiologies, diagnoses, and treatments is beyond the scope of this discussion. Information on this subject is contained elsewhere in this book and in other literature.[4-7] Briefly, voice and speech dysfunction may be due to trauma (brain, face, neck, chest), exposure to toxins and pollution, cerebrovascular accident, voice abuse, cancer, psychogenic disorders, and other causes. This chapter concentrates on the consequences of voice and speech dysfunction and also synthesizes information introduced in previous writings.[2,8,9]

Evaluation

Evaluation of a person with speech or voice complaints begins with a thorough history. Inquiry should include questions regarding the patient's professional and avocational vocal needs and habits, voice use patterns, problems prior to the onset of the current complaint, the time and apparent cause of the onset of voice and speech dysfunction, and any evaluations and interventions that have been tried to improve voice function. It is also essential to obtain information about environmental irritants and pollution, which may impact the voice greatly.[6] The voice may be impaired not only by mucosal irritants and inhalant toxicity, but also by any substances that decrease lung function or neurologic function (including neurotoxins such as heavy metals). However, a thorough history must include information about virtually all body systems, because maladies almost anywhere in the body may be causally related to voice complaints. The details of a comprehensive voice and speech history, and physical examination are beyond the scope of this brief chapter and may be found in other literature[7] and elsewhere in this book. The physical examination should include thorough evaluation of the structures in the head and neck and evaluation of other parts of the body, as appropriate, based on history and physical assessment of the patient. A thorough evaluation of voice and speech is also mandatory.

For the purposes of this chapter, it should be assumed that the evaluation of voice and speech involves an assessment of a person's ability to produce phonation and articulate speech, and does not involve assessment of content, language, or linguistic structure. At the present time, there is no single, universally accepted measure to quantify voice or speech function. Therefore, the standard of practice requires the use of a battery of tests.

Various tests and objective measures of voice have been clinically available since the late 1970s. Tests such as strobovideolaryngoscopy, acoustic analysis, phonatory function assessment, and laryngeal electromyography (EMG) are recognized as appropriate and useful in the evaluation of speech and voice disorders.[10-14] Some or all of these tests may be necessary in selected cases to determine the severity of a voice disorder and establish the presence of organic versus nonorganic voice and/or speech impairment and disability.

Evaluation of voice requires visualization of the larynx by a physician trained in laryngoscopy (usually an otolaryngologist) and determination of a specific medical cause for the voice dysfunction. Assessment of voice quality, frequency range, intensity range and endurance, pulmonary function, and function of the larynx as a valve (airflow regulator) can be performed easily and inexpensively. Normative values for these assessments have been established in the literature and are discussed elsewhere in this book.[7,11,14] More sophisticated techniques to quantify voice function (spectrography, inverse filtering, etc) may be helpful in selected cases. Slow-motion assessment of vocal fold vibration using strobovideolaryngoscopy (an established procedure that was first described more than 100 years ago) is often medically necessary to establish an accurate diagnosis.

In keeping with standard practice to establish the presence and amount of impairment and disability, a battery of tests is required to determine audibility, intelligibility, and functional efficiency of voice and speech. Audibility permits the patient to be heard over background noise. Intelligibility is the ability to link recognizable phonetic units of speech in a manner that can be understood. Functional efficiency is the ability to sustain voice and speech at a rate and for a period of time sufficient to permit useful communication.

Many approaches are available for speech assessment, most of which are described in standard speech-language pathology textbooks.[4] However, for the purposes of determining impairment and disability, the method recommended in the AMA *Guides* is employed most commonly.[2] This assessment protocol uses "The Smith House" reading paragraph, which reads as follows:

Larry and Ruth Smith have been married nearly fourteen years. They have a small place near Long Lake. Both of them think there's nothing like the country for health. Their two boys would rather live here than any other place. Larry likes to keep some saddle horses close to the house. These make it easy to keep his sons amused. If they wish, the boys can go fishing along the shore. When it rains, they usually want to watch television. Ruth has a cherry tree on each side of the kitchen door. In June they enjoy the juice and jelly.

The patient is placed approximately 8 feet from the examiner in a quiet room. The patient is then instructed to read the paragraph so that the examiner can hear him or her plainly and so that the patient can be understood. Patients who cannot read are asked to count to 100 (and should be able to do so in under 75 seconds). Patients are expected to be able to complete at least a 10-word sentence in one breath, sustain phonation for at least 10 seconds on one breath, speak loudly enough to be heard across the room, and maintain a speech rate of at least 75 to 100 words per minute. The advantages of the system described in the *Guides* are simplicity, and wide application for disability determination. However, this approach does not take advantage of many standardized speech evaluation tests, of technology for better quantification, or of techniques available to help identify psychogenic and intentional voice and speech dysfunction. These advanced methods should be used at least when the results of simple confrontation testing are unconvincing or equivocal; ideally they should be used in all cases. In addition, it does not address the issue of workers whose native language is something other than English. No specific passages have been assigned for various languages. However, appropriate passages may be drawn from the phoniatric or speech-language pathology literature of appropriate countries and used by a medical examiner whose command of the specific language is sufficient to permit valid and reliable interpretation of the patient's responses.

In most respects, the medical evaluation of a person sent for medical/legal purposes or independent medical evaluation (IME) is the same thorough examination that should be performed for all patients with voice and speech disorders. However, for medical-legal purposes, it is important for physicians to be certain that they thoroughly understand the occupational needs and demands of the patient. One schoolteacher's professional vocal needs may be very different from those of another schoolteacher, even in the same school district. Similar differences occur among all voice professionals including singers, telephone operators, and many others whose occupations depend on voice and speech. Understanding the individual circumstances is essential in formulating an accurate, rational, and defensible opinion regarding causation and consequences of a voice and/or speech problem. All such information must be thoroughly documented, and the rationale for the physician's conclusions must be apparent.

There is a substantial difference in physician responsibilities for the patient at the conclusion of a medical-legal encounter compared with patients evaluated medically only. Ordinarily, we are accustomed to providing our patients with information, diagnoses, treatment recommendations, and to ordering appropriate studies. Such communication is not appropriate in many medical/legal settings; and the physician, patient, and referring professional (often an attorney) may be better served by having the physician's conclusion communicated in writing in a formal medical-legal report. The physician should be careful not to express opinions until they have been formed to a reasonable degree of medical certainty. This often requires gathering of additional information (eg, work records), which may not be available at the time of the initial examination.

Great care should be taken to avoid expressing opinions prematurely, because retracting them later can be confusing and awkward and can impugn the physician's medical and legal credibility. Formulating accurate conclusions that can be supported is important to help establish what happened and its consequences and, in some cases, to support recommendations for patient assistance. For example, people in vocally intensive occupations (schoolteachers, stockbrokers) who require voice surgery and/or extensive voice therapy may be well served by a leave of absence, acquisition of assistive devices (eg, microphones), and other modifications in performance routine that may have an unexpectedly great impact on their work environment and job security.

Judgments regarding short- and long-term disability issues may have profound effects on both individual lives and businesses; in some cases they may require an employer to pay a disabled worker the equivalent of many years' salary, on top of the cost associated with replacement of the employee. Such recommendations should be made firmly when appropriate and should never be made when they are not truly medically necessary (particularly prolonged leaves of absence). Formulating accurate and fair opinions in these matters requires thorough understanding of all relevant facts and often reflection and review on the part of the physician.

Suggested Criteria for Determining Voice and/or Speech Impairment

An appropriate determination of voice-related disability requires a comprehensive understanding of voice science and medicine, legal definitions and issues, and consideration of the vocal needs of each individual with voice and/or speech impairment.

For the purposes of classifying voice and/or speech impairment and disability, audibility, intelligibility, and functional efficiency must be taken into account. Audibility permits the patient to be heard over background noise. It generally reflects the condition of the voice. Disability determination should be based on subjective and objective assessments of voice and speech, on reports pertaining to the patient's performance in everyday living and occupational situations, and on instruments such as the Vocal Handicap Index.[15] The reports or evidence should be supplied by reliable observers. For the nonprofessional voice user, the standard of evaluation should be the normal speaker's performance in average situations for everyday living. For the professional voice user, the standard of evaluation is the expected performance in professional and everyday situations of comparable voice professionals. Table 99–1 summarizes suggested voice and speech impairment criteria, modified in part from those set forth in the AMA *Guides*. In evaluating functional efficiency, *everyday speech communication* should be interpreted as including activities of daily living and also the routine voice and speech requirements of the patient's profession. A judgment is made regarding the patient's speech and voice capacity with regard to each of the three columns of the classification chart (Table 99-1). The degree of impairment of voice and/or speech is equivalent to the greatest percentage of impairment recorded in any one of the three columns of the classification chart.

For example, a particular patient's voice/speech impairment is judged to be the following: Audibility, 10% (Class 1); Intelligibility, 50% (Class 3), and Functional Efficiency, 30% (Class 2). This patient's voice/speech impairment is judged to be equivalent to the greatest impairment, 50%.

Converting an impairment of voice and speech into impairment of the whole person requires knowledge of the individual's occupational voice and speech requirements. These may be divided into three classes, as follows. (Note that these criteria are this author's recommendations and are not yet accepted AMA guidelines.)

Table 99–1. Voice and Speech Impairment Guide.

Classification	Audibility	Intelligibility	Functional Efficiency
Class 1 0%-14% speech impairment	Can produce voice of intensity sufficient for *most* of the needs of everyday speech communication, although this sometimes may require effort and occasionally may be beyond patient's capacity.	Can perform *most* of the articulatory acts necessary for everyday speech communication, although listeners occasionally ask the patient to repeat, and the patient may find it difficult or impossible to produce a few phonetic units.	Can meet *most* of the demands of articulation and phonation for everyday speech communication with adequate speed and ease, although occasionally the patient may hesitate or speak slowly.
Class 2 15%-34% speech impairment	Can produce voice of intensity sufficient for *many* of the needs of everyday speech communication; is usually heard under average conditions; however, may have difficulty in automobiles, buses, trains, stations, restaurants, etc.	Can perform *many* of the necessary articulatory acts for everyday speech communication. Can speak name, address, etc and be understood by a stranger, but may have numerous inaccuracies; sometimes appears to have difficulty articulating.	Can meet *many* of the demands of articulation and phonation for everyday speech communication with adequate speed and ease, but sometimes gives impression of difficulty, and speech may sometimes be discontinuous, interrupted, hesitant, or slow.
Class 3 35%-59% speech impairment	Can produce voice of intensity sufficient for *some* of the needs of everyday speech communication, such as close conversation; however, has considerable difficulty in such noisy places as listed above; the voice tires rapidly and tends to become inaudible after a few seconds.	Can perform *some* of the necessary articulatory acts for everyday speech communication; can usually converse with family and friends; however, strangers may find it difficulty to understand the patient, who often may be asked to repeat.	Can meet *some* of the demands of articulation and phonation for everyday speech communication with adequate speed and ease, but often can sustain consecutive speech only for brief periods; may give the impression of being rapidly fatigued.
Class 4 60%-84% speech impairment	Can produce voice of intensity sufficient for a *few* of the needs of everyday speech communication; can barely be heard by a close listener or over the telephone, perhaps may be able to whisper audibly but has no louder voice.	Can perform a *few* of the necessary articulatory acts for everyday speech communication; can produce some phonetic units; may have approximations for a few words such as names of own family members; however, unintelligible out of context.	Can meet a *few* of the demands of articulation and phonation for everyday speech communication with adequate speed and ease, such as using single words or short phrases, but cannot maintain uninterrupted speech flow; speech is labored, rate is impractically slow.
Class 5 85%-100% speech impairment	Can produce voice of intensity sufficient for *none* of the needs of everyday speech communication.	Can perform *none* of the articulatory acts necessary for everyday speech communication.	Can meet *none* of the demands of articulation and phonation for everyday speech communication with adequate speed and ease.

Class 1: Voice/speech impairment should not result in significant change in ability to perform necessary occupational functions. Little or no voice/speech required for most daily occupational requirements. Examples: manuscript typist, data-entry clerk, copy editor.

Class 2: Voice/speech is a necessary component of daily occupational responsibilities, but not the principal focus of the individual's occupation. Impairment of voice or speech may make it difficult or impossible for the individual to perform his or her occupation at his or her preimpairment level. Examples: stockbroker, non-trial attorney, supervisor in a noisy shop.

Class 3: Voice/speech is the primary occupational asset. Impairment seriously diminishes the individual's ability to perform his or her job or makes it impossible to do so. Examples: classroom teacher, trial attorney, opera singer, broadcast announcer.

Table 99–2 is intended as a guideline for converting the percentage of voice and/or speech impairment to percentage impairment of the whole person.

The "Worth" of a Voice

Although improved, standardized guidelines for the estimation of vocal impairment and disability such as

Table 99-2. Speech Impairment Related to Impairment of the Whole Person.

% Speech Impairment	% Impairment of the Whole Person Occupational Class 1	% Impairment of the Whole Person Occupational Class 2	% Impairment of the Whole Person Occupational Class 3
0	0	0	0
5	2	4	5
10	4	8	10
15	5	10	15
20	7	14	20
25	9	18	25
30	10	20	30
35	12	24	35
40	14	28	40
45	16	32	45
50	18	36	50
55	19	38	55
60	21	42	60
65	23	46	65
70	24	48	70
75	26	52	75
80	28	56	80
85	30	60	85
90	32	64	90
95	33	66	95
100	35	70	97

those proposed above may be helpful, no such guidelines are universally applicable to each individual case. If such guidelines are accepted by the AMA *Guides*, they may come to govern voice impairment and disability determination in workers' compensation cases and jurisdictions that include speech and voice within their workers' compensation statutes. In other jurisdictions, and in situations in which the vocal impairment is not causally related to employment, legal redress for voice impairment is generally determined under tort law. In these cases, a judge or jury determines the degree of impairment and disability and the value of compensation, generally based on expert testimony. Reference to documents such as the AMA *Guides* may be included, but many other factors are introduced into testimony to help the judge or jury establish whether a loss is compensable (someone was at fault) and, if so, the amount of compensation that is appropriate. Malpractice actions are generally handled in this fashion; and malpractice suits for dysphonia occur frequently. In some cases, they are (arguably) justified. As recently as 2001, this author reviewed actions in which "vocal cord stripping" was used in young professional singers as the first treatment for vocal nodules, and the surgery resulted in profound, bilateral vocal fold scar. In such instances, arguments frequently center on the singer's true artistic skill and potential for life earnings (determination of damages). Other cases involve famous, established singers for whom enormous earning ability is well-documented, and financial losses in the millions are relatively easy to estimate. In such cases, arguments focus on issues of informed consent, accuracy of diagnosis, appropriateness of surgery, and whether the dysphonia was caused by a deviation from the standard-of-care or was simply a recognized complication such as unfavorable scar.

In all such instances, otolaryngologists have an obligation to their profession and the public. As distasteful as medical-legal aspects of voice disorders may be, we must be prepared to evaluate them honestly and dispassionately. Our evaluation should draw on all of the scientific, clinical, and technological advances that have enhanced the practice of laryngology/voice and should be influenced by an awareness of the standard of practice in impairment and disability determination as set forth in publications such as the AMA *Guides*.

We must be prepared to recognize that dysphonia may result in substantial disability and loss of earnings for many of our patients. When such problems occur as an unavoidable consequence of surgery, we must be prepared to help juries and judges understand the unpredictabilities of surgery. However,

when they occur because of deviations or violations of the standard-of-care, we must also be willing to recognize that the patient may be entitled to compensation in accordance with our country's legal system. We must also recognize that, to some extent, the pressures exerted by the medical-legal climate have worked to improve the standard-of-care and still exert pressure on our profession to remain current with the latest advances and changes in the state-of-the-art care. Maintaining currency is particularly important in a rapidly evolving discipline such as laryngology/voice.

Case Reports

Case 1 is a 42-year-old, female, former teacher, now an elementary school guidance counselor, who returned to work 7 years ago following a 10-year hiatus. Within the first month, she experienced a sudden onset of hoarseness. She continued to work for several months before seeking medical attention. Initial evaluation by an otolaryngologist revealed inflamed vocal folds and nodules, and relative voice rest for 4 days was recommended. She had no improvement in her voice. She then saw a speech therapist weekly for 2 years with no improvement. She then underwent excision of bilateral vocal fold masses. Her voice improved for 6 months, after which her hoarseness returned. She was again diagnosed with recurrent vocal fold nodules and gastroesophageal reflux disease.

She was referred to this author (RTS) 2 years following surgery with complaints of constant hoarseness and voice fatigue. She was unable to project her voice well and unable to sing, although she would have liked to. She had been treated for gastroesophageal reflux disease for the past year. She had year-round allergy symptoms but stated they were now better controlled since she started receiving injections.

Physical examination revealed a moderately hoarse and breathy voice. Strobovideolaryngoscopy revealed a broad-based, solid, white mass of her right vocal fold with a fibrotic mass of the left vocal fold; arytenoid erythema and edema consistent with gastroesophageal reflux disease; bilateral superior surface varicosities and scarring were apparent on stroboscopic visualization. Laryngeal EMG revealed mild bilateral superior laryngeal nerve paresis. No neuromuscular junction abnormalities were noted. Objective voice evaluations were completed and revealed decreased intensity, phonation time, harmonic-to-noise ratio, acoustic measures, and s/z ratio.

There was no improvement in the appearance of her vocal fold lesions following 6 weeks of aggressive medical treatment for the reflux laryngitis disease.

Voice therapy was unsuccessful over the 6-week period despite excellent compliance by the patient. The patient was taken to the operating room for excision of the bilateral lesions. Biopsy revealed adult-onset laryngeal papillomatosis, not nodules as had been diagnosed by her previous physician.

The patient required two subsequent laryngeal operations within 1 year in an attempt to eradicate disease and improve her phonatory function. She will continue to require ongoing surveillance by a laryngologist for recurrence of papillomata and surveillance for the development of laryngeal carcinoma. She will require ongoing voice therapy and treatment for her reflux disease. When she is able to return to work, she will require a personal amplification system to help with vocal projection. Her vocal prognosis is guarded. Her impairment would be noted as 60% to 84% (Class 4).

Case 2 is a 38-year-old male factory worker who has worked at the same chemical plant for 20 years. He started in the rubber division and 10 years later switched to the plastics and chemical division. He was working in a management position, stating he was responsible for everything that blows up. He suffered an inhalation injury 2 years ago resulting from heavy exposure to vinyl chloride fumes when three reactors malfunctioned. He underwent microlaryngoscopy and excision of bilateral vocal fold polyps 1 year after this injury. His voice improved after surgery, and he remained out of work for approximately 6 weeks following surgery. One month after returning to work, he was exposed to anhydrous ammonia fumes and experienced immediate dyspnea and sudden and severe hoarseness. He underwent a second microlaryngoscopy and vocal fold polypectomy. He attempted to return to work but became aphonic after 3 days.

He reported voice deterioration after voice use and any exposure to fumes, perfumes, smoke, and gasoline and that his hoarseness was now associated with shortness of breath. He also experienced chronic globus sensation. He was undergoing psychological counseling for stress-related problems secondary to his voice problems, and he also had to quit smoking.

His voice was harsh, hoarse, slightly breathy, and pressed. Strobovideolaryngoscopy revealed bilateral vocal fold scarring, decreased mucosal wave, hypervascularity, and mucosal irregularities. Objective voice measures revealed marked abnormalities in harmonic-to-noise ratio, shimmer, and maximum flow rate.

This individual had a mucosal vocal fold injury secondary to inhalation of noxious fumes, initially vinyl chloride, and airway hyperactivity causing dysphonia and dyspnea. Additional surgery was recommended. The vocal fold mucosa had never returned to normal

nor had his voice quality. Five years, later he developed progressive dysplastic vocal fold changes (leukoplakia).

This case illustrates the scope of the shortcomings of the *Guides'* current rating system. It does not take into account significant, medically proven symptom fluctuation or specific occupational vocal requirements. When this patient is at home, protected from fumes or pollution, he would be rated Class 3 on the basis of audibility. Once he enters the work environment, or many other everyday settings, his impairment becomes a Class 5. Considering the impact on his life and employability, it is reasonable to assign him a Class 5 rating.

Case 3 is a 28-year-old male singer and songwriter. He developed vocal difficulties 1 year ago while recording an album. He had been singing and performing rock and roll for 10 years with no prior vocal difficulties. While recording his album, he experienced loss of midrange, decreased volume, breathiness, and hoarseness. He was not ill at the time. Three months later he was diagnosed with a left vocal fold polyp, and surgical excision of the lesion was performed the following month. The patient had additional complaints of his voice being worse is the morning, frequent throat clearing, and a globus sensation. He was given advice concerning control of his reflux laryngitis symptoms and placed on a reflux protocol. He remains unhappy with his vocal progress to date.

Strobovideolaryngoscopy revealed a right vocal fold mass, left vocal fold scar, reflux laryngitis, and superior laryngeal nerve paresis. The mass and scar were typical sequelae of hemorrhage, as suggested by his history of sudden voice change while recording. Examination of his singing voice revealed excess tension in the jaw and tongue, hoarseness, and decreased range. Laryngeal EMG was recommended and revealed a 20% decrease in function of the left superior laryngeal nerve. Additionally, he had abnormalities in electroglottography (EGG) quasi-open quotient, AC flow, minimal flow, maximum flow rate, s/z ratio, maximum phonation time, and acoustic measurements.

This case illustrates an important shortcoming of the current rating system. According to the current method, he would be rated Class 2 on the basis of audibility. Yet, as a professional singer, he is totally disabled from this work-related injury. A classification scheme that considered the individual's professional voice needs would classify him as Class 5.

Conclusion

As the field of laryngology/voice evolves over time, considerations of voice impairment and disability also are evolving. All laryngologists should be familiar with these developments, as well as substantive developments in medical, surgical, and post-surgical voice management. Physicians must be extremely diligent about obtaining all of the facts before arriving at a diagnosis and rendering an opinion. Misdiagnoses of voice and speech disorders are common, and somewhat understandably so, because of the dramatic recent advances in the standard of voice and speech care. Nevertheless, misdiagnosis is serious for both medical and medical-legal reasons and can generally be avoided. Information on the latest techniques in voice evaluation is available through The Voice Foundation (1721 Pine Street, Philadelphia, Pa 19103), the literature cited in this article, and many other sources. In medical-legal settings, it is advisable for physicians to consider not only the standard of care, but moreover the state-of-the-art. They should also complement their medical expertise with a reasonable understanding of legal issues, including not only definitions of impairment and disability, but also the legal theories and jurisdiction under which a case is being managed. Such knowledge will enhance our abilities to help not only our patients' voices, but also each patient as a person.

References

1. World Health Organization. *International Classification of Functioning, Disability and Health.* Geneva, Switzerland: WHO; 2001.
2. *Guides to the Evaluation of Permanent Impairment.* 5th ed. Chicago, Ill: American Medical Association; 2001.
3. Sataloff RT. Otolaryngological (ENT) impairment. In: Demeter SL, Andersson GBJ, eds. *Disability Evaluation.* 2nd ed. St. Louis, Mo: Mosby-Yearbook, Inc; 2003:512–530.
4. Aronson A. *Clinical Voice Disorders.* 3rd ed. New York, NY: Thieme Medical Publishers; 1990.
5. Rubin J, Sataloff RT, Korovin G, Gould WJ. *The Diagnosis and Treatment of Voice Disorders.* New York, NY: Igaku-Shoin Medical Publishers, Inc; 1995.
6. Sataloff RT. The impact of pollution on the voice. *Otolaryngol Head Neck Surg.* 1992;106(6):701–705.
7. Rubin JS, Sataloff RT, Korovin GS. *Treatment of Voice Disorders.* 2nd ed. Clifton Park, NY: Delmar Thompson Learning; 2003
8. Sataloff RT. Voice and speech impairment and disability. In: Sataloff RT. *Professional Voice: Science and Art of Clinical Care.* 2nd ed. San Diego, Calif: Singular Publishing Group, Inc; 1997:795–801.
9. Sataloff RT, Abaza MM. Impairment, disability and other medical/legal aspects of dysphonia. *Otolaryngol Clin North Am.* 2000;33:1143–1152.
10. Baken RJ. *Clinical Measurement of Speech and Voice.* Boston, Mass: College-Hill Press; 1987.
11. Hirano M. *Clinical Examination of the Voice.* New York, NY: Springer-Verlag; 1981.
12. Sataloff RT, Spiegel JR, Carroll LM, et al. Strobovideolaryngoscopy in professional voice users: results and clinical value. *J Voice.* 1988;1(4):359–364.
13. Sataloff RT, Spiegel JR, Hawkshaw MJ. Strobovideolaryngoscopy: results and clinical value. *Ann Otol Rhin Laryngol.* 1991;100(9):725–727.
14. Sataloff RT. The human voice. *Sci Am.* 1992;267(6):108–115.
15. Benninger MS, Gardener GM, Jacobson BH, Grywalski C. New dimensions in measuring voice treatment outcomes. In: Sataloff RT. *Professional Voice: The Science and Art of Clinical Care.* 2nd ed. San Diego, Calif: Singular Publishing Group, Inc; 1997:789–794.

100

Voice: Legal Considerations

Judith A. Gic

Voice care specialists, like other medical professionals, can be caught up in a variety of patient-related legal issues. These run the gamut from seeking a specialist's evaluation of vocal disability for purposes of obtaining benefits (disability insurance, workers' compensation, etc) to attacking that specialist's quality of care in a medical negligence lawsuit. Among law-based relationships falling somewhere in between might be a specialist's involvement in helping a voice-injured employee come to agreement with his or her employer on a reasonable accommodation. A multitude of roads connect patients to voice specialists, and medical negligence is only one of them.

In fact, voice specialists are probably more likely to be involved in legal issues on behalf of their patients than against them. That probability arises from the significance of the voice to a vast array of human endeavors. Highly paid singers do not define the realm of professional voice users. Anyone who communicates for a living (eg, radio and television news announcers, teachers, and trial litigators) relies on a healthy voice. Furthermore, even those who generally are not understood to communicate for a living, to a large degree, still vocalize as a regular part of work or just plain living. For most people, the world is a chattering, noisy place of their own making. Does the value of a voice vary with each owner? Would Callas have elected to sacrifice her voice in light of a diagnosis of laryngeal cancer? Does a lifelong smoker value having a voice any less than a diva committed to stressing her voice throughout her lifetime?

These questions prompt us to reflect on the importance of the voice to everyone and to realize that any person without a voice is diminished significantly. According to the American Medical Association's *Guides to the Evaluation of Permanent Impairment*, a voice or speech impairment will, depending on its severity, result in a whole-person impairment rating of up to 35%, without regard for the person's profession[1] (see chapter 99). Consequently, the chronic impairments that drive patients to seek out a voice specialist are likely to affect them in broader ways, including ways that have legal implications.

Of course, voice specialists must also be ever mindful of the possibility of legal claims against them by their patients. Voice is key to ways that individuals project themselves into their worlds, so a patient with a voice problem may also endure a great deal of anxiety as he or she works to accept a degradation in vocal ability. Regardless of whether the voice specialist is thought to have caused the problem or is thought to have done an inadequate job of fixing it, there is a potential for liability. Liability for professional negligence affecting vocal ability arises under the same laws and principles that govern liability for negligence affecting other aspects of bodily health. In this regard, there is nothing special about the voice; and therefore, those who specialize in care of the voice should have a general awareness of the legal precedents.

Therefore, this chapter will point out some of the legal aspects of voice problems by surveying situations (and, where appropriate, legal cases) where the involvement of voice care specialists may help patients as litigants and, on the opposite end, where the quality of care has been an issue between them.

Workers' Compensation

In *Buford v Standard Gravel Co,*[2] the plaintiff prevailed on a claim for permanent and total disability benefits. His first on-the-job injury occurred in 1981 when he was working on an oil derrick. A piece of rig equipment broke loose and struck Buford on the throat, crushing his larynx and causing chronic hoarseness and reduced volume. Beginning about 7 years after that accident, he suffered two back injuries and based his claim for permanent and total disability benefits on those two back injuries plus the injury to his voice. Somewhat problematic was the fact that no permanent disability percentage had been assigned to Buford following the larynx injury in 1981. (This is not entirely surprising, because even now "there is no single, acceptable, proven test that will measure objectively the degrees of impairment due to the many varieties of voice disorders."[3]) Even so, there was no evidence that Buford's voice quality had declined any further in the time between the accident and the application for benefits; in other words, all of his voice problems were the result of the on-the-job accident. Evidence from vocational rehabilitation specialists showed that Buford's back injuries prevented him from performing his job as a welder (and various other trades for which he was reasonably suited) and that his voice problems precluded an alternative career as a welding instructor: "Buford cannot speak to a class for thirty to forty minutes at a time because of his throat injury, and he can only talk loud enough for a class to hear him "if they were quiet."[4] The case report does not disclose whether or to what extent any voice specialist evaluated Buford as part of the vocational rehabilitation process, but it is clear that this was a situation appropriate for a voice specialist to examine the patient and to provide expert medical opinion on his degree of vocal disability.

A fractured larynx was also among the plaintiff*s injuries in *Barbaglia v General Motors Acceptance Corporation,*[5] where the plaintiff was involved in an on-the-job auto accident. (Since this case was decided in 1973, seat belts and airbags have reduced all types of auto accident injuries, including upper body injuries from striking the steering wheel.) The fracture left the plaintiff with "permanent residual hoarseness."[6] Based on the fracture and his other injuries, he applied for workers' compensation benefits and received a 5% permanent partial disability rating. The judge based the disability rating only on injuries to the plaintiff's legs and ignored the injuries to his larynx and ribs. The plaintiff appealed and won a higher rating, 25%, based on the injuries that the lower court had ignored. He appealed again, seeking a higher rating, but the Nebraska Supreme Court affirmed the 25% rating. The case report clearly discloses only that the plaintiff's treating physician testified on his behalf; the record is not clear on whether that physician was a voice care specialist or whether any medical professional other than the treating physician was called to testify. This, like Buford, was a case where expert opinion from a voice

care specialist would have been appropriate and helpful. Indeed, a dissenting judge who would have voted in favor of finding Barbaglia totally disabled noted that Barbaglia's "permanent hoarseness . . . is certainly a disabling function insofar as speaking is concerned."[7] Assuming there was no voice care specialist to testify, the presence of one might have aided the dissenting judge's view to prevail.

Other Benefits

Other types of insurance benefits besides workers' compensation insurance may be at stake for a voice-injured plaintiff. Where the accident or injury is not work-related, the plaintiff may be able to claim benefits under a disability policy, such as an employer-provided policy covered by the Employee Retirement Income Security Act (ERISA) or a self-provided policy.

In such cases, the voice care specialist's involvement would be similar to that of other medical professionals treating an insured with a disability. In general, the insurer predicates payment of benefits on receipt of an application for payment of benefits from the insured individual. A part of the application typically is reserved for use by the insured's physician, who is expected to provide objective and accurate information about the extent of the insured's disabling condition, such as when it first manifested, its severity, its expected duration, and its effect on the insured's ability to work. Because the insured agrees to disclosure of such information as part of the insurance application process, it does not impinge on doctor-patient confidentiality. Insurance companies generally also expect benefit applicants to sign release documents enabling them to obtain copies of the insured's medical records. Of course, any other contact between the insurance company and the physician would have to be patient-approved.

In contentious cases, the voice care specialist's involvement may go beyond merely providing documents and turn into providing testimony. Testimony generally would involve whether the voice problem was caused by an act, occurrence, or similar liability trigger covered by the policy, as well as whether the degree of the problem was sufficiently severe to satisfy the policy's definition of a disabling condition. For example, many disability policies provide short-term disability benefits for a condition that prevents the insured from performing the substantial duties of his or her regular occupation, but restrict long-term disability benefits to those unable to perform the duties of any occupation. The insured's attorney may turn to the insured's physician in search of an expert opinion on the parameters of the disability so as to better understand whether the insured can satisfy such definitions.

Personal Injury

In personal injuries that damage the larynx, voice care specialists may be consulted to give expert opinion on how the injury caused the damage that the plaintiff claims, as well as on the degree of injury or disability. For example, in *McGrath v Irving*,[9] the plaintiff sued for damages, including total laryngectomy, alleging that they were caused in part by the defendant's negligence in an auto accident. McGrath alleged that she inhaled glass during the accident and that this caused an epidermoid carcinoma of the larynx, necessitating the laryngectomy. The defendant challenged the theory of cancer causation resting on the inhalation of glass (something one might also do now; but it is only fair to keep in mind the early 1960's context of this case). The plaintiff presented expert testimony from McGrath's treating physician, who was also a member of the department of laryngology-bronchoesophagology at Temple University. He testified that the inhaled glass "accelerated development or growth of . . . [the] cancer."[9] The jury accepted the voice specialist's opinion as evidence of causation and awarded damages to the plaintiff, which the appellate court affirmed.

The universe of the personal injuries affecting the voice is extremely broad, and may even include neurological impairments more properly classified as difficulties with speech rather than voice. For example, in *Meunstermann v United States*,[10] the court found that negligent failure to perform a cesarian delivery caused the fetus to suffer a stroke resulting in, among other things, a permanent difficulty in speaking. In *Greynolds v Kurman*,[11] a cerebral angiogram performed without informed consent caused a stroke resulting in global aphasia. In *Silvestri v Smallberg*,[12] the court affirmed $1.25 million for past and future pain and suffering based in part on "garbled speech" resulting from a stroke proven to have resulted from the defendant's failure to perform a lumbar puncture. Even in such cases, voice care specialists may be appropriate sources of expert opinion on the causation and, particularly, the degree of the patient's voice and/or speech injury for purposes of giving the jury an adequate basis for assessing damages.

Reasonable Accommodation

Federal disability law (primarily the Americans with Disabilities Act) and state laws in a variety of states prohibit employment discrimination against the disabled. They also affirmatively require employers to provide reasonable accommodations to disabled employees who would not otherwise be able to perform their jobs. For example, suppose that the plaintiff is a grocery store cashier with a significantly reduced (by whatever cause) ability to project volume. Grocery store checkout lines are not quiet places, and cashiers may at any point have need to speak to a customer (besides providing an obligatory greeting and thank you), request assistance from a manager, and so on.

If the employer shows that it wants to terminate the cashier because of the voice problem, a voice care specialist may become involved at two stages. First, the specialist may assist the patient in documenting the existence of a disability. Employers are not required simply to accept an employee's assertion of disability; the disability may need to be proven. Second, once the employer has accepted the existence of a disability, the employer may be required to work with the employee on crafting a reasonable accommodation that would enable him or her to perform at least the job's essential functions without imposing an undue hardship on the employer. Because these statutory requirements are situation-specific and not clear-cut, expert opinion from the employee's voice care specialist may help the employer better understand the exact nature of the employee's limitations and how they can be addressed. For example, the specialist may be able to say that the cashier's volume problem is progressive over an 8-hour shift but may be alleviated by ready access to liquids. Although the employer might not allow other cashiers to have beverages at their workstations, the specialist's opinion may obligate the employer to allow the voice-disabled employee to do so in aid of his or her job. The voice care specialist may have to provide similar evidence in a judicial proceeding should the employer terminate the cashier.

Medical Negligence

The prospect of negligence liability, and its cost, are probably most obvious to otolaryngologists in the case of professional voice users, the most famous recent case being the malpractice claim of singer Julie Andrews. Andrews sued two voice specialists and a New York City hospital after she failed to recover her singing voice following surgery to remove masses from her vocal folds; she eventually settled for an undisclosed sum.[13] Among professional voice users, even a minor loss of vocal ability can translate into a significant decrease in earnings.

However, as noted above, almost everyone who works relies to some degree on his or her voice. For example, in *Coffin v Board of Supervisors of Louisiana State University*,[14] the plaintiff was a telephone switchboard operator who sued for chronic hoarseness and poor voice quality after a panendoscopy that was intended to explore her bronchi, esophagus and larynx. After a resident had had difficulty inserting the bronchoscope and esophagoscope, the attending otolaryngologist inserted the endoscope and observed a tear of the right piriform sinus. Emergency surgery ensued, after which the evidence showed that the patient never recovered her normal voice. The trial court concluded, and the appellate court affirmed, that the plaintiff's "vocal cords and voice box were severely traumatized by [the resident's] negligence in the ramming of both the bronchoscope and endotracheal tube down Mrs. Coffin's throat."[15] The defendant's theory of causation, which the courts rejected, proposed that her hoarseness resulted from 24 years of smoking and two procedures, subsequent to the panendoscopy and emergency surgery, to remove leukoplakia from the vocal folds.

In another case, *Fiumefreddo v McLean*,[16] the plaintiff was another apparently ordinary voice user (although his actual livelihood was not disclosed in the Court's opinion). He suffered permanent paralysis of a vocal fold as a result of damage to the recurrent laryngeal nerve during a thymectomy intended to treat myasthenia gravis. The jury rendered a verdict in favor of the two defendants, but the trial court reversed and remanded for a new trial because of an error in the jury instructions. Expert medical testimony established that injury to the nerve should not occur during a thymectomy absent a deviation from the standard of care, and so the plaintiff argued that the jury should have been instructed that it was allowed to infer the occurrence of negligence from the fact of the injury. The court agreed. (The result of the subsequent trial, if any, was not published.)

Assessing damages for personal injuries is always difficult, and no less so than when the voice is involved. Because of the posture in which Fiumfreddo went to the appeals court, there was no discussion about the proper amount of damages. But in Coffin, the appellate court affirmed two types of voice-related damages awarded by the trial court. First, the plaintiff received about $171,819 for lost wages and lost earning capacity. (Note that the injury occurred in 1984 and the appellate decision was rendered in 1993.) "There is evidence that she can no longer function as a telephone or switchboard operator, receptionist, or in other occupations which require frequent oral communications . . . . In his opinion {ie, that of a vocation-

al rehabilitation expert}, it would be difficult for Coffin to find employment in a competitive job market due to both her unpleasant voice and her age."[17] Second, the plaintiff also received a general damage award that included $50,000 specifically to compensate her for the distress arising out of the "[p]ermanent damage to voice, past and present loss of quality of life due to diminished voice quality."[18]

The defendant argued that the second damage award impermissibly duplicated the lost earnings award; the court disagreed. "There is no bar to Coffin's ability to recover damages, in addition to economic loss, for the physical damage to her vocal cords and larynx (voice box) or for the loss in her quality of life."[19] The evidence supporting this award was testimony describing Coffin's voice as "gravelly, abnormal, severely hoarse. On occasion, Coffin opens her mouth to say something and no voice comes out, or she begins talking or singing and her voice leaves."[19]

The court's reliance on such imprecise language as "gravelly, abnormal, severely hoarse" reflects the previously noted fact that "[a]t this time there is no single, acceptable, proven test that will measure objectively the degrees of impairment due to the many varieties of voice disorders."[20] The AMA Guides group symptoms of voice disorders into the categories of "abnormal volume (voice fatigue, weakness, or low sound intensity), abnormal control (pitch and/or melodic variation), and/or abnormal quality (hoarseness, harshness, or breathiness)."[20] In other words, the court's use of such terms is consistent with what medicine has supplied up to this point.

The imprecision of voice impairment measurement injects a certain degree of unpredictability in assessing the value of voice injuries. Aside from the difficulty of putting a dollar value on the injury (a difficulty that exists in all personal injury cases), there is the difficulty of defining the extent of the injury, especially in the absence of recorded evidence of the patient's voice before the alleged negligence. For this reason, otolaryngologists should consider obtaining voice samples from patients before procedures that could endanger the voice.

Conclusion

Voice care specialists pride themselves in providing comprehensive care for patients with voice disorders. It is widely recognized that care includes attending not only to physical problems of the vocal folds, but also to their consequences for daily activities and quality of life. In many cases, these important patient concerns may include legal issues. In order to help their patients, it is important for voice care specialists to be familiar with the scope of legal problems encountered by patients with voice disorders and to be willing to provide expert, objective medical opinions when called upon to do so.

References

1. Cocchiarella L, Andersson GBJ. *Guides to the Evaluation of Permanent Impairment.* Chicago, Ill: AMA Press; 2000:265.
2. *Buford v Standard Gravel Co.* 5 SW3d 478 (Ark App 1999).
3. Cocchiarella L, Andersson GBJ. *Guides to the Evaluation of Permanent Impairment.* Chicago, Ill: AMA Press; 2000: 264.
4. *Buford v Standard Gravel Co,* 5 SW3d 481 (Ark App 1999).
5. *Barbaglia v General Motors Acceptance Corp,* 209 NW2d 353 (Neb 1973).
6. *Barbaglia v General Motors Acceptance Corp,* 209 NW2d 354.
7. *Barbaglia v General Motors Acceptance Corp,* 209 NW2d 356 (Spencer J., dissenting).
8. *Barbaglia v General Motors Acceptance Corp,* 265 NY2d 376 (NY App Div 1965).
9. *McGrath v Irving,* 265 NYS2d 378.
10. *Meunstermann v United States,* 787 F Supp 499 (DC Md 1992).
11. *Greynolds v Kurman,* 632 NE2d 946 (Ohio Ct App 1993).
12. *Silvestri v Smallberg,* 637 NYS2d 115 (NY App Div), aff'd, 648 NYS2d 870 (NY 1996).
13. Available at: http://www.hollywood.com/news/details/article/312981 and http://news.bbc.co.uk/hi/english/enterainment/newsid_565000/565852.stm Accessed Nov 15, 2001.
14. *Coffin v Board of Supervisors of Louisiana State University,* 620 So 2d 1354 (La Ct App 1993).
15. *Coffin v Board of Supervisors of Louisiana State University,* 620 So. 2d 1360.
16. *Fiumefreddo v McLean,* 496 NW2d 226 (Wis Ct App 1993).
17. *Coffin v Board of Supervisors of Louisiana State University,* 620 So 2d 1366.
18. *Coffin v Board of Supervisors of Louisiana State University,* 620 So 2d 1367.
19. *Coffin v Board of Supervisors of Louisiana State University,* 620 So 2d 1362.
20. Cocchiarella L, Andersson GBJ. *Guides to the Evaluation of Permanent Impairment.* 5th ed. Chicago, Ill: AMA Press; 2000:264.

101

Voice and Forensics

Harry F. Hollien

Although many practitioners in clinical areas carry out research that is both timely and sophisticated, much of the knowledge basic to their speciality is provided by individuals who are primarily scholars and/or scientists. Thus, otologists and audiologists are supported (in part, anyway) by psychoacousticians and auditory physiologists. So too are speech pathologists and laryngologists consumers of much of the material produced by phoneticians (specialists, who are often referred to, in this part of the world anyway, as voice and/or speech scientists). As you might expect, the latter group (the phonetic scientists) interfaces with yet other groups of professionals (ie, engineers, linguists, psychiatrists, specialists in diving, etc); they do so for a variety of practical and scientific reasons. In turn, they learn from these other specialists—about problems, about behaviors, about methods—just as they do from the clinical speech and hearing professionals. This cross-fertilization can be both rich and valuable.

The focus of this chapter is about one of these relationships, one where phonetic scientists have been challenged by the needs and problems of several groups of interrelated practitioners and have been able to respond by drawing on their talents, training, and experience. The area(s) to which I am referring are the forensic sciences. The practitioners in question are primarily law enforcement and/or intelligence personnel, attorneys, and jurists. Phoneticians interface with these professionals in much the same manner as they have with laryngologists, speech/voice pathologists, and voice teachers. In fact, the relationship between phonetics and forensics has grown so much over the past 20 to 30 years that there is now a subspecialty within the phonetic sciences called forensic phonetics. Recently, I described this area in a book, *The Acoustics of Crime*, [1] as well as in a number of articles

and chapters.[2-5] Moreover, this specialty now has its own society; it is called the International Association of Forensic Phonetics (IAFP). We publish a journal in collaboration with forensic linguists (they started their society before we did); it is called *Forensic Linguistics: The International Journal of Speech, Language and the Law* and it is published by the University of Birmingham (Edgbaston, Birmingham B15, 2TT, UK). The current IAFP officers also can be contacted at that address.

But what is forensic phonetics and what does it do for those specialties cited above? First, it serves them in traditional ways by providing information and testing relationships; it also provides support just as it does for the clinical areas of speech and voice. In any event, forensic phonetics can be defined as a professional specialty based on the utilization of current knowledge about the communicative processes—including the development of specialized techniques and procedures—for the purpose of meeting certain of the needs of legal groups and law enforcement agencies. Although many of these developments and approaches also can be used to assist military, industrial, and security organizations, the forensic phonetics interface is primarily with the criminal justice and judicial systems. As such, it constitutes one of the practical applications of the phonetic sciences; and, as stated, it also has led to the development of specialized techniques, equipment, and approaches in support of their needs.

Forensic phonetics consists of two general areas. One involves the electroacoustical analysis of speech and voice signals that have been transmitted and stored; the other involves the analysis (both physical and perceptual) of communicative behaviors. The first area is focused on problems such as the proper transmission and storage of spoken exchanges, the authentication of tape recordings, the enhancement of speech on tape recordings, speech decoding, legal transcripts, and similar problems. The second major area involves issues such as the identification of speakers, the process of obtaining information relative to the physical and/or psychological states of a talker (stress, psychosis, intoxication, are examples), and the analysis of speech for evidence of deception or authorship. This chapter will not cover all of these areas—much less still others that are associated with this specialty but on a secondary basis (for listings, see Hollien[1]). Rather, the focus here will be on just three of the content areas: (1) the accurate processing and decoding of speech/voice (for forensic purposes, of course), (2) the identification of speakers from voice, and (3) the detection of (certain) behavioral states by analysis of speech/voice.

Although the reasons for such activities should become obvious after the cited areas are reviewed, it might be useful to briefly describe some of the extant problems. First, it should be noted that a surprisingly large percentage of all human (oral) discourse occurs in situations other than those that are "face-to-face" in nature. For example, in Western Europe, and especially in North America, a significant proportion of the total number of spoken messages will occur over telephone links, radio, television, or the Internet. Moreover, much of this speech—plus a percentage of the face-to-face exchanges—is tape-recorded or electronically stored by some other technique. To illustrate, a large number of organizations systematically record all or most of their incoming telephone calls (plus many of those outgoing); and this practice is being adopted by many other groups (ie, by security agencies, industry, schools, hospitals, and so on). Of yet greater importance: (1) the extent (and sophistication) of electronic surveillance is expanding, (2) many legal and law enforcement interviews are captured by multiple recording systems, and (3) most (acoustic) activities in courtrooms are being recorded. Note also that many of the procedures already developed by forensic phoneticians can be utilized to enhance these activities and also to aid in the solution of crimes (already committed); prevent crimes that are being planned; ensure the accuracy of legal records; assist decision makers during trials; and so on. It would now appear timely to consider the selected issues, and their current solutions, in some detail.

Problems with Speech Fidelity

Without a doubt, intelligible, accurate speech (whether "live" or stored) is important to many groups; included in this long list are law enforcement agencies, other units within the criminal justice system, and the courts. For example, the effectiveness of many detectives would be sharply reduced if suddenly they could no longer utilize tape recordings for surveillance, during interrogation, and/or for record keeping. Indeed, it is possible that analysis of signals stored on tape recordings ranks among the more powerful of the tools that investigators currently have at their disposal. On the other hand, any degradation of the intelligibility and/or quality of these signals (by distortion, noise, interference, etc) can create problems (sometimes severe) with the aforementioned surveillance, interrogations, investigations, and so on. With specialized knowledge about the problems, plus effective processing procedures, the amount of information captured and utilized can be substantial.

Sources of Difficulty

The tape recordings generated for legal and law enforcement purposes are rarely high fidelity; indeed, they often (very often it seems) are of rather limited quality. The two main sources of this difficulty are distortion and noise. Both result primarily from use of inadequate equipment, poor recording techniques, or events occurring in the acoustic environment within which the tape recordings were made[1,6-8] The degradation of speech intelligibility by and within equipment can result from: (1) reduction of signal bandwidth, (2) harmonic distortion, (3) system noise, and (4) intermittent masking/reduction/elimination of the target sounds. The equipment employed in the field is rarely laboratory quality but rather consists of body bugs, telephones, line taps, suction cup pickups, and so on. Although most of the transducers and systems employed provide for the adequate transfer of speech (the frequency band necessary for good speech intelligibility rarely exceeds 200–4000 Hz), degradation will develop rapidly if these conditions are combined. For example, when noise is added to target speech recorded with inexpensive or very small tape recorders, the end result is speech that is not intelligible enough for easy decoding or, perhaps, any decoding at all. Poorly maintained, or inappropriately used, equipment often can lead to problems of this type. Finally, although very slow recording speeds permit a great deal of information to be captured on small reels of tape, intelligibility will be degraded; because too much material is crowded into very small areas of magnetic space; even small distortions, when added, can result in sharply debased messages.

Noise, even by itself, can be a culprit also; and it takes many forms.[1,8] One such source is "forensic noise" (ie, competing speech, music, and so on). However, the more common types of noise can be: (1) broadband or narrow band, (2) that with a natural frequency or frequencies (60 Hz hum for example), or (3) steady-state or intermittent. It can result from friction sources (ie, the wind, clothing movement, fans/blowers), radio transmission, vehicle operation, explosions, and so on. Some of the effects of noise can be mitigated by the elimination of the part of its spectrum that exists outside of the functional speech range (ie, below 350 Hz and above 3500 Hz). So too can noises, which have "natural frequencies," be countered as often their "narrow frequency band" effect can be eliminated or reduced even if it is located within the speech range. Intermittent or impact noise—street noise, gunshots, video games, bells, horns, explosions, doors closing, and so on—can obscure speech but usually only on an intermittent basis. Because these impact noises (as well as their sources) are extremely variable, it is virtually impossible to list them all.

Finally, although it is not practical to describe all of the potential problems that can reduce speech intelligibility, suffice to say they are legion. But, even so, can speech be enhanced for listening and/or decoded for forensic purposes? In many cases, it can.

Remedies

First, it should be acknowledged that a number of scientists and engineers have been developing fairly sophisticated machine techniques designed to reconstruct degraded speech. They employ approaches such as bandwidth compression, cross channel correlation, mean least squares analysis, all-pole models, group delay functions, linear adaptive filtering, linear predictive coefficients, cepstrum techniques, deconvolution, and so on.[9-14] However, many of these techniques, at this time, do not appear to be functionally easy to apply in the forensic milieu; most are complex, time consuming, and costly. In any case, they will not be reviewed to any great extent in this chapter; rather the procedures to be described will include some of the more practical and easily applied approaches currently in use.[1,6-8,15]

A General Procedure

Reasonably good techniques are available to upgrade tape recordings for decoding purposes. The initial step is to protect the "original" tape recording by making a good quality copy. This approach will reduce deterioration due to tape breakage, accidental erasure, stretching, and twisting or friction wear to the recording oxide. Imagine the problems that would be encountered if important evidence in a criminal case was thus compromised.

Second, the examiner will listen to the tape recording one or more times before attempting to process it.

This procedure permits development of a good working knowledge of its contents as well as of the types of interference and degradation that exist. By this process, strategies can be designed to counter the problems found.

It often will be necessary to apply frequency biasing and filtering techniques. They may be understood by observation of the hardware systems found in Figure 101–1. It will be noted that, even if digital in nature, the filtering often will be conducted in stages rather than in a single pass. Moreover, the phased approach will avoid the need to cascade a large number of filters into a single equipment array; because when filters are used in series, signal reduction can be severe; and they must be isolated from each other to avoid interaction effects.

Another issue, just how acoustic energy patterns affect human hearing (and ultimately that of the decoders) also is important. It has long been known that energy at lower frequencies will tend to mask that at higher frequencies, whereas energy at higher frequencies will not affect lower ones but rather will act as a distraction. Thus, frequencies occurring below the speech band will mask it to the greatest extent. Fortunately, this low-frequency noise often can be removed (to some extent) by good filtering techniques. Finally, even though its presence can be quite annoying, noise above 3000 Hz will not tend to mask speech very much; however, the irritation it creates can be reduced either by analog or digital filtering.

Filtering Techniques

A brief consideration of how filtering is accomplished might prove useful (see again Fig 101–1). As is well known, analog filtering is the easiest to use. In its simplest form, it can be referred to as biasing or equalization; and such circuits often are found on tape recorders, amplifiers, or home audio systems. However, comb and notch filters are more powerful. For example, if spectral analysis shows that a noise source is producing a relatively narrow band of high energy at or around a specific frequency, a notch filter centering on that frequency may be employed to reduce its debilitating effect. Notch filters with a center frequency around 60 Hz are particularly helpful in reducing the speech-masking effects of AC "hum." Comb filters consist of a series of separately controllable notch filters arrayed in a systematic sequence from low frequencies to high. They can be used to continuously modify the spectrum of a signal by selectively attenuating undesirable frequency bands. For example, they can be operated simultaneously as a bandpass filter (350–3500 Hz) and one or more notch filters; or it can

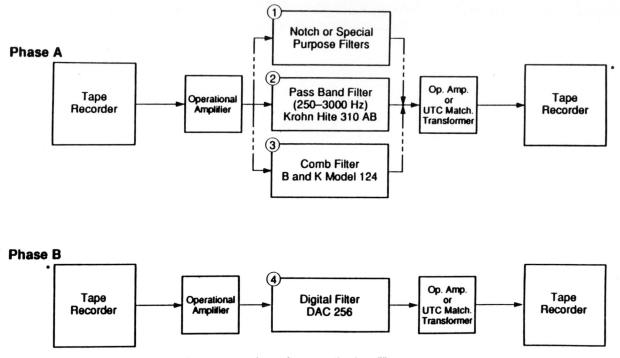

Fig 101–1. This block diagram demonstrates how analog and/or digital filtering can be accomplished. The three analog filters (1-3) can be used singly or cascaded; however, they would not be employed in parallel (as shown). A typical configuration would be to place a comb filter and a digital filter (both isolated) in a series.

be cascaded with other units to increase the filtering effects of the total system.

An important class of filters is digital in nature. Basically, these filters digitize the signal a set number of times each second (say, 20 K). They then determine the energy bands throughout the spectrum and remove the unwanted frequencies. Of course, this process is somewhat more complicated than just described. One example should suffice. A common unit provides two modes of automatic operation. It employs a 256th order filter that rapidly designs its own characteristics to remove unwanted noise by adaptive predictive deconvolution. It works best for linear noise (many noise signals are predictable) but can process nonlinear signals by "short-time correlation." The second (more powerful) mode feeds the noise to one of the unit's channels as a reference and the same noise plus the target speech to the other. The process then becomes one of adaptive noise cancellation. Incidentally, all of the digital filtering techniques can be carried out either by appropriate hardware or by computer software. In practice, digital filtering can be very helpful, especially when analog filters fail to remove enough of the unwanted interference. On the other hand, digital ap-

proaches can create problems also (ie, the resulting signal can be distorted or add what sounds like an echo). It must be remembered, also, that filtering techniques may not work all that well if the noise exists *within* the speech frequency band. In such cases, other techniques plus skilled human decoders must be applied.

Variable-Speed Tape Recorders

Variable-speed tape recorders sometimes can be useful in upgrading speech intelligibility; the process can be accomplished by means of hardware or computer software. Approaches of this type exist in two classes: (1) where only a simple (often manual) increase or decrease in recorder speed is possible and (2) where expansion and compression circuits have been added so that the tape speed can be altered with minimal disruption of the speech spectra. The first procedure is especially useful when the speed of the original tape recorder has been varied for some reason. In the second instance, the perceived pitch of the talker's voice is altered but his or her articulatory characteristics change but little. Manipulations of both of these systems can be especially effective when they are combined with filtering.

In Summary

Many techniques can be used to enhance the speech stored on tape recordings. The preceding paragraphs sketched out only a few. Suffice it to say that they must be applied robustly if messages are to be decoded and transcribed. The second stage is the actual decoding.

Speech Decoding and Transcripts

The subsequent phase in the extraction of utterances and messages from distorted tapes involves speech decoding. Although these procedures are well established, some of the situations wherein problems are encountered will be discussed briefly. As stated earlier, difficulties often result from: (1) tape recordings being made under less than optimal conditions, (2) recordings that are the product of electronic surveillance, (3) dialogue or utterances that were recorded under less than ideal conditions, and (4) material inadvertently added to a tape recording that was being made for other purposes. Although the relevant speech in these cases *may* be comprehendible, such is not always the case (even after enhancement). In those instances, formal decoding will have to be applied with trained personnel attempting to accurately reproduce the recorded speech in written form.[16,17] It must be added that the decoders will face not only the channel or system distortions described above but also speaker-related problems. Difficulties of this type can result from a number of intended and inadvertent behaviors by the talker or talkers. They include: (a) disguise (almost always intentional), (b) dialects and foreign languages, (c) variation in speech rate (often unintended), (d) effects of stress or fear, (e) effects of alcohol/drugs/ health states, and (f) additional speakers, and/or interruptions by other speakers. Although the existence of these conditions may not be a problem, any of them can increase degradation of speech intelligibility and make decoding more difficult. As with system distortions, these factors should be identified early and dealt with individually. For example, the use of specialized decoders for foreign language dialects sometimes is warranted. Note also that efficient and accurate decoding requires that the cited professionals be exposed to formal training primarily in phonetics and linguistics.

Noise and Masking

It must be assumed, of course, that the masking effects of noise already have been mitigated insofar as is pos-

sible; the residue, thus, may or may not create problems for the decoder. For one thing, the effects of noise may not always be as debilitating as might be expected; and speech often can be understood even in the presence of rather intense nonspeech signals. This phenomenon is due largely to the internal redundancy of language and the structure of an utterance. Thus, if the competing noise (especially if broadband) is *only* twice as intense as the speech, the spoken message often will remain intelligible or nearly so. Even more surprising, the intensity of the interference signal sometimes can reach a level as much as four times greater than that of the speech (depending on the type of noise, of course) before it completely destroys intelligibility. Thus, the problem often is that noise is more of a distraction than a block to comprehension; and it may not prevent efficient decoding especially if the transcriber is well trained.

An issue closely related to noise and masking involves human capabilities for sensory processing of an auditory nature. Of these, three factors are of particular importance; they are (1) foreground-background processing, (2) binaural listening, and (3) auditory illusions (especially those related to speech). Foreground-background processing is best illustrated by the picture where a white vase can be observed in the middle of a figure (foreground) and that silhouettes of two (identical) people facing each other can be seen at the sides. In audition, the parallel process involves a person's ability to attend selectively to particular elements within a heard stimulus (the so-called "cocktail party" effect). In the case of speech in noise, the human auditor often can focus on the speech and relegate the noise to the background—at least to some extent. As would be expected, much of this processing occurs at the cortical level; it is aided by binaural listening and directional hearing. It also is one of the reasons humans tend to make better speech decoders than do machines.

Binaural listening simply means that the auditor hears the signal simultaneously in both ears (it does not have to be stereophonic also). All that is necessary to appreciate this procedure is to alternately listen to some speech first through a single earphone and then through two. It often is surprising how much recorded conversations will be enhanced when a switch is made to good quality binaural earphones.

Speech decoders also are aided by auditory "illusions." Indeed, no special training is necessary here as most people have learned naturally to process distorted or partly heard speech. Although much of the relevant processing of this type takes place at the cortical level, the nonlinearities in the hearing modality also contribute. One thing that happens is that listeners intuitively learn to fill in those parts of speech that are distorted or missing; they do so by attending to coarticulation and the characteristics of the linguistic environment in which utterances are heard. For example, a vowel and its transitions alone often can provide enough information to permit a decoder to correctly "hear" missing consonants (and, hence, the entire word); certain speech sounds within a word can be obliterated (or replaced by noise) and still be understood; and a talker's fundamental frequency is perceived even though it has not been passed to the listener because of limited frequency response (of a telephone, say). Actually, there is no mystery about these auditory illusions[18] as their nature is lawful; they depend partly on the neurophysiological structure of the listener's ear, partly on training, and partly on his or her experience. In any case, they serve to aid an individual involved in a difficult speech decoding task.

Linguistic Elements

Basic knowledge about the segmentals (vowels, consonants) and other speech elements is a fundamental part of the decoder's repertoire. Indeed, comprehension of phoneme place and manner will provide the decoder with many useful insights. And, to be effective, decoders also must be familiar with both word structure and the characteristics of word boundaries.[19,20] As you know, linguistic rules exist for word structure (just as they do for sentence structure); and these rules provide important information about what a word might be (or should be) when it cannot be heard clearly. Moreover, knowledge about word boundaries is important; it bears especially on spectrography when utilized to provide a visual picture of an utterance. A solid understanding of word and phoneme boundaries/characteristics is especially important when the decoding task is particularly challenging.

Second, analysis of the linguistic stress patterns exhibited by a speaker also can be helpful in the preparation of accurate transcripts. The many nonlinguistic gestures a person uses to enhance the meaning of a message are well known.[21,22] Speakers employ suprasegmentals (or paralinguistic elements) to create emphasis; included are variation in speaking fundamental frequency, phoneme/syllable/word duration, vocal intensity, and so on. Familiarity with these features and how they affect speech can provide important clues when transferring heard discourse into written form. Finally, knowledge about the nature and characteristics of dialects,[23-25] either foreign or regional, also can be important. For example, recognition of a specific dialect can provide an assist when it is necessary to correctly link each of the speakers heard on a tape to the messages they produce.

Coarticulation refers to the production of oral speech; it describes how each speech sound uttered affects those near it. Specifically, it can be said that, when an individual moves from one speech sound to another, the position of the articulators for the first sound, modifies the placement precision of the articulators for the second sound. So too does the position the articulators take for the second phoneme affect the first; and these modifications extend out to several phonemes—and in both directions. However, the greater the distance between the speech sounds, the smaller the effect. As would be expected, these differences in articulatory movements also change the acoustic characteristics of a phoneme. Thus, the vowel /u/ is slightly different acoustically if it is preceded by a /d/ than if it is led by an /m/. In turn, the /m/ is modified if succeeded by an /i/ rather than the /u/. In any event, these relationships can be exploited to enhance decoding efficiency.

The Mechanics of Decoding

To understand how the speech found on degraded tape recordings is decoded and turned into a written transcript, it also is necessary to understand something about the mechanics of the decoding process itself. First of all, if the method utilized by the decoder does not involve thorough and structured techniques—or if he or she is not properly trained—the product probably will be inadequate or worse. In short, it is important to employ a thorough and systematic approach to decoding if the transcript is to be reasonably accurate and essentially unchallengeable.

Because the techniques associated with good decoding are rather extensive, only a very brief review will be provided. First, the decoder will listen to the entire tape recording on good quality equipment. This approach involves more than simple familiarization; it also permits a log to be initiated, difficult material to be identified, proper names to be learned, and any idiosyncratic characteristic of the recording noted. This listening process then is repeated as the decoders begin transcript development. As you might expect, the decoder simply starts at the beginning and reproduces the heard utterances in sequence. Codes are used to indicate (1) where questions exist, (2) where decoding may be possible but is questionable, and (3) when words are inaudible or unintelligible. It is necessary to continue (and replicate) this process until no further improvement in the written transcript can be made.

The most common approach to the decoding task is simply to have a trained, experienced individual carry it out. However, a somewhat more efficient approach is to have one decoder develop the transcript and then have a second review and refine it. Perhaps the best approach of all is to have two different decoders complete the task independently and then have yet a third verify the work and/or resolve any disagreements. Although this (third) approach is a little cumbersome and expensive, it is sometimes necessary when the challenge presented is severe and an accurate transcript is critical. An example involves recordings associated with aircraft disasters (CVR or cockpit tapes). Instances that are less critical but still of some importance are when the speech captured involves "street talk," foreign languages, or dialects; if the material is highly technical; or if it contains language not familiar to ordinary decoders.

Once the listening procedure is complete and a reasonable transcript has been developed, it is necessary to apply the cited codes in order to identify the talkers, problem portions of the transcript, and other events. Also, the decoder should identify each talker by number (or by name, if possible) and by sex. Specialized systems of this type have been developed[17]; their use is mandatory if the transcript is to clearly describe all of the events contained on the tape recording. Finally, as has been implied, proper names are often quite difficult to decode. That is, although speech and language are internally redundant—and markedly affected by text and coarticulation, there is little-to-no external information inherently associated with a proper name. However, information external to the material on the tape recording may provide an assist here.

Once the decoding process has been completed and the confusions resolved, the entire document should be structured in final form and carefully evaluated for errors. The potency of the written word, as applied to the criminal justice system, is not to be underestimated. Juries, for example, can be powerfully influenced by a transcript. Thus, the messages and information found on a tape recording must be established as accurately and fairly as possible.

Finally, it must be noted that the efficient decoding of distorted or masked speech involves not only the tasks described above. It also demands a good understanding of the law enforcement milieu and the criminal justice system.

Speaker Identification

Almost every adult who enjoys normal hearing has had the experience of recognizing some unseen speaker (usually, but not always, someone familiar to them) solely from listening to his or her voice. It probably was from this common, everyday experience that the concept of speaker identification was born. However, references to it in novels, comic strips, movies, and especially television have resulted in distortion of its basic nature. Indeed, many people believe that: (1) law enforcement can identify a talker from his voice and do so both easily and infallibly, (2) "voiceprints" are the direct equivalent of fingerprints, and so on. But what is the reality here? Well, it now should be clear that, although many of the cited opinions are gross exaggerations, there is *some* basis for them. A short review follows.

Definitions

Speaker identification is one of two different types of speaker recognition, the other being speaker verification. Specifically, it is defined as the task of identifying an unknown speaker from samples of his or her voice. This process can be a rather difficult one, primarily because it often must be accomplished in the face of system distortions (reduced bandpass, noise, distortion, etc) and/or speaker distortions (stress, disguise, impairments, etc). Worse yet, the talker usually is uncooperative—especially if there is a crime involved. In other instances, a match is not possible at all, either because the unknown talker is not among the suspects or the tape recordings of the unknown voice are simply too poor to be of any use.

Speaker verification, on the other hand, involves subjects who want to be recognized. Here, high quality equipment and sophisticated processing techniques can be used; and many reference samples of the talker's speech are available or can be obtained. Speaker verification is employed to permit a person access to secure areas, to bank by telephone, to communicate with (verifiable) personnel in space capsules or other remote locations, and so on. As is obvious, speaker verification poses a much less formidable challenge than does speaker identification. As a matter of fact, the verification problem would be solved if valid speaker identification were to become possible.

Problems

The first problem is a basic one. Anyone who attempts to develop speaker identification will discover that it is not yet known if the speech/voice of each individual is so unique that it will always be different from that of any other person. Nor, has it been unassailably established that *intersubject* speaker variability will always be greater than *intrasubject* variability. Fortunately, these problems are not controlling, because there already are ways to accomplish reasonably good identification, especially within the boundaries offered by the forensic environment.

As you probably noted from the introduction, the operational problems faced can be sorted into two categories: (1) system distortions and (2) difficulties with speakers. System distortion occurs as a result of occurrences such as reduced frequency response (eg, telephone transmissions), noise, distortions, interruptions, and so on. In these cases, some of the information about the talker can be lost or is masked; and, just as in speech decoding, such reductions increase the difficulty of achieving correct identification.

Second, difficulties with speakers also can be debilitating. As would be expected, many criminals experience fear, anxiety, or some sort of stresslike emotions when they commit a crime. The usual consequence is a change in one or more of their speaking characteristics. The effects of ingested drugs, alcohol, or health states (such as a bad cold) also can interfere with the identification process. Worst of all, the unknown talker may attempt voice disguise.

On the other hand, there are conditions or events which suggest that identification/differentiation among voices is possible. For one thing, it has been postulated[1,26-31] that a given individual's speech signal contains features that are sufficiently unique and consistent to that person that, at least, some successful identifications can be carried out. Indeed, both available data and logic permit the assumption that certain elements within a talker's speech tend to be relatively idiosyncratic as a result of that person's anatomy, physiology, and motor control plus the habituated speech patterns they employ. Further, social, economic, geographic, and educational factors as well as maturation level, psychological/physical states, sex, and intelligence also tend to affect speech in relevant ways. Obviously, when these factors are combined, they can create a fairly unique cluster of features. In turn, it has been established that, if a number of these features are measured, it will be possible (in many instances anyway) to successfully discriminate among talkers on the basis of the resulting composite analysis or (structured) profile. Thus, although there may be no single attribute within a person's speech that is of sufficient strength and uniqueness to permit differentiation, the use of a group of features can permit successful recognition.

Some History

Primitive efforts in the area of voice recognition probably antedate recorded history, and such attempts have been continued down through the millennia.

There was a relevant trial in an English court several hundred years ago, and speaker identification admissibility in the United States may be traced as far back as 1904 (Mack vs Florida[32]). Even so, the issue is a complex one for, as it turns out, it matters who is testifying and in what court. For example, some courts will permit witnesses to "identify" a speaker (from voice judgments) only if they can satisfy the presiding jurist that they really know that person. This approach is a reasonable one; as it is consistent with relevant research. That is, if a witness has been in close contact with a speaker for a long period of time, he or she probably can recognize the speaker's voice—and be fairly accurate in doing so. Moreover, many courts also permit a qualified specialist to render an opinion after comparing a sample of the unknown talker's speech (usually from an evidence tape) to an appropriate exemplar recording. Here, the professional conducts an examination and then decides if two talkers are involved or only one. But, before either of these approaches is described, yet a third type of aural-perceptual speaker identification should be considered; it involves *earwitness* lineups or "voice parades."

Earwitness Identification

An earwitness lineup (or a voice parade) usually involves a person who has heard, but has not seen, another individual who is otherwise not known to him. Later (usually, very much later), he or she is asked to remember what that person sounded like and attempt to identify a suspect as the individual involved in the original confrontation. Ordinarily, this type of lineup is conducted by law enforcement agents. What happens is that an administrator inserts an exemplar (provided by the suspect) into a group of 3 to 6 recorded speech samples obtained from other people. The witness is then required to listen to all of the samples and make a choice among them as to which one was the perpetrator. However, this approach has come under some fire in the past,[1,33,34] because it exhibits several problems. For example, sometimes the suspect's exemplar is compared to speech uttered by individuals who speak in quite a different manner than he does; in other instances, ambient cues exist on the tape. Either of these occurrences can result in false positives. Second, some administrators attempt to base their procedures on those drawn from eyewitness identification, a procedure that parallels earwitness lineups in some ways but is quite different in others. Problems with witness memory/emotions and/or with conditions existing at the time of the confrontation are numerous and can add to the complexity of the process. Extensive reviews of these and related issues are available.[33,35-37]

Moreover, research in this area is continuing and additional information is being generated[35,38-41]; so too are guidelines as to how valid auditory lineups may be structured.[7,36] Finally, the operational criteria to follow have been developed to mitigate the cited difficulties; a fairly detailed description of them is found in Hollien.[27]

An appropriate structuring of earwitness lineups may be best understood by consideration of the following outline:

Definition: An earwitness lineup is a procedure where a witness who has heard, but not seen, a suspect attempts to pick his or her voice from a field of voices.

Parity: The procedure must be conducted in a manner that is scrupulously fair to both the earwitness(es) and the suspect(s). Accurate records must be kept of all phases of the procedure.

Validity: The witness must demonstrate that he or she has adequate hearing and that he or she attended to the speaker's voice at a level that would permit identification. Witnesses should be told that the suspect may or may not be present in the lineup and that only one suspect will be evaluated at a time.

Procedure: All samples should be recorded with as good acoustic fidelity as is possible; they should be presented in an identical manner. The same or similar speech should be used, samples should be of equal length, ambient background should be parallel for all samples, and so on. Utterances should be of neutral material. Between five and eight foils or distractor speakers should be used. Each of them should be similar to the suspect with respect to age and dialect plus social, economic, and educational status. The suspect's voice can be described to the foil talkers, but they must not have heard it. Once a tape recorded "lineup" has been developed, a series of 2 to 3 mock trials should be carried out with 4 to 6 dispassionate individuals as listeners. If they consistently identify the suspect as the target (even though they have never heard his voice), the lineup tape must be restructured.

Presentation: The witness(es) should then listen to the tape and be asked to identify (or not identify) one of the samples as the person they originally heard. However, they should be reassured that it is not *necessary* to make a selection. Two appropriate approaches are available for presentation purposes.

The first is referred to as the "serial" approach. Here, the suspect's speech sample is embedded among several other samples (produced by the foil or distractor talkers). The samples are played in sequence and the witness makes a judgment. The entire tape may be replayed as structured or with the order of the individual samples rearranged. This procedure may be applied either to assist the witness in making a decision or to establish the reliability of the witness' judgments.

The second of the two procedures has been named the "sequential" approach; it is best understood by consideration of Figure 101–2. In this case, two small rooms are used with the first containing the witness (A), the administrator (D), and a video camera (E); the second is the site of a TV monitor (F) and observers (G). Each of the samples is recorded on its own tape (C), and these tapes are provided to the witness one at a time (in any order). Once all of them have been played, the witness may request—and play—any or all of them, and in any order desired.

Reasonably good judgments are possible using either procedure, but the second appears to be the most powerful.

The Aural-Perceptual Approach

This section will focus on the aural-perceptual approach to speaker identification; it also will feature the forensic phonetician rather than the lay listener who either attempts to identify familiar speakers or participates in an earwitness lineup. Also briefly reviewed are what is, or is not, considered possible; the strengths and weaknesses of several approaches and how the forensic phonetician can develop appropriate skills. But, first, what research can be used in support of the aural-perceptual approach to speaker identification?

The first of the modern studies[42] in this area is a classic. In this case, a psychologist (McGehee) became interested in the subject from her observations of Charles Lindbergh's voice identification of Bruno Hauptmann (the man who was convicted of kidnaping the Lindbergh baby). Her procedures paralleled what Lindbergh did; that is, she had her auditors listen to an individual and then attempt to identify him within a group of other talkers of the same sex and do so at various latencies (1 day to 5 months). McGehee reported that the percentage of correct identifications was quite high initially but that falloff in accuracy was gradual but steady—from 83% correct identification the day after exposure to only 13% after about 5 months. To a great extent, contemporary research substantiates McGehee's general findings; that is, it appears that untrained individuals can make fairly good aur-

Fig 101–2. A graphic display of the "sequential" approach to earwitness identification. A is the witness, B = a tape recorder, C = the tape recordings, D is the administrator, E = the videocam, F = the TV monitors, and G shows observers.

al-perceptual identifications initially but this level cannot be sustained.

Although the answers to all potential questions are not available even today, a number of key studies have been carried out; hence some models can be constructed. Early examples include Bricker and Pruzansky[43] who reported high levels of correct identification when they used *sentences* as stimuli. Thus, it appears that, although identification accuracy is possible, it is correlated with sample size and duration. It also has been established that the identification task can be degraded by such things as increasing the number of speakers to be identified, substituting whispered for normal speech, recording the sample under degraded speaking conditions, varying speech materials, and so on. When these conditions exist, a listener's performance tends to deteriorate somewhat. Either that or they need very long speech samples. Moreover, these

relationships apparently interfere even with identification of even known speakers.[1,27,44-46] It also has been reported that speaker disguise, presence of dialects, subjects who sound alike, and high noise levels can operate to reduce identification accuracy[1,26,27,30,47-54]— as can (possibly anyway) the presence of stress and other emotions.

On the other hand, it has been demonstrated that there are many elements within the speech signal, which serve to permit accurate identifications. Indeed, people use processing of this type to make the many day-to-day identifications they do, and the accuracy of the techniques they use has been confirmed by research. What they do is attend to those features or events that consistently occur within any utterance. The processing of these natural speech characteristics (most of them are suprasegmentals) also forms the basis of most of the formal aural-perceptual (and some machine) approaches used to identify speakers. What are some of these features? One is speaking fundamental frequency level or SFF[1,27,55-58]; perceptually this attribute is heard as pitch level and variability. A second includes vowel formant frequencies, ratios, and transitions.[27,58-60] Third, attempts have been made[55,58] to compare the relative importance of the source (voice) and vocal tract (articulators) for these purposes; it was found that both of them contribute—and do so additively. In addition, phonemic effects on the identification task have been investigated. It has been reported that, although the level of correct perceptual identification varies as a function of the vowel produced, consonant-vowel transitions, vocal tract turbulence, and inflections, these elements, nonetheless, can be used to identify speakers.[30,59,61] Finally, voice quality, speech prosody/timing, and other features all appear to interrelate with the identification process. In short, quite a number of natural speech features can be used to support the aural-perceptual speaker identification process. They are particularly effective when used in groups (ie, in the development of profiles).

The summation that follows is based on—and complements—the relationships cited above, especially those that are positively associated with the perceptual identification task. First, speakers known to the listener are the easiest to identify by voice; and accuracy here can be quite high. Second, if the listener's familiarity with a talker's speech is reinforced occasionally, levels of correct identification can be sustained. Third, larger and better speech samples lead to more accurate aural-perceptual identifications. Fourth, good quality samples aid in the identification process. Fifth, although listeners can be variable in their ability to make accurate judgments, some are naturally quite good at it. Sixth, listeners appear to be successful in using a number of the natural features that are found within speech/voice. And finally, phonetic training appears to aid in successful identifications, especially if the practitioner is a trained/experienced forensic phonetician.

As was suggested in the preceding paragraph and especially by item six above, a number of natural speech features can be employed for identification purposes. They are formalized as follows.

Speaking Fundamental Frequency or Heard Pitch. The parameters here are general pitch level (high, medium, low) as well as the variability and patterning of pitch usage. Many individuals exhibit habituated pitch patterns that can aid the listener in the identification task.

Articulation. The focus in this instance is (especially) on idiosyncratic phoneme production. The controlling word here is idiosyncratic; because, to be useful in identification, an individual's phoneme production must be, in some manner, a little different from that of other speakers.

General Voice Quality. There is little doubt that the general quality of a sound-producing mechanism aids in its identification. Many aspects of voice quality are useful here (eg, the use of vocal fry is an example).

Prosody. This parameter set involves how an individual's speech timing, or temporal patterning, affects the ability to identify him or her from voice. It is well known that auditors listen to how slow, or fast, a person talks; how smooth or choppy the presentation is; and so on. Thus, speech timing and melody provide cues about identity.

Vocal Intensity. Although limited data are available on vocal intensity, its usage is thought to be a viable recognition feature. However, in practice, it is difficult to assess absolute intensity; because even small environmental changes can result in marked variations in energy level. Nevertheless, it is theorized that evaluation of variability patterns can be useful.

General Speech. Several general speech features also are important. Although the main focus here is on segmentals; they also include attributes such as (1) dialect, (2) unusual use of linguistic stress, (3) idiosyncratic language patterns, (4) speech impediments, and (5) idiosyncratic pronunciations. These features extend beyond the simple articulatory or prosody considerations discussed above and can provide robust cues for the recognition of speakers.

All of the above vectors will be used as the basis of a structural approach to aural-perceptual speaker identification; it will be described later in this chapter.

Applied Research

A substantial corpus of applied research is available; it also is relevant to this discussion. Most of it is based on the fact that people who identify each other by voice do so only after carrying out auditory and cognitive processing of the heard signal. Questions can be asked then if people exist who can organize and effectively use these processes (it appears that forensic phoneticians can do so) and what are some of the elements in the forensic milieu that can affect it.

One study carried in response to these questions was conducted by Shirt[62] who studied the ability of general phoneticians (not specialists) to make identification judgments. She developed a test based on 74 recorded voices provided her by the British Home Office; she then asked 20 phoneticians and an equal number of untrained controls to carry out three fairly difficult identification tasks. She found that, although the best control did as well as the phoneticians, the phoneticians (overall) were fairly accurate and did a rather better job than the untrained subjects. Moreover, neither of the groups was permitted to utilize any kind of structured analysis procedure; and the phoneticians were not trained in the forensic sciences.

Koester[63] also reported that his (general) phoneticians did very much better than his untrained controls in several experiments where they attempted to identify people they knew; again unstructured procedures were used. Not one of Koester's phoneticians made even a single error in the entire experiment. These studies, plus field evidence, suggest that phoneticians can meet the identification challenge rather effectively even when not allowed more than a brief exposure to a voice. It also appears that they can do even better if they are familiar with forensics, trained to task, and operate in a structured manner.

Many of the issues reviewed above have been challenged (especially in the legal setting). Accordingly, we carried out a series of studies to test several of the criticisms. In the first,[48] we attempted to estimate listeners' ability to resist the effects of talker disguise and stress and assess the importance of listeners being acquainted with the talkers. Speakers were 10 adult males who had recorded speech samples under normal conditions as well as those of stress (electric shock) and free disguise. The three classes of listeners were individuals who knew the talkers very well, did not know them but were trained to recognize their voices, and neither knew the talkers nor understood

English (they also received training, however). The identification task itself was a very difficult one. As may be seen in Figure 101–3, listeners who knew the talkers performed best and the non-English-speaking auditors did the worst. Moreover, it was found that the normal and stress conditions were not very different from each other; whereas the disguised productions resulted in significantly fewer correct identifications. Thus, although it appears possible that listeners who know speakers can identify them even under very difficult conditions, it is sometimes possible to fool them (ie, by means of disguise). We also found it was possible to train lay listeners (at least some of them) to recognize talkers at a reasonable level of accuracy.

In another experiment, we studied the effects of stress and/or arousal on speaker identification.[64] The question asked here was: Will the victims of a crime perform better than people who are not stressed by such events? In this instance, young women were pre-screened for potential sensitivity to stressors and sorted into two groups: the 20 most susceptible to stress and the 20 least likely to be threatened (controls). The "stress" group was presented 10 minutes of violent video stimuli (attacks on women, rape scenes, death of children) while a male voice read a threatening commentary; the controls saw a pastoral video sequence while hearing a male voice read neutral to supportive material. Their arousal (or lack of it) during the experiment was verified by a standard polygraph technique. Later, speaker recognition (of the male voice) was carried out. The aroused women did better at identifying the talker than did the controls. Thus, it appears that fear/stress/arousal can upgrade a person's ability to correctly identify speakers from their voices.

In a third investigation, we studied speaker identification primarily by contrasting earwitness and eyewitness identification.[65] Specifically, visual and aural-perceptual identifications were made of a simulated crime from sets of photographic and tape-recorded exemplars. Auditors were law school students divided into groups who attempted identifications at various times after a simulated crime took place. The results demonstrated that visual identifications can be quite accurate, less so for speaker identification. Among the other findings were those that supported the position that earwitness testimony should be viewed by judges and juries with some caution. On the other hand, current research[35] demonstrates that witnesses often can apply specific sensory processes to make reasonably good judgments.

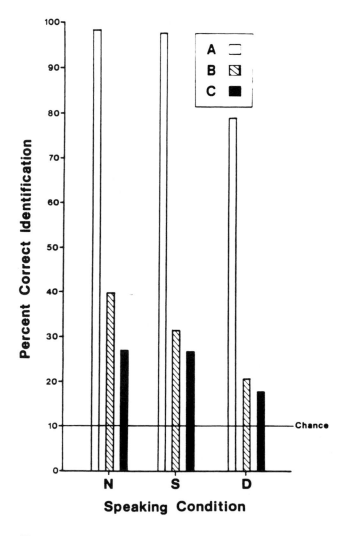

Fig 101–3. The mean (correct) identification of 10 talkers speaking under the conditions of: N = normal, S = stress, and D = disguise. Three listener groups consisted of: A = individuals who knew the talkers very well, B = listeners who did not know the talkers but who were trained to recognize them, and C = those who were trained similarly but did not know either English nor the talkers. The task was to name each speaker for all six of his presentations out of a total of 60.

The Use of Specialists

Let us return to consideration of the forensic phonetician. Although it has been suggested that even untrained individuals can sometimes carry out speaker identification (if they have natural talent and conditions are favorable), many others cannot do so at any reasonable level of effectiveness. Thus, it would appear hazardous to rely on such individuals. Rather, it would appear that identification tasks should be directed to specialists (ie, people who have extensive and relevant training and experience in their area). Indeed, forensic phoneticians have demonstrated the ability to conduct effective speaker identification even when their judgments are based only on heard stimuli. They can do so if adequate speech samples are available and they employ structured analysis techniques. However, to be considered competent, the specialist also should be able to specify his or her identification rates, demonstrate extensive graduate training in the phonetic sciences (especially in forensic phonetics), have some experience, and provide defensible identification procedures and strategies. What are some of the approaches employed by these particular professionals?

Many phoneticians attempt to determine if the suspect is or is not the perpetrator by aural-perceptually contrasting their speech segmentals (ie, the speech sounds they make, how they use phonemes to construct spoken words, dialects, etc). Such approaches are successful in many instances, especially if the practitioner establishes robust evaluation criteria and can demonstrate the attributes listed in the preceding paragraph. On the other hand, this approach is quite subjective; and its elements tend to be difficult to quantify. A superior approach is to place these techniques in a role that supports more sophisticated methods — such as one based on the suprasegmentals (ie, the natural speech features described both above and, yet again, below. A procedure of this type follows.

An Approach

Of course, the manner in which any identification approach is conducted (ie, just how the speech samples are judged for a match or a nonmatch and how the responses are quantified) is of greatest importance. Accordingly, a suggested procedure (see also Hollien and Hollien[66]) follows. As you might expect, its focus is on the suprasegmentals (ie, the assessment of voice, prosody, frequency patterns, vocal intensity, voice quality, and others); and they, in turn, are supplemented by segmental analysis. The approach permits reasonable quantification and rigor to be achieved, because its application is based on a structured evaluation system. Approaches of this type have been shown to be reasonably successful; the especially useful ones permit confidence level estimates to be generated.

The first step in the process is to obtain multiple speech samples of the unknown (evidence tape) and known (exemplar) speakers and place them in pairs on an evaluation tape. The pairs are played repeatedly, and comparisons are made of one speech parameter at a time. As may be seen from consideration of Figure 101–4, up to 20 parameters may be compared. To reiterate, one parameter at a time is assessed (eg, pitch

patterns); and the process is continued until a judgment can be made. The next parameter is then assessed, and the process replicated until all possible (parameter) comparisons have been completed. At that time, an overall judgment is made. Subsequently, the entire process is independently repeated a number of times.

As can be seen from consideration of Figure 101–4, judgments are made on a 10-point scale; and the likelihood that the two samples are produced by the same speaker can be assessed on the basis of the individual parameter judgments and, especially, by the overall mean. If the collected scores fall between 0 and 3, a match cannot be made; and it may be said that the samples undoubtedly were produced by two different people (see Fig 101–5). If the overall mean scores fall between 7 and 10, a reasonably robust match has been made (Fig 101–6). Scores between 4 and 6 are generally considered neutral but actually are a little on the positive side. For example, if the mean score for 14 sets of evaluations (carried out 3 times overall for a total of 42 assessments) proves to be 5.8 (or 58%), a low-level match has been made; it is one that is not particularly compelling but, nevertheless, is on the positive side. Moreover, it would hardly permit the argument to be made that the samples were produced by two different people. Incidentally, if foil talkers are used, the confidence level can be raised substantially, especially if the mean scores are polarized (ie, 0–3 or 7–10).

In summary, data are now available about people's ability to make aural-perceptual speaker identifications and much of it is positive. For example, it has been demonstrated that (1) most auditors use strategies involving natural speech features for this purpose, (2) specialized training will aid in task success, and (3) some people are better at it than are others. It also is known that elements such as noise, distortion, very short speech samples, and large groups of talkers can degrade the effectiveness of the process. In any case, even though aural-perceptual approaches to speaker identification have some limitations, fairly good results can be expected if the task is highly structured and if the auditors are well-trained professionals who are able to demonstrate reasonably good competency.

The "Voiceprint" Problem

The procedure referred to as "voiceprints" has been pretty much discredited; hence, description of this so-called "method" of speaker identification will not be included in this chapter. If the reader is interested in learning the history of this approach, the controversies surrounding it, and its demise, he or she can consult

```
                    FORENSIC COMMUNICATION ASSOCIATES
  Case Name:                                              FCA REF:


                Aural-perceptual Approach to Speaker Identification
            Score Sheet   -- 0 = U-K least alike; 10 = U-K most alike

  1. PITCH                                                   SCORE  RANGE
       a. Level            0 . . . . 5 . . . . . 10

       b. Variability      0 . . . . 5 . . . . . 10

       c. Patterns         0 . . . . 5 . . . . . 10

  2. VOICE QUALITY
       a. General          0 . . . . 5 . . . . . 10

       b. Vocal Fry        0 . . . . 5 . . . . . 10

       c. Other            0 . . . . 5 . . . . . 10

  3. INTENSITY
       a. Variability      0 . . . . 5 . . . . . 10

  4. DIALECT
       a. Regional         0 . . . . 5 . . . . . 10

       b. Foreign          0 . . . . 5 . . . . . 10

       c. Idiolect         0 . . . . 5 . . . . . 10

  5. ARTICULATION
       a. Vowels           0 . . . . 5 . . . . . 10

       b. Consonants       0 . . . . 5 . . . . . 10

       c. Misarticulations 0 . . . . 5 . . . . . 10

       d. Nasality         0 . . . . 5 . . . . . 10

       e. Other            0 . . . . 5 . . . . . 10

  6. PROSODY
       a. Rate             0 . . . . 5 . . . . . 10

       b. Speech Bursts    0 . . . . 5 . . . . . 10

       c. Other            0 . . . . 5 . . . . . 10

  7. OTHER
       a. Nonfluencies     0 . . . . 5 . . . . . 10

       b. Speech Disorders 0 . . . . 5 . . . . . 10
           MEAN                                           ___  ___
```

Fig 101–4. A copy of the form developed for use with the suprasegmental speaker identification approach being described.[45,51]

the relevant chapter in either of the author's books on forensic phonetics.[1,27] Large bibliographies of original sources are listed there also.

Machine/Computer Approaches

The speaker recognition issue changes radically when efforts are made to apply modern technology to the problem. Indeed, with the seeming limitless pow-

er of electronic hardware and computers, it would seem that solutions should be but a step away. Yet such is not actually the case. For one thing, authors such as Hecker[26] insist that no machines are both as sensitive and as powerful (for these purposes) as is the human ear. What Hecker means by "the ear" is, of course, the entire auditory (sensory) system coupled to the brain with all its sophisticated memory and cognitive functions. On the other side of the issue are

```
                    FORENSIC COMMUNICATION ASSOCIATES
    Case Name: State vs. Jane Doe                    FCA REF: 1491

           Aural-perceptual Approach to Speaker Identification
           Score Sheet  -- 0 = U-K least alike; 10 = U-K most alike
```

			SCORE	RANGE
1. PITCH				
a. Level	0 X=====X . 5 10		2	1-3
b. Variability	0 . . X . 5 10		3	3
c. Patterns	0 . X==X . 5 10		2	2-3
2. VOICE QUALITY				
a. General	0 . . X======X 10		4	3-5
b. Vocal Fry	0 . . . . 5 X . . . 10		6	6
c. Other	0 . . . . 5 10		NA	NA
3. INTENSITY				
a. Variability	0 . X==X . 5 10		3	2-3
4. DIALECT				
a. Regional	0 X==X . . 5 10		1	1-2*
*IMPORTANT				
b. Foreign	0 . . . . 5 10		NA	NA
c. Idiolect	0 . . . . 5 10		NA	NA
5. ARTICULATION				
a. Vowels	0 . . . . X==X . . . 10		5	5-6
b. Consonants	0 . X=====X 5 10		3	2-4
c. Misarticulations	0 X . . . 5 10		1	1*
U shows a /d/ for /th/ substitution				
d. Nasality	0 . . . . X==X . . . 10		6	5-6
e. Other	0 . . . . 5 10		NA	NA
6. PROSODY				
a. Rate	0 . . . . X 5 10		4	4
b. Speech Bursts	0 . . X==X 5 10		3	3-4
c. Staccato (K only)	0 X=====X . 5 10		2	1-3
7. OTHER				
a. Nonfluencies	0 . . . . 5 10		NA	NA
b. Speech Disorders				
MEAN	0 . . . . 5 10		NA	NA
*Double Weight	Mean of three runs; no foils.		29%	25-35%

Fig 101-5. Display of the evaluation of a woman who, as it turns out, was not the criminal.

scientists who argue that, due to burgeoning technology, machines/computers can be made to operate just as efficiently. They probably can, but the task is not an easy one.

First some perspectives. As you might expect, the best way to develop a machine-based speaker identification method is to establish some type of system and test it. For example, a group of vectors or relationships might be chosen and then researched on the basis of the model found in Figure 101–7. As may be seen, the first step is to formulate a vector; the second is to test its ability to discriminate a particular talker from among a fairly large group of talkers. If successful, the work could then proceed; if not, changes would have to be made to the vector's parameters (or parts) and the initial evaluation process replicated. The next stage would be to experiment with the vector where distortions, such as limited bandpass, noise, and/or

```
                    FORENSIC COMMUNICATION ASSOCIATES
        Case Name: State vs. John Doe                    FCA REF: 1475

                Aural-perceptual Approach to Speaker Identification
                Score Sheet  -- 0 = U-K least alike; 10 = U-K most alike

                                                            SCORE   RANGE
        1. PITCH
            a. Level            0 . . . . . 5 . X=====X 10    8      7-9

            b. Variability      0 . . . . . 5 X==X . . 10     7      6-7

            c. Patterns         0 . . . . . 5 . X==X . 10     7      7-8

        2. VOICE QUALITY
            a. General          0 . . . . . 5 . X=====X 10    8      7-9

            b. Vocal Fry        0 . . X=====X . . . . 10      4      3-5
            Slightly more fry by U
            c. Other            0 . . . . . 5 . . . . 10      NA     NA

        3. INTENSITY
            a. Variability      0 . . . . . 5 X=======X 10    7      6-9

        4. DIALECT
            a. Regional         0 . . . . . 5 . X=====X 10    8      7-9

            b. Foreign          0 . . . . . 5 . . . . 10      NA     NA

            c. Idiolect         0 . . . . . 5 . . X==X 10     9      8-9
            Both "Lilt"
        5. ARTICULATION
            a. Vowels           0 . . . . . 5 X=====X . 10    7      6-8

            b. Consonants       0 . . . . . 5 X=====X . 10    7      6-8

            c. Misarticulations 0 . . . . . 5 . . . . X 10    9      9
            BOTH
            d. Nasality         0 . . . . X=======X . . 10    6      4-7

            e. Other            0 . . . . . 5 . . . . 10      NA     NA

        6. PROSODY
            a. Rate             0 . . . . . 5 . X=====X 10    8      7-9
            RELATIVELY FAST
            b. Speech Bursts    0 . . . . . 5 X==X . . 10     6      6-7

            c. CHOPPY           0 . . . . . 5 . . X . 10      8      8

        7. OTHER
            a. Nonfluencies     0 . . . . . 5 . . . X 10      9      9
            Show similar articulation problems
            b. Speech Disorders 0 . . . . . 5 . . . . 10      NA     NA

            MEAN          Neither of two foils matched U or K.
                                                            74%    66-81%
```

Fig 101–6. Assessment of a male suspect who was the perpetrator in question.

talker variation, are present. A fourth phase would be to attempt to increase the power of the system by combining the vectors with each other. The research now would become much more complex, because it would be necessary to compare all potential combinations of vectors and then repeat the procedures for the various types of distortions. And, this process would have to be replicated each time the system was upgraded.

The final phase would be to test the procedure in the field. In this instance, either one of two approaches could be utilized. The first involves the solution of simulated crimes generated under fieldlike conditions and the second application of the system to real-life cases. Either approach should provide useful information about the validity and efficiency of the method, but both have their limitations. For example, even well-designed (simulated) cases are a little artificial and only roughly parallel real-life situations. On the other hand, the use of actual investigations permits only nonscientific confirmation of the results (ie, confessions, convictions, etc); and observations such as these cannot really be substituted for scientific data.

Summary of Approach to the Problem

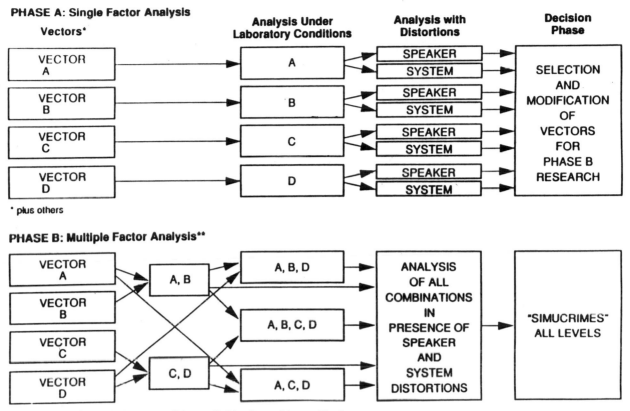

Fig 101-7. Model providing the basis for comprehensive development of a semi-automatic speaker identification system (SAUSI).

Nevertheless, the data obtained can be used to demonstrate if the procedure is of merit or if it is lacking. Finally, although there may be no single parameter or vector that is so robust, or so all-encompassing, that it permits efficient identifications to be made under any and all conditions, a profile approach (ie, one involving a group of vectors) should counter this problem.

Research on Machine Methods

It should be remembered that the focus of this discussion is on speaker identification not speaker verification. The verification task, while formidable, is relatively straightforward in nature. Unless an imposter is present, the talkers are cooperative; and the speech samples are both highly controlled and can be continually updated. Thus, few of the problems associated with the identification task are encountered in the verification domain. Unfortunately, most of the research carried out has been on verification; and this situation is probably due to the fact that it presents the lesser

challenge of the two and that such a system (if valid and effective) would be wildly rewarding (ie, financially). The irony is that, if the speaker identification problem can be met, the speaker verification task would be immediately solved also. Nevertheless, relatively few scientists work in the identification area even though it is of high social consequence.

A number of potentially useful research programs in speaker identification have been initiated by researchers who employed relatively large groups of vectors or factors.[29,67-74] These approaches have included linear prediction, recognition by synthesis, (signal) axis crossings, cross correlation, probability density estimations, cepstrum methods, neural nets, and so on. A number of them were, at least, partly successful; others showed high potential for success if upgrades or modified procedures had been introduced. Unfortunately, very few of these research programs were sustained (note that most of them occurred before the 1990s). A more extensive review of these approaches—plus detailed description of two that were (ie, those of Wojciech Majewski and Robert Rodman) can be found in the author's book *Forensic Voice Identification*.[27]

What happened subsequently was that the general thrust shifted toward verification. An exception to the trend is a program being carried out at the University of Florida.[1,27,56,57,60,75-82] The subject of this program is called SAUSI or Semiautomatic Speaker Identification; it is among the very few efforts that are both extensive and long-term. It should provide a good example as to how the standards cited above can be applied to research of this nature. Also provided will be details of an operational approach to speaker identification.

Natural Speech Vectors

The first step in the development of SAUSI was to identify and evaluate a number of parameters found within the speech signal, ones that had the potential of being effective identification cues. It was determined very early that traditional approaches to signal processing were lacking (due to the many distortions associated with forensics); hence, the "natural" features cited above were adopted. This decision was stimulated by the results from early experiments, the aural-perceptual literature, and the realization that people routinely process heard speech using just such features.

The Profile Concept

A second perspective emerged early in system development. It had been noted that no single vector (applied by itself) seemed able to provide a high level of correct identification for all of the many types of degraded speech encountered in the forensic milieu. In response, those being studied at that particular time were combined into a single test. However, it also was discovered that adding too many features sometimes resulted in a reduction in success. This situation is caused by the process wherein a developing system will improve as relevant parameters are added until it reaches asymptote. At that point, further additions result in movement onto the negative slope of the curve and, as stated, an ultimate reduction in success occurs. This problem was confounded by yet a second one—that of targets being sought in multidimensional space—and it too proved to be a formidable one. We responded by normalizing the data and then using two-dimensional profiles (ie, where all vectors were represented but on an equal basis). The normalization process helped materially by preventing the dominance of a particular vector simply because its calculated values were greater than those of the others; and the profile approach proved robust because it allowed the simultaneous evaluation of many relationships. It also permitted internal validation and "rotations";

that is, we were able to test samples of the unknown speaker, the target talker (the "known"), and a group of foils or controls against the basic reference sample of the "unknown" and do so all at the same time. We used this approach; because, to be valid, a method must show that the unknown talker's test sample is the best match for his (or her) own reference set. Finally, we could use the procedure to carry out multiple replications (rotations) and combine them to provide the basis for a final decision.

The SAUSI Vectors

The natural speech vectors tested, and ultimately adopted, were suggested by our research and that of Stevens.[30] A full description of these vectors may be found in *Acoustics of Crime*[1] and *Forensic Voice Identification*,[27] and they will be briefly reviewed here.

Long-Term Speech Spectra (LTS). Power spectra have been utilized extensively as speaker identification cues.[1,11,27,52,58,75-78,81,83-87] They appear to provide an effective index of general voice quality. Moreover, it has been found that this vector is resistant to the effects of speaker stress and to limited pass band conditions; however, it does not function particularly well when talkers disguise their voices. LTS analysis involves determining the energy levels for all frequencies throughout the spectrum as a function of time. By this means, the influence of individual phonemes is removed; and general voice quality is reflected. The analysis procedure employs Euclidean distance comparisons for all subjects at multiple points along the frequency curve. The data are then normalized and assessed both directly and as a part of the profile.

Speaking Fundamental Frequency (SFF). As with aural-perceptual approaches, the perception of the fundamental frequency of voice (F_0 or SFF) has been shown to be a fairly good cue for speaker recognition.[1,27,56,72,77,84,88,89] The robustness of SFF appears to have been yet further upgraded by use of a 30-parameter SFF vector (ie, for SAUSI). To be specific, the parameters making up this vector include SFF geometric mean and standard deviation plus the number frequencies in each of 30 semitone intervals (or "bins"). When normalized, these parameters make up a vector, which is used to compare speaking fundamental frequency level, variability, and patterns across subjects in much the same manner as does LTS.[57,79]

Vowel Formant Tracking (VFT). Much use has been made of vowel formant center frequencies, bandwidths, and transitions by individuals using time-frequency-amplitude spectrographic techniques in speaker identification.[1,27,30,31,44,46,47,77,90,91] While that approach was not a particularly sophisticated one (especially when used alone as in "voiceprints"), interpretation of the relevant research suggests that vowel formants definitely are important speaker identification cues (especially when obtained by modern methods). In any case, the VFT parameter is based on the measurement of the center frequencies of the first three formants of several long vowels and calculation of the ratios among them. It now appears that F_1 and F_2 are especially good indicators of speaker identity and appear to be resistant to many kinds of distortion. The software approach utilized consists of preprogrammed vowel formant windows and a vector of 28 parameters. As with the others, VFT is first evaluated separately and then as part of the SAUSI profile.

Temporal Analysis (TED). Relatively little speaker identification research has focused on any of the temporal parameters that can be extracted from the speech wave; there are but few exceptions.[27,57,60,75,76,80,82,92] Nevertheless, strong logic suggests that certain speaker-related prosodic elements can be extracted and used for recognition purposes. For example, given the hypothesis that talkers differ with respect to the temporal factors of speech (ie, in syllables, words, phrases, sentences), it is possible that the time a person takes to produce a specific amount of connected discourse will be useful in the identification task. The approach here involves an energy detection and assessment computer program. The speech energy bursts (and related) are identified and timed as a function of the amount of energy present. The several resulting parameters are merged into a vector and processing/analysis proceeds as with the others.

These vectors (plus several others) have been tested individually and in combination a large number of times in the laboratory and in the field—where attempts were made to "solve" simulated, but structured, crimes. Many experiments—both successful and unsuccessful—were carried out; and most of the basic information about SAUSI has been generated by these 40 to 50 studies. Moreover, the uniqueness of the features was tested differentially under normal and distorted speaking conditions. Finally, when a vector (or cluster of vectors) began to show potential, the research effort was shifted to the field. At that time, the forensic model was invoked and the profile approach applied. It should be remembered that the SAUSI approach addresses the very severe limitations imposed on the identification task by the forensic model (ie, one referent; one test sample within a field of competing samples). This rather harsh research design forces matches (or nonmatches) to be made from a fairly large collection of voices (6–25 in number) on the basis of either the bioequivalence[93] or nearest neighbor statistical procedure. To compensate for this challenge, the rotation approach referred to above is applied; that is, each profile is generated (using the same speakers but different samples) several times and the analyses replicated. The final continuum usually consists of the data from 3 to 5 rotations and includes a summation of all vectors. Hence, any decision is based on several million individual comparisons (factors, parameters, vectors, rotations).

Application

As more and more research was completed, it became increasingly apparent that the mass of data generated by a SAUSI analysis needed to be organized for better interpretation. The first step was to display it as seen in Figure 101–8. This approach assisted the operator in coping with the differential robustness of the vectors

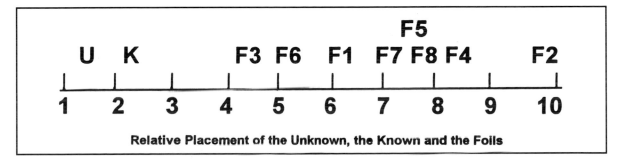

Fig 101–8. Printout of a single SAUSI trial (with F = 8). Note that the unknown-vs-unknown comparison validated the run and that K = U.

as a function of the type of degradation to the signal. As can be seen, the relationships among the unknown talker and the foils are presented for each normalized vector and for the combined vectors. This approach proved satisfactory for system analysis; it also facilitated the decision-making identification process.

The way speakers are evaluated further may be best understood by observation of Figures 101–9 and 101–10. In the first case, the identification of the unknown (U) is sought within a field that also consists of a known talker and controls (foils). The data seen actually are based on several cases where our four mul-

```
Unknown Reference    C:\SAUSI\E3
Unknown Test         C:\SAUSI\E3
Known                C:\SAUSI\E3
Foil  1              C:\SAUSI\E3
Foil  2              C:\SAUSI\E3
Foil  3              C:\SAUSI\E3
Foil  4              C:\SAUSI\E3
Foil  5              C:\SAUSI\E3
Foil  6              C:\SAUSI\E3
Foil  7              C:\SAUSI\E3
Foil  8              C:\SAUSI\E3
Foil  9              C:\SAUSI\E3
Foil 10              C:\SAUSI\E3
Foil 11              C:\SAUSI\E3
```

	LTS	TED	SFF	VFT	SUM
Unknown test	1.0000	1.4818	1.0000	1.0000	1.0000
Known	1.5323	1.0000	1.2836	1.2292	1.1686
Foil 1	3.8862	7.8851	3.9469	2.6166	5.1448
Foil 2	6.1144	4.4177	9.5805	3.1202	6.6102
Foil 3	9.1714	5.4474	5.2633	3.4391	6.6367
Foil 4	9.0549	5.5074	10.0000	10.0000	10.0000
Foil 5	5.9006	3.4713	7.0671	2.0996	5.2058
Foil 6	6.1824	10.0000	9.5805	4.6620	8.7621
Foil 7	9.7969	3.5349	9.5805	3.6224	7.5982
Foil 8	7.6665	8.2456	7.4505	4.4635	7.9845
Foil 9	10.0000	5.4801	9.5805	4.7024	8.5640
Foil 10	8.6318	7.4416	5.8762	4.4418	7.5553
Foil 11	4.0598	4.7911	6.3774	2.7540	5.0393

Fig 101–9. A continuum providing normalized data for the unknown, the known, and 11 foil speakers.

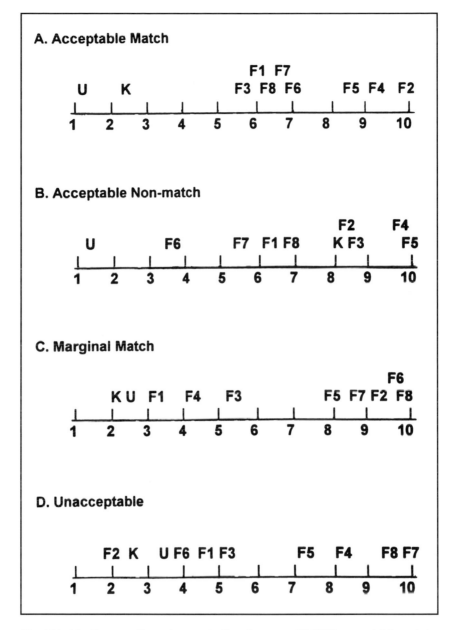

Fig 101–10. Four continua demonstrating degrees of SAUSI acceptable matches to acceptable nonmatches.

tidimensional vectors were normalized and then plotted on a two-dimensional continuum. As may be seen in Figure 101–9, the unknown was chosen as himself and then clearly identified as the known talker. Note also, the data shown in Figure 101–10. Here, a number of matches and nonmatches are contrasted.

At present, the SAUSI system operates fairly well and does so even in most forensic situations. Nevertheless, presentation of data from a recent series of experiments would appear useful; they may be found in Figure 101–11. The first of these experiments, done in 1988, involved a large number of subjects but only laboratory samples (ie, high fidelity). Note that none of the individual vectors provided 100% correct identification. The second part of this project (not shown) was designed to test the proposition that SAUSI would eliminate a known speaker if he was not also the unknown; it did so and at a level of 100% correct elimination. The second set of experiments done in 1993 also involved a large number of subjects; but this

Conditions and Study	Vectors				
	TED	LTS	SFF	VFT	SUM
A. High Fidelity					
Hollien	62	88	68	85	90
Hollien et al	63	100	100	100	100
Jiang	82	100	80	100	100
B. Noise					
Hollien et al	64	90	77	92	100
Jiang	76	94	76	96	100
C. Telephone Passband					
Hollien et al	55	92	90	88	98
Jiang	58	100	90	96	100

Fig 101–11. Summary data from three major projects evaluating the SAUSI vectors under three environmental conditions. Values are percent correct identification of 25 or more adult male speakers; all samples were subjected to three complete rotations.

time, separate replications were carried out for high fidelity, noise, and telephone passband (Hollien et al[80] and unpublished). As can be seen, this 1993 upgrading of the vectors resulted in marked improvement for all conditions.

In 1995, Jiang[60] further upgraded the SAUSI vectors and then ran a replication of the 1993 experiment. As can be seen from consideration of Figure 101–11, correct identifications were strikingly higher for all conditions; and the correct identification level reached 100% for the summed rotations; it did so even for the two degraded conditions. The overall improvement reported is judged to be due to (1) the upgrading of vector design, (2) better equipment and processing procedures, and (3) insights from both research and field experience.

In summary, virtually all of the research carried out on SAUSI was designed to reflect the forensic model; thus, the system has been tested under rather stringent conditions. The overall results indicate that the strength of an individual vector varies somewhat from situation to situation. Indeed, although no one vector has individ-

ually provided consistently high levels of correct identification under any and all conditions, they appeared to compensate for one another, especially when rotated and combined into a normalized two-dimensional profile.

Detecting Stress, Intoxication, and Other Behaviors

Many attempts have been made to detect behavioral states from voice (ie, those resulting from emotions, stress, psychosis, intoxicants, deception, fatigue, and so on). Much of that effort has lacked scientific rigor; and some of it has not even been legitimate. Nonetheless, honest inquiry focused on the several cited conditions has resulted in some useful information. However, to review all of these issues would require a chapter (each); and attempts to condense all of them into this section just might be counterproductive. Accordingly, the only areas to be considered here will be stress and intoxication—plus their effect on speech and voice. They are nicely illustrative; but if you wish to investigate the nature and effects of the other conditions, you should consult the basic literature.

Psychological Stress in Voice

To understand how a person is feeling just from hearing his or her voice is not very easy to do. Yet, there are times when an individual has little else to go on to determine the talker's state and what action he might be intending. Unfortunately, although it can be said that at least some of the relationships between vocal behaviors and psychological stress are known or suspected, many of them are rather tenuous. But is the determination of stress in voice important anyway? Yes, it undoubtedly is, especially with respect to certain types of direct interaction among people. For one thing, it often is important to monitor the potential for stress in personnel who are physically separated from a base or control site (ie, pilots, astronauts, aquanauts, police officers, and others) irrespective of the message content of the spoken interchange. It also can be desirable for a worker at a crisis control center to be able to tell if the caller actually plans to commit suicide or merely wants to talk about it. Are there vocal cues that will aid a patrolman in quickly determining if the perpetrator is about to attack—or others that will warn him of a specific danger during a household disturbance? In short, there are many instances wherein speaker-based information about the stress states of an individual would be quite helpful; and the needs of legal and law enforcement personnel rank high in this regard.

Perspectives

First, it should be noted that the term stress denotes a negative psychological state rather than one that reflects emotions in general. Although it may be just as important to determine when a person is happy as it is to know if he or she is angry, anxious, or fearful, the "reading" of negative emotions is more appropriate in the forensic situation. Moreover, much of the research that has been carried out in these areas has been either on stress or psychosis.

What is psychological stress? Is it fear; is it anger; is it anxiety? Scherer[94,95] suggests that, in general, this problem appears to result from "the lack of a precise specification and description of the emotional state underlying the vocal expression, independent of whether it is induced, posed, or studied naturalistically." This is a fair statement indeed, and one that suggests the scope of the definition problem. Of course, in

laboratory experiments, stress often is identified in terms of the applied stressor. This type of definition is not particularly useful in the real world, however; because, even though the stimuli are described, the emotion(s) or the stress being felt tends to be unknown. Moreover, when various emotions are specifically identified for research purposes, they often are simulated by actors,[1,96,97] an approach that is used primarily because it is rarely possible to record a person's speech while he or she is experiencing full blown stress states and then again under normal speaking conditions.

A third problem, and one which is perhaps more serious than the first two, relates directly to the level of stress. The question is not just "is stress present," but also what is its severity? Thus, no matter how research on stress is approached, both its presence and level should be included. Only detection is ordinarily studied, and virtually all of the research findings to date have omitted level. Moreover, most investigations have been conducted without the application of rigorous controls. It is little wonder, then, that many contradictions and substantial variability appear among the reported data.

Definitions

Back to definitions. The first step in understanding stress is to define it and to do so at a *level* of specificity beyond those suggested above. A reasonable definition, then, would be as follows. Stress, when experienced, reflects some sort of psychological state—especially one that constitutes a response to a threat.[97-99] On the other hand, stress may be induced either internally or externally with "adaptive or coping behavior required"[95,101]; or it may not be "imposed" at all but rather constitute a state where an individual "responds" to stressful conditions. In any event, we define stress as a "psychological state which results as a response to a perceived threat and is accompanied by the specific emotions of fear and anxiety."[1,97,102-104]

When the restrictions implied by this definition are considered, it might seem that the materials to follow would be of somewhat limited use in the forensic milieu. To illustrate, before it is possible to tell if a person's voice is exhibiting stress, it might be necessary to learn something about how he or she sounds under ordinary circumstances. Moreover, the need to make a judgment may come and go so quickly that formal analysis would fall in the difficult-to-impossible category. Yet, it often *is* possible to establish reasonable insights about the stress being experienced by another person and do so by assessment of their vocal characteristics. How is this possible?

The Speaking Correlates of Stress

It has long been accepted that listeners can, indeed, identify some emotions (including stress) from speech samples alone and do so at reasonably high levels of accuracy.[95-97,101,103,105-108] For example, several authors[96,105] have reported that identifications can fall in the 80 to 90% correct range. Of course, most of this research was carried out on "emotions" as portrayed (vocally) by actors, and it may be possible that they created some sort of artificial stereotypes. However, data have been reported,[104,109,110] which can be used to argue that it also is possible to specify the emotions that actually are being experienced. More importantly, if it is possible to discover felt emotions simply by listening to a talker's voice, it also should be possible to identify the relevant acoustical and temporal parameters (within the voice signal) that correlate with these percepts. Indeed, several such features have been identified.

Speaking Fundamental Frequency

Changes in heard pitch or speaking fundamental frequency (SFF or F_0) appear to correlate with psychological stress when it is being experienced. For example, years ago when Fairbanks and Pronovost[96] carried out research with actors, they found that the SFF level was raised for the emotions of fear and anger but not so for others; this relationship tends to be supported by most current studies.[94,106,108,111] Other researchers[108,110] have analyzed the real-life emotions of pilots when in danger and control tower operators under pressure. These talkers also have exhibited a rise in SFF as a function of increased stress. On the other hand, not all authors support this relationship; some[96] found only slight increases in SFF/F_0 as a function of stress, and others[112,113] report mixed results. However, it does appear that moderate to substantial increases in F_0 level usually correlate with the presence of psychological stress. To be useful, however, baseline data ordinarily should be compared to that resulting from the stressful situation. Fundamental frequency variability appears to be a much poorer predictor of stress than does SFF level. Data in this regard are not very orderly; indeed almost any position can be argued—that SFF variability may increase; may decrease, may not change, or may vary from speaker to speaker.[95-97,101,108,111] Thus, a metric of this type probably would not be useful for legal or law enforcement groups (at this stage anyway)

The Intensity of Voice

Vocal intensity is another acoustic parameter that, at least to some extent, correlates with the presence of psychological stress. However, only one group[97] has reported measurements of "absolute" intensity. They found positive correlations, and other investigators[94,108,114] pretty much agree even though they used relative measures. Thus, while inconsistencies occur, the best evidence is that vocal intensity often is increased as a function of stress.

Speech Timing

Identification of the prosodic speaking characteristics related to stress has proven to be a fairly complex process. For example, although some authors indicate that fear and anger appear typified by rapid speaking rates, as well as by short phonatory pauses,[94] others[97,108] tend not to agree. On the other hand, there is a temporal pattern shift that appears to correlate with rise in stress and does so on a fairly universal basis. It is that fewer speech bursts occur when a person speaks while experiencing that emotion. Hence, angry or fearful individuals appear to speak in longer utterances (bursts) than they would ordinarily. Finally, a rather important finding reported in this area is that nonfluencies correlate positively with stress states.

A Model

The above discussion focused on stress rather than on emotions in general. This approach was taken because psychological stress is of primary interest to law enforcement and related agencies. In any event, appropriate data have been combined into a predictive model of the vocal correlates of psychological stress, which is found in Figure 101–12. The patterns seen can be used to (potentially) determine what happens when most people speak under conditions of psychological stress. Specifically, the several shifts that can be expected include the following: (1) speaking fundamental frequency will be raised, (2) nonfluencies will increase, (3) vocal intensity will rise moderately, (4) speech rate will increase slightly, and (5) the number of speech bursts will be reduced. However, it should be remembered that, although this pattern will occur for most people, some individuals will not exhibit it (ie, the cited shifts). Moreover, because the observed characteristics take place as change from neutral speaking characteristics, information of this type will be of greatest value in the criminal justice setting when contrasts can be made to reference profiles.

Detection of Deception

This area (ie, the detection of behavioral states from speech analysis) cannot be concluded without at least a

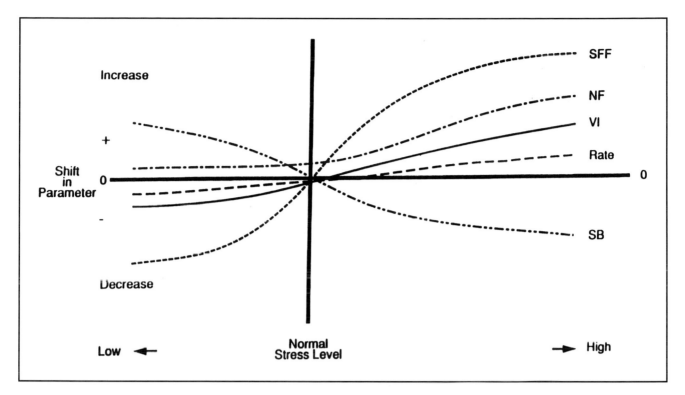

Fig 101–12. A model of the most common shifts in the voice and speech of a person who is experiencing psychological stress. SFF refers to speaking fundamental frequency, NF refers to noninfluencies, VI refers to vocal intensity, and SB refers to the number of speech bursts per unit of time.

passing reference to the so-called "psychological stress evaluators." It is claimed that these devices can be used to detect both stress and lying from voice assessment. I will not develop this issue to any great extent, but a couple of comments would appear germane.

First, if one is going to use a machine to detect lying, there must be a human lie response (ie, a measurable physiological or psychological event that always occurs when a person lies). Lykken says there is no such animal[115] but then so would simple logic. Second, individuals who market "systems" or devices that they purport are able to detect lying from elements within the voice indicate that they utilize the micro-tremors (or subsonic frequencies) of a human's vocal muscles for such purposes.[1] Are there any studies to support their claims? Not really; indeed the contrary is true[1,103,116-118] In any event, there is a great deal of mystery about how these devices actually work and whether they can validly perform any of the tasks their proponents claimed possible. Based on the available evidence, it can only be concluded that these systems are of no value in the detection of deception—or even of stress. It might even be concluded that using them constitutes fraudulent behavior. If you are interested in this area, you might find it useful to read the references cited.

Alcohol-Speech Relationships

Almost anyone who is asked to do so probably would describe the speech of an inebriated talker as "slurred," "misarticulated," or "confused." But, do commonly held stereotypes of this type square with the results studies have reported? More importantly, are there data to suggest that it is possible to determine a person's sobriety solely from analysis of his or her speech? Unfortunately, few relevant research projects have been carried out in the past and, hence, not a great deal of research has been reported.[119-125] Worse yet, many of those publications are limited in scope. Recently, however, interest in the area has been increasing. Moreover, although only a few of the early authors provided experimental data (ie, many of their presentations were anecdotal, reviews of other research or somewhat tangential to the issue), current efforts tend to be more rigorous in nature.[85,119-140] Please note that Chin and Pisoni's book[131] provides a good general review of this topic.

Underlying Research

It has been demonstrated that the consumption of even moderate amounts of alcohol can result in fairly substantial changes in human behavior. Cognitive function can be impaired,[132,133] as can sensory-motor performance.[132-136] Because the speech act represents the output of a number of high level integrated systems (sensory, cognitive, motor), it is not anomalous to assume that this process may also be susceptible to the influence of extraneous factors such as alcohol consumption. To be specific, it is well known that the oral production of any language involves the use of multiple sensory modalities, high level cortical functioning, complex cognitive processing, and a whole series of central and peripheral motor acts. Interruptions or insults to any of the links in this chain may result in disruptions of, or impairment in, the flow of speech and language.[137] Moreover, the component elements in this system are lawful in their interactions. For example, the speech- signal contains features that can be utilized to identify the specific physiological processes involved in its production. Further, they can interact with each other in ways that provide information about such features as speaker identity and the emotional states being experienced.[1,27] Thus, it would appear legitimate to assume that alcohol consumption also can be reflected in the voice/speech of the talker.

Specific Speech-Intoxication Relationships

Without question, research on the effects of intoxication on much of human behavior is difficult to conduct; and it now appears that study of the alcohol-speech relationships can be numbered among the more severe of these challenges. Indeed, the investigators who have researched the correlations between motor speech and ethanol consumption have experienced substantial problems in designing and conducting studies that exhibit acceptable precision. However, a few relationships already appear to be emerging from their efforts.

Some investigators have focused on the quality of the speech on an "intoxicated-sober" continuum. For example, when certain of them[120,121] had their subjects speak when sober and intoxicated, they found that articulation was degraded, speech rate slowed, and perception of intoxication states increased. Pisoni and Martin[130] also demonstrated that listeners could identify a talker when drunk or when sober, at least 62 to 74% of the time. Degradations in morphology and/or syntax, have been found to occur[124] as have articulatory problems.[121,122] However, the preeminent focus here (see above plus Johnson et al[85] and Natale et al[120]) appears to have been on the paralinguistic features of speech. Prior to our work (see below), various authors predicted that speaking fundamental frequency level, although variable, often is lowered and SFF variabili-

ty can be increased; speaking rate often is slowed; the number and length of pauses is often increased; and amplitude or intensity levels are sometimes reduced. Our research (plus that of the Pisoni group[130]) has validated some of these reports, clarified others, and added to the relevant database. We found that some of the confusions that occurred early on appear related to difficulties in procedure.

Application Difficulties

The basic problem with virtually all of the data reported in the older literature is that they were quite variable. Yet, Klingholz et al[119] appear to believe that they can account for many of these inconsistencies on the basis of inadequate and/or differing research designs. They indicate that the substantial variation observed probably is due to nonobjective measurements of blood alcohol level (BAL), too high a BAL, the use of too few (intoxicated) subjects, and/or analyses that were only qualitative. Most of these observations undoubtedly are correct. But, even after completing their own research, these authors point out that "intoxicated individuals can be falsely classified as sober" (and vice versa) on the basis of the "acoustic analysis" of speech. Moreover, they did not list all of the problems found in the research they reviewed; that is, few if any of the investigators controlled for drinking habits, intoxication level, increasing versus decreasing BAL, or effort. Nor did they employ blind controls who ingested placebos or contrast the effects of alcohol with those resulting from other physiological or psychological states.[125-128] Specifically, any number of (other) behavioral states—stress, fatigue, depression, effort, emotions, and speech/voice disorders—could complicate attempts to determine intoxication level from speech analysis. Further, it may not be possible to make valid judgments unless the target utterances can be compared with a profile of that person's speech when sober.

Our Research Program

Recognizing the confusions and contradictions associated with the intoxication-speech dilemma, we have developed a research program that attempts to resolve some of the conflicts and/or hopefully provide remedies.[126-128] Although currently ongoing, our efforts already have led to solutions for at least some of the problems.

First, the methodological approach we utilized was designed to upgrade the precision of the traditional procedures used to induce acute alcohol intoxication. Instead of administering heavy doses of ethanol—

based on body weight, sex, and so on—our subjects received lighter doses (80-proof rum or vodka) mixed with a soft drink (orange juice, cola) plus Gatorade. The subjects drank at their own pace but breath concentration levels (BrAC) were measured at 10- to 15-minute intervals throughout the experiment. Efficiency was increased by this approach with nausea and discomfort sharply reduced; further, serial measurements were permitted and intoxication level could be highly controlled. Relatively large groups of subjects were studied and all subjects participated in all procedures (ie, all of those in their particular experiment). Figure 101–13 graphically portrays how the intoxication level was tracked for one of the subjects. The "windows" or intoxication levels (ascending or descending) at which speech was studied included (among others) BrAC 0.00 (sober), BrAC 0.04-0.05 (mild), BrAC 0.08-0.09 (legal), and BrAC 0.12-0.13 (severe).

Subjects were carefully selected on the basis of 27 behavioral and medical criteria. After training, they were required to repeatedly produce four types of speech under a variety of conditions and intoxication levels; included were a standard 98-word oral reading passage, articulation test sentences, a set of diadochokinetic gestures, and extemporaneous speech. Standard "drinking practice" evaluations were applied to classify subjects as light, moderate, or heavy drinkers. As may be deduced from the above descriptions, our procedures were very carefully carried out for all conditions and at all levels. Analysis included auditory processing by listeners (drunk-sober, intoxication level, etc), acoustic analysis of the signal, and various classification/sorting (behavioral) tests.

Current Findings

A number of relationships already have emerged from this program of research. First, it appears that auditors of all types are able to detect the presence of intoxication from listening to the talkers' speech and voice; and they can do so at rather high levels of accuracy. On the other hand, they are not so facile at determining the level of intoxication. Although they were able to discriminate among the levels, they tended to overestimate speaker impairment for individuals who were only mildly (to moderately) intoxicated and underestimate the level of involvement for those more severely involved[126] (see also Fig 101–14). Second, it appears possible to accurately simulate rather severe levels of intoxication and even reduce the percept of intoxication if the individual attempts (while inebriated) to sound sober.[125] Moreover (and surprisingly), there seem to be only minor gender differences and few-to-

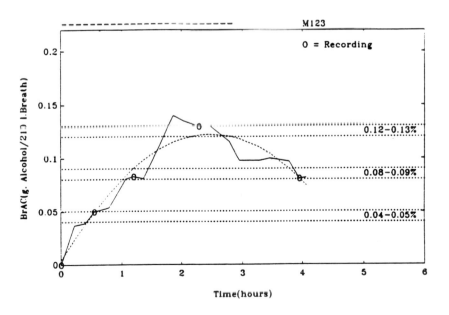

Fig 101–13. A plot of changes in intoxication level as a function of ingesting ethanol. The curve demonstrates a subject's progress relative to increasing levels of intoxication from the beginning to the completion of the experimental portion of a trial (BrAC was not always recorded after the primary run). Note that the speech samples were recorded while the speaker was in each of the windows. The smooth curve is a second order polynomial.

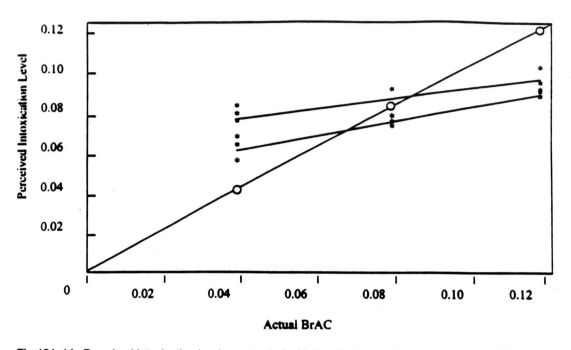

Fig 101–14. Perceived intoxication levels contrasted with the physiologically measured levels (45-degree line with circles) from sober to severely intoxicated (BrAC 0.12-0.13). Four studies are combined for the top set (35 speakers, 85 listeners) and two for the lower set (36 speakers, 52 listeners). Note the overreaction to the speech of people who are mildly intoxicated and the underrating of those who were seriously inebriated.

none for drinking level (light, moderate, heavy). Perhaps the most powerful data to date are those obtained from large groups of subjects in the "primary" investigations (see Figure 101–15). As can be seen, they show at least some shifts for all of the speaking characteristics measured excepting vocal intensity. First, note that speaking fundamental frequency (heard pitch) is raised (not lowered) with increases in intoxication level; this is a relationship suggested by clinicians but not by previous researchers.[138] Most notable of all is the nearly universal slowing down of speech as intoxication increases and the sharp rise of the number of nonfluencies for the same conditions. Perhaps the most striking relationship of all is this last one (see again, Fig 101–15). The correlation here is a very powerful one, and the pattern seen in the figure has been confirmed by several of our more recent studies. In short, patterns are emerging that permit the prediction of the speech/voice behaviors in a large proportion of those individuals who become intoxicated from ingesting ethanol. Finally, we also have broken some new ground as we have discovered that a small group of subjects account for virtually all of the departures from main patterns (we are now studying these deviations also). Finally, although the impact of these findings on the forensic milieu is not yet clear, it very well could prove to be a useful one.

Conclusion

Attempts have been made to describe several of the elements that make up a fairly new and still developing discipline of forensic phonetics. Some areas central to the field are well established; others still operate to create somewhat fuzzy boundaries. Among the topics clearly within the scope of forensic phonetics are (1) the enhancement and decoding of speech on tape recordings, (2) the authentication of tape recordings, (3) speaker identification (if not verification), and (4) the detection of a number of behavioral states from voice/speech analysis. Other elements may or may not be relevant also; only time will tell. In any event, just as with all relatively new fields, much is to be learned about what can and cannot be accomplished by application of the methods and procedures proposed and in use. Fortunately, appropriate baseline materials have been established by relevant practitioners and scientists situated both in America and Europe. These concepts and procedures are being upgraded and extended.

Acknowledgments The research described in this chapter was supported primarily by the National Institutes of Health, the Office of Naval Research, the US Army Research Office, the Justice Department, the Dreyfus Foundation,

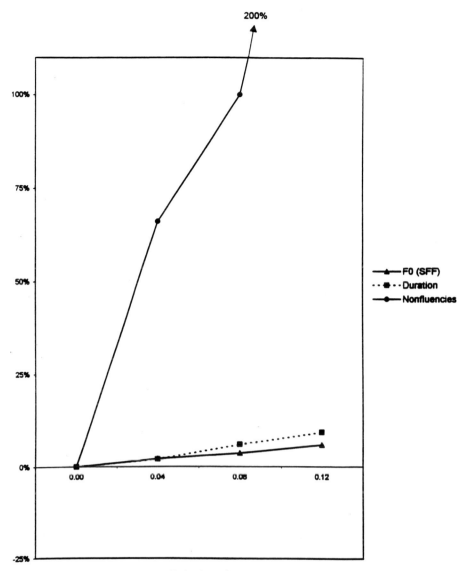

Fig 101–15. The shifts in several parameters as a function of increasing intoxication. The increase in F_0 and reduction in speaking rate (increased duration) are statistically significant. However, they are dwarfed by the dramatic shift in nonfluencies.

and the University of Florida. Grateful thanks is extended to all of them.

References

1. Hollien H. *The Acoustics of Crime.* New York, NY: Plenum; 1990.
2. Hollien H. Forensic phonetics: a new dimension to the phonetic sciences. In: *Festchrift fur Otto von Essen.* Hamburg, Germany: Phonetische Beitrage; 25:157–190.
3. Hollien H. Forensic communication: an emerging specialty. *Criminal Defense.* 1983;10:22–29.
4. Hollien H. The phonetician as a speech detective. In: Casagrande J, ed. *The Linguistic Connection.* New York, NY: University Press of America; 1983:101–132.
5. Hollien H. Forensic phonetics. In: Siegal JA, ed. *Encyclopedia of Forensic Sciences.* San Diego, Calif: Academic Press; 2000:1243–1254.
6. Dean JD. The work of the Home Office tape laboratory. *Police Res Bull.* 1980;35:25–27.
7. Hollien H. Noisy tape recordings in forensics. *ESCA Proceedings, Speech Processing in Adverse Conditions* (Nice, France). 1992:167–170.
8. Hollien H., Fitzgerald JT. Speech enhancement techniques for crime lab use. *Proceedings of the International*

Conference Crime Countermeasures (Oxford, UK). 1977:21–29.

9. Bloch SC, Lyons PW, Ritterman SI. Enhancement of speech intelligibility by "blind" deconvolution. *Proceedings of the Carnahan Conference on Crime Countermeasures (Lexington, Ky). 1977:167–174.*

10. Le Bouquin-Jeannes R. Enhancement of speech degraded by coherent and incoherent noise using a cross-spectral estimator. *IEEE Trans Speech Audio Processing.* 1997;5:404–420.

11. Lee KY. Speech enhancement based on neutral predictive hidden Markov models. *Signal Processing.* 1998;65:373–381.

12. Lim JS, Oppenheimer AV. Enhancement and bandwidth comprehension of noisy speech. *Proc IEEE.* 1979;67:1586–1604.

13. Paul JE, Reames JB, Woods RC. Real-time digital laboratory enhancement of tape recordings. *Proceedings of the Institute of Acoustics. Part I: Police Applications Speech and Tape Recording Analysis.* 1984;6:1–11.

14. Wan EA. Removal of noise from speech using the dual EKF algorithm. *Proceedings of the International Conference on Acoustics, Speech, and Signal Processing, ICASSP, Piscataway, NY,* 1998:181:384.

15. Blain BJ. Tape recording enhancement. *Police Res Bull.* (London, UK Home Office), 1980;35:22–24.

16. Hollien PA. Utilization of blind decoders in phonetics. In: Cohen A, Broecke M, eds. *Tenth International Congress of Phonetic Sciences.* Dordrecht, Holland: Foris Publications; 1983:532.

17. Hollien PA. An update on speech decoding. *Proceedings of the Institute of Acoustics. Part I: Police Applications of Speech and Tape Recording Analysis.* 1984:33–40.

18. Warren RM, Warren PR. Auditory illusions and confusions. *Sci Am.* 1970;223:30–36.

19. Osberger MJ. A comparison between procedures used to locate speech segment boundaries. *J Acoust Soc Amer.* 1979;50:225–228.

20. Peterson GE, Lehiste I. Duration of syllable nuclei in English. *J Acoust Soc Am.* 1960;32:693–703.

21. Aull AM, Zue VW. Lexical stress determination and its application to large vocabulary speech recognition. *IEEE Proc. ICASSP.* 1985;CH218:1549–1552.

22. Cutler A, Foss DJ. On the role of sentence stress in sentence processing. *Lang Speech.* 1977;20:1–10.

23. Bolinger D, Sears DA. *Aspects of Language.* 3rd ed. New York, NY: Harcourt Brace Jovanovich; 1981.

24. Taylor DS. Non-native speakers and the rhythm of English. *Int Rev Appl Ling Lang Teach.* 1981;19:219–226.

25. van Coestsem F, Hendricks R, McCormick S. Accent typology and sound change. *Lingua.* 1981;53:293–315.

26. Hecker MHL. Speaker Recognition: *An Interpretative Survey of the Literature.* ASHA Monograph No 16. Washington, DC: ASHA; 1971.

27. Holien H. *Forensic Voice Identification.* London, UK: Academic Press; 2002.

28. Kuenzel HJ. *Spechererkennung.* Heidelberg, Germany: Kriminalistik; 1987.

29. Nolan JF. *The Phonetic Basis of Speaker Recognition.* Cambridge, UK: Oxford University Press; 1983.

30. Stevens KN. Sources of inter- and intra-speaker variability in the acoustic properties of speech sounds. *Proceedings of the Seventh International Congress of Phonetic Sciences.* Montreal, Canada; 1971:206–232.

31. Tosi O. *Voice Identification: Theory and Legal Applications.* Baltimore, Md: University Park Press; 1979.

32. Mack vs State of Florida. 54 Fla. 55, 44 So. 706 (1907), citing 5, *Howell's State Trials,* 1186.

33. Broeders APA. Earwitness identification: common ground, disputed territory and uncharted areas. *Forensic Linguistics.* 1996;3:1–13.

34. Michel JF. Use of a voice lineup. Presented at the Annual Meeting of the American Academy of Forensic Sciences; Feb 1980; New Orleans, La. Abstract 937(A).

35. DeJong G. Earwitness characteristics and speaker identification accuracy. Unpublished Ph.D. dissertation, University of Florida, Gainesville, Fla.

36. Hollien H, Huntley R, Kuenzel H, Hollien PA. Proposal for earwitness lineups. *Forensic Linguistics.* 1995;2:143–154.

37. Yarmi AD. Earwitness speaker identification. *Psychol Publ Policy Law.* 1995;1:792–816.

38. Bull R, Clifford BR. Earwitness voice recognition accuracy. In: Wells GL, Loftus E, eds. *Earwitness Testimony: Psychological Perspectives.* Cambridge, UK: Cambridge University Press; 1984.

39. Clifford BR. Memory for voices: the feasibility and quality of earwitness evidence. In: Bostock L, ed. *Evaluating Witness Evidence.* Clifford, NY: John Wiley and Sons; 1984.

40. Kuenzel H. On the problem of speaker identification by victims and witnesses. *Forensic Linguistics.* 1994;1:45–58.

41. Yarmey AD. Verbal, visual, and voice identification of rape suspect under different levels of illumination. *J Appl Psychol.* 1986;71:363–370.

42. McGehee F. The reliability of the identification of the human voice. *J Gen Psychology.* 1937;17:249–271.

43. Bricker P, Pruzansky S. Effects of stimulus content and duration on talker identification. *J Acoust Soc Am.* 1966;40:1441–1450.

44. Carbonell JR, Stevens KN, Williams CE, Woods B. Speaker identification by a matching-from-samples technique. *J Acoust Soc Am.* 1965;40:1205–1206.

45. Huntley RA. Listener skill in voice identification. Presented at the American Academy of Forensic Sciences; February 1992; New Orleans, La. Abstract 105(A).

46. Stevens KN, Williams CE, Carbonell JR, Woods D. Speaker authentication and identification: a comparison of spectrographic and auditory presentation of speech materials. *J Acoust Soc Am.* 1968:44:1596–1607.

47. Endres W, Bambach W, Flosser G. Voice spectrograms as a function of age, voice disguise, and voice imitation. *J Acoust Soc Am.* 1971;49:1842–1848.

48. Hollien H, Majewski W, Doherty ET. Perceptual identification of voices under normal, stressed, and disguised speaking conditions, *J Phonetics.* 1982;10:139–148.

49. Hollien H, Schwartz R. Speaker identification utilizing noncontemporary speech. *J Forensic Sci.* 2001;46:63–67.

50. Houlihan K. The effects of disguise on speaker identification from sound spectrograms. In: Hollien H, Hollien P, eds. *Current Issues in the Phonetic Sciences: Proceedings of the IPS-77 Congress*; Miami Beach, Florida; 17–19 December 1977. Amsterdam, The Netherlands: J Benjamins; 1979:811–820.

51. Kuenzel HJ. Field procedures in forensic speaker identification. *Proceedings of the 12th International Congress of Phonetic Sciences*. Aix-en-Provence, France: Université de Provence; 1991.

52. McGlone RE, Hollien PA, Hollien H. Accoustic analysis of voice disguise related to voice identification. *Proceedings of the International Conference on Crime Countermeasures*. Oxford, UK; July 25–27, 1977:31–35.

53. Pollack I, Pickett JM, Sumby WH. On the identification of speakers by voice. *J Acoust Soc Am*. 1989;26:403–412.

54. Reich AR, Duke JE. Effects of selected vocal disguise upon speaker identification by listening. *J Acoust Soc Am*. 1979;66:1023–1028.

55. Compton AJ. Effects of filtering and vocal duration upon the identification of speakers aurally. *J Acoust Soc Am*. 1963;35L1748–1752.

56. Hollien H, Majewski W, Hollien PA. Analysis of F_0 as a speaker identification technique. *Proceedings of Eighth International Congress of Phonetic Sciences. Abstract of Papers*. 1975:337.

57. Jiang M. Fundamental frequency vector for a speaker identification system. *Forensic Ling*. 1996;1:45–58.

58. LaRiviere CL. Contributions of fundamental frequency and formant frequencies to speaker identification. *Phonetica*. 1975;31:185–197.

59. Iles M. Speaker identification as a function of fundamental frequency and resonant frequencies, Unpublished doctoral dissertation, University of Florida. Gainesville, Fla.

60. Jiang M. Experiments on a speaker identification system. Unpublished doctoral dissertation, University of Florida, Gainesville, Fla.

61. Kuenzel HJ, Koester JP. Measuring vocal jitter in forensic speaker identification. Presented at the American Academy of Forensic Sciences; 1992; New Orleans, La. Abstract 113–114(A).

62. Shirt M. An auditory speaker recognition experiment. *Proceedings of the Institute of Acoustics. Part 1, Police Applications of Speech, Tape Recording Analysis*. London, UK: Documenta Acustica; 1984:71–74.

63. Koester JP. Auditive Spechererkennung bei Experten und Naiven. In *Festschrift Wangler*. Hamburg, Germany: Helmut Buske, AG; 1981;52:171–180.

64. Atwood W, Hollien H. Stress monitoring by polygraph for research purposes. *Polygraph*. 1986;15:47–56.

65. Hollien H, Bennet GT, Gelfer MP. Criminal identification comparison: aural vs. visual identifications resulting from a simulated crime. *J Forensic Sci*. 1983;28:208–221

66. Hollien H, Hollien PA. Improving aural-perceptual speaker identification techniques. In: Braum A, Koester JP, eds. *Studies in Forensic Phonetics*. Trier, Wissenschaftlicher Verlag; 1995;64:87–64.

67. Atal BS. Effectiveness of linear prediction characteristics of the speech wave for automatic speaker identification and verification. *J Acoust Soc Am*. 1974;55:1304–1312.

68. Bakis R, Dixon NR. Toward speaker-independent recognition-by-synthesis. *IEEE Proc, ICASSP*. 1982:566–569.

69. Basztura CS, Majewski W. The application of long-term analysis of the zero-crossing of a speech signal in automatic speaker identification. *Arch Acoust*. 1978;3:3–15.

70. Broderick PK, Paul JE, Rennick RE. Semi-automatic speaker identification system. In: *Proceedings of the 1975 Carnahan Conference on Crime Countermeasures; Lexington, Ky*; 1975:37–45.

71. Bunge E. Automatic speaker recognition system auros for security systems and forensic voice identification. *Proceedings of the International Conference on Crime Countermeasures*; Oxford, UK; 1977:1–8.

72. Edie J, Sebestyen GS. Voice identification general criteria. Report RADC-TDR-62-278. New York, NY: Rome Air Development Centre, Air Force Systems Command, Griffiss AFB; 1972.

73. Fredouille C, Bonastre JF. Use of dynamic information and second order statistical methods in speaker identification. *RLA2C*. Avignon, France. 1998;3:50–54.

74. Schwartz R, Roncos S, Berouti M. The application of probability density estimation to text-independent speaker identification. *Proceedings of the ICASSP*. 1982:1649–1652.

75. Doherty ET. An evaluation of selected acoustic parameters for use in speaker identification. *J Phonetics*. 1976;4:321–326.

76. Doherty ET, Hollien H. Multiple factor speaker identification of normal and distorted speech. *J Phonetics*. 1978;6:1–8.

77. Hollien H. The profile approach to speaker identification. *Proceedings of the 12th International Congress on Phonetic Sciences (ICPhS)*; Aix en Provence, France; 1991:396(A).

78. Hollien H. The future of speaker identification: a model (Plenary). *Proceedings of the 13th International Congress on Phonetic Sciences (ICPhS)*. vol 3, 138–145. Stockholm, Sweden; August 1995.

79. Hollien H, Jiang M, The challenge of effective speaker identification (Keynote). *Proceedings RLA2C*. Avignon, France; 1998:2–9.

80. Hollien H, Jiang M, Kuenzel H. Upgrading the SAUSI Prosody (TED) Vector, In: Braun A, Koester J-P, eds. *Studies in Forensic Phonetics*. Trier, Wissenschaftlicher Verlag; 1993;64:98–108.

81. Hollien H, Majewski W. Speaker identification by long-term spectra under normal and distorted speech conditions. *J Acoust Soc Amer*. 1977;62:975–980.

82. Johnson CC, Hollien H, Hicks JW Jr. Speaker identification utilizing selected temporal speech features. *J Phonetics*. 1984;12:319–327.

83. Hollien H. Consideration of guidelines for earwitness lineups. *Forensic Linguistics*. 1996;3:14–23.

84. Hollien H, Gelfer MP, Huntley R. The neutral speech vector concept in speaker identification. In: Borowski

VA, Koester JP, eds. *Neue Tendenzen in der Anger-wandten Phonetik.* Hamburg, Germany: Helmut Buske Verlag; 1990;62:71–87.

85. Johnson K, Pisoni D, Bernacki R. Do voice recordings reveal whether a person is intoxicated? *Phonetica.* 1990;47:215–237.

86. Zalewski J, Mejewski W, Hollien H. Cross-correlation between long-term speech spectra as a criterion for speaker identification. *Acustica.* 1975;34:20–24.

87. Hollien H, Hicks JW Jr, Oliver LH. A semiautomatic system for speaker identification. *Neue Tendenzen in der angerwandten Phonetik.* Hamburg, Germany: Helmut Buske Verlag; 1990:62:89–106.

88. Jassem W, Steffen-Batog M, Czajka S. Statistical characteristics of short-term average F_0 distribution as personal voice features. In: Jassem W, ed. *Speech Analysis and Synthesis.* vol 3. Warsaw, Poland: Pa'nstwowe Wydawn; 1973:209–228.

89. Wolf JJ. Efficient acoustic parameters for speaker recognition. *J Acoust Soc Am.* 1972;51:2044–2055.

90. Koval S, Krynov S. Practice of usage of spectral analysis for forensic speaker identification. *Proceedings of the Workshop Reconassaince du Locuteur et Ses Spplications Commerciale et Criminalistique (RLAC2);* Avignon, France; April 20–23, 1998:136–140.

91. Paoloni A, Pierucci P, Ragazzini S. Improving automatic formant tracking for speaker identification. *RLA2C;* Avignon, France; 1998;1:24–27.

92. Onellet P, Tadj C, Dumouchel J-P. Dialog and prosodic models for text-independent speaker identification. *RLA2C;* Avignon, France. 1998;2:41–44.

93. Hsu JC, Hwang J, H-K, Ruberg S. Confidence intervals associated with tests of bioequivalence. *Biometrika.* 1994;81:103–114.

94. Scherer KR. Vocal affect expression: a review and a model for future research. *Psychol Bull.* 1985;99:143–165.

95. Scherer KR. Voice, stress and emotion. In: Appley H, Trumbull R, eds. *Dynamics of Stress: Physiological, Psychological, and Social Perspectives.* New York, NY: Plenum Press; 1986:157–179.

96. Fairbanks G, Provovost W. An experimental study of the pitch characteristics of the voice during the expression of emotion. *Speech Monogr.* 1939;6:87–104.

97. Hicks JW Jr, Hollien H. The reflection of stress in voice-1: understanding the basic correlates. *Proceedings of the Carnahan Conference on Crime Countermeasures; Lexington, Ky;* 1981:189–194.

98. Appley MH, Trumbull R. On the concept of psychological stress. In: Appley MH, Trumbull R, eds. *Psychological Stress: Issues in Research.* New York, NY: Meredith Publishing Co; 1967.

99. Howard R. Neurophysiological studies of stress, arousal and anxiety. In: Spielberger CD, Sarason IG, eds. *Stress and Anxiety.* 1991;13:178–191.

100. Murray IR, Arnott JL. Toward the simulation of emotion in synthetic speech: a review of the literature on the human emotion. *J Acoust Soc Am.* 1993;93:1097–1108.

101. Scherer KR. Vocal indicators of stress. In: Darby J, ed. *Speech Evaluation in Psychiatry.* New York, NY: Grune & Stratton; 1981:171–187.

102. Hollien H. Vocal indicators of psychological stress. In: Wright F, Bahn C, Rieber RW, eds. *Forensic Psychology and Psychiatry.* New York, NY: New York Academy of Sciences; 1980:47–72.

103. Hollien H, Geisson L, Hicks JW Jr. Voice stress evaluators and lie detection. *J Forensic Sci.* 1987; 32:405–418.

104. Hollien H, Saletto JA, Miller SK. Psychological stress in voice: a new approach. *Studia Phonetica Posnaniensia.* 1993;4:5–17.

105. Liberman P, Michaels SB. Some aspects of fundamental frequency and envelope amplitude as related to emotional content of speech. *J Acoust Soc Am.* 1962;34: 922–927.

106. Scherer KR. Personalities markers in speech. In: Scherer KR, Giles H, eds. *Social Markets in Speech.* Cambridge, UK: Cambridge University Press; 1979:147–209.

107. Stepffen-Batog M, Madelska L, Katulska K. The role of voice timbre, duration, speech melody and dynamics in the perception of the emotional coloring of utterances. *Studia Phonetika Posnaniensia.* 1993;4:73–92.

108. Williams CE, Stevens KN. Emotions and speech: some acoustical correlates. *J Acoust Soc Am.* 1972;2:1238–1250.

109. Kuroda I, Fujiwara O, Okamura N, Utsuki N. Method for determining pilot stress through analysis of voice communication. *Aviat Space Environ Med.* 1976;47:528–533.

110. Williams CE, Stevens KN. On determining the emotional state of pilots during flight: an exploratory study. *Aerospace Med.* 1969;40:1369–1372.

111. Cummings K, Clements M. Analysis of glottal waveforms across stress styles. *Proc IEEE, ICASSP.* CH 2847: 369–372.

112. Asparoukhov O, Boyanov B. Computer analysis of speech patients under preoperative stress. *Acustica.* 1994; 80:412–414.

113. Hecker MHL, Stevens KN, von Bismarck G, Williams CE. Manifestations of task-induced stress in the acoustic speech signal. *J Acoust Soc Am.* 1968;44:993–1001.

114. Friedhoff AJ, Alpert M, Kurtzberg RL. An electroacoustic analysis of the effects of stress on voice, *J Cardiovasc Nurs.* 1964;11:266–272.

115. Lykken DT. *A Tremor in the Blood: Uses and Abuses of the Lie Detector.* New York, NY: McGraw-Hill, Inc; 1981.

116. Kubis J. *Comparison of Voice Analysis and Polygraph as Lie Detection Procedures.* Aberdeen Proving Ground, Md: US Army Land Warfare Laboratory; 1973.

117. McGlone RE. Tests of the psychological stress evaluator (PSE) as a lie and stress detector. *Proceedings of the International Conference on Crime Countermeasures; Lexington, Ky;* 1975:83–86.

118. McGlone RE, Hollien H. Partial analysis of the acoustic signal of stressed and unstressed speech. *Proceedings of the Carnahan Conference on Crime Countermeasures; Lexington, Ky;* 1976:19–21.

119. Klingholz F, Penning R, Liebhardt E. Recognition of low-level of alcohol intoxication from speech signal. *J Acoust Soc Am.* 1988;84:929–935.

120. Natale M, Kanzler M, Jaffe J. Acute effects of alcohol on defensive and primary-process language. *J Addict.* 1980;15:1055–1067.

121. Sobell L, Sobell M. Effects of alcohol on the speech of alcoholics, *J Speech Hear Res.* 1972;15:861–868.

122. Sobell L, Sobel M, Coleman R. Alcohol-induced dysfluency in nonalcoholics, *Folia Phoniatr* (Basel). 1982;34:316–323.

123. Trojan F, Kryspin-Exner K. The decay of articulation under the influence of alcohol and paraldehyde. *Folia Phoniatr.* 1968;20:217–238.

124. Chin SB, Large N, Pisoni D. Effects of alcohol on the production of words in context: a first report. Report 21. Bloomington, Ind: Speech Research Laboratory, Indiana University.

125. Hollien H, DeJong G, Martin CA. Production of intoxication states by actors: perception by lay listeners. *J Forensic Sci.* 1998;43:1153–1162.

126. Hollien H, DeJong G, Martin CA, Schwartz R, Liljegren K. Effects of ethanol intoxication on speech suprasegmentals. *J Acoust Soc Am.* 2001;110:3198–3206.

127. Hollien H, Martin CA. Conducting research on the effects of intoxication on speech. *Forensic Linguistics.* 1996;3:101–127.

128. Hollien H, Liljegren K, Martin CA, DeTong G. Production of intoxication states by actors: acoustic and temporal characteristics. *J Forensic Sci.* 2001;46:68–73.

129. Pisoni DB, Hathaway SN, Yuchtman M. Effects of alcohol on the acoustic-phonetic properties of speech. In: *Alcohol, Accidents and Injuries.* Pittsburgh, Pa: Society of Automotive Engineers; 1986:131–150.

130. Pisoni, DB, Martin CS. Effects of alcohol on the acoustics-phonetic properties of speech: perceptual and acoustic analyses. *Alcohol Clin Exp Res.* 1989;13:577–587.

131. Chin SB, Pisoni D. *Alcohol and Speech.* San Diego, Calif: Academic Press; 1997.

132. Arbuckle T, Chaikelson J, Gold D. Social drinking and cognitive function revisited. *J Stud Alcohol.* 1994;55:352–361.

133. Hindmarch I, Kerr JS, Sherwood N. The effects of alcohol and other drugs on psychomotor performance and cognitive function, *Alcohol Alcohol.* 1991;26:71–79.

134. Connors GJ, Maisto SA. Effects of alcohol, instructions and consumption rate on motor performance. *J Stud Alcohol.* 1980;41:509–517.

135. Moskowitz H, Burns M. Effects of rate of drinking on human performance. *J Stud Alcohol.* 1976;37:598–605.

136. Oei T, Kerschbaumer DM. Peer attitudes, sex, and the effects of alcohol on simulated driving performance, *Am J Drug Alcohol Abuse.* 1990;16:135–146.

137. Netsell R. Speech motor control: theoretical issues with clinical impact. In: Berry WR, ed. *Clinical Dysarthria.* San Diego, Calif: College-Hill Press; 1983:1–19.

138. Cooney O, McGuigan K, Murphy P, Conroy R. Acoustic analysis of the effects of alcohol on the human voice. *J Acoust Soc Am.* 1998; 103:2895.

102

Controversy in the Care of the Singer and Professional Voice Users

Clark A. Rosen and Kimberly M. Steinhauer

A multitude of controversial subjects surrounds the medical care of singers and professional voice users. These controversies typically arise from a paucity of definitive, scientific information regarding the use of the vocal mechanism during a variety of situations. The scarcity of rigorous, experimental testing of the professional voice has relegated voice care to an art form equally as complex and mysterious as that of performing an art song. The purpose of this chapter is to highlight the controversies in order to provide a dialogue for future research and to heighten the awareness of voice care professionals who deal daily with these issues; however, as is the nature of controversy, identifying the issues is the easy first step in a long complicated process of resolution.

Choral Versus Solo Singing

Choral singing is viewed in a negative light frequently within the area of medical care of the singer. Often, the voice care professional recommends that the patient limit or withdraw from choral singing, regardless of the diagnosis and treatment plan. This overtly disapproving approach regarding choral singing stems mostly from anecdotal incidents whereby choral singers report an increase in dysphonia during or after rehearsal. Another source is the laryngologist's past patient experience of caring for singers who have developed a voice problem related to choral singing. It is important to note that a significant selection bias exists in this type of approach, because the laryngologist cannot possibly know the number of countless choral singers who never developed a voice problem. Similarly, when a singer develops a vocal injury from solo singing, the negative connotation that is applied to choral singers is not applied to solo singers.

There are multiple reasons for voice complaints associated with choral singing, including competition with the neighboring choral singer by trying to match intensity and voice quality and oversinging as a result of the decreasing ability to monitor one's voice in the large group (Lombard effect). However, the most serious risk factor in developing vocal injury occurs when the choir member follows a choral conductor who does not fully understand the intricate details, demands, and needs of a singer. All too frequently, choral conductors have an instrumental background and may not fully understand the technical aspects of singing.[1] Inexperienced choral conductors will place inappropriate expectations and demands on the choral singer to achieve a specific vocal quality or "color," which can be potentially damaging to the singer. Therefore, the tendency for choral singers to oversing, compete, or develop injurious singing techniques or habits frequently has led voice care professionals to view choral singing negatively.

A variety of potential difficulties associated with choral singing must be considered carefully when advising singers; however, there are significant advantages to choral singing that must not be dismissed. The advantages include the development of musicianship, ear training, and an esprit de corps that one misses as a soloist. An additional benefit is the positive professional development associated with choral singing (ie, exposure and financial reward). When addressing the appropriateness of a singer's participation or continuation in choral singing activities, the pros and cons need to be balanced. This decision-making process must incorporate the vocal experience of the conductor, maturity of the singer, and a healthy collaboration between the choral director and private singing teacher.[2]

Surgery for Singers and Professional Voice Users

A widespread misconception among singers and singing teachers concludes that a singer will never return to full vocal function following vocal fold surgery. This grave error has led many vocalists to end their careers prematurely, fearing that surgery will not improve their singing voices. Furthermore, significant morbidity and loss of professional development have occurred from this fallacy; because many singers delay surgery and, as a result, lose income.

Singers, singing teachers, speech-language pathologists, and otolaryngologists must be informed that the appropriate use of surgery to improve the voice (specifically phonomicrosurgery for benign vocal fold lesions) usually can restore a singer's voice to its premorbid condition; however, complete recovery of the singing voice depends on a multitude of factors, including compliance of the patient and expertise of the voice care team. Surgery must be reserved until all nonsurgical rehabilitative treatment options have been exhausted. It is reasonable to state that a "specialist of specialists" should perform surgery on the singer and professional voice user. These surgeons have a great deal of training and expertise in this type of highly specialized voice surgery. In addition to finding the right surgeon, the best results typically are achieved by working closely with a voice team that should, at a minimum, be comprised of an otolaryngologist specializing in voice care (laryngologist), a speech-language pathologist specializing in voice care, and a singing voice specialist.

Laser Versus Cold Steel Phonomicrosurgery

The debate between laser surgery versus "cold steel" surgery of the vocal fold has continued for over a decade. The crux of the debate rests on which surgical technique is best to achieve optimal voice results. Several key concepts need to be understood to assist in the framing of this controversy.

Laser and cold steel surgery are methods used to cut tissue but are not actual operative philosophies or surgical techniques. Most importantly, it is essential to recognize that the surgeon behind the instrument (laser or cold steel) is usually the essential component to surgi-

cal success. Thus, excellent results can most often be obtained with either laser or cold steel if the surgeon understands the appropriate use of the technique, uses good judgment, and has a high degree of skill.[3]

The history behind this controversy arose when the laser was developed and was touted as a panacea for laryngeal surgeons. The enthusiasm for the laser was driven, in part, by the "if it is new and high-tech, it must be better" concept and by the companies selling the laser. Another attractive aspect of the laser was the "no instrument in the laryngoscope" aspect to the laser surgery. If one performs laryngeal surgery through a small laryngoscope, the laser affords the surgeon the ability to make incisions in the vocal fold without having to have an instrument within the already crowded and narrow laryngoscope operating space. Similarly, if a surgeon has difficulty controlling his nondominant hand during bimanual surgery, the laser could be an advantage from a precision and control aspect.

The risks of laser surgery of the vocal fold arise from the fact that the laser works by vaporizing tissue using extreme heat. The heat associated with laser use can cause significant thermal injury to adjacent areas of the vocal fold. This injury results in scar formation within the vocal fold. The other disadvantages of laser surgery include cost and airway fire risk. The laser used most frequently for surgery of the vocal fold is the carbon dioxide (CO_2) laser. This laser has been through several generations of development of laser delivery methods (micromanipulator) and requires routine maintenance. An essential aspect to this controversy is the availability of the most recent micromanipulator that delivers a laser spot size of about 0.3 mm. No laser surgery of the vocal fold for benign disease should be performed that does not have this level of micromanipulator and is not regularly maintained. Many hospitals in the United States of America purchased a CO_2 laser a decade or more ago and have not continued proper maintenance. Therefore, many CO_2 lasers are dated in their technology and not properly maintained. Furthermore, laser surgery of the vocal folds requires special skill, knowledge, and maintenance of these skills by the surgeon. If the surgeon does not regularly use the laser, the outcome can be disastrous.

For the majority of phonomicrosurgerical procedures, the present principles and techniques negate the advantages of the laser. This includes the use of large-bore laryngoscopes, miniaturized cold steel instruments, and specialized training for the nondominant hand. Thus, cold steel phonomicrosurgery is usually the preferred technique for precise, accurate microsurgery of the vocal fold.[4] There are still indications for laser surgery, but most laryngologists consider them rare and for highly specialized situations.

Voice Rest

Significant debate exists regarding voice rest for singers and professional voice users. Some individuals feel that healthy professional voice users are served best by having regularly scheduled periods of "voice rest." Also, when a minor voice problem does occur in a heavy voice user, there is much controversy regarding the utility of voice rest.

An important issue regarding voice rest involves the use of scheduled breaks to prevent vocal fatigue or injury in the healthy voice professional (eg, a 20-minute silent period for the school teacher, abstaining from singing during the opening hymn for the minister, or preperformance quiet meditation for the singer). The benefits of this practice may be correlated with positive physical and/or psychological effects. Despite the widespread use of this practice and the positive anecdotal results, the mechanism underlying the positive effects of voice rest are unknown.

Another controversy regarding voice rest for the singer and professional voice user concerns the prescription of voice rest during vocal malady. Arguments have been made for the use of voice rest to allow the temporary inflammation of the vocal folds associated with medical illness to subside. In contrast, equally impassioned arguments have been made for appropriate and controlled voice *use* to facilitate healing associated with vocal fold swelling and/or the postoperative condition.[5,6] Specifically, the use of vocal fold high-amplitude, low impact vocal tasks has been likened to rehabilitative stretching and exercises that are used in sports medicine rehabilitation.

Future research will address much of the unknown aspects regarding voice rest controversies. Until then, the art of medicine must invoke the psychological profile, experience level, and physical diagnosis of the professional voice user to determine the appropriate use(s) of voice rest.

Age and Maturational Development of the Voice

The voice care professional is often asked to make a decision or give an opinion regarding the duration and type of singing obligations young singers should assume. This area of great controversy arises most notably when factors such as style of singing, amount of singing, and age of the singer are implicated as causes of a vocal injury. Specifically, this section highlights both the psychological and physical issues young singers may confront as they embark on a performing career.

Unequivocal guidelines for decisions regarding vocal performance are inappropriate due to the different psychological and physical rates of development of young singers. An 8-year-old girl may be able to manage multiple performances per week with very little psychological trauma; however, a 15-year-old boy may experience significant psychological difficulties and negative repercussions from a single, monthly performance.

This area is complicated further by the anecdotally documented but poorly understood physical development of the operatic female singer, who does not fully develop vocally until the third decade of life. It is important to remember that, even though the 22-year-old female singer is physically an adult, vocally she is not. Thus song selection, vocal demands, and training must be adjusted with this in mind.

Young boys endure adolescent voice changes that can have a great impact on both their physical and psychological ability to perform during this time period. This is another example of a time period in a singer's development that may require special consideration. One study found that boys at these time periods did well with vocal training.[7] This study has not been replicated and runs contrary to current opinion and dogma.

Little research has explored the physical impact of singing on the vocal mechanism of the young performer. In addition, the small amount of anecdotal information used in directing singers and their families in the development of young voices is based on Western European classical musical styles (bel canto is acceptable, however, belting is not). The overlying principle guiding development in young performers should involve nurturing the singer, while simultaneously avoiding injury or inhibition of the growth of the singer (see chapter 27).

Incidence, Importance, and Impact of Laryngopharyngeal Reflux Disease (LPRD) on Singers and Professional Voice Users

In the last decade, there has been an upsurge in the recognition of the impact of laryngopharyngeal reflux disease on a variety of voice disorders (ie, vocal fold nodules, vocal fold granulomas, etc). This has been especially noted in singers and professional voice users, because a multitude of factors in this group may make them more prone to laryngopharyngeal reflux disease. In addition, any minor changes that occur to the voice from LPRD may affect singers to a greater degree. The controversy within this subject matter involves the unknown true incidence and impact of this disease on singers and professional voice users. The majority of information that we have about the impact of LPRD on the development of voice disorders is anecdotal and descriptive. Thus, the present philosophy of many laryngologists is to treat singers and professional voice users as if they have LPRD even without definitive diagnosis; because the diagnostic process is costly, time-consuming, and can often lead to a quagmire of results. To proceed without definitive diagnosis is simpler, and the negative sequelae of not treating can be significant.

The difficulties and controversies that arise with LPRD in this patient population stem from our limited knowledge base regarding baseline incidence of LPRD, lack of understanding of the pathophysiology of LPRD as related to voice disorders, and lack of definitive diagnostic testing. The impact of laryngopharyngeal reflux disease was previously underrecognized in laryngology and most likely is presently overrecognized and, therefore, overdiagnosed and overtreated.

The direct impact of LPRD on the voice is difficult to assess fully on physical examination or diagnostic testing. We are often left to rely on anecdotal reports of patients' symptoms that can be biased due to a poorly controlled situation, as well as to a possible placebo effect and empiric treatment. Specific questions regarding the impact and incidence of laryngopharyngeal reflux disease in singers and professional voice users include:

1. What is the direct mechanism(s) of LPRD affecting voice production in this population?
2. What is the incidence of LPRD in singers, and is it higher or lower than in nonsingers?
3. How does one accurately identify significant, active LPRD?

The latter will lead to more appropriate treatment recommendations and minimize expensive and possibly complicated treatment for disorders that are not present.

The most common problems in this area have been that it appears that any type of history of having reflux irritation to the larynx results in changes to the posterior aspect of the larynx (posterior laryngitis), and these changes do not resolve quickly or at all. Therefore, when a singer is evaluated for a nonspecific voice problem, and these changes are identified on laryngeal examination, the common assumption is that the patient's voice problem is due to LPRD when, in fact, these physical examination findings are a holdover from a past experience. This typical patient may have no active laryngopharyngeal reflux disease, and his or her voice problem may be due to a separate matter. This can lead to delayed diagnosis and missed diagnosis, which are not helpful to the patient or to the overall cost of health care.

Instrumental Music and Singing

Often the laryngologist is asked to address the possible detrimental situation of a young singer who also plays a wind instrument. Because most wind instruments do not use the larynx as an articulator, there should generally not be a problem with singers also playing a wind instrument. There are anecdotal experiences of a variety of wind instruments, specifically of flute and French horn, using the larynx as a possible articulator, which in theory could impact the singing voice. More important than the wind instrument's use of the larynx as another level of articulation is the role of the musculature in the instrumental music production and the negative impact of the wind instrumental music playing on the singing voice. Specifically, it is hypothesized that excessive neck tension created or developed during the instrumental music playing could lead to difficulties with the singing voice. This could occur due to the importance of a full range of motion and relaxation in the laryngeal musculature for normal voice production. As with singers, such problems with tension are less likely to occur with highly skilled instruments (see chapter 41). When there is a question regarding the negative aspects of instrumental music on the singing voice, one can evaluate the larynx during instrumental music playing with the flexible nasopharyngoscope and see the degree of laryngeal tension and laryngeal articulation during playing. Furthermore, often laryngeal massage, neck muscle relaxation exercises, and vocal warm-up exercises can be used to release any built-up stress and tension in this region following instrumental music playing prior to the onset of singing.

Singing Styles

A universal question surfacing within each voice evaluation addresses the patient's repertoire. The answer the voice care professional prefers to hear most often is "classical." This reply may mislead the voice care professional into a false state of comfort, just as the reply of "popular" music may mislead the same professional into a false state of discontent. The connotations for classical singing are as enigmatic and varied as those for popular singing; thus, the use of the label "legitimate" as synonymous for classical singing should not imply that any other style is "illegitimate."[8] Singing Wagnerian classic operatic arias may be just as stressful on the laryngeal mechanism as singing a Rolling Stones' classic rock ballad.

Research has shown that the production of different voice qualities relies on a dynamically changing vocal mechanism.[9-13] Yet, voice treatment has embraced the techniques biased toward Western European classical singing (ie, that of the early art song). The voice care professional must evaluate and treat the patient according to demands of the specialized repertoire by highlighting the associated burdens and risks, without unduly frightening the patient.

Typically, power singing (true operatic singing and belting) is associated with vocal injury in both the immature and adult singer who, thereafter, feels branded with the negative stigma of being "damaged goods." Yet, in athletics, such as football, physical injury is to be expected and is dealt with respectfully. We, as the comfortable audience, are thrilled by the power singer who takes risks to provide full dramatic impact. We, as voice care professionals, should provide the highest and most sophisticated quality of treatment to ensure that these performers may walk the vocal tightrope for our enjoyment in the many years to come. After all, longevity in a career is not reserved specifically for the bel canto singer. Lasting success crosses the borders of musical style due to smart choices by the performer and by those who provide the advice—from the managers and agents to the voice care professional.

Sports Medicine and Vocal Medicine

Several areas of vocal medicine frequently use the guiding principles of sports medicine as a basis to make decisions. Specifically, management of vocal performance, vocal training and rehabilitation from vocal injury often cite or use a sports medicine/exercise physiology paradigm (see chapter 79). The essential question regarding this area of controversy is: How valid are these various analogies?

The most reasonable and reliable example of this parallel thinking is the psychological approach and care of the singer and professional voice user with respect to performance. Because the mental aspects of performance are the same or similar for singing and pitching, it is reasonable for voice care professionals to use this area of sports medicine as a guide or basis.

The leap of faith between sports medicine and vocal medicine becomes greater when one attempts to apply training techniques of sports medicine to singing. Until research is done to validate these methods for singers, one needs to be very careful when vocal training methods are proposed based on the principles of athletic training. Our knowledge base regarding the muscular system of the vocal tract and how learning in this region is organized is too limited to assume that training techniques that are used to shoot a basketball will be appropriate for vocal training.

Recently, principles of exercise physiology and sports medicine have been applied to the approaches of care of injuries of the vocal mechanism.[14] In particular, recent research in sports medicine has demonstrated an advantage to mobilization of the musculoskeletal region in question following an injury instead of the traditional immobilization approach. Thus, after knee surgery, the knee is promptly (within hours) mobilized instead of being placed in a cast. Is a similar approach to a vocal injury (ie, vocal fold edema following singing, vocal fold hemorrhage, or vocal fold surgery) appropriate? It is important that voice care professionals proceed with a rational, scientific-based approach to voice care and not just accept the transference of philosophy from one field to another without careful consideration and rigorous testing. Great concern exists regarding the use of sports medicine/exercise physiology principles in designing programs for the care of the injured lamina propria of the vocal fold. The lamina propria is a unique area of the body and certainly has great differences in composition and metabolism in comparison with large, striated muscle groups of the body.

Conclusion

A substantial number of controversial areas exist regarding the medical care of singers and professional voice users. Many of these areas of controversy stem from lack of scientific understanding and/or ethical limitations regarding the testing of certain hypotheses. The field of care for the professional voice is moving from antidotal medicine to teleological medicine toward scientific medicine. The first step in this progression is the essential question: Why does this happen, and why is it treated in this fashion? From that stepping-stone, the field will move forward to provide singers and professional voice users with improved care.

References

1. Smith B, Sataloff RT. *Choral Pedagogy*. San Diego, Calif: Singular Publishing Group; 2000:3–12,105–169.

2. Edwin R. The good, the bad, and the ugly: singing teacher-choral director relationships. *J Singing*. 2001; 57(5):53–54.

3. Benninger MS. Micro-dissection or microspot CO2 laser for limited vocal fold benign lesions: a prospective randomized trial. *Laryngoscope*. 2000;110(2 Pt 2):1–17.

4. Zeitels SM. Laser versus cold instruments for microlaryngoscopic surgery. *Laryngoscope*. 1996;106(5 Pt 1):545–552.

5. Verdolini K, Zeitels SM, Maniotis A, Desloge RB, Hillman RE. Role of mechanical stress in tissue recovery subsequent to acute phonotrauma. Paper presented at the Twenty-Eighth Annual Symposium: Care of the Professional Voice; June 1999; Philadelphia, Pa.

6. Spiegel JR, Emerich K, Abaza MM, Sataloff RT. Voice rest after phonosurgery: current concepts of post–operative management. Paper presented at the Twenty-Eighth Annual Symposium: Care of the Professional Voice; June 15, 1999; Philadelphia, Pa.

7. Blatt IM. Training singing children during the phases of voice mutation. *Ann Otol Rhinol Laryngol*. 1983;92(5, Pt 1):462–468.

8. Delp R. From the president: now that the belt voice has become legitimate. *J Singing*. 2001;57 (5):1–2.

9. Colton RH, Estill J. Elements of voice quality: perceptual, acoustic and physiological aspects. In: Lass N, ed. *Speech and Language: Advances in Basic Research and Practice*. New York, NY: Academic Press; 1981.

10. Schutte HK, Miller DG. Belting and pop, nonclassical approaches to the female middle voice: some preliminary considerations. *J Voice*. 1993;7(2):142–150.

11. Sundberg J. *The Science of the Singing Voice*. Dekalb: Northern Illinois University Press; 1987.

12. Titze IR. *Principles of Voice Production*. Englewood Cliffs, NJ: Prentice Hall; 1994.

13. Zemlin WR. *Speech and Hearing Science: Anatomy and Physiology*. 4th ed. Boston, Mass: Allyn & Bacon; 1997.

14. Verdolini K, Ronan D, Saxon K. Mechanisms of wound healing: implications for the exercise hypothesis in voice therapy. Paper presented at the Twenty-Ninth Annual Symposium: Care of the Professional Voice; June 2000; Philadelphia, Pa.

103

Voice Horizons

John S. Rubin and Robert Thayer Sataloff

Communication is central to, and representative of, the human condition. Throughout history the speaking and singing voice have been objects of reverence, joy, and, at times, fear. Even in some societies where physical fitness and prowess were emphasized, for example, Sparta, the singing voice had a major role. Yet, appreciating the voice is not the same as understanding it. Unraveling the mystery of the human voice has been a slow process until the last quarter of the 20th century.

In the modern era of basic science and clinical research, it is hardly surprising that studies of vocal function and vocal health have been interdisciplinary in nature; and this shift in approach has been responsible for great progress. Pioneering researchers have drawn primarily from their own fields of expertise, such as medicine, physics, speech sciences, engineering, and so on. Initially, they brought to the fledgling field of voice a strong basis in physics and mathematics, thereby favoring the areas of acoustical analysis and signal processing, aerodynamics, and computer modeling.

Anatomists have supplied a strong foundation in cross-sectional anatomy and myology of the vocal folds and in the central connections and neural pathways responsible for speech and song. Recently, genetics and the cellular biology underlying laryngeal injury and repair have been emphasized.[1] Understanding aging has also come to the forefront through public demand, including studies on ways to delay the effects of advancing years on all body systems and functions, including the larynx and voice.

Physiologists have investigated the biomechanics of the vocal tract, including the mechano- and chemoreceptors. Much has been gleaned recently on the basic, but complex, function of structures such as the cricoarytenoid joint, for example. Endocrinolo-gists have advanced the concept that the larynx acts very much as a steroid-receptor organ, with receptors to testosterone and estrogen, as well as with early responses to changes in the thyroid axis. Pedagogists have emphasized research into vocal techniques, not uncommonly fusing the physical (eg, breathing techniques) with the emotional-spiritual components of voice production.

When considering the horizons of laryngology, certain caveats need to be expressed. The authors recognize that there are always resource limitations, (generally inadequate funding) and that voice research in general still lags behind research in many other communications disorders due to a shorter research history. Yet, we also recognize the profound importance of voice for transmitting an individual's ideas and emotions and the potentially devastating effects that a voice disorder can have on patients' quality of life and ability to earn a living. In addition, we recognize the potentially serious systemic medical disorders that may present with laryngeal manifestations but are still often unrecognized by most physicians and lay people.

A useful point of reference, when discussing the future, is the recent past. In 1995, a National Strategic Research Plan[2] for voice research in the United States identified certain specific short-term research priorities. Areas of importance that were identified included: (1) cellular and molecular biology; (2) hormonal effects (mechanisms and sites of action); (3) human development (including embryology, effects of aging on the voice, and genetic transmission of vocal characteristics); (4) neural and vascular factors affecting voice function (and dysfunction); (5) laryngeal biomechanics and respiratory functions and their effects on phonation; (6) the impact of upper digestive tract function and dysfunction on the larynx and pharynx (mechanical and vagal reflex mechanisms); and (7) epidemiology of voice disorders.

Even more recently, throughout the United States and Europe, there has been a move in medicine toward evidence-based outcomes research and a focus on patient satisfaction. To that end, quality of life indicators have been brought to the fore. The concepts of impairment, handicap, and disability, and indices devised to rate them, have had a significant impact on both medical care and the distribution of medical resources. These important issues undoubtedly will play a major role in shaping the next generation of voice research.

The authors believe that this patient-oriented move toward evidence-based outcomes medicine is a very positive step. Together with the research areas identified in the 1995 United States National Strategic Research Plan, and with other areas of research discussed elsewhere in this book and in other literature, these areas represent extremely important pieces of the puzzle that must be completed if we are to understand how the human voice works, why it fails, or how it can be repaired. We believe that the growing appreciation for the societal importance of the voice, the impact of good and expeditious voice care, and the potentially high cost (human and economic) of unsuccessful voice care will lead to the availability of resources sufficient to answer many of the questions posed in this chapter and many more that we do not have space to address.

What then are the horizons of the field? Where is the urgency implicit in clinical need? These questions will determine the next generation of voice research, in concordance with public will and with national and international spending patterns for research.

To answer these questions, and possibly identify others, a thorough review was performed of articles published in the *Journal of Voice* in the 3 years (1998-2000) subsequent to publication of the second edition of this book. The *Journal of Voice* was selected because of its established position as a premier interdisciplinary peer-reviewed journal that involves specialists in virtually all fields related to voice. Of 178 articles reviewed, the major categories of topics included: aerodynamics and acoustics, 44 (25%); clinical voice problems, 35 (20%); surgical issues, 16 (9%); perceptual/profiles, 15 (8%); neurolaryngology, 13 (7%); laryngeal/vocal fold imaging, 12 (7%); biomechanics, 11 (6%); aging, 7 (4%); reflux/upper aerodigestive issues, 6 (3%); psychology, 5 (3%); outcomes measurements 5 (3%); molecular/cellular, 4 (2%); pedagogy, 2 (1%), historical, 2 (1%); and other, 1 (1%). Only a few of these articles will be discussed specifically in this chapter, although all of them, along with the larger world body of voice literature, have influenced our vision of the future of voice care.

Physics and mathematics have dominated the basic science publications in voice research and most likely will continue to do so in the near future. However, there are still significant deficits in our knowledge base and ability to document laryngeal function. The large number of clinically related papers attests to the importance of information designed to improve our abilities to manage the serious, subtle, or overt problems that are inherent to the larynx.

The relative paucity of molecular/cellular research is, perhaps, a matter of concern. The articles are of high quality, however; and the degree of interest throughout the field of voice in the initial results garnered through them suggests that such studies are likely to increase quickly, providing that a secure funding base can be obtained. Such studies have already (and perhaps to a surprising degree) had a profound impact on how surgeons approach the larynx and how scientists think about the larynx. In the authors' opinion, laryngeal molecular and cellular research, now and in the future, should be supported strongly by the voice community.

Let us now review categorically the near-term priorities for laryngeal research identified in the National Strategic Research Plan [2]

Cellular and Molecular Biology

Interest was stimulated in this area by the works of pioneers in the field, such as Hirano's seminal work on the layered structure of the vocal fold.[3,4] This work has gained significant momentum through the ongoing contributions of Gray and colleagues.[1,5-7] Questions deserving of further investigation are legion. These include, at first examination: the genetic makeup of the laryngeal substrata; distribution of molecular markers throughout the epithelium; expression of proteins necessary for cell-to-cell interactions (eg, the cadherins and other integrins);[8-10] molecular changes leading to disease, both benign and malignant; and immunohistochemical and ultrastructural investigations of the epithelium, basement membrane, and layers of the lamina propria. These have been championed by researchers such as Gray et al[1,11] and Sato.[12]

Hormonal Effects (Mechanisms and Sites of Action)

There has been extensive interest in the larynx as a hormone target organ. The role of sex hormones has recently been investigated by Abitbol et al[13] and others. The changes in the larynx due to thyroid axis disorders are well recognized.[14] Additional research regarding the nature and location of hormone receptors and of end-organ mechanisms of response to hormonal manipulations (ie, premenstrual and perimenopausal changes and changes in circulating thyroid hormones) may offer ways of blocking adverse effects when hormonal fluctuation or dysfunction is inevitable and possibly produce methods of reversing hormone-related voice changes. It also seems possible that hormonal factors may be operative in vocal fold problems that have gender-specific predilection. For example, it is generally agreed that vocal fold nodules are more common in children and adult females. Reinke's edema appears to occur mainly in adult women. Mechanical reasons have generally been presumed, but these remain unproven; and possible hormone contributions have not been studied adequately.

Human Development (Including Embryology, Effects of Aging on the Voice, and Genetic Transmission of Vocal Characteristics)

The voice changes throughout life. Laryngeal structure and function deteriorate with advancing age, particularly at advanced age, which compromises the cellular, structural, and neural-muscular integrity of the laryngeal system. Control of voice relies not only on the vocal folds, but also on a delicate balance of pulmonary function and laryngeal and articulator activity; and these in turn depend on the functional integrity of the neural, endocrine, and skeletal systems.[15,16]

A review of age-related changes affecting the larynx includes changes in cartilages, articular surfaces, ligaments, and supporting structures, and the true vocal folds. Changes in the laryngeal cartilages include complete ossification by the eighth decade, and often by the sixth decade. This ossification leads to decreased flexibility of cartilages.[17,18] Changes in the articular surfaces include thinning surface and irregularities.[17,19,20]

Changes in the ligaments include loosening of the joint capsules, breakdown in collagen fiber organization, and thinning of elastic fibers.[21-24] Changes in the supporting structures occur in the conus elasticus including waviness, fragmentation, and separation, and changes in connective tissue septae with disorganization.[25-28]

Changes in the true vocal fold include edema of the mucosa, but mainly changes in the lamina propria. Hirano found decrease in density and thinning of the superficial and intermediate layers, collagenous thickening with loss of linearity, and an increase of fibrosis

of the deep layer.[30] The likely effects of these changes on the voice include changes in apposition, pitch, and vocal fold vibration.

Cricoarytenoid articular changes can lead to glottal insufficiency.[17] Stiffer, thinner vocal folds will vibrate more rapidly, perhaps with less amplitude.[17] This is consistent with data that F_0 in men increases after the sixth decade.[16,31] Changes in compliance and elasticity of the lamina propria lead to asynchronous vibrations and incomplete closure thus allowing air to escape during sound production. This leads to aperiodicity.[17]

Changes in the vocal ligament may cause irregularities in vocal fold vibration, which are perceivable as roughness[33-35] and are measured as abnormally high perturbation factors or F_0 variability.[17,32-35] Atrophy of laryngeal muscles could lead to bowing of the vocal folds and weakness. All of the above may lead to increased breathiness and a strained tense voice with changes in voice pitch and resonance, the perceptual correlate of the "elderly" voice.[33]

Published studies on voice changes in elderly versus younger subjects have demonstrated the following findings in the elderly: pitch changes, irregularities in vocal fold vibration, glottal incompetency (air loss and breathiness), voice production changes associated with laryngeal tension, pitch breaks, roughness, hoarseness, harshness, changes in vibrato, development of a tremolo, decreased breath control, and vocal fatigue.[29,31,32,34-36]

It is clear that there is now a substantial body of information in the geriatric literature substantiating physiologic changes that could disrupt the normal process of speech and voice production, and it is not difficult for even inexperienced listeners to reliably categorize speakers as "young" or "old."[37,38] Surprisingly, however, relatively few data are available that correlate the loss of voice with communicative skills of the aging process.[39]

Even less information is available on the potential benefit of speech therapy in vocal rehabilitation of elderly speakers. There is, however, no question but that individual differences in fitness may have a direct impact on the aging voice and that fitness may be improved through vocal rehabilitation with exercise or lifestyle changes.[40-42] In fact, when discussing altered parameters of function, the degree of interindividual variability must be kept in mind.[40]

In a recently published study in the *Journal of Voice*, Decoster and Debruyne examined the voices of radio broadcasters on a longitudinal basis, comparing their voices at 30-year intervals.[43] Recent reviews by Linville and Sataloff have summarized the most current research and clinical management of the effects of age on the voice.[44,45] However, further studies clearly are required to examine prospectively voice-related age changes and to look at the possible communication and psychological benefits obtainable through modification with vocal rehabilitation. Given the continued increase in our society of elderly individuals, such studies should be a research priority.

Neural and Vascular Factors Effects on Voice Function (and Dysfunction)

Investigations into the neural and vascular factors affecting voice production are crucial to advancing our knowledge and understanding of neurolaryngology. Such studies can be considered on a peripheral (laryngeal) and central (supravagal) level. Peripherally, mechanoreceptors and chemoreceptors have been identified throughout the laryngeal mucosa, muscles, the trachea, and the lungs. A body of research is available that focuses on the mucosal receptors.[46-53] Further research is necessary, particularly on the laryngeal and tracheal receptors and their functions and phonatory control. Collapse of transmural pressure receptors in the upper airway has been associated with enhancement of inspiratory activity.[54,55] These receptors may be of particular importance in sudden infant death syndrome.[56] They may also be important in mediating the laryngeal response to systemic and local disease and thus worthy of further research.

Our knowledge of neurolaryngeal feedback controls is rudimentary. Ventilatory inhibition occurs during speech,[57] and there is a clear link between lung pressure and control of inspiration during vocalization.[58] Given the fact that many clinical problems (not the least being dystonia and tremor) appear to be due to defective neural control, any research that sheds light on the anatomy and pathophysiology of the control systems should be of great value to both clinicians and general public. Information on the nature of relevant neurotransmitters, neural interconnections, and controls has the potential to provide us with controllable (and reversible) pharmacological intervention far more sophisticated and specific than agents such as botulinum toxin, our current first-line treatment at the level of the end organ in several of these disorders.

The neural control of voice, in speech or in singing, is still not well understood. As noted by Smith,[59] "while there have been advances in knowledge of neurological control of vocalization, it is readily apparent that there is little information on the laryngeal pathophysiology of many neurological disorders." It has been established that stimulation of the periaqueductal gray region in the midbrain elicits vocalization.[60] This area may be responsible for the in-

tegration of laryngeal and respiratory muscle patterns used in vocalizations, as well as for integration of emotional content.[61]

Many neurological disorders affect the voice either early or late in their course. As one example, Parkinson's disease, a nigrostriatal disorder characterized by dopamine deficiency, is common, occurring in 1% of individuals over the age of 60 and 0.1% under that age.[62] At least 89% of the 1.5 million individuals afflicted with Parkinson's disease in the United States have a voice disorder with characteristics of reduced loudness, monotone, hoarseness, and tremor.[62] Hypoadduction of the vocal folds and bowed vocal folds have been observed early in the disorder.[59,63]

It is clear that further research into the entire field of neurolarygology is necessary.

Laryngeal Biomechanics, Respiratory Mechanisms, and Their Effects on Phonation

It has been more than 30 years since Hast published his landmark study on the physiology of the cricothyroid muscle, yet the biomechanics of the larynx are still poorly understood.[64] There has been much more research on laryngeal mucosa than on the laryngeal gesture. Many investigators have linked prolonged mechanical misuse and overuse of the larynx with laryngeal dysfunction and injury. Furthermore, many studies have demonstrated marked improvement through mechanical manipulation utilizing voice therapy (as discussed in preceding chapters) and other techniques.[65] The biomechanics of the laryngeal muscles and skeleton link the inherent properties of the larynx to the gestures that control phonation.[66] Further investigations of laryngeal biomechanics are needed, with emphasis on the development of models to recognize and quantify biomechanical dysfunction and to restore optimal use of laryngeal structures. One such model has been developed by Harris and others.[65,67,68]

Additional work is also needed to clarify the rotational dynamics of the arytenoid cartilage and cricoarytenoid joint and to develop techniques with abilities to measure movements in this region objectively. Such measurements should eventually be applicable to frequency and intensity changes, laryngeal efficiency, and progress in vocal training. In chapter 9, Letson described important new insights into this area, including the vertical component of motion of the arytenoid cartilage that can be overlooked when examining the larynx clinically from the "bird's eye" position that we assume during stroboscopy.

Additionally, research should be encouraged in muscle physiology, in areas such as the metabolic requirements of laryngeal muscles[69] and their fatigue resistance,[66,70] the relationships and functional implications of fast and slow-twitch fibers in laryngeal muscles,[71] and the applicability of sports medicine studies in exercise physiology to laryngeal habilitation and rehabilitation (as discussed by Schneider et al in chapter 79).

In general, computer models created to study laryngeal biomechanics and computer-generated analyses of the effects of various laryngeal configurations on phonation have been beneficial as both research and educational tools.[72] Additional computer research should be encouraged and supported.

It must be remembered that the mass and the expenditure of muscular energy in the larynx are much smaller than those of the muscles supporting respiration. Thus, further biomechanical research is required into the forces generated by the intercostals, diaphragm, abdominal, and back muscles. Bowden, Hixon, Dickson, and others have pioneered this subject, but more research is indicated.[73-75] Research, such as the recent collaboration of Thorpe et al,[76] in which an interdisciplinary team of scientists, speech-language therapists, and singing teachers investigated rib cage position, abdominal motions, and acoustical output of professional opera singers, are seminal to advances in the field, and should be supported.

The Impact of Upper Digestive Tract Dysfunction on the Larynx and Pharynx (Mechanical and Vagal Reflex Mechanisms)

This area continues to generate research interest. The larynx is known to be subject to injury by esophageal reflux, yet our understanding of the interrelationship is still poorly defined. Laryngopharyngeal reflux is clearly a very different disorder than gastroesophageal reflux.[77] To investigate, 24-hour ambulatory pH monitoring has been used increasingly.[77,78] Normative databases for proximal probes in esophageal pH monitoring have been developed recently.[79-81] The concept of a reflux area index has been described to incorporate the number and duration of episodes of reflux.[82] This appears to be a useful indicator of proximal reflux severity. Further investigations on this indicator are needed. More research is also required into the potential role of reflux in such diverse areas as chronic cough, asthma, sudden infant death syndromes, sleep disorders, and common otolaryngologic disorders such as tonsillitis, irritable airway, chronic sinusitis, subglottic stenosis, and others.

Epidemiology of Voice Disorders

The relationships of various potentially carcinogenic factors for laryngeal cancer can require extensive investigation. Cancer of the larynx represents 2.3% of all malignant tumors in males and 0.4% in females, excluding basal and squamous cell carcinomas of the skin.[83] The National Cancer Institute estimates that cancer of the larynx accounts for approximately 1.3% of all new cancer diagnoses and 0.83% of all cancer deaths in the United States,[84] representing approximately 11,000 new cases per year.[83-84] The incidence peaks in the sixth and seventh decades of life.[83] The larynx and hypopharynx are by far the most common sites of head-and-neck squamous cell carcinoma (HNSCC) in the western world.[85]

Known risk factors for laryngeal cancer include tobacco and alcohol use/abuse, industrial exposure to toxins (asbestos, mustard gas, petroleum products, and others), viral agents, radiation exposure, and laryngeal papilloma.[83] There is also some consideration that gastroesophageal reflux may be a significant cofactor.[86] Laryngeal tumors are twice as common in heavily industrialized areas.[85]

Viral agents, especially the human papilloma virus (HPV) and the Epstein-Barr virus (EBV),[83,85,87] have been considered as possible cofactors associated with head-and-neck cancer. Cigarette smoking and alcohol consumption are the two strongest etiological factors for the development of HNSCC and of cancer of the larynx, both independently and synergistically.[83,85]

Occupational exposure to toxic substances is a significant and not satisfactorily researched potential cofactor. For example, in Spain, 4% of cancer deaths are attributed to occupational cancer; over 3 million workers (25.4% of employees) are exposed to potential carcinogens and laryngeal carcinoma incidence is high,[88] yet knowledge of specific problems of occupational cancer in Spain is scarce. Recently, many case control studies have identified a variety of hazardous agents as potentially participating in the development of neoplasia of the larynx or chronic laryngitis.

Maier and Tisch, in their Heidelberg case control study,[89] found that chronic consumption of alcohol and tobacco increased the relative risk of squamous cell carcinoma of the larynx independently in a dose-dependent manner. The majority of cancer patients were found to be blue-collar workers who are exposed to a variety of hazardous working materials such as polycyclic aromatic hydrocarbons, cement dust, metal dusts, asbestos, varnish, lacquer, and others. Environmental exposure to airborne carcinogens like fossil fuel single stove emissions may increase the relative risk of laryngeal cancer. Diesel fumes were associated with laryngeal cancer in one study.[90]

Szeszenia-Dabrowska, in their analysis of malignant neoplasms in Poland from 1971 to 1994, recognized that, in occupational diseases, cancer of the larynx occurred in 25.5% of workers, with asbestos dust, ionizing radiation, chromium and its compounds, and benzidine being the most common causes.[91] Asbestos has been associated with laryngeal carcinoma and hyperplastic laryngitis by several investigators.[92-95] Nickel and chromate dust are principal inorganic chemicals that can cause lesions in the nose, larynx, lung, and paranasal sinuses.[85] Sulfuric acid mist exposure has been associated with an increased risk of development of laryngeal cancer,[96,97] as has fluoride dust.[98]

From the above, it is obvious that further far-reaching epidemiological studies involving the workplace are necessary. Furthermore, as health care providers, we need to be active in continuing to raise public appreciation of the risks of smoking on the larynx and the importance of smoking cessation.

Outcomes Research and Quality of Life

Although not identified specifically in the 1995 review, quality of life issues and outcomes have become seminal in many clinicians' approach to patients with voice problems. The World Health Organization views health to encompass physical, mental, and social states of being.[99] Yet, the study of outcomes is a new area for voice.[100] A patient's perception of the severity of his or her problem can now be assessed using one of several voice-specific outcome measures. The Voice Handicap Index developed by Jacobson and colleagues is one such instrument,[101] and appears to be, perhaps, more specific for our cohort of patients than the previously described medical outcomes instrument study, a short form, 36-item, general health survey otherwise known as the SF-36.[102,103]

Studies of this type are in their infancy and will undoubtedly develop rapidly. These studies emphasize the impact of the voice problem on the affected individual; as such, they are very important. The next step may well be development of new tools, or utilization of present tools on a cross-cultural basis, as the world becomes more and more a global community.

Clinical Practice and Research

Our ability to care for patients presenting with voice problems has changed dramatically in recent years, mainly due to advances in basic research.[104] All of the research discussed above (as well as the many important research considerations not discussed) impact directly on the clinical care of voice patients.

The need to diagnose voice disorders more accurately, and to assess treatment outcomes, has led to the widespread use of clinical voice laboratories. Although advances have been made in our ability to measure voice function objectively, a great deal more research in this area is needed. The authors suspect that advances in voice assessment may be limited by not only current technology, but also our paradigm for voice assessment. Research efforts may develop an entirely new approach to voice assessment, perhaps using different technology such as signal detection methods from the aerospace industry and self-educating neuronets. In the coming years, we anticipate substantial changes and improvements in our ability to analyze acoustic and aerodynamic features of voice and continued improvements in radiological imaging technology, as well.

In addition, our patients' needs have driven clinical research. Considering surgical techniques, examples include the continued interest in implantable and injectable materials (eg, autologous collagen), for vocal fold medialization; the development of animal models (eg,, the use of Lactosorb in a rabbit larynx)[105-107]; continued interest in methods and materials to treat or reduce vocal fold scarring and granulation formation (eg, the agent mitomycin[108]); and many others.

Clinicians are becoming concerned more actively with preventive voice care. We anticipate that this will assume an even greater role in the future. Preventive programs in the near future should include early detection efforts such as vocal evaluations and education in the schools and the workplace. Studies will be necessary to determine the efficacy of such programs and their cost-effectiveness prior to widespread implementation.

Interdisciplinary Collaboration

This text and its first two editions have emphasized the major advances in voice medicine made possible through interdisciplinary collaboration. The importance of voice care teams is now well recognized throughout the world. The value, relevance, and impact on the practice of the laryngologist and speech-language pathologist are clear. Similar benefits exist for singing teachers, acting teachers, and others involved in professional voice use and training. We have witnessed expanded interactions in nonmedical settings in the past decade and anticipate that they will continue. Foundations such as the Voice Foundation in the United States, the British Voice Association in the United Kingdom, the Australian Voice Foundation in Australia, and others appear to act as catalysts for multidisciplinary learning, teaching, and training. Physicians and voice scientists are now serving as faculty and or advisers in more nonmedical organizations, and singing voice teachers and voice therapists are becoming actively involved in medical settings.

A new era is evolving in voice pedagogy and education for singers; voice training for actors and other speakers has begun to follow suit. This should result in additional pedagogical research on the applications of scientific and medical knowledge on voice training and benefit the training of voice educators. The consequent advances undoubtedly will be as exciting for voice teachers as they have been for physicians and speech-language therapists. They should improve substantially the quality and consistency of voice training.

It appears that the evaluation and development of sports medicine and sports science is an appropriate analogy for voice. Advances in sports performance have resulted in large part from the application of scientific information, principles, and technology by far-sighted coaches. Similarly, systematic application of analogous information by skilled voice teachers may lead to the discovery of new performance levels in the healthy voice. This may yet be the most exciting horizon in voice research, as well as in other areas of Arts Medicine.

Conclusion

A review of the recent history of the field of voice care illuminates the importance of inter- and multidisciplinary fellowship. We believe that the level of accomplishments over the past two or three decades will be maintained in the coming years. The field is poised on the brink of a technological explosion, with rapidly improving methodology for investigation, documentation, and treatment.

Clearly, the willingness of specialists from the diverse backgrounds relevant to voice disorders to communicate and collaborate has led to this rapid expansion in the knowledge base. Voice research must continue. It will undoubtedly do so through the combination of scientific curiosity and clinical need.

In this chapter we have identified only a few of the interesting and pressing problems. There are many more that we have not mentioned and more still that have not yet been recognized. We have faith that they will be addressed and supported in clinics and laboratories and that they will lead to a whole new chapter of

pressing issues in time for the following edition of this text.

References

1. Gray SD. Cellular physiology of the vocal folds. *Otolaryngol Clin North Am.* 2000;33(4):679–697.
2. *National Strategic Research Plan.* Bethesda MD: US Dept of Health and Human Services; Publication NIH 95–3711. 1995:261–306.
3. Hirano M. Structure of the vocal fold in normal and disease states. Anatomical and physical study. *ASHA.* 1981; 11:11–30.
4. Hirano M. Phonosurgical anatomy of the larynx. In: Ford CN, Bless DM, eds. *Phonosurgery.* New York, NY: Raven Press; 1991:25–43.
5. Gray SD, Hirano M, Sato K. Molecular and cellular structure of vocal fold tissue. In: Titze IR, ed. *Vocal Fold Physiology: Frontiers in Basic Science.* San Diego, Calif: Singular Publishing Group Inc; 1993:1–23.
6. Gray SD, Pignatari SN, Harding P. Morphologic ultrastructure of anchoring fibers in normal vocal fold basement membrane zone. *J Voice.* 1994;8:48–52.
7. Gray SD, Titze IR, Chan R, et al. Vocal fold proteogylcans and their influences on biomechanics. *Laryngoscope.* 1999;109:845–854.
8. Dorudi S, Hanby AM, Poulsom R, et al. Level of expression of E-cadherin mRNA in colorectal cancer correlates with clinical outcome. *Br J Cancer.* 1995;71:614–616.
9. Dorudi S, Sheffield JP, Poulsom R, et al. E-cadherin expression in colorectal cancer: an immunohistochemical and in situ hybridization study. *Am J Pathol.* 1993:142(4):981–986.
10. Marshall JF, Rutherford DC, McCartney AC, et al. Alpha v beta 1 is a receptor for vitronectin and fibrinogen, and acts with alpha 5 beta 1 to mediate spreading on fibronectin. *J Cell Sci.* 1995;108:1227–1238.
11. Gray SD, Hirano M, Sato K. Molecular and cellular structure of vocal fold tissue. In: Titze IR, ed. *Vocal Fold Physiology: Frontiers in Basic Science.* San Diego, Calif: Singular Publishing Group Inc; 1993:1–23.
12. Sato K. Functional fine structurues of the human vocal fold mucosa. In: Rubin JS, Sataloff RT, Korovin GS, eds. *Diagnosis and Treatment of Voice Disorders.* 2nd ed. Clifton Park, NY: Delmar Thomson Learning; 2003:41–48.
13. Abitbol J, Abitbol P, Abitbol B. Sex hormones and the female voice. *J Voice.* 1999;13:424–426.
14. Simpson CB, Fleming DJ. Medical and vocal history in the evaluation of dysphonia. *Otolaryngol Clin North Am.* 2000;33:719–729.
15. Gould WJ, Rubin JS. Special considerations for the professional voice user. In: Rubin JS, Sataloff RT, Korovin G, Gould WJ, eds. *Diagnosis and Treatment of Voice Disorders.* Tokyo/New York: Igaku-Shoin Medical Publishers; 1995; 424–435.
16. Ringel RL, Chodzko-Zajko WJ. Vocal indices of biological age *J Voice.* 1987;1(1):31–37.
17. Kahane JC. Connective tissue changes in the larynx and their effects on voice. *J Voice.* 1987;1(1):27–30.

18. Zenker W, Zenker A. Ueber die regelund der stimmilippen-spannung durch von aussen eingreifende menchanismen. *Folia Phoniatr.* 1960;12:1–36.

19. Kahn A, Kahane JC. India ink pinprick assessment of age-related changes in the cricoarytenoid joint (CAJ) articular surfaces. *J Speech Hear Res.* 1986;29:536–543.

20. Kahane JC, Hammons J. Developmental changes in the articular cartilage of the human cricoarytenoid joint. In: Baer T, Harris K, Sasaki C, eds. *Vocal Physiology.* San Diego, Calif: College-Hill Press; 1987:14–18.

21. Segre R. Senescence of the voice. *Eye Ear Nose Throat Mon.* 1971;50:223–233.

22. Hommerich KW. Der alternde larynx: Morphologische aspekt. *Hals Nasen Ohrenaerzte.* 1972;20:115–120.

23. Kofler D. Histopathologische veranderingen an altereskehlkopf. *Monatssche Ohrenkeilk Laryngorhinol* (Wein). 1932;66:1468–1472.

24. Ferreri G. Senescence of the larynx. *Ital Gen Rev Oto-Rhino-Laryngol.* 1959;1:640–709.

25. Kahane JC. Age related changes in the elastic fibers of the adult male ligament. In: Lawrence V, ed. *Transcripts of the 11th Symposium: Care of the Professional Voice.* New York, NY: The Voice Foundation; 1982;116–122.

26. Kahane JC. Postnatal development and aging of the human larynx. *Semin Speech Lang.* 1983;4:189–203.

27. Kahane JC. A survey of age-related changes in the connective tissues of the human adult larynx. In: Bless DM, Abbs JH, eds. *Vocal Fold Physiology. Contemporary Research and Clinical Issues.* San Diego Calif, College-Hill Press; 1983:44–49

28. Kahane JC, Stadlan EM, Bell JS. A histomorphological study of the aging male larynx. *ASHA.* 1979;20:747.

29. McGlone RE, Hollien H. Vocal pitch characteristics of aged white women. *J Speech Hear Res.* 1963;6:164–170.

30. Hirano M, Kurita S, Nakashima T. Growth, development and aging of human vocal folds. In: Bless DM, Abbs JH, eds. *Vocal Fold Physiology. Contemporary Research and Clinical Issues.* San Diego Calif: College-Hill Press; 1983:22–43.

31. Hollien H, Shipp T. Speaking fundamental frequency and chronological age in males. *J Speech Hearing Res.* 1972;15:155–159.

32. Wilcox KA, Horii YH. Age and changes in vocal jitter. *J Gerontol.* 1980;35:194–198.

33. Ryan WJ, Burk KW. Perceptual and acoustic correlates of aging in the speech of males. *J Commun Disord.* 1974; 7:181–192.

34. Ryan WJ, Capadano HL. Age perception and evaluative reactions toward adult speakers. *J Gerontol.* 1978;33:98–102.

35. Ptacek PH, Sander EK, Manoley W, et al. Phonatory and related changes with advanced age. *J Speech Hear Res.* 1966;9:353–360.

36. Hartman DE, Danahuer JL. Perceptual features of speech for males in four perceived age decades. *J Acoust Soc Am.* 1976;59:713–715.

37. Shipp T, Hollien H. Perception of the aging male voice. *J Speech Hear Res.* 1969;12:703–710.

38. Linville SE. Acoustic-perceptual studies of aging voice in women. *J Voice.* 1987;1(1):44–48.

39. Morris RJ. Brown WS Jr., Age-related voice measures among adult women. *J Voice.* 1987;1(1):38–43.

40. Finch CE, Schneider EL. *Handbook of the Biology of Aging.* 2nd ed. New York, NY: John Wiley; 1985.

41. Spirduso WW. Physical fitness in relation to motor aging. In: Mortimer JA, Pirizzolo FJ, Maletta GJ, eds. *The Aging Motor System.* New York, NY: Praeger Publishers; 1982:120–151

42. Fries JF, Crapo LM. *Vitality and Aging.* San Francisco, Calif: Freeman; 1981.

43. Decoster W, Debruyne F. Longitudinal voice changes: facts and interpretation. *J Voice.* 2000;14 (2):184–193.

44. Linville SE. Vocal aging. *Curr Opin Otolaryngol Head Neck Surg.* 1995;3:183–187.

45. Sataloff RT, Vocal aging. *Curr Opin Otolaryngol Head Neck Surg.* 1998;421–428.

46. Boggs DF, Bartlett D. Chemical specificity of a laryngeal apneic reflex in puppies. *J Appl Physiol.* 1982;53:455–462.

47. Davis PJ, Bartlett D, Luschei ES. Coordination of the respiratory and laryngeal systems in breathing and vocalization. In: Titze IR, ed. *Vocal Fold Physiology: Frontiers in Basic Science.* San Diego, Calif: Singular Publishing Group Inc; 1993:189–226.

48. Boushey HA, Richardson PS, Widdicombe JG, Wise JCM. The response of laryngeal afferent fibers to mechanical and chemical stimuli. *J Physiol.* 1974;240:153–175.

49. Davis PJ, Nail BS. Quantitative analysis of laryngeal mechanosensitivity in the cat and rabbit. *J Physiol.* 1987; 388:467–485.

50. Mathew OP, Sant'Ambrogio G, Fisher JT, Sant'Ambrogio FB. Laryngeal pressure receptors. *Respir Physiol.* 1984; 54:259–268.

51. Testerman RL. Modulation of laryngeal activity by pulmonary changes during vocalization in cats. *Exp Neurol.* 1970;29:281–297.

52. Sant'Ambrogio G, Mathew OP, Fisher JT, Sant'Ambrogio FB. Laryngeal receptors responding to transmural pressure, airflow, and local muscle activity. *Respir Physiol.* 1983;54:317–330.

53. Sant'Ambrogio G, Brambilla-Sant'Ambrogio F, Mathew OP. Effect of cold air on laryngeal mechanoreceptors in the dog. *Respir Physiol.* 1986;64:45–56.

54. Mathew OP. Upper airway negative-pressure effects on respiratory activities of upper airway muscles. *J Appl Physiol.* 1984;56:500–505.

55. Mathew OP, Farber JP. Effect of upper airway negative pressure on respiratory timing. *Respir Physiol.* 1983;54: 259–268.

56. Benninger MS, Schwimmer C. Functional neurophysiology and vocal fold paresis. In: Rubin JS, Sataloff RT, Korovin GK, Gould WJ, eds. *Diagnosis and Treatment of Voice Disorders.* New York, NY: Igaku-Shoin Medical Publishers; 1995;105–121.

57. Gelfer C, Harris K, Collier R, Baer T. Is declination actively controlled? In: Titze IR, Scherer RC, eds. *Vocal Fold Physiology: Biomechanics, Acoustics and Phonatory Control.* Denver, Colo: The Denver Center for the Performing Arts; 1983:113–116.

58. Garrett JD, Luschei ES. Subglottic pressure modulation during evoked phonation in the anesthetized cat. In: Baer T, Sasaki C, Harris K, eds. *Laryngeal Function in Phonation and Respiration.* Boston, Mass: College-Hill Press; 1987:139–153.

59. Smith ME, Ramig LO. Neurological disorders and voice. In: Rubin JS, Sataloff RT, Korovin G, Gould WJ, eds. *Diagnosis and Treatment of Voice Disorders.* Tokyo/New York: Igako Shoin Medical Publishers; 1995:203–224.

60. Bandler R. Brain mechanisms of aggression as recorded by electrical and chemical stimulation: suggestion of a central role for the midbrain periaqueductal gray region. In: Epstein A, Morrison A, eds. *Progress in Psychobiology and Physiological Psychology.* vol 13. New York, NY: Academic Press; 1988:67–153.

61. Davis P, Zhang SP, Winkworth A, Bandler R. Neural control of vocalization: respiratory and emotional influences. *J Voice.* 1996;10:23–38.

62. Logemann JA, Fisher HB, Boshes B, Blonsky ER. Frequency and occurrence of vocal tract dysfunctions in the speech of a large sample of Parkinson's patients. *J Speech Hear Disord.* 1978;43:47–57.

63. Gracco C, Marek K. Laryngeal manifestations of early Parkinson's disease: data characterizing stage of disease and severity of symptoms. Presented at the Conference of Motor Speech Disorders; March 1994; Sedona, Ariz. .

64. Hast MH. Mechanical properties of the cricothyroid muscle. *Laryngoscope.* 1965;75:537–548.

65. Harris T, Lieberman J. The cricothyroid mechanism, its relation to vocal fatigue and voice dysfunction. *J Voice.* 1993;3:89–96.

66. Cooper DS, Partridge LD, Alipour-Haghighi F. Muscle energetics, vocal efficiency and laryngeal biomechanics. In: Titze IR, ed. *Vocal Fold Physiology: Frontiers in Basic Science.* San Diego, Calif: Singular Publishing Group Inc; 1993:37–92.

67. Rubin JS, Lieberman J, Harris TM. Laryngeal manipulation. *Otolaryngol Clin North Am.* 2000;33(5):1017–1034.

68. Harris T. Laryngeal mechanisms in normal function and dysfunction. In: Harris T, Harris S, Rubin JS, Howard DM, eds. *The Voice Clinic Handbook.* London: Taylor and Francis Group/Whurr Publishers; 1998:64–87.

69. Cooper DS, Rice DH. Fatigue resistance of canine vocal fold muscle. *Ann Otol Rhinol Laryngol.* 1990;99:228–233.

70. Cooper DS, Pinczower E, Rice DH. Laryngeal intramuscular pressures. *J Acoust Soc Am.* 1990;88 (suppl 1):S151.

71. Sanders I. The microanatomy of the vocal folds. In: Rubin JS, Sataloff RT, Korovin GS, Gould WJ, eds. *Diagnosis and Treatment of Voice Disorders.* Tokyo/New York: Igaku Shoin Medical Publishers; 1995:70–85.

72. Titze IR, Talkin DT. A theoretical study of the effects of various laryngeal configurations on the acoustics of phonation. *J Acoust Soc Am.* 1979;66:60–74.

73. Bowden REM, Scheuer JL. Weight of abductor and adductor muscles of the human larynx. *J Laryngol Otol.* 1960;74:971–980.

74. Hixon TJ. Kinematics of the chest wall during speech production: volume displacements of the rib cage, abdomen and lung. *J Speech Hear Res.* 1973;16:78.

75. Dickson DR, Maue-Dickson W. *Anatomical and Physiological Bases of Speech.* Boston, Mass: Little, Brown and Co; 1982.

76. Thorpe CW, Cala SJ, Chapman J, Davis PJ. Patterns of breath support in projection of the singing voice. *J Voice.* 2001;15(1):86–104.

77. Sataloff RT, Castell DO, Katz PO, Sataloff DM. *Reflux Laryngitis and Related Disorders.* San Diego, Calif: Singular Publishing Group Inc; 1999;1–112.

78. Koufman JA. The otolaryngologic manifestations of gastroesophageal reflux (GERD): a clinical investigaton of 225 patients using ambulatory 24-hour pH monitoring and an experimental investigation of the role of acid and pepsin in the development of laryngeal injury. *Laryngoscope.* 1991:101(4, suppl 53):1–78.

79. Vincent DA Jr, Garrett JD, Radionoff SL, et al. The proximal probe in esophageal pH monitoring: development of a normative database. *J Voice.* 2000;14(2):247–254.

80. Dobhan R, Castell DO. Normal and abnormal proximal esophageal acid exposure: results of ambulatory dual-probe pH monitoring. *Am J Gastroenterol.* 1993:88(1): 25–29.

81. Jacob P, Kahrilas PJ, Herzon G. Proximal esophageal pH-metry in patients with reflux laryngitis. *Gastroenterology.* 1991;100:305–310.

82. Vandeplas Y, Franckx-Goosens A, Pipeleers-Marichal M, et al. Area under pH 4: advantages of a new parameter in the interpretation of esophageal pH monitoring data in infants. *J Pediatr Gastroenterol Nutr.* 1989;9(1): 34–39.

83. Thawley SE, Cysts and tumors of the larynx. In: Paparella MM, Shumrick DA, Gluckman JL, Meyerhoff WL, eds. Otolaryngology. *Vol III. Head and Neck.* Philadelphia, Pa: WB Saunders Co; 1991;2307–2369.

84. Young JL, Asire AJ, Polltell ES. SEER program Cancer incidence and mortality in the United States 1973–1976. BHEW Publication (NIH)78-1837. Washington DC: US Government Printing Office; 1978.

85. Watkinson JC, Gaze MN, Wilson JA, eds. *Stell & Maran's Head and Neck Surgery.* 4th ed. Oxford, England: Butterworth Heineman; 2000:1–9.

86. Koufman J. Gastroesophageal reflux and voice disorders. In: Rubin JS, Sataloff RT, Korovin G, Gould WJ, eds. *Diagnosis and Treatment of Voice Disorders.* Tokyo/New York: Igaku Shoin Medical Publishers; 1995:161–175.

87. Sugar J, Vereczkey I, Toth J. Some etio-pathogenetic factors in laryngeal carcinogenesis. *J Environ Pathol Toxicol Oncol.* 1996;15:195–199.

88. Gonzalez CA, Agudo A. Occupational cancer in Spain. *Environ Health Perspect.* 1999;107(suppl 2):273–277.

89. Maier H, Tisch M. Epidemiology of laryngeal cancer: Results of the Heidelberg case-control study. *Acta Otolaryngol Suppl.* 1997;527:160–164.

90. Muscat JE, Wynder EL. Tobacco, alcohol, asbestos and occupational risk factors for laryngeal cancer. *Cancer.* 1992;69:2244–2251.

91. Szeszenia-Dabrowska N, Strzelecka A, Wilczynska U, Szymczak W. Occupational neoplasms in Poland in the years 1971–1994. *Med-Pr.* 1997;48:1–14.

92. Podol'skaia EV. [Precancerous conditions of the larynx in workers exposed to dust and their prevention.] *Vestn-Otorinolaringol.* 1989;2:67–69.

93. Landrigan PJ, Nicholson WJ, Suzuki Y, Ladou J. The hazards of chrysotile asbestos: a critical review. *Ind Health.* 1999;37:271–280.

94. Vejlupkova J, Lebedova J. Diseases caused by asbestos. *Prakt Lek.* 2000;80:441–446.

95. Gustavsson P, Jakonsson R, Johansson H, et al. Occupational exposures and squamous cell carcinoma of the oral cavity, pharynx, larynx, and oesophagus: a case-control study in Sweden. *Occup Environ Med.* 1998;55:393–400.

96. Soskolne CL, Zeighami EA, Hanis NM, et al. Laryngeal cancer and occupational exposure to sulfuric acid. *Am J Epidemiol.* 1984;120:358–369.

97. Steenland K. Laryngeal cancer incidence among workers exposed to acid mists. *Cancer Causes Control.* 1997;8:34–38.

98. Grandjean P, Olsen JH, Jensen OM, et al. Cancer incidence and mortality in workers exposed to fluoride. *J Natl Cancer Inst.* 1992;84:1903–1909.

99. World Health Organization. *International Classification of Impairments, Disabilities and Handicaps: A Manual of Classification Relating to the Consequences of Disease.* Geneva, Switzerland: World Health Organization; 1980:25–43.

100. Murry T, Rosen CA. Outcome measurements and quality of life in voice disorders. *Otolaryngol Clin North Am.* 2000;33(4)905–916.

101. Jacobson BH, Johnson A, Grywalsky C, et al. The Voice Handicap Index (VHI): development and validation. *J Voice.* 1998;12:540–550.

102. List MA, Ritter-Sterr C, Lansky SB. A performance status scale for head and neck patients. *Cancer.* 1990;66:564–569.

103. Ware JE, Sherbourne CD. The MOS 36-item short form health survey (SF-36). Conceptual framework and item selection. *Med Care.* 1992;30:473–483.

104. Sataloff RT. Rational thought: the impact of voice science upon voice care. (G. Paul Moore Lecture). *J Voice.* 1995;9(3):215–234.

105. Dufresne AM, Lafreniere D. Soft tissue response in the rabbit larynx following implantation of LactoSorb (PLA/PGA copolymer) prosthesis for medialization laryngoplasty. *J Voice.* 2000;14(3):387–397.

106. Remacle M, Lawson G, Keghian J, Jamart J. Use of injectable autologous collagen for correcting glottic gaps: initial results. *J Voice.* 2000;14(4):280–288.

107. Ford CN, Staskowski PA, Bless DM. Autologous collagen vocal fold injection: a preliminary clinical study. *Laryngoscope.* 1995;105:944–948.

108. Rahbar R, Valdez TA, Shapshay SM. Preliminary results of intraoperative mitomycin-C in the treatment and prevention of glottic and subglottic stenosis. *J Voice.* 2000;14:282–286.

104

Education in Laryngology: Rising to Old Challenges

Robert Thayer Sataloff

Introduction and Historical Perspective

As we enter the new millennium, it seems appropriate to ask whether education in laryngology and voice has kept pace with the remarkable clinical and technological advances of the last 2 decades. Throughout the history of otolaryngology, considerable time and thought have been devoted to educational issues. The founders of the American Laryngological Association (ALA) were deeply concerned with training in laryngology. This was the subject of Louis Elsberg's Presidential Address at the first meeting of the ALA on June 10, 1879 in New York.[1] Elsberg began teaching laryngology in 1861, and he established the first training clinic affiliated with any institution in 1863 at the University of the City of New York. By 1879, when the ALA was formed, Elsberg reported that there were 25 laryngology teachers in American medical schools. Elsberg's extraordinary address (57 published pages) provides a fascinating review of the history of laryngology and culminates with a section entitled "Laryngological Instruction." Elsberg reviewed the mission of laryngology, and of the ALA in particular, as being not only to develop greater knowledge and skills, but also to disseminate them and raise the standard of care and education. Elsberg's address to the second meeting of the ALA was delivered by Jacob Solis-Cohen, in Elsberg's absence.[2] Elsberg dedicated this entire address to specific training issues, including requirements for basic science and clinical knowledge that should be acquired before physicians in training were permitted to care for patients. He was an advocate for both undergraduate and graduate education in laryngology and even proposed instruction in comparative laryngology to enhance the understanding of the human larynx through study of other species. In his Presidential Address before the fourth meeting of the ALA, Frederick Knight emphasized the same concerns. He observed, "it will be a great gain when every physician feels he must own a laryngoscope. A more important point for us here arises, how we can make him use it intelligently; how all men who graduate from our medical schools shall be given a little available knowledge of laryngology during their precious time of pupilage."[3(p4)] Knight stressed the importance of both didactic education and laboratory and clinical training. He also recognized the expense of medical training and called for endowment of medical schools to support education, an uncommon notion in his day. In addition, Knight offered specific recommendations for the teaching of laryngology within the medical school curriculum, even courageously calling for an extension of the duration of medical study. In Birmingham, England, in 1890, John St. Swithin Wilders addressed the section of laryngology and rhinology of the British Medical Association in "On the Teaching of Laryngology."[4] He, too, emphasized the importance of educating all physicians in the fundamentals of laryngology and use of the laryngoscope and raised concerns about specialty hospitals, especially those that were not used by medical students in their education. He stressed the importance of laryngological edu-

Reprinted with minor modifications from *Annals of Otology, Rhinology and Laryngology* (1999;108[11]:1046–1052), with permission. (The 1999 Daniel C. Baker Lecture to the American Laryngological Association)

cation within general hospitals "which profess to educate students" and even raised an extremely controversial call "that no more special hospitals will be founded."[4(p377)]

Concerns about laryngology and its place in medical education were highlighted again in Henry L. Swain's Presidential Address to the twenty-third meeting of the ALA, in which he called for specific time within the medical school curriculum for courses in our field.[5] Since that time, training issues have been addressed sporadically. For example, in 1906, Knight[6] reviewed the state of training in laryngology, highlighting the proliferation of instrumentation. Reflecting back on Elsberg's day, Knight noted that, "the meagre armamentarium offered in the olden time is in striking contrast with the vast collection of apparatus now at our command. It is not certain that the enormous multiplication of instruments in recent years brings marked advantage."[6(p 840)] It would be interesting to hear his perspective if he were alive today amid technological developments that make his own armamentarium look meager indeed.

Thomas J. Harris[7] addressed the complex issues of postgraduate training in laryngology in an insightful paper read before the ALA in 1913. Residency programs as we know them had not yet been developed. Harris emphasized the importance of undergraduate preparation, trainee selection, basic science education (particularly anatomy and pathology), postgraduate courses, and supervised clinical experience. He also advocated the establishment of a minimum postgraduate training time for qualification in otolaryngology. Skillern, writing in *JAMA* in "Post-graduate Work in Laryngology," echoed these concerns, noting that, "prior to 1918, practically no under-graduate teaching on a systematic and comprehensive scale had been successfully carried out in this country."[8(p1145)] Skillern observed that, "the aspiring young laryngologist became of the opinion that once the submucous resection and the enucleation of the tonsil were mastered, he forthwith had become a full-fledged and competent specialist."[8(p1145)] At that time, a 6-week course was typical for specialty training in otolaryngology. He called for more rigorous and longer training in otolaryngology and instruction in subspecialty areas such as laryngology and otology.

In the years following these early papers devoted to education in laryngology, only a few authors have returned to this important subject. Milligan[9] argued that insufficient time was devoted to laryngology in the undergraduate medical school curriculum in Britain. Dean[10] devoted his 1925 ALA Presidential Address to the teaching of undergraduate laryngology, and Layton[11] addressed undergraduate and post-graduate education in 1940. In 1966, Alford[12] wrote an excellent review of the evolution of undergraduate and graduate medical training in the United States, the development of standards and quality control, and the effects of the evolving medical educational milieu on residency training in otolaryngology. Bailey[13] provided interesting insights into the early years of the introduction of laryngology as a component of otolaryngology training for medical students in the same issue of the *Laryngoscope* in which Alford's article was published. Thirty-three years later, the training of medical students in laryngology remains an important and challenging issue, as does the education of the general public on the importance of laryngological and related disorders; but they are beyond the scope of this paper, which is devoted to postgraduate training in laryngology. Currently, Medline lists more than 300 articles that address training in otolaryngology. However, specific laryngology and voice training issues are rarely mentioned in these publications; and when they are, they usually focus on the teaching of indirect laryngoscopy to medical students. Considering the historical importance of laryngology to the development of otolaryngology, it is surprising how little has been written about teaching this challenging subspecialty, especially in recent years.

In addition to concerns about curricular issues, laryngologists have been interested in the many practical aspects of teaching clinical laryngology. For example, before the advent of video-monitored laryngoscopy, a variety of devices were conceived to allow trainees to see the larynx during examinations performed by their mentors. Most involved the use of mirrors, such as Lukens' demonstroscope[14] in 1929 and a device developed at the Mayo Clinic around 1960 that attached a shortened laryngeal mirror to a headlight with a reflecting mirror.[15] It is also worth remembering that the laryngeal mirror itself was originally introduced as a training device, albeit for singers, by singing teacher Manuel Garcia in 1854.[16] A great many other clever devices have been introduced before and since that time that have enhanced diagnosis, treatment, and training in laryngology.[17]

As early as 1936, Francis LeJeune reported that, "the motion picture film has been found of inestimable value in teaching the younger student clinical pathology of the larynx."[18(p492)] LeJeune's fascinating report indicates that he not only recognized the educational value of motion pictures in teaching laryngoscopy and laryngeal surgery, but also that he learned from his studies. His careful observations of the larynx led him to advocate "carrying out sharp dissection with the laryngeal knife for the removal of the growth. Such a procedure usually ensures a smooth, straight cord when healed." Nevertheless, because of the cumbersome equipment, the delay necessary to develop the film, and the time-consuming nature of motion picture laryngoscopy, this technology was not utilized widely in laryngology clinics. However, in the late 1950s and early 1960s, von Leden and Moore established a voice clinic and used high-speed motion pictures extensively in clinical care and laryngeal research.[19-22] They also described the importance of television as a teaching device in otolaryngology.[19] The application of an operating microscope to direct laryngoscopy improved not only surgical management but also training. Tardy[23] was among the first to highlight the importance of combining the microscope with a color television camera in his 1972 article "Microscopic Laryngoscopy: Teaching Techniques." He advocated television display of laryngeal surgery for the purpose of enhancing training by allowing everyone in the operating room to see what the surgeon was doing. In addition to describing the value of new technology (microscope-assisted laryngoscopy and color television monitoring), Tardy showed photo documentation of magnified laryngeal polyp resection using techniques considerably more delicate than the "stripping" technique popular at the time. This insightful article specifically listed the teaching value of televised microscopic laryngeal surgery and called for its use in residency programs. Although today Tardy's observations seem obvious, it should be remembered that, at the time, some respected otolaryngologists and educational institutions still considered even the microscope (television monitoring aside) superfluous for mastoid surgery, let alone laryngoscopy; and many laryngologists still believed that laryngoscopy could be performed perfectly well while holding an unsuspended laryngoscope with one hand and using instruments only in the other. Tardy's work was an important early step toward improving both physician education and patient care. Even so, it took a while to catch on. For example, at the University of Michigan, the first camera for the otolaryngology department's microscope was not purchased until 1978. Even then, it was ordered by Dr. A.C.D. Brown of the department of anesthesia so that the anesthesiologist could see the surgical field during mastoid surgery, rather than by the otolaryngology department to enhance otological and laryngological training. In retrospect, such lengthy delay in acquiring television monitors from so venerable a training program seems hard to fathom. Hence, it behooves each of us entrusted with the training of young otolaryngologists to reflect upon whether we are guilty of perpetrating similar unfathomable delays at our own institutions today.

Since 1975 (in English in 1977), when Hirano described the layered structure of the vocal fold, laryn-gology has enjoyed unprecedented growth.[24] Great advances in our understanding of the anatomy and physiology of phonation have been paralleled by technological developments for voice quantification and outcomes assessment.[25] These advances have resulted in dramatic improvement in the standard of care for all patients with laryngologic disorders; and due largely to exceptional interdisciplinary collaboration, they have affected clinical care remarkably quickly. Stimulated by meetings such as the Voice Foundation's Annual Symposium on Care of the Professional Voice, founded by Wilbur James Gould, Hans von Leden, and others in 1972, laryngologists, speech-language pathologists, basic science researchers, singing teachers, acting teachers, performers, and others have worked together to advance knowledge and enhance patient care. They have developed a common language, posed questions of practical value in the clinic and studio, and developed an interdisciplinary paradigm for answering important questions through valid, reliable research. Much of this research has been reported at meetings of the ALA and of the American Broncho-Esophagological Association (ABEA), the Voice Foundation symposia, and dozens of other similar meetings that have evolved over the last 2 decades. Because of the interdisciplinary nature of many of these meetings and research efforts, and the collaborative, penetrating discussions that occur among professionals of different disciplines at such meetings, even the most esoteric scientific advances are promulgated quickly. Their practical importance is probed at the time of their presentation, and new discoveries are applied to patient care throughout the world within days after such meetings end.

Although the sheer amount of new information, equipment, diagnostic and therapeutic approaches, and surgical advancements is exciting, it has also created inconsistencies among training programs in the United States and throughout the world. Advances have been integrated piecemeal into various educational programs at different rates and to different degrees. Now that laryngology and voice is well established as a subspecialty, it seems timely to reflect on what we have learned, what anyone finishing a residency in otolaryngology or a fellowship in laryngology and voice should be expected to know, and how we can best teach these essentials. The development and adoption of training guidelines for laryngology and voice should be encouraged not only to help program directors, but also to ensure reasonable consistency in minimal basic knowledge among graduates from all programs, with the end result being a consistently high level of care for laryngological patients. However, the rapid and successful evolution of our field highlights the need to consider more than just facts and skills as we develop training priorities. We should also try to impart an enthusiasm for the kind of interdisciplinary creativity that was responsible for our current evolution as a field and to encourage and inspire similar academic and clinical creativity.

Residency Training

Although laryngology (including voice, speech, swallowing, and related disorders) constitutes only one segment of otolaryngology, it is particularly important, for several reasons. First, laryngological problems are common. Estimates of the incidence of voice disorders in school-age children range, for example from 6 to 23%.[26] Although there are no reliable, valid data on the incidence of voice disorders in the adult population, they are probably as prevalent as they are in children; and they may be even more common in elderly adults who are also more likely to develop neurological disorders with related voice, speech, and swallowing abnormalities. Most of our graduates will be called on to care for patients with laryngological disorders and to educate colleagues (including primary care physicians) on the proper diagnosis and treatment of laryngeal problems. Second, the standard of care and state-of-the-art for management of voice disorders have changed dramatically and continuously throughout the 1980s and 1990s.[27] The diagnostic techniques, methods of documentation, and imperative for outcomes assessment that are now standard were nonexistent just a few years ago. Some surgical techniques that were routine in the 1970s are now considered negligent; and newer surgical techniques that replaced them in the 1980s are already obsolete. If we do not make a concerted effort to ensure that our residents are fully aware of these developments and their practical implications, they may provide outdated treatment; and both they and their patients will suffer the consequences.

Providing such training is especially difficult in laryngology because of the speed with which the field has developed. It is certainly not possible for all otolaryngologists, or even all academic otolaryngologists, to keep up with all developments in all fields within our specialty. There are many programs in which laryngology is managed and taught by general otolaryngologists, or by head and neck cancer surgeons without special training in the modern clinical and research aspects of laryngology. However, if every training program in the United States had the desire and funds to hire an experienced and/or fellowship-trained laryngologist today, there would not be

enough to supply all of the positions. Therefore, at least until the number of laryngologists has caught up with the number needed, we must be especially diligent about defining expected areas of basic knowledge.

Details of a recommended curriculum are beyond the scope of this paper. However, suggestions have been articulated at least in preliminary form. One such document was developed by the Speech, Voice and Swallowing Committee of the American Academy of Otolaryngology. However, to date, no proposal has been accepted by the bodies that guide residency training in otolaryngology.

The thoughts that follow constitute only a broad overview of my vision of minimum residency requirements with regard to substantive knowledge and clinical skill. They are offered not as definitive recommendations but rather to encourage dialog and an eventual consensus. This chapter concentrates on voice, because voice is the most advanced and complex division of laryngology at present and to limit the length of this chapter. A similar model should be applied to training in the management of swallowing disorders and selected speech and language disorders.

Basic Science

Comprehensive knowledge of relevant anatomy, physiology, and pathology is required for insightful diagnosis and expert treatment of laryngological patients. Every trainee should be familiar with the layered microanatomy of the vocal fold, characteristics of its basement membrane, neuromuscular anatomy (including the latest concepts in fiber composition and subspecialization within given muscles), laryngeal aging (from embryology to death), and the nature and importance of supraglottic and infraglottic components of the vocal tract. Neurolaryngology has emerged as a new field and is vitally important to the clinician. Just as neurotology has expanded our scope of training in otology, so must neurolaryngology in laryngology. Training should include elements of neuroanatomy and neurophysiology that seemed irrelevant until recently. Every graduate of a residency should also be familiar with the intricacies of voice physiology, including respiration, infraglottic power-source functions, details of sound production at the level of the vocal folds, and the resonator functions of the supraglottic vocal tract. Understanding each component of the anatomy and physiology is not simply an academic exercise. Such knowledge allows the clinician to perform a "systems analysis" on the voice, determine which components are malfunctioning or misfunctioning, and establish diagnoses and treatment paradigms rationally.[28] Moreover, just as we expect our trainees to understand audiograms and how to interpret them, every trainee should be familiar with instrumentation for objective voice quantification and should be able to interpret data generated from voice laboratories. They should also be familiar with instruments for outcomes assessment in patients with voice disorders.[28]

Research

Research is an essential component of any postgraduate training program. Ultimately, at its best, research is the means by which we figure out how to improve the condition of patients whom we cannot help now. Each resident should receive training in research methodology and should have practical experience with basic and/or clinical research. Such training is essential not only to teaching incisive interpretation of the literature, but also to developing the ability to formulate precise questions relevant to the practice of laryngology and to design rational paths toward their answers. Good research training should help solidify the dissatisfaction all physicians feel about our limitations, and it should encourage our lifelong curiosity and an unwillingness to accept the limitations of our knowledge. Research should become a vital tool of daily practice through which we advance the boundaries of our speciality and enhance the care of our patients.

Diagnosis and Medical Management

Residents should master details of the comprehensive, multisystem history required for patients with voice disorders, with special techniques for physical examination, and be familiar with the many other special considerations that must be taken into account when caring for voice professionals. They should be able to recognize not only obvious laryngological problems, such as benign and malignant vocal fold lesions, but also less obvious lesions and related disorders. Graduates of our residencies should be able differentiate voice dysfunctions emanating from the infraglottic or supraglottic vocal tract, as well as laryngeal manifestations of systemic disease (reflux, thyroid disease, and many others). They should also gain experience in performing and interpreting strobovideolaryngoscopy and be familiar with the application of other diagnostic tests, including acoustic analysis, airflow assessment, laryngeal electromyography, and others. In addition, otolaryngology residents should receive specific training in the principles and practice of voice therapy, and they should spend at least some time observing therapy performed by an expert speech-language pathologist. Sufficient knowledge should be imparted to allow any laryngologist to determine whether a specific speech-language pathologist is providing his or her patient with appropriate, safe, and beneficial therapy. Physicians who refer their patients to speech-language pathologists cannot fulfill this basic obligation unless they have a reasonable understanding of the indications for referral, the techniques utilized by modern voice therapists, and the expected duration and progress of therapy. Ideally, residents should also be given an opportunity to work with a multidisciplinary voice team. It is also essential, of course, for trainees to be familiar with medical treatment of voice disorders, including the vocal consequences of various medications prescribed by otolaryngologists and other physicians (iatrogenic dysphonias).

In addition, we must prepare our trainees for "special situations," for example, complex problems such as laryngeal trauma, vocal fold scarring, and arytenoid dislocations that often require special expertise and/or rapid diagnosis and management. High-performance professional voice users also pose special challenges, obligations, and risks with which any practicing otolaryngologist should be familiar in order to avoid well-meaning but potentially costly treatment errors.

Surgery

Otolaryngology boasts an excellent tradition of teaching surgical skills. Prior to performing neck surgery on humans, residents have been instructed on the anatomy and physiology of neck structures, and pathophysiology; and they have performed neck dissections on cadavers. They have also generally observed or assisted in numerous similar surgical procedures. The training tradition is even more consistent and rigorous for surgery of the temporal bone. Temporal bone laboratory dissection with professorial instruction and supervision is required in most programs before residents are entrusted with surgical care of human ears. Unfortunately, the same systematic approach to teaching of surgical skills is often not applied to laryngeal surgery in most institutions. Laryngeal endoscopy, microscopic voice surgery, and phonosurgery (including framework surgery) are amenable to a similar thorough and systematic approach to training. In addition to instruction in anatomy and physiology of phonation, examination and quantification of voice function, outcomes assessment, alternatives to surgery, and timing of surgery before operating, the resident should have a thorough knowledge of surgical instrumentation (traditional and laser). Practice under supervision in laryngeal dissection laboratories (similar to temporal bone laboratories) and periods of observation in the operating room should precede resident surgery on human larynges. Attention to surgical technique and ergonomics is essential because of the technical difficulties involved in maintaining perfect control of the tips of long laryngeal instruments. Indeed, laryngeal microsurgery may well be approached conceptually as ear surgery with longer instruments. Resident surgery on patients should be supervised closely and should follow a planned progression from simple to complex cases; and it should be recognized that microdissection of the vibratory margin of the vocal fold may be more challenging technically than some seemingly "larger" cases such as laryngectomy. Results from resident's surgery should be comparable to those achieved by professorial faculty. Training should also include criteria for determining which cases should not be performed by inexperienced or occasional laryngeal surgeons and guidelines for referral to tertiary care laryngologists.

Special Considerations

In addition to providing training in facts and skills, attention must be paid to the art of patient care. This is extremely important in the management of all patients, and acutely important when caring for high-performance voice professionals.

Residents in otolaryngology and fellows in laryngology and voice should also be imbued with curiosity about the many questions that remain unanswered. They should receive historical information about the development of our field, and exposure to voice professionals in other disciplines such as speech-language pathologists, singing teachers, and arts-medicine specialists in other fields.

Fellowship Training

Fellowship programs in laryngology have proliferated recently in response to clinical and academic demand, but they have existed for many years. For example, Dr. Hans von Leden and the late Dr. Wilbur James Gould have trained fellows since the 1950s and 1960s, among them such distinguished individuals as Drs. Minoru Hirano and Nobuhiko Isshiki. This author began providing such training in 1981; and since that time, fellows have included not only laryngologists, but also speech-language pathologists and singing teachers. If our specialty is to provide enough practitioners to meet the need for high caliber laryngology and voice care teams, then we must participate in advanced training both for physicians and for professionals in other disciplines who will constitute the interdisciplinary teams of the future.

Although no formal guidelines for fellowship training have been accepted or implemented to date, they may be anticipated in the near future. A draft document has been developed by Dr. Robert Ossoff, this author, and other members of the Ad Hoc Committee on Laryngology Fellowship of the ALA. The need for quality control and some standardization in minimum experience in fellowship programs will hopefully lead to further action on this document or a similar set of guidelines in the near future.

Creative Thought

Interdisciplinary opportunities for creativity in medicine still offer the potential for excitement, joy, and innovation in daily practice.[29] The current advances in laryngology were inspired by interest in the problems of professional voice users, particularly opera singers; but this trend in laryngology was not isolated. Modern voice medicine is but one component of a larger field of arts-medicine that offers similar interdisciplinary team care for pianists, string players, dancers, wind instrumentalists, and others.[30] The arts-medicine aspects of laryngology are exciting for at least two reasons that should be addressed in any training program. First, performers and artists place critical demands on their bodies, and they do not have the usual tolerance for incomplete cures. An injured finger that returns to 98% normal function may be adequate even for a microsurgeon, but it is not adequate for a premier pianist. That extra 2% separates the famous artist from those who have not quite reached the "top." Arts-medicine patients force us to redefine "normal" much more narrowly, and they challenge our abilities to recognize, quantify, and restore physiological perfection. Much of the fun and many of the ideas that have helped advance laryngology and voice have come from close interactions with such patients, as well as with speech-language pathologists, voice scientists, singing teachers, acting teachers and other colleagues, all of whom provide insights useful in clinical practice. Second, arts-medicine provides physicians with an opportunity to work closely with professionals and educators in the arts and humanities. The arts and medicine are inherently similar in many ways. However, through our educational process, physicians too often lose sight of the importance of the arts to our practices, and there is a movement in medical education to correct this deficiency. Arts-medicine offers the clinician a chance to work and think with colleagues in related fields, such as artists and performers, and to find new solutions to complex problems. It also may afford us with the inspiration and opportunity to study one of the performing arts. In our quest to master the science and art of healing, we can learn much from our colleagues in the arts and humanities that will help our insight, sensitivity, and ability to empathize. Such interactions also help us keep us from being trapped intellectually by existing paradigms and allow us to approach questions with a broader vision, creating new solutions to problems that seem insurmountable within the compartmentalized framework of our traditional training, and even allowing us to create new fields of medicine.

Conclusion

Laryngologists of the future will be ideally positioned to thrive as sophisticated diagnosticians, surgeons, and scientists; but they will also have exceptional opportunities to remain "physicians" in the truest and broadest sense. It is incumbent upon us to offer training environments that will not merely provide skills, but also kindle and nurture curiosity, creativity, and broader vision. In these days of economic and legal crises, medicine has precious few reminders of the reasons why most of us were inspired to become doctors. For the last 2 decades, modern laryngology has been built on such enthusiasm and practicing it has been a daily joy. We must ensure that the next generation will not have to settle for anything less. If we are successful, 20 years from now, our practice will look as crude as Elsberg's methods seems to us today; and we will have accomplished our mission as educators and left behind training centers filled not only with information, but also with inspiration and imagination.

References

1. Elsberg L. Presidential Address to the First Meeting of the American Laryngological Association. *Trans Am Laryngol Assoc.* 1879;1:33–90.
2. Elsberg L. Presidential Address to the Second Meeting of the American Laryngological Association. *Trans Am Laryngol Assoc.* 1880;2:3–11.
3. Knight F. Presidential Address to the Fourth Meeting of the American Laryngological Association. *Trans Am Laryngol Assoc.* 1882;4:2–11.
4. Wilders JSS. On the teaching of laryngology. *Br Med J.* 1890;2:376–377.
5. Swain HL. Laryngology and its place in medical education: Presidential Address to the Twenty-Third Meeting of the American Laryngological Association. *Trans Am Laryngol Assoc.* 1901;23:1–17.
6. Knight CH. The teaching of laryngology, then and now. *Laryngoscope.* 1906;160:840–843.
7. Harris TJ. The training of the specialist. *Ann Otol Rhinol Laryngol.* 1913;22:475–481.
8. Skillern RH. Post-graduate work in laryngology. *JAMA.* 1921;77:1145–1146.
9. Milligan W. The rise and progress of laryngology: its relation to general medicine and its position in the medical curriculum. *Brit Med J.* 1922;1:547–551.
10. Dean LW. The teaching of undergraduate laryngology. *Laryngoscope.* 1925;35:735–741.
11. Layton TB. The aims and methods of teaching laryngology. *J Laryngol Otol.* 1940;55:495–502.
12. Alford BR. The age of the medical education revolution. *Laryngoscope.* 1996;106:801–804.
13. Bailey BJ. Laryngology education at the turn of the century. *Laryngoscope.* 1996;106:797–800.
14. Ridpath RF. Diseases of the larynx. In: Jackson C, Coates GM, eds. *The Nose, Throat, and Ear and Their Diseases.* Philadelphia, Pa: WB Saunders; 1929:736–744.
15. Shahrokh DK, Devine KD. A teaching device for residents in laryngology. *Arch Otolaryngol.* 1961;74:234–235.
16. Garcia M. Observations on the human voice. *Proc R Soc Lond.* 1855;7:397–410.
17. Zeitels SM. Premalignant epithelium and microinvasive cancer of the vocal fold: the evolution of phonomicrosurgical management. *Laryngoscope.* 1995;105(3, Pt2):1–51.
18. LeJeune FE. Motion picture study of laryngeal lesions. *Surg Gynecol Obstet.* 1936;62:492–495.
19. Moore P, von Leden H. Television in otolaryngology and other specialties—a new teaching device. *JAMA.* 1959;169:1976–1980.
20. von Leden H. Laryngeal physiology: cinematographic observations. *J Laryngol Otol.* 1960;74:705–712.
21. Moore GP, White FD, von Leden H. Ultra high speed photography in laryngeal physiology. *J Speech Hear Disord.* 1962;27:162–171.
22. von Leden H, Le Cover M, Ringel RL, Isshiki N. Improvements in laryngeal cinematography. *Arch Otolaryngol.* 1966;83:482–487.
23. Tardy ME Jr. Microscopic laryngology: teaching techniques. *Laryngoscope.* 1972;82:1315–1322.
24. Hirano M. Structure and vibratory pattern of the vocal folds. In: Sawashinma N, Cooper FS, eds. *Dynamic Aspects of Speech Production.* Tokyo, Japan: University of Tokyo Press; 1977:13–24.
25. Sataloff RT. The human voice. *Sci Am.* 1992;267:108–115.
26. National Strategic Research Plan of the National Institute on Deafness and Other Communication Disorders, 1991, 1992, 1993. NIH publication No. 95–3711. Bethesda, Md: US Department of Health and Human Services; 1995:270.
27. Sataloff RT. Rational thought: the impact of voice science upon voice care *J Voice.* 1995;9:215–234.
28. Benninger MS, Gardner GM, Jacobson BH, Grywalski C. New dimensions in measuring voice treatment outcomes. In: Sataloff, RT. *Professional Voice: The Science and Art of Clinical Care.* 2nd ed. San Diego, Calif: Singular Publishing Group; 1997:789–794.
29. Sataloff RT. Interdisciplinary opportunities for creativity in medicine. *Ear Nose Throat J.* 1998;77:530–533.
30. Sataloff RT, Brandfonbrener A, and Lederman, R eds. *Performing Arts Medicine.* 2nd ed. San Diego, Calif: Singular Publishing Group; 1998.

105

Interdisciplinary Opportunities for Creativity in Medicine

Robert Thayer Sataloff

In the Hippocratic oath, we swear: *"I will keep pure and holy both my life and my art."* From time to time, it behooves us to reflect on our lives in medicine and to assess not only whether we have remained true to our original mission, but also whether our profession still provides viable possibilities for altruistic, creative practice.

Observations at different stages of medical education reveal disturbing trends. Premedical students are usually enthusiastically committed to helping mankind, not only by aiding one patient at a time, but also by advancing medical science. Physicians who have been in practice for a number of years speak much more often of malpractice crises, overhead expenses, managed care, and the changing politics of medical practice.

In the last few years, more and more young, successful doctors have begun seeking alternative careers—out of medicine. The purpose of this chapter is not to analyze the educational and cultural factors that turn so many bright-eyed, idealistic premeds into so many jaded, pragmatic doctors (nearly all of us have our own theories). Certainly, the demands of our profession make it hard enough for most of us to keep up with the necessities of patient care and running our practices. Stimulating, novel ideas and imaginative new approaches to medical treatment are often not a part of our daily routine. Yet, many of us expected that they would be. This author believes that it is still possible and preferable to incorporate creativity into everyday practice. This can be accomplished with slight adjustments in philosophy and traditional practice methods. Interdisciplinary teamwork is a particularly satisfactory approach.

For hundreds of years, medical doctors have practiced alone. For some, especially in earlier times, this was to protect their mystique and insecurities. For others, isolation was a consequence of specialization. This is not a new phenomenon. Herodotus (484-424 BC) wrote:

The art of medicine in Egypt is thus exercised: one physician is confined to the study and management of one disease; there are of course a great number who practice this art; some attend to the disorders of the eyes, others to those of the head, some take care of the teeth, others are conversant with all diseases of the bowels; whilst many attend to the cure of maladies which are less conspicuous.[1]

The old tradition continues today, even in most university settings and multispecialty groups. Although doctors work together under the same roof and talk together in the same conference rooms, they rarely truly think together and work together as a unit. It is even more rare for them to interact with nonphysicians in a meaningful way.

However, in the last several years, an encouraging number of new interdisciplinary teams have emerged. They are important not merely because of their advances in medical treatment, but also because of their changes in thinking, cooperation, and approaches to caring for patients. This collaboration has resulted in new opportunities for creative approaches to medical problems, approaches that were not possible to adopt from the parochial posture of isolated specialists.

The Team Approach

The team concept in medicine is certainly not entirely new. For example, in-depth cooperation among internists and surgeons made cardiac surgery and renal transplantation possible. More recently, cooperation among radiologists and neurosurgeons has resulted in intraoperative ultrasound localization of brain lesions, invasive radiologic treatment of stenoses and aneurysms, and other major advances that have improved safety and decreased morbidity. Sports medicine has combined the skills and insights of various specialists to revolutionize the care of professional athletes. Selected spinal cord injury "teams" have combined the talents of neurosurgeons and orthopedic surgeons, operating on the same patient at the same time, along with the skills of psychiatrists, physical therapists, psychologists, speech-language pathologists, and others. Such collaboration results in a dialogue and subtle refinements of ideas that are rare for the physician working alone.

Learning to work together, being open to different ideas and approaches, and being prepared to make time to talk with a colleague are among the most important requirements of the interdisciplinary team. The physicians must replace egotistical prerogatives with genuine, open curiosity. This posture allows a fresh approach to old problems, armed with new perspectives and divested of the boundaries of traditional specialties and their limitations.

The author is fortunate enough to be involved with two such interdisciplinary teams. They keep the practice of medicine exciting and vital. The newest frontier in otology is the ear-brain interface, the skull base. It was an unexplored boundary full of vital structures that represented the limits of otolaryngology, coming from below, and the end of neurosurgery, coming from above. Unraveling the mysteries of the "no-man's-land" of the skull base became possible only in the last 3 decades because of the interdisciplinary specialty of neurotology. This subspecialty started in Los Angeles, in the early 1960s for the treatment of acoustic neuromas and glomus tumors. It led to the development of the cochlear implant, surgical cures for vertigo, and other advances. Most recently, it also has led to major new developments in the treatment of previously "unresectable" malignancies of the temporal bone.

Our team includes not only a neurotologist (the author) and neurosurgeon, but also an ophthalmologist, internist, general surgeon, anesthesiologist, psychiatrist, nurse, rehabilitation specialist, and others attuned to the special problems of these patients and their prolonged surgeries. Consequently, since 1980, we have been able to develop new techniques to resect areas that have not been resected before; to manage anesthesia safely for more than 30 hours, when necessary; and to return patients to their homes, self-sufficient and in reasonably good condition. Moreover, every time we do such a case, we find new ways to do it better the next time. Occasionally, we find techniques to do more things that we thought were not possible. Such interactions help keep the fun in medical practice.

Arts-Medicine

Not all creative teamwork has to involve 30-hour operations and critically ill patients. The interdisciplinary speciality of arts-medicine has also evolved remarkably since its introduction in the 1980s. There is already an International Arts-Medicine Association, headquartered in Philadelphia, and there are arts-medicine clinics and conferences in several states. This field is exciting for a variety of reasons. First, performers and artists place extreme demands on their bodies and do not have the usual tolerance for incomplete cures. An injured finger that returns to 98% normal function may be adequate even for a microsurgeon, but it is not adequate for a premier pianist. That extra 2% separates the famous artist from the artist who has not quite reached the "top." The author has been involved extensively with the treatment of singers and other professional voice users since the late 1970s. Learning how to recognize, define, and treat subtleties of voice pathology that are not even mentioned in most residencies has been a daily challenge and joy. Much of the fun and many of the ideas have come from close collaboration with speech-language pathologists, singing teachers, acting-voice teachers, voice scientists, and other colleagues, all of whom provide insights useful in clinical practice. Second, arts-medicine provides physicians with an opportunity to work closely with professionals in the arts and humanities. Not all "interdisciplinary opportunities" need to be among medical disciplines.

Arts and medicine are inherently similar in many ways. However, through our educational process, physicians too often lose sight of the importance of arts and humanities in our practices. There is a movement in medical education to correct this problem, and art-medicine offers the clinician a chance to work and think with colleagues in related fields, with artists and performers, and to find new solutions to complex problems. It also may afford inspiration and opportunity to study one of the arts.

As A.M. Harvey wrote in his book, *The Principles and Practice of Medicine,* "The principal complaint which patients make about modern scientific medicine is the failure of physicians to communicate with them adequately."[2] Tolstoy observed that, "Art is the human activity having for its purpose the transmission to others of the highest and best feelings to which men have risen."[3] In our quest to master the science and art of healing, we can learn from our colleagues in the arts and humanities much that will help our insight, sensitivity, and ability to empathize.

True interdisciplinary study provides endless opportunities for the enrichment of the practice of medicine with creative insights. Whether we work with tertiary care surgeons to resect the "unresectable" or with poets to find new ways to hear and talk with our distraught patients, medicine remains a viable option for the imaginative, creative physician who still wants the same exciting challenges and opportunities he or she wanted as a sophomore in college. We need only refuse to accept anything less.

References

1. Herotodus. *Histories.* Book 2:84.
2. Harvey AM, Osler W. *The Principles and Practice of Medicine.* New York, NY: McGraw-Hill; 1988.
3. Tolstoy L. *What is Art?* 1896:chap 8.

106

Physicians Studying Voice and the Arts

Robert T. Sataloff

Much has been said in this book about the necessity for interdisciplinary education. Speech-language pathologists, acting teachers, and singing teachers clearly need to study anatomy, physiology, and basic health maintenance of the voice. Singing teachers need to learn about the singing voice. Speech-language pathologists benefit from singing study, voice scientists need to understand clinical problems and priorities, and so forth. At the most practical level, the reasons why a laryngologist should study voice are obvious. Through singing lessons, speech lessons, and personal performance experience, we acquire terminology, experience, and understanding that cannot be achieved in other ways; this makes us better doctors. Without such training, the laryngologist can compensate to some degree by reading and study, but he or she never acquires quite the same expertise or patient rapport as the physician who has also experienced the discipline of musical development and the ecstasy and terror of public performance.

However, there may be even more compelling reasons for physicians to study the arts in general. Many of the most rewarding joys of subspecializing in voice or other areas of arts-medicine come from the interdisciplinary opportunities for creativity and the philosophical influence of our colleagues in the humanities. It is wise and rewarding for physicians to recognize the importance of the study of the arts in making us not only better doctors, but also better people.

A modern poet has characterized the personality of art and the personality of science as follows: "Art is I: Science is We."[1(p997)]

Since its earliest days, medicine has concerned itself with refining its understanding of the truths of science and art and applying their universal wisdom to the care of people. This implies an obligation for the physician to understand more about life than just the particulars of body function with which our science is concerned. We must expand our parochial vision into a broad understanding of humanity. One of the most obvious and accessible avenues to such philosophical breadth is the combination of medical studies with the study of the arts.

"Only through art can we get outside ourselves and know another's view of the universe which is not the same as ours and see landscapes which would otherwise have remained unknown to us like the landscapes of the moon. Thanks to art, instead of seeing a single world, our own, we see it multiply until we have before us as many worlds as there are original artists."[2] David, daVinci, Shakespeare, Bach, and others of their stature have remained vital because of the depth and universality of their visions of life. Understanding their messages enriches our entire being and gives new light to our own vision. Moreover, the process of learning to understand their wisdom teaches us how to perceive another's view—the art of understanding. As physicians, we must believe that there are as many "original artists" as there are people in the world; and it is the art of our profession to see what they see and to care for them accordingly.

"The principal complaint which patients make about 'modern scientific medicine' is the failure of physicians to communicate with them adequately."[3] What they are trying to tell us is not that they want more information, but that they want more humanity. "Art is the human activity having for its purpose the transmission to others of the highest and best feelings to which men have risen."[4] This fundamental caring is what we fail to communicate. This is especially curious, since it is the emotion that draws so many of us to medicine and makes it so much more fulfilling for us than the laboratory sciences. As Hippocrates observed: "Where there is love of man, there is also love of the art."[5] If we are to master the art of medicine, study of the arts may provide invaluable help, for to have the love is not enough. We must learn to understand it and to communicate it to our patients so that they feel it. This is where our science fails; and without this art, we are about as comforting as a well-programmed computer—and not nearly so efficient.

In addition to more abstract wisdom, study of the arts reveals a rather reassuring similarity of methods among the arts and sciences, as well as a similarity of goals.

He who would do good to another must do it in minute particulars:
General good is the plea of the scoundrel, hypocrite and flatterer,
For art and science cannot exist but in minutely organized particulars.[6]

Both science and art seek universal truths; both seek the "I" and "We," and both recognize that the substance of great truths is smaller truths. Only their perspectives differ. Moreover, mastery of these differences may well be the substance of the genius that allows a few people occasionally to see that which has been before all of us all of the time, but has been missed.

We swear in the Hippocratic Oath: "I will keep pure and holy both my life and my art." In our quest to mas-

ter the science and art of healing, we will do well to pay attention to the nature of the lives and world with which we live and especially to art, the science of the study of that nature. "It is art that makes life, makes interest, makes importance, for our consideration and application of these things, and I know no substitute whatever for the force and beauty of its process."[7(p279)]

It is somewhat comforting, somewhat humbling to consider one final truth:
All nature is but art unknown to thee,
All chance, direction which thou canst not see;
All discord, harmony not understood;
All partial evil, universal good;
And, spite of pride, in erring reason's spite,
One truth is clear, Whatever is, is right.[8]

References

1. Bernard C. *Bull NY Acad Med IV.* 1928;1V:997.
2. Proust M. O'Brien J, ed. *The Maxims of Marcel Proust.* New York: Columbia University Press, 1948;24:235.
3. Harvey AM, Johns RJ, Owens AH, Ross RS. *The Principles and Practice of Medicine,* 18th ed. New York: Appleton-Century-Crofts; 1972:2.
4. Tolstoy L. *What is Art?* 1898, Chapter 8.
5. Hippocrates. *Precepts.* Chapter 1.
6. Blake W. *Jerusalem.* Chapter 3, Sec. 55.
7. James H. Letter to H.G. Wells, July 10, 1915.
8. Pope A. An essay on man. Epistle 1:289.

Suggested Reading List

(See also "Suggested Readings" and "References" listed in individual chapters.)

1. Abitbol J. *Atlas of Laser Voice Surgery.* San Diego, Calif: Singular Publishing Group, Inc; 1994.
2. Andrea M, Dias O. *Atlas of Rigid and Contact Endoscopy in Microlaryngeal Surgery.* Philadelphia, Pa: Lippincott-Raven; 1995.
3. Andrews ML. *Voice Therapy for Children.* San Diego, Calif: Singular Publishing Group, Inc; 1991.
4. Andrews ML. *Manual of Voice Treatment.* San Diego, Calif: Singular Publishing Group, Inc; 1994.
5. Appleman DR. *The Science of Vocal Pedagogy.* Bloomington, Ind: Indiana University Press; 1967.
6. Aronson AE. *Clinical Voice Disorders,* 2nd ed. New York, NY: Thieme Medical Publishers, Inc; 1985.
7. *ASHA.* American Speech-Language-Hearing Association. Rockville, Md 20852.
8. Baer T, Sasaki C. *Laryngeal Function in Phonation and Respiration.* San Diego, Calif: Singular Publishing Group, Inc; 1994.
9. Baken RJ, Orlikoff RT. *Clinical Measurement of Speech and Voice.* 2nd ed. San Diego, Calif: Singular Publishing Group; 2000.
10. Baken RJ, Daniloff RG. *Readings in Clinical Spectrography of Speech.* San Diego, Calif: Singular Publishing Group, Inc; 1991.
11. Behlau M. *Voz.* Rio de Janeiro, Brazil: Livaria e Editora Revinter; 2001.
12. Behlau M, Pontes P. *Avaliacao e Tratemento das Disfonias.* Sao Paulo, Brazil: Editora Lovise; 1995
13. Benjamin BNP. *Diagnostic Laryngology: Adults and Children.* Philadelphia, Pa: WB Saunders; 1990.
14. Benjamin BNP. *Endolaryngeal Surgery.* London, England: Martin Dunitz; 1998.
15. Benninger MS, Jacobson BH, Johnson AF. *Vocal Arts Medicine.* New York, NY: Thieme Medical Publishers, Inc; 1994.
16. Berry C. *The Actor and the Text.* New York, NY: Applause Theatre Books; 1987.
17. Berry C. *The Voice and the Actor.* New York, NY: Macmillan General References; 1973.
18. Blitzer A, Brin MF, Sasaki CT, Fahn S, Harris KS. *Neurologic Disorders of the Larynx.* New York, NY: Thieme Medical Publishers, Inc; 1992.
19. Boone DR. *Is Your Voice Telling on You? How to Find and Use Your Natural Voice.* San Diego, Calif: Singular Publishing Group, Inc; 1994.
20. Borden G, Harris K. *The Speech Primer.* Baltimore, Md: Williams and Wilkins; 1980.
21. Brodnitz F. *Keep Your Voice Healthy.* Boston, Mass: College Hill Press; 1988.
22. Brodnitz F. *Vocal Rehabilitation: A Manual.* Rochester, Minn: American Academy of Ophthalmology and Otolaryngology; 1991.
23. Brown OL. *Discover Your Voice: How to Develop Healthy Voice Habits.* San Diego, Calif: Singular Publishing Group; 1996.
24. Brown WS, Vinson BP, Crary MA. *Organic Voice Disorders: Assessment and Treatment.* San Diego, Calif: Singular Publishing Group; 1996.
25. Bunch M. *Dynamics of the Singing Voice. Disorders of Human Communication 6.* New York, NY: Springer-Verlag; 1982.
26. Butcher P, Elias A, Raven R. *Psychogenic Voice Disorders and Cognitive-Behavior Therapy.* San Diego, Calif: Singular Publishing Group, Inc; 1994.
27. Case JL. *Clinical Management of Voice Disorders.* San Diego, Calif: Singular Publishing Group, Inc; 1991.
28. Castell DO: *The Esophagus.* 2nd ed. Boston, Mass: Little Brown and Co; 1995.
29. Colton R, Casper J. *Understanding Voice Problems.* Baltimore, Md: Williams & Wilkins; 1990.
30. Conable B, Conable W. *How to Learn the Alexander Technique: A Manual for Students.* Columbus, Ohio: Andover Road Press; 1991.
31. Costa Olival H, Duprat A, Eckley CA. *Laringologia Pediatrica.* Sao Paulo, Brazil: Roca; 1999.
32. Crelin EF. *The Human Vocal Tract.* New York, NY: Vantage Press; 1987.
33. Critchley M, Henson RA. *Music and The Brain.* London: William Heinemann Medical Books Limited; 1977.
34. Dal Vera R, ed. *Standard Speech and Other Contemporary Issues in Professional Voice and Speech Training.* Voice and Speech Trainers Association, Inc; 2000.

1514   PROFESSIONAL VOICE: THE SCIENCE AND ART OF CLINICAL CARE

35. Dal Vera R, ed. *The Voice in Violence: And Other Contemporary Issues in Professional Voice and Speech Training.* New York, NY: Applause Theatre Books; 2001

36. Dal Vera R, Colaianni L, eds. *Standard Speech: Essays on Voice and Speech.* New York, NY: Applause Theatre Books; 2001.

37. Davis PJ, Fletcher NH. *Vocal Fold Physiology: Controlling Complexity and Chaos.* San Diego, Calif: Singular Publishing Group; 1996.

38. Dedo HH. *Surgery of the Larynx and Trachea.* Philadelphia, Pa: BC Decker; 1990.

39. Dejonckere PH. *Vibrato.* San Diego, Calif: Singular Publishing Group, Inc; 1988.

40. Doyle PC. *Foundations of Voice and Speech Rehabilitation Following Laryngeal Cancer.* San Diego, Calif: Singular Publishing Group, Inc; 1994.

41. Ferlito A. *Neoplasms of the Larynx.* London, UK: Churchill Livingston; 1993.

42. Ferlito A. *Diseases of the Larynx.* London, UK: Arnold; 2000.

43. Ford CN, Bless DM. *Phonosurgery: Assessment and Surgical Management.* New York, NY: Raven Press; 1992.

44. Fried NP. *The Larynx: A Multidisciplinary Approach.* 2nd ed. St. Louis, Mo: CV Mosby; 1996.

45. Fujimura O. *Vocal Fold Physiology: Voice Production, Mechanisms, and Functions.* vol 2. New York, NY: Raven Press; 1988.

46. Gauffin J, Hammarberg B. *Vocal Fold Physiology: Acoustic, Perceptual, and Physiological Aspects of Voice Mechanisms.* San Diego, Calif: Singular Publishing Group; 1991.

47. Gleck J. Chaos. New York, NY: Penguin Books; 1987.

48. Gould WJ, Lawrence VL. *Surgical Care of Voice Disorders. Disorders of Human Communication 8.* New York, NY: Springer-Verlag; 1984.

49. Gould WJ, Sataloff RT, Spiegel JR. *Voice Surgery.* St. Louis, Mo: CV Mosby; 1993.

50. Green MCL, Mathieson L. *The Voice and Its Disorders.* San Diego, Calif: Singular Publishing Group, Inc; 1994.

51. Hamptom, M, Acker B, eds. *The Vocal Vision: Views on Voice.* New York, NY: Applause Theatre Books; 1997.

52. Hirano M. *Clinical Examination of the Voice. Disorders of Human Communication 5.* New York, NY: Springer-Verlag; 1981.

53. Hirano M, Bless DM. *Videostroboscopic Examination of the Larynx.* San Diego, Calif: Singular Publishing Group, Inc; 1993.

54. Hirano M, Sato K. *Histological Color Atlas of the Human Larynx.* San Diego, Calif: Singular Publishing Group, Inc; 1993.

55. Hixon T. *Respiratory Function in Speech and Song.* Boston, Mass: College-Hill Press; 1988.

56. Hollien H. *The Acoustics of Crime.* New York, NY: Plenum Publishing; 1990.

57. Isshiki N. *Phonosurgery—Theory and Practice.* New York, NY: Springer-Verlag; 1989.

58. Jackson C. Jackson CL. *Diseases and Injuries of the Larynx.* New York, NY: Macmillan & Co; 1942.

59. Johnson TS, ed. *Prevention of Voice Disorders. Seminars in Speech and Language.* New York, NY: Thieme Medical Publishers; 1991.

60. *Journal of Singing.* Clifton Park, NY: Delmar Thomson Learning.

61. *Journal of Voice.* Clifton Park, NY: Delmar Thomson Learning.

62. Kahane JC, Folkins JF. *Atlas of Speech and Hearing Anatomy.* Columbus, Ohio: Charles E. Merrill Publishing Co; 1984.

63. Karnell MP. *Videoendoscopy.* San Diego, Calif: Singular Publishing Group, Inc; 1994.

64. Kent, RD *Reference Manual for Communicative Sciences and Disorders: Speech and Language.* Austin, Tex: Pro-Ed; 1994.

65. Kirchner JA. *Atlas on the Surgical Anatomy of Laryngeal Cancer.* San Diego, Calif: Singular Publishing Group; 1998.

66. Koschkee DL. *Voice Care in the Medical Setting.* San Diego, Calif: Singular Publishing Group, Inc; 1995.

67. Kotby MN. *The Accent Method of Voice Therapy.* San Diego, Calif: Singular Publishing Group, Inc; 1994.

68. Laukkanen A. *On Speaking Voice Exercises.* Tampere, Finland: University of Tampere; 1995.

69. Lessac A. *The Use and Training of the Human Voice: A Practical Approach to Speech and Voice Dynamics.* 3rd ed. New York, NY: McGraw Hill Humanities/Social Sciences/Languages; 1997.

70. Lindestadt P. *Electromyographic and Laryngoscopic Studies of Normal and Disturbed Voice Function.* Stockholm, Sweden: Huddinge University; 1994.

71. Linthicum FH Jr, Schwartzman JA. *An Atlas of Micropathology of the Temporal Bone.* San Diego, Calif: Singular Publishing Group, Inc; 1994.

72. Ludlow CL, Cooper JA. *Genetic Aspects of Speech and Language Disorders.* New York, NY: Academic Press; 1983.

73. Mandel S, Sataloff RT, Schapiro S. *Minor Head Trauma: Assessment, Management and Rehabilitation.* New York, NY: Springer-Verlag; 1993.

74. Mathieson L, Baken RJ. *Green & Mathieson's The Voice & Its Disoders.* London: Whurr Publishers; 2001.

75. *Medical Problems of Performing Artists.* Philadelphia, Pa: Hanley & Belfus. (journal)

76. Miller R. *The Structure of Singing: System and Art in Vocal Technique.* New York, NY: Schirmer Books; 2001.

77. Moore GP. *Organic Voice Disorders.* Englewood Cliffs, NJ: Prentice-Hall, Inc; 1971.

78. Moriarty J. *Diction.* Boston, Mass: EC Schirmer Music Company; 1975.

79. Morrison M, Rammage L, Nicol H, Pullan B, May P, Salkeld L. *The Management of Voice Disorders.* San Diego, Calif: Singular Publishing Group, Inc; 1994.

80. Nair G. *Voice: Tradition and Technology.* San Diego, Calif: Singular Publishing Group; 1999.

81. Orlikoff RF, Baken RJ. *Clinical Voice and Speech Measurement.* San Diego, Calif: Singular Publishing Group, Inc; 1993.

82. Peacher G. *Speak to Win.* New York, NY: Bell Publishing; 1985.

83. Pickett JS. *The Sounds of Speech Communication.* Baltimore, Md: University Park Press; 1980.

84. Prater RJ, Swift RW. *Manual of Voice Therapy.* San Diego, Calif: Singular Publishing Group, Inc; 1984.

85. Proctor TF. *Breathing, Speech and Songs*. New York, NY: Springer-Verlag; 1980.

86. Sataloff J, Sataloff RT, Vassallo LA. *Hearing Loss*. Philadelphia, PA: JB Lippincott; 1980.

87. Rodenburg P. *The Actor Speaks: Voice and the Performer*. New York, NY: St. Martin's Press; 2000.

88. Rosen DC, Sataloff RT. *Psychology of Voice Disorders*. San Diego, Calif: Singular Publishing Group; 1997.

89. Rossol M. *The Artist's Complete Health and Safety Guide*. 2nd ed. New York, NY: Allworth Press; 1994.

90. Rubin J, Sataloff RT, Korovin G. *Diagnosis and Treatment of Voice Disorders*. 2nd ed. Albany, NY: Delmar Thomson Learning; 2002.

91. Sataloff RT. *Vocal Health and Pedagogy*. San Diego, Calif: Singular Publishing Group; 1998.

92. Sataloff RT. *Voice Perspectives*. San Diego, Calif: Singular Publishing Group; 1998.

93. Sataloff RT. *Embryology and Anomalies of the Facial Nerve*, New York, NY: Raven Press; 1991.

94. Sataloff RT. *Professional Voice: The Science and Art of Clinical Care*. New York, NY: Raven Press; 1991.

95. Sataloff RT, Branfonbrener A, Lederman RJ. *Performing Arts Medicine*. 2nd ed. San Diego, Calif: Singular Publishing Group; 1998.

96. Sataloff RT, Castell DO, Katz PO, Sataloff DM. *Reflux Laryngitis and Related Disorders*. 2nd ed. San Diego, Calif: Singular Publishing Group; 1999.

97. Sataloff RT, Hawkshaw MJ. *Chaos in Medicine: Source Readings*. San Diego, Calif: Singular Publishing Group; 2000.

98. Sataloff RT, Hawkshaw JM, Spiegel JR. *Atlas of Laryngoscopy*. San Diego, Calif: Singular Thomson Learning; 2000.

99. Sataloff RT, Mandel S, Mañon-Espaillat R, Heman-Ackah YD, Abaza M. *Laryngeal Electromyography*. Clifton Park, NY: Thomson Delmar Learning; 2003.

100. Sataloff RT, Sataloff J. *Occupational Hearing Loss*. New York, NY: Marcel Dekker; 1987.

101. Sataloff RT. The Human Voice. *Sci Am*. 1992;267(6):108-115.

102. Sataloff RT, Sataloff J. *Hearing Loss*. 3rd ed. New York, NY: Marcel Dekker; 1993.

103. Sataloff J, Sataloff RT. *Occupational Hearing Loss: Source Readings*. San Diego, Calif: Singular Publishing Group, Inc; 1996.

104. Sataloff RT, Titze IR. *Vocal Health and Science*. Jacksonville, Fla: The National Association of Teachers of Singing; 1991.

105. Saxon KG, Schneider CM. *Vocal Exercise Physiology*. San Diego, Calif: Singular Publishing Group, Inc; 1994.

106. Seikel JA, King DW, Drumright DG. *Anatomy and Physiology for Speech, Language, and Hearing*. San Diego, Calif: Singular Publishing Group; 1997.

107. Silver CE, Ferlito A. *Surgery for Cancer of the Larynx and Related Structures*. 2nd ed. Philadelphia, Pa: WB Saunders; 1996.

108. Silver CE, Rubin JS. *Atlas of Head and Neck Surgery*. 2nd ed. New York, NY: Churchill Livingstone; 1999.

109. Smith B, Sataloff RT. *Choral Pedagogy*. San Diego, Calif: Singular Publishing Group; 2000.

110. Spandorfer M, Curtis SD, Snyder J. *Making Art Safely*. New York, NY: John Wiley and Sons; 1996.

111. Stemple JC. *Voice Therapy: Clinical Studies*. 2nd ed. San Diego, Calif: Singular Publishing Group; 2000.

112. Stemple JC, Glaze LE, Klaben BG. *Clinical Voice Pathology: Theory and Management*. 3rd ed. San Diego, Calif: Singular Publishing Group; 1999.

113. Stemple J, Gerdman BK. *Clinical Voice Pathology*. San Diego, Calif: Singular Publishing Group, Inc; 1994.

114. Sundberg J. *The Science of the Singing Voice*. DeKalb, Ill: Northern Illinois Press; 1987.

115. Sundberg J, Nord L, Carlson R. *Music, Language, Speech and Brain*. London, UK: Macmillan Press; 1991.

116. Ternström S. *Acoustics for Choir and Orchestra*. Stockholm, Sweden: Royal Swedish Academy of Music; 1986.

117. Thurman L, Welch G. *Body, Mind and Voice: Foundations of Voice Education*. Collegeville, Minn: The Voice Care Network; 2000.

118. Titze IR. *Vocal Fold Physiology: Frontiers in Basic Science*. San Diego, Calif: Singular Publishing Group; 1983.

119. Titze IR. *Principles of Voice Production*. Inglewood Cliffs, NJ: Prentice Hall; 1994.

120. Titze IR, Scherer R. *Biomechanics, Acoustic and Phonatory Control*. New York, NY: Raven Press; 1983.

121. Tucker H. *The Larynx*. 2nd ed. New York, NY: Thieme Medical Publishers Inc; 1993.

122. Tucker H. *Surgery for Phonatory Disorders*. New York, NY: Churchhill Livingstone; 1981.

123. Urrutia G-T, Marco IC. *Diagnostico Y Tratamiento De Los Trastonos De La Voz*. Madrid, Spain: Sociedad Espanola de Otorrinolaringologia y Patologai Cervico Facial; 1996.

124. Utterback AS. *Broadcast Voice Handbook*. Chicago, Ill: Bonus Books; 1995.

125. Vennard W. *Singing: The Mechanism and the Technic*. New York: Carl Frisher, Inc; 1967.

126. Weinstein JS, Laccourreye O, Brasnu D, Laccourreye H. *Organ Preservation Surgery for Laryngeal Cancer*. San Diego, Calif: Singular Publishing Group; 2000.

127. Zeitels SM. *Atlas of Phonomicrosurgery and Other Endolaryngeal Procedures for Benign and Malignant Disease*. San Diego, Calif: Singular Thomson Learning; 2001.

128. Zemlin WR. *Speech and Hearing Science: Anatomy and Physiology*. Englewood Cliffs, NJ: Prentice-Hall; 1988.

Vocal Fold Physiology Series

Under the auspices of The Voice Foundation, 1721 Pine Street, Philadelphia, Pennsylvania.

1. Baer T, Sasaki C, Harris KS. *Laryngeal Function in Phonation and Respiration.* San Diego, Calif: College-Hill Press; 1991.
2. Bless DM, Abbs H. *Vocal Fold Physiology: Contemporary Research and Clinical Issues.* San Diego, Calif: College-Hill Press; 1983.
3. Fujimura O. *Vocal Physiology: Voice Production, Mechanisms, and Functions.* San Diego, Calif: Singular Publishing Group, Inc; 1988.
4. Fujimura O, Hirano M. *Vocal Fold Physiology: Voice Quality Control.* San Diego, Calif: Singular Publishing Group, Inc; 1994.
5. Gauffin J. Hammarberg B. *Vocal Fold Physiology: Acoustic, Perceptual, and Physiological Aspects of Voice Mechanisms.* San Diego, Calif: Singular Publishing Group, Inc; 1991.
6. Hirano M, Kirchner JA, Bless DM. *Neurolaryngology: Recent Advances.* San Diego, Calif: Singular Publishing Group, 1991.
7. Kirchner JA. *Vocal Fold Histopathology.* San Diego, Calif: College Hill Press; 1986.
8. Stevens KN, Hirano M. *Vocal Fold Physiology.* Tokyo: Tokyo University Press; 1981.
9. Sundberg J. *The Science of Musical Sounds.* New York, NY: Academic Press; 1991.
10. Titze IR. Vocal *Fold Physiology: Frontiers in Basic Science.* San Diego, Calif: Singular Publishng Group, Inc; 1993.
11. Titze IR, Scherer RC. *Vocal Fold Physiology: Biomechanics, Acoustics and Phonatory Control.* Denver, Colo: Denver Center for the Performing Arts; 1983.

Glossary

This glossary has been developed from the author's experience and also from a review of glossaries developed by Johan Sundberg (personal communication, June 1995), Ingo Titze (*Principles of Voice Production*, Englewood, NJ: Prentice-Hall, 1994:330–338), and other sources. It is difficult to credit appropriately contributions to glossaries or dictionaries of general terms, as each new glossary builds on prior works. The author is indebted to colleagues whose previous efforts have contributed to the compilation of this glossary.

AAO–HNS: American Academy of Otolaryngology-Head and Neck Surgery

AIDS: Acquired Immune Deficiency Syndrome

abduct: To move apart, separate

abduction quotient: The ratio of the glottal half-width at the vocal processes to the amplitude of vibration of the vocal fold

abscess: Collection of pus

absolute jitter (Jita): A discrete measure of very short term (cycle-to-cycle) variation of the pitch periods expressed in microseconds. This parameter is dependent on the fundamental frequency of the voicing sample. Therefore, normative data differs significantly for men and women. Higher pitch results in lower Jita

absolute voice rest: Total silence of the phonatory system

acceleration: The rate of change of velocity with respect to time (measured in millimeters per square second mm/s^2)

acoustic power: The physical measure of the amount of energy produced and radiated into the air per second (measured in watts)

acoustical zero decibels: 0.0002 microbar

actin: A protein molecule that reacts with myosin to form actinomysin, the contractile part of a myofilament in muscle

acting-voice trainer: (1) *See* **Voice Coach**; (2) A professional with specialized training who may work with injured voices as part of a medical voice team in an effort to optimize speaking voice performance

Adam's apple: Prominence of the thyroid cartilage, primarily in males

adduct: To bring together, approximate

affricate: Combination of plosive and fricative consonants such as /dʒ/

allergy: Bodily response to foreign substances or organisms

alto: (*See* **Contralto**)

alveolar ridge: The bony ridge of the gum into which the teeth insert

AMA: American Medical Association

amplitude: Maximum excursion of an undulating signal from the equilibrium; the amplitude of a sound wave is related to the perceived loudness; mostly it is expressed as a logarithmic, comparative level measure using the decibel (dB) unit

amplitude perturbation quotient (APQ): A relative evaluation of short term (cycle-to-cycle) variation of peak-to-peak amplitude expressed in percent. This measure uses a smoothing factor of 11 periods

amplitude spectrum: A display of relative amplitude versus frequency of the sinusoidal components of a waveform

amplitude to length ratio: The ratio of vibrational amplitude at the center of the vocal fold to the length of the vocal fold

amplitude tremor: Regular (periodic) long-term amplitude variation (an element of vibrato)

amplitude tremor frequency (Fatr): This measure is expressed in Hz and shows the frequency of the most intensive low-frequency amplitude-modulating component in the specified amplitude-tremor analysis range

amplitude tremor intensity index (ATRI): The average ratio of the amplitude of the most intensive low-frequency amplitude modulating component (amplitude tremor) to the total amplitude of the analyzed sample. The algorithm for tremor analysis determines the strongest periodic amplitude modulation of the voice. This measure is expressed in percent

anabolic steroids: Primarily male hormones, increase muscle mass and may cause irreversible, masculinization of the voice. Anabolic steroids help cells convert simple substances into more complex substances, especially into living matter

anisotropic: Property of a material that produces different strains when identical stresses are applied in different directions

antagonist (muscle): An opposing muscle

anterior: Toward the front

anterior commissure: The junction of the vocal folds in the front of the larynx

antibiotic: Drug used to combat infection (bodily invasion by a living organism such as a bacteria or virus). Most antibiotics have action specifically against bacteria

anticoagulant: Blood thinner; agent that impairs blood clotting

antinodes: The "peaks" in a standing wave pattern

antihistamine: Drug to combat allergic response

aperiodic: Irregular behavior that has no definite period; is usually either chaotic or random

aperiodicity: The absence of periodicity; no portion of the waveform repeats exactly

aphonia: The absence of vocal fold vibration; this term is commonly used to describe people who have "lost their voice" after vocal fold injury. In most cases, such patients have very poor vibration, rather than no vibration; and they typically have a harsh, nearly whispered voice

appendix of the ventricle of Morgagni: A cecal pouch of mucous membrane connected by a narrow opening with the anterior aspect of the ventricle. It sits between the ventricular fold in the inner surface of the thyroid cartilage. In some cases, it may extend as far as the cranial border of the thyroid cartilage, or higher. It contains the openings of 60 to 70 mucous glands, and it is enclosed in a fibrous capsule, which is continuous with the ventricular ligament. Also called *appendix ventriculi laryngis*, and *laryngeal saccule*

aria: Song, especially in the context of an opera

arthritis: Inflammation of joints in the body

articulation: Shaping of vocal tract by positioning of its mobile walls such as lips, lower jaw, tongue body and tip, velum, epiglottis, pharyngeal sidewalls, and larynx

articulators: The structures of the vocal tract that are used to create the sounds of language. They include the lips, teeth, tongue, soft palate, and hard palate

arytenoid cartilages: Paired, ladle-shaped cartilages to which the vocal folds are attached

arytenoid dislocation: A condition frequently causing vocal fold immobility or hypomobility due to separation of the arytenoid cartilage from its joint and normal position atop the cricoid cartilage

ASHA: American Speech-Language-Hearing Association

aspirate: Speech sound characterized by breathiness

aspirate attack: Initiation of phonation preceded by air, producing /h/

aspiration: (1) In speech, the sound made by turbulent airflow preceding or following vocal fold vibration, as in /hɑ/. (2) In medicine, refers to breathing into the lungs substances that do not belong there such as food, water, or stomach contents following reflux. Aspiration may lead to infections such as pneumonia, commonly referred to as *aspiration pneumonia*

asthma: Obstructive pulmonary (lung) disease associated with bronchospasm, and difficulty expiring air

atmospheric pressure: The absolute pressure exerted by the atmosphere, usually measured in millimeters of mercury (mmHg)

atresia: Failure of development. In the case of the larynx, this may result in fusion or congenital webbing of the vocal folds, or failure of development of the trachea

atrophy: Loss or wasting of tissue. Muscle atrophy occurs, for example, in an arm that is immobilized in a cast for many weeks

attractor: A geometric figure in state space to which all trajectories in its vicinity are drawn. The four types of attractors are (1) *point,* (2) *limit cycle,* (3) *toroidal,* and (4) *strange.* A point trajector draws all trajectories to a single point. An example is a pendulum moving toward rest. A limit cycle is characteristic of periodic motion. A toroidal attractor represents quasiperiodic motion (often considered a subset of periodic motion). A strange attractor is associated with chaotic motion

back vowel: A vowel produced by pulling the tongue posteriorly, with relation to its neutral position

bands: Range of adjacent parameter values; a frequency band is an ensemble of adjacent frequencies

band pass filter: Filter that allows frequencies only within a certain frequency range to pass

baritone: The most common male vocal range. Higher than bass and lower than tenor. Singer's formant around 2600 Hz

basement membrane: Anatomic structure immediately beneath the epithelium

bass: (*See* **Basso**)

bass baritone: In between bass and baritone. Not as heavy as basso profundo, but typically with greater flexibility. Must be able to sing at least as high as F_4. Also known as *basso cantante* and *basso guisto.* Baritones with bass quality are also called *basse taille*

basso: Lowest male voice. Singer's formant around 2300–2400 Hz

basso profundo: Deep bass. The lowest and heaviest of the bass voices. Can sing at least as low as D_2 with full voice. Singer's formant around 2200–2300 Hz. Also known as *contra-basso*

bel canto: Literally means "beautiful singing." Refers to a method and philosophical approach to singing voice production

benchmark: The standard by which other similar occurrences are judged

benign tumors: Tumors that are not able to metastasize or spread to distant sites

Bernoulli's principle: If the energy in a confined fluid stream is constant, an increase in particle velocity must be accompanied by a decrease in pressure against the wall

bifurcation: A sudden qualitative change in the behavior of a system. In chaos, for example, a small change in the initial parameters of a stable (predominantly linear) system may cause oscillation between two different states as the nonlinear aspects of the system become manifest. This transition is a bifurcation

bilabial covering: Using the lips to constrict the mouth opening and "cover" the sound. This technique is used commonly by young singers in the form of slight vowel distortion to attenuate upper harmonics and make a sound richer and less brash.

bilateral: On both sides

bilateral vocal fold paralysis: Loss of the ability to move both vocal folds caused by neurologic dysfunction

biomechanics: The study of the mechanics of biological tissue

bleat: Fast vibrato, like the bleating of a sheep

body: With regard to the vocal fold, the vocalis muscle

Boyle's law: In a soft-walled enclosure and at a constant temperature, pressure and volume are inversely related

bravura: Brilliant, elaborate, showy execution of musical or dramatic material

break: (*See* **Passagio**)

breathy phonation: Phonation characterized by a lack of vocal fold closure; this causes air leakage (excessive airflow) during the quasi-closed phase, and this produces turbulence that is heard as noise mixed in the voice

bronchitis: Inflammation of the bronchial tubes in the lungs

bronchospasm: Forceful closing of the distal airways in the lungs

bruxism: Grinding of the teeth

bulimia: Self-induced vomiting to control weight

butterfly effect: Refers to the notion that in chaotic (nonlinear dynamics) systems a minuscule change in initial condition may have profound effects on the behavior of the system. For example, a butterfly flapping its wings in Hong Kong may change the weather in New York

cancer: An abnormality in which cells no longer respond to the signals that control replication and growth. This results in uncontrolled growth and tumor formation, and may result in spread of tumor to distant locations (metastasis)

carrier: (1) In physics, a waveform (typically a sinusoid) whose frequency or amplitude is modulated by a signal. (2) In medicine, a person who is colonized by an organism (typically bacteria such as streptococcus or pneumococcus), but who has no symptoms or adverse effects from the presence of the organism.

Nevertheless, that carrier is able to transmit the organism to other people in whom it does cause a symptomatic infection

cartilage: One of the tissues of the skeleton; it is more flexible than bone

cartilage of Wrisberg: Cartilage attached in the mobile portion of each aryepiglottic fold

cartilage of Santorini: Small cartilage flexibly attached near the apex of the arytenoid, in the region of the opening of the esophagus

castrato: Male singer castrated at around age 7 or 8, so as to retain alto or soprano vocal range

category: Voice type classified according to pitch range and voice quality; the most frequently used categories are bass, baritone, tenor, alto, mezzosoprano, and soprano, but many other subdivisions of these exist

caudal: Toward the tail

central vowel: A vowel produced with the tongue at or near neutral position

chaos: A qualitative description of a dynamic system that seems unpredictable, but actually has a "hidden" order. Also a mathematical field that studies fractal geometry and nonlinear dynamics

chaotic behavior: Distinct from random or periodic behavior. A chaotic system *looks* disorganized or random but is actually deterministic, although aperiodic. It has sensitive dependence on initial condition, has definite form, and is bounded to a relatively narrow range (unable to go off into infinity)

chest voice: Heavy registration with excessive resonance in the lower formants

coarticulation: A condition in which one phoneme influences the production of phonemes before and after it, resulting commonly in degradation of the quality and clarity of the surrounding sounds

cochlea: Inner ear organ of hearing

coefficient of amplitude variation (vAm): This measure, expressed in percent, computes the relative standard deviation of the peak-to-peak amplitude. It increases regardless of the type of amplitude variation

coefficient of fundamental frequency variation (vF$_0$): This measure, expressed in percent, computes the relative standard deviation of the fundamental frequency. It is the ratio of the standard deviation of the period-to-period variation to the average fundamental frequency

collagen: The protein substance of the white (collagenous) fibers of cartilage, bone, tendon, skin, and all of the connective tissues. Collagen may be extracted, processed, and injected into the vocal fold to treat various abnormalities

collagenase: An enzyme that catalyzes the degradation of collagen

coloratura: In common usage, refers to the highest of the female voices, with range well above C$_6$. May use more whistle tone than other female voices. In fact, coloratura actually refers to a style of florid, agile, complex singing that may apply to any voice classification. For example, the bass runs in Händel's *Messiah* require coloratura technique

complex periodic vibration: A sound that repeats regularly. A pattern of simultaneously sounding partials

complex sound: A combination of sinusoidal waveforms superimposed upon each other. May be complex periodic sound (such as musical instruments) or complex aperiodic sound (such as random street noise)

complex tone: Tone composed of a series of simultaneously sounding partials

component frequency: mathematically, a sinusoid; perceptually, a pure tone. Also called a *partial*

compression: A deformation of a body that decreases its entire volume. An increase in density

concert pitch: Also known as *international concert pitch*. The standard of tuning A$_4$. Reference pitch has changed substantially over the last 200 to 300 years

condensation: An increase in density

constructive interference: The interference of two or more waves such that enhancement occurs

contact ulcer: A lesion with mucosal disruption most commonly on the vocal processes or medial surfaces of the arytenoids. Caused most commonly by gastroesophageal reflux laryngitis and/or muscular tension dysphonia

contrabasso: (*See* **Basso profundo**)

contraction: A decrease in length

contralto: Lowest of the female voices. Able to sing F$_3$ below middle C, as well as the entire treble staff. Singer's formant at around 2800–2900 Hz

conus elasticus: Fibroelastic membrane extending inferiorly from the vocal folds to the anterior superior border of the cricoid cartilage. Also called the *cricovocal ligament*. Composed primarily of yellow elastic tissue. Anteriorly, it attaches to the minor aspect of the thyroid cartilage. Posteriorly, it attaches to the vocal process of the arytenoids

convergent: With regard to glottal shape, the glottis narrows from bottom to top

corner vowels: (ɑ), (i), and (u); vowels at the corners of a vowel triangle; they necessitate extreme placements of the tongue

corticosteroid: Potent substances produced by the adrenal cortex (excluding sex hormones of adrenal origin) in response to the release of adrenocorticotropic hormone from the pituitary gland, or related substances. Glucocorticoids influence carbohydrate, fat, and protein metabolism. Mineralocorticoids help regular electrolyte and water balance. Some corticosteroids have both effects to varying degrees. Corticosteroids may also be given as medications for various effects, including anti-inflammatory, antineoplastic, immune suppressive, and ACTH secretion suppressive effects, as well as for hormone replacement therapy

countertenor: Male voice that is primarily falsetto, singing in the contralto range. Most countertenors are also able to sing in the baritone or tenor range. Countertenors are also known as *contraltino* or *contratenor*

cover: (1) In medicine, with regard to the vocal fold, the epithelium and superficial layer of lamina propria. (2) In music, an alteration in technique that changes the resonance characteristics of a sung sound, generally darkening the sound

cranial nerves: Twelve paired nerves responsible for smell, taste, eye movement, vision, facial sensation, chewing muscles, facial motion, salivary gland and lacrimal (tear) gland secretions, hearing, balance, pharyngeal and laryngeal sensation, vocal fold motion, gastric acid secretion, shoulder motion, tongue motion, and related functions

creaky voice: The perceptual result of subharmonic or chaotic patterns in the glottal waveform. According to IR Titze, if a subharmonic is below about 70 Hz, creaky voice may be perceived as pulse register (vocal fry)

crescendo: To get gradually louder

cricoid cartilage: A solid ring of cartilage located below and behind the thyroid cartilage

cricothyroid muscle: An intrinsic laryngeal muscle that is used primarily to control pitch (paired)

crossover frequency: The fundamental frequency for which there is an equal probability for perception of two adjacent registers

cycle: One complete set of regularly recurring events

cysts: Fluid-filled lesions

damp: To diminish, or attenuate an oscillation

damped oscillation: Oscillation in which energy is lost during each cycle until oscillation stops

decibel: One tenth of a bel. The decibel is a unit of comparison between a reference and another point. It has no absolute value. Although decibels are used to measure sound, they are also used (with different references) to measure heat, light, and other physical phenomena. For sound pressure, the reference is 0.0002 microbar (millionths of one barometric pressure). In the past, this has also been referred to as 0.0002 $dyne/cm^2$, and by other terms

decrescendo: (*See* **Diminuendo**)

deformation: The result of stress applied to any surface of a deformable continuous medium. Elongation, compression, contraction, and shear are examples

dehydration: Fluid deprivation. This may alter the amount and viscosity of vocal fold lubrication and the properties of the vocal fold tissues themselves

destructive interference: The interference of two or more waves such that full or partial cancellation occurs

dialect: A variety of a spoken language, usually associated with a distinct geographical, social, or political environment

diaphragm: A large, dome-shaped muscle at the bottom of the rib cage that separates the lungs from the viscera. It is the primary muscle of inspiration and may be co-activated during singing

diminuendo: To get gradually softer

diphthong: Two consecutive vowels occurring in the same syllable

displacement: The distance between two points in space, including the direction from one point to the other

displacement flow: Air in the glottis that is squeezed out when the vocal folds come together

diuretic: A drug to decrease circulating body fluid generally by excretion through the kidneys

divergent: With regard to the vocal folds, the glottis widens from bottom to top

dizziness: A feeling of imbalance

dorsal: Toward the back

down-regulation: Decreased gene expression, compared with baseline

dramatic soprano: Soprano with powerful, rich voice suitable for dramatic, heavily orchestrated, operatic roles. Sings at least to C_6

dramatic tenor: Tenor with heavy voice, often with a suggestion of baritone quality. Suitable for dramatic roles that are heavily orchestrated. Also referred to as *tenora robusto*, and *helden tenor*. The term helden tenor (literally "heroic" tenor) is used typically for tenors who sing Wagnerian operatic roles

dynamics: (1) In physics, a branch of mechanics that deals with the study of forces that accelerate object(s). (2) In music, it refers to changes in the loudness of musical performance

dysmenorrhea: Painful menstrual cramps

dyspepsia: Epigastric discomfort, especially following meals; impairment of the power or function of digestion

dysphonia: Abnormal voicing

dysphonia plica ventricularis: Phonation using false vocal fold vibration rather than true vocal fold vibration. Most commonly associated with severe muscular tension dysphonia Occasionally may be an appropriate compensation for profound true vocal fold dysfunction

dystonia: A neurological disorder characterized by involuntary movements, such as unpredictable, spasmodic opening or closing of the vocal folds

edema: Excessive accumulation of fluid in tissues, or "swelling"

elastic recoil pressure: The alveolar pressure derived from extended (strained) tissue in the lungs, rib cage, and the entire thorax after inspiration (measured in Pascals)

electroglottograph (EGG): Recording of electrical conductance of vocal fold contact area versus time; EGG waveforms have been frequently used for the purpose of plotting voice source analysis

electromyograph (EMG): Recording of the electric potentials in a muscle, which are generated by the neural system and which control its degree of contraction; if rectified and smoothed the EMG is closely related to the muscular force exerted by the muscle

elongation: An increase in length

embouchure: The shape of the lips, tongue, and related structures adopted while producing a musical tone, particularly while playing a wind instrument

endocrine: Relating to hormones and the organs that produce them

endometriosis: A disorder in which endometrial tissue is present in abnormal locations. Typically causes excessively painful menstrual periods (dysmenorrhea) and infertility

epiglottis: Cartilage that covers over the larynx during swallowing

epilarynx: A region bordered by the rim of the epiglottis and the glottis synonymous with epiglottal tube. This resonating region is considered by some to be the site of origin of the singer's formant

epithelium: The covering, or most superficial layer, of body surfaces

erythema: Redness

esophagus: Tube leading from the bottom of the pharynx to the stomach; swallowed food is transported through this structure

expansion: A deformation of a body such that the entire volume increases

extrinsic muscles of the larynx: The strap muscles in the neck, responsible for adjusting laryngeal height and for stabilizing the larynx

Fach (German): Literally, job specialty. It is used to indicate voice classification. For example, lyric soprano and dramatic soprano are different Fachs

false vocal folds: Folds of tissue located slightly higher than and parallel to the vocal folds in the larynx

falsetto: High, light register, applied primarily to men's voices singing in the soprano or alto range. Can also be applied to women's voices

fibroblasts: Cells responsible in part for the formation of scar in response to tissue injury

fibrosis: Generally refers to a component of scar caused by cross-linking of fibers during a reactive or a reparative process

flat singing: Usually refers to pitch (frequency) lower than the desirable target frequency. Sometimes also used to refer to a singing style devoid of excitement or emotional expression

flow: The volume of fluid passing through a given cross-section of a tube or duct per second; also called volume velocity (measured in liters per second)

flow glottogram: Recording of the transglottal airflow versus time, ie, of the sound of the voice source. Generally obtained from inverse filtering, FLOGG is the acoustical representation of the voice source

flow phonation: The optimal balance between vocal fold adductory forces and subglottic pressure, producing efficient sound production at the level of the vocal folds

flow resistance: The ratio of pressure to flow

fluid: A substance that is either a liquid or a gas

fluid mechanics: The study of motion or deformation of liquids and gases

flutter: Modulation in the 10–12 Hz range

F_0: Fundamental frequency

F_0–tremor frequency (Fftr): This measure is expressed in Hz and shows the frequency of the most intensive low-frequency F_0 modulating component in the specified F_0 tremor analysis range

F_0–tremor intensity index (FTRI): The average ratio of the frequency magnitude of the most intensive low-frequency modulating component (F_0 tremor) to the total frequency magnitude of the analyzed sample. The algorithm for tremor analysis determines the strongest periodic frequency modulation of the voice. This measure is expressed in percent

focal: Limited to a specific area. For example, spasmodic dysphonia may be focal (limited to the larynx), or part of a group of dystonias that affect other parts of the body such as the facial muscles or muscles involved in chewing

force: A push or pull; the physical quantity imparted to an object to change its momentum

forced oscillation: Oscillation imposed on a system by an external source

formant: Vocal tract resonance; the formant frequencies are tuned by the vocal tract shape and determine much of the vocal quality

formant tuning: A boosting of vocal intensity when F_0 or one if its harmonics coincides exactly with a formant frequency

front vowel: A vowel formed by displacing the tongue anteriorly, with regard to its neutral position

functional residual capacity (FRC): Lung volume at which the elastic inspiratory forces equal the elastic expiratory forces; in spontaneous quiet breathing exhalation stops at FRC

fractal: A geometric figure in which an identical pattern or motif repeats itself over and over on an ever-diminishing scale. Self-similarity is an essential characteristic

fractal dimension: Fractal dimensions are measures of fractal objects that can be used to determine how alike or different the objects are. Box counting algorithms and mass-radius measurement are two common approaches to determining fractal dimension. The fractal dimension represents the way a set of points fills a given area of space. It may be defined as

the slope of the function relating the number of points contained in a given radius (or its magnification) to the radius itself. For example, an object can be assessed under many magnifications. The coast of Britain can be measured, for example, with a meter stick or a millimeter stick, but the latter will yield a larger measure. As magnification is increased (smaller measuring sticks), a point will be reached at which small changes in magnification no longer significantly affect length. That is, a plot of coastline length versus magnification reaches a plateau. That plateau corresponds to fractal dimension. The more irregular the figure (eg, coastline), the more complex and the more space it occupies, hence, the higher its fractal dimension. A perfect line has a fractal dimension of 1. A figure that fills a plane has a fractal dimension of 2. Fractal dimension cannot be used alone to determine the presence or absence of chaotic behavior

frequency analysis: Same as spectrum analysis

frequency tremor: A periodic (regular) pitch modulation of the voice (an element of vibrato)

fricative: A speech sound, generally a consonant, produced by a constriction of the vocal tract, particularly by directing the airstream against a hard surface, producing noisy air turbulence. Examples include *s* produced with the teeth, *s* produced with the lower lip and upper incisors, and *th* produced with the tongue tip and upper incisors

frontal (or coronal) plane: An anatomic plane that divides the body into anterior and posterior portions; across the crown of the head

functional voice disorder: An abnormality in voice sound and function in the absence of an anatomic or physiologic organic abnormality

fundamental: Lowest partial of a spectrum, the frequency of which normally corresponds to the pitch perceived.

fundamental frequency (F_0): The lowest frequency in a periodic waveform; also called the first harmonic frequency

gas: A substance that preserves neither shape nor volume when acted upon by forces, but adapts readily to the size and shape of its container

gastric: Pertaining to the stomach

gastric juice: The contents of the stomach, ordinarily including a high concentration of hydrochloric acid.

gastroesophageal reflux (GER): The passage of gastric juice in a retrograde fashion from the stomach into the esophagus. These fluids may reach the level of the larynx or oral cavity, and may be aspirated into the lungs

gastroesophageal reflux disease (GERD): A disorder including symptoms and/or signs caused by reflux of gastric juice into the esophagus and elsewhere. Heartburn is one of the most common symptoms of GERD. (*See* also **Laryngopharyngeal reflux**)

genomics: The study of genes (genetic material) made up of DNA, and located in the chromosomes of the nuclei of cells in an organism.

glide: A written consonant that is produced as a vowel sound in transition to the following vowel. Examples include: /j/ and /w/

glissando: A "slide" including all possible pitches between the initial and final pitch sounded. Similar to portamento and slur

globus: Sensation of a lump in the throat

glottal: At the level of the vocal folds

glottal chink: Opening in the glottis during vocal fold adduction, most commonly posteriorly. It may be a normal variant in some cases

glottal resistance: Ratio between transglottal airflow and subglottal pressure; mainly reflects the degree of glottal adduction

glottal stop (or click): A transient sound caused by the sudden onset or offset of phonation

glottal stroke: A brief event in which air pressure is increased behind the occluded glottis and then released, more gently than following a glottal stop. Glottal strokes are used to separate phonemes in linguistic situations in which running them together might result in misunderstanding of the meaning

glottis: Space between the vocal folds. (*See* also **Rima glottitis**)

glottis respiratoria: The portion of the glottis posteriorly in the region of the cartilaginous portions of the vocal folds

glottis vocalis: The portion of the glottis in the region of the membranous portions of the vocal folds

grace days: Refers to a former contractual arrangement, especially in European Opera Houses, in which women were permitted to refrain from singing during the premenstrual and early menstrual portions of their cycles, at their discretion

granuloma: A raised lesion generally covered with mucosa, most commonly in the region of the vocal

process or medial surface of the arytenoid. Often caused by reflux and/or muscle tension dysphonia

halitosis: Bad breath

harmonic: A frequency that is an integer multiple of a given fundamental. Harmonics of a fundamental are equally spaced in frequency. Partial in a spectrum in which the frequency of each partial equals n times the fundamental frequency, n being the number of the harmonic

harsh glottal attack: Initiating phonation of a word or sound with a glottal plosive

head voice: A vocal quality characterized by flexibility and lightness of tone. In some classifications, it is used to designate a high register of the singing voice

hemorrhage: Rupture of a blood vessel. This may occur in a vocal fold

hertz: Cycles per second (Hz) (named after Gustav Hertz)

high pass filter: Filter which only allows frequencies above a certain cutoff frequency to pass; the cutoff is generally not abrupt but, rather, gentle and is given in terms of a roll-off value, eg, 24 dB/octave

histogram: Graph showing the occurrence of a parameter value; thus, a fundamental frequency histogram shows the occurrence of different fundamental frequency values, eg, in fluent speech or in a song

Hooke's law: Stress in proportion to strain; or, in simpler form, force is proportional to elongation

hormones: Substances produced within the body that affect or control various organs and bodily functions

hyoid bone: A horseshoe-shaped bone known as the "tongue bone." It is attached to muscles of the tongue and related structures, and to the larynx and related structures

hyperfunction: Excessive muscle effort for example, pressed voice, muscle tension dysphonia

hypernasal: Excessive nasal resonance

hypofunction: Low muscular effort, for example, soft breathy voice

hyponasal: Deficient nasal resonance

hypothyroidism: Lower than normal output of thyroid hormone. This condition is referred to commonly as an "underactive thyroid," and often results in malaise, weight gain, temperature intolerance, irregular menses, muffling of the voice, and other symptoms

Hz: (*See* **Hertz**)

impotence: The inability to accomplish penile erection

in vitro: Outside the living body, for example, an excised larynx

in vivo: In the living body

incompressibility: Property of a substance that conserves volume in a deformation

inertia: Sluggishness; a property of resisting a change in momentum

inferior: Below

infertility: The inability to accomplish pregnancy

infraglottic: Below the level of the glottis (space between the vocal folds). This region includes the trachea, thorax, and related structures

infraglottic vocal tract: Below the level of the vocal folds. This region includes the airways and muscles of support (Infraglottic is synonymous with subglottic)

infrahyoid muscle group: A collection of extrinsic muscles including the sternohyoid, sternothyroid, omohyoid, and thyroid muscles

insertion: The point of attachment of a muscle with a bone that can be moved by the muscle

intensity: A measure of power per unit area. With respect to sound, it generally correlates with perceived loudness

interarytenoid muscle: An intrinsic laryngeal muscle that connects the two arytenoid cartilages

intercostal muscles: Muscles between the ribs

interval: The difference between two pitches, expressed in terms of musical scale

intrinsic laryngeal muscles: muscles within the larynx responsible for abduction, adduction, and longitudinal tension of the vocal folds

intrinsic pitch of vowels: Refers to the fact that in normal speech certain vowels tend to be produced with a significantly higher or lower pitch than other vowels

inverse filtering: Method used for recovering the transglottal airflow during phonation; the technique implies that the voice is fed through a computer filter that compensates for the resonance effects of the supraglottic vocal tract, especially the lowest formants

inverse square law: Sound intensity is inversely proportional to the square of the distance from the sound source

IPA: International Phonetic Alphabet (*See* **Appendix I**)

isometric: Constant muscle length during contraction

iteration: In mathematics, the repetitive process of substituting the solution to an equation back into the same equation to obtain the next solution

jitter: Irregularity in the period of time of vocal fold vibrations; cycle-to-cycle variation in fundamental frequency; jitter is often perceived as hoarseness

jitter percent (Jitt): A relative measure of very short term (cycle-to-cycle) variation of the pitch periods expressed in percent. The influence of the average fundamental frequency is significantly reduced. This parameter is very sensitive to pitch variations

juvenile papillomatosis: A disease of children characterized by the clustering of many papillomas (small blisterlike growths) over the vocal folds and elsewhere in the larynx and trachea. Papillomatosis may also occur in adults, in which case the adjective *juvenile* is not used. The disease is caused by human papilloma virus

keratosis: A buildup of keratin (a tough, fibrous protein) on the surface of the vocal folds

kinematics: The study of movement as a consequence of known or assumed forces

kinetic energy: The energy of matter in motion (measured in joules)

klangfarbe: Tone color, referring to vocal quality

labiodental: A consonant produced by bringing the lower lip in contact with the upper front teeth

lag: A difference in time between one point and another

lamina propria: With reference to the larynx, the tissue layers below the epithelium. In adult humans, the lamina propria consists of superficial, intermediate, and deep layers

laminar: Smooth or layered; in fluid mechanics, indicating parallel flow lines

laminar flow: Airflow in smooth layers over a surface (as differentiated from irregular, or turbulent flow)

laryngeal saccule: (*See* **Appendix of the Ventricle of Morgagni**)

laryngeal sinus: (*See* **Ventricle of Morgagni**)

laryngeal ventricle: Cavity formed by the gap between the true and false vocal folds

laryngeal web: An abnormal tissue connection attaching the vocal folds to each other

laryngectomy: Removal of the larynx. It may be total, or it may be a "conservation laryngectomy," in which a portion of the larynx is preserved

laryngitis: Inflammation of laryngeal tissues

laryngitis sicca: Dry voice

laryngocele: A pouch or herniation of the larynx, usually filled with air and sometimes presenting as a neck mass. The pouch usually enlarges with increased laryngeal pressure as may occur from coughing or playing a wind instrument.

laryngologist: Physician specializing in disorders of the larynx and voice, in most countries. In some areas of Europe, the laryngologist is primarily responsible for surgery, while diagnosis is performed by phoniatricians

laryngomalacia: A condition in which the laryngeal cartilages are excessively soft and may collapse in response to inspiratory pressures, obstructing the airway

laryngopharyngeal reflux (LPR): A form of gastroesophageal reflux disease in which gastric juice affects the larynx and adjacent structures. Commonly associated with hoarseness, frequent throat clearing, granulomas, and other laryngeal problems, even in the absence of heartburn

laryngospasm: Sudden, forceful, and abnormal closing of the vocal folds

larynx: The body organ in the neck that includes the vocal folds. The "voice box"

larynx height: Vertical position of the larynx; mostly measured in relation to the rest position

larynx tube: Cavity formed by the vocal folds and the arytenoid, epiglottis, and thyroid cartilages and the structures joining them

laser: An acronym for *light amplification by stimulated emission of radiation*. A surgical tool using light energy to vaporize or cauterize tissue

lateral: Toward the side (away from the center).

lateral cricoarytenoid muscle: Intrinsic laryngeal muscle that adducts the vocal folds through forward rocking and rotation of the arytenoids (paired)

LD50: In determining drug toxicity, the LD50 is the amount of the substance that will cause death in 50% of test specimens (lethal dose for 50%)

lesion: In medicine, a nonspecific term that may be used for nearly any structural abnormality

legato: Smooth, connected

leukoplakia: A white plaque. Typically, this occurs on mucous membranes, including the vocal folds

level: Logarithmic and comparative measure of sound intensity; the unit is normally dB

lied: Song, particularly art song

lift: (*See* **Passagio**)

ligament: Connective tissue between articular regions of bone

linear system: A system in which the relation between input and output varies in a constant, or linear, fashion

lingual: Related to the tongue

linguadental: A consonant produced by bringing the tongue in contact with the teeth

linguapalatal: A consonant produced by bringing the tongue in contact with the hard palate

lip covering: Altering lip shape to make a sound less brash or bright, and "rounder" or more "rich"

liquid: A substance that assumes the shape of its container, but preserves its volume

loft: A suggested term for the highest (loftiest) register; usually referred to as *falsetto voice*

logistic map: A simple quadratic equation that exhibits chaotic behavior under special initial conditions and parameters. It is the simplest chaotic system

Lombard effect: Modification of vocal loudness in response to auditory input. For example, the tendency to speak louder in the presence of background noise

long-term average spectrum (LTAS): Graph showing a long-time average of the sound intensity in various frequency bands; the appearance of an LTAS is strongly dependent on the filters used

longitudinal: Along the length of a structure

longitudinal tension: With reference to the larynx, stretching the vocal folds

loudness: The amount of sound perceived by a listener; a perceptual quantity that can only be assessed with an auditory system. Loudness corresponds to intensity, and to the amplitude of a sound wave

low pass filter: Filter which allows only frequencies below a certain frequency to pass; the cutoff is generally not at all abrupt but gentle and is given in terms of a roll-off value, eg, 24 dB/octave

LTAS: An acronym for long-term-averaged spectrum

lung volume: Volume contained in the subglottic air system; after a maximum inhalation following a maximum exhalation the lung volume equals the vital capacity

lyric soprano: Soprano with flexible, light vocal quality, but one who does not sing as high as a coloratura soprano

lyric tenor: Tenor with a light, high flexible voice

malignant tumor: Tumors that have the potential to metastasize, or spread to different sites. They also have the potential to invade, destroy, and replace adjacent tissues. However, benign tumors may have the capacity for substantial local destruction, as well

Mandelbrot's set: A series of two equations containing real and imaginary components that, when iterated and plotted on a two-dimensional graph, depict a very complex and classic fractal pattern

mandible: Jaw

marcato: Each note accented

marking: Using the voice gently (typically during rehearsals) to avoid injury or fatigue

masque (mask): "Singing in the masque" refers to a frontal tonal placement conceptualized by singers as being associated with vibration of the bones of the face. It is generally regarded as a healthy placement associated with rich resonant characteristics and commonly a strong singer's formant (or "ring")

mechanical equilibrium: The state in which all forces acting on a body cancel each other out, leaving a zero net force in all directions

mechanics: The study of objects in motion and the forces that produce the motion

medial (or mesial): Toward the center (midline or midplane).

melisma: Two or more notes sung on a single syllable

menopause: Cessation of menstrual cycles and menstruation. Associated with physiologic infertility

menstrual cycle: The normal, cyclical variation of hormones in adult females of child-bearing age, and bodily responses caused by those hormonal variations

menstrual period: The first part of the menstrual cycle, associated with endometrial shedding and vaginal bleeding

messa di voce: Traditional exercise in Italian singing tradition consisting of a long prolonged crescendo and diminuendo on a sustained tone

metastasis: Spread of tumor to locations other than the primary tumor site

mezza voce: Literally means "half voice." In practice, means singing softly, but with proper support

mezzo soprano: Literally means "half soprano." This is a common female range, higher than contralto but lower than soprano

middle (or mixed): A mixture of qualities from various voice registers, cultivated in order to allow consistent quality throughout the frequency range

middle C: C_4 on the piano keyboard, with an international concert pitch frequency of 261.6 Hz

millisecond: One thousandth of a second; usually noted ms. or msec

modulation: Periodic variation of a signal property; for example, as vibrato corresponds to a regular variation of fundamental frequency, it can be regarded as a modulation of that signal property

motor: Having to do with motion. For example, motor nerves allow structures to move

motor unit: A group of muscle fibers and the single motor nerve that activates the fibers

mucocele: A benign lesion filled with liquid mucus

mucolytic: A substance that thins mucous secretions

mucosa: The covering of the surfaces of the respiratory tract, including the oral cavity and nasal cavities, as well as the pharynx, larynx, and lower airways. Mucosa also exits elsewhere, such as on the lining of the vagina

mucosal tear: With reference to the vocal folds, disruption of the surface of the vocal fold. Usually caused by trauma

mucosal wave: Undulation along the vocal fold surface traveling in the direction of the airflow

modulation: The systematic change of a cyclic parameter, such as amplitude or frequency

momentum: Mass times velocity; a quantity that determines the potential force that an object can impart to another object by collision

muscle fascicles: Groups of muscle fibers enclosed by a sheath of connective tissue

muscle fibers: A long, thin cell; the basic unit of a muscle that is excited by a nerve ending

muscle tension dysphonia: Also called muscular tension dysphonia. A form of voice abuse characterized by excessive muscular effort, and usually by pressed phonation. A form of voice misuse

mutational dysphonia: A voice disorder. Most typically, it is characterized by persistent falsetto voice after puberty in a male. More generally, it is used to refer to voice with characteristics of the opposite gender

myasthenia gravis: A neuromuscular junction disease associated with fatigue

myoelastic-aerodynamic theory of phonation: The currently accepted mechanism of vocal fold physiology. Compressed air exerts pressure on the undersurface of the closed vocal folds. The pressure overcomes adductory forces, causing the vocal folds to open. The elasticity of the displaced tissues (along with the Bernoulli effect) causes the vocal folds to snap shut, resulting in sound.

myofibril: A subdivision of a muscle fiber; composed of a number of myofilaments

myofilament: A microstructure of periodically arranged actin and myosin molecules; a subdivision of a myofibril

myosin: A protein molecule that reacts with actin to form actinomycin, the contractile part of a myofilament

nasal tract: Air cavity system of the nose

NATS: National Association of Teachers of Singing

natural oscillation: Oscillation without imposed driving forces

neoplasm: Abnormal growth. May be benign or malignant

nervous system: Organs of the body including the brain, spinal cord, and nerves. Responsible for motion, sensation, thought, and control of various other bodily functions

neurotologist: Otolaryngologist specializing in disorders of the ear and ear-brain interface (including the skull base), particularly hearing loss, dizziness, tinnitus, and facial nerve dysfunction

neutral vowel: A vowel produced in the center of the oral cavity.

nodes: The "valleys" in a standing wave pattern

nodules: Benign growths on the surface of the vocal folds. Usually paired and fairly symmetric. They are generally caused by chronic, forceful vocal fold contact (voice abuse)

noise: Unwanted sound

noise-to-harmonic ratio (NHR): A general evaluation of noise percent in the signal and includes jitter, shimmer, and turbulent noise

nonlinear dynamics: (*See also* **Chaos** and **Chaotic Behavior**) The mathematical study of aperiodic, deterministic systems that are not random and cannot be described accurately by linear equations. The study of nonlinear systems whose state changes with time

nonlinear system: Any system in which the output is disproportionate to the input

objective assessment: Demonstrable, reproducible, usually quantifiable evaluation, generally relying on instrumentation or other assessment techniques that do not involve primarily opinion, as opposed to subjective assessment

octave: Interval between two pitches with frequencies in the ratio of 2:1

off-glide: Transition from a vowel of long duration to one of short duration

olfaction: The sense of smell, mediated by the first cranial nerve

on-glide: Transition from a sound of short duration to a vowel of longer duration

onset: The beginning of phonation

open quotient: The ratio of the time the glottis is open to the length of the entire vibratory cycle

oral contraceptive: Birth control pill

organic disorder: A disorder due to structural malfunction, malformation, or injury, as opposed to psychogenic disorders

organic voice disorder: Disorder for which a specific anatomic or physiologic cause can be identified, as opposed to psychogenic or functional voice disorders

origin: The beginning point of a muscle and related soft tissue

oscillation: Repeated movement, back and forth

oscillator: With regard to the larynx, the vibrator that is responsible for the sound source, specifically the vocal folds

ossicle: Middle ear bone

ossify: To become bony

ostium: Opening

otolaryngologist: Ear, nose, and throat physician

otologist: Otolaryngologist specializing in disorders of the ear

overtone: Partial above the fundamental in a spectrum

ovulation: The middle of the menstrual cycle, associated with release of an ovum (egg), and the period of fertility

palatal: Related to the palate (*See* also **Linguapalatal**)

papillomas: Small benign epithelial tumors that may appear randomly or in clusters on the vocal folds, larynx, and trachea and elsewhere in the body. Believed to be caused by various types of human papillomavirus (HPV), some of which are associated with malignancy

parietal pleura: The outermost of two membranes surrounding the lungs

partial: Sinusoid that is part of a complex tone; in voiced sounds, the partials are harmonic implying that the frequency of the *n*th partial equals *n* times the fundamental frequency

particle: A finite mass with zero dimensions, located at a single point in space

pascal (Pa): International standard unit of pressure; one newton (N) per meter squared (m^2)

Pascal's law: Pressure is transmitted rapidly and uniformly throughout an enclosed fluid at rest

pass band: A band of frequencies minimally affected by a filter

passaggio (Italian): The break between vocal registers

period: (1) In physics, the time interval between repeating events; shortest pattern repeated in a regular undulation; a graph showing the period is called a waveform. (2) In medicine, the time during the menstrual cycle associated with bleeding and shedding of the endometrial lining

period doubling: One form of bifurcation in which a system that originally had x period states now has 2x periodic states, with a change having occurred in response to a change in parameter or initial condition

period time: In physics, duration of a period

periodic behavior: Repeating over and over again over a finite time interval. Periodic behavior is governed by an underlying deterministic process

peristalsis: Successive contractions of musculature, which cause a bolus of food to pass through the alimentary tract

perturbation: Small disturbances or changes from expected behavior

pharyngocele: A pouch or herniation of part of the pharynx (throat), commonly fills with air in wind players

pharynx: The region above the larynx, below the velum and posterior to the oral cavity

phase: (1) The manner in which molecules are arranged in a material (gas, liquid, or solid); (2) the angular separation between two events on periodic waveforms

phase plane plot: Representation of a dynamic system in state space

phase space: A space created by two or more independent dynamic variables, such as positions and velocities, utilized to plot the trajectory of a moving object

phase spectrum: A display of the relative phases versus frequency of the components of a waveform

phonation: Sound generation by means of vocal fold vibrations

phoneme: A unit of sound within a specific language

phonetics: The study of speech sounds

phonetogram: Recording of highest and lowest sound pressure level versus fundamental frequency that a voice can produce; phonetograms are often used for describing the status of voice function in patients. Also called *voice range profile*

phoniatrician: A physician specializing in diagnosis and nonsurgical treatment of voice disorders. This specialty does not exist in American medical training, where the phoniatrician's activities are accomplished as a team by the laryngologist (responsible for diagnosis and surgical treatment when needed) and speech-language pathologist (responsible for behavioral voice therapy)

phonosurgery: Originally, surgery designed to alter vocal quality or pitch. Now used commonly to refer to all delicate microsurgical procedures of the vocal folds

phonotrauma: Vocal fold injury caused by vocal fold contact during phonation, associated most commonly with voice abuse or misuse

phrenic nerve: The nerve that controls the diaphragm. Responsible for inspiration. Composed primarily of fibers from the third, fourth, and fifth cervical roots

piriform sinus: Pouch or cavity constituting the lower end of the pharynx located to the side and partially to the back of the larynx. There are two, paired pyriform sinuses in the normal individual

pitch: Perceived tone quality corresponding to its fundamental frequency

pitch matching: Experiment in which subjects are asked to produce the pitch of a reference tone

pitch period perturbation quotient (PPQ): A relative evaluation of short term (cycle-to-cycle) variation of the pitch periods expressed in percent

pleural space: The fluid-filled space between the parietal and visceral pleura

plosive: A consonant produced by creating complete blockage of airflow, followed by the buildup of air pressure, which is then suddenly released, producing a consonant sound

Poincaré section: A graphical technique to reveal a discernable pattern in a phase plane plot that does not have an apparent pattern. There are two kinds of Poincaré sections

polyp: A sessile or pedunculated growth. Usually unilateral and benign, but the term is descriptive and does not imply a histological diagnosis

posterior: Toward the back

posterior cricoarytenoid muscle: An intrinsic laryngeal muscle that is the primary abductor of the vocal folds (paired)

power: The rate of delivery (or expenditure) of energy (measured in watts)

power source: The expiratory system including the muscles of the abdomen, back, thorax, and the lungs. Responsible for producing a vector of force that results in efficient creation and control of subglottal pressure

power spectrum: Two-dimensional graphic analysis of sound with frequency on the x axis and amplitude on the y axis

prechaotic behavior: Predictable behavior prior to the onset of chaotic behavior. One example is period doubling

pressed phonation: Type of phonation characterized by small airflow, high adductory force, and high subglottal pressure. Not an efficient form of voice production. Often associated with voice abuse, and common in patients with lesions such as nodules

pressure: Force per unit area

prevoicing: Phonation that occurs briefly before phonation of a stop consonant

prima donna: Literally means "first lady." Refers to the soprano soloist, especially the lead singer in an opera

primo passaggio: "The first passage"; the first register change perceived in a voice as pitch is raised from low to high

proteomics: The study of proteins

psychogenic: Caused by psychological factors, rather than physical dysfunction. Psychogenic disorders may result in physical dysfunction or structural injury

pulmonary system: The breathing apparatus including the lungs and related airways

pulse register: The extreme low end of the phonatory range. Also know as *vocal fry* and *Strohbass*, characterized by a pattern of short glottal waves alternating with larger and longer ones, and with a long closed phase

pure tone: Sinusoid. The simplest tone. Produced electronically. In nature, even pure-sounding tones like bird songs are complex

pyrotechnics: Special effects involving combustion and explosion, used to produce dramatic visual displays (similar to fireworks), indoors or outdoors

pyrosis: Heartburn

quadrangular membrane: Elastic membrane extending from the sides of the epiglottic cartilage to the corniculate and arytenoid cartilages. Mucosa covered. Forms the aryepiglottic fold and the wall between the piriform sinus and larynx

quasiperiodic: A behavior that has at least two frequencies in which the phases are related by an irrational number

radian: The angular measure obtained when the arc along the circumference of the circle is equal to the radius

radian frequency: The number of radians per second covered in circular or sinusoidal motion

random behavior: Action that never repeats itself and is inherently unpredictable

rarefaction: A decrease in density

recurrent laryngeal nerves: The paired branches of the vagus nerve that supply all of the intrinsic muscles of the larynx except for the cricothyroid muscles. The recurrent laryngeal nerves also carry sensory fibers (feeling) to the mucosa below the level of the vocal folds

reflux: (*See* **Gastroesophageal Reflux** and **Laryngopharyngeal Reflux**)

reflux laryngitis: Inflammation of the larynx due to irritation from gastric juice

refractive eye surgery: Surgery to correct visual acuity

registers: Weakly defined term for vocal qualities; often, register refers to a series of adjacent tones on the scale that sound similar and seem to be generated by the same type of vocal fold vibrations and vocal tract adjustments. Examples of register are vocal fry, modal, and falsetto; but numerous other terms are also used

regulation: The events by which a protein is produced or destroyed, and the balance between these two conditions

Reinke's space: The superficial layer of the lamina propria

relative average perturbation (RAP): A relative evaluation of short-term (cycle-to-cycle) variation of the pitch periods expressed in percent

relative voice rest: Restricted, cautious voice use

resonance: Peak occurring at certain frequencies (resonance frequencies) in the vibration amplitude in a system that possesses compliance, inertia, and reflection; resonance occurs when the input and the reflected energy vibrate in phase; the resonances in the vocal tract are called *formants*

resonator: With regard to the voice, refers primarily to the supraglottic vocal tract, which is responsible for timbre and projection

restoring force: A force that brings an object back to a stable equilibrium position

return map: Similar to phase plane plot, but analyzed data must be digital. This graphic technique represents the relationship between a point and any subsequent point in a time series

rhinorrhea: Nasal discharge; runny nose

rhotic: A vowel sound produced with r-coloring.

rima glottitis: The space between the vocal folds. Also known as the glottis

roll-off: Characteristics of filters specifying their ability to shut off frequencies outside the pass band; for example, if a low pass filter is set to 2 kHz and has a roll-off of 24 dB/octave, it will alternate a 4 kHz tone by 24 dB and a 8 kHz tone by 48 dB

rostral: Toward the mouth (beak)

sagittal: An anatomic plane that divides the body into left and right sides

sarcoplasmic reticulum: Connective tissue enveloping groups of muscle fibers

scalar: A quantity that scales, or adjusts size; a single number

second passaggio: "The second passage"; the second register change perceived in a voice

semicircular canal: Inner ear organ of balance

semi-vowel: A consonant that has vowel-like resonance

sensory: Having to do with the feeling or detection of other nonmotor input. For example, nerves responsible for touch, proprioception (position in space), hearing, and so on

sharp singing: Singing at a pitch (frequency) higher than the desirable target pitch

shimmer: Cycle-to-cycle variability in amplitude

shimmer percent: Is the same as shimmer dB but expressed in percent instead of dB. Both are relative evaluations of the same type of amplitude perturbation but they use different measures for this result: either percent or dB

simple harmonic motion: Sinusoidal motion; the smoothest back and forth motion possible

simple tone: (*See* **Pure Tone**)

singer's formant: A high spectrum peak occurring between about 2.3 and 3.5 kHz in voiced sounds in Western opera and concert singing. This acoustic phenomenon is associated with "ring" in a voice, and with the voices ability to project over background noise such as a choir or an orchestra. A similar phenomenon may be seen in speaking voices, especially in actors. It is known as the *speaker's formant*

singing teacher: Professional who teaches singing technique (as opposed to Voice Coach).

singing voice specialist: A singing teacher with additional training, and specialization in working with injured voices, in conjunction with a medical voice team

sinus of Morgagni: Often confused with ventricle of Morgagni. Actually, the sinus of Morgagni is not in the larynx. It is formed by the superior fibers of the superior pharyngeal constrictor as they curve below the levator veli palatini and the eustachian tube. The space between the upper border of the muscle and the base of the skull is known as the sinus of Morgagni, and is closed by the pharyngeal aponeurosis

sinusitis: Infection of the paranasal sinus cavities

sinusoid: A graph representing the sine or cosine of a constantly increasing angle; in mechanics, the smoothest and simplest back-and-forth movement, characterized by a single frequency, an amplitude, and a phase; tone arising from sinusoidal sound pressure variations

sinusoidal motion: The projection of circular motion (in a plane) at constant speed onto one axis in the plane

skeleton: The bony or cartilaginous framework to which muscle and other soft tissues are attached

smoothed amplitude perturbation quotient (sAPQ): A relative evaluation of long-term variation of the peak-to-peak amplitude within the analyzed voice sample, expressed in percent

smoothed pitch perturbation quotient (sPPQ): A relative evaluation of long-term variation of the pitch period within the analyzed voice sample expressed in percent

soft glottal attack: Gentle glottal approximation, often obtained using an imaginary /h/

soft phonation index (SPI): A measure of the ratio of lower frequency harmonic energy to higher frequency harmonic energy. If the SPI is low, then the spectral analysis will show well-defined higher formants

solid: A substance that maintains its shape, independent of the shape of its container

soprano acuto: High soprano

soprano assoluto: A soprano who is able to sing all soprano roles and classifications

sound level: Logarithmic, comparative measure of the intensity of a signal; the unit is dB

sound pressure level (SPL): Measure of the intensity of a sound, ordinarily in dB relative to 0.0002 microbar (millionths of 1 atmosphere pressure)

sound propagation: The process of imparting a pressure or density disturbance to adjacent parts of a continuous medium, creating new disturbances at points farther away from the initial disturbance

source-filter theory: A theory that assumes the time-varying glottal airflow to be the primary sound source and the vocal tract to be an acoustic filter of the glottal source

source spectrum: Spectrum of the voice source

spasmodic dysphonia: A focal dystonia involving the larynx. May be of adductor, abductor, or mixed type. Adductor spasmodic dysphonia is characterized by strain-strangled interruptions in phonation. Abductor spasmodic dysphonia is characterized by breathy interruptions

speaker's formant: (*See* **Singer's formant**)

special sensory nerves: Nerves responsible for hearing, vision, taste, and smell

spectrogram: Three-dimensional graphic representation of sound with time on the x axis, frequency on the y axis, and amplitude displayed as intensity of color

spectrograph: The equipment that produces a spectrogram

spectrum: Ensemble of simultaneously sounding sinusoidal partials constituting a complex tone; a display of relative magnitudes or phases of the component frequencies of a waveform

spectrum analysis: Analysis of a signal showing its partials

speech-language pathologist: A trained, medically affiliated professional who may be skilled in remediation of problems of the speaking voice, swallowing, articulation, language development, and other conditions

speed: The rate of change of distance with time; the magnitude of velocity

spinto: Literally means *pushed* or *thrust*. Usually applies to tenors or sopranos with lighter voice than dramatic singers, but with aspects of particular dramatic excitement in their vocal quality. Enrico Caruso was an example

spirometer: A device for measuring airflow

stable equilibrium: A unique state to which a system with a restoring force will return after it has been displaced from rest

staccato: Each note accented and separated

standard deviation: The square root of the variance

standing wave: A wave that appears to be standing still; it occurs when waves with the same frequency (and wavelength) moving in opposite directions interfere with each other

state space: In abstract mathematics, the area in which a behavior occurs

stent: A device used for shape, support, and maintenance of patency during healing after surgery or injury

steroid: Steroids are potent substances produced by the body. They may also be consumed as medications. (*See* **Anabolic steroids, Corticosteroids**)

stochastic: Random from a statistical, mathematical point of view

stop band: A band of frequencies rejected by a filter; it is the low region in a filter spectrum

strain: Deformation relative to a rest dimension, including direction (eg, elongation per unit length)

strain rate: The rate of change of strain with respect to time

stress: Force per unit area, including the direction in which the force is applied to the area

striking zone: The middle third of the musculomembranous portion of the vocal fold; the point of maximum contact force during phonatory vocal adduction

stroboscopy: A technique that uses interrupted light to simulate slow motion. (*See* also **Strobovideolaryngoscopy**)

strobovideolaryngoscopy: Evaluation of the vocal folds utilizing simulated slow motion for detailed evaluation of vocal fold motion

Strohbass (German): "Straw bass"; another term for *pulse register* or *vocal fry*

subglottal: Below the glottis

subglottal pressure: Air pressure in the airway immediately below the level of the vocal folds. The unit most commonly used is centimeters of water. That distance in centimeters that a given pressure would raise a column of water in a tube

subglottic: The region immediately below the level of the vocal folds

subharmonic: A frequency obtained by *dividing* a fundamental frequency by an integer greater than 0

subjective assessment: Evaluation that depends on perception and opinion, rather than independently reproducible quantifiable measures, as opposed to objective assessment

sulcus vocalis: A longitudinal groove, usually on the medial surface of the vocal fold

superior: above

superior laryngeal nerves: Paired branches of the vagus nerve that supply the cricothyroid muscle and supply sensation from the level of the vocal folds superiorly

support: Commonly used to refer to the power source of the voice. It includes the mechanism responsible for creating a vector force that results in efficient subglottic pressure. This includes the muscles of the abdomen and back, as well as the thorax and lungs; primarily the expiratory system

supraglottal: Above the glottis, or level of the vocal folds

supraglottic: (1) Above the level of the vocal folds. This region includes the resonance system of the vocal tract, including the pharynx, oral cavity, nose, and related structures. (2) Posterior commissure. A misnomer. Used to describe the posterior aspect of the larynx (interarytenoid area), which is opposite the anterior commissure. However, there is actually no commissure on the posterior aspect of the larynx

suprahyoid muscle group: One of the two extrinsic muscle groups. Includes the stylohyoid muscle, anterior and posterior bellies of the digastric muscle, geniohyoid, hyoglossus, and mylohyoid muscles

temporal gap transition: The transition from a continuous sound to a series of pulses in the perception of vocal registers

temporomandibular joint: The jaw joint; a synovial joint between the mandibular condyle and skull anterior to the ear canal

tenor: Highest of the male voices, except countertenors. Must be able to sing to C_5. Singer's formant is around 2800 Hz

tenore serio: Dramatic tenor

testosterone: The hormone responsible for development of male sexual characteristics, including laryngeal growth

thin voice: A term used by singers to describe vocal weakness associated with lack of harmonic richness. The voice often also has increased breathiness, noise, and weakness and is commonly also described as "thready"

thoracic: Pertaining to the chest

thorax: The part of the body between the neck and abdomen

thready voice: (*See* **Thin voice**)

thyroarytenoid muscle: An intrinsic laryngeal muscle that comprises the bulk of the vocal fold (paired). The medial belly constitutes the body of the vocal fold

thyroid cartilage: The largest laryngeal cartilage. It is open posteriorly and is made up of two plates (thyroid laminae) joined anteriorly at the midline. In males, there is a prominence superiorly known as the "Adam's apple"

tidal volume: The amount of air breathed in and out during respiration (measured in liters)

timbre: The quality of a sound. Associated with complexity, or the number, nature, and interaction of overtones

tonsil: A mass of lymphoid tissue located near the junction of the oral cavity and pharynx (paired)

tonsillitis: Inflammation of the tonsil

tracheal stenosis: Narrowing in the trachea. May be congenital or acquired

tracheoesophageal fistula: A connection between the trachea and esophagus. May be congenital or acquired

trajectory: In chaos, the representation of the behavior of a system in state space over a finite, brief period of time. For example, one cycle on a phase plane plot

transcription: Converting the message in DNA to messenger RNA

transfection: Infection by naked viral nucleic acid

transglottal flow: Air that is forced through the glottis by a transglottal pressure

transition: With regard to the vocal fold, the intermediate and deep layers of lamina propria (vocal ligament)

translation: Using messenger RNA to make proteins

transverse: Refers to an anatomic plane that divides the body across. Also used to refer to a direction perpendicular to a given structure or phenomenon such as a muscle fiber or airflow

tremolo: An aesthetically displeasing, excessively wide vibrato (*See* **Wobble**). The term is also used in music to refer to an ornament used by composers and performers

tremor: A modulation in activity

trill: In early music (Renaissance) where it referred to an ornament that involved repetition of the same note. That ornament is now referred to as a *trillo*

trillo: Originally a trill, but in recent pedagogy a rapid repetition of the same note, which usually includes repeated voice onset and offset

triphthong: Three consecutive vowels that make up the same syllable

tumor: A mass or growth

turbulence: Irregular movement of air, fluid, or other substance, which causes a hissing sound. White water is a typical example of turbulence

turbulent airflow: Irregular airflow containing eddies and rotating patterns

tympanic membrane: Eardrum

unilateral vocal fold paralysis: Immobility of one vocal fold, due to neurological dysfunction

unstable equilibrium: The state in which a disturbance of a mechanical system will cause a drift away from a rest position

unvoiced: A sound made without phonation, and devoid of pitch; voiceless

upregulation: Increased gene expression, compared with baseline

variability: The amount of change, or ability to change

variance: The mean squared difference from the average value in a data set

vector: A quantity made up of two or more independent items of information, always grouped together

velar: Relating to the velum or palate

velocity: The rate of change of displacement with respect to time (measured in meters per second, with the appropriate direction)

velopharyngeal insufficiency: Escape of air, liquid or food from the oropharynx into the nasopharynx or nose at times when the nasopharynx should be closed by approximation of the soft palate and pharyngeal tissues

velum: The area of the soft palate and adjacent nasopharynx.

ventral: Toward the belly

ventricle of Morgagni: Also known as *laryngeal sinus*, and *ventriculus laryngis*. The ventricle is a fusiform pouch bounded by the margin of the vocal folds, the edge of the free crescentic margin of the false vocal fold (ventricular fold), and the mucous membrane between them that forms the pouch. Anteriorly, a narrowing opening leads from the ventricle to the appendix of the ventricle of Morgagni

ventricular folds: The "false vocal folds," situated above the true vocal folds

ventricular ligament: A narrow band of fibrous tissue that extends from the angle of the thyroid cartilage below the epiglottis to the arytenoid cartilage just above the vocal process. It is contained within the false vocal fold. The caudal border of the ventricular ligament forms a free crescentic margin, which constitutes the upper border of the ventricle of Morgagni

ventricular phonation: (*See* **Dysphonia plica ventricularis**)

vertical phase difference: With reference to the vocal folds, refers to the asynchrony between the lower and upper surfaces of the vibratory margin of the vocal fold during phonation

vertigo: Sensation of rotary motion. A form of dizziness

vibrato: In classical singing, vibrato is a periodic modulation of the frequency of phonation. Its regularity increases with training. The rate of vibrato (number of modulations per second) is usually in the range of 5–6 per second. Vibrato rates over 7–8 per second are aesthetically displeasing to most people, and sound "nervous." The extent of vibrato (amount of variation above and below the center frequency) is usually one or two semitones. Vibrato extending less than ±0.5 semitone are rarely seen in singers although they are encountered in wind instrument playing. Vibrato rates greater than two semitones are usually aesthetically unacceptable, and are typical of elderly singers in poor artistic vocal condition, in whom the excessively wide vibrato extent is often combined with excessively slow rate

viscera: The internal organs of the body, particularly the contents of the abdomen

visceral pleura: The innermost of two membranes surrounding the lungs

viscoelastic material: A material that exhibits characteristics of both elastic solids and viscous liquids. The vocal fold is an example

viscosity: Property of a liquid associated with its resistance to deformation. Associated with the "thickness" of a liquid

vital capacity: The maximum volume of air that can be exchanged by the lungs with the outside; it includes the expiratory reserve volume, tidal volume, and inspiratory reserve volume (measured in liters)

vocal cord: Old term for vocal fold

vocal fold (or cord) stripping: A surgical technique, no longer considered acceptable practice under most circumstances, in which the vocal fold is grasped with a forceps, and the surface layers are ripped off

vocal fold stiffness: The ratio of the effective restoring force (in the medial-lateral direction) to the displacement (in the same direction)

vocal folds: A paired system of tissue layers in the larynx that can oscillate to produce sound

vocal fry: A register with perceived temporal gaps; also known as *pulse register* and Strohbass. (*See* **Pulse register**)

vocal ligament: Intermediate and deep layers of the lamina propria. Also forms the superior end of the conus elasticus

vocal tract: Resonator system constituted by the larynx, the pharynx and the mouth cavity

vocalis muscle: The medial belly of the thyroarytenoid muscle

vocalise: A vocal exercise involving sung sounds, commonly vowels on scales of various complexity

voce coperta: "Covered registration"

voce mista: Mixed voice (also voix mixed)

voce di petto: Chest voice

voce sgangherata: "White" voice. Literally means immoderate or unattractive. Lacks strength in the lower partials

voce di testa: Head voice

voce piena: Full voice

voice abuse: Use of the voice in specific activities that are deleterious to vocal health, such as screaming

voice box: (*See* **Larynx**)

voice coach: (1) In singing, a professional who works with singers, teaching repertoire, language pronunciation, and other artistic components of performance (as opposed to a singing teacher, who teaches technique); (2) The term voice coach is also used by acting-voice teachers who specialize in vocal, bodily, and interpretive techniques to enhance dramatic performance

voice misuse: Habitual phonation using phonatory techniques that are not optimal and then result in vocal strain. For example, speaking with inadequate support, excessive neck muscle tension, and suboptimal resonance. Muscular tension dysphonia is a form of voice misuse

voice range profile: (*See* **Phonetogram**)

voice rest: (*See* **Absolute voice rest, relative voice rest**)

voice source: Sound generated by the pulsating transglottal airflow; the sound is generated when the vocal fold vibrations chop the airstream into a pulsating airflow

voice turbulence index (VTI): A measure of the relative energy level of high frequency noise

voiced: A language sound made with phonation, and possessing pitch.

voiceless: (*See* **Unvoiced**)

volume: "Amount of sound," best measured in terms of acoustic power or intensity

vortex theory: Holds that eddys, or areas of organized turbulence, are produced as air flows through the larynx and vocal tract

Vowel color: refers to vowel quality, or timbre, and is associated with harmonic content

Waldeyer's ring: An aggregation of lymphoid tissue in the pharynx, including the tonsils and adenoids

waveform: A plot of any variable (eg, pressure, flow, or displacement) changing as time progresses along the horizontal axis; also known as a time-series

wavefront: The initial disturbance in a propagating wave

wavelength: The linear distance between any point on one vibratory cycle and a corresponding point of the next vibratory cycle

whisper: Sound created by turbulent glottal airflow in the absence of vocal fold vibration

whistle register: The highest of all registers (in pitch). It is observed only in females, extending the pitch range beyond F_6

wobble: Undesirable vibrato, usually with vibrato rate of 2 to 4 Hz, and extent greater than ± 0.5 semitone (*See also* **Tremolo**)

xerostomia: Dry mouth

Young's modulus: The ratio between magnitudes of stress and strain

Appendix I

International Phonetic Alphabet

	English	Italian	Latin	French	German
Vowels					
[i]	meet, key	chi	Filio	qui, cygne	liebe, ihn, wir
[e]	—	—	—	parlé, nez, parler, parlerai	Seele, geben, Weh
[I]	mitt, hit	—	—	—	mit, sitzen
[e²]	chaotic	vero	—	—	Tränen
[ɛ]	bed	bello	requiem	belle, avait, mai, tête seine	Bett, hätte
[ɛ̄]	—	—	—	sein, pain, fin, faim, thym	—
[a]	—	—	—	voilà la salade	—
[ɑ]	father	alma	mala	âme	Vater, Mahler
[ɑ̃]	—	—	—	enfant, champ, Jean, paon	—
[ɔ]	jaw	morte	Domine	sortir, aura	Dorn
[o²]	rowing	nome, dolce	—	—	—
[U]	foot	—	—	—	Mutter
[o]	—	—	—	rose, ôter, pot, beau, faut, écho	Rose, tot, froh
[ö]	—	—	—	fond, ombre	—
[u]	moon	luna	unum	fou	Uhr, Buch, tun
[y]	—	—	—	tu, flûte, eût	früh, Tür
[Y]	—	—	—	—	Glück
[ø]	—	—	—	peu, berceuse	schön
[œ]	—	—	—	cœur, fleur	können
[œ̃]	—	—	—	parfum, défunt	—
[ə]	Rita, oven	—	—	je, faisant, parlent (forward–use lips)	lieben
[ɛ̃]	—	—	—	—	Liebe
[æ]	cat	—	—	—	—
[ɜ]	first	—	—	—	—
[ʌ]	cup	—	—	—	—
Consonants: Fricatives					
[f]	father, physic	fuori	fecit	fou, phare	Vater, Phantasie
[v]	visit	vecchio, Wanda	vestrum	vent, wagon	Weg
[ʃ]	shine (bright)	lascia (Bright)	sciote	charme (dark)	schön, Stadt Spass (dark)
[ʒ]	Asia (bright)	—	—	je, givre (dark)	—
[s]	simple, receive	seno, questo	salutare	soixante, cent, leçon, jasmin	essen, Fenster, Haus

	English	Italian	Latin	French	German
[Z]	roses, zoo	rosa, sdegno	—	rose, azure	Seele, unser, Rose
[θ]	three	—	—	—	—
[ð]	this	vado	—	—	—
[ʕ]	human	—	—	—	ich, recht
[x]	—	—	—	—	Nacht, doch, such
[h]	house, who	—	—	—	Haus, lebhaft

Consonants: Nasals

	English	Italian	Latin	French	German
[m]	mother	mamma	mortuus	maman	Mutter, nahm
[n]	nose	naso	nescio	nez	nein, Nase (dental)
[ɲ]	onion	ognuno	agnus	oignon, agneau	—
[ŋ]	ring, thank	sangue, anche	—	—	Ring, Dank

Consonants: Lateral and trilled

	English	Italian	Latin	French	German
[l]	liquid	largo, alto	alleluia	large, fatal	links, alte, also
[ɫ]	milk	—	—	—	—
[r]	three	rosa, orrore	rex	roucoule	Retter, irre

Consonants: Affricates

	English	Italian	Latin	French	German
[tʃ]	cheer, pitch, cenere	cielo,	cibo, coelo, caeca	—	plätschert
[dʒ]	joy, George	gioia, gemo	pange, regina	—	—
[ts]	cats	zio, senza	gratias, justitia	—	Zimmer, Spitz
[dz]	leads	azzuro, bonzo	azymis	—	—

Consonants: Plosives

	English	Italian	Latin	French	German
[p]	pepper (explosive)	papa (dry)	peccata (dry)	papa, absent (dry)	Paar, lieb (explosive)
[b]	bow	bada	beata	bas	Bett
[t]	tent (sharp, alveolar)	tutto (dry, dental)	terra, catholicam (dry, dental)	tantot (dry, dental Palatalized before [l][y][j][ɥ]) tire, tu tiens, tuer	Tante, Grund, Thau (sharp, alveolar)
[d]	dead (alveolar)	doppio (dental)	Domine (dental)	dindon (dental; palatalized before [i][y][j][ɥ]) dire, dure, Dieu, réduit	decken (alveolar)
[k]	cat, chorus, quick (explosive)	come, ecco, chioma, che, questo (dry)	credo, bracchio (dry) mihi	comment, qui, choeur (dry, except before [i][y][j][ɥ])	Kunst, Qual, chor, Tag (explosive)
[g]	give grande, gonfia	gamba,	gaudebit	gauche, grande	geben, General

Glides, diphthongs, and triphthongs

	English	Italian	Latin	French	German
[j]	yes (no buzz)	ieri (no buzz)	ejus (no buzz)	bien, moyen	Jahr
[w]	west	guarda	qui, linguis	oui	—
[ɥ]	—	—	—	nuit	—
[ʎ]	lute	gl'ochhi	—	—	—
[ɑ:i]	mine, high	mai	Laicus	—	—
[ɑ:I]	mine, high	—	—	—	mein, Hain
[aj]	—	—	—	corail	—
[ɛ:i]	say, mate	sei	mei	—	—

	English	Italian	Latin	French	German
[ɛːl]	say, mate	—	—	—	—
[ɛj]	—	—	—	soleil	—
[œj]	—	—	—	denuil	—
[uj]	—	—	—	fenouil	—
[oːu]	grow	—	—	—	—
[ɔːi]	boy	poi	—	—	—
[ɔːl]	boy	—	—	—	—
[ɔːy]	—	—	—	—	treu, träumen
[ɑːu]	cow	aura	laudamus	—	—
[ɑːU]	cow	—	—	—	Tau
[ɑːo]	—	—	—	—	Tau
[ɛːə]	air	—	—	—	—
[lːə]	ear	—	—	—	—
[ɔːə]	ore	—	—	—	—
[Uːə]	sure	—	—	—	—
[ɑːiə]	fire	—	—	—	—
[ɑːuə]	our	—	—	—	—
[ɔːyə]	—	—	—	—	Feuer

Modified from Moriarty J. *Diction*. Boston, Mass: EC Schirmer; 1975:257–263, with permission.

Appendix IIa

PATIENT HISTORY: SINGERS
Robert Thayer Sataloff, M.D., D.M.A.
1721 Pine Street
Philadelphia, PA 19103

NAME _____ AGE _____ SEX _____ RACE _____

HEIGHT _____ WEIGHT _____ DATE _____

VOICE CATEGORY: _____ soprano _____ mezzo-soprano _____ alto
_____ tenor _____ baritone _____ bass

(If you are not currently having a voice problem, please skip to Question #3.)

PLEASE CHECK OR CIRCLE CORRECT ANSWERS

1. How long have you had your present voice problem?

   Who noticed it?

   [self, family, voice teacher, critics, everyone, other _____]

   Do you know what caused it? Yes _____ No _____

   If yes, what?

   Did it come on slowly or suddenly? Slowly _____ Suddenly _____
   Is it getting: Worse: _____ , Better _____ , Same _____

2. Which symptoms do you have? (Please check all that apply.)
   _____ Hoarseness (coarse or scratchy sound)
   _____ Fatigue (voice tires or changes quality after singing for a short period of time)
   _____ Volume disturbance (trouble singing) softly _____ loudly _____
   _____ Loss of range (high _____ low _____)
   _____ Change in classification (example: voice lowered from soprano to mezzo)
   _____ Prolonged warm-up time (over ½ hr to warm up voice)
   _____ Breathiness
   _____ Tickling or choking sensation while singing
   _____ Pain in throat while singing
   _____ Other: (Please specify)_____
   _____
   _____

3. Do you have an important performance soon? Yes _____ No _____
   Date(s): _____

4. What is the current status of your singing career?
    Professional _____   Amateur _____

5. What are your long-term career goals in singing?
    [ ] Premier operatic career
    [ ] Premier pop music career
    [ ] Active avocation
    [ ] Classical
    [ ] Pop
    [ ] Other (_____)
    [ ] Amateur performance (choral or solo)
    [ ] Amateur singing for own pleasure

6. Have you had voice training?   Yes _____   No _____
    At what age did you begin?

7. Have there been periods of months or years without lessons in that time?   Yes _____   No _____

8. How long have you studied with your present teacher?

    Teacher's name:
    Teacher's address:

    Teacher's telephone number:

9. Please list previous teachers and years during which you studied with them.

10. Have you ever had training for your speaking voice?   Yes _____   No _____
    Acting voice lessons?   Yes _____   No _____
    How many years?
    Speech therapy?   Yes _____   No _____
    How many months?

11. Do you have a job in addition to singing?   Yes _____   No _____

    If yes, does it involve extensive voice use?   Yes _____   No _____

    If yes, what is it? [actor, announcer (television/radio/sports arena), athletic instructor, attorney, clergy, politician, physician, salesperson, stockbroker, teacher, telephone operator or receptionist, waiter, waitress, secretary, other _____

12. In your performance work, in addition to singing, are you frequently
    required to speak?   Yes _____   No _____
    dance?   Yes _____   No _____

13. How many years did you sing actively before beginning voice lessons initially?

14. What types of music do you sing? (Check all that apply.)
    _____ Classical   _____ Show
    _____ Nightclub   _____ Rock
    _____ Other: (Please specify.) _____
    _____

15. Do you regularly sing in a sitting position (such as from behind a piano or drum set)?
    Yes _____   No _____

16. Do you sing outdoors or in large halls, or with orchestras? (Circle which one.)   Yes _____   No _____

17. If you perform with electrical instruments or outdoors, do you use monitor speakers? (Circle which one).
    Yes _____   No _____

    If yes, can you hear them?   Yes _____   No _____

18. Do you play a musical instrument(s)?   Yes _____   No _____
    If yes, please check all that apply:
    _____ Keyboard (piano, organ, harpsichord, other _____)
    _____ Violin, viola
    _____ Cello
    _____ Bass
    _____ Plucked strings (guitar, harp, other _____)
    _____ Brass
    _____ Wind with single reed
    _____ Wind with double reed
    _____ Flute, piccolo
    _____ Percussion
    _____ Bagpipe
    _____ Accordion
    _____ Other: (Please specify)._____   _____

19. How often do you practice?
    Scales: [daily, few times weekly, once a week, rarely, never]

    If you practice scales, do you do them all at once, or do you divide them up over the course of a day?
    [all at once, two or three sittings]

    On days when you do scales, how long do you practice them?
    [15 ,30,45,60,75 ,90,105,120, more] minutes

    Songs: [daily, few times weekly, once a week, rarely, never]

    How many hours per day?
    [½,1,1½,2,2½,3,more]

Do you warm up your voice before you sing? Yes _____ No _____

Do you cool down your voice when you finish singing? Yes _____ No _____

20. How much are you singing at present (total including practice time) (average hours per day)?

Rehearsal: _____

Performance: _____

21. Please check all that apply to you:

_____ Voice worse in the morning

_____ Voice worse later in the day, after it has been used

_____ Sing performances or rehearsals in the morning

_____ Speak extensively (e.g. , teacher, clergy, attorney, telephone work)

_____ Cheerleader

_____ Speak extensively backstage or at postperformance parties

_____ Choral conductor

_____ Frequently clear your throat

_____ Frequent sore throat

_____ Jaw joint problems

_____ Bitter or acid taste, or bad breath first thing in the morning

_____ Frequent "heartburn" or hiatal hernia

_____ Frequent yelling or loud talking

_____ Frequent whispering

_____ Chronic fatigue (insomnia)

_____ Work around extreme dryness

_____ Frequent exercise (weight lifting, aerobics)

_____ Frequently thirsty, dehydrated

_____ Hoarseness first thing in the morning

_____ Chest cough

_____ Eat late at night

_____ Ever used antacids

_____ Under particular stress at present (personal or professional)

_____ Frequent bad breath

_____ Live, work, or perform around smoke or fumes

_____ Traveled recently: When: _____

Where: _____

Eat any of the following before singing?

_____ Chocolate   _____ Coffee

_____ Alcohol   _____ Milk or ice cream

_____ Nuts   _____ Spiced foods

Other: (Please specify.)

_____ Any specific vocal technical difficulties? [trouble singing soft, trouble singing loud, poor pitch control, support problems, problems at register transitions, other] Describe other:

_____ Any problems with your singing voice recently prior to the onset of the problem that brought you here? [hoarseness, breathiness, fatigue, loss of range, voice breaks, pain singing, other] Describe other:

_____ Any voice problems in the past that required a visit to a physician? If yes, please describe problem(s) and treatment(s): [laryngitis, nodules, polyps, hemorrhage, cancer, other]
Describe other:

22. Your family doctor's name, address, and telephone number

23. Your laryngologist's name, address, and telephone number:

24. Recent cold?   Yes _____   No _____

25. Current cold?   Yes _____   No _____

26. Have you been exposed to any of the following chemicals frequently (or recently) at home or at work? (Check all that apply.)

_____ Carbon monoxide   _____ Arsenic
_____ Mercury   _____ Aniline dyes
_____ Insecticides   _____ Industrial solvents (benzene, etc.)
_____ Lead   _____ Stage smoke

27. Have you been evaluated by an allergist?   Yes _____   No _____

If yes, what allergies do you have:
[none, dust, mold, trees, cats, dogs, foods, other]
(Medication allergies are covered elsewhere in this history form.)
If yes, give name and address of allergist:

28. How many packs of cigarettes do you smoke per day?

Smoking history
_____ Never
_____ Quit. When? _____
_____ Smoked about _____ packs per day for _____ years.
_____ Smoke _____ packs per day. Have smoked for _____ years.

29. Do you work or live in a smoky environment?   Yes _____   No _____

30. How much alcohol do you drink? [none, rarely, a few times per week, daily]
If daily, or few times per week, on the average, how much do you consume? [1,2,3,4,5,6,7,8,9,10, more] glasses per [day, week] of [beer, wine, liquor].

Did you formerly drink more heavily?   Yes _____   No _____

31. How many cups of coffee, tea, cola, or other caffeine-containing drinks do you drink per day?

32. List other recreational drugs you use [marijuana, cocaine, amphetamines, barbiturates, heroin, other]:

33. Have you noticed any of the following? (Check all that apply)

_____ Hypersensitivity to heat or cold

_____ Excessive sweating

_____ Change in weight: gained/lost _____ lb in _____ weeks/ _____ months

_____ Change in skin or hair

_____ Palpitation (fluttering) of the heart

_____ Emotional lability (swings of mood)

_____ Double vision

_____ Numbness of the face or extremities

_____ Tingling around the mouth or face

_____ Blurred vision or blindness

_____ Weakness or paralysis of the face

_____ Clumsiness in arms or legs

_____ Confusion or loss of consciousness

_____ Difficulty with speech

_____ Difficulty with swallowing

_____ Seizure (epileptic fit)

_____ Pain in the neck or shoulder

_____ Shaking or tremors

_____ Memory change

_____ Personality change

For females:

Are you pregnant?	Yes _____	No _____
Are your menstrual periods regular?	Yes _____	No _____
Have you undergone hysterectomy?	Yes _____	No _____
Were your ovaries removed?	Yes _____	No _____
At what age did you reach puberty?	_____	
Have you gone through menopause?	Yes _____	No _____
If yes, when?		

34. Have you ever consulted a psychologist or psychiatrist?   Yes _____   No _____

Are you currently under treatment?   Yes _____   No _____

35. Have you injured your head or neck (whiplash, etc.)?   Yes _____   No _____

36. Describe any serious accidents related to this visit.

None _____

37. Are you involved in legal action involving problems with your voice?   Yes _____   No _____

38. List names of spouse and children:

39. Brief summary of ear, nose, and throat (ENT) problems, some of which may not be related to your present complaint.

PLEASE CHECK ALL THAT APPLY

_____ Hearing loss   _____ Ear pain
_____ Ear noises   _____ Facial pain
_____ Dizziness   _____ Stiff neck
_____ Facial paralysis   _____ Lump in neck
_____ Nasal obstruction   _____ Lump in face or head
_____ Nasal deformity   _____ Trouble swallowing
_____ Mouth sores   _____ Excess eye skin
_____ Jaw joint problem   _____ Excess facial skin
_____ Eye problem
_____ Other: (Please specify.)

40. Do you have or have you ever had:
_____ Diabetes   _____ Seizures
_____ Hypoglycemia   _____ Psychiatric therapy
_____ Thyroid problems   _____ Frequent bad headaches
_____ Syphilis   _____ Ulcers
_____ Gonorrhea   _____ Kidney disease
_____ Herpes   _____ Urinary problems
_____ Cold sores (fever blisters)   _____ Arthritis or skeletal problems
_____ High blood pressure   _____ Cleft palate
_____ Severe low blood pressure   _____ Asthma
_____ Intravenous antibiotics or diuretics   _____ Lung or breathing problems
_____ Heart attack   _____ Unexplained weight loss
_____ Angina irregular heartbeat   _____ Cancer of (_____)
_____ Other heart problems   _____ Other tumor (_____)
_____ Rheumatic fever   _____ Blood transfusions
_____ Tuberculosis   _____ Hepatitis
_____ Glaucoma   _____ AIDS
_____ Multiple sclerosis   _____ Meningitis
_____ Other illnesses: (Please specify.)

41. Do any blood relatives have:
_____ Diabetes   _____ Cancer
_____ Hypoglycemia   _____ Heart disease
_____ Other major medical problems such as those above. Please specify:

42. Describe serious accidents unless directly related to your doctor's visit here.

    _____ None
    _____ Occurred with head injury, loss of consciousness, or whiplash
    _____ Occurred without head injury, loss of consciousness, or whiplash
    Describe:

43. List all current medications and doses (include birth control pills and vitamins).

44. Medication allergies
    _____ None   _____ Novocaine
    _____ Penicillin   _____ Iodine
    _____ Sulfa   _____ Codeine
    _____ Tetracycline   _____ Adhesive tape
    _____ Erythromycin   _____ Aspirin
    _____ Keflex/Ceclor/Ceftin   _____ X-ray dyes
    _____ Other: (Please specify.)

45. List operations
    _____ Tonsillectomy (age _____)
    _____ Appendectomy (age _____)
    _____ Adenoidectomy (age _____)
    _____ Heart surgery (age _____)
    _____ Other: (Please specify.)

46. List toxic drugs or chemicals to which you have been exposed:
    _____ Lead
    _____ Streptomycin, Neomycin, Kanamycin
    _____ Mercury
    _____ Other: (Please specify.)

47. Have you had x-ray *treatments* to your head or neck (including treatments for acne or ear problems as a child, treatments for cancer, etc.)?
    Yes _____   No _____

48. Describe serious health problems of your spouse or children.
    _____ None

Appendix IIb

PATIENT HISTORY: PROFESSIONAL VOICE USERS
Robert Thayer Sataloff, M.D., D.M.A.
1721 Pine Street
Philadelphia, PA 19103

NAME _____ AGE _____ SEX _____ RACE _____
HEIGHT _____ WEIGHT _____ DATE _____

1. How long have you had your present voice problem? _____

    Who noticed it?

    Do you know what caused it? Yes ____   No _____

    If so, what?

    Did it come on slowly or suddenly? Slowly _____   Suddenly _____

    Is it getting: Worse _____, Better _____, Same _____

2. Which symptoms do you have? (Please check all that apply.)
    _____ Hoarseness (coarse or scratchy sound)
    _____ Fatigue (voice tires or changes quality after speaking for a short period of time)
    _____ Volume disturbance (trouble speaking)   softly _____   loudly _____
    _____ Loss of range (high _____, low _____)
    _____ Prolonged warm-up time (over ½ hr to warm up voice)
    _____ Breathiness
    _____ Tickling or choking sensation while speaking
    _____ Pain in throat while speaking
    _____ Other: (Please specify.)_____

    _____   _____
    _____   _____

3. Have you ever had training for your speaking voice?
        Yes _____   No _____

4. Have there been periods of months or years without lessons in that time? Yes _____   No _____

1549

5. How long have you studied with your present teacher?
   Teacher's name: _____
   Teacher's address: _____
   Teacher's telephone number:_____

6. Please list previous teachers and years during which you studied with them:

7. Have you ever had training for your singing voice? Yes _____   No _____
   If so, list teachers and years of study:

8. In what capacity do you use your voice professionally?
   _____ Actor
   _____ Announcer (television/radio/sports arena)
   _____ Attorney
   _____ Clergy
   _____ Politician
   _____ Salesperson
   _____ Teacher
   _____ Telephone operator or receptionist
   _____ Other: (Please specify.)

9. Do you have an important performance soon?   Yes _____   No _____
   Date(s): _____

10. Do you do regular voice exercises?   Yes _____   No _____
    If yes, describe:

11. Do you play a musical instrument?   Yes _____   No _____
    If yes, please check all that apply:
    _____ Keyboard (piano, organ, harpischord, other _____)
    _____ Violin, viola
    _____ Cello
    _____ Bass
    _____ Plucked strings (guitar, harp, other _____)
    _____ Brass
    _____ Wind with single reed
    _____ Wind with double reed
    _____ Flute, piccolo
    _____ Percussion
    _____ Bagpipe
    _____ Accordion
    _____ Other: (Please specify.) _____

12. Do you warm up your voice before practice or performance?   Yes _____   No _____

    Do you cool down after using it?   Yes _____   No _____

13. How much are you speaking at present (average hours per day)?
    _____ Rehearsal   _____ Performance   _____ Other

14. Please check all that apply to you:
    _____ Voice worse in the morning
    _____ Voice worse later in the day, after it has been used
    _____ Sing performances or rehearsals in the morning
    _____ Speak extensively (e.g. , teacher, clergy, attorney, telephone work)
    _____ Cheerleader
    _____ Speak extensively backstage or at postperformance parties
    _____ Choral conductor
    _____ Frequently clear your throat
    _____ Frequent sore throat
    _____ Jaw joint problems
    _____ Bitter or acid taste; bad breath or hoarseness first thing in the morning
    _____ Frequent "heartburn" or hiatal hernia
    _____ Frequent yelling or loud talking
    _____ Frequent whispering
    _____ Chronic fatigue (insomnia)
    _____ Work around extreme dryness
    _____ Frequent exercise (weight lifting, aerobics)
    _____ Frequently thirsty, dehydrated
    _____ Hoarseness first thing in the morning
    _____ Chest cough
    _____ Eat late at night
    _____ Ever used antacids
    _____ Under particular stress at present (personal or professional)
    _____ Frequent bad breath
    _____ Live, work, or perform around smoke or fumes
    _____ Traveled recently: When:_____ _____
                          Where: _____

15. Your family doctor's name, address, and telephone number:

16. Your laryngologist's name, address, and telephone number:

17. Recent cold?   Yes _____   No _____

18. Current cold?   Yes _____   No _____

19. Have you been evaluated by an allergist?   Yes _____ No _____
    If yes, what allergies do you have:
    [none, dust, mold, trees, cats, dogs, foods, other, _____]
    (Medication allergies are covered elsewhere in this history form.)
    If yes, give name and address of allergist:

20. How many packs of cigarettes do you smoke per day?
    Smoking history
    _____ Never
    _____ Quit. When? _____
    _____ Smoked about ____ packs per day for ____ years.
    _____ Smoke ____ packs per day. Have smoked for ____ years.

21. Do you work or live in a smoky environment?   Yes _____ No _____

22. How much alcohol do you drink? [none, rarely, a few times per week, daily] If daily, or few times per week, on the average, how much do you consume? [1, 2, 3, 4, 5, 6, 7, 8, 9, 10, more] glasses per [day, week] of [beer, wine, liquor]

    Did you formerly drink more heavily?   Yes _____ No _____

23. How many cups of coffee, tea, cola, or other caffeine-containing drinks do you drink per day?

24. List other recreational drugs you use [marijuana, cocaine, amphetamines, barbiturates, heroin, other _____
    _____]

25. Have you noticed any of the following? (Check all that apply)
    _____ Hypersensitivity to heat or cold
    _____ Excessive sweating
    _____ Change in weight: gained/lost _____ lb in _____
                     weeks/ _____ months
    _____ Change in your voice
    _____ Change in skin or hair
    _____ Palpitation (fluttering) of the heart
    _____ Emotional lability (swings of mood)
    _____ Double vision
    _____ Numbness of the face or extremities
    _____ Tingling around the mouth or face
    _____ Blurred vision or blindness
    _____ Weakness or paralysis of the face
    _____ Clumsiness in arms or legs
    _____ Confusion or loss of consciousness
    _____ Difficulty with speech
    _____ Difficulty with swallowing

_____ Seizure (epileptic fit)
_____ Pain in the neck or shoulder
_____ Shaking or tremors
_____ Memory change
_____ Personality change

For females:

Are you pregnant?	Yes _____	No _____
Are your menstrual periods regular?	Yes _____	No _____
Have you undergone hysterectomy?	Yes _____	No _____
Were your ovaries removed?	Yes _____	No _____
At what age did you reach puberty?	_____	
Have you gone through menopause?	Yes _____	No _____

26. Have you ever consulted a psychologist or psychiatrist?
    Yes _____   No _____

    Are you currently under treatment?   Yes _____   No _____

27. Have you injured your head or neck (whiplash, etc.)?
    Yes _____   No _____

28. Describe any serious accidents related to this visit.
    None _____

29. Are you involved in legal action involving problems with your voice?
    Yes _____   No _____

30. List names of spouse and children:

31. Brief summary of ear, nose, and throat (ENT) problems, some of which may not be related to your present complaint.

_____ Hearing loss	_____ Ear pain
_____ Ear noises	_____ Facial pain
_____ Dizziness	_____ Stiff neck
_____ Facial paralysis	_____ Lump in neck
_____ Nasal obstruction	_____ Lump in face or head
_____ Nasal deformity	_____ Trouble swallowing
_____ Nose bleeds	_____ Trouble breathing
_____ Mouth sores	_____ Excess eye skin
_____ Excess facial skin	_____ Eye problem
_____ Jaw joint problem	
_____ Other (Please specify.)	

32. Do you have or have you ever had:

_____ Diabetes

_____ Hypoglycemia

_____ Thyroid problems

_____ Syphilis

_____ Gonorrhea

_____ Herpes

_____ Cold sores (fever blisters)

_____ High blood pressure

_____ Severe low blood pressure

_____ Intravenous antibiotics or diuretics

_____ Heart attack

_____ Angina

_____ Irregular heartbeat

_____ Other heart problems

_____ Rheumatic fever

_____ Tuberculosis

_____ Glaucoma

_____ Multiple sclerosis

_____ Other illnesses: (Please specify.)

_____ Seizures

_____ Psychiatric therapy

_____ Frequent bad headaches

_____ Ulcers

_____ Kidney disease

_____ Urinary problems

_____ Arthritis or skeletal problems

_____ Cleft palate

_____ Asthma

_____ Lung or breathing problems

_____ Unexplained weight loss

_____ Cancer of (_____)

_____ Other tumor (_____)

_____ Blood transfusions

_____ Hepatitis

_____ AIDS

_____ Meningitis

33. Do any blood relatives have:

_____ Diabetes

_____ Hypoglycemia

_____ Cancer

_____ Heart disease

_____ Other major medical problems such as those above. Please specify:

34. Describe serious accidents *unless* directly related to your doctor's visit here.

_____ None

_____ Occurred with head injury, loss of consciousness, or whiplash

_____ Occurred without head injury, loss of consciousness, or whiplash Describe:

35. List all current medications and doses (include birth control pills and vitamins).

36. Medication allergies

_____ None

_____ Penicillin

_____ Sulfa

_____ Novocaine

_____ Iodine

_____ Codeine

_____ Tetracycline   _____ Adhesive tape
_____ Erythromycin   _____ Aspirin
_____ Keflex/Ceclor/Ceftin   _____ X-ray dyes
_____ Other: (Please specify.)

37. List operations:
    _____ Tonsillectomy   _____ Appendectomy
           (age _____)   (age _____)
    _____ Appendectomy   _____ Heart surgery
           (age _____)   (age _____)
    Other: (Please specify.)

38. List toxic drugs or chemicals to which you have been exposed:
    _____ Lead   _____ Streptomycin, Neomycin, Kanamycin
    _____ Mercury   _____ Other: (Please list.)

39. Have you had x-ray _treatments_ to your head or neck (including treatments for acne or ear problems as a
    child), treatments for cancer, etc.?
    Yes _____   No _____

40. Describe serious health problems of your spouse or children.
    _____ None

Appendix IIc

PATIENT HISTORY: SINGERS
Robert Thayer Sataloff, M.D. , D.M.A.
1721 Pine Street
Philadelphia, PA 19103

NAME _____ AGE _____ SEX _____ RACE _____

HEIGHT _____ WEIGHT _____ DATE _____

VOICE CATEGORY: _____ soprano   _____ mezzo-soprano   _____ alto

                    _____ tenor   _____ baritone   _____ bass

(If you are not currently having a voice problem, please skip to Question #3.)

PLEASE CHECK OR CIRCLE CORRECT ANSWERS

1. How long have you had your present voice problem?

    [1,2,3,4,5,6,7,8,9,10, more]
    [hours, days, weeks, months, years]

    Who noticed it?

    [self, family, voice teacher, critics, everyone, other _____]

    Do you know what caused it?
    [Yes _____   No _____]

    If yes, what? [a cold, yelling, excessive talking, singing, surgery, other _____]

    Did it come on slowly or suddenly?
    [Slowly _____   Suddenly _____]

    Is it getting: Worse _____ , Better _____ , Same _____

2. Which symptoms do you have? (Please check all that apply.)
    _____ Hoarseness (coarse or scratchy sound)
    _____ Fatigue (voice tires or changes quality after singing for a short period of time)
    _____ Volume disturbance (trouble singing) softly _____   loudly _____
    _____ Loss of range (high _____   low _____)
    _____ Change in classification (example: voice lowered from soprano to mezzo)
    _____ Prolonged warm-up time (over ½ hr to warm up voice)
    _____ Breathiness
    _____ Tickling or choking sensation while singing

---

*English language questionnaire was modified to a yes/no and circled answers format to allow comparison with foreign language translations that follow.

_____ Pain in throat while singing
_____ Other: (Please specify.) _____
_____

3. Do you have an important performance soon?   Yes _____   No _____
   Date(s): _____

4. What is the current status of your singing career?   Professional _____   Amateur _____

5. What are your long-term career goals in singing?
   [ ] Premier operatic career_____
   [ ] Premier pop music career
   [ ] Active avocation
   [ ] Classical
   [ ] Pop
   [ ] Other (_____)
   [ ] Amateur performance (choral or solo)
   [ ] Amateur singing for own pleasure

6. Have you had voice training?   Yes _____   No _____   At what age did you begin? (Circle)
   [2,3,4,5,6,7,8,9,10,11,12,13,14,15,16,17,18,19,20,21,22,23,24,25,26,27,28,29,30,35,40,45,50,55,60,65,70,75,80,85]

7. Have there been periods of months or years without lessons in that time?   Yes _____   No _____

8. How long have you studied with your present teacher?
   [1,2,3,4,5,6,7,8,9,10,11,12,13,14,15,16,17,18,19,20,21,22,23,24,25, more]

   [weeks, months, years]

   Teacher's name:
   Teacher's address:

   Teacher's telephone number:

9. Please list previous teachers and years during which you studied with them:

10. Have you ever had training for your speaking voice?   Yes _____   No _____
    Acting voice lessons?   Yes _____   No _____
    How many years?   [Less than one, 1–5, 6–10, more]
    Speech therapy?   Yes _____   No _____   How many months?
                                                           [1,2,3,4,5,6,7–12, more]

11. Do you have a job in addition to singing?
    Yes _____   No _____

If yes, does it involve extensive voice use?
     Yes _____   No _____

If yes, what is it? [actor, announcer (television/radio/sports arena), athletic instructor, attorney, clergy, politician, physician, salesperson, stockbroker, teacher, telephone operator or receptionist, waiter, waitress, secretary, other _____]

12. In your performance work, in addition to singing, are you frequently required to speak?
     Yes _____   No _____   dance? Yes _____   No _____

13. How many years did you sing actively before beginning voice lessons initially?
    [2,3,4,5,6,7,8,9,10,11,12,13,14,15,16,17,18,19,20,21,22,23,24,25, more]

14. What types of music do you sing? (Check all that apply.)
    _____ Classical   _____ Show
    _____ Nightclub   _____ Rock
    Other: (Please specify.) _____

15. Do you regularly sing in a sitting position (such as from behind a piano or drum set)?
     Yes _____   No _____

16. Do you sing outdoors or in large halls, or with orchestras? (Circle which one.)   Yes _____   No _____

17. If you perform with electrical instruments or outdoors, do you use
    monitor speakers?   Yes _____   No _____
    If yes, can you hear them?   Yes _____   No _____

18. Do you play a musical instrument(s)?   Yes _____   No _____
    If yes, please check all that apply:
    _____ Keyboard (piano, organ, harpischord, other _____)
    _____ Violin, viola
    _____ Cello
    _____ Bass
    _____ Plucked strings (guitar, harp, other _____)
    _____ Brass
    _____ Wind with single reed
    _____ Wind with double reed
    _____ Flute, piccolo
    _____ Percussion
    _____ Bagpipe
    _____ Accordion
    _____ Other: (Please specify.) _____

19. How often do you practice?
    Scales: [daily, few times weekly, once a week, rarely, never]

If you practice scales, do you do them all at once or do you divide them up over the course of a day?
[all at once, two or three sittings]

On days when you do scales, how long do you practice them?
[15,30,45,60,75,90,105,120, more] minutes

Songs: [daily, few times weekly, once a week, rarely, never]

How many hours per day?
[½,1,1½,2,2½,3, more]

Do you warm up your voice before you sing? _____ Yes _____ No

Do you cool down your voice when you finish singing? _____ Yes _____ No

20. How much are you singing at present (total, including practice time)
(average hours per day)?
Rehearsal: [½,1,1½,2,2½,3,4,5,6,7,8,9,10]
Performance: [½,1,1½,2,2½,3,4,5,6,7,8]

21. Please check all that apply to you:
_____ Voice worse in the morning
_____ Voice worse later in the day, after it has been used
_____ Sing performances or rehearsals in the morning
_____ Speak extensively (e.g., teacher, clergy, attorney, telephone work)
_____ Cheerleader
_____ Speak extensively backstage or at postperformance parties
_____ Choral conductor
_____ Frequently clear your throat
_____ Frequent sore throat
_____ Jaw joint problems
_____ Bitter or acid taste, or bad breath first thing in the morning
_____ Frequent "heartburn" or hiatal hernia
_____ Frequent yelling or loud talking
_____ Frequent whispering
_____ Chronic fatigue (insomnia)
_____ Work around extreme dryness
_____ Frequent exercise (weight lifting, aerobics)
_____ Frequently thirsty, dehydrated
_____ Hoarseness first thing in the morning
_____ Chest cough
_____ Eat late at night
_____ Ever used antacids
_____ Under particular stress at present (personal or professional)
_____ Frequent bad breath
_____ Live, work, or perform around smoke or fumes
_____ Traveled recently: When: _____
                 Where: _____

Eat any of the following before singing?

_____ Chocolate	_____ Coffee
_____ Alcohol	_____ Milk or ice cream
_____ Nuts	_____ Spiced foods

Other: (Please specify.)

_____ Any specific vocal technical difficulties?
[trouble singing softly, trouble singing loudly, poor pitch control, support problems, problems at register transitions, other] Describe:

_____ Any problems with your singing voice recently prior to the onset of the problem that brought you here?
[hoarseness, breathiness, fatigue, loss of range, voice breaks, pain singing, others] Describe:

_____ Any voice problems in the past that required a visit to a physician? If yes, please describe problem(s) and treatment(s):
[laryngitis, nodules, polyps, hemorrhage, cancer, other] Describe:

22. Your family doctor's name, address, and telephone number:

23. Your laryngologist's name, address, and telephone number:

24. Recent cold?   Yes _____   No _____

25. Current cold?   Yes _____   No _____

26. Have you been exposed to any of the following chemicals frequently (or recently) at home or at work? (Check all that apply.)

_____ Carbon monoxide   _____ Arsenic
_____ Mercury   _____ Aniline dyes
_____ Insecticides   _____ Industrial solvents
_____ Lead   (benzene, etc.)
_____ Stage smoke

27. Have you been evaluated by an allergist?   Yes _____   No _____
If yes, what allergies do you have:
[none, dust, mold, trees, cats, dog, foods, other _____]
(Medication allergies are covered elsewhere in this history form.)

If yes, give name and address of allergist:

28. How many packs of cigarettes do you smoke per day?

Smoking history
_____ Never
_____ Quit. When?
_____ Smoked about [less than ½, ½, 1, 1½, 2, 2½, 3, more] per day for [1,2,3,4,5,6,7,8,9,10,11–15, 16–20,21–25,26–30,31–35,36–40,41–45,46–50, more] years
_____ Smoke [less than ½, ½, 1, 1½, 2½, 3, more] per day for [1,2,3,4,5,6,7,8,9,10,11–15,16–20,21–25,26–30,31–35,36–40,41–45,46–50, more] years

29. Do you work in a smoky environment?   Yes _____   No _____

30. How much alcohol do you drink? [none, rarely, a few times per week, daily] [1,2,3,4,5,6,7,8,9,10, more] glasses per [day, week] of [beer, wine, liquor]

    Did you formerly drink more heavily?   Yes _____   No _____

31. How many cups of coffee, tea, cola, or other caffeine-containing drinks do you drink per day? [0,1,2,3,4,5,6,7,8,9,10]

32. List other recreational drugs you use [marijuana, cocaine, amphetamines, barbiturates, heroin, other _____ _____]

33. Have you noticed any of the following? (Check all that apply)
    _____ Hypersensitivity to heat or cold
    _____ Excessive sweating
    _____ Change in weight: gained/lost _____ lb in _____
                         weeks/ _____ months
    _____ Change in skin or hair
    _____ Palpitation (fluttering) of the heart
    _____ Emotional lability (swings of mood)
    _____ Double vision
    _____ Numbness of the face or extremities
    _____ Tingling around the mouth or face
    _____ Blurred vision or blindness
    _____ Weakness or paralysis of the face
    _____ Clumsiness in arms or legs
    _____ Confusion or loss of consciousness
    _____ Difficulty with speech
    _____ Difficulty with swallowing
    _____ Seizure (epileptic fit)
    _____ Pain in the neck or shoulder
    _____ Shaking or tremors
    _____ Memory change
    _____ Personality change

    For females:

    Are you pregnant?   Yes _____   No _____
    Have you undergone hysterectomy?   Yes _____   No _____
    Were your ovaries removed?   Yes _____   No _____
    Are your menstrual periods regular?   Yes _____   No _____
    At what age did you reach puberty?
    [7,8,9,10,11,12,13,14,15,16,17,18,19,20]
    Have you gone through menopause?   Yes _____   No _____

    If yes, when? [presently; 1,2,3,4,5,6,7,8,9,10, more] years ago

34. Have you ever consulted a psychologist or psychiatrist?
         Yes _____   No _____
    Are you currently under treatment?   Yes _____   No _____

35. Have you injured your head or neck (whiplash, etc.)?   Yes _____   No _____

36. Describe any serious accidents.

37. Are you involved in legal action involving problems with your voice?
    Yes _____ No _____

38. List names of spouse and children:

39. Brief summary of ear, nose, and throat (ENT) problems, some of which may not be related to your present complaint.

    Please check all that apply:

    _____ Hearing loss   _____ Ear pain
    _____ Ear noises   _____ Facial pain
    _____ Dizziness   _____ Stiff neck
    _____ Facial paralysis   _____ Lump in neck
    _____ Nasal   _____ Lump in face
            obstruction   or head
    _____ Nasal deformity   _____ Trouble
    _____ Mouth sores   swallowing
    _____ Jaw joint   _____ Excess eye
            problem   skin
    _____ Eye problem   _____ Excess facial
    _____ Other: (Please specify.)   skin

40. Do you have or have you ever had:

    _____ Diabetes   _____ Seizures
    _____ Hypoglycemia   _____ Psychiatric therapy
    _____ Thyroid problems   _____ Frequent bad
    _____ Syphilis   headaches
    _____ Gonorrhea   _____ Ulcers
    _____ Herpes   _____ Kidney disease
    _____ Cold sores (fever   _____ Urinary problems
            blisters)   _____ Arthritis or skeletal
    _____ High blood pressure   problems
    _____ Severe low blood   _____ Cleft palate
            pressure   _____ Asthma
    _____ Intravenous antibiotics   _____ Lung or breathing
            or diuretics   problems
    _____ Heart attack   _____ Unexplained weight
    _____ Angina   loss
    _____ Irregular heartbeat   _____ Cancer of (_____)
    _____ Other heart problems   _____ Other tumor (_____)
    _____ Rheumatic fever   _____ Blood transfusions
    _____ Tuberculosis   _____ Hepatitis
    _____ Glaucoma   _____ AIDS
    _____ Multiple sclerosis   _____ Meningitis
    _____ Other illnesses: (Please specify.)

41. Do any blood relatives have:
    _____ Diabetes   _____ Cancer
    _____ Hypoglycemia   _____ Heart disease
    _____ Other major medical problems such as those above.
             Please specify:

42. Describe serious accidents *unless* directly related to your doctor's visit here.
    _____ None
    _____ Occurred with head injury, loss of consciousness, or whiplash
    _____ Occurred without head injury, loss of consciousness, or whiplash
             Describe:

43. List all current medications and doses (include birth control pills and vitamins).

44. Medication allergies
    _____ None   _____ Novocaine
    _____ Penicillin   _____ Iodine
    _____ Sulfa   _____ Codeine
    _____ Tetracycline   _____ Adhesive tape
    _____ Erythromycin   _____ Aspirin
    _____ Keflex/Ceclor/Ceftin   _____ X-ray dyes
    _____ Other: (Please specify.)

45. List operations:
    _____ Tonsillectomy   _____ Adenoidectomy
            (age _____)   (age _____)
    _____ Appendectomy   _____ Heart surgery
            (age _____)   (age _____)
    _____ Other: (Please
            specify.)

46. List toxic drugs or chemicals to which you have been exposed:
    _____ Lead   _____ Streptomycin, Neomycin, Kanamycin
    _____ Mercury   _____ Other: (Please specify.)

47. Have you had x-ray *treatments* to your head or neck (including treatments for acne or ear problems as a child, treatments for cancer, etc.)?   Yes _____   No _____

48. Describe serious health problems of your spouse or children.

    _____ None

Arabic Version of Appendix IIc

تاريخ المرضى: المغنيين

روبرت تاير ساتالوف، م.د، د.م.أ

١٧٢١ شارع باين

فيلادلفيا، بنسلفانيا ١٩١٠٣

الاسم ———————————— السن ——— الجنس ——— العرق ——— الطول ————

الطول ———————————— الوزن ———————— التاريخ ————————

تصنيف الصوت: ——— مثل صوت المرأة عالي ——— صوت عالي متوسط ——— آلتو (عالي)

——— تينور (مشدود) (وتري) ——— باريتون (جهير) ——— باس رخيم

(اذا حاليا لا تعاني من مشكلة في الصوت انتقل الى السؤال الثالث.)

الرجاء وضع اشارة أو دائرة على الاجوبة الصحيحة

١- منذ متى وانت تعاني من مشكلة الصوت الحالية؟

[١،٢،٣،٤،٥،٦،٧،٨،٩،١٠، أكثر]

[ساعات، أيام، أسابيع، شهور، سنوات]

من لاحظ المشكلة؟

[نفسي، العائلة، مدرس الصوت، النقاد، الجميع، غيرهم ———]

هل تعرف سبب المشكلة؟

[——— نعم ——— لا]

اذا نعم ما هو السبب؟ [برد، صريخ، اطالة في الكلام، غناء، جراحة، غيرها]

هل حصلت المشكلة تدريجيا أم فجأة؟

[تدريجيا ———، فجأة ———]

هل الحالةتسوء ——— تتحسن ——— لاتتغير ——— ؟

٢- اي العلامات موجودة عندك ؟ (ضع اشارة على الجميع اذا كان ينطبق)

——— خشونة (صوت خشن أو مجروح)

——— تعب (الصوت يتعب أو النوعية تتغير بعد الغناء لفترة قصيرة)

——— اضطراب علو (مشكلة غناء) انخفاض ——— ارتفاع ———

——— ضياع الحدود (عالي ——— منخفض ———)

——— تغير في التصنيف (مثلا: الصوت ينخفض من الصوت العالي الى المتوسط)

——— فترة تهيئة طويلة (اكثر من ١/٢ ساعة لتهيئة الصوت)

——— ضياع النفس

——— دغدغة أو شعور اختناق اثناء الغناء

_____ ألم في الحنجرة اثناء الغناء

_____ غيرها (ارجو التحديد) _____

_____

٣- هل عندك حفل تأدية قريبا؟ _____ نعم _____ لا

التاريخ: _____

٤- ماهو وضعك الحالي المهني بالنسبة الى الغناء؟ _____ احتراف _____ هواية

٥- ما هي اهدافك الطويلة الامد بالنسبة لمهنة الغناء؟

_____ اوبرا نوع اول [ ]

موسيقى شعبية نوع اول صاخبة [ ]

هواية ناشطة مهنة احترافية [ ]

كلاسيكي [ ]

شعبي [ ]

غيرها (_____) [ ]

تأدية هواة (كورال أو سولو) [ ]

غناء هواية لارضاء النفس [ ]

٦- هل حصلت على تدريب صوتي؟ _____ نعم _____ لا في أي عمر بدأت؟ (ضع دائرة)

[٨٥،٨٠،٧٥،٧٠،٦٥،٦٠،٥٥،٥٠،٤٥،٤٠،٣٥،٣٠،٢٩،٢٨،٢٧،٢٦،٢٥،٢٤،٢٣،٢٢،٢١،٢٠،١٩،١٨،١٧،١٦،١٥،١٤،١٣،١٢،١١،١٠،٩،٨،٧،٦،٥،٤،٣،٢]

٧- هل تخلل ذلك مدة شهور أو سنوات بدون دروس؟ _____ نعم _____ لا

٨- كم امضيت مع مدرسك الحالي؟

[١،٢،٣،٤،٥،٦،٧٨،٩،١٠،١١،١٢،١٣،١٤،١٥،١٦،١٧،١٨،١٩،٢٠،٢١،٢٢،٢٣،٢٤،٢٥ ،اكثر]

[اسابيع، شهور، سنوات]

اسم المدرس:

عنوان المدرس:

رقم هاتف المدرس:

٩- الرجاء ادراج اسماء المدرسين السابقين والسنوات التي درست خلالها عندهم:

١٠ هل حصلت على تدريب بالنسبة للصوت الكلامي؟ _____ نعم _____ لا

دروس صوتية تمثيلي _____ نعم _____ لا

كم سنة؟ [اقل من واحد، ١-٥، ٦-١٠، اكثر]

علاج كلامي؟ _____ نعم _____ لا كم عدد الشهور؟

[١،٢،٣،٤،٥،٦،٧-١٢، اكثر]

١١ هل لديك عمل آخر بالاضافة الى الغناء؟

_____ نعم _____ لا

اذا نعم، هل يتطلب استخدام الصوت بكثرة؟

_____ نعم _____ لا

اذا نعم، ما هو؟ [ممثل، معلن (تليفيزيون، راديو، ميدان الرياضة)، معلم رياضة، محامي، سياسي، طبيب، بائع، بائع اسهم، مدرس، عامل تليفون أو استقبال، جرسون، سكرتير، غيرها _____]

١٢– هل يتطلب عملك منك الكلام بكثرة؟

_____ نعم _____ لا   الرقص؟ _____ نعم _____ لا

١٣– كم سنة غنيت قبل ان تتلقى دروساً في الصوت؟

[٢،٣،٤،٥،٦،٧،٨،٩،١٠،١١،١٢،١٣،١٤،١٥،١٦،١٧،١٨،١٩،٢٠،٢١،٢٢،٢٣،٢٤،٢٥ أو اكثر]

١٤– ما هي انواع الموسيقى التي تغني؟ (ضع اشارة على كل ما ينطبق)

_____ كلاسيكية   _____ عرض

_____ نادي ليلي   _____ روك

غيرها (ارجو التحديد): _____

١٥– هل تغني بتكرار وانت في وضع جلوس (مثلا من وراء بيانو أو تشكيلة طبول)

_____ نعم _____ لا

١٦– هل تغني في الخلاء أو في قاعات كبيرة أو مع أوركسترا؟ (ضع دائر على أي واحدة) _____ نعم _____ لا

١٧– اذا كنت تؤدي مع الالات كهربائية في الخلاء هل تستخدم سماعات مؤشرة؟   _____ نعم   _____ لا

اذا نعم، هل تستطيع سماعهم؟ _____ نعم   _____ لا

١٨– هل تلعب آلة موسيقية؟ _____ نعم _____ لا

اذا نعم ضع اشارة على كل ما ينطبق:

_____ مفاتيح (بيانو، اورغن، بيان قيثاري، غيرها _____)

_____ كمنجة، كمان

_____ فيولونسيل تشيلو (كمنجة كبيرة)

_____ باس طبل

_____ وتريات (جيتار، قيثار، غيرها _____)

_____ آلة النفخ النحاسية

_____ آلة نفخ بلسان

_____ آلة نفخ بلسانين

_____ مزمار السرناي ناي صغير

_____ آلات النقر

_____ مزمار القربة

_____ اكورديون

_____ غيرها (الرجاء التحديد)

١٩– كم مرة تتدرب؟

المؤشر: [يوميا، عدة مرات في الاسبوع، مرة في الاسبوع، نادرا، ابدا]

اذا كنت تتدرب على المؤشرات، هل تقوم بها كلها دفعة واحدة ام تقسمها على مدار اليوم؟

[دفعة واحدة، جلستين أو ثلاث]

في الايام التي تقوم بها بالمؤشرات، كم تمضي في التدريب

[١٥،٣٠،٤٥،٦٠،٧٥،٩٠،١٠٥،١٢٠، اكثر] دقيقة

اغنيات: [يوميا، عدة مرات في الاسبوع، مرة في الاسبوع، نادرا، ابدا]

كم ساعة في اليوم؟

[١٠،١/٢، ٢، ١/٢ ١، ٢،٣،١/٢، اكثر]

هل تهيء صوتك قبل الغناء؟   نعم ـــــــ لا ـــــــ

هل تهيء صوتك بعد الغناء؟   نعم ـــــــ لا ـــــــ

٢٠- كم هو الوقت الذي تمضيه في الغناء حاليا (بما يتضمن التدريب)

(متوسط الساعات في اليوم)

تدريب: [١٠،١/٢، ٢، ١/٢ ١، ٢،٣،٤،٥،٦،٧،٨،٩،١٠ ١/٢]

اداء: [٨،٧،٦،٥،٤،٣،٢ ١/٢ ١، ٢، ١/٢ ١٠،١/٢]

٢١- الرجاء وضع اشارة على كل ما ينطبق عليك:

ـــــــ الصوت اسوء في الصباح

ـــــــ الصوت اسوء بعد الصباح بعد استعماله

ـــــــ اغني اداءً أو تديبا في الصباح

ـــــــ اتكلم بكثرة (مثلا مدرس، محامي، عمل هاتفي الخ..)

ـــــــ قائد فرق تشجيع

ـــــــ اتكلم بكثرة خلف الكواليس أو حفلات تقديم

ـــــــ مايسترو كورال

ـــــــ انظف الحنجرة عدة مرات

ـــــــ الم حنجرة متكرر

ـــــــ مشاكل في مفاصل الحنك

ـــــــ طعم حموضة في الفم أو رائحة كريهة في الفم عند الصباح

ـــــــ حرقة او فتق

ـــــــ صريخ متكرر او بصوت مرتفع

ـــــــ همس متكرر

ـــــــ تعب مزمن (ارق)

ـــــــ عمل حول جفاف

ـــــــ تدريب متكرر (رفع اثقال، لياقة بدنية، الخ..)

ـــــــ عطش متكرر، جفاف

ـــــــ خشونة في الصوت اول شيء في الصباح

ـــــــ سعال صدري

ـــــــ اكل متأخر في الليل

ـــــــ استعمل حبوب مهضمة

ـــــــ تحت ضغط حاليا (شخصي أو مهني)

ـــــــ رائحة فم كريهة متكررة

ـــــــ اعيش، اعمل أو اوؤدي حول دخان أو أبخرة

ـــــــ سافرت مؤخرا: متى: ـ_____

أين: ـ_____

آكل اي من الاتي قبل الغناء؟

ـــــــ شوكولاتة	ـــــــ قهوة
ـــــــ كحول	ـــــــ حليب أو أيسكريم
ـــــــ جوزيات مكسرات	ـــــــ طعام مبهّر حار

غيرها (ارجو التحديد):

ـــــــــ اي صعوبة فنية محددة بالنسبة للصوت؟

[صعوبة في الغناء بنعومة، صعوبة بالغناء بصوت مرتفع، ضعف سيطرة حدة الصوت، صعوبة في الدعم، صعوبة في انتقالات التأشير، غيرها] صف أو وضّح:

ـــــــــ اي صعوبات بصوتك الغنائي مؤخراً قبل الصعوبة الاخيرة التي جاءت بك الى هنا؟

[خشونة، انقطاع نفس، تعب، ضياع الحدود، تقطع في الصوت، الم في الغناء، غيرها] صف أو وضّح:

ـــــــــ اي صعوبات في الصوت فيما مضى مما استدعى زيارة الطبيب؟ اذا نعم الرجاء أوصف الصعوبات والعلاج

[التهاب الحنجرة، غدد، اورام غشاء مخاطي، نزيف، سرطان، غيرها] صف أو وضّح:

٢٢- اسم طبيب العائلة والعنوان ورقم الهاتف

٢٣- ما اسم طبيب الحنجرة، عنوانه ورقم الهاتف

٢٤- رشح مؤخراً؟   ـــــــــ نعم   ـــــــــ لا

٢٥- رشح حالي؟   ـــــــــ نعم   ـــــــــ لا

٢٦- هل تعرضت للمواد الكيميائية التالية بتكرار أو مؤخراً في البيت أو العمل؟
(ضع اشارة حول كل ما ينطبق)

ـــــــــ زرنيخ   ـــــــــ اول اكسيد الكاربون
ـــــــــ الصبغ الانيليني   ـــــــــ الزئبق
ـــــــــ مذيبات صناعية (بنزين، الخ)   ـــــــــ مبيدات حشرية
                                        ـــــــــ رصاص
                                        ـــــــــ دخان المسرح

٢٧- هل تم تشخيصك من قبل طبيب حساسية؟   ـــــــــ نعم   ـــــــــ لا
اذا نعم، ما هي الحساسيات التي عندك:
[لاشئ، غبار، عفن، شجر، قطط، كلاب، طعام، غيرها ـــــــــــــــــــ]
(علاجات الحساسية متناولة في موضع آخر من هذا البيان التاريخي.)
اذا نعم، اسم وعنوان طبيب الحساسية:

٢٨- كم علبة سجائر تدخن في اليوم؟
تاريخ التدخين
ـــــــــ ابدا
ـــــــــ تركت. متى؟
ـــــــــ دخنت كمية [اقل من نصف واحد، نصف واحد، واحد، واحد ونصف، اثنين، اثنين ونصف، ثلاثة، اكثر] في اليوم لمدة
[١،٢،٣،٤،٥،٦،٧،٨،٩،١٠،١١-١٥،١٦-٢٠،٢١-٢٥،٢٦-٣٠،٣١-٣٥،٣٦-٤٠،٤١-٤٥،٤٦-٥٠، اكثر] سنوات
ـــــــــ أدخن كمية [اقل من نصف واحد، نصف واحد، واحد، واحد ونصف، اثنين، اثنين ونصف، ثلاثة، اكثر] في اليوم لمدة
[١،٢،٣،٤،٥،٦،٧،٨،٩،١٠،١١-١٥،١٦-٢٠،٢١-٢٥،٢٦-٣٠،٣١-٣٥،٣٦-٤٠،٤١-٤٥،٤٦-٥٠، اكثر] سنوات

٢٩- هل تعمل في اجواء مدخنين؟   ـــــــــ نعم   ـــــــــ لا

٣٠– كم تشرب من الكحول؟ [لاشئ، نادراً، مرات قليلة في الاسبوع، يومياً [١،٢،٣،٤،٥،٦،٧،٨،٩،١٠، اكثر]

اكواب في [اليوم، الاسبوع] من [البيرة، النبيذ، ليكور]

هل كنت تشرب اكثر من ذلك ؟ ــــــ نعم ــــــ لا

٣١– كم كوبا من القهوة، الشاي، الكولا، او غيرها مما يحتوي على الكافايين تشرب في اليوم
[٠،١،٢،٣،٤،٥،٦،٧،٨،٩،١٠]

٣٢– ادرج المخدرات الاخرى التي تستعمل؟ [ماريجوانا، كوكايين، امغيتامين، البربيتوريك، هيروين، غيرها ــــــــــــ]

٣٣– هل لاحظت اي من الاتي؟ (ضع اشارة على كل ما ينطبق)
ــــــ حساسية للحرارة أو البرد
ــــــ تعرق مكثف
ــــــ تغير في الوزن: زيادة/نقصان ــــــ   باوند في ــــــ في ــــــ اسابيع/شهور
ــــــ تغير في الجلد أو الشعر
ــــــ خفقان في القلب
ــــــ تغيرات عاطفية
ــــــ رؤية مزدوجة
ــــــ عدم الرشاقة في اليدين والرجلين
ــــــ التحير او غياب الوعي
ــــــ صعوبة في الكلام
ــــــ صعوبة في البلع
ــــــ نوبة صرع
ــــــ تخدر الوجه والاطراف
ــــــ دغدغة حول الفم والوجه
ــــــ رؤية مغبشة أو عميان
ــــــ ضعف أو شلل في الوجه
ــــــ الم في العنق او الكتف
ــــــ رجفة
ــــــ تغير في الذاكرة
ــــــ تغير في الشخصية

للإناث

هل انت حامل؟   ــــــ نعم   ــــــ لا
هل اجريت عملية استئصال للرحم؟   ــــــ نعم   ــــــ لا
هل ازلت المبيضات؟   ــــــ نعم   ــــــ لا
هل عادتك الشهرية منتظمة؟   ــــــ نعم   ــــــ لا
في اي عمر بلغت؟
[٧،٨،٩،١٠،١١،١٢،١٣،١٤،١٥،١٦،١٧،١٨،١٩،٢٠]
هل بلغت حد انقطاع الطمث؟   ــــــ نعم   ــــــ لا

اذا نعم، متى؟ [حاليا،١،٢،٣،٤،٥،٦،٧،٨،٩،١٠، اكثر] سنة مضت

٣٤– هل ذهبت الى طبيب نفساني أو أخصائي نفسي؟
ــــــ نعم ــــــ لا
هل انت الان تحت العلاج؟   ــــــ نعم ــــــ لا

٣٥– هل جرحت رأسك أو عنقك (ضربة سوط، الخ..)   ــــــ نعم ــــــ لا

٣٦- صف اي حوادث خطرة أو جدية لها علاقة بهذه الزيادة؟

٣٧- هل انت معني بامور قانونية تتعلق بمشاكل حول صوتك؟
　　　　—— نعم —— لا

٣٨- ما اسم الزوج(ة) والاولاد

٣٩- تاريخ موجز عن مشاكل الاذن والانف والحنجرة. بعض منها قد لا ينطبق على شكواك الحالية:

ارجو وضع دائرة على كل ما ينطبق:

—— وجع اذن	—— ضياع السمع
—— وجع وجه	—— اصوات في الاذن
—— عنق جامد	—— دوخة
—— ورم في العنق	—— شلل وجهي
—— ورم في الوجه أو الرأس	—— انسداد انفي
—— صعوبة في البلع	—— تشوه في مجرى الانف
—— زيادة في جلد العين	—— اوجاع فم
—— زيادة في جلد الوجه	—— مشاكل مفاصل الحنك
	—— مشاكل عين
	—— غيرها (الرجاء التحديد)

٤٠- هل تشكو او شكوت فيما مضى من:

—— نوبات صرع	—— السكري
—— علاج نفساني	—— نقص السكر
—— أوجاع رأس متكررة صداع	—— مشاكل الغدة الدرقية
—— قرحة	—— سفليس
—— امراض الكلوة	—— السيلان
—— امراض مجاري البولية	—— القوباء (هيربس)
—— مشاكل عظمية والتهاب المفاصل	—— قروح البرد (قروح الحرارة)
—— الشق الحلقي	—— ضغط دم مرتفع
—— التهاب رئوي	—— ضغط دم منخفض
—— مشاكل تنفس ورئة	—— مضادات حيوية خلال الوريد
—— نقص وزن غير مفسرة	—— ذبحة قلبية
—— سرطان (——————)	—— الذبحة اللوزية
—— اورام اخرى (——————)	—— دقات قلب غير منتظمة
—— تغيير دم	—— امراض قلب اخرى
—— التهاب الكبد	—— حرارة روماتيزية
—— ايدز (فيروس غياب المناعة)	—— سل
—— التهاب السحايا	—— الماء الازرق في العين
	—— تصلب الانسجة
	—— امراض اخرى (الرجاء التحديد)

٤١- هل احد اقربائك بالدم يعاني من:

‏_____ السكري   _____ السرطان

‏_____ نقص في السكر   _____ امراض القلب

‏_____ اي امراض اخرى رئيسية مثل المذكور اعلاه.

الرجاء التحديد:

٤٢- صف حوادث رئيسية الا اذا كانت تتعلق بزيارتك للطبيب هنا.

‏_____ لا شئ

‏_____ حصل مع جرح في الرأس، غياب الوعي، أو ضرب السوط

‏_____ حصل بدون جرح في الرأس، غياب الوعي، أو ضرب السوط

صف:

٤٣- ضع لائحة بجميع الادوية الحالية التي تتناولها (بما في ذلك حبوب منع الحمل والفيتامينات)

٤٤- حساسية من الادوية التالية

‏_____ لا شيء   _____ نوفوكاين

‏_____ بنسيلين   _____ ايودين

‏_____ سولفا   _____ كوديين

‏_____ تيتراسيكلين   _____ شريط لاصق

‏_____ اريثرومايسين   _____ اسبيرين

‏_____ كلفكس/سيكلور/سفتين   _____ اصبغة صور الاشعة

‏_____ غيرها (الرجاء التحديد)

٤٥- حدد العمليات

‏_____ عملية استئصال اللوز   _____ عملية استئصال الزائدة الانفية

(سن: _____)   (سن: _____)

‏_____ عملية استئصال الزائدة   _____ عملية جراحة القلب

(سن: _____)   (سن: _____)

‏_____ غيرها (الرجاء التحديد)

٤٦- حدد اي الكيماويات أو السموم التي تعرضت لها

‏_____ الرصاص   _____ ستربتومايسين، نيومايسين، كانامايسين

‏_____ الزئبق   _____ غيرها (الرجاء التحديد)

٤٧- هل اخذت اشعة علاجية لرأسك أو عنقك (بما يتضمن علاجات حب الشباب أو اوجاع الاذن وانت طفل) (علاجات السرطان الخ..)؟   _____ نعم   _____ لا

٤٨- صف الامراض الرئيسية لزوجك واولادك

‏_____ لا شيء

Chinese Version of Appendix IIc

Translated by Dr. Li Guoqi
翻译：李国琦
病史：歌唱演员
Robert Thayer Sataloff，医学博士，音乐艺术博士
1721 Pine Street
Philadelphia, PA 19103
U.S.A.

姓名 _____ 年龄 _____ 性别 _____ 种族 _____

身高 _____ 体重 _____ 日期 _____

噪音类别 _____ 女高音 _____ 女中音 _____ 女低音
         _____ 男高音 _____ 男中音 _____ 男低音

（现在若无噪音问题，请从第3个问题开始。）

请在合适的答案上打勾或划圈

1. 你现在的噪音问题已有多长时间了？

[1，2，3，4，5，6，7，8，9，10，10以上]
[小时，天，星期，月，年]

谁发现的？
[自己，家庭成员，噪音教师，评论家，所有的人，其它 _____]

你知道原因吗？
[知道 _____ 不知道 _____]

若知道，原因是[感冒，大声喊叫，谈话过多，唱歌，手术，其它 _____]

是突然发生的还是缓慢发生的？
[缓慢 _____ 突然 _____]

变化：恶化 _____，好转 _____，无变化

2. 你有何症状？（划出所有适用于你的症状。）
_____ 声音嘶哑（声音粗糙或沙哑）
_____ 疲劳（只演唱很短时间后即感噪音疲劳或音质改变）
_____ 音量紊乱（响度问题） 柔声 _____ 高声 _____
_____ 音域变窄（高音 _____ 低音 _____ ）
_____ 分类改变（例如，噪音由女高音变为女中音）
_____ 适应时间延长（噪音适应时间超过1/2小时）
_____ 喘息声
_____ 演唱时有酥痒或哽息感
_____ 演唱时喉咙疼痛
_____ 其它症状（请说明。）_____

_____

3. 你最近有重要演出吗？   有 _____ 无_____

  日期 _____

4. 你现在的演唱活动属于：   专业 _____ 业余 _____

5. 你演唱的长远目标是
   [ ] 主要从事歌剧演出
   [ ] 主要从事流行音乐演出
   [ ] 积极的业余爱好
   [ ] 古典音乐
   [ ] 流行歌曲
   [ ] 其它[_____]
   [ ] 业余演出（合唱或独唱）
   [ ] 业余演唱，自我娱乐

6. 你进行过嗓音训练吗？   训练过 _____ 未训练过 _____ 从何年龄开始训练？（请圈出）
   [2,3,4,5,6,7,8,9,10,11,12,13,14,15,16,17,18,19,20,21,22,23,24,25,26,27,28,30,35,45,50,55,60,65,70,75,80,85]

7. 你从那时起有束长达数月或数年的间断训练？   有 _____ 无 _____

8. 你从师现在的老师有多长时间了？
   [1,2,3,4,5,6,7,8,9,10,11,12,13,14,15,16,17,18,19,20,21,22,23,24,25,25   以上]

   [星期，月，年]

   老师的姓名：
   老师的地址：

   老师的电话号码：

9. 请列出你以前老师的姓名及你向其学习的年限

10. 你进行过语言嗓音训练吗？   训练过 _____ 未训练过 _____
    演出发音课程？   是 _____ 否 _____
    多少年？   [少于一年，1-5，6-10，更长]
    讲话疗法？   是 _____ 否 _____ 多少月？
                                [1,2,3,4,5,6,7-12，更长]

11. 除演唱外，你有其它工作吗？
    有 _____ 无 _____

    如果有，此工作是否用嗓音较多？
    是 _____ 否 _____

若是，是何工作？[演员，播音员（电视／电台／体育现场），运动员教练，律　师，牧师，政治家，医生，售货员，股票经纪人，教师，电话接线员或接待员　，服务员，女服务员，秘书，其它 _____]

12. 在你演出时，除唱歌外，是否经常要求你讲话？
　　是 _____ 否 _____ ;　跳舞？是 _____ 否 _____

13. 在参加嗓音训练课程前，你已经演唱了多少年？
　　[2,3,4,5,6,7,8,9,10,11,12,13,14,15,16,17,18,19,20,21,22,23,24,25,25　以上]

14. 你演唱何类音乐？（标出所有适用于你者）
　　_____ 古典　　　　　　　　　　　_____ 表演
　　_____ 一夜总会　　　　　　　　　_____ 摇滚
　　_____ 其它（请说明。）_____

15. 你经常用坐姿唱歌吗？（例如边弹钢琴边唱或是边演奏架子鼓边唱）？
　　是 _____ 否 _____

16. 欠在户外或大厅，或与交响乐队一起演唱吗？
　　（圈出哪一种条件。）　　是 _____ 否 _____

17. 如果你用电子乐器或是在户外演出，
　　你使用监听喇叭吗？　　是 _____ 否 _____
　　若用，你能听到吗？　　能 _____ 不能 _____

18. 你演奏乐器吗？　演奏 _____ 不演奏 _____
　　_____ 键盘乐器（钢琴，风琴，大键琴，其它 _____ ）
　　_____ 小提琴，中提琴
　　_____ 大提琴
　　_____ 贝司
　　_____ 拨弦乐器（吉他，竖琴，其它是 _____ ）
　　_____ 铜管乐器
　　_____ 单簧管
　　_____ 双簧管
　　_____ 长笛，短笛
　　_____ 打击乐
　　_____ 风笛
　　_____ 手风琴
　　_____ 其它乐器（请说明。）_____

19. 你练习的频度是：
　　音阶：[每天，每周数次，每周一次，很少练习，从不练习]

如果你练习音阶，你是一次练完还是在一天的课程中分成几次练习？
[一次练完，分成两、三次练习]

练习音阶时，每天练习多长时间？
[15,30,45,60,75,90,105,120,120以上]分钟

歌唱：[每天，每周数次，每周一次，很少练习，从不练习]

每天多少小时？
[1/2,1,1 1/2,2,2 1/2,3,3以上]

你演唱前是否练声？　是 ＿＿＿＿＿　否 ＿＿＿＿＿

你演唱后是否遛嗓？　是 ＿＿＿＿＿　否 ＿＿＿＿＿

20. 目前的演唱时间（包括练习）每天平均几小时？
   练习：[1/2,1,1 1/2,2,2 1/2,3,4,5,6,7,8,9,10]
   表演：[1/2,1,1 1/2,2,2 1/2,3,4,5,6,7,8]

21. 勾出所有适用于你的项目：
   ＿＿＿＿＿ 早晨声音变坏
   ＿＿＿＿＿ 用声后下午声音变坏
   ＿＿＿＿＿ 上午歌唱演出或彩排
   ＿＿＿＿＿ 大量说话（例如，教师，牧师，律师，电话接线员等）
   ＿＿＿＿＿ 啦啦队长
   ＿＿＿＿＿ 在后台或演出后聚会时大量说话
   ＿＿＿＿＿ 合唱队指挥
   ＿＿＿＿＿ 经常清理喉咙
   ＿＿＿＿＿ 经常咽喉疼痛
   ＿＿＿＿＿ 下颌关节功能紊乱
   ＿＿＿＿＿ 嘴内发苦，发酸或是起床后口臭
   ＿＿＿＿＿ 经常烧心或食管裂孔疝
   ＿＿＿＿＿ 经常叫喊或大声说话
   ＿＿＿＿＿ 慢性疲劳（失眠）
   ＿＿＿＿＿ 在极端干燥的环境工作
   ＿＿＿＿＿ 经常锻炼（举重，技巧等）
   ＿＿＿＿＿ 经常口渴，脱水
   ＿＿＿＿＿ 早晨感觉声音嘶哑
   ＿＿＿＿＿ 咳嗽
   ＿＿＿＿＿ 夜间很晚吃饭
   ＿＿＿＿＿ 曾用过抗酸制剂
   ＿＿＿＿＿ 目前有特别压力（个人的或工作上的）
   ＿＿＿＿＿ 经常口臭
   ＿＿＿＿＿ 在烟雾环境下居住，工作或演出
   ＿＿＿＿＿ 最近旅行　何时 ＿＿＿＿＿＿＿＿＿＿＿＿＿＿＿＿＿＿＿＿＿＿＿＿＿＿＿＿＿
   　　　　　　　　　　何地 ＿＿＿＿＿＿＿＿＿＿＿＿＿＿＿＿＿＿＿＿＿＿＿＿＿＿＿＿＿

在演唱前吃下列食品吗？
   ＿＿＿＿＿ 巧克力　　　　　＿＿＿＿＿ 咖啡
   ＿＿＿＿＿ 酒　　　　　　　＿＿＿＿＿ 牛奶或冰淇淋
   ＿＿＿＿＿ 坚果　　　　　　＿＿＿＿＿ 辛辣食品

其它（请说明。）

_____ 有无特殊发声技巧困难？
[柔声音量问题，高声音量问题，高音控制困难，支撑点问题，改变音域困难 ，其它]
说明：
_____ 除此次来就诊的问题外，你近来有无演唱发声困难？
[声音嘶哑，气促，疲劳，音域变窄，发音问题，演唱疼痛，其它]
说明：
_____ 过去有无需要去看医生的发声问题，匿有请描述问题及治疗经过。
[咽炎，声带结节，声带息肉，出血，癌症，其它]
说明：

22. 你家庭医生的姓名，住址及电话号码：

23. 你的咽喉科医生的姓名，住址及电话号码：

24. 最近感冒过吗？   是 _____   否 _____

25. 正在患感冒吗？   是 _____   否 _____

26. 在家中或工作时，你经常（或最近）暴露于下列化学物质中吗？（划出所 有适用者。）

_____ 一氧化碳	_____ 砷
_____ 汞	_____ 苯胺染料
_____ 杀虫剂	_____ 工业溶剂（苯等）
_____ 铅	
_____ 舞台烟雾	

27. 你由过敏专家检查过吗？   检查过 _____   未检查过 _____
若检查过，你对何物过敏？
[不过敏，灰尘，霉菌，树木，猫，狗，食物，其它 _____]
过敏药物在本表别处另有说明。）

匿   检查过，请写出过敏专家的姓名及住址：

28. 你每天吸多少包香烟？

吸烟史
_____ 从不吸烟
_____ 已戒掉。何时戒的？
_____ 戒烟前每天吸[不到半包，半包，一包，一包半，两包，两包半，三包，三包 以上]，共吸了[1,2,3,4,5,6,7,8,9,10,11-15,16-20,21-25,26-30,31-35,36-40,41-45,46-50,50 以上]年
_____ 现在每天吸[不到半包，半包，一包，一包半，两包，两包半，三包，三包以 上]，共吸了[1,2,3,4,5,6,7,8,9,10,11-15,16-20,21-25,26-30,31-35,36-40,41-45,46-50,50 以上]年

29. 你在有烟雾的环境中工作吗？   是 _____   否 _____

30. 你饮多少酒类？[从不，很少，每周几次，每天] [1,2,3,4,5,6,7,8,9,10,10以上][天，周]
    [啤酒，葡萄酒，白酒]

    你以前曾更严重地饮酒吗？   是 _____   否 _____

31. 你每天饮多少杯咖啡，茶，可乐或其它含咖啡因的饮料？[1,2,3,4,5,6,7,8,9,10,10以上]

32. 列出其它你用过的药物[大麻，可卡因，安非他命类，巴比妥类，海洛因，   其它 _____]

33. 你发现有下列情况吗？
    _____   对冷或热过度敏感
    _____   出汗过多
    _____   体重改变：在 _____ 周／ _____ 月之内
              增加／减少 _____ 磅
    _____   皮肤或毛发变化
    _____   心悸
    _____   情绪不稳定
    _____   复视
    _____   面部或肢体麻木
    _____   嘴周或面部刺痛
    _____   视力模糊或丧失
    _____   面部活动减弱或麻痹
    _____   肢体活动困难
    _____   意识紊乱或丧失
    _____   讲话困难
    _____   吞咽困难
    _____   癫痫
    _____   颈，肩部疼痛
    _____   震颤
    _____   记忆力改变
    _____   个性改变

    女性：

    你正在怀孕吗？   是 _____ 否 _____
    你作过子宫切除吗？   是 _____ 否 _____
    你的双侧卵巢切除了吗？   是 _____ 否 _____
    你的月经周期规则吗？   是 _____ 否 _____
    你初潮的年龄是
    [7,8,9,10,11,12,13,14,15,16,17,18,19,20]   是 _____ 否 _____
    你是否已经绝经？   是 _____ 否 _____

如果已经绝经，什么时候？[现在；1,2,3,4,5,6,7,8,9,10，更多] 年前

34. 你是否看过心理医生或精神病医生？
    是 _____ 否 _____
    你现在正接受治疗吗？   是 _____ 否 _____

35. 你的头部或颈部受过伤吗（ ）？   是 _____ 否 _____

36. 说明任何严重事故。

37. 你曾因嗓音而卷入过法律纠纷吗？
    是 _____ 否 _____

38. 请列出配偶和子女的名字：

39.耳鼻喉科问题简短总结，其中有些问题可能与你现在的主诉无关。

                    请划出所有适用于你的项目。

_____ 听力下降	_____ 耳痛
_____ 耳鸣	_____ 面部疼痛
_____ 晕眩	_____ 颈部僵硬
_____ 面瘫	_____ 颈部肿块
_____ 鼻塞	_____ 头、面部肿块
_____ 鼻部畸型	_____ 吞咽困难
_____ 嘴痛	_____ 眼睑松弛
_____ 下颌关节问题	_____ 面部皮肤松弛
_____ 眼睛问题	
_____ 其它:（请说明。）	

40. 你是否患或曾患过：

_____ 糖尿病	_____ 癫痫
_____ 低血糖	_____ 精神病
_____ 甲状腺疾病	_____ 经常严重头痛
_____ 梅毒	_____ 溃疡
_____ 淋病	_____ 肾脏疾病
_____ 泡疹	_____ 小便困难
_____ 冰伤（烫起水泡）	_____ 骨胳，关节疾病
_____ 高血压	_____ 腭裂
_____ 严重的低血压	_____ 哮喘
_____ 静脉注射抗菌素或利尿剂	_____ 肺部或呼吸道疾病
_____ 心脏病发作	_____ 不明原因的体重减轻
_____ 心绞痛	_____ （ _____ ）癌
_____ 心律不齐	_____ 其它肿瘤（ _____ ）
_____ 其它心脏疾病	_____ 输血
_____ 风湿热	_____ 肝炎
_____ 结核	_____ 爱滋病
_____ 青光眼	_____ 脑膜炎
_____ 多发性硬化症	
_____ 其它疾病（请说明。）	

41. 和你有血缘关系的亲戚有下列疾病吗？
　　_____ 糖尿病　　　　　　　_____ 癌症
　　_____ 低血糖　　　　　　　_____ 心脏病
　　_____ 其它类似上述所列的严重疾病（请说明病名）

42. 请描述你所遇到的严重事故（不包括你此次来就诊路上发生的事故）
　　_____ 从没发生过事故
　　_____ 发生过事故并伴有善受伤，意识丧失或颈部受伤
　　_____ 发生过事故但无头部受伤，意识丧失或颈部受伤
　　事故过程：

43. 列出你正在使用的药物及剂量（包括避孕药及维生素）。

44. 过敏药物
　　_____ 无　　　　　　　　　_____ 努夫卡因
　　_____ 青霉素　　　　　　　_____ 碘
　　_____ 磺胺类　　　　　　　_____ 可待因
　　_____ 四环素　　　　　　　_____ 胶布
　　_____ 红霉素　　　　　　　_____ 阿司匹林
　　_____ 先锋/Ceclor/Ceftin　　_____ X线造影剂
　　_____ 其它（请说明药名）

45. 手术史
　　_____ 扁桃体切除术
　　　　　　（年龄 _____ ）
　　　　　　　　　　　　　　　　_____ 肾上腺切除术
　　_____ 阑尾切除术
　　　　　　　　　　　　　　　　　　　（年龄 _____ ）
　　　　　　（年龄 _____ ）
　　　　_____ 其它手术（请说明。）　_____ 心脏手术
　　　　　　　　　　　　　　　　　　　（年龄 _____ ）

46. 列出你接触过的毒性药物或化学药品
　　_____ 铅　　　　　　　_____ 链霉素，新霉素，卡那霉素
　　_____ 汞　　　　　　　_____ 其它（请说明）

47. 你头颈部做过X线治疗吗？（包括孩子童时粉刺或耳部疾病的治疗，癌症治疗等）
　　做过在 _____ 未做过在 _____

48. 请描述你的配偶或子女的严重健康问题。
　　_____ 无

French Version of Appendix IIc

Translated by Patricia Le Foll

PASSE MEDICAL: CHANTEURS
Robert Thayer Sataloff, M.D., D.M.A.
1721 Pine Street
Philadelphia, PA 19103
U.S.A.

NOM _____ AGE ____ SEXE _____ NATIONALITÉ _____
TAILLE _____ POIDS _____ DATE _____

TYPE DE VOIX : _____ soprano _____ mezzo soprano _____ alto
_____ tenor _____ baryton _____ basse

(Si vous n'avez pas de problème de voix courant, veuillez passer à la question n° 3)

VEUILLEZ COCHER OU ENTOURER LA REPONSE CORRESPONDANT A VOTRE CAS :

1. Depuis combien de temps avez-vous votre problème de voix actuel ? 1, 2, 3, 4, 5, 6, 7, 8, 9, 10, plus [heure(s), jour(s), semaine(s), mois, an(s)]

   Qui l'a remarqué ?
   Moi-même, ma famille, le professeur de vocalises, les critiques, tout le monde, autre _____

   En connaissez vous la cause ? Oui _____ Non _____

   Si oui, donnez la cause : vous avez attrapé froid, crié, trop parlé, chanté, subi une intervention chirurgicale, autre _____

   Est-ce arrivé progressivement ou subitement ? Progressivement _____ Subitement _____

   Quelle est la situation actuelle ? Pire _____ , meilleure _____ , sans changement _____

2. Quels sont vos symptômes ? (Veuillez indiquer tout élément se rapportant à votre cas)
   _____ Enrouement (sons rauques ou grêles)
   _____ Fatigue (la voix se fatigue ou sa qualité change après avoir chanté pendant une courte période de temps)
   _____ Trouble du volume sonore (difficulté pour chanter : doucement _____ , fort _____)
   _____ Perte d'intensité dans les gammes hautes _____ basses _____
   _____ Changement de classification (par exemple : la voix passe de soprano à mezzo)
   _____ Allongement de la période de mise en train vocale (plus d'une demi-heure pour préparer la voix)
   _____ Problème de respiration
   _____ Sensations de chatouillement ou d'étouffement en chantant
   _____ Douleur dans la gorge en chantant
   _____ Autre (veuillez préciser :) _____

3. Avez-vous un important tour de chant bientôt ? Oui _____ Non _____
   Date(s) : _____

4. Quel est votre statut habituel de chanteur ?   Professionnel _____   Amateur _____

5. Quels sont vos objectifs de carrière à long terme ?
   _____ Chanteur d'opéra de premier rang
   _____ Chanteur de musique populaire de premier rang
   _____ Activité secondaire régulière
   _____ Chanteur classique
   _____ Chanteur populaire
   _____ Autre (précisez : _____)
   _____ Tours de chant amateurs (chorale ou solo)
   _____ Chanteur amateur pour la satisfaction personnelle

6. Avez-vous suivi une formation pour développer la voix ? Oui _____   Non _____

   A quel âge l'avez-vous commencée ? (Entourez :)
   2, 3, 4, 5, 6, 7, 8, 9, 10, 1l, 12, 13, 14, 15, 16, 17, 18, 19, 20, 21, 22, 23, 24, 25, 26, 27, 28, 29, 30, 35, 40, 45, 50, 55, 60, 65, 70, 75, 80, 85

7. Y a-t-il eu des mois ou des années sans leçons depuis ? Oui _____   Non _____

8. Depuis combien de temps étudiez-vous avec votre professeur actuel ?
   1, 2, 3, 4, 5, 6, 7, 8, 9, 10, 11, 12, 13, 14, 15, 16, 17, 18, 19, 20, 21, 22, 23, 24, 25, plus
   [semaine(s), mois, an(s)]

   Nom du professeur :
   Adresse du professeur :

   N° de téléphone du professeur :

9. Veuillez énumérer, ci-dessous, le nom des professeurs précédents et les années pendant lesquelles vous avez étudié avec eux :

10. Avez-vous déjà reçu un entraînement pour votre voix de conversation ? Oui _____   Non _____
    Cours de voix pour la comédie ? Oui _____   Non _____
    Combien d'années ? Moins d'une, 1–5, 6–10, plus
    Séances pour trouble de la langue ? Oui_____ Non _____
    Combien de mois ? 1, 2, 3, 4, 5, 6, 7–12, plus

11. Exercez-vous un autre métier en parallèle à votre activité de chanteur ? Oui _____   Non _____

    Si oui, cette autre occupation nécessite-t-elle un emploi intensif de la voix ? Oui _____   Non _____

    Si oui, quel métier est-ce ? Acteur, présentateur (de télévision, à la radio, sur les terrains de sport), professeur d'éducation physique, avocat, prêtre, politicien, médecin, représentant, agent de change, professeur, standardiste ou réceptionniste, serveur, serveuse, secrétaire, autre : _____

12. Lors de vos tours de chant, en plus de votre chant, vous est-il fréquemment nécessaire de parler ?
    Oui _____   Non _____   De danser ? Oui _____   Non _____

13. Pendant combien d'années avez-vous chanté régulièrement avant de commencer les cours pour la voix ?
    2, 3, 4, 5, 6, 7, 8, 9, 10, 11, 12, 13, 14, 15, 16, 17, 18, 19, 20, 21, 22, 23, 24, 25, plus

14. Quels types de musique chantez-vous ? (Veuillez indiquer tout élément se rapportant à votre cas)
    _____ pour des représentations classiques   _____ pour des spectacles
    _____ pour les discothèques   _____ pour le rock
    autre (veuillez préciser : _____)

15. Chantez-vous généralement en position assise (comme derrière un piano ou une batterie) ?
    Oui _____   Non _____

16. Chantez-vous à l'extérieur, dans de grandes salles, ou avec des orchestres ? (Entourez) Oui _____   Non _____

17. Si vous effectuez votre tour de chant avec des instruments électriques ou à l'extérieur, utilisez-vous des haut-parleurs ? Oui _____   Non _____   Si oui, pouvez-vous les entendre ? Oui _____   Non _____

18. Jouez-vous d'un ou de plusieurs instruments de musique ? Oui _____   Non _____

    Si oui, veuillez cocher le ou les instruments :
    _____ Instruments à touches (piano, orgue, clavecin, autre : _____)
    _____ violon, alto
    _____ violoncelle
    _____ basse
    _____ instruments à cordes non frottées (guitare sèche, harpe, autre : _____)
    _____ cuivres
    _____ instruments à vent à une anche
    _____ instruments à vent à double anche
    _____ flûte, piccolo
    _____ percussions
    _____ cornemuse
    _____ accordéon
    _____ autre (veuillez préciser : _____)

19. Quand faîtes-vous des gammes ?
    _____ quotidiennement
    _____ quelques fois par semaine
    _____ une fois par semaine
    _____ rarement
    _____ jamais

    Si vous faîtes des gammes, les faîtes-vous toutes en une fois ou bien les répartissez-vous tout au long de la journée ? [Toutes en une fois, en deux ou trois parties]

    Les jours pendant lesquels vous faîtes des gammes, pendant combien de temps le faîtes-vous ?
    [15, 30, 45, 60, 75, 90, 105, 120, plus, minutes]

    Quand pratiquez-vous le chant ?
    [Quotidiennement, quelques fois par semaine, une fois par semaine, rarement, jamais]

    Combien d'heures par jour ?
    [0,5, 1, 1,5, 2, 2,5, 3, plus]

    Faîtes-vous des exercices de voix avant de chanter ? Oui _____   Non _____

Faîtes-vous des exercices de voix après le chant ? Oui _____ Non _____

20. Combien de temps (heures) consacrez-vous au chant actuellement (en comprenant l'entraînement, en temps moyen par jour) ?

Répétitions : 0,5, 1, 1,5, 2, 2,5, 3, 4, 5, 6, 7, 8, 9, 10

Tours de chant : 0,5, 1, 1,5, 2, 2,5, 3, 4, 5, 6, 7, 8

21. Veuillez indiquer, ci-après, tout élément vous concernant :
_____ voix plus mauvaise le matin
_____ voix plus mauvaise en fin de journée, après pratique vocale
_____ effectue répétitions et tours de chant le matin
_____ parle beaucoup (professeur, prêtre, avocat, au téléphone, au travail, etc.)
_____ animateur
_____ parle beaucoup en coulisses ou aux soirées après les tours de chant
_____ chef de chorale
_____ râcle souvent ma gorge
_____ fréquents maux de gorge
_____ problèmes articulaires de la mâchoire
_____ goût amer ou aigre, mauvaise haleine au réveil
_____ fréquentes brûlures d'estomac ou hoquets
_____ crie souvent ou parle fort
_____ chuchote souvent
_____ fatigue chronique (insomnie)
_____ travail en des lieux très secs
_____ fais de l'exercice physique régulièrement (poids, aérobic, etc.)
_____ souvent assoiffé, déshydraté
_____ enrouement au réveil
_____ toux venant de la poitrine
_____ mange tard le soir
_____ ai pris des remèdes contre les acidités
_____ suis particulièrement tendu(e) en ce moment (pour des raisons personnelles ou professionnelles)
_____ ai souvent mauvaise haleine
_____ vis, travaille, ou chante en des lieux avec fumée ou vapeur
_____ ai voyagé récemment, quand : _____ , où : _____
Avant de chanter, mange du _____ chocolat
_____ des noisettes
_____ de la glace
_____ de la nourriture épicée
_____ de l'alcool
_____ du café
_____ du lait
autre : _____

Avez-vous des difficultés vocales techniques quelconques ?

Difficulté à chanter doucement, difficulté à chanter fort, difficulté à contrôler un accord, problèmes de soutien, difficultés avec les modulations, autre (décrivez) : _____

Avez-vous eu des problèmes récemment avec votre voix de chanteur, préalablement au problème qui vous amène ?
Enrouement, problème de respiration, fatigue, perte d'intensité, voix cassée, douleur en chantant, autre (décrivez) : _____

Avez-vous déjà eu des problèmes de voix qui vous ont amené(e) à voir un médecin ? Si oui, veuillez décrire le ou les problème(s) et son ou leur(s) traitement(s) : laryngite, nodules, polypes, hémorragie, cancer, autre (décrivez) : _____

22. Nom, adresse et téléphone de votre médecin traitant :

23. Nom, adresse et téléphone de votre laryngologiste :

24. Avez-vous attrapé froid récemment ? Oui _____ Non _____

25. Avez-vous un rhume actuellement ? Oui _____ Non _____

26. Avez-vous déjà été exposé(e) à l'un des produits chimiques suivants fréquemment ou récemment à la maison ou au travail (veuillez indiquer tout élément vous concernant) ?
    _____ monoxyde de carbone   _____ arsenic
    _____ mercure   _____ colorants azoïques
    _____ insecticides   _____ solvants industriels (benzine, etc.)
    _____ plomb
    _____ fumées de scène

27. Avez-vous reçu le diagnostic d'un spécialiste des allergies ? Oui _____ Non _____

    Si oui, quelles sont vos allergies ? Aucune, à la poussière, à la moisissure, aux arbres, aux chats, aux chiens, à certains aliments, autre : _____
    (Les allergies à certains médicaments sont traitées ultérieurement dans ce questionnaire médical)

    Si oui, veuillez indiquer le nom et l'adresse du spécialiste des allergies :

28. Combien de paquets de cigarettes fumez-vous par jour ?
    Histoire de votre consommation de cigarettes :
    _____ jamais
    _____ ai arrêté, quand ? _____
    _____ fumais environ : moins d' 0,5, 0,5, 1, 1,5, 2, 2,5, 3, plus par jour pendant 1, 2, 3, 4, 5, 6, 7, 8, 9, 10, 11–15, 16–20, 21–25, 26–30, 31–35, 36–40, 41 45, 46–50, plus an(s)
    _____ fume moins de 0,5, 0,5, 1, 1,5, 2, 2,5, 3, plus par jour pendant 1, 2, 3, 4, 5, 6, 7, 8, 9, 10, 11–15, 16–20, 21–25, 26–30, 31–35, 36–40, 41–45, 46–50, plus an(s)

29. Travaillez-vous dans un entourage de fumeurs ? Oui _____ Non _____

30. Dans quelle mesure buvez-vous de l'alcool?
    Pas du tout, plusieurs fois par semaine, tous les jours
    1, 2, 3, 4, 5, 6, 7, 8, 9, 10, plus, verres par jour, semaine
                    de bière, vin, liqueurs

    Vous est-il arrivé de boire davantage dans le passé d'une façon habituelle ? Oui _____   Non _____

31. Combien de tasses de café, thé, ou de verres de coca-cola ou autre boisson contenant de la caféine buvez-vous
    par jour ? 0, 1, 2, 3, 4, 5, 6, 7, 8, 9, 10

32. Veuillez énumérer ci-après les autres drogues auxquelles vous vous adonnez : marijuana, cocaïne, amphéta-
    mines, barbituriques, héroïne, autre : _____

33. Avez-vous remarqué l'un des phénomènes suivants (indiquez tout élément vous concernant) :
    _____ hypersensibilité au froid ou à la chaleur
    _____ transpiration excessive
    _____ changement de poids : prise/perte de poids : _____ kilos
                            en _____ semaines, _____ mois
    _____ changement observé au niveau de la peau, des cheveux
    _____ palpitations cardiaques
    _____ trouble de l'équilibre émotionnel (changements d'humeur)
    _____ vision double
    _____ insensibilité du visage ou des extrêmités
    _____ picotement de la bouche ou du visage
    _____ vision trouble ou cécité
    _____ faiblesse ou paralysie du visage
    _____ maladresse des bras ou des jambes
    _____ troubles de la conscience ou perte de conscience
    _____ problèmes d'élocution
    _____ difficulté à avaler
    _____ crises (crises d'épilepsie)
    _____ douleur dans le cou ou dans l'épaule
    _____ tremblements ou frémissements
    _____ troubles de la mémoire
    _____ changement de personnalité

    Pour les femmes :

    Etes-vous enceinte ? Oui _____   Non _____

    Avez-vous eu une hystérectomie ? Oui _____   Non _____
    Vous a-t-on enlevé les ovaires ? Oui _____   Non _____
    Avez-vous un cycle régulier ? Oui _____   Non _____
    A quel âge avez-vous atteint la puberté ? 7, 8, 9, 10, 11, 12, 13, 14, 15, 16, 17, 18, 19, 20
    Avez-vous eu votre ménopause ? Oui _____   Non _____
        Si oui, quand ? En ce moment _____
        ou: y-a-t-il 1, 2, 3, 4, 5, 6, 7, 8, 9, 10, plus, an(s)

34. Avez-vous déjà consulté un psychologue ou un psychiatre ? Oui _____   Non _____

    Etes-vous actuellement sous traitement ? Oui _____   Non _____

35. Vous êtes-vous blessé(e) à la tête ou au cou (coup du lapin, etc.) ? Oui _____   Non _____

36. Veuillez décrire tout accident sérieux qui vous serait arrivé :

37. Etes-vous en procès pour des problèmes de voix ? Oui _____   Non _____

38. Nom de votre conjoint(e) et enfant(s) :

39. Bref résumé de votre histoire médicale, dont certains aspects peuvent n'avoir aucune relation avec votre problème actuel :

    VEUILLEZ COCHER TOUT ELEMENT VOUS CONCERNANT :

    _____ perte de l'ouïe   _____ problème ophtalmologique
    _____ sons dans l'oreille   _____ autre (précisez : _____)
    _____ vertiges   _____ douleur dans l'oreille
    _____ paralysie faciale   _____ douleur de la face
    _____ obstruction nasale   _____ cou raide
    _____ plaies buccales   _____ excès de membrane oculaire
    _____ problème articulaire de la mâchoire   _____ excès épidermique sur le visage
    _____ ganglion dans le cou
    _____ ganglion sur le visage ou la tête
    _____ difficulté d'absorption

40. Avez-vous ou avez-vous eu :
    _____ du diabète   _____ des crises d'apoplexie
    _____ de l'hypoglycémie   _____ des soins psychothérapiques
    _____ des problèmes de thyroïdes   _____ des ulcères
    _____ la syphilis   _____ une maladie rénale
    _____ des gonorrhées   _____ de l'arthrose ou des problèmes de squelette
    _____ de l'herpès   _____ des blessures du palais
    _____ des gerçures ou des boutons de fièvre   _____ de l'asthme
    _____ de l'hypertension   _____ des problèmes de respiration ou de poumons
    _____ une baisse importante de tension   _____ une perte de poids inexpliquée
    _____ des injections intraveineuses d'antibiotiques _____ un cancer de _____
            ou de diurétiques   _____ autre tumeur _____
    _____ une crise cardiaque   _____ une hépatite
    _____ une angine   _____ des transfusions de sang
    _____ un battement cardiaque irrégulier   _____ le SIDA
    _____ d'autres problèmes cardiaques   _____ la méningite
    _____ une fièvre rhumatismale
    _____ la tuberculose
    _____ un glaucome
    _____ une sclérose multiple
    _____ autre(s) problème(s) ?
            Précisez :

41. Est-ce que l'un de vos parents a :
    _____ du diabète   _____ un cancer
    _____ de l'hypoglycémie   _____ une maladie cardiaque
    _____ un autre problème médical évoqué dans la liste précédente, précisez :

42. Décrivez les accidents sérieux dont vous avez été victime, à moins qu'il ne soit directement lié au problème qui vous amène ici :
    _____ aucun
    _____ est arrivé avec blessure à la tête, perte de conscience, ou "coup du lapin"
    _____ est arrivé sans blessure à la tête, perte de conscience, ni "coup du lapin"
    Décrivez :

43. Enumérez tous vos médicaments en cours, ainsi que leur quantité (y compris la pillule contraceptive et les vitamines) :

44. Allergies médicamenteuses :
    _____ aucune   _____ novocaïne
    _____ pénicilline   _____ iodine
    _____ sulfamides   _____ codéine
    _____ tétracycline   _____ aspirine
    _____ érythromycine   _____ colorants pour les rayons X
    _____ Keflex, Ceclor, Ceftine   _____ sparadrap
    _____ Autre, précisez :

45. Enumérez les interventions chirurgicales :
    _____ amygdalectomie (âge : _____)   _____ enlèvement d'une tumeur
    _____ appendicite (âge : _____)   _____ de glandes (âge : _____)
    _____ opération cardiaque (âge : _____)
    _____ Autre, précisez :

46. Enumérez les drogues toxiques ou les produits chimiques auxquels vous avez été exposé(e) :
    _____ plomb   _____ streptomycine, néomycine, kanamycine
    _____ mercure   _____ Autre précisez : _____

47. Avez-vous eu des traitements aux rayons X pour votre tête ou votre cou (y compris les traitements pour l'acné ou les problèmes d'oreilles en tant qu'enfant, les traitements pour le cancer, etc.) ? Oui _____   Non _____

48. Décrivez les problèmes médicaux importants de votre conjoint(e) ou de votre ou vos enfant(s), s'il y a lieu :

German Version of Appendix IIc

Translated by Deike Stroebel, M.D.

PATIENTENANAMNESE: SÄNGER
Robert Thayer Sataloff, M.D., D.M.A.
1721 Pine Street
Philadelphia, PA 19103
U.S.A.

Name _____ Alter (i.J.) _____ Geschlecht _____

Stamm _____ Grösse _____ Gewicht _____ Datum _____

Stimmlage: _____ Sopran _____ Mezzosopran _____ Alt
_____ Tenor _____ Bariton _____ Bass

(Wenn Sie zur Zeit kein Stimmproblem haben, gehen Sie bitte direkt zur Frage Nr. 3.)

BITTE KREUZEN ODER UMKREISEN SIE DIE FÜR SIE ZUTREFFENDEN ANTWORTEN:

1. Wie lange haben Sie Ihr jetziges Stimmproblem schon ?
   (1,2,3,4,5,6,7,8,9, 10, länger)
   (Stunden, Tage, Wochen, Monate, Jahre)

   Wer hat es zuerst bemerkt?
   (Sie selbst, Familie, Gesangslehrer, Kritiker, alle, andere Personen _____)

   Kennen Sie die Ursache?
   (Ja _____ Nein _____)

   Wenn ja, welche? (Erkältung, Schreien, exzessives Sprechen,
   Singen, Operation, andere Ursachen _____)

   Begann Ihr Stimmproblem langsam oder trat es plötzlich auf?
   (langsam _____, plötzlich _____)

   Wie ist der Verlauf bisher?: Schlechter _____ Besser _____ Unverändert _____

2. Welche Symptome haben Sie? (Bitte kreuzen Sie alle für Sie zutreffenden Antworten an.)
   _____ Heiserkeit (rauhe oder kratzige Stimme)
   _____ Ermüdungszeichen (Stimme ermüdet oder ändert sich in der Qualität, nachdem Sie kurze Zeit
   gesungen haben.)
   _____ Lautstärke-probleme (erschwertes Singen) bei _____ leisem Singen _____ lautem Singen
   _____ Verlust an Tonumfang (hohe Töne _____ , tiefe Töne _____)
   _____ Änderung der Stimmlage (z.B. Stimmlage verändert sich von Sopran zu Mezzosopran)
   _____ Verlängerte Aufwärmphase (über ½ Stunde)
   _____ Hauchige Stimme
   _____ Kratzen im Hals oder Engegefühl beim Singen
   _____ Halsschmerzen beim Singen

_____ Andere Symptome (Bitte beschreiben Sie sie): _____

_____

3. Haben Sie in nächster Zeit ein wichtiges Konzert?   Ja _____   Nein _____
   Termindaten: _____

4. Singen Sie zur Zeit geruflich _____ oder als Amateur _____?

5. Was sind die langfristigen Ziele Ihrer Gesangskarriere?
   _____ Opernsänger mit Premierenvorstellungen
   _____ Popsänger mit Premierenvorstellungen
   _____ nebenberufliche Gesangstätigkeit
   _____ Klassischer Gesang
   _____ Popmusik
   _____ Andere Ziele (_____)
   _____ Amateurveranstaltungen (Chor oder Solo)
   _____ Amateursingen zum eigenen Vergnügen

6. Hatten Sie Gesangsunterricht?   Ja _____   Nein _____
   In welchem Alter haben Sie damit begonnen? (Bitte Zutreffendes umkreisen)
   (2, 3, 4, 5, 6, 7, 8, 9, 10, 11, 12, 13, 14, 15, 16, 17, 18, 19, 20, 21, 22, 23, 24, 25, 26, 27, 28, 29, 30, 35, 40, 45, 50, 55, 60, 65, 70, 75, 80, 85)

7. Gab es monate—oder jahrelange Unterbrechungen des Gesangsunterrichts?   Ja _____   Nein _____

8. Wie lange arbeiten Sie schon mit Ihrem jetzigen Lehrer zusammen? (1, 2, 3, 4, 5, 6, 7, 8, 9, 10, 11, 12, 13, 14, 15, 16, 17, 18, 19, 20, 21, 22, 23, 24, 25, länger)
   (Wochen, Monate, Jahre)

   Name Ihres Gesangslehrers:
   Adresse:

   Telefonnummer:

9. Bitte geben Sie Ihre früheren Lehrer an und wieviele Jahre Sie mit ihnen studiert haben:

10. Hatten Sie jemals Sprachunterricht?   Ja _____   Nein _____
    Sprachunterricht für Schauspieler?   Ja _____   Nein _____
    Wieviele Jahre? (weniger als 1 Jahr, 1–5 Jahre, 6–10 Jahre, länger)
    Hatten Sie jemals eine logopädische Behandlung?   Ja _____   Nein _____
    Wenn ja, wieviele Monate? (1, 2, 3, 4, 5, 6, 7–12, länger)

11. Üben Sie einen Beruf zusätzlich zu Ihrer Gesangstätigkeit aus?   Ja _____   Nein _____

    Wenn ja, wird Ihre Stimme dabei sehr beansprucht?   Ja _____   Nein _____

    Wenn ja, welchen Beruf üben Sie aus ? (Schauspieler/in, Ansage/in - in TV, Radio, Sportarena), Sportlehrer/in, Rechtsanwalt/wältin, geistliche, Politiker/in, Arzt/Ärztin, Verkäufer/in, Börsenmakler/in, Lehrer/in, Telephonist/in, Kellner/in, Sekretär/in, anderer Beruf
    _____)

12. Müssen Sie bei Ihrem Auftreten, neben dem Gesang, vermehrt Sprechen?   Ja _____   Nein _____
    Tanzen?   Ja _____   Nein _____

13. Wieviele Jahre haben Sie aktiv gesungen, bevor Sie Sprachunterricht genommen haben?
    (1, 2, 3, 4, 5, 6, 7, 8, 9, 10, 11, 12, 13, 14, 15, 16, 17, 18, 19, 20, 21, 22, 23, 24, 25, mehr)

14. Welche Musikrichtungen singen Sie?
    (Bitte kreuzen Sie alle zutreffenden an)
    _____ Klassik _____ Showmusik _____ Nachtklub _____ Rockmusik
    Andere (Welche?: _____
    _____)

15. Singen Sie regelmässig in einer sitzenden Position (wie z.B. am Klavier oder Schlagzeug)?
    Ja _____   Nein _____

16. Singen Sie im Freien, in grossen Hallen, oder mit Orchester?
    Ja _____   Nein _____ (Bitte umkreisen Sie das Zutreffende)

17. Benützen Sie einen Lautsprecher? Wenn Sie Auftritte mit elektronischen Instrumenten oder im Freien haben?
    Ja _____   Nein _____
    Wenn ja, können Sie ihn hören?   Ja _____   Nein _____

18. Spielen Sie ein Musikinstrument?   Ja _____   Nein _____
    Wenn ja, bitte kreuzen Sie alle für Sie zutreffenden Instrumente an:
    _____ Tasteninstrument (Klavier, Orgel, Cembalo, andere_____)
    _____ Violine, Viola
    _____ Cello
    _____ Bass
    _____ Zupfinstrument (Gitarre, Harfe, andere _____)
    _____ Blechblasinstrument
    _____ Blasinstrument mit einem Blatt
    _____ Blasinstrument mit zwei Blättern
    _____ Querflöte, Piccoloflöte
    _____ Schlagzeug
    _____ Dudelsack
    _____ Akkordeon
    _____ Andere Instrumente (welche?: _____)

19. Wie oft üben Sie?
    Tonleitern: (täglich, mehrmals in der Woche, einmal in der Woche, selten, nie)

Wenn Sie Tonleitern üben, üben Sie alle auf einmal oder verteilen Sie sie über die gesamte Übungsdauer? (alle auf einmal, in 2 oder 3 Teilen)

Wenn Sie Tonleitern üben, wie lange?
(15, 30, 45, 60, 75, 90, 105, 120, mehr Minuten)

Lieder: (täglich, mehrmals in der Woche, einmal in der Woche, selten, nie)

Wieviele Stunden am Tag üben Sie ?
(½, 1, 1½, 2, 2½, 3, mehr)

Wärmen Sie Ihre Stimme auf bevor Sie singen?   Ja _____   Nein _____

Wärmen Sie Ihre Stimme nach dem Singen ab?   Ja _____   Nein _____

20. Wie lange singen Sie zur Zeit (einschliesslich der Übungszeit, Durchschnittliche Stundenanzahl/Tag)?
Übung: (½, 1, 1-½, 2, 2-½, 3, 4, 5, 6, 7, 8, 9, 10)
Aufführungen: (½, 1, 1-½, 2, 2-½, 3, 4, 5, 6, 7, 8)

21. Bitte kreuzen Sie alles an, was auf Sie zutrifft:
_____ Stimmeist schlechter vormittags
_____ Stimme ist schlechter später am Tag (nach Gebrauch)
_____ Gesangsaufführungen- oder Proben am Morgen
_____ Vermehrtes Sprechen (z.B., Lehrer, Geistlicher, Anwalt, Arbeit am Telephon, etc.)
_____ Anführer beim Anfeuern (z.B. Sportveranstaltungen)
_____ Vermehrtes Sprechen hinter der Bühne oder auf Parties nach der Vorstellung
_____ Chorleiter
_____ Häufiges Räuspern
_____ Häufige Halsschmerzen
_____ Kiefergelenksprobleme
_____ Bitterer, saurer Geschmack oder schlechter Atem nach dem Aufwachen
_____ Häufiges Sodbrennen oder Hiatushernie
_____ Häufiges Schreien oder lautes Sprechen
_____ Häufiges Flüstern
_____ Chronische Müdigkeit (Schlaflosigkeit)
_____ Arbeit unter extremer Trockenheit
_____ Häufige sportliche Tätigkeit (Gewichtheben, Aerobic, etc.)
_____ Häufiges Durstgefühl, Dehydration
_____ Heiserkeit am frühen Morgen
_____ Husten
_____ Mahlzeiten in den späten Abendstunden
_____ Einnahme von Antazida
_____ Besondere Belastungssituation zum jetzigen Zeitpunkt (persönlich oder beruflich)
_____ Häufig schlechter Atem
_____ Ständig rauchige Umgebung oder sonstige
            Abgase (privat, beruflich, bei Aufführungen)
_____ Sind Sie in letzter Zeit verreist?: Wann?: _____
            Wohin?:

Nehmen Sie vor dem Singen etwas zu sich, z.B.:
_____ Schokolade   _____ Kaffee
_____ Alkohol   _____ Milch oder Eiskrem

_____ Nüsse   _____ Scharf gewürzte Speisen
_____ andere Speisen (welche?): _____

Haben Sie bestimmte technische Schwierigkeiten beim Singen? (erschwertes Singen an leisen Stellen, erschwertes Singen an lauten Stellen, schwache Tonhöhenkontrolle, Atemstützeprobleme, Probleme bei Tonlagenübergang, andere Probleme?) _____

Haben Sie in letzter Zeit andere Probleme beim Singen bemerkt, abgesehen von dem Problem, das Sie hierherführte? (Heiserkeit, Luftnot, Ermüdung, Verlust an Tonumlang, Stimmzusammenbruch, schmerzhaftes Singen, andere Probleme, (welche? _____)

Hatten Sie in letzter Zeit gesundheitliche Probleme in die einen Arztbesuch erforderten? Wenn ja, bitte beschreiben Sie die Probleme und ggf. Behandlungen: (Laryngitis, Knötchen, Polypen, Blutungen, Krebs, andere Probleme: _____)

22. Name, Adresse and Telefonnummer Ihres Hausarztes:

23. Name, Adresse, und Telefonnummer Ihres Hals-Nasen-Ohren Arztes:

24. Waren Sie in letzter Zeit erkältet?   Ja _____   Nein _____

25. Sind Sie zur Zeit erkältet?   Ja _____   Nein

26. Waren (oder sind) Sie häufiger den folgenden Chemikalien ausgesetzt?
    (zuhause oder beruflich)
    _____ Kohlenmonoxide   _____ Arsen
    _____ Quecksilber   _____ Anilinfarbstoffe
    _____ Insektizide   _____ Industrielle Lösungsmittel (Benzol, etc.)
    _____ Blei
    _____ Bühnenrauch

27. Wurden Sie bei einem Allergologen ausgetestet?   Ja _____   Nein _____

    Wenn ja, welche Allergien haben Sie?:
    (keine, Staub, Schimmelpilze, best. Baumarten, Katzen, Hunde,
    Lebensmittel, andere _____)
    (Die Medikamente werden später im Fragebogen erfasst werden)

    Wenn ja, bitte geben Sie der Name und die Adresse des Allergologen an:_____

28. Wieviel rauchen Sie täglich?

    Raucheranamnese:
    _____ Schon immer Nichtraucher
    _____ Nichtraucher seit wann? _____
    _____ Habe geraucht (Packungen: weniger als ½, 1, 1½, 2, 2½, 3, mehr) pro Tag über (Jahre: 1, 2, 3, 4, 5, 6, 7, 8, 9, 10, 11–15, 16 20, 21–25, 26–30, 31–35, 36–40, 41–45, länger)

_____ Rauche derzeit (Packungen: weniger als ½, 1, 1½, 2, 2½, 3, mehr) pro Tag über (Jahre: 1, 2, 3, 4, 5, 6, 7, 8, 9, 10, 11–15, 16–20, 21–25, 26–30, 31–35, 36–40, 41–45, 46–50, länger)

29. Arbeiten Sie in einer Umgebung, in der geraucht wird? Ja _____ Nein _____

30. Wie oft und wieviel Alkohol trinken Sie?
(garnicht, selten, ein paar Mal/Woche, täglich)
(1, 2, 3, 4, 5, 6, 7, 8, 9, 10, mehr) Gläser (Bier, Wein, Likör) pro (Tag, Woche)

Haben Sie früher einmal mehr getrunken? Ja _____ Nein _____

31. Wieviele Tassen Kaffee, Tee, Cola oder anderer koffeinhaltiger Getränke trinken Sie pro Tag?
(1, 2, 3, 4, 5, 6, 7, 8, 9, 10)

32. Welche Entspannungsdrogen nehmen Sie ein? (Marihuana, Kokain, Amphetamine, Barbiturate, Heroin, andere _____)

33. Haben Sie folgende Zeichen an sich selber festgestellt?
(Bitte kreuzen Sie alle zutreffenden an)
_____ Überempfindlichkeit gegunüber Hitze oder Kälte
_____ Verstärktes Schwitzen
_____ Gewichtsänderung: zugenommen/abgenommen _____ Pfund in _____ Wochen/
_____ Monaten
_____ Haut- oder Haarveränderung
_____ Herzflattern oder -rasen
_____ Emotionale Labilität (Stimmungsschwankungen)
_____ Doppeltsehen
_____ Taubheitsgefühl im Gesicht oder an den Extremitäten
_____ Kribbeln um dem Mund herum oder im Gesicht
_____ Unscharfes Sehen oder Blindheit
_____ Schwäche oder Lähmung im Gesicht
_____ Schwerfälligkeit in Armen oder Beinen
_____ Bewußtseinsverwirrung oder- verlust
_____ Sprachschwierigkeiten
_____ Schluckbeschwerden
_____ Epileptischer Anfall
_____ Nacken- oder Schulterschmerzen
_____ Zittern oder Tremor
_____ Gedächtnisveränderung
_____ Persönlichkeitsveränderung

Sonderfragen für Frauen:

Sind Sie schwanger? _____ Ja _____ Nein

Ist Ihre Periode regelmässig? Ja _____ Nein _____
Hatten Sie eine Hysterektomie (Gebärmutterentfernung)? Ja _____ Nein _____
Wurden bei Ihnen die Eierstöcke entfernt? Ja _____ Nein _____
In welchem Alter erreichten Sie die Pubertät?
(7, 8, 9, 10, 11, 12, 13, 14, 15, 16, 17, 18, 19, 20)
Sind sie in der Wechseljahren? Ja _____ Nein _____

Wenn ja, seit wann? (seit kurzem, seit 1, 2, 3, 4, 5, 6, 7, 8, 9, 10, mehr Jahren)

34. Haben Sie jemals einen Psychologen oder Psychiater aufgesucht?   Ja _____   Nein _____
    Befinden Sie sich zur Zeit in Behandlung? Ja _____   Nein _____

35. Haben Sie eine Kopf- oder Halsverletzung durchgemacht (Schlendertrauma, etc.)? Ja _____   Nein _____

36. Beschreiben Sie ggf. durchgemachte ernstere Unfälle.

37. Sind sie in ein Gerichtsverfahren bezüglich Ihrer Stimmeprobleme verwickelt? Ja _____   Nein _____

38. Name des/der Ehegatten/gattin und der Kinder:

39. Kurze Zusammenstellung der Hals-, Nasen- oder Ohrenprobleme, welche möglicherweise nicht mit Ihren
    derzeitigen Beschwerden zusammenhängen:

    BITTE KREUZEN SIE ALLE ZUTREFFENDEN ANTWORTEN AN:

    _____ Hörverlust   _____ Ohrenschmerzen
    _____ Ohrengeräusche   _____ Gesichtsschmerzen
    _____ Schwindel   _____ Steifer Nacken
    _____ Gesichtslähmung   _____ Schwellung im Nacken
    _____ Obstruktion im Nasenbereich   _____ Schwellung im Gesichts - oder Kopfbereich
    _____ Nasenverformung   _____ Erschwertes Schlucken
    _____ Wunden oder Entzündungen im   _____ Über-hängende Augenlider
            Mundbereich   _____ Vermehrte Faltenbildung im Gesicht
    _____ Kiefergelenksprobleme
    _____ Augenprobleme
    _____ Andere Probleme (welche?)

40. Haben oder hatten Sie jemals:
    _____ Diabetes   _____ Krampfanfall/epileptischer Anfall
    _____ Hypoglykämie   _____ Psych. Behandlung
    _____ Schilddrüsenprobleme   _____ gehäuft starke Kopfschmerzen
    _____ Syphilis   _____ Magen/Darmgeschwür
    _____ Gonorrhoe   _____ Nierenerkrankung
    _____ Herpes   _____ Harnblasenproblem
    _____ Erfrierungen/Rostbeulen   _____ Gelenkbeschwerden
    _____ Bluthochdruck   _____ Lippen-Kiefer-Gaumenspalte
    _____ Ausgeprägte Hypotonie   _____ Asthma
    _____ Intravenöse Behandlung mit   _____ Lungen-oder Atemproblem
            Antibiotika oder Diuretika   _____ Ungeklärter Gewichtsverlust
    _____ Herzinfarkt   _____ Krebs (welchen? _____)
    _____ Angina pectoris   _____ Anderer Tumor (_____)
    _____ Unregelmässiger Herzschlag   _____ Blutübertragung
    _____ Andere Herzprobleme   _____ Hepatitis
    _____ Rheumatisches Fieber   _____ AIDS

_____ Tuberkulose   _____ Meningitis

_____ Glaukom

_____ Multiple Sklerose

_____ Andere Erkrankungen (welche?):

41. Haben Ihre Blutsverwandten Erkrankungen?:

_____ Diabetes   _____ Krebs

_____ Hypoglykämie   _____ Herzerkrankung

_____ Andere grössere gesundheitliche Probleme (welche?)

42. Bitte beschreiben Sie schwere Unfälle, sofern sie nicht direkt mit Ihrem heutigen Arztbesuch zusammen-hängen.

_____ Keine

_____ Unfälle mit Kopfverletzungen, Bewusstseinsverlust, oder Schleudertrauma

_____ Unfälle ohne Kopfverletzungen, Bewusstseinsverlust, oder Schleudertrauma _____

_____)

43. Bitte geben Sie alle Medikamenten in der zur Zeit eingenommenen Menge an (einschliesslich Antibabypille und Vitaminpräparaten)

44. Bestehen bei Ihnen Allergien auf bestimmte Medikamente:

_____ keine   _____ Novokain

_____ Penizillin   _____ Jod

_____ Sulfonamide   _____ Kodein

_____ Tetracyclin   _____ Pflaster

_____ Erythromycin   _____ Aspirin

_____ Cefalosporine   _____ Röntgenkontrastmittel

_____ Andere Medikamente (welche?):

45. Geben Sie Operationen an:

_____ Tonsillektomie (im Alter von _____ Jahren)

_____ Appendektomie (im Alter von _____ Jahren)

_____ Adenoidektomie (im Alter von _____ Jahren)

_____ Herzoperationen (im Alter von _____ Jahren)

_____ Andere Operationen (welche?):

46. Listen Sie die Medikamente oder Chemikalien auf, denen Sie ausgesetzt waren:

_____ Blei   _____ Streptomycin, Neomycin, Kanamycin

_____ Quecksilber   _____ Andere (welche):

47. Hatten Sie eine Strahlenbehandlung im Kopf- oder Halsbereich (eingeschlossen Aknebehandlung, Bestrahlung bei Ohrenproblemen im Kindesalter, Krebstherapie, etc.)?   Ja _____   Nein _____

48. Bitte beschreiben Sie ernsthafte gesundheitliche Probleme Ihres Ehegatten/gattin oder Ihrer Kinder.

_____ keine

Greek Version of Appendix IIc

Translated by Georgia Generalis
ΙΑΤΡΙΚΟ ΠΛΗΡΟΦΟΡΙΑΚΟ ΣΗΜΕΙΩΜΑ ΑΣΘΕΝΗ: ΤΡΑΓΟΥΔΙΣΤΕΣ
Robert Thayer Sataloff, M.D., D.M.A.
1721 Pine Street
Philadelphia, PA 19103
U.S.A.

ΟΝΟΜΑ _____ ΗΛΙΚΙΑ _____ ΦΥΛΛΟ _____ ΦΥΛΗ _____

ΥΨΟΣ _____ ΒΑΡΟΣ _____ ΗΜΕΡ/ΝΙΑ _____

ΚΑΤΗΓΟΡΙΑ ΦΩΝΗΣ: _____ ΥΨΙΦΩΝΟΣ _____ ΜΕΤΖΟ ΣΟΠΡΑΝΟ _____ ΧΑΜΗΛΟΦΩΝΟΣ
_____ ΤΕΝΟΡΟΣ _____ ΒΑΡΥΤΟΝΟΣ _____ ΜΠΑΣΟΣ

(Εάν κατά το παρόν δεν έχετε πρόβλημα φωνής, παρακαλείθτε να αφήσετε ασυμπλήρωτη την Ερώτηση υπ. αριθ. 3)

ΠΑΡΑΚΑΛΕΙΣΘΕ ΝΑ ΣΗΜΕΙΩΣΕΤΕ ΝΑ ΚΛΕΙΣΕΤΕ ΣΕ ΚΥΚΛΟ ΤΗ ΣΩΣΤΗ ΑΠΑΝΤΗΣΗ

1. Πόσο καιρό έχετε το παρόν φωνητικό πρόβλημα;

    [1, 2, 3, 4, 5, 6, 7, 8, 9, 10, περισσότερο]
    [ώρες, ημέρες, εβδομάδες, μήνες, έτη]

    Ποιός το πρόσεξε;

    [εσείς, οικογένεια, δάσκαλος φωνής, κριτικός, όλοι, άλλος _____]

    Γνωρίζετε την αιτία;
    [Ναι ____   Όχι ____]

    Εάν ναι, ποια είναι; [κρύωμα, κραυγή, πολή ομιλία, τραγούδι, εγχείρηση, άλλη αιτία _____]

    Το πρόβλημα παρουσιάστηκε σιγά-σιγά ή ξαφνικά;
    [Σιγά-σιγά _____, Ξαφνικά _____   ]

    Νιώθετε: Χειρότερα _____, Καλλίτερα _____, ή το ίδιο _____]

2. Τι συμπτώματα έχετε; (σημειώστε το κατάλληλο)
    _____ Βραχνάδα (άριθμη φωνή)
    _____ Κόπωση (κουρασμένη ή αλλαγή ποιότητας φωνής μετά από μικρή διάρκεια τραγουδιού)
    _____ Προβλήματα με το τραγούδι απαλά _____   δυνατά _____
    _____ Χάσιμο είρους (ψηλά _____   χαμηλά _____)
    _____ Αλλαγή ταξινομήσεως της φωνής (παράδειγμα: η φωνή χαμηλώνει από υψίφωνα σε mezzo).
    _____ Παρατεταμένες ρρόβες (προθέρμανση φωνής για μισή ώρα)
    _____ Αναπνοή
    _____ Αίσθημα γαργαλίσματος ή καταπνίξεως κατά την ώρα του τραγουδιού.
    _____ Πόνος στο λαιμό κατά την ώρα του τραγουδιού.

_____ Άλλη αιτία (περιγράψτε ακριβώς) _____

_____

3. Έχετε να δώσετε σπουδαία παράσταση σύντομα;   Ναι _____   Όχι _____
   Ημερομηνίες: _____

4. Περιγράψτε τη σταδιοδρομία σας στο τραγούδι: Επαγγελματική _____   Ερασιτεχνική _____

5. Ποια είναι η μελλοντική σας σταδιοδρομία στο τραγούδι;
   [ ] Πρεμιέρα σε Όπερα
   [ ] Πρεμιέρα σε μοντέρνα μουσική (pop music)
   [ ] Επαγγελματική απασχόληση
   [ ] Κλασική
   [ ] Μοντέρνα
   [ ] Άλλη [_____]
   [ ] Ερασιτεχνική παράσταση (χορωδία ή μόνος/-η)
   [ ] Τραγουδώντας ερασιτεχνικά για δική σας ευχαρίστηση.

6. Έχετε πάρει μαθήματα φωνητικής;   Ναι _____   Όχι _____   Σε ποια ηλικία αρχίσατε; (σημειώστε)
   [2,3,4,5,6,7,8,9,10,11,12,13,14,15,16,17,18,19,20,21,22,23,24,25,26,27,28,29,30,35,40,45,50,55,60,65,70,75,80,85]

7. Υπήρξαν χρονικές περίοδοι μηνών ή ετών που δεν πήρατε μαθήματα;   Ναι _____   Όχι _____

8. Πόσον καιρό σπουδάζετε με τον παρόντα δάσκαλο;
   [2,3,4,5,6,7,8,9,10,11,12,13,14,15,16,17,18,19,20,21,22,23,24,25, περισσότερο]

   [εβδομάδες _____   μήνες, _____   έτη _____]

   Όνομα δασκάλου: _____
   Διεύθυνση δασκάλου: _____
   Τηλέφωνο δασκάλου: _____

9. Ονομάσετε τους δασκάλους και τα χρόνια κατά τη διάρκεια των οποίων σπουδάσατε μαζί τους.

10. Έχετε πάρει μαθήματα ορθοφωνίας (ομιλίας);   Ναι _____   Όχι _____
    Μαθήματα ηθοποιίας - Φωνής;   Ναι _____   Όχι _____
    Πόσα χρόνια;   [λιγότερα από ένα, 1-5, 6-10, περισσότερα]
    Θεραπεία λόγου;   Ναι _____   Όχι _____   Πόσους μήνες;
                                                    [1, 2, 3, 4, 5, 6, 7-12, περισσότερους]

11. Έχετε άλλη εργασία επιπλέον του τραγουδιού;
    Ναι _____   Όχι _____

    Εάν ναι, απαιτεί πολύ τη χρησιμοποίηση της φωνής σας;
    Ναι _____   Όχι _

Εάν ναι, τι είδους εργασία; (ηθοποιός, εκφωνητής/εκφωνήτρια τηλεοράσεως, ραδιοφώνου, αθλητικά), εκπαίδευση αθλητών, δικηγόρος, εκκλησιαστική απασχόληση, πολιτικός, ιατρός, πωλητής, χρηματιστής, δάσκαλος, τηλεφωνητής ή υπάλληλος υποδοχής, σερβιτόρος/-α, γραμματέας, άλλο _____

12. Κατά παράστασή σας, επιπλέον του τραγουδιού, χρειάζεται και να μιλάτε;
    Ναι _____   Όχι _____.   Χορεύετε; Ναι _____   Όχι _____

13. Πόσα χρόνια τραγουδούσατε πριν αρχίσετε μαθήματα φωνής;
    [2,3,4,5,6,7,8,9,10,11,12,13,14,15,16,17,18,19,20,21,22,23,24,25,περισσότερο]

14. Τί είδους μουσική τραγουδάτε; (σημειώστε)
    _____ Κλασική   _____ Θέαμα
    _____ Νυχτερινό κέντρο   _____ Μοντέρνο (Rock)
    _____ Άλλο (αναφέρετε συγκεκριμένα) _____

15. Συνηθίζετε να τραγουδάτε καθισμένος/-η (όπως στο πιάνο ή τύμπανα);
    Ναι _____   Όχι _____

16. Τραγουδάτε σε υπαίθριους χώρους, αίθουσες με ορχήστρες; (σημειώστε)   Ναι _____   Όχι _____

17. Εάν δίνετε παράσταση με ηλεκτρικά όργανα ή στο ύπαιθρο, χρησιμοποιείτε κατευθυνόμενα
    μεγάφωνα;   Ναι _____   Όχι _____
    Εάν ναι, μπορείτε να τα ακούσετε;   Ναι _____   Όχι _____

18. Παίζετε μουσικό/-ά όργανο/-α;   Ναι _____   Όχι _____
    Εάν ναι, σημειώστε το κατάλληλο:
    _____ Πλήκτρα (πιάνο, όργανο, άλλο _____)
    _____ Βιολί, βιόλα
    _____ Βιολοντσέλο
    _____ Μπάσο
    _____ Έγχορδα (Κιθάρα, άρπα, άλλο _____)
    _____ Σάλπιγγα
    _____ Φύσημα με μονό αυλό
    _____ Φύσημα με διπλό αυλό
    _____ Φλάουτο, μικρό φλάουτο
    _____ Κρουστό
    _____ Γκάιντα
    _____ Ακορντεόν
    _____ Άλλο (περιγράψτε) _____

19. Πόσο συχνά εξασκείστε;
    Κλίμακες: [καθημερινά, μερικές φορές την εβδομάδα, μια φορά την εβδομάδα, σπάνια, ποτέ]

    Εάν εξασκείστε στις κλίμακες, τις κάνετε όλες συγχρόνως ή τις χωρίζετε κατά τη διάρκεια της ημέρας; [όλες συγχρόνως, σε δύο ή τρεις εξασκήσεις]

Τις ημέρες που εξασκείστε με κλίμακες, για πόσο χρόνο εξασκείστε με αυτές;
[15, 30, 45, 60, 75, 90, 105, 120, περισσότερο] λεπτά

Τραγούδια: [καθημερινά, μερικές φορές την εβδομάδα, μια φορά την εβδομάδα, σπάνια, ποτέ]

Πόσες ώρες την ημέρα;
[½, 1, 1½, 2, 2½, 3, περισσότερες]

Κάνετε φωνητική παράδοση πριν τραγουδήσετε;   Ναι _____   Όχι _____

Κάνετε φωνητική μετάβαση όταν σταματήσετε το τραγούδι;   Ναι _____   Όχι _____

20. Πόσο τραγουδάτε τώρα (συμπεριλαμβανομένου και του χρόνου εξασκήσεως) κατά μέσο όρο την ημέρα;
Πρόβες: [½, 1, 1½, 2, 2½, 3, 4, 5, 6, 7, 8, 9, 10]
Παράσταση: [½, 1, 1½, 2, 2½, 3, 4, 5, 6, 7, 8]

21. Σημειώστε αυτά που σας αφορούν:
_____ Η φωνή χειροτερεύει το πρωί
_____ Η φωνή χειροτερεύει αργότερα την ημέρα μετά τη χρησιμοποίησή της.
_____ Παραστάσεις τραγουδιού ή πρόβες το πρωί
_____ Μιλάτε πολύ; (π.χ. δάσκαλος, κληρικός, δικηγόρος, τηλέφωνο, εργασία, κλπ.)
_____ Συμμετοχή σε ομάδα που παρασύρει τον κόσμο σε ζητωκραυγές και σε ενθουσιασμό
_____ Μιλάτε εκτενέστερα πίσω από τη σκηνή ή σε πάρτι μετά τις παραστάσεις
_____ Διευθυντής χορωδίας
_____ Καθαρίζετε συχνά το λαιμό σας
_____ Συχνά ερεθισμένος λαιμός
_____ Προβλήματα αρθρώσεως ομιλίας
_____ Πικρή ή ξινή γεύση, ή κακοσμία του στόματος το πρωί
_____ Συχνές καούρες ή ισοφαγοκήλη
_____ Συχνές κραυγές ή δυνατή ομιλία
_____ Συχνά ψιθυρίσματα
_____ Χρόνια κόπωση (αϋπνία)
_____ Δουλεύετε σε ξηρό περιβάλλον
_____ Συχνή γυμναστική (βάρη, αερόμπικς, κλπ.)
_____ Συχνή δίψα, αφυδάτωση
_____ Βραχνάδα το πρωί
_____ Βήχας θώρακα
_____ Τρώτε αργά το βράδι
_____ Έχετε χρησιμοποιήσει αντιόξινα φάρμακα
_____ Κάτω από ιδιαίτερο άγχος προς το παρόν (προσωπικό ή επαγγελματικό)
_____ Συχνή κακοσμία στόματος
_____ Ζείτε, εργάζεστε, ή δίνετε παραστάσεις σε περιβάλλον με καπνούς ή αναθυμιάσεις;
_____ Ταξιδέψατε πρόσφατα;   Πότε; _____
                                  Πού; _____

Τι τρώτε από τα παρακάτω πριν τραγουδήσετε;
_____ Σοκολάτα   _____ Καφέ
_____ Οινοπνευματώδη   _____ Γάλα ή Παγωτό
_____ Ξηρούς καρπούς   _____ Καυτερά φαγητά

Άλλα (σημειώστε)

_____ Φωνητική δυσκολία τεχνικής φύσεως;

[Προβλήματα με το σιγανό τραγούδι, προβλήματα τραγουδώντας δυνατά, πρόθηκα ελέγχου ύψουγ (συχνότητας) πρόβλημα ενισχύσεως (βοήθειας), πρόβλημα αλλαγής ρυθμού, άλλα]
Περιγράψτε:

_____ Είχατε άλλο φωνητικό πρόβλημα στο τραγούδι πριν από το παρόν πρόβλημα για το οποίο είστε σήμερα εδώ;

[βραχνάδα, αναπνοή, κούραση, πόνος όταν τραγουδάτε, άλλα] Περιγράψτε:

_____ Είχατε προβλήματα στο παρελθόν που απαιτούσαν επίσκεψη σε γιατρό; Εάν ναι, παρακαλώ περιγράψτε τα προβλήματα και τις θεραπείες:

[λαρυγγίτιδα, όγκος, πολύποδας, αιμορραγία, καρκίνος, άλλα] Περιγράψτε:

22. Όνομα, διεύθυνση και αριθμός τηλεφώνου του οικογενειακού σας γιατρού:

23. Όνομα, διεύθυνση και αριθμός τηλεφώνου του λαρυγγολόγου σας.

24. Είχατε κρύωμα στο πρόσφατο παρελθόν;   Ναι _____   Όχι _____

25. Είστε κρυωμένος/-η τώρα;   Ναι _____   Όχι _____

26. Έχετε εκτεθεί συχνά (ή πρόσφατα) στα παρακάτω χημικά στο σπίτι ή στην εργασία σας;
(σημειώστε το κατάλληλο)

_____ μονοξείδιο του άνθρακα   _____ αρσενικό
_____ υδράργυρος   _____ χρωστική ανιλίνη
_____ εντομοκτόνο   _____ βιομηχανικά διαλυτικά υγρά
_____ μόλυβδος   (βενζίνη, κλπ.)
_____ καπνός σκηνής
(διακοσμητικός καπνός σκηνής)

27. Έχετε εξεταστεί για αλλεργίες;   Ναι _____   Όχι _____
Εάν ναι, τι αλλεργίες έχετε;
[καμία, σκόνη, μούχλα, δέντρα, γάτες, σκύλοι, τροφές, άλλα _____]
(οι αλλεργίες σε φάρμακα καλύπτονται σε άλλη σελίδα)

Δώστε το όνομα και τη διεύθυνση του γιατρού

28. Πόσα πακέτα τσιγάρα καπνίζετε την ημέρα;

(Ιστορικό καπνίσματος)
_____ Ποτέ
_____ Σταμάτησα να καπνίζω. Πότε;
_____ Κάπνιζα περίπου [λιγότερο από μισό πακέτο, μισό, ένα, ενάμισι, δύο, δυόμισι, τρία, περισσότερα] την ημέρα για [1, 2, 3, 4, 5, 6, 7, 8, 9, 10, 11-15, 16-20, 21-25, 26-30, 31-35, 36-40, 41-45, 46-50, περισσότερα] χρόνια.
_____ Καπνίζω περίπου [λιγότερο από μισό πακέτο, μισό, ένα, ενάμισι, δύο, δυόμισι, τρία, περισσότερα] την ημέρα για [1, 2, 3, 4, 5, 6, 7, 8, 9, 10, 11-15, 16-20, 21-25, 26-30, 31-35, 36-40, 41-45, 46-50, περισσότερα] χρόνια.

29. Δουλεύετε σε περιβάλλον που έχει καπνό;   Ναι _____   Όχι _____

30. Πόσα οινοπνευματώδη ποτά πίνετε;   [κανένα, σπανίως, μερικές φορές την εβδομάδα, κάθε μέρα]
    [1, 2, 3, 4, 5, 6, 7, 8, 9, 10, περισσότερα] ποτήρια την [ημέρα, εβδομάδα] [μπύρα, κρασί, ποτό]
    Πίνατε περισσότερο στο πδρελθόν   Ναι _____   Όχι _____

31. Πόσα φλιτζάνια καφέ, τσάι, κόκα-κόλα ή άλλα ποτά με καφεΐνη πίνετε την ημέρα;
    [0, 1, 2, 3, 4, 5, 6, 7, 8, 9, 10]

32. Αναφέρετε άλλα ψυχοφάρμακα που χρησιμοποιείτε [μαριχουάνα, κοκαΐνη, αμφεταμίνες,
    βαρβιτουρικά, ηρωίνη, άλλα _____]

33. Έχετε παρατηρήσει τίποτε από τα ακόλουθα; (σημειώστε)
    _____ Υπερευαισθησία στη ζέστη ή στο κρύο
    _____ Υπερβολικό ίδρωμα
    _____ Αλλαγή στο βάρος;   πήρατε/χάσατε _____ κιλά (λίβρες)
                                  σε _____ εβδομάδες/ _____ μήνες
    _____ Αλλαγή στο δέρμα ή τα μαλλιά
    _____ Ταχυπαλμία (φτερούγισμα) της καρδιάς
    _____ Ψυχική αστάθεια (αλλαγέτ στη διάθεσή σας)
    _____ Διπλή όραση
    _____ Μούδιασμα του προσώπου ή των άκρων
    _____ Τσούξιμο γύρω από το στόμα ή το πρόσωπο
    _____ Θάμπωμα της ορατότητας ή τύφλωση
    _____ Αδυναμία ή παράλυση του προσώπου
    _____ Αδεξιότητα στα χέρια ή στα πόδια
    _____ Σύγχυση ή χάσιμο των αισθήσεων
    _____ Δυσκολία στην ομιλία
    _____ Δυσκολία όταν καταπίνετε
    _____ Σπασμοί (επιληπτικοί σπασμοί)
    _____ Πόνος στο λαιμό ή στον ώμο
    _____ Κλόνισμα - τρεμούλιασμα
    _____ Αλλαγή στη μνήμη
    _____ Αλλαγή προσωπικότητας

    Για γυναίκες

    Είστε έγκυος;   Ναι _____   Όχι _____
    Έχετε υποστεί υστερεκτομή;   Ναι _____   Όχι _____
    Έχετε βγάλει τις ωοθήκες σας;   Ναι _____   Όχι _____
    Είναι οι περίοδοί σας κανονικές στην έμμηνο ροή τους;   Ναι _____   Όχι _____
    Σε ποια ηλικία φθάσατε στη σεξουαλική ωριμότητα;
    [7, 8, 9, 10, 11, 12, 13, 14, 15, 16, 17, 18, 19, 20]
    Έχει σταματήσει η έμμηνος περίοδός σας;   Ναι _____   Όχι _____

    Εάν ναι, πότε; [την παρούσα χρονική περίοδο; 1, 2, 3, 4, 5, 6, 7, 8, 9, 10 χρόνια πριν]

34. Έχετε ποτέ συμβουλευτεί ψυχολόγο ή ψυχίατρο;
    Ναι _____   Όχι _____
    Εισαστε πρόσφατα υπό θεραπεία;   Ναι _____   Όχι _____

35. Έχετε τραυματιστεί ποτέ στο λαιμό ή στο κεφάλι; (απότομη κίνηση, κλπ.)   Ναι _____   Όχι _____

36. Περιγράψτε οποιοδήποτε σοβαρό ατύχημα.

37. Είστε υπό νομική - δικαστική αγωγή για το πρόβλημα της φωνής σας;
Ναι _____ Όχι _____

38. Αναφέρετε ονόματα συζύγου και παιδιών:

39. Αναφέρετε περιληπτικά ωτορινολαρυγγολογικά προβλήματα μερικά από τα οποία ίσως δεν έχουν καμία σχέση με τα παράπονα του παρόντος.

ΠΑΡΑΚΑΛΕΙΣΤΕ ΝΑ ΣΗΜΕΙΩΣΕΤΕ ΑΥΤΑ ΠΟΥ ΣΑΣ ΑΦΟΡΟΥΝ

_____ Χάσιμο ακοής (κώφωση)
_____ Βοή στ' αυτιά
_____ Ζαλάδες
_____ Παράλυση προσώπου
_____ Φράξιμο της μύτης
_____ Παραμόρφωση της μύτης
_____ Ερέθισμα του στόματος
_____ Προβλήματα σιαγόνας
_____ Προβλήματα με την όραση
_____ Άλλα: (παρακαλείστε να αναφερθείτε συγκεκριμένα)

_____ Πόνος αφτιών
_____ Πόνος προσώπου
_____ Σκληρός αυχένας
_____ Όγκος στο λαιμό
_____ Όγκος στο πρόσωπο ή στο κεφάλι
_____ Πρόβλημα κατάποσης
_____ Υπερβολικό δέρμα στα μάτια.
_____ Υπερβολικό δέρμα στο πρόσωπο

40. Έχετε ή είχατε στο παρελθόν:

_____ Διαβήτη
_____ Υπογλυκαιμία
_____ Προβλήματα θυρεοειδή αδένα
_____ Σύφιλη
_____ Βλεννόροια
_____ Έρπης
_____ Άφθες
_____ Υψηλή πίεση
_____ Επικίνδυνα χαμηλή πίεση
_____ Ενδοφλέβεια ανυθιοτικά η διουρημκά
_____ Προβλήματα πνευμόνων και αναπνοής
_____ Έμφραγμα
_____ Φλόγωση του λαιμού
_____ Αρρυθμία
_____ Άλλα προβλήματα της καρδιάς
_____ Ρευματισμούς των άκρων (Ρευκαυμό ωρετύ)
_____ Φυματίωση

_____ Γλαύκωμα
_____ Πολλαπλή σκλήρωση (Σκλώρωσμ κατά ηλάκας)
_____ Άλλες ασθένειες, προσδιορίστε:
_____ Σπασμούς
_____ Ψυχοθεραπείu
_____ Συχνοί μεγάλοι πονοκέφαλοι
_____ Έλκος
_____ Νεφροπάθειες
_____ Ουρολογικά προβλήματα
_____ Αρθριτικά
_____ Λαγόχειλο
_____ Άσθμα
_____ Ανεξήγητο χάσιμο βάρους
_____ Καρκίνο του (_____)
_____ Άλλοι όγκοι
_____ Μεταγγίσεις αίματος
_____ Ηπατίτιδα
_____ Έιτζ (AIDS)
_____ Μηνιγγίτιδα

41. Έχει κανένας εξ αίματος συγγενής σας:
_____ Διαβήτη   _____ Καρκίνο
_____ Υπογλυκαιμία   _____ Καρδιοπάθεια
_____ Άλλα μεγάλα ιατρικά προβλήματα όπως τα παραπάνω. Παρακαλείστε να προσδιορίσετε:

42. Περιγράψτε σοβαρά ατυχήματα εκτός και αν σχετίζονται άμεσα με την επίσκεψη στο γιατρό σας εδώ.
_____ Κανένα
_____ Συνέβη μαζί με τον ταυματισμό της κεφαλής, χάσιμο των αισθήσεων ή απότομο τράνταγμα στον αυχένα
_____ Συνέβη χωρίς τραυματισμό της κεφαλής, χάσιμο των αισθήσεων ή σπάσιμο του λαιμού. Περιγράψτε:

43. Αναφέρετε όσα φάρμακα παίρνετε πρόσφατα και τις δόσεις (συμπεριλαμβανομένων των αντισυλληπτικών χαπιών και βιταμινών)

44. Αλλεργία στα φάρμακα:
_____ Καμία   _____ Νοβοκαΐνη
_____ Πενικιλίνη   _____ Ιώδιο
_____ Σούλφα   _____ Κοδεΐνη
_____ Τετρακυκλίνη   _____ Κολλητική ταινία
_____ Ερυθρομυκίνη   _____ Ασπιρίνη
_____ Κέφλερ/Σέκλορ/Σέρφτιν
_____ Ακτίνες
_____ Άλλα, παρακαλείστε να προσδιορίσετε

45. Αναφέρετε εγχειρήσεις
_____ Αμυγδαλεκτομή   _____ Κρεατάκια
       (ηλικία ____)   (ηλικία ____)
_____ Σκωληκοειδίτιδα   _____ Εγχείρηση καρδιάς
       (ηλικία ____)   (ηλικία ____)
_____ Άλλα, προσδιορίστε:

46. Αναφέρετε τοξικά ναρκωτικά ή χημικά στα οποία έχετε εκτεθεί:
_____ Μόλυβδος   _____ Στρεπτομυκίνη, Νεομυκίνη,
_____ Υδράργυρος   Καναμυκίνη
                                  _____ Άλλα, προσδιορίστε:

47. Έχετε κάνει ακτινοθεραπείες στο κεφάλι ή στο λαιμό σας (συμπεριλαμβανομένης της θεραπείας για ακμή ή πρόβλημα αφτιών στην παιδική σας ηλικία, θεραπεία για καρκίνο, κλπ.);
       Ναι ____   Όχι ____

48. Περιγράψτε σοβαρά προβλήματα υγείας του/της συζύγου ή των παιδιών:
_____ Κανένα

Hebrew Version of Appendix IIc

תולדות הפציינט: זמרים
דר' רוברט ט. סטלוף, דר' לרפואה, דר' למוסיקה
רח. פיין 1721
פילדלפיה, פנסילבניה 19103

שם_____ גיל_____ מין_____ מוצא_____

גובה_____ משקל_____ תאריך_____

קטגורית הקול: סופרן_____ מצו סופרן_____ אלט_____
טנור_____ בריטון_____ בס_____

(במידה ואין לך בעית קול עכשוית, עבור לשאלה מס. 3.

סמן בבקשה את התשובות הנכונות

1. כמה זמן קיימת הבעיה הנוכחית?
(1,2,3,4,5,6,7,8,9,10)
(שעות, ימים, שבועות, חדשים, שנים)
מי הבחין בבעיה?
(אני, בני משפחה, מורה לשירה, מבקרים, כולם, אחרים_____)
האם ידוע לך מה גרם לבעיה?
(כן_____ לא_____)
אם כן, מה הגורם? (הצטננות, צעקות, דיבור מוגזם בכמותו, שירה, ניתוח,
אחר_____)
האם הבעיה הופיעה באופן הדרגתי או פתאומי?
הדרגתי_____ פתאומי_____
האם המצב נהיה: יותר גרוע_____ יותר טוב_____ ללא שינוי_____

2. איזה תסמינים יש לך? (בבקשה סמן)
____ צרידות (קול מחוספס או צורמני)
____ עייפות (הקול מתעייף או משתנה באיכותו לאחר שירה במשך זמן קצר)
____ הפרעה בעצמה (קושי לשיר) בשקט_____ בקול רם_____
____ ירידה במנעד (גבוה_____ נמוך_____)
____ שינוי בקטגורית הקול (לדוגמא: הקול יורד מסופרן למצו סופרן)
____ זמן חימום מוארך (דרושות יותר מ-30 דקות לחמם את הקול)
____ נשיפתיות
____ תחושה של דגדוג או מחנק בזמן השירה
____ כאב בגרון בזמן השירה
____ אחר (נא לציין_____)

3. האם יש לך הופעה חשובה בקרוב? כן_____ לא_____
תאריך(ים)_____

4. מהו המצב הנוכחי של קריירת השירה שלך?
מקצוען_____ חובב_____

5. מהן המטרות רחוקות הטווח של קריירת השירה שלך?
____ קריירה בשירת אופרה בראש וראשונה
____ קריירה במוסיקת פופ בראש וראשונה
____ תחביב
____ שירה קלסית
____ פופ
____ אחר (_____)
____ ביצוע חובב (מקהלה או סולו)
____ שירה חובבת לתענוג אישי

6. האם למדת פיתוח קול? כן _____ לא _____ באיזה גיל התחלת ללמוד _____

7. האם היו במשך הזמן תקופות של חודשים או שנים ללא שעורים בפיתוח קול ?

כן _____לא _____

8. כמה זמן הנך לומד אצל המורה הנוכחי?
(1,2,3,4,5,6,7,8,9,10,11,12,13,14,15,16,17,18,19,20,21,22,23,24,25, יותר)
(שבועות, חודשים,שנים)
שם המורה _____
כתובת _____
טל. _____

9. ציין את שמות מוריך הקודמים וכמה זמן למדת:

10. האם קבלת אימון לקול הדיבור שלך? כן _____ לא _____
האם קבלת אימון לקול המשחק שלך? כן _____ לא _____
כמה שנים? (פחות משנה, 1- 5 , 6-10 , יותר)
האם קבלת טיפול בדיבור? כן _____ לא _____
כמה חודשים?(1,2,3,4,5,6,7-12, יותר)

11. האם יש לך עיסוק אחר בנוסף לשירה?
כן _____ לא _____
אם כן, האם העיסוק דורש שימוש רב בקול?
כן _____ לא _____
אם כן, מהו העיסוק? {שחקן, קריין (טלויזיה/ רדיו/ זירת ספורט), מאמן אתלטיקה, עורך דין, איש דת, פוליטיקאי, רופא, איש מכירות, סוכן בורסה, מורה, מרכזן, פקיד קבלה, מלצר, מכיר, אחר}.

12. בעת ההופעות, בנוסף לשירה,האם הנך נדרש לעתים קרובות לדבר? כן _____ לא _____
לרקוד? כן _____ לא _____

13. כמה שנים שרת באופן פעיל לפני שהתחלת בשעורים לפיתוח קול?
(1,2,3,4,5,6,7,8,9,10,11,12,13,14,15,16,17,18,19,20,21,22,23,24,25,יותר)

14. איזה סוגי מוסיקה אתה שר?
קלסית _____
מועדוני לילה _____ הצגות _____
אחר (נא לציין) _____ רוק _____

15. האם הנך שר בדרך כלל במצב ישיבה (כמו מאחורי פסנתר או מערכת תופים)? כן _____
לא _____

16. האם אתה שר בחוץ או באולמות גדולים, או עם תזמורת? כן _____ לא _____
סמן היכן.

17. במידה ואתה מופיע עם כלים חשמליים, או בחוץ, האם אתה משתמש במוניטורים?
כן _____ לא _____
אם כן, האם אתה יכול לשמוע אותם? כן _____ לא _____

18. האם אתה מנגן בכלי נגינה? כן _____ לא _____
אם כן, סמן:
מקלדת (פסנתר, אורגן, צ'מבלו, אחר _____) _____
כינור, ויולה _____
צ'לו _____
בס _____

_____ כלי פריטה (גיטרה, נבל, אחר _____ (

_____ כלי נשיפה ממתכת

_____ כלי נשיפה מעץ עם עלה יחיד

_____ כלי נשיפה מעץ עם עלה כפול

_____ חליל- צד, פיקולו

_____ כלי הקשה

_____ חמת-חלילים

_____ אקורדיון

_____ אחר (נא לציין)

19. באיזו תדירות הנך מתאמן?

סולמות: (יום יום, מס' פעמים בשבוע, לעתים נדירות, אף פעם)

אם הנך מתאמן בסולמות, האם אתה מבצע אותם בפעם אחת או מחלק למספר פעמים במשך היום? (בפעם אחת, שתיים או שלוש פעמים)

בימים בהם הנך מבצע סולמות, במשך כמה זמן הנך מתאמן?
(15,30,45,60,75,90,105,120, יותר) דקות

שירים: (יום יום, מס. פעמים בשבוע, פעם בשבוע, לעתים נדירות, אף פעם)

כמה שעות ביום?
(½ , 1 , 1½ , 2 , 2½ , 3, יותר)

האם אתה מחמם את קולך לפני שאתה שר? כן _____ לא _____

האם אתה מרגיע את הקול כשאתה מסיים לשיר? כן _____ לא _____

20. כמה זמן הנך מקדיש כעת לשירה (סה"כ, כולל זמן האימונים, ממוצע שעות ליום)?

חזרות: (½ , 1 , 1½ , 2 , 2½ , 3 , 4 , 5 , 6 , 7 , 8 , 9 , 10)

הופעות: (½ , 1 , 1½ , 2 , 2½ , 3 , 4 , 5 , 6 , 7 , 8)

21. נא לסמן את המתאים לך:

_____ הקול גרוע יותר בבוקר

_____ הקול גרוע מאוחר יותר ביום, אחרי שימוש בו

_____ שר בהופעות או חזרות המתקיימות בבוקר

_____ מדבר באופן אינטנסיבי (לדוגמא - מורה, איש דת, עורך דין, משתמש הרבה בטלפון)

_____ מעודדת

_____ מדבר הרבה מאחורי הקלעים או במסיבות לאחר הופעות

_____ מנצח מקהלות

_____ מכחכח לעתים תכופות

_____ כאבי גרון תכופים

_____ בעיות במפרקי הלסת

_____ טעם מר או חומצי, או ריח רע מהפה בעת הקימה בבוקר

_____ צרבת תכופה או בקע סרעפתי

_____ צעקות תכופות או דיבור בקול רם

_____ דיבור בלחש לעתים קרובות

_____ עיפות כרונית (נדודי שינה)

_____ עבודה בסביבה יבשה באופן קיצוני

_____ תרגול תכוף – הרמת משקולות, התעמלות אירובית

_____ צמא לעתים קרובות, מיובש

_____ צרוד כאשר מתעורר בבוקר

_____ שיעול מסיבה ריאתית

_____ אוכל בשעות הלילה המאוחרות

_____ שימוש בנוגדי חומציות, גם בעבר

_____ מצוי במתח לאחרונה (אישי או מקצועי)

_____ ריח רע מהפה, תדיר

_____ גר, עובד או מופיע בסביבת עשן או אדים

_____ נסיעה רחוקה בעת האחרונה: מתי _____

לאן _____

אוכל או שותה אחד מן הדברים הבאים לפני שירה:

שוקולד_____   _____חלב או גלידה

אלכוהול_____   _____מזון מתובל

אגוזים_____   _____קפה

אחר: (פרט)

_____קשיים קוליים מיוחדים בטכניקה: (קושי לשיר בשקט, בקול רם, שליטה דלה בגובה קול, שליטה דלה בתמיכה נשימתית, במעבר בין רגיסטרים, אחר) תאר:

_____בעיות בקול השירה בעת האחרונה לפני הופעת הבעיה שהביאה אותך לכאן (צרידות, נשיפתיות, התעיפות, ירידה בטווח, שבירת קול, כאב בשירה, אחר) תאר:

_____בעית קול בעבר אשר הצריכה ביקור אצל רופא? אם כן, נסה לתאר את הבעיה(ות) והטיפולים: (דלקת גרון, יבלות, פוליפים, שטף דם, סרטן, אחר) תאר:

22. שם רופא המשפחה, כתובת ומספר טלפון:

23. שם רופא א.א.ג, כתובת ומספר טלפון:

24. האם סבלת מהצטננות בעת האחרונה? כן_____ לא_____

25. האם הנך מצונן כעת? כן _____ לא _____

26. האם נחשפת לאחד או יותר מן החומרים הבאים לעתים קרובות (או לאחרונה) בבית או בעבודה? (סמן)

חד תחמוצת הפחמן_____   _____ארסן

כספית_____   _____צבעי אנילין

קוטלי מזיקים_____   _____ממיסים תעשייתיים (בנזין וכו')

עופרת_____   _____עשן במה

27. האם נבדקת ע"י אלרגולוג? כן _____ לא_____

אם כן, אילו אלרגיות יש לך?

(אין, אבק, עובש, עצים, חתולים, כלבים, סוגי מזון, אחר_____)

(התיחסות לאלרגיה לתרופות מופיעה במקום אחר בשאלון)

אם כן, ציין שם, כתובת ומספר הטלפון של האלרגולוג.

28. כמה חפיסות סיגריות הנך מעשן ביום?

תולדות העישון:

_____לא עישנתי מעולם

_____הפסקתי (ציין מתי)

עישנתי בערך _____ חפיסות ליום, במשך _____ שנים.

מעשן _____ חפיסות ליום. מעשן מזה _____ שנים.

29. האם אתה עובד בסביבה מלאת עשן? כן_____ לא _____

30. כמה אלכוהול הנך שותה? (בכלל לא, לעתים נדירות, מספר פעמים בשבוע, יום יום) (1,2,3,4,5,6,7,8,9,10, יותר) כוסות ב (יום, שבוע) של (בירה, יין, ליקר).

האם בעבר שתית יותר? כן _____ לא _____

31. כמה כוסות של קפה, תה, קולה, או משקאות אחרים המכילים קפאין הנך שותה במשך היום?_____

32. במידה והנך משתמש בסמים, ציין (מריחואנה, קוקאין, אמפטמינים, ברביטורטים, הרואין, אחר_____)

33. האם שמת לב לאחד או לכמה מן הדברים הבאים? סמן:

_____ רגישות יתרה לחום או לקור

_____ הזעה מרובה

_____ שינויים במשקל: עליתי/ ירדתי _____ ק"ג ב _____ שבועות/ _____ חודשים

_____ דפיקות לב

_____ חוסר יציבות רגשית (שינויים במצב הרוח)

_____ ראייה כפולה

_____ חוסר תחושה בפנים או בגפיים

_____ עקצוץ מסביב לפה או לפנים

_____ טשטוש ראייה או עוורון

_____ חולשה או שיתוק של הפנים

_____ תחושת כבדות בזרועות או ברגליים

_____ בלבול או איבוד הכרה

_____ קושי בדיבור

_____ קושי בבליעה

_____ התקף אפילפטי

_____ כאב בצוואר או בכתף

_____ רעד

_____ שינוי בזכרון

_____ שינוי באישיות

לנשים:

האם את בהריון? כן _____ לא _____

האם עברת כריתת רחם? כן _____ לא _____

האם השחלות שלך הוצאו? כן _____ לא _____

האם מחזור הוסת שלך סדיר? כן _____ לא _____

באיזה גיל קבלת וסת ראשונה?

(20,19,18,17,16,15,14,13,12,11,10,9,8,7)

האם הנך מקבלת עדיין את המחזור? כן _____ לא _____

אם לא, מתי הוא נפסק? (כעת, לפני 1,2,3,4,5,6,7,8,9,10 יותר) שנים

34. האם התיעצת בעבר עם פסיכולוג או פסיכיאטר? כן _____ לא _____

האם הנך נמצא כעת בטיפול? כן _____ לא _____

35. האם נפגעת בראש או בצוואר (צליפת שוט וכדומה)? כן _____ לא _____

36. תאר תאונות רציניות במידה והיו _____

37. האם אתה נתון במעורבות משפטית הקשורה לבעיית הקול שלך?

38. רשום את שמות בת/ בן הזוג והילדים _____

39. תמצית קצרה של בעיות אף אוזן גרון, חלקן יכול לא להיות קשור לבעייתך העכשוית אנא סמן:

_____ ירידה בשמיעה   _____ כאב בפנים

_____ כאב אזניים   _____ צוואר "תפוס"

_____ טינטון   _____ שיתוק בפנים

_____ סחרחורת   _____ גוש, נפיחות בעורף

_____ חסימה באף   _____ גוש, נפיחות בפנים או בראש

_____ דפורמציה באף   _____ קושי בבליעה

_____ פצעים בפה   _____ עודף עור בעין

_____ בעיה בפרק הלסת   _____ עודף עור בפנים

_____ בעיות עיניים   _____ אחר (נא לציין)

40 . אילו מהבאים יש לך כעת, או היו לך בעבר :

התקפים אפילפטיים_____	סכרת_____
טיפולים פסיכיאטריים_____	היפוגליקמיה_____
כאבי ראש תכופים_____	בעיות בבלוטת התריס_____
כיבים_____	עגבת_____
מחלת כליות_____	זיבה_____
בעיות במערכת השתן_____	הרפס_____
בעיות במערכת השלד או דלקת_____	שלפוחיות חום_____
מפרקים_____	יתר לחץ דם_____
חך שסוע_____	לחץ דם נמוך מאוד_____
גנחת_____	מתן תוך ורידי של_____
בעיות נשימה וריאות_____	אנטיביוטיקה או תרופות_____
איבוד משקל בלתי מוסבר_____	משתנות_____
סרטן ב(_____) _____	התקף לב_____
גידול אחר ב(_____) _____	תעוקת לב_____
עירוי דם_____	דופק לא סדיר_____
דלקת כבד_____	בעיות לב אחרות_____
איידס_____	שגרון_____
דלקת קרום המח_____	שחפת_____
טרשת נפוצה_____	גלאוקומה_____
	מחלות אחרות (אנא ציין)_____

41. האם ישנם קרובי משפחה הסובלים מ:

סרטן_____	סכרת_____
מחלת לב_____	היפוגליקמיה_____
	בעיות רפואיות רציניות כנ"ל._____
	אנא צייַן:_____

42. תאר תאונות רציניות שאינן קשורות לביקורך העכשוי אצל הרופא כאן.

אין_____

_____התאונה קרתה עם פגיעת ראש, איבוד הכרה, או צליפת שוט.

_____התאונה קרתה ללא פגיעת ראש, איבוד הכרה או צליפת שוט.

תאר:_____

43. נא לרשום את כל התרופות הנלקחות על ידך כעת ומינונן (כולל גלולות למניעת הריון ויטמינים).

44. אלרגיה לתרופות

נובוקאין_____	אין_____
יוד_____	פניצילין_____
קודאין_____	סולפה_____
אגד מדבק_____	טטרציקלין_____
אספירין_____	אריתרומיצין_____
חומר ניגודי ברנטגן_____	קפלקס/צקלור_____
אחר (נא לציין_____) _____	צפטין_____

45. צייַן ניתוחים אשר עברת

כריתת אדנואידים_____	כריתת שקדים_____
גיל(_____)	(גיל_____)
ניתוח לב_____	כריתת המעי העוור_____
גיל(_____)	(גיל_____)
	אחר (נא לציין)_____

46. ציין סמים רעילים או כימיקלים שהיית חשוף להם:

עופרת_____   _____סטרפטומיצין, נאומיצין, קנמיצין

כספית_____   אחר (נא לציין)_____

47. האם קבלת טיפול קרינתי לאזור הראש או הצוואר (כולל טיפולים באקנה או בעיות באוזן בילדות, טיפול בסרטן וכדומה)?   כן_____   לא_____

48. נא לתאר בעיות בריאות רציניות של בן/בת זוגך או ילדיך.

אין_____

Italian Version of Appendix IIc

Translated by Gian Mazzoni

STORIA DEL PAZIENTE: CANTANTI
Robert Thayer Sataloff, M.D., D.M.A.
1721 Pine Street
Philadelphia, PA 19103
U.S.A.

NOME _____ ETÀ _____ SESSO _____ RAZZA _____

STATURA _____ PESO _____ DATA _____

CATEGORIA DELLA VOCE:

_____ Soprano _____ Mezzo Soprano _____ Alto

_____ Tenore _____ Baritono _____ Basso

(Se non ha problemi di voce in questo momento, risponda incominciando dalla domanda #3)

CERCHIARE LA RISPOSTA CORRETTA:

1. Da quanto tempo ha questo problema di voce?
   [1, 2, 3, 4, 5, 6, 7, 8, 9, 10, più a lungo]
   [ore, giorni, settimane, mesi, anni]

   Chi si è accorto del il problema?
   [lei, un familiare, il maestro di voce, critici, tutti, altri _____]

   Sa da cosa è causato? [si _____ no _____]

   Se la risposta è si, qual'è la causa? [raffreddore, gridare, parlare troppo, canto, chirurgia, altro _____]

   Il problema si è manifestato con l'andar del tempo o sull'istante? [andar del tempo _____ sull'istante _____]

   Sta: Peggiorando _____ , Migliorando _____ , Rimane lo stesso _____

2. Che sintomi ha? (Marchi tutti i sintomi.)
   _____ Voce rauca
   _____ Fatica (la voce si stanca oppure cambia di qualità dopo aver cantato per un breve periodo di tempo)
   _____ Problemi di volume (problemi mentre canta _____ a voce bassa _____ a voce piena
   _____ Perdita di banda di frequenze (alte _____ basse _____)
   _____ Cambio di voce (per esempio: voce abbassata da soprano a mezzo soprano)
   _____ Prolungamento del tempo necessario per riscaldare la voce (più di mezz'ora)
   _____ Mancanza di fiato
   _____ Solletico o sensazione di strangolamento mentre canta
   _____ Dolore mentre canta
   _____ Altri sintomi (per favore specifichi): _____
   _____
   _____

3. Deve dare un concerto?   Si _____   No _____
   Data: _____

4. Lei è un cantante?
   Di professione _____   Dilettante _____

5. A lungo termine, quali sono le sue mete?
   [   ] Carriera lirica
   [   ] Carriera nella musica pop
   [   ] Vocazione attiva
   [   ] Classica
   [   ] Pop
   [   ] Altro (_____)
   [   ] Prove dilettanti (corale o solo)
   [   ] Canto dilettante per piacere personale

6. Ha avuto lezioni di voce?   Si _____   No _____ A che età ha incominciato?
   [2, 3, 4, 5, 6, 7, 8, 9, 10, 11, 12, 13, 14, 15, 16, 17, 18, 19, 20, 21, 22, 23, 24, 25, 26, 27, 28,29,30,35,40,45,50,55,60, 65, 70, 75, 80, 85]

7. Ci son stati periodi di mesi o anni senza lezioni durante questo tempo?   Si _____   No _____

8. Da quanto tempo studia con il suo corrente maestro? [1, 2, 3, 4, 5, 6, 7, 8, 9, 10, 11, 12, 13, 14, 15, 16, 17, 18, 19, 20, 21, 22, 23, 24, 25, di più]   [settimane, mesi, anni]

   Nome del maestro:
   Indirizzo:

   Numero di telefono:

9. Altri maestri con i quali ha studiato e le date:

10. Ha avuto lezioni di voce parlata?   Si _____   No _____
    Lezioni di recitezione?   Si _____   No _____
    Per quanti anni? [Meno di uno, 1–5, 6–10, di più]
    Logoterapia?   Si _____   No _____   Quanti mesi? [1, 2, 3, 4, 5, 6, 7–12, di più]

11. Ha un, altra professione?   Si _____   No _____
    Se si, usa la voce molto?   Si _____   No _____
    Se si, che professione? [attore, annunciatore (televisione/radio/campi sportivi), istruttore atletico, avvocato, prete, politico, dottore, commesso, agente di cambio, maestro, telefonista, cameriere, cameriera, segretaria, altro _____]

12. Nel suo lavoro, oltre al canto, deve parlare frequentemente? Si _____ No _____
    Deve ballare? Si _____ No _____

13. Per quanti anni ha cantato prima di iniziare lezioni? [2, 3, 4, 5, 6, 7, 8, 9, 10, 11, 12, 13, 14, 15, 16, 17, 18, 19, 20,21, 22, 23, 24, 25, di più]

14. Che tipo di musica canta?
    _____ Classica   _____ Show
    _____ Nightclub   _____ Rock
    _____ Altro (per favore specificare): _____

15. Regolarmente canta seduto (per esempio al pianoforte)? Si _____ No _____

16. Canta all'aperto, in saloni, o con orchestra? (cerchia la parola corrispondente) Si _____ No _____

17. Se canta all'aperto o con accompagnamento di strumenti amplificati, usa altoparlanti di monitoraggio?
    Si _____ No _____
    Se si, li può sentire? Si _____ No _____

18. Suona un strumento musicale? Si _____ No _____
    Se si, indichi quale o quali strumenti:
    _____ strumenti a tastiera (piano, organo, arpicordo, altro _____)
    _____ Violino, viola
    _____ Cello
    _____ Basso
    _____ Chitarra, arpa, altro _____
    _____ Ottoni
    _____ Strumenti a fiato a canna singola
    _____ Strumenti a fiato a canna doppia
    _____ Flauto, piccolo
    _____ Strumenti di percussione
    _____ Zampogna
    _____ Fisarmonica
    _____ Altro (specifichi): _____

19. Con che frequenza si esercita? Scale musicali: [giornalmente, qualche volta alla settimana, una volta alla settimana, raramente, mai]

    Se si esercita mediante le scale musicali, queste vengono effettuate in una sessione oppure vengono divise durante il corso della giornata? [tutte insieme, due o tre sedute]
    Nei giorni in cui si praticano le scale musicali, per quanto tempo vengono effettuate?
    [15, 30, 45, 60, 75, 90, 105, 120, di più] minuti

    Canzoni: [giornalmente, qualche volta alla settimana, raramente, mai]

    Quante ore al giorno? [½, 1, 1½, 2, 2½, 3, di più]

Effettua il riscaldamento della voce prima di cantare?   Si _____   No _____

Viene effettuato un periodo di raffreddamento al termine?   Si _____   No _____

20. Quanto tempo canta in questo periodo (totale, incluso il tempo di esercizio, media giornaliera)?
    prova: [½, 1, 1½, 2, 2½, 3, 4, 5, 6, 7, 8, 9, 10]
    esibizione: [½, 1, 1½, 2, 2½, 3, 4, 5, 6, 7, 8]

21. Segni tutto ciò che le si addice:
    _____ Voce peggiore al mattino
    _____ Voce peggiore più tardi nel giorno, dopo averla usata
    _____ Prove o esibizioni canore nel mattino
    _____ Parla per periodi di tempo prolungati (i.e. maestro, prete, avvocato, telefono, lavoro)
    _____ Cheerleader (sostenitore)
    _____ Parla a lungo dietro le quinte o a riunioni dopo l'esibizione
    _____ Direttore del coro
    _____ Si schiarisce la gola frequentemente
    _____ Mal di gola frequente
    _____ Problemi alla giuntura delle mascelle
    _____ Palato amaro o acido, o alito cattivo di prima mattina
    _____ Frequente acidità di stomaco o ernia iatale
    _____ Grida o parla ad alta voce frequentemente
    _____ Sussurra frequentemente
    _____ Affaticamento cronico (insonnia)
    _____ Lavora in luoghi secchi
    _____ Esercizio fisico di frequente
    _____ Sete di frequente, disidretezione
    _____ Rauco di prima mattina
    _____ Tosse bronchiale
    _____ Mangia tardi la sera
    _____ Ha mal usato antiacidi
    _____ È particolamente stressato in questo periodo (per ragioni personali o professionali)
    _____ Alito cattivo con molta frequenza
    _____ Vive, lavora o si esibisce in locali dove c'è fumo
    _____ Ha viaggiato recentemente: Quando: _____
            Dove: _____

Mangia una o più delle seguenti cose prima di cantare?
_____ Cioccolata   _____ Caffè
_____ Alcoolici   _____ Latte o gelato
_____ Noci   _____ Alimenti piccanti
Altro (specifichi): _____

_____ difficoltà tecniche vocali specifiche? [problema con il canto a messe voce, problema con il canto a piena voce, poco controllo del "tono", problema nell'accompagnamento vocale, problema con la trasposizione di registro, altro] Descriva:

_____ Ha recentemente avuto dei problemi di voce prima dell'inizio del disturbo che l'ha condotta qui? [voce rauca, mancanza di fiato, affaticamento, perdita di "frequenze" interruzione della voce, dolore mentre canta, altro] Descriva:

_____ Ha avuto problemi nel passato per i quali ha dovuto consultare un medico? Se si, descriva il problema e la terapia: [laringite, noduli, polipi, emorragia, cancro, altro] Descriva:

22. Indichi nome, indirizzo e numero di telefono del suo medico di famiglia:

23. Indichi nome, indirizzo e numero di telefono del suo otorino:

24. Ha avuto recentemente un raffreddore?   Si _____   No _____

25. Ha attualmente il raffreddore?   Si _____   No _____

26. È stato frequentemente (o recentemente) esposto a qualcuna delle seguenti sostanze chimiche: (segni tutto ciò
e pertinente)

_____ Monossido di carbonio   _____ Arsenico
_____ Mercurio   _____ Coloranti di anilina
_____ Insetticidi   _____ Solventi industriali (benzene, etc.)
_____ Piombo
_____ Fumo

27. Si è sottoposto alla visita di un allergologo?   Si _____   No _____

Se si, di quali allergie lei soffre: [nessuna, polvere, muffa, piante, gatti, cani, cibi, altro _____]
(le allergie ai farmaci sono trattate in un altro punto di questo questionario)

Se si, indichi nome ed indirizzo dell'allergologo a cui si è rivolto:

28. Quanti pacchetti di sigarette fuma al giorno?

Sua storia come fumatore
_____ Mai
_____ Ha smesso. Quando?
_____ Fumava circa [meno di metà, metà, una, una e mezza, due, due e mezza, tre, tre e mezza, di più]
al giorno per [1, 2, 3, 4, 5, 6, 7, 8, 9, 10, 11–15, 16–20, 21–25, 26–30, 31–35, 36–40, 41–45, 46–50, di più]
anni.
_____ Fuma [meno di metà, metà, una, una e mezza, due, due e mezza, tre, di più] al giorno per [1, 2, 3, 4, 5,
6, 7, 8, 9, 10, 11–15, 16–20, 21–25, 26–30, 31–35, 36–40, 41–45, 46–50, di più] anni.

29. Lavora o vive in un ambiente dove si fuma?   Si _____   No _____

30. Quanti alcoolici consume in medie? [mai, raramente, poche volte alla settimana, giornalmente] [1, 2, 3, 4, 5, 6,
7, 8, 9, 10, di più] bicchieri al [giorno, settimana] di [birra, vino, liquori]

Beveva in misura maggiore?   Si _____   No _____

31. Quante tazze di caffè, tè, cola, o altre bevande contenenti caffeina beve in un giorno? [0, 1,2,3,4,5,6,7, 8, 9, 10]

32. Elenchi eventuali droghe o farmaci che lei usa [mariuana, cocaina, amfetaminici, barbiturici, eroina, altro
_____]

33. Ha notato alcune delle seguenti manifestazioni? (Segni quello che descrive le sue manifestazioni)
_____ Ipersensibilità al caldo o al fredda
_____ Sudore eccessivo
_____ Cambiamenti in peso aumento/diminuizione _____ Kg in _____
settimane/ _____ mesi
_____ Cambiamenti della pelle o dei capelli
_____ Palpitazioni cardiache
_____ Labilità emozionale (cambi di umore)
_____ Sdoppiamento della vista
_____ Torpidità della faccia o delle estremità
_____ Formicolio alla bocca o alla faccia
_____ Visione sfuocata o cecità
_____ Debolezza o paralisi della faccia
_____ Goffagine nelle braccia o nelle gambe
_____ Sintomi di confusione o perdita di consapevolezza
_____ Difficoltà nel parlare
_____ Difficoltà in inghiottire
_____ Attacchi epilettici
_____ Dolori al collo o alle spalle
_____ Tremori
_____ Perdita di memoria
_____ Cambiamenti di umore

Per le donne

È incinta? Si _____ No _____
Si è sottoposta ad isterectomia? Si _____ No _____
Si è sottoposta ad intervento di rimozione delle ovaia? Si _____ No _____
Ha un ciclo menstruale regolare? Si _____ No _____
A quanti anni ha avuto la prima menstruazione? [7, 8, 9, 10, 11, 12, 13, 14, 15, 16, 17, 18, 19, 20]
È già in menopausa? Si _____ No _____
Se si, da quanti anni? [adesso; 1, 2, 3, 4, 5, 6, 7, 8, 9, 10, di più] anni fa.

34. È mai ricorso ad un psicologo o ad un psichiatria? Si _____ No _____
È attualmente in cura? Si _____ No _____

35. Ha avuto danni alla testa o al collo? Si _____ No _____

36. Descriva ogni incidente serio che ha avuto.

37. Ha qualche azione legale in atto a causa di problemi connessi alla sua voce? Si _____ No _____

38. Elenchi il nome del suo coniuge e dei figli:

39. Breve sommario di problemi otorinolaringoiatrici, alcuni dei quali possono anche non essere collegati al suo attuale disturbo.

    Segni tutto cio che è pertinente

_____ Perdita uditiva	_____ Altro (specifichi):
_____ Sensazione di rumore nelle orecchie	_____ Dolore alle orecchie
_____ Vertigini	_____ Dolore facciale
_____ Paralisi facciale	_____ Collo rigido
_____ Ostruzione nasale	_____ Gromulo al collo
_____ Deformità nasale	_____ Gromulo in faccia o testa
_____ Piaghe alla bocca	_____ Problemi con l'inghiottire
_____ Problemi alla giunzione mandibolare	_____ Pelle agli occhi in eccesso
_____ Problemi agli occhi	_____ Pelle facciale in eccesso

40. Soffre o ha mai sofferto di:

_____ Diabete	_____ Epilessia
_____ Ipoglicemia	_____ Ricorso a terapia psichiatrica
_____ Problemi alla tiroide	_____ Frequenti attacchi di cefalea
_____ Sifilide	_____ Ulcere
_____ Gonorrea	_____ Artrite o problemi ossei
_____ Herpes	_____ Cleft palate
_____ Piaghe	_____ Asma
_____ Ipertensione arteriosa	_____ Problemi respiratori o polmonari
_____ Ipotensione arteriosa	_____ Inspiegabile perdita di peso
_____ Assunzione di antibiotici o diuretici in vena	_____ Cancro a (_____)
_____ Attacchi cardiaci	_____ Altri tumori
_____ Angina	_____ Trasfusioni sanguigne
_____ Battito cardiaco irregolare	_____ Epatite
_____ Altri problemi cardiaci	_____ AIDS
_____ Febbre reumatica	_____ Menengite
_____ Tubercolosi	
_____ Glaucoma	
_____ Sclerosi multipla	
_____ Problemi di reni o urinari	
_____ Problemi all'apparato	
_____ Altre malattie (si prega di specifícare):	

41. Ha storia di familiari consanguinei con:

_____ Diabete	_____ Cancro
_____ Ipoglicemia	_____ Problemi cardiaci

    _____ Altri gravi problemi medici di entità para a quelli precedentemente indicati. Si prega di specificare:

42. Descriva incidenti gravi da lei avuti, eccetto quelli direttamente riferibili alla sua attuale visita medica.

    _____ Nessuno

    _____ Incidente con trauma cranico, perdita di coscienza o contusione al collo

    _____ Incidente senza trauma cranico, perdita di coscienza o contusione al collo

    Descriva:

43. Elenchi tutte le medicine che attualmente assume e le relative dosi (includere la pillola anticoncezionale e le vitamine):

44. Allergie farmacologiche:
    _____ Nessuna
    _____ Penicillina
    _____ Sulfamidici
    _____ Tetraciclina
    _____ Eritromicina
    _____ Keflex/Ceclor/Ceftin
    _____ Altro (si prega di specifícare):

    _____ Novocaina
    _____ Iodina
    _____ Codeina
    _____ Cerotti
    _____ Aspirina
    _____ Coloranti radiologici

45. Interventi chirurgici
    _____ Tonsillectomia (età _____)
    _____ Appendicite (età _____)
    _____ Altro (si prega specificare):

    _____ Adenoidi (età _____)
    _____ Chirurgia cardiaca (età _____)

46. Elenchi le sostanze tossiche o gli agenti chimici a cui è stato esposto:
    _____ Piombo
    _____ Mercurio

    _____ Streptomicina, Neomicina, Canamicina
    _____ Altro (specifichi):

47. Si è mai sottoposto a terapio radiante per problemi alla testa o all collo (incluse cure per l'acne, problemi uditivi infantili, terapia per il cancro, etc.)?   Si _____   No _____

48. Descriva seri problemi di salute del suo coniuge o dei suoi figli.

    _____ Nessuno

Japanese Version of Appendix IIc

Translated by Kazuhiko Shoji, M.D.
病歴：歌手
Robert Thayer Sataloff, M.D., D.M.A.
1721 Pine Street
Philadelphia, PA 19103
U.S.A.

氏名 _____ 年齢 _____ 性別 _____ 人種 _____

身長 _____ 体重 _____ 日付 _____

声域： _____ ソプラノ   _____ メゾソプラノ   _____ アルト
_____ テノール   _____ バリトン   _____ バス

（もし現在、声に異常がなければ問3に進んで下さい。）

適当な答にチェックするか丸で囲んで下さい。

1. どれだけの期間、声の異常が続いていますか？

   [1,2,3,4,5,6,7,8,9,10, それ以上]
   [時間，日，週，月，年]

   だれが異常に気づきましたか？

   [自分自身，家族，声楽の先生，批評家，誰もが，その他 _____]

   原因が何か分かりますか？
   [はい _____　いいえ _____]

   もし、わかるならば、原因は何ですか？[風邪，叫んだこと，しゃべりすぎ，歌唱，手術，その
   他 _____]

   症状は急におこりましたか？
   [徐々に _____ ，急に _____]

   症状は：悪化している _____ ，改善している _____ ，変わらない _____ ，

2. どんな症状がありますか？（該当するものすべてにチェックしてください。
   _____ 嗄声（しわがれ声）
   _____ 疲労（声が疲れる，つまり短い時間歌った後で声の質が変わる）
   _____ 声量のみだれ _____ 小声で歌った時 _____ 大声で歌ったとき
   _____ 音域の減少（高音域 _____ 低音域 _____ ）
   _____ 声域の変化（例：ソプラノからメゾソプラノに変わった）
   _____ ウォーミングアップ時間の延長（声をウォーミングアップするのに30分以上かかる）
   _____ 息がもれるような声になる
   _____ 歌っているときにむずがゆい感じがしたり，締め付けられるような感じがする

_____ 歌っているときにのどの痛みを感じる
_____ その他（具体的に）：_____
_____

3. 近々大事な公演をひかえていますか？   はい _____ いいえ _____
   日付：_____

4. 歌手としてあなたは現在   プロ _____   アマチュア _____

5. 歌手としてあなたの最終目標は？
   [ ] 最高のオペラ歌手
   [ ] 最高のポップミュージック歌手
   [ ] 活動的な副業
   [ ] クラッシック
   [ ] ポップ
   [ ] その他[_____]
   [ ] アマチュアとして公演する（コーラスもしくはソロで）
   [ ] 自分で楽しむだけのアマチュア

6. 声楽の訓練を受けましたか？   はい _____ いいえ _____   何才で始めましたか？
   （まるで囲んで下さい。）[2, 3, 4, 5, 6, 7, 8, 9, 10, 11, 12, 13, 14, 15, 16, 17, 18, 19, 20, 21, 22, 23, 24,
   25, 26, 27, 28, 30, 35, 40, 45, 50, 55, 60, 65, 70, 75, 80, 85]

7. 数ヵ月もしくは数年レッスンなしですごした期間がありましたか？   はい _____ いいえ
   _____

8. 現在の先生の下でどれだけの期間学んでいますか？
   [1, 2, 3, 4, 5, 6, 7, 8, 9, 10, 11, 12, 13, 14, 15, 16, 17, 18, 19, 20, 21, 22, 23, 24, 25 それ以上]

   [週，月，年]

   先生の名前：
   住所：

   電話番号：

9. 以前の先生の名前とその先生の下で学んだ期間を書いて下さい。

10. 会話の声のトレーニングを受けた事がありますか？   はい _____ いいえ _____
    演劇の声のレッスンは？   はい _____ いいえ _____
    何年？   [1年以下、1-5, 6-10, それ以上]
    言語訓練は？   はい _____ いいえ _____
                                                   [1, 2, 3, 4, 5, 6, 7-12, それ以上]

11. 歌手以外の仕事をしていますか？
    はい _____ いいえ _____

もし、しているなら、特によく声を使う仕事ですか？
　　はい ＿＿＿＿＿　　いいえ ＿＿＿＿＿

はい　の場合その仕事は何ですか？ [俳優、アナウンサー（テレビ／ラジオ／スポーツ競技場），
スポーツインストラクター，弁護士，政治家，医者，セールスマン，証券ブ ローカー，教師，
電話交換手，電話受付係り，ウェイター，ウェイトレス，秘書，その他 ＿＿＿＿＿＿＿＿＿＿]

12. 公演では歌う事以外に頻繁にしゃべらなければなりませんか？
　　はい ＿＿＿＿＿　　いいえ ＿＿＿＿＿　　　　頻繁に踊りますか？　　はい ＿＿＿＿＿　　いいえ ＿＿＿＿＿

13. 初めて声楽のレッスンを受ける前に何年間活発に歌っていましたか？
　　[2, 3, 4, 5, 6, 7, 8, 9, 10, 11, 12, 13, 14, 15, 16, 17, 18, 19, 20, 21, 22, 23, 24, 25 それ以上]

14. どのような種類の歌を歌っていますか？（該当するものすべてにチェックしてください。）
　　＿＿＿＿＿　クラッシック　　　　　　　　　＿＿＿＿＿　ショー
　　＿＿＿＿＿　ナイトクラブ　　　　　　　　　＿＿＿＿＿　ロック
　　＿＿＿＿＿　その他（具体的に）：＿＿＿＿＿＿＿＿＿＿＿＿＿＿＿＿＿＿＿＿＿

15. 通常座って歌っていますか？（ピアノやドラムセットなどを演奏しながら）
　　はい ＿＿＿＿＿　　いいえ ＿＿＿＿＿

16. あなたは（野外で、大きなホールで、オーケストラといっしょに）歌っていますか？（該当するものをまるで囲んで下さい。）　　はい ＿＿＿＿＿　　いいえ ＿＿＿＿＿

17. 野外での演奏や電気楽器と一緒に公演するときはモニター
　　スピーカーを使用しますか？　　　　　　　　　　　　　　はい ＿＿＿＿＿　　いいえ ＿＿＿＿＿
　　はい　の場合、モニタースピーカーの音が聞こえますか？　　はい ＿＿＿＿＿　　いいえ ＿＿＿＿＿

18. 楽器を演奏しますか？　　はい ＿＿＿＿＿　　いいえ ＿＿＿＿＿
　　はい　の場合、該当するものをすべてチェックして下さい。
　　＿＿＿＿＿　キーボード（ピアノ、オルガン、ハープシコード、その他 ＿＿＿＿＿＿＿＿＿＿＿）
　　＿＿＿＿＿　バイオリン、ビオラ
　　＿＿＿＿＿　チェロ
　　＿＿＿＿＿　コントラバス
　　＿＿＿＿＿　撥弦楽器（ギター、ハープ、その他 ＿＿＿＿＿＿＿＿＿＿＿＿＿＿＿＿＿＿）
　　＿＿＿＿＿　金管楽器
　　＿＿＿＿＿　シングルリードの管楽器
　　＿＿＿＿＿　ダブルリードの管楽器
　　＿＿＿＿＿　フルート、ピッコロ
　　＿＿＿＿＿　パーカッション
　　＿＿＿＿＿　バグパイプ
　　＿＿＿＿＿　アコーディオン
　　＿＿＿＿＿　その他（具体的に）：＿＿＿＿＿＿＿＿＿＿＿＿＿＿＿＿＿＿＿＿＿

19. 練習の頻度は？
　　音階発声練習：[毎日，週に2〜3回，週に1回，たまに，全くしない]

それは、一度にしますかそれとも1日に2〜3回にわけてしますか？
[一度にする，2〜3回に分けてする]

1日にどのくらい練習しますか？
[15, 30, 45, 60, 75, 90, 105, 120, それ以上] 分

歌曲：[毎日，週に2〜3回，週に1回，たまに，全くしない]

1日に何時間練習しますか？
[1/2, 1, 1 1/2, 2, 2 1/2, 3 それ以上]

歌う前に声のウォーミングアップをしますか？　　　はい _____　いいえ _____

歌い終わった後に声のウォーミングダウンをしますか？　　　はい _____　いいえ _____

20. 現在どのくらい歌っていますか？（練習を含む総時間）（一日の平均時間）
リハーサル：[1/2, 1, 1 1/2, 2, 2 1/2, 3, 4, 5, 6, 7, 8, 9, 10]
公演中：[1/2, 1, 1 1/2, 2, 2 1/2, 3, 4, 5, 6, 7, 8, 9, 10]

21. 該当する項目をすべてチェックして下さい：
_____　午前中に声が悪い
_____　声を使った後、1日の後半に声が悪い
_____　午前中に公演するかリハーサルをする
_____　よく話す（例えば先生、聖職者、電話関係の仕事、弁護士、等）
_____　応援団（チアリーダー）
_____　舞台裏や公演後のパーティーでよくしゃべる
_____　コーラスの指揮者
_____　せきばらいをよくする
_____　しばしばのどが痛くなる
_____　顎の関節がおかしい
_____　朝一番に苦みや酸味を感じる、もしくは口臭がある
_____　胸焼けがたびたびする
_____　頻繁に叫んだり大きな声でしゃべる
_____　たびたびささやき声を出す
_____　慢性的に疲れ易い
_____　極端に乾燥した場所で働く
_____　たびたび運動する（ウェイトリフティング、エアロビクス、等）
_____　しばしばのどが乾いたり、脱水状態になる
_____　朝一番に嗄声がある
_____　咳がでる
_____　夜遅くものを食べる
_____　制酸剤を飲んだ事がある
_____　現在特別なストレスがある（個人的もしくは職業上の）
_____　よく口臭がある
_____　タバコその他の煙のなかで生活したり働いたり公演したりする
_____　最近旅行した：いつ：_____
　　　　　　　　　　どこへ：_____

歌う前に以下のもののうちどれを飲食しますか？
_____　チョコレート　　　　　_____　コーヒー
_____　アルコール　　　　　　_____　ミルクまたはアイスクリーム
_____　ナッツ　　　　　　　　_____　スパイシーな食物

その他（特定して下さい）：

_____ なにか技術的に特に困ったことはありますか？
[小声で歌いにくい、大きな声で歌いにくい、音程をコントロールしにくい、音域の移行が難しい、その他]記載してください：

_____ ここを受診した原因となった異常が生じる前に最近歌声になんらかの問題があった
[しわがれ声、息が漏れるような声、声の疲労、音域が狭くなった、声が割れた、歌うと痛みがあった、その他]記載してください：

_____ 病院を受診しなければならなかったような声の異常は過去にありましたか？もし、あったならばそれと治療を記載してください：
[喉頭炎、声帯結節、声帯ポリープ、出血、癌、その他]記載してください：

22. ファミリードクターの名前、住所、電話番号：

23. かかりつけの喉頭専門医の名前、住所、電話番号：

24. 最近、風邪をひきましたか？   はい _____   いいえ _____

25. 今、風邪をひいていますか？   はい _____   いいえ _____

26. つぎに挙げる化学物質にひんぱんに（もしくは最近）家や仕事場でさらされましたか？
（該当するもの全てをチェックして下さい）

_____	一酸化炭素	_____	ヒ素
_____	水銀	_____	アニリン系色素
_____	殺虫剤	_____	有機溶剤
_____	鉛		（ベンジン等）
_____	舞台用の煙		

27. アレルギーの専門医にかかった事がありますか？   はい _____   いいえ _____
はいと答えた方は、何のアレルギーですか：
[ない、ほこり、カビ、猫、犬、食餌、その他、_____]
（薬のアレルギーはこの用紙の別の項で尋ねます）

はいと答えた方は、アレルギー専門医の氏名、住所を教えて下さい：

28. 一日に何箱タバコを吸いますか？

喫煙歴
_____ ない
_____ やめた。いつ？
_____ だいたい1日に[半箱以下、半箱、1箱、1箱半、2、2箱半、2、それ以上] [1, 2, 3, 4, 5, 6, 7, 8, 9, 10, 11-15, 16-20, 21-25, 26-30, 31-35, 36-40, 41-45, 46-50, それ以上]年間吸っていた。
_____ だいたい1日に[半箱以下、半箱、1箱、1箱半、2、2箱半、3、それ以上] [1, 2, 3, 4, 5, 6, 7, 8, 9, 10, 11-15, 16-20, 21-25, 26-30, 31-35, 36-40, 41-45, 46-50, それ以上]年間吸っている。

29. 煙の多い環境で働いていますか？   はい _____   いいえ __

30. どの程度お酒を飲みますか？[飲まない、まれに、1週間に2～3回、毎日][ビール、ワイン、リキュール]をグラスに[0, 1, 2, 3, 4, 5, 6, 7, 8, 9, 10, それ以上]杯ぐらい

　　以前はより大量の飲酒をしていましたか？　　　はい＿＿＿＿＿＿　　いいえ＿＿＿＿＿＿

31. コーヒー、紅茶、コーラなどカフェインを含んだ飲物を一日に何杯飲みますか？
　　[0, 1, 2, 3, 4, 5, 6, 7, 8, 9, 10]

32. 他に娯楽で使用しているドラッグを挙げて下さい[マリファナ、コカイン、アンフェタミン、バルビツレート、ヘロイン、その他＿＿＿＿＿＿＿＿＿＿＿＿＿＿＿＿＿＿＿＿＿＿＿＿]

33. 以下の症状がありますか？（該当するものすべてにチェックしてください）
　　＿＿＿＿＿　高温、寒冷に特に敏感
　　＿＿＿＿＿　汗をよくかく
　　＿＿＿＿＿　体重の変化：増／減＿＿＿＿＿　週／月で＿＿＿＿＿　ポンド
　　＿＿＿＿＿　肌や髪の変化
　　＿＿＿＿＿　動悸
　　＿＿＿＿＿　感情の起伏が大きい
　　＿＿＿＿＿　ものが二重に見える
　　＿＿＿＿＿　顔面や手足のシビレ
　　＿＿＿＿＿　口の回りや顔面がヒリヒリする
　　＿＿＿＿＿　ものがボヤけて見えたり、目が見えない
　　＿＿＿＿＿　顔面の麻痺
　　＿＿＿＿＿　手足の動きがぎこちない
　　＿＿＿＿＿　意識の混乱や意識消失
　　＿＿＿＿＿　しゃべりにくい
　　＿＿＿＿＿　飲み込みにくい
　　＿＿＿＿＿　てんかん発作
　　＿＿＿＿＿　首や肩の痛み
　　＿＿＿＿＿　ふるえ
　　＿＿＿＿＿　記憶力の変化
　　＿＿＿＿＿　人格の変化

女性のみ答えて下さい：
　　　　　妊娠していますか？　　　　　　　　　はい＿＿＿＿＿　いいえ＿＿＿＿＿
　　　　　子宮切除を受けましたか？　　　　　　はい＿＿＿＿＿　いいえ＿＿＿＿＿
　　　　　卵巣を摘出されましたか？　　　　　　はい＿＿＿＿＿　いいえ＿＿＿＿＿
　　　　　月経は周期的ですか？　　　　　　　　はい＿＿＿＿＿　いいえ＿＿＿＿＿
　　　　　初潮は何才でしたか？
　　　　　[7, 8, 9, 10, 11, 12, 13, 14, 15, 16, 17, 18, 19, 20]
　　　　　閉経しましたか？　　　　　　　　　　はい＿＿＿＿＿　いいえ＿＿＿＿＿
はい　ならいつですか？[今；1, 2, 3, 4, 5, 6, 7, 8, 9, 10 それ以上]年前

34. 精神科医や精神分析医を受診した事がありますか？
　　　　はい＿＿＿＿＿＿　いいえ＿＿＿＿＿＿
　　　　今、治療を受けていますか？　　　はい＿＿＿＿＿　いいえ＿＿＿＿＿

35. 頭部や首にケガをした事がありますか？（ムチウチ等）　　　はい＿＿＿＿＿　いいえ＿＿＿＿＿

36. 大きな事故を記載してください。

37. あなたの声の問題に関連した訴訟に関与していますか？
はい ＿＿＿＿ いいえ ＿＿＿＿

38. 配偶者および子供の名前を書いて下さい：

39. 耳鼻科の病気（あるものがあるとは限らないかもしれません）の要約該当するものすべてをチェックしてください

＿＿＿＿ 難聴 　　　　＿＿＿＿ 耳の痛み
＿＿＿＿ 耳なり 　　　＿＿＿＿ 顔の痛み
＿＿＿＿ めまい 　　　＿＿＿＿ 肩こり
＿＿＿＿ 顔面の麻痺 　＿＿＿＿ 首の腫れ物
＿＿＿＿ 鼻づまり 　　＿＿＿＿ 顔面や頭の腫れ物
＿＿＿＿ 鼻の変形 　　＿＿＿＿ 嚥下困難
＿＿＿＿ 口の痛み 　　＿＿＿＿ まぶたの皮膚の過多
＿＿＿＿ 顎の関節の異常 ＿＿＿＿ 顔の皮膚の過多
＿＿＿＿ 目の異常
＿＿＿＿ その他：（具体的に）

40. 現在以下の病気があるか以前あった：

＿＿＿＿ 糖尿病 　　　　　　＿＿＿＿ てんかん
＿＿＿＿ 低血糖 　　　　　　＿＿＿＿ 精神治療
＿＿＿＿ 甲状腺疾患 　　　　＿＿＿＿ 偏頭痛
＿＿＿＿ 梅毒 　　　　　　　＿＿＿＿ 潰瘍
＿＿＿＿ 淋病 　　　　　　　＿＿＿＿ 腎疾患
＿＿＿＿ ヘルペス 　　　　　＿＿＿＿ 尿路疾患
＿＿＿＿ 熱の花 　　　　　　＿＿＿＿ 関節炎か骨の異常
＿＿＿＿ 高血圧 　　　　　　＿＿＿＿ 口蓋裂
＿＿＿＿ 高度の低血圧 　　　＿＿＿＿ 喘息
＿＿＿＿ 抗生剤か利尿剤の注射 ＿＿＿＿ 肺、呼吸の障害
＿＿＿＿ 心臓発作 　　　　　＿＿＿＿ 原因不明の体重減少
＿＿＿＿ 狭心症 　　　　　　＿＿＿＿ 癌（＿＿＿＿＿＿＿＿＿）
＿＿＿＿ 不整脈 　　　　　　＿＿＿＿ 他の腫瘍（＿＿＿＿＿＿＿）
＿＿＿＿ 他の心臓疾患 　　　＿＿＿＿ 輸血
＿＿＿＿ リウマチ熱 　　　　＿＿＿＿ 肝炎
＿＿＿＿ 結核 　　　　　　　＿＿＿＿ エイズ
＿＿＿＿ 緑内障 　　　　　　＿＿＿＿ 髄膜炎
＿＿＿＿ 多発性硬化症
＿＿＿＿ 他の病気、具体的に：

41. 家族歴：

_____ 糖尿病   _____ 癌
_____ 低血糖   _____ 心疾患
_____ その他、上に挙げたような大きな病気を具体的に書いて下さい：

42. ここを受診した理由と直接関係ない重大な事故を記載して下さい。

_____ なし
_____ 頭部の外傷、意識消失やムチうちを伴った事故
_____ 頭部の外傷、意識消失やムチうちを伴わない事故
記載してください：

43. 現在服用している薬とその用量を記載してください（避妊用ピルとビタミン剤を含む）

44. 薬物アレルギー

_____ なし   _____ ノボカイン
_____ ペニシリン   _____ ヨード
_____ サルファ剤   _____ コデイン
_____ テトラサイクリン   _____ ばんそうこう
_____ エリスロマイシン   _____ アスピリン
_____ ケフレックス／   _____ X線造影剤
セクロール／セフチン
_____ その他、具体的に：

45. 手術歴

_____ 扁桃腺摘出   _____ アデノイド
（ _____ 才）   （ _____ 才）
_____ 虫垂切除   _____ 心臓手術
（ _____ 才）   （ _____ 才）
_____ その他、具体的に：

46. あなたがさらされたことのある毒薬、劇物を挙げて下さい。

_____ 鉛   _____ ストレプトマイシン／ネオマ
_____ 水銀   イシン／カナマイシン
_____ その他、具体的に：

47. 頭や首にX線治療を受けた事がありますか？（子供の頃のニキビや耳の病気に対する治療を含む、癌の治療等で）   はい _____   いいえ _____

48. あなたの配偶者や子供の重大な健康上の問題点を記載してください。

_____ なし

Korean Version of Appendix IIc

Translated by in Min Young, M.D.
환자 병력: 성악가/가수
Robert Thayer Sataloff, M.D., D.M.A.
1721 Pine Street
Philadelphia, PA 19103
U.S.A.

성명 _____ 나이 _____ 성별 _____ 인종 _____

신장 _____ 몸무게 _____ 날짜 _____

음성종류: _____ 소프라노 _____ 메조-소프라노 _____ 알토
_____ 테너 _____ 바리톤 _____ 베이스

(현재 음성에 문제가 없으시면 항목 3번으로 가십시오.)

1. 얼마동안 음성문제를 가시고 계셨습니까?

   (1, 2, 3, 4, 5, 6, 7, 8, 9, 10 이상)
   (시간, 일, 주, 개월, 년)

   누가 처음 문제를 발견하였습니까?

   (본인, 가족, 음악선생, 비평가, 모든주위사람, 그외 _____)

   문제의 원인을 아십니까?
   예 _____ 아니오 _____

   원인을 아신다면 디음 중 무엇입니까?

   (감기, 고함을 질렀음, 과대한 대화, 노래, 수술, 기타 _____)

   문제가 이떻게 발생했습니까!
   서서히 _____ 갑자기 _____

   상태는 점점 나빠지고 있음, _____ 좋아지고 있음, _____ 변동없음 _____

2. 어떤 징후를 가지고 계십니까? (관련되는 징후를 모두 체크하십시오)
   _____ 목쉰소리 (거칠음 또는 할퀴는듯한 소리)
   _____ 피로 (짧은시간 노래후에 목소리가 변하거나 성대가 금방 피로해진다)
   _____ 음량징해 (노래부르기가 힘늘어짐) 조용히 부를때   크게 부를때
   _____ 음역상실 (고음 저음)
   _____ 연습시간이 길어짐 (반시간 이상의 연습)
   _____ 성량부족 (숨이 차움)
   _____ 노래하는 동안 간지럽거나 숨이 막힘

_____ 노래하는 동안 인후에 통증이 생김

_____ 그 외 (자세히 기입하십시오) _____

_____

3. 중요한 공연이 곧 있을 예정입니까?   예 ____ 아니오____

   날짜: _____

4. 현재 귀하의 음악활동은 다음 어느것에 속합니까?   전문가 ____ 아마츄어 ____

5. 귀하 음악활동의 장기적인 계획은 어느것입니까?

   [ ] 오페라계에서의 주역

   [ ] 대중 음악계에서의 주역

   [ ] 부업으로서 활발한 활동

   [ ] 고전음악

   [ ] 대중가요

   [ ] 그외 (_____)

   [ ] 아마츄어 활동(합창 또는 독창)

   [ ] 취미로서의 아마츄어 활동

6. 음악레슨을 받은 적이 있습니까?   예 ____ 아니오____ 몇살때 시작? (해당 숫자에 동그라미로 표시)

   [2,3,4,5,6,7,8,9,10,11,12,13,14,15,16,17,18,19,20,21,22,23,24,25,26,27,28,30,35,40,45,50,55,60,65,70,80,85]

7. 레슨받는동안 몇개월 또는 몇년간의 공백 기간을 가진적이 있습니까?   예 ____ 아니오____

8. 현재의 음악교사와는 몇년간 같이 공부하였습니까?

   [1, 2, 3, 4, 5, 6, 7, 8, 9, 10, 11, 12, 13, 14, 15, 16, 17, 18, 19, 20, 21, 22, 23, 24, 25, 이상]

   주, 월, 년

   음악교사 이름:

   음악교사 주소:

   음악교사 전화번호:

9. 그동안에 사사받았던 모든 음악교사들의 이름과 배웠던 년수를 기록해주십시오:

10. 평소 말소리를 고치기위한 음성레슨을 받은적이 있습니까?   예 ____ 아니오____

    연기발성 레슨?   예 ____ 아니오____

    얼마동안? 1년미만,   1-5년 , 6-10년, 10년이상

    언어 장애 교정요법?   예 ____ 아니오____ 몇개월동안?

    1,2,3,4,5,6,7-12개월, 그 이상

11. 노래(성악)이외의 다른 직업을 가지고 있습니까?

    예 ____ 아니오____

    만약 그렇다면 목소리를 많이 사용하는 직업입니까?

    예 ____ 아니오____

대답이 "예"라면 귀하의 직업은 다음중 무엇입니까?(연기자, 아나운서(텔리비젼/라디오/스포츠중계), 운동선수 코치나 트레이너, 변호사, 목사, 정치가, 의사, 영업사원, 증권 중개인, 교사, 전화교환원 또는 예약접수자, 웨이터, 웨이트레스, 비서 그외 _____)

12. 공연시 노래(성악)이외에 자주 얘기를 해야합니까?
      예 _____ 아니오_____ 춤을 추어야 합니까?   예 _____ 아니오_____

13. 음성레슨을 시작하기 이전 몇년동안 노래를 부르셨습니까?
    [2, 3, 4, 4, 5, 6, 7, 8, 9, 10, 11, 12, 13, 14, 15, 16, 17, 18, 19, 20, 21, 22, 23, 24, 25, 년 이상]

14. 어떤 종류의 음악을 하십니까? (해당사항 모두 기입)
    _____ 클래식   _____ 쇼 음악 (뮤지컬이나 방송용 쇼)
    _____ 나이트클럽용 음악   _____ **Rock**
    _____ 그외 (자세하게 설명) _____

15. 앉아서 자주 노래를 하십니까?(예를 들어 피아노나 드럼뒤에 앉아있는 경우)
      예 _____ 아니오_____

16. 야외에서 혹은 대형 홀에서 혹은 오케스트라와 노래를 부르십니까? (해당사항 하나에 표시)   예 __ 아니오__

17. 야외에서나 전자악기를 사용해서 공연할 때
    모니터 스피커를 사용하십니까?   예 _____ 아니오_____
    "예"라면 스피커에서 나오는 소리를 들을수 있습니까?   예 _____ 아니오_____

18. 악기를 사용하십니까?   예 _____ 아니오_____
    "예"라면 해당사항에 모두 표시해주십시오:
    _____ 키보드(피아노, 올갠, 하프시코드, 그외 _____)
    _____ 바이올린, 비올라
    _____ 첼로
    _____ 배스
    _____ 줄이 있는 현악기(기타, 하프, 그외 _____)
    _____ 관악기
    _____ 리드(**reed**)가 하나인 관악기
    _____ 리드(**reed**)가 두개인 관악기
    _____ 플룻, 피콜로
    _____ 타악기류
    _____ 백파이프
    _____ 아코디온
    _____ 그외:(자세하게 설명) _____

19. 일마나 자주 연습을 하십니까?
    연습량: (날마다, 1주일에 몇번, 1주일에 한번, 아주 가끔, 전혀 않함)

    정해진 연습량이 있다면 한꺼번에 다 또는 여러번 나누어서 하십니까?
    한꺼번에 디,   2-3번 나누어서

연습을 할때는 몇분 동안 하십니까?
(15, 30, 45, 60, 75, 90, 105, 120, 이상) 분

노래하는 횟수: [매일, 1주일에 몇번, 1주일에 한번, 아주 가끔, 전혀 않함]

하루에 몇시간 노래하십니까?
½, 1½, 2, 2½, 3시간, 3시간이상

노래하기전에 성대푸는 연습을 하십니까?   예 ____ 아니오 ____

노래후에 성대다듬는 연습을 하십니까?   예 ____ 아니오 ____

20. 현재 얼마나 노래를 하고 계십니까? (연습시간 포함)
   (하루 평균수치)
   리허설 시: ½, 1, 1½, 2, 2½, 3, 4, 5, 6, 7, 8, 9, 10
   공연시: ½, 1, 1½, 2, 2½, 3, 4, 5, 6, 7, 8

21. 다음 중 해당사항에 모두 표시해 주십시오.
   _____ 아침에 목소리 상태가 더 나빠짐
   _____ 오후나 저녁때 목소리 상태가 더 나빠짐
   _____ 아침에 공연이나 리허설을 한다
   _____ 얘기를 많이 한다 (예: 교사, 목사, 변호사, 전화교환원등)
   _____ 치어리더/치어걸
   _____ 공연후 파티나 무대뒤에서 얘기를 많이 한다
   _____ 합창단 지휘자
   _____ 자주 가래를 뱉는다
   _____ 자주 목이 붓고 아프다
   _____ 턱관절에 이상이 있다
   _____ 아침에 일어났을 때 시거나 쓴 입맛 또는 구취가 심하다.
   _____ 가슴이 아프거나 탈장이 자주 됨
   _____ 소리를 자주 지르거나 크게 얘기를 함
   _____ 자주 귓속말을 함
   _____ 만성 피로 (불면증)
   _____ 매우 건조한 곳에서 근무
   _____ 자주 운동을 함 (역도나 보디빌딩 또는 에어로빅)
   _____ 자주 목이 마르고 탈수현상이 생김
   _____ 아침에 목이 쉰다
   _____ 기침이 가슴으로부터 밀려온다
   _____ 저녁 늦게 식사를 한다
   _____ 제산제를 사용한 적이 있다
   _____ 현재 스트레스 받는 상황에 처해있다(집 또는 직장에서)
   _____ 자주 구취가 생긴다
   _____ 담배연기나 가스냄새가 나는 곳에서 살거나 근무 또는 공연한다
   _____ 최근에 여행한 적이 있다: 언제: _____
                                    어디로: _____

노래하기 전 다음 중 어떤 음식을 드십니까?
   _____ 초콜렛   _____ 커피
   _____ 술   _____ 우유나 아이스크림
   _____ 땅콩류   _____ 매운 음식
그외: (자세히 설명)

_____ 노래 테크닉 중 특별하게 불편은 느끼는 것은?
[조용히 부를 때, 크게 부를 때, 음성조절할 때, 음성을 지속할 때, 전조부분일 때, 그외] 자세히 설명:

_____ 현재의 증상이 생기기전 노래할 때 목소리에 이상이 있었습니까?
[목이 쉼, 성량부족, 피로, 음역상실, 음성변성, 노래중 통증, 그외] 자세히 설명:

_____ 과거에 목소리문제로 의사를 방문한 적이 있습니까? 그렇다면 그 문제와 치료에 대해 자세히
서술하십시오.
[후두염, 경결종, 폴립스, 출혈, 암, 그외]: 자세히 설명:

22. 주치의 이름과 주소 및 전화번호:

23. 인후과 담당의사의 이름과 주소 및 전화번호:

24. 최근에 김기에 걸린적이 있습니까?   예 _____ 아니오_____

25. 현재 감기에 걸려있습니까?   예 _____ 아니오_____

26. 자주 혹은 최근에 집에나 직장에서 다음 열거된 화학제품에 노출된 적이 있습니까?
(해당사항 모두에 표시)

_____ 일산화탄소   _____ 비소
_____ 수은   _____ 아닐린 물감
_____ 납   _____ 공업용 용해제
_____ 삼충제   (벤젠외 기타)
_____ 무대용 스모크

27. 알레르기 전문의에게 치료나 상담을 받은 직이 있습니까?   예 _____ 아니오_____
그렇다면 어떤 알레르기를 갖고 있습니끼?
[없다, 먼지, 곰팡이, 나무, 고양이, 개, 음식, 그외 _____   ]
(약에 대한 알레르기는 다른섹션에 포함되어 있습니다)
대답이 "예"라면 알레르기 전문의의 이름과 주소 및 전화번호를 기입하십시오.

28. 하루에 남배 넟갑을 피우십니까!
흡연 기록
_____ 담배를 안피움
_____ 담배를 끊었음. 끊은 시기:
_____ 하루에 [½이하, ½, 2, 2½, 3, 3갑 이상]을 [1, 2, 3, 4, 5, 6, 7, 8, 9, 10, 11–15, 16–20, 21–25,
26–30, 31–35, 36–40, 41–45, 46–50, 이상]년 동안 피웠었다.
_____ 하루에 [½2이하, ½, 2, 2½, 3, 3갑 이상]을 [1, 2, 3, 4, 5, 6, 7, 8, 9, 10, 11–15, 16–20, 21–25,
26–30, 31–35, 36–40, 41–45, 46–50, 이상]년 동안 피어오고 있다.

29. 흡연환경 속에서 근무하십니까?   예 _____ 아니오_____

30. 술은 얼마나 드십니까? [전혀 안한다. 아주 가끔, 일주일에 몇번, 매일] [하루, 한주]에 [1,2...10, 10잔 이상]의
[맥주, 와인, 위스키]를 마신다.

과거에 술을 더 많이 드셨습니까?   예 _____ 아니오_____

31. 하루에 몇잔의 커피, 홍차, 콜라 또는 다른 카페인이 힘유된 음류를 드십니까?
[0, 1, 2, 3, 4, 5, 6, 7, 8, 9, 10잔]

32. 향략용 약제를 사용하고 계시면 자세히 기록하십시오. [마리화나, 코케인, 각성제(암페타민), 수면제(바르비투르),
아편 그외]

33. 다음 증상 중 해당사항이 있습니까? (해당사항 모두에 표시)
_____ 더위 또는 추위에 민감함
_____ 땀을 과다하게 흘림
_____ 몸무게에 변화가 있음: 몸무게가 늘었음/줄었음 _____ 파운드 _____
_____주 _____개월 사이에
_____ 피부나 머리칼에 변화가 옴
_____ 심장이 뛰거나 심하게 고동침
_____ 감정변화(기분의 기폭이 심함)
_____ 물체가 둘로 보임
_____ 얼굴이나 수족에 무감각이 옴
_____ 입 근처나 얼굴이 얼얼해 옴
_____ 물체가 확실히 보이지 않거나 시력을 일음
_____ 얼굴에 마비가 옴
_____ 팔다리가 평소처럼 움직여지지 않음
_____ 의식을 일거나 정신상태가 혼미해짐
_____ 언어 장애
_____ 음식을 삼키기가 어려움
_____ 경련(간질병 발작)
_____ 목이나 어깨에 통증이 옴
_____ 몸이 떨리거나 수족이 흔들림
_____ 기억력 감소
_____ 성격 변화

여성일 경우:

임신 중이십니까?   예 _____ 아니오_____
제왕 절개수술을 받은적이 있습니까?   예 _____ 아니오_____
난소가 제거되었습니까?   예 _____ 아니오_____
월경은 정상입니까?   예 _____ 아니오_____
사춘기를 몇살때 맞았습니까?   예 _____ 아니오_____
[7, 8, 9, 10, 11, 12, 13, 14, 15, 16, 17, 18, 19, 20살]
폐경이 되었습니까?

대답이 "예" 라면 [현재, 1, 2, 3, 4, 5, 6, 7, 8, 9, 10] 년 전에

34. 심리학 전문의나 정신과 의사를 만나 보신적이 있습니까?
예 _____ 아니오_____
현재 치료중에 있습니까?   예 _____ 아니오_____

35. 머리나 목을 다친 적이 있습니까? (차사고를 당했을 때 목이 흔들린 경우 등)   예 _____ 아니오_____

36. 심각한 사고를 당했었다면 모두 기록하십시오.

37. 음성문제로 인해 법적상황에 처해있습니까?
    예 _____ 아니오_____

38. 배우자와 자녀들의 이름을 기록하십시오.

39. 귀나 코 또는 목의 이상이 있는 경우 간단히 실명하십시오. 그 증세는 현재 귀하의 문제에 관련이 안될수도
    있습니다.

                    해당 사항 모두를 표시하십시오.

    _____ 청각장해.   _____ 이통
    _____ 귀에서 잡음이 들림   _____ 아부통 안면통증
    _____ 어지러움   _____ 경부경적(목이 굳어짐)
    _____ 안면신경마비   _____ 경부의 혹
    _____ 비강폐쇄   _____ 안부두부의 혹
    _____ 기형적인 비강구조   _____ 음식을 삼키기가 어려움
    _____ 턱관절의 이상   _____ 과다한 눈주의 피부
    _____ 시각이상   _____ 과다한 얼굴피부
    _____ 그외: (자세히 설명)

40. 다음 증세를 가지고 계시거나 과거에 가진적이 있습니까?

    _____ 당뇨병   _____ 발작 - 간질
    _____ 당과소증   _____ 정신치료
    _____ 갑상선 질환   _____ 빈빈한 두통
    _____ 매독   _____ 위궤양
    _____ 인질   _____ 신장질환
    _____ 수포진   _____ 비뇨문제
    _____ 송기(물십)   _____ 관절염 또는 골격문제
    _____ 고혈압   _____ 언청이
    _____ 심한 저혈압   _____ 천식
    _____ 정맥주사 용 항생제나 이뇨제   _____ 폐 또는 호흡 질환
    _____ 심장마비   _____ 이유없는 체중감소
    _____ 협심증   _____ 암 (종류:)
    _____ 불규칙한 심장박동   _____ 종양 (종류:)
    _____ 그외 심장문제   _____ 수혈
    _____ 류마티스 열   _____ 간염
    _____ 결핵   _____ 에이즈
    _____ 녹내장   _____ 뇌막염
    _____ 다발성경화증
    _____ 기타 질병 (자세히 설명)

41. 친척이나 가족중 다음 질병을 갖고 있는 분이 있으면 표시해 주십시오.

　　_____ 당뇨병　　　　　　　　　　　_____ 암
　　_____ 저혈당증　　　　　　　　　　　_____ 심장병
　　_____ 기타 건강문제.
　　　　　자세히 기입하십시오:

42. 현재의 증세와 직접 관계는 없으나 과거 사고를 당한 경우가 있다면 설명해 주십시오.

　　_____ 없음
　　_____ 뇌의 손상, 의식상실 또는 윕래쉬(차사고중 뒤에서 받혀 목이 흔들렸을때)의 증상이 있었음.
　　_____ 뇌의 손상, 의식상실 또는 윕래쉬(차사고중 뒤에서 받혀 목이 흔들렸을때)의 증상이 없었음.
　　　　　기타(자세히 기입):

43. 현재 사용하고 있는 모든 약제와 그 분량을 기입하십시오 (피임약과 비타민제 포함)

44. 알레르기용 약:

　　　　　_____ 없음　　　　　　　　　　　_____ 노보케인
　　　　　_____ 페니실린　　　　　　　　　　_____ 옥소(**Iodine**)
　　　　　_____ 술파제(**Sulfa**)　　　　　　　_____ 코데인 (**Codeine**)
　　　　　_____ 테트라싸이클린　　　　　　　　_____ 반창고
　　　　　_____ 에리스로마이신　　　　　　　　_____ 아스피린
　　　　　_____ 케플렉스/시클로어/세푸틴　　　_____ 엑스레이 광선염료
　　　　　_____ 기타(자세히 기입):

45. 다음과 같은 수술을 받았다면 표시하십시오.

　　　　　_____ 편도선 절제술　　　　　　　　_____ 아테노이드 절제술
　　　　　　　　(나이 _____)　　　　　　　　　　(나이 _____)
　　　　　_____ 맹장수술　　　　　　　　　　　_____ 심장수술
　　　　　　　　(나이 _____)　　　　　　　　　　(나이 _____)
　　　　　_____ 기타
　　　　　　　　(자세히 기입)

46. 다음과 같은 특성약품이나 화약품에 노출된 적이 있으면 표시하십시오.

　　　　　_____ 납 (연)　　　　　　　　　　　_____ 스트랩토마이신, 네오마이신,
　　　　　_____ 수은　　　　　　　　　　　　　　　케나마이신
　　　　　　　　　　　　　　　　　　　　　　_____ 기타(자세히 기입):

47. 뇌나 목에 엑스레이 광선치료를 받은 적이 있습니까? (어렸을때의 여드름이나 귀 치료 또는 암치료 등 포함)
　　예 _____ 아니오_____

48. 배우자 또는 자녀들이 갖고있는 건강문제가 있다면 자세히 기입해주십시오.

　　_____ 없음.

Polish Version of Appendix IIc

Translated by Victoria Fullam and B. Janusz Kaczmarski
HISTORIA PACJENTA: ŚPIEWACY
Robert Thayer Sataloff, M.D., D.M.A.
1721 Pine Street
Philadelphia, PA 19103
U.S.A.

IMIĘ I NAZWISKO _____ WIEK _____ PŁEĆ _____ RASA _____

WZROST _____ WAGA _____ DATA _____

KATEGORIA GŁOSU: _____ sopran _____ mezzosopran _____ alt

_____ tenor _____ baryton _____ bas

(Jeżeli obecnie nie masz problemu z głosem, opuść pytania numer jeden i dwa)

PODKREŚL POPRAWNE ODPOWIEDZI

1. Jak długo masz obecny problem z głosem ?

[1, 2, 3, 4, 5, 6, 7, 8, 9, 10, więcej]
[godziny, dni, tygodnie, miesiące, lata]

Kto zwrócił na to uwagę?

[Ja sam, rodzina, nauczyciel śpiewu, krytycy, wszyscy, inni]

Czy znasz powód ?
[Tak _____ Nie _____]

Jeżeli tak, jaki ? [przeziębienie, krzyczenie, nadmierne mówienie, śpiewanie, operacje, inny _____]

Czy problem pojawił się zwolna czy nagle ?
[Zwolna _____ Nagle _____]

Czy problem: Pogarsza się _____ Polepsza się _____ lub jest taki sam _____ ?

2. Jakie są symptomy ? (Podkreśl wszystkie , które masz)
_____ Ochrypłość (i szorstki dźwięk)
_____ Zmęczenie (głos się męczy lub zmienia jakość po śpiewaniu przez krótki czas).
_____ Zakłócenie siły głosu trudności śpiewaniu cicho _____ , głośno _____
_____ Strata zakresu: wysokiego _____ , niskiego _____ .
_____ Zmiana klasyfikacji na przykład: głos obniżył się od sopranu do mezzosopranu.
_____ Przedłużony czas na rozgrzanie się ponad 1/2 godziny, żeby rozgrzać głos.
_____ Za dużo powietrza w głosie.
_____ Uczucia łaskotania lub duszenia się podczas śpiewania.
_____ Ból w gardle podczas śpiewania

_____ Inne (wyszczególnij) :_____

_____

3. Czy będziesz miał wkrótce ważne wykonanie ?   Tak _____   Nie _____
   Data(y): _____

4. Jaki jest obecny status Twojej kariery śpiewaczej ?   Zawodowy _____   Amatorski _____

5. Jakie są Twoje zamierzenia w karierze śpiewaczej na dłuższą metę ?
   [ ] Kariera solowo– operowa.
   [ ] Solowa Kariera w muzyce rozrywkowej.
   [ ] Jako uboczne zajęcie rozrywkowe.
   [ ] Muzyka poważna.
   [ ] Muzyka rozrywkowa.
   [ ] Inne (_____)
   [ ] Amatorskie wykonania (chóralne lub solowe).
   [ ] Amatorskie śpiewanie dla własnej przyjemności.

6. Czy miałeś lekcje śpiewu ? Tak ____ Nie ____. W którym wieku zaczynałeś mieć lekcje (Podkreśl)
   [2, 3, 4, 5, 6, 7, 8, 9, 10, 11, 12, 13, 14, 15, 16, 17, 18, 19, 20, 21, 22, 23, 24, 25, 26, 27, 28, 30, 35, 40, 45,
   50, 55, 60, 65, 70, 80, 85]

7. Czy w tym czasie były miesiące lub lata bez lekcji ?   Tak _____   Nie _____

8. Jak długo studiujesz u obecnego nauczyciela śpiewu ?
   [1, 2, 3, 4, 5, 6, 7, 8, 9, 10, 11, 12, 13, 14, 15, 16, 17, 18, 19, 20, 21, 22, 23, 24, 25, więcej]

   [tygodnie, miesiące, lata]

   Imię i nazwisko nauczyciela śpiewu
   Adres nauczyciela śpiewu

   Numer telefonu nauczyciela śpiewu

9. Zestaw listę poprzednich nauczycieli i lata w których studiowałeś u nich:

10. Czy miałeś kiedykolwiek lekcje ćwiczenia głosu mówionego?   Tak _____   Nie _____
    Lekcje ćwiczenia głosu dla aktorów ?   Tak _____   Nie _____
    Przez ile lat ?   [Mniej niż jeden, 1–3, 6–10, więcej]
    Terapię mówcy ?   Tak _____   Nie _____
    Przez ile miesięcy ?   [1, 2, 3, 4 ,5, 6, 7–12, więcej]

11. Czy pracujesz oprócz śpiewania ?
    Tak _____   Nie _____

    Jeżeli tak, czy praca wymaga nadmiernego używania głosu ?
    Tak _____   Nie _____

Jeżeli tak, jaka jest ta praca ? [Lektor, mówca (w telewizji, w radiu, na stadionie sportowym), nauczyciel sportu, prawnik, duchowny, polityk, lekarz, sprzedawca, makler giełdowy, nauczyciel, telefonistka lub recepcjonistka, kelner, kelnerka, sekretarka, inna]

12. W ramach pracy wykonywane, poza śpiewaniem, czy musisz często
mówić ? Tak _____ Nie _____ tańczyć ? Tak _____ Nie _____

13. Przez ile lat aktywnie śpiewałeś przed rozpoczęciem lekcji śpiewu ?
[2, 3, 4, 4, 5, 6, 7, 8, 9, 10, 11, 12, 13, 14, 15, 16, 17, 18, 19, 20, 21, 22, 23, 24, 25, więcej]

14. Jakie rodzaj muzyki śpiewasz ? Podkreśl wszystkie dotyczące:
_____ Muzyka poważna   _____ Muzyka nocnych klubów
_____ Muzyka teatralna   _____ Muzyka rokowa
_____ Innc (wyszczcgólnij) _____

15. Czy regularnie śpiewasz w pozycji siedzącej, np. przy fortepianie lub przy zestawie perkusyjnym ?
Tak _____ Nie _____

16. Czy śpiewasz na otwartych przestrzeniach lub na dużych salach lub z orkiestrami ? (Podkreśl które)
Tak _____ Nie _____

17. Jeżeli występujesz z instrumentami electroniczna lub na terenie otwartym, czy używasz głośników
podsłuchowych?   Tak _____ Nie _____
Jcżcli tak, czy je słyszysz ? Tak _____ Nie _____

18. Czy grasz na instrumencie muzycznym (instrumentach muzycznych) ?   Tak _____ Nie _____
Jeżeli tak, podkreśl wszystkie na których grasz:
_____ Klawiszowe (Fortepian, organy, klawesyn, inne _____)
_____ Skrzypce, Altówka
       Wiolonczela
_____ Kontrabas
_____ Strunowe szarpane (Gitara, Harfa, inne _____)
_____ Dęte blaszane
_____ Dęte drewniane z pojedynczym stroikiem
_____ Dęte drewniane z podwójnym stroikiem
_____ Flet, piccolo
_____ Perkusja
_____ Kobza
_____ Akordeon
_____ Inne (wyszczególnij): _____

19. Jak często ćwiczysz ?
Gamy: [codziennie, parę razy w tygodniu, raz w tygodniu, rzadko, nigdy]
Jeżeli ćwiczysz gamy, czy ćwiczysz wszystkie na raz lub czy rozdzielasz je w ciągu dnia ?
[wszystkie na raz, na dwie lub trzy sesje]

W dniach kiedy ćwiczysz gamy, jak długo ćwiczysz ?
[15, 30, 45, 60, 15, 90, 105, 120, więcej] minut

Pieśni: [codziennie, parę razy w tygodniu, raz w tygodniu rzadko, nigdy]

Ile godzin dziennie ?
[½, 1½, 2½, 3, więcej]

Czy rozgrzewasz głos przed śpiewaniem ?   Tak _____   Nie _____

Czy ochładzasz głos po zakończeniu śpiewania ?   Tak _____   Nie _____

20. Ile obecnie śpiewaszpodaj ogólną sumę zawierającą czas ćwiczenia
(przeciętna ilość godzin dziennie):
Na próbach: [½, 1, 1½, 2, 2½, 3, 4, 5, 6, 7, 8, 9, 10]
Na wykonaniach : [½, 1, 1½, 2, 2½, 3, 4, 5, 6, 7, 8]

21. Podkreśl wszystkie Ciebie dotyczące:
_____ Masz głos w gorszym stanie rano.
_____ Masz głos w gorszym stanie później w ciągu dnia, po użyciu.
_____ Śpiewasz na wykonaniach lub próbach rano.
_____ Mówisz dużo (np. jako nauczyciel, duchowny, prawnik, praca telefoniczna, itd.)
_____ Działasz jako wodzirej (na meczach sportowych).
_____ Mówisz dużo za kulisami lub na przyjęciach po wykonaniach.
_____ Jesteś dyrygentem chóralnym.
_____ Często chrząkasz.
_____ Często masz anginę (gardła).
_____ Masz problemy ze stawem szczękowym.
_____ Masz gorzki lub kwaśny smak lub cuchnący oddech rano.
_____ Często masz palenie w żołądku lub przepuklina około przełyku
_____ Często krzyczysz lub głośno mówisz.
_____ Często mówisz szeptem.
_____ Masz chroniczne zmęczenie (bezsenność)
_____ Pracujesz w skrajnie suchych warunkach.
_____ Często ćwiczysz fizycznie (podnoszenie ciężarów, itp.)
_____ Często jesteś spragniony, odwodniony.
_____ Masz rano ochrypłość.
_____ Masz kaszel klatki piersiowej.
_____ Jesz późno w nocy.
_____ Czy kiedykolwiek zażyłeś środki zobojętniające kwas żołądkowy.
_____ Czy jesteś obecnie pod szczególnym stresem (osobistym lub zawodowym)
_____ Często masz cuchnący oddech.
_____ Mieszkasz, pracujesz, występujesz w pobliżu dymów lub oparów.
_____ Podróżowałeś niedawno   Kiedy _____
                            Gdzie _____

Czy jesz coś z następujących produktów przed śpiewaniem ?
_____ Czekoladę   _____ Lody lub mleko
_____ Kawę   _____ Orzechy
_____ Alkohol   _____ Pikantne potrawy
Inne (wyszczególnij)

_____ Czy masz jakieś specyficzne trudności wokalno-techniczne ?
[problem ze śpiewaniem cicho, problem ze śpiewaniem głośno, niedobra kontrola wysokości tonu, problemy z podparciem, problemy z przejściem z rejestru do rejestru, inne] Opisz:

_____ Czy miałeś niedawno jakieś problemy ze śpiewaniem przed początkiem problemu, który spowodował obecne badanie lekarskie ?
[ochrypłość, za dużo powietrza w głosie, zmęczenie, strata zakresu, przerw w głosie, ból podczas śpiewania, inne] Opisz:

_____ Czy miałeś jakieś problemy z głosem w przeszłości, które wymagałyby badania lekarskiego ?
Jeżeli tak, opisz problem i badania:
[zapalenie krtani, guzki, polipy, krwotoki, rak, inne] Opisz:

22. Imię i nazwisko, adres i numer telefonu Twojego lekarza domowego.

23. Imię i nazwisko, adres i numer telefonu Twojego laryngologa.

24. Czy byłeś niedawno przeziębiony ?   Tak _____   Nie _____

25. Czy obecnie jesteś przeziębiony ?   Tak _____   Nie _____

26. Czy byłeś często (lub niedawno) wystawiony na następujące chemikalia w domu lub w pracy ?
(Podkreśl wszystkie dotyczące)

_____ Tlenek węgla   _____ Arszenik
_____ Rtęć   _____ Farby anilinowe
_____ Środek do tępienia owadów   _____ Rozpuszczalniki przemysłowe i
_____ Ołów   benzynowe, itd.
_____ Dym do efektów scenicznych

27. Czy byłeś badany przez specjalistę od chorób alergicznych ?   Tak _____   Nie _____
Jeżeli tak, jakie masz alergie
[żadne, kurz, pleśń, kwitnące drzewa, koty, psy, jedzenie, inne _____]
[Pytania o alergiach na lekarstwa znajdują się dalej na tej ankiecie]

Jeżeli tak, podaj imię, nazwisko i adres specjalistów od chorób alergicznych.

28. Ile paczek papierosów palisz dziennie ?

Historia palenia
_____ Nigdy
_____ Przestałem. Kiedy ?
_____ Paliłem około [mniej niż połowę, połowę, jedną, półtorej, dwie, dwie i pół, trzy, więcej] paczki dziennie przez [1, 2, 3, 4, 5, 6, 7, 8, 9, 10–15, 16–20, 21, 25, 26–30, 31–35, 36–40, 41–45, 46–50, więcej] lat
_____ Palę [mniej niż połowę, połowę, jedną, półtorej, dwie, dwie i pół, trzy, więcej] paczek dziennie przez [1, 2, 3, 4, 5, 6, 7, 8, 9, 10, 11–15, 16–20, 21–25, 26–30, 31–35, 36–40, 41–45, 45–50, więcej] lat

29. Czy pracujesz w otoczeniu zadymionym ?   Tak _____   Nie _____

30. Ile alkoholu pijesz ? [żaden, rzadko, parę razy w tygodniu, codziennie] [1, 2, 3, 4, 5, 6, 7, 8, 9, 10] szklanki [dziennie, w tygodniu] [piwa, wina, mocnych trunków]

    Czy kiedyś więcej piłeś ?   Tak _____   Nie _____

31. Ile kubków kawy, herbaty, coli, lub innych napojów kofeinowych pijesz dziennie ? [0, 1, 2, 3, 4, 5, 6, 7, 8, 9, 10]

32. Zestaw listę innych używek, które zażywasz: [marihuanę, kokainę, amfetaminę, barbiturany, heroinę, inne _____]

33. Czy zwróciłeś uwagę na następujące [Podkreśl wszystkie Ciebie dotyczące] :
    _____ Nadwrażliwość na gorąco lub zimno
    _____ Nadmierne pocenie się
    _____ Zmianę wagi: przytyłem/schudłem _____ kg w ciągu _____ tygodni/_____ miesięcy
    _____ Zmiany skórne lub w owłosieniu
    _____ Palpitacje (migotanie) serca
    _____ Skoki nastroju
    _____ Dwojenie widzenia
    _____ Drętwienie twarzy lub kończyn
    _____ Mrowienie wokół ust lub na twarzy
    _____ Zamglony wzrok lub ślepota
    _____ Słabość lub paraliż twarzy
    _____ Niezręczność rąk lub nóg
    _____ Zażenowanie lub strata przytomności
    _____ Trudności w mówieniu
    _____ Trudności z przełykaniem
    _____ Ataki epilepsji
    _____ Ból w karku lub w ramioniach
    _____ Wstrząsy lub drżenia
    _____ Zmiany pamięci
    _____ Zmiany osobowości

    Dla kobiet:

    Czy jesteś w ciąży ?   Tak _____   Nie _____
    Czy miałaś usuniętą macic ?   Tak _____   Nie _____
    Czy jajniki były usuwane ?   Tak _____   Nie _____
    Czy okresy są regularne ?   Tak _____   Nie _____
    W którym wieku doszłaś do dojrzałości płciowej ?
    [7, 8, 9, 10, 11, 12, 13, 14, 15, 16, 17, 18, 19, 20]
    Czy już przeszłaś menopauzę ?   Tak _____   Nie _____
Jeżeli tak, kiedy ? [obecnie, 1, 2, 3, 4, 5, 6, 7, 8, 9, 10, więcej] lat temu.

34. Czy kiedykolwiek radziłeś się ze psychiatry lub psychologa ?
    Tak _____   Nie _____

    Czy obecnie chodzisz na badania ?   Tak _____   Nie _____

35. Czy skaleczyłeś głowę lub kark (przez sztywny kark, itd.?]   Tak _____   Nie _____

36. Opisz wszystkie poważne wypadki .

37. Czy jesteś zaangażowany w akcje prawne dotyczące problemów związanych z głosem ?
   Tak _____ Nie _____

38. Zestaw listę imion i nazwisk małżonki i dzieci:

39. Podaj krótkie podsumowanie ENT (uszy, nos, garało) problemów uszy, nos garało nie dotyczyć Twojego obecnego problemu.
                PODKREŚL WSZYSTKIE DOTYCZĄCE

_____ Strata słuchu   _____ Ból ucha

_____ Szmery w uszach   _____ Ból twarzy

_____ Zawroty głowy   _____ Sztywny kark

_____ Paraliż twarzy   _____ Guz w karku

_____ Zatykanie w nosie   _____ Guz na twarzy lub w na

_____ Deformacja nosa   głowie

_____ Owrzodzenie w ustach   _____ Trudności z połykaniem

_____ Problem z stawem   _____ Nadmierna ilość skóry na
        szczękowym   powiece oka

_____ Problem z oczami   _____ Nadmierna ilość skóry na

_____ Inne (wyszczególnij)   twarzy

40. Czy masz lub kiedykolwiek miałeś ?:

_____ Cukrzycę   _____ Napady

_____ Za mało cukru we krwi   _____ Leczenic psychiatryczne

_____ Problemy z tarczycą   _____ Częste silne bóle głowy

_____ Syfilis   _____ Wrzody żołądkowe

_____ Rzeżączkę   _____ Chorobę nerek

_____ Herpes   _____ Problemy dróg moczowych

_____ Pęcherzyk na wardze   _____ Artretyzm lub problemy z układem

_____ Nadciśnienie   kostnym

_____ Poważnie podciśnienie   _____ Rozszczepione podniebienie

_____ Antybiotyki lub lekarstwo   _____ Astmę
        moczopędne podawane dożylnie   _____ Problemy z płucami lub

_____ Zawał serca   oddychaniem

_____ Anginę (serca)   _____ Niewytłumaczalne chudnięcie

_____ Nieregularne bicie serca   _____ Rak (czego) (_____)

_____ Inne problemy z sercem   _____ Inny guz (czego) (_____)

_____ Ostry gościec stawowy   _____ Transfuzję krwi

_____ Gruźlicę   _____ Zapalenie wątroby

_____ Jaskrę   _____ AIDS

_____ Stwardnienie rozsiane (sklerozę)   _____ Zarclenie błony mózgowej

_____ Inne choroby (wyszczególnij)

41. Czy jacyś krewni mają :

_____ Cukrzycę   _____ Rak

_____ Za mało cukru we krwi   _____ Chorobę serca

_____ Inne poważne problemy zdrowotne
jak powyżej (wyszczególnij)

42. Opisz poważne wypadki, *jeżeli nie* odnoszą się bezpośrednio do [Twojej wizyty lekarskiej tutaj]

_____ Żadne

_____ Wydarzyły się z obrażeniem głowy, z stratą przytomności lub porażenia szyi (wypadek samochodowy)

_____ Wydarzyły się bez obrażeń głowy, bez straty przytomności lub porażenia szyi (wypadek samochodowy)

43. Zestaw listę wszystkich lekarstw, które obecnie zażywasz wraz z dawkami i włączając w to tabletki przeciwko zapłodnieniu i witaminy.

44. Alergie na lekarstwa

_____ Żadne   _____ Nowokaina

_____ Penicylina   _____ Jodyna

_____ Leki sulfonamidowe   _____ Kodeina

_____ Tetracyklina   _____ Przylepiec – plazterkí

_____ Erytromycyna   _____ Aspiryna

_____ Keflex/Ceclor/Ceftin   _____ Barwniki do prześwietleń

_____ Inne , wyszczególnij   rentgenowskich

45. Zestaw listę operacji

_____ Wycięcie migdałków: _____ Wycięcie trzeciego migdałka

(wiek _____)   _____ Operacje na serce

_____ Wycięcie wyrostka robaczkowego   (wiek _____)

(wiek_____)

_____ Inne, wyszczególnij

46. Zestaw listę lekarstw toksycznych lub chemikalii na które byłeś narażony:

_____ Żadne   _____ Streptomycyna, Neomycyna,

_____ Ołów   Kanamycyna

_____ Rtęć   _____ Inne, wyszczególnij

47. Czy miałeś leczenie promieniami Rentgena głowy lub karku (zawierające leczenie trądzijiku lub problemów z uszami jako dziecko, leczenie raka, itd.?)   Tak _____   Nie _____

48. Opisz poważne problemy zdrowotne małżonki lub dzieci

_____ Żadne

Portuguese Version of Appendix IIc

Histórico do Paciente: Cantores

Translated by Deborah Feijó Andrade, S.L.P., M. Sc.

Robert Thayer Sataloff, M.D., D.M.A.
1721 Pine Street
Philadelphia. PA 19103 – U.S.A.

Nome _____ Idade _____ Sexo _____ Raça_____

Altura _____ Peso _____ Data _____

Classificação de Voz:

_____ soprano _____ mezzo-soprano _____ contralto

_____ tenor _____ barítono _____ baixo

(Se atualmente você não apresenta nenhum problema de voz, por favor passe para a pergunta 3)

POR FAVOR, MARQUE AS RESPOSTAS CORRETAS:

1. Há quanto tempo você apresenta o seu problema atual de voz ?
   [1,2,3,4,5,6,7,8,9,10 ou mais]
   [horas, dias, semanas, meses, anos]

   Quem percebeu o problema ?
   [eu mesmo, família, professor de voz, críticos, todos, outros _____]

   Você sabe o que causou o problema ? [Sim _____ Não _____]

   Se a resposta foi sim, o que foi ? [um resfriado, gritar, falar muito, cantar, cirurgia, outros _____]

   O problema foi progressivo ou apareceu de repente ?
   [Progressivo _____ de repente _____]

   O problema está: piorando _____ , melhorando _____ , estável _____

2. Quais os sintomas que você apresenta (por favor, marque todos os que se aplicam):
   _____ Rouquidão (som áspero ou arranhado)
   _____ Fadiga (cansaço vocal ou mudança de qualidade vocal depois de cantar por um curto período de tempo)
   _____ Distúrbio de volume (dificuldade de cantar) fraco _____ forte _____
   _____ Perda de extensão vocal (agudo _____ grave _____)
   _____ Mudança na classificação (ex.: voz mudou de soprano para mezzo)
   _____ Necessidade de aquecimento prolongado (mais de meia hora para aquecer a voz)
   _____ Soprosidade
   _____ Sensação de coceira ou engasgo enquanto canta
   _____ Dor na garganta enquanto canta
   _____ Outros: (Por favor, especifique quais são) _____

3. Você tem alguma apresentação importante em breve ?   Sim _____   Não _____

    Data(s): _____

4. Qual é o atual *status* da sua carreira ?   Profissional _____   Amador _____

5. Quais são os seus objetivos, a longo-prazo, em sua carreira como cantor ?

    [   ] Lírico profissional (ópera)

    [   ] Popular profissional

    [   ] Semi-profissional

    [   ] Clássico

    [   ] Popular

    [   ] Outros [_____]

    [   ] Amador (coralista ou solista)

    [   ] Amador para divertimento próprio

6. Você teve treinamento vocal ?   Sim _____   Não _____ Com quantos anos começou ? _____

    [2,3,4,5,6,7,8,9,10,11,12,13,14,15,16,17,18,19,20,21,22,23,24,25,26,27,28,29,30,35.40.45,50,55,60,65,70,75,80,85]

7. Durante este tempo houve períodos de meses ou anos sem aulas de canto ? Sim _____ Não _____

8. Há quanto tempo você estuda com o seu atual professor de canto ?

    [1, 2, 3, 4, 5, 6, 7, 8, 9, 10, 11, 12, 13, 14, 15, 16, 17, 18, 19, 20, 21, 22, 23, 24, 25, mais]

    [semanas, meses, anos]

    Nome do professor:

    Endereço do professor:

    Telefone do professor:

9. Faça uma lista com o nome dos professores com quem você já estudou e os anos em que estudou com cada um deles:

10. Você já fez algum treinamento de voz falada ?   Sim _____   Não _____

    Aula de teatro ?   Sim _____   Não _____

    Por quantos anos ?   [menos que 1 ano, 1-5, 6-10, mais]

    Terapia fonoaudiológica ?   Sim _____   Não _____

    Por quantos meses ?   [1,2,3,4,5,6,7-12, mais]

11. Você tem alguma outra atividade profissional além de cantar ?   Sim _____   Não _____

    Se sua resposta é sim, esta atividade envolve uso extensivo de voz ?   Sim _____   Não _____

    Se sua resposta é sim, qual é a atividade ? [ator/atriz, locutor(a) (televisão, rádio, estádio), instrutor(a) esportivo, advogado(a), clérigo, político(a), médico(a) , vendedor(a), operador(a) de pregão, professor(a) , telefonista ou recepcionista, garçom/ garçonete, secretário(a), outros _____)

12. Na sua atividade, além de cantar, você também é freqüentemente requisitado a falar ?
    Sim _____ Não _____ e a dançar ?   Sim _____   Não _____

13. Por quanto anos você cantou ativamente antes de ter aulas de canto ?
    [1,2,3,4,5,6,7,8,9,10,11,12,13,14,15,16,17,18,19,20,21,22,23,24,25, mais]

14. Que tipo de músicas você canta ? (marque todos os que sejam aplicáveis.)
    _____ Clássico   _____ Espetáculos
    _____ Boate   _____ Rock

15. Você em geral canta sentado ? (em um piano ou bateria)

16. Você canta ao ar livre, em grandes salas de concerto ou com orquestras ? (marque qual deles)
    Sim _____   Não _____

17. Se você canta com instrumentos eletrônicos ou ao ar livre, você usa caixas de retorno ?
    Sim _____   Não _____

18. Você toca algum instrumento musical ?   Sim _____   Não _____

    Se a resposta for sim, marque o que se aplica:
    _____ Teclado (piano, órgão, cravo, outros _____)
    _____ Violino, Viola
    _____ Violoncelo
    _____ Contrabaixo
    _____ Cordas percutidas (guitarra, harpa, outros, _____)
    _____ Metais
    _____ Instrumento de sopro com palheta simples
    _____ Instrumento de sopro com palheta dupla
    _____ Flauta, Flautim
    _____ Instrumentos de percussão
    _____ Gaita de foles
    _____ Acordeão
    _____ Outros: (Especifique qual instrumento) _____

19. Com que freqüência você pratica ?
    Escalas: [diariamente, algumas vezes por semana, raramente, nunca]

    Se você pratica escalas, você as faz todas de uma vez ou as divide durante o período de um dia ?
    [Todas de uma vez, dividido em dois ou três momentos do dia]

    Nos dias em que você faz escalas, por quanto tempo você pratica ? [15, 30, 45, 60, 75, 90,105, 120, ou mais] minutos?

    Canções: [diariamente, algumas vezes por semana, raramente, nunca]

    Quantas horas por dia ? [½, 1, 1½, 2, 2½, 3, mais]

    Você aquece a sua voz antes de cantar ?   Sim _____   Não _____

    Você desaquece a voz quando acaba de cantar ?   Sim _____   Não _____

20. Quanto você canta atualmente ? (o total, incluindo o tempo em que você pratica) (média de horas por dia) ?
Ensaio: [½, 1, 1½, 2, 2½, 3, 4,5,6,7,8,9,10]
Apresentação: : [½, 1, 1½, 2, 2½, 3, 4,5,6,7,8]

21. Por favor, marque o que se aplica a você:
_____ Voz rouca pela manhã.
_____ Voz rouca ao fim do dia, depois de usar por muito tempo.
_____ Apresentações ou ensaios pela manhã.
_____ Falar excessivamente (ex.: professor, religioso, advogado, telefonista).
_____ Chefe de torcida.
_____ Falar extensivamente nos camarins ou em festas após apresentações .
_____ Regente de coral.
_____ Pigarros constantes.
_____ Dores de garganta freqüentes.
_____ Problema na articulação mandibular.
_____ Gosto amargo ou ácido, ou mau hálito ao acordar.
_____ Azia freqüente ou hérnia de hiato.
_____ Gritar ou falar alto com freqüência.
_____ Sussurrar com freqüência.
_____ Fadiga crônica (insônia).
_____ Trabalhar em ambientes extremamente secos.
_____ Exercícios freqüentes (musculação, exercícios aeróbicos).
_____ Sentir muita sede, sentir-se desidratado.
_____ Rouquidão pela manhã.
_____ Tosse peitoral.
_____ Comer tarde da noite.
_____ Uso freqüente de anti-ácidos.
_____ Encontra-se sob algum tipo de estresse atualmente (pessoal ou profissional).
_____ Freqüentemente tem mau hálito.
_____ Vive, trabalha ou atua em locais com fumaça .
_____ Viajou recentemente: Quando: _____
                    Para onde: _____

Você come ou bebe algum destes alimentos antes de cantar ?
_____ Chocolate   _____ Café
_____ Álcool   _____ Leite ou sorvete
_____ Nozes   _____ Comida picante ou condimentada

Outros: (especifique) _____

_____ Alguma dificuldade técnica específica ao usar a voz ?
         [dificuldade em cantar fraco, dificuldade em cantar forte, deficiência em controlar a freqüência, difi-
         culdade no suporte respiratório, dificuldades na transição de registros, outros]? Descreva

_____ Algum problema recente com a sua voz cantada, anterior a este problema que o trouxe agora ao con-
         sultório ? (rouquidão, soprosidade, fadiga, per

_____ Algum problema de voz no passado que requisitou consulta médica ? Se a resposta for sim, por
         favor descreva o(s) problema(s) e o(s) tratamento(s): [laringite, nódulos, pólipos, hemorragia, câncer,
         outros] Descreva:

22. O nome, endereço e telefone do seu médico (clínico ou médico da família):

23. O nome, endereço e telefone do seu laringologista:

24. Algum resfriado recente ?   Sim _____   Não _____

25. Está resfriado no momento ?   Sim _____   Não _____

26. Você esteve exposto a algum dos agentes químicos abaixo freqüentemente (ou recentemente) em casa ou no trabalho ? (Marque o que se aplica).
    _____ Monóxido de carbono   _____ Arsênico
    _____ Mercúrio   _____ Corante de anilina
    _____ Inseticidas   _____ Solventes industriais
    _____ Chumbo   (benzeno)
    _____ Fumaça artística, gelo seco

27. Você já foi avaliado por um alergista?   Sim _____   Não _____
    Se a resposta for sim, que alergias você apresenta:
    [nenhuma, poeira, mofo, árvores, gato, cachorro, alimentos, outros _____]
    (Alergias a medicações estão incluídas em outro questionário)

    Se a resposta for sim, dê o nome e o endereço do alergista:

28. Quantos maços de cigarro você fuma por dia ?

    Histórico do seu hábito de fumar:
    _____ Nunca
    _____ Deixou de fumar. Quando ?
    _____ Fumou [menos que _, 1, 1_, 2, 2_, 3, ou mais] maços por dia por [1, 2, 3, 4, 5, 6, 7, 8, 9, 10, 11-15, 16-20, 21-25, 26-30, 31-35, 36-40, 41-45, 46-50, mais] anos.
    _____ Fuma [menos que _, 1, 1_, 2, 2_, 3, ou mais] maços por dia por [1, 2, 3, 4, 5, 6, 7, 8, 9, 10, 11-15, 16-20, 21-25, 26-30, 31-35, 36-40, 41-45, 46-50, mais] anos.

29. Você trabalha em ambiente com fumaça ?   Sim _____   Não _____

30. Quanto de bebida alcóolica você bebe ? [nenhuma, raramente, algumas vezes por semana, diariamente] [1,2,3,4,5,6,7,8,9,10, mais] copos por [dia, semana] de [cerveja, vinho, uísque]

    Você já consumiu mais bebida alcóolica do que consome hoje ?   Sim _____   Não _____

31. Quantas xícaras/copos de café, chá, refrigerante ou outras bebidas que contenham cafeína você bebe por dia ? [0,1,2,3,4,5,6,7,8,9,10]

32. Faça uma lista com outras drogas que você usa
    [maconha, cocaína, anfetaminas, barbitúricos, heroína, outras _____]

33. Você já percebeu algum dos sintomas abaixo ? (Marque todos que se aplicam)
    _____ Hipersensitividade ao calor e ao frio
    _____ Suor excessivo
    _____ Mudança de peso: ganho/perda _____ libras em _____ (1)
              (cada libra equivale a 453 gramas ou 0,453 quilos)
    _____ Mudanças na pele ou cabelo
    _____ Palpitação no coração
    _____ Labilidade emocional (mudança de humor)
    _____ Visão dupla
    _____ Dormência na face ou nas extremidades
    _____ Coceira ao redor da boca ou da face
    _____ Visão turva ou cegueira
    _____ Fraqueza ou paralisia facial
    _____ Perda do controle dos movimentos dos braços ou das pernas
    _____ Confusão mental ou perda de consciência
    _____ Dificuldade de fala
    _____ Dificuldade para engolir
    _____ Convulsões (Epilepsia)
    _____ Dor no pescoço ou ombros
    _____ Tremores
    _____ Alterações de memória
    _____ Mudança de personalidade

    Para mulheres:

    Você está grávida ?   Sim _____   Não _____
    Realizou histerectomia ?   Sim _____   Não _____
    Teve os ovários removidos ?   Sim _____   Não _____
    Seus períodos menstruais são regulares   Sim _____   Não _____
    Com quantos anos atingiu a puberdade ?
    [7,8,9,10,11,12,13,14,15,16,17,18,19,20]
    Você já passou da menopausa ?   Sim _____   Não _____

    Se a resposta for sim, quando [atualmente; 1,2 3,4,5,6,7,8,9,10, ou mais] anos atrás.

34. Você já consultou um psicólogo ou psiquiatra ?   Sim _____   Não _____
    Atualmente você está em tratamento ?   Sim _____   Não _____

35. Você já machucou o pescoço ou cabeça (com movimentos bruscos e repentinos de cabeça) ?
    Sim _____   Não _____

36. Descreva qualquer acidente sério que já tenha sofrido.

37. Você está envolvido em alguma ação judicial que envolva o seu problema de voz?   Sim _____   Não _____

38. Escreva o nome do seu cônjuge e filhos:

39. Breve sumário de problemas de ouvido, nariz e garganta. Alguns deles podem não estar relacionados com o seu problema atual.

Marque todos os que se aplicam:

_____ Perda de audição   _____ Dor de ouvido
_____ Ruídos do ouvido   _____ Dor facial
_____ Tonteiras   _____ Tensão no pescoço
_____ Paralisia facial   _____ Caroço do pescoço
_____ Obstrução nasal   _____ Caroço na face
_____ Deformidades   ou cabeça
nasais   _____ Dificuldade de
_____ Dor na língua   deglutição
_____ Problema na articulação   _____ Excesso de pele
da mandíbula   nos olhos
Problemas oculares   _____ Excesso de pele
_____ Outros: (especifique)   na face

40. Você tem ou já teve:
_____ Diabetes   _____ Convulsões
_____ Hipoglicemia   _____ Terapia psiquiátrica
_____ Problemas de tireóide   _____ Dores de cabeça freqüentes
_____ Sífilis   _____ Úlceras
_____ Gonorréia   _____ Doenças renais
_____ Herpes   _____ Problemas urinários
_____ Gripe e febre acompanhados   _____ Artrite ou problemas ósseos de lesões de pele
_____ Pressão alta   _____ Fissura palatina
_____ Antibióticos ou diuréticos   _____ Asma intravenosos
_____ Ataque cardíaco   _____ Problemas pulmonares ou respiratórios
_____ Angina   _____ Perda de peso sem razão
_____ Batimentos cardíacos   _____ Câncer de (_____) irregulares
_____ Outros problemas de coração   _____ Outros tumores (_____)
_____ Febre reumática   _____ Transfusão de sangue
_____ Tuberculose   _____ Hepatite
_____ Glaucoma   _____ AIDS
_____ Esclerose Múltipla   _____ Meningite
_____ Outras doenças (especifique)

41. Algum parente consangüíneo tem:
_____ Diabetes   _____ Câncer
_____ Hipoglicemia   _____ Doenças cardíacas
_____ Outros problemas médicos sérios como os indicados acima ?
Por favor, especifique:

42. Descreva os acidentes sérios que sofreu, que não estejam diretamente relacionados com a sua consulta de hoje.
_____ Nenhum
_____ Acidente com ferimentos na cabeça ou perda de consciência.
_____ Acidente sem ferimentos na cabeça ou perda de consciência
Descreva:

43. Faça uma lista de todos os medicamentos que você está tomando no momento incluindo as dosagens (inclua pílulas anticoncepcionais e vitaminas)

44. Alergia a medicamentos:
    _____ Nenhum   _____ Novocaina
    _____ Penicilina   _____ Iodo
    _____ Sulfa   _____ Codeína
    _____ Tetraciclina   _____ Fita adesiva
    _____ Eritromicina   _____ Aspirina
    _____ Keflex/Ceclor/Ceftin   _____ Contraste para radiografia
    _____ Outros: (especifique)

45. Faça uma lista de cirurgias:
    _____ Amigdalectomia   _____ Adenoidectomia
           (Idade _____)   (Idade _____)
    _____ Apendicite   _____ Cirurgia cardíaca
           (Idade _____)   (Idade _____)
    _____ Outra: (especifique)

46. Faça uma lista de drogas tóxicas e substâncias químicas a que você tenha sido exposto:
    _____ Chumbo   _____ Estreptomicina, neomicina,
    _____ Mercúrio   _____ Outros: (especifique)

47. Você já fez algum *tratamento* com raios X em sua cabeça ou pescoço (incluindo tratamento para acne ou problemas de ouvido quando criança, tratamentos para câncer, etc.) ? Sim _____   Não _____

48. Descreva qualquer problema sérios de saúde com o seu cônjuge ou filhos.
    _____ Nenhum

(1) I added the equivalent of kilos in pounds to facilitate portuguese speakers, once that they usually use kilos to measure weight.

Romanian Version of Appendix IIc

Translated by Lumi Shapp
Istoricul pacientului: cântăreţi
Robert Thayer Sataloff, M.D., D.M.A.
1721 Pine Street
Philadelphia, PA 19103
U.S.A.

Numele _____ Vârsta _____ Sexul _____ Naţionalitatea _____

Înâlţimea _____ Greutatea _____ Data _____

Categoria vocală _____ soprană _____ mezzosoprană _____ altistă
_____ tenor _____ bariton _____ bas

(Dacă nu aveţi probleme vocale în prezent, treceţi direct la întrebarea nr.3)

BIFAŢI ORI ÎNCERCUIŢI RĂSPUNSURILE CORECTE:

1. De cât timp aveţi problema actuală cu vocea?

(1,2,3,4,5,6,7,8,9,10, mai mult)
(ore, zile, săptămâni, luni, ani)

Cine a detectat-o?
(însuşi, familia, profesorul de voce, criticii muzicali, toată lumea, alţii _____)

Cunoaşteţi cauza?
(Da _____ Nu _____)

Dacă da, care anume? (o răceală, ţipat, vorbire excesivă, cântatul, intervenţie chirurgicală, altele _____)

S-a ivit treptat ori pe neaşteptate?
(treptat _____, brusc _____)

Problema devine din ce în ce mai: dificilă _____ uşoară _____ staţionară _____ ?

2. Ce fel de simptome aveţi? (Bifaţi tot ce se aplică.)
_____ Răguşeală (sunet răguşit ori zgâriat)
_____ Oboseală (vocea oboseşte sau îşi schimbă calitatea după cântat de scurtă durată)
_____ Perturbări de volum (probleme în timpul cântatului) _____ încet _____ tare
_____ Pierderea întinderii (înalt _____ jos _____)
_____ Schimbări de clasificare (ca de exemplu: vocea coboară de la soprană la mezzo)
_____ Încălzire prelungită (peste 1/2 oră încălzire a vocii)
_____ Exces de aer în timpul cântatului
_____ Senzaţie de gâdilătură sau înnecare în timpul cântatului
_____ Durere în gât în timpul cântatului
_____ Altele (specificaţi): _____

3. Aveți un spectacol important în viitorul apropiat?   Da _____ Nu _____
     Data _____

4. Care este statutul dvs. actual în cariera vocală?   Profesionist _____ Amator _____

5. Care vă sunt planurile de viitor în privința cântatului?

   [ ]   Cântăreț de operă de carieră

   [ ]   Cântăreț de muzică ușoară de carieră

   [ ]   Cântăreț de profesie carieră secundară

   [ ]   Cântăreț clasic

   [ ]   Muzică ușoară

   [ ]   Altele _____

   [ ]   Cântăreț amator (coral, solist)

   [ ]   Cântăreț amator pentru plăcerea personală

6. Ați avut antrenament vocal?   Da _____ Nu _____ La ce vârstă ați început? (încercuiți)
[2, 3, 4, 5, 6, 7, 8, 9, 10, 11, 12, 13, 14, 15, 16, 17, 18, 19, 20, 21, 22, 23, 24, 25, 26, 27, 28, 29, 30, 35, 40, 45, 50, 55, 60, 65, 70, 75, 80, 85]

7. Ați trecut prin perioade de luni sau ani fără a lua lecții în tot acest timp?   Da _____ Nu _____

8. De cât timp studiați cu profesorul dvs. actual?
(1, 2, 3, 4, 5, 6, 7, 8, 9, 10, 11, 12, 13, 14, 15, 16, 17, 18, 19, 20, 21, 22, 23, 24, 25, peste)

(săptămâni, luni, ani)

Numele profesorului:
Adresa profesorului:

Numărul de telefon:

9. Enumerați profesorii din trecut și anii între care ați studiat cu fiecare:

10. Ați luat vreodată lecții pentru vocea vorbită ?   Da _____ Nu _____
    Lecții de actorie?   Da _____ Nu _____
    Câți ani?   (Mai puțin de un an, 1-5, 6-10, mai mult)
    Lecții de corectarea vorbirii?   Da _____ Nu _____ Câte luni?
                                        (1, 2, 3, 4, 5, 6, 7-12, mai mult)

11. Aveți vreo ocupație în afara cântatului?
    Da _____ Nu _____

    Dacă da, necesită folosirea excesivă a vocii?
    Da _____ Nu _____

Dacă da, ce profesie anume (actor, crainic - de televiziune / radio / sportiv / stadion -, antrenor de atletism, avocat, preot, politician, medic, vânzător, profesor, operator la telefoane, recepționist, chelner, secretar, altele _____)

12. În ceea cc privește munca dvs., în afara cântatului, vi se întâmplă deseori să vi se ceară să vorbiți?
    Da _____ Nu _____ dansați?   Da _____ Nu _____

13. Câți ani ați cântat în mod activ îmainte de a începe să luați lecții de voce?
    [2, 3, 4, 5, 6, 7, 8, 9, 10, 11, 12, 13, 14, 15, 16, 17, 18, 19, 20, 21, 22, 23, 24, 25 peste]

14. Ce fel de muzică cântați? (Bifați toate care se aplică)
    _____ Clasică   _____ Revistă
    _____ Bar   _____ Ușoară
    _____ Altele (specificați): _____

15. Cântați de obicei așezat (de exemplu la pian sau tobe)?   Da _____ Nu _____

16. Cântați în aer liber sau săli spațioase, ori cu orchestră? (încercuiți una dintre ele) Da _____ Nu _____

17. Când vă produceți cu instrumente electrice sau în aer liber,
    vă folosiți de megafoane?   Da _____ Nu _____
    Dacă da, le și auziți? Da _____ Nu _____

18. Cântați la vreun instrument? Da _____ Nu _____
    Dacă da, încercuiți toate cele de mai jos care se aplică:
    _____ Claviatură (pian, orgă, harpă, altele _____)
    _____ Vioară, violă
    _____ Violoncel
    _____ Contrabas
    _____ Corzi de ciupit (ghitară, harpă, altele _____)
    _____ Alămuri
    _____
    _____
    _____ Flaut, picolină
    _____ Percuție
    _____ Cimpoi
    _____ Acordeon
    _____ Altele (specificați ce anume) _____

19. Cât de frecvent exersați?
    Vocalize: (zilnic, de câteva ori pe săptămână, rareori, niciodată)

    Când vocalizați, cântați toate gamele deodată sau cu pauze în decursul zilei?
    (toate deodată, două sau trei ședințe)

În zilele când faceți vocalize, cât timp exersați?
(15,30,45,60,75,90,105,120 mai mult) minute.

Cântece: (zilnic, de câteva ori pe săptămână, odată pe săptămână, rareori, niciodată)

Câte ore pe zi?
(½, 1, 1½, 2, 2½, 3, peste)

Vă încălziți vocea înainte de a cânta?   Da _____ Nu _____

Vă opriți în mod treptat când terminați de cântat?   Da _____ Nu _____

20. Cât de mult cântați la ora actuală?
(totalul să includă exersarea) (număr mediu de ore pe zi)
Repetiții: (½, 1, 1½, 2, 2½, 3, 4, 5, 6, 7, 8, 9, 10)
Spectacole: (½, 1, 1½, 2, 2½, 3, 4, 5, 6, 7, 8)

21. Marcați tot ce se aplică situației dvs.:
_____ Voce deteriorată dimineața
_____ Voce înrăutățită în timpul zilei, după folosire
_____ Cânt în spectacole sau repetiții în cursul dimineții
_____ Vorbesc exagerat de mult (ex: profesor, preot, avocat, la telefon, cu serviciul, etc.)
_____ Vorbesc prea mult în spatele scenei sau la petreceri după spectacol
_____ Dirijez un cor
_____ Tușesc frecvent
_____ Am probleme cu încheietura maxilarului
_____ Am un gust amar sau acru ori miros în gură când mă trezesc din somn
_____ Adeseori am "arsuri"
_____ Adesea strig și vorbesc cu voce tare
_____ Șoptesc în mod frecvent
_____ Oboseală cronică (insomnie)
_____ Muncesc în aer foarte uscat
_____ Exersez mult (ridic greutăți, fac gimnastică, etc.)
_____ Adesea mi-e sete și sunt deshidratat
_____ Sînt răgușit dis-de-dimineață
_____ Tușesc din piept
_____ Mănânc noaptea târziu
_____ Folosesc anti-acizi
_____ Mă aflu în prezent într-o stare de tensiune (acasă sau la serviciu)
_____ Adesea îmi pute gura
_____ Trăiesc, lucrez sau cânt într-o atmosferă plină de fum, fumuri sau gaze
_____ Călătorii recente: Când _____
                          Unde _____

Ce anume mâncați (beți) înainte de a cânta?
_____ Ciocolată _____ Cafea
_____ Alcool _____ Lapte sau înghețată
_____ Nuci _____ Mâncăruri picante

Altele (specificați)

_____ Dificultăți anume în tehnica vocală?

(dificultăți la cântatul cu voce înceată, cu voce tare, lipsă de control al tonului, probleme de suport, probleme de trecere de la un registru la altul, altele) Descrieți:

_____ Anumite probleme recente la cântat înainte de problema curentă care v-a determinat să veniți aici?

(rãgușealã, exces de aer, oboseală, pierdere de registru, voce spartă, dureri în timpul cântatului, altele) Descrieți:

_____ Anumite probleme din trecut care au necesitat vizite la doctor? Dacă da, descrieți problema și tratamentul:

(laringită, noduri, polipi, hemoragie, cancer, altele) Descrieți:

22. Numele medicului dvs. de familie, adresa și numărul de telefon:

23. Numele laringologului dvs., adresa și numărul de telefon:

24. Ați suferit vreo răceală recentă?   Da _____ Nu _____

25. Sînteți răcit în prezent?   Da _____ Nu _____

26. Ați fost expus la vreuna din următoarele substanțe chimice în mod frecvent (sau recent) acasă sau la lucru? (Înscmnați toatc carc sc aplică)

    _____ monoxid de carbon   _____ arsenic

    _____ mercur   _____ vopsele de anilină

    _____ insecticide   _____ solvenți industriali

    _____ plumb   (benzină, etc.)

    _____ fum de scenă

27. Ați făcut analize pentru alergii vreodată?   Da _____ Nu _____

Dacă da, ce fel de alergii aveți?

(niciuna, la praf, la mucegai, la copaci, la pisici, la câini, la mâncare, altele _____)

(Alergiile la medicamente vor fi enumerate mai jos)

Dacă da, notați numele și adresa medicului alergist:

28. Câte pachete de țigări fumați pe zi?

Istoricul fumatului:

_____ Niciodată

_____ M-am lăsat. Când?

_____ Am fumat aproximativ (mai pîțin de jumătate, o jumătate una, una și jumătate, două, două și jumătate, trei, mai mult) pe zi timp de (1, 2, 3, 4, 5, 6, 7, 8, 9, 10, 11-15, 16-20, 21-25, 26-30, 31-35, 36-40, 41-45, 46-50, peste) ani.

_____ Acum fumez (mai puțin de jumătate, o jumătate, una una și jumătate, două, două și jumătate, trei mai mult) pe zi timp de (1, 2, 3, 4, 5, 6, 7, 8, 9, 10, 11-15, 16-20, 21-25, 26-30, 31-35, 36-40, 41-45, 46-50, peste) ani.

29. Lucrați într-un mediu de fumători?   Da _____ Nu _____

30. Ce cantități de alcool consumați? (de loc, rareori, de câteva ori pe săptămână, zilnic) (1, 2, 3, 4, 5, 6, 7, 8, 9, 10, sau mai mult) pahare pe (zi, săptămână) de (bere, vin, spirt)

   Ați consumat mai mult alcool în trecut?   Da _____ Nu _____

31. Câte cești de cafea, ceai, cola sau alte băuturi care conțin cafeină beți pe zi?
   (0, 1, 2, 3, 4, 5, 6, 7, 8, 9, 10)

32. Enumerați orice alte droguri pe care le folosiți (marijuana, cocaină, amfetamină, barbiturice, heroină, altele _____)

33. Ați observat unele din următoarele (notați toate care se aplică)
   _____ Sensibilitate exagerată la căldură sau frig
   _____ Transpirație excesivă
   _____ Schimbări în greutate: câștig / pierdere _____ Kg
                                     în timp de _____ săptămâni / _____ luni
   _____ Schimbări la piele sau păr
   _____ Palpitații la inimă
   _____ Schimbări bruște de dispoziție
   _____ Vedere dublă
   _____ Amorțeală a feței sau extremităților
   _____ Tremur în jurul gurii sau feței
   _____ Vedere încețoșată sau orbire
   _____ Slăbicîune sau paralizie a feții
   _____ Stângăcie a membrelor
   _____ Confuzie sau pierderea cunoștinței
   _____ Dificultăți la vorbire
   _____ Dificultăți la înghițit
   _____ Crize de epilepsie
   _____ Dureri la ceafă sau în umeri
   _____ Tremurături
   _____ Schimbări de memorie
   _____ Schimbări în personalitate

   Pentru femei:
   Sînteți însărcinată?   Da _____ Nu _____
   Ați avut o histerectomie?   Da _____ Nu _____
   Ați avut ovarele scoase?   Da _____ Nu _____
   Aveți menstruația regulată?   Da _____ Nu _____
   La ce vârstă ați ajuns la pubertate?
   (7, 8, 9, 10, 11, 12, 13, 14, 15, 16, 17, 18, 19, 20)
   Ați trecut de menopauză?   Da _____ Nu _____
Dacă da, când? (în prezent; 1, 2, 3, 4, 5, 6, 7, 8, 9, 10, peste) ani în urmă

34. V-ați consultat vreodată un psiholog sau psihiatru?
        Da _____ Nu _____
   Sînteți în tratament în prezent?   Da _____ Nu _____

35. V-ați rănit vreodată capul, ceafa, gâtul?   Da _____ Nu _____

36. Descrieți eventuale accidente grave.

37. Sînteți cumva implicat în acțiuni legale în legătură cu vocea dvs.?
    Da _____ Nu _____

38. Enumerați soț, soție, copii?

39. Prezentați un scurt rezumat al problemelor de O.R.L., chiar dacă nu se relatează direct la problema curentă.

MARCAȚI TOATE CARE SE APLICĂ

_____ Pierderea auzului

_____ Zgomote în ureche

_____ Amețeli

_____ Pareză facială

_____ Nas infundat

_____ Diformitate a nasului

_____ Bube la gură

_____ Probleme de încheietura maxilarului

_____ Probleme de ochi

_____ Altele (specificați):

_____ Dureri în ureche

_____ Dureri pe față

_____ Înțepenire a gâtului

_____ Nod în gât

_____ Nod în față sau cap

_____ Greutate la înghițit

_____ Exces de piele pe ochi

_____ Exces de piele pe față

40. Aveți sau ați avut vreodată:

_____ Diabet

_____ Hipoglicemie

_____ Probleme de tiroidă

_____ Sifilis

_____ Blenoragie

_____ Herpes

_____ Herpes pe gură

_____ Hipertensiune arterială

_____ Hipotensiune arterială

_____ Antibiotice sau diuretice intravenoase

_____ Atac de cord

_____ Anghină pectorală

_____ Inima neregulată

_____ Alte probleme cu inima

_____ Febră reumatică

_____ Tuberculoză

_____ Glaucomă

_____ Scleroză în plăgi

_____ Alte boli, specificați:

_____ Crize epileptice

_____ Psihoterapie

_____ Dureri de cap puternice și frecvente

_____ Ulcer

_____ Boli de rinichi

_____ Probleme urinare

_____ Artrită sau probleme osoase

_____ Gură de lup

_____ Astmă

_____ Probleme respiratorii sau de plămâni

_____ Pierderi inexplicabile de greutate

_____ Cancer al
    (_____)

_____ Tumoare la
    (_____)

_____ Transfuzie de sânge

_____ Hepatită

_____ SIDA

_____ Meningită

_____ Scleroză în plăci

_____ Alte boli, specificați:

41. Rude ale dvs. de sânge au:
_____ Diabet   _____ Cancer
_____ Hipoglicemie   _____ Boli de inimă
_____ Alte probleme de sănătate serioase ca cele de mai sus.
Specificați:

42. Descrieți accidente grave afară de cele ce se relatează în mod specific la vizita dvs. aici:
_____ Niciunul
_____ A rezultat în rănire la cap, pierderea cunoștinței sau rănirea cefii
_____ Nu a rezultat în rănire la cap, pierderea cunoștinței sau înțepenirea cefii
Descrieți:

43. Enumerați orice medicație curentă inclusiv dozele (includeți anticoncepționale și vitamine)

44. Alergii la medicamente:

_____ Niciuna   _____ Novocaină
_____ Penicilină   _____ Iodină
_____ Sulfați   _____ Codeină
_____ Tetraciclină   _____ Aspirină
_____ Keflex / Ceclor / Ceftin _____ Vopsele de radiografie
                                  _____ Altele (specificați):

45. Enumerați operații chirurgicale:

_____ Amigdalită   _____ Polipi
(vârsta _____)   (vârsta _____)
_____ Apendicită   _____ Inimă
(vârsta _____)   (vârsta _____)
_____ Altele
(specificați):

46. Enumerați droguri sau chimicale toxice la care ați fost expus:

_____ Plumb   _____ Streptomicină, Neomicină,
_____ Mercur   Kanamicină
                                  _____ Altele (specificați): _____

47. Ați avut tratament cu raze la cap sau gât (includeți tratament pentru coșuri sau probleme cu urechile în copilărie, tratament pentru cancer, etc.) ?   Da _____ Nu _____

48. Descrieți probleme grave de sănătate ale copiilor, soției, soțului:
Niciuna

Russian Version of Appendix IIc

Translated by Valentina Markovsky, M. D.
История Болезни: Певцы
Revised by Mikhail Vaysberg
Robert Thayer Sataloff, M. D., D. M. A.
1721 Pine Street,
Philadelphia, PA 19103
U. S. A.

Фамилия, имя _____Возраст _____ пол _____национальность _____
Рост _____   Вес _____   Число _____

Голосовые категории: _____ Сопрано _____ Меццо-сопрано _____ Альт
                       _____ Тенор   _____ Баритон   _____ Бас

(Если вы не имеете жалоб на голос, пожалуйста, пропустите вопросы 1, 2, 3)

Пожалуйста, отметьте или обведите правильные ответы.

1. Как долго или сколько времени вы жалуетесь на голос?
   [1, 2, 3. 4, 5, 6, 7, 8, 9, 10, или больше] [часов, дней, недель, месяцев, лет]
   Кто это заметил?
   [сами, семья, учитель пения, критики, кто-то еще]
   Знаете ли, что вызвало проблемы с голосом?
   Да_____   Нет_____

   Если да, что? [холод, кричание, длительная речь, пение, операция, что-то еще]

   Как это произошло?
   [постепенно_____   внезапно _____]

   На данный момент ваше состояние?   [хуже ___, лучше___ или без перемен___]

2. Какие жалобы у вас? (Пожалуйста, отметьте все подходящие ответы)
   _____ Охриплость (грубый или скрипящий звук)
   _____ Проблема с объёмом (проблема пения)   тихо _____, громко_____
   _____ Усталость (усталость голоса или изменение качества голоса после пения,
          короткое время)
   _____ Потеря амплитуды (высокие ноты _____, низкие ноты_____)
   _____ Изменение в тембре (пример: голос снижается от сопрано до меццо)
   _____ Длительная подготовка к пению (больше чем полчаса, чтобы подготовить голос
          к пению)
   _____ Шипящий голос (нехватка воздуха)
   _____ Щекотание или чувство удушья во время пения

_____Боль в горле во время пения

_____Другие проблемы (пожалуйста, объясните)_____

_____

3. Запланировано ли у вас важное выступление скоро?   Да _____ Нет _____

   Когда: _____

4. Какой вы певец сейчас?   Профессиональный _____   Любительский_____

5. Какие у вас планы на будущее вашего пения?
   [ ] Сольная карьера
   [ ] Оперная карьера
   [ ] Популярная музыка
   [ ] Классическая
   [ ] Народно-фольклорная и современная
   [ ] Другие (_____)
   [ ] Любительские выступления (хор или соло)
   [ ] Любительское пение для собственного удовольствия

6. Брали ли вы уроки пения?   Да _____ Нет _____

   В каком возрасте вы начали? (Обведите кругом:
   2, 3, 4, 5, 6, 7, 8, 9, 10, 11, 12, 13, 14, 15, 16, 17, 18, 19, 20, 21, 22, 23, 24, 25, 26, 27, 28, 29, 30,
   40, 45, 50, 55, 60, 65, 70, 75, 80, 85)

7. Были ли периоды месяцев или лет без уроков в это время? Да _____ Нет _____

8. Как долго вы занимаетесь с вашим настоящим учителем? (Подчеркните:
   1, 2, 3, 4, 5, 6, 7, 8, 9, 10, 11, 12, 13, 14, 15, 16, 17, 18, 19, 20, 21, 22, 23, 24, 25, больше)
   (недель, месяцев, лет)

   Фамилия учителя:

   адрес:

   номер телефона:

9. Пожалуйста, перечислите учителей и сколько лет вы занимались с ними:

10. Вы когда-нибудь тренировались разговорной речи? Да _____ Нет _____
    Уроки актерского мастерства (голос):   Да _____ Нет _____
    Сколько лет?   [меньше чем 1 год, 1-5 лет, 6-10 лет, больше]
    Голосовая терапия: Да _____ Нет _____
                                                Сколько месяцев? (1, 2, 3, 4, 5, 6, 7-12, больше)
11. Есть ли у вас работа кроме пения?
        Да _____ Нет _____
    Если да, требует ли ваша работа голосовых напряжений?
        Да _____ Нет _____

Если да, ваша профессия (актер, диктор (телевидение/радио, спортивный комментатор), спортивный тренер, адвокат, священник, политический деятель, врач, продавец, сток-брокер, учитель, оператор телефонной станции, секретарь, официант, другие):

12. В вашей работе, в дополнение к пению, часто ли вам приходится разговаривать?
    Да _____ Нет _____ или танцевать? Да _____ Нет _____

13. Сколько лет вы активно пели, перед тем как начали уроки пения?
    (2, 3, 4, 5, 6, 7, 8, 9, 10, 11, 12, 13, 14, 15, 16, 17, 18, 19, 20, 21, 22, 23, 24, 25, больше)

14. Какую музыку вы поете (пометьте)?
    _____ Классическая   _____ Ночной клуб
    _____ Представление   _____ Рок-н-ролл
    Другие (объясните)_____

15. Вы регулярно поете сидя (играя на пианино или барабане)?
    Да _____ Нет _____

16. Поете ли вы на открытом пространстве
    (Да _____ Нет _____), в больших залах (Да _____ Нет _____)
    или с оркестром (Да _____ Нет _____)?
    (Обведите один из них.)

17. Если вы выступаете с электрическими инструментами или на открытом пространстве, используете ли вы громкоговорители?
    Если да, можете ли вы слышать их? Да _____ Нет _____

18. Вы играете на музыкальных инструментах?
    Если да, пожалуйста, укажите:
    _____ Клавиатура (пианино, орган, клавесин, др.)
    _____ Скрипка
    _____ Виолончель
    _____ Бас
    _____ Струнные инструменты (гитара, клавесин, др.)
    _____ Медный духовой инструмент
    _____ Духовой инструмент (с одним или двумя язычками)
    _____ Флейта, пикалло
    _____ Ударные инструменты
    _____ Волынка
    _____ Аккордеон
    _____ Другие (пожалуйста, объясните: _____)

19. Как часто вы упражняетесь?
    (ежедневно, несколько раз в неделю, раз в неделю, редко, никогда)
    Гаммы (ежедневно, несколько раз в неделю, раз в неделю, редко, никогда)

    Когда вы играете гаммы, тренируете ли вы их все сразу или разбиваете их в течение дня?
    (Все сразу или за 2-3 раза)

В те дни, когда вы играете гаммы, сколько времени вы упражняетесь?
[15, 30, 45, 60, 75, 90, 105, 120, больше минут]

Песни (ежедневно, несколько раз в неделю, раз в неделю, редко, никогда)

Сколько часов в день?
[1/2, 1, 11/2, 2, 21/2, 3, больше]

Согреваете ли вы голос перед пением?   Да _____ Нет _____

Охлаждаете ли вы голос после окончания пения?   Да_____ Нет _____

20. Сколько времени вы поете в настоящее время (включая репетиции и упражнения)?
(среднее количество часов в день)
Репетиция: (1/2, 1, 11/2, 2, 21/2, 3,, 4, 5, 6, 7, 8, 9, 10)
Представление или выступление: (1/2, 1, 11/2, 2, 21/2, 3, 4, 5, 6, 7, 8)

21. Пожалуйста, отметьте следующие состояния, если вы наблюдаете их у себя:
_____Голос хуже утром
_____Голос хуже в конце дня после использования
_____Голосовые выступления или репетиции утром
_____Длительное использование разговорного голоса (учитель, адвокат, телефон, на работе)
_____Массовик
_____Интенсивно говорите за кулисами или на бенефисе
_____Дирижер хора
_____Часто прочищаете свое горло
_____Часто болит горло
_____Проблемы с челюстным суставом
_____Горький или кислый вкус или запах изо рта рано утром, когда вы просыпаетесь
_____Частые отрыжки или изжога или околопищеводная грыжа
_____Часто кричите или громко разговариваете
_____Часто шепчете
_____Хроническая усталость (бессонница)
_____Работа в условиях повышенной сухости
_____Частые упражнения спортом (поднятие тяжестей, художественная гимнастика и т. д.)
_____Постоянная жажда, обезвоживание
_____Охриплость, когда просыпаетесь
_____Глубокий кашель
_____Прием пищи поздно вечером
_____Употребление лекарств для снижения кислотности желудка
_____Стрессовое состояние в настоящее время (на личной или служебной почве)
_____Частый плохой запах изо рта
_____Живете, работаете или выступаете в условиях дыма или газа
_____Путешествовали недавно: Когда?_____
Куда?_____

Едите ли перед пением?
_____ Шоколад   _____ Кофе
_____ Алкоголь   _____ Молоко или мороженое
_____ Орехи   _____ Острую пищу

Что-нибудь еще (назовите):

_____ Какие-либо технические вокальные трудности? (проблемы петь мягко, проблемы петь громко, плохой контроль, проблема поддержания голоса, проблемы при перемене регистра голоса, другие). Опишите:

_____ Какие-либо другие проблемы с пением, возникшие до проблем с голосом, что привели вас к врачу (охриплость, одышка, усталость, потеря интенсивности, прерывание голоса, [боль во время пения, другие]) Опишите:

_____ Были ли у вас в прошлом проблемы с голосом, которые требовали посещения врача? Если да, то опишите, пожалуйста, эти проблемы и полученное вами лечение (ларингит, узелки, полипы, кровотечение, рак, другие). Опишите:

22. Имя, фамилия, адрес и номер телефона вашего семейного врача:

23. Имя, фамилия, адрес и номер телефона вашего ларинголога:

24. Были ли вы простужены в недавнее время?   Да _____   Нет _____

25. Простужены ли вы сейчас?   Да _____   Нет _____

26. Подвергались ли вы частому (или недавнему) воздействию следующих химических веществ дома или на работе? (Отметьте все, которые относятся к вам)

_____ Окись углерода		_____ Мышьяк	
_____ Ртуть		_____ Анилиновые красители	
_____ Инсектициды		_____ Промышленные	
_____ Свинец		растворители (бензол и т. п.)	
_____ Сценический дым			

27. Осматривал ли вас аллерголог?
Если да, какие аллегории у вас:
(никаких, пыль, плесень, деревья, кошки, собаки, пищевые продукты, другие)
Если да, напишите фамилию и адрес врача.

28. Сколько пачек сигарет вы курите в день?
История курения:
_____ Никогда
_____ Бросил. Когда?
_____ Курил около (меньше чем полпачки, полпачки, одну, одну с половиной, две, две с половиной, три и больше) в день в течение (1, 2, 3, 4, 5, 6, 7, 8, 9, 10, 11-15, 16-20, 21-25, 26-30, 31-35, 36-40, 41-45, 46-50, больше) лет.
_____ Курю (меньше чем полпачки, полпачки, одну, одну с половиной, две, две с половиной, три и больше) в день в течение (1, 2, 3, 4, 5, 6, 7, 8, 9, 10, 11-15, 16-20, 21-25, 26-30, 31-35, 36-40, 41-45, больше) лет.

29. Вы работаете в накуренных помещениях?   Да _____   Нет _____

30. Как часто вы употребляете спиртные напитки (несколько, редко, несколько раз в неделю, ежедневно) [1, 2, 3,4, 5, 6, 7, 8, 9, 10, больше] стаканов в [день, неделю) (пива, вина, крепких напитков)

  Вы пили больше раньше? Да _____ Нет _____

31. Сколько чашек кофе, чая, колы или других напитков, содержащих кофеин, Вы выпиваете ежедневно?

32. Перечислите другие наркотики, которые вы употребляете (марихуана, кокаин, амфетамины, барбитураты, героин, другие):

33. Замечали ли вы что-нибудь из ниже перечисленного (отметьте, если да):
 _____ Сверхчувствительность к теплу или холоду
 _____ Чрезмерное потение
 _____ Изменение в весе (прибавление/потеря) Сколько кг/фунтов за _____ недель, _____ месяцев)
 _____ Изменения в коже или волосах
 _____ Сердцебиение
 _____ Эмоциональная неустойчивость (изменения настроения)
 _____ Двойное зрение
 _____ Онемение лица и конечностей
 _____ Нервный тик или покалывание вокруг рта или на лице
 _____ Неуклюжесть рук или ног
 _____ Помутнение или потеря сознания
 _____ Трудности с речью
 _____ Трудности с глотанием
 _____ Судороги (эпилептические припадки)
 _____ Боль в плече или шее
 _____ Дрожание или трясучка
 _____ Изменение памяти
 _____ Изменение характера

Для женщин:
Ваши менструальные циклы регулярны?   Да _____ Нет _____
Вы беременны?   Да _____ Нет _____
Удалена ли у вас матка?   Да _____ Нет _____
Удалены ли яичники?   Да _____ Нет _____
В каком возрасте вы начали менструировать?
[7, 8, 9, 10, 11, 12, 13, 14, 15, 16, 17, 18, 19, 20]
Наступила ли менопауза?   Да _____ Нет _____

Если да, когда? [сейчас, 1, 2, 3, 4, 5, 6, 7, 8, 9, 10, больше] лет назад

34. Вы когда-нибудь консультировались у психолога или психиатра?
  Да _____ Нет _____
  Находитесь ли вы под наблюдением сейчас? Да _____ Нет _____

35. Были ли у вас травмы головы или шеи?   Да _____ Нет _____

36. Опишите серьёзные катастрофы или аварии, относящиеся к этому визиту:
  _____ Никаких

37. Вовлечены ли вы в судебный процесс, связанный с проблемами вашего голоса?
  Да _____ Нет _____

38. Напишите имена супруга или супруги и детей:

39. Коротко перечислите проблемы с ухом, горлом, носом, которые могут быть не связаны с вашими настоящими жалобами.

Пожалуйста, отметьте нижеследующее:

_____ Потеря слуха	_____ Боль в ушах
_____ Шум в ухе	_____ Лицевая боль
_____ Головокружение	_____ Затруднение движения шеи
_____ Лицевой паралич	_____ Опухоль на шее
_____ Заложен нос	_____ Опухоль на лице или голове
_____ Изменение формы носа	_____ Проблемы с глотанием
_____ Язвы во рту	_____ Излишняя кожа вокруг глаз
_____ Проблемы с челюстным суставом	_____ Излишняя кожа на лице
_____ Проблемы с глазами	_____ Другие (опишите)

40. У вас есть или когда-нибудь были:

_____ Диабет	_____ Психотерапия
_____ Гипогликемия	_____ Частые сильные головные боли
_____ Проблемы со щитовидной железой	
_____ Сифилис	_____ Язвы
_____ Гонорея	_____ Болезни почек
_____ Вирус-герпес	_____ Мочеиспускательные проблемы
_____ Простудные болячки	
_____ Повышенное давление/пониженное давление	_____ Артрит или суставные проблемы
_____ Внутривенные антибиотики или диуретики	_____ Расщепление верхнего неба
	_____ Астма
_____ Судороги	_____ Легочные или дыхательные проблемы
_____ Инфаркт	
_____ Инсульт	_____ Необъяснимая потеря веса
_____ Боли в груди	_____ Рак ( )
_____ Проблемы с сердцем	_____ Другие опухоли ( )
_____ Туберкулёз	_____ Переливания крови
_____ Рассеянный склероз	_____ Гепатит
_____ Ревматическая лихорадка	_____ СПИД
_____ Аритмия	_____ Менингит
_____ Глаукома	_____ Другие заболевания

41. Ваши близкие родственники страдают:

   _____ Диабетом

   _____ Гипогликемией

   _____ Раком

   _____ Сердечными болезнями

   _____ Другими серьезными медицинскими проблемами:

   Пожалуйста, опишите:

42. Опишите серьезные аварии или травмы (кроме тех, что относятся к вашему визиту):

   _____ Не было

   _____ Сопровождались травмой головы, потерей сознания, травмой шеи

   _____ Без травмы головы, без потери сознания, без травмы шеи

   Опишите:

43. Перечислите все лекарства и дозировки (включая противозачаточные и витамины), которые Вы принимаете сейчас:

44. Аллергии к лекарствам:

   _____ Нет

   _____ Пенициллин   _____ Йод

   _____ Сульфапрепараты   _____ Кодеин

   _____ Тетрациклин   _____ Пластырь

   _____ Эритромицин   _____ Аспирин

   _____ Кефлек/Секлор/Сефтин   _____ Контрасты для рентгена

   _____ Новокаин   _____ Другие (назовите):

45. Перечислите операции:

   _____ Удаление аденоидов

   (возраст_____)

   _____ Удаление миндалин   _____ Операция на сердце

   _____ Удаление аппендицита   _____ Другие

   (возраст_____)   (опишите):

46. Перечислите токсичные вещества, если вы подвергались их воздействию:

   _____ Свинец   _____ Стрептомицин, неомицин,

   _____ Ртуть   канамицин

   _____ Другие (назовите):

47. Получали ли вы облучение в области головы или шеи (включая лечение угрей или ушные детские проблемы, лечение рака и т. д.)?   Да _____ Нет_____

48. Опишите серьезные проблемы со здоровьем ваших детей или супруга (супруги):

Spanish Version of Appendix IIc

Translated by Sara Casoy

HISTORIA DEL PACIENTE: CANTANTES
Robert Thayer Sataloff, M.D. , D.M.A.
1721 Pine Street
Philadelphia, PA 19103
U.S.A.

NOMBRE _____ EDAD _____ SEXO _____ RAZA _____

ESTATURA _____ PESO _____ FECHA _____

CATEGORÍA DE LA VOZ:

_____ Soprano _____ Mezzo Soprano _____ Alto

_____ Tenor _____ Barítono _____ Bajo

(Si actualmente usted no tiene ningún problema vocal, por favor omita las preguntas 1 y 2.)

MARQUE LA RESPUESTA CORRECTA

1. ¿Cuánto tiempo hace que padece de su problema vocal?
   [1, 2, 3, 4 , 5, 6, 7 , 8, 9, 10, más]
   [horas, días, semanas, meses, años]

   ¿Quién le dijo que tenia el problema?
   [usted mismo, su familia, su profesor, críticos, otros _____]

   ¿Sabe usted que le pudo causar el problema?
                    [Sí _____   No _____]

   Si la respuesta es sí, ¿qué cree usted pudo causarlo?
   [un resfriado, gritar, hablar en exceso, cantar, cirugía, otros _____]

   ¿Comenzó a sentir estos síntomas de repente o gradualmente?
   [Gradualmente _____   De repente _____]

   ¿Cómo se siente ahora?: Peor _____ , Mejor _____ , Igual _____ ?

2. ¿Qué síntomas usted presenta? (Por favor marque todos los que se relacionen con su estado.)
   _____ Ronquera (emision áspera o irregular)
   _____ Fatiga (cansancio vocal o cambios de cualidad después de haber cantado por un corto período de tiempo)
   _____ Cambios en el volumen de la voz (Problemas al cantar) Bajo _____   Fuerte _____
   _____ Pérdida del registro (alto _____   bajo _____)
   _____ Cambios de clasificación (por ejemplo: de soprano a mezzo)
   _____ Tiempo prolongado de vocalización o calentamiento de la voz (más de media hora)
   _____ Voz con mucha pérdida de aire

_____ Sensación de cosquiello o obstrucción mientras está cantando
_____ Dolor en la garganta mientras está cantando
_____ Otros: (Especifique.) _____

3. ¿Va a tener usted una actuación importante pronto?

    [Sí _____ No _____]

    Fecha(s): _____

4. ¿A qué nivel está su entrenamiento como cantante?

    Profesional _____ Amateur _____

5. ¿Cuáles son sus aspiraciones como cantante?
    [ ] Cantante operístico
    [ ] Cantante de música moderna pop
    [ ] Como pasatiempo frequente
    [ ] Classico
    [ ] Popular
    [ ] Otros
    [ ] Actuaciones no profesionales (coral o solista)
    [ ] Canta para su propia distracción

6. ¿Ha recibido usted entrenamiento vocal?

    Sí _____ No _____. A qué edad usted comenzó?

    (Encierre en un círculo.)

    [2, 3, 4, 5, 6, 7, 8, 9, 10, 11, 12, 13, 14, 15, 16, 17, 18, 19, 20, 21, 22, 23, 24, 25, 26, 27, 28, 29, 30, 35, 40, 45, 50, 55, 60, 65, 70, 75, 80, 85]

7. ¿Ha tenido usted períodos de tiempo en los cuales no ha recibido lecciones de canto?

    [Sí _____ No _____]

8. ¿Por cuánto tiempo ha estado usted estudiando con su profesor actual?

    [1, 2, 3, 4, 5, 6, 7, 8, 9, 10, 11, 12, 13, 14, 15, 16, 17, 18, 19, 20, 21, 22, 23, 24, 25, más]

    [semanas, meses, años]

    Nombre de su profesor:

    Dirección de su profesor:

    Número de teléfono:

9. Por favor escriba el nombre de sus previos profesores y los años que usted estudió con ellos:

10. ¿Ha tenido usted entrenamiento para su voz hablada?

    [Sí _____ No _____]

    ¿Lecciones de voz para actuación?

    [Sí _____ No _____]

    Cuántos años? [menos de uno, 1–5, 6–10, más]

    ¿Terapia de habla (logopedia)? Sí _____ No _____ ¿Cuántos meses?

    [1, 2, 3, 4, 5, 6, 7–12, más]

11. ¿Además del canto; desempeña usted otro tipo de trabajo?

    Sí _____ No _____

Si su respuesta es sí, utiliza usted extensivamente su voz?   Sí _____   No _____

[Actor, presentadero, locutor (T.V./radio/deportes), instructor deportivo, abogado, religioso, político, vendedor, corredor de bolsa, profesor, telefonista o recepcionista, camarero, camarera, secretaria, otros _____]

12. ¿En el desempeño de su trabajo, además de cantar, utiliza su voz con mucha frecuencia?
    Sí _____   No _____
    ¿usted baila?   Sí _____   No _____

13. ¿Cuántos años estuvo usted cantando activamente antes de comenzar sus lecciones de canto?
    [2, 3, 4, 5, 6, 7, 8, 9, 10, 11, 12, 13, 14, 15, 16, 17, 18, 19, 20, 21, 22, 23, 24, 25, más]

14. ¿Qué tipo de música usted canta?
    _____ Clásica   _____ Presentaciones públicas
    _____ Club Nocturno   _____ Rock (música moderna)
    _____ Otros: (Especifique.)

15. ¿Canta usted regularmente sentado (detrás de un piano, o instrumentos de percusión)?
    Sí _____   No _____

16. ¿Canta usted en espacios abiertos o en grandes salas de concierto o con orquesta?
    Sí _____   No _____

17. ¿Si usted realiza sus presentaciones con instrumentos eléctricos o en espacios abiertos, usa usted monitores?
    Sí _____   No _____
    Si su respuesta es sí, puede usted escucharlos?
    Sí _____   No _____

18. ¿Ejecuta usted algún instrumento musical?   Sí _____   No _____
    Si su respuesta es afirmativa por favor marque cuál o cuales:
    _____ Teclados (piano, órgano, clavicordio, otros _____)
    _____ Metales
    _____ Violin, Viola
    _____ Violoncelo
    _____ Contrabajo
    _____ Instrumentos de cuerda (guitarra, arpa, otros _____)
    _____ Instrumentos de viento de caña sencilla
    _____ Instrumentos de viento de caña doble
    _____ Flauta, piccolo
    _____ Percusión
    _____ Gaita
    _____ Acordión
    _____ Otros: (Especifique.) _____

19. ¿Cuánto a menudo usted practica?
    Escalas: [diariamente, algunas veces a la semana, una vez a la semana, esporadicamente, nunca]
    ¿Si usted practica escalas, las hace todas a la vez o las divide en el transcurso del día?
    [todas a la vez, dos o tres sesiones]
    ¿En los días que usted hace escalas, cuánto tiempo las práctica?
    [15, 30, 45, 60, 75, 90, 105, 120, más] minutos

Canciones: [diariamente, algunas veces a la semana, una vez a la semana, esporadicamente o nunca]
¿Cuántas horas al día?
[½, 1½, 2, 2½, 3, más]
¿Vocaliza usted antes de cantar? _____ Sí _____ No
¿Vocaliza usted ligeramente su voz cuando termina de cantar? _____ Sí _____ No

20. ¿Actualmente cuánto tiempo usted canta? (Total, incluso el tiempo de práctica en horas por día)
Ensayos: [½, 1, 1½, 2, 2½, 3, 4, 5, 6, 7, 8, 9, 10]
Funciones: [½ 1, 1½, 2, 2½, 3, 4, 5, 6, 7, 8]

21. Por favor marque los cosas con los cuales usted se siente relacionado (a):
_____ muy mala voz en la mañana
_____ muy mala voz en el transcurso del diá, después de haberla usado
_____ Funciones o ensayos en la mañana
_____ Hablar continuamente (profesor, clérigo, abogado, telefonista, trabajo, etc.)
_____ Animador de equipo deportivo (escuela, universidad, etc.)
_____ Hablar excesivamente fuera del escenario o en fiestas después de haber terminada la función
_____ Director de Coro o coral
_____ Usted trata de limpiar com trequencia la tiema en la gargomta?
_____ Frecuente mal de garganta
_____ Problemas con la mandíbula
_____ Siente sabor amargo y ácido, o mal aliento al levantarse en las mañanas
_____ Frecuente acidez o hernia de hiato
_____ Frecuentemente grita o habla muy fuerte
_____ Frecuentemente habla susurrando
_____ Fatiga crónica (insomnio)
_____ Trabaja en un ambiente extremadamente seco
_____ Realiza ejercicios físicos con mucha frecuencia (levantamiento de pesos, aeróbicos, etc)
_____ Frecuente resequedad y deshidratación
_____ Ronquera en la mañana
_____ Tos de pecho
_____ Comer a altos horas de la noche
_____ Uso de Antiácidos
_____ Se encuentra bajo alto tension nerviosa o presiones (personal o profesional)
_____ Mal aliento frecuentemente
_____ Vive, trabaja, o canta en lugares donde se fume, o presencia de vapores
_____ Recientes viajes: Cuándo: _____
            Dónde: _____
¿Come o bebe cualquiera de los siguientes productos antes de cantar?
_____ Chocolate   _____ Café
_____ Alcohol   _____ Leche o helados
_____ Mani   _____ Comidas con muchos condimentos
Otros: (Especifique.)
_____ ¿Alguna dificultad o problema técnico vocal?
       [problemas al cantar suave, problemas al cantar a plena voz, pobre control de la entonación, problemas
       de apoyo, problemas de cambio de registros, otros] describa:
_____ ¿Ha tenido usted algún malestar vocal, antes de comenzar el problema que le trajo aqui?
       [ronquera, aire en la voz, fatiga, pérdida de registro, la voz se corta, dolor al cantar, otros] Describa:

_____ ¿Cualquier otro problema vocal que requirió su vista a un médico o especialista? Si la respuesta es sí, por favor describa el (o los) problema(s) y el tratamiento(s).
[laringitis, nódulos, pólipos, hemorragias, cancer, otros] Describa:

22. Nombre del médico familiar, dirección, y número telefónico:

23. Nombre de su otorrinolaringologo, dirección, y número telefónico:

24. ¿Ha tenido usted algun sesfuado recientemente? Sí _____ No _____

25. ¿Resfuado actual? Sí _____ No _____

26. ¿Ha estado usted, reciente o frecuentemente en su trabajo o en su casa, expuesto a cualquiera de los siguientes productos químicos?
    _____ Monóxido de carbon   _____ Arsénico
    _____ Mercurio   _____ Anilina
    _____ Insecticidas   _____ Solventes industriales
    _____ Gasolina (con plomo)   (benzina, etc)
    _____ Humo de cigarrillo

27. ¿Ha sido usted evaluado por un especialista en alergias?
                    Sí _____ No _____
    Si responde afirmativamente, a qué cosa es usted alérgico:
    [ninguno, polvo, moho, árboles, gatos, perros, comidas, otros _____]
    (Medicamentos a los cuales es usted alérgico y están incluidos en la historia médica de su especialista.)
    Si responde afirmativamente, por favor escriba el nombre y la dirección de su alergista:

28. ¿Cuántas cajas de cigarrillos usted fuma al día?
    Historia del fumador
    _____ Nunca
    _____ Dejó de fumar. ¿Cuándo?
    _____ Fumada cerca de [menos de la mitad, la mitad, una, una y media, dos, dos y media, tres, más] al día
        por [1, 2, 3, 4, 5, 6, 7, 8, 9, 10, 11–15, 16–20, 21–25, 26–30, 31–35, 36–40, 41–45, 46–50, más] años
    _____ Fuma cerca de [menos de la mitad, la mitad, una, una y media, dos, dos y media, tres, más] al día
        por [1, 2, 3, 4, 5, 6, 7, 8, 9, 10, 11–15, 16–20, 21–25, 26–30, 31 35, 36–40, 41–45, 46–50, más] años

29. ¿Trabaja usted en un lugar donde se fume?
                    Sí _____ No _____

30. ¿Cuanto alcohol usted bebe? [nada, raramente, algunas veces por semana, diariamente] [1, 2, 3, 4, 5, 6, 7, 8, 9, 10, más] vasos al [dia, semana] de [cerveza, vino, licor]
    ¿Acostumbra a usted beber más que ahora? Sí _____ No _____

31. ¿Cuántas tazas de café, té, cola, o otras bebidas que contienen cafcina, usted toma al día?
    [0, 1, 2, 3, 4, 5, 6, 7, 8, 9, 10]

32. Señale otras drogas que usted usa [marihuana, cocaina, anfetaminas, barbitúricos, heroina, otros _____]:

33. ¿Ha observado en usted cualquiera de los siguientes cambios? (Marque todas las que se relacionen con usted)
    _____ Hipersensibilidad al color o frío

_____ Transpiración excesiva

_____ Cambios en el peso: ganancia/perdida _____ libras _____ kilos

en _____ semanas/ _____ meses

_____ Cambios en la piel o el pelo

_____ Rápida palpitación de el corazón

_____ Cambios de estados emocionales

_____ Doble visión

_____ Entumecimiento o insensibilidad en la cara o en las extremidades

_____ Hormiguillo alrededor de la boca o la cara

_____ Visión borrosa o poca visión

_____ Parálisis facial

_____ Torpeza en brazos o piernas

_____ Pérdida del conocimiento

_____ Dificultad al hablar

_____ Dificultad al tragar

_____ Ataque epiléptico

_____ Dolor en el cuello y los hombros

_____ Espasmos o temblores

_____ Cambios en la memoria

_____ Cambios en la personalidad

Para el sexo femenino:

¿Está usted embarazada? Sí _____   No _____

¿Ha sufrido una histerectomía? Sí _____   No _____

¿Sus ovarios fueron removidos? Sí _____   No _____

¿Es regular su periodo menstrual? Sí _____   No _____

¿A qué edad usted alcanzó la pubertad?

[7, 8, 9, 10, 11, 12, 13, 14, 15, 16, 17, 18, 19, 20]

¿Está usted en periódo menopáusico? Sí _____   No _____

¿Si su respuesta es afirmativa, cuándo ocurrió?

[ahora; 1, 2, 3, 4, 5, 6, 7, 8, 9, 10, más] años

34. ¿Ha usted consultado un psiquiatra o psicólogo?

Sí _____   No _____

¿Está usted envuelto en tratamiento?

Sí _____   No _____

35. ¿Se ha lastimado usted su cuello o su cabeza?

Sí _____   No _____

36. Describa cualquier accidente(s) serio(s).

37. ¿Está usted envuelto en acciones legales relacionadas con su problema vocal?

Sí _____   No _____

38. Escriba los nombres de su esposa/epsoso y sus hijos:

39. Resumen de problemas relacionados con oídos, nariz, y garganta, algunos de los cuales puedan no estar relacionados con su presente malestar.

Por favor marque todos con los que usted se sienta relacionado:

_____ Pérdida de la audición   _____ Dolor en los oídos

_____ Ruidos en el oído   _____ Dolor en la cara

_____ Vértigos   _____ Cuello rígido
_____ Parálisis facial   _____ Hinchazón o bulto en el cuello
_____ Obstrucción nasal   _____ Hinchazón o bulto en la cara o la cabeza
_____ Deformidad nasal   _____ Problemas para tragar
_____ Dolor en la boca   _____ Exceso de piel en los ojos
_____ Problemas en la mandíbula   _____ Exceso de piel en la cara
_____ Problemas oculares
_____ Otros: (Especifique.)

40. Padece usted o padeció de algunas de los siguientes problemas:
_____ Diabetes   _____ Convulsiones
_____ Hipoglicemia   _____ Terapia psiquiátrica
_____ Problemas con la   _____ Frecuentes dolores de cabeza
        tiroides   _____ Úlceras
_____ Sífilis   _____ Enfermedades en los riñones
_____ Gonorrea   _____ Artritis o problemas en los huesos
_____ Herpes   _____ Palatosquisis—tisura del paladar
_____ Ampollas causadas por   _____ Asma
        fiebre alta   _____ Problemas pulmonarios o
_____ Alta presión circulatoria   respiratorios
_____ Severa baja presión   _____ Inexplicable pérdida de peso
        circulatoria   _____ Cancer de (_____)
_____ Antibióticos intravenosos   _____ Otros tumores (_____)
        o diuréticos   _____ Transfusiones de sangre
_____ Ataque al corazón   _____ Hepatitis
_____ Angina   _____ SIDA
_____ Latidos irregulares del   _____ Meningitis
        corazón
_____ Otros problemas
        cardíacos
_____ Fiebre reumática
_____ Tuberculosis
_____ Glaucoma
_____ Esclerosis multiple
_____ Otras enfermedades:
        (Especifique.)

41. Algunos de sus familiares tienen:
_____ Diabetes   _____ Cancer
_____ Hipoglicemia   _____ Enfermedades cardiovasculares
_____ Otras enfermedades o graves problemas médicos:
        (Por favor especifique)

42. Describa accidentes serios que usted no halla relatado en su visita al doctor.
_____ Ninguno
_____ Daños en la cabeza, o pérdida del conocimiento, o traumatismo cervical
_____ Sin daños en la cabeza o pérdida del conocimiento, o traumatismo cervical
Describa:

43. Escriba los nombres y las dosis de los medicamentos que actualmente está usando (incluya pastillas anticonceptivas y vitaminas).

44. Alergia a medicaciones.
    _____ Ninguna   _____ Novocaina
    _____ Penicilina   _____ Iodina
    _____ Sulfatos   _____ Codeina
    _____ Tetraciclina   _____ Cinta adhesiva
    _____ Eritromicina   _____ Aspirina
    _____ Keflex/Ceclor/Ceftin _____ Rayos X
    _____ Otros: (Especifique.)

45. Operaciones a las que ha sido sometido(a):
    _____ Extracción de las amigdalas (edad _____)
    _____ Extracción del apéndice (edad _____)
    _____ Extracción de adenoides (edad _____)
    _____ Cirugía del corazón (edad _____)
    _____ Otros: (Especifique.)

46. Marque las drogas tóxicas o químicos a los cuales usted halla sido expuesto:
    _____ Plomo   _____ Estreptomicina, neomicina, kanamicina
    _____ Mercurio   _____ Otras: (Especifique.)

47. ¿Ha sido usted tratado con rayos X en su cabeza o cuello (incluya tratamientos par acne o problemas del oído cuando era niño, tratamientos por cancer, etc)?
    Sí _____   No _____

48. Describa serios problemas de salud de su esposa esposo e sus hijos.
    Ningún _____

Swedish Version of Appendix IIc

Translated by Rolt Leanderson
SJUKHISTORIA: SÅNGARE
Robert Thayer Sataloff, M.D., D.M.A.
1721 Pine Street,
Philadelphia, PA 19103
U.S.A.

NAMN _____ _____ ÅLDER _____ KÖN _____ RAS _____

LÄNGD _____ VIKT _____ DATUM _____

RÖSTLÄGE _____ sopran _____ mezzosopran _____ alt
_____ tenor _____ baryton _____ bas

(Om Du inte för närvarande har röstproblem, fortsätt på fråga 3)

VAR VÄNLIG RINGA IN DE TILLÄMPLIGA SVAREN

1. Hur länge har Du haft ditt nuvarande rostproblem?

   (1, 2, 3, 4, 5, 6, 7, 8, 9, 10, eller längre)
   (timmar, dagar, veckor, månader, år)

   Vem observerade detta?

   (Du själv, familjen, röstpedagog, kritiker, alla, andra _____)

   Är Du medveten om orsaken?
   (Ja ____ Nej ____)

   Om ja, vilken? (Forkylning, rop och skrik, för mycket prat, sång, kirurgi, annat _____)

   Kom det långsamt eller plötsligt?
   (Långsamt _____ plötsligt _____)

   Håller det på att bli: Sämre _____ , Bättre _____ , eller Oförändrat _____ ?

2. Vilka symtom har Du? (Kryssa för allt tillämpligt.)
   _____ Heshet (grov eller skrapig klang)
   _____ Trötthet (rösten tröttnar och förändrar
   kvalitet efter en kort tids sjungande)
   _____ Problem med olika röststyrka (under sång) svagt _____ starkt _____
   _____ Minskat röstomfång (på höjden _____ , på djupet _____)
   _____ Ändrad rösttyp (exempel: sopran blir mezzosopran)
   _____ Förlängd uppsjungningstid (över 1/2 timme för att få igång rösten)
   _____ Läckage i rösten
   _____ Irritations eller krampkänsla under sång

_____ Smärta i strupen under sång

_____ Annat (Ange så detaljerat som möjligt) _____

_____

3. Har Du en viktig föreställning eller konsert snart?   Ja _____ Nej _____

Datum: _____

4. Vilken är Din nuvarande typ av sångkarriär?   Professionell _____ Amatör _____

5. Vilken är den långsiktiga målsättningen i Din sångkarriär?

[ ] operasolist

[ ] popsångare (solist)

[ ] hobbyaktivitet

[ ] klassisk sång

[ ] popsång

[ ] annan sång (_____)

[ ] amatörkonserter (kör eller solo)

[ ] amatörsång för eget nöjes skull

6. Har Du skolat Din röst?   Ja _____ Nej _____ Vid vilken ålder började Du? (Ringa in)
[2,3,4,5,6,7,8,9,10,11,12,13,14,15,16,17,18,19,20,21,22,23,24,25,26,27,28,29,30,35,40,45,50,55,60,65,70,75,80,85]

7. Har det funnits perioder (månader eller år då) Du inte tagit lektioner under denna tid? Ja _____ Nej _____

8. Hur länge har Du studerat för din nuvarande sånglärare?
[2,3,4,5,6,7,8,9,10,11,12,13,14,15,16,17,18,19,20,21,22,23,24,25]

(veckor, månader, år)

Lärarens namn:
Lärarens adress:
telefonnr:

9. Var god uppge tidigare lärare och det år Du studerade hos dem?

10. Har Du någonsin skolat Din talröst?   Ja _____ Nej _____
Teaterlektioner?   Ja _____ Nej _____
Hur många år?   (Mindre än 1, 1–5, 6–10, fler)
Har Du fått-behandling för Dintalröst?   Ja _____ Nej _____ Hur många månader?
                                             (1, 2, 3, 4, 5, 6, 7–12, fler)

11. Har Du yrkesarbete vid sidan om Din sång?
Ja _____ Nej _____

Om ja, innebär det röstansträngning?
Ja _____ Nej _____

Om ja, vilket är detta? (skådespelare, hallåman—TV/radio/idrottsvenemang—gymnastiklärare, advokat, präst, politiker, läkare, försäljare, börsmäklare, lärare, telefonist eller receptionist, kypare, sekreterare, annat _____)

12. När Du uppträder, måste Du då tala jämsides med sången?
Ja _____ Nej _____   Dansa? Ja _____ Nej _____

13. Hur många år sjöng Du aktivt innan Du började ta sånglektioner?
[2,3,4,5,6,7,8,9,10,11,12,13,14,15,16,17,18,19,20,21,22,23,24,25, fler]

14. Vilken typ av sång utövar Du? (Kryssa för alla alternativ.)
_____ Klassisk   _____ Show
_____ Night Club   _____ Rock
Annan (V g specificera): _____

15. Sjunger Du regelbundet i sittande ställning? (vid piano eller slagverk)
Ja _____ Nej _____

16. Sjunger Du utomhus i stora lokaler eller med orkestrar? (Ringa in vilket)   Ja _____ Nej _____

17. Om Du uppträder tillsammans med elektriska instrument eller utomhus,
får har Du då hjälp av högtalare?   Ja _____ Nej _____
Om ja, kan Du höra dem?   Ja _____ Nej _____

18. Spelar Du musikinstrument?   Ja _____ Nej _____
Om ja, ange viket:
_____ Klavértinstrument (piano, orgel, cembalo, annat _____)
_____ Violin, viola
_____ Cello
_____ Bas
_____ Knäppinstrument (gitarr, harpa, annat _____)
_____ Bläckblås
_____ Träblås med enkelt rör blad
_____ Träblås med dubbelt blad
_____ Flöjt, piccola
_____ Slagverk
_____ Säckpipa
_____ Dragspel
_____ Annat (V g auge vilket): _____

19. Hur ofta övar Du?
Skalor: (dagligen, några gånger per vecka, en gång i veckan, sällan, aldrig)

Om Du övar skalor, utför Du då alla på en gång eller delar upp dem i perioder under dagen?
(Alla på en gång, 2 eller 3 tillfällen)

Hur länge övar Du de dagar, då Du tränar skalor?
(15, 30, 45, 60, 75, 90, 105, 120, fler) minuter

Sånger: (dagligen, några gånger i veckan, en gång i veckan, sällan eller aldrig)

Hur många timmar om dagen?
(½, 1, 1½, 2, 2½, 3, fler)

Värmer Du upp rösten innan Du skall sjunga?   Ja _____ Nej _____

Varvar Du ner efter sångövningen?   Ja _____ Nej _____

20. Hur mycket sjunger Du för närvarande
(inkl övningstid, antal timmar per dag)?
Repetitioner: (½, 1, 1½, 2, 2½, 3, 4, 5, 6, 7, 8, 9, 10,)
Sång inför publik: (½, 1, 1½, 2, 2½, 3, 4, 5, 6, 7, 8)

21. Var god kryssa för allt som gäller Dig:
_____ Rösten sämre på morgonen
_____ Rösten sämre senare på dagen efter den har använts
_____ Sångframträdanden eller repetitioner på morgonen
_____ Talröstansträngning (t ex lärare, präst, advokat, telefon, osv)
_____ Cheerleader
_____ Intensivt pratande bakom scenen eller vid partys efter föreställningar
_____ Körledare
_____ Konstant harklingsbehov
_____ Ständigt ont i halsen
_____ Besvär från käklederna
_____ Syrlig eller bitter smak i munnen, el dålig andedräkt på morgonen
_____ Ofta halsbränna
_____ Måste skrika eller tala starkt
_____ Måste viska starkt och ofta
_____ Kronisk trötthet allmänt (sömnsvårigheter)
_____ Arbete i extremt torra lokaler
_____ Tränar ofta (tyngdlyftning, styrketräning o s v)
_____ Ofta törstig
_____ Morgonhes
_____ Hosta (som utlöses från lungorna)
_____ Sena måltider
_____ Måste använda syraneutraliserande mediciner
_____ Befinner mig i stressituation f n (personlig eller i yrket)
_____ Ofta dålig andedräkt
_____ Måste leva, arbeta eller framträda i rökiga, dammiga lokaler
_____ Har rest mycket nyligen. När: _____
                                        Vart: _____

Jag äter följande innan jag sjunger?
_____ Choklad   _____ Kaffe
_____ Alkohol   _____ Mjölk eller glass
_____ Nötter   _____ Kryddad mat
Annat (V g specificera):

_____ Någon eller några speciella tekniska sångsvårigheter?
(problem med att sjunga mjukt och svagt, starkt, dålig tonhöjdskontroll, problem med stödet, problem med registerövergångar, annat. Beskriv: _____)

_____ Besvär med sångrösten tidigare, innan det nu aktuella problemet började?
(heshet, läckage, trötthet, försämring av omfånget, registerbrott, smärta vid sång, annat. Beskriv: _____)

_____ Röstproblem tidigare som krävde besök hos läkare?
Om ja, beskriv detta eller dessa, liksom behandlingen.
(stämbandsinflammation, knutor, polyper, blödning, tumör på stämbanden, annat. Beskriv: _____)

22. Har Du någon läkare Du brukar gå till? Vill Du i så fall uppge hans namn, adress och telefonnr:

23. Var god lämna motsvarande uppgifter betr Din ev röstdoktor:

24. Varit förkylt nyligen?   Ja _____ Nej _____

25. Pågående förkylning?   Ja _____ Nej _____

26. Har Du utsatts för något eller några av följande kemiska ämnen ofta (eller nyligen) hemma eller på arbetet. (Kryssa för allt som gäller)

_____ Koloxid   _____ Arsenik
_____ Kvicksilver   _____ Anilinfärger
_____ Insektsmedel   _____ Lösningsmedel
_____ Bly   _____ Teaterrök

27. Har Du konsulterat en allergolog?   Ja _____ Nej _____
Om ja, vad är Du allergisk mot:
(Damm, mögel, växter, trädslag, katt, hund, födoämnen, annat _____)
(Medicinering för allergi tas upp på annan plats i formuläret)

Om ja, var god uppge namn och adress på allergispecialisten:

28. Hur många paket cigaretter röker Du per dag?

Rökvanor
_____ Aldrig
_____ Har slutat, när?
_____ Jag rökte cirka (mindre än ½, 1, 1½, 2, 2 ½, 3, eller mer per dag) under (1, 2, 3, 4, 5, 6, 7, 8, 9, 10-15, 16-20, 21, 25, 26–30, 31–35, 36–40, 41–45, 46–50, eller mer) år, sedan (1, 2, 3, 4, 5, 6, 7, 8, 9, 10-15, 16-20, 21, 25, 26–30, 31–35, 36–40, 41–45, 46–50, eller mer) år.
_____ Jag röker (mindre än ½, 1, 1½, 2, 2½, 3, eller mer) per dag sedan (1, 2, 3, 4, 5, 6, 7, 8, 9, 10-15, 16-20, 21, 25, 26–30, 31–35, 36–40, 41–45, 46–50, eller mer) år.

29. Arbetar Du i rökig miljö?   Ja _____ Nej _____

30. Hur mycket alkohol dricker Du? (Ingen, sällan, ett par gånger i veckan, dagligen)
(1, 2, 3, 4, 5, 6, 7, 8, 9, 10, eller mer) glas per dag eller vecka av (öl, vin eller sprit)

Har Du tidigare druckit mera?   Ja ____ Nej ____

31. Hur många koppar kaffe, te, Coca cola eller annan kaffeininnehållande dryck dricker Du per dag?
(1, 2, 3, 4, 5, 6, 7, 8, 9, 10)

32. Använder Du någon annan medicin som påverkar nervsystemet? (Marijuana, kokain, amfetamin,
barbiturater, heroin, annan _____)

33. Har Du något av följande symtom? (Fyll i det tillämpliga)
_____ Överkänslighet för värme eller kyla
_____ Kraftig svettning
_____ Förändringar i vikt: Ökat/minskat _____ kg på _____ veckor/eller månader
_____ Hud eller hårförändringar
_____ Snabba svängningar i humöret
_____ Dubbelseende
_____ Domningskänsla i ansiktet eller armar och ben
_____ Känsla av krypningar eller skälvningar runt munnen eller i ansiktet
_____ Oskarp syn eller blindhet
_____ Svaghet eller förlamning i ansiktet
_____ Fumlighet i armar och ben
_____ Förvirring eller nedsatt medvetande
_____ Svårigheter med talet
_____ Sväljningssvårigheter
_____ Anfall (epilepsiliknande)
_____ Smärta i nacke eller skuldror
_____ Darrning eller skakning i kroppen
_____ Minnesförändringar
_____ Personlighetsförändringar

För kvinnor:

Är Du gravid?   Ja ____ Nej ____
Har Du fått livmodern borttagen?   Ja ____ Nej ____
Är Dina äggstockar bortopererade?   Ja ____ Nej ____
Är mensperioderna regelbundna?   Ja ____ Nej ____
När fick Du första menstruationen?
(7, 8, 9, 10, 11, 12, 13, 14, 15, 16, 17, 18, 19, 20 år)
Har Du gått igenom klimakteriet?   Ja ____ Nej ____

Om ja, när? (för närvarande, 1, 2, 3, 4, 5, 6, 7, 8, 9, 10, flera) år sedan.

34. Har Du någonsin konsulterat en psykolog eller psykiater?
Ja ____ Nej ____
Går Du i psykoterapi?   Ja ____ Nej ____

35. Har Du skadat huvud- eller nacke (t ex pisksnärtskada)?   Ja ____ Nej ____

36. Beskriv ev olycksfall Du varit utsatt för!

37. Har Ditt röstproblem fått juridiska konsekvenser?
    Ja _____ Nej _____

38. Var god ange namn på hustru och barn:

39. Kort sammanfattning av åkommor inom öron-, näs-, hals-regionen som kan vara relaterade till Ditt röstproblem.

VAR GOD MARKERA DET TILLÄMPLIGA

_____ Hörselskada

_____ Öronsusningar

_____ Yrsel

_____ Ansiktsförlamning

_____ Nästäppa

_____ Näsdeformering

_____ Munsår

_____ Problem med käkleden

_____ Ögonproblem

_____ Annat: (Specificera!)

_____ Öronvärk

_____ Ansiktssmärtor

_____ Stel nacke

_____ Svulst i nacken

_____ Svullnad i ansikte eller huvud

_____ Sväljningssvårigheter

_____ Påsar under ögonen

_____ Överskott av ansiktshud

40. Har Du eller har Du någonsin haft:

_____ Sockersjuka

_____ Lågt blodsocker

_____ Sköldkörtelproblem

_____ Syfilis

_____ Gonorré

_____ Herpes

_____ Feberblåsor

_____ Högt blodtryck

_____ Väsentligt för lågt BT

_____ Fått antibiotikum eller vattendrivande intravenöst

_____ Hjärtattacker

_____ Ont i hjärtat (angina)

_____ Oregelbundna hjärtslag

_____ Andra hjärtproblem

_____ Reumatisk feber

_____ Tuberkulos

_____ Glaukom (för högt ögontryck)

_____ MS

_____ Andra åkommor, v g specificera:

_____ Anfall av olika slag

_____ Psykologisk, psykiatrisk beh.

_____ Upprepad svår huvudvärk

_____ Magsår

_____ Njursjukdom

_____ Urinvägsproblem

_____ Åkommor i leder och benstomme

_____ Kluven gom

_____ Astma

_____ Lungsjukdom eller andn. problem

_____ Oförklarlig viktförlust

_____ Cancer i _____

_____ Annan tumör _____

_____ Blodtransfusioner

_____ Hepatit

_____ AIDS

_____ Hjärnhinneinflammation

41. Har någon av Dina släktingar:

_____ Sockersjuka   _____ Cancer

_____ Lågt blodsocker   _____ Hjärtsjukdom

_____ Andra betydande medicinska problem (se ovan)? V g specificera:

42. Beskriv allvarliga olycksfall som inte har direkt samband med Ditt aktuella problem.

_____ Inga

_____ Olycksfall med huvudskada, medvetandeförlust eller "pisksnärt"

_____ Olycksfall utan huvudskada, medvetandeförlust eller "pisksnärt"

Beskriv:

43. Ange alla de mediciner Du tar för närvarande och i vilka doser (inkl P-piller och vitaminer):

44. Medicinallergier:

_____ Ingen   _____ Novacaine

_____ Pc   _____ Jod

_____ Selfa   _____ Kodein

_____ Tetracycline   _____ Salicylsyra

_____ Erytromycin   _____ Röntgenkontrast

_____ Keflex/Ceftin   _____ Tape (kontaktallergi)

_____ Andra: (V g specificera)

45. Genomgångna operationer:

_____ Tonsillektomi   _____ Skrapning bakom näsa

(ålder _____)   (ålder _____)

_____ Blindtarmsop   _____ Hjärtkirurgi

(ålder _____)   (ålder _____)

_____ Annat:

(V g specificera)

46. Lista på gifter eller kemikalier som Du kan ha varit utsatt för:

_____ Bly   _____ Streptomycin, neomycin

_____ Kvicksilver   kanamycin

                                     _____ Annat: (V g specificera)

47. Har Du fått röntgenbehandlingar mot huvud eller nacke? (inklusive behandlingar för akne eller öronproblem, behandling för cancer el dyl)   Ja _____ Nej _____

48. Beskriv allvarliga sjukdomar som drabbat hustru eller barn

_____ Inga

_____ Ange vilka:

Yiddish Version of Appendix IIc

גטשיקטע פון פאציענט: זינגערס
דר. ראבערט ט. סאָטאלאָף מ.ד., ד.מא.
פיין גאס
פילאדעלפיה, פא. 19103

נאמען _____//_____ עלטער _____ מאן _____ פרוי _____ ראסע _____

הויך _____ געוויכט _____ דאטום _____.

שטימען קאטעגאריע: סאפראנא   מעצא סאפראנא

אלטא   טענאר   באריטאן   באס

אויב איר האט ניט קיין פראבלעם יעצט מיט אייער שטימע, ביטע היפט אריבער צו פראגע 3.

ביטע, צייכנט אן אדער מאכט א קרייז ארום ריכטיקן ענטפער

1. ווי לאנג האט איר א פראבלעם מיט אייער שטימע?

[1, 2, 3, 4, 5, 6, 7, 8, 9, 10, אדער מער]

[שטונדן, טעג, וואכן, מאנאטן, יארן]

ווער האט עס באמערקט?

[אליין, פאמיליע, לערער פאר זינגען, קריטיקער, יעדער איינער, אנדערע]

צו ווייסט איר וואס האט עס פאראורזאכט?

[יא   ניין]

אייב יא, וואס איז די סבה? א פארקילונג, שרייען, צו פיל ריידן, זינגען, אן אפעראציע, אנדערע

האט עס פאסירט לאנגזאם אדער פלוצלונג?

[לאנגזאם   פלוצלונג]

ווערט עס ערגער   בעסער   אדער די זעלבע

2. וועלכע סימטאמען האט איר? אונטערשרייכט אלע וואס פאסן.

_____ הייזעריקייט, (שארשקעדיקער קלאנג,)

_____ מידקייט, (די שטימע ווערט מיד נאכן זינגען א קורצע צייט)

_____ (שוועריקייטן אין זינגען)

_____ פארלוסט פון עומפאנג (הויך, נידעריג)

_____ ענדערונג אין קלאסיפיקאציע,ווי צום ביישפיל פון סאפראנא צו מעצא

_____ פארלענגערונג פון צוגרייטונג פון דער שטימע, איבער א האלבע שעה

      אטעמען

_____ א געפיל פון קיצלען אדער ווערגן בשעת זינגען

_____ שמערצן אין האלז ביים זינגען

_____ אנדערע ביטע אויסרעכענען _____

3. האט איר א וויכטיקן קאנצערט אין גיכן?   יא _____ ניין _____
דאטום _____

4. וואס איז אייער איצטיקע פאזיציע אין אייער זינגען   פראפעסיאנעלע _____ אמאטארישע _____

5. וואס זיינען אייערע צוקונפיקע צילן אין זינגען.
[ ] קאריערע אין אפערע
[ ] הויפטזעכליך אין פאפולערערע מוזיק
[ ] אקטיווע נעבנבאשעפטיקונג
[ ] קלאסישע
[ ] פאפולערע
[ ] אנדערע
[ ] אמאטארישע פארשטעלונג כאר אדער סאלא
[ ] אמאטארישער זינגען פארן אייגענעם פארגעניגען

6. האט איר געהאט שולונג אין זינגען?   יא ____ ניין ____ ווי אלט זייט איר געווען ווען איר האט אנגעהויבן?
(2, 3, 4, 5, 6, 7, 8, 9, 10, 11, 12, 13, 14, 15, 16, 17, 18, 19, 20, 21, 22, 23, 24, 25, 26, 27, 28, 30, 35, 40, 45, 50, 55, 60, 65, 70, 75, 80, 85)

7. זיינען געווען פעריאדן פון מאנאטן אדער יארן אן אונטעריכטן אין זינגען?   יא _____ ניין _____

8. ווי לאנג לערנט איר ביי אייער איצטיקן לערער?
(1, 2, 3, 4, 5, 6, 7, 8, 9, 10, 11, 12, 13, 14, 15, 16, 17, 18, 19, 20, 21, 22, 23, 24, 25) אדער מער
[וואכן, מאנאטן, יארן]

נאמען פון לערער
אדרעס פון לערער
לערערס טעלעפאן נומער

9. ביטע גיט אן פריערדיקע לערער און די יארן וואס איר האט ביי זיי געלערנט.

10. האט איר ווען געהאט שולונג פאר אייער שטימע צו ריידן?   יא _____ ניין _____
אינטעריכטונג אין שטימע פאר בימה פארשטעלונגען?   יא _____ ניין _____
וויפיל יארן?   (ווייניגער ווי א יאר 1-5, 6-10, מער)
טעראפי אין ריידן?   יא _____ ניין _____ וויפיל מאנאטן?
(1,2,3,4,5,6,7-12, מער)

11. האט איר א באשעפטיקונג א חוץ זינגען?
יא _____ ניין _____

אויב יא, פארלאנגט עס אינטענסיווע באנוצונג פון שטימע?
יא _____ ניין _____

אויב יא, וואס איז עס? (אקטיאר, אנאנסירער (טעלעוויזשן/ ראדיא / ספארט) אינסטרוקטאר פאר
אטלעטיקע, אדוואקאט, גייסטליכע, פאליטיקער, דאקטויפער, פארקויפער, מעקלער פון ווערט פאפירן, לערער,
טעלעפאניסט, אדער סעקרעטאר ביים ענטפאנגען מענטשן, קעלנער, סעקרעטאר, אנדערע

‏12. ביים דורכפירן אייער ארבעט, אין צוגאב פון זינגען, דארפט איר אויך אפט ריידן?

‏יא _____ ניין _____ טאנצן? יא _____ ניין _____

‏13. וויפיל יארן האט איר אקטיוו געזונגען איידער איר האט אנגעהויבן מיט אונטערריכטונג פון זינגען.

‏(2, 3, 4, 5, 6, 7, 8, 9, 10, 11, 12, 13, 14, 15, 16, 17, 18, 19, 20, 21, 22, 23, 24, 25, מערער)

‏14. וועלכע מוזיק זינגט איר?

‏_____ קלאסיש			פארשטעלונג _____

‏_____ נאכט קלוב			מאדערנע (ר̄ק) _____

‏_____ אנדערע

‏_____ ביטער אנגעבן גענוי _____

‏15. זינגט איר געוויינליך אין א זיצנדיקע פאזיציע (אזוי ווי הינטער א פיאנא אדער א באראבאן?

‏יא _____ ניין _____

‏16. זינגט איר אין דרויסן אדער אין א גרויסן זל, אדער מיט̄ן ארקעסטער? (צייכנט אן וועלכער).

‏יא _____ ניין _____

‏17. אויב איר באנוצט עלעקטרישע אינסטרומענטן אדער אין דרויסן,

‏באנוצט איר אן אנזאגער לויטשפרעכער? יא _____ ניין _____

‏אויב יא, קענט איר זיי העו̄ן? יא _____ ניין _____

‏18. שפילט איר אויף א מוזיקאלישן אינסטרומענט? יא   ניין

‏אויב יא, אונטערשטרייכט אלע וואס פאסן!

‏_____ פיאנא, ארגאן, האַרפסיקארד, אנדערע

‏_____ פידל, וויאלא

‏_____ טשעלא

‏_____ באס

‏_____ גיטאו̄ , האַרפע, אנדערע

‏_____ מעש אינסטרומענט

‏_____ ווינד אינסטרומענט מיט איין רעה̄ר

‏_____ ווינד אינסטרומענט מיט דאפלטן רעהר

‏_____ פלייט, פיקאלא

‏_____ באראבאנעם

‏_____ ז̄ק פייף

‏_____ אקארדיאן

‏_____ אנדערע (רעכנט אויס)

‏19. ווי אפט פראקטיצירט איר?

‏סקאלעס (טעגליך, איייניקע מאל א וואך, איינמאל א וואך, דעלטן, קינמאל)

‏אויב איר פראקטיצירט סקאלעס, מאכט איר זיי מיט אמאל, אדער צעטיילט איר זיי אין משך פון טאג?

‏(אלע מיטאמאל, צוויי אדער דריי מאל)

‏אין טעג ווען איר זינגט סקאלעס, ווי לאנג פראקטיצירט איר זיי?

‏15, 30, 40, 60, 75, 90, 105, 120, אדער מער מינוטן.

לידער: (טעגליך, עטלעכע מאל א וואך, איינמאל א וואך, זעלטן, קיינמאל)

וויפיל שעה א טאג?

(1/2, 1, 1.1/2, 2, 2.1/2, 3 מערער)

איבט איר איין די שטימע איידער איר זינגט?   יא _____ ניין _____

נאכן ענדיקן זינגען לאזט איר אפ די שטימע לאנגזאם?   יא _____ ניין _____

20. וויפיל זינגט איר יעצט (איינגערעכנט איבונגס צייט) (דורכשניטליך שעה א טאג?)

איבונגסצייט: (1/2, 1, 1.1/2, 2, 2.1/2, 3, 4, 5, 6, 7, 8, 9, 10)

פארשטעלונג (1/2, 1, 1.1/2, 2, 2.1/2, 3, 4, 5, 6, 7, 8)

21. ביטע צייכנט אפ, וואס פאסט צו אייך:

_____ שטימע ערגער אין דער פרי

_____ שטימע ערגער שפעטער אין טאג, נאך דעם ווי איר האט איר גענוצט

_____ זינגען פארשטעלונגען אדער רעפעטיציעס אין דער פרי

_____ ריידן א סך (צום ביישפיל, לערער, גייסטליכער, אדוואקאט, טעלעפאן, ארבעט, א.א.וו.)

_____ אויפמונטערונג פירער

_____ פיל ריידן הינטער די קוליסן, אדער נאך א פארשטעלונג באנקעט

_____ דיריגענט פון א כאר

_____ אויסריייניקן די האלז אפט

_____ אפטע הייזעריקייט

_____ פראבלעמען מיטן באקן ביין

_____ ביטערער אדער זויערער טעם, אדער שלעכטער ריח אין דער פרי

_____ אפטער הארץ ברעננעניש, אדער ברוך אין שידוואנט

_____ אפט שרייען אדער הויך ריידן

_____ אפט שושקענען

_____ כראנישע מידקייט (שלאפלאזיקייט)

_____ ארבעט ביי עקסטרעמער טרוקנקייט

_____ אפטע איבונגען (הויבן שווערע געוויכטן, עראביקס, א.א.וו.)

_____ אפטע דורשטיקייט, אויסגעטריקנט

_____ הייזעריקייט די ערשטע זאך אין דער פרי

_____ הוסטן פון הארצן, ברוסט קאסטן,

_____ עסן שפעט ביי נאכט

_____ זיך באנוצט מיט רפואות, פאר זויערקייט אין מאגן

_____ אונטער א באזונדערן דרוק צום מאמענט (פערזענליך אדער פראפעסיאנעל)

_____ אפטער שלעכטער ריח אין מויל

_____ לעבט, ארבעט אדער שטעלט פאר ארום רויך אדער רויכערען

_____ ארומגעפארן לעצטנס: ווען: _____

ווי _____

געגעסן די פאלגענדע עסן פארן זינגען?

שאקאלאד _____   קאפע _____

אלקאהאל _____   מילך אדער אייס קרים (מאראזשענע) _____

ניס _____   שארפע עסן _____

אנדערע (ביטע רעכנט אויס):

_____ ספעציעלע שוועריקייטן מיט דער שטימע?

(שוועריקייטן צו זינגען שטילערהייט, שוועריקייטן זינגען הויך, ניט גענוגדיקן קאנטראל,

פראבלעמען מיט אונטערשטיצונג, פראבלעמען ביים איבערגאנג, אנדערע) באשרייבט:

_____ פראבלעמען מיט דער זינגעדיקער שטימע לעצטנס, פאר דער פראבלעם וואס האט אייך
געבראכט אהער?
[הייזעריקייט, פראבלעמען מיט אטעמען, מידקייט, פארלוסט פון פארנעם, די שטימע ברעכט,
שמערצן ביים זינגען, אנדערע] באשרייבט:

_____ פראבלעמען מיט דער שטימע אין דער פארגאנגענהייט, וועלכע האט פארלאנגט א וויזיט ביים
דאקטאר? אויב יא, ביטע באשרייבט די פראבלעמען און די באהאנדלונג:
[הייזעריקייט (ענטצינדונג), noclules פאליפן, בלוטונג, רק (קענסער), אנדערע], באשרייבט:

22. דער נאמען פון אייער דאקטאר, אדרעס און טעלעפאן נומער:

23. דער נאמען פון אייער האלז ספעציאליסט (לארינגאלאג) אדרעס און טעלעפאן נומער:

24. א פארקילונג ניט לאנג צוריק?   יא _____   ניין _____

25. א פארקילונג יעצט?   יא _____   ניין _____

26. זייט איר געוווען אויסגעשטעלט צו די פאלגענדע כעמיקאלן: אפט (אדער נישט לאנג צוריק) אין שטוב
אדער ביי דער ארבעט?
(אונטערשטרייכט אלע וואס פאסן)
_____ קוילו מאנאקסייד   _____ ארסעניק
_____ קוועק זילבער   _____ אנילין פארב
_____ פאר אינסעקטן   _____ אינדוסטריעלע פארדינונג שטאף
_____ בליי   (בענזין א.א.וו.)
_____ רויך פון סצענע

27. זייט איר געווארן אונטערזוכט פון אן אלערדזשיסט?   יא _____   ניין _____
אויב יא, וועלכע אלערגיעס האט איר:
[קיינע שיווייב, מיכל, ביימער, קעץ, הינט, עסנווארג , אנדערע _____]
(אלערגיע פון מעדיצין איז באשריבן אין אן אנדער פלאץ אין די געשיכטע פארם)
אויב יא, גיט און דעם נאמען פון אייער אלערגיע דאקטאר:

28. וויפיל פעקלאך ציגארעטן רויכערט איר א טאג?
_____ געשיכטע פון רייכערן
_____ קיינמאל ניט
_____ אויפגעהארט, ווען?
_____ האט גערויכערט אומגעפער [וויייניקער ווי א האלבן, א האלבן, איינעם, אנדערהאלבן, צוויי,
צוויי און א האלב, דריי, מערער] יעדן טאג פאר:
(1, 2, 3, 4, 5, 6, 7, 8, 9, 10, 11-15, 16-20, 21-25, 26-30, 31-35, 36-40, 41-45,
46-50, מערער) יארן

29. ארבעט איר אין א פאררויכערטער אומגעבונג?   יא _____   ניין _____

‫30. וויפיל אלקאהאל טרינקט איר? (קיינמאל, זעלטן, עטלעכע מאל א וואך, יעדן טאג [1, 2, 3, 4, 5, 6,‬
‫7, 8, 9, 10, מערער] גלעזער א [טאג, א וואך] אדער [ביר, וויין, ליקער]‬

‫האט איר געטרונקען מערער? יא _____ ניין _____‬

‫31. וויפיל קוביקעס מיט קאפע, טיי, קאלא אדער אנדערע געטראנקען וואס אנטהאלטן קאפעאין טרינקט איר‬
‫א טאג? [0, 1, 2, 3, 4, 5, 6, 7, 8, 9, 10]‬

‫32. שרייבט אויס אנדערע בארואיקענדנע מעדיצין נעמט איר [מאריאואנא, קאקאאין, אמפעטאמינס, שלאף‬
‫פילן, העראאין אנדערע _____ [‬

‫33. האט איר באמערקט די פאלגענדע? [צייכנט אפ די וואס פאסן]‬
‫_____ באזונדערע פילבארקייט צו הייצ אדער קעלט‬
‫_____ אויסערארדענטליכער שוויצן‬
‫_____ ענדערונג אין געוויכט: צוגענומען/פארלארן _____ פונט, אי _____ וואכן/מאנאטן‬
‫_____ ענדערונג אין הויט אדער האר‬
‫_____ הארץ קלאפעניש פון הארצן‬
‫_____ עמאציאנעלע אויסברוכן (ענדערונגען אין שטימונג)‬
‫_____ דאפעלטער זעען‬
‫_____ אפנעמען פון געזיכט אדער הענט אדער פיס‬
‫_____ שטעכן (זעכצער) ארום מויל אדער געזיכט‬
‫_____ נישט קלארער זען אדער בלינדהייט‬
‫_____ שוואכקייט אדער פאראליז פון געזיכט‬
‫_____ אומגעשיקטקייט אין הענט אדער פיס‬
‫_____ צוטומלונגקייט אדער פארלוסט פון באוווסטזיין‬
‫_____ שוועריקייטן מיט ריידן‬
‫_____ שוועריקייטן ביים שלינגען‬
‫_____ אנפאלן פון עפילעפסיע‬
‫_____ שמערצן אין קארק (האלדז) אדער שולטער‬
‫_____ ציטערן אדער קאנוווילסיעס‬
‫_____ ענדערונג אין זכרון‬
‫_____ ענדערונג אין פערזענליכקייט‬

‫פאר פרויען:‬

‫זייט איר שוואנגער? יא _____ ניין _____‬
‫דורכגעמאכט אן אפעראציע פון ארויסנעמען די געבערמוטער? יא _____ ניין _____‬
‫האט מען באזייטיקט אייער אייערשטאק? יא _____ ניין _____‬
‫האט איר רעגולערע מענסטרואיציעס? יא _____ ניין _____‬
‫אין וועלכן עלטער האט איר זיך אנוויקלט געשלעכטליך? (געקראגן מענסטרואיציע)‬
‫7, 8, 9, 10, 11, 12, 13, 14, 15, 16, 17, 18, 19, 20‬
‫זייט איר שוין דורך מענאפאז? יא _____ ניין __‬
‫אויב יא, מיט וויפל יאר צוריק [יעצט, 1, 2, 3, 4, 5, 6, 7, 8, 9, 10, מערער.‬

‫34. האט איר ווען געזען א פסיכיאטער אדער א פסיכאלאג? יא _____ ניין _____‬

‫זייט איר יעצט אונטער באהאנדלונג? יא _____ ניין _____‬

‫35. האט איר פארוווינדעט איינוד קאפ אדער קארק (וויפלעש, א.א.וו.) ? יא _____ ניין _____‬

36. באשרייבט וועלכע ערנסטע קאטאסטראפעס.

37.זייט איר פארמישט אין לעגאלע פראבלעמען מיט אייער שטימע?   יא _____ ניין _____

38. רעכנט אויס נעמען פון אייער מאן/פרוי און קינדער:

39. קורצער סך הכל פון אייערע אויערן, נאז און האלדז פראבלעמען, פון וועלכע קענען נישט זיין פארבונדן מיט אייער יעצטיגן פראבלעם

ביטע אפצייכענען די וואס איז נוגע אייך

שמערצן אין אויער	_____	פארלוסט פון געהער	_____
שמערצן אין געזיכט	_____	א טומל אין די אויער	_____
שטייפער געניק	_____	שווינדל	_____
געשוויולסט אין געניק	_____	פאראליז אין געזיכט	_____
געשוויולסט אין געזיכט אדער קאפ	_____	פארשטאפונג פון נאז	_____
שוועריקייטן צו שלינגען	_____	דעפארמירטער (קרומער) נאז	_____
צופיל הויט איבער די אויגן	_____	(געשוויר) ארויסשלאק אין מויל	_____
צופיל הויט איבערן געזיכט	_____	פראבלעמען מיטן באקן-ביין	_____
		פראבלעמען מיט אויגן	_____
		אנדערע (ביטע רעכנט אויס)	_____

40. האט איר יעצט, אדער האט איר וען געהאט:

ספאזמען	_____	דיאבעטיס (צוקער)	_____
פסיכישע טעראפי	_____	היפאגלייסעמיא (ווייניג צוקער)	_____
אפטע שווערע קאפשמערצן	_____	פראבלעמען מיטן טייראיד	_____
		(שילד דריזע)	
(אלסערס) מאגן געשווירן	_____	סיפיליס	_____
נירן קראנקייט	_____	גאנארעא	_____
פראבלעמען מיט אורין	_____	הערפעס	_____
ארטרייטיס, אדער פראבלעמען	_____	אויסשלאג פון פאו קיילונג	
פון סקעלעט		(געוואורן פון פארקילונג)	
געשפאלטענער גומען	_____	הויכער בלוט דרוק	_____
אסטמא	_____	ערנסטער נידעריקער בלוט דרוק	_____
לונג אדער אטמונג פראבלעמען	_____	אנטיביאטיקס אין וועגע (אדערן)	_____
פארלוסט פון וואג וואס האט	_____	אדער דיורעטיקס	
נישט קיין דערקלערונג		(מעדיצין ארויסצוציען וואסער)	
ראק (קענסער) פון	_____	הרץ אטאק	_____
אנדערע געשוויולעכץ	_____	אנגינא (הארץ אנטצינדונג)	_____
בלוט איבערגוס (טראנזיציע)	_____	ניט רעגולערער הארץ קלאפן	_____
העפאטאיטיס	_____	אנדערע הארץ פראבלעמען	_____
איידס	_____	רומאטישער פיבער	_____
מארך ענטצינדונג	_____	טובערקולאז, שווינדזוכט	_____
		גלוקאמא	
		פילפאכיקער סקלעראז	
		אנדערע קראנקייטן, ביטע אויסרעכענען:	_____

41. צו האבן איירע בלוט פארוואנטע:

_____ דיאבעטיס (צוקער) _____ קענסער (רֱק)

_____ היפאגלייסעמיא _____ הארץ קראנקייט

_____ אנדערע מעדיצינישע פראבלעמען, אזוי ווי אויבן דערמאנט, ביטע אויסרעכענען:

42. באשרייבט ערנסטע אומגליקספאלן (עקסידענטס) נישט דירעקט פארבינדן מיטן וויזיט ביים דאקטאר דא:

_____ קיינע

_____ פאסירט מיט ווונדן אין קאפ, פארלוסט פון באוויסטזיין, פארווינדונג אין נאקן

_____ האט פאסירט אנע פארווינגונג פון קאפ, פארלוסט פון באוווסטזיין, פארוווונדונג אין נאקן, באשרייבט:

43. רעכנט אויס אלע מעדיצינען און דאזע (אריינרעכענענדיק געבורט קאנטראל פילן און וויטאמינען).

44. אלערגיע מעדיצן:

_____ נאוואקאין	_____ קיינע	
_____ יאד	_____ פעניצילין	
_____ קאדעאין	_____ סולפא	
_____ קלעפעדיקע לייקאפלאסט	_____ טעטראסיקלין	
_____ אספירין	_____ עריטראמייסין	
_____ פארבן צו רענטגען	_____ קעפלעקס/סעקלאר/סעפטין	
	_____ אנדערע, רעכנט אויס	

45. _____ רעכנט אויס אפעראציעס (עלטער _____)

_____ פאליפן אפאראציע (עלטער _____)

_____ הארץ אפעראציע (עלטער _____)

_____ אפענדיציט אפעראציע (עלטעֶר _____)

46. רעכנט אויס גיפטיקע מעדיצין אדער כעמיקאלן צו וועלכע איר זייט געווען אויסגעשטעלט:

_____ בליי _____ מטרעפטאמייסין, נעאמייסין, קאנאמייסין

_____ קוועקזילבער _____ אנדערע, רעכנט אויס:

47. האט איר געהאט רענטגען אויפֿן קאפ אדער נאקן (אריינגערעכנט באהאנדלונג פאר עקנע אדער אויערן פראבלעמען אלס קינד) _____ יא _____ ניין

48. באשרייבט ערנסטע געזונדהייטס פראבלעמען פון אייער מאן/פרוי אדער קינדער.

_____ קיינע

Appendix IIIa
Reading Passages

A classic passage including all the speech sounds of English.

The Rainbow Passage

When the sunlight strikes raindrops in the air, they act like a prism and form a rainbow. The rainbow is a division of white light into many beautiful colors. These take the shape of a long round arch, with its path high above, and its two ends apparently beyond the horizon. There is, according to legend, a boiling pot of gold at one end. People look but no one ever finds it. When a man looks for something beyond his reach, his friends say he is looking for the pot of gold at the end of the rainbow.

An all voiced passage.

Marvin Williams

Marvin Williams is only nine. Marvin lives with his mother on Monroe Avenue in Vernon Valley. Marvin loves all movies, even eerie ones with evil villains in them. Whenever a new movie is in the area, Marvin is usually an early arrival. Nearly every evening Marvin is in row one, along the aisle.

A general purpose passage useful for evaluating hard glottal attack, phrasing, and nasal resonance.

Towne-Heuer Vocal Analysis Reading Passage

If I take a trip this August, I will probably go to Austria. Or I could go to Italy. All of the places of Europe are easy to get to by air, rail, ship or auto. Everybody I have talked to says he would like to go to Europe also.

Every year there are varieties of festivals or fairs at a lot of places. All sorts of activities, such as foods to eat, sights to see occur. Oh, I love to eat ices seated outdoors! The people of each area are reported to like us . . . the people of the U.S.A. It is said that that is true except for Paris.

Aid is easy to get because the officials are helpful. Aid is always available if troubles arise. It helps to have with you a list of offices or officials to call if you do require aid. If you are lost, you will always be helped to locate your route or hotel. The local police will assist you, if they are able to speak as you do. Otherwise a phrase book is useful.

I have had to have help of this sort each trip abroad. However, it was always easy to locate. Happily, I hope, less help will be required this trip. Last trip every hotel was occupied. I had to ask everywhere for flats. Two earlier trips were hard because of heat or lack of heat at hotels.

On second thought, I may want to travel in autumn instead of in August. Many countries can be expensive in the summer months and much less so in autumn. November and December can make fine months for entertainment in many European countries. There may be concerts and musical events more often than during the summer. Milan, Rome, and Hamburg, not to mention Berlin, Vienna, and Madrid are most often mentioned for music.

Most of my friends and I wouldn't miss the chance to try the exciting, interesting, and appetizing menus at most continental restaurants. In many European countries food is inexpensive and interestingly prepared. Servings may be small but meals are taken more often so that there is no need to go hungry.

Maritime countries make many meals of seafood, such as mussels, clams, shrimp, flounder, and salmon or herring. Planning and making your own meals cannot be done even in most small, inexpensive hotels. One must eat in the dining room or in restaurants. Much fun can be had meeting the local natives during mealtimes. Many of them can tell you where to find amusing and interesting shops and sights not mentioned in tour manuals.

Appendix IIIb

Laryngeal Examination

Speaking Voice

Range: ____ Soprano ____ Alto ____ Tenor ____ Baritone ____ Bass

Pitch variability: ____ Normal ____ Decreased ____ Increased

Excess tension: ____ Normal ____ Minimal ____ Moderate ____ Severe

____ Tongue

____ Neck

____ Face

Support: ____ Good ____ Deficient

Volume: ____ Appropriate ____ Soft ____ Loud

Volume variability: ____ Appropriate ____ Diminished ____ Excessive

Quality: ____ Normal ____ Hoarse ____ Breathy

____ Fatiguable ____ Diplophonic

Rhythm: ____ Normal ____ Slow ____ Fast ____ Spasmodic

____ Stuttering ____ Dysarthric

Habits: ____ Throat clearing ____ Coughing

Other:

Singing Voice

Stance: ____Balanced, proper   ____Balanced, weight back   ____Unbalanced

                   ____Knees locked

Breathing: ____Nasal, unobstructed

                   ____Nasal, partially obstructed

                   ____Oral Chest (excessive)

                   ____Abdominal (proper)

Excess tension: ____Face   ____Lip   ____Jaw   __Neck   ____Shoulders   ____Tongue

Tongue tension: ____Corrects easily   ____Does not correct easily

Support: ____Present   ____Practically absent

                   ____Effective   ____Ineffective

                   ____Initiated after the tone

Laryngeal position: ____Stable   ____Alters   ____High   ____Low

Mouth opening: ____Appropriate   ____Decreased   ____Excessive

Vibrato: ____Regular   ____Irregular   ____Rapid   ____Tremolo

Range: ____Soprano   ____Alto   ____Tenor   ____Baritone   ____Bass

Register changes: ____Controlled   ____Uncontrolled

Quality: ____Premier   ____Professional   ____Amateur   ____Pathologic

                   ____Hoarse   ____Breathy   ____Fatiguable   ____Diplophonic

Technical errors present: ____In all registers   ____Low   ____Middle   ____High

Pitch: ____Accurate   ____Inaccurate

Appendix IVa
Laryngologist's Report

PATIENT OFFICE
(215) 545-3322
FAX: (215) 790-1192
office@phillyent.com

Sataloff Institute for Voice & Ear Care

ADMINISTRATIVE OFFICE
(215) 732-6100
FAX: (215) 545-3374
rtsataloff@phillyent.com

February 10, 2004

Re: John Doe

To Whom It May Concern:

I had the pleasure of seeing John Doe in the office today. He is a 25-year-old actor performing the lead role with a national touring company now performing at the Walnut Street Theater. He is concerned about his voice. He denies any voice loss but complains of frequent sore throat and voice fatigue. Recently he has found his voice is gravelly and lower than his normal range. He is concerned about "crackling sounds." One month ago, he saw a physician who diagnosed him with laryngopharygeal reflux and started him on Aciphex twice daily. Last week he developed a globus sensation that lasted all day. He also reports a bitter taste upon awakening, throat clearing and "post nasal drip." He has been seen by several other physicians over the past two years and has been told he has dust allergy and reflux. He wants reassurance that he is not "destroying" his voice. He is not singing at this time and is acting full-time. He has had acting training in college and some singing training, as well. However, the singing training in college left him with a sore throat, and he reports that he has discounted his training from college because he does not believe it was of high quality. He has also had acting lessons in school and some after graduation. He is currently performing eight shows per week. He is on stage for the entire two and one half hours. He has been performing in this show since Christmas 2003. He does not play musical instruments, and he is not exposed to noxious fumes.

Mr. Doe reports a past medical history of microhematuria in childhood, prostratitis, depression and intermittent tightness in his chest for many years. He finds the chest tightness can last for two days at a time and then abates for as long as two years.

Mr. Doe reports a past surgical history of extraction of four impacted wisdom teeth five years ago.

His current medications include Aciphex twice daily, Zyrtec and Nasonex. He denies any medication allergies but reports environmental allergies to mold, dust and dogs. He is a life-long non-smoker, drinks no caffeinated beverages and consumes one alcoholic beverage per week.

Page 2
February 10, 2004
Re: John Doe

His tympanic membranes and hearing were normal. Examination of the nose was normal. Examination of the oral cavity and pharynx revealed diminished gag reflex on the left. Examination of the neck was normal. Laryngeal examination was completed by strobovideolaryngoscopy and a copy of that report is attached. FEEST revealed slightly decreased sensation side of the larynx on the left. During conversational speech, his voice was pressed but not hoarse. During speaking, he had jaw and tongue tension and inadequate support. Brief singing evaluation revealed excessive tension in the tongue and jaw and suboptimal support technique. Voice team evaluation will be performed, and reports will be attached to this letter.

I have asked Mr. Doe to continue on his Aciphex twice daily for control of his laryngeal reflux and have added Zantac 300 mg at bedtime to his regimen. I have given him prescriptions for selected blood tests and referred him to Dr. Steven Mandel for a laryngeal EMG. He will be evaluated by my voice team, and I have asked him to follow up with me after completion of his testing for his reflux, paresis, vocal fold mass, and muscle tension dysphonia.

With best regards.

Very truly yours.

Robert T. Sataloff, M.D., D.M.A.

RTS/jb

Enclosure

cc: Mr. John Doe

Appendix IVb

Strobovideolaryngoscopy Report

PATIENT OFFICE
(215) 545-3322
FAX: (215) 790-1192
office@phillyent.com

Sataloff Institute for Voice & Ear Care

ADMINISTRATIVE OFFICE
(215) 732-6100
FAX: (215) 545-3374
rtsataloff@phillyent.com

REPORT OF OPERATION: John Doe

DATE: February 10, 2004

PRE-OPERATIVE DIAGNOSIS:	1. Dysphonia
POST-OPERATIVE DIAGNOSIS:	1. Left vocal fold paresis 2. Left vocal fold fibrotic mass 3. Right vocal fold contact cyst or pseudocyst 4. Laryngopharyngeal reflux
PROCEDURE:	Laryngoscopy with magnification, strobovideolaryngoscopy, and complex voice analysis and synchronized electroglottography including sensory testing.
SURGEON:	Robert T. Sataloff, M.D., D.M.A.

Anesthesia: Topical
Rigid Endoscope: Kay-70

Flexible Laryngoscope: Olympus ENF-L3

Stroboscope: Kay-4

Procedure: The patient was taken to the special procedure room and prepared in the usual fashion. The laryngoscope was inserted, and suspended from the video system for magnification and documentation. Testing was performed at several frequencies and intensities. Initial examination was performed using continuous light. The findings were as follows:

Voice: Normal

Page 2
February 10, 2004
Re: John Doe

Supraglottic Hyperfunction: Moderate with decreased anterior-posterior distance and decreased lateral distance. It did improve with voluntary increase in pitch.

Right vocal fold abduction, adduction and longitudinal tension: Normal

Left vocal fold abduction was normal; adduction was slightly sluggish; and longitudinal tension was mildly decreased.

Arytenoid Joint Movement: Normal

Dysdiadochokinesis: Absent

Laryngeal EMG: Was recommended

CT: Not recommended

MRI: Not recommended

Arytenoids: Moderately erythematous and mildly edematous, right greater than left.

Posterior laryngeal cobblestoning (pachydermia): Absent

Right true vocal fold color: Normal, without significant varicosities.

Left true vocal fold color: Normal, without significant varicosities.

Masses and other Vibratory Margin Irregularities: The patient has a left vocal fold paresis and a left fibrotic mass in the striking zone that is about 3 mm in length at its base and has mild underlying stiffness. He also has a right contralateral cyst verses pseudocyst at the contact point. There is also stiffness at its base.

Other Significant Structural Lesions: Absent

Vocal Fold Vibrations: Symmetric in amplitude and phase

Periodicity: Regular

Glottic Closure: Intermittently incomplete anterior and posterior to the mass(es).

Vocal process height: Equal

Page 3
February 10, 2004

Amplitude of Right Vocal Fold: Minimally decreased
Amplitude of Left Vocal Fold: Mildly decreased
Minimally-to-mildly decreased

Wave Form of Right Vocal Fold: Minimally-to-mildly decreased
Wave Form of Left Vocal Fold: Mildly decreased

Right musculomembranous vocal fold vibratory function: Slightly hypodynamic in the middle one-third.

Left musculomembranous vocal fold vibratory function: Hypodynamic in the middle one-third

EGG: Revealed peak skewing. This indicates increased adduction, suggestive of pressed phonation.

The procedure concluded without complication

Robert T. Sataloff, M.D., D.M.A.

RTS/jb

Appendix IVc

Objective Voice Analysis and Laryngeal Electromyography

Robert Thayer Sataloff, MD, DMA
Objective Voice Assessment

Patient: John Doe   **Date of Birth**: xx-xx-xx   **Age**: 25
Occupation: actor   **Date of Evaluation**: 02-10-04   **Physician**: Dr. RTS
Diagnosis: Left vocal fold paresis, Laryngeal reflux, Small bilateral masses of the vocal folds, MTD
Hoarseness rating:Grade: 4 mm Roughness: 6.5 mm Breathiness: 3.5 mm Asthenia: 2.5 mm Strain: 4 mm

Acoustic Assessment

Conversation   (name, date, age)   **Reading** (M. Williams Passage)
Mean Frequency: 107.23 Hz   Mean Frequency: 105.55 Hz
Mean Intensity: 73.21 dBSPL   Mean Intensity: 73.58 dBSPL
Reading Time: 17.91 sec   Total Voiced Time: 11.25sec   % voiced: 62.814 %
Physiological Frequency Range of Phonation   **Singing Frequency Range**
Low = 73.5 Hz (*1/period*)   Low = _ Hz (*1/period*)
High= 412.15 Hz (*1/period*)   High= _ Hz (*1/period*)
Semitone Range (STR) = 29.84589 ST   Norm = 33-36 ST, (Hollien, Dew, Philips 1971)

Perturbation Measures

5 Token /a/:   Please see attached printout with graph.
Fo(M85-155Hz;F143-235Hz)-108.375 Hz;**Jitter%**(M0.5389;F0.633)-0.447%;**RAP%**(M 0.345; F 0.378)-0.267%;
Shimmer% (M 2.523; F 1.977)- 1.288 %; **NHR** (M 0.122; F 0.112)- 0.147 ; **STD** (M 3.3; F 2.5)- 0.992

Spectrography

Sustained /i/ (Spectrogram) ; Yanagihara Hoarseness Rating Type: Type I
Type I= harmonic components mixed with noise in F1 and F2

Aerodynamic assessment

Spirometry: FVC = 115(%)   FEV 1.0 = 75(%)   FEF (25%-75%) = 33(%)
Mean Flow Rate (MFR): 329.4376 mls/sec
Maximum Phonation Time /a/ = 16.36 sec (mean); the best- 18.84 sec   **S/Z ratio:** 1.1763034
(WNL females= 25.7 sec; WNL males=34.6 sec)   *(WNL range 0.8-1.29)*

Glottal Efficiency Profile

Mean Flow Rate
| 49 | 69 | 89------------112--------------136 | 156 | 256.................**X** |

S/Z RATIO
| 0.2 | 0.4 | 0.8------------1.07------**X**-------1.29 | 2.2 | 4.4 |

Maximum Phonation Time
| 40 | 33 | 28.7-----------25.7-------------22.5 | **X** 15 | 9.0 |

Recording/Analysis Equipment: TASCAM DAP1 DAT recorder, KAY model 4302 head-mount microphone at 15 cm., KAY Multi-Speech Model 3700 (MDVP Advanced 5105, Real-Time Spectrogram 5121) Schiller SP-10 Spirometer).

Page 2
February 10, 2004
Operative Report (cont'd)
Robert Thayer Sataloff, M.D., D. M. A.
re: John Doe

ACOUSTIC PROFILE (SPOKEN) /ɑ/

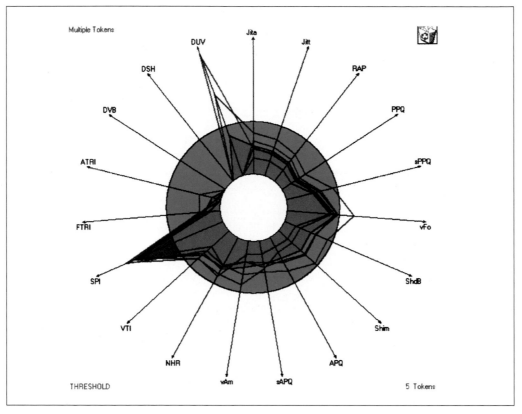

Page 3
February 10, 2004
OBJECTIVE VOICE ANALYSIS: John Doe

MDVPreport: Voice Report

Token 2

Parameter	Name	Value	Unit	Norm(f)	STD(f)	Thresh
Average Fundamental Frequency	Fo	108.375	Hz	243.973	27.457	
Mean Fundamental Frequency	MFo	108.366	Hz	241.080	25.107	
Average Pitch Period	To	9.228	ms	4.148	0.432	
Highest Fundamental Frequency	Fhi	111.164	Hz	252.724	26.570	
Lowest Fundamental Frequency	Flo	105.204	Hz	234.861	28.968	
Standard Deviation of Fo	STD	0.992	Hz	2.722	2.115	
Phonatory Fo-Range in semi-tones	PFR	2		2.250	1.060	
Fo-Tremor Frequency	Fftr	4.167	Hz	3.078	1.964	
Length of Analyzed Sample	Tsam	3.750	s	3.000	0.000	
Absolute Jitter	Jita	41.230	us	26.927	16.654	83.200
Jitter Percent	Jitt	0.447	%	0.633	0.351	1.040
Relative Average Perturbation	RAP	0.267	%	0.378	0.214	0.680
Pitch Perturbation Quotient	PPQ	0.253	%	0.366	0.205	0.840
Smoothed Pitch Perturbation Quotient	sPPQ	0.553	%	0.532	0.220	1.020
Fundamental Frequency Variation	vFo	0.916	%	1.149	1.005	1.100
Shimmer in dB	ShdB	0.113	dB	0.176	0.071	0.350
Shimmer Percent	Shim	1.288	%	1.997	0.791	3.810
Amplitude Perturbation Quotient	APQ	0.986	%	1.397	0.527	3.070
Smoothed Ampl. Perturbation Quotient	sAPQ	2.212	%	2.371	0.912	4.230
Peak-to-Peak Amplitude Variation	vAm	6.847	%	10.743	5.698	8.200
Noise to Harmonic Ratio	NHR	0.147		0.112	0.009	0.190
Voice Turbulence Index	VTI	0.047		0.046	0.012	0.061
Soft Phonation Index	SPI	27.227		7.534	4.133	14.120
Fo-Tremor Intensity Index	FTRI	0.333	%	0.304	0.156	0.950
Degree of Voice Breaks	DVB	0.000	%	0.200	0.100	1.000
Degree of Sub-harmonics	DSH	0.000	%	0.200	0.100	1.000
Degree of Voiceless	DUV	0.000	%	0.200	0.100	1.000
Number of Voice Breaks	NVB	0		0.200	0.100	0.900
Number of Sub-harmonic Segments	NSH	0		0.200	0.100	0.900
Number of Unvoiced Segments	NUV	0		0.200	0.100	0.900
Number of Segments Computed	SEG	124		92.594	0.000	
Total Number Detected Pitch Periods	PER	405		713.188	0.000	

Report Date: Feb. 10, 2004 Tuesday   Name: John Doe   Age & Gender: 25 years, male

Page 4
April 27, 1995
OBJECTIVE VOICE ANALYSIS: John Doe

SPECTROGRAPHIC ANALYSIS
KAY ELEMETRICS
DSP SONA-GRAPH 5500

POWER SPECTRUM (TOP) AND NARROW BAND SPECTRUM (BOTTOM) FOR /ɑ/:

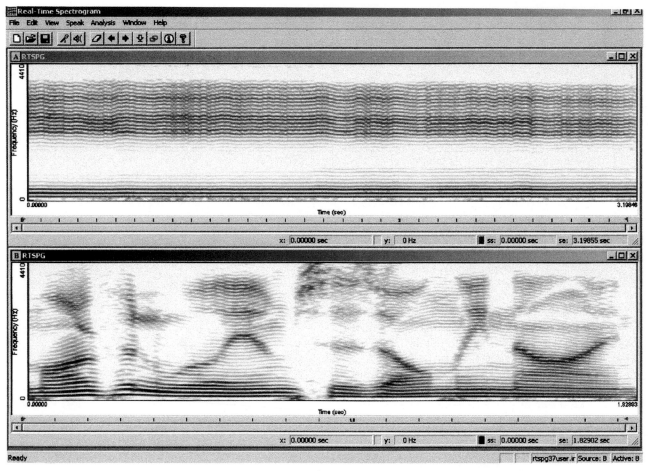

Report Date: Feb. 10, 2004 Tuesday   Name: John Doe   Age & Gender: 25 years, male

Page 5
OBJECTIVE VOICE ANALYSIS: John Doe

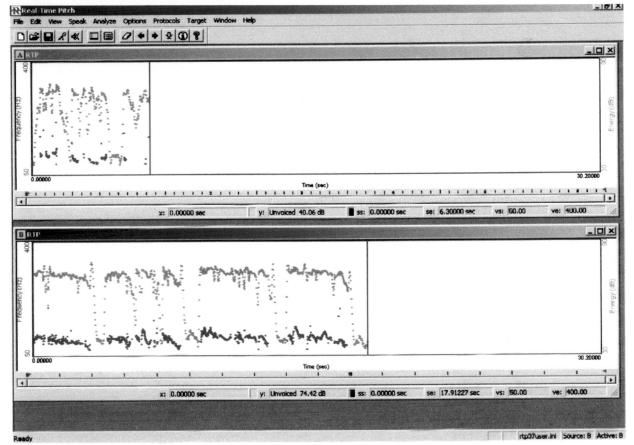

Report Date: Feb.10, 2004 Tuesday   Name: John Doe   Age & Gender: 25 years, male

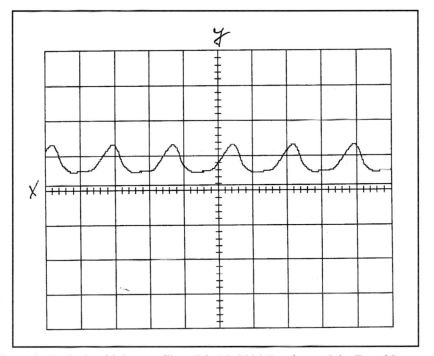

Oscilloscopic Analysis with inverse filter: Feb. 10, 2004 Tuesday;   John Doe, 25 years, male

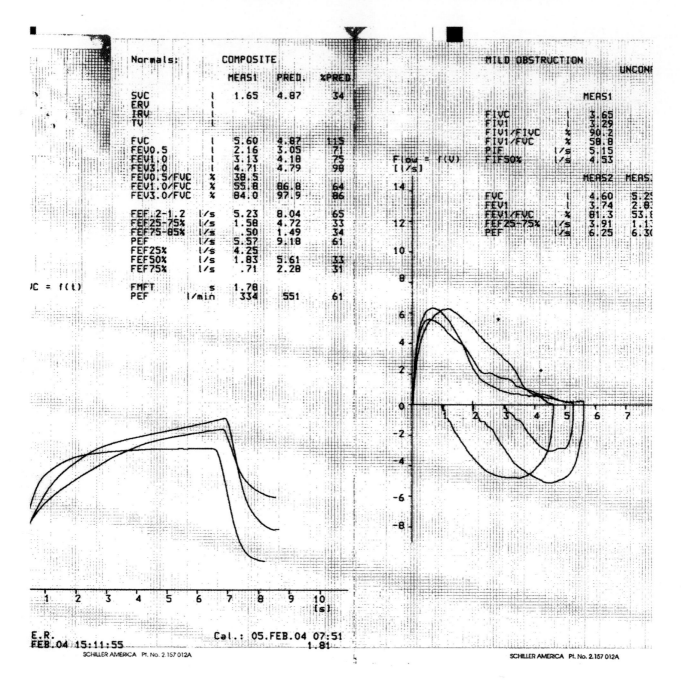

Normals:		COMPOSITE		
		MEAS1	PRED.	%PRED
SVC	l	1.65	4.87	34
ERV	l			
IRV	l			
TV	l			
FVC	l	5.60	4.87	115
FEV0.5	l	2.16	3.05	71
FEV1.0	l	3.13	4.18	75
FEV3.0	l	4.71	4.79	98
FEV0.5/FVC	%	38.5		
FEV1.0/FVC	%	55.8	86.8	64
FEV3.0/FVC	%	84.0	97.9	86
FEF.2-1.2	l/s	5.23	8.04	65
FEF25-75%	l/s	1.58	4.72	33
FEF75-85%	l/s	.50	1.49	34
PEF	l/s	5.57	9.18	61
FEF25%	l/s	4.25		
FEF50%	l/s	1.83	5.61	33
FEF75%	l/s	.71	2.28	31
FMFT	s	1.78		
PEF	l/min	334	551	61

VC = f(t)

Flow = f(V)
[l/s]

MILD OBSTRUCTION   UNCON

		MEAS1
FIVC	l	3.65
FIV1	l	3.29
FIV1/FIVC	%	90.2
FIV1/FVC	%	58.8
PIF	l/s	5.15
FIF50%	l/s	4.53

		MEAS2	MEAS
FVC	l	4.60	5.2
FEV1	l	3.74	2.8
FEV1/FVC	%	81.3	53.6
FEF25-75%	l/s	3.91	1.1
PEF	l/s	6.25	6.3

E.R.
FEB.04 15:11:55

Cal.: 05.FEB.04 07:51
1.81

Robert Thayer Sataloff, M.D., D.M.A.
1721 Pine Street
Philadelphia, PA 19103-6771

Graduate Hospital

Tenet

Professor, Otolaryngology-Head & Neck Surgery
Director, Jefferson Arts Medicine Center
Conductor, Thomas Jefferson University Choir
Thomas Jefferson University

Chairman, Otolaryngology-Head & Neck Surgery
Graduate Hospital
Adjunct Professor, Otorhinolaryngology-HNS
The University of Pennsylvania

PATIENT OFFICE
(215) 545-3322
FAX: (215) 790-1192
office@phillyent.com

Sataloff Institute for Voice & Ear Care

ADMINISTRATIVE OFFICE
(215) 732-6100
FAX: (215) 545-7813
rtsataloff@phillyent.com

Interpretations of Findings:

Objective voice assessment reveals the following: Values of NHR (noise to harmonic ratio), SPI (soft phonation index), and MFR (mean flow rate) were all noticeably above the accepted normal limits, while Jitter %, RAP % (relative average perturbation), Shimmer %, STD (standard deviation of fundamental frequency), MPT (maximum phonation time), and mean frequencies of both conversational and reading voice samples as well as semitone range for the physiologic frequency, fell bellow or at the lowest possible level of the appropriate amplitude for these parameters. Oscilloscopic analysis with inverse filter demonstrates an epiglottic gap in the amount of 200 mls of escaping air. Spectrography reveals increase noise above 2.2 kHz in the area of F1 and F2.

Acoustic measures demonstrate moderately low mean Fundamental frequencies of conversational and reading (Marvin Williams's passage) voice samples and reduced semi-tone range. The combination of decreased perturbation measures of Jitter %, RAP %, Shimmer %, and STD as well as increased SPI and NHR reveals the existence of moderate irregularity of vocal fold vibration in sustained phonation and are consistent with the diagnosis of tension dysphonia due to unilateral vocal fold paresis and small, bilateral masses on the vocal folds. Spectrographic analyses of sustain vowel /i/ reveal decreased intensity of harmonics and increased noise elements chiefly in the formant region of the vowels. This correlates to perceptual measures of decreased oral resonance and is consistent with acoustic measures showing mild to moderate irregularity of vocal fold vibration.

Low MPT measures and abnormally high mean Flow rate denote inadequate glottal closure. This correlates with the diagnosis of unilateral vocal fold paresis. Oscilloscope measures with inverse filter further indicate insufficient glottal closure.

Decreased physiologic frequency range (pitch range) and low-average speaking F0 correlates with perceptual measures of increased strain and supports the diagnosis of muscle tension dysphonia. In addition, a few short, irregular periods of contraction and instability are seen on the spectrographic representation of sustained phonation. This finding is consistent with the diagnosis of muscle tension dysphonia as well.

Pulmonary function measurements demonstrate lung capacity at the upper levels of normal limits for this age, gender, height, and weight. However, low levels of FEV1.0/FVC and FEF25-75% at 64% and 33%, respectively, indicate mild obstructive changes at the end of expiration.

Dimiter Dentchev (M.D., Ph.D)

Chairman, Board of Directors
The Voice Foundation
Editor-in-Chief
Journal of Voice
215-735-7999

Chairman, Board of Directors
American Institute for Voice and Ear Research
215-735-7487

Philadelphia Ear, Nose & Throat Associates
Robert Thayer Sataloff, M.D., D.M.A.
Joseph R. Spiegel, M.D., F.A.C.S.
Karen M. Lyons, M.D.
web: www.phillyent.com

NEUROLOGY AND NEUROPHYSIOLOGY ASSOCIATES, P.C.

Ramon Mañon-Espaillat, M.D.
Clinical Professor of Neurology
Jefferson Medical College
Epilepsy and Sleep Disorders

Steven Mandel, M.D.
Clinical Professor of Neurology
Jefferson Medical College
Neuromuscular Diseases

Olga A. Katz, M.D., PhD.
Instructor of Neurology
Jefferson Medical College
Clinical Neurophysiology

xx/xx/xx

Robert Sataloff, M.D.
1721 Pine Street
Philadelphia, PA 19103

Reference: **John Doe**
               DOB: xx/xx/xxxx
               Evaluation Date: x/x/xx

Dear Dr. Sataloff:

HISTORY: I had the pleasure of seeing John Doe in the office on xx/xx/xx for a neurological consultation and electrodiagnostic studies.

He is a 25-year-old gentleman who reports difficulty with his voice. He has noted some hoarseness and projection difficulties.

He has been on a number of medications, including Zyrtec, Aciphex, Nasonex, and ranitidine.

He does not drink alcohol and does not smoke cigarettes. He is not receiving any therapy.

He has a history of hayfever.

Family history is noncontributory for neurological disease.

The patient has completed a patient history form and this form was reviewed in the presence of the patient as this note was being dictated.

1015 Chestnut Street • Suite 810 • Philadelphia, PA 19107
151 Fries Mill Road • Suite 506 • Turnersville, NJ 08012
Phone: (215) 574-0075   Fax: (215) 627-8208 • NJ Phone: (856) 228-0006
E-Mail: steven.mandel@mail.TJU.EDU

Page 2
John Doe
Evaluation Date: x/x/xx

EXAMINATION: He was awake and alert, answering appropriately. He had no obvious aphasia or dysarthria. He had no motor deficits. No tremors, dysmetria, or bruits were detected. Position and vibratory sense were normal.

Based upon his complaints, electrodiagnostic studies were obtained.

Prior to performing electrodiagnostic studies, "Consent for Electrodiagnostic Testing" was signed by the patient in my presence with the consent form present in the patient's chart.

LARYNGEAL EMG: Accessory nerve stimulation revealed normal latency and amplitude responses with repetitive stimulation study being normal. Needle EMG examination demonstrated approximately 80-90% recruitment response from left cricothyroid. Right cricothyroid, vocalis, and posterior cricoarytenoid muscles appeared to be normal. There was poor relaxation at rest and findings consistent with muscular tension dysphonia.

IMPRESSION: The above electrical studies indicate mild left superior laryngeal nerve paresis with muscular tension dysphonia. There is no evidence to indicate any neuromuscular junction abnormalities.

This note was dictated in the presence of the patient so as to insure the accuracy of the history provided by the patient. The patient has verbalized understanding as to the contents of this letter.

Thank you for allowing me to participate in the care of your patient. If you have any questions regarding the contents of this report or any other issues related to the care of this patient, please do not hesitate to contact me.

Sincerely,

Steven Mandel, M.D.

SM/ac

Patient Name: _____John Doe_____   Date: __2|10|04__

Voice Handicap Index (VHI)
(Jacobson, Johnson, Grywalski, et al.)

Instructions: These are statements that many people have used to describe their voices and the effects of their voices on their lives. Check the response that indicates how frequent you have the same experience.

Never=0 points; Almost never=1point; Sometimes=2 points; Almost Always=3 points; Always=4 points	Never	Almost Never	Sometimes	Almost Always	Always
F1. My voice makes it difficult for people to hear me.	✓				
P2. I run out of air when I talk.	✓				
F3. People have difficulty understanding me in a noisy room.	✓				
P4. The sound of my voice varies throughout the day.				✓	
F5. My family has difficulty hearing me when I call them throughout the house.	✓				
F6. I use the phone less often than I would like.			✓		
E7. I'm tense when talking with others because of my voice.			✓		
F8. I tend to avoid groups of people because of my voice.	✓				
E9. People seem irritated with my voice.		✓			
P10. People ask, "What's wrong with your voice?"	✓				
F11. I speak with friends, neighbors, or relatives less often because of my voice.	✓				
F12. People ask me to repeat myself when speaking fact-to-face.	✓				
P13. My voice sounds creaky and dry.			✓		
P14. I feel as through I have to strain to produce voice.			✓		
E15. I find other people don't understand my voice problem.				✓	
F16. My voice difficulties restrict my personal and social life.			✓		
P17. The clarity of my voice is unpredictable.		✓			
P18. I try to change my voice to sound different.			✓		
F19. I feel left out of conversations because of my voice.	✓				
P20. I use a great deal of effort to speak.		✓			
P21. My voice is worse in the evening.			✓		
F22. My voice problem causes me to loss income.	✓				
E23. My voice problem upsets me.				✓	
E24. I am less out-going because of my voice problem.		✓			
E25. My voice makes me feel handicapped.		✓			
P26. My voice "gives out" on me in the middle of speaking.	✓				
E27. I feel annoyed when people ask me to repeat.	✓				
E28. I feel embarrassed when people ask me to repeat.	✓				
E29. My voice makes me feel incompetent.		✓			
E30. I'm ashamed of my voice problem.				✓	

P Scale **23**   F Scale **14**   E Scale **25**   Total Scale **62**

Please **Circle** the word that matches how you feel your voice is today.   1. Normal (2. Mild   3. Moderate) 4. Severe

Appendix IVd
Speech-Language Pathologist's Report

INITIAL VOICE EVALUATION

Name: John Doe

Date of evaluation: 2/10/04

D.O.B.: XX/XX/XX

History: John Doe is a 25-year-old professional actor, currently performing the lead role in a touring company of "XXXXX XXXXX" at the Walnut Street Theatre in Philadelphia. He comes to this office with complaints of gravelly vocal quality, loss of range, and vocal fatigue. Mr. Doe reports that he has experienced voice problems since college, where he majored in theatre, but indicates that his problems have become more evident now that he has been cast in several major roles. He reports that the show opened in December of 2003, and adds that he is onstage for almost the entire 2_ hour duration of this show. Mr. Doe relates that he uses physical warm-ups for prior to performing, but that he is not confident in the vocal training he has received and avoids using vocal warm-ups for fear of fatiguing his voice before going onstage. Mr. Doe adds that he recently saw a physician who made a diagnosis of reflux and prescribed Aciphex twice daily.

Laryngovideostroboscopy performed by Dr. Robert Sataloff today revealed left vocal fold paresis, a left vocal fold fibrotic mass, a right vocal fold cyst vs. pseudocyst, and reflux. Laryngeal EMG was ordered to confirm vocal fold paresis. Dr. Sataloff asked Mr. Doe to continue Aciphex for symptoms of reflux and added Zantac 300 mg at bedtime. Mr. Doe's medical history is reportedly otherwise significant for microhematuria in childhood, prostatisis, allergies, and depression.

Medications: Aciphex, Zantac, Zyrtec, Nasonex

Allergies:

Vocal Hygiene: Mr. Doe reportedly drinks 8 glasses of water daily. He reports occasional consumption of caffeinated soda and frequent consumption of cranberry juice. He denies tobacco use. Mr. Doe admits to frequent throat clearing. He indicates that he avoids using his voice in an extreme fashion when he is not on stage, but is concerned that he may be forced to yell frequently if he has to return to waiting tables between acting jobs. He received some acting voice training as an undergraduate theatre major, but indicates that he had not found the training to be helpful,

Oral Mechanism Exam: The oral mechanism exam was unremarkable

Objective Evaluation: May be found under separate cover.

Subjective Evaluation: During conversational speech, Mr. Doe presented with intermittent hoarseness and occasional glottal fry and posterior tone placement at the ends of sentences. Tone placement was otherwise anterior, and occasionally hypernasal. Excessive tension was visible in the jaw, and his tone quality was suggestive of decreased pharyngeal space and tongue base tension. Mr. Doe demonstrated a tendency to sit with his sternum depressed and to utilize a shallow abdominal breathing technique with minimal rib cage expansion. Breath support was judged to be insufficient to promote maximal vocal resonance and freedom. On reading the Towne-Heuer Vocal Analysis reading passage, he produced 18% of hard glottal attacks (7-23% is considered to be in the normal range).

Doe, John
Voice Evaluation
Page 2 of 2

Trial Therapy: Vocal hygiene issues were discussed with an emphasis on adherence to a reflux protocol. Trial therapy focused on the reduction of excessive tension in the jaw and tongue and more efficient use of abdominal breath support. Jaw massage and relaxation exercises were introduced and resulted in increased volume and resonance during the production of open-vowel words. Tongue stretches and speech with tongue extension were practiced, and subsequent cueing for anterior tongue placement resulted in a more anterior, less pressed technique. Instruction in abdominal breath support was initiated. The patient accessed a much freer vocal production when encouraged to allow expansion of the rib cage upon inhalation rather than attempting to hold his rib cage fixed in place while breathing abdominally. An audiotape of these exercises was provided to the patient for home practice.

Impressions and Recommendations: John Doe is a professional actor who presents with intermittent hoarseness, decreased range, and vocal fatigue secondary to bilateral vocal fold masses, vocal fold paresis, and lack of adequate vocal technique to allow for successful compensation. Mr. Doe would benefit from voice therapy to promote the reduction of his vocal fold masses and improved voice quality and endurance through the establishment of a more efficient, well-supported vocal technique.

The following are the projected goals of the aforementioned therapy:

1. Establishment of improved posture and spinal alignment to promote greater efficiency of breathing and support.
2. More effective use of abdominal breathing and support in conversational speech.
3. Consistent use of frontal tone focus and increased oropharyngeal space to improve vocal tone quality, ease, and efficiency.
4. Elimination of excessive muscle tension in jaw and tongue.
5. Practice of exercises designed to address laryngeal nerve paralysis.

A course of 8 voice therapy sessions, 60 minutes in duration, is recommended to address these goals. Prior to the completion of such therapy, Mr. Doe will be referred back to Dr. Sataloff for re-evaluation and the need for further treatment assessed. Mr. Doe is an intelligent and motivated patient. Based upon his response to trial therapy, the prognosis for improved voice quality and function with compliance to a course of voice therapy is considered good.

Shirley Gherson, CCC-SLP

Appendix IVe
Singing Voice Specialist's Report

VOCAL STRESS ASSESSMENT

Patient: John Doe
Date of Evaluation: February 18, 2004

John Doe is a 25-year-old professional actor who has been experiencing his current vocal complaints of vocal fatigue, a "gravelly-sounding" vocal quality, loss of vocal range and general vocal unreliability during the recent run of a high-level professional play in which he plays the lead role. Mr. Doe states that he has a history of these vocal complaints dating back to college, and he believes that they are now more evident as the demands of his career have increased. His recent lead role requires extensive voice use for most of the show, approximately 3 hours. He was examined by an ENT physician who diagnosed reflux and prescribed Aciphex. Mr. Doe was evaluated by Dr. Robert T. Sataloff on February 10, 2004 who diagnosed left vocal fold paresis, a left vocal fold fibrotic mass, a right vocal fold contact cyst or pseudocyst and laryngopharyngeal reflux.

Mr. Doe has been acting since childhood but does not believe that he has ever received adequate training in voice production and vocal health for his speaking voice. He is not a singer and has had no significant training for his singing voice. For the past two years, when not involved in a production, he has been supplementing his income by working about 20 hours a week in the kitchen of a Hard Rock Café. He acknowledges talking on the phone "a lot."

Mr. Doe denies using tobacco products and rarely drinks alcoholic beverages. He exercises regularly and considers his general health to be good. His regular medications include daily Zyrtec and Nasonex for allergies, as well as Aciphex BID and 300 mg of Zantac at night for his reflux.

During the intital singing evaluation, Mr. Doe demonstrated the following technical patterns: mid-abdominal inhalation and breath support efforts; excessive muscular tension in the regions of the jaw and tongue; reduced oral resonance space; audibly suggested muscle tension in the region of the pharynx. His approximate singing range was C2-C5, with only falsetto present above E4. Mr. Doe presented with an average bari-tenor singing voice that matched pitch well and was pleasant in quality. His conversational speaking voice was moderately pressed with a generally posterior tone placement.

This session continued with efforts to release some of the counterproductive compensatory muscle tension in Mr. Doe's jaw and tongue. Gentle tongue stretching

Page 2
February 18, 2004
Vocal Stress Assessment (continued)
Re: John Doe

exercises as well as verbal cues with tactile jaw massage proved effective. We then focused on utilizing this more relaxed musculature on simple singing exercises (5-1, 1-5-1 and 135875421 on lip trills, A2-D#4 and 3-1 on \baɪbaɪ\ with the resulting voice showing more freedom of production as well as a more balanced resonance quality. Mr. Doe recognized these changes and will practice daily with a cassette tape of this session until he can return for a follow-up session, hopefully in one week.

Mr. Doe is an extremely intelligent and compliant patient who appears highly motivated to improve his vocal quality and endurance. It is likely that his current vocal complaints are related to a combination of causes including reflux, vocal fold masses, vocal fold paresis and a less-than-optimum level of vocal technique and conditioning necessary to meet the rigorous vocal demands of a busy acting career. Regular singing voice sessions (in conjunction with voice therapy) focused on identifying and eliminating counterproductive compensatory muscle tension, establishing a more efficient and reliable breath management system and encouraging more anterior tonal placement may allow Mr. Doe to access more of his vocal potential with less strain. More efficient vocal production may lead to some spontaneous reduction of his vocal fold masses. Strict reflux control may also prove to be a necessary component to his recovery strategy.

Thank you for allowing me to participate in his care.

Sincerely yours,

Margaret Baroody, M.M.
Singing Voice Specialist

Appendix IVf

Acting Voice Specialist's Report

ACTING VOICE EVALUATION

Name: John Doe   **Date of evaluation:** 2/10/04

                                                 Date of birth:

History: John Doe is a 25-year-old professional actor, currently performing the lead role in a touring company of "XXXXX XXXXX" at the Walnut Street Theatre in Philadelphia. He comes to this office with complaints of a gravelly voice quality, loss of range, and vocal fatigue. Mr. Doe reports that he has experienced vocal problems since college, where he majored in theatre, but indicates that his problems have become more evident now that he has been cast in several major roles. He reports that he is onstage for almost the entire 2_ hour duration of this show, and that his character often serves as narrator or to comment on the action of the play to the audience. He adds that the show opened in December of 2003. Mr. Doe relates that he uses physical warm-ups prior to performing, but that he is not confident in the vocal training he has received and avoids using vocal warm-ups for fear of fatiguing his voice before going onstage. Mr. Doe adds that he recently saw a physician who made a diagnosis of reflux and prescribed Aciphex twice daily.

Laryngovideostroboscopy performed by Dr. Robert T. Sataloff today revealed left vocal fold paresis, a left vocal fold fibrotic mass, a right vocal fold cyst vs. pseudocyst, and reflux. Laryngeal EMG was ordered to confirm the vocal fold paresis. Dr. Sataloff asked Mr. Doe to continue Aciphex for symptoms of reflux and added Zantac 300 mg at bedtime. Mr. Doe's medical history is reportedly otherwise significant for microhematuria in childhood, prostatitis, and depression.

Evaluation of Vocal Technique: During conversational speech, Mr. Doe demonstrated a mildly pressed, posteriorly placed voice produced with inadequate breath support and reduced oropharyngeal space. When asked to demonstrate his vocal production for this particular role (and when observed in performance at the theatre), he demonstrated a more anteriorly placed, but mildly nasal and pressed voice. The use of a "Brooklynese" accent in his current role intensified hypernasality. Vocal hyperfunction was judged to be exacerbated by jaw tension, restricted rib cage expansion, laryngeal tension, head/neck misalignment, and decreased oropharyngeal space.

Vocal Exercises Given: Because the patient was evaluated in the afternoon prior to a performance, today's work focused primarily on introducing a vocal warm-up combining physical movement to free the upper body and rib movement and vocal work to promote increased airflow and space. An arm-swing warm-up utilizing lip trills on glides and lip trills elided into spoken words and text resulted in freer, more resonant vocal production. The patient reported that his voice felt easier to produce and yet stronger than it has recently. These exercises were recorded on audiotape and provided to the patient for home practice.

Doe, John
Acting Voice Evaluation
Page 2 of 2

<u>Impressions and Recommendations:</u> John Doe is a 25-year-old actor, who presents with a pressed, inadequately supported voice, secondary to bilateral vocal fold masses, left vocal fold paresis, and reflux. His vocal training has not prepared him to effectively compensate for laryngeal weakness or injury. He would benefit from acting voice sessions designed to assist the patient in preparing himself for performance with warm-ups to promote the reduction of upper body tension, improved alignment, and increased jaw relaxation and oropharyngeal space during voice production. It has also been recommended that the patient receive concurrent speaking voice therapy

and singing voice sessions to address vocal techniques in conversational speech and promote greater vocal endurance and strength.

Mr. Doe is a very pleasant and motivated patient. It is a privilege to participate in his care.

Michelle Horman, CCC-SLP
Acting Voice Specialist

Appendix Va

Outline for Daily Practice

I. Warm-up and cool-down routine

    A. Stretch/relaxation exercises:

        1. Head/neck range of motion

        2. Shoulder rolls and shrugs

        3. Facial massage

        4. Tongue stretch

    B. Vocalises (which are provided by the singing specialist)

    C. Speaking exercises:

        1. Easy speech breathing exercises: "Candle blowing," /s/, /ʃ/, /h/-/ɑ/, /m/, /ɑ/

        2. Oral resonance warm up: "ng-ah"

        3. Connected speech: Counting

        4. Monitoring sites of tension: /f-v/, /s-z/, /θ-ð/, /ʃ-dʒ/

        5. Bridging exercises:

            a. Sliding block scale for /m/

            b. Spoken "vocalises"

            c. Lip trills

        6. Quiet breathing exercise

II. Additional daily practice:

    The target areas are addressed systematically.

    A. Breath control and support

    B. Phrasing

    C. Easy onset and blending techniques

    D. Oral resonance

    E. Tone focus and vocal placement

    F. Loudness/projection

    G. Speaking rate, rhythm, and intonation

III. Carryover practice:

    A. Application of specific goals in ongoing speech

    B. Transition from structured to spontaneous

    C. Stress management strategies

Appendix Vb
Sample Phrases

THREE SYLLABLES IN LENGTH

Put it on.

Tell me how.

Walk around.

Did you know?

Juicy peach.

Yes and no.

Do you know?

Crunchy apple.

Put them down.

What's your name?

Come over here.

Not right now.

Time to go.

Close your eyes.

Fine report.

Read the book.

Who is it?

Pick it up.

Take a nap.

Good evening.

FOUR SYLLABLES IN LENGTH

Pleased to meet you

You'd like it there.

The sun was bright.

Fill it up, please.

How much is it?

He knows the way

The train was late.

Maybe later.

Cream and sugar.

Bread and butter.

Salt and pepper.

Toast and butter.

Pie and coffee.

Needle and thread.

Turkey and cheese.

Nice to meet you.

That's fine for now.

Don't tease the dog.

Beth arrived late.

This is enough.

FIVE SYLLABLES IN LENGTH

Where are they going?

The concert was great.

Turn off the iron.

SIX SYLLABLES IN LENGTH

That's a good idea.

Ted wants to come along.

Put everything away.

FIVE SYLLABLES IN LENGTH
(continued)

The book was stolen.

Tip the waiter well.

When is he finished?

Flowers need water.

Will she be here soon?

The oven is on.

The tea is steeping.

Yes, that's fine with me.

The phone is ringing.

Play the clarinet.

Let's consider it.

They enjoyed the song.

SEVEN AND EIGHT SYLLABLES IN LENGTH

The weather in August is hot.

I love sleeping late on Sundays.

What time can you come for dinner?

We will probably start at six.

The top of this jar is stuck.

Would you help me open it, please?

I can't remember the number.

Please give it to me again.

What shall we have for dessert?

Pie and ice cream sound delicious.

What are you doing after work?

Be careful not to go too fast.

The snowfall was light that year.

Our guests will arrive at nine.

They ate breakfast at the diner.

SIX SYLLABLES IN LENGTH
(continued)

He can phone us later.

She bought it somewhere else.

Leave the window open.

Place it down carefully.

Come over and see us.

The children were playing.

The fire alarm rang.

The switch is over there.

Let me know when he calls.

They moved to the mountains.

The spectators were pleased.

The puppy is playful.

NINE AND TEN SYLLABLES IN LENGTH

Lisa bought some vegetables for dinner.

He wears a 16 and a half collar.

I will be happy to meet with you.

They all went skiing for the holiday.

The bakery smells simply delicious.

There are four bedrooms on the top floor.

After the rain, the air smelled earthy.

Have you been to the theater lately?

Summer at the seashore is popular.

TEN, ELEVEN, AND TWELVE SYLLABLES IN LENGTH

City buses are often crowded and noisy.

He avoided making eye contact while riding on the bus.

Don't forget to turn off the lights and lock the door.

Oh no, I think I left my keys inside.

We usually go boating each summer.

The car was badly damaged by the crash.

Fortunately, there were no injuries.

Sally loves to go swimming in the lake.

She was reminded not to go too far.

Distilled water tastes much better than tap.

Appendix Vc

Frontal Placement Words

till	town	teal
tot	test	tips
lash	style	still
tall	team	hall
ten	mile	Bill
leash	swell	toad
much	lot	tell
tie	tip	net
latch	least	leap
dial	bell	top
smile	loft	loud
snowfall	town hall	distill
livid	low tide	windmill
tinfoil	vowel	man-made

Appendix Vd
H/Vowel Minimal-Pairs

had-add	hall-all	hold-old
head-Ed	hit-it	home-ohm
hone-own	ho-oh	his-is
hay-ay	hat-at	hand-and
hear-ear	hitch-itch	hi-I

Appendix Ve
Vowel-Initiated Words

LONG VOWELS IN ENGLISH

/ɑ/	/o²/	/ɑ:I/	/i/
odd	oath	aisle	eat
octet	oat	eye	east
object	oak	ice	each
obtuse	old	idle	eek
octopus	oboe	I've	eager
operate	okay	Irish	Ethan
otter	only	iota	enough
obligate	overt	item	even

SHORT VOWELS IN ENGLISH

/æ/	/ɛ/	/I/	/ʌ/
as	end	in	up
at	ever	is	ugh
ask	effort	if	ugly
after	educate	ill	uplift
apple	elephant	id	upset
attitude	enemy	image	utmost
avenue	elegant	issue	under
accident	envy	inactive	unlock
accent	entertain	indent	usher

Appendix Vf

Phrases for Blending

fall over	go into	put upon
leave on	the only	lose it
see it	the other	win it
do it	not even	that's enough
put on	not any	leave open
down under	cold as	one of
not old	the ice	she's ill
look at	he's ill	then add
the end	yes and	so it
high up	one at	Sue is

Appendix Vg
Phrases to Practice Easy Onset and Blending

Elliot ate an apple and allowed Andrew another.

Each and every avenue is open at eight o'clock.

Over on Aston Avenue is an open air amphitheater.

I am in agreement in every aspect of our association.

Alan's attitude is overly obnoxious.

In April, Addie always attends an extravaganza in Arizona.

Alice openly acknowledges an aversion to avocados.

Exercise is an important and energizing activity.

Amanda is in Alabama at an annual event.

It is eleven o'clock already, and all of us are anxiously awaiting Ellen's arrival.

Eliminating additives is advisable.

Is Emily afraid of an eerie effigy?

Eddie is outdoors on an icy evening.

Actually, I am aware of all the errors in Adam's arithmetic assignment.

Every evening in autumn our area orchestra attempts to entertain an uninterested audience of adolescents.

Appendix Vh

Homographs

refuse-refuse   contrast-contrast

compound-compound   content-content

converse-converse   commune-commune

console-console   minute-minute

project-project   object-object

Appendix Vi

Open-Vowel Words

/ɑ/	/æ/	/ɑːI/	/ɑu/
top	map	tie	power
hot	match	reply	town
pocket	hot	side	found
deposit	flag	fire	coward
probable	sad	line	tower
knock	bag	fine	without
shot	cash	confide	house
doctor	cast	tired	how
father	happen	height	loud
garage	mash	rhyme	flower

1. Talking too much
2. Talking too loudly
3. Talking too rapidly
4. Talking while moving vigorously
5. Talking while lifting, bending, or moving arms
6. Taking the "teacher's voice" out of the classroom
7. Shouting and yelling excessively to distant people
8. Talking over classroom, cafeteria, barroom noise
9. Inappropriate use of the telephone
10. Inappropriate emphasis on vowel onset words
11. Jerky revisions to phrases and sentences
12. Use of fillers, Uh-huh, OK, and Uhm, etc.
13. Singing or talking in the car
14. Inadequate sleep or rest
15. Excessive talking at sports events
16. Exposure to dust
17. Exposure to fumes from cleaning products
18. Exposure to primary or secondary tobacco smoke
19. Exposure to dry air
20. Poor acoustics in the classroom
21. Poor ventilation in the classroom
22. Lack of hydration (don't drink enough water)
23. Use of cough drops with menthol, mint, or anesthetics
24. Alcohol
25. Smoking
26. Caffeine (coffee, tea, Coke, Pepsi, Mountain Dew, chocolate)
27. Spicy foods
28. Acidic foods
29. Dairy products
30. Over-the-counter decongestants and antihistamines
31. Cough medicines
32. Aspirin/Ibuprofin
33. Mouthwash
34. Mints
35. Asthma inhalers
36. Poor breath support
37. Excessive chest breathing
38. Too big a breath
39. Too small a breath
40. Abrupt voice onset
41. Excessive tension in voice or throat
42. Too high or low a pitch to the voice
43. Too closed or tense jaw
44. High tongue position and tongue tension
45. Reduced use of tongue in forming words with jaw substitution
46. Poor tone focus, voice "in throat"
47. Facial tension
48. Poor posture, bent from waist
49. Neck tension
50. Speaking with jaw thrust or constriction

51. Unresolved stress

Other_____

_____

_____

_____

_____

_____

_____

Appendix VI

Checklist of Vocal Abuse for Teachers

Please circle the following statements if they are appropriate to you. Please add any additional items particular to your life or setting.

Vocal Abuse/Misuse Items

1. Talking too much
2. Talking too loudly
3. Talking too rapidly
4. Talking while moving vigorously
5. Talking while lifting, bending, or moving arms
6. Taking the "teacher's voice" out of the classroom
7. Shouting and yelling excessively to distant people
8. Talking over classroom, cafeteria, barroom noise
9. Inappropriate use of the telephone
10. Inappropriate emphasis on vowel onset words
11. Jerky revisions to phrases and sentences
12. Use of fillers, Uh-huh, OK, and Uhm, etc.
13. Singing or talking in the car
14. Inadequate sleep or rest
15. Excessive talking at sports events
16. Exposure to dust
17. Exposure to fumes from cleaning products
18. Exposure to primary or secondary tobacco smoke
19. Exposure to dry air
20. Poor acoustics in the classroom
21. Poor ventilation in the classroom
22. Lack of hydration (don't drink enough water)
23. Use of cough drops with menthol, mint, or anesthetics
24. Alcohol
25. Smoking
26. Caffeine (coffee, tea, Coke, Pepsi, Mountain Dew, chocolate)
27. Spicy foods
28. Acidic foods
29. Dairy products
30. Over-the-counter decongestants and antihistamines
31. Cough medicines
32. Aspirin/Ibuprofin
33. Mouthwash
34. Mints
35. Asthma inhalers
36. Poor breath support
37. Excessive chest breathing
38. Too big a breath
39. Too small a breath
40. Abrupt voice onset
41. Excessive tension in voice or throat
42. Too high or low a pitch to the voice
43. Too closed or tense jaw
44. High tongue position and tongue tension
45. Reduced use of tongue in forming words with jaw substitution
46. Poor tone focus, voice "in throat"
47. Facial tension
48. Poor posture, bent from waist
49. Neck tension
50. Speaking with jaw thrust or constriction
51. Unresolved stress

Other_____

_____

_____

_____

_____

_____

_____

Index

A

Abdominal anatomy, 1:167, 1:169
Abetalipoprotcinemia, 2:892
Abillify, 2:565
Abortifacients, 1:338–339
Abscess
   retropharyngeal, 2:819
   tonsillar, 2:818–819
Academy of Vocal Arts, Philadelphia, 2:1041–1042
Accent method therapy, 2:967
Acetaminophen, 2:912, 2:946
Acetazolamide, 2:851
Acetylcysteine, 2:667
Achalasia, 2:603, 2:604, 2:940
Acid-hyperfusion test, 2:607
Acidosis, 2:892
Aciphex, 2:911
Acoustic analysis
   in clinical voice laboratory, 1:379–382
   in singing studio, 2:1042–1043
Acoustic neuroma, 2:516, 2:517, 2:866
Acrodermatitis chronic atrophicans, 2:811
Acromegaly, 2:546–547, 2:812
Acting, 1:327
   and facial paralysis, 2:860–861
   and hearing loss, 2:694
   and nutrition, 2:659–680, *See* Nutrition
   occupational hazards, 1:340–341
   overview, 1:339–341
   personality subtype, 2:559
   and pollution, 2:732–733
   and professional consultation, 1:341
   and sleep, 2:681–688, *See also* Sleep
   vocal demands on, 1:340
   voice evaluation, 1:350–352
   voice stressors, 1:339–341
Acting-voice trainers, 2:492–493, 2:505–506
   alignment evaluation, 2:1056
   articulator isolation, 2:1056

   and assessment, 2:1055–1056
   and awareness, habitual, 2:1053
   body tension evaluation, 2:1056
   and breath, 2:1053, 2:1056
   educational approaches for, 2:1052–1055
   efficacy, 2:1059–1060
   evaluation, 2:1056
   and forward placement, 2:1056
   and injured voices, 2:1054–1055
   and learning modes, 2:1051
   Lessac system, 2:1053–1054
   Linklater method, 2:1053
   in medical setting, 2:1055–1057, 2:1059–1060
   and patient history, 2:1055–1056
   relaxation, 2:1056
   Skinner approach, 2:1052–1053, 2:1058
   training overview, 2:1051–1052
   and treatment, 2:1057
Actinomyces as pathogenic, 2:797
Actinomyces israelii, 2:817
Actinomycosis, 2:485, 2:812
Actors' Equity Association, 1:339, 1:340, 2:761, 2:762, 2:766, 2:770
Acupuncture, 2:918
Acyclovir, 2:841, 2:909, 2:947, 2:949
ADD (attention deficit disorder), 2:914
Adenine arabinoside, 2:841
Adenoidectomy, 2:719
Adenoid hypertrophy, 2:725
Adenoma, pituitary, 2:546
Adenopathy, 2:817, 2:818
Adenosine triphosphate (ATP), 2:684
Adenovirus, 2:821
α-adrenergic agonists, 2:603
β-adrenergic agonists, 2:603
Adrenocorticosteroids, 2:926
Adrenocorticotropic hormone (ACTH), 2:547, 2:892, 2:906, 2:914
Aerobic conditioning, 2:503
Aerobics, 1:329

confidential voice therapy, **2:**966
counseling, **2:**961
and dehydration, **2:**970
and environmental noise, **2:**970
exercises
  bridging, **2:**977–978
  carryover, **2:**983
  cool-down, **2:**981, **2:**1091
  guided imagery, **2:**981
  meditation, **2:**981
  onset, **2:**973–974
  oral resonance, **2:**974–975
  projection, **2:**976
  prosody, **2:**976, **2:**977
  quieting response, **2:**981
  range of motion, **2:**979–981
  voice placement, **2:**975–976
  warm-up, **2:**981, **2:**1091
functional integration (FI), **2:**968
and glottal attack harshness, **2:**973–974
glottal fry, **2:**976
and grunting, **2:**969
head/neck alignment, **2:**980–981
holistic approach, **2:**961–962
inhalational phonation, **2:**968
injured voice training, **2:**1032–1035
instrumentation use, **2:**984
Lee Silverman Voice Treatment (LVST), **2:**967
level four, **2:**981–982
level one, **2:**969–970
level three, **2:**978–981
level two, **2:**970–978
loudness *versus* projection, **2:**976
and loud talking, **2:**969–970
mechanics, breath/support, **2:**972
muscular tension evaluation, **2:**965
and noisy vocalization, **2:**969
optimal pitch therapy, **2:**967
oral/facial evaluation, **2:**965
overview, **2:**961–962
patient history, **2:**963–964
phonation evaluation, **2:**964–965
phrasing, **2:**972
pitch, **2:**977–978
postsurgical, **2:**612
preoperative therapy, **3:**1139
professional/everyday carryover, **2:**962
and professional needs, **2:**961
progress monitoring, **2:**962
prosody, **2:**965, **2:**976–977
quiet breathing, **2:**972
recitative training, **2:**978
and recommendations, therapist, **2:**966
referral to specialists, **2:**981–982
reflexive techniques, **2:**968
relaxation, **2:**978–981
resonant voice therapy, **2:**966–967
respiration evaluation, **2:**964
safe voice/speech skills during, **2:**962

screaming, **2:**1053–1054
and screaming, **2:**969–970
self-massage, **2:**980
sex change/gender reassignment, **3:**1361–1362
singing evaluation, **2:**965–966
singing lessons, concurrent, **2:**983–984
and sleep/rest, **2:**970
strategies of, **2:**982
and sulcus vocalis, **3:**1176
and talking excessively, **2:**970
team, interdisciplinary, **2:**611, **2:**612, **2:**962–963,
    2:1427–1432, **3:**611, **3:**612, **3:**962–963, **3:**1427–1432
and throat clearing, **2:**969
tone focus, **2:**975–976
training principles, **2:**1088–1089
trial therapy, **2:**966
vegetative techniques, **2:**968
and vocal fold hemorrhage, **2:**1023
and vocal fold motion, **2:**487
for vocal fold nodules, **2:**488
vocal fold paralysis/paresis, **2:**879–880
vocal fold polyps, **2:**489
and vocal fold scar, **3:**1309–1310
and vocal hygiene, **2:**969–970
voice evaluation, **2:**963
voice placement, **2:**975–976
and whispering, **2:**969
and yelling, **2:**969–970
Voice trainers
and vocal abuse, **2:**955
Voice training, **1:**327, **1:**328
Volume problems, **1:**327
Vomiting, **2:**501, **2:**541, **2:**547, **2:**566, **2:**673, **2:**759, **2:**866,
    2:906, **2:**916, **2:**931, *See also* Regurgitation
and dietary supplements, **2:**917
from supplements, **2:**917
as symptom, **2:**602–603
von Leden, Hans, **1:**5
VOT (voice onset time) and age, **2:**500

W

Waldeyer's ring, **2:**712
Wallenberg's syndrome, **2:**855, **2:**889
Wallerian degeneration, **2:**875
Warfarin, **1:**407, **2:**564, **2:**625
Warm-up, vocal, **2:**606, **2:**607, **2:**981, **2:**989
Waterbrash, **2:**603
Webs, *See* Laryngeal webs
Wechsler Adult Intelligence Scale-Revised (WAIS-R),
    2:504
Wegener's granulomatosis, **2:**491, **2:**517, **2:**800–802, **2:**812,
    2:821
Weightlifting, **1:**329
Weight management, **2:**666
Weight table, **2:**658
Wellbutrin, **2:**564
Whey protein dietary supplements, **1:**226
Whiplash, cervical, **2:**863

ISBN 1-59756-001-4